Weldons

ENCYCLOPAEDIA OF NEEDLEWORK

A Practical Guide to Needlecraft in all its Varieties compiled and edited by Weldons Needlework Experts

With nearly 2,000 Illustrations and Complete Index

Published by arrangement with Weldons Ltd.

THE WAVERLEY BOOK CO., LTD.
Farringdon Street, London. E.C.4

CONTENTS

The Complete Index to every detail of the Encyclopedia, printed at the end of the book, should always be consulted when immediate reference is desired to any particular item or illustration.

Foreword

NEEDLE and thread have traced for themselves down the ages a history every bit as interesting as that chronicled by pen or brush. Fashions and fancies, new crafts and crazes have sprung up from time to time, but needlework has gone steadily onward—varying its form and adapting itself to the changing needs of succeeding generations.

This Encyclopaedia of Needlework deals with its subject in all its phases, taking the worker step by step—by means of actual photographs, clear descriptions, explanatory diagrams, simplified charts and other methods of illustration—from the choice of materials for particular pieces of work, right through to the last stitches used in making up the finished article.

Needlework offers great scope for originality—a fact which makes a tremendous appeal to the enlightened woman of to-day. There are intriguing old designs from which to copy, new ones to create, and thanks to the skill and science of modern manufacturing processes, the means of being able to give expression to colour-sense in the fullest meaning of the term.

Each worker will find something of interest, whether she has time to devote to the intricacies of lace-making or needle-painting, or merely wishes to experience the thrill of fingering her own handiwork in the jumper she wears or the rugs which cover her floors—two very popular sections of this book that should make a practical appeal to all who are unable to devote time to needlework in the strictest sense. The busiest housewife and mother will also find chapters of the greatest use to her—plain sewing, darning, mending and so on.

The expert and the novice alike will find that the manner of writing and the choice of illustrations have been planned with a view to giving them the very best information in the most interesting and useful manner, yet without the usual dullness of a textbook.

You will not find the latest fads and passing fashions of a mere season in these pages. On the contrary, this Encyclopaedia has been so compiled that it will not date, and it will be found just as useful in years to come as it is to-day.

Weldons paper patterns and transfer designs mentioned in this book may be obtained through your needlework shop or direct from Weldons Ltd., 30 Southampton Street, Strand, London, W.C.2. Please note that only those for which a number is given are available.

Enquiries regarding needlework in this book should be addressed to Eileen Maxwell, Needlework Dept., Weldons Ltd., 30 Southampton Street, Strand, London, W.C.2.

EMBROIDERY

BOOK I

APPLIQUÉ. CANVAS EMBROIDERIES. LINEN EMBROIDERIES. CUT WORK. DRAWN THREAD. WHITE EMBROIDERIES.

INTRODUCTION AND EMBROIDERY STITCHES

Stitches play the most important part in embroidery, as by the choice of the right stitch one expresses correctly the subject chosen for embroidering. A serious worker should make a study of old needlework of past centuries in order to ensure that the stitches used are in keeping with the style of design. The tools used for embroidery are few, but special care should be taken when choosing them.

Needles—Only the best needles should be used, as inferior needles are apt to be rough through not being clearly cut. For most kinds of embroidery long-eyed needles are used, but for darned netting and canvas embroidery needles with blunt points, known as tapestry needles are used. One should be careful to avoid working with bent needles as these are apt to make crooked stitches which spoil the work. Good needles seldom bend!

The size of the needles used for each piece of work depends on the stoutness of the thread. The needles should be just large enough to allow the thread to pass through the material easily.

Thimbles.—Two thimbles of a good make are needed for frame embroidery, and only one when work is done in the hand. Thimbles should always be smooth so that they will not catch in the threads and make the finished work rough. For frame work they are worn on the middle finger of each hand.

Scissors should always be sharp and have good points. For Church Embroidery a strong, sharp pair, and for fine work a small pair of very sharp embroidery scissors should be used, otherwise one cannot get clean edges. There are some embroidery scissors with one blade pointed and the other rounded. These are very useful for cutting material from lace or net, as the rounded end will not pierce the net. A large pair of cutting-out shears is always useful for cutting material that cannot be torn.

Frames are a great help in embroidery as they keep the work taut and prevent it from puckering. Though frames are a little more trouble at first, after a little practice the worker will be loath to do without them. There are several types of frames which are used, varying according to the piece of work chosen.

Tambour Frames are often quite satisfactory for small pieces of work. These are usually two circles of smooth wood, fitting closely one inside the other, but sometimes they are made of iron or other metal, and these should be covered with strips of flannel or baize wound tightly and neatly round them, and stitched into place. Wooden frames, when they have become loose by long usage, can also be treated in the same way. It is essential that they fit well, and that there is only just enough room for the inner hoop to pass through the outer one. The fabric to be embroidered is placed over the small hoop, the other hoop then being pressed down over the material on to the smaller to hold the work taut.

It is sometimes advisable to put a piece of interlining between the work and the outer hoop to prevent the work from being rubbed.

Another method is to tack the silk to be worked firmly to a cotton or linen in the frame. This allows the silk to come over the outside of the frame and prevents it from spoiling. Before working cut away the linen or cotton from under the part of the silk to be worked. Fig. 1 shows three different tambour frames, any of which can be used, the screw frame being perhaps the most satisfactory.

There is another type of tambour frame, which can be fixed to a table. The frame can then be adjusted in a position most convenient to the worker, so that both hands are left free for the embroidery. This can be seen clearly in Fig. 2. Fig. 3 shows another type of clamp frame.

Fig. 4 shows the most useful frame for embroidery. It consists of two round

ROUND FRAMES

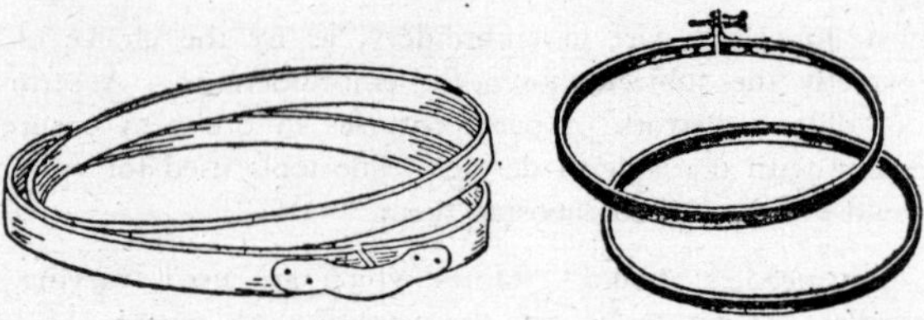

TAMBOUR Round spring frame. Round frame with screw. **FRAMES**

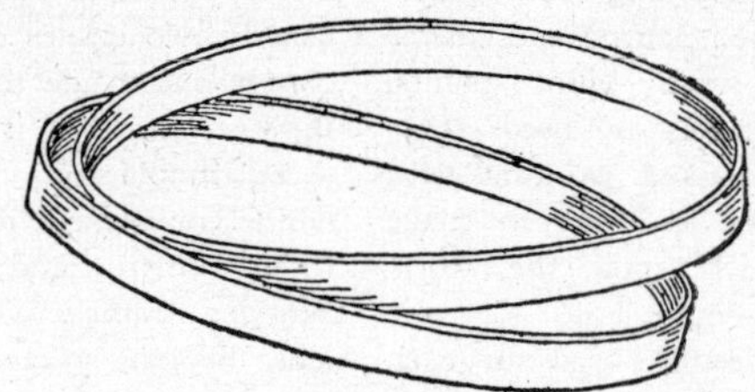

Fig. 1

Plain round frame.

Left: **Fig. 2.** A frame clamped to a table.

Below: A variation of the fixed frame.

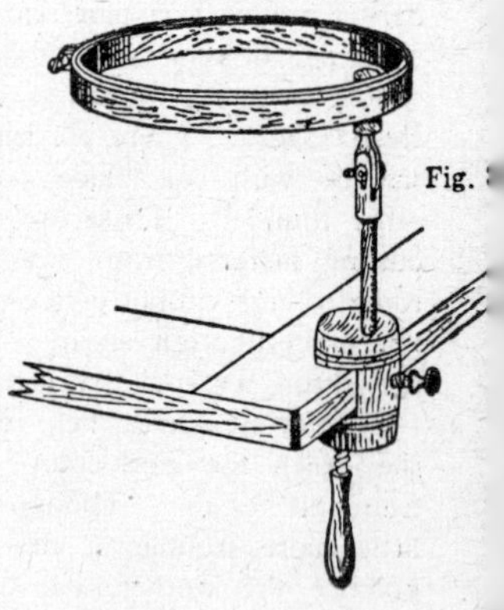

Fig. 3

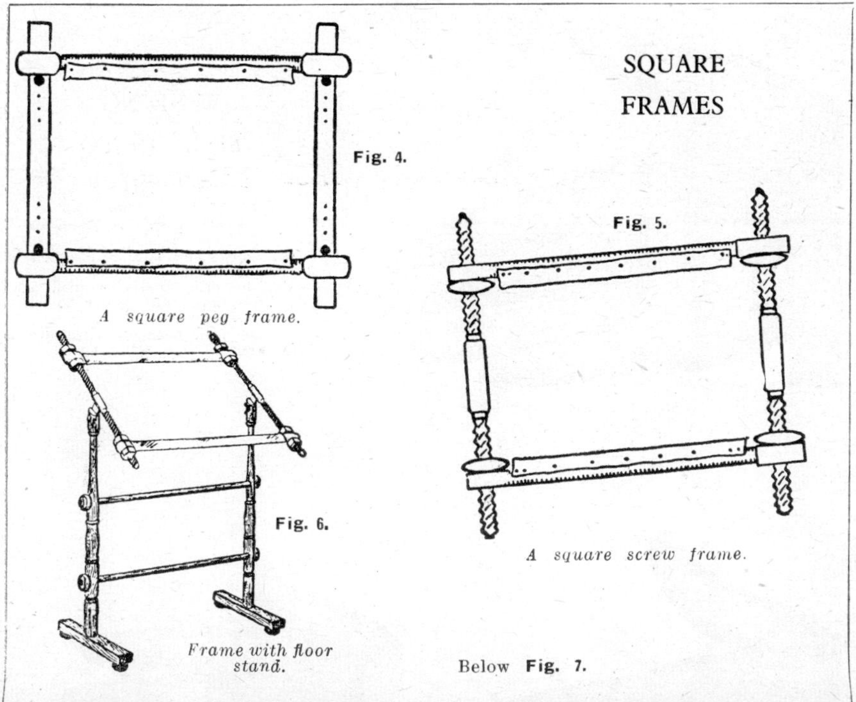

A square peg frame.

A square screw frame.

Frame with floor stand.

Below **Fig. 7.**

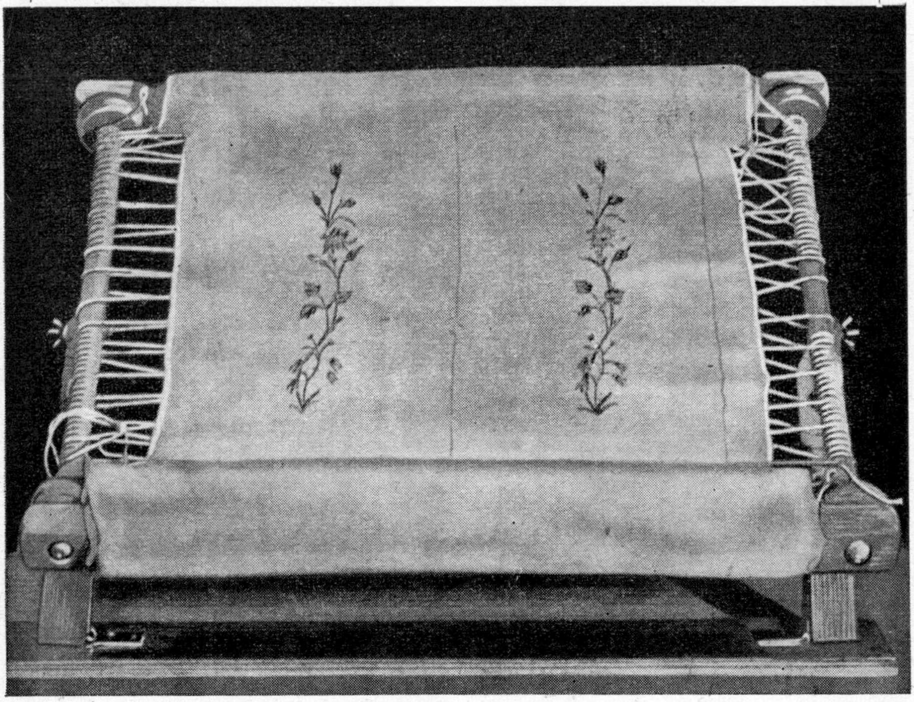

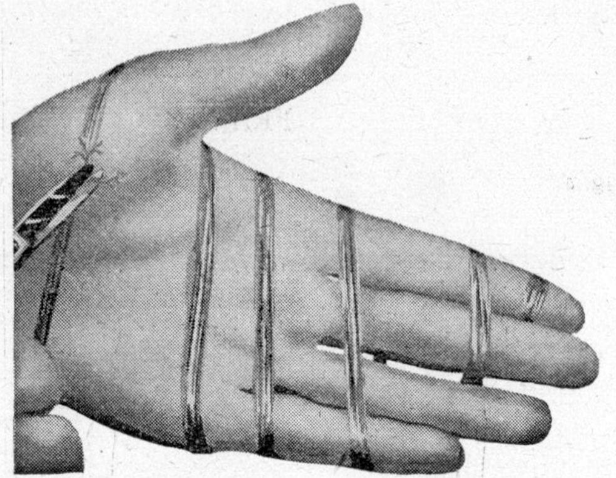

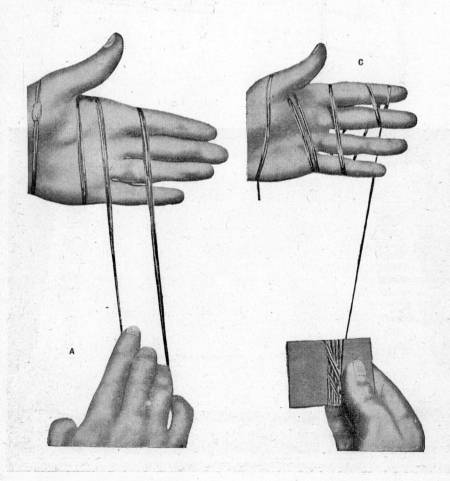

WINDING SILK ON TO A CARD

(*a*) shows the silk being wound on to the hand.

(*b*) the silk firmly wound and the knot being cut ready to wind on to the card.

(*c*) the silk being wound on to the card.

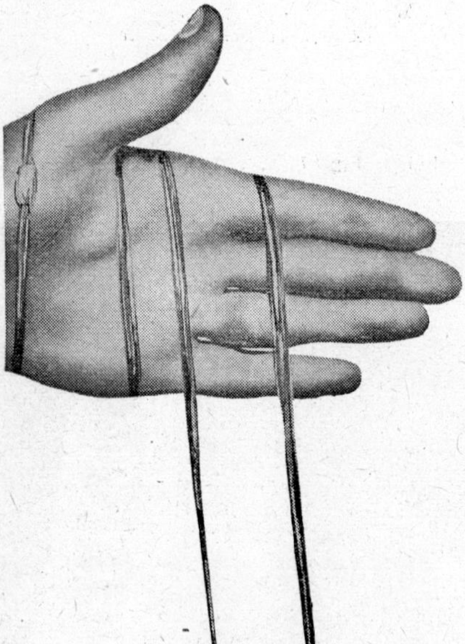

B

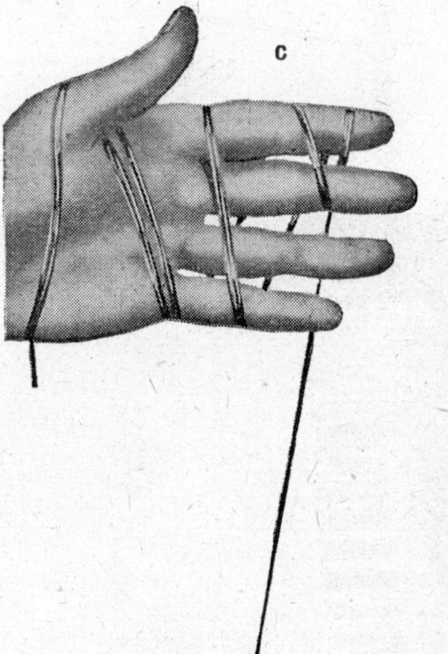

C

A

pieces of wood which have a mortise at each end. Strips of webbing are securely nailed along these, extending the full length of the wood between the mortises—and to this the work is sewn with stout thread or thin string.

For the sides of the frame two flat pieces of wood with holes pierced at regular intervals are used: these pass through the mortises, and the width of the frame is adjusted and the work kept tightly stretched by means of metal pins which are inserted in the holes by each mortise.

Fig. 5 shows another variety of this type of frame, which has, in place of the flat laths with metal pins, wooden screws with movable nuts.

In the screw frames the sides consist of long wooden screws which screw through holes in the rollers, and there are separate screw nuts to hold the rollers in the position required.

The size of the frame is measured by the webbing and will accommodate a piece of work of this width or narrower. If the material is longer than the depth of the fully-extended frame, the extra length is rolled on to the rollers.

A fixed stand for the frame is often used, and this is very convenient, though not an absolute necessity.

Fig. 6 shows a frame fixed to a floor stand. These are not always practical as they need plenty of space. Fig. 7 shows a frame which can be stood on a table or stool. But the most usual way for large frames is to use trestles. These are adjustable and can be fixed to the height and angle required by the worker.

Small frames can be rested on a table and held in position by a weight.

How to Frame up a Piece of Work.—The selvedge side of the material must be put at right angles to the main bars of the frame.

If the selvedge is used it should be cut through at intervals, then find the centre of the webbing and mark it with a pin. Make certain the edge of the material is quite straight (if possible draw a thread of the material) and turn it under about ½ inch on to the wrong side. Find the centre of the material and place it to the centre of the webbing (which has already been marked with a pin). Pin, then oversew the work firmly into position, beginning from the centre and working out to the sides. The work can be sewn either with thick cotton used double or with thread, according to the kind of material being framed.

Make quite certain that the two sides of the material are quite equally stretched. This can be tested by putting in the arms and sliding the main bars together. This is most important for large pieces of work.

Before putting in the sides of the frame, roll any surplus length on to the lower roller, first covering it with a protective layer of soft material or tissue paper. Now fix in the two arms, and stretch. Sew a piece of webbing about ½ an inch in (this varies according to the material used), along the exposed sides of the work, thread a carpet needle with strong string, and brace, going down into the webbing and up under the arm, then over, and down into the webbing. When this has been done along both sides, fix the string at one end at either side and tighten up the string evenly. The frame should then be taut and ready for working. Fig. 7 shows the finished work ready for pressing.

In church embroidery and other large pieces which need to be particularly taut and which are worked on a linen ground, it is advisable to make a hem at each side over a stout piece of string and not use webbing, as this is stronger. The work is then braced in exactly the same way as described above.

Transferring the design.—There are several methods of doing this, but the most usual is the **pounce method.** For this a pricking of the design is made in the following way. Trace design on to tracing paper, then place this, right side down, over two thicknesses of blanket or cloth, putting a piece of good quality tissue paper between the tracing and the blanket. Prick closely along all the lines, using a No. 9 sewing needle which, for comfort, can be fixed into a wooden handle. When you lift the tracing and tissue paper from the blanket, you will find the design clearly defined in pricked outline on the tissue paper. The tracing paper is discarded and the tissue paper pricking used for the transferring. Place the tissue on the material to which the design is to be transferred, making sure that the rough side is uppermost, as the smooth side will lie more closely to the material. The fact of reversing the design before pricking ensures that it will be the right way round on the material.

Pin the pricking firmly in position or secure with weights. Make sure that the paper lies absolutely smoothly on the fabric.

A pounce is then rubbed through the holes—this is a fine powder that will pass easily through the holes and so leave a dotted line on the material. French chalk can be used as it will not harm the material and will give a white dotted line on dark fabrics. For lighter fabrics mix the French chalk with a little powdered charcoal or washing blue. To apply the pounce, roll up tightly a narrow strip of flannel (bandage fashion) and stitch the end to prevent it unrolling. Dip the end of this pad in the pounce and rub the pounce through the holes. Finally, lift the pricking carefully from the material when you will find the design reproduced in a fine dotted line. Gently blow away any surplus pounce from the material, then paint over the dotted line with blue watercolour paint to make it permanent. Use a fine sable brush, working with the tip only and keeping the brush in an upright position. On silk or satin use watercolour or a hard pencil.

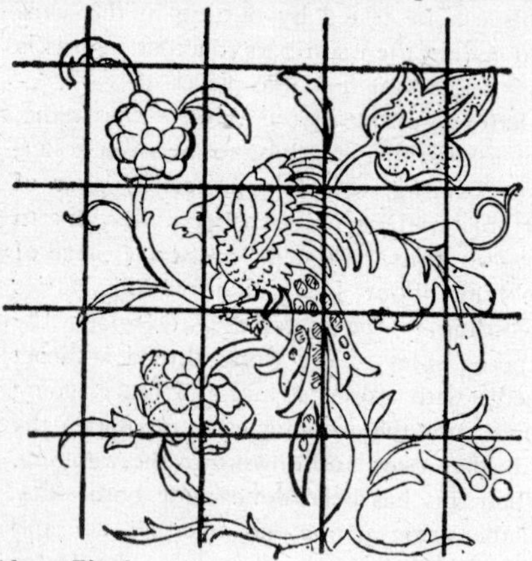

Above **Fig. 8.**

Fig. 8 shows the original size of the design with the squares drawn over it.

In Fig. 9 the squares and design are shown with both ¼″ larger.

Fig. 9.

Tracing Method.—For fine white work or semi-transparent material outline your drawing in Indian ink on cartridge paper and leave it several hours to dry, then place the material over the drawing and trace with a hard pencil.

Transfers are very useful as they can easily be cut about and adjusted as one requires. Transfers can be obtained in blue or yellow print, though today they are mostly blue. Blue is used on light materials and yellow on brown or dark materials.

Place the transfer with the shiny side on to the material and use a moderately hot iron. (The heat of the iron can be tested by cutting off the wording or number of the transfer and placing it on a piece of similar material.) Some materials do not take the transfer as readily as others. When this happens place a cloth over the material and run the iron over that. This will flatten the surface for the time being, and if the transfer is applied quickly it should take quite easily.

Transfer Inks can be bought, which are quite useful as one is not always able to buy the exact design one requires. The design is traced on to tracing paper, and then outlined in transfer ink and, when dry, transferred to the material in the usual way. These inks are not always available, so a substitute can be made out of ordinary washing blue and fine sugar. Powder enough blue to fill a flat teaspoonful, and add three flat teaspoonfuls of sugar and one of water. Mix these well together so that the grain of the sugar disappears completely. With a fine sable brush paint round the outline and leave to dry—then transfer in the usual way.

Taking off the Design by Rubbing.—Frequently, when copying embroidery designs, it is possible to transfer an impression by rubbing. This also applies to lace, for some of the best designs are to be found in lace specimens. This can be done with the help of a heel ball and fairly thin tracing paper.

Place the tracing paper over the lace or embroidery and steady it with weights or drawing pins. Then rub the heel ball gently over this. The outline will only be faint, but this is a guide and can be pencilled over quite easily and adapted for the embroidery. The method of adapting a border with the aid of mirrors is explained in the chapter on cross stitch.

To Enlarge or Reduce a Design.—This is done with the help of squares and is very useful, as a design is frequently either too large or too small.

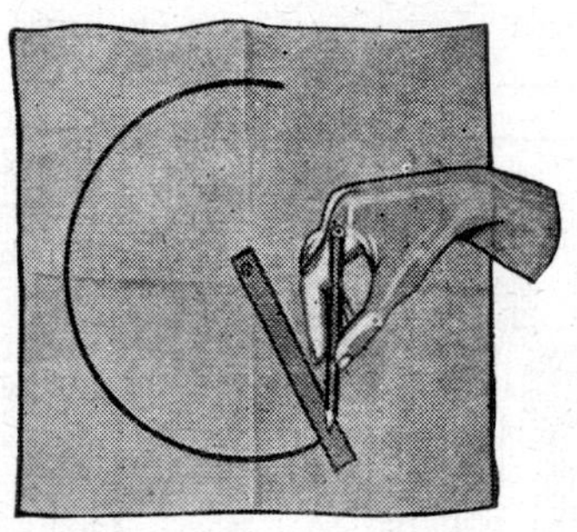

Fig. 10.—Showing a simple way to draw a circle.

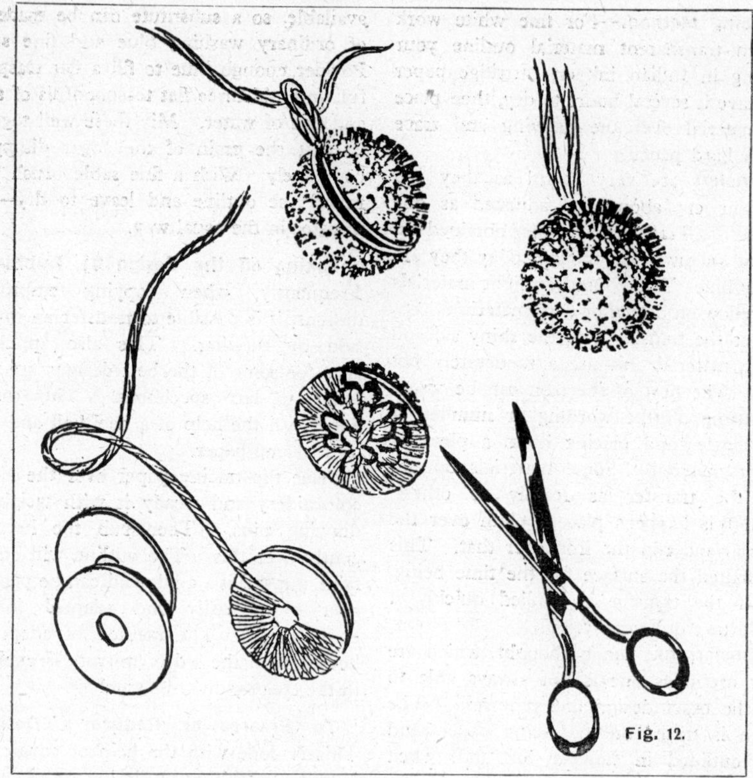

Fig. 11 shows a simple method of making and knotting a fringe.
In Fig. 12 the diagrams show so clearly the different stages for making pompoms that no further explanation is required.

Either draw or trace the design on to squared paper or draw even squares over the design, and then trace on to the tracing paper.

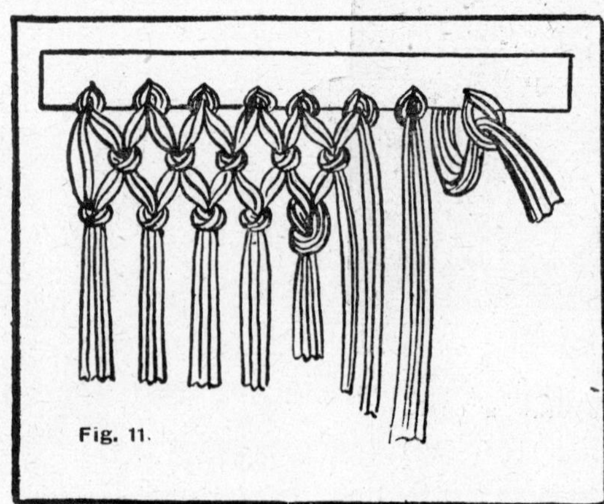

To enlarge a design take a piece of paper and mark it out in squares $\frac{1}{4}$ inch larger than the present design, so that if the squares are $\frac{1}{2}$ inch make them $\frac{3}{4}$ inch down each side. This can be done in whatever proportion is required. Then follow the lines of the pattern, square by square, either making them larger or smaller according to whether the design is being enlarged or reduced. This can be seen in Figs. 8 and 9. Now the design is ready to be traced off and either pricked or transferred.

Sometimes a large circle has to be

marked on the material. This is not always easy to draw accurately. A good plan is shown in Fig. 10 Fold the material in four and, in order to obtain a horizontal and perpendicular fold, mark the place where the creases cross the centre. A strong slip of paper is fastened to the centre with a pin, half the diameter of the circle required is measured off, and the paper is pierced at this point with a sharp pencil and the circle drawn.

Washing and ironing.—It is not possible to wash all embroideries, but for those that are washable use pure soap or good soap flakes. Dissolve the soap or flakes in hot water and add sufficient cold to make it lukewarm. Now dip the work in and out of the water, but do not rub. Rinse well in warm water and leave to dry. When still damp place a thick blanket on a table, over which place a cloth. Lay the right side of the embroidery on to this and place another cloth on the back, and with a hot iron, iron carefully. The embroidery when dry should have a raised appearance and not be flattened out.

For **Embroidery Paste**—see chapter on Appliqué.

Fringes, tassels, Pompoms and Cords are frequently needed for finishing work Below are simple directions for making.

Fringes—A simple fringe is made as follows: Take two threads, double them, and draw the looped ends up through the edge of the material. Pass the cut ends through the loop and draw tight. Knot similar groups of threads all along the edge of the material, and knot the threads together below the material, then comb out the fringe and cut the ends level. Fig. 11.

Tassels—Wind the thread round a card, bind the strands together at one end and cut through at the other, then bind the doubled strands firmly round just below the top. The tassel can be left like this or the top can be ornamented with a cap of buttonhole stitch if desired.

For **pompoms** follow the diagrams in Fig. 12.

To Make a Cord.—Cut several strands of thread three times the length required, and twist tightly together until they begin to kink, then fold in half and twist again to form a firm cord. The tighter the threads are twisted, the more even and firm the cord will be.

STITCHES

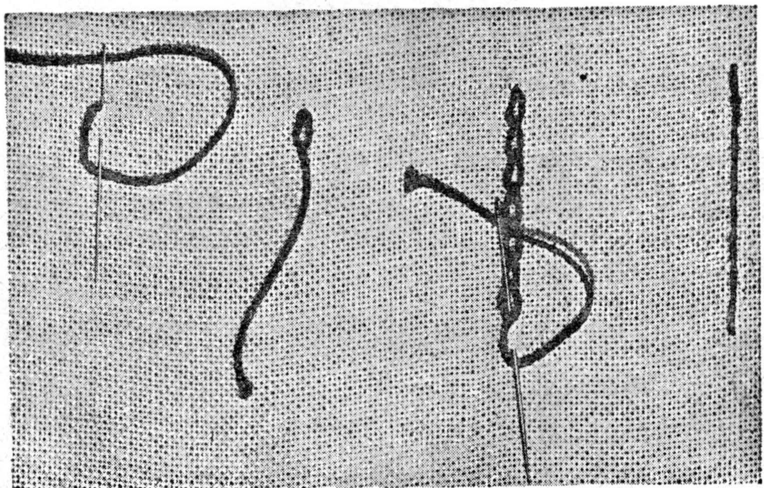

Fig. 14.—SIMPLE CHAIN STITCH

Fig. 13.

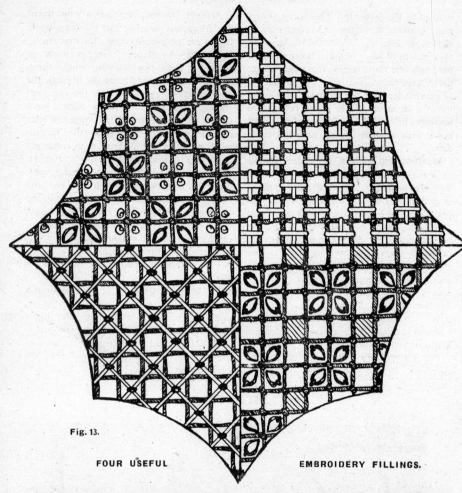

FOUR USEFUL EMBROIDERY FILLINGS.

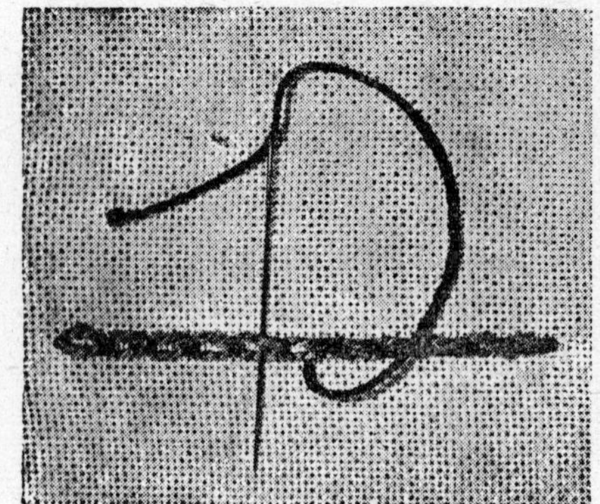

Fig. 15. OVERSEWN CHAIN

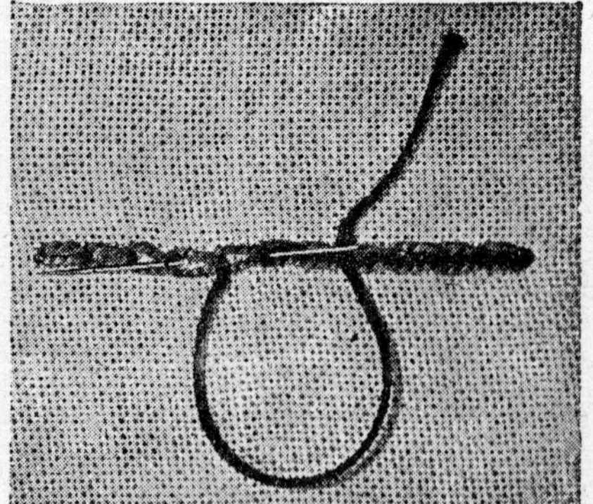

Fig. 16. BACK STITCHED CHAIN

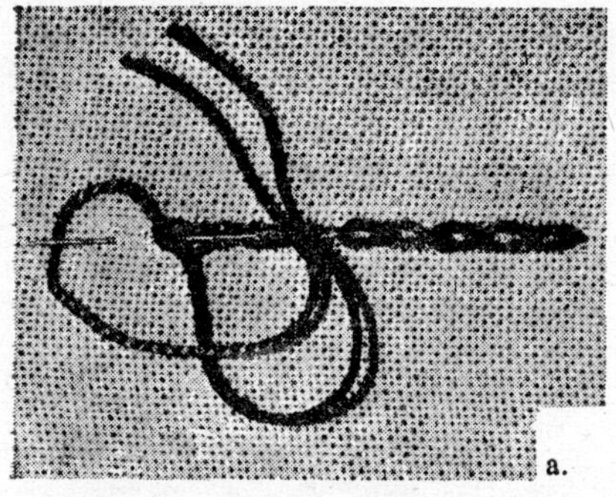

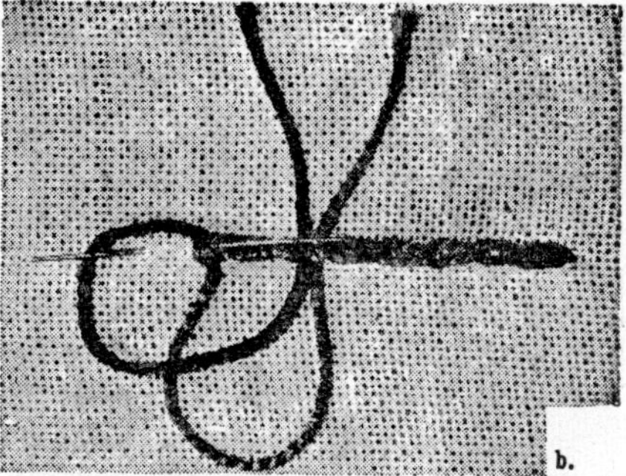

Fig. 17 (a, b, and c). **THREE VARIATIONS OF MAGIC CHAIN.**

Magic Chain—is worked with two threads of different colours threaded into one needle. Begin working in exactly the same way as simple chain stitch, keeping only one colour under the needle to the left, the other being on the right. See illustration. Pull the needle through and an ordinary chain stitch is formed in one colour.

The second stitch is worked exactly like the first, this time reversing the colours. It will be noticed in working that the thread to be used, automatically comes out to the left-hand side alternating each time. If, when the stitch is finished the contrasting colour shows on the top, a gentle pull will make it disappear — hence the name magic chain.

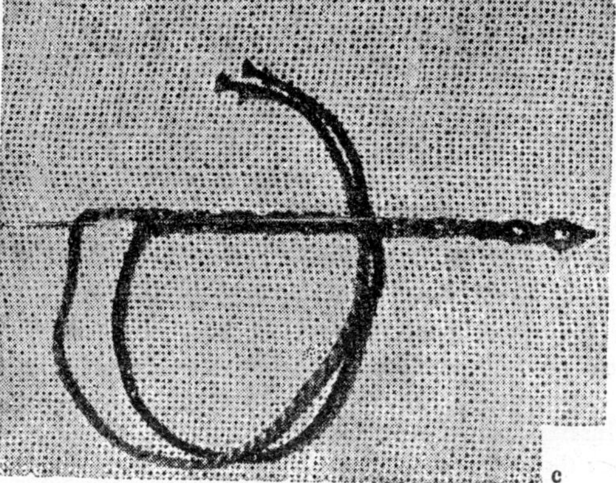

This stitch can be varied in many ways such as working two stitches in one colour, and then two in the other, or three in one and two in the other colour, and so on.

Fig. 18. **DOUBLE CHAIN STITCH.** The working can be followed clearly in the illustration.

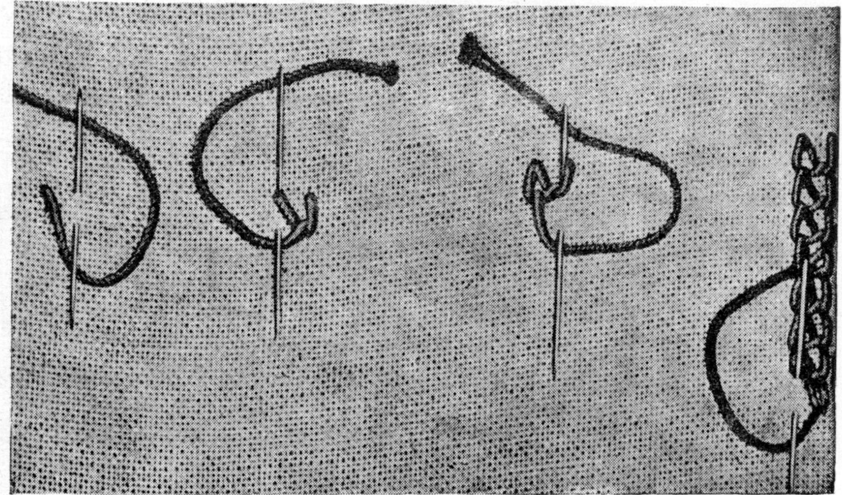

Simple Chain Stitch is principally used as an outline stitch and is worked from right to left.

To Work.—Bring the needle up from the back, at the top of the line down which it is to be worked. Hold the thread down on the material towards the left, then insert the needle in exactly the same place it first came up, bringing it out a short distance farther on. Fig. 14. The distance depends on the purpose to which the stitch is put. The thread is kept behind the needle and is then drawn up firmly. This forms the chain. Insert the needle in the hole out of which the thread has just come, and repeat as before for the length required, always keeping the stitch the same length. On the reverse side a backstitch is formed. *To fasten off*, take the needle through to the wrong side just beyond the last stitch and fasten into the backs of the stitches.

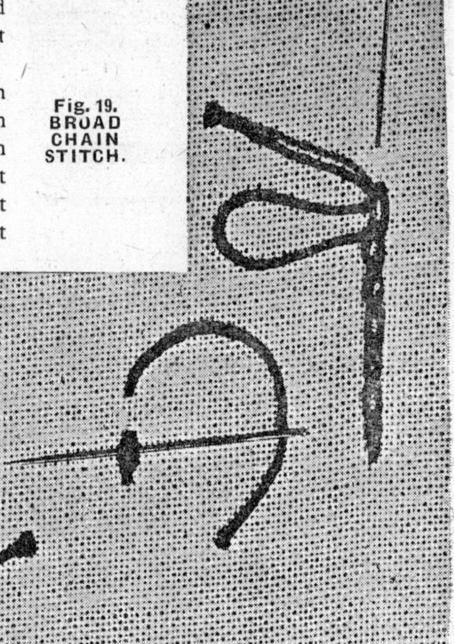

Fig. 19. BROAD CHAIN STITCH.

Oversewn Chain Stitch.—First, outline the design in simple chain stitch. When this is done oversew the chain stitch in either a contrasting thread or the same colour. This is quick and easy to work and is effective when finished. The thread used for oversewing does not go through the material except at the beginning and fastening off. The oversewn stitch lies over the join of each chain stitch. Fig. 15.

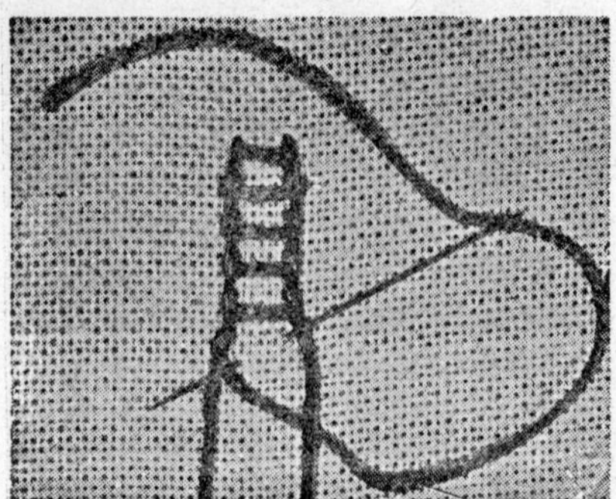

FIG. 21. SINGALESE CHAIN STITCH.

Back Stitched Chain.—A row of simple chain stitch is worked first, and down the centre of this back stitch is worked. This can be done either in the same colour or in a contrasting shade. Fig. 16.

Broad Chain Stitch is not worked like

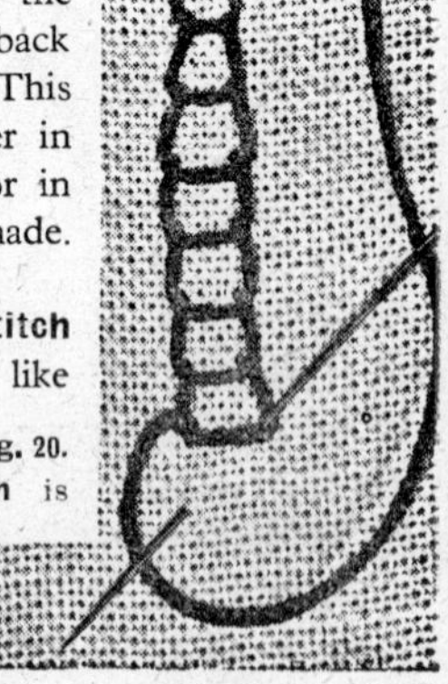

Fig. 20.

Open Chain Stitch is useful for regular broadening ones; the working can be followed from the illustration.

simple chain stitch. It has a tightly plaited appearance and is much firmer. Thick thread should be used and the stitches should be taken close together, otherwise it would be too like simple chain stitch.

Bring the needle out on the traced line, make a short running stitch and bring the needle out again as if a second running stitch is to be made, but, instead, pass the needle through the loop from right to left and insert it alongside the last stitch, bringing it out a little farther along the line. Pass the needle under the chain loop just made and insert the needle against the last stitch, bringing it out a little farther on. In passing the needle under the stitch care must be taken not to take up any ground material. Fig. 19.

Singalese Chain Stitch is worked like open chain except that it is in two colours, one of which is twisted in and out along the edges. Bring a dark thread out at the top of each outer line and let them lie loosely on the material. With the lighter thread work open chain stitch over the dark threads. Bring the needle up on the left side just below the dark thread and a little inside of it. Keep the working thread under the two dark threads and insert the needle on the opposite edge a little inside the darker thread, bringing it out on the left edge, then pull the loop through. The needle is in position for the second stitch. If the dark threads work loose, pull them tight before taking them through to fasten off.

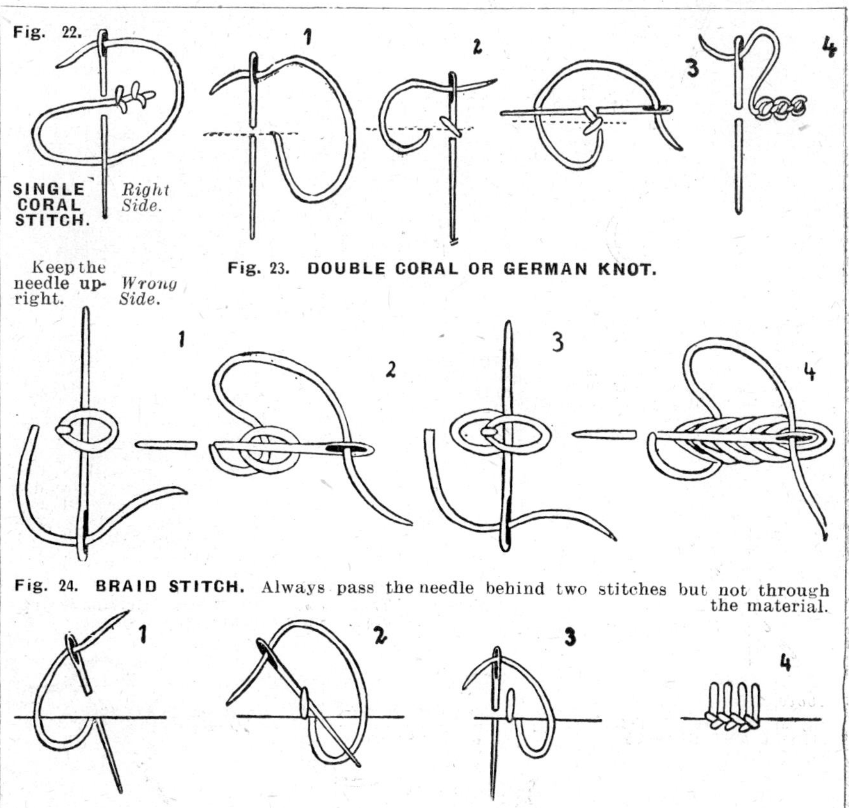

Fig. 22. SINGLE CORAL STITCH.

Fig. 23. DOUBLE CORAL OR GERMAN KNOT.

Fig. 24. BRAID STITCH. Always pass the needle behind two stitches but not through the material.

Fig. 25. PLAITED EDGE STITCH. In Diagram 2 the needle does not go through the material.

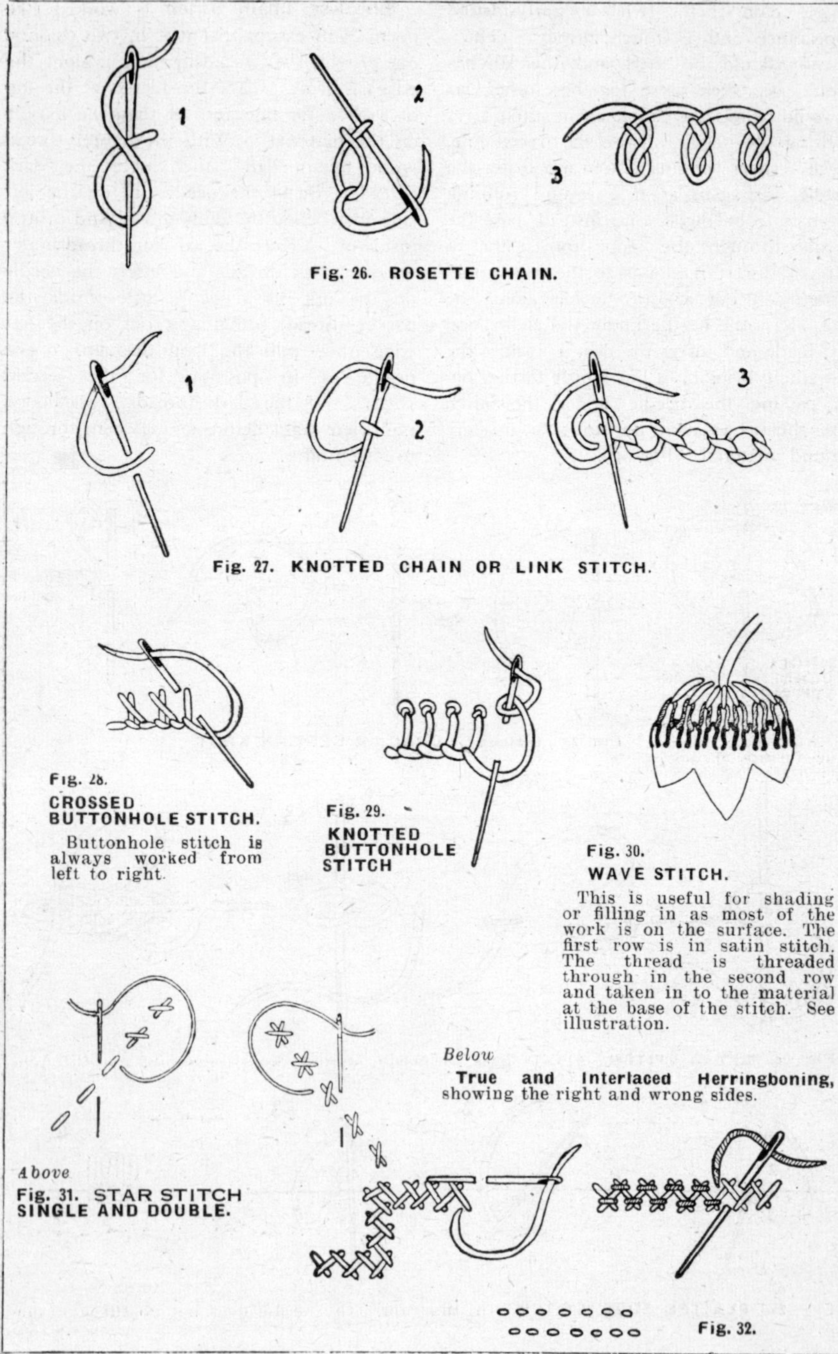

Fig. 26. ROSETTE CHAIN.

Fig. 27. KNOTTED CHAIN OR LINK STITCH.

Fig. 28.
CROSSED BUTTONHOLE STITCH.

Buttonhole stitch is always worked from left to right.

Fig. 29.
KNOTTED BUTTONHOLE STITCH

Fig. 30.
WAVE STITCH.

This is useful for shading or filling in as most of the work is on the surface. The first row is in satin stitch. The thread is threaded through in the second row and taken in to the material at the base of the stitch. See illustration.

Above
Fig. 31. STAR STITCH SINGLE AND DOUBLE.

Below
True and Interlaced Herringboning, showing the right and wrong sides.

Fig. 32.

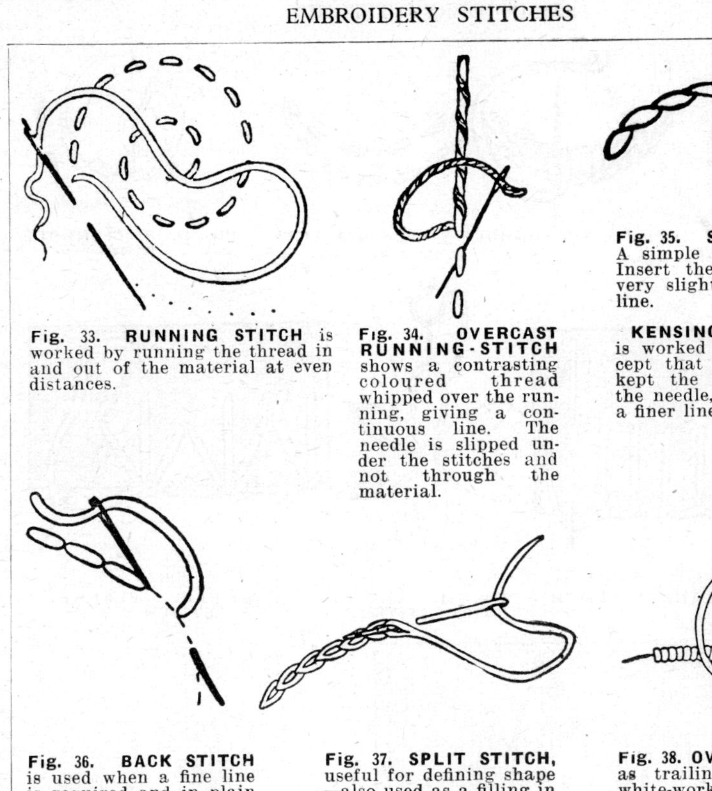

Fig. 33. RUNNING STITCH is worked by running the thread in and out of the material at even distances.

Fig. 34. OVERCAST RUNNING-STITCH shows a contrasting coloured thread whipped over the running, giving a continuous line. The needle is slipped under the stitches and not through the material.

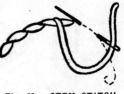

Fig. 35. STEM STITCH. A simple outline stitch. Insert the needle at a very slight angle to the line.

KENSINGTON STITCH is worked the same, except that the thread is kept the other side of the needle, thus forming a finer line.

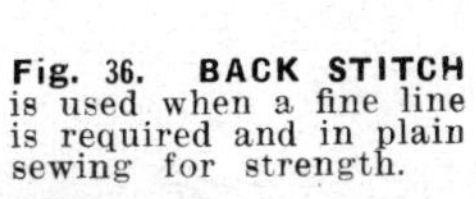

Fig. 36. BACK STITCH is used when a fine line is required and in plain sewing for strength.

Fig. 37. SPLIT STITCH, useful for defining shape—also used as a filling in Old English embroidery.

Fig. 38. OVERCAST, used as trailing outlines in white-work and sewing lace on to lingerie.

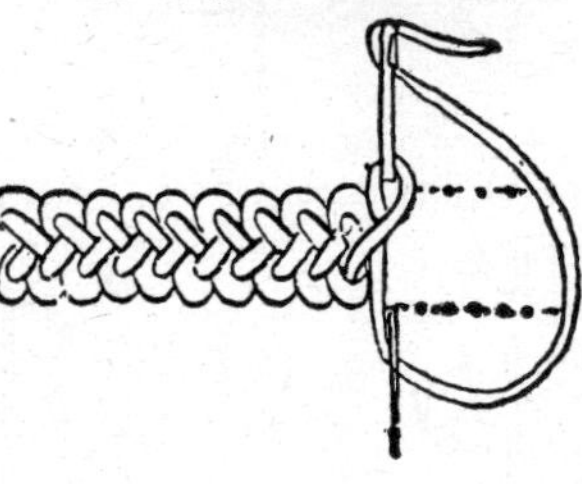

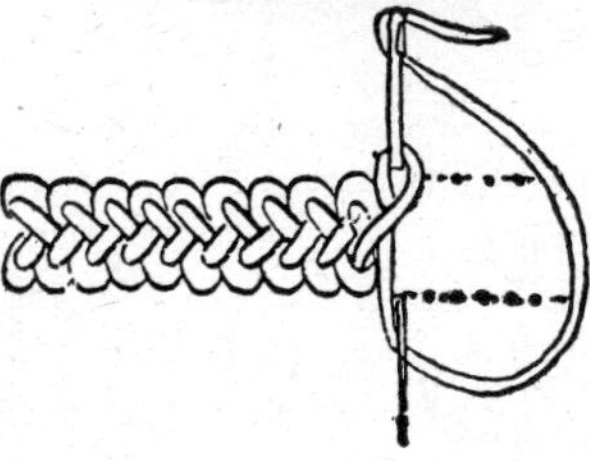

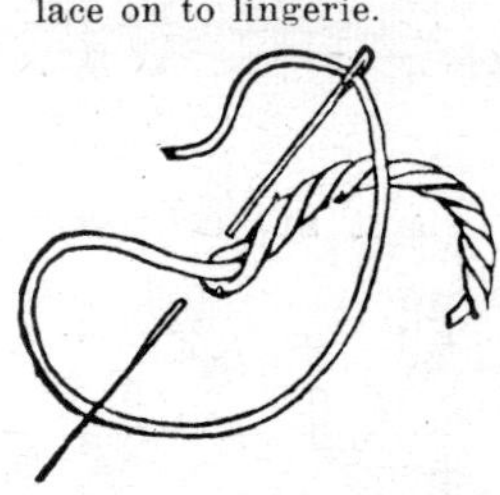

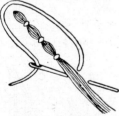

Fig. 39. COUCHING, a quick economical stitch used for outlines, especially in appliqué.

Fig. 40. CABLE PLAIT.

Fig. 41. ROPE STITCH.

Fig. 42. CABLE STITCH.

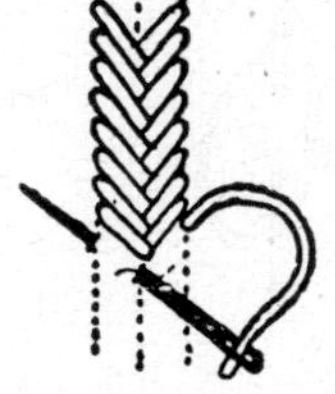

Fig. 43. FISH BONE.

Fig. 44. KNOT STITCH.

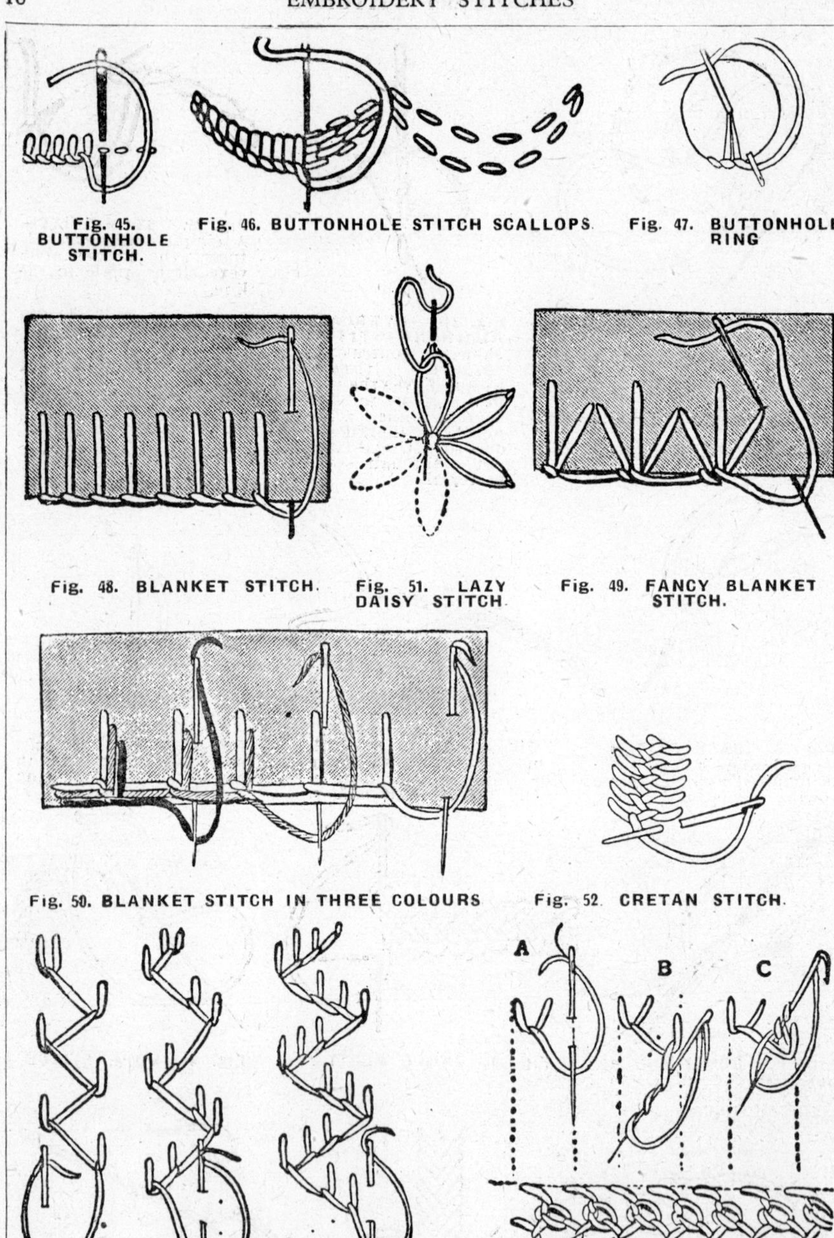

Fig. 45. BUTTONHOLE STITCH.

Fig. 46. BUTTONHOLE STITCH SCALLOPS.

Fig. 47. BUTTONHOLE RING

Fig. 48. BLANKET STITCH.

Fig. 51. LAZY DAISY STITCH.

Fig. 49. FANCY BLANKET STITCH.

Fig. 50. BLANKET STITCH IN THREE COLOURS

Fig. 52. CRETAN STITCH.

Fig. 54. THORN STITCH

Fig. 53. FEATHER STITCH. (Three varieties)

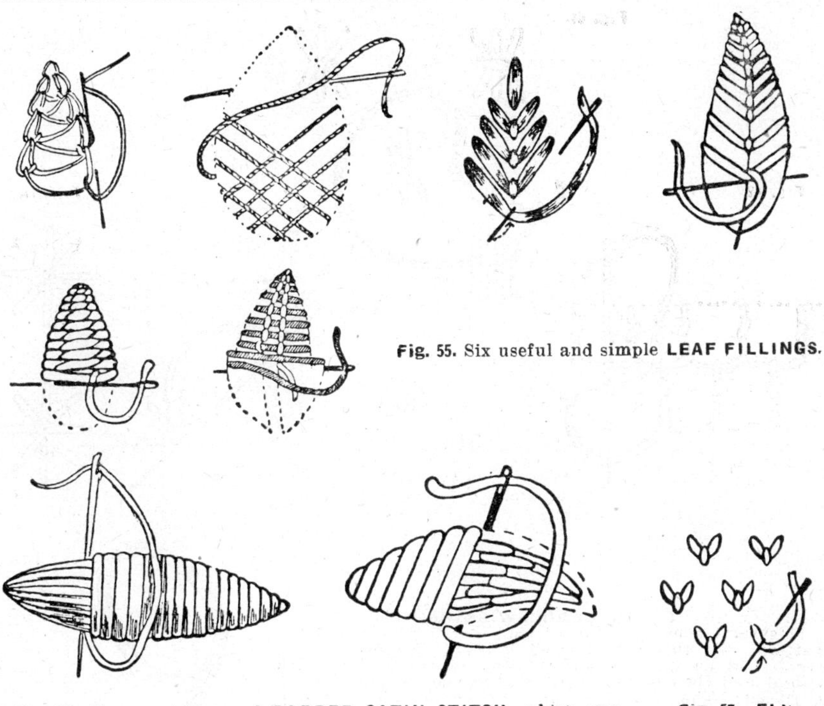

Fig. 55. Six useful and simple **LEAF FILLINGS.**

Fig. 56. Two variations of **PADDED SATIN STITCH,** which can also be used for Leaf Fillings.

Fig. 57. FLY STITCH.

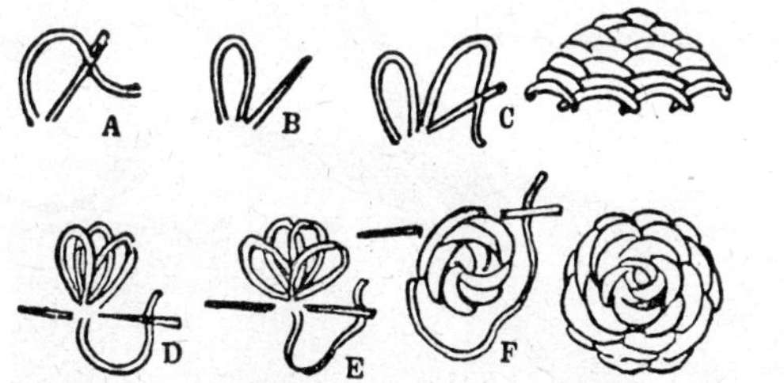

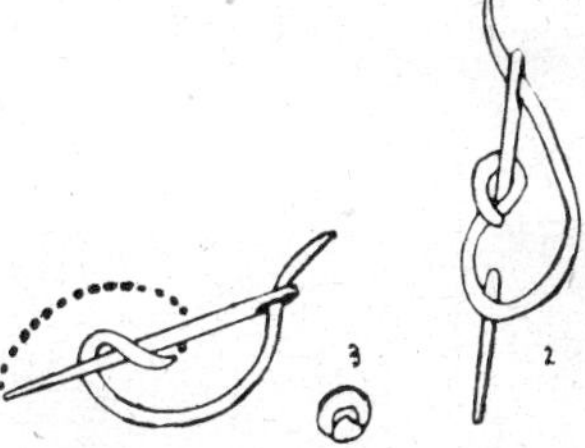

Fig. 58. RAISED OR BANKSIA ROSES. Use firm embroidery silk or cotton. Bring out needle from wrong side, insert again to form first loop, which should be about ½ inch in height, as seen on upper left side of diagram. Bring up needle again, and form a second loop in same way, as shown by diagram, then a third and fourth loop. These form the heart of the rose. Take a small back stitch close to the four loops to hold them securely in place. Now work long stem stitches round centre, as shown in lower part of diagram toward right-hand side, the first row being nearly as high as centre loops. Work next petal row outside the first and a little lower, and so on until rose is finished. On extreme right is seen a completed rose, and above the side view of rose shows how it stands out from material.

Fig. 59. FRENCH KNOT.

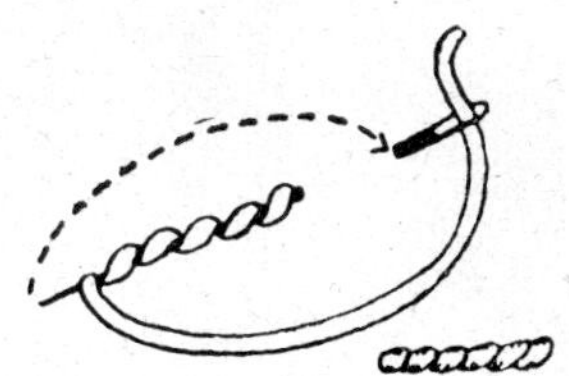

Fig. 60. BULLION STITCH.

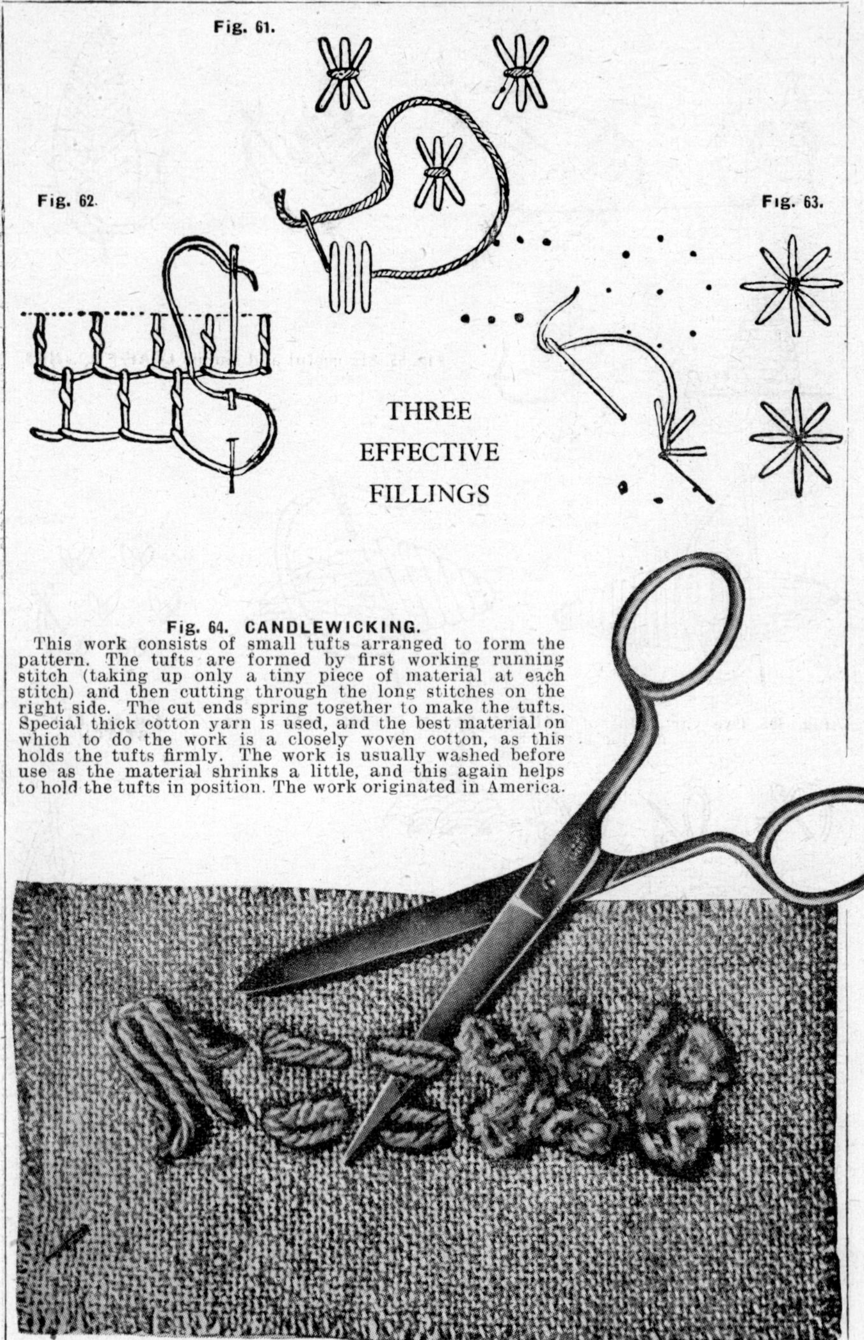

Fig. 64. CANDLEWICKING.

This work consists of small tufts arranged to form the pattern. The tufts are formed by first working running stitch (taking up only a tiny piece of material at each stitch) and then cutting through the long stitches on the right side. The cut ends spring together to make the tufts. Special thick cotton yarn is used, and the best material on which to do the work is a closely woven cotton, as this holds the tufts firmly. The work is usually washed before use as the material shrinks a little, and this again helps to hold the tufts in position. The work originated in America.

APPLIQUÉ

Appliqué is the method of embroidery in which material of one kind or colour is cut and sewn to another, the applied material taking the place of what would otherwise be stitchery. No other form of embroidery is quite so boldly decorative, and yet it is so quick and simple to do that it makes an immediate appeal to all who love to turn out pretty colourful effects, without having very much time to devote to the work.

Most of the colour effect is gained by the use of the superimposed materials, which are cut to form shapes, or the parts of a scene built up from several pieces, and stitchery is only used to hold them to the ground material, connect them together, and decorate them very slightly.

This is not a new idea in needlework, as it was practised in the Middle Ages, long before the many threads which we now have at our disposal were obtainable, yet its fascination persists.

As with other kinds of decorative needlework, appliqué has many variations. Appliqué with Embroidery, Blind Appliqué, Figure Appliqué, and Motif Appliqué are just a few. All the stitches necessary for this type of work will be found in the section "Embroidery Stitches."

Materials for Appliqué Work.—Any kind of material can be used for the groundwork. Firm materials are always best for appliqué work as they leave a clean edge when cut. Satin is apt to roll and has to be handled carefully. Velvet, taffeta, shantung, firm cotton materials, and linen being favourites. Russian crash is also used a great deal, and plush and brocade are well in the running for larger surfaces such as bed-spreads, curtains, etc. Oil baize, or, to use its more popular name, American cloth, Lancaster cloth—a material of the same nature—oiled silk, etc., used for such things as bathroom and kitchen curtains, as well as felt, which can be used for any number of purposes, are particularly suitable for appliqué, as they have the advantage that their non-fray edges need not be completely covered, thus saving a great deal of labour.

The appliquéd parts of the work can be of the same or different material, providing that it is of a similar texture, and that it is firmly woven—this meaning that cotton voile, which is of a slightly "elastic" type of weave, is not the best fabric for use on such a firm ground as velvet

Materials of several kinds can be combined quite well in the same piece of work, as, for example, taffeta on velvet or plush, linen or crash on other firm cotton fabrics, net on silk (particularly suitable for lingerie and other dainty articles), or cretonne on plain linen or on materials such as casement cloth or even art canvas.

The threads used to outline the applied materials vary according to the texture of the latter. Silk and artificial silk can both be used on silk, artificial silk, velvet, plush, and even linen grounds, the thickness suiting the weight of the material.

On cotton foundations, cotton and mercerised threads are suitable, and on linen, mercerised and silk threads. Embroidery wools are also used, and these are particularly effective for really bold designs, or for special effects such as appliquéd animals and birds, when the appearance of fur or feathers is desired.

Cords and braids are also used for outlining the applied materials, but this type of work is more often found in older specimens, when there was not nearly such a range of threads for working.

General hints on Appliqué.—Most of the more general appliqué work can be done in the hand, though for large areas such as bedspreads, curtains and screens, the material is best stretched in a frame. Different varieties of embroidery frames are shown in the introductory chapter of this book. Full instructions for the use of the frames and details for mounting the work will also be found there.

Materials inclined to pull out of shape or fray easily, can be thinly pasted over the back and left to dry before cutting. To

Fig. 1. Examples of net and lace appliqué especially suitable for lingerie

make a good paste for this purpose, take three tablespoonfuls of flour and as much powdered resin as will lie on a shilling. Well mix with half a pint of cold water, pour into an iron saucepan, and stir with an old wooden spoon until it boils. Boil for five minutes, stirring continually to prevent burning, and use when quite cold again.

A number of the finer kinds of material are better for being backed with either very thin, smooth tissue paper, or muslin. This is done in the following manner, with paste made from wheat flour (this drying quicker than any other) well strained beforehand to remove any lumps. Spread the paste on the paper or muslin with a brush, taking care that it is only just liquid enough to make the backing and material adhere neatly together. It must never be wet enough to penetrate to the right side of the material, where it would cause unsightly damp spots to appear.

When the paste has been carefully brushed on to the paper or muslin, lay your material on it, care being taken to keep it flat. Press with a clean cloth or rolling-pin wound in linen, always keeping the way of the material. Do not leave any lumps or bulges between the layers as this will spoil the look of the work. Now cover a clean pastry or drawing-board, or a table that is not in general use, with several layers of uncreased white paper. Lay your lined materials upon this, and cover with several more sheets of the white paper. Lay a second board upon these, and weight it down with weights, stones, or other heavy objects, to act as a press. Leave until it is quite dry.

Even the most delicate of materials treated in this way can be successfully used for appliqué work. Plush and velvet are not in the least injured by the treatment, but in dealing with fabrics of this nature, the side with the pile must be placed on to the white paper, and the lining that has just been pasted, put on to the back and pressed down. If, when the entire work is completed, any parts of the velvet or plush seem to be a little flattened, these can easily be restored by steaming—that is holding the wrong side of the material close to the spout of a fast-boiling kettle, so that the steam penetrates through the material, raising the pile.

When framing up for appliqué, the frame must be quite slack until all the pieces to be applied are sewn in position. The design cut out is first pinned into position and then stitched neatly with small stitches, using a thread to match the piece applied. This being done, tighten the frame and begin working the outline, either by couching, satin stitch or whatever the case may be.

When overlapping occurs in a design leave $\frac{1}{4}$-inch margin on the under piece to allow for giving when the frame is tightened. If the pieces are to be oversewn at the edge, cut out and leave about 1/16 inch beyond the outline.

If the material is thin, then it is as well to sew it down before cutting out. Pin the pieces of the design into place, then backstitch round the outlines, keeping the stitch fairly slack. The edges are cut away afterwards for outlining.

N.B. In all appliqué, work all the pieces that come underneath first, so that there is an unbroken line on top.

Appliqué with Embroidery.—This is the most usual form of appliqué work. In this type, the applied portions of material are held down to the backing with embroidery stitches, and their details also put in in stitchery—as, veins in leaves, the inner petals and stamens of flowers, the features on figures, and so on.

Again, this type of work sub-divides into two methods, both of which give practically the same effect, but are chosen according to the type of design which is selected, or the texture of the materials employed in carrying it out.

First Method.—This is preferable for materials which fray easily. To work, two copies of the same transfer are needed, one for ironing on to the background, and the other for cutting up and transferring to the appliqué materials. The pieces are then roughly cut out and neatly tacked and then buttonhole stitched into place, a close variety of the stitch being used for very fine

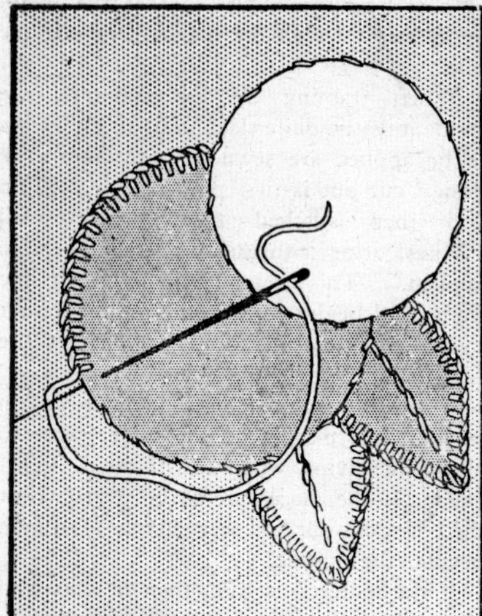

Fig. 2. Showing the second method of working appliqué, only one copy of the design being needed.

materials, or for such fabrics as voile or net, but a wider one for firmer materials, to give a lighter effect, though care must be taken that no rough edges are left to show after the material is cut away.

The edging completed, the top material must be neatly cut away, right up to the purl edge of the buttonholing, with sharp, finely pointed scissors. All detail work must be embroidered in after the cutting out is finished.

Second Method.—By this method, only one copy of the transfer is needed, and this is ironed off into place on the appliqué material. The appliqué portions are then cut out and used as paper patterns for marking the position on the background material. As each piece is cut out, lay it exactly over the corresponding shape on the background material, and pin or lightly tack it into place, taking care that it lies perfectly flat and unwrinkled. To help with this part of the task, especially for large pieces of applied material, it is a good plan to put a thin coating of a fairly dry paste over the centre of the background. Do not put the paste anywhere near the edges of the design, or it will be troublesome to force the needle through later. Also, do not put the paste on to the applied pieces themselves, as it will cause unsightly bulges and puckers.

When everything is in place, buttonhole neatly into position, using matching or contrasting threads (Fig. 2).

Other stitches and methods used for outlining this work are couching, satin stitch, long and short edge, and Japanese gold and cords. Fine cord can also be used on the thicker materials such as silk or velvet, and is especially good for large areas, such as curtains, pram covers, Church work and so on, where a bold effect is desired.

If couching is used, see that the laid thread is thick enough to cover and protect the edges, and for this method you will find that several thicknesses of a moderate thread laid side by side will give a much neater and flatter finish than a single very thick thread. Embroidery wool used double is an excellent medium, while rug wool, a good make of 8-ply, or even fine rug wools are also quite satisfactory, especially for big and bold designs.

Raised satin stitch—i.e. a satin stitch worked over a padding of threads—with a fine silk cord outline is effective for large flowers.

All couching threads, cords, and Japanese

Fig. 3.—A specimen of Blind Applique

gold must be pulled through to the wrong side with a large needle. When the work is completed, these threads are trimmed, and pasted down with a small piece of tissue paper over them to keep them secure. This, naturally, would only apply when the work is to be lined.

Blind Appliqué.—This is the name given to the kind of appliqué which is not embroidered, except for very small details, but which is secured to the background with blind stitch or back stitch. It is an extremely popular form of needlework in the United States, from whence we have learned the art.

It is particularly suited to designs in plain material, and needs no embroidery. It is also easily the best form of appliqué for patterned materials where the charm of decorative stitchery would be lost.

It is the simplest and by far the quickest form of this kind of needlework, and it is therefore the best to use for large pieces, such as curtains, bedspreads, portières, screens, and so on.

Cut out each piece of material to be appliquéd, with narrow turnings, and pin or tack into position, being sure that the pins or tacking threads are not very near the edges, or they will impede the progress of the work when it comes to stitching the portions into place. Use sewing cotton in a matching shade for working, and slip stitch all round on to the foundation, tucking the spare edges under as you go, either with the point of the needle, or with your finger and thumb.

Fig. 3 shows blind appliqué—pinned into position and partly slip stitched. This type of appliqué work must be extremely well pressed after it is finished, or there will be ugly little ridges where the tucked-under edges are not quite level.

Figure Appliqué is done in much the same way, though the stitch most generally used is satin stitch, finely worked. All the

Fig 4.

Appliquéd in simple buttonhole stitch, the details such as eyes, mouth and hair being embroidered

FOR THE NURSERY

under pieces are put on first, care being taken that the satin stitch is kept even, as cord is seldom used as an extra outline. All embroidered details are worked, if possible, when the outline is completed.

Appliqué and embroidery combined can be used to great advantage in the working of coats-of-arms, for, being varied in design, there is good scope for it. Cloth of gold used in small quantities is a favourite background, but it has to be handled carefully on account of fraying.

Motifs in Appliqué. — Ready-made motifs in lace, suitable for use on dainty lingerie, children's clothes and blouses, look quite attractive if applied with either matching or contrasting silk. It is advisable to use matching silk where there are several applied pieces, or a contrasting shade for added effect when only very small pieces are to be laid on (Fig. 1).

Appliqué for Lingerie.—Iron off the selected design on to the material, and at the back of it tack a piece of double net large enough to extend well beyond the edge of the pattern. In some cases it is better to put the net *over* the material, the design showing through for working, as net is more easily cut away invisibly on the right side than material. This, however, should be according to the design, and the worker will quickly discover which is the easiest and most satisfactory method for her to use on her own particular piece of work.

Work the outlines of the design in either overcast or buttonhole stitch—if the latter, arrange the purl edges to come inwards, and slightly pad first by working running stitches along the lines. Any wide parts that are a feature of the design, such as the body of the butterfly in Fig. 1, look most effective if worked in satin stitch.

When the embroidery is completed, cut away the unwanted material on one side and the net that is not required on the other.

When making net hems, such as those

A novel idea for an afternoon tea cloth Gay flower-baskets are appliquéd on to the corners to form pockets to slip the sprigged napkins into.

Fig. 5.

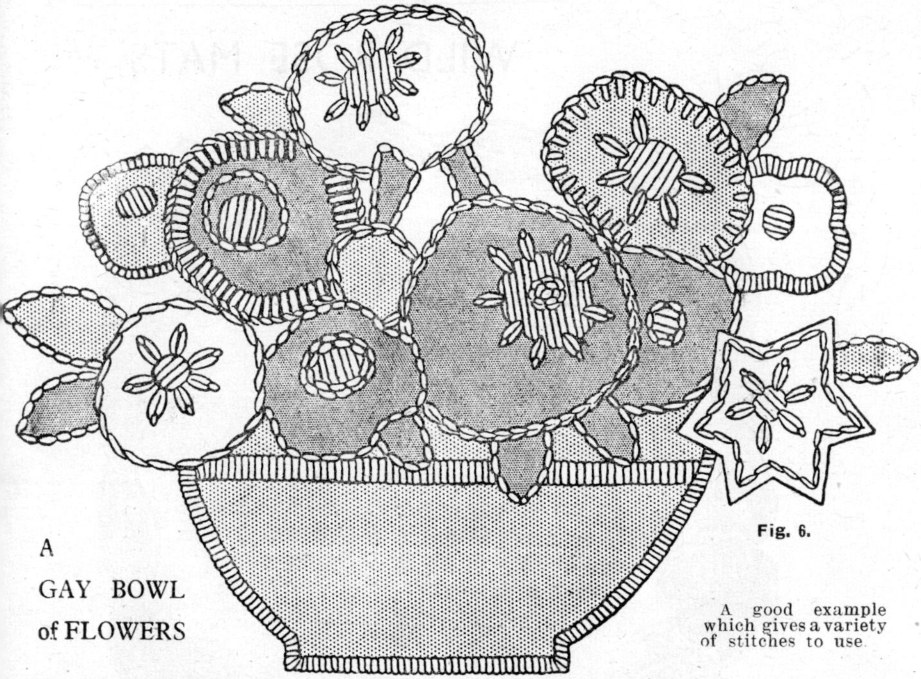

A GAY BOWL of FLOWERS

Fig. 6.

A good example which gives a variety of stitches to use.

featured in the illustrations given in Fig. 1, the net should run with the taut way of it running along the hem, otherwise the latter will stretch out of shape very easily.

Just as a suggestion, écru, or a deep cream shade net always looks better than white. It has a certain "depth" which seems to lend quality and tone to the garment on which it is used, and can look delightful on all pastel shades, and on white itself.

This form of appliqué is most useful on washing silk, artificial silk, lingerie crépe, nylon, crépe de chine, and other lightweight silk materials used for underwear of all kinds.

The second type of appliqué used for lingerie is mostly employed where a dull-backed satin is the material from which the garments are made The applied pieces are merely the reverse (or dull) side of the material, attached to the right (or shiny) side with matching or contrasting silk thread (See also chapter on Punch Work.)

The stitching should be very fine—either buttonholing (this being the best stitch to use where the edge of the appliqué forms the edge of the garment), or close satin stitch.

Design for a Teacloth.—Here baskets of flowers are appliquéd in each corner to hold the tea napkins (Fig. 5).

Materials are $1\frac{5}{8}$ yards of 45-inch linen, $\frac{1}{4}$ yard of 36-inch linen of each of the following, buttercup yellow and marigold orange, and $\frac{1}{8}$ of a yard of tan. Two skeins each of orange, yellow, fawn and green stranded cotton, and three copies of Weldon's Transfer No. 8932, price 4d. each, post free.

Cut a 45-inch square of linen, and make a hem-stitched hem all round. Also cut four 11-inch squares for the napkins. Transfer one of the large baskets on to each corner of the cloth, also the baskets only on to the tan linen, and some flowers on to the yellow and some on to the orange material.

(a)

WILD ROSE MATS

Fig. 7.

Worked in pink and green on linen, this delightful design makes an excellent luncheon mat. (a) and (b) show the first stages of pinning and tacking the applied pieces

(b)

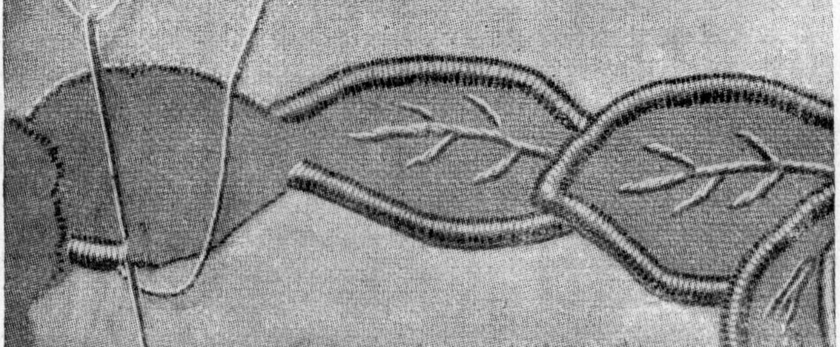

Fig. 8.

Fig. 8 shows the detail for working the leaves The outlines are worked in fine buttonhole stitch, the veins being afterwards worked in stem stitch

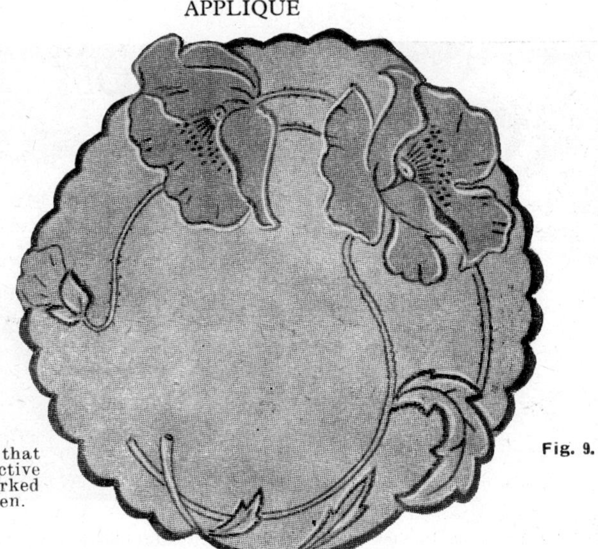

Another uesign that makes an attractive finger-bowl mat, worked in scarlet and green.

Fig. 9.

Using the fawn thread, buttonhole stitch along the top of the basket on the tan linen, with the purl edge outwards. Work the upright lines in couch stitch, the cross lines in straight stitches, and the band round the neck of the basket in two rows of buttonholing fitted one into the other. Now cut out the baskets close up under the edge of the buttonholing, and along the transfer line at the edge. Tack over the baskets on the cloth, and buttonhole from one side of the top, round the bottom to the other, so that the open top of the basket forms a pocket.

Cut out the flowers, tack over those transferred on to the cloth, and work round them in buttonhole stitch of the same colour. Work the centres in French knots and straight stitches; the leaves in satin stitch and the stems in overcast stitch directly on the linen with green. Work two rows of buttonhole stitch fitted one into the other with fawn for the handles, and embroider the bow in satin stitch, shading it with yellow and orange.

For the napkins, arrange groups of the flowers in one corner of each, about $\frac{3}{4}$ of an inch in from the edge, and pencil in some stalks. Work flowers in the same way as those on the cloth, then cut round the top of each group, and finish the napkins with a narrow hemstitched hem, as seen in the illustration.

A Cushion Cover or Table Runner.—Bowls of flowers are always good subjects for appliqué work, as they provide a splendid chance of using up odd scraps of gaily coloured material. The design comes from Weldon's Transfer No. 17024, price 1s., post free.

The design looks attractive in felt appliqués, stitched down with gaily coloured wools (Fig. 6).

Coloured canvas, hessian or heavy linen makes a splendid background, and on to this (having previously cut it to the size required), iron the transfer. Should the surface be very rough, however, transfer the design by the pounce method, or by tracing with carbon paper. Next, trace each flower and the bowl separately on to pieces of coloured felt, and tack these over the corresponding parts on the ground material.

Work round the outlines in buttonhole stitch, chain stitch, satin stitch or back stitch. The flower centres are in the same

Fig. 10.
A delightful three-piece Duchesse Set, attractively embroidered with inlay work, built up from the simple outlines shown on the next page.

stitches, and lazy-daisy stitches are added to make stamens.

The material for the bowl should be cut to shape and tacked over the transferred outline on the background. It should then be invisibly hemmed, and, to make it stand out well, the edges should be stitched over with wool of a contrasting shade, either in buttonhole stitch with the purl edge outwards, or in close overcasting.

Appliqué should always be well pressed on the wrong side under a damp cloth after it is completed.

Wild Rose Dinner Mats.—Materials needed are: 1 yard of cream coloured linen 54 inches wide, $\frac{3}{8}$ yards of green and rose-pink linen 36 inches wide, 14 skeins of green and six of pink stranded cotton to match the linens exactly, one skein of black and one of gold.

Trace the design on to the cream linen, then trace the flowers and leaves. Cut out the leaves, pin, and then tack them into position on to those corresponding on the cream linen, as shown in Fig. 7a. Sew round the edges in green cotton to match, as they come under the flowers. Fix the roses in position and sew round them Diagram 7b shows the leaves being tacked into position. Take two threads of the green silk in the needle, start working a close buttonhole stitch round all the leaves that come underneath and then work those that come on top (Fig. 8).

Work a vein down the centre of the leaves in stem stitch. Work the roses in the same way. The rose centres are worked by taking one thread of black and one of gold and working a few lines in the centre, with French knots, as the photograph shows clearly.

Press the work well and cut round the edges with a sharp pair of scissors. Work the centre and small mats in the same way.

Finger Bowl Mat worked in organdie. The work is prepared in the same way as above—a pale cream organdie being used. Scarlet and green are used for the poppy mat.

Pin and tack the material for the flowers and leaves into position. Work round the flowers in satin stitch except on the outside edge, where buttonhole stitch should be used. The stems and centres are then worked. Using silk on the organdie gives added life to the set.

Sabrina Work.—This consists of cutting from coloured velvets, satins, cloth or washing materials, whole flowers, single petals, leaves or conventional patterns.

These are then attached to coloured cloth or linen backgrounds with wide-apart buttonhole stitch, such parts of the design too small to be cut and appliquéd being worked direct on to the background, using either chain or stem stitch.

Bedspreads, curtains, borders, portières and so on look most effective in this type of work.

First select the design—choosing small fruit, leaves or flowers with tendrils. Iron it off into position on the material, and also on to thin cardboard. Cut out the cardboard shapes. The materials to be applied are then cut by these shapes, or, if preferred, they may be cut direct by ironing off the various flowers, etc., from the transfer on to the respective fabrics.

Lightly tack each motif on to its correct position on the background material, and using a thread which matches each particular motif in colouring, attach it to the foundation with wide-apart buttonhole stitch. Work tendrils, etc., with silk in chain stitch, and finish flower centres with French knots or satin stitch, as the size and type of the work demands.

Inlay Work.—Inlaid, or Inlay Work is yet another form of appliqué, and in ancient times it was greatly used for church hangings and ecclesiastical vestments. Nowadays it is mostly seen on the Continent, particularly in France, from which country the modern version seems to have originated.

In reality, it is a reversed form of appliqué —instead of the design being cut out and applied to a background, the ground fabric is cut away to a definite pattern, to show a different coloured lining beneath. In more complicated pieces, both background and pattern are cut out and laid on an *entire* foundation, and as this most nearly conforms to the original idea of the work, we will deal with that method first.

The outline which is used to build up the design of the Duchesse Set given on the previous page.

Fig. 11.

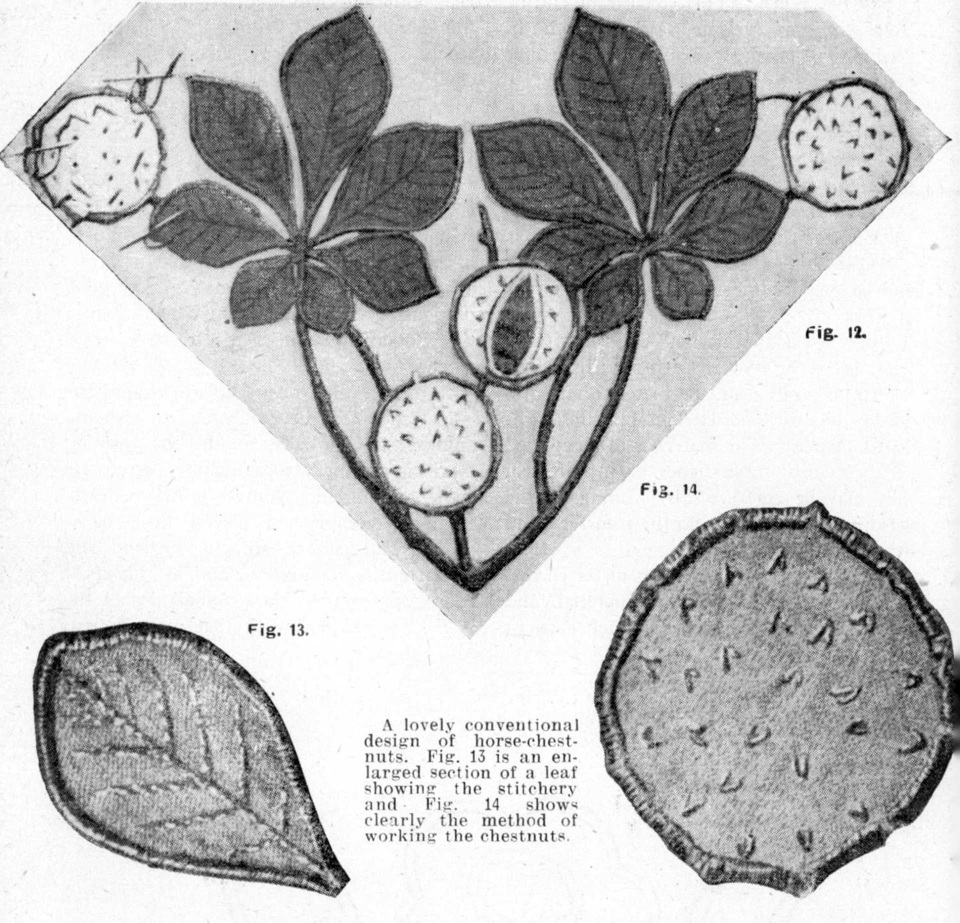

A lovely conventional design of horse-chestnuts. Fig. 13 is an enlarged section of a leaf showing the stitchery and Fig. 14 shows clearly the method of working the chestnuts.

Start work by stitching a piece of holland or stout linen in a frame, to form the background. This may be removed when the work is completed, or, if required, may be left to give extra strength. The materials for the background and pattern must first be cut out, and it is a good plan to cut these together as they have to fit in much in the same way as the pieces of a jig-saw puzzle are joined together.

The fabrics for this type of work must be of a texture which will not easily fray, leather being responsible for much of the old-time work, though it is little used to-day. If the materials are of different textures, the thinner should be backed with fine linen or stout muslin to make it equal in strength to the thicker.

After the materials are cut out, they are placed in position on the prepared holland, and tacked to it very firmly. All edges are then joined by overcast stitch, which must not, of course, be allowed to penetrate the foundation.

When all the pieces have been joined, the stitches must be covered with a finishing cord or braid, and then removed from the backing if desired.

A Duchesse Set in Inlay Work.—For the amateur who is anxious to try this form of needlework, we suggest that the

A really lovely design for Inlay work taken from the Victoria and Albert Museum. The ground is red plush, and the appliqué was originally tinsel cloth, with the centres left in plush. The outlining is in gold couching.

simplified version be experimented with first.

Designs of a fairly conventional type are most suited to Inlay Work, and care should be taken to select those which do not depend on a variety of colouring for their attraction. Simple, straightforward outlines are a great essential when choosing them, as intricate twists and turns are exceedingly difficult to cut out satisfactorily, and the finished work is apt to look "bitty" and ragged.

We suggest, therefore, that the beginner starts on a design such as is depicted in Fig. 10, building up a delightful pattern from the outlines of flowers and leaves in Fig. 11—which can be traced off with carbon paper, arranged either according to individual choice, or as illustrated, to make an attractive table runner.

Materials needed are: 1½ yards of natural-coloured linen or fine crash 18 inches wide, ½ a yard of the orange colour in the same width, as well as two skeins each of stranded cotton in orange and bright green.

The runner should be just under 54 inches long, and between 13 and 18 inches wide, according to requirements.

Cut the orange linen in half, and line the two ends of the runner only, by cutting it ½ an inch less in width, so that the ends of the natural-coloured linen can be neatly

AN HISTORIC EXAMPLE

An old piece of Inlay appliqué from the Victoria and Albert Museum. It is worked in green and stone colour with deep yellow couching thread round the edges.

Fig. 16.

turned over its raw edges. The edges of the runner should be all turned in and tacked down.

Build up your design from the pieces given in this chapter, trace it on to the natural linen with carbon paper, placing it so that the outermost point of the design is at least $1\frac{1}{2}$ inches in from the edge of the runner at all points, though more plain linen can be allowed if desired.

To work the inlay, with the point of a very sharp pair of scissors, poke a hole through one of the leaves, piercing the natural linen only. Now cut away the natural linen inside the outline of the leaf. Before cutting away any more of the design, roughly overcast the natural-hued outlines to the orange material which is revealed beneath. This overcasting can be quite widely spaced, but it is a necessary precaution as the linen edges may begin to fray before the embroidery is begun.

The embroidery itself is done in close buttonhole stitch, keeping the purl edge along the cut outline, and making the stitches the depth of the double lines on the design.

When cutting out a flower, pin or tack down the centre which is to remain, and cut away all round the outer edge of the centre.

Overcast both flower outline and centre before beginning to embroider, and work the centre with the buttonhole stitch to the outside. This can then be filled in with French knots or satin stitch (the latter not being quite so dainty in appearance as the knots). The flowers and centres are, of course, buttonholed with the orange cotton, and three threads in the needle are sufficient for the work throughout.

The turned-in and tacked edges of the runner can be machine hem-stitched in either orange or green, or they can be given a buttonhole border, either in one of the colours, or a combination of the two —for example, green buttonhole stitches ½ an inch in height and ½ an inch apart, between which are orange buttonhole stitches, ¼ of an inch in height.

Take out all tacking threads and press the work on the wrong side over a thick ironing blanket. The rest of the runner should afterwards be pressed, a damp cloth being used if necessary, to remove any creases caused during the process of embroidery.

For Fig. 21 the work is tacked carefully together all round the outside edges of the design. Couch round the outline with several strands of filoselle and stitch down with a thread of contrasting colour. The same colour may also be used to stitch it down if preferred.

In the method shown here, the material is cut away afterwards. This is quite good for buttonhole or satin stitched edges, but is not to be recommended for couching if there is to be any washing done to the article, as tacking under the couching is not strong enough for hard wear. The method explained below is more suitable for that.

For Fig. 22 put in tacking lines to keep the leaf flat and in the exact position required, then with cotton matching the appliquéd piece, hem the edges invisibly, making no turnings, and finish with slanting satin stitch. In Fig. 23 the same method has been used, but instead of

Fig. 17.

Another section of the Museum piece shown on the opposite page. With a little adaptation this would make a glorious design for a cushion or Portière.

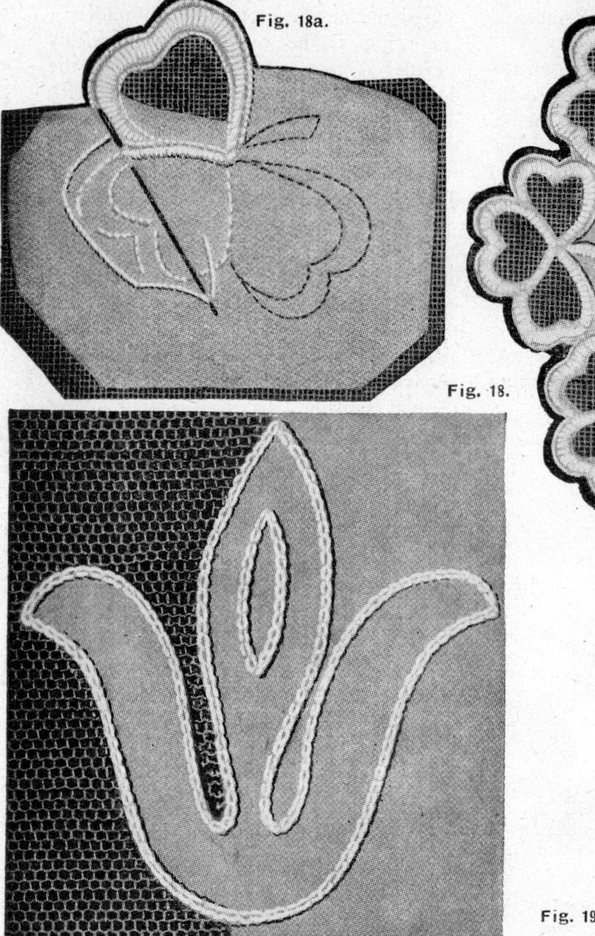

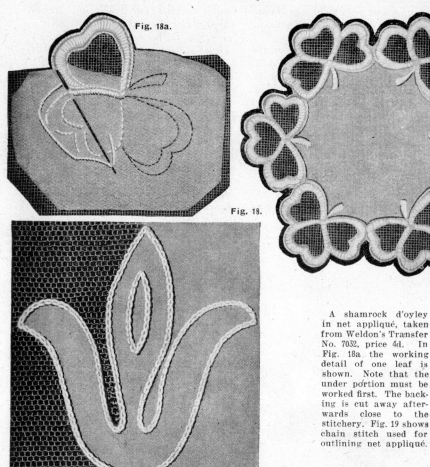

Fig. 18a.

Fig. 18.

Fig. 19.

A shamrock d'oyley in net appliqué, taken from Weldon's Transfer No. 7032, price 4d. In Fig. 18a the working detail of one leaf is shown. Note that the under portion must be worked first. The backing is cut away afterwards close to the stitchery. Fig. 19 shows chain stitch used for outlining net appliqué.

plain satin stitch, it is satin stitched over cord.

In Fig. 12 a corner of a conventional design of chestnuts and leaves in appliqué, is given. Fig. 13 shows a leaf which is buttonholed round the edge with the veining in stem stitch. Fig 14 shows one of the chestnuts in actual size. The edge is buttonholed and the centre is filled in with fly stitch. The open sections of the chestnuts are worked in white satin stitch. The stems are worked in very close satin stitch in brown.

Appliqué on Net.—For this kind of appliqué the design is outlined in chain stitch on white or coloured opaque material, the outside of the chain stitch being carefully cut away after the work is finished, leaving the design in relief on the net. When bold and clear designs are chosen the effect is particularly good. Appliqué on net can be used for borders and insertions on curtains, bedspreads, cushions, etc. It is also suitable as dress trimming, for which a finer net is used.

First trace the design on to firm white calico or stiff paper, and if the lines are not distinct enough, go over them in Indian ink and leave to dry. Tack the net over the design smoothly and firmly, then tack the lawn in position on top. The

Fig. 20.

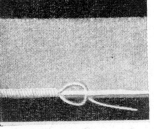

Above is a really lovely leaf design in net appliqué worked in chain stitch. Cretonne may be used instead of lawn, by cutting out the design and appliquéing it to the net in the same way. Below is one method of couching, by tacking down several threads of Filoselle in a contrasting colour, while Figs. 22 and 23 show two more ways of appliqué. Fig. 22 on the left, shows slanting satin stitch over tacking, and Fig. 23, below, shows close satin stitch over a fine cord.

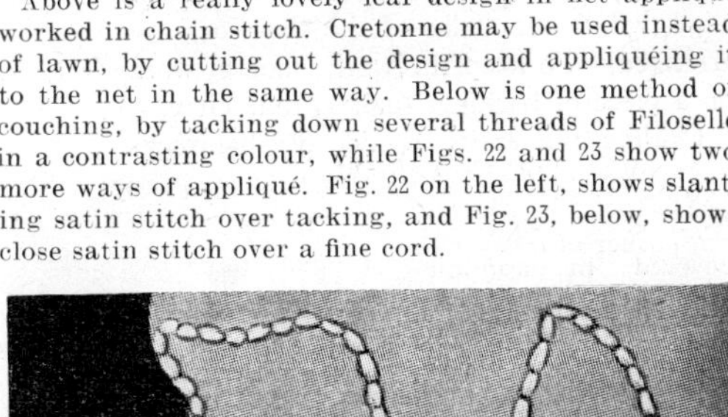

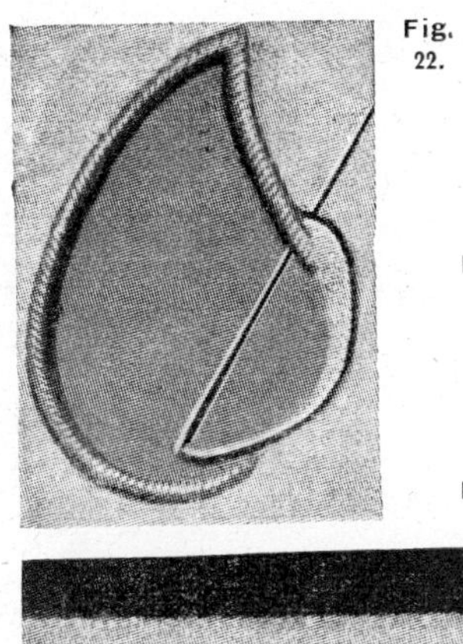

Fig. 22.

Fig. 21.

Fig. 23.

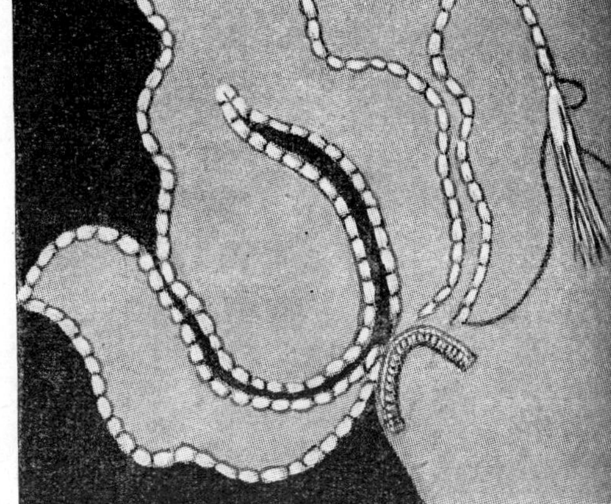

outlines of the design should show clearly through both lawn and net.

Then with a medium-sized mercerised cotton outline the whole design and all important markings in chain stitch.

When the work is finished, take a sharp pair of scissors and carefully cut away the lawn round the outside of the design.

Fig. 19 shows a small piece of appliqué net in process of working and the opaque material being cut away.

D'Oyley in net appliqué.—The method of working this is very simple when applied to punch worked designs because, instead of working the design or background in punched work, the net can be placed over and, when embroidered, the material cut away from underneath. Strong washing net is used, of round mesh, or the coarser square fillet mesh net with linen

For Fig. 18 lawn and fine washing net are used and medium-sized white embroidery cotton. First of all trace your design on the lawn. Lay the net smoothly over the entire design and tack the net and lawn together, tacking the net slightly beyond the extreme outlines of the design as in Fig. 18a. This also shows how to arrange the net over the design on the lawn with a second row of tacking along the inner edge, where the stalks of the shamrock are arranged. To keep the work smooth, work on a piece of backing, such as toile cirée.

Outline the entire border of shamrocks in small running stitches, taking them through both lawn and net, and then work in double buttonhole stitch. Work the right and left sections of the shamrocks first, starting at the base of the stalk and working up to where the side section joins the central portion, which is worked last, starting at the base of the stalk and working all round it to the starting point.

When all the leaves are finished, the net must be cut away from the centre of the d'oyley very carefully on the right side, just under the purl edge of the stitchery. Work the shamrock stalks in satin stitch, taking the stitches across from side to side. With a pair of lace scissors and holding the d'oyleys on the wrong side, cut the lawn carefully away from under the shamrock leaves and both net and lawn beyond the outer purl edge of the d'oyley.

Fig. 24.

A corner of a coverlet covered in appliqué motifs, in gay red, yellows and greens, on a pale yellow ground. The tendrils are embroidered in fine black thread. By courtesy of the Victoria and Albert Museum

ASSISI WORK

A Brief History of Assisi Work.—Assisi, that little Italian village immortalised by the memory of St. Francis, is also renowned for its beautiful embroidery, the charm of which has persisted through the ages.

For century after century, the pious sisters flocked to the secluded convents of this peaceful retreat, and following the example of Chiara degli Scifi, divided their days between work and prayer. Whilst their gentle hearts murmured silent Te Deums, their clever and seemingly tireless fingers fashioned exquisite pieces of linen embroidery for use in the churches, work which has character and charm entirely its own.

Many of the present-day Italian churches still proudly retain in their sacristies, permeated with incense and mystery, innumerable treasures of ecclesiastical linen worked by these nuns of early times, and the embroidery is so delicately perfect as to appear fashioned by the hands of fairies rather than those of mortal women!

The beautiful legend of St. Francis supplied a great source of inspiration for these humble workers, so it is not strange to find that many of their wonderful pieces of work bear motifs and characters taken from incidents and episodes in the life of the Saint, similar to those depicted in the frescoes and mural decorations of Giotto and Simon Martini.

For scores of years the little village of Assisi jealously guarded its legacy of art, happy in its peace, proud in its memories, and rich in its poverty—for, in the skilful needlework of those unknown religious sisters, it had created, and was still creating, a perfect manifestation of beauty.

But as time went on, the peasants began to introduce touches of the same kind of embroidery into their homes and on to their personal apparel, and women, finding that it gave them an outlet for their energies together with a real chance of earning money and thus helping their men-folk in the struggle for existence, which, in that poor neighbourhood, was continuous, studied the art of this kind of embroidery with great diligence.

One of the nobility, the Contessa di Brazza, who foresaw with great clarity of vision that Italy as a whole needed to be roused from the welter of worldliness into which it had sunk, urged on and encouraged the women in their new venture, kindling in them the desire to create beauty in needlework, which should be handed down to the generations to come.

Each town created a type of work peculiar to itself: and Assisi, following the example of her sister towns, developed the kind of embroidery that had been her own for long centuries.

A band of women, presided over by a Madame Maria Bartocci Rossi, who was ably assisted by her daughter, Madame Chiarina Rossi Buzi, delved among the archives of famous old patrician families, searched tirelessly in the ancient convents, and in the sacristies of the principal churches as well as the tiny country chapels, and copied with absolute precision the primitive designs of the thirteenth and fourteenth centuries, characterised by their extreme simplicity of line, and others of the fifteenth and sixteenth centuries, which had developed a more perfect type of beauty from the earliest specimens.

The linen they used was woven in the palest shade of ivory, to resemble that used in earlier days, and there was no breaking away from the traditional colours of past years—scarlet and blue—nor was the plan of these newer designs allowed to lose its charming simplicity of character.

Thus, step by step, the secret of this wonderful work spread gradually out of Assisi, out of Italy, and into the world of which the originators knew so little.

Now it is found almost everywhere, and although nowadays no one can afford to devote the time and patience to it as did those nuns of Assisi, yet, in effect, the work is none the less beautiful.

A Description of the Nature of Assisi Work.—In the sheer simplicity of design lies one of the chief charms of Assisi work, for, of course, the people who first created it had little opportunity for studying draughtsmanship, and sought their inspiration from the primitive drawings which decorated the churches, in most of which the lovely legend of St. Francis was depicted in one or other of its many and varied forms.

The embroidery was done entirely by the counted thread, so that the outlines were necessarily very simple, a characteristic to which we still conform to-day.

The design is merely outlined, and then the background filled in with cross-stitch.

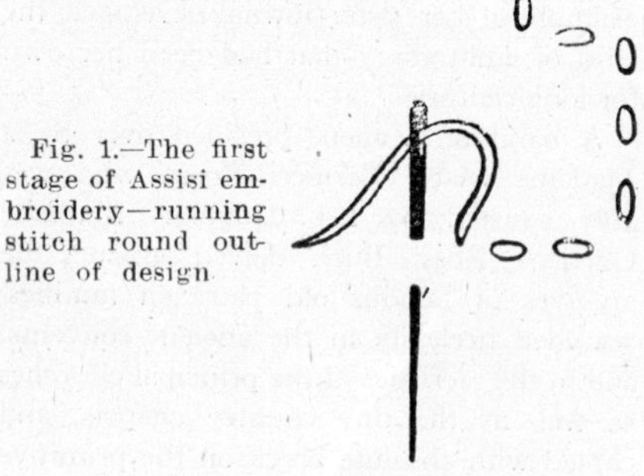

Fig. 1.—The first stage of Assisi embroidery—running stitch round outline of design

Materials for Assisi Work.—Now, as in former days, this type of embroidery looks its best on deep ivory or cream linen, and it should be worked with cotton threads in scarlet and china blue, though orange and black are a combination which are frequently met with in more modern pieces.

It is easiest to work this embroidery from a chart.

Method of Working the Embroidery.—There are only three simple parts to the working of Assisi embroidery, the outlining of the pattern making the first two, and the filling in of the background the third.

The outline has the appearance of backstitch, but it is in reality two rows of running stitch, the first going alternately over and under two threads, and the second

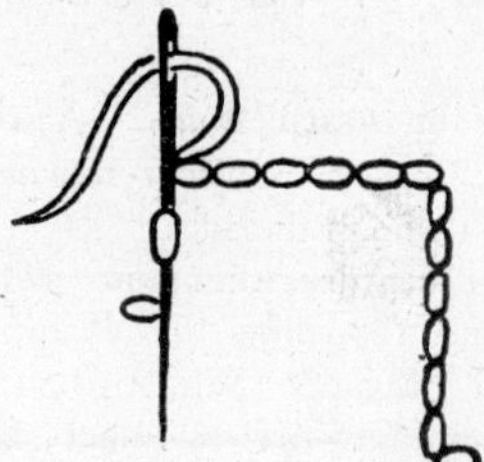

Fig. 2.—The second stage—a second row of running stitch filling in the spaces left by the first row, to make continuous line.

working back and filling in the spaces, so that a continuous line is formed.

When this part is completed, the linen round the pattern is filled in with cross-stitch, half of each stitch being made first, as in Needlework-Tapestry (see Fig. 20, page 300) and then the crossing stitches being worked on top, care being taken that all the stitches go the same way, in order to preserve the uniformity of the work when completed.

A Table Runner in Assisi Work.—The handsome design on this lovely runner is typical of Assisi work, the Dragon Rampant being a very favourite subject, and appearing in any number of the old pieces.

Heavy cream art linen, sold in widths of 18, 36, 45, and 54 inches, is used to make the runner, which should be 50 inches long, and for which ½ a yard of the 54-inch width is sufficient. In this case, orange and black are really decorative, but for those who prefer to adhere firmly to the old-time tradition, blue and red is equally attractive.

Mark out the centre of each end of the runner with a tacking thread, then outline the pattern in the double running stitch, as previously described. The edge of each little square represents one stitch (or two

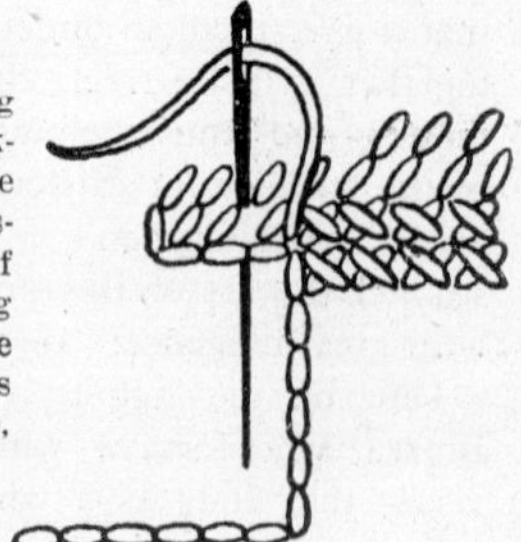

Fig. 3.—Filling in the background of the work with cross-stitch—half of each stitch being made first, the crossing stitches worked on top, all one way.

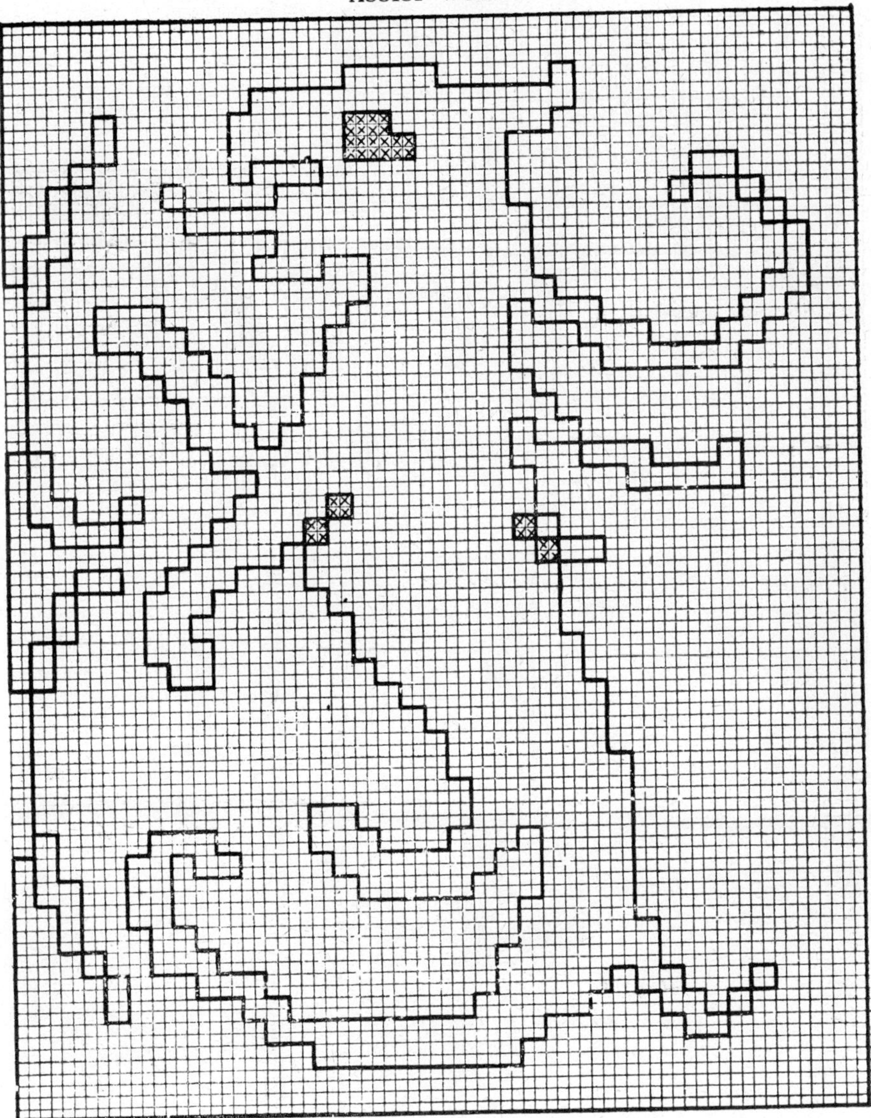

This chart shows half the design for the Table Runner described on the previous page—the opposite side being worked in reverse, so that the Dragons are facing each other.

threads of the linen), and the background squares each equal one cross to go over two threads in height and width. You will find it perfectly simple to follow the design from the clear chart given here.

When the embroidery is completed, finish the sides of the runner with a narrow hem, and the ends with a wider one. Press the work on the wrong side under a damp cloth.

This design is also effective on cushions and chair-backs, while those who have only a little time to devote to the work, will find the bordering alone most attractive on

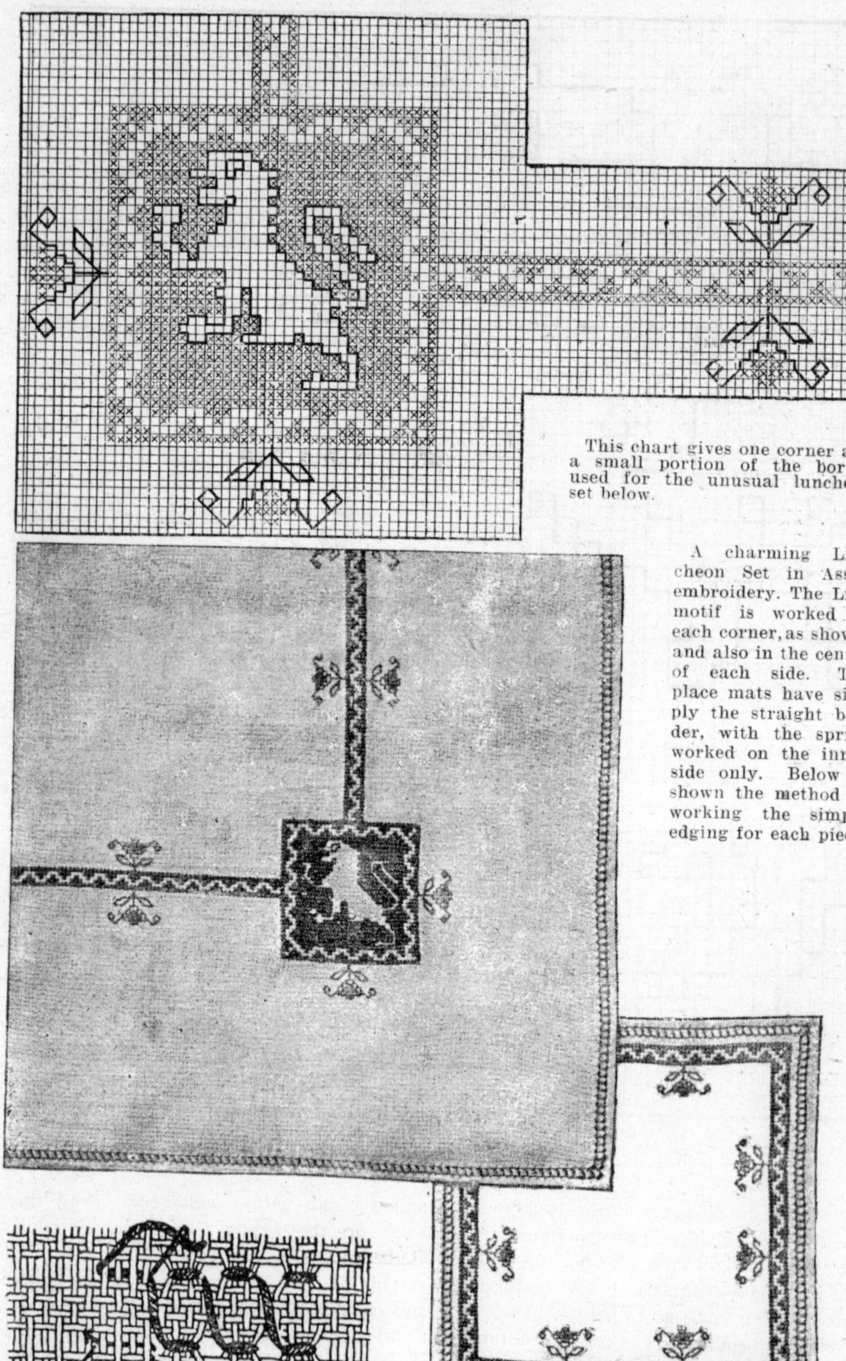

This chart gives one corner and a small portion of the border used for the unusual luncheon set below.

A charming Luncheon Set in Assisi embroidery. The Lion motif is worked in each corner, as shown, and also in the centre of each side. The place mats have simply the straight border, with the sprigs worked on the inner side only. Below is shown the method of working the simple edging for each piece.

An attractive Table Runner with ends of Assisi embroidery.

runners, cloths, and even for the lower edges of plain cream linen casement curtains.

A Luncheon Set.—In this example the design is left plain and the background filled in with cross-stitch, whilst dainty little sprigs are worked at intervals in back-stitch and cross-stitch combined.

The original set was fashioned in a deep cream hand-made linen, and the embroidery done with untwisted embroidery cotton in a deep shade of china blue, the thickness of the working thread being equal to that of the thread of the material.

When following the chart, each cross must be made over two threads in height and width, and the back stitches which make the little sprigs are also worked over two threads.

The centre piece is 31 inches square, and

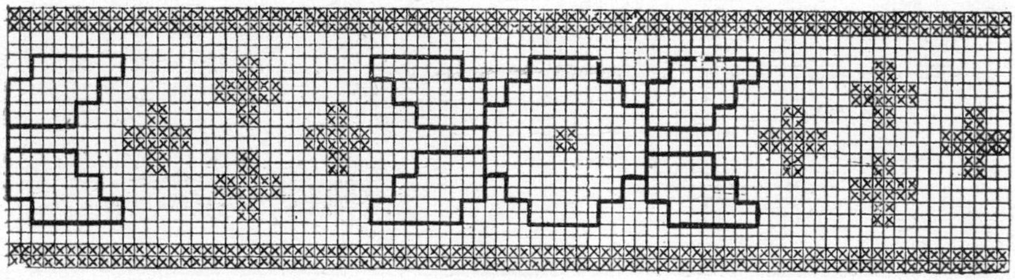

A section of the chart needed for working the border of the Table Runner shown above

A reproduction of a large piece of Assisi embroidery which, although it appears so complicated, is, in reality, simplicity itself—worked in the easy manner fully described in this section—the main motifs merely outlined, and the background filled in with ordinary cross-stitch.

has the lion motif worked at each corner and at the centre of each side, and these motifs are connected with the simple cross-stitch border decorated with sprigs, worked as previously mentioned.

The same border is worked round the 7-inch square mats but with the sprigs on the inner side only. Half an inch should be allowed for turnings, and the narrow border worked $5\frac{1}{4}$ inches from the raw edge on the centre piece, and about $\frac{7}{8}$ of an inch on the place mats.

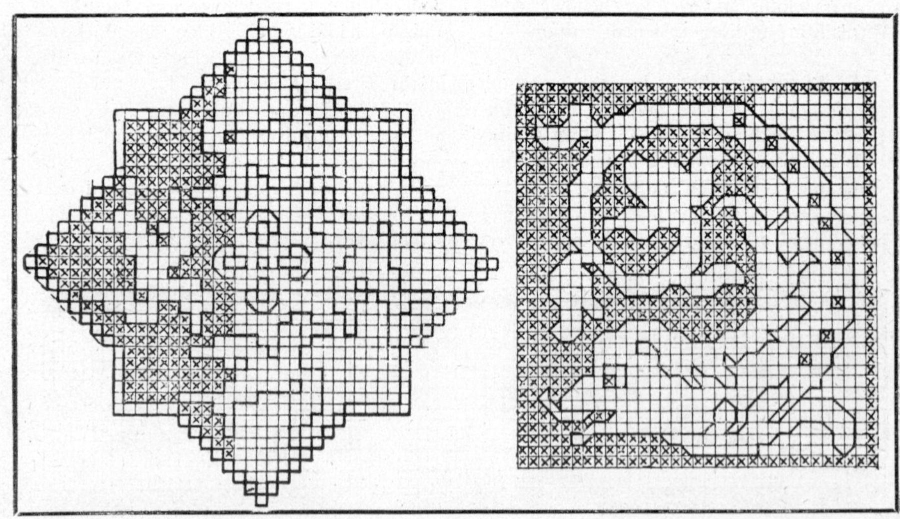

Two simple motifs for Assisi work, showing how easy they are to plan. The originals were drawn on graph paper with ten squares to the inch.

Fig. 4.—Four borders for Assisi Work.

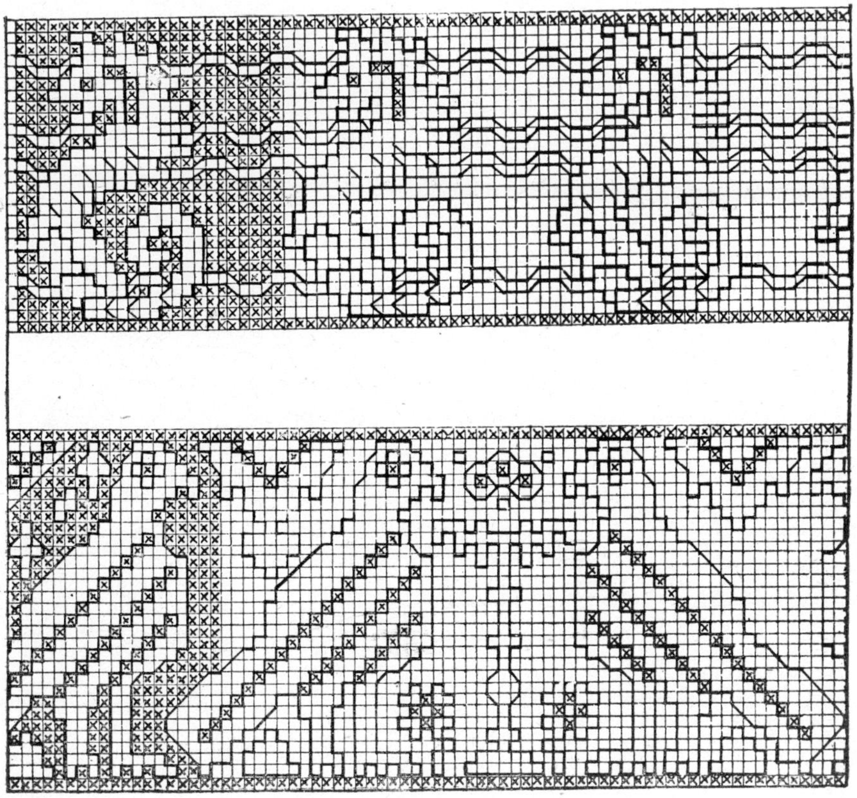

The simple edging round each piece is made by drawing out two threads of the linen, leaving four threads between along each side, then working in the stitch shown in the diagram along the spaces and across the threads between. An $\frac{1}{8}$ of an inch wide hem finishes the edges of both the centre piece and the place mats.

Some Examples of Charts for Assisi Work.—The simple little illustrations in Fig. 4 show how to build up easy-to-follow charts from which to work attractive Assisi embroidery.

They are shown drawn on ordinary graph paper which has eight squares to the inch, and it is easy to see what a simple matter it is to work out designs of this nature, according to individual choice, remembering all the time that simplicity should be the keynote of the pattern, and that the introduction of animals—particularly lions, dragons and griffins, and birds of the eagle variety—are most in keeping with the traditional nature of this type of work.

Four simple little borders are shown, and these can be used to link up either of the simple motifs, or others can be planned to suit the particular piece of work which is being embroidered.

In each case, a part of the background has been finished with crosses, to show just how it will appear when worked—the actual pattern left plain, and the background filled in with simple cross-stitch, as has already been fully described in the preceding pages.

BEAD WORK

This craft, which was so popular in the mid-Victorian period, can be divided into roughly five classes: needle and thread bead work, which is used for decorating canvas, making necklaces and evening bags; knitted and crochet work, which is used for the same purposes; loom work by which some necklaces, bracelets and borders for table-runners, etc., are made, and lastly, novelty bead work under which heading come the bead embroiderings on dresses, evening cloaks, etc., and wooden-bead table-mats.

Materials for Bead Work.—Originally the beads used for dress ornamentation were more like jewels than the type of bead we know to-day. They were of many kinds, and were foiled at the back, which greatly increased their brilliancy. They were mostly cut like real stones, and whilst some were used without any setting, others were mounted in gilt claws which were provided with holes, through which the needle was passed to form the stitches which held the gem to the foundation.

If beads possess very small holes, it is better to damp the end of the thread, rounding it between the finger and thumb, and pass it through the holes in the manner of threading a needle. Then thread on the needle at the other side, to pass it through the foundation material.

Period gems may be had in forms to resemble diamonds, rubies, topazes, opals, sapphires, aquamarines, and emeralds, whilst turquoises and pearls are usually represented by the more modern type of rounded bead. Some of the gems were round and rose-cut, some lozenge-shaped, some hexagonal, others square, the lozenge-shaped crystals often being known as "fish-tails."

For modern work, when the old type of jewels are used, the unset variety with two tiny holes in them is the best, as they do not stand up so prominently above the surface as those with the metal settings.

For use on cotton materials, the smooth kind of stone is always to be preferred to the cut surface type.

The old type of jewelled embroidery was not merely confined to replicas of gems. There were also small pieces of mother-of-pearl, pierced to allow for the passage of a needle, and specially prepared for the work. These were either square, round or lozenge-shaped, the latter being a particular favourite. Scraps of coral were also largely used, as well as iridescent sequins and spangles. These latter are quite often used in modern work, especially for evening bags, and they should never be employed scantily—to be really effective they need massing together or arranging so that they overlap like fish scales.

Modern varieties are numerous. There are wooden beads, Venetian necklet and flower beads, flat glass discs for threading between smaller beads to give greater length to a necklace, tubes (used a great deal for dress trimming), large glass beads and bugles, diamanté, imitation jade, amber and coral: beads of papier maché and other composition substances, beads of cork, of leather, and chromium.

Bead Needles run from sizes 8 to 16, and have elongated eyes which allow the passage of a thicker thread, although the actual needle is finer than the finest darning needle. Metal beads, which usually have larger holes than the other kinds, can easily be threaded with a No. 9 or 10 head needle, but in buying for working with beads of other types, it is best to take a specimen to the shop, in order to obtain the correct size.

For Necklet Threading special cards of silk in white and colours are sold, with a threading wire attached to one end. The sizes of this range generally from 4 to 8, the lower number being the finest. Little cards of necklet wire in gold and silver, medium size only, are sold for threading heavy beads; whilst wooden and leather beads can often be threaded on coloured, very thin twine, to give them a really artistic effect

Fig. 1.—An attractive design for a bag, ready stencilled in colour on double thread canvas

Groundwork Material for Bead Embroidery.—Rich fabrics, such as velvet, satin, plush, and brocade, are excellent grounds if they are suitable to the article being fashioned.

Cotton materials of a durable nature are also largely used, net, muslin, stout gauze (both tinsel and silk) being attractive.

A great deal of bead embroidery is worked on canvas of the two-thread variety.

For all ordinary types of bead embroidery, unless the directions give a special make of thread, strong linen thread or silk twist should be used, and often a thread of an entirely different colour from the bead is effective, as, for example, seed pearls strung on deep pink silk twist, take on depth, red under a number of light-tinted glass beads gives a warm glow, and blue often gives a metallic lustre.

Many kinds of gold thread are also employed in bead embroidery, and as there are a number of different shades of this, it is always advisable to take specimen beads when buying, in order to obtain the right shade.

Needle and Thread Bead Work is mostly used for evening bags, purses, and so on, and designs can be bought ready stamped on canvases of varying sizes, or an ordinary transfer can be used in conjunction with two-thread canvas. When buying the beads for this type of work, get a size that will just cover the mesh, so that the canvas will not show when the embroidery is finished. If they are too large the work will not set flat.

Coloured cross-stitch designs serve for bead work, unless one is competent enough to work out a design for oneself. The amateur should naturally begin with

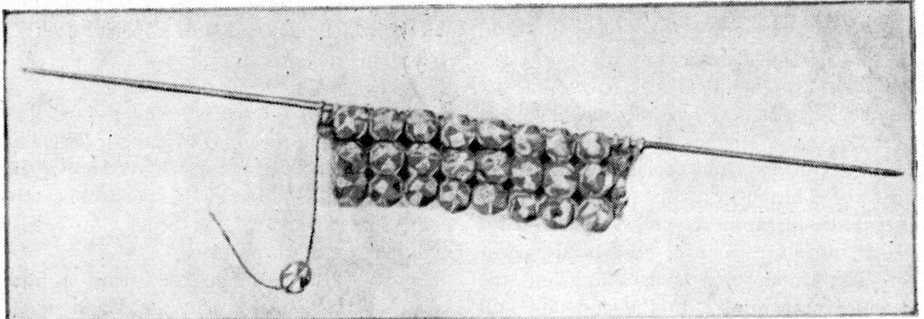

Fig. 2.—A specimen of knitted bead work—in straight rows.

quite a simple design, until she gets used to sewing the beads on to the canvas. Beads are obtainable in various sizes and most colours, including gold and steel specimens. Very fine and soft canvas is specially made for bead work, costing a few shillings a yard, but being wide, a small piece goes a long way. Bead work on canvas is quite simple. The fine canvas referred to should be obtained and the beads sewn in position separately.

Bead work on canvas is done in rows from left to right. Join the thread on the wrong side, then bring up the needle at the left-hand lower corner of the mesh. Thread on a bead and pass the needle down through the upper right-hand corner and up again through the mesh right underneath, making a stitch like the first half of a cross-stitch with a bead resting on it. (Fig. 3.)

Bead work on canvas is frequently used for evening bags, purses, etc. A stitch similar to the first half of a cross-stitch is used, and the beads placed so that no canvas shows.

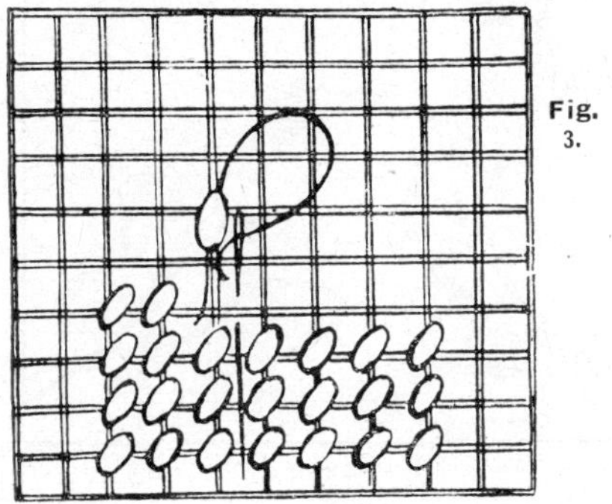

Fig. 3.

When the end of the row is reached, pass the needle and thread through the meshes just under the beads, to get back to the left-hand side. The alternative is to fasten off at the end of each row, as each new row must begin from the left-hand side. The pattern must be followed in each row, the colours and outline of the shape of the bag being clearly indicated on the stencilled canvas.

Care should be taken to avoid pulling the thread too tightly, as the canvas, through soft and pliable, can so easily be unduly stretched. The beads should be arranged to preserve a good line.

Tiny seed pearls, rather sparsely intermingled with " diamonds " make a charming evening bag. Another idea is to work a bag in deepening shades of one colour, i.e. pink deepening into crimson.

If a canvas of the design required cannot be bought, then the pattern can be pencilled out first on graph paper with the same number of holes to the inch as the canvas, and the design followed from this. A repetition of the same design could be worked on the corner of a tulle veil, using the lightest and smallest make of pearls that it is possible to obtain.

Knitted Bead Work.—Thread the beads on stout silk, and then decide whether a plain bag or one that will be gathered on a mount, is required, so that enough stitches are allowed when casting on. Naturally the first kind is the easiest for the beginner, and small pochettes or envelope-shaped purses can be made easily.

For a bag with stripes cast on any number of stitches divisible by 6 with 3 over for edge stitches, which are knitted plain. Knit two rows plain without any beads. Third row: slip 1, knit 1, * put the needle in the next stitch in position for plain knitting, then push up a bead against the last stitch and finish knitting the stitch; repeat from * to the end and knit plain the last stitch, without a bead. Knit the next row without beads. If threaded correctly, there should now be 3 beads of the same colour to begin each row, thus keeping the striping intact.

If knitting in a special pattern this should be worked out first on paper, and then the beads threaded in the correct order before beginning to work. The bag should be lined with silk, the knitted piece without beads at each side, being used for turnings

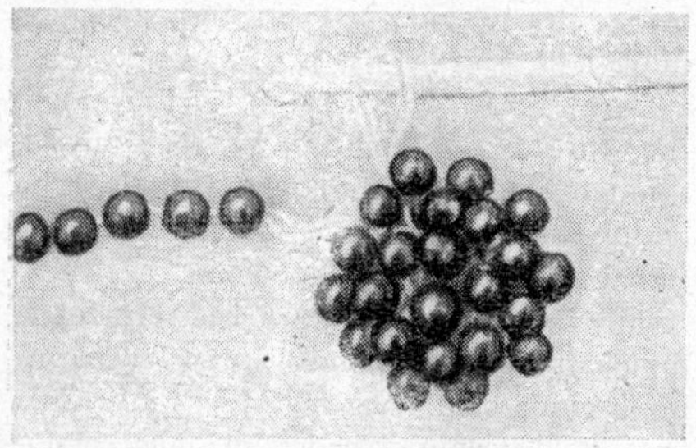

Fig. 4. The beginning of a crochet bead bag showing the right side and how the beads are first threaded on to the Sylko. This sample is especially worked with large beads and contrasting thread to show the working more clearly

Crochet Bead Work.—For square or oblong bags, it is best to work in rounds after the manner of a stocking, beginning with a ring of crochet chain according to the width of bag required, and working from the outside, so that the beads can easily be held in position. (Fig. 4.)

Another attractive design is made by working two large circular pieces of bead crochet, and joining them with a strip of the work about 8 beads wide to form a side piece, which gives greater capacity to the bag. Instructions for a bag of this type are given below.

Unwind the thread, winding it carefully on to an empty reel, and slipping it between the thumb and finger to feel any knots. If these are left, and they happen to be too large for the hole of the beads, the beads will not slip down on them.

Sylko No. 8 can be used with a fine bead needle, a steel crochet hook and small beads. If, for any reason such as choice of colour, larger beads are used, then fewer decreasings must be done, in order to keep the work flat. A whole bunch of beads can be passed on, and when all the beads are used up the thread can be broken, another ball threaded, and the two threads joined by a knot at the back of the work, close up to the last bead.

An attractive design would be 25 pearl and 25 silver beads alternately threaded. (The stitches needed are fully explained in the crochet section of this book.)

To work: make 4 chain stitches and join into a ring by slip stitching into the first stitch. 1st round: * 1 double crochet into the ring, push up a bead close against this stitch, and repeat from * five times. 2nd round: 2 double crochet in each stitch all round, always pushing up a

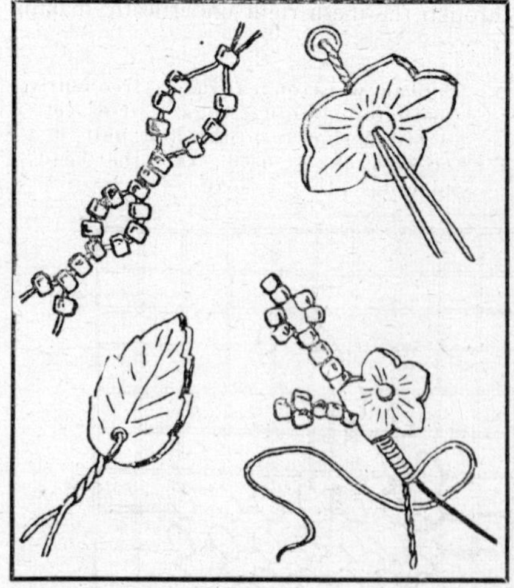

Fig. 5. Detail for making the necklace on the facing page.

A lovely necklace fashioned from glass beads made to resemble delicately-tinted flowers and leaves. On the opposite page are clear diagrams showing how to wire the leaves and flowers and thread the tiny connecting beads.

bead after each stitch and taking up the back loop of the double crochet. The beads will appear on the side of the work that is away from you. Sew a piece of white cotton to indicate the first stitch of the round, as it is most important to preserve the uniformity of the rounds.

Do three more rounds like the second. 6th round: * 1 double crochet into first stitch, 2 double crochet into next stitch, and repeat from * all round. In the case of bigger beads, increase in every fifth stitch. 7th round: 1 double crochet in each stitch. Now repeat the last two rounds until the circle is big enough to fit the top. The work must lie quite flat: if worked too loosely the circle will "flare" a little, but this can easily be remedied by working an extra plain round or two without any increasings. If worked too tightly the circle may curl in, and in this case, an extra increase round, with two double crochet in each stitch will soon set it right.

When the circle is big enough, work a few rounds of plain double crochet without beads at one end, to form the part that will fit into the metal top, and if the latter happens to be oval, a few extra rounds can be worked with short rows in the middle, to shape it.

Complete two circles, work a narrow strip, with about five beads in each row as follows: After working one row of beads and double crochet as just described, turn and slip stitch back along all the stitches just worked, to get to the opposite end of the work once more. Then repeat a row of beads and a slip stitch row until the strip is long enough to go round the lower portion of the circle, from hinge to hinge of the clasp.

Before sewing up the beaded portions, cut out a lining of silk, satin or other suitable material, allowing at least $\frac{1}{4}$ of an inch extra all round for turnings. Sew these together, then sew the narrow beaded strip on to the strip of silk, with oversewing. Slip the lining portion between the two beaded circles, so that the wrong sides of each are together. Oversew the top of the bag and the lining together, then sew on the metal mount with strong linen thread, thus: join the thread on the wrong side, push up through the first hole from wrong to right side, thread a bead on the needle, then push the needle back through the same hole: repeat this with each hole in the mount. When the end of the clasp is reached, draw up the sides of the bag a little to close them, and fasten off securely.

Loom Bead Work.—The loom is a simple wooden construction made in three sizes. (Fig. 7.) The medium loom, about $11\frac{1}{2}$ by $7\frac{1}{2}$ inches, is chiefly used for making necklets, purses and bags. On this size, a bag about 7 inches wide can be made, but it is best to work wide designs in strips, taking 20 to 40 beads, according to size, and afterwards joining the strips together by threading in and out of the beads on the edges of the strips.

Extra long bead needles can be bought for wide designs, and any cross-stitch or tapestry pattern can be followed, as there is no preliminary threading of the beads, each being taken up as needed, row by row, according to the pattern decided on.

Ordinary strong linen thread or silk twist is the best to use for loom work. First prepare the warp threads, allowing some inches over the length of the intended article. Cut the threads in separate lengths, allowing one more thread than there are beads for ordinary flat weaving, as in the case of a bag. The loom is always placed with the spool away from the worker, as shown in the illustration.

To set the warp, tie all the threads together at one end, and secure them on one of the nails on the spool at the top of the loom. Then place the threads in rotation on the notches of the first bridge, and carry each thread down to the corresponding notch on the second bridge. When all the warp threads are set, draw them down firmly, pass them through one of the holes at the end of the loom and push in the little peg to keep these threads perfectly taut. Then wind the remaining length of thread round the end of the loom and the pegs.

Take the weaving thread which should be of the same kind as the warp thread and thread it into the needle. Tie it at the top of the first left-hand warp thread. Thread the full number of beads for the first row, pass the needle from left to right under the warp threads, and push a bead up into position between each warp. When there are too many beads to keep on the needle, let them slip down the thread, push them in position and hold under the warp threads with the forefinger of the left hand.

The beads should be pushed well up between the threads, so that the latter do not come over the needle when passing back.

Take the needle in the right hand and pass it back from right to left through all the beads, taking care that the needle keeps above the warp threads to the end of the row. Draw the thread up firmly. The passing of the thread under and over the work makes a selvedge on both edges. When the loom is full, wind the work round the spool away from you, but leave a little of the work to project over the top bridge, as the threads can now only be pressed down into the notches on the lower bridge. If they were passed down the upper bridge, a gap would occur in the work. Secure the ends firmly round the pegs again before

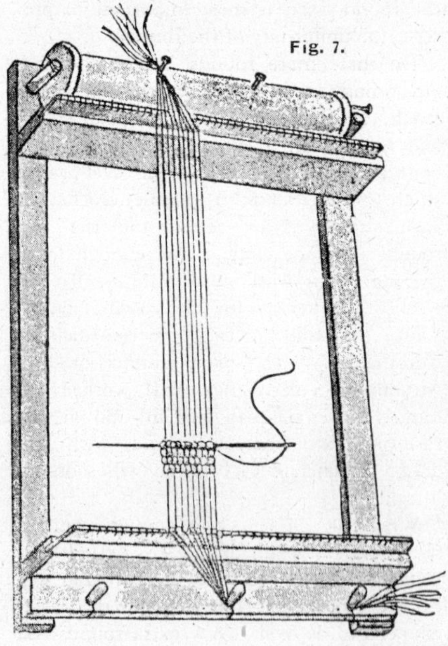

The simplest form of loom for bead work.

Fig. 8. The Single Daisy chain. Diagrams A to D show how various sections of the chain are threaded.

beginning to weave afresh. At the left-hand side of the spool you will find three holes, into one of which a loose nail must be passed to keep the spool in position when working, so as to keep the warp threads taut: they must not be allowed to slacken at all during the process of working.

When sufficient has been woven, fasten all ends securely.

Necklaces can be fashioned by weaving on the smallest size loom, and using only tiny beads, which are most generally sold by the hank. This form of woven bead work can also be used as a bordering, sewn neatly in rows across the ends of a plain brocade table runner, or other articles of that kind where a little weight is needed for added effect.

How to Make a Single Daisy chain and necklet.—Small loom beads will be required, with large openings, and large beads, strong " cut garnet " bead thread, bead needles, metal clasp, and a small piece of wax, which should be rubbed along the thread before beginning the necklet.

Daisy chains are started with a length of bead thread, having a needle at either end, so that they are worked from each side. A small weighted cushion is useful for pinning the chain to as it is worked.

Select beads of three colours—white for the daisy, with, say a green bead for the centre, and green, blue or pink beads between. Any selection of colours may be used as desired. Take a length of thread, place a needle on each end, thread one white bead, draw thread through until bead is in the middle; put left-hand needle in right-hand side of bead, and right-hand needle in left-hand side of bead. This crosses the thread and makes a firm beginning. (Fig. 9a.)

* Now thread seven more white beads on left-hand needle, making eight altogether, put left-hand needle through right-hand

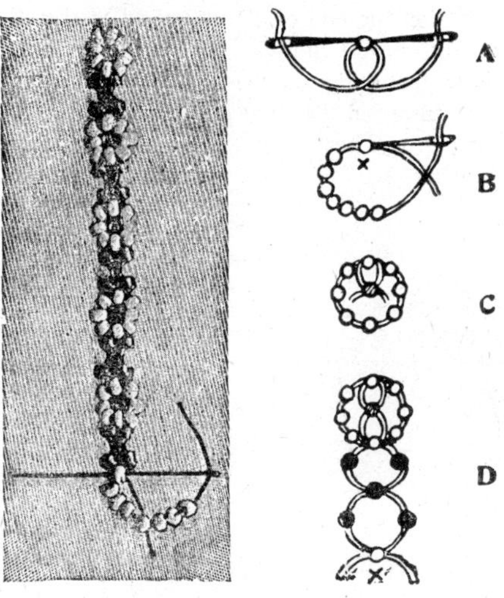

Fig. 9

side of first bead once more; this forms a ring, and the two cottons are hanging one on each side of the first bead. (B, Fig. 9.) Next thread a green bead to form the middle of the daisy, threading it from both sides as the first bead (C, Fig. 9), then put left-hand needle through left-hand side of the middle white bead on the opposite side of the daisy, and bring it out on the right side, and the right-hand needle through the right-hand side of the same bead and bring it out on the left side. This crosses the threads again and the daisy is complete. Next thread a blue bead on each side, then a single blue bead, with the threads crossed as before. Now a blue bead on each thread again. (D, Fig. 9.) For the second daisy, thread one white bead through each side with both needles crossing thread as before, and continue working from * for the length required, but containing an uneven number of daisies, as the loops of beads are started from the lowest middle bead of the centre daisy. Sew the clasp neatly to the ends and then pass a length of thread (about ½ yard) through the lowest middle bead of the centre daisy, and leave half of the thread hanging on either side, make the thread firm by passing the left needle through the right side of the bead, and bringing it out on the left side again.

Fasten the end of about ½ yard of thread to the lowest middle bead of the third daisy (counting in the middle one) from the centre, on the right and left sides of the necklet. There are now four threads hanging, two on the left side, and two on the right side of the necklet. Thread nine beads on each of the two centre threads, and ten beads on each of the outside threads. * Now connect the two left-hand threads by threading one more bead and crossing the thread through it as above. Put one more bead on each thread, then cross the threads again, through the top middle bead of the daisy which comes next; make the daisy as usual, and leave two threads hanging. Repeat from * on the right side, only calling the left-hand threads, right-hand threads; when this is done, there are, once more, four threads hanging. Thread nine beads on each of the two middle threads, one more to cross the threads, one more on each thread to make the daisy, pass both threads through a long tubular bead, make another daisy, and tie the threads firmly at the bottom to fasten off.

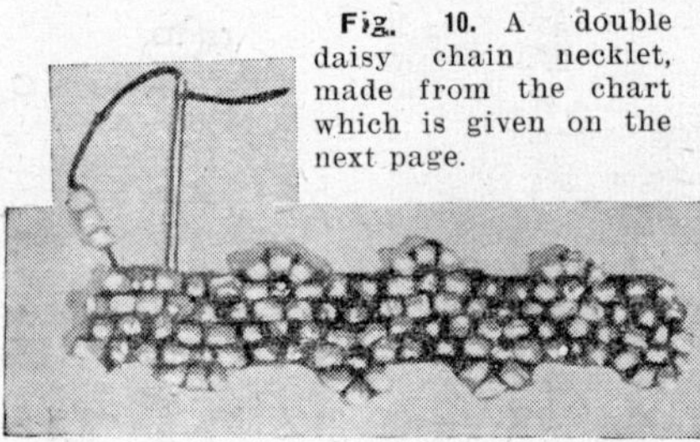

Fig. 10. A double daisy chain necklet, made from the chart which is given on the next page.

Now proceed with the right-hand side. ** On the single thread on that side, thread twenty-four beads, and pass the needle and thread through the middle lowest bead of the fourth daisy on the right-hand side (counting in the middle one), thread on nine beads. Fasten a length of thread to the lowest middle bead of the sixth daisy on the right-hand side, thread ten beads, one more to cross these two threads, one more on each of these two threads, make a daisy; on the two threads which are now hanging, thread sixteen beads on the one nearest the centre, and finish off through the lowest bead of the fourth daisy. Thread twenty-two beads on the remaining thread, and fasten off through the lowest middle bead of the seventh daisy.

Take a short length of thread, and pass it through the lowest middle bead of the first hanging daisy on the right-hand side of the centre, pass both ends through a long tubular bead, then make a daisy as usual, and finish off neatly. Repeat from ** for the left-hand side. Fig. 8 shows the necklet completed.

The Double Daisy Chain is also easy; except where the outside petals of the daisies are threaded and attached to the main body of the chain, it is worked up and down. One bead is threaded at a time, after which the needle is passed through another bead, thus holding the last one threaded in position. Beads of three different colours are selected, one colour for the background (which may be called the ground bead), one for the flower colour and one bead of a different colour for the centre of each daisy—white daisies with yellow hearts and green grounds, or forget-me-not blue flowers with yellow or gold hearts and white, green or gold ground. Yellow daisies with black hearts are effective. Ordinary small beads are used, but they must be uniform in size and shape, and have fairly large and free openings, as the thread has to be passed through some of them twice. In Fig. 11 each black circle represents a ground bead; the white circles, the flower beads; and the shaded circle, the heart or centre of each daisy. As strong a thread as the beads will permit should be used, allowing for the second passing of the needle. If the thread is liable to kink or knot, do not take too long a piece, and to begin, tie the thread firmly round the first bead. When joining on a fresh length of thread, finish off the previous thread by making a few button-hole stitches on the thread which passed between the last two beads, and join on the new thread by tying it on to the last bead.

Begin by threading two ground, two flower, and one heart bead as seen in Fig. 11. These are Nos. 1, 2, 3, 4, and 5. Hold this group of five between the thumb

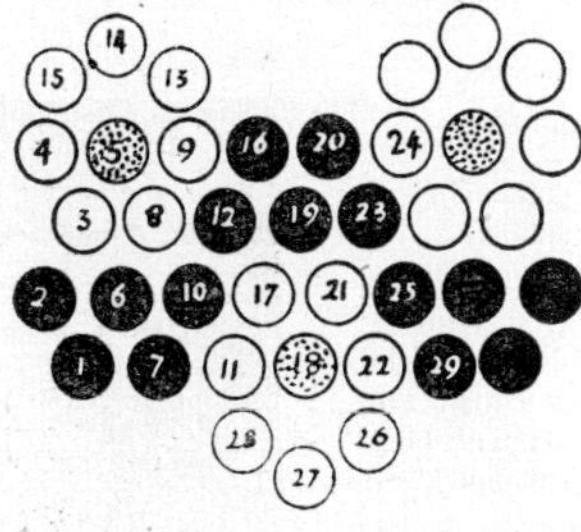

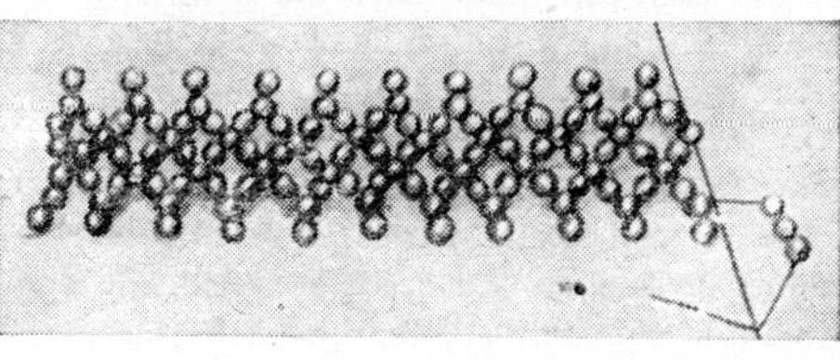

Fig. 11. Follow this chart for making the double daisy chain necklet. **Fig. 12** (right) shows an attractive bead chain which can be used in a variety of ways

and first finger of the left hand, No. 1 bead being towards you, and No 5 away from you, and missing No. 4, pass the needle downwards through No. 3. Thread No. 6 (ground bead) and pass the needle downwards through No. 1 Still holding the work in the same position, thread No. 7 (ground bead) and pass upwards through No. 6; thread No. 8 (flower bead), pass up through No. 5 (centre bead); thread No. 9 (flower bead), pass down through No. 8; thread No. 10 (ground bead), pass down through No. 7 (ground bead); thread No. 11 (flower bead), pass up through No. 10 (ground bead); thread No. 12 (ground bead), pass up through No. 9 (flower bead).

Then thread Nos. 13, 14, 15 (flower beads), pass down through Nos. 4 and 3 (flower beads) and on round through Nos. 8 and 9, which finishes the first daisy

Thread No. 16 (ground bead), * pass down through No. 12 (ground bead); thread No. 17 (flower bead), pass down through No. 11 (flower bead); thread No. 18 (centre bead), pass up through No. 17 (flower bead); thread No. 19 (ground bead), pass up through No. 16 (ground bead); thread No. 20 (ground bead), pass down through No. 19 (ground bead); thread No. 21 (flower bead), pass down through No. 18 (centre bead); thread No. 22 (flower bead), pass up through No. 21 (flower bead); thread No. 23 (ground bead), pass up through No. 20 (ground bead); thread No. 24 (flower bead), pass down through No. 23 (ground bead); thread No. 25 (ground bead), pass down through No. 22 (flower bead).

Then thread flower beads Nos. 26, 27, and 28, pass up through Nos. 11 and 17, and on round through Nos. 21 and 22. This finishes the second flower.

Thread No. 29 (ground bead), pushing it up to the work. Turn the work over, and it will be seen that this 29th bead is in the same position as No. 16 (ground bead) (Fig. 10). * Repeat from * to *, turning the work over to the reverse side between each repetition, until you have sufficient length of the daisy chain worked. Fig. 10 shows the double daisy chain in the working.

A Bead Chain.—This is attractive in any colour, either as a necklet, bracelet, or even as dress-trimming. Thread eight beads (A, Fig. 13) fastening the first bead on very securely, then pass the needle back through the seventh bead from bottom (B, Fig. 13), thread three more beads (C, Fig. 13), pass the needle through the fourth bead (D, Fig. 13), thread three beads (E. Fig. 13), pass the needle back through the middle of

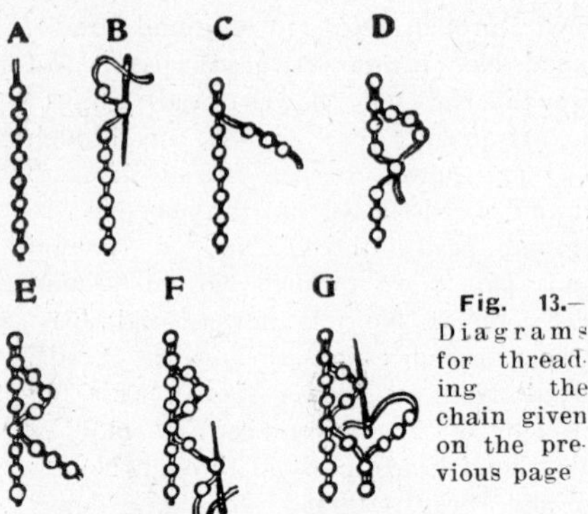

Fig. 13.—Diagrams for threading the chain given on the previous page

the three just threaded (F. Fig. 13), thread three beads and pass the needle through the fourth bead from the top (G, Fig. 13). Turn the chain over and the beads will be in the position of F, Fig. 13; proceed from F to G each time, and make the chain any length desired. Fig. 12 shows the chain in the process of working.

In Fig. 14 is another dainty bead chain, using two kinds of beads. To make this, round and oval beads are needed. Different colours of small round beads are used, say, white for the daisy, green for its centre, and mauve for the beads on each end of the daisy and on each side of the blue oval bead. Two needles are required as for the others. Thread the oval bead first through one hole, taking care to bring the thread half-way through, to have an even length of thread on both sides. * Thread the bead through the second hole, the right-hand hole with the right-hand thread, and the left-hand hole with the left-hand thread; now thread three small mauve beads on each thread, then cross the threads through one small white bead; next thread seven more small white beads on the left-hand side, and finish the daisy as described for the single daisy chain, proceeding from B in Fig. 9. Next cross the thread in the first hole of the next oval bead, and continue from * for the length required. Fig. 14 shows the chain in the process of being worked

Other Uses for Bead Work.—Bead Embroidery can be used for small motifs, on evening cloaks and wraps, or the ends of long chiffon or georgette scarves.

The designs should not be elaborate and not too heavily laden with the beads. Having chosen a simple pattern, a needle is threaded with stout but firm silk to match the article on which the embroidery is placed, and a secure knot made on the wrong side. A bead is then placed over every dot on the design (which can be ironed off from a special bead-design transfer). This is done by passing the needle—which should be a fine one in order that it does not injure the material—up through the centre of the first dot, threading on a bead, then passing

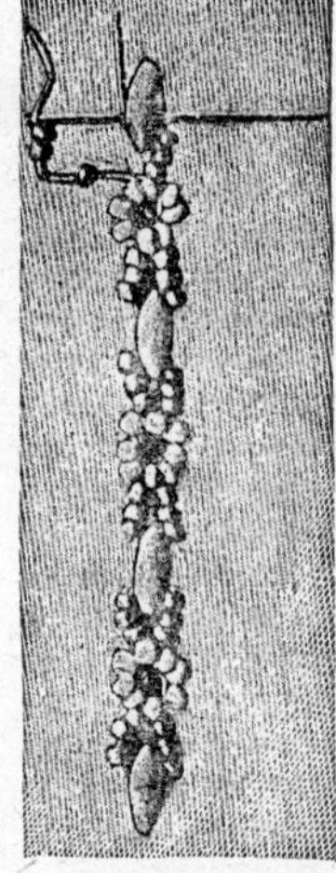

Fig. 14. Another dainty bead necklet in which round and oval beads are combined. Different coloured small round beads are used for the daisies and surrounding beads.

the needle down again right under the bead, either through the same hole if the material is fairly strong, or immediately next door to it for more flimsy fabrics. The cotton passes along at the back of the work, and the needle is put up again through the second dot, and the process repeated until every dot on the design is covered by a bead.

Bead Berry Embroidery.—Berry Embroidery with beads, as shown in Figs. 15 and 16 is a combination of embroidery and beading. The foliage and stems are embroidered, and the berries, such as blackberries, raspberries, mulberries, ivy, and rowan berries, are beaded. The illustration, showing the detail of the berry spray, indicates the manner of working. Select a firm material, such as Roman satin, cloth, art serge, or thick silk for the foundation; suitable shades of lustre thread, flax thread or embroidery silks for the stitchery; and wooden or glass beads in natural colours for the berries. This design can be used for tea-cosies, cushions, handbags, or dress-trimmings. The foliage is worked in Embroidery cotton, No. 8, in five shades of meadow green, and three of dull brownish red. Purplish black Tosca wooden beads are sewn on for the berries.

Fig. 16. A really decorative spray of beads which lend weight to shaded silk embroidery.

Use long and short stitches for the leaves, working from the edge of the leaf slantwise towards the centre vein. The same stitch is used for the branch; for the knots and thorns, the direction must be varied to correspond with the form and preserve a rugged appearance. The stalks are in stem stitch, in medium and dark green, with touches of brownish red. Beads are sewn on for the berries with strong cotton, each bead being secured with a back stitch.

Fig. 15 shows a border, suitable for dress or blouse trimming, or for a table cover or blotter. The berries are worked

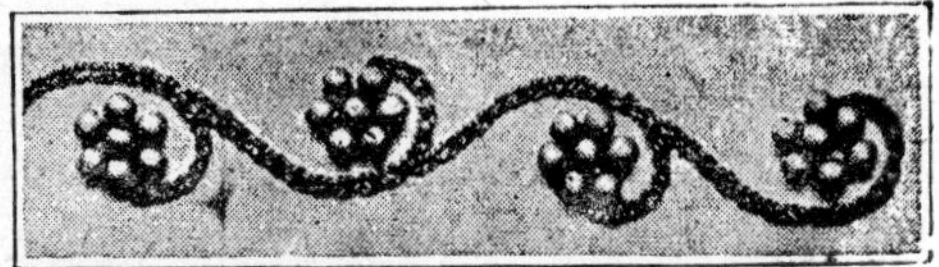

Fig. 15. Beads used as berries make a charming combination with silk embroidery, for a border.

exactly the same as in Fig. 16. The connecting lines are worked in chain stitch.

BEAD CURTAINS

Materials Required.—A bar of wood, a ball or two of coloured string and a supply of beads and bugles.

Only one bar of wood, from which depends the string of threaded beads, is needed for each curtain, but it must be ¾ inch to 1 inch thick, and pierced with holes at regular intervals, about three holes to every inch, or eighteen holes in a 6-inch length. The holes must be sufficiently large to take the string passed through them; and the bar of wood will vary in length according to the width of the curtain to be made. After the holes are pierced, the bars should be painted to suit the room. These bars can be made to order by a carpenter.

Beads are obtainable in hanks or packets, in a wide range of colours—white glass, milky white, light and dark amber, several shades of blue, green, red, coral, lemon, and opal; the transparent beads are the best for curtain work because the light filters through them. The "pea" size is chiefly used, although in many patterns a small, flat bead can be introduced with good effect. The small beads are likewise useful to place as a finish at the ends of the strings, to prevent the larger beads from slipping over the knot.

Bugles, or tubular beads, are in different lengths, both opaque and transparent, and hollow, to admit the string passing through. These are splendid for curtains and may be freely used, as they are light-weighted, and the transparent ones very light and sparkling.

Bead and macramé string is passed through the beads and bugles to suspend

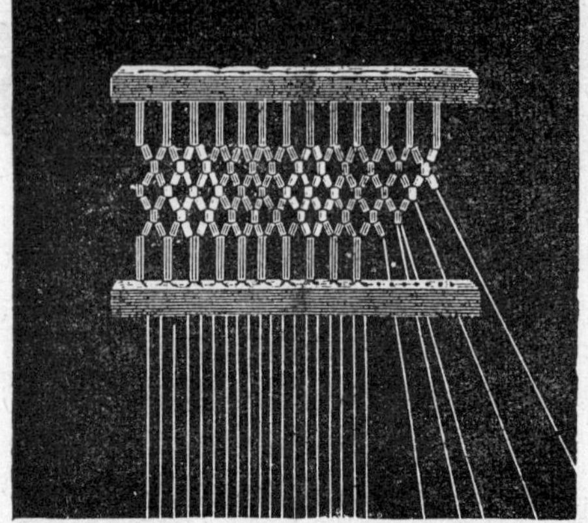

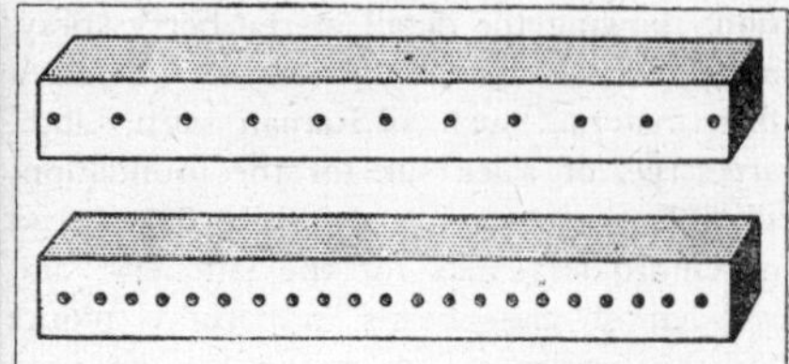

Fig. 24. On the left is honeycomb insertion, in the making, and above, two bars are shown, the top one with holes spaced far apart, and the bottom one with more holes to the inch.

them in lengths hanging from the bar. In some patterns the string is not visible, being completely covered by beads and bugles; but in others certain lengths of string are left visible, and form a part of the design.

How to Thread the Strings on to the Bar.—The material procured, the strings must be arranged on the bar of wood. When cutting the strings, allow a little more than double the length of curtain when finished, because some is taken up in passing through the bar, and some may be used in knots. For a curtain 1 yard in length, cut 2 yards 6 inches of string; for one 2 yards long, cut 4 yards 6 inches; for a 3-yard length cut 6 yards 8 inches; always double, because the cut string makes two working strings. The number of strings depends upon the width of pattern, or the purpose for which the curtain is used. Cut several, and add more as needed. Place the bar of wood on the table, and, beginning on the left-hand side, pass the first string up through the first hole, and down through the second hole; pass the second string up through the third hole, and down through the fourth hole; and so on, always drawing the string through till both ends are equal. There will now be a string hanging from every hole, and it is on these that the bugles and beads are threaded. At the top of the bar there is a line of string, like running stitches, passing from hole to hole; drive a tin-tack through each "stitch" of string into the bar to keep it from slipping. Then thread the beads and bugles in accordance with the pattern selected. Any surplus length of string is clipped off after the last knot is tied. It is awkward to make a neat join if the string falls short of the length.

The Vandyke Pattern.—(Fig. 18.)—A bar of wood pierced with holes, a supply of yellow string, some light gold beads and

Fig. 18.—A simple patterned bead curtain.

some pale transparent blue beads, milky-white bugles and peacock-blue bugles are needed. To start with, cut the string into pieces the length necessary for the work, and place them on the bar, allowing 16 strings for the width of a Vandyke, and 1 string over to keep the pattern even.

1*st String*.—Thread one peacock-blue bugle, and one gold bead, push close to the bar, and confine them by tying a knot on the string; * thread one white bugle and one blue bead, and push up to within 1¼ inches of the knot (that is, leaving 1¼ inches of string visible), and hold into position with a knot; thread one peacock-blue bugle and one gold bead, and push up to within 1¼ inches of the former knot, and hold in position with a knot; repeat from * to the end of the string, where secure the whole with two knots, one tied over the other. 2*nd String*.—Thread as before, one peacock-blue bugle and one gold bead; push up, but not close to the bar, leave ¼ inch of string between the bar and the bugle, and tie a knot; then proceed from * to * the same as on the first string; and in beginning ¼ inch lower, each bugle and each bead down the string will hang relatively lower than those on the first string. This makes the Vandyke.

3*rd String*.—Leave ¾ inch of string visible just below the bar, and carry on with the bugles and beads as before. 4*th String*.—Leave 1 inch of string below the bar, and carry on with the bugles and beads as before. 5*th String*.—Leave 1¼ inches of string below the bar and carry on with the bugles and beads in continuation of the Vandyke. 6*th String*.—Leave 1½ inches of string below the bar, and carry on with the bugles and beads in continuation of the Vandyke; this is the lowest point. 7*th String*.—The Vandyke now rises gradually; this string is therefore to be worked to correspond with the fifth string. 8*th String*.—The same as the fourth string. 9*th String*.—The same as the third string. 10*th String*.—The same as the second string. 11*th String*.—The same as the first string. 12*th String*.—Thread three gold beads, push up close to the bar and knot in place. * Thread one white bugle and one blue bead, and push up to within 1¼ inches of the knot, and hold in position with a knot; thread one peacock-blue bugle and one gold bead, and push up to within 1¼ inches of the former knot, and tie a knot, and repeat from * to the end of the string, where finish with a double knot as usual. 13*th String*.—Begin with two gold beads, push close to the bar and knot in place, and proceed then as from * to * on the previous string. 14*th String*.—Begin with one gold bead knotted up close to the bar and continue as from * to * on the previous string; this is the highest point of the Vandyke. 15*th String*.—The Vandyke now slopes gradually downwards; work this string like the thirteenth string. 16*th String*.—Work this string the same as the twelfth string. 17*th String*.—This must correspond with the first string. Continue from the second string to the seventeenth string inclusive; and repeat the same for the width of the curtain.

Fig. 19.—Diamond pattern.

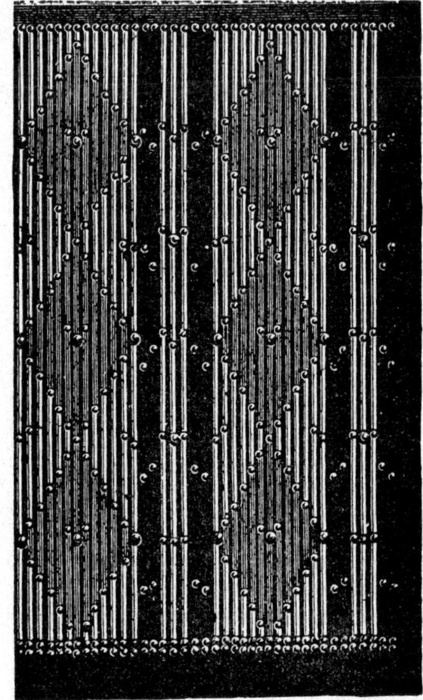

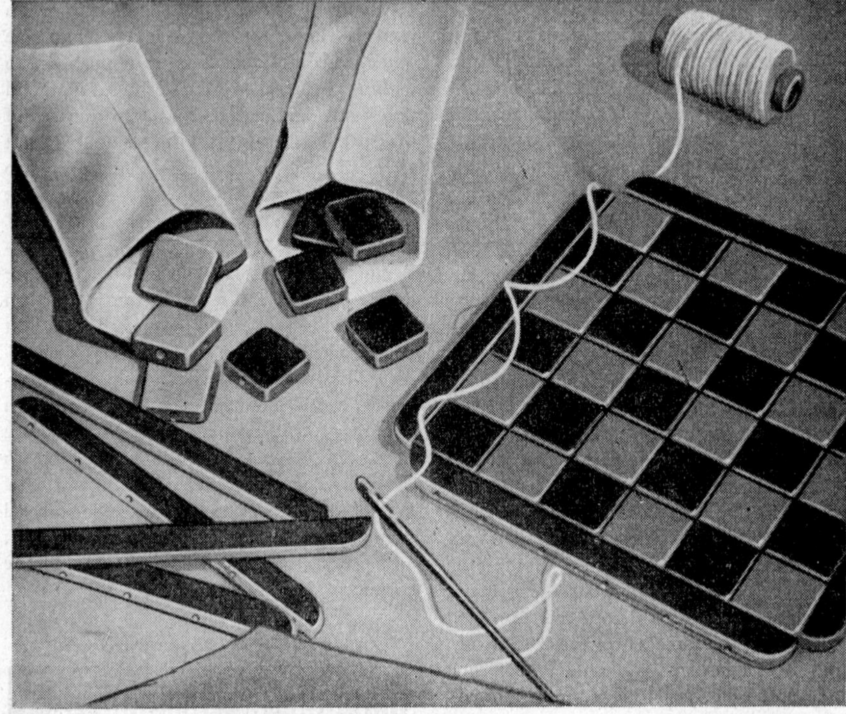

Fig. 20.—Novelty beads are used to make these useful and decorative table mats. Full instructions for making are given in this chapter.

Diamond Patterned Curtain.—The size of the curtain when finished is 3 feet 6 inches wide and about 3 feet deep. The wooden bars are $\frac{3}{4}$ inch thick wood, and measure 3 feet 6 inches from end to end. The top bar is pierced with 53 holes, all at regular intervals, and the lower bar has 106 holes closer together. Materials needed for working are: Two balls of string, one bundle each of red, purple and yellow, and two bundles of white reeds, and a hank each of amber, opal and porcelain blue beads, pea size, and a hank of large blue beads.

Prepare for working by cutting 53 lengths of 2 yards each; thread these in the top bar in the manner explained previously, and there will be 10 working strings for the manipulation of the honeycomb insertion.

Honeycomb Insertion (Fig. 17) is worked with $\frac{1}{3}$ sections of white and $\frac{1}{8}$ sections of purple reeds, which should be prepared beforehand. **1st row.**—Thread $\frac{1}{3}$ white reed on the 1st string on the left-hand side of the top bar, another $\frac{1}{3}$ white reed on the 2nd and 3rd strings together, and the same on every 2 threads together to the end, where there will be $\frac{1}{3}$ white reed on the last string to correspond with the beginning. **2nd row.**—Thread $\frac{1}{8}$ white reed on each of the three first strings, * $\frac{1}{8}$ purple reed on each of the two next strings, and $\frac{1}{8}$ white reed on each of the four following strings, and repeat from * to end. **3rd row.**—Thread $\frac{1}{8}$ white reed on the 1st and 2nd strings together, $\frac{1}{8}$ purple reed on the 3rd and 4th strings together and on the 5th and 6th strings together, $\frac{1}{8}$ white reed on the two following strings together. Repeat from *. **4th row.**—Thread $\frac{1}{8}$ white reed on each of the two first strings and $\frac{1}{8}$ purple reed on each of the four following strings.

BEAD WORK ON PARCHMENT

AN ANCIENT PIECE OF CHURCH WORK

Fig. 21.

By courtesy of the Victoria and Albert Museum.

Repeat. **5th row.**—Thread $\frac{1}{8}$ white reed on the 1st string, then $\frac{1}{8}$ purple reed on every two strings together to the end, with $\frac{1}{8}$ white reed on the last string singly. **6th row.**—Same as 4th row. **7th row.**—Same as 3rd row. **8th row.**—Same as 2nd row. **9th row.**—Thread $\frac{1}{3}$ white reeds to correspond with the 1st row. This finishes the insertion. Pass the strings in regular consecutive order through the holes of the second bar.

For the Diamond Stripes.—Sections of red and white reeds are used in forming the diamonds, as $\frac{1}{3}$, $\frac{2}{3}$, $\frac{1}{4}$, $\frac{1}{2}$ and $\frac{3}{4}$ which must all

VERY EARLY CHURCH WORK IN BEADS ON PARCHMENT

By courtesy of the Victoria and Albert Museum.

Fig. 22.

Fig. 23.

be accurately cut. Begin with the **1st string** on the left-hand side. Thread one amber bead and one dark purple reed alternately until six of each are threaded, finish with two amber beads and tie the string in a firm knot. **2nd string.**—Thread one opal bead and one yellow reed alternately until six of each are threaded, add two beads and secure with a knot. **3rd and 4th strings.**—The same as the 2nd string. **5th and 6th strings.**—Same as the 1st string. **7th string.**—Thread one amber bead, * one white reed, one blue bead, one white reed, one opal bead, and repeat from * twice, put on one more opal bead and tie a knot. **8th string.**—Thread one amber bead, 5/6 white reed, * one blue bead, $\frac{1}{3}$ red reed, one blue bead, one $\frac{2}{3}$ white reed, repeat from * once, one blue bead, $\frac{1}{3}$ red reed, one blue bead, $\frac{3}{4}$ white reed, two amber beads and fasten off. **9th string.**—Thread one amber bead, $\frac{2}{3}$ white reed, * one blue bead, $\frac{3}{4}$ red reed, one blue bead, $1\frac{1}{3}$ white reeds, repeat from * once, one blue bead, $\frac{3}{4}$ red reed, one blue bead, $\frac{2}{3}$ white reed, two amber beads and

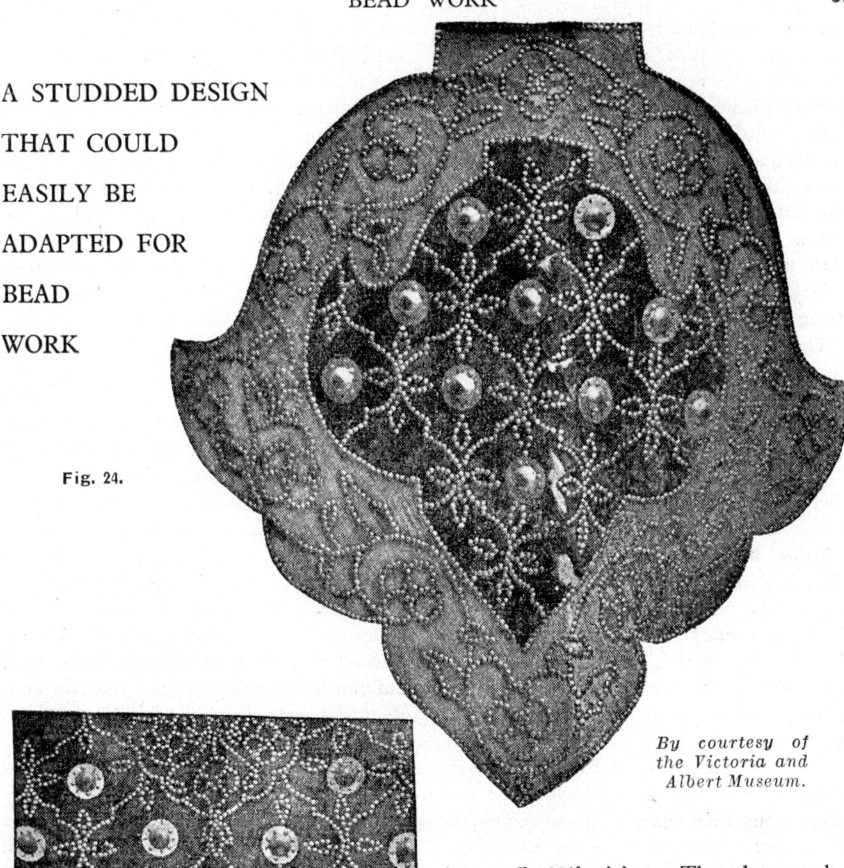

A STUDDED DESIGN THAT COULD EASILY BE ADAPTED FOR BEAD WORK

Fig. 24.

By courtesy of the Victoria and Albert Museum.

fasten off. **10th string.**—Thread one amber bead, $\frac{1}{2}$ white reed, * one blue bead, one red reed, one blue bead, one white reed, repeat from * once, one blue bead, one red reed, one blue bead, $\frac{1}{2}$ white reed, two amber beads and fasten off. **11th string.**—Thread one amber bead, $\frac{1}{3}$ white reed, * one blue bead, $1\frac{1}{3}$ red reeds, one blue bead, $\frac{3}{4}$ white reed, repeat from * once. One blue bead, $1\frac{1}{3}$ red reeds, one blue bead, $\frac{1}{3}$ white reed, two amber beads and fasten off. **12th string.**—Thread one amber bead, $\frac{1}{4}$ white reed, * one blue bead, $\frac{3}{4}$ red reed, one opal bead (this should come level with the blue bead on the 7th string), $\frac{3}{4}$ red reed, one blue bead, $\frac{1}{2}$ white reed (not quite half), repeat from * twice, ending with $\frac{1}{8}$ white reed instead of $\frac{1}{2}$, add two amber beads and fasten off. **13th string.**—Thread one amber bead, a little less than $\frac{1}{8}$ white reed * one blue bead, one red reed, one large blue bead, one red reed, repeat from * to end, add two blue beads and fasten off. **14th string.**—Same as 12th string. Now work in reverse order until the 19th string is threaded as the 7th. **20th and 21st strings.** —As 5th and 6th strings. **22nd, 23rd and 24th strings.**—Thread opal beads and yellow reeds, as 2nd, 3rd and 4th strings. **25th and 26th strings.**—As 5th and 6th strings. Repeat from 7th string to the 26th string four times, which finishes the curtain.

The large beads on the 13th string denote the centres of the diamonds, and if these occupy more than their allotted space and so prevent the ordinary sized blue bead from coming level with the middle of the ½ white reed on the 12th string, each red reed must be shortened a little.

Table Mats of flat Wooden Beads.—Materials required: Eighteen flat square red beads (almost an inch square), 18 flat square black beads, exactly the same size as the red, 4 long black wooden side pieces, 1 special bead threading needle, and a reel of wooden-bead twine are needed.

Arrange the beads into the check design seen in Fig. 20, and place the side pieces along each edge. Thread the needle with about 2 yards of twine and knot about 2 inches from the end. Begin at the right-hand bottom corner. Run the needle through the right-hand hole in the side piece, then thread it up through the red and black beads which make the first row of checks on the right-hand side. Finish the row by running the needle through the end hole in the top side piece—from the inside this time. Pull twine taut, but do not strain or cut.

Now thread downwards through the second row of beads, first threading through the second hole in the top side piece. The needle will come out of the last black bead in exactly the right place to go easily through the corresponding hole in the lower side piece. Again pull the twine taut and do not cut it.

Continue alternately threading up and down through the remaining four rows of beads to the bottom left-hand corner. Do not cut the twine yet, as the threading process must be repeated back in the same way, through the same beads as a strengthening precaution.

To do this, run the needle through the second hole from the left in the lower side piece (your thread last came out of the extreme left-hand hole). Run the needle back through the second row of beads from the left, and continue working back through the beads and side pieces as before, until you reach the second hole from the right in the bottom side piece. See that the twine is evenly taut through the whole mat, and then tie the 2-inch end of twine left at the beginning to the end with which you have been working, knotting very, very tightly and securely.

The mat is now half finished, and to complete it, rethread the needle with 2 yards of twine, then thread through the holes which run across the beads—at right angles to the previous way of working. Thread back through these beads as well, and finish the mat by tying the two ends of this piece of twine together, just as detailed for the first rows.

The parchment specimens show how beads were used in Church work at a very early date. Each bead is sewn on separately so that if one comes loose they do not all come undone. The outline of the face in Fig. 22 is a different colour from the lips, for which different shaped, slightly larger beads are used. These beads are used again to show the colour on the cheek. In this way shading is done with beads of various sizes and colours instead of with silks.

In Fig. 21 there are many different coloured beads of various kinds used to form the designs on the robe. The hair, too, is in various shades.

Fig. 23 is a contrast to the other two examples as only two kinds of beads are used.

Figs. 24 and 25 are quite different from those mentioned above. These are excellent designs, which with a little adaptation would be suitable for an evening bag. Instead of the large flat metal studs, sequins or bead clusters could be used. The large

Fig. 26.

From the Victoria and Albert Museum.

shield in the circle could be replaced by a simple monogram or even a different scrolled design.

Fig. 26 shows part of a Sicilian seventeenth-century Altar Frontal in silver gilt, silks and corals on cloth of silver. Split and satin stitch and couched gold work are used.

The figure on the right-hand side is worked in silk, the floor in squares of satin stitch, and the patterned roof in rows of couched gold. For the small pillars, corals and passing thread over cardboard strips are used. The corals are all sewn on separately to make them secure.

The large pillars, starting from the top, have a crown-shaped piece which has a background of cloth of gold on which the design is worked in crinkled plate gold surrounded by two rows of corals. The first tier is in plate, then come two rows of coral, one of plate, then a border of passing thread over cardboard, then coral again, then a narrower tier in passing thread, and then corals again which form the surrounding for the base of the pillar which is worked in plate again. The panel down either side of the pillars is worked on a blue ground the design being in gold.

The background for the vase is of cloth of silver. The vase itself is worked in raised plate and outlined in cord. Little circles of corals are worked along the edge. The leaves at the mouth are worked in a green and gold twisted thread, the flowers and leaves in corals, crinkled plate and raised plate.

BLACK WORK

Black work was first known in this country in the reign of Henry VIII and was also much used in Elizabethan times. It is sometimes known as Spanish work, and is believed to have come over to England with Catherine of Aragon.

This type of work is usually done on a white linen ground in fine black silk. The designs used are nearly always made up of scrolls of vine leaves and bunches of grapes, which are filled in with various small fillings. The designs were not drawn on to the materials but were done solely by the counted thread, and much ingenuity was displayed in the varied forms of the patterns. It will be noticed that the stems and outlines are always in a heavier stitch.

In some pieces the patterns which form the fillings for the leaves are all different. These patterns can first be designed on squared paper and then copied on to the linen. They must always be worked accurately to look well.

In the following specimens such stitches as back, chain, braid, buttonhole, satin, coral, are used.

Unfortunately the silk in the original pieces has perished and in consequence the fillings are not all as clear as they might otherwise be. In order to illustrate the type used, some of the most interesting fillings have been reworked in a slightly thicker silk, so that they give the worker a clearer idea of the formation of the stitches.

It is easier to use a frame for Black Work as the material should be taut in order to facilitate the counting of the threads.

This type of embroidery looks very striking worked on curtains, bedspreads, round the edges of day pillows, and on large surfaces.

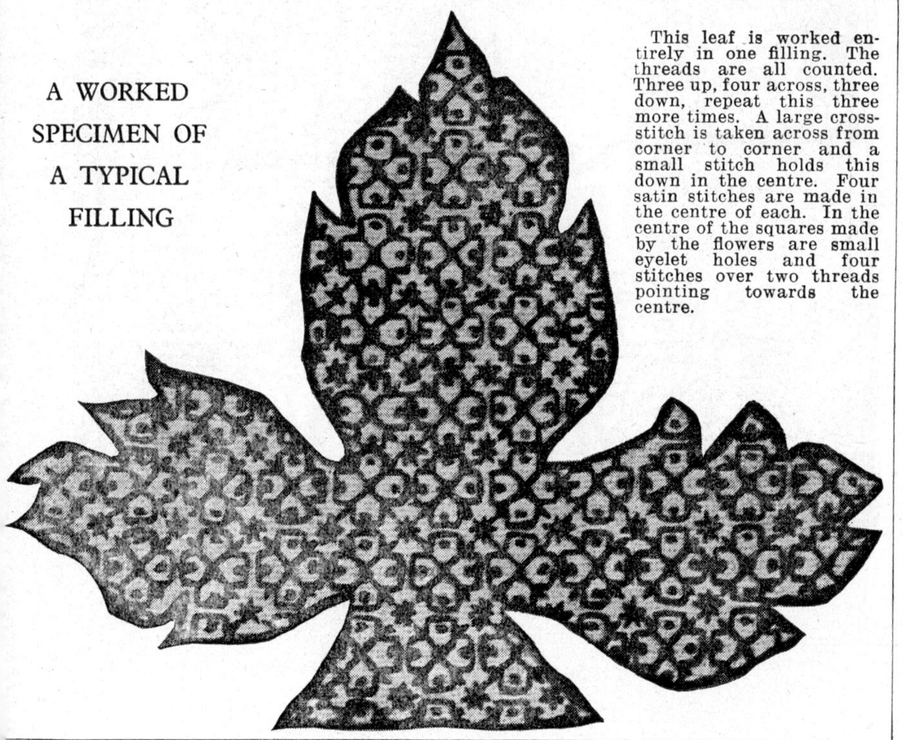

A WORKED SPECIMEN OF A TYPICAL FILLING

This leaf is worked entirely in one filling. The threads are all counted. Three up, four across, three down, repeat this three more times. A large cross-stitch is taken across from corner to corner and a small stitch holds this down in the centre. Four satin stitches are made in the centre of each. In the centre of the squares made by the flowers are small eyelet holes and four stitches over two threads pointing towards the centre.

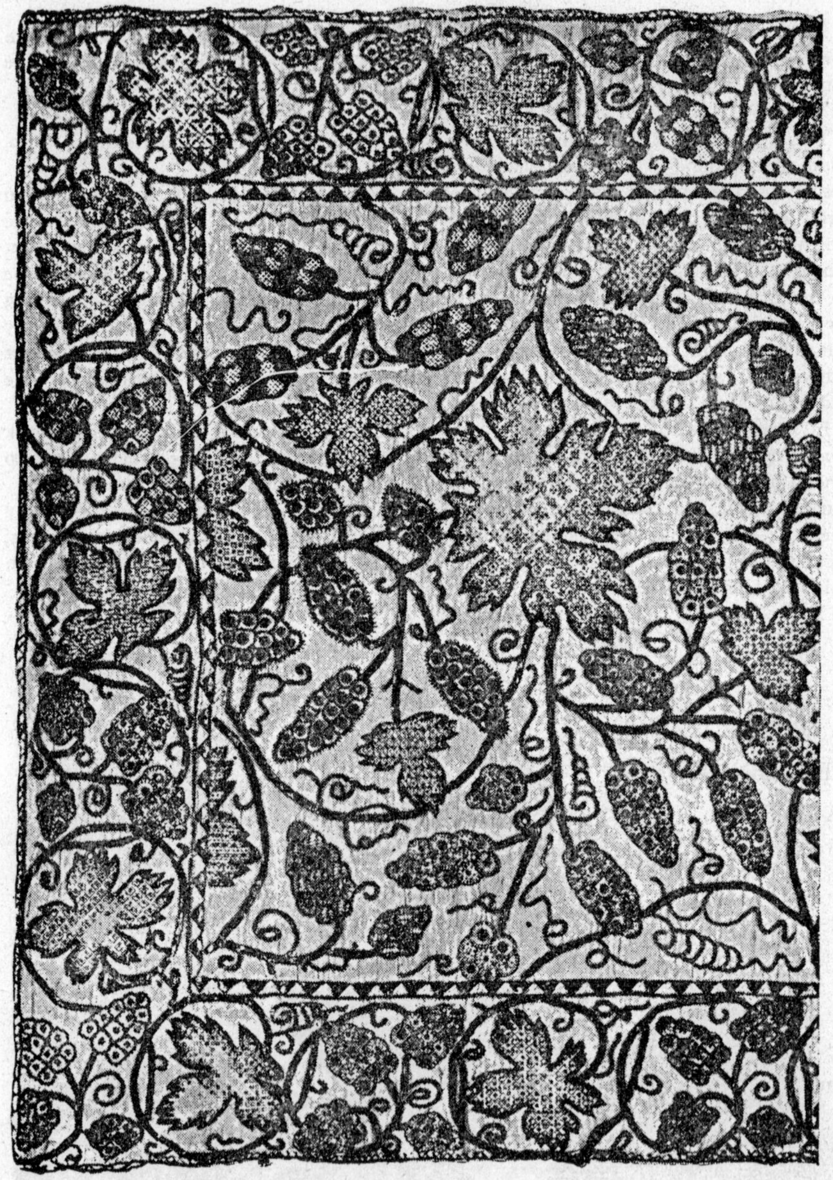

Reproduced by the courtesy of the Victoria and Albert Museum.

A 16TH CENTURY CURTAIN

Worked in silk on linen in braid, chain, back, coral and buttonhole stitches.

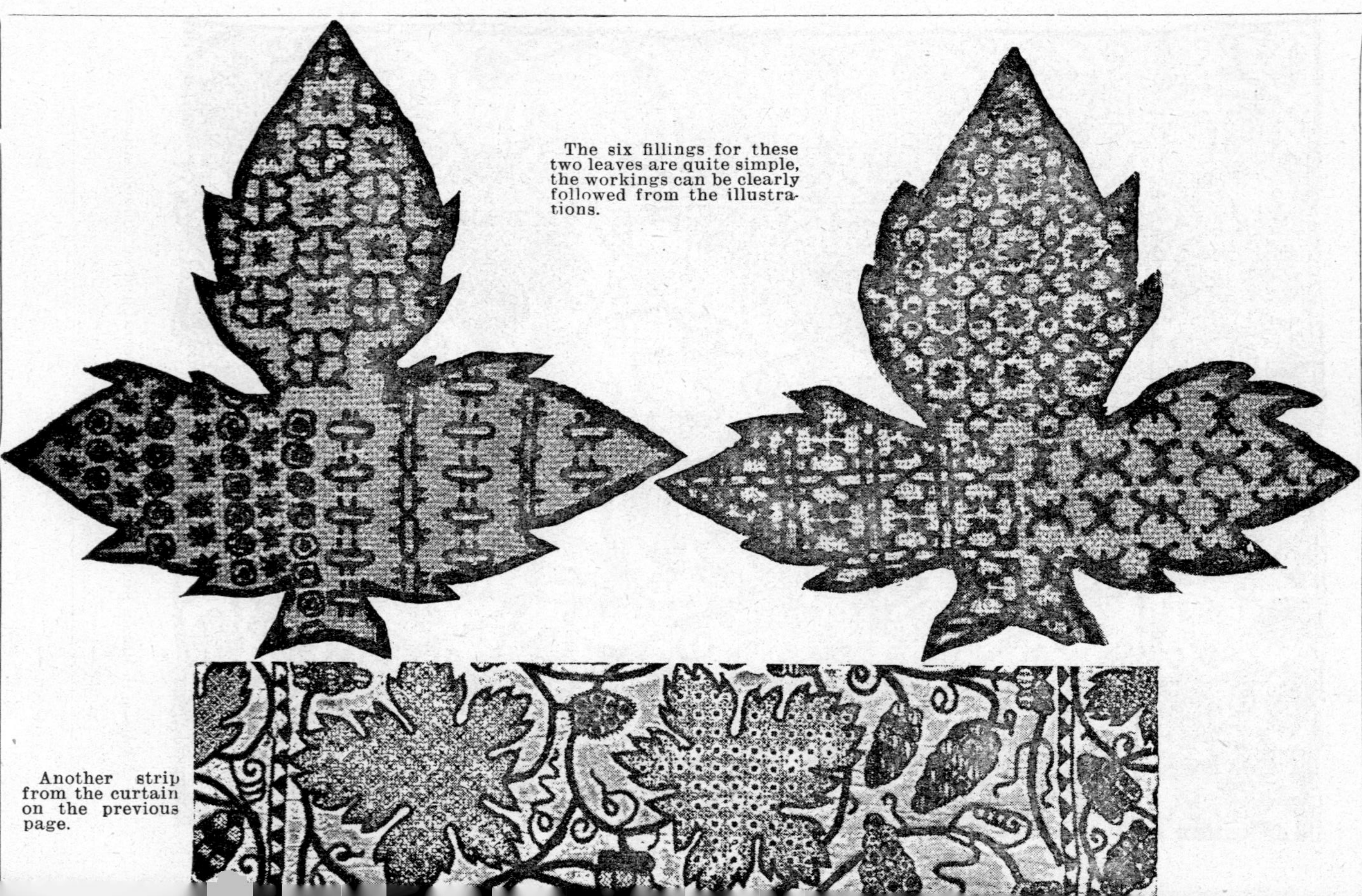

The six fillings for these two leaves are quite simple, the workings can be clearly followed from the illustrations.

Another strip from the curtain on the previous page.

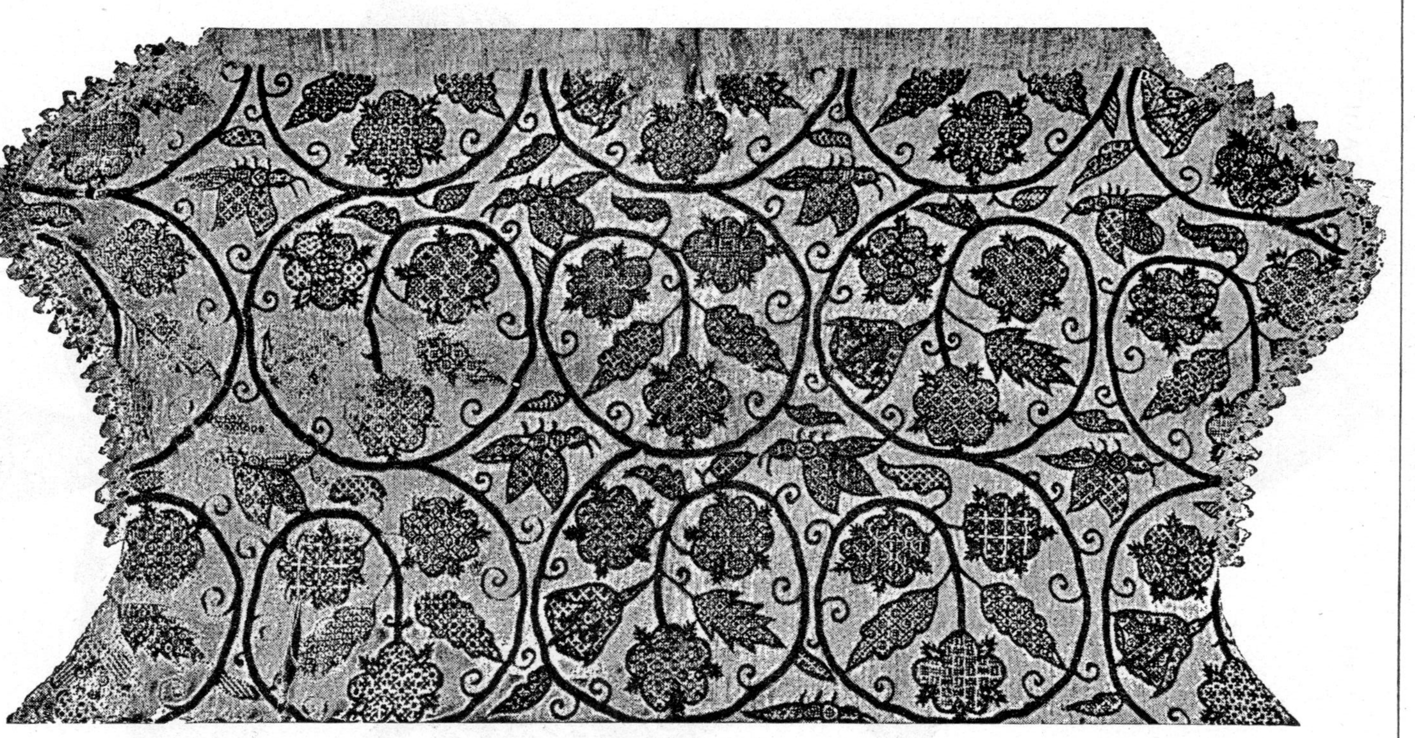

From the Victoria and Albert Museum.

Reproduced by kind permission of Mrs. Grubbe.

A WOMAN'S HEADDRESS

THREE MORE EXAMPLES

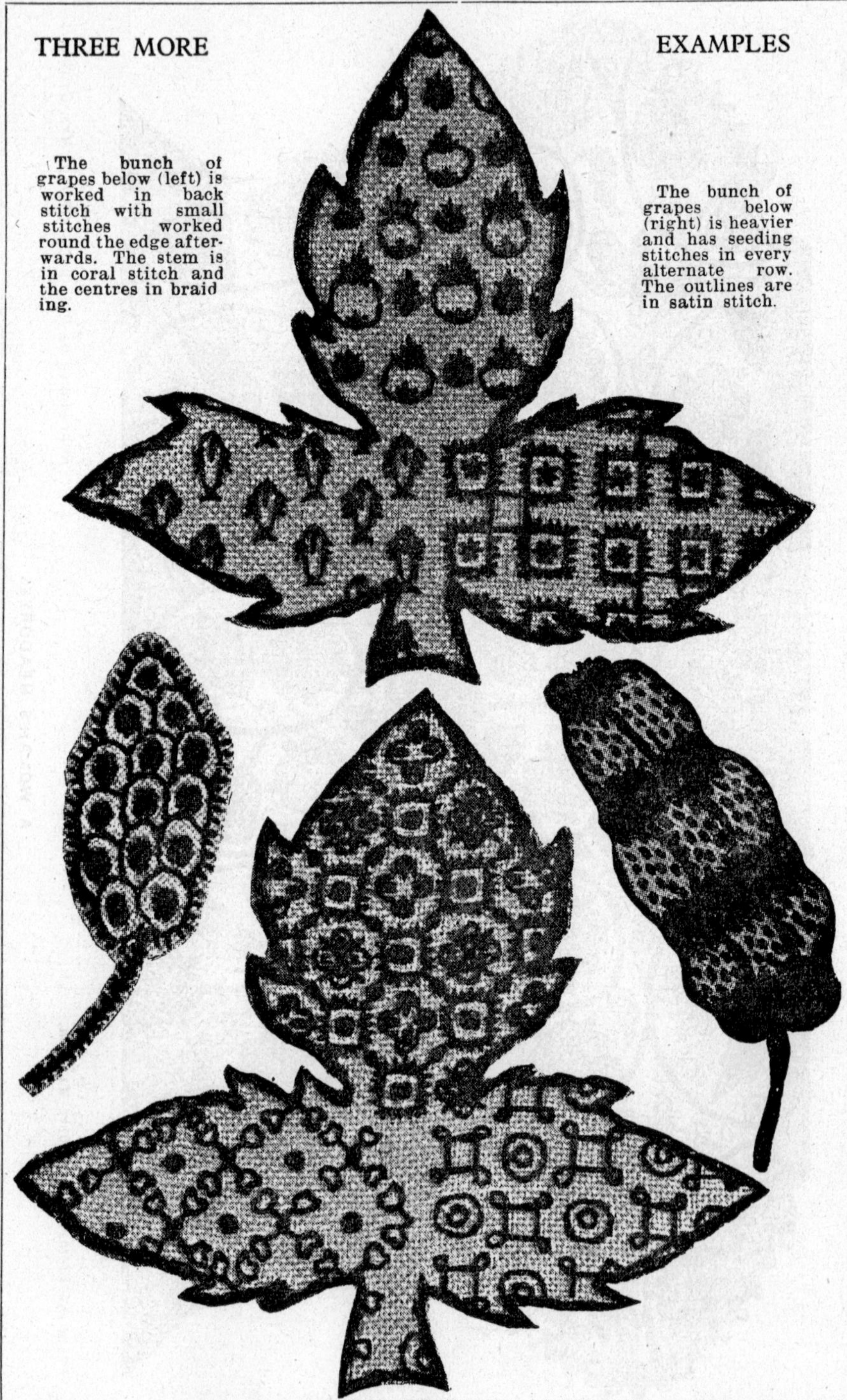

The bunch of grapes below (left) is worked in back stitch with small stitches worked round the edge afterwards. The stem is in coral stitch and the centres in braiding.

The bunch of grapes below (right) is heavier and has seeding stitches in every alternate row. The outlines are in satin stitch.

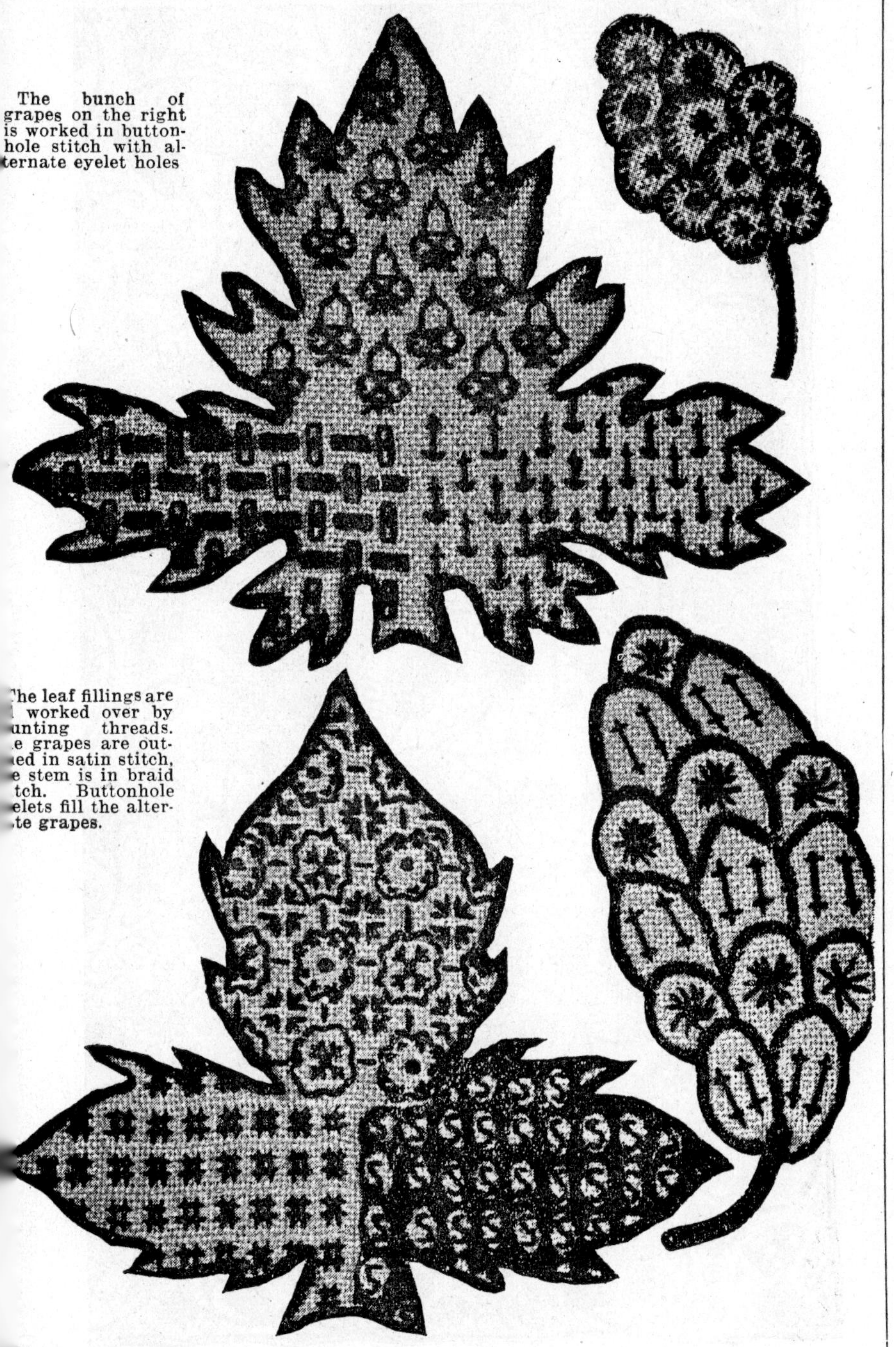

The bunch of grapes on the right is worked in buttonhole stitch with alternate eyelet holes

The leaf fillings are worked over by unting threads. e grapes are outed in satin stitch, e stem is in braid tch. Buttonhole elets fill the alterte grapes.

Reproduced by courtesy of the Victoria and Albert Museum

16TH CENTURY PILLOW SLIP

Reproduced by courtesy of the Victoria and Albert Museum

BRAIDING

Braiding is a form of needlework occasionally used for decorating cushion covers, runners, chair-backs, etc.

Braids are composed of plaited threads, and among the more familiar types are boot and shoe laces, costume braids, Prussian bindings, cords and gimps used in upholstery, tinsel galons, and fancy artificial silk braids. Most of these can be had either flat or in the tubular form.

Braid work has been used throughout the ages and is to be found used with embroideries in most countries. It is chiefly used as a trimming when much embroidery is not wanted.

Costume braids, as they used to be called, were formerly made of worsted or mohair, but they can now be obtained in silk, cotton and artificial silk mixtures, suitable for embroidery work of all varieties. Many braids have a groove running down the centre which makes it an easy matter to stitch the braid trimming to any kind of fabric background.

Braids can be bought in widths of from ¼ of an inch to 9 and even 12 inches, the latter kind not being very greatly used.

For some purposes tape, either white or coloured, can be used in the same manner as braid and applied to the same type of designs.

How to do Braid Work.—Braiding on costumes and dresses usually implies the binding off cuffs, collar and revers with a fine make of braid, to neaten the edges and give a special finish.

Fancy braiding is the attaching of braid to a groundwork material in a set design previously marked on the fabric, outlining the design completely and forming an effective and hard-wearing trimming.

Iron off the selected braiding transfer into position on the material, then lay the braid along the design, inch by inch, attaching it with small running stitches along the centre groove, as shown in the illustration. When the design is complete the end of the braid can be made neat by threading it through the eye of a large darning or crewel needle, and passing it through to the wrong side, where it can be securely sewn down with tiny stitches. If the braid is too coarse to go through the eye of the needle, it can be sewn to the eye, and pulled through very carefully, afterwards attaching it as just described.

Braid work of all kinds must be well pressed on the wrong side after it is finished, and if it is a very elaborate pattern, it is improved by being left under heavy weights for some time after it is completed.

Sewing on Flat or Tubular Braid.—Flat and tubular braids are sewn down from right to left. Fasten the braid neatly at the right-hand side—by pulling it through from the back with the aid of a large crewel needle, holding it down in front of you on to the line on to which it is to be sewn. Bring the needle up so that it catches the braid close to the lower edge, insert the needle into the material as closely as possible to where it was brought out. Take a slanting stitch about ⅜ of an inch long, bringing out the needle through both material and braid, quite close up to the lower edge.

Sewing on Soutache Braid.—There are two ways of attaching soutache braid. The simpler method is to hold the braid flat over the line of the transferred design, and sew through the centre of the soutache, taking a very short stitch on the right side, and quite a long one on the underside, being careful not to pull the thread too tightly, or you will cause the braiding to pucker up in an unsightly manner.

If using a design with many sharp curves, however, it is better to use the second method of braiding, which consists of sewing on the braid so that it stands upright. Hold the braid in front of you over the line of the design as before, but keeping it upright instead of flat. Fasten the braid securely at the right-hand side of the work, and bring the needle up through the material, just catching the lower edge of the braid. Insert the needle as near as

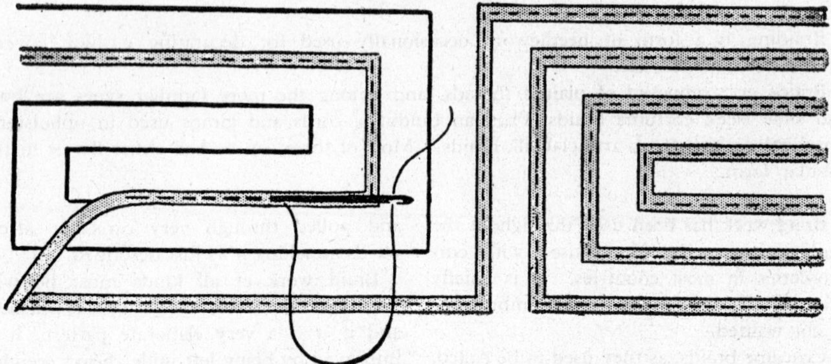

Fig. 1.—SEWING ON BRAID IN GREEK KEY PATTERN

possible to where you brought it out and take a stitch about $\frac{1}{4}$ of an inch long. Bring the needle out through material and lower edge of braid firmly but without puckering.

Braids with woven designs and figures were much used for vestments. These braids took the place of embroidery and were very effective, being much less costly and simple to apply.

The method used was very easy, as, the design tacked into position, one only had to hem round the edges as invisibly as possible, at the same time making it secure.

Narrow braids of this type were also used for trimming men's and women's clothes. Many plaited braids were used, gold or silver threads plaited with silk or wool were great favourites. These were sewn on in the same manner, as invisibly as possible.

Plaited Braids were also used in the early seventeenth century for purse strings.

Most designs for braid work are very simple. The two methods have already been described. Care must be taken when sewing the braid on rounded corners, to ease it in carefully on the inner side, so as to allow it to lie flat on the outer edge.

Fig. 2 shows clearly the larger stitches being taken on the outside and the smaller ones on the inside.

Threads for Braiding.—The thread used for sewing down the braid may be either of the same colour as the braid itself, thus making it invisible, or it may be made an additional decoration by being of a different colour, and placed visibly across to form chequering or some simple pattern.

For places where the braid work has to be especially neatened it is always wisest to unravel a little of the braid and use an actual strand of this as the sewing thread. Corners and sharp curves also need special care and attention, with extra stitches here and there, and a strand of the braid itself is the best medium for these stitches.

Fig. 2.—SEWING BRAID ON CURVES

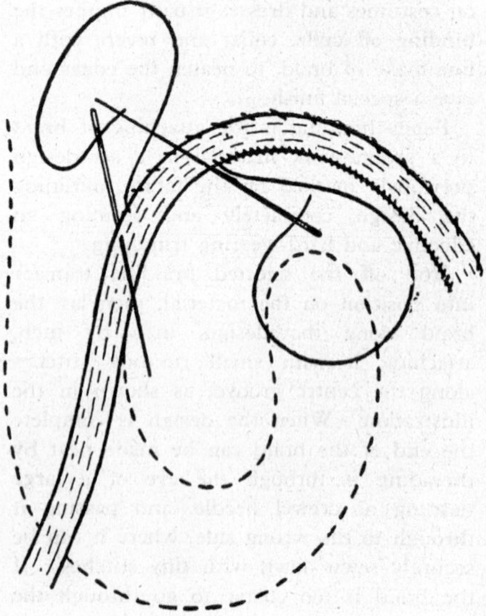

BRODERIE ANGLAISE

Of the very many kinds of beautiful white embroidery, Broderie Anglaise, or English White Embroidery, is one of the most lovely, and as the stitches needed for its execution are few, it is especially useful for embroidering house linen, dainty personal wear, and even children's clothes. It was originally Czecho-Slovakian peasant embroidery and was brought to England in the ninth century.

As the work is done entirely with a thread to match the material (or with only one thread, though it is occasionally of a contrasting colour, such as cinnamon brown on écru, or china blue on white), there are no difficult questions of colour blending to be dealt with, and once the embroidery is started, the worker can go straight ahead, and will find it extremely restful to do.

The Appearance of Broderie Anglaise.—Designs for Broderie Anglaise have a wealth of small but very simple detail, as the work consists of eyelets, both oval and round, which are finely stitched along the edges. Sometimes a design consists entirely of these open eyelets, but sometimes parts of it are cut and others worked solidly in satin stitch. Stems and scrolls which connect the various parts of the design are usually worked in overcast or stem stitch, and chain stitch is also sometimes introduced.

Many designs for Broderie Anglaise have bows, spirals, and other motifs in them, worked in what is known as Ladder Work, which, as its name implies, has little bars worked from side to side, which hold together the outlines when the material between has been cut away.

In some of the more elaborate pieces of this work will be found other stitches, such as French knots and various kinds of fillings, and the working of these is fully described in the part of this book devoted to embroidery stitches.

Scalloping makes a very suitable edging for articles worked in Broderie Anglaise, but hem-stitching can also be combined with this type of embroidery most effectively.

Materials for Broderie Anglaise.—The implements are few, but they must be of a good and reliable make. Ordinary embroidery needles, of a size that will take the thread smoothly and easily, are, of course, the first essential. A very sharp pair of scissors is an absolute necessity for snipping eyelet holes and scalloped edges, and an embroidery stiletto is used for piercing the smaller holes.

Good materials are essential, and they must be smooth and even, without any tendency to fraying, or much of the work will be wasted. For house linen, fine linen is the ideal fabric, while for lighter and smaller articles such as handkerchief sachets, baby's cushion covers, underwear and baby clothes, linen lawn, cambric and muslin are good materials to choose.

Lawn and nainsook are both suitable for underwear embroidered in this way, and Broderie Anglaise is also seen a great deal on crêpe de Chine, jap silk, and other varieties of washing silks. This form of embroidery, combined with satin stitch and scalloping, can also be effectively introduced on fine flannel and nun's veiling.

Working threads vary according to the material chosen, and the fineness or coarseness of the thread should be according to the weight of the material to be embroidered. It is always advisable to take the material to the shop when buying the cotton, as there is such a large range of thicknesses, that it will be far easier to see the most suitable size to be bought.

Mercerised embroidery threads are the most generally employed on linen and cotton materials, and they can be obtained in the floss or twisted varieties. Floss and mercerised embroidery cotton are ideal threads, and Coton à Broder is also recommended. Linen thread is also a suitable medium, especially for house linen, such as towels, sheets and pillow-slips—linen floss being the first choice.

A fine twisted embroidery silk is best for use on crêpe de Chine and other silk fabrics; and for embroidery on flannel or other light-weight woollen grounds, a specia variety of thread known as Flannel Silk should be employed.

Broderie Anglaise is usually worked in the hand, but for the more solid forms, in which a good deal of satin stitch and other stitches are introduced, a tambour frame is to be recommended.

Work on muslin or very fine lawn is inclined to pucker, and to prevent this, it should be tacked over glazed linen or toile cirée, which can be bought at most art needlework shops and good stores.

How to Work

Eyelet holes play the most important part in this form of embroidery.

Eyelets.—Each hole should be first outlined in small running stitches exactly on the tracing, large holes being outlined with a double row of running stitches. Cut the hole across, and across again, with pointed scissors, turn the four points of the material to the wrong side with the needle, and overcast as in Fig. 1. The less material taken up, the better the shape of the hole. Cut off the ragged edges of the material on the wrong side. Small holes should not be cut but pierced with the stiletto, and the edge overcast. When working long-shaped holes (Fig. 2) or oval eyelets, as they are often called, care must be taken to round the lower portion nicely and to make the upper portion well pointed.

Do not on any account start a new thread whilst working an eyelet; in fact, if possible, one thread should be used for both the running and the overcasting, the latter being begun after the running is done, without cutting off.

In working shaded holes, or **Shadow Eyelets** as they are also called, where the lower rounded portion is embroidered with a wider stitch than the upper, it is often advisable to work the former portion first, then the latter, taking care to graduate the stitches evenly (Fig. 3). But these must not be too heavily padded, for if they are, it is difficult to keep them a good shape, and the effect is spoiled. Buttonhole stitch is again often employed instead of overcasting, if preferred by the worker.

Three-cornered holes are worked in the same way as oval or round eyelets, care being taken to keep the shape (Fig. 4).

Do not crowd the stitches when working eyelets, as this quickly spoils the shape and the effect is poor. Aim at placing the stitches so that they lie evenly side by side.

When an eyelet is completed, fasten off by running the thread along in the back of the last few stitches, and snip it off close to the embroidery.

In some pieces of work, particularly if the material is flimsy and perhaps liable to fray if stretched or pulled during use or washing, the eyelets can be buttonhole stitched instead of overcast, the eyelet being prepared as previously described, then worked with buttonhole stitch, the purl edge being either on the outside or inside edge of the hole, though the same direction must be maintained throughout the whole piece of work.

Another way of working a round or oval shadow eyelet is to pad it in the same way as before, working the narrow edge in overcast stitch and the wider in buttonhole stitch. Fig. 5 shows the working in the different stages of the shaded holes with buttonhole and overcast edge. This is effective, especially when used for a

Fig. 1
HOW TO CUT EYELETS

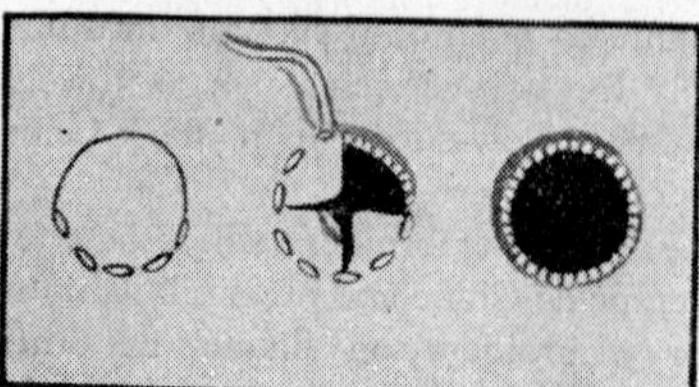

Fig. 2
OVAL EYELETS

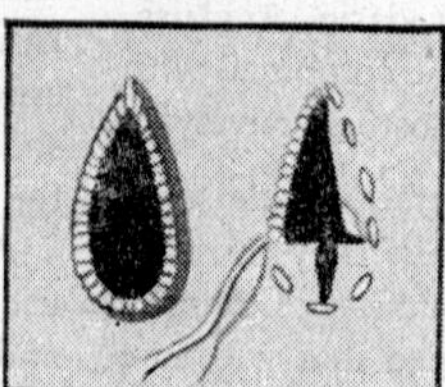

Fig. 3
SHADOW EYELETS

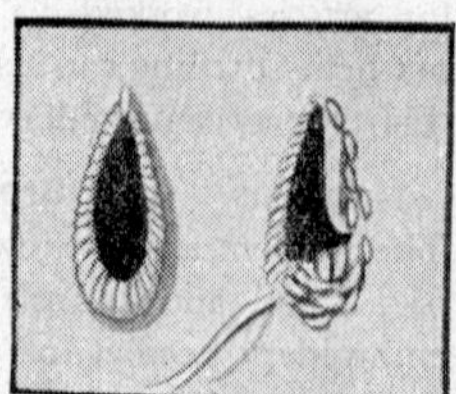

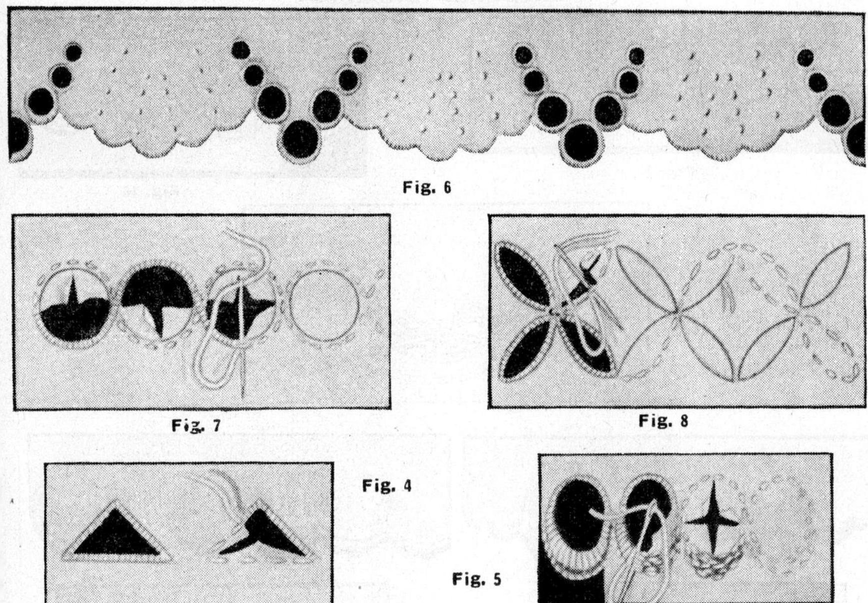

Fig. 6

Fig. 7

Fig. 8

Fig. 4

Fig. 5

scalloped border with eyelet holes. Fig. 6 is a good example.

When working a row or chain of holes (Fig. 7) the top of the one hole and the bottom of the next should be worked alternately in wave fashion; or else the tops of all the holes should first be worked and then the bottoms. This makes a better connection between the individual holes. In the so-called "cucumber-seed" pattern, Fig. 8, the whole figure is outlined in this "wave" method, and each hole is then embroidered separately. In this way any risk of the material tearing away at the juncture of any two holes is avoided. If the holes actually form the edge of any piece of work, their outside edges should be outlined several times and then worked round in buttonhole stitch, the upper portions of the holes being embroidered afterwards.

Buttonhole Stitch is mostly used for finishing the edges of a piece of work, and is always done the same way, in whatever kind of design. First of all the upper and lower edges of the tracing are run round, then the centre is padded, and thirdly, the buttonhole stitch is worked right across, working from left to right. This can be done either in the hand or sewn on to toile cirée. The needle is inserted vertically above the upper contour and brought out directly below the lower (Fig. 9) keeping the thread under the needle point, thus making a purl edge. For scallops such as those in Figs. 10 and 11, where the lower contour is longer than the upper one, the stitches must be close together along the upper edge and rather more spread out along the lower one, but they must always touch each other. The thread must not be drawn too tight, or else the material will pucker. The stitches should get smaller towards the point of the scallop. Small, flat scallops or wavy curves can be padded with one or two rows of running-stitches; deeper curves may be padded with chain stitch (Figs. 11 and 12). The outlines must be entirely covered. A scallop and hole can be worked together (Fig. 13). Each thread should be both started and finished off on the right side of the work by means of a few running

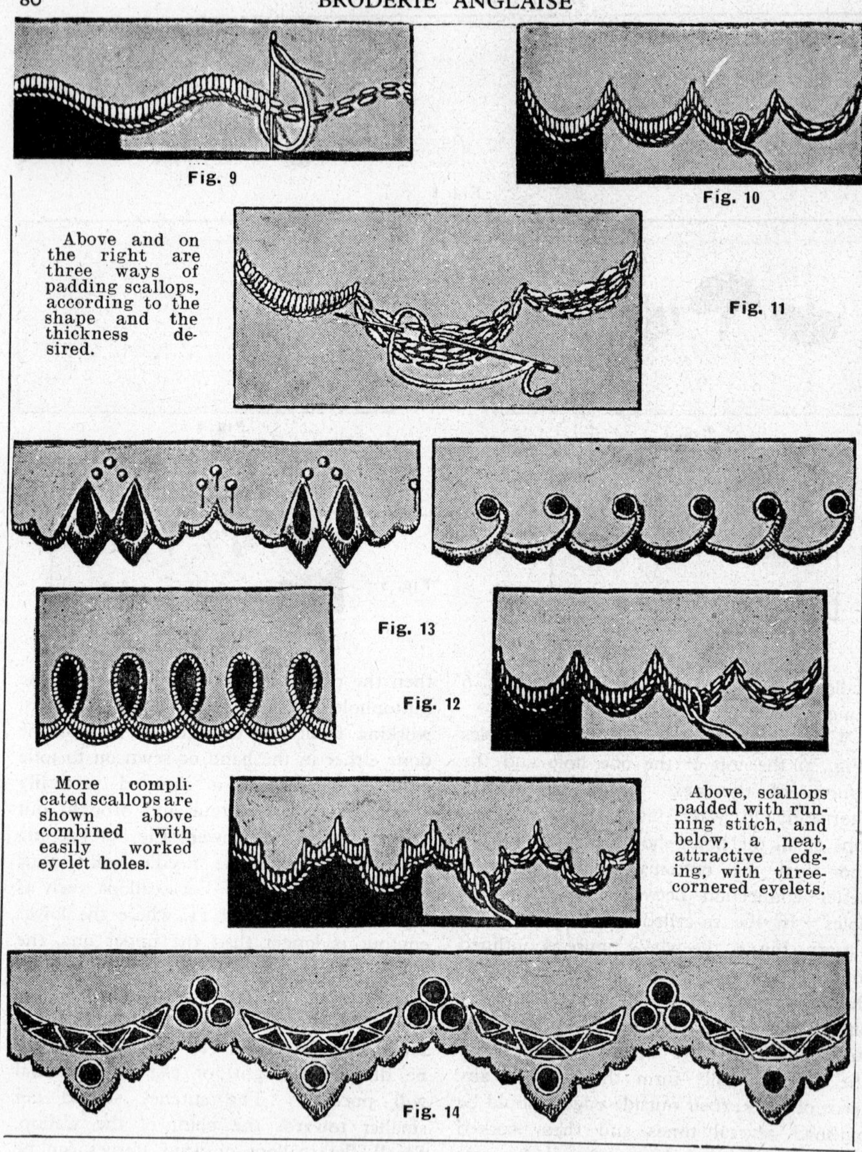

Fig. 9

Fig. 10

Fig. 11

Above and on the right are three ways of padding scallops, according to the shape and the thickness desired.

Fig. 13

Fig. 12

More complicated scallops are shown above combined with easily worked eyelet holes.

Above, scallops padded with running stitch, and below, a neat, attractive edging, with three-cornered eyelets.

Fig. 14

stitches, and when beginning a new thread, run a few stitches, and then bring the needle up through the last loop of the old thread. When finished the material must be cut away carefully quite close to the buttonholed edge.

As has been mentioned before, parts of Broderie Anglaise designs are worked solidly, and the choice as to which parts to cut and which to leave lies with the worker, though in many cases the most effective arrangement is obvious

For the solid embroidery, **Satin Stitch** is generally used, in both unpadded and raised varieties. Here again a little practice shows which kind is the most suitable to use, but as a rule the padded kind should be employed when the design is to be brought into prominence, and the unpadded kind for less important parts of the design.

For spots, which figure so largely in this type of embroidery, the fully padded stitch is best. Larger sections to be worked in satin stitch should be padded all over with running stitch; the padding may be made light or heavy as desired. The satin stitching in this case is worked across the narrow way of the space, and may go directly at right angles to the design, or be slightly slanting.

In satin stitch or raised embroidery, great care must be taken to keep the stitches close to each other, leaving no spaces. Work from left to right and usually from top to bottom. The outlines must be worked first, and then be filled in with large running stitches worked one into the other, taking care that the stitch is always larger on the right side of the work, so that the embroidery has a raised effect, and the padding stitches are always in a direction contrary to the embroidery stitches. For straight bars, and for all raised embroidery, there must be several layers of foundation stitches in the centre. When working dots in satin stitch, after outlining with small running stitches they should be padded twice, making the top layer of padding rather larger than the bottom one, thus obtaining the raised effect (Figs. 15 and 16). The dot is then embroidered, starting with the middle stitch and working the top and bottom half of it with an equal number of stitches. Dots are often outlined after working with back or stem stitch. In all curved forms the embroidery is worked towards the middle, Fig. 17 (showing small spray outlines, etc.), and when working sprays the leaves must be worked before the stalk.

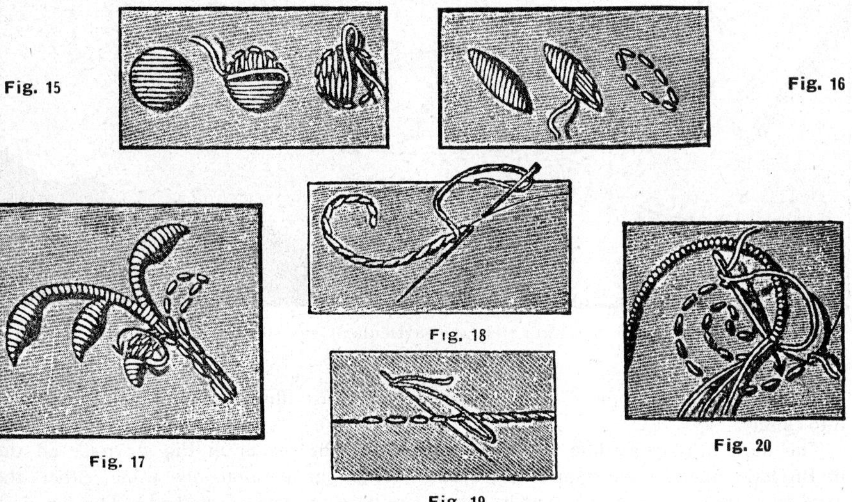

Fig. 15 Fig. 16 Fig. 17 Fig. 18 Fig. 19 Fig. 20

Throughout one piece of work there should be a definite system for the direction of the satin stitching. For instance, spots on a border can have the stitches either worked level with the edge of the material, or in the opposite direction: in a trail of spots, the stitches can all be worked lengthways, following the line of the trail: in a flower they can all radiate towards the centre, and so on. Where the design repeats, use the same formation throughout every repeat. Unless care is taken over this, the finished result of the work is apt to

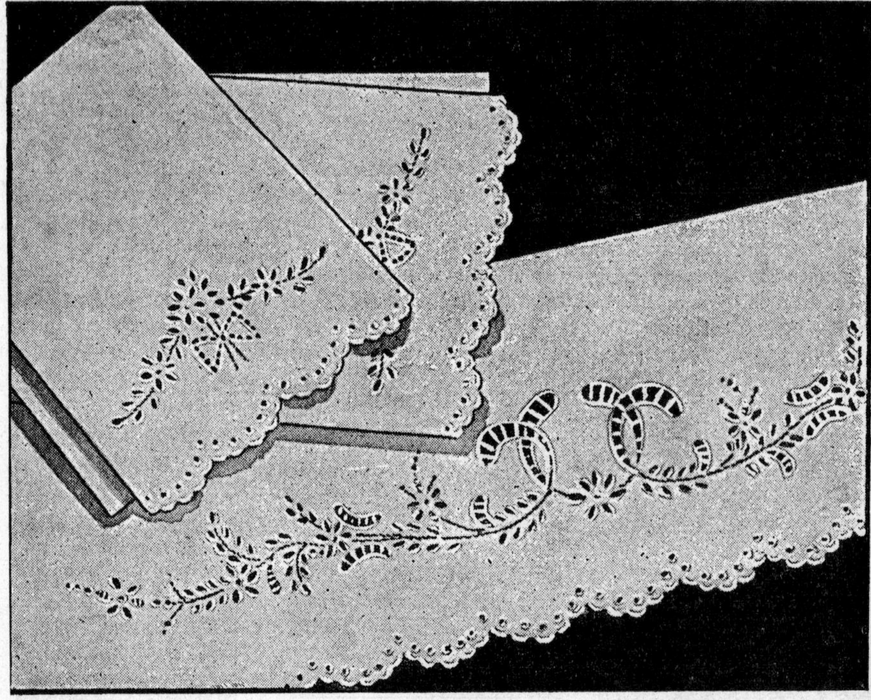

Fig. 21.—Neat designs that are particularly suitable for bed linen

look carelessly "scrappy" when looked into closely.

The most satisfactory **line stitches** used in Broderie Anglaise are stem stitch, overcast stitch and chain stitch. Others, such as back stitch, are sometimes employed, but the first three are quite adequate, and the best effects are usually obtained when the embroidery is kept simple. Of the three, overcast is the richest, and is most in keeping with the style of the embroidery as a whole. For very fine lines stem stitching is suitable, and chain stitching makes a good continuous line.

Stems worked in stem stitch or overcast stitch are padded with a line of run or back stitches, or worked over one or more loose threads held along the outline (Figs. 18, 19, and 20) In either case the appearance of fine cord is obtained.

A few specimens of Broderie Anglaise which are particularly suitable for the beginner, are illustrated here and on the next page.

For the border in Fig. 22 trace off the design in position, by using either the pounce or transfer method. The detail of the stitchery is clearly indicated. The eyelets are worked in satin stitch, the battlemented border being in slanting satin stitch. This border would be particularly suitable for a towel or bed linen. The design dates back to Napoleon's time when it was fashion's latest idea for petticoats.

Fine huckaback or linen is the best material to choose, and either of these may be bought by the yard.

A towel with hemstitched ends can be bought machine-made, or the hemstitching done by hand. Use fine embroidery cotton for working and a slightly thicker thread for padding

For working the bed linens as suggested above use a Coton à Broder The

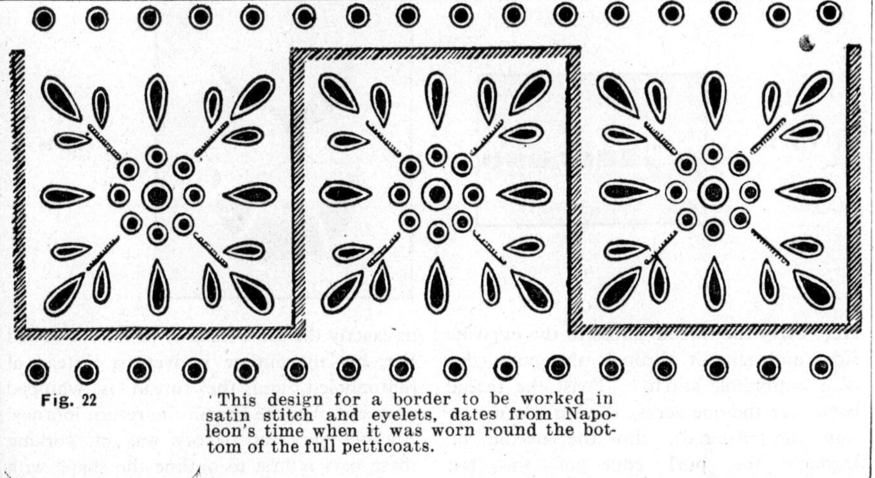

Fig. 22 This design for a border to be worked in satin stitch and eyelets, dates from Napoleon's time when it was worn round the bottom of the full petticoats.

flowers and leaves should be in eyelet holes, the stems in stem stitch, and the bows in ladderwork, making either the twisted or button-holed variety of bars. The scalloping should be in buttonhole stitch.

Ladder Work.—As has been mentioned previously, more elaborate designs in Broderie Anglaise are often combined with Ladder work—Venetian Ladder Work, as it is often called, having a very charming effect, which is exceedingly easy and quick to work. The work consists of shapes buttonholed or overcast along the edges, with bars to connect the two outlines, the material between the bars being carefully cut away.

There are four methods of working the bars, all of which are clearly shown in the diagrams on this page. They are:

1. Twisted Bars (Fig. 23).
2. Buttonhole Bars (Fig. 24).
3. Darned Bars (Fig. 25).
4. Overcast Bars (Fig. 26).

To work **Twisted Bars,** first outline the space with even running stitch, then buttonhole stitch along one side and down the other side until the first bar is reached.

WORKED BARS

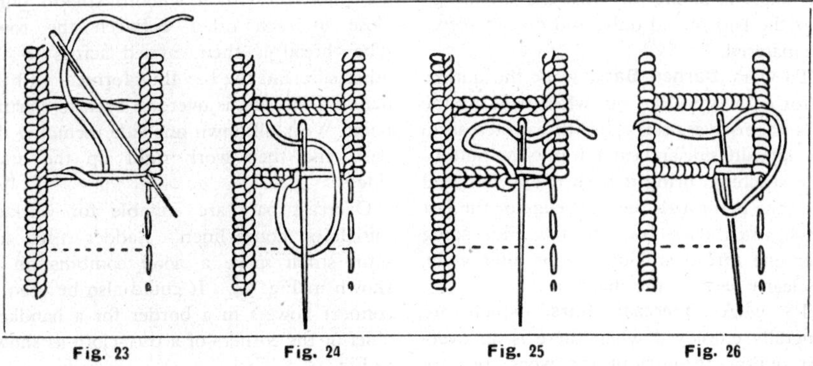

Fig. 23 Fig. 24 Fig. 25 Fig. 26

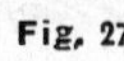
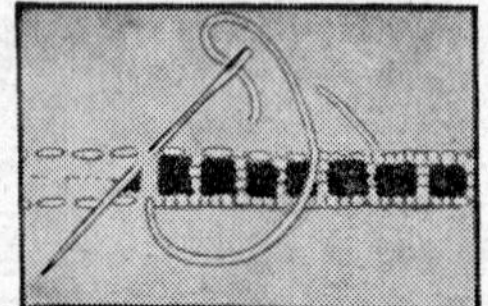

Fig. 27

Fig. 28

Here carry the thread across to the opposite side, and take it through the purl edge of a buttonhole stitch. Twist the thread back over the one across the bar (do not go into the material), slip the needle up through the purl edge of the last buttonhole stitch made, and continue buttonhole stitching until the next bar is reached. Work each bar in the way just described.

Twisted bars can also be worked with overcast stitch as Fig. 26 clearly shows. They are made and embroidered when the outlining is done. The hole is then cut and the edges of the material turned back with the needle, and the shape closely overcast all round, as in the case of holes. When large patterns have to be worked they are sewn down on to toile cirée or glazed linen or mounted in a frame.

To work **Buttonhole Bars,** work as for the Twisted Bar, but instead of twisting the thread back over the one laid across the space, buttonhole stitch over it, as seen in the diagram, taking care that the stitches go over the laid thread only, and do not pierce the material.

To work **Darned Bars,** work the outline as for a Twisted Bar, but when working the bars themselves, carry the thread across to the opposite side and catch it into the buttonhole stitching, bring it back to the first end and take it through the purl edge of the last stitch, then darn back to the end, going over one thread and under one alternately, as clearly seen in the diagram.

To work **Overcast Bars,** which are generally employed when there is an overcast outline throughout the work, prepare in exactly the same manner as for a Twisted Bar, but the outline is overcast instead of buttonholed, and the thread is whipped over and over the bar on the return journey. Another very satisfactory way of working these bars is first to outline the shape with running stitches, then, when working the first side of the overcasting, to carry the thread either once or three times across each bar is as it is reached, overcast the laid threads, and continue overcasting the outlining until the next bar is reached. Complete by overcasting the second outline.

When the outlining and bars are completed, carefully cut away the material behind the bars, using very sharp scissors. To cut the material close up to the stitching, turn the work on to the back and trim away the edges from under the purl edge.

The overcast bars shown in Fig. 27 are more difficult to execute. A thread is drawn in the material, a row of running stitches is made down each side, two holes are punched with a smooth stiletto fairly close to each other between the rows. The thread is then carried across to the other side and the bar thus formed, and the material threads, is overcast back to starting point. Work all down one side including the bars, and then work right up the other side.

Overcast bars are suitable for working initials on house linen. Ladder stitch and satin stitch make a good combination as shown in Fig. 34. It could also be used to connect flowers in a border for a handkerchief or the corners of a tray-cloth as shown in Fig. 35

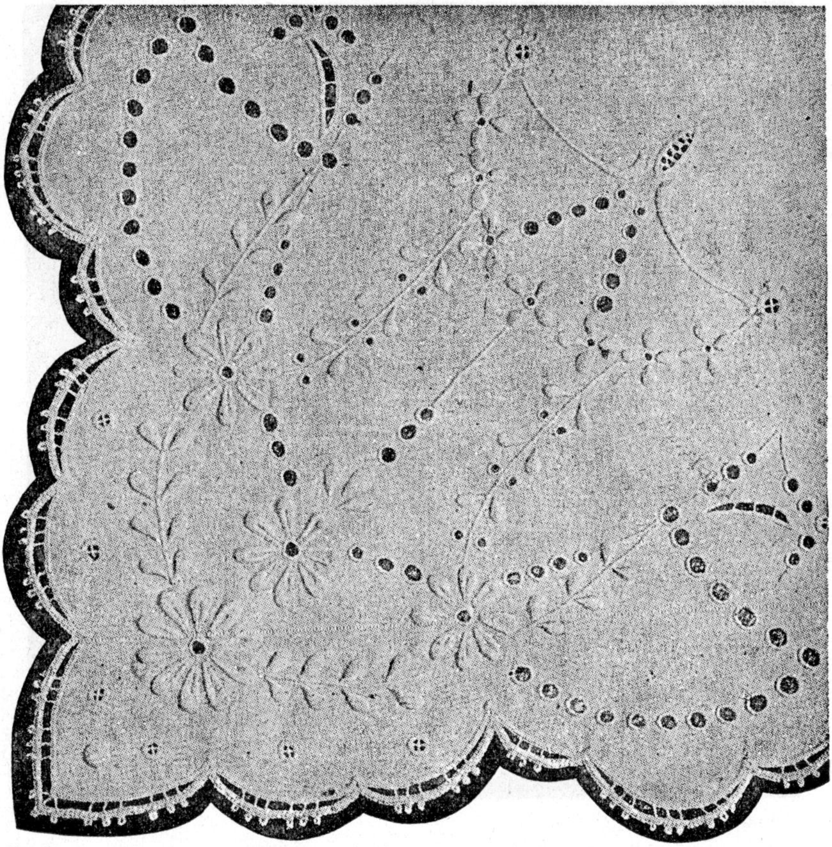

Fig. 29

A LOVELY CLOTH

Fig. 29a shows how the small twisted eyelet fillings near the edge are worked, and Fig. 29b gives the working detail of the picot border.

An Afternoon Teacloth.—(Fig. 30).—For the large squares the working can easily be followed from Fig. 31. Outline the square with running stitches and buttonhole with the purl edge inside; also run and buttonhole the edge of the shaped inner section (purl edge outside) and as each bar is reached, carry the thread to the outer square, and secure it in the outer edge, twist back and continue buttonholing to the next bar. When finished the material is cut away from under the purl edges.

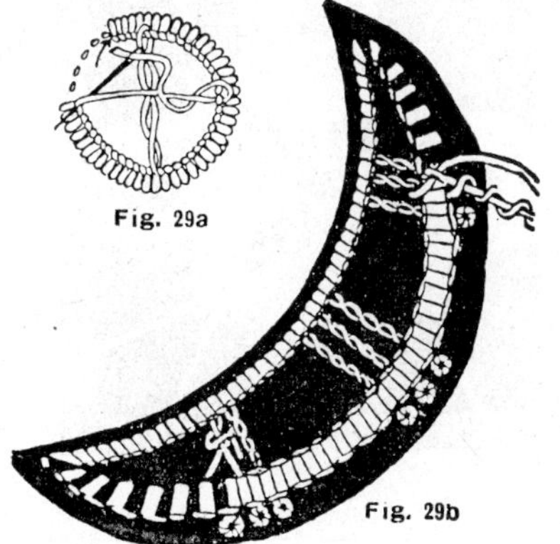

Fig. 29a

Fig. 29b

Work the scalloping with ordinary

Fig. 30

FOR AFTERNOON TEA

Fig. 31

Fig. 32

Fig. 33

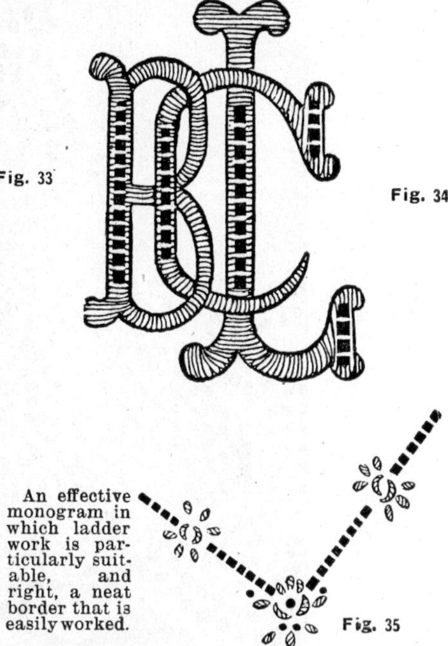

Fig. 34

An effective monogram in which ladder work is particularly suitable, and right, a neat border that is easily worked.

Fig. 35

buttonhole stitch, first of all outlining it with ordinary running stitches.

In Fig. 33 the combination of overcast eyelets, square buttonholed eyelets, ladder work and the introduction of herringbone stitch as a filling for the oval leaves and flower petals, is a change from raised satin stitch, and makes an effective piece of work.

For the ladder work, first outline in

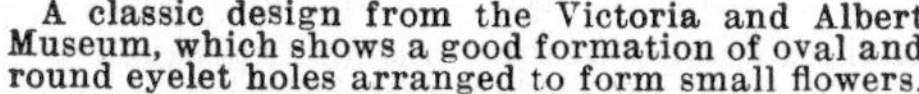

A classic design from the Victoria and Albert Museum, which shows a good formation of oval and round eyelet holes arranged to form small flowers.

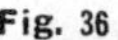

Fig. 36

Fig. 37

A lovely design, reproduced by kind permission of the Victoria and Albert Museum, made up of oval eyelet holes arranged to form circles and feathery fronds. Especially good are the two diamonds one either side of the circle.

running stitches, then one side is buttonholed, and also the second side to the first bar, then take the thread across to the first side, secure it in the purl edge and twist back. Continue buttonholing to the next bar.

Each small square is outlined in running stitches. Then buttonhole two sides and the third side to the bar, carry the thread across and secure it in the purl edge of the first side and twist back. Continue buttonholing until the bar is reached on the fourth side, take the thread through the first bar and secure it in the purl edge of the second side, twist back and finish the buttonholing. When the work is finished the material can be cut from under the buttonholed edges of the ladder section and the squares.

Work all the oval and round eyelets in overcast stitch, first outlining them in running stitch and piercing a hole with a stiletto for the circles, and cutting a slit with a sharp pointed pair of scissors for the ovals.

Work the flower petals and leaves in herringbone stitch, just inside each outline. Each petal is afterwards outlined in stem-stitch. Fig. 32 shows clearly the working of these stitches. The stems are also worked in stem-stitch. Fig. 33 shows an enlarged section of the working.

CANVAS BRAIDING

Canvas Braiding is a simple method of decorating large surfaces of canvas, and is very effective in comparison with the amount of trouble and material expended on the work.

Materials required for Canvas Braiding.—Ivory Canvas and canvas needles with blunt points; a coarse and fine thread—coarse for the braiding thread and a finer for overcasting. A coarse canvas will take a stout make of braiding thread, a finer canvas a finer thread; but the thread should completely hide the set of holes over which it is placed, as that gives the work a raised or braided appearance.

For the braiding or foundation thread a twisted thread is good. The braiding thread is kept in position with small stitches worked in a finer embroidery thread. These stitches are worked in some bright-coloured thread or silk, and from the line of holes directly above the braiding thread into the lines directly below it. The majority of braiding designs are suited to one colour only, and to use two or three shades spoils its simplicity.

The Method of Working.—When overcasting the braiding thread, the small stitches must be taken in routine; when the needle goes down through one of the lower holes it is inexpedient to bring it out again in the same set of holes for the next stitch; it should come out through the upper row. This prevents the canvas pulling out of shape, which it is apt to do when the stitches are not worked regularly.

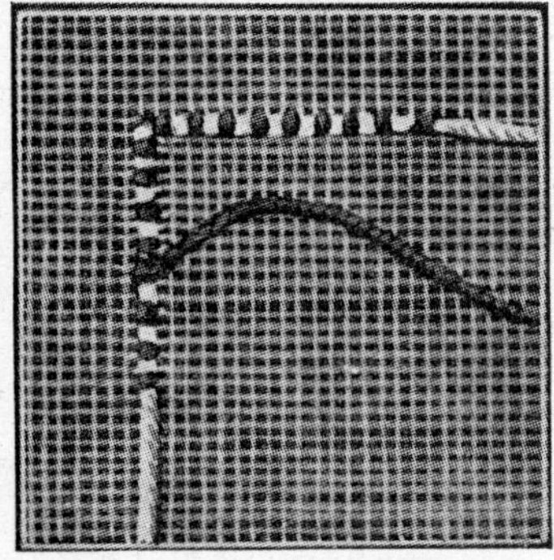

Fig. 1.—Ordinary overcasting stitch in which the braiding thread covers one row of holes and the finer thread is worked in small, plain stitches.

Draw the coarse braiding thread through the needle, bring it up from under the canvas through one of the holes directly on the line it is to follow; this prevents having rough ends on the right side of the work.

To finish off, the braiding thread is taken down through the last hole in the canvas on the line it is following. The loose ends can be cut fairly short, and secured on the reverse side with a stitch or two.

The Stitches Used.—Fig. 1 shows the ordinary overcasting stitch when the braiding thread covers one row of holes, and the finer thread is worked in small plain stitches, leaving a space of one hole between each stitch, so that the braiding thread shows between. Turn the braiding thread square at the corners, take a stitch across the corner going down into the same hole as the last stitch. Then start working down the next side taking the first stitch down into the same hole as the last two stitches. This makes a good corner.

Fig. 2 has only a single braiding thread and the small stitches are worked in pairs over it. This change gives a distinctive character to the design, making it more important and solid in appearance. It will be seen that two holes are left between each set of stitches. This way is best when the work is done in a long straight line, as the edge of a border; but when this stitch is used in a twisted pattern, where the lines cross and recross one another, it will be found necessary to leave only one hole between the double stitches. The corner is easily turned with two sets of stitches, the inner two meeting in the same hole.

Crossed Overcasting as shown in Fig. 3 is very simple. The overcasting stitches

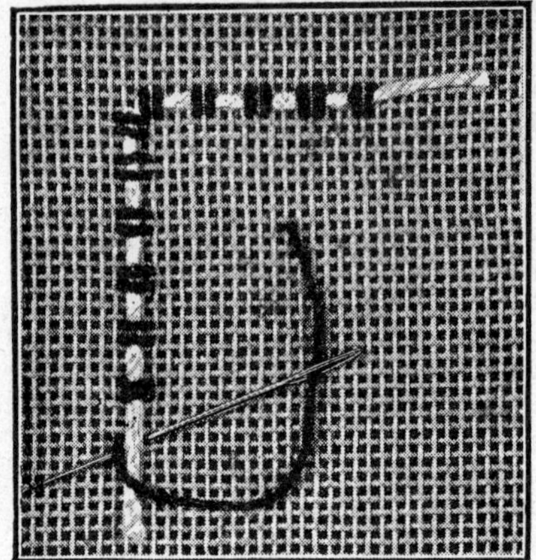

Fig. 2.—A single braiding thread, with small stitches over it, worked in pairs.

are crossed as in ordinary cross-stitch. In order to get them square it must be borne in mind that one hole of the canvas is covered by the braiding thread and that therefore these stitches must miss one hole on the opposite side of the thread, and the needle must go down through the third hole: that is, three holes are occupied each way of the square. The corner is turned with two sets of crossed stitches placed diagonally, as shown in Fig. 3. One hole is left between the stitches.

Fig. 4. A double braid that matches **Fig. 2.** It is worked in the same way, the second row of overcast stitches alternating with the first.

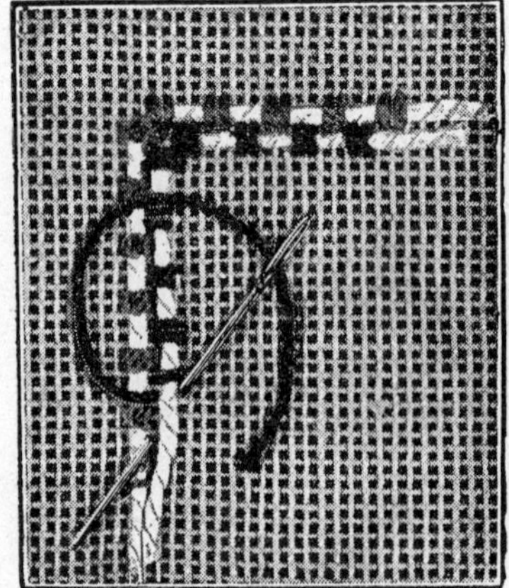

Fig. 4 is a double braid intended to match Fig. 2 and is worked over two under threads in the same way. The interval of the two holes with the one thread is used for the stitches belonging to the other; in this way they work in and out of one another, and so preserve a perfect regularity. For this reason there must be left two holes between the sets of stitches. The corner looks elaborate, but is really quite simple. The outer braiding thread is carried on one set of stitches further than the inner one, which leaves it plenty of room to turn the corner in exactly the same way as that used by the inner braiding thread, explained before.

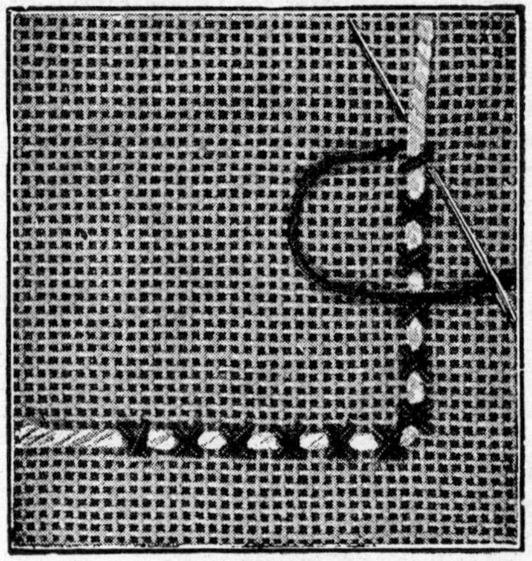

Fig. 3. The overcasting stitches are crossed like ordinary cross-stitch. The corner is turned with two sets of crosses placed diagonally.

Zigzag Overcasting.—In Fig. 5 slanting (that is, diagonal) stitches alone are used, which give the work a very light effect. These stitches are worked in such a manner as to produce a series of V-shaped lines along the braiding thread. They go first in one direction, then in the other; each hole serves for two stitches or, in other words, they start and finish from the same hole. Bring the needle up under the thread, and three holes in front of where you wish to start the work, then insert the needle three holes beyond where it was first inserted and above the thread, bringing it out four holes further along, and still above the thread. Now insert the needle in the starting hole and bring it out four holes further along below the thread and so on. The corner is turned by turning the braiding thread sharply, and then securing it with no less than three stitches, all of which meet in the centre hole above the thread. This holds the corner in place and the effect of the stitch at the extreme point of the angle is particularly good.

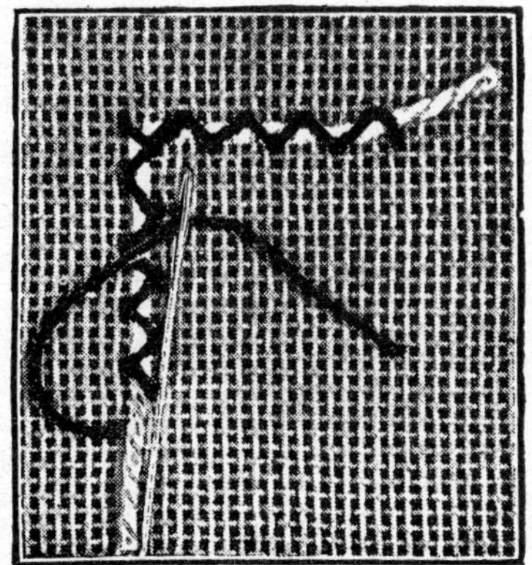

Fig. 5. Slanting or diagonal stitches are worked to produce a series of V-shaped waves over the braiding thread.

Castellated Pattern.—The upper line is worked first so as to give a correct indication where the second line is to be placed, worked on canvas cut straight with the grain of the material. Fig. 6 shows the design finished.

Fig. 7.—A border design consisting of tiny squares each side of which has three sets of double stitches.

Start with three cross-stitches (an interval of one hole between them); then turn sharply upwards and work three more stitches; turn to the right and work three more; then downwards and work three more. At this point another turn—to the right—brings the braiding thread into position for restarting these instructions. When a sufficient strip of the castellated line has been worked, the inner line is introduced into the pattern. Count three holes downwards into the canvas below the lower part of the first stitch, bring up the needle through the fourth hole, place the braiding thread along the line of the fifth and work four stitches in a straight line from left to right. Turn upwards and work four stitches (this brings the lower line up inside the first one); turn and work four stitches down again.

A Useful Border Design shown in Fig. 7. The little squares have three sets of double stitches on each side. There is a space of two holes between each. The double lines on either side of the row of squares are set at an interval of three clear holes between themselves and the inner row of squares. The double lines have the stitches done alternately, as shown in Fig. 4, not one above the other.

An Effective Insertion is shown in Fig. 8. Work five double stitches, laying the braiding thread horizontally along the canvas; turn upwards and work five more stitches; turn left and work four stitches;

Fig. 6.—Castellated pattern worked in cross-stitches, the upper line being worked first.

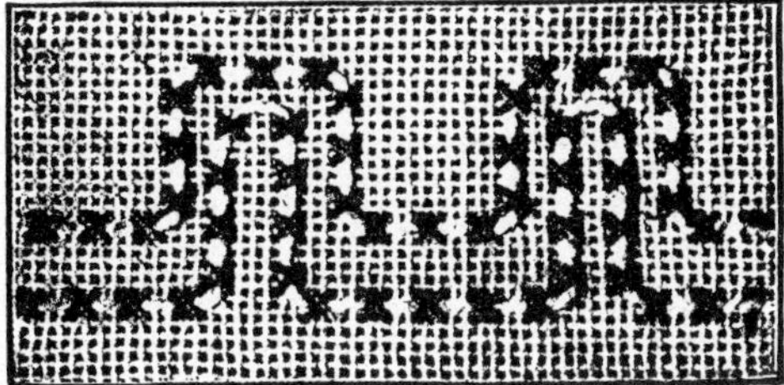

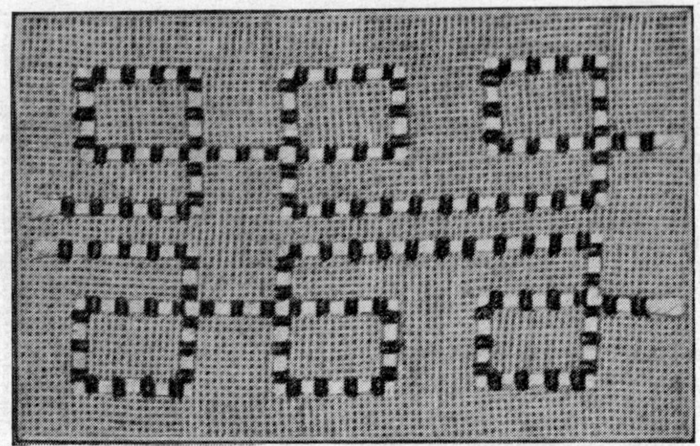

Fig. 8. A very simple pattern that makes an effective border or insertion, the overcast stitches being worked in pairs.

turn downwards and work three stitches; turn to the right and work eleven; turn upwards and work three stitches; turn to the left and work four; turn downwards and work five; turn to the right and work eleven stitches. At this point the braiding thread is in position to turn upwards, and so start the next double twist. A space of two holes is left between each stitch. This forms the upper part of the pattern. The lower part is merely the same design reversed, with an interval of three holes left between the two halves where the long line of eleven stitches is set. This is quite a simple pattern to follow, and can be worked very quickly.

CANVAS EMBROIDERY

"Canvas Work" is the name given to a form of stitching done on canvas or coarse linen. In early days the stitches used were known as cushion stitches. These stitches were worked over a number of threads at a time, and so covered the ground quickly. This work being quick to do and effective when finished, soon became popular.

The work is practically everlasting if care is taken over the washing and cleaning of it, and it may be employed for most of the purposes to which cross-stitch is suitable—as well as a variety of others. It makes charming table and tray cloths, nightdress cases, sideboard runners, chair backs and cushions, and even bedspreads and curtains.

Materials for Canvas Embroidery.—The material employed for this type of embroidery is a single-thread canvas, known as French canvas, Zanzibar canvas, Persian canvas, Heligoland canvas, tammy cloth, or Congress canvas—the latter name being the most usual.

It is always the greatest economy to buy the best quality, for though the cheaper kinds of canvas look quite well when they are new, the stiffness is often excessive, and when this wears or washes out, as it quickly does, they become poor and flimsy looking.

Pure linen canvas is never over-stiff, and thus it not only looks well to the very last but it falls into soft and graceful folds if needed. The width of the canvas varies, the general widths being 27 inches, 36 inches and 54 inches.

There are also several kinds of fancy materials which are used for this work, such as net canvas, a canvas divided into squares and stripes, and often mixed with bands of open-work or imitation drawn thread work. These are attractive when embroidered, but as the pattern must be put into a certain prescribed space, there is more trouble in getting one that will exactly fit into so small an area, and consequently there is less choice.

For chair backs, sideboard cloths, and so on, a canvas is woven the necessary width, and enriched with shaded stripes in subdued colourings, alternating with the plain ones. This material is especially rich looking when well worked in brilliant Oriental colourings.

Cotton is generally used for the embroidery, and this may be either the inexpensive knitting variety, or ivory embroidery cotton. Zanzibar cream, white, coloured, or unbleached embroidery cotton is also a good choice, and white or coloured crochet cottons are necessary when the threads have to be pulled rather tightly.

The size of the cotton must depend on the coarseness or fineness of the canvas, a good rule being that it should be of such a size as will exactly fit the open spaces between the meshes of the material. Except in special instances, it is not necessary to employ such thick cotton that the meshes of the canvas become dragged out of place by it. Silk is only used when the canvas is very fine and the stitches very small.

The worker will quickly find the advantage of using blunt needles, and those employed for rugs, chenille embroidery, and tapestry are all suitable. The eye must be large enough to take the thread without fraying it.

General Hints on Canvas Embroidery.—This work is one of the few kinds of embroidery in which a very long needleful of thread is an advantage rather than a hindrance. This is more especially the case when the pattern involves very long stitches, as a short needleful would very quickly be used up.

In working such a pattern as this it is quite often convenient to begin the design with a very long thread and to draw it through to half its length. Work the one end until it is used up, then continue the pattern in the opposite direction with the long end that was left unused at first. This, of course, cannot be done with every design as it is not always possible to work in both directions.

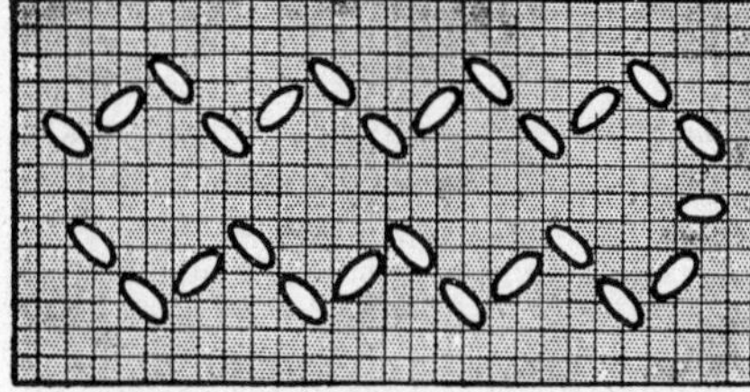

INCORRECT

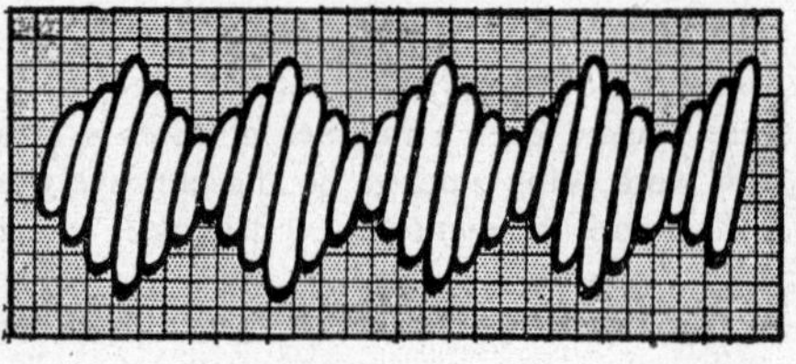

CORRECT

Figs. 1 and 2. Long stitch, with the wrong side worked correctly and incorrectly.

The wrong side of the work should be almost as neat as the right; in fact, with a little care and forethought, it is quite possible to make some patterns reversible.

The neatest way of beginning and ending a needleful of thread, is simply to run the ends between the stitches, or to run the thread in between the meshes of the canvas in some part that will, later on, be covered with the stitchery.

Some workers prefer to join the new thread to the old with a weaver's knot, but this, though not very untidy, is still sufficiently so to prevent the wrong side of the work from being shown. It is as well to note, right from the beginning, that a knot must on no account be used when starting a fresh needleful.

Designs for Canvas Embroidery.—There are a number of cross-stitch patterns which can be perfectly well worked in Long Stitch on a single-thread canvas. Of course, only the more solid designs in cross-stitch will serve the purpose, as, if more slender patterns were attempted, the effect would only be straggling, as the stitches would have to be carried over so small a number of threads of the canvas.

When adapting a cross-stitch pattern, the worker must first settle the number of threads of her canvas that she will consider as equal to one cross-stitch.

The Stitches used for Canvas Embroidery.—The most commonly used stitch for canvas embroidery is Long Stitch, which is *not* the same as the long stitch used in art needlework, but is exactly like ordinary satin stitch. Hence, as much cotton rests on the wrong side of the work as upon the right.

The right and the wrong way of working Long Stitch—shown from the back of the work—is shown in Figs. 1 and 2.

As a general rule, the stitches must be drawn up only so as to lie perfectly flat upon the canvas: if allowed to be too loose, they will only serve as traps to catch in everything with which they come in contact, and the work will soon be frayed and untidy. If, on the other hand, they are too tight, the work will be puckered and drawn out of place.

Open-work effects can be gained with very little trouble. On single thread canvas, all that is necessary is to draw the stitches very tightly, so that the loosely woven meshes become drawn together.

The other main stitch used for this type of embroidery is Short Stitch (or, as it is sometimes called, Straight Stitch). This is worked by taking the first stitch diagonally from left to right, over a certain number of threads.

Cross-stitch is occasionally used with long stitch, in its many varieties of Leviathan, Greek, and slanting cross-stitch.

Sometimes the design is partly executed in plain and fancy darning: sometimes darning stitches are carried over long stitches, thus enabling the work to be improved by a lattice work of colour.

Occasionally the whole of the background is filled in with small stitches, which throw the bolder design into good relief very effectively.

The worker must hold the material so that the threads are quite straight, for if they are drawn in the least degree slanting, the stitches will rest irregularly upon the canvas.

It should be noted that all the designs and patterns given in the following pages, and more especially those in which the stitches are rather short, may be worked upon silk, satin, and any other material of which it is not possible to count the threads, by tacking a piece of canvas of the required size over the richer fabric, and working over it, being careful that the stitches go right through both materials. The stitches must be drawn up rather more tightly than if they were worked on the canvas alone, and when all the embroidery is finished, the threads of the canvas must be carefully pulled away one by one, leaving the embroidery exactly the same in appearance as though it had been executed directly upon the silk or satin.

When the work is finished, it can be greatly improved by being laid, wrong side uppermost, on a thick ironing blanket between two folds of damp linen. A warm iron should then be passed over the uppermost cloth until it is dry.

Simple Designs.—Fig. 3 shows Long Stitch worked as a border, showing just how simple yet how attractive it can be.

To form the line of vandykes of the two sizes given in Fig. 3 the first stitch is taken over two threads, the second over three, and the following stitches over four and five. The next three stitches are carried over four, three, two, thus completing one of the smaller vandykes. In making the next point, the number of threads taken up is increased to seven, as the vandyke is larger, then the stitches are taken over six, five four, three and two threads, and the next small vandyke is made as described before. A narrow insertion may be made of a double set of vandykes such as these; the second set is worked along the straight edge of the first row, and corresponds exactly with the vandykes that were first worked.

Battlemented Vandyke is another version of Long Stitch, and it is extremely useful for working along the straight edge of a design.

The longest stitches in this pattern are taken over eleven threads of the canvas (except when the material is very fine the stitches will not set well if taken over a greater number). Begin by working three stitches over five threads of the canvas in the manner shown by the position of the needle in Fig. 4. * Take three stitches over eight threads, then three over eleven. This brings the work to the top of the vandyke. Make three stitches over eight threads, then three over five, and repeat from * until a sufficient length of vandykes is produced.

Long Stitch Grouped into Squares is shown in Fig. 5. This design consists of squares, each made up of four triangles, which fit closely together, allowing no canvas to be visible between them.

This arrangement is particularly satisfactory when a large surface has to be covered, and gives an effect similar to that

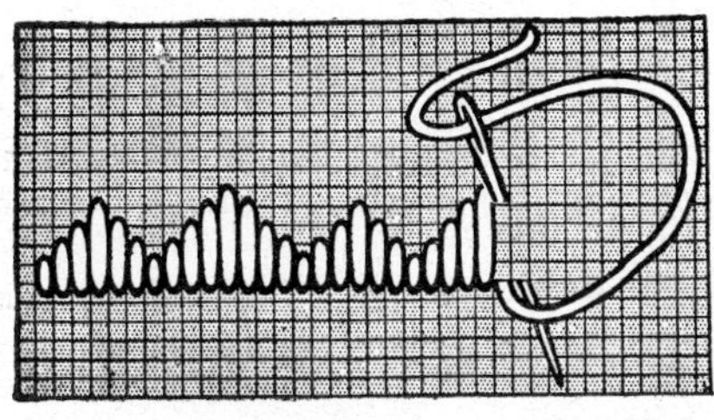

Fig. 3. LONG STITCH WORKED AS A BORDER

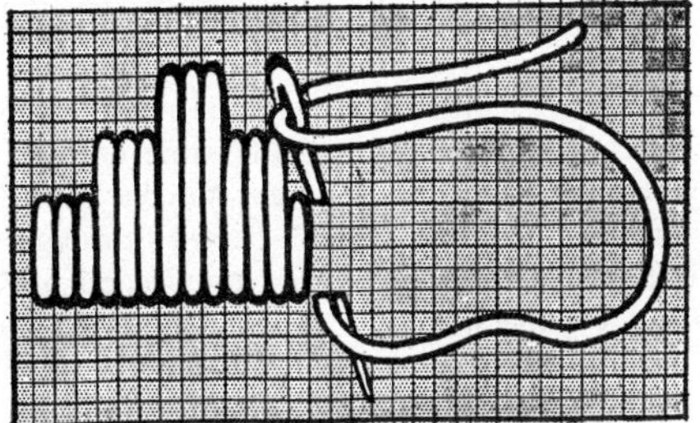

Fig. 4. BATTLEMENTED VANDYKE

of quilting. Such squares may be placed in rows of three, five, or seven, or may be grouped so as to fill squares or oblong spaces.

Each triangle is worked thus: Make fifteen stitches over two, three, four, five, six, seven, eight, nine, eight, seven, six, five, four, three, and two threads respectively, taking care that one end of each stitch is in line with the others, thus forming one straight edge. Make a second triangle in the same way, so that the slanting end of the first eight stitches is taken through the same holes in the canvas that the last eight stitches of the previous triangle were passed through. The third triangle fits into the second one in the same way, and the fourth should fit exactly into the space left after the first three have been worked.

In arranging a row of these squares, they should be placed side by side, the straight edge of one triangle fitting against the corresponding straight edge in the next square.

Varieties of Short Stitch are illustrated in Figs. 6, 7, 8, and 9, and all these arrangements can be used in different types of work, and can be altered and re-arranged to fit any original design.

They often serve as boundary lines between narrow insertions which go to make up a wide border, or they can be used to act as a heading to a pointed pattern. Again, they can be employed to mark out the sides of a square or oblong pattern.

In working Fig. 9, * make three satin stitches, each over three upright threads of the canvas, then three stitches over nine upright threads arranging them so that the first three stitches just worked lie next to the centre of the latter: repeat from * for the length required.

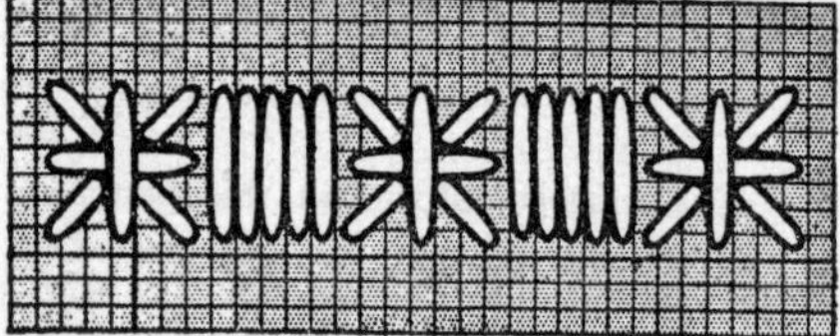

Fig. 6. SHORT STITCH

Fig. 5 LONG STITCH GROUPED IN SQUARES

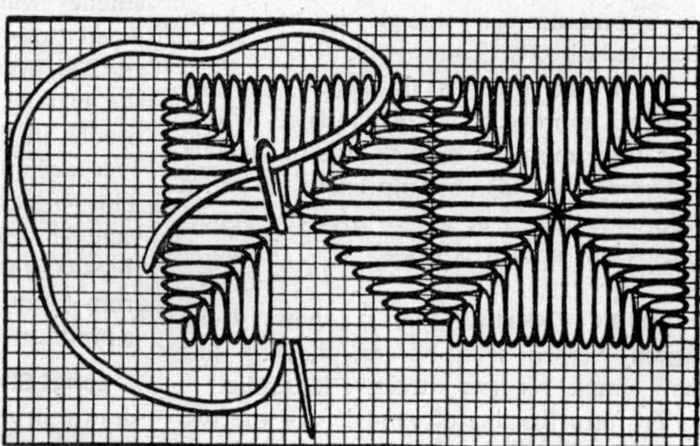

Fig. 7. SHORT STITCH

To work Fig 8, * make five stitches side by side over three upright threads of canvas, then pass the needle up from the wrong side, three threads below the bottom of the last-worked stitch and one to the right, pass it over three threads, the top of the stitch coming on a level with the bottom of the previous stitches, work two more stitches by the side of this and over three threads in height, bring the needle down three theads as above, and work five stitches side by side over three threads. Now pass the needle up three threads and one to the right and work three stitches side by side over three threads, the first one coming on a level with the top of the previous stitches. Repeat from *.

cross-stitches) over four threads of canvas in height, thus: * bring the needle out where the bottom of the stitch is to be, count four threads to the left, then four threads in an upright direction, put the needle into the work and bring it out by the side of the hole at which it came out before. Make another stitch by the side of the first one, and a third and fourth at the side of that. After the fourth stitch, bring the needle out exactly below the top of it, but four threads lower down. Work four stitches as before described, repeating from *.

When a sufficient number have been worked to fill the length required, begin again at the right-hand end, and work a straight satin stitch over four threads of

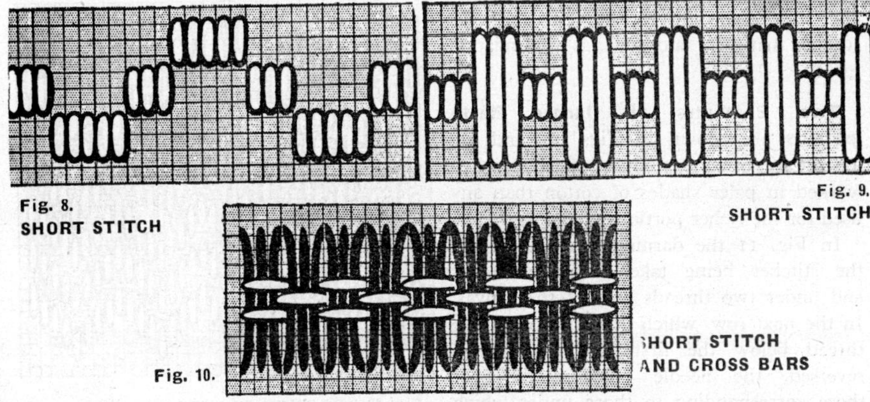

Fig. 8. SHORT STITCH

Fig. 9. SHORT STITCH

Fig. 10. SHORT STITCH AND CROSS BARS

Fig. 6 shows Short Stitch combined with Leviathan Cross-stitch, and is worked in the following manner. Take the first stitch diagonally from left to right over six threads of canvas, make a similar stitch from right to left, then make a stitch from left to right over six threads and exactly between the two first worked stitches; finally work a similar straight stitch in an upright direction.

* Work five upright satin stitches over-six upright threads, putting the first into the holes of the canvas which come immediately next to the cross-stitch, then make another Leviathan cross-stitch, and repeat from * as required.

For the design shown in Fig. 7 begin at the right-hand end of the work, and make four slanting satin stitches (just like half

D*

canvas, putting it into the hole at the bottom of the last stitch of the first group and the first stitch of the second group, thus connecting the clusters. Work a similar line along the top of the first two groups, and continue all along the line.

A Combination of Short Stitch and Cross Bars is featured in Fig. 10. This is worked as a series of straight stitches in a dark colour over ten threads of canvas. They should all be kept perfectly even, and no one stitch should be drawn any tighter than its fellows. Three rows of darning are then worked over this first set of stitches, using a lighter shade of thread.

In each row, three stitches are taken, then three left, in the usual manner of darning; in the next row, the needle is

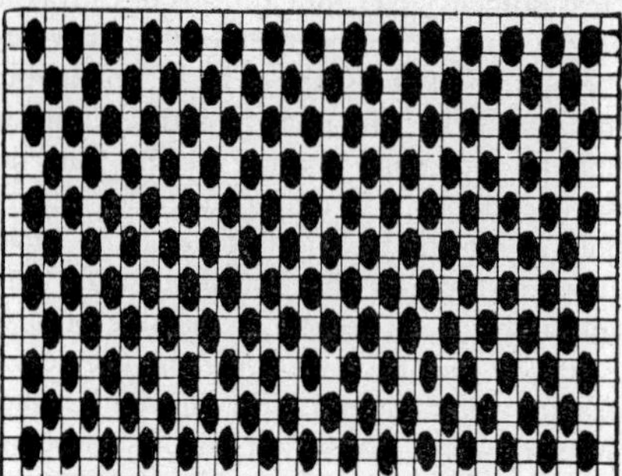

Fig. 11.—DARNED BACKGROUND

passed *over* those threads *under* which it was taken in the preceding row. The third row is exactly like the first. The darning may, of course, be increased to any width and size, according to the length of the stitches that were laid down as a foundation for it.

Two Examples of Darned Backgrounds are shown in Figs. 11 and 12. These are often extremely effective when worked in paler shades of cotton than any used for the richer portions of the work.

In Fig. 11 the darning is quite simple, the stitches being taken alternately over and under two threads only of the canvas. In the next row, which is worked only one thread below the first, the stitches are reversed, the needle being taken over those corresponding to those under which it passed in the first row.

In Fig. 12 the darning is arranged to form a simple chevron pattern. This way the canvas may be darned so as to form diaper patterns, checks, quiltings, stars, battlements, and many others.

Fig. 13.
BACKGROUND WORKED IN SQUARES

Two work the chevrons, each stitch is taken over three threads, under one, this single stitch being one thread lower down than the last for five rows, after which the picked-up stitch is one higher than the preceding set for five more rows.

A Background in Squares is simpler to work than the two patterns above. To make the squares, a stitch is taken across four threads of the canvas in each of the four directions, and a number of squares worked close together forms the open network seen in Fig. 13.

Striped Embroidery may be worked all over the canvas as a background or can be

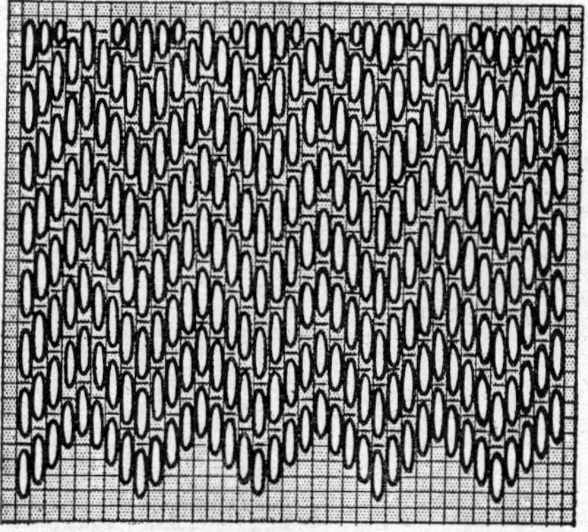

Fig. 12.—DARNED BACKGROUND IN WAVES

arranged as a border. For the vandykes work five upright stitches over five threads of canvas, each one being one thread higher than the last, * then work four stitches each one thread lower than the last, then four, each one thread higher and repeat from * till a sufficient number of zigzags are made. For the spots, take the second coloured cotton, bring the needle out four threads below the tip of one of the vandykes, work an upright stitch over two threads, pass the needle under two threads in a straight line towards the left, make another upright stitch also over two threads, pass the needle again under two threads towards the left and make a third short stitch. After this stitch, bring the needle along two threads and down two threads, and make a short stitch over two threads in a downward direction. This stitch should be on a level with the second-worked short stitch. Continue thus to make the short stitches to follow the zigzag lines, and always two threads below the vandykes. Next work a second set of vandykes just two threads below the dots or six threads below the first made vandykes, and continue until the background is covered. Fig. 14 shows clearly the finished effect.

A Narrow Border of Solid Filling.—Fig. 15 shows the finished border very clearly. A detail of one of the small squares in the middle of the stripe is given in

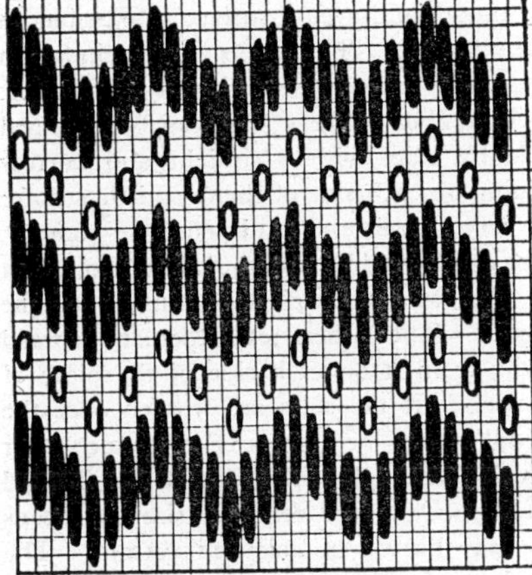

Fig. 14.—STRIPED EMBROIDERY

Fig. 16 and plainly shows the way in which the stitches of each triangle fit in together to make the square, leaving just enough of the canvas free to take the small cross-stitch in the centre. This is worked over a square of two threads of canvas, and should be a different colour from the rest.

Beyond this very closely worked middle band is one thread of canvas, beyond which comes a straight row of cream-coloured stitches over six threads, and beyond them again a coloured vandyke, the stitches covering from two to eight threads. Along the single thread of canvas are run two rows of darning, alternately two threads being taken and two left. In the second row, those threads taken up in the first row are left, thus causing the stitches to alternate.

Fig. 15.—NARROW BORDER OF SOLID FILLING AND CHART

Back stitch used as an Openwork Stitch.—Most workers will want to know how to get an openwork effect as they will like to combine that with the closer stitches. Open-work stitch is worked in the same way as close and thick Long Stitch, the difference being that stronger cotton is required to withstand the tight workmanship needful to draw the loose threads of material together.

The stitch shown in Fig. 17 is popular. It consists merely of back stitches taken over each side of a square of canvas formed of three threads of the material. The stitches are taken in such a sequence that as far as possible the cotton lies diagonally or slantwise across the back of the square. This is to avoid giving a solid appearance to the holes, which would happen were the cotton to be passed beneath them on the wrong side. This stitch may be used to fill almost any shaped space.

Fig. 16.—DETAIL OF ONE OF THE CENTRE WHEELS IN Fig. 15.

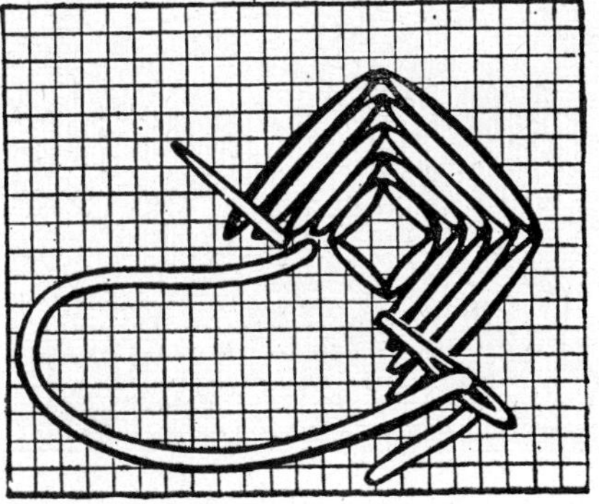

Fig. 17.—OPEN-WORK BACK STITCH

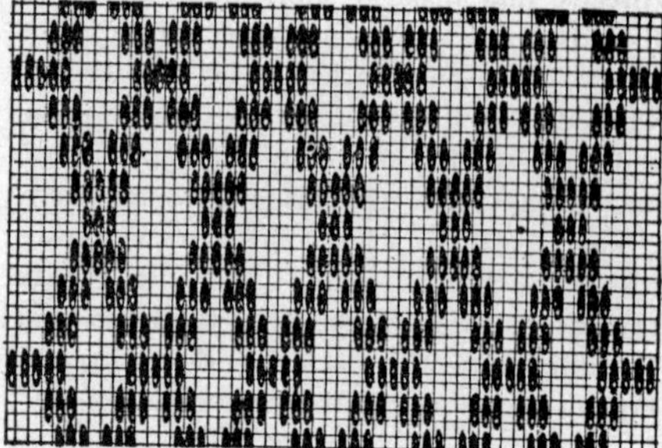

Fig. 18.—NETWORK EMBROIDERY

Network Embroidery is depicted in Fig. 18, and this is appropriate to large pieces of embroidery only, as it is somewhat solid and heavy in effect. The stitches themselves are quite small, being taken over three threads of the canvas. They are all arranged in sets of three or five, so this pattern has the advantage of being executed with very little counting.

It will be noticed that the design consists of alternate large and small lozenges, which can easily be filled in with a small star if it is wanted entirely closed. This grounding is particularly suitable for the centre of such an article as a tea-cloth.

A Star ornamented with Holbein Stitch is shown in Fig. 19, and this again is suited more especially to the rather large pieces of work.

Fig. 19. STAR ORNAMENTED WITH HOLBEIN STITCH

The pattern is one which requires careful execution in order that the rather large expanse of close stitches may present as smooth and even a surface as possible on the right side. The scrolls of Holbein Stitch are a very important feature of this square.

A number of these stars can be arranged side by side, with a straight and narrow edging on each side of them, and thus make a very handsome and effective border. The corner will be easy to manage too, if one of the stars be placed exactly in the angle. The others can then be spread along from it on each side of the piece of canvas. If the stars are worked over the middle of a bed coverlet or some other equally large area, this should be divided into spaces of the required size by means of run threads of coloured cotton. The meshes of the canvas must be carefully counted, in order that all the spaces are of exactly the same size. The middle of the star should correspond with the precise place where the guide lines meet and cross each other. After all the stars are finished the guide-lines should, of course, be pulled out carefully.

The star shown here is begun in the middle. Work first with white cotton, and make seven stitches over one, three, five, seven, nine, eleven, and thirteen threads. Work a stitch above the last of these, over seven threads, six of which are above the end of the previous stitch and one beyond. Make seven more of these stitches, each over seven threads, and each one advancing one thread beyond the preceding stitch.

Then make a stitch over eight threads, two of which are beyond those covered by the previous stitch, work six more of these stitches one above the other, then eight stitches over seven threads, each one covering one thread further to the left than the last one, work seven stitches over thirteen, eleven, nine, seven, five, three, and one to correspond with those made in beginning this open lozenge. Work down the second side in the same way, making eight slanting stitches over seven threads, seven straight stitches over eight threads, and eight more slanting stitches, the last of which brings the work back to the triangle with which this lozenge was begun.

Work three more of these shapes in the same way with the white cotton, then fill in the spaces between them with short stitches of blue cotton, and fill in the centres of the lozenges themselves with stitches of blue taken across in the same direction as the white and passed over the space and down through the same holes through which one end of these white stitches were drawn. This done, take a third colour of cotton, or a darker shade of blue, begin in one of the corners of the star, work five diagonal stitches over three threads of canvas, and trace out the scrolls each stitch of which is taken over three threads also. Make each set of scrolls in the same way, thus completing the star.

A Border and Corner for a carving-cloth, tray-cloth, or other purposes is shown in Fig. 20, the original being worked in pale blue embroidery cotton and with white knitting cotton on coarse écru canvas. It is not a difficult pattern to work, but requires attention owing to the absence of long straight rows of stitching, the pattern being formed of somewhat broken lines, which gives it its light and dainty appearance.

Fig. 20.
BORDER FOR A CLOTH

Begin with the outermost vandyke in blue, work three upright stitches side by side over six threads, work a tiny square of three stitches over three threads above these, putting the bottom of the first stitch into the hole next to that through which the top of the last stitch was placed. Make three more of these little squares, then another group of three stitches over six threads. Continue this all along the border

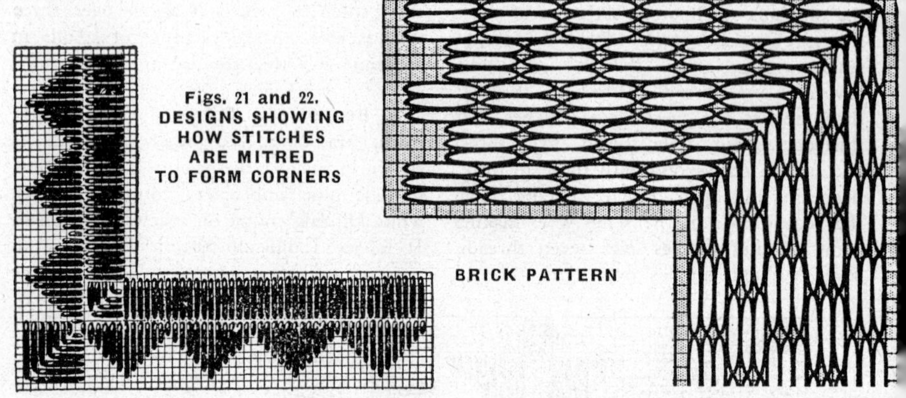

Figs. 21 and 22. DESIGNS SHOWING HOW STITCHES ARE MITRED TO FORM CORNERS

BRICK PATTERN

Fill in the vandykes with a sort of arrow head pattern in white. Begin at the right-hand end, the blue vandykes towards the worker. Take one stitch over six threads, three threads removed from the six blue upright stitches, one stitch over seven, the top of the stitch being on a level with the preceding one, then work a stitch over eight and one over nine threads in the same way. Bring the needle down three threads, work three stitches over seven, eight and nine threads, bring the needle down again, work three more stitches, bring the needle down three threads, take a stitch over seven threads, bring the needle down one thread, make another stitch over seven threads, take the needle up one thread, make a stitch over seven threads, work thus in sets of three to correspond with the first part of the arrow head design.

In the middle make a tiny square of four stitches of white cotton over four

Figs. 23 and 24. THE SAME BORDER WORKED IN LONG STITCH AND CROSS-STITCH

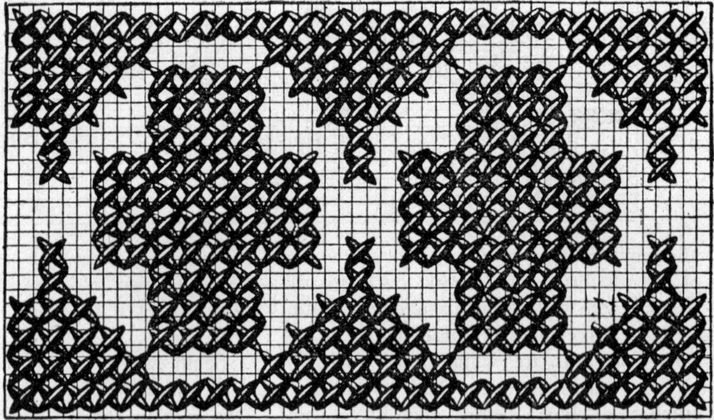

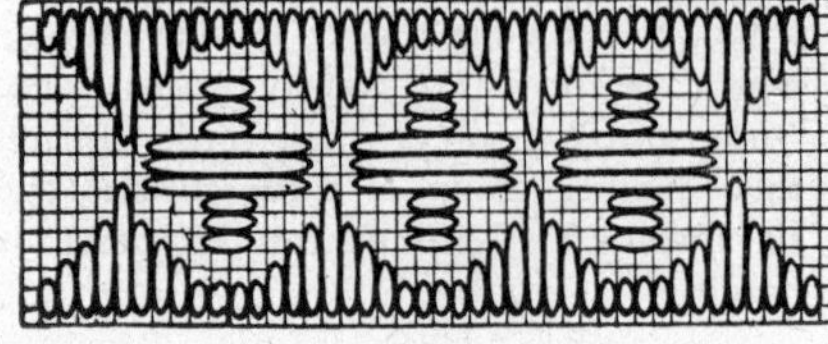

threads of canvas each way; beyond these work four similar stitches over four threads.

Now take the blue cotton, start from the right-hand corner of one of these squares, make a stitch horizontally over nine threads, then one over eight, seven, six, five, four, three, two and one. One end of all these stitches must slant, the other be kept quite straight, and four upright threads of canvas are left free between each arm of the cross. An irregular vandyke is worked with white cotton beyond these stars.

Begin between two of the stars. Count three threads beyond the slanting end of the arm of the star, * make three upright stitches over seven threads, bring the needle up three threads from the bottom of these three stitches, and work eleven stitches each over seven threads and each one thread higher than the last; after the last one, bring the needle down three threads and work five stitches over seven threads, then repeat from *.

In the spaces between these vandykes, work a small square of upright stitches over one, three, five, three, and one thread. Beyond this row of points is worked another set with blue to correspond with the first. * Count five threads up from the group of five stitches at the top of the vandyke, work five stitches over these and over five threads, then pass the needle up two threads and work three upright stitches over five threads. Work three more similar groups of three, each two threads lower than the last, then one stitch instead of three and also over five.

Next, work four more groups like the last, but slanting upwards instead of downwards, and repeat from *.

The corner is managed in much the same way as the rest of the pattern, but the white square is larger, the stitches in the middle being taken over two threads and gradually increasing until the largest extends over ten. This square is surrounded by six triangles instead of four, the shortest stitches being taken over one thread, and the longest over nine.

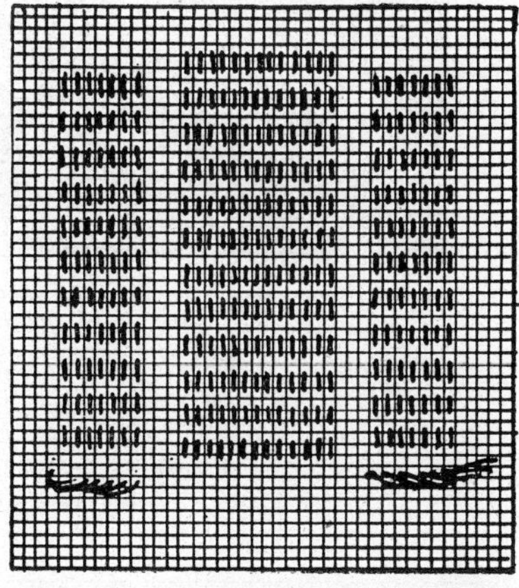

Fig. 25.
Herringbone variation makes an attractive change. When cut, this stitch resembles a rug stitch. The neat and simple appearance of the wrong side is seen in the smaller illustration.

Designs showing how Stitches are Mitred together to form corners are illustrated in Figs. 21 and 22. This is sometimes a little troublesome to the inexperienced worker, but it is a good plan to run a black thread in and out of those holes of the material which form the exact angle of the corner, and to work on first one side of this thread, then on the other, until the two sets of stitches meet exactly in the corner, that is in the holes through which the black thread has been run.

No. 21 shows a very simple corner for a border of the vandyke type. Work the outside row of vandykes, then turn the corner by placing the first stitch of the

Fig. 26. An attractive piece of Rococo work which is reproduced by kind permission of the Victoria and Albert Museum.

Fig. 27. The 5 stages of working Rococo stitch. Start as in the right-hand top sketch, then follow the diagrams towards the left.

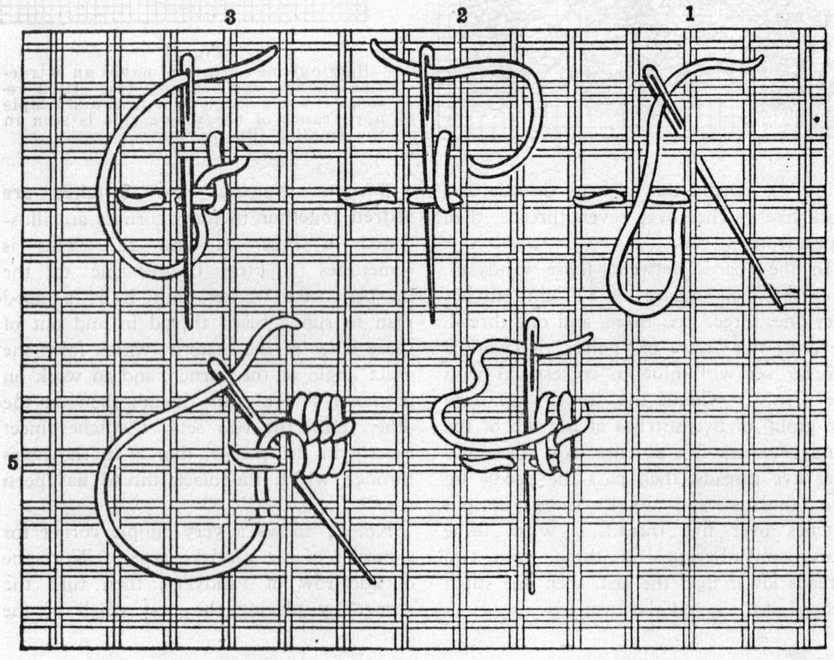

next point into one of the holes into which the last stitch of the previous vandyke was placed, and so that the two stitches set at right angles to one another. To fill the corner which is still vacant between these two vandykes, work two more stitches so as to form a small square, above these work six stitches over three, four, five, six, seven, and eight threads. The slanting ends of this triangle of stitches must be towards the corner, not towards the rest of the border. Make a second triangle in exactly the same way, arranging the stitches so that the slanting ends fit into the same holes through which those of the preceding triangle were passed. The square space left between the two rows of straight stitches inside these vandykes is filled with an arrow-head shape, in which four stitches are taken over two, three, four, and five threads, a second set of stitches being worked to correspond with them, and fitting into the same holes at the corner.

Fig. 22 shows the manner of arranging the corner for what is known as a Brick

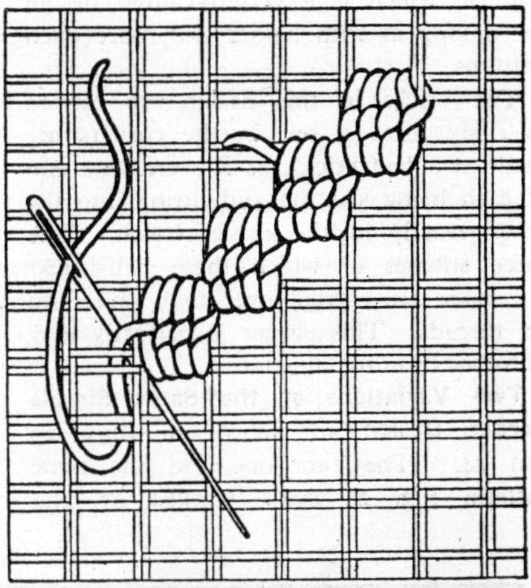

Fig. 27a.

Fig. 28. A delicate design in Rococo stitch, reproduced by permission of the Victoria and Albert Museum. Above, the last stages of working the stitch.

Pattern, which is a very favoured design for mixing in with bolder and more open patterns.

The bricks in this design are carried over six threads, but in the corners are made two half-bricks, as it were, one end of each being slanting and fitting into the other exactly in the corner holes. The three stitches of which these half-bricks are made are carried over four, five, and six threads. This corner is perfectly easy to follow from the illustration.

Two Variations of the Same Simple Border Design are shown in Figs. 23 and 24. They are one and the same pattern, Fig. 23 being worked in long stitch, and Fig. 24 being carried out in simple cross-stitch (the working of which is fully described in the section of this book devoted to that subject).

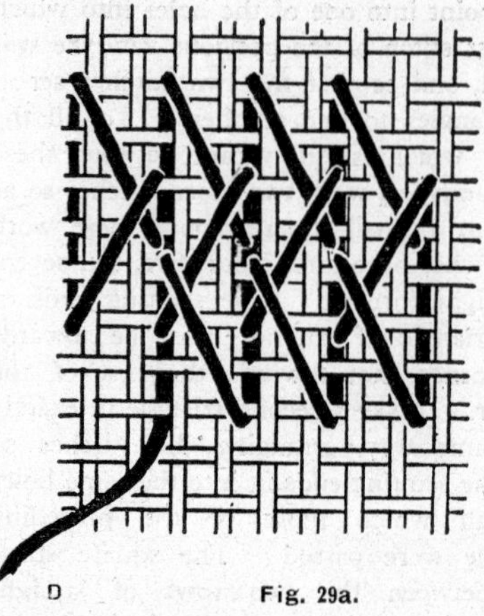

Fig. 29a.

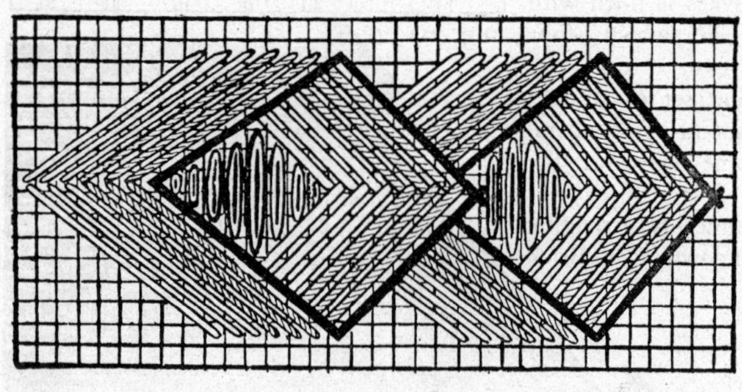

Fig. 29. TWO SIMPLE STITCHES

It must be noticed that the cross-stitch works out to a much larger scale than the long stitch, the reason for this being that the cross-stitch requires to be taken over two threads of the canvas, where one is sufficient for the other method of working this simple but charming little pattern.

A Herringbone variation is worked over single or double thread canvas in wool. Work one row of ordinary herringbone. Start at the top left-hand corner, bring the needle out in the usual way, then three holes to the right and four threads down, take up two threads on the needles, take the needle up over four threads, three holes to the right, take up two threads, and continue in the usual way, leaving one thread between each stitch. For the next row start immediately above the last one, so that the stitches lie on those just made, but work one thread above and one below. Work thus all along the row. Work four more rows in like manner, taking the herringbone over two more stitches each time. For the second pattern, start the first row of herringbone eight threads lower down and work in the same way as before. See Fig. 25.

Work as many rows as required, but these two rows complete a pattern. Cut through the centre of the rows with the exception of the first row worked. The two centre rows will stand upright back to back, and form a sloping wall at either side. This makes a fascinating pattern. To secure the back, paste over it with embroidery paste, as explained before.

Rococo Stitch is not used frequently, but is very effective and was seen a great deal in earlier work. It is most suitable for small articles. It is nearly always worked in silk on soft double thread canvas, the horizontal threads of which were stouter than the upright threads. No canvas should show between the stitches.

Small, regular holes are made over the surface with this stitch; in consequence light backgrounds should be chosen, as they show up the stitch more clearly. Very simple designs are used as will be seen from Fig. 26.

To start working run the thread between the lower threads of canvas, take the needle down one hole lower, take it up over two threads and out one hole lower, take it up over two threads and out one hole to the right and one hole lower. (Fig. 27, Dia. 1.) Cross over the stitch just made and bring the needle out one hole to the left and one thread lower down. Take it up over two threads, bring it out one thread lower, cross the stitch (Diagrams 3 and 4) and continue as before. Four stitches should fill each hole, but more can be made if necessary.

Fig. 27a is worked in diagonal rows, from right to left, starting at the top right-hand corner. Each stitch must be pulled tightly to make the required holes.

A good example of rococo work that is easy to follow is shown in Fig. 28.

It is worked on a background of creamy green. For the bigger of the two sprays, the first two rows are in dark red, the next two in light red, and the centre in yellow. The rest is in green.

For the second spray there is a triangular piece in yellow, then two rows in light red and two in dark and the centre in green. The spray on the side has a cross of one row of rococo in dark steel. The stitches round that are in dark red.

The large diamonds round each spray are in a dark greeny blue, and the centre of the small diamonds in yellow.

The stitch in Fig. 29 is worked on single thread canvas in three shades of brown and one of cherry. Starting with the lightest brown, bring the needle up at A, count seven holes to the right and seven threads down, take the needle down in the 7th hole. Bring the needle up one thread higher, count seven holes to the left and seven threads down. Take the needle down again at B. Start each row, one hole to the right. Work three rows in light brown, three in mid, and one in dark brown, making seven rows in all.

Fig. 30. A USEFUL BORDER

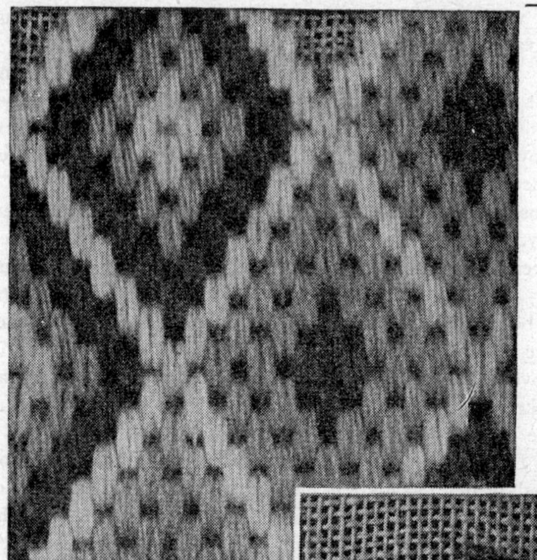

FOUR USEFUL AND DECORATIVE STITCHES

Fig. 31. A neat and useful design for large areas—worked on single thread canvas.

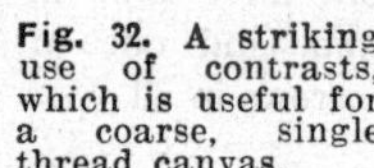

Fig. 32. A striking use of contrasts, which is useful for a coarse, single thread canvas.

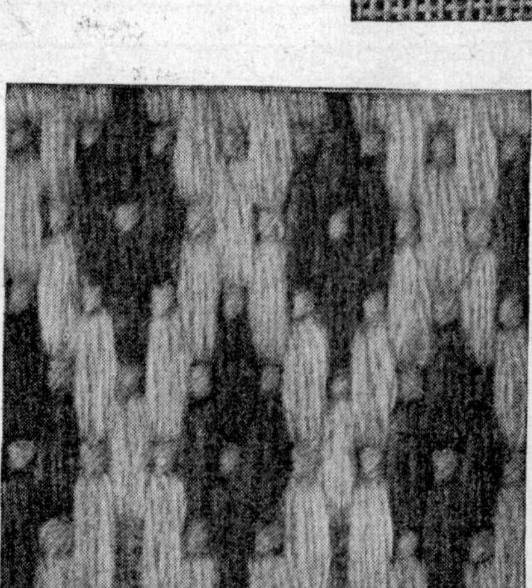

Fig. 33. A simple and effective design—worked on double thread canvas.

Fig. 34. A very simple background stitch.

Now with the dark brown, bring the needle up at D, count seven holes to the left and seven threads down and take the needle down in the seventh hole. Bring the needle up and take it down into the last stitch, C. This forms the square. Work in the same way as before, only take a stitch to the left each time instead of to the right, ending with the light brown on the edge. Work the square in the centre in cherry satin stitch. This completes the pattern which can be repeated as required.

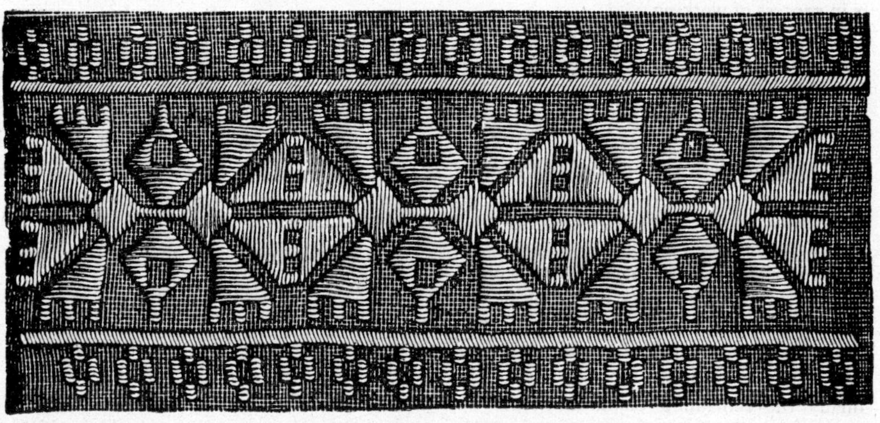

Fig. 35.

TWO EASILY WORKED BORDERS

Fig. 36.

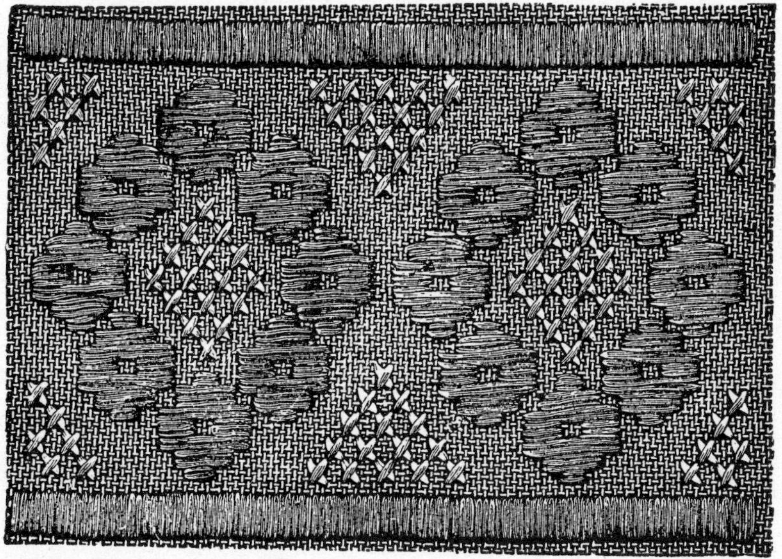

Fig. 29a shows an attractive interlacing stitch on single thread canvas. This consists of stitches slanting over 2 threads in width and 4 threads in height, with an upright stitch on the back; each successive row is laced for 2 threads over the base of the previous row. In the diagram the third row is in process of working.

Fig. 30 is a useful border worked in cream, gold and light brown. The working can be followed easily from the illustration.

Fig. 31 is a fascinating stitch to work and makes a handsome all-over patterning for stool and chair seats. It is worked on single thread canvas in pairs of stitches over 6 threads in height, each new pair rising 3 threads higher than the previous pair. It is worked with 4 shades of the same colour, darkest in the centre of the lightest diamonds, then the next shade, then the third shade, then the lightest shade which is continued to form a trellis all over the canvas; finally the remaining diamond shapes are filled with light, medium and dark, working from centre to edge.

Fig. 32 is a simple Vandyke stitch on single thread canvas; for the dark stripes all stitches go over 4 threads, each successive stitch rising or falling one thread. The lighter stripes go over three threads and rise or fall one thread.

Another easy and effective stitch is shown in Fig. 33. This is worked on double thread canvas 11 holes to the inch. The pattern consists of groups of 3 stitches, over 5 double threads in height, each group worked 3 rows higher than the group to its left. The stitches are worked into both the large and small holes, the dark ones forming a diamond pattern as shown in the illustration. The tiny spaces between the groups are filled with cross-stitch in a medium shade.

The canvas stitch in Fig. 34 was often used as a background in old embroideries, and is easily worked.

Fig. 35 is worked all in one colour on very fine canvas. The largest stitches are carried over 15 threads, the shortest over 2.

Fig. 36 is worked in two shades of one colour or two contrasting shades, whichever the worker prefers. The cross-stitches are more elongated than square, going over 4 threads in height and 3 in width.

CHENILLE EMBROIDERY

Chenille embroidery originated in France and derives its name from the resemblance its round fluffy threads have to the bodies of caterpillars. During the eighteenth century it was fashionable at the French Court and many pieces worked by Marie Antoinette are still preserved. From there it came to England where it was much used. It is so soft that when well worked it looks like painting on velvet.

There are two kinds of chenille—the fine or *Chenille à broder*—which is soft and not wired, and was used in the old work, and *Chenille ordinaire,* a coarse chenille which was used for couching on the surface of material, or passed through large holed canvas or gold and silver perforated cardboard.

Trace the design on the material and work in a frame. The needles used should have wide eyes and sharp points. Chenille should be used in short lengths and the background can be worked in Filoselle or wool. This makes a good contrast.

Chenille worked in several shades can be most effective. If carefully worked the finished effect is that of a painting. A moss rose is a good subject to choose. Chenille is worked in the same way as silk; keeping the pile in one direction as far as possible.

Chenille can also be laid over the surface and secured at intervals with the same colour silk. This is only suitable for heavy materials, as for starting and finishing each

AN 18TH CENTURY CHENILLE EMBROIDERED WAISTCOAT

Reproduced by kind permission of the Victoria and Albert Museum.

Reproduced by kind permission of the Victoria and Albert Museum.

thread, a hole has to be made in the material with a stiletto and the chenille pulled through to the wrong side and there secured.

Chenille ordinaire can be worked over large open meshed canvas, in satin stitch, forming many varied patterns.

Chenille on perforated gold and silver cardboard is very simple and can be worked up to form crosses, stars and wheels. The cardboard should be backed with linen to prevent it breaking away in the process of working. Using a needleful of Chenille, pass backwards and forwards through the cardboard, as if it were canvas. Two or three contrasting colours look well for this kind of Chenille embroidery.

Chenille embroidery is used in embroidered pictures together with silk and paint as shown on the previous page. In this excellent museum piece the face, arms and hands are painted in water-colour to give a more natural effect. The Shepherd Boy's coat is shaded in chenille thread, three shades of a rich red being used. The shading gives the rounded effect of the arm beneath.

The Shepherdess's skirt is also worked in chenille. As the illustration shows, part of it is worked in straight lines and part is curved to show the drapery, which is also accentuated by the shading.

The bark of the tree is in chenille, too. Chenille gives a warm velvety look to a picture and adds depth, too. The rest of the picture is worked in silk shading,

AN ENLARGED SECTION OF THE WAISTCOAT

for the directions of working which, see the chapter on Silk Shading.

The eighteenth century waistcoat, a section of which is given in this chapter, was worked on a background of old gold ribbed silk in beautiful shades of chenille. The enlarged section gives a clear idea of the shading. All the chenille was couched, using a silk the exact shade to sew it down. In this way the stitches are unnoticeable.

The large leaf up the centre is worked with a light yellow-green chenille round the outside, gradually becoming darker towards the centre. The vein and stalk are in a light shade. The same shades of green are used throughout, sometimes dark on the outside and light in the centre, and sometimes vice versa. These shades blend in well with the coloured chenille flowers and give a light appearance throughout.

The flower in the bottom left-hand corner of the design is worked in pale pink at the outside, shading gradually to puce in the centre.

The flower at the right-hand bottom corner is worked in deep crimson merging to salmon-pink in the centre. The flower above is worked in salmon-pink in the outside to crimson in the centre. The calyx is in light green on the outside and dark in the centre. The star flowers are worked in shades of blue embroidery silk and make a good contrast to the chenille.

CROSS-STITCH

The very simplicity of working—only one stitch being used throughout the work—has made cross-stitch embroidery a firm favourite for all time. Originating in Russia, Norway, and Germany, and also in Italy where the far-famed Assisi work is but a variation of it, this class of needle-craft is even more popular to-day than ever before because of the ease and speed with which it can be worked, and the charming effects which can be produced.

Cross-stitch does not require any very great experience of embroidery on the part of the worker, as the beauty of the work depends chiefly on regularity, and a good choice of colours.

Cross-stitch is suitable for the decoration of all kinds of household articles, such as short curtains, cushions, bed-spreads, guest towels, luncheon sets, tea cosies, tea and tray cloths, duchesse sets, runners, and in fact almost everything to which the addition of simple embroidery lends an added beauty; and blouses, children's frocks, and pinafores, overalls, etc., look charming when worked with floral designs or quaint birds, animals, or other devices in the same quick-way stitchery.

Owing to the general construction of the stitch, the embroidery looks its best if the design is rather formal, and of a patterned and "repeat" kind. This, however, is not an absolute essential of the work, and many lovely cross-stitch designs are of a floral nature, and often shaded in a fairly elaborate way. For these it is often possible to obtain colour charts, showing exactly where to place each shade. If these are not available, it will save much time during the process of working, if the colours which are intended to be used, are put on a spare copy of the transfer, or on the plain design with coloured chalks or crayons, so that there is before you a clear key as to the arrangement of the shades.

Methods of Working.—The most straightforward way of working a cross-stitch design is, of course, with the aid of a transfer. Transfers are now readily obtainable with the cross-stitches ready marked for working. Sometimes, however, when a coarse, rough, or hairy-surfaced material is being used, even the very best transfer cannot be clearly seen; in fact, in a number of cases it will often not even come off on to the fabric. Then it is best to tack a piece of canvas firmly round the edges on to the material allowing the canvas to be larger than the design, as it is apt to fray. The work is then done over threads of the canvas into the material underneath, and after completion the canvas threads are drawn out as shown clearly in Fig. 1. Always keep the stitches fairly tight, as it must be remembered, when the threads are pulled out, the work will appear much looser.

The third alternative to the use of a transfer, is to work on a coarse material in which the threads can be easily counted. For this method it is best to work from a chart, or, of course, stitches can be counted from a cross-stitch design transfer equally well.

Materials Required for Cross-stitch Embroidery.—Practically any kind of material can be used for cross-stitch needlework, the method of working being adapted to the nature of the fabric employed. Thus, for fine materials, silks, soft linens, lawns, muslins, etc., it is best to use a transfer; for velvets, velours, rough serges, and so on, the canvas method is most satisfactory; and for the counting method, canvas, scrim, Hardanger cloth, fairly coarse linen or tweed, or huckaback are by far the best.

For work done on an open ground such as canvas, coarse linens, etc., just mentioned, wool needles with blunt points and long eyes should be used; but for work on a close ground, good crewel needles are the most suitable.

The working thread may be of linen, wool, mercerised cotton, or silk, and care should be taken to select a weight of thread

Fig. 1. CROSS-STITCH WORKED OVER CANVAS

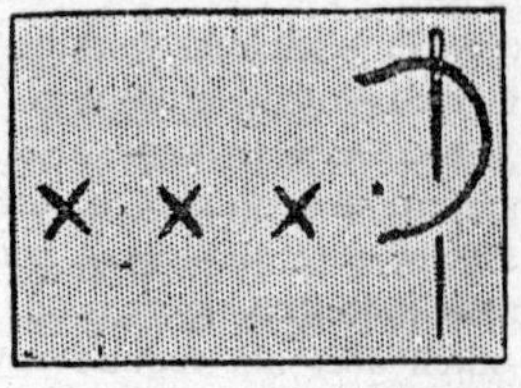

Fig. 2. HOW TO WORK CROSS-STITCH

most suited to the fabric on which it is to be used—that is, not using a very heavy make of embroidery wool on a fine linen or silk, or using a fine crewel thread or mercerised cotton on a heavy ground when it will become insignificant and "spidery."

The thread should be drawn tightly throughout—linen threads being pulled more tightly than wool, or the work will have a loose, untidy appearance when finished.

How Cross-Stitch is Worked.—From the left-hand corner of one of the squares bring up the needle and cotton, then in a slanting direction, that is, taking it across the square to the top of the right-hand side, next pass the needle through and down (this forming the first or under part of the stitch); then bring the needle up through the lower right-hand corner in readiness for making the upper stitch, as shown in Fig. 2. Then take the needle across to the top left-hand corner of the square, and pass it through, when you have formed the complete stitch.

When beginning a thread on an open ground, an oblique half-stitch is made under the first cross-stitch, as clearly seen in Fig. 3; on close materials a few preliminary stitches are made, but the work should never be started with a knot. Every stitch should take up the same number of threads each way.

In doing cross-stitch, each stitch can be completed as just described, although some people prefer to do all the under stitches first, then cross them all afterwards. In either case all stitched must be crossed the one way in order to preserve the uniformity of the work. This is shown quite clearly in Fig. 4.

Fig. 5 shows double cross-stitch very clearly. It is worked over two threads, and a straight cross lies over the oblique one.

It must be remembered that it is less easy to work a plain ground, than a patterned one. Though the back of the work is not the same as the front in appearance, it affects the look of the front of the work if the stitches at the back are not even and all in the same direction.

Double-sided Cross-stitch (Fig. 6), makes crosses on both sides of the material. It requires an extra stitch on the right side from the centre hole upwards to the left, to bring the thread into the correct position for making the second stitch on the wrong side. Each complete cross must be finished before the next is started. The appearance of the stitch is exactly the same as that in Fig. 4 on both sides of the material. This stitch was the original and earliest Italian variety of working.

When working cross-stitch try not to start all your rows one under the other, as this is inclined to make a ridge which spoils the look of your work.

Two technical points which are important in working cross-stitch are: if you are doing a difficult design, it should be started in the centre and worked outwards: and the ground work should be started at the lower left-hand corner.

Bright peasant colours are the best to use for cross-stitch embroidery, as pastel shades are apt to give an insipid effect except for very dainty articles of personal attire.

When your embroidery is finished, pay special attention to the pressing of it. This must be done on the *wrong* side of the work and over a damp cloth (of the non-fluffy variety) with a hot iron.

The Adaptability of Cross-stitch.—Most cross-stitch and tapestry designs are interchangeable, as the working stitches are so similar. In fact, many embroidery designs of a fairly formal type can be turned into cross-stitch ones without much trouble. To do this, take a spare copy of the transfer, or make a tracing of it on paper through a black carbon sheet. With a sharply pointed pencil fill in the design with crosses of a suitable size, keeping them all the same size and in regular rows as far as possible. If the design is to be worked in several colours, mark the crosses with crayons of the correct shade. When embroidering, use the cross-stitched paper as a chart, either putting in the crosses by eye if the design is small and simple, or laying canvas over the material, as already described, and copying the chart on that, cutting and pulling away the canvas threads when the embroidery is completed.

Cross-stitch patterns can readily be adapted to fit shapes other than those for which they were designed, and a simple method of arranging a corner from a straight border, is to place a mirror on the most suitable motif: the reflection thus produced being an exact reproduction in the opposite direction, can be drawn on to graph paper (see Fig. 8). If a square is required two mirrors are used instead of one, both meeting at the back line. These are placed at right angles to each other and diagonally across the border.

It is slightly more difficult to make a curved border from a straight one, but with a little care it can be managed quite well in the following way. Tack a square piece of canvas over the curved opening, then mark its outline on to the canvas in

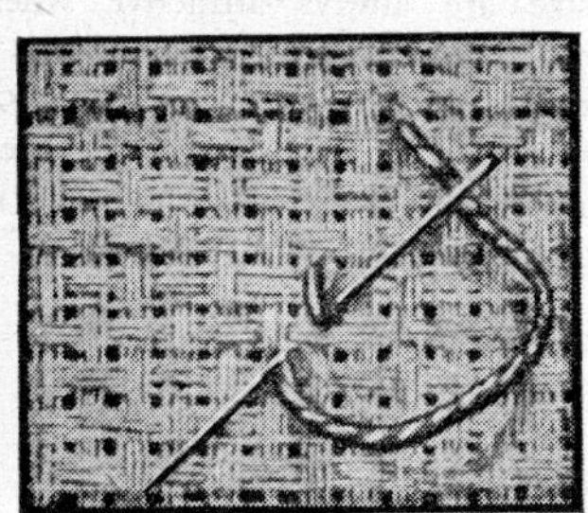

Fig. 3. BEGIN THIS WAY

THREE KINDS OF CROSS-STITCH

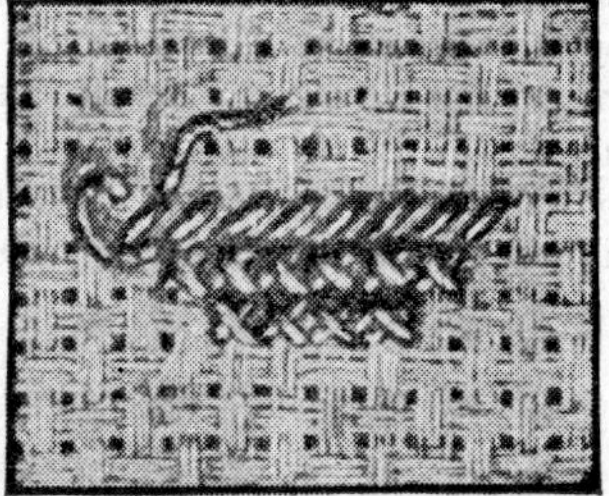

Fig. 4. SIMPLE CROSS-STITCH

Fig. 5. DOUBLE CROSS-STITCH OR LEVIATHAN STITCH

Fig. 6. DOUBLE SIDED CROSS-STITCH

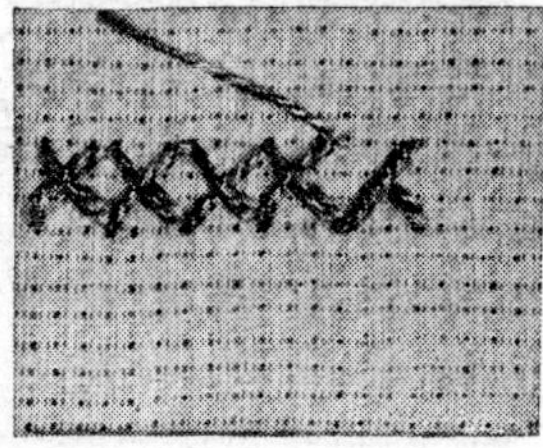

Fig. 7

ADAPTING A STRAIGHT BORDER TO CURVES

pencil, and work a plain line of cross-stitch along it. The stitches will arrange themselves in line, sometimes level, and sometimes above or below one another. In working the second outline, the width of the pattern is kept as nearly as possible, and the requisite space is obtained by setting the design out in separate sections, which are afterwards joined by slightly altering the motifs, making them wider at the bottom and narrower at the top. Fig. 7 shows clearly the method used.

Cross-stitch may, instead of forming a design in itself, be used as a background for it, completely filling in all the space not occupied by it. When it is thus used, the design is of a formal and decidedly conventional type, and it is first outlined in back stitching before the cross-stitches are added. This particular form of cross-stitch embroidery is best known as Assisi Work, which has been fully explained and illustrated in an earlier section of this book.

Cross-stitch may also be used as a light filling for large monograms or parts of a small design which is outlined in some simple outlining stitch. In this case the crosses do not appear on the transfer, but are put in by the worker by eye.

Plain Hemstitched Handkerchiefs of a suitable size are always attractive when embroidered in dainty cross-stitch motifs.

The simple forget-me-not wreath (Fig. 9) is very easy to start on. You will want three colours, blue, yellow, green. A filoselle is the best thread to use.

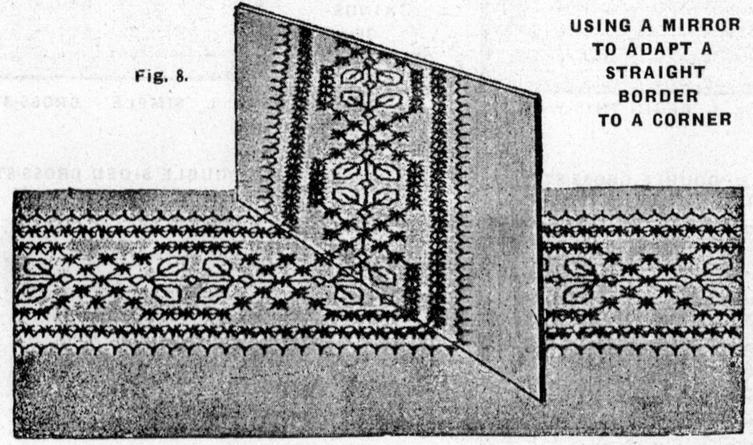

Fig. 8.

USING A MIRROR TO ADAPT A STRAIGHT BORDER TO A CORNER

To work the cross-stitch, just tack a small piece of fine canvas—it should have about 20 threads to the inch—in one corner of the handkerchief. You will find it quite easy to work from this chart. It is quite a simple matter to pull out the threads of canvas when the work is finished. Then press the finished embroidery on the wrong side under a damp cloth with a hot iron.

The Nursery Table-cloth.—(Fig. 10). The nursery cloth is worked on 54-inch linen in embroidery cottons of the gayest colours. You will need $1\frac{1}{4}$ yards of linen, the back must have the monkeys worked the reverse way. The charts showing the little cactus plants at either end of the camel design are given here.

The key to the chart for the camel shows where to work the different colours which are as follows: (1) black, (2) emerald, (3) buttercup, (4) sandy-brown, (5) scarlet, (6) royal blue.

The chart for the Donkey side of the cloth is given in Fig. 13. This has a different key for the colours, which are as follows: (1) black, (2) emerald, (3) sandy-brown, (4) scarlet, (5) buttercup, (6) grey.

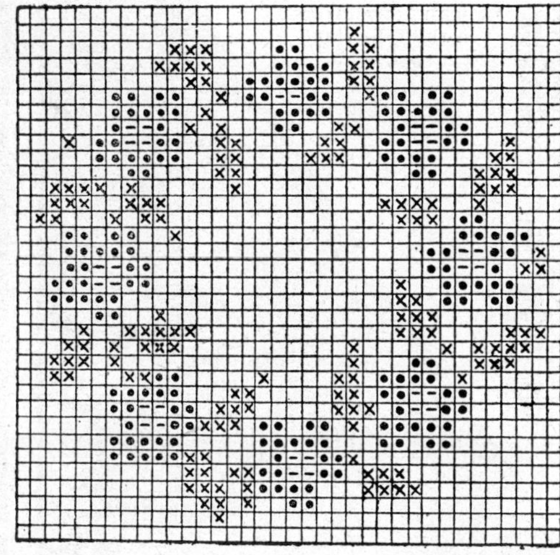

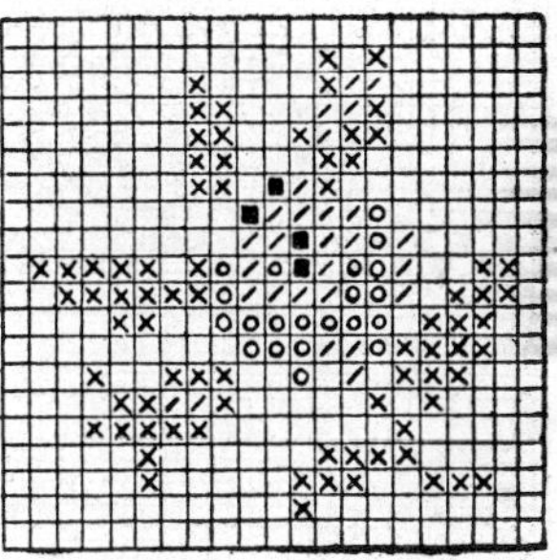

• BLUE
– YELLOW
× GREEN
■ DARK PINK
o MID PINK
/ LIGHT PINK

Fig. 9. FORGET-ME-NOTS

vhich allows for a good hem all round. The vork is done over single thread canvas 10 holes to the inch). The two pairs of pposite sides have the same design on nem.

The canvas is tacked into position over ne piece to be embroidered, and the design worked through both linen and canvas, ne canvas being drawn away, thread by read, after the embroidery is completed.

In Fig. 12 is a clear working chart of the Camel" side of the cloth. To save space, ne tree is shown only once. The tree nown is the one that is worked in front of ne camel on the cloth above: the tree at

Each square of the chart represents one cross-stitch on the linen, so it is necessary only to count the number of squares with the same key sign to know the exact placing of the different colours.

The border of the cloth is worked thus: the two inside rows in emerald and the two outside rows in black. An inch to an inch-and-a-half-wide hem is turned down beyond the last cross-stitch and hemmed neatly on the wrong side.

The embroidery completed, the whole cloth should be well pressed on the wrong side under a damp cloth, with a hot iron. This brings the design up well.

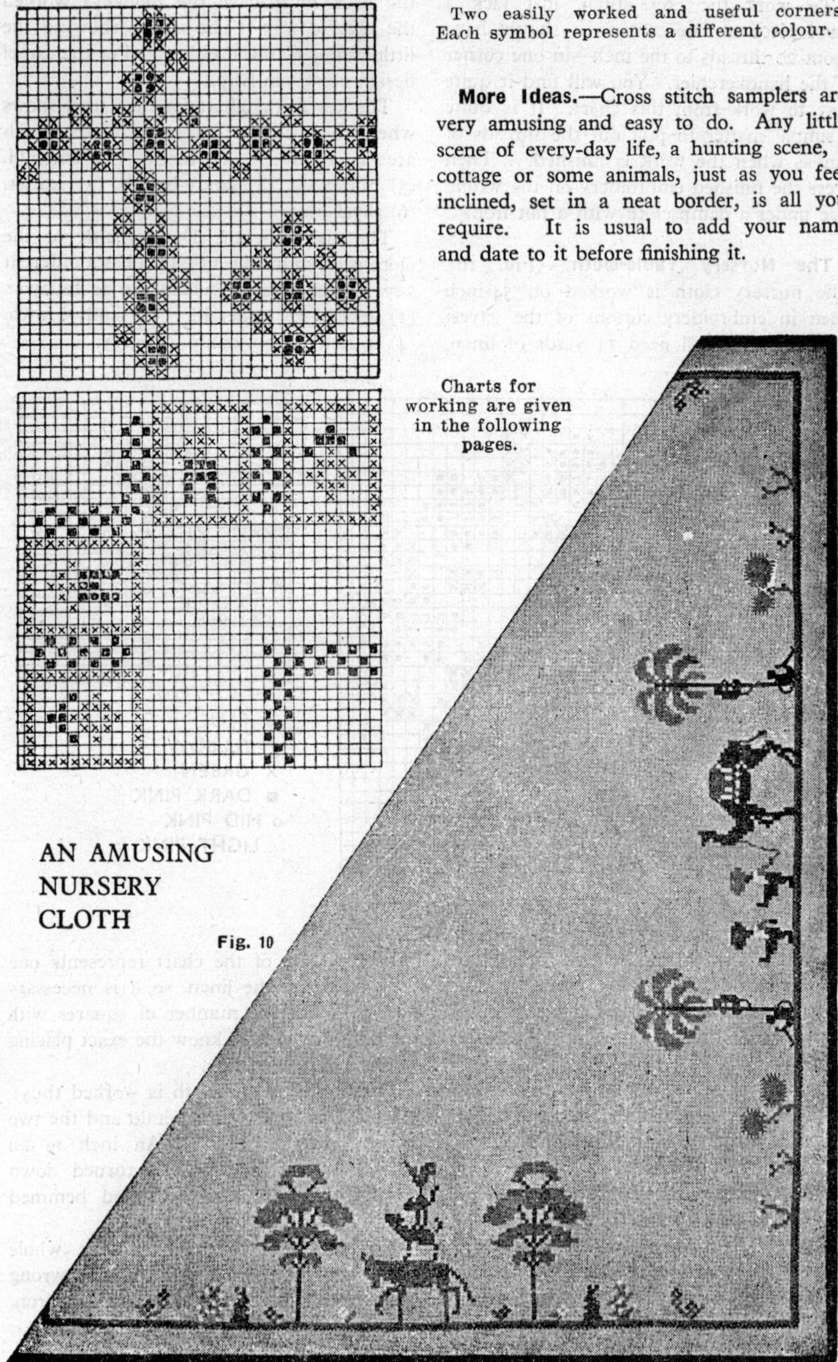

Two easily worked and useful corners. Each symbol represents a different colour.

More Ideas.—Cross stitch samplers are very amusing and easy to do. Any little scene of every-day life, a hunting scene, a cottage or some animals, just as you feel inclined, set in a neat border, is all you require. It is usual to add your name and date to it before finishing it.

Charts for working are given in the following pages.

AN AMUSING NURSERY CLOTH

Fig. 10

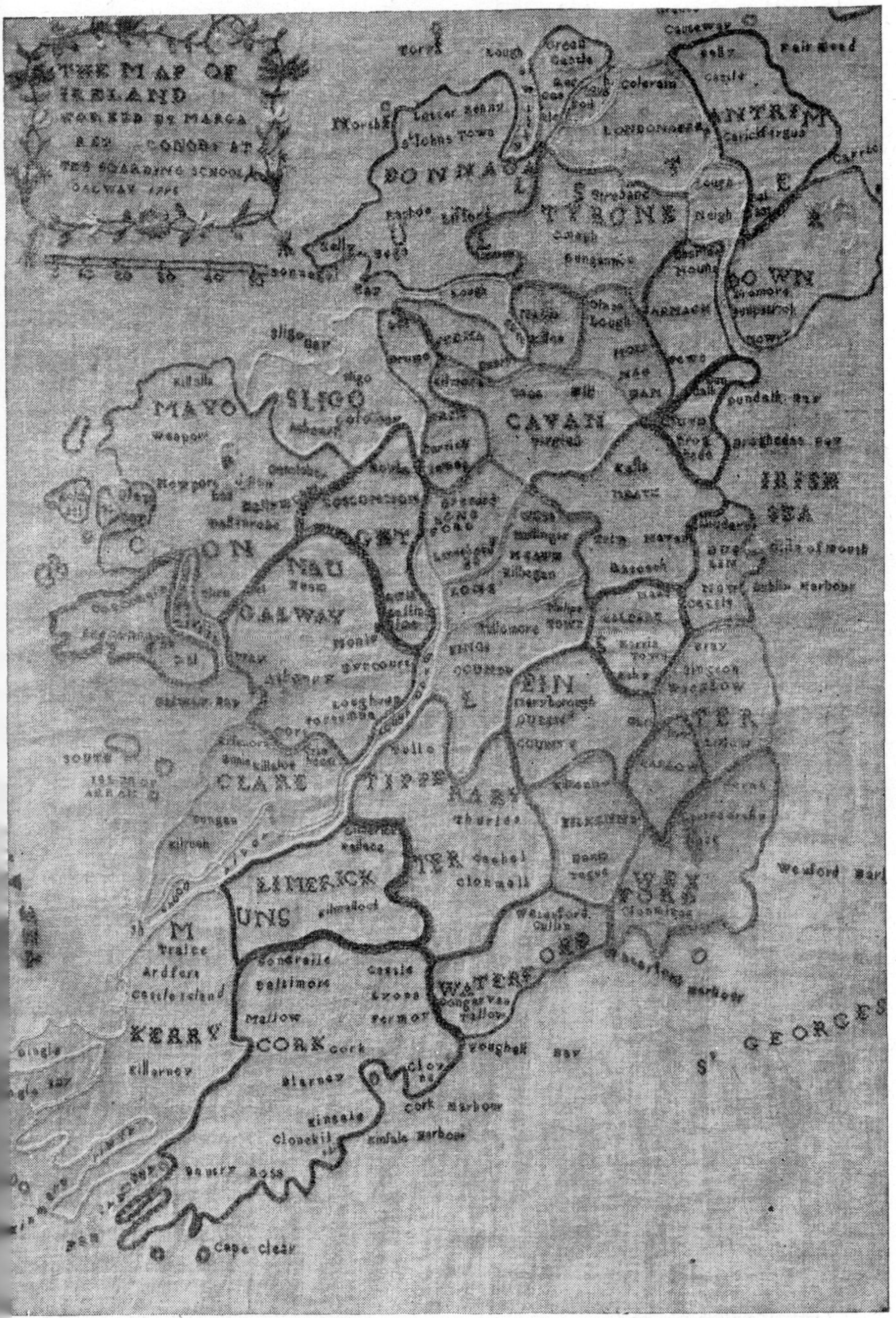

A novel idea, which makes a variation from the usual type of sampler, this beautifully worked map of Ireland has all the lettering worked in cross-stitch. The county boundaries are in fine chain stitch. Reproduced by permission of the Victoria and Albert Museum.

CHART FOR WORKING THE NURSERY CLOTH

Here is the detailed chart for working the nursery cloth given on the preceding pages. Each square represents one stitch. The colours are (1) black, (2) emerald, (3) buttercup, (4) sandy-brown, (5) scarlet, (6) royal blue. Diagrams A—E show in detail the working of the little cactus plants that are scattered round the border.

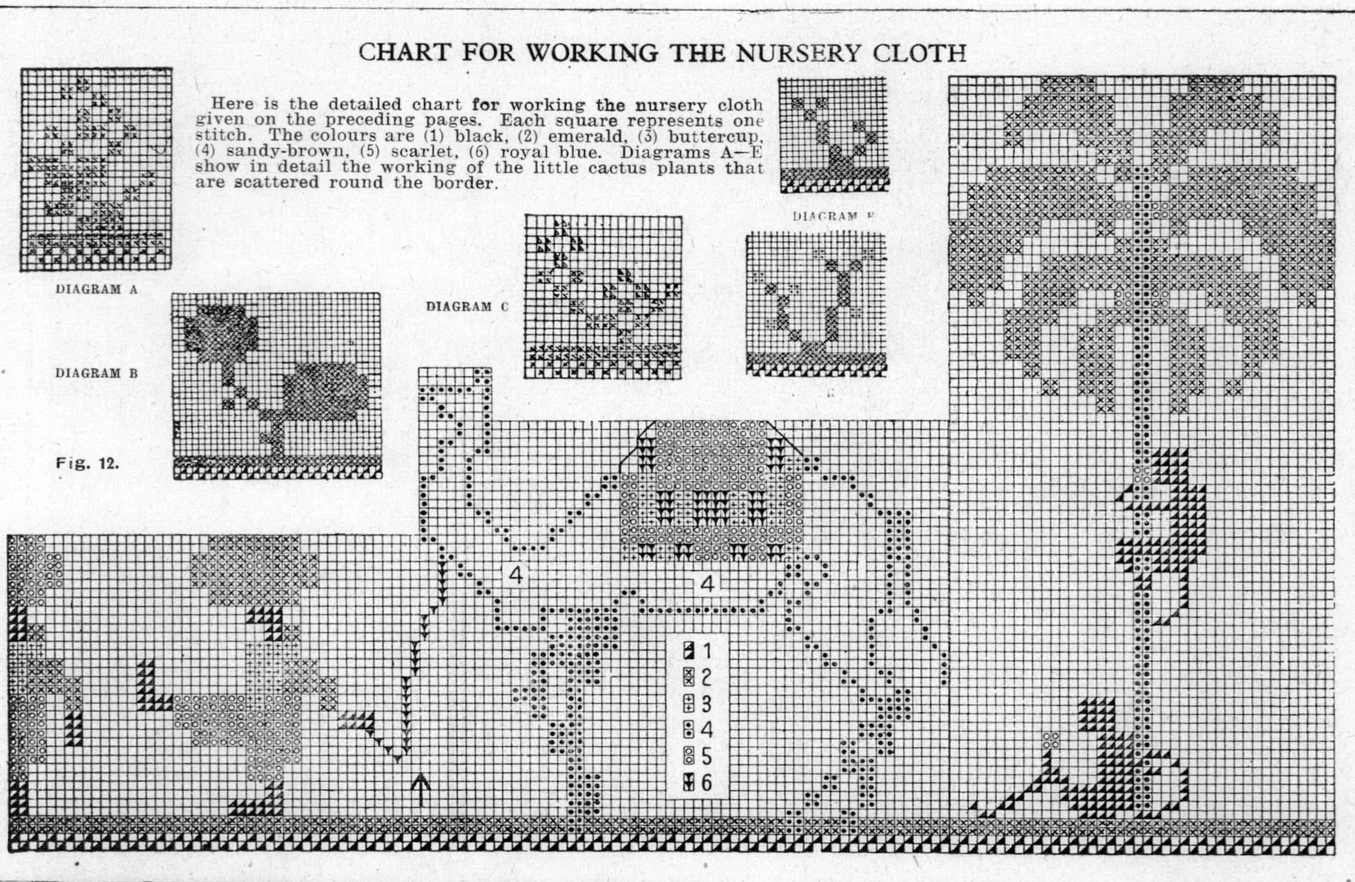

Fig. 12.

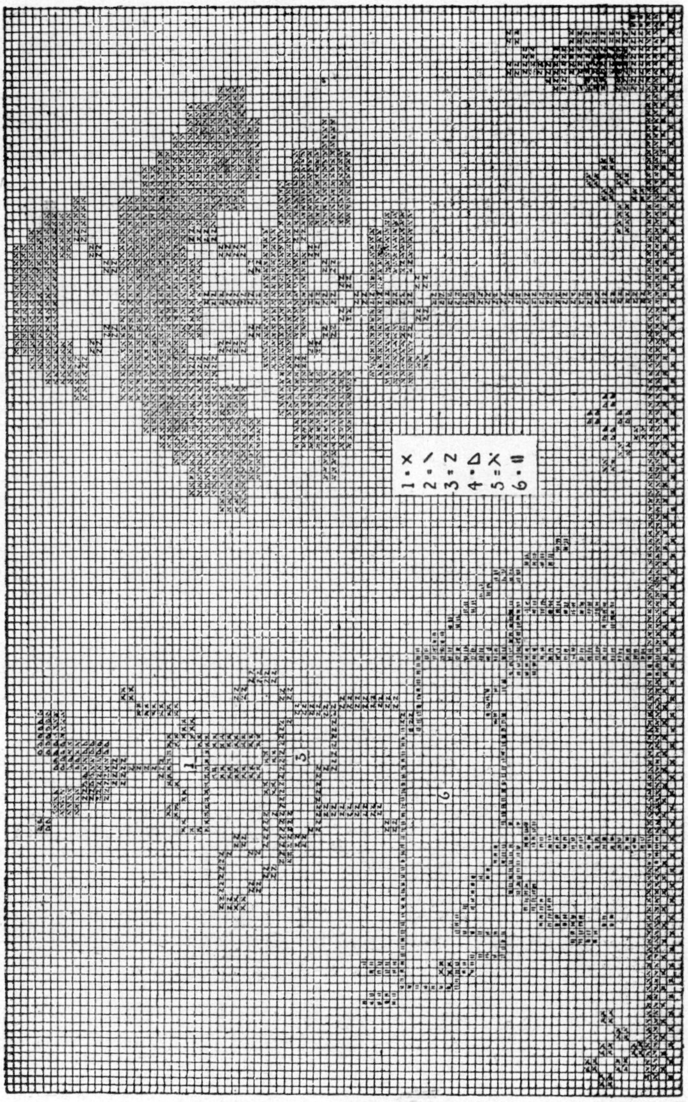

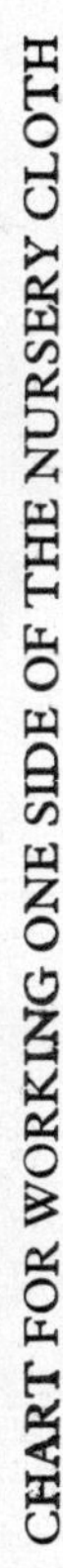

Fig. 13.

CHART FOR WORKING ONE SIDE OF THE NURSERY CLOTH

Fig. 14. This quickly-worked and effective cushion is in brown, green, scarlet, gold and royal. A chart for working half the central design is given on the previous page.

Greek-Isle peasant cross-stitch. A matching motif is shown on the following pages.

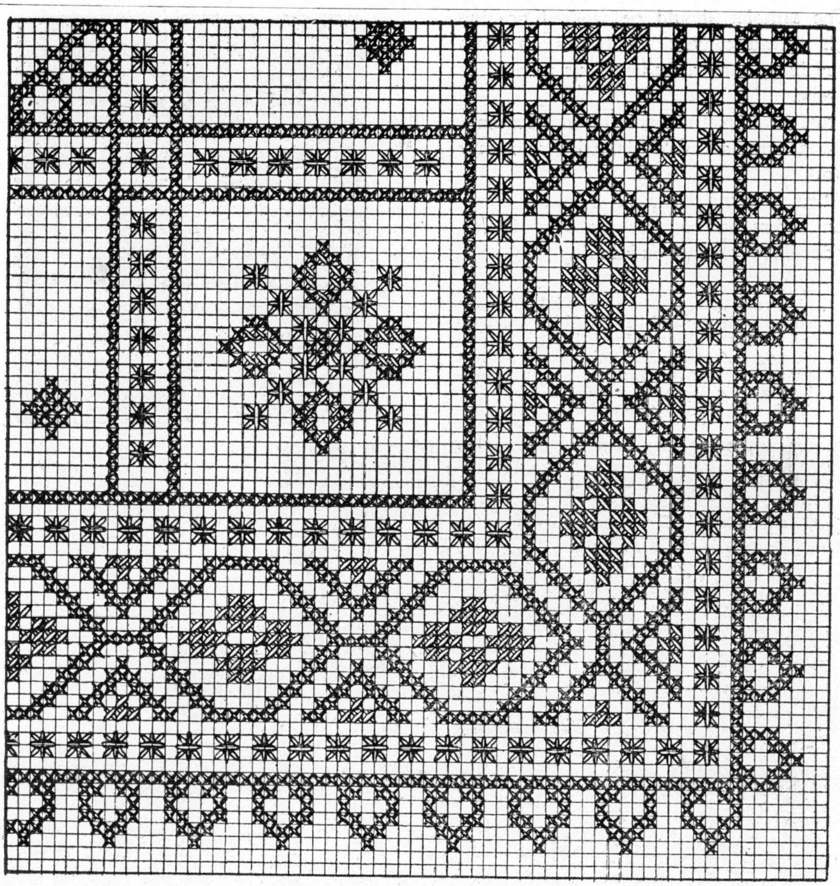

Fig. 15. CROSS-STITCH AND LEVIATHAN STITCH

A striking design for a cloth worked in two colours. Double cross-stitch on Leviathan stitch (details for working are shown in Fig. 5 at the beginning of the chapter) is used as a contrast in the border and in the diamonds in the square. With this chart as a guide it is possible to work directly on to the material. The design below makes a charmingly neat border.

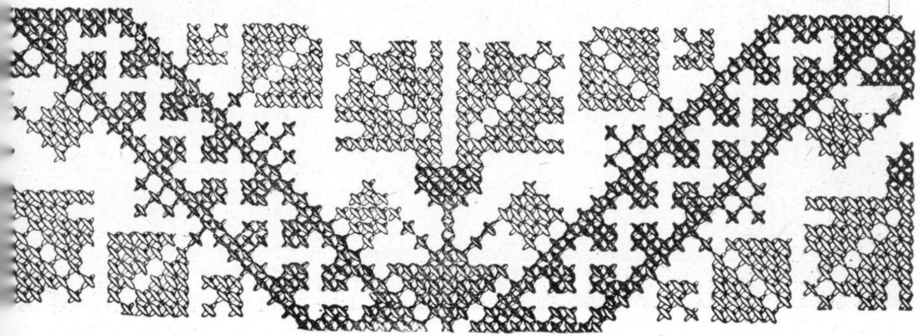

The sampler should be worked on fine single thread canvas, which has 19 holes to the inch, and worked in four threads of Filoselle.

Cross-stitch pictures worked in black on a white ground are most effective and easy to work.

When marking linen or blankets cross-stitch letters and figures are very useful. For details see chapter on initials.

Fig. 16.

A lovely specimen of Greek-Isle peasant cross-stitch worked in reds, blues, greens and black. Reproduced by kind permission of the Victoria and Albert Museum. Above, Fig. 16, shows very clearly how Holbein stitch can be combined with cross-stitch.

Fig. 15 shows a border for a cloth worked in cross-stitch and double cross-stitch in two shades of silk. Using Fig. 15 as a guide you could work directly on to your material.

In Fig. 16 is a border showing Holbein or half-stitch. It is also known as Italian stitch or outline stitch and is often used with cross-stitch. Figs. 1 and 2, Page 38 show exactly how Holbein stitch is done. It must be worked with great regularity and both sides must be exactly alike.

All stitches must be perfectly horizontal and of equal length, and worked in short stitches in single stitch, so arranged that the outline be covered in straight lines, all of which must meet or join perfectly, turning if required at the end of each stitch.

Holbein work, which dates back from the time of Holbein, is most decorative and useful for table-cloths, towels, etc., worked in cotton, or if on richer materials, silk. Fig 16. can be worked in two colours, keeping the cross-stitch to the darker shade.

A lovely Chinese design worked in cross-stitch and Holbein stitch in black on white cotton. Reproduced by kind permission of the Victoria and Albert Museum.

A delicate Chinese design worked in cross-stitch. The spiky veins are single threads couched down at intervals. The border is particularly adaptable. Below, another corner of the same design. Animals, butterflies and insects are used a great deal in Oriental designs. Reproduced by kind permission of the Victoria and Albert Museum.

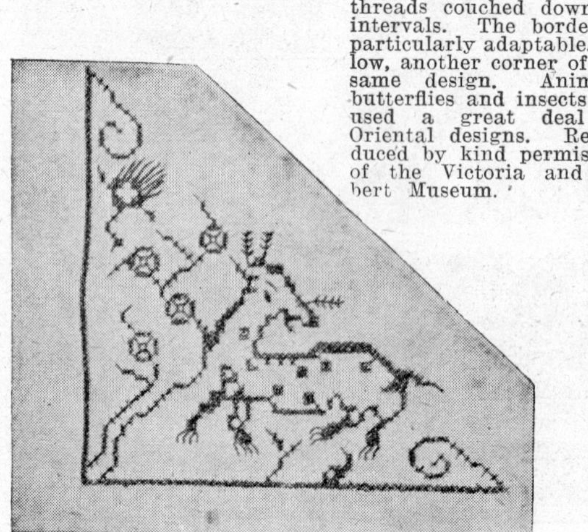

DRAWN THREAD WORK

Drawn thread work is carried out by drawing threads from a suitable material and ornamenting the open strand with fancy stitches.

This work is by no means new. The very earliest fancy work that was ever invented consisted of drawing certain threads out of linen material and weaving them with a needle round and about the remaining threads to form a pattern. There is no doubt that the embroidery of fine linen mentioned in Scripture as being used for the vestments of the priests and the hanging of the Temple was worked by drawn threads in various fancy stitches.

As time went on, drawn thread work was introduced into European countries, workers became skilful, fabrics were varied and improved. Good embroidery was done in Greece, Italy, Russia, Germany and Spain, under the designation of *Punto tirato* (threads drawn one way of the material), *Punto tagliato* (threads drawn both ways—across and across), *Opus tiratum* (fancy open stitches, Dresden Point, lace stitches), and other names, more especially indicative of the locality in which a particular form of work started.

Towards the end of the sixteenth century the art of embroidering on linen was taken up in England by members of the Royal Household, who being clever in lacemaking, introduced lace stitches intermingled with drawn thread work to enrich their clothes and house-linen. Reticella stitches and point lace stitches, such as *Point de Bruxelles, Point de Venise, Point D'Esprit, Point Tiré,* and many others have thus been gradually incorporated with drawn thread work, and are now used as a filling for cut out spaces, corners, and other purposes.

Drawn thread work can be used for lingerie, handkerchiefs, sheets, tray and teacloths, towels, night-dress cases, and other household requisites.

Materials Required.—Linen is most suitable, and can be obtained in a variety of colours and qualities. There are numerous widths, 36-inch, 45-inch, and 72-inch being the most useful for table linens.

Linen canvas, cambric, lawn, heavy Jap silks and crêpe de Chine can also be used. On no account choose cheap material with roughness and irregularity in the texture or the threads will not draw properly, and when drawn some will be thicker than others, making the insertions uneven in width, i.e. the warp threads will be wider than the weft threads, or vice versa. This is fatal to the exactitude of the work especially when forming a perfect square.

For working, the thread drawn out of the material was once used, but now linen threads in white or colour are used. Lace thread is also used for drawn thread work, and can be bought in white and neutral shades.

The thread should be the same size as the thread drawn from the linen. In some patterns the same thread is used throughout, but for others a variation is made by using a thick thread for some portions of the pattern. Charming effects may be obtained with coloured linen and tinted or shaded threads.

Crochet cotton, either white or coloured, may be introduced for the coarser parts of the work, for running lines of "crossing" or *Punto tirato* knots, and for such prominent parts of the patterns as spinning wheels, spiders, and stars. Frequently, fast dyed embroidery silks in shades of colour are introduced into marginal fancy-stitching with pleasing effect.

Other essentials for drawn thread work are crewel needles or short darners, a pair of sharp, finely pointed embroidery scissors, and in some cases, a frame.

Drawn thread work is very durable and will wash and clean well time after time, provided the best materials are used and care is taken in working to secure all edges of the solid linen properly, and to run in the ends of all the working threads. Most especially care must be taken in the formation of corners and such open spaces in solid linen, where the threads that are to be drawn have first to be cut so as not to interfere with the marginal texture of the linen itself. For instance, supposing an insertion of a depth of sixteen threads is required to go along the side of a cloth without extending to the extreme width of the material, cut across the sixteen threads, perfectly straight with a finely pointed pair of scissors, at the place where the top of the insertion should stop. Cut across exactly the same sixteen threads at the opposite end. Then raise the cut threads one by one with the point of the needle to get a small end by which to draw out the rest of the thread. The edges so cut are generally strengthened with buttonhole stitching.

Before cutting the linen, draw a thread and cut along the drawn thread line, thus giving a straight edge with the grain of the material. When preparing drawn thread patterns, measure the spaces and draw a single thread to mark them, taking care to cut the threads where required. (Fig. 1.)

Fig. 1.

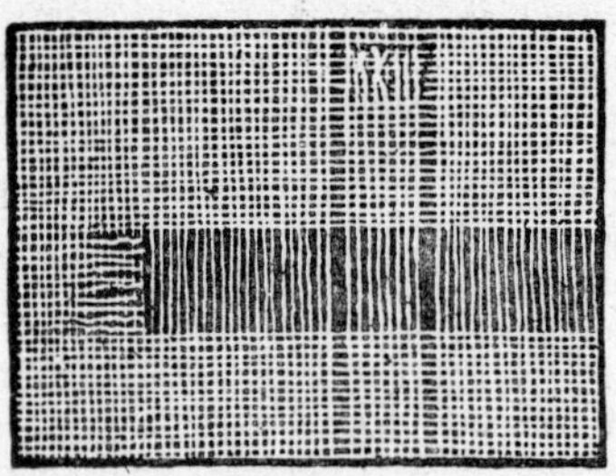

Draw a single thread to mark the outline of spaces to be drawn, as in Fig. 1. At the corners where warp and weft threads are withdrawn, or where bands of hemstitching are required, buttonhole the edge of the linen (Fig. 2).

Fig. 2.

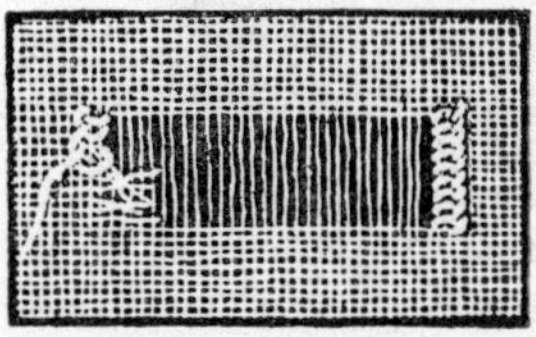

Otherwise the linen will have a drawn appearance beyond the pattern.

At the corners where the warp and the weft threads are both withdrawn, or where bands of hem-stitching are required, the edge of the linen should be buttonholed. (Fig. 2.) This may be done at the same time as the hemstitching.

Although much of the simpler drawn thread work can be done in the hand, a frame is necessary for more complicated work. The double row of hemstitching must always be worked in the hand before putting the work on a frame. If the threads are drawn out in one direction only, the work is known as hemstitching, and when both warp and weft threads are removed, as insertion.

STITCHES USED

Simple Hemstitch is used for handkerchiefs, sheets and other linen articles which sometimes need an ornamental hem. The hem, of course, varies in width according to its use.

For handkerchiefs, the hem should be about an inch wide. For this, draw out four threads of the material at a distance of $2\frac{1}{8}$ inches from the margin of all four sides of the material, to allow for the hem turning in. By reason of the two open lines of drawn threads crossing each other at each end of the fabric a little square is formed at the corner. The turn of the hem must be folded exactly to lie perfectly level with the upper edge of the drawn open threads, to which it is sewn in process of hemstitching.

For sheets, a wider hem is generally allowed, usually from three to four inches on best fine linen sheets, but a two-inch hem, or even a one-inch, will be enough for sheets in ordinary use. As the hem in this instance will not be carried down the sides, a drawing of five or six threads at a suitable distance from the top and bottom of the sheet will suffice.

Hemstitching, Method 1. — Figure 3. In this example the hem is turned down on the right side of the material. The stitching is worked from right to left along the upper edge of the drawn open threads. The hem may, of course, be turned on the wrong side, but as the fabric for handkerchiefs and sheets usually has both sides alike, the fold is not unsightly.

(*N.B.* In these instructions the working thread is termed "cotton" to avoid confusion with the threads of the material.) Thread the needle and secure the end of the cotton inside the fold of the hem at the extreme right-hand side of the piece of material, and, holding the hem over the first finger of the left hand, bring the needle and cotton out two threads above the fold of the hem. Insert the needle between the open threads directly under the place the cotton is brought out, and, passing it from right to left, take up three open threads on the needle and draw the cotton through. Insert the needle in the same place as before, but in a slightly upward direction to pass through the hem in position (as in Fig. 3) and bring it out two threads above the fold of the hem, straight above the cotton of the stitch just worked and three threads to the left of where the cotton was first brought out, and draw the cotton through. * Insert the needle from right to left to take up the next three threads of drawn open linen and draw the cotton through. Insert the needle in the same place, but turning it in a slightly upward direction through the hem, bring it out straight above the fold of the hem and three threads to the left of where the cotton was before brought out. As shown in Fig. 3, draw the cotton through, and repeat from * to end of the line of drawn open threads.

There are two motions to every stitch; the first is taken from right to left in the drawn open threads and the second confines the group of drawn threads in a cluster, secures the hem, and brings the cotton in position for working the next stitch. Care should be taken to make every stitch perfectly true and regular and to draw the cotton close, but not so tight that it puckers the material.

This hem-stitch is used extensively in drawn thread embroidery to strengthen the upper and lower edge of nearly all openwork insertions. It may be made as deep as desired and while it forms a strengthening ornamental overcast stitch on the margin of solid linen, it at the same time confines a certain number of open threads in clusters (of two, three, four, six or eight in a cluster) according to the requirements of the pattern that is to be worked.

Hemstitching, Method 2.—Fig. 4. This hemstitch resembles the one above and can be used for the same purposes, but it is worked slightly differently, the stitches slanting obliquely instead of being upright and the two components of each stitch being entwined together.

Draw out four threads of linen and turn down a hem as in Fig. 3. The hemstitching is worked from right to left. Secure the end of the cotton inside the fold of the hem at the right-hand side of the material, hold the hem over the first finger of the left hand and bring up the needle and cotton in the hem two threads above the fold. * Hold the cotton under the left thumb, insert the needle in the open insertion two threads to the right from where the cotton is brought out in the hem, and take four open threads in the needle as shown in Fig. 4 and passing the needle above the cotton held by the left thumb, draw the cotton through in a sort of buttonhole stitch loop. Insert the needle in the space at the left of the cluster of threads just drawn together and bring it out in the hem two threads above the fold and four threads to the left of the last stitch in the hem and draw the cotton through. Repeat from *.

This method clusters four threads together in each stitch and the stitch in the

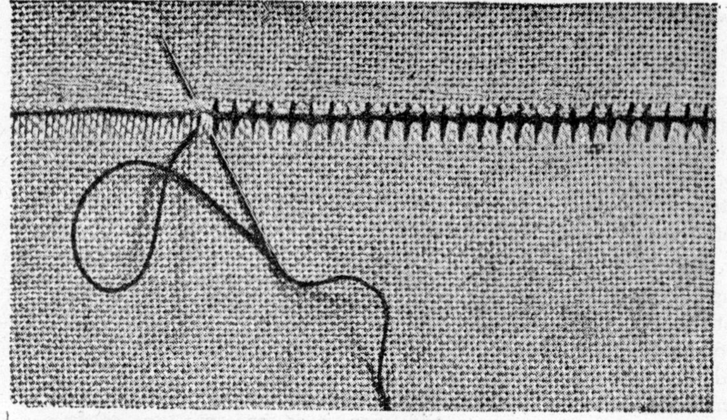

THREE WAYS OF HEM-STITCHING

Fig. 3.—SIMPLE HEMSTITCH

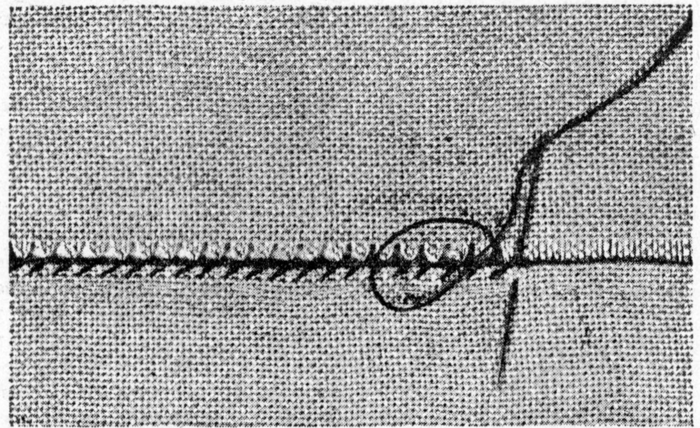

Fig. 4. ANOTHER WAY OF WORKING SIMPLE HEMSTITCH

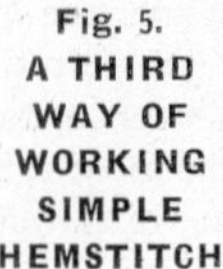

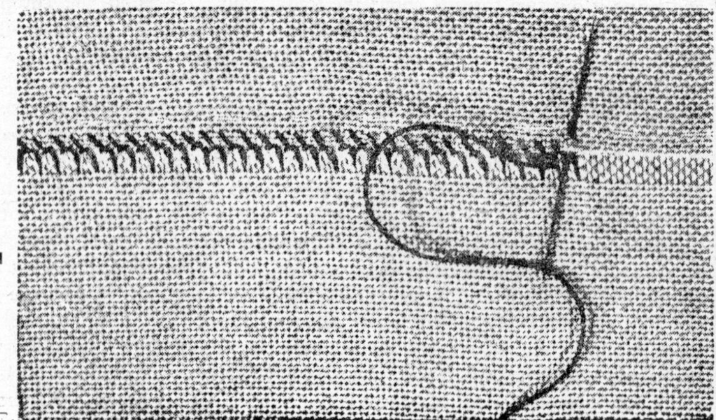

Fig. 5. A THIRD WAY OF WORKING SIMPLE HEMSTITCH

hem always emerges above the middle of a cluster.

Hemstitching, Method 3.—Fig. 5. This stitch is worked from left to right and the stitches slant obliquely. As it is attractive and easily worked many people prefer it to the two previous stitches.

Prepare the material by drawing out four threads and turn down a hem as before. Secure the end of cotton inside the fold of the hem at the extreme left-hand corner of the material, hold the hem over the finger of the left hand and bring up the needle and cotton in the hem, two threads above the fold. * Insert the needle from right to left to take up three open threads, bringing the needle out exactly under the cotton that comes out of the hem, and draw the cotton through. Insert the needle in the same space of open threads and bring it up perpendicularly two threads above the fold of the hem in the position represented in Fig. 5 which is three threads distant from the last stitch in the hem, and draw the cotton through. Repeat from *, taking three threads further to the right in each consecutive stitch.

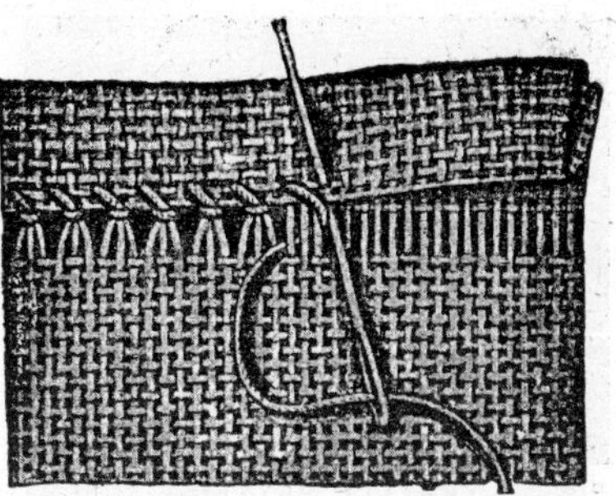

Showing hemstitch as in Fig. 5, sewing down a hem with the hemstitching.

Open Hemstitch Insertion. — The open hemstitch insertion shown in Fig. 6 is made by working a line of simple hemstitch along both the upper and lower edges of an insertion of drawn threads; this method of hemstitching forms the foundation of numerous elaborate patterns and serves a twofold purpose, as it not only strengthens each margin of solid linen, but it also keeps the open threads in even, regular clusters.

Start by drawing out eight threads Work from left to right. Secure the end of the cotton with which you intend working on the left-hand side of the linen near the upper edge of the drawn thread insertion, by small invisible stitches on the wrong side of the material. Bring the needle and cotton out three threads above the open insertion and insert the needle between the open threads directly under the place where the cotton is brought out. Slant it from right to left, take up three open threads in the needle, and draw the cotton through. Insert the needle in the same place but in a slightly upward direction, and bring it out three threads above the open insertion straight above the cotton of the stitch just worked, and three threads to the right of where the cotton was first brought out, and draw the cotton through. This is practically the same as simple hemstitch (Fig. 4), but here the stitches are deeper as they cover three threads of the solid linen instead of two. It is also better adapted for fancy purposes. Continue working in the same manner to the end of the line of drawn open threads drawing the cotton close, but not too close to pucker the linen. Care should be taken to keep the same number of threads in each cluster, or the bars will be irregular. When the end of the line is reached fasten off the cotton securely by running the end in through some of the worked stitches. Turn the work so that the edge of the open work insertion, which was at the top, is now at the bottom and repeat the hemstitch, taking up the same clusters

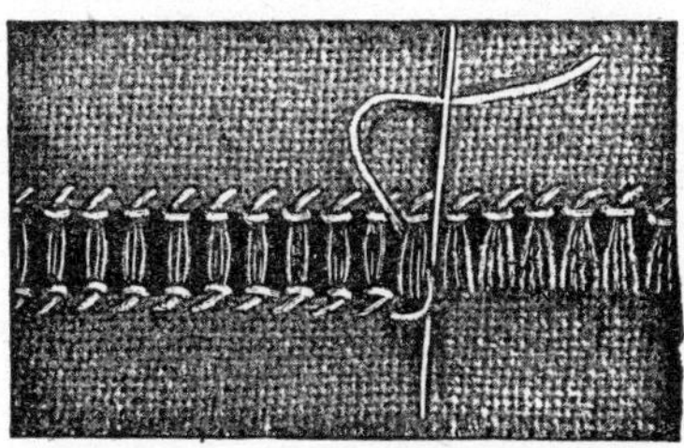

Fig. 6.—OPEN HEMSTITCH INSERTION

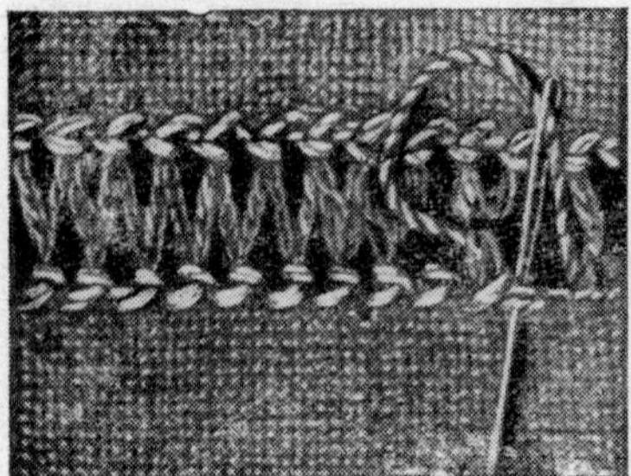

Fig. 7.—TRELLIS PATTERN INSERTION

of threads which you took in the first row. The counting will not be difficult, as the stitches of the first row will have made a little parting in the open threads between the clusters, to indicate where to place the clusters of the second row.

The art of forming groups and clusters is of very great importance in drawn thread work and particular attention must always be paid to the working of the first row, for upon this, the whole beauty of the work depends, and sometimes a slight inaccuracy will throw out a whole pattern.

Trellis Hemstitch.—The trellis hemstitch, as shown in Fig. 7, is produced by taking up half of one cluster and half of the one following when stitching the second edge.

A variation of this trellis insertion can be made by drawing out a greater number of threads and grouping six or eight threads (it must always be an even number) in a cluster.

Single Crossing.—This is a favourite stitch as it produces a good effect at the cost of very little labour. Prepare the insertion by drawing out eight, ten or twelve threads or any even number and work the hemstitch along the top and bottom edge, grouping the open threads in straight regular clusters of three threads in a cluster, and taking the stitches two threads deep in the margin of the solid linen. When this is done proceed to "cross" the threads, like this:—

Thread the needle with a length of cotton sufficient to run from end to end of the row of drawn open threads (the cotton can be joined with a knot if the insertion is too long to take a single thread, but knots look so bad that it is advisable to avoid them where possible). Secure the end of the cotton at the right-hand side of the material with a small invisible stitch at the back of the outer margin of the linen to the right beyond the drawn threads, if these threads have been cut to form an outer margin. If not it must be tied in a knot in the middle of the first cluster of open threads. Then, keeping the needle and cotton on the right side of the work, put the needle from left to right, under the second cluster from the cotton, pointing the needle away from you, lift it slightly and bring the point of the needle round so as to take up the first cluster from right to left, and turn the needle to bring the first cluster of threads up clear to the left of the second cluster. This brings the two clusters of threads "crossed" upon the needle. Draw the cotton through and proceed to cross every two clusters in the same way. Fig. 8 shows the crossing in the working very clearly. The cotton should run easily, exactly midway along the centre of the insertion, and must not be drawn too tightly.

A delightful effect can be made by drawing out enough threads to make the insertion an inch or an inch and a half wide, and running a piece of narrow ribbon through, instead of cotton, as shown in Fig. 9.

When ribbon is run into any article which needs washing, it is as well to remove it before washing. The best plan is to unsew the ribbon at one end where it is stitched to the work, and secure the ribbon

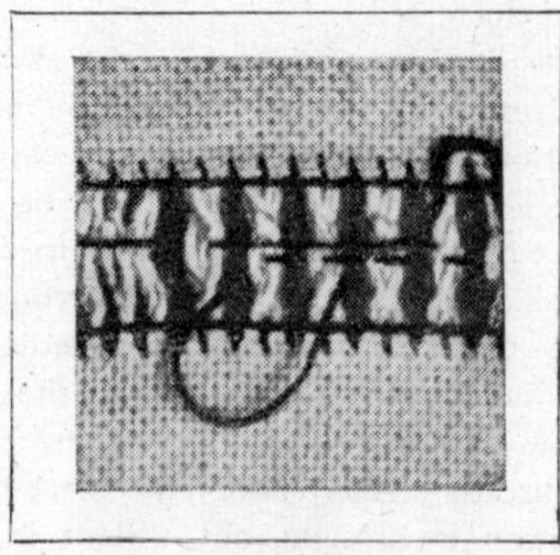

Fig. 8.—SINGLE CROSSING INSERTION

to a string of stout crochet cotton or white pipingcord, then to unstitch the other end of the ribbon and pull that so as to draw out the whole length of ribbon and leave the cotton in its place. The ends of the cotton must be sewn down, and when ready to insert the ribbon again, unpicked and secured to the end of the ribbon and drawn

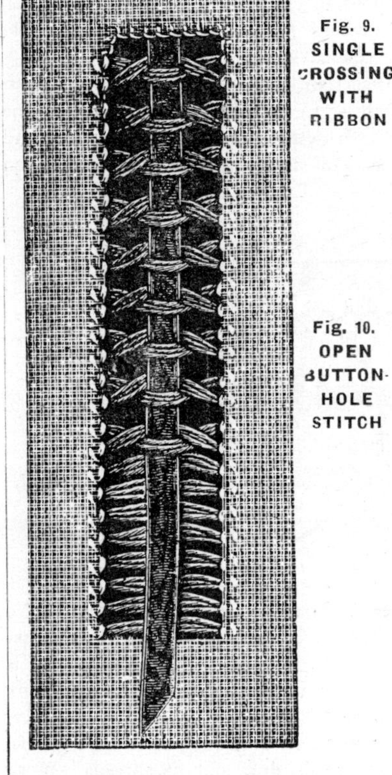

Fig. 9. SINGLE CROSSING WITH RIBBON

into position again. This saves the trouble of recrossing all the strands.

Open Buttonhole Stitch is occasionally used to strengthen the edges of drawn thread insertions and it makes a pretty variation from hemstitch in which the horizontal stitches lie straight along the edge of the open threads and the teeth project as it were, into the solid linen, so in open buttonhole stitch the horizontal stitches lie in a straight line upon the solid linen and the teeth bind a certain number of open threads into clusters.

Draw out eight threads. Work from left to right, going first along the lower edge of the insertion. Secure the cotton on the left-hand side of the material close by the lower edge of the insertion, and bring up the needle and cotton in the margin of the solid linen two threads below the edge of the open insertion. * Hold the cotton under the left thumb, insert the needle in the open insertion above the place from where the cotton is springing and holding it in a downward direction slanting from left to right, bring the point out two threads below the edge of the open insertion and four threads from the place where the last

Fig. 10. OPEN BUTTONHOLE STITCH

stitch is already worked, according to the position shown in Fig. 10. Repeat from * to the end of the row and fasten off. Turn the work so that the buttonhole stitches now come at the top, and the unworked edge at the bottom. Work again in the same way, clustering the threads together in regular clusters of four threads in a cluster, as shown in the illustration.

Insertion of Cross-Stitch and Spike Stitch.—This is an effective stitch for ornamenting the edges of an insertion and it may at any time be used as a substitute for hem-stitch.

For this example, eight threads are drawn out. It is worked from left to right along the lower edge of drawn open threads. Secure the cotton on the wrong side of the fabric and bring up the needle and cotton in the solid linen two threads below the edge of the insertion. Insert the needle

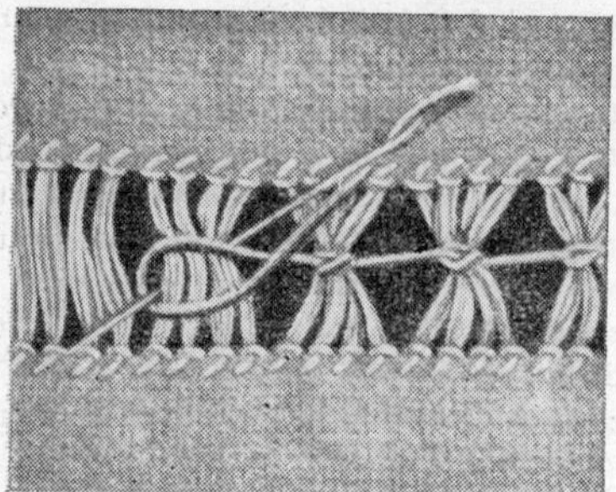

Fig. 12.—DRAWN THREAD KNOTS

between the open threads just above the cotton and bring it out with the point towards you two threads below the place it was first brought out, that is, in the solid linen four threads below the edge of the insertion and draw the cotton through. * Insert the needle from right to left to take up four of the drawn threads bringing up the needle in the space where last inserted, and draw the cotton through. Insert the needle, point away from you, four threads below the insertion and four threads from the bottom of the first half of the cross-stitch and bring it up in the open insertion where the first half of the cross-stitch is worked as shown in Fig. 11, and draw the needle and cotton through. Insert the needle two threads below the insertion, point towards you and bring it straight down two threads lower, i.e. in the same place where a cross-stitch is already worked, and repeat from *. A tiny straight stitch called a spike-stitch will be seen between each cross-stitch.

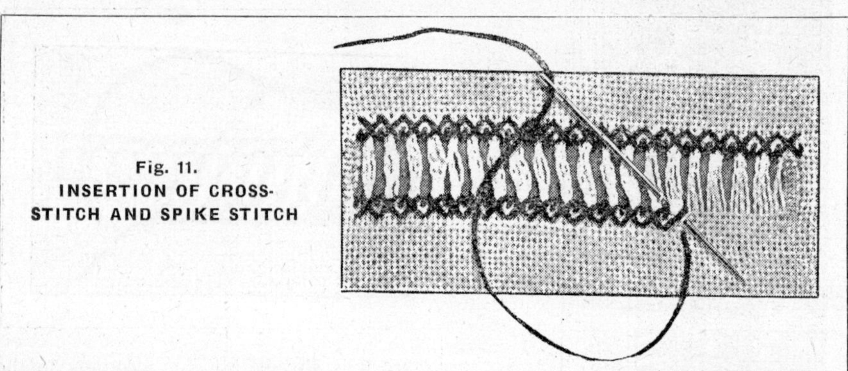

Fig. 11.
INSERTION OF CROSS-STITCH AND SPIKE STITCH

When one side of the work is done, turn the material and work along the opposite side, keeping the threads in regular clusters.

Fig. 12 gives a clear illustration of the drawn thread knot or *Punto Tirato* knot as it is sometimes called. Begin, as shown, by making a loop with the working thread, then pass the needle under the strands to be knotted together and through the loop. It is quite simple and quick to do and looks very effective when done.

Insertion of Hemstitch and Cross-stitch is more elaborate than any of the previous examples as it is rather wider and consists of two insertions of drawn open threads separated from each other by a strip or bar of solid threads on which cross-stitches are worked. Nevertheless, it is quite easy to do and is useful for many purposes.

To work it, draw out six threads, leave three threads, draw out six threads. Work hemstitch along the top edge and bottom edge as shown in the illustration, grouping four threads together in a cluster and taking the stitches two threads deep into the margin of the solid linen. The same four threads are grouped together in the second row like the first row of the hemstitching. Careful counting is essential or the trellis pattern will not be formed correctly. The cross-stitches which are designed to occupy the whole surface of the three solid threads in the centre of the insertion are worked in the first instance straight along from left to right and then back from right to left, and in process of working they sub-divide the clusters and thereby produce the trellis pattern. Secure the end of the cotton on the wrong side of the fabric on the left-hand side of the piece of work and bring up the needle and cotton in between the second and third threads of the first cluster below the three-thread bar. Insert the needle in between the second and third threads of the second cluster above the bar and bring it out between the second and third threads of the second cluster above the bar. Bring it out again between the second and third threads of the third cluster below the bar, and draw the cotton through and so on, sub-dividing each cluster in regular order to the end. Work back inserting the needle in exactly the same position (note the position of the needle in Fig. 13), and you will have a row of crosses on the right side of the linen and a neat line of small perpendicular stitches on the wrong side.

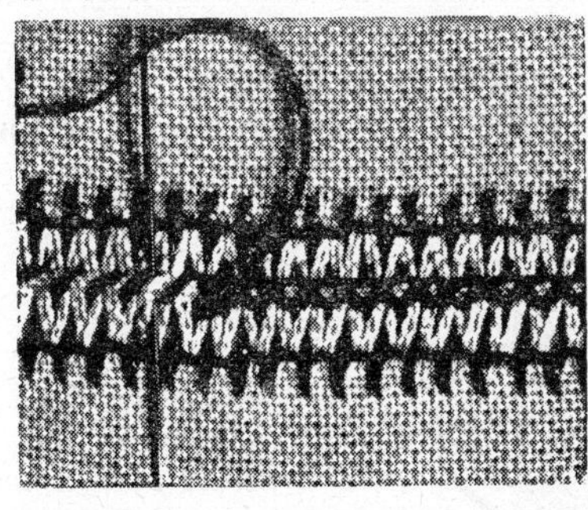

Fig. 13.
INSERTION OF HEM-STITCH AND CROSS-STITCH

Insertion of Double-Herringbone.—Fig. 14 shows an insertion suitable for a straight border or for square articles where the work is not required to go to the extreme ends of the material but stops short at a certain place to form a corner, where the threads that are to be drawn out are first of all cut away to ensure an inch or more margin of solid linen outside the insertion, the corner spaces being afterwards filled up with small wheels or stars. To work the insertion of double-herringbone draw out five threads, and leave three threads, draw out thirteen, leave three, draw out five.

Begin with the herringbone stitch, working from left to right over the top bar of three linen threads. Attach the end of the cotton securely at the left-hand side in the threads comprising the top bar, insert the needle from right to left to take up the six first threads of the wide-open insertion and draw the cotton through. Insert the needle from left to right in the top narrow insertion, and omitting the three first threads to the left, take up the six following threads and draw the cotton through. Insert the needle again to take up the same six threads and draw the cotton through. * Insert the needle from right to left to take up the six next threads of the wide insertion and draw the cotton through. Insert the needle in the same position again and draw the cotton through. Insert the needle to take up the next six threads of the top narrow insertion and draw the cotton through. Insert the needle again in the same position and draw the cotton through

Fig. 14.—INSERTION OF DOUBLE HERRINGBONE

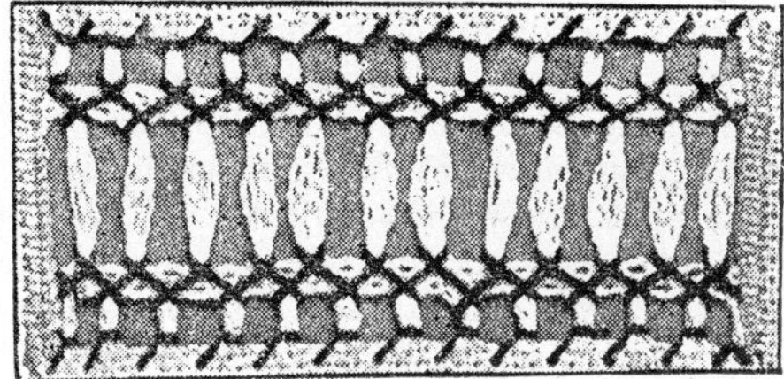

and repeat from *. This process confines six threads in each cluster and forms a series of interlaced herringbone stitches above the three-thread bar of solid linen, as shown in the illustration, while the only stitches visible on the wrong side of the work are those which hold each cluster of six threads together. When the first row is completed, turn the work and proceed similarly along the other bar of three solid threads, taking up the same six threads in a cluster along the centre insertion as in the first row, so that the clusters stand upright. Complete the insertion by working a row of hemstitch along the upper and lower edge of the insertion as shown in the illustration, grouping four threads in a cluster and taking the stitches two threads deep into the margin of the solid linen. Especial care should be taken to group the self-same threads into clusters along the lower edge of the insertion as those at the top. The binding stitch is worked from left to right. Secure the end of the needleful of cotton by making a small stitch on the wrong side of the fabric to the left of the lowest bar of solid linen threads. Bring up the needle and cotton in the lowest row of the drawn-open threads to the left of the first cluster. Insert the needle from right

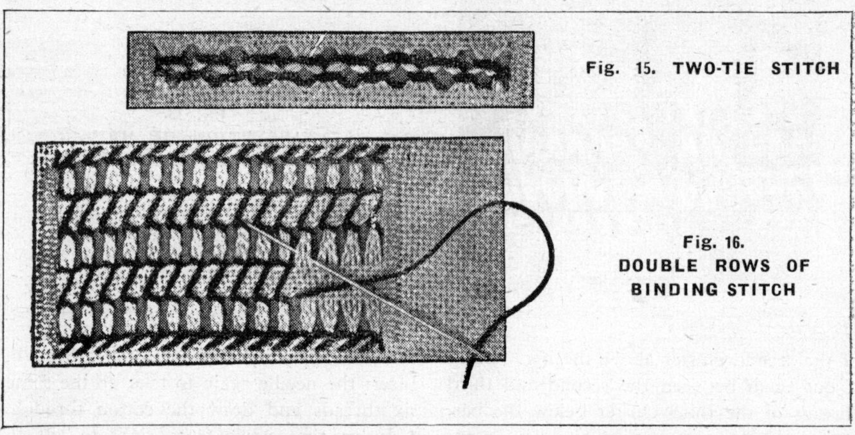

Fig. 15. TWO-TIE STITCH

Fig. 16. DOUBLE ROWS OF BINDING STITCH

lower edge of the drawn-open threads, taking up the same six threads that have already been grouped together in the course of herringboning, and making the stitches two threads deep into the margin of the solid linen.

Binding Stitch is used as a decorative embroidery over a narrow line or bar of solid linen threads between two rows of drawn open threads, and while it "binds," or holds in place the threads of the bar to be ornamented, it at the same time groups into clusters the drawn open threads on each side. A simple insertion composed of binding stitch is shown in Fig. 16, and the stitch may also be used in combination with other drawn thread stitches. To work Fig. 16 draw out six threads, leave six threads, draw out six, leave six, draw out six. Work a row of hemstitch at the upper to left to take up the first cluster of threads, bringing out the point of the needle in the same space as the cotton was just drawn up and draw the cotton through. Hold the cotton under the left thumb, insert the needle from right to left to take up the same four threads in the middle open row and draw the cotton through. Insert the needle to the right of the stitch just worked in the middle row and, placing it in a downward direction, bring it out in the lowest row to the right of the stitch already worked there. * Insert the needle from right to left to take up the next four threads of the lowest open row, as shown in Fig. 16, and draw the cotton through. Hold the cotton under the left thumb to keep it from getting twisted, insert the needle from right to left to take up the same four threads in the middle row, and draw the cotton through.

Insert the needle to the right of the stitch just worked in the middle row and bring it out in the lowest row to the right of the stitch that is worked there and draw the cotton through. Repeat from * to the end of the row. Draw the cotton rather tightly each time to keep the stitches close together in a straight, even line. Turn the work and proceed with the other row of binding stitch in the same way.

Two-tie Stitch is popular for a narrow insertion round handkerchiefs and other articles and is sometimes used by itself, as shown in Fig. 15, and sometimes in combination with other drawn thread insertions. Though apparently quite simple, great exactness must be observed in working to get the ties in a straight, even row.

Draw out eight threads to make about the width of $\frac{3}{8}$ of an inch of drawn open insertion. Work from left to right. Bring up the needle to the left of the first drawn thread, then insert the needle from right to left to take up eight of the drawn open threads one-third below the top of the insertion. Draw the cotton through. Take up the eight threads again in the same place and draw the cotton through; take up the last four threads from right to left, one-third above the lower edge of the insertion and draw the cotton through. Take up the next four threads to the right with the four threads you last took up, eight threads in all, and draw the cotton through. Take up the next four threads to the right with the four threads you last took up—eight threads in all—and draw the cotton through. Take up the eight threads again in the same place and draw the cotton through. Take up the last four threads from right to left one-third below the top of the insertion, and draw the cotton through. Take up the next four threads to the right with the four threads you last took up—eight threads in all—and draw the cotton through. Take up the eight threads again in the same place and draw the cotton through. Continue thus working a double tie one-third from the bottom and from the top, alternately. Draw the cotton moderately tight, and make all the ties at even distance from the margin of the solid linen, at the same time keeping the cotton as it passes from tie to tie, at the back of the clustered threads.

Forming a Corner by cutting out threads and leaving a margin of solid linen on the outside of the material:—

Take a piece of linen the size desired. Suppose the margin of the cloth is to be two inches deep all round. Mark this depth at the corners either by running in a thread of coloured cotton or by a line └ with a black-lead pencil. Begin at one corner, count eighteen threads both ways from the angle. Raise the cut threads one by one with the needle point and draw out all the eighteen threads both ways of the material, cutting them again where they meet the cotton or line at the opposite corners. Repeat as before and when complete there will be a square space as in Fig. 17 and an insertion of drawn open threads will be seen from corner to corner on all four sides of the fabric.

Hemstitching Insertion and overcasting the corner. Fig. 18 shows how to continue the corner once the threads have been drawn as in Fig. 17. Both edges of the drawn open insertion are strengthened with a row of hemstitching, grouping three threads in a cluster and taking the stitches four threads deep into the margin of solid linen. The corner is worked in ordinary buttonhole stitch overcasting, taking a stitch six threads deep into each alternate thread of the linen.

Corner Fillings Method 1.—Figs. 21 and 22 show Spider's Web or Wheels. To work the corner carry four threads across the open space formed by cutting the threads as in Fig. 17, two threads from the centre of the open strands, and two others diagonally from one corner to another (see Fig. 22). Carry the fourth thread to the centre only, then knot the threads together as shown in the diagram and darn the centre to the required size. Now carry the fourth thread across the remaining space and continue the stitching in the new direction as shown in Fig. 22.

Another Insertion.—Fig. 21. The threads must be drawn to the width of

A beautiful example from the Victoria and Albert Museum of white embroidery and drawn thread work. The embroidery is in satin stitch in very fine silk on cotton, and was worked in Persia in the late eighteenth or early nineteenth century.

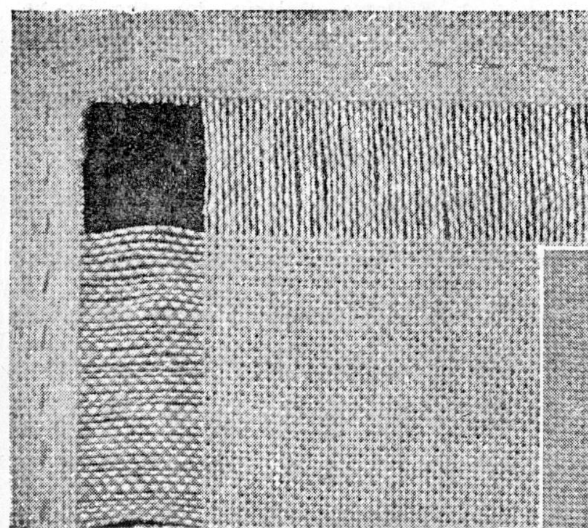

Fig. 17.

Fig. 17 shows how a corner is made so that a solid margin of linen is on the outside of the material. The edges are buttonholed, as shown below. When worked in self-coloured thread they will be scarcely visible.

TWO EASILY WORKED CORNERS

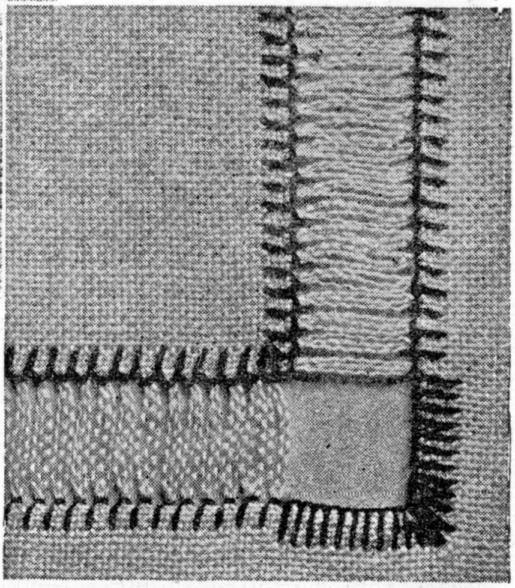

Fig. 18.

On the right, a more elaborate corner is shown, with threads alternately left and drawn so that a design can be worked through them.

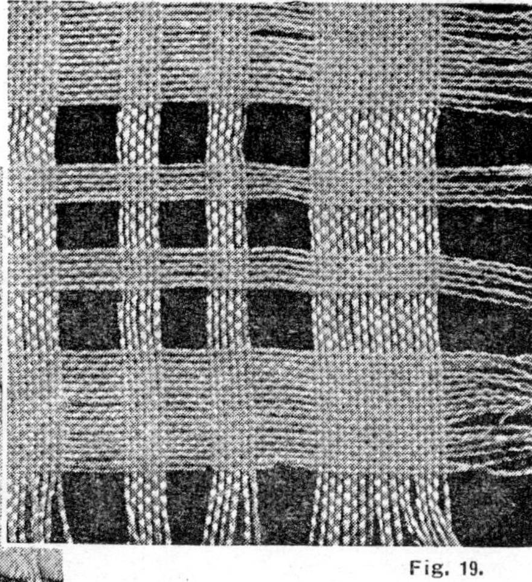

Fig. 19.

Single crossing insertion can be worked through the drawn threads, as shown on the left. A knot is tied in each square to secure the thread.

Fig. 20.

Fig. 21. INSERTION IN KNOT-STITCH. A SPIDER'S WEB

about $\frac{3}{4}$ of an inch and the strands divided into sets of six by hemstitching both edges. Three strands of one cluster and three of the next are then caught together down the centre with drawn thread knots. The Spider's Web corner is worked here.

Corner Fillings, Method 2.—The number of threads to be drawn depends, of course, upon the pattern, but the same number of threads must always be drawn out each way. Count, say, forty threads from the margin of the material, take the needle, raise the forty-first thread a little way from the margin, draw it out. Draw out seven more threads in the same way. Leave the following six threads, draw out another six threads, leave six threads, draw out eight threads. Do the same along the other three sides. Unravel the outer margin of twenty-three threads to form a fringe and you will have four drawn corners as shown in Fig. 19, together with an open insertion along each side of the material ready to embroider in any pattern.

A Suitable Pattern for the above Corner.—Hemstitch the edges for durability. After unravelling the threads to form a fringe there are eighteen solid threads left between the fringe and the first open insertion, and eighteen solid threads likewise between the two open insertions. Thread a needle with a long length of rather coarse cotton. Tie the end of the cotton in a firm knot round the first six threads of the open insertion, leaving an end sufficient to hang to the depth of the fringe, and proceed to cross the threads over three (see Fig. 8). Then carry the crossing to the end of the row and finish by tying the cotton in a firm knot round the last six threads, leaving an end to hang the depth of the fringe. Work the other line of insertion on the same side of the cloth in the same way. Proceed similarly along the other sides of the material, but tie a knot as the cotton of the previous working is crossed. This is to keep the two cottons in place as they cross each other in the centre of each square, and is best managed by keeping the thumb of the left hand on the cotton until the knot has been drawn exactly into the centre of the square. Fig. 20 shows the worked corner.

Chequered Insertion.—Suitable for a border on sideboard covers, etc. Draw out eight threads to form the upper space of open threads, leave twenty-one threads for the chequers. Draw out eight threads for the lower space of open threads, then subdivide the insertion still further to complete the formation of the squares of solid linen and to get the line of drawn threads between

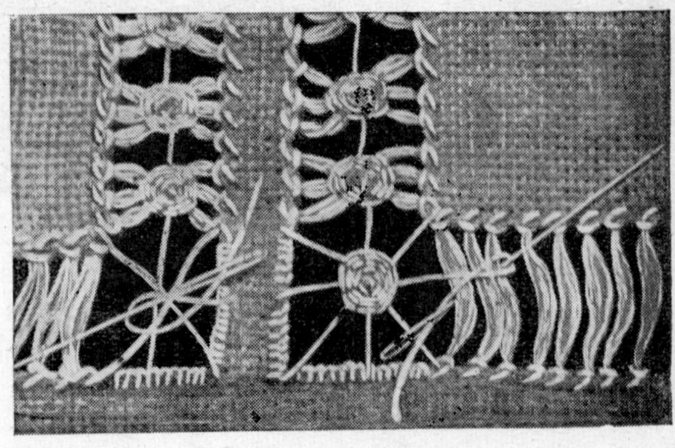

Fig. 22.

How to make a Spider's Web in the corner. On the left the threads are being taken across, and in the large section the web is finished.

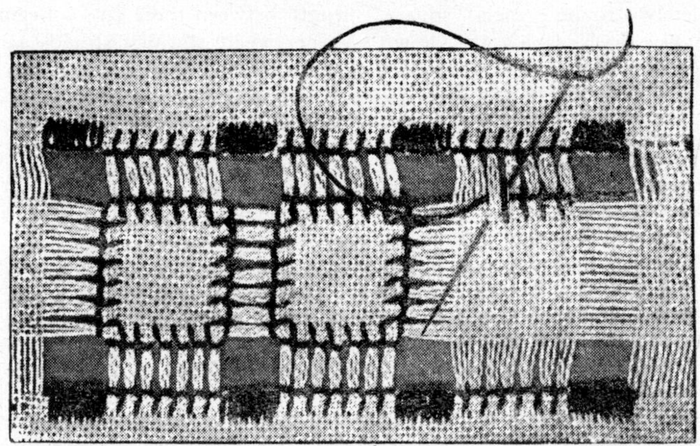

Fig. 23. CHEQUERED INSERTION

each chequer. This is done by cutting away and drawing out certain threads perpendicularly across the insertion, thus: cut eight threads away along both top and bottom edges and draw them out. * Leave twenty-one threads for a chequer, cut away eight threads along both the top and bottom edge and draw them out. Repeat from * for the length required. Start working at the right-hand top corner. Work eight ordinary buttonhole stitches into the solid linen along the top edge of the small cut-away space. Work seven hemstitches subdividing the twenty-one drawn open threads into seven clusters of three threads a cluster, and continue to the end of the row. Then turn the work upside down and work the opposite edge in the same way. Then

Fig. 24. DOUBLE CROSS PATTERN

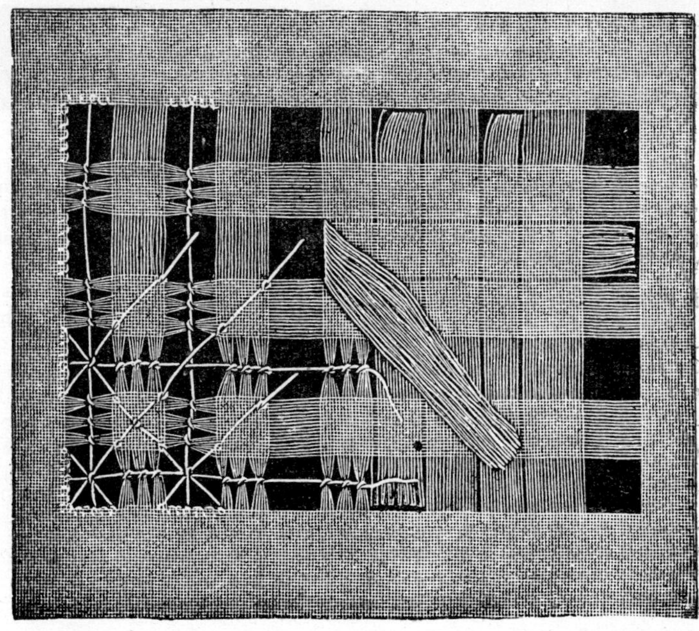

work completely round each square, chequer with hemstitch, taking the drawn threads in clusters of three, which gives seven clusters on each side of the square as shown in Fig. 23. A dainty finish is made by embroidering a sprig in each or every alternate square.

Double Cross Pattern is a specimen of a class of little patterns in which the whole of the background is drawn into regular squares and which, consequently form useful centres or borders.

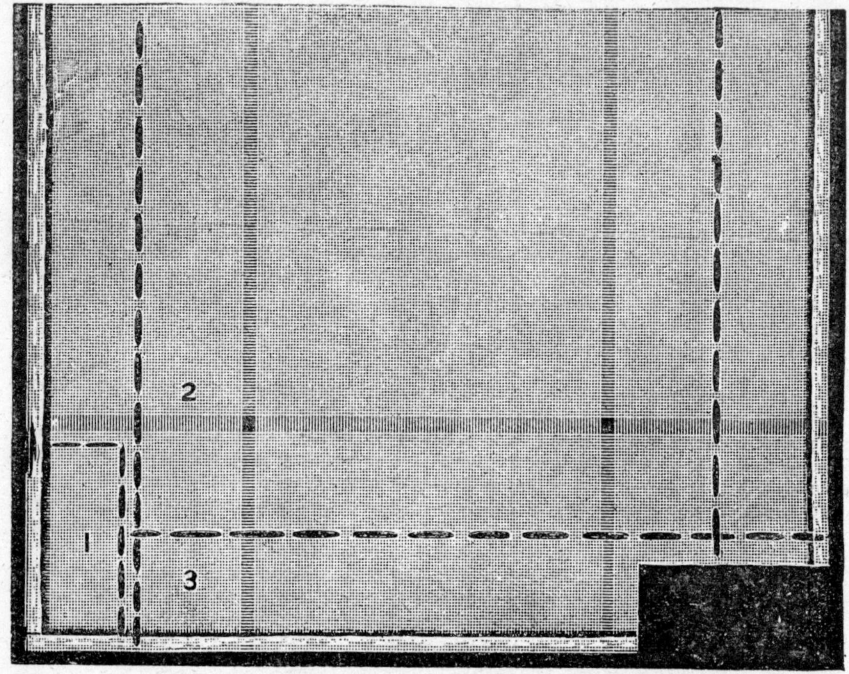

Fig. 25. HOW TO CUT A CORNER FOR HEMSTITCHING

Always begin the work at least half an inch within the hem. The hemstitching may be worked into the first band of embroidery, but it is preferable to leave a margin between them.

Plan out how much of the material is to be drawn, cut through fifteen strands and pull one of these as a measuring thread for the rest of the pattern. Just before reaching the end, cut through the same fifteen threads and draw them out along their whole length between these cuts. Begin from the corner where the first strands were clipped and cut fifteen of the open strands there. Measure with one of these threads by drawing it nearly as far as the work is to extend and cut the other ends of this second set of fifteen threads. Draw them out. There are now two bands of half-drawn stitches at right angles with each other and meeting at the corner with an open square. Measure each band of half-drawn stitches into sets of fifteen strands each. Alternately leave and cut one of these sets along the whole length of the work, ending with fifteen cut strands to form another corner. (That this may be arranged was the object of not at first extending the work to the extreme limit of the surface to be covered, as all the clipping would then have been done along the outer edge of the strands, nearest the hem.) When all the threads are drawn out the whole surface will be equally divided into open, half-drawn and solid or linen squares. Oversew or buttonhole the cut edges of the squares with fine thread. For the rest of the work, thread coarser than that of the material may be used.

Begin on the right-hand side of the work in the exact middle of the buttonholing along one side of the open square. Secure the working thread firmly there, * bring it down to the nearest half-drawn square, knot fifteen strands of this into three groups, each one enclosing five threads and putting the knots at equal distances apart, carrying on the working thread still in the same direction and repeat from * down the entire length of the work. Finish off, after crossing the last open square by a few stitches worked into the exact middle of the buttonholing opposite the starting-point. Run an exactly similar line of stitching down across each set of open squares along the whole of the work in the same direction. Now put lines down all the bands of open squares, in an opposite direction, so that they cross the first working threads in the middle of every open square. Start again, this time from the extreme outer corner of an open square, secure the working thread there, and bring it across diagonally to the opposite angle, thus: ** make a tiny chain stitch in the nearest corner of the next solid square, cross the square and make another similar stitch in the opposite corner of it, cross the next open square and repeat from ** all across. After passing over the last open square fasten off in the buttonholed corner.

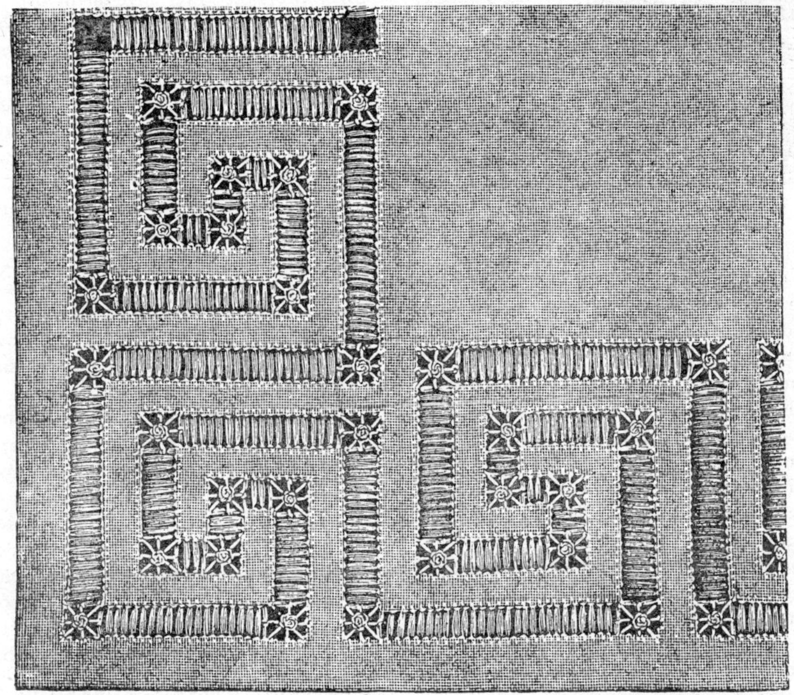

Fig. 26. GREEK KEY PATTERN WITH CORNER

Run lines like this over the whole work, across all the open squares in the same direction. One last set of threads now goes across and across all the surface in a reverse way to the last working threads, and crossing with them each thread is secure in the corner of an open square. * Bring the cotton half-

Fig. 27. POINT D'ESPRIT WORKED OVER HALF THE DRAWN THREADS

way down across the nearest open square, there knot it in with the three threads that already cross it, pass down again to the nearest corner of the next solid square, secure there with a small stitch, pass to the middle of this square, knot the exact centre of the one long stitch already in position, go on to the lower corner of the same solid square, make a small stitch there and then repeat from the last *. Fig. 24 shows the working clearly. It is sometimes elaborated by working with the last thread a small lace wheel or spider in the centre of each open square, round and round the stitches which cross it after these have been knotted. In any case, as soon as that knot is made and the thread carried on to the next solid square, the knot in the open square forms the centre of eight little spokes branching outwards to the sides and corners.

How to Hemstitch a Corner.—Either of the varieties of hemstitching can be used. The raw edges of the linen should be turned down narrowly once on the wrong side as for ordinary hemming, and tacked, then beyond this margin from three to five strands should be drawn out along all four sides of the work at double the distance from the turned-down edges that the width of the completed hem is to be. At each corner, to lessen some of the extra thickness formed by the meeting of the two hems, cut the whole of the little section inside the black lines and marked 1 completely away, as the lower right-hand corner shows in Fig. 25. Fold the hem on the left-hand side of Fig. 25 in half at the upright black line so that the hem edge meets the margin of the upright drawn strips. Then fold along the horizontal black line, so that the turned-down edge below 3 meets the lower edge of the drawn-work band below 2. Work hemstitching through the double sets of drawn strands formed by folding from the left side inwards and from the bottom edge upwards, and neatly stitch together the folded material to the extreme left-hand side from the drawn work band above, down to what is now the extreme lower left-hand corner of the hem.

When the corner is passed, work along the hemmed edge as usual. When ready to prepare the next corner hold it in the position shown in the diagram, cut away the section 1, and proceed as before until the whole hem is complete.

Greek Key Pattern with Corner makes a splendid border for a tea-cloth and is shown worked with a corner that makes it useful along four sides of any square or oblong as well. The surface to be decorated must be planned out in squares, which ought first to be marked by sticking pins through the linen to the lace pillow or soft pad beneath.

Begin planning the border an inch within

Fig. 28. POINT D'ESPRIT WORKED OVER THE ENTIRE LINE OF DRAWN THREADS

the hem of the cloth which it is to surround. Start from the left-hand bottom corner, remembering that the half-drawn bands which form the pattern, as well as the linen lines between them, are all twenty strands wide. From the corner draw a band extending as far as seven squares (140 strands) to the right. Starting again from the same corner, form an open square there by cutting twenty strands and drawing these along the other edge of the cloth for nine squares (180 strands). Cut the last twenty strands upwards for seven squares only, as this comprises the corner. For the corner, cut the uppermost of these last strands and draw for seven squares to the left, five down, three from left to right, and five squares upwards, three to the right and five squares down. Draw for a distance of seven squares to the left and cut an open square there. This forms the extreme corner. Turn the work, and along the next edge of the cloth, draw upwards for nine squares then repeat from the first * of these strands to form another open square and draw them for another nine squares parallel with the first cut band. If the cloth is held with the corner to the worker's right, the last cut band will appear upright to the left of it. * Cut the top twenty strands and draw to the left for a length of nine squares, cut there for an open square and draw downwards for seven squares (140 strands). Cut the lowest twenty of these and draw five squares (100 strands) to the right. Cut the uppermost twenty and draw up for three squares, cut the uppermost twenty and draw to the left for three squares, cut the last twenty and draw upwards for three squares, cut the uppermost twenty and draw from left to right for five squares. Cut the top square and draw down for seven, cut the lowest and draw to the left for nine squares, cut the last twenty strands and draw upwards for nine squares and repeat from * until the next corner has to be worked. As much space must be left for that as would be occupied by one repeat of the pattern. When the last repetition is made, care must be taken to draw the last twenty until the fourth and last corner is being planned. Having cut upwards for this seven instead of nine squares as before described, draw seven to the left, five down, three from left to right, three up, three from left to right, five down, and the last band will meet at the bottom in the original strip of seven squares length with which the work was first started from extreme corner.

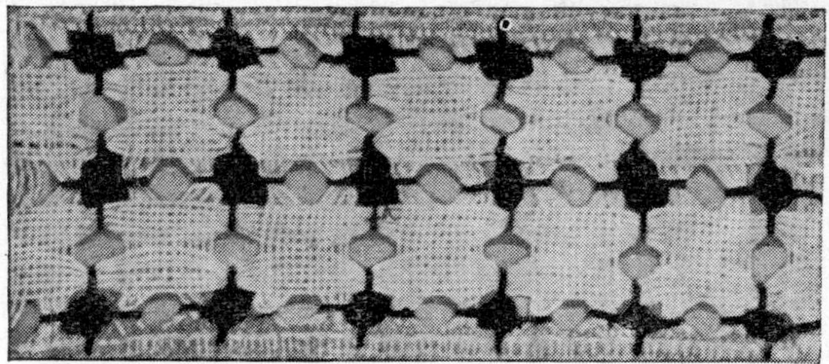

Fig. 29. A SAMPLE OF THE STITCH USED ON A HANDKERCHIEF

The actual embroidery, as will be seen from Fig. 26, is very simple to do. Buttonhole the cut edges of the open squares which appear at every angle of the pattern and cluster all the half-drawn threads into groups of five strands each by hem-stitching along both edges of the band. In every open square work a wheel with thread three times as coarse as that used for the hem-stitching. First bring a diagonal line of this thread across the square from corner to corner, another line from the middle of the linen edge to the centre of the first group beyond, and knot it there; then a third line to cross with this from the middle of the opposite cluster, knot there and bring a last thread from a vacant corner to the

Fig. 30. POINT TIRE

exact centre. There knot all the other threads and work round the seven spokes three times, working alternately over and under them. Pass the needle through a stitch of the outer circle opposite the vacant corner. Bring the thread to that corner, thus making the eight spokes of the wheel. Finish off neatly.

Point D'Esprit: showing the effect of loops worked over half the line of drawn threads. *Point D'esprit* is a light open stitch peculiar to *Guipure D'art* and it is equally well adapted to drawn thread work, as it makes a good all-over pattern for filling spaces where the threads are drawn both ways from the material, which consequently is transformed into a surface of square open spaces intersected with columns of open threads and small square blocks of solid linen. Dainty articles are worked in this stitch, for if fine linen and lace thread are used, the effect is equal to the best lace work.

In Fig. 27 the stitches of *Point D'esprit* are looped round half the open threads that separate the square open spaces and the loops draw these threads aside and a diamond-shaped opening is formed, as seen in the diagram. Remove threads both warp and weft way of the material selected, drawing out, say, twelve threads and leaving intact the same number as you draw out. The drawn out thread must be cut away to make a margin of solid linen round the outside of the open pattern. The fabric now has a variety of squares, an open square space, a solid square, a square of upright and vertical threads.

Point D'esprit can be worked either in straight lines row by row or diagonally across and across. Begin by making a knot or a small invisible stitch at the back of the solid linen, bring the needle and cotton up

Fig. 31.—CORNER AND BORDER OF POINT TIRE AND CHEQUERS

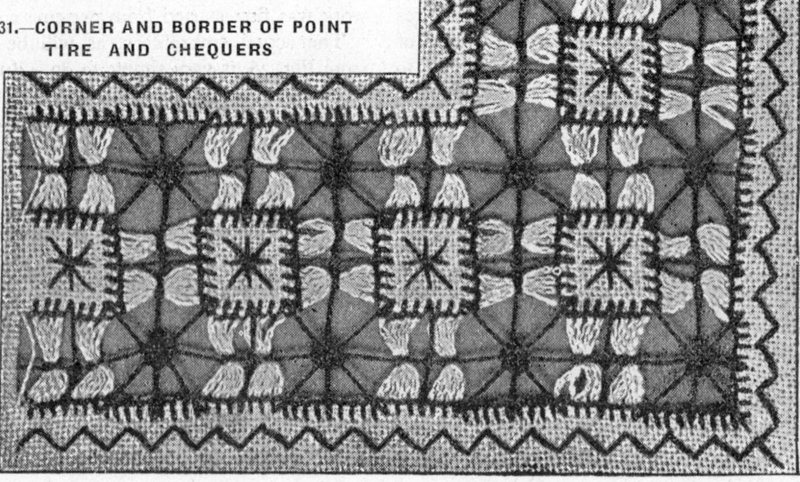

in the centre of one of the square open spaces (preferably a corner space), hold the cotton under the thumb of the left hand, insert the needle downwards in the centre of the bar of twelve open threads, turning the point towards you, and bring it out in the open space to form a loose button-hole stitch loop, and draw the cotton till the threads of the loop lie across each other in the middle of the open space. Work a similar loop on each of the other three sides of the open space, looping always into six threads, which, in the present instance, is half the number of open threads. Then pass the needle under the first thread of cotton (not the loop stitch) and draw the cotton through and so twist the cotton round each thread which connects the loops of *Point D'esprit.* Finally join evenly and return the needle to the wrong side of the fabric and slip it invisibly along to the next open square space. It will be rather puzzling to a novice to get all the four loops shaped exactly alike, and the same size, but attention and practice will make perfect.

Point D'Esprit (2) showing the effect of loops worked over the entire line of drawn threads. The working of this example is simpler than the preceding one, because here the loops are worked over the entire line of drawn threads, and therefore, when once the fabric is properly pre-

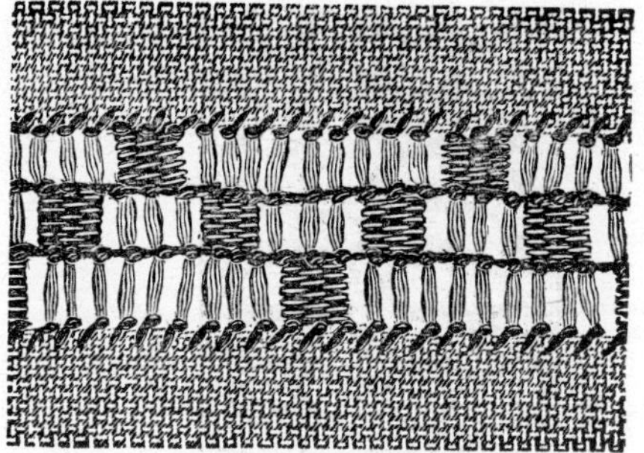

Fig. 32. POINT DE REPRISE

pared, there is no further counting of threads. Also there are no twisted stitches worked round the cotton in the centre of the point. Arrange for the pattern by drawing threads out both ways across the material, six threads to be drawn away, six threads to be left, alternately. The drawn away threads must be cut by a marginal line to make a frame of solid linen round the outside of the pattern. Work the *Point D'esprit* stitch to fill each alternate square open space, taking the loops over all six of the open threads, as shown in Fig. 28. The loops thus made draw the six open threads towards the *Point D'esprit*—thus each alternate square open space is transformed into a circular space. Fig. 29 shows a border for a handkerchief. It is as well to work the drawn thread border before working the pattern.

Point Tire.—This is a lacy stitch. As will be seen from Fig. 30 more threads

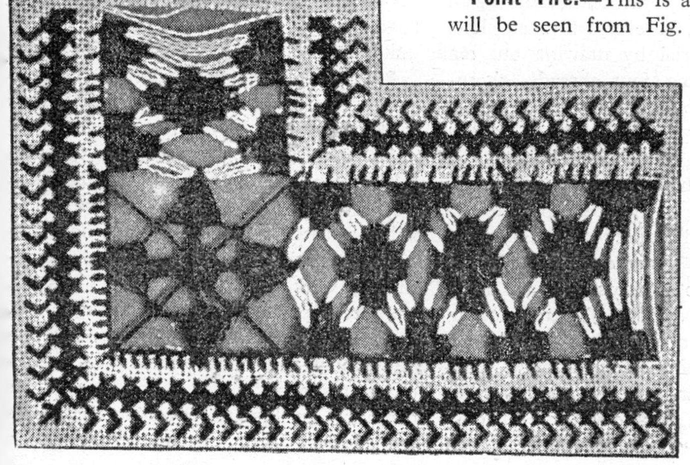

Fig. 33.—LOZENGE PATTERN BORDER AND CORNER

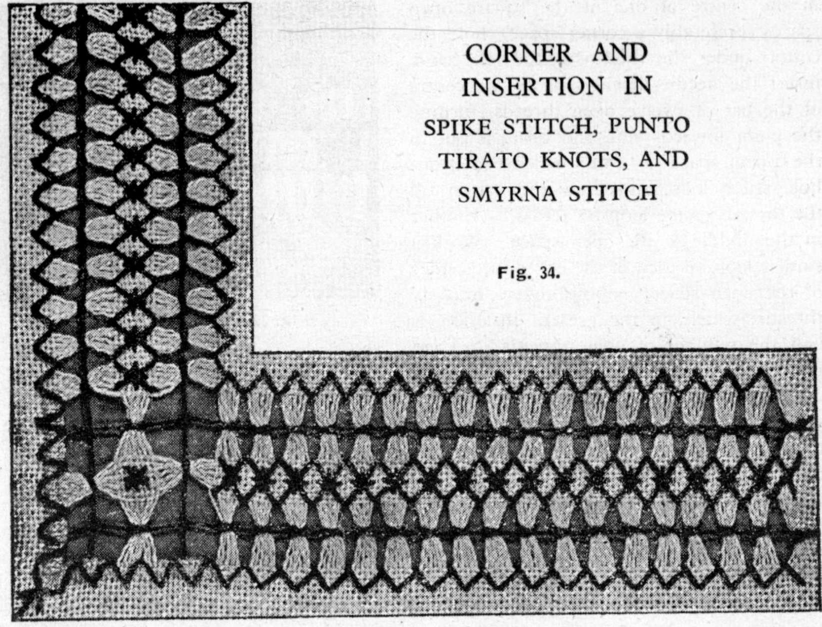

CORNER AND INSERTION IN SPIKE STITCH, PUNTO TIRATO KNOTS, AND SMYRNA STITCH

Fig. 34.

are drawn from the material than are left in, which makes the open squares larger than the closed ones. The open square spaces are traversed diagonally with cotton, and a small knot tied in the centre of each open space to retain the cotton in position. In the first diagonal line of cotton every small closed square is dotted with a small spider or wheel. This is not worked in the succeeding diagonal line, but occurs again in the next, and in every alternate line. Prepare the material by drawing out ten threads and leaving four threads, alternately, both ways of the material, arranging the drawn threads so as to leave a margin of solid linen as a frame round the outside of the pattern. Then, beginning at a corner, carry a cotton across the open space to the first small closed square in a diagonal direction, work a spider or tiny wheel on the square, and go on across the next space to the next small square. There work in the same way, then proceed to the opposite side (or corner) of the foundation. Continue working a line of cotton across every open space in the same direction, but only form spiders in each alternate row. When these lines are worked all over the material in this direction, work in the opposite direction and wherever the second cotton crosses the first, a *Punto Tirato* knot is tied in the exact centre of each open square. If joins are made in the working cotton they must be made at the back of one of the small closed squares, the ends being hidden. Fig. 31 shows very clearly a border in *Point Tiré* and chequers. All the stitches have already been described so it should be quite easy to follow.

Point de Reprise border. This is one of the stitches which, in common with many other lace stitches, has been introduced into drawn thread work. It is a thick stitching and is worked in the same way as ordinary darning. The same stitch is used in darned patterns and it is applied to the same purpose in drawn-thread work. All geometrical designs, vandykes, pyramids, stars, oblongs, etc., may be used. The darning passes in and out through two or more threads or clusters of threads, according to the pattern that is chosen. In Fig. 32 *Point de Reprise* is carried over three clusters of threads in a vandyked pattern, and can be used as a tray-cloth border.

Prepare the border by drawing out sixteen or eighteen threads one way of the material. Work hemstitching along each edge of the open threads, grouping three threads in a cluster and taking the stitches two threads deep into the margin of solid linen. Next divide the open insertion into three equal spacings, by working a row of *Punto Tirato* knots one-third distance from the top edge of the insertion, and a second row of knots one-third from the bottom edge, as in the illustration, knotting together the same three threads as are already grouped in the clusters. Each cluster must be kept perfectly straight, therefore the knot must be drawn to just the right degree of tightness each time.

For the *Point de Reprise*—begin at the top right-hand corner, securing the end of the cotton in the margin of the material. Pass the needle over the first cluster, take up the second cluster and draw the cotton through. * Point the needle from left to right and pass it under the third cluster, over the second and under the first, and draw the cotton through. Repeat from * until the space is filled with darned stitches. Then pass the needle under the *Punto Tirato* cotton and darn in like manner over the next three clusters in the middle space. Then over three clusters in the lower space. Slip the needle up to darn

Fig. 36.

Below is an attractive cushion in weave stitch and lace stitch. Above is a full-size section showing the details of working.

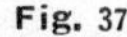

Fig. 37.

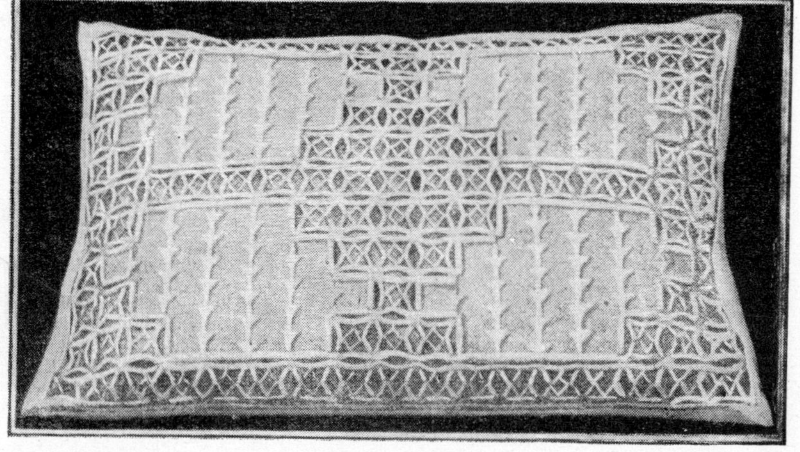

Fig. 38.—GREEK KEY INSERTION

in the middle space again, then darn again in the upper space, and so on, up and down, to the end of the row. Each space must be filled closely and evenly. The cotton should not be drawn tight, for, as shown in the diagram, the clusters of three threads must retain their original upright position.

PUNTO TIRATO

Point de Reprise is often worked over only two clusters of threads and to do this pass the needle over the first cluster and take up the second and then pass the needle back over the second cluster, take up the first and continue to do so, forwards and backwards until the space is full. Fig. 33 shows a border worked in *Point de Reprise.*

Fig. 39.—ANOTHER INSERTION FROM THE SAMPLER

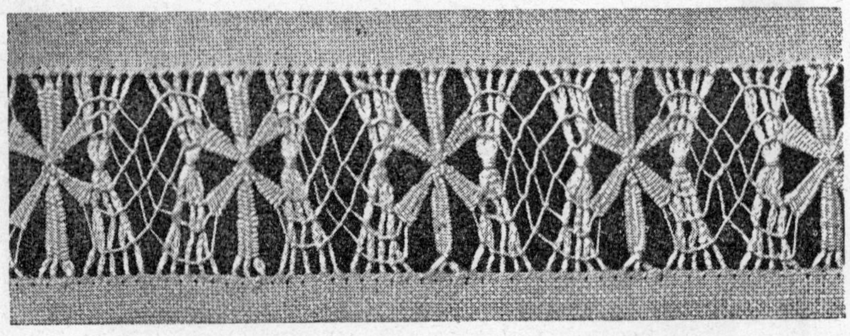

Fig. 40.

A beautiful sampler in White Work finished with four different drawn thread borders. Notice particularly the four motifs in the corners. Full details for working the embroidery are given in the chapter on White Work. Worked by Mary A. Caraman

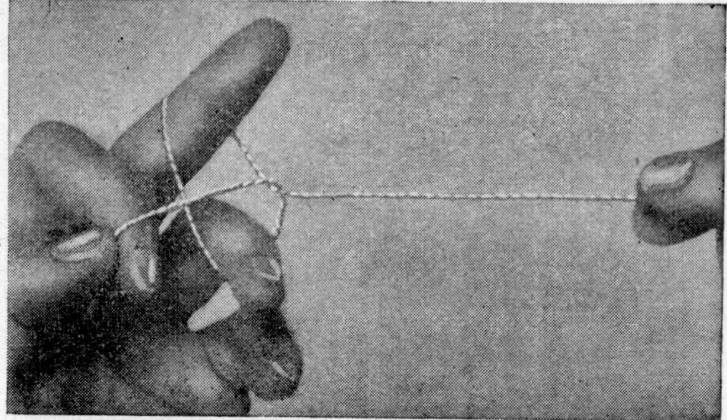

Fig. 41.

Fig. 42.

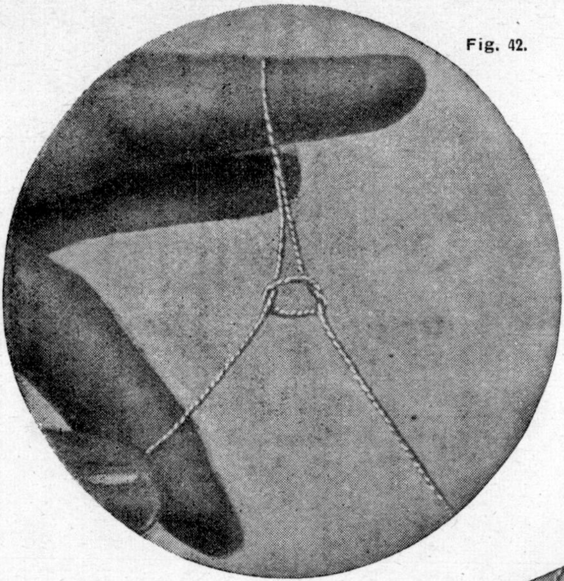

It is not always possible to use one thread only throughout a border, so when threads have to be joined, follow the directions given for working this lace knot, and the threads will never come undone.

Fig. 43.

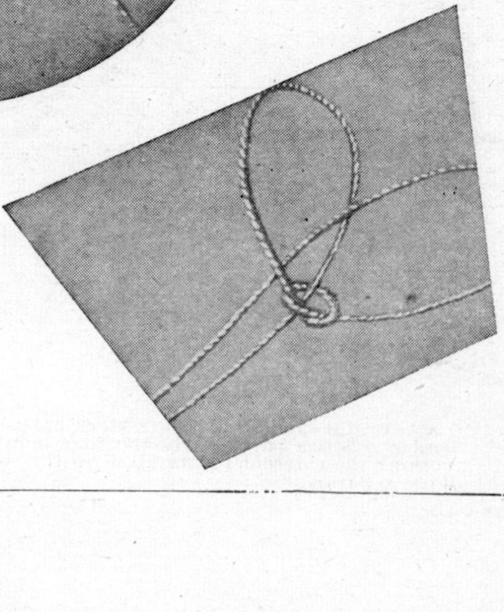

JOINING TWO THREADS WITH A LACE KNOT

Corner Insertion in Spike stitch, Punto Tirato Knots, and Smyrna stitch.—This corner and border shows how several stitches can be combined effectively to form a pattern. Mark off a certain portion of the material for a margin outside the drawn thread work. Then, beginning at the corner, cut across ten threads each way of the angle, leave eight threads, cut across ten threads. The same threads must be cut at each of the other corners, and drawn out from one corner to another. To ensure fitting the pattern in evenly, draw and work of the material, bring the needle and cotton in the solid linen three threads each way above the insertion. Insert the needle in the open space at the corner and bring it out in an upward direction in the same place where it was brought out to begin with and draw the cotton through. * Insert the needle in the small space to the left between the clusters and, passing it in an upward direction, bring it out over the centre of the cluster of threads and five threads above the insertion, and draw the cotton through. Insert the needle in the

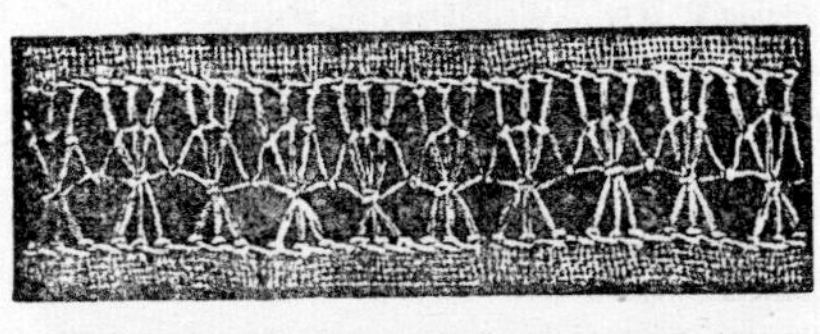

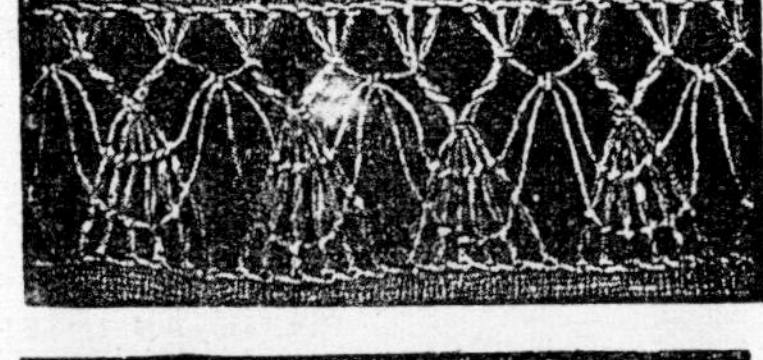

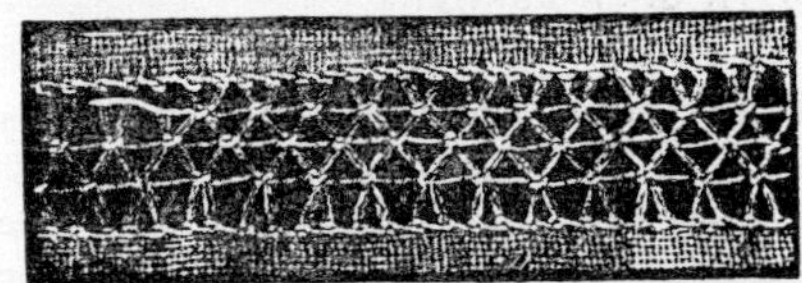

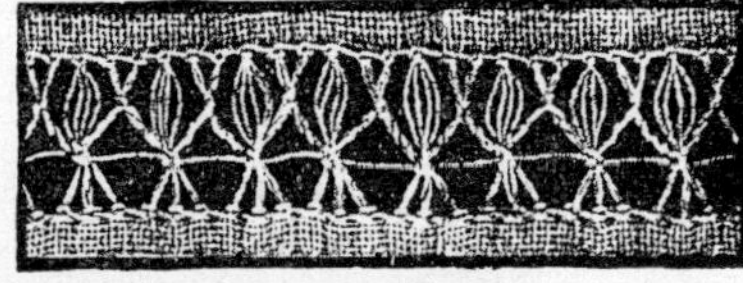

Fig. 44.

FIVE DRAWN THREAD INSERTIONS

nearly the length of the two sides first, if all the corners are to look the same. Work *Punto Tirato* knots from margin to margin of the material along the centre of each insertion of drawn open threads together in a cluster, excepting at the corner where it crosses a previous row of cotton in the middle of an open square. A row of spike-stitch is arranged as a border on each side of the drawn thread insertion. Work this from right to left, holding the insertion towards you. Begin on the inside edge by the corner. Secure the end of the cotton by an invisible stitch at the back same place as before, and bring it out in the same place. Repeat from *. Work the same Spike stitch round the outer margin of the insertion. The Smyrna stitch, which occupies the bar of eight solid threads in the centre of the insertion may be executed in two different ways. One way is to work two rows of the spike-stitches, just described, in such a way that the stitches meet together in the form of a cross, and then put a small crossed stitch over the junction of the spike stitches. Another way is to make an ordinary large cross-stitch to cover all the solid threads.

Fig. 45.—AN INSERTION WITH OPEN CORNERS

It is covered with a small cross-stitch shown in the illustration.

Design for a Cushion.—The pattern is easily built up as the drawn part consists of squares. For the band, which runs along the centre of the cushion, eighteen threads are drawn out and between the sixth and seventh threads on either side of this, slits are cut in the linen along eighteen threads leaving twelve threads between each. These threads are then drawn and the sets of twelve remaining across the insertion are darned into two bars and the loose threads along the sides into single bars.

When this band is worked in, the whole pattern can be quite easily built up, all the cut edges being overcast with satin stitch over six threads.

Round the whole of the outside of the design a row of cross-stitch is worked, each cross being over a square of six threads, and this is outlined again in satin stitch. In the four solid sections of linen inside the design, rows of arrowhead shapes are

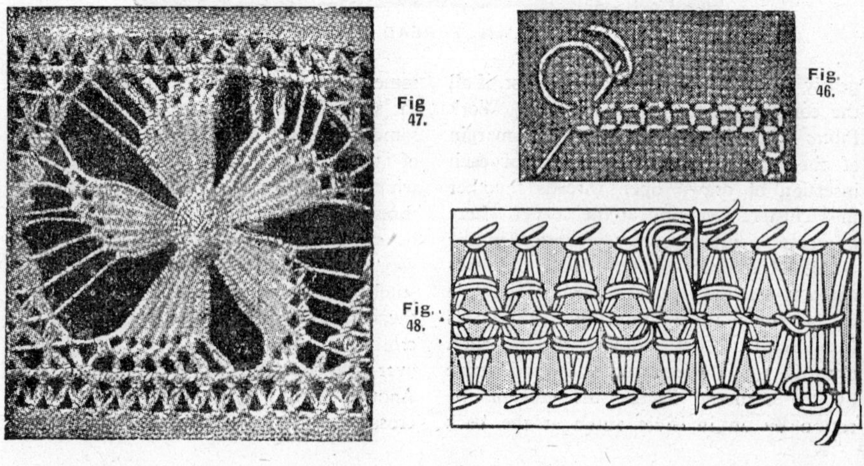

Fig. 47.

Fig. 46.

Fig. 48.

Fig. 48.

Fig. 50.

Fig. 51.

Fig. 49.—A delicately worked runner for which details of the fillings are given here and on the opposite page. Fig. 48 shows the enlarged detail for the narrow border and the centre photograph above shows four of the motifs, while in the bottom figure the corner is very clearly shown. Fig. 47 shows still another corner motif, and Fig. 46 shows how to work the stitch that is used for the corners.

worked in satin stitch on stems of back stitch. Each row is worked exactly over the point between two bars in the border, each back stitch going over six threads of linen. The satin stitch is worked on either side of this as shown in Fig. 36. Fig. 37 shows the cushion complete.

Knotting Drawn Threads which is the foundation of a number of borders is quite simple to do. *E.g. Greek Key Border.* Draw forty threads to make a border along all four sides of the work. Then hemstitch both edges, taking up three threads each time. Frame up the work in the usual way.

Fig. 52. **AN EFFECTIVE CORNER**

Before knotting the threads weave under and over the first two clusters at either end of the row. This makes a foundation to which the threads for knotting can be attached. This design needs eight knotted rows or lines which have to be evenly placed. Start at the top left-hand corner and knot down one row at a time, making sure that the knot is firm, and remembering to keep the squares square. When all the threads are knotted and fastened off, start darning with a blunt needle keeping it always in the same direction. Start at the top left-hand corner, one square from the top and one from the edge. Work * over the first threads, under the second, over the third, for the first row. Under the third, over the second and under the first for the second. Repeat from * until there are enough rows to fill in between the bars (about five times more should be enough). This is done down five more squares. For the sixth darn in and out in the same manner over eighteen threads. The corner has now been turned. Turn the next corner, darn over and under three threads for three squares upwards. The next row, turn and work along eight threads. Next square, over three threads, the following square over eight threads, then over three threads, then over eighteen again. This completes one key. Continue for as many as required. See Fig. 38.

It will not be possible to work the whole border with one thread, so join with a lace knot.

To make a **Lace Knot,** take the new thread on your left hand between the thumb and first finger, and take the thread over the next two fingers, and between the first and second fingers. Now pull your second finger back, bringing the knot between the second and third fingers. The second finger now pulls the thread through, slipping it off the third. This forms a loop. Still keeping the loop over the second finger, and the thread between the thumb and first finger and the other end towards the right

Fig. 53.—A CHILD'S DRESS EMBROIDERED WITH HEMSTITCHING AND DRAWN THREAD SQUARES

A DAINTY CHILD'S FROCK

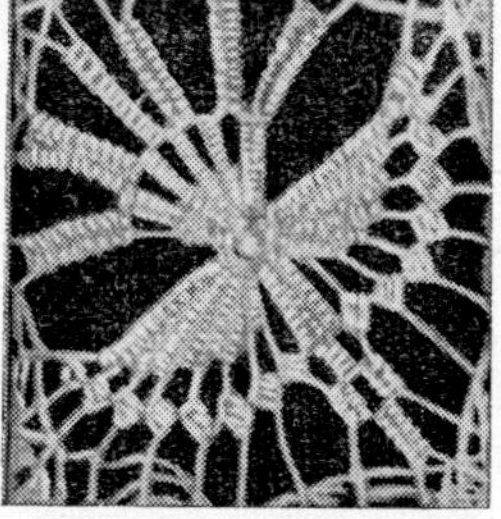

Fig. 54.

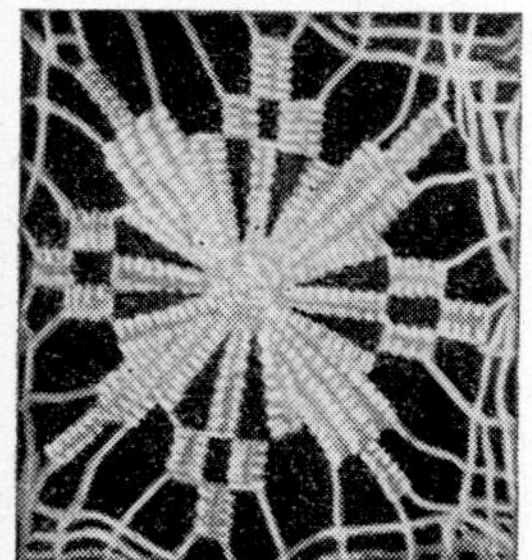

Fig. 56.

THREE OF THE INSERTIONS USED

Fig. 55.

(this is the one to be worked with) place the old thread through the loop and catch it between the first and second finger. Draw the thread up tight, taking the old thread and the one between the thumb and first finger, in one hand and pull tightly. If this knot is made correctly it will not come undone. It is quite safe to cut the threads up close. This knot, though difficult to master, is most useful in embroidery. Figs. 41-43 show the working of this knot.

Teneriffe Drawn Thread derives its name from its similarity to Teneriffe Lace. Fig. 49 shows a runner in this work. The method of working is much the same as already explained, the threads being knotted into patterns, and darned into elaborate designs.

A piece of linen 36 inches long and 18 inches wide is required to make the runner, and linen thread is used for working. When working the insertion leave about six inches of thread at the beginning of each row before tying the first knot, also at the end after the last knots. These threads will be required for the corners.

Two inches from the edge threads are drawn to a depth of half an inch and along this space is worked the border shown in Fig. 48.

At the corners the linen is buttonholed where it is cut to draw out the threads, and this is outlined with the stitch in Fig. 46. The threads used for working the border are carried to the opposite side of the corner where they are fastened into the buttonholing at equal spaces and are darned in the pattern in Fig. 51. Three-quarters of an inch above this border, the space for the wide insertion is arranged, by drawing six threads, leaving four, drawing threads to a width of 2 inches, leaving four threads, and drawing six. The stitch shown in Fig. 46 is worked tightly over both sets of four threads of linen that remain, so that the threads across the border are formed into straight clusters of four. Each side of the insertion is then hemstitched, each stitch taking two threads from one cluster and two from the next. The beginning of the work in the centre of the insertion is done in ten rows as follows:—

From left to right:—

1st row: Knot clusters together in sets of eight just above the centre.

2nd row: Knot clusters together in sets of eight just below the centre.

3rd row: Just above the first knot, knot together the first four clusters, then the next four, skip the next eight and carry the thread across to the other side of the centre where knot together the first four and then the second four clusters of threads of the third set of eight. Continue in this way to the end, forming a wavy line.

4th row: As 3rd row starting below the first knot and working alternately above and below the centre as before, so that this wavy line crosses the first.

5th and 6th rows: Knot the first three clusters together, the next two and the last three of the group, miss the next cluster of eight, then work as before on the opposite side of the centre and repeat to end.

7th and 8th rows: Knot alternate clusters of eight into four groups of two, first one side, then the other side of the centre.

9th and 10th rows: Knot the first cluster alone, then the next six into pairs and the last one alone, working alternately above and below the centre on alternate groups.

The clusters of eight left between the sets of knots are now darned into patterns, of which there are seven in all, shown in Figs. 47, 50 and 51, and these are arranged as seen in the illustration.

The corners of the wide insertion are buttonholed and outlined with the stitch in Fig. 46. The butterfly is darned on the threads coming from the knots in the insertion, these threads being carried to the opposite side of the corner and fastened into the purl edge of the buttonholing.

The narrow insertion shown in Fig. 48 is repeated $\frac{3}{4}$ of an inch inside the wide insertion and also across either end of the rectangle so formed, dividing off a square at each end.

In the centre of each square, threads are drawn both ways, leaving about $\frac{3}{4}$ of an inch of linen all round. This is buttonholed round and outlined with the stitch in Fig. 48, then sixteen threads are laid across

COVER IN DRAWN THREAD WORK COMBINED WITH WHITE WORK. Persian.

the spaces either way and a star is darned on them. The method of forming the star which should have seven points in all, is clearly shown in Fig. 47. The cloth is finished with an edging of pillow lace

Figs 45 and 52 show clearly some corners to work.

The intricately worked cover on the previous page shows how effective drawn work is combined with fine white work. The embroidery is done in silk on cotton in satin stitch, the unusual eight-petalled star flower being the main motif. The design which is reproduced by kind permission of the Victoria and Albert Museum, is Persian, and dates from the late eighteenth or early nineteenth century

A novel and most unusual way of working Initials is shown below. Almost any of the fillings given in this chapter would be suitable, but the simpler the design the better the effect. When the threads have been drawn the whole outline should be buttonholed. The E below is worked in single crossing. The corners may be left with a simple knot as in the illustration or decorated with a small wheel or spider. The N is worked in a simple square stitch, drawing out two threads and leaving two threads which are afterwards whipped; the D is in knot stitch.

N.B.—Many of the illustrations in this chapter are worked in black mercerised cotton, so that the working shows up more clearly.

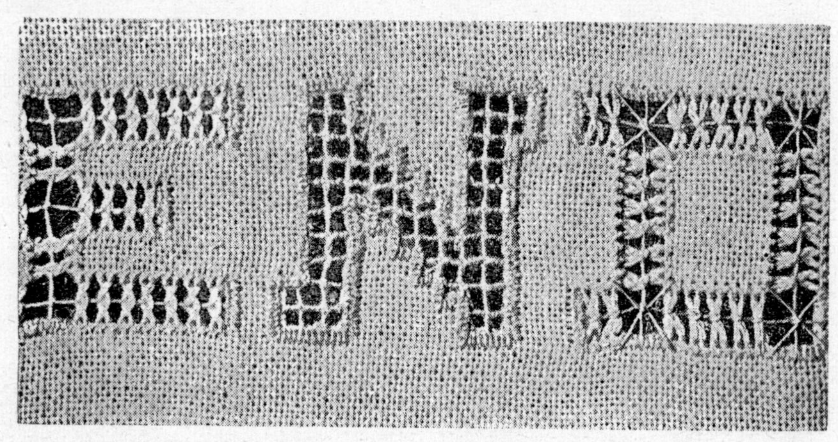

SIMPLY DESIGNED INITIALS IN DRAWN THREAD WORK

ECCLESIASTICAL EMBROIDERY

Embroidery in gold is perhaps one of the oldest kinds worked in England. There are records of its being taught in the tenth century when it was much used for Church vestments.

From an early date much Church embroidery was done in convents, though often it was executed by men as well. In Belgium amongst other places, to this day, a great deal of Church embroidery is done by men, and it is taught as a craft at a very early age.

A great deal of early English Church embroidery was sent abroad. Until the middle of the fourteenth century great progress was made, but then, owing to the unrest and trouble both at home and abroad little work was done. However, when it was revived, its standard was not quite as high as before compared with that done abroad. Church work has always been a favourite embroidery and requires much practice and skill.

Materials required.—Only the best materials should be used in Church embroidery. Gold embroidery can seldom be worked on a silk material only, as gold thread being heavy, the silk is not strong enough. A backing of good unbleached linen (the chemical used to bleach linen is apt to ruin the gold), not loosely woven, should be used. Brocade, satin, and moiré silk are all suitable, and velvet may also be used.

Japanese gold is the most suitable thread as it seldom tarnishes. The qualities and sizes of this vary. Japanese gold is wound on silk, which is usually of an orange shade. The brighter and deeper the orange silk, the better the quality of the gold. This should always be looked at before buying and is easily noticeable, as all Japanese gold is in skeins and the two ends are usually visible. Silver can also be bought in various sizes, but is much more apt to tarnish. Fig. 1 shows a few of the different sizes in gold and one in silver. There is an aluminium thread now made which does not tarnish. Gold and aluminium cords of

Fig. 1.—JAPANESE GOLD AND SILVER

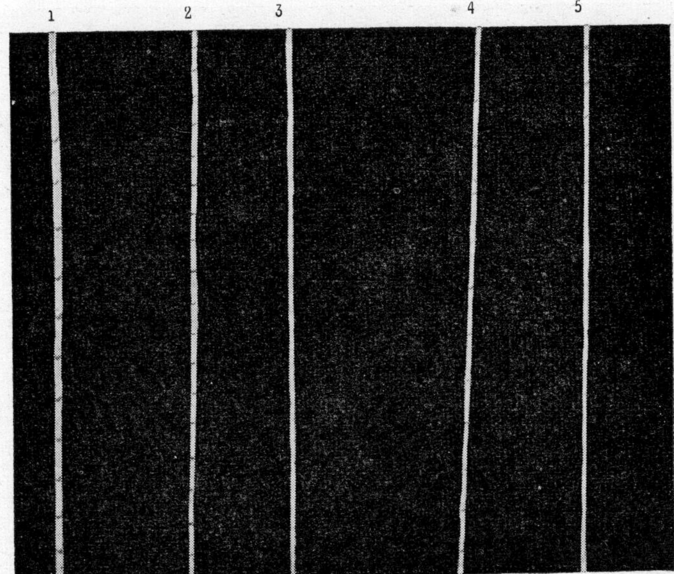

1-4 SHOW VARIOUS THICKNESSES IN GOLD, No. 5 THICKNESS OF SILVER THREAD

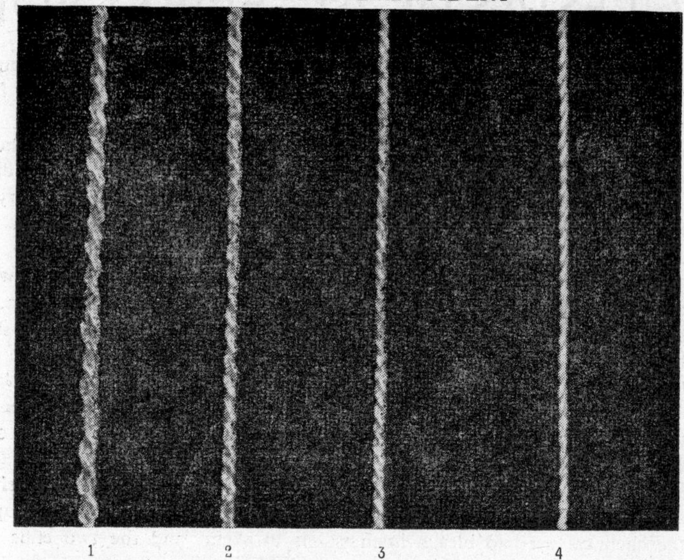

Fig. 2. CORDS

various sizes are used as outlines (Fig. 2).

Other threads used are:

Plate is a flat strip of metal which can be obtained in various widths, though 1/16 of an inch is the most useful.

Passing Thread is a bright, smooth

Fig. 3. OTHER THREADS USED

PLATE ROUGH PURL PEARL PURL WIRE CHECK CHECK PURL SMOOTH PURL

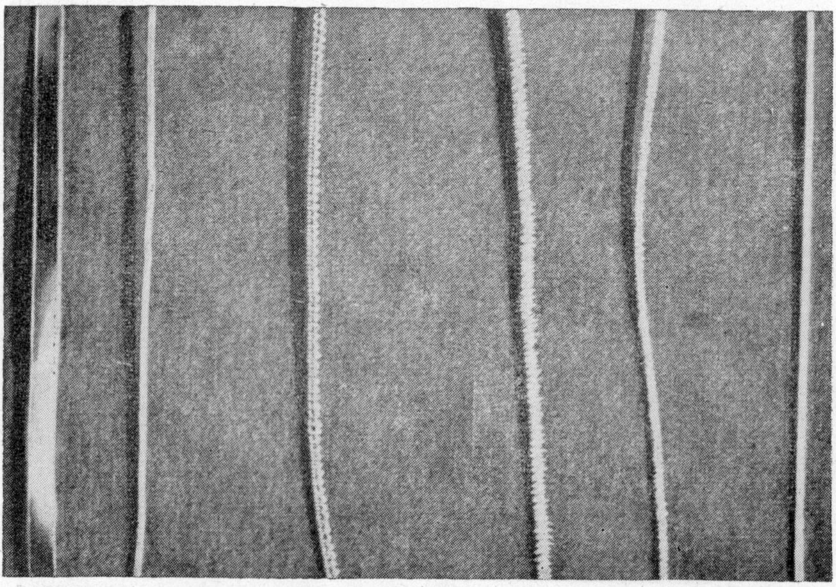

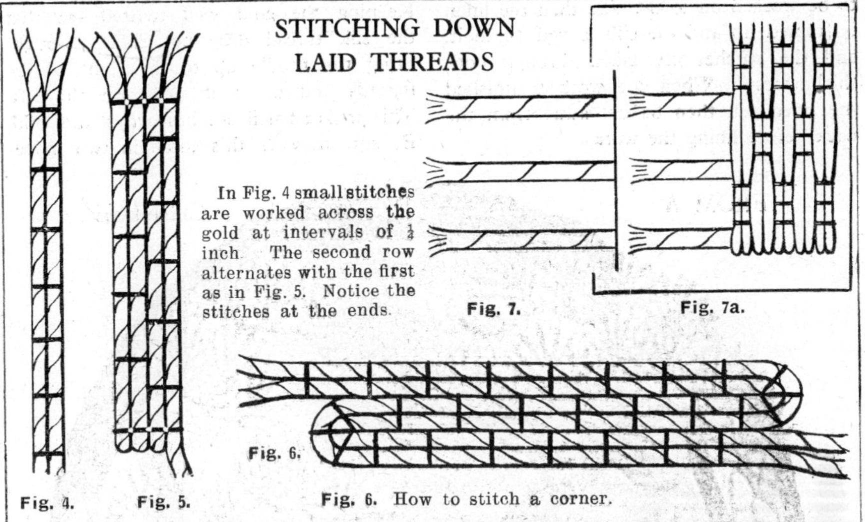

In Fig. 4 small stitches are worked across the gold at intervals of ¼ inch. The second row alternates with the first as in Fig. 5. Notice the stitches at the ends.

Fig. 4. Fig. 5. Fig. 6. How to stitch a corner.

thread which resembles a gold wire. This, like Japanese gold, is also wound on a silk thread, only it is much tighter. It can be had in various sizes.

Purl resembles a smooth, hollow tube of metal which is very elastic and pliable. It is made in lengths about 1 yard long and is cut into small pieces, as required, with a sharp knife or scissors. Some of the different kinds of purl are:—check, wire check, smooth and rough purl.

Check purl sparkles and is bright. It is made of flattened wire so that parts of it catch the light.

Wire check is the same, but as it is made of the round wire, is duller and of a deeper yellow.

Smooth purl is flat gold wire, which, owing to its being spun spirally, gives it a bright polished look.

Rough purl.—For this the wire has been rounded, which makes it look more yellow and duller in colour.

Bullion is a name which is given to purl of large sizes.

Pearl purl is made in the same spiral tube-like way as ordinary purl, but the gold wire had first been hollowed out, the convex side being the one exposed, which makes it look like small gold beads. This is often used for outlining. Fig. 3 shows some of the different kinds.

Horsetail is a fine, strong thread used for couching down the gold. It is obtainable in various colours.

Padding for gold work is usually a soft yellow linen thread and for silver, white or grey is used. A thin felt is used for raised work, and thin cardboard. A yellow macramé string is also used.

Jewels of different kinds are used as a finish to church work, seed pearls being very suitable.

Materials needed are: A piece of wax; a stiletto made entirely of metal, of which one end is quite flat; two thimbles and a sharp pair of scissors; a small flat tray lined with soft felt when using purl; Floss silk, which has a natural division through the centre, should only half the thickness be required; Filoselle and Filo floss and Chenille are also used. A stout embroidery frame should always be used. Ordinary fine embroidery needles should be used for the silk and a very much coarser one for pulling the gold through.

To Work.—Frame up the work in the usual way. If the embroidery is to be appliquéd, work it on to the linen and then appliqué on to the silk. But if it is to be worked on to the silk, then the linen is framed up and the silk tacked on to it, and the stitches are taken through both thicknesses. When the work is finished the linen can then be cut away from the back before lining the work.

Keeping the gold well twisted (so that the silk thread does not show through) bring the needle up to the right of the threads and insert it again on the left. This makes small stitches across the gold. Be sure to work this stitch in two move-

FROM A CHINESE

Reproduced by kind permission of the Master of Campion Hall, Oxford.

Fig. 8.

If gold has never been worked with before it is easiest to start on a design with straight lines. First wax the horsetail, then thread it in a very fine needle, then make two small stitches in the linen which will afterwards be covered by the gold thread (two threads of gold are used at once), bring the needle out on the outline and make a small stitch over one thread of gold leaving about one inch beyond, secure this by taking two small stitches in the material, then take a stitch over the second gold thread as closely as possible to the first and secure it in the same way.

ments; work these stitches across the gold at intervals of about $\frac{1}{4}$ of an inch apart as shown in Fig. 4. Continue in this way until the end of the row and finish off the threads in the same way as at the start, leaving about one inch before cutting the gold. This thread is later pulled through to the wrong side. The second row is started in the same way. The needle is brought up to the right again, half-way between the stitch of the previous row, and inserted again to the left of the two threads, close up to the first row, leaving no space between the rows. These stitches are spaced as in the first row as can be seen in Fig. 5. These two rows are repeated alternately for the length required, thus forming a brick stitch. Care must be taken to keep the stitches straight and even, as on this depends the beauty of the work If working on a curved line or circle the stitches at the beginning and end of each which becomes the outside one, make a small stitch in the centre and then one at the side. This secures the threads and makes them lie flat, continue now in the usual way over both threads (Fig. 6). The threads at the beginning and end are pulled through to the wrong side with a large needle.

EMPEROR'S ROBE

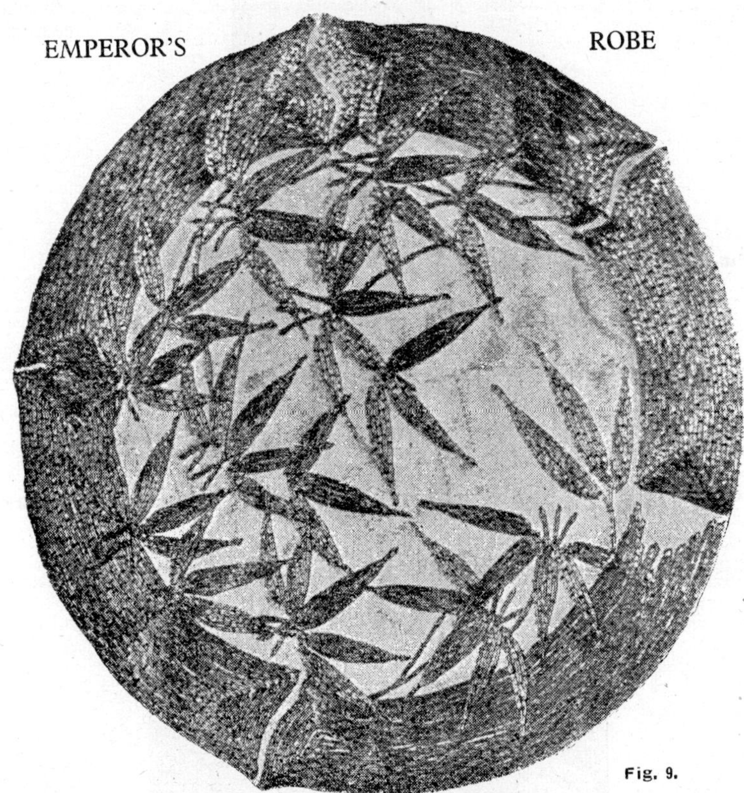

Fig. 9.

row follow the outline, each becoming shorter.

Gold embroidery is always worked on the surface, and here is another method of turning the thread, though this way is not always possible. The first two threads are secured as before but at the end of the row and each following row, turn it thus: Make a small stitch over each thread at the end of the row, then turn the outside thread (which, in this row becomes the inside one) and make another small stitch over this. Now with the inside thread

Purl is stitched on as if one were sewing beads. The purl is cut into pieces of the required size and placed on a tray (the hands should touch it as little as possible as it tarnishes very easily). A very fine embroidery needle and horsetail are used to sew it down, and the flat end of the stiletto is useful to help it into position.

String is often used under gold to raise it and various patterns can be worked. The string is first waxed, then stitched alternately from side to side with small stitches, and laid according to the design chosen.

A
CELTIC
STOLE

WORKED BY
MARY A.
CARAMAN

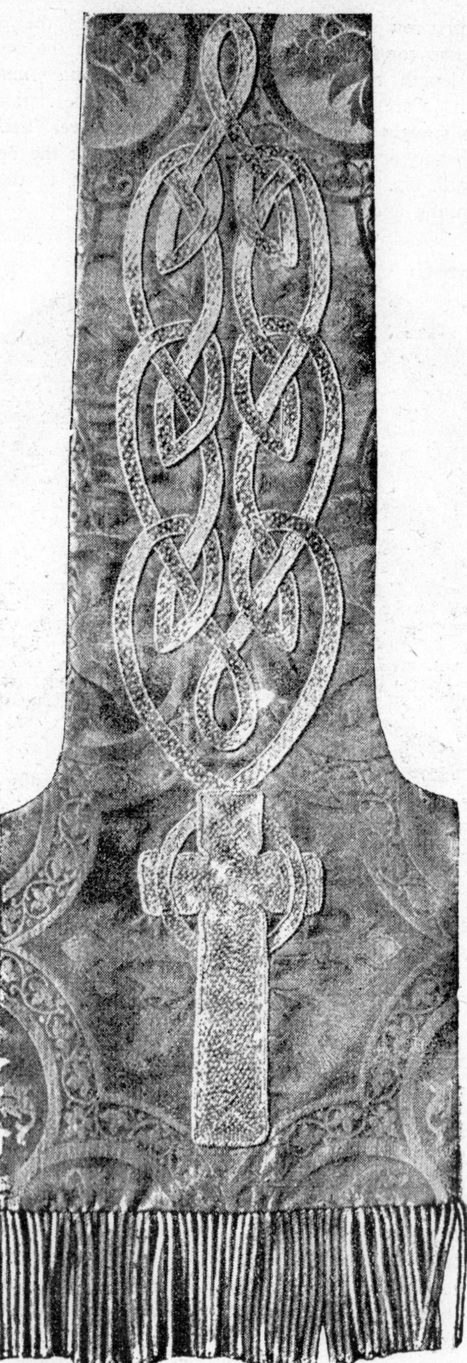

Fig. 10.

COPYRIGHT DESIGN

Fig. 11. A CROSS WORKED OVER CARD

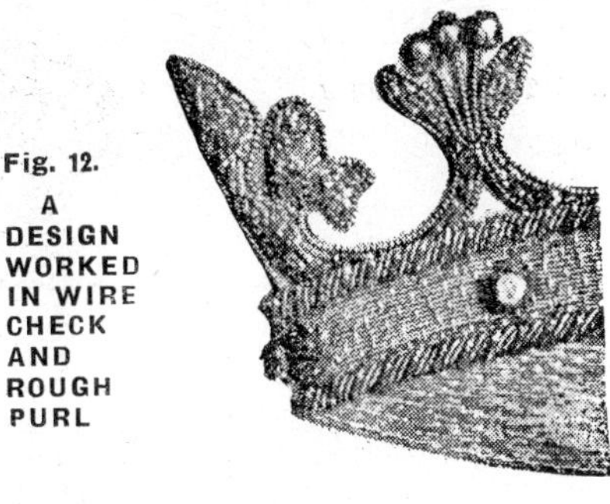

Fig. 12. A DESIGN WORKED IN WIRE CHECK AND ROUGH PURL

Fig. 7 shows how the string is first stitched down, Fig. 7a the couching over it.

Another method of working gold when a raised effect is needed, is to work it over a padding of felt. Cut the felt the size and shape required and cut several pieces, still keeping the shape but decreasing in size. Sew the smallest piece in the middle of the design, stitching it right round. Over this sew the next piece in like manner and so on until the top piece is reached. This covers all the others and leaves a neatly padded shape well raised in the middle and sloping to either side. Japanese gold is worked over this in the usual way. Here are a few different

Fig. 14. GOLD WORKED OVER STRING

Fig. 19.

ABOVE, THE POPE'S COAT OF ARMS, AND BELOW, A DESIGN WORKED OVER STRING

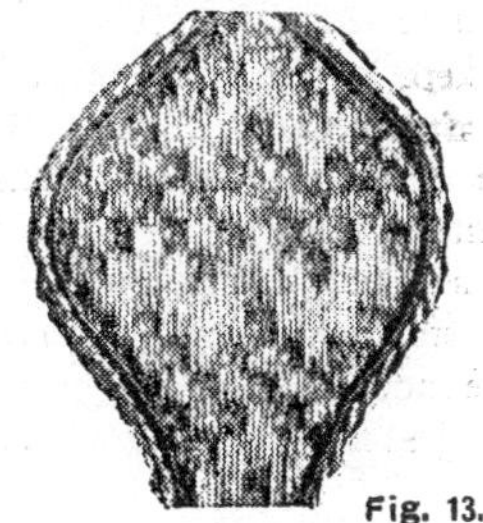

Fig. 13.

A CROSS
in Italian Shading

Fig. 15.

WORKED BY

MARY A. CARAMAN

ways of working up gold, which can be clearly followed from the various designs chosen

Designs from an Emperor's robe.—Fig. 8 is a design worked in flat gold directly on to the silk. The shapes must be well kept in the working as it is not outlined afterwards by a cord. This piece is worked in fine gold and is stitched down with bright red horsetail.

Fig. 9 is a heavier piece worked in deep gold and stitched in bright red horsetail. It will be noticed how the gold is taken round at the corners, always keeping the shape, and that some of the leaves are worked over the circle. Notice particularly the regularity of the stitches.

The Celtic Stole in Fig. 10 is worked on an emerald green brocade. The scroll is worked in gold and outlined with an aluminium cord, the cross in gold with three rows of aluminium round the edge, and a circle of aluminium in the centre. A gold cord is worked round the outline of the cross with an aluminium one beyond that. It will be noticed that the shape of the cross is kept by working the gold round and keeping a decided line on turning the corners. This stole was worked directly

Fig. 16.

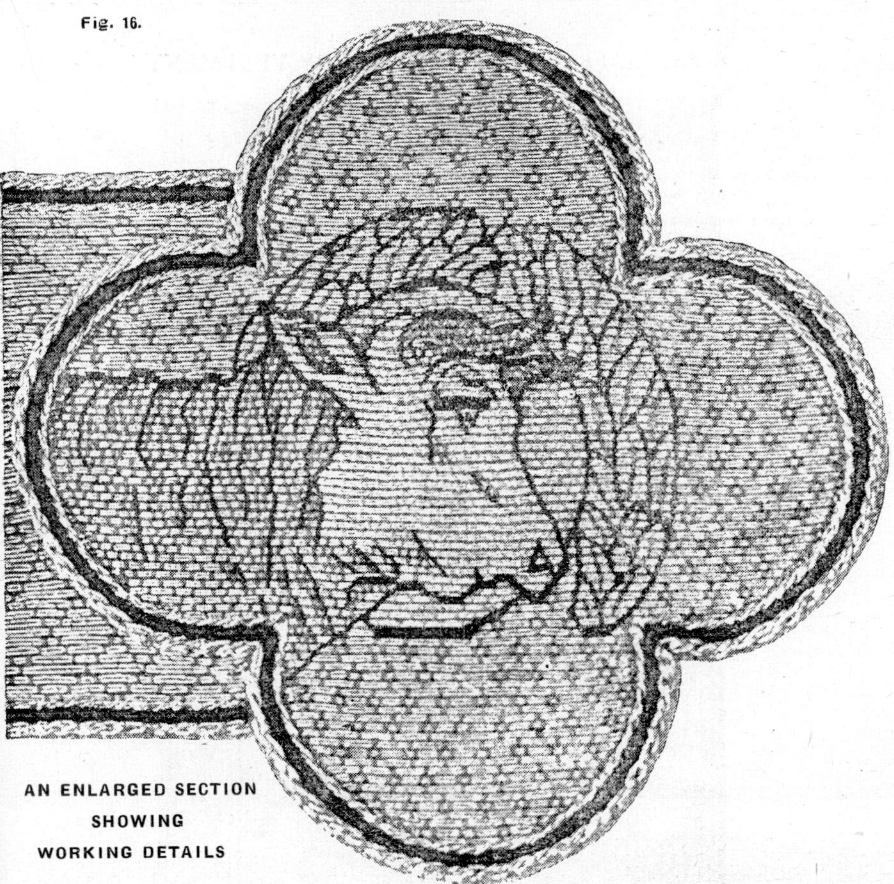

AN ENLARGED SECTION SHOWING WORKING DETAILS

on to the silk. It has a fringe of gold and aluminium.

A cross which is worked over cardboard in passing thread is shown in Fig. 11. The ends are worked in wire check. It is all outlined in a very fine pearl purl.

Fig. 12 is a section showing wired check and round purl used alternately to form two borders. The left-hand upper section is first padded, then wire check is worked over it, finally being outlined in pearl purl. The jewels are set in wire check.

Fig. 13 shows a section of a design worked over string.

The IHS in Fig. 14 shows two more different ways of working gold over string. A fine gold is used which gives the I and H the appearance of being worked in basket-stitch. A gold cord is worked round the outline. For the S the string is spaced evenly, the stitches being taken at either side of it so that it stands out in contrast to the flatness of the gold between

A cross worked in Italian shading, with the arms in diamond pattern is shown in Fig. 15. The cross was first traced on the linen and then the gold was worked across the arms to form the diamonds. Quite a fine gold was used and it was stitched in orange horsetail. The four figures representing the four Evangelists were worked in a finer gold still—again various coloured horsetails were used. A reddish

A PANEL FROM A 16TH CENTURY VESTMENT

Fig. 17.

Reproduced by kind permission of the Master of Campion Hall, Oxford.

AN EARLY ENGLISH 14TH CENTURY VESTMENT

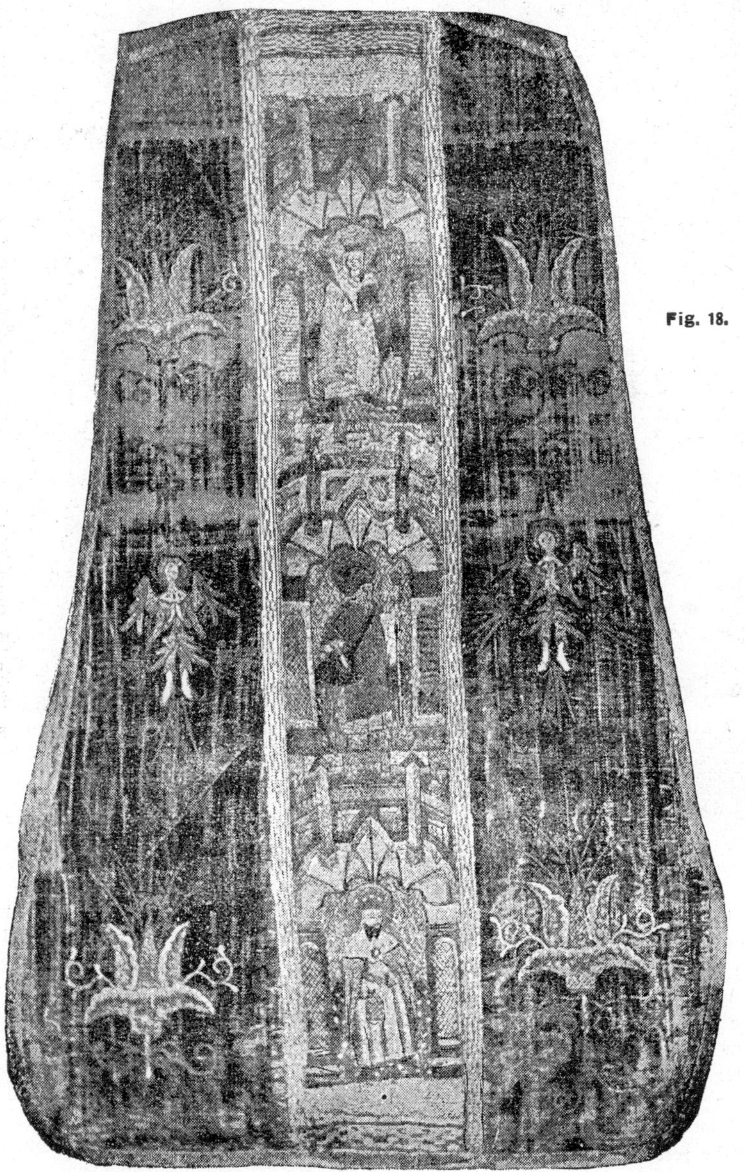

Fig. 18.

Reproduced by kind permission of the Master of Campion Hall, Oxford.

A BURSE IN SILKS ON WHITE SATIN. SEED PEARLS ARE USED ROUND THE RIM OF THE CHALICE

shade was used for the outlines, with a browny grey for the shadows. The faces were worked in yellow to make them look light, while the haloes were in orange. The backgrounds were in bright blue diamonds and the outline was worked by taking stitches close together, in some cases over one thread of gold only.

The IHS in the centre is also in Italian shading. The outline for this is in a brighter red and the roundness is arrived at with the shading—this time also in red. The high light is obtained by stitching down the rest of the gold in yellow horse-tail. The background is in a very fine close brick-stitch. There is a fine gold cord round the edge, then one in deep red silk with a coarser gold on the outside. Fig. 16 gives a very much enlarged view of one of the corners and shows the working very clearly.

A panel of a sixteenth-century vestment in Italian shading is shown in Fig. 17. It is also worked over very fine gold in various colours. The robe is most beautifully shaded in greens as can be seen by the lifelike appearance of the folds. The cloak, too, is equally well done in shades of pink. The houses and clouds can be seen in the background. The designs at the top and bottom and the pink roses in the border are worked in Italian shading, while the leaves are in raised gold.

The English fourteenth-century vestment shown in Fig. 18, on page 173, is beautifully embroidered. The faces specially are well worked. The lowest figure is thought to be St. Edward the Confessor.

Fig. 19 is a coat of arms appliquéd in cloth of gold. This material is not at all easy to work as it frays a great deal. It is outlined in gold and then has a split stitch round the edge in nigger brown. The cord and tassels are worked in silk, the three balls are worked in shades of red in Italian shading over silver, and the keys are worked in Italian shading while the ends of the mitre are embroidered.

Finishing the work.—When a piece of work is completed it is as well to secure the ends as an extra precaution. This can be done by pasting a piece of tissue paper over the back of the design, making sure all the ends are quite flat.

If the design is to be appliquéd to the silk do not outline it on the linen ground. Cut the linen to about 1/16 of an inch from the design and appliqué it on to the silk. Trim the material and sew a cord round the edge to hide the linen. In some cases a silk and then a gold cord are necessary, or, if preferred, chenille may be couched down instead of the silk cord.

When this is done, as in the case of a stole, join the silk at the back of the neck and appliqué a small cross in the same way. Then press the stole on the wrong side, but do not use a damp cloth unless it is really necessary as some silks leave water marks which would spoil the look of the work.

If the design is worked directly on to the silk, it is usually advisable to cut the linen away from the back, as this often becomes drawn and puckers the silk between the embroidery; then press the work on the wrong side as described above Next join the material at the back of the neck if this has not already been done, and work a smaller cross in the centre.

Then cut a piece of linen the exact shape and size the stole is required when finished. Place the embroidered silk face downwards on the table and carefully tack the lining to it. (Do not seam the linen at the back of the neck, but cut it so that the two pieces meet and catch-stitch them together. In this way they will be much flatter.)

Now turn the silk over the linen, taking care to keep the edges even. When both sides have been pinned or tacked as far as the embroidery it is as well to see if the design is still in the centre, and if not it should be adjusted before going any further. When it is tacked all round, herringbone the two lightly together, taking care that no stitches show through on to the right side.

The silk should now lie very smoothly over the linen, then the fringe is attached to the ends; this can either be fixed between the edges of the two materials, or if preferred and the heading is handsome enough, it can be left on the right side. But whichever method is chosen the fringe should be securely sewn with very small running stitches.

The next step is the lining. This should be of silk, satin or good quality sateen. The emerald green stole in Fig. 10 was lined with emerald green. The same colour as the silk upon which the stole is worked usually looks best for a preaching stole. Join the lining at the back of the neck and press the seam well. Then tack it carefully down the centre, taking care not to spoil the embroidery. Leave good turnings and tack the lining on to the front as near the edge as possible, without the lining showing through to the front. Then slip stitch the edges together, taking small stitches. Now remove the tackings and give the stole a final press with a hot iron, placing a dry cloth between the lining and the iron so as not to leave any marks.

This is only one way of making up stoles and should be found quite easy even if this has never been done before.

The most important thing in making up Church Embroidery is accuracy. Most pieces are made up in the same way only varying in shape. Cardboards are used for burses, and bracing threads are used for the two outside pieces, being taken in both directions to keep the silk taut. The same thing is done for the lining over the other two cardboards, four being used in all. The front and the lining are joined separately to the back and the lining. The two bottom pieces are oversewn firmly together and down each side buttonholed loops are used at intervals, about three to a side. This allows the burse to close easily. A cord can be put round the front of the burse and so hiding the under-join completely. This is the easiest method for one who has not done it before. The more complicated method is to put gussets in both sides in place of the buttonholed loops described above.

FAGGOTTING
AND INSERTION STITCHES

Faggotting is both useful and ornamental. The general principle of the work is the joining of two pieces of material by means of an insertion stitch. A great variety of stitches can be introduced.

Most materials can be used for this work, though silk, satin, linen and cotton are the most suitable. Faggotting is often used to join seams of either lingerie or thick materials in conjunction with hand embroidery.

The thread used varies according to the material or the purpose for which the faggotting is required. A twisted silk, broriche, and sewing silk, and in some cases stranded cotton and wool can be used.

The method of working is very simple. First of all turn under the raw edges as if for an ordinary hem and tack. These edges can be hemmed or slip stitched, or if a narrow hem, they can be left just tacked, as the faggot stitch will keep the edges together. The stitches should always be made as invisible as possible.

For double articles, such as collars or cuffs, the two pieces may be joined on the wrong side and then turned. When this is done, press well before joining.

The two edges to be joined are then tacked at an even distance apart on a piece of stiff paper or *toile cirée*. This distance varies according to the material used or the use to which the faggotting is put. Whatever its purpose the spacing must always be regular and the same tension kept throughout in working any faggot stitch.

The more elaborate type of faggotting is known as **Rouleau work,** for which a good washing satin is perhaps the easiest material to manage. For this, crossway strips have to be made into rouleaux, which are afterwards twisted and interlaced into patterns, and tacked on to brown paper. The spaces are filled in with faggot stitches, so that when the work is taken off the brown paper, it is securely held together. These strips must not be cut on the straight or by the thread, but on the direct cross. For this, the material has to be cut at an angle of forty-five degrees to the warp or weft. Cut as for bias binding (see page 532). Three-quarters of an inch is the smallest possible size strip one should cut, but strips from 1 inch to 1¼ inches are the more usual. Trim all the ends of the strips to make one straight length. The seams should lie in the same direction, so that the way of the grain of the material is the same throughout.

To make the Rouleau, the long strip just joined is folded with the right side inside, and machined to below the edge of the fold. (This is for the smallest rouleau.) This is the only part of the work which is not done by hand. An important point to remember is, that when machining, the folded strip should be stretched as much as possible, otherwise when pulled later, the stitching will snap and come undone. If the tension of the stitch is not too tight it should be quite easy.

Trim the raw edges, allowing a wider edge for material that frays. To turn the rouleau on to the right side place a blunt tipped darning needle into the open end of the fold as far as the eye. It must now be joined to the satin in order to draw it through. To do this, thread a fine needle with some strong cotton and sew the satin to the darning needle very firmly. (This needle turns the rouleau inside out and has to withstand strong pulling.) Having fixed the satin to the needle, push the needle along, holding the top of the fold, so that the raw edges do not fray in the process (Fig. 1). Continue pulling until all the material has come through (Fig. 2). Press the rouleau and

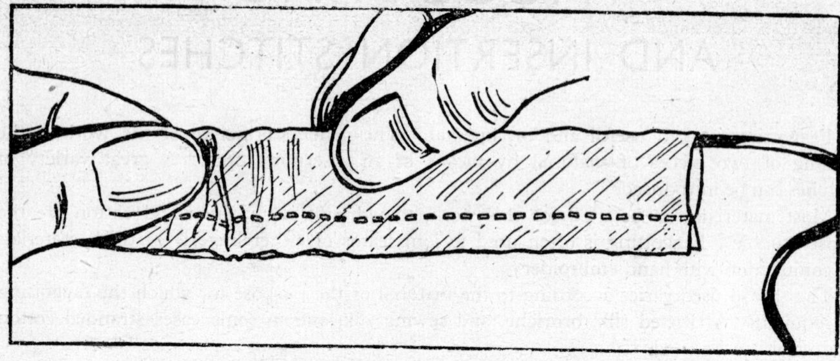

Fig. 1. After machining, the satin is drawn through to the right side with the help of a needle which is fixed to the satin and then pushed along.

keep it well stretched being careful not to get it twisted. It is now ready for use.

Mark out the design on brown paper and tack the rouleau on to it, and iron the brown paper on the back in order to flatten it before working.

Shell Rouleau is a variation. The rouleau is prepared in the usual way, the shells being made before tacking on to the brown paper. With a double thread of sewing silk to tone with the rouleau bring out the needle in the middle of the rouleau on the right side, as shown in Fig. 3. Put the needle vertically behind the rouleau and not through it, with the thread underneath the needle in the same way as for blanket stitch (Fig. 4). Pull the thread through, upwards and towards you and draw up tightly (Fig. 5). When pulling, take hold of the thread away from the needle in order not to rub the thread against the eye. Then, pass the needle horizontally through the centre of the fold, putting it in on the right of the knot just made, and bringing it out again $\frac{1}{4}$ of an inch further to the left (Fig. 6).

Fig. 7 shows the finished rouleau with its shell-like scallops. These can be made fuller and fluffier than in the illustration.

Fig. 2. Pull the thread until all the rouleau has been turned on to the right side. Press with a warm iron and keep well stretched, being careful not to twist it.

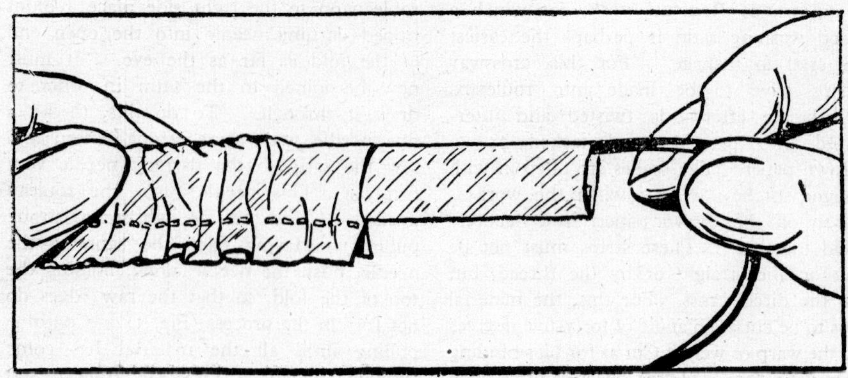

SHELL ROULEAU

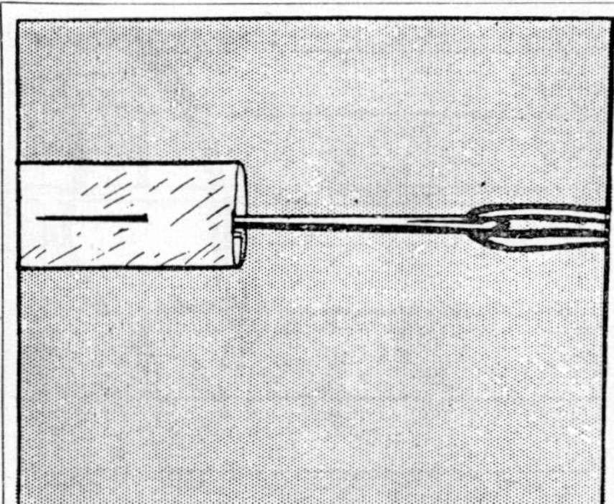

Fig. 3.

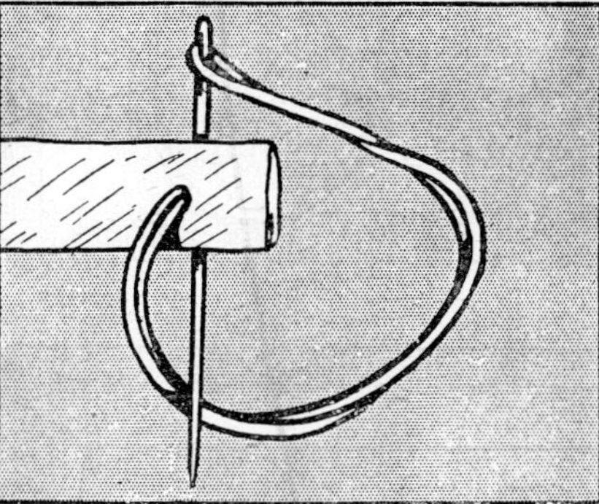

Fig. 4.

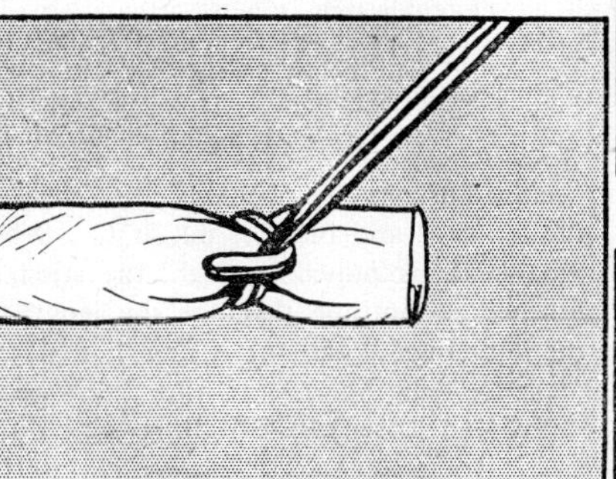

Fig. 5

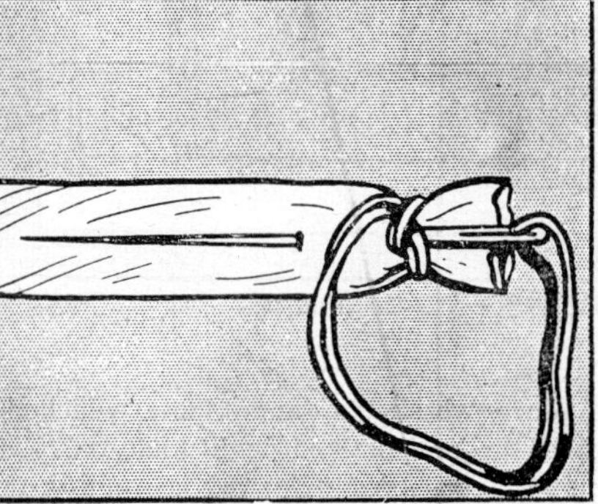

Fig. 6.

Follow these easy stage diagrams for making Shell Rouleau. The scallops should be full, so that the stitches are scarcely visible on the right side. **Fig. 7** shows the wrong side of a narrow shell rouleau.

Fig. 7.

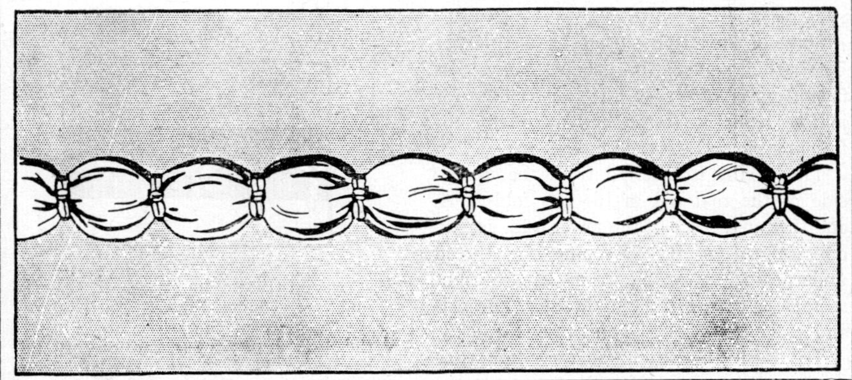

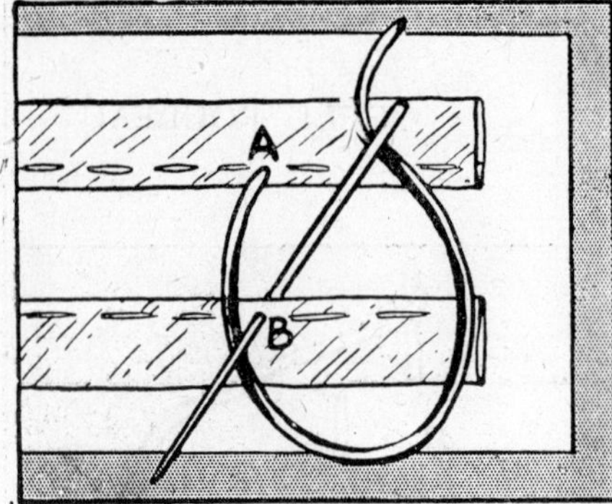

Fig. 8.

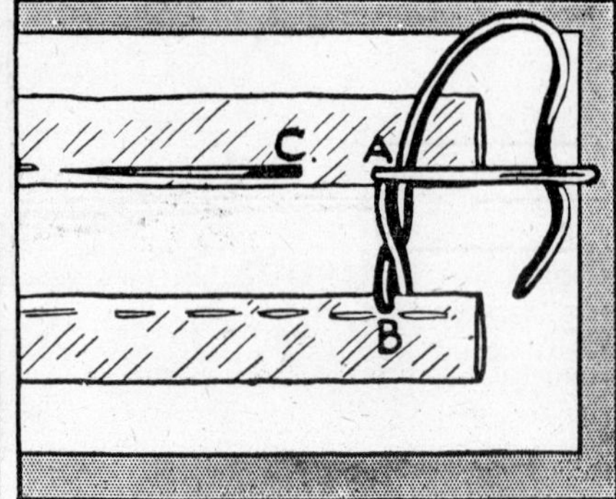

Fig. 9.

Faggot stitch is most often used for joining hems or seams. Figs. 8 and 9 show the working and Fig. 10 the finished stitch

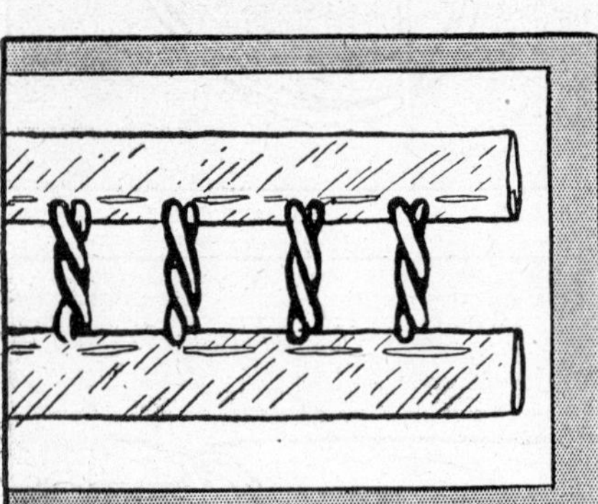

Fig. 10.

When working a satin blouse, which is going to be trimmed with rouleau, it is quite a good idea to make the rouleau of the crêpe side instead of the satin to get an effect of contrast.

Some of the stitches used for faggotting: The stitch which is usually known as faggotting is very easy. It can be used for joining hems or seams, and is suitable for fine lingerie and dresses (Figs. 8-10).

The needle is inserted from the underside of the material in the top fold at A, and then in a piece of the lower fold, exactly opposite A, at B. Keeping the thread underneath the needle from left to right as seen in Fig. 8, pull it through, upwards and away from you. This is done quickly.

To finish the stitch, at the same time getting it in position for the next, put the needle horizontally through the edge of the top fold and bring it out at C. When the needle is pulled through, the stitch is finished. Continue this, for the length of the join (Figs. 9 and 10).

Twisted Insertion Stitch is very quick and easy to do. The needle is inserted from the under-side of the material on the lower side, and then is taken across to the upper side, inserting it from underneath as before (Fig. 11). To make the twist, put the needle under the thread from right to left as in Fig. 12. Twist the point again from left to right inserting it in the lower edge (Fig. 13). The movement done in Figs. 12 and 13 is all in one, but is shown separately here to make it clearer.

Fig. 13.

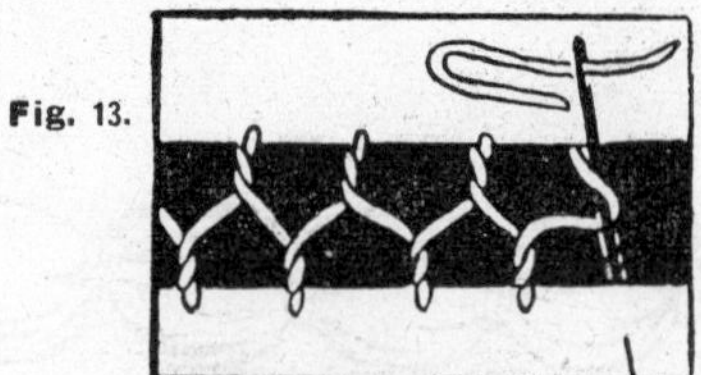

Twisted Insertion stitch is quickly and easily done. Figs. 11 and 12 show the working of the stitch and Fig. 13 the last stage. The motion of the needle in Figs. 12 and 13 should be done in one movement

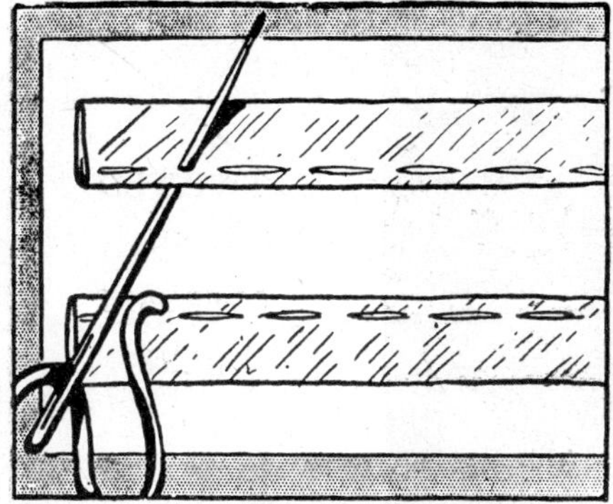

Fig. 11.

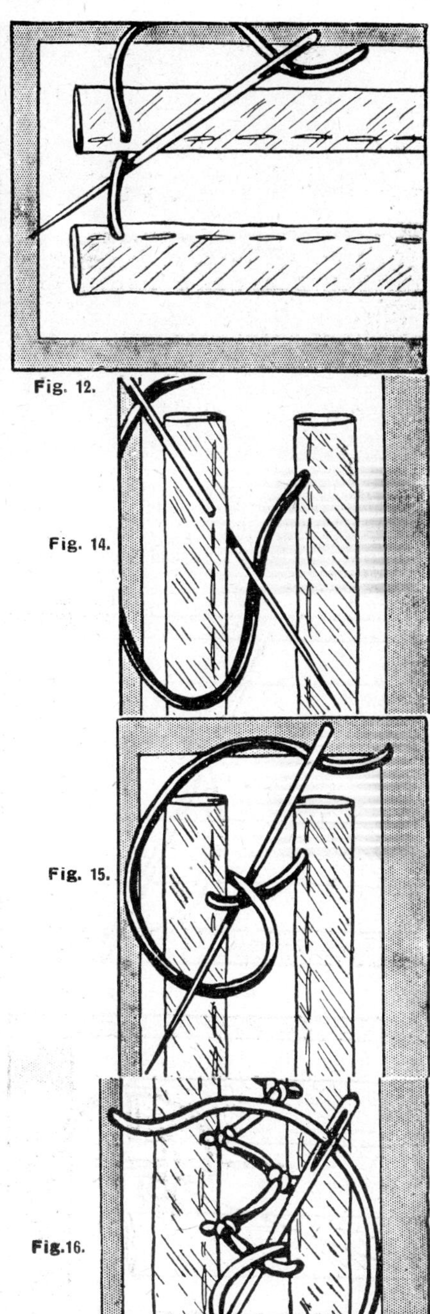

Fig. 12.

Fig. 14.

Fig. 15.

Fig. 16.

The three bottom diagrams on the right (**Figs. 14, 15 and 16**) show the working of Knotted Insertion stitch. Care is needed in pulling the knots tight.

Knotted Insertion Stitch needs care in pulling the knots tight and keeping the thread between at an even tension. This will be quite easily followed from Figs. 14, 15 and 16.

Laced Insertion Stitch is excellent for joining squares of material which have been embroidered for bedspreads or runners. The squares are first edged with a braid edging or buttonhole, and the join made by weaving a contrasting coloured thread in and out of the stitch heads as shown in Fig. 17.

Twisted Bars. Begin working from left to right as in Fig. 18. Insert the needle into the lower hem, then take it up and down into the upper hem, twist the needle three times round the bar, before inserting

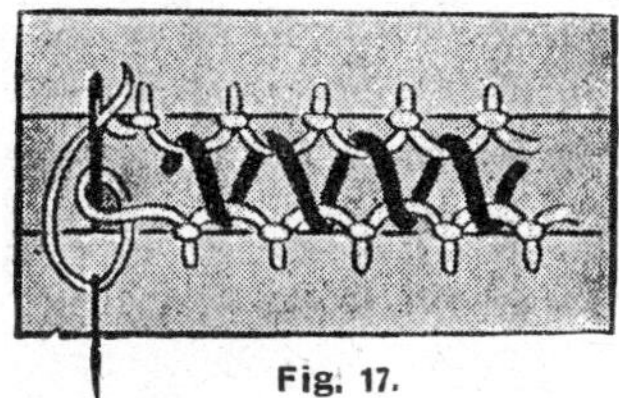

Fig. 17.

Laced Insertion stitch is very good for joining two embroidered pieces of material together. The contrasting lace thread makes a decorative finish to a useful stitch

TWISTED AND OVERCAST BARS

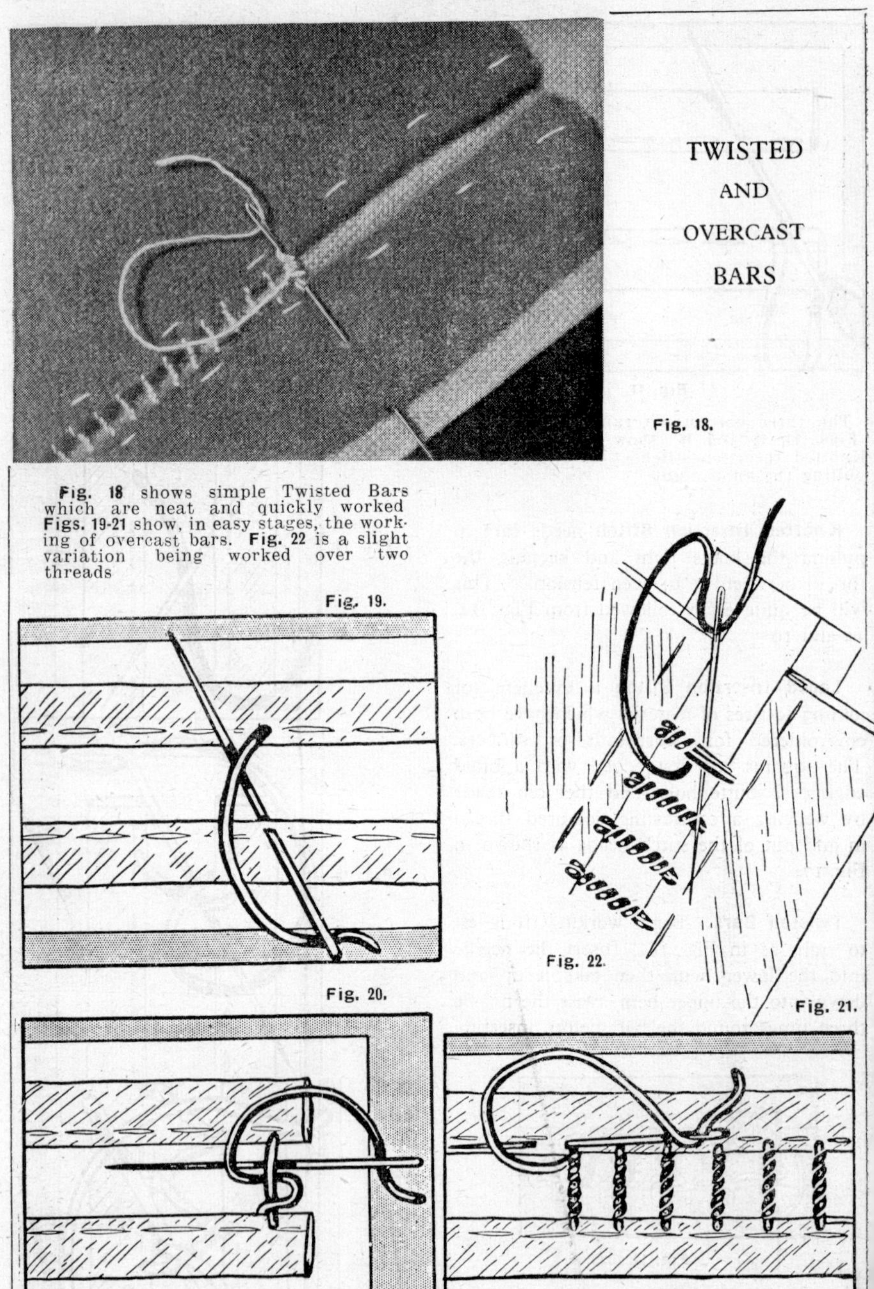

Fig. 18.

Fig. 18 shows simple Twisted Bars which are neat and quickly worked **Figs. 19-21** show, in easy stages, the working of overcast bars. **Fig. 22** is a slight variation being worked over two threads

Fig. 19.

Fig. 20.

Fig. 21.

Fig. 22.

TRELLIS STITCH AND RUNNING SHEAF

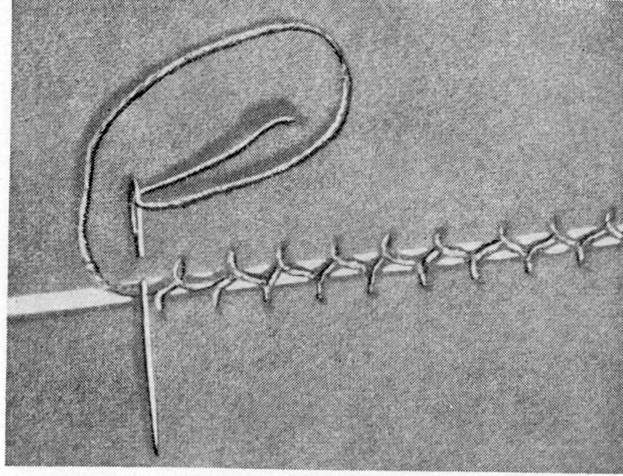

Fig. 26.

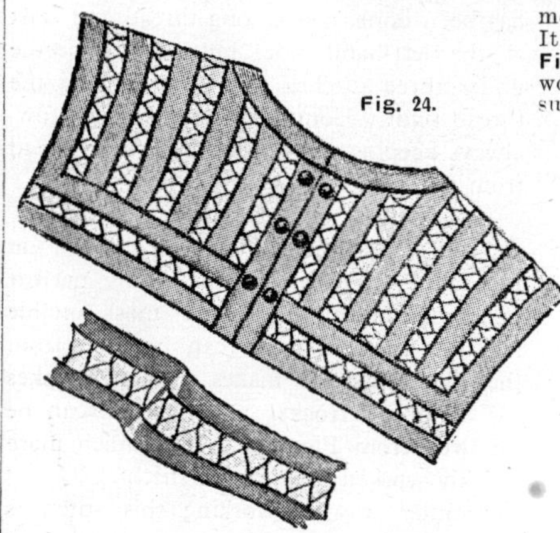

Fig. 24.

Trellis Insertion in **Fig. 24** is one of the most useful stitches for joining rouleaux. It is attractive used on a child's yoke as in **Fig. 24. Fig. 25** shows the simplicity of the working, while **Fig. 26** gives a variation suitable for thicker material.

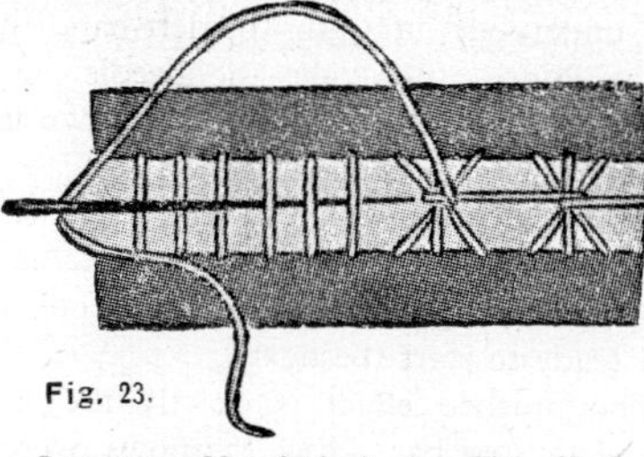

Fig. 23.

Running Sheafstitch in **Fig. 23** is attractive and very simple. Plain faggotting is divided into groups of three by a crosswise thread. Plaited Insertion in **Fig. 27** is more complicated, but can easily be followed from the diagrams.

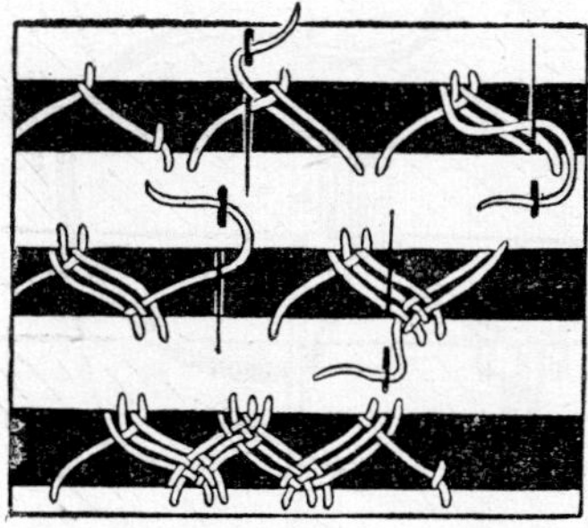

Fig. 27.

Fig. 25.

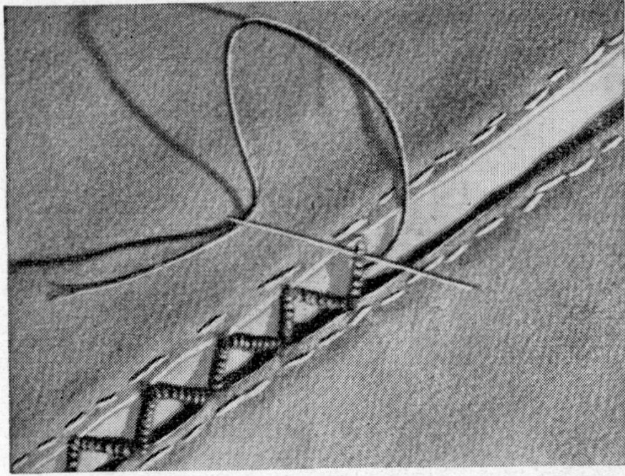

Fig. 28.

Zig-zag Buttonholed Insertion is both attractive and strong. The buttonholing is done over two diagonal threads, the whole being worked from left to right

the needle in under the hem at the bottom. Tighten the thread that has been loosened while twisting, and pull the needle through.

Overcast Bars.—Insert the needle from the under-side up into the left-hand side to be joined, then take the needle across to the right and insert the needle down into the material as shown in Fig. 19.

In Fig. 20 the needle is seen overcasting the bars, and in Fig. 21 the needle is slipped through the edge to finish one bar and ready to start the next

The finished effect is exactly the same as the twisted bar. Fig. 22 shows overcast bars worked over two strands.

Running Sheaf Stitch in Fig. 23 is useful. The two materials are first joined with ordinary faggot stitch. When this has been done, take a long thread and start at the left-hand side, putting the needle under three stitches and then drawing the thread tight. Continue thus along the row, always keeping the needle under the thread from the last stitch

Trellis Insertion Stitch is shown in Fig. 24. It is useful for joining narrow bands of rouleau and is really most suitable for thin materials. As can be seen from the illustration, it makes attractive yokes for children's frocks. This stitch can be followed from Fig. 25. It is much more quickly worked than faggot stitch

Another way of working this stitch is shown in Fig. 26. It is here worked on a coarser material with a thicker thread.

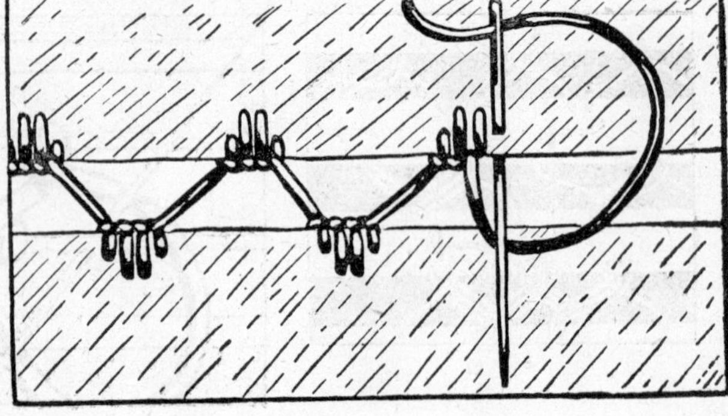

Grouped Buttonhole Insertion is effective and is extremely simple to work. There are several variations. depending on the number and position of the buttonhole stitches. Tailor's buttonholes may also be used

Fig. 29.

It is worked from right to left, always keeping the silk to the left of the needle.

Plaited Insertion Stitch is not as easy as those described above. The diagrams in Fig. 27 simplify it considerably. It can be worked in two colours if preferred.

over and under the threads at the lower edge, and insert it into the upper side, keeping the thread behind the needle as before. Continue working as above for the length required.

Zig-zag Buttonholed Insertion (Fig. 28) is worked from left to right. Insert the

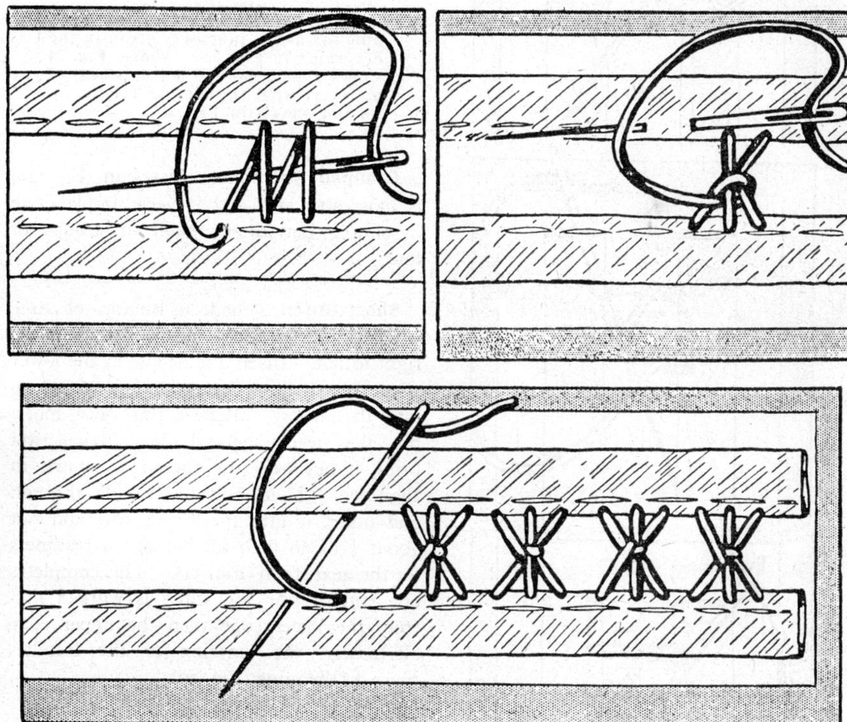

Figs. 30-32 show clearly the stages of working Sheaf stitch. As the stitch is worked first from the lower edge and then from the upper edge alternately, the crossing of the bundles must do the same.

Two or three rows, one under the other, can be worked as a trimming. Work from left to right, and insert the needle in the lower hem, and, keeping the thread to the right, take the needle down into the upper edge. Then take the needle down into the lower edge a little further to the right, under the first stitch and down into the upper edge towards the left, over the first stitch. Take it down into the lower edge towards the left. Now put the needle

needle at the lower edge, take it across to the upper edge and insert it $\frac{1}{4}$ of an inch to the right. Now bring it back and put it in where the first stitch was taken. Bring it out again and buttonhole along the two strands up to the upper edge. Bring the thread down to the lower edge, $\frac{1}{2}$ inch away from the previous stitch on that edge, take the thread back to the upper edge and buttonhole down as before. Continue in this way for the length required.

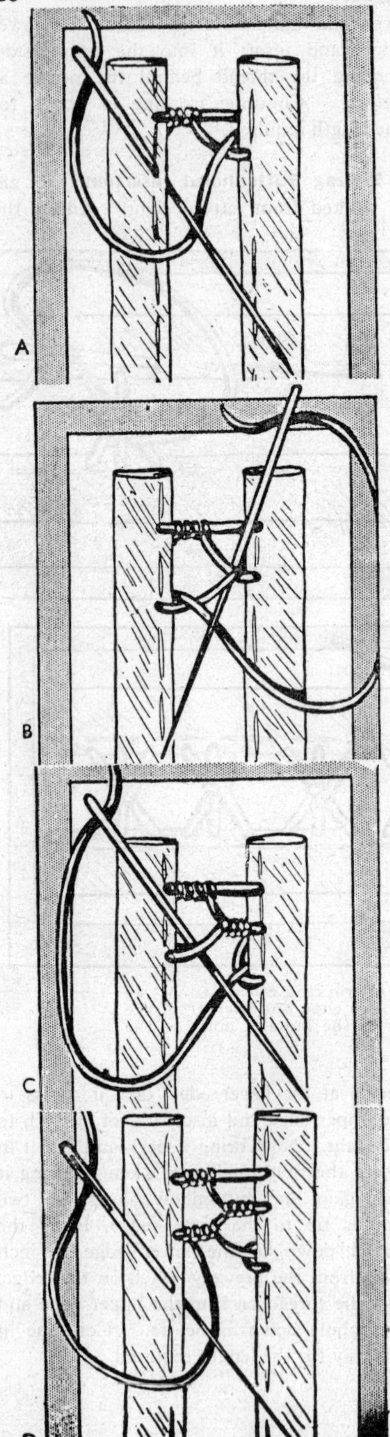

Right.

Fig. 34.

The working of an insertion suitable for heavy fabrics is given in the diagrams in **Fig.** 33. Above, **Fig.** 34 shows a neat way of joining lace to material with the simple Trellis Insertion shown in Fig. 24.

Grouped Buttonhole Insertion (Fig. 29) is most attractive and is very simply done in simple buttonhole stitch in groups of four.

Sheaf Stitch is made in bundles of three stitches tied together and is worked from right to left. Insert the needle in the lower edge, take it down into the upper and up into the lower. Repeat this once more, put the needle behind the stitches and bring it out over the thread as shown in Fig. 30. Then pull the needle through and insert it into the upper row and out about $\frac{1}{4}$ of an inch further on in readiness for the next stitch (Fig. 31). This completes one stitch. As the stitch is worked first from the lower edge then the upper edge alternately, the crossing of the bundles must do the same (Fig. 32).

A more complicated insertion suitable only for heavier materials is shown in the diagrams in Fig. 33. Bring the needle out

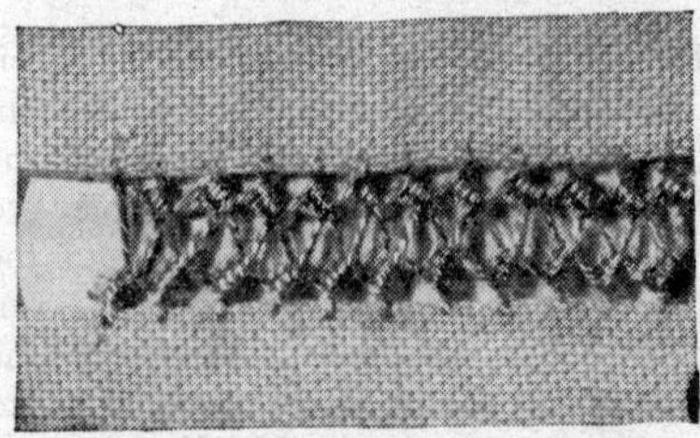

Fig. 33. Above is a finished section of the insertion. On the left are shown the working diagrams.

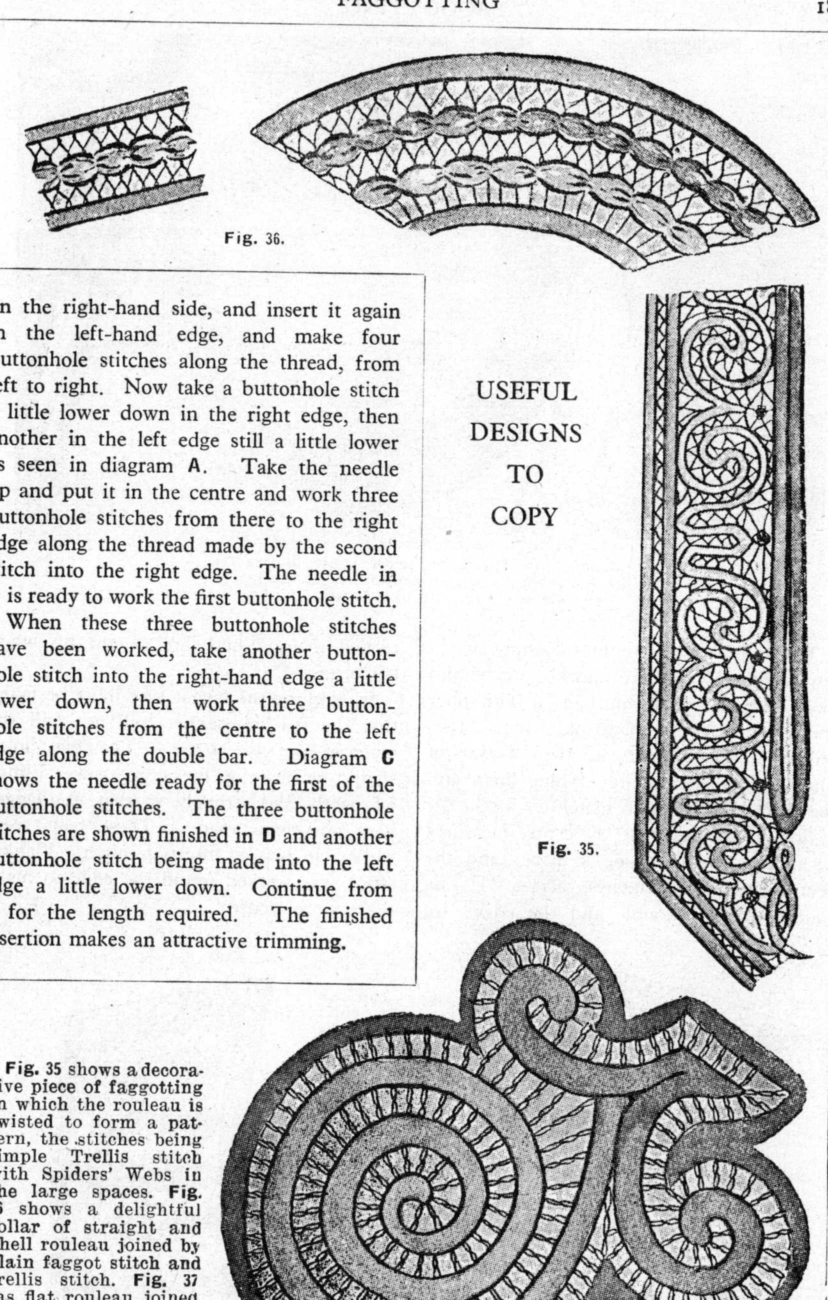

Fig. 36.

on the right-hand side, and insert it again in the left-hand edge, and make four buttonhole stitches along the thread, from left to right. Now take a buttonhole stitch a little lower down in the right edge, then another in the left edge still a little lower as seen in diagram **A**. Take the needle up and put it in the centre and work three buttonhole stitches from there to the right edge along the thread made by the second stitch into the right edge. The needle in **B** is ready to work the first buttonhole stitch.

When these three buttonhole stitches have been worked, take another buttonhole stitch into the right-hand edge a little lower down, then work three buttonhole stitches from the centre to the left edge along the double bar. Diagram **C** shows the needle ready for the first of the buttonhole stitches. The three buttonhole stitches are shown finished in **D** and another buttonhole stitch being made into the left edge a little lower down. Continue from **B** for the length required. The finished insertion makes an attractive trimming.

USEFUL DESIGNS TO COPY

Fig. 35.

Fig. 35 shows a decorative piece of faggotting in which the rouleau is twisted to form a pattern, the stitches being simple Trellis stitch with Spiders' Webs in the large spaces. **Fig.** 36 shows a delightful collar of straight and Shell rouleau joined by plain faggot stitch and Trellis stitch. **Fig.** 37 has flat rouleau joined with twisted faggotting.

Fig. 37.

Simplicity is the keynote of these decorative table mats which are so economically made out of a few skeins of silk and bias binding.

Table Mats made of bias binding and a few skeins of silk are quickly made and look effective when finished. The ones shown above were made of ½-inch cotton binding used double, in two shades of blue. The centres are of blue linen and the threads in tones to match.

For the smallest mat, the centre measures 2¼ inches, the next one 3 inches and the centre piece 6¾ inches across. The rounds are cut double and the edges are turned in, and both are caught up when faggotting.

In working the faggot care must be taken that the stitches neither pull nor frill the material out of shape. The bias joins should be made on the wrong side. Finish off neatly and strongly so that the faggot does not come apart. These mats were worked in twisted insertion stitch. Blanket stitch was worked round the edge to make them more secure.

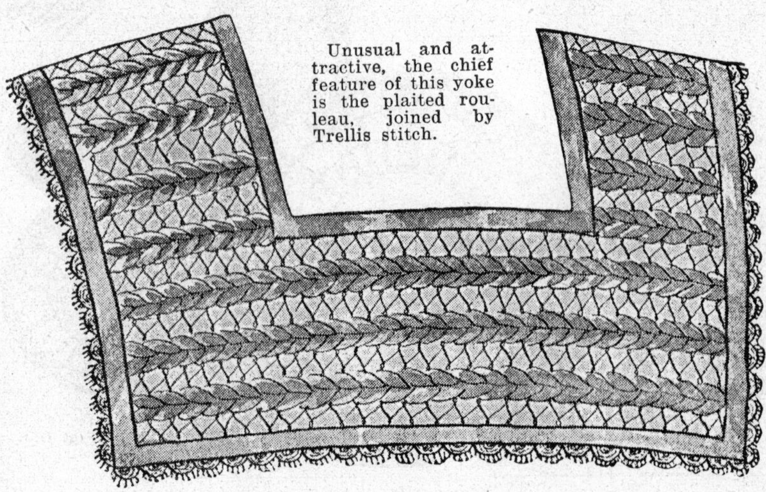

Unusual and attractive, the chief feature of this yoke is the plaited rouleau, joined by Trellis stitch.

HARDANGER EMBROIDERY

Modern Hardanger is of Norwegian origin, deriving its name from the city of Hardanger (pronounced Hardonger). It is also much worked in Denmark and Sweden.

The original Hardanger embroidery is very old, being done in ancient times in Asia and Persia, worked in silk on a kind of gauze netting. It was expensive and considered a very valuable and decorative needlework.

Hardanger work is durable, easily done and not trying to the sight. It requires careful working so that the stitches are placed quite evenly and the squared effect of the design maintained throughout. This embroidery is distinctive in style, this being due to the fact that the designs are always worked on squares. Whether they are large or small the same number of threads must be covered each way, or the character of the design is spoilt. Drawn thread work is largely introduced, usually as a means of dividing the work into open squares which may afterwards be decorated with lace stitches or patterns in darning stitch.

In making cuffs, collars, yokes, etc., it is essential to fit them in paper or lining before cutting the material. The beginner should practise before doing a piece of work such things as the drawing of threads, the working of squares and how to cut the canvas, as the work cannot be unpicked. The first thing to do when starting a piece of work is to overcast the edges of the material to prevent fraying. Care must be taken when cutting the openings between stitches.

After cutting four threads close to the oversewing, carefully draw them out, making exact squares of four threads each way. Never make the mistake of cutting first. Work first and cut last, otherwise the material will ravel and become worthless in working. Be sure to cut the thread evenly to form a square.

Materials required.—The foundation

Fig. 1. THREE BORDER STITCHES

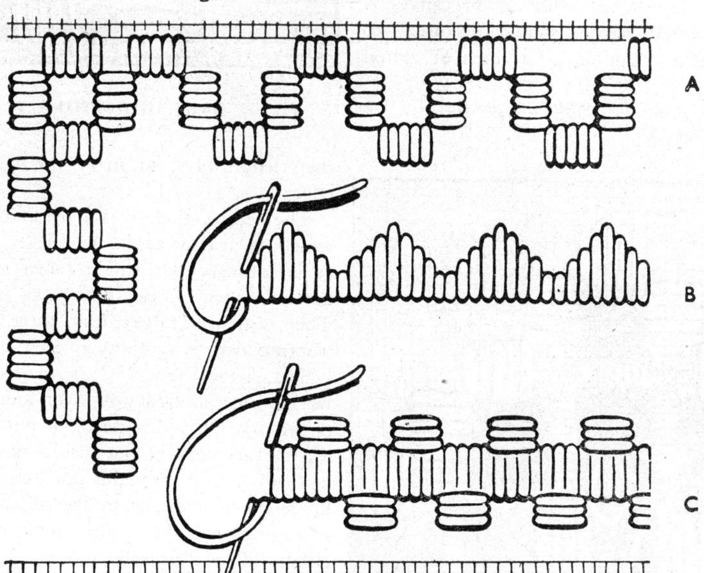

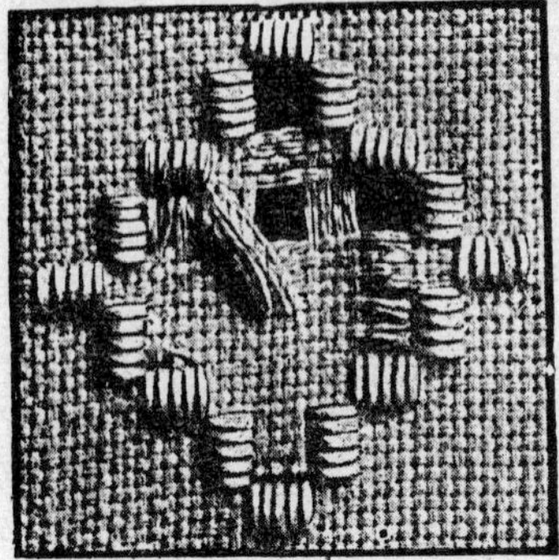

Fig. 2. DRAWING THREADS AND WORKING SATIN STITCH SQUARES

material should have an even texture, i.e. both warp and weft thread should be of the same thickness and easy to draw. Most suitable, therefore, are Hardanger, Java, and congress canvas, all the coarser makes of linen and some cotton fabrics of coarse, even texture. The working thread for lace stitches and darning or weave stitch should be of the same thickness as those of the foundation material, but as a rule the satin stitch is worked in a rather coarser thread. Any good linen thread, mercerised cotton or twisted embroidery thread would be suitable. When working on canvas, a blunt-pointed needle should be used for the stitchery, but on finer linen or cotton material an ordinary crewel needle of a suitable size to take the thread is used. Very sharp pointed scissors are needed for cutting the canvas or linen between the blocks. Various stitches are used for the solid parts, including satin, overcast, back and cross-stitch.

Three Border Stitches are shown in Fig. 1. The first, A, is the turret or battlement edging which is much used. It is simply satin or flat stitch taken over two, three or four stitches, and worked in groups of five stitches, first widthways, then lengthways, to make the battlement edge.

Fig. 3. BARS IN DARNING STITCH

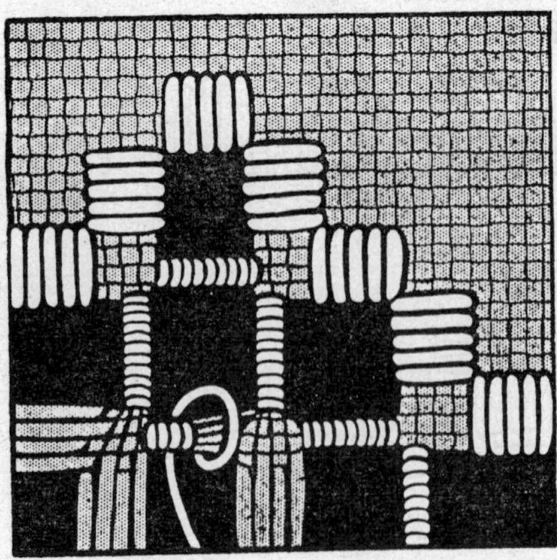

Fig. 4.—TWISTED BARS

The centre stitch B is a pyramid border, which is useful as it is quickly worked. It is satin or flat stitch, taken over two threads, then three, four, five and six. Then decreased to five, four, three and two, working two twos between each pyramid.

The lower design C is in flat stitch, worked in a straight row over four threads of the material. The needle is put in at the top of the work in the thread next to the last stitch and brought out four threads lower down and one to the left as clearly shown in Fig. 1. The small blocks at either side of this solid row are worked in the reverse way to the row itself, that is across, over four threads and three or four stitches deep, leaving a space of four threads between each block. The upper row of blocks alternates with the lower.

Always start the work by outlining the design with satin stitch, as shown in Fig. 2. Each of these stitches should be taken over four threads, and every square should contain five stitches, which means that the last stitch of a vertical row and the first of a horizontal row respectively finish and begin in the same weave crossing.

After all the edges are outlined thus,

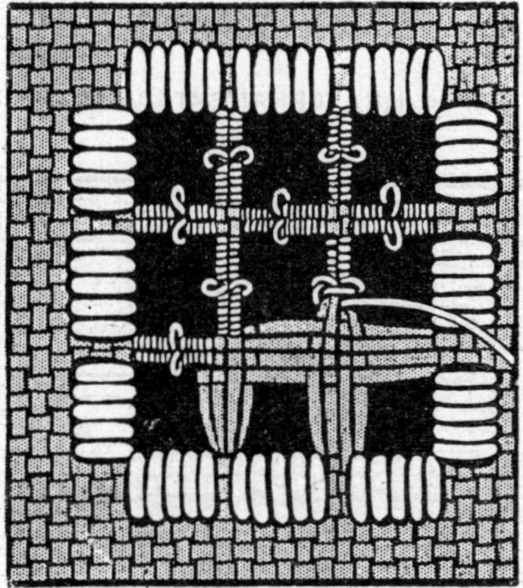

Fig. 6.—DRAWING UP THREAD OF PICOT

start to cut and draw the threads to form the open squares. This has to be done in both directions, alternately drawing four threads and leaving four threads. The threads which are left are worked with darning or weave stitches into bars (Fig. 3). This is done by taking the needle first under two threads and then over two from one side to the other. Another way of working the bars is shown in Fig. 4. This consists of twisting the working thread round and round the carrying thread—this is overcast stitch. Picots can be made according to Figs. 5, 6 and 7 by making a loop with the working thread. In Fig. 7 it is enlarged to show clearly the working of the **picots.** The weaving is the same as

Fig. 5.—SIMPLE PICOT

before, over two and under two, but when the centre of each bar is reached then make a picot each side thus: Pass the needle under the working thread, and pass the needle through the loop, as shown in the illustration. In Fig. 8 the picot is made by twisting the thread round the needle. Picots should always be made in the middle of the bars.

The Star Pattern in Fig. 9 shows the twisted lace filling stitch, which here is carried from one corner to another across

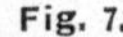

Fig. 7.

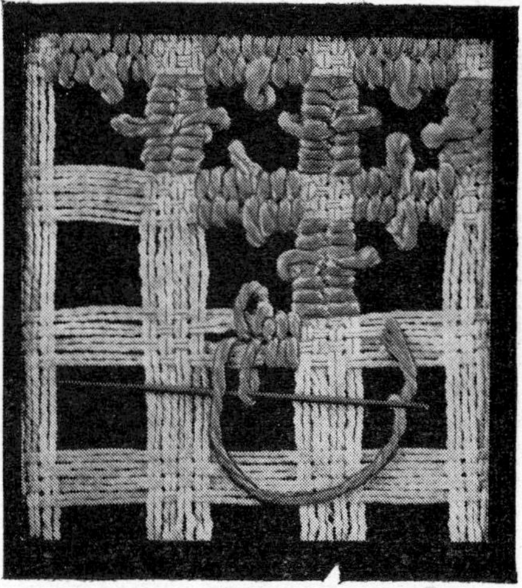

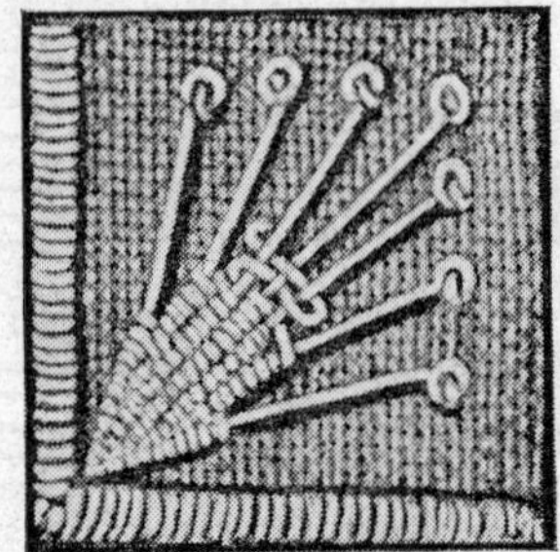

Fig. 12.—DARNING OVER LOOSE THREADS

Fig. 13.—BORDER DESIGN IN HARDANGER BACK-STITCH

Fig. 10 (left).—ORNAMENTED DIAMOND

Fig. 9 (above).—STAR PATTERN

Fig. 8 (left).—METHOD OF WORKING A TWISTED PICOT

Fig. 16

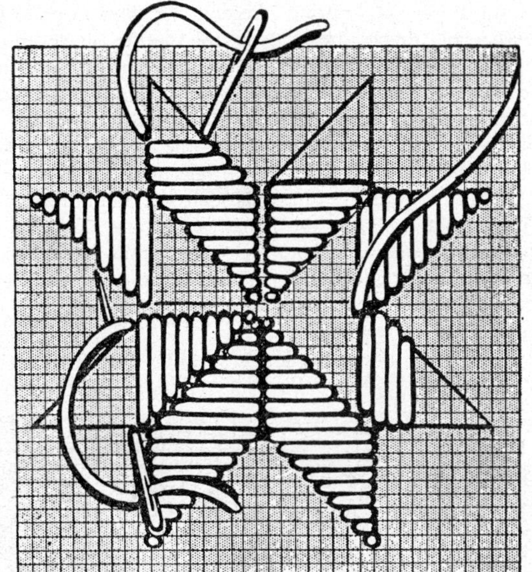

EIGHT-POINTED STAR

Fig. 15
CROSS IN FISHBONE STITCH

Fig. 14.
FANCY BACK-STITCH BORDER

the square, while the satin stitches round the edge are graduated to give a star-like appearance.

In the **ornamented diamond** (Fig. 10) the centre is the same as the star pattern but the satin stitches are different. The stitches grow gradually larger to the centre, then decrease, each side being worked alike. Each stitch takes another thread of canvas, then decreases in the same way.

A Flower Design.—Details for which are shown in Fig. 12. Carry seven threads fanwise from a given point across the square, and end each of these threads with a French knot, then with darning stitch fill in the flower at the base, working first over seven, then over five, and then over three threads.

Back Stitching is often used as a border for the more difficult designs in Hardanger embroidery. Fig. 13 shows it in the working. It is worked on the slant of the canvas, both rows of stitchery are worked at the same time, from the underside of the embroidery, each stitch is taken across three threads. Fig. 14 shows a line motif and how to work it in back stitch. It is shown in Fig. 21 as a connection between two open motifs. The holes are caused partly by the pull of the thread while working, and partly by bringing up the needle twice through the same hole.

A Cross in Fishbone Stitch is an extremely useful filling for centres and is simple to work. Bring the needle up from the wrong side and make a stitch in a diagonal direction over three or four threads of canvas towards the left. Bring the needle back to the hole exactly below that from which the first stitch was started; make another stitch across three or four threads, putting it into the hole exactly below that in which the first stitch was finished. Continue to work these slanting stitches one below the other, until the line is long enough. Then begin again at the top of the line, and work a similar set of stitches slanting from left to right. One end of each of these stitches must pass through the same hole as the corresponding stitch in the first line. The other three arms are worked in the same way. (Fig. 15.)

Fig. 17.—OVERCAST AND LACE STITCH

The Eight-pointed Star is a feature of Hardanger embroidery. First mark the canvas for the centre of the star. Place the canvas quite flat on the table, and put a pin in the centre. Make a line with a pencil, nine threads long; make another the reverse way to form a cross, and between each line make another line. Thus making eight lines all radiating from the centre. The threads must be counted to get each line true.

The section at the right-hand of the star (Fig. 16) is arranged by bringing up the threaded needle from the centre of the star. Pass it down between the first and second mesh to the right, bring the needle up one mesh above the centre second mesh, pass it down between the second and third mesh to the right. Bring up the needle above the centre, pass it down between the third and fourth mesh, and so continue until nine threads are covered, thus finishing one half of a section. Bring the needle up on the tenth mesh, skip one mesh to the right, put the needle through the ninth mesh, and reduce one mesh each time, until you come to the top or point, thus completing one section. The other seven sections are worked in the same way.

For the Insertion Pattern shown in Fig. 17, draw out six threads and leave

Fig. 18.—DARNING STITCH INSERTION

six, divide the latter into sets of three each, and work them with fine thread into bars. Fill the small squares with lace stitches as seen from the illustration.

Another Useful Filling, in Fig. 18, needs eight threads drawing out and four leaving. After the bars have been made in the usual way, carry two threads diagonally across the square and work in the wheel in darning stitch. Take four threads across each of the small squares and darn them to match the outside lines.

In Fig. 19 the ground is prepared by drawing six threads out and leaving six. The corner filling consists of five to six rows of darning stitches, with the spider's web in the centre in lace stitch.

Fig. 19.—DARNING AND LACE STITCH

Fig. 20.—A LEAF SHAPE

A Decorative Motif much used in Hardanger embroidery is the leaf shape shown in Fig. 20. This shape may be either used as a filling for open squares or can be placed on a trellised ground as seen in Fig. 28. When preparing the foundation threads for the leaf, the two outside threads are held in a curved position by pins, which are removed after the darning is finished. By this method a full shape is secured.

Two stitches often used in Hardanger embroidery are the **plain loop and the picot loop.** These are made by covering the carrying thread with so-called single shuttle stitches, such as are used in tatting. They are quite easy to make as can be seen from Fig. 22.

In the first movement, a loop stitch is made over the foundation threads, and in the second, the needle is brought under the foundation threads, upwards. For the picots proceed in the same way, but at regular intervals making small loops in the thread and holding it firmly until the next stitch is made.

Single Shuttle Stitch is shown in Fig. 22, and in Fig. 23 is shown the shuttle stitch with the picot. Both these stitches are effective either for decorating open spaces or outlining large shapes. Shuttle stitches are much used in Hardanger embroidery on coarse linen; a strong mercerised cotton is used for working them.

Fig. 21.—A BORDER DESIGN

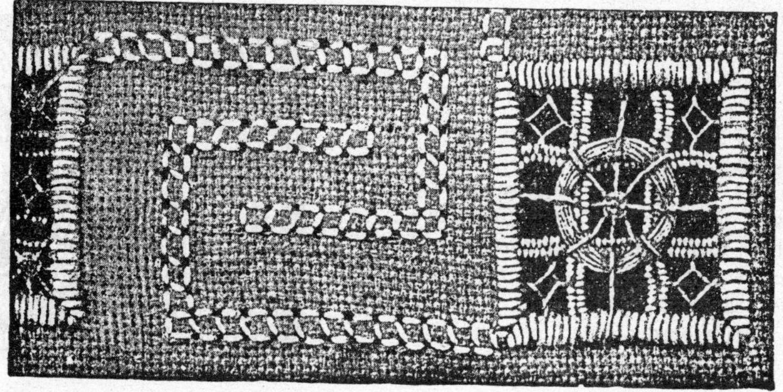

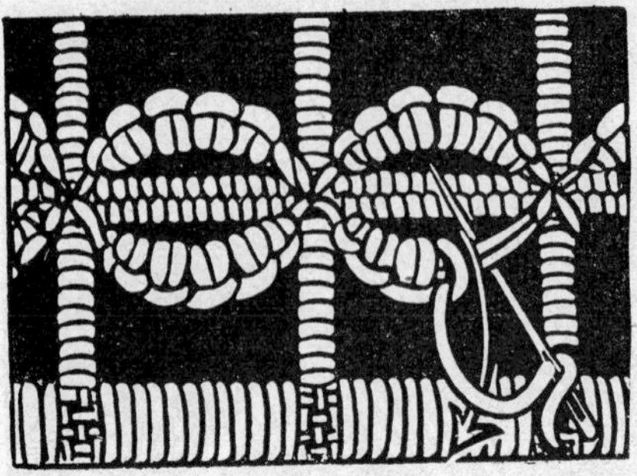

Fig. 22. SINGLE SHUTTLE STITCH

canvas in two thicknesses of cotton, the finer being used for darning the bars.

The outside edge is buttonholed over four threads, the squares (four threads wide) having their outer edge worked in plain overcast stitch, taken over four threads.

The bars are darned two over and two under, then in the centre of each bar and on one side only a picot is made. A satin stitch diamond centres the cut work and is worked as follows: one stitch over two threads, one stitch over four threads, the next over six, the next over eight, the next over ten, the next over twelve. Then

Fig. 24. OPEN WORK SQUARE

An Open work Square as shown in Fig. 24 is suitable either as an insertion or, with three put together in triangular fashion, makes a good corner. It consists of a square of four holes each way, worked diamond ways. First outline the drawn squares with flat stitch taken over four threads, with five stitches in a row. The drawn squares are done with the weaving stitch (over two, under two) then nine squares filled in with a twisted lace stitch. The border round is described earlier in this chapter.

Fig. 25 is a border much used in Hardanger embroidery. It is worked on Java

Fig. 23.—SHUTTLE STITCH WITH PICOT

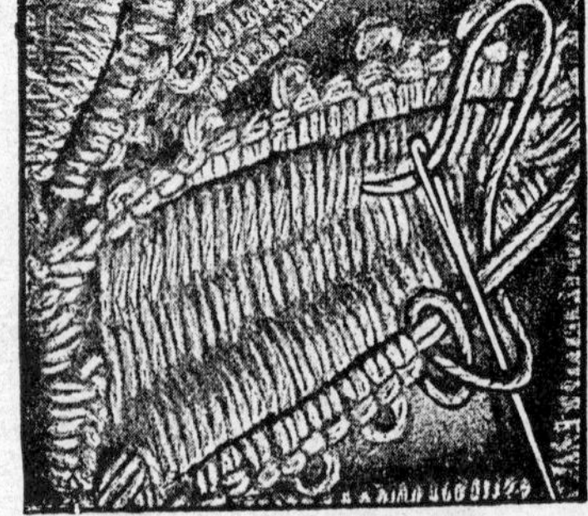

decrease in the same way. This pattern can be worked as a deep border by repeating it several times, in which case a heading is not necessary.

For a small border as shown in the illustration a heading is quite effective. For the heading work a line of satin stitch over two, three or four threads as preferred, and in the centre of the half diamond put a half-diamond in satin stitch.

get the best effect, the embroidery should be worked in a frame.

Fig. 26 shows a practical method of dividing the threads and marking the corners of the squares. After laying out the work in this way, the outlining can be done quickly and easily, as all further counting is unnecessary and mistakes in the cutting and drawing out are impossible. Special attention must be shown to the corner lines, which serve as a guide for the whole lay-out.

Fig. 25. A USEFUL DECORATIVE BORDER

Fig. 28 shows single shuttle-stitch, lace stitch, overcast bars and woven bars, with the leaf worked over the squares as already described for Fig. 15.

Fig. 27 shows **another insertion** which is simple yet effective. It is worked on coarse linen and the one shown here is three and a quarter inches wide. The embroidery is in flat or satin stitch, the cut work is in weaving stitch (over two threads, under two) and some of the squares are filled in with lace stitch.

When coarse canvas has to be embroidered the design used is often very elaborate, being made up of lace fillings and motifs worked in darning stitch. To

For **the star pattern insertion** in Fig. 29, prepare the ground by drawing four groups of eight threads, leaving four threads lengthways, then draw groups of eight, leaving four crossways. The edges are closely

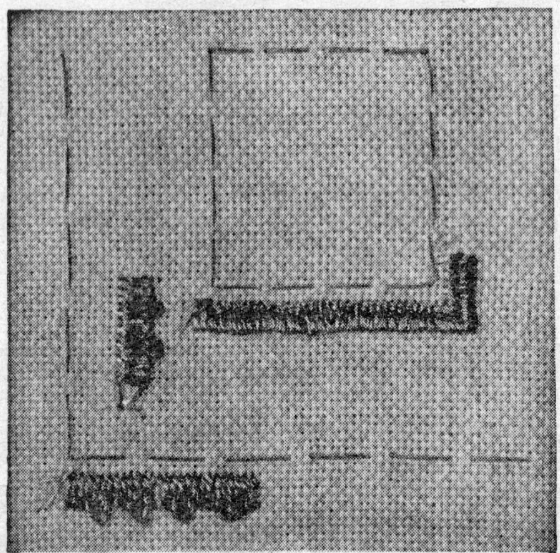

Fig. 26. LAYING OUT AND MARKING THE WORK

worked with buttonhole stitch, and the loose threads with darning stitch to form the dividing bars. Now proceed with the star pattern, which is worked over four open squares, alternately on either side of the insertion. Foundation threads are carried diagonally across the squares, six from the right-hand side and six from the left, crossing in the centre. They should each have the thread twisted back to the starting-point to give strength. Start the darning from the centre, first in spider's web pattern, and afterwards working outwards over each set of threads. The four squares between each of the star shapes have twisted lace stitches worked from the centre of each dividing bar.

A Key Pattern Insertion (Fig. 30.) The original is about 6 inches wide and is worked on strong Hardanger canvas. For the open squares, draw four threads each way and leave four between. These are darned into bars for the background.

The pattern is outlined on either side with satin stitch taken over four threads, and the space between is filled with cross-stitch. The edges of the insertion have turrets worked in satin stitch. Each thread is worked over four threads in width,

Fig. 27. A SIMPLE YET CHARMING DESIGN

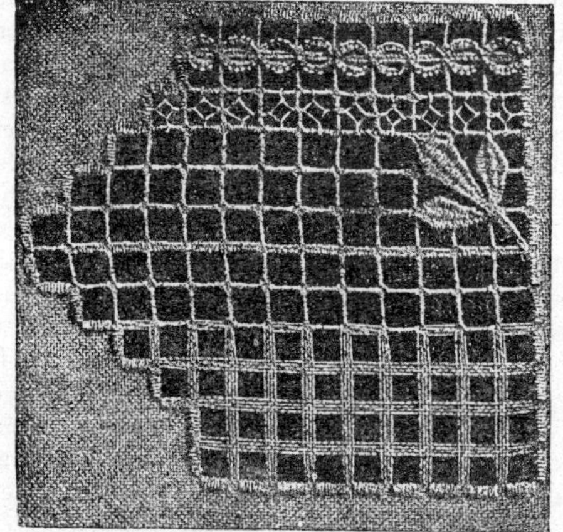

Fig. 28.

SINGLE SHUTTLE-STITCH, LACE STITCH, OVERCAST AND WOVEN BARS

and alternately over four and eight in height.

A Maltese Cross design as shown in Fig. 31 should be worked on Java canvas. Draw the threads to within four threads of both straight edges, which are about 10 inches long, work a tiny drawn thread insertion and finish off the slanting side with a row of fancy back stitching as seen in the illustration. The working of the pattern is begun by doing the outlining with satin stitch taken over four threads, after which four threads are drawn and four left in for the open work squares. These latter threads are then darned into bars and the open squares decorated with lace filling stitches. Upon this background rest three large crosses worked in satin stitch with open work fillings, which are obtained by alternately drawing two threads and leaving two in both directions, leaving a diamond shape in each centre, which is afterwards worked in satin stitch. The triangular border along the slanting side is composed of satin stitch worked in squares over four threads.

Fig. 29. STAR PATTERN INSERTION

A Tea-cloth Design is shown in Fig. 33. Measuring twenty inches square it could be worked on canvas or linen. The design is so clearly reproduced that very little explanation is needed. The entire border of sixteen half-diamonds along either side, with a square corner, is worked in buttonhole stitch, the drawn thread work being outlined with flat stitch which also forms the half-diamonds and blocks just above the vandyked border.

The cut work is done in thick over-casting to give a corded effect.

Fig. 32 is eleven inches in width, and is worked on Java canvas in two thicknesses of cotton, the finer cotton being used for the bar fillings in the cut work. This is easily followed from the illustration.

An afternoon teacloth in Hardanger embroidery is practical as it wears well. Fig. 37 is a good example. A coarse linen or fine Hardanger canvas is most satisfactory. The cloth can be made any size according to the number of repeats.

In beginning the work, the position for one side of the border should be marked with a line of tacking. Above this slits are cut in the linen along twelve threads, missing eight threads between each, and a second set cut exactly opposite, but twenty threads above. The cut threads are then drawn, also twelve threads lengthways in the centre of the line between the slits. Either side of this insertion is satin stitched over four threads. Each group of threads remaining across the spaces is darned into bars and those along either side into single bars, a loose buttonhole stitch being worked into the centre of each of the bars forming the squares before the darning of the fourth bar is complete, so that a thread is laid across each corner as seen in Fig. 36. Above this insertion the linen is divided into sections as seen from the illustration, with satin stitch bars over four threads.

Each small square encloses forty-four threads, and each large square covers the space of nine small ones.

Fig. 30. KEY PATTERN INSERTION

The large squares are outlined with the narrow insertion first described, the small square in the centre of each being worked in the same way as an all-over pattern, but nine threads are drawn and eight left instead of twelve and eight as in the borders.

For the openwork squares draw groups of four threads leaving four threads between each, and darn the remaining threads into bars working a picot on either side in the centre of each.

The remaining small squares have two sets of four threads drawn either way in the centre, leaving a cross of four threads which are darned into bars, then a thread is laid diagonally across each tiny space

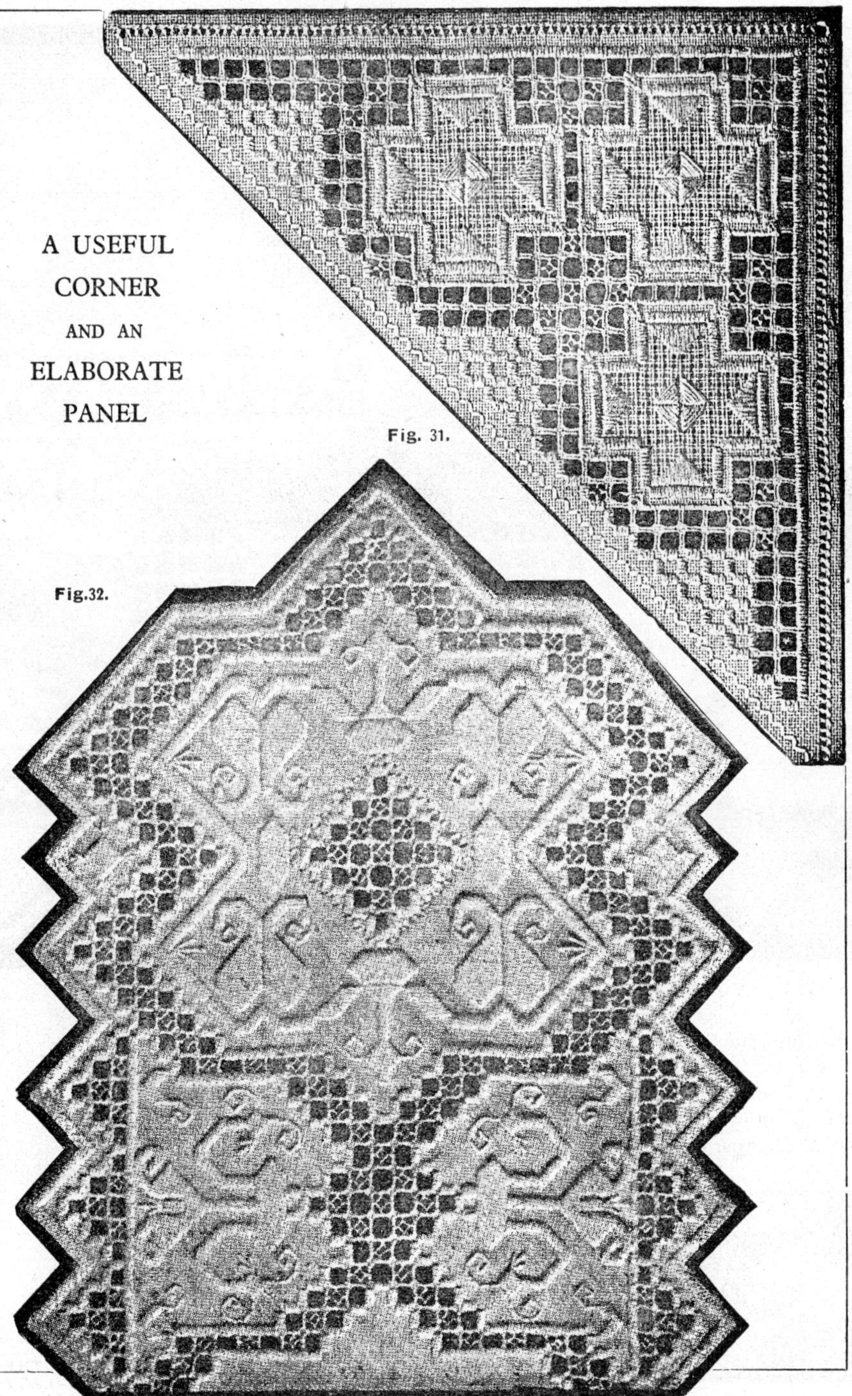

A USEFUL CORNER AND AN ELABORATE PANEL

Fig. 31.

Fig.32.

Fig. 33. AN UNUSUAL FLOWER DESIGN ARRANGED IN A CORNER

and satin stitch worked all round as shown in Fig. 36.

The hem of the cloth is finished with the insertion shown in Fig. 35. Fig. 37 shows a corner of the completed cloth.

Fig. 34.

Fig. 35. LEFT, THE INSERTION FOR THE CLOTH IN Fig. 38, AND ABOVE, A LACY FILLING

Fig. 37. A LOVELY TEACLOTH

AN ENLARGED SECTION

Fig. 36.

Fig. 38. A USEFUL SQUARE

The design in Fig. 38 shows a section of a handsomely embroidered strip for a table runner. The material is Java canvas, and the embroidery is worked with Sylko No. 5 and No. 8, the finer thread being used for the bar fillings.

Two lines of fish-bone stitch form the border, between which is a design with serrated edges worked in groups of three stitches over six threads. Fig. 34 shows the working for the lacy bar fillings.

HEDEBO EMBROIDERY

Hedebo work is a form of white work which was done by the Danish peasants on white linen. This white linen was first woven by the peasants who then decorated it with this work for their underclothes and household linen.

The Danish name for this work is Hedebosyning, but it is more generally known as Hedebo work, deriving its name from Heden, a heath, and Bo, to live, which suggests that it is the work of people who live on a heath.

The work is done mostly on linen, but occasionally cambric and muslin are used. The working thread should be linen or mercerised cotton of various sizes to suit the texture of the material used. It is advisable to tack the material on to toile cirée in order to keep it taut for working.

For the openwork parts of the design the material is entirely cut away and afterwards filled in with a great variety of lace stitches.

The solid parts of the embroidery, which usually take the form of leaves are worked in satin stitch, as in Broderie Anglaise, and the various eyelets and dots found in that work are also used.

Buttonhole edgings are another feature of Hedebo work. These finish both straight and scalloped edges. The little pyramid shapes give particular charm to this work.

Hedebo Buttonhole Stitch differs slightly from ordinary buttonhole stitch, but it is quite simple. It should always be worked from left to right, unless the pattern necessitates its being worked otherwise.

To work the stitch put the needle in from the wrong side and bring it out about $\frac{1}{8}$ inch below the edge, and draw the thread up, leaving a small loop, and pass the needle from the back to the front, through the loop, and draw the thread up evenly, as seen in Figs. 1 and 2.

The stitches should not be too close together or the purl edge will not lie flat, and there will be no room for the insertion of the next row of buttonhole stitches. To join a new thread, pass the needle through the loop of the last-made stitch before drawing it up tightly, keep both the ends of thread together as shown in Figs. 3 and 4.

How to work an open shape is shown in Fig. 5. Before buttonholing the edges, outline them with a row of small running stitches, then cut away the material inside the running stitches and turn the edges back to the wrong side. With the needle, cover the edge of the shape with a row of well-spaced buttonhole stitches, then continue as illustrated, by working a row of open buttonholing into the purl edge of the first row. Then oversew the loops of the last row and finish with another row of buttonholing. The right-hand square of Fig. 5 shows the oversewing and last row of buttonholing being done.

Figs. 6 and 7 illustrate the method of working **oval or leaf shapes** which form a great feature of this work. The edges are

Figs. 1-4 show the working of Hedebo buttonhole stitch.

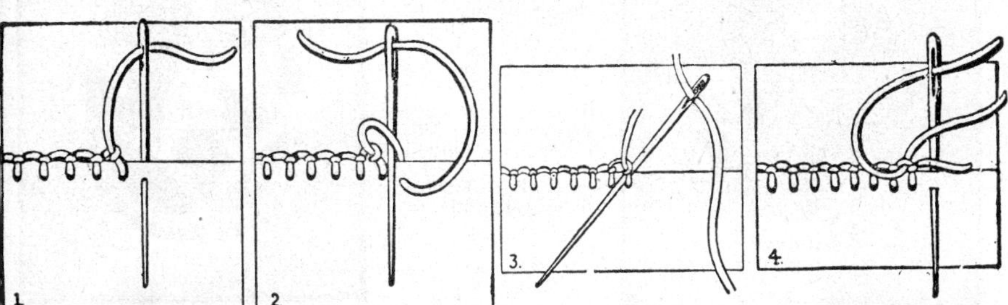

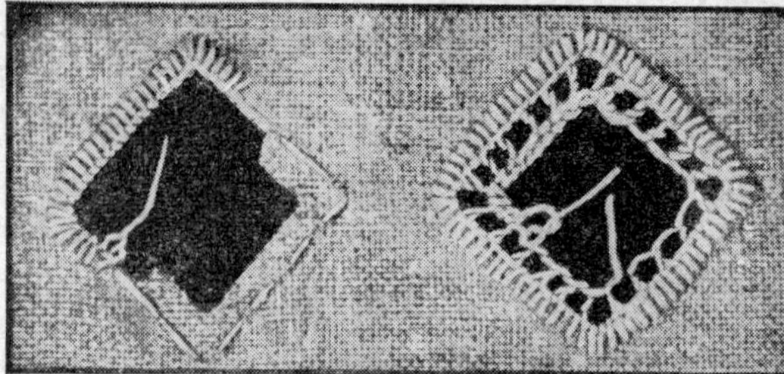

Fig. 5.

Two details in working an open shape. The edges are first outlined, then buttonholed, the shape being built on to this foundation.

first secured with buttonhole stitches, starting at the cross and working in the direction of the arrow. Fig. 6 shows the filling started. This consists in carrying, in the direction of the arrow, three threads backwards and forwards to form the foundation for the little pyramid as a filling for the pointed end of the shape. Buttonhole these threads, going back neatly to the beginning, and then continue buttonholing to and fro till the pyramid is finished. The first row of the pyramid should consist of eight stitches, the second of 7 and so on, dropping a stitch in every row. The working thread is then brought back with small invisible stitches from the point of the pyramid to its base, ready for continuing buttonholing the edge of the shape. Work a row of open buttonhole stitches into the rounded edge of the shape, oversew back and buttonhole as for an open shape. Make a large loop by carrying a thread backwards and forwards three times and buttonhole it up to O, then work the second pyramid, and the third and fourth, all in their proper position and joined together at their points as shown in Fig. 7. Fasten off the thread at the edge.

The edgings in Figs. 8 and 9 are worked without a tracing straight into the edge of the material, which should first be turned in. If working on a curved edge, a line of runstitch should be worked first to give the strength. For Fig. 8, pyramid edging is worked in four rows. First secure the edges with buttonhole stitch, then make a row of open buttonhole stitch into the purl edge of the first row, taking up about every third loop. Oversew, then buttonhole closely over the edges of this row, to form the foundation of the pyramids. For these work six buttonhole stitches into the

Fig. 6.

Two stages in the working of oval or leaf shapes which form one of the main features of Hedebo work. Fig. 6 shows the filling started and Fig. 7 the beginning of the final pyramid.

Fig. 7.

first six of the previous row, turn, and, missing the first stitch, work five stitches, then turning each time, work four, three, two and one stitch respectively which brings the pyramid to a point. Slip stitch invisibly down the side of the pyramid, miss two buttonhole stitches of the foundation row, work the next and following pyramids in the same manner.

The picot loop edging in Figs. 9 and 9a is worked on a closely buttonholed foundation, which is made into the edge of the material. When this is finished, make the small loops by carrying a thread backwards and forwards four times. To get the four threads all the same length they should be very firmly held down throughout the working and the beginner will find it an advantage to use a pair of scissors or a stiletto for the purpose, but after some practice the worker will have no difficulty in holding the threads over the first finger of the left hand. Cover the loops closely with buttonholing, then make a second loop and buttonhole as far as the centre. Now carry three threads across to the centre of the first loop and buttonhole back to where the buttonholing of the second loop was left off, and finish by buttonholing the other half of the second loop. The picots should be added while buttonholing the loops, thus: Pin out a small loop between two buttonhole stitches and hold securely on the pin, bring up the needle from the wrong side through the last but one buttonhole stitch (Fig. 9) then buttonhole the little loop, withdraw the pin and insert the needle in its place, draw the thread up tightly and secure it in the last buttonhole stitch on the wrong side of the work.

Fig. 10 shows four methods of filling Hedebo circles, which are quite simple and easy to follow from the illustration. They consist mainly of pyramids and buttonhole stitch. When once the method of working is mastered it will be found that an endless variety of fillings may be worked by different arrangements of buttonhole stitch, which is the foundation for all this work.

The Table Centre (Fig. 11) is worked on white linen with a medium sized thread for the buttonhole edges and solid embroidery, and a fine linen thread for the lace fillings. The four flower baskets forming the elaborate motif in the centre of each repeat of the design have most exquisite stitching used to good effect in the detail of the baskets, and as a filling for some of the flowers. The satin-stitch leaves make a good contrast to the open work. The circular border of cut-work and dots, together with the cut-work

Fig. 8.

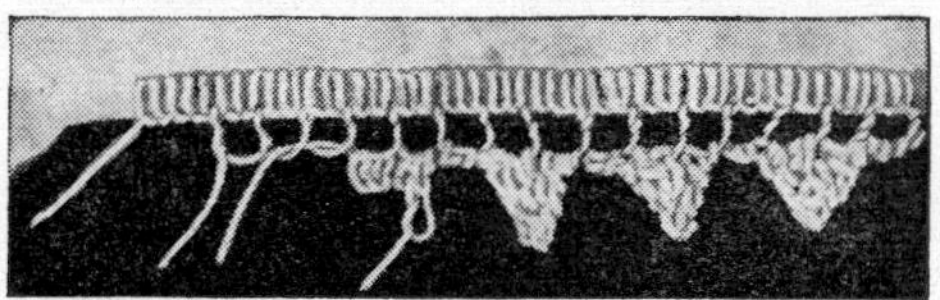

These edgings are worked straight into the edge of the material without a tracing. For Fig. 8 pyramid edging is worked in four rows and for Fig. 9 large buttonholed loops form the main decoration.

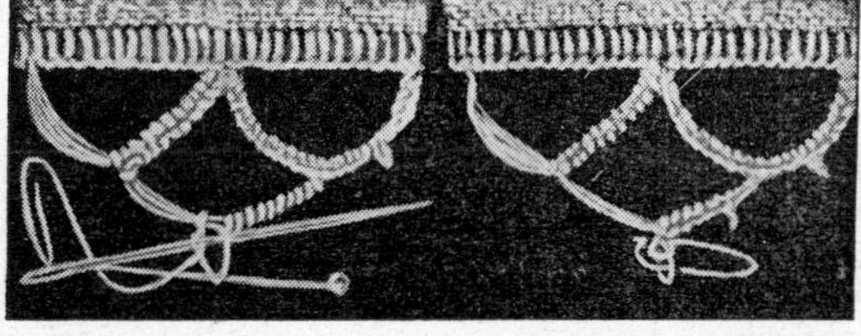

Fig. 9. Fig. 9a.

Fig. 11. A dainty d'oyley or table centre worked on white linen. Satin-stitch makes an effective contrast to the open work.

circles between the large motifs, completes the design. The outer edge which is scalloped to fit the design is finished off with a pyramid lace, bridged by buttonhole loops at the edge, while the space between the large curves, is effectively filled with groups of loops worked in tiers and finished with a pyramid edging.

A Cloth (Fig. 12), the centre motif of which, with its well-defined shapes, is particularly characteristic of Hedebo embroidery. The lace stitches filling the ovals will

Fig. 10.

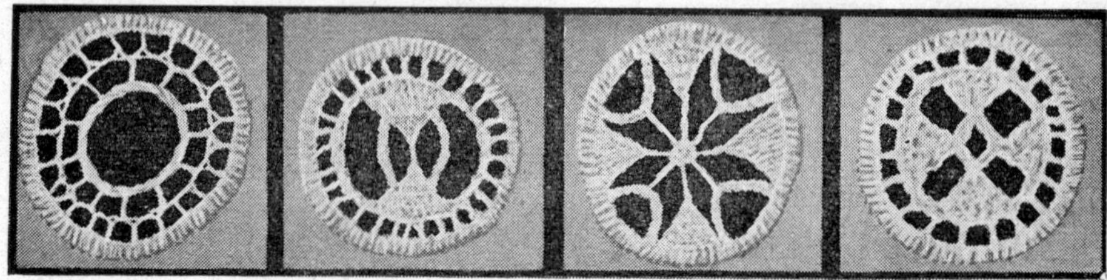

be seen to suggest the circle, and care must be taken to keep this line when working. The elongated spots between the ovals at each corner are overcast eyelets. Small circles are arranged in each scallop to form a square, and each of these has a spider's web filling. The outer scalloped edge is finished with a pyramid edging. The lace stitch used as a filling for the ovals is shown in detail in Fig. 13. Start by buttonhole stitching half of the shape, then carry a thread across the point of the oval and oversew it back, cover it with two rows of buttonholing, oversewing them each time back to the starting-point. Now work two buttonhole bars from the outer edge to the centre of the open buttonholing, and a bar with three tiny pyramids between at the top.

Fig. 12 is an unusual design for a cloth which is particularly characteristic of Hedebo embroidery. For details of the lace stitch used in the oval, see Fig. 13.

The Cosy (Fig. 14) is most effective worked on a fine lawn, with a medium-sized mercerised cotton and a fine linen thread for the filling stitches.

The embroidery shows very fine lace stitching giving almost the effect of lace insertions let into the lawn. The large motifs at the lower corners and in the centre are filled with patterns consisting of pyramids, squares and stars with twisted connecting threads and buttonholed loops. The smaller holes have spiders worked in them. It is impossible to give all the directions for working these, but any one who has studied the methods of working already described will not find it difficult either to copy these from the illustration or to work others that will be equally effective. The eyelets are in overcast stitch, and the leaves connecting the cutwork in satin-stitch.

Fig. 14.—An elaborate tea-cosy worked on a fine lawn. So fine is the embroidery that it resembles lace.

The scalloped edges are first buttonholed round, then a row of open buttonhole stitch is added, after which a border of rings connected by loops is worked in the centre of each scallop. To make these loops, wind the thread several times round a pencil or stiletto, so that they will all be the same size. Fix the end securely. Then slip the ring off the pencil and buttonhole closely over the ring of padding. The rings are attached to each other with a firm stitch as they are finished. When six have been worked they are fixed to the foundation of open buttonhole stitch with another line of close buttonhole securing each ring with two, or three stitches (Fig. 15). Now work a spider's web into each ring, leaving the centre open, complete the edging with five buttonholed loops, with picots in the centre of each scallop and small pyramids between each scallop.

A star, made up of pyramids, the foundation of which is a ring of buttonhole stitch, is a filling often used in Hedebo embroidery, being quite easy to work. Begin with a circle with forty-two buttonhole

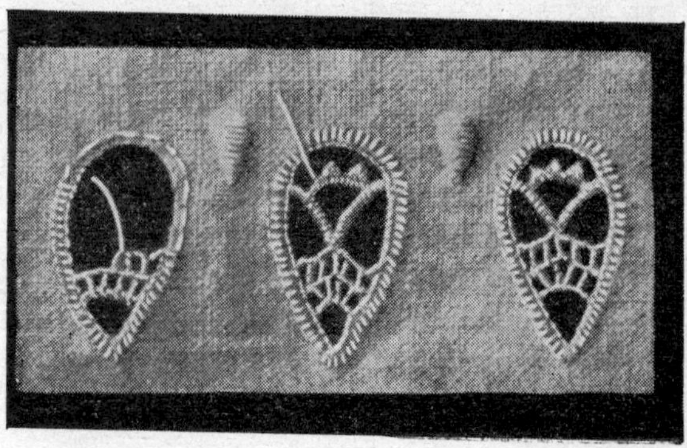

Fig. 13.

Fig. 15.

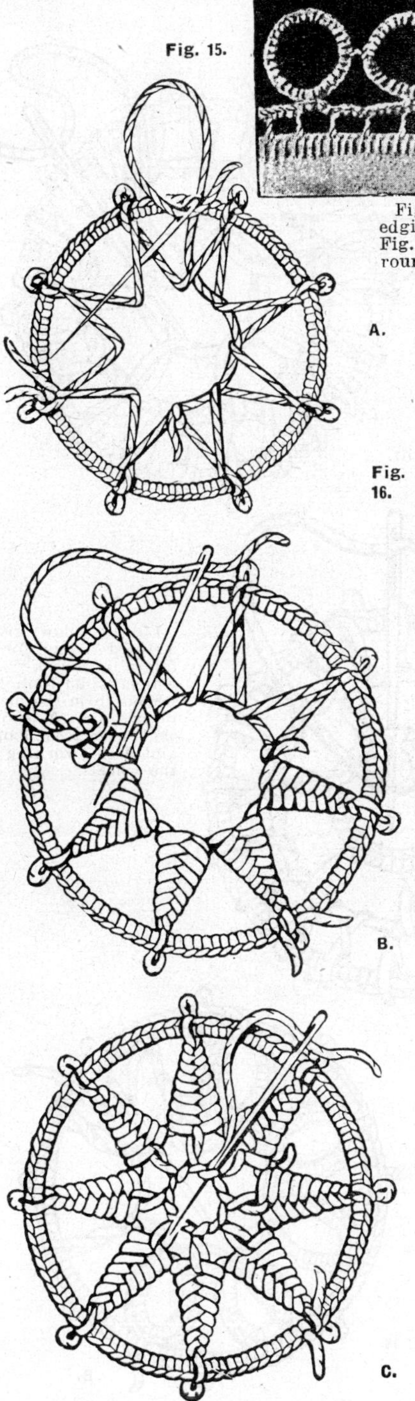

Fig. 15 shows in detail the working of the lace edging of the tea-cosy. The three diagrams in Fig. 16 show a Hedebo stitch worked in a tatted round.

A.

Fig. 16.

B.

C.

stitches worked closely on to it, six stitches are allowed for the base of each pyramid, with one stitch between. Work each pyramid in the usual way.

Another variety of this work consists of several lace stitches worked on crochet and Tatting foundations and are made as follows: Make a round of tatting or double crochet, the size of the space to be filled, and ornament the edge with picots. Tack this round on *toile cirée* and fill it in with various lace stitches. For Fig. 16, fill a round of tatting loops with eight long loops. Draw them together at the base to form a circle. Take the thread through them in the way shown in A. Then run the thread up to where one of the loops starts and darn it backwards and forwards as in Point de Reprise, to fill in the form of a vandyke as shown in B. Fill in all the loops in this way, then work eight short loops in the centre of the circle and draw together at their base.

Another filling is shown in Fig. 17.

For Fig. 18 make a wheel of eight long loops in a tatted round interlaced thus: Fasten the thread into the tatted round and take it as a loose thread to the eighth part of the round. Fasten it to the tatting and return down it, twist the cotton round the straight thread for $\frac{3}{4}$ the distance down. Take the thread to the next division of the round and repeat this until a wheel is formed, twisting the thread round the first stitch as a finish as shown in A. To finish make an oval of each arm of the wheel and work over it with buttonhole stitch. Form the foundation of the oval with a thread, which is passed through the top and bottom part of the twisted thread and work in the twisted thread to be one side of the oval.

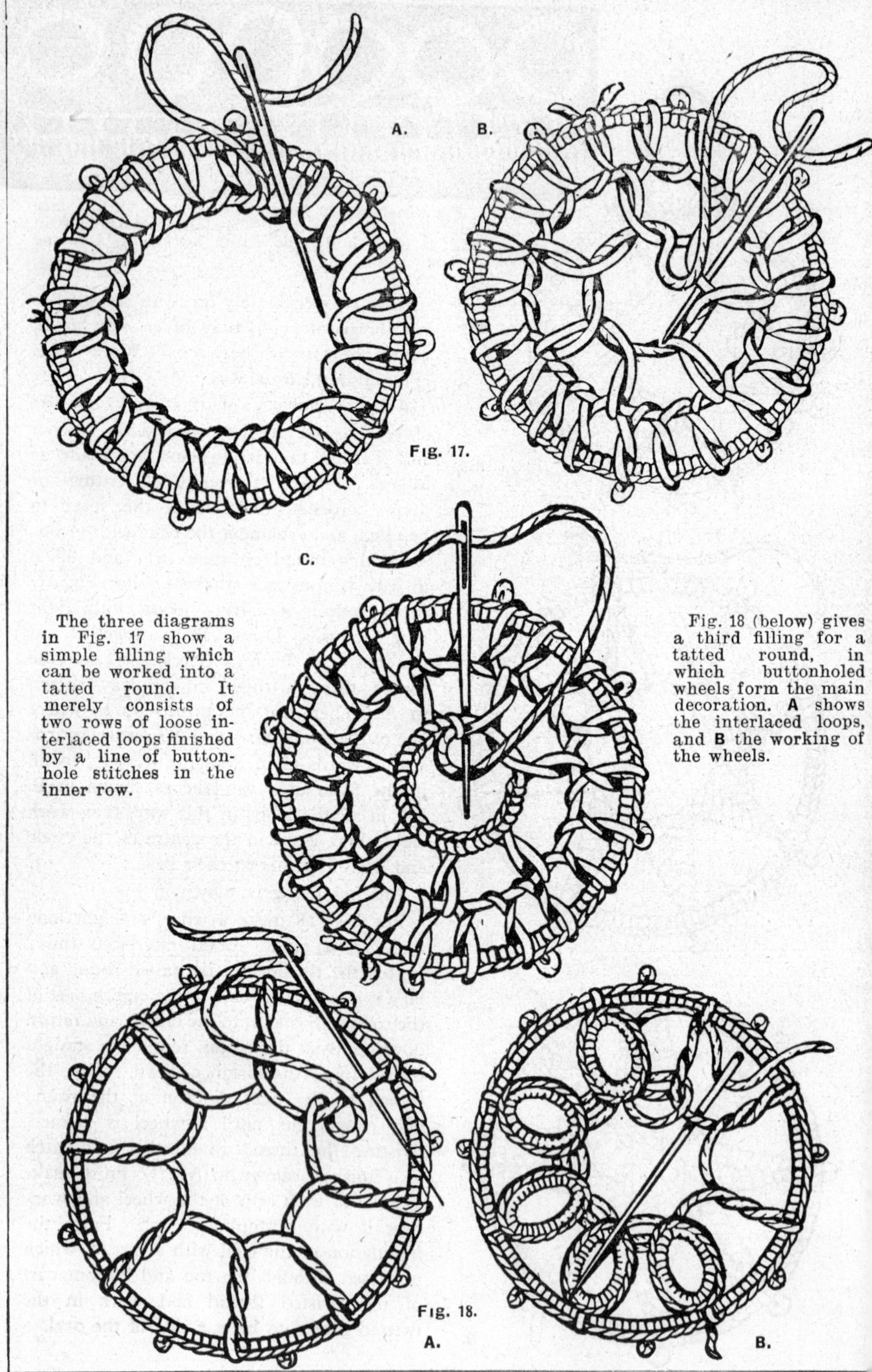

Fig. 17.

Fig. 18.

The three diagrams in Fig. 17 show a simple filling which can be worked into a tatted round. It merely consists of two rows of loose interlaced loops finished by a line of buttonhole stitches in the inner row.

Fig. 18 (below) gives a third filling for a tatted round, in which buttonholed wheels form the main decoration. **A** shows the interlaced loops, and **B** the working of the wheels.

HUCKABACK DARNING

With simple darning stitch, an endless variety of designs can be worked on huckaback linen. At one time it was much used for men's waistcoats, and is always popular because it is quick and easy to do.

Materials required:—a good quality huckaback linen of medium sized weaving; Filoselle or mecerised stranded cotton, consisting of twelve to fifteen strands; and fairly long, blunt embroidery needles.

To Work.—Fig. 1 shows clearly the method of working, which really consists of darning the silk in and out of the raised bars, taking two at a time, according to the design selected, in the huckaback cloth.

Fig. 2 shows a pattern simply composed of rows of plain darning in a dark shade of thread and one zigzag row in a lighter shade, then two rows of dark thread repeated for the length required.

With little practice one can vary the stitches in many effective ways. Fig. 3 is worked in two shades, in Twisted Stitch. For this pattern the fabric must be turned so that the double thread runs up the work instead of across. Bring the needle through the fabric on the left side of the double thread and pass the needle under the double thread, from right to left and under the next stitch above, from right to left, and continue to the end of the row. Work another similar row in the lighter shade and the next in the darker shade. Miss two rows of threads and start the pattern again. Fig. 4 shows a pattern in which two different coloured silks are used. With the darker thread work a perpendicular row of plain darning stitches, i.e. take up the double thread, but do not pass the needle through to the other side of the fabric but merely under the fabric threads. Now take the

Fig. 1 shows a method of working, which consists of darning the silk in and out of the raised bars.

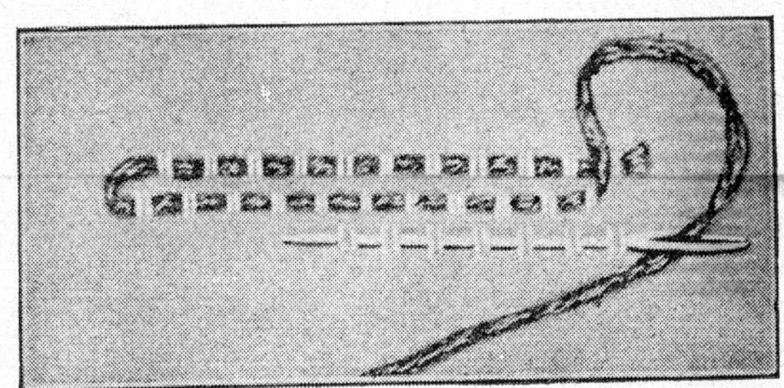

Fig. 1.

Fig. 2.

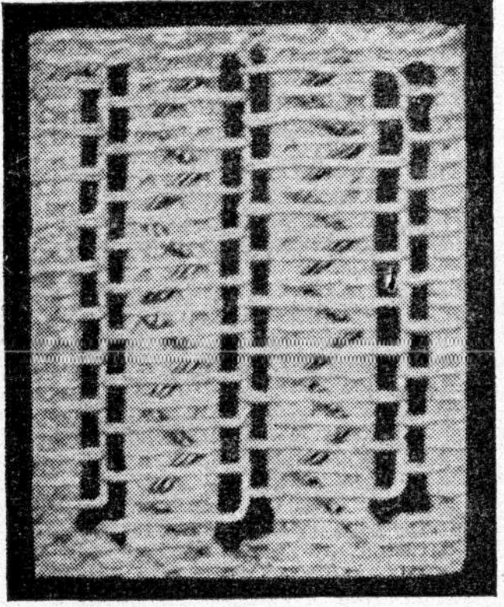

Fig. 2 is a simple pattern in two shades—dark and light. Fig. 3 is worked in twisted stitch, again in two contrasting colours.

Fig. 3.

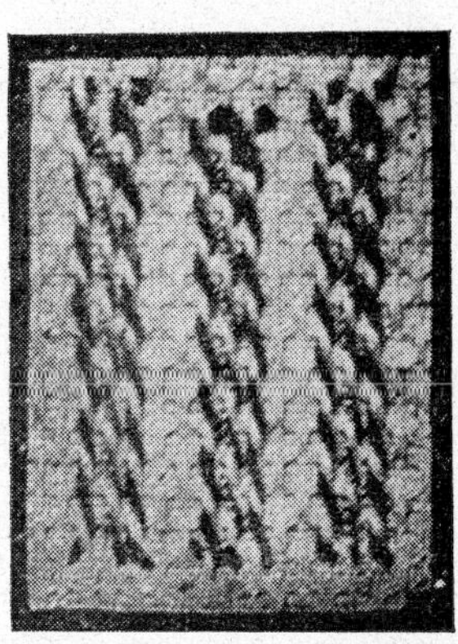

Fig. 4.

Fig. 5.

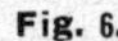

Fig. 6.

Fig. 4 is worked entirely on the right side, the stitches not piercing to the wrong side at all. Figs. 5 and 6 show two more methods of darning.

light silk, miss one row of threads, place the needle in the top thread in the next row, and pass it obliquely to the left under six double threads and again pass the needle obliquely to the left under six threads. Continue straight down the fabric in this manner, but the last time only pass the needle under three stitches, turn and work up three stitches in the opposite direction. Then again start working under six double threads and so crossing the sloping line worked in the first row.

Figs. 5 and 6 give two more methods of darning. These all over patterns make attractive cushion-covers, pochettes, etc., and are quick and easy to work.

HUNGARIAN POINT OR FLORENTINE STITCH

This work is of ancient origin, and was first done to any great extent in England during the sixteenth century. This was before the general use of upholstered furniture. Cushions, often covered with Florentine needlework, were used to soften the hard seats of stools and benches. The work reappeared at intervals during the succeeding eras.

In the early work such colours as dull pinks, greens and brown are usually to be found. Two or three colours only were used in one piece, introducing the many intermediary shades.

The patterns are built up by the stitches which are upright and, in many instances, go over the same number of threads throughout the one piece of work. Usually, too, one stitch encroaches upon the next, most often by half its depth, and so the curiously shaded and entirely distinct patterns are formed. Most of the designs are arranged so that when one row has been put in, practically all the counting is finished, for subsequent rows follow the same as the first and it is only necessary to be sure that one picks up the right number of threads. Single thread canvas is used, and wools, silks or mercerised cottons. Wool and silk are sometimes used together.

The work is usually counted from a chart. Diagram 9 shows clearly the working in a piece just started.

Fig. 8 was worked on single thread canvas of 18 holes to the inch, in 4 shades of dull blue, grey, green and old rose. Take every stitch over six threads of canvas, put in one row first, using the chart as a guide, in darkest green. When this row is worked, it is very simple to work the others as follows: after the darkest green row, one row each of mid, light and lightest green; one row each in lightest, light, mid and dark blue; one row each darkest, mid, light and lightest rose; one row each lightest, light, mid and dark green; one row each dark, mid, light and lightest blue; one row each lightest, light, mid and dark rose. Repeat all the rows in this order as required.

The design in Fig. 11 is worked on single thread canvas (22 holes to the inch) in stranded cottons—four shades of olive green and four shades of old rose. Three strands are used at a time, and it is worked in upright stitches over four threads of the canvas. It is shaded upwards from light to dark green, then light to dark rose.

Fig. 12 is worked on single thread canvas with tapestry wools, using mulberry for the dark vandykes, then 4 shades of moss-green, and 3 of mauve, and a little blue.

To work: Make all stitches upright over 4 threads, taking each new stitch two threads higher or lower than the previous stitch. With dark mulberry work 8 stitches upwards and 8 stitches downwards alternately, right across canvas. Inside the lower points, work one dark blue stitch and above this a light blue one, then fill in a light blue stitch each side, thus forming a tiny all-blue diamond. Repeat these blue diamonds 4 threads below the lowest points of the mulberry vandykes. Below the mulberry vandykes, work one very light green stitch at top and six down each side, then with light, mid and dark green in turn, fill in 3 similar rows below; with the medium green, fill in the remaining stitches above the blue diamonds now reached. With lightest mauve, work 2 rows right across immediately below the green vandykes, then one row of mid mauve and one row of dark mauve. This completes one repeat of the pattern which now starts again with the dark mulberry stripe fitted into the last row.

Fig. 13 is in vandykes and blocks of brick stitch varying in width, which gives the effect of waves. It is worked over six threads of canvas in fifteen shades of three

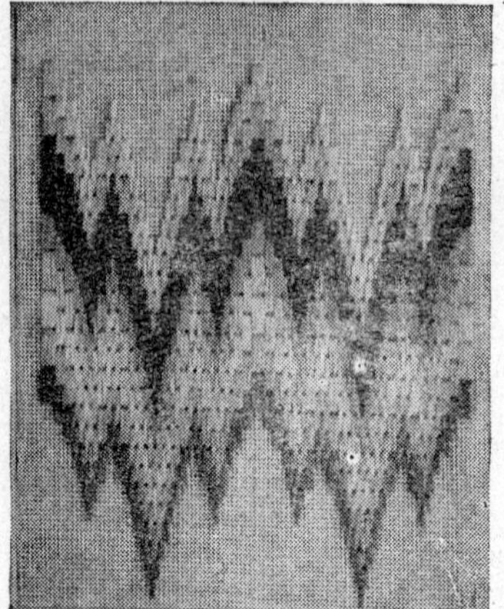

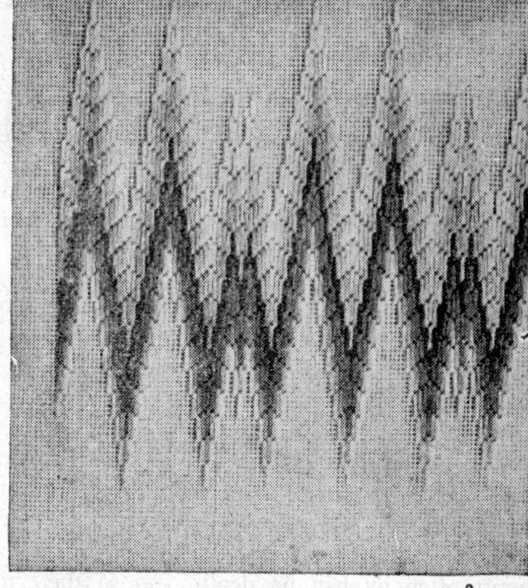

2

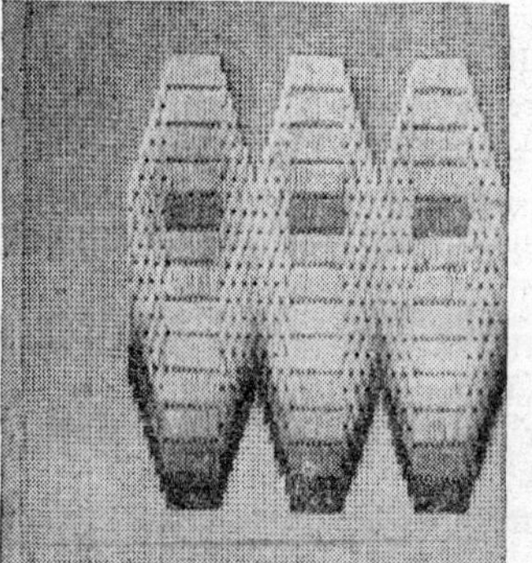

3

colours. Seven greens are used, 6 reds and one white. Fig. 13 is worked in wool, the stitch across each block of stitches in the wave is worked in silk. The one colour is taken up through the block of brick stitches, along the vandykes and up through the next block.

To work.—Start with the darkest shade of green at the bottom left-hand corner

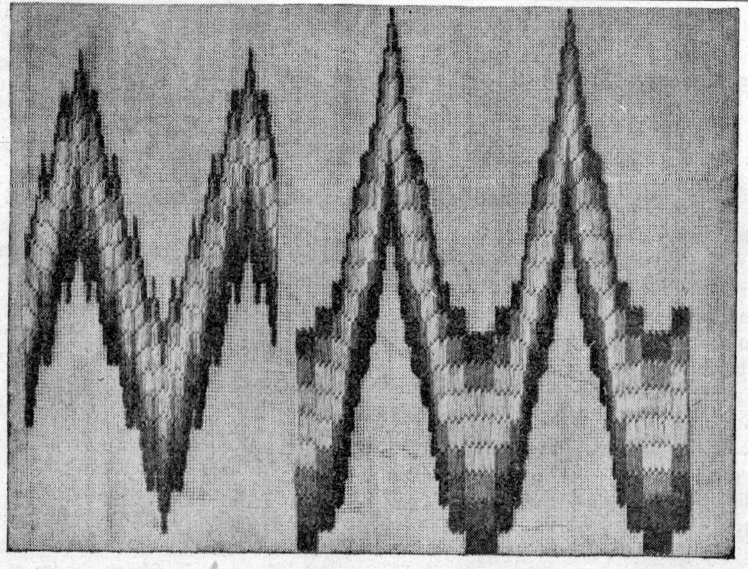

4

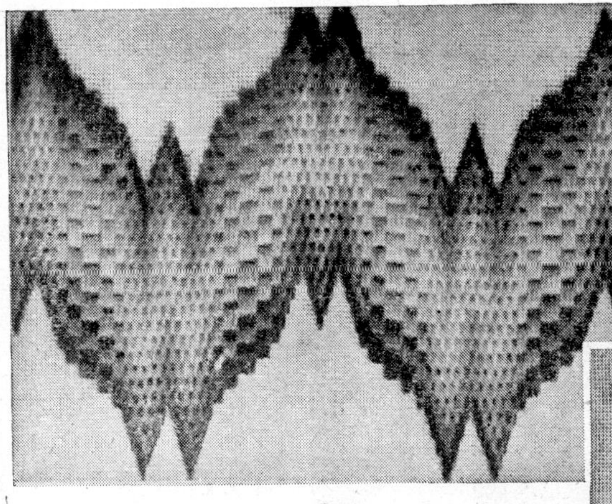

SEVEN
SIMPLE
DESIGNS
TO COPY

and work upwards and across. Each block is worked in upright stitches going over six threads of canvas. * The first block consists of three stitches, the next, four, starting three holes higher up each time, then five, six, five, four, three and two stitches. Now start the vandyke which continues on from the wave. * * Work eight upright blocks of two stitches over six threads of canvas. Now eight upright blocks downwards as seen from

6

7

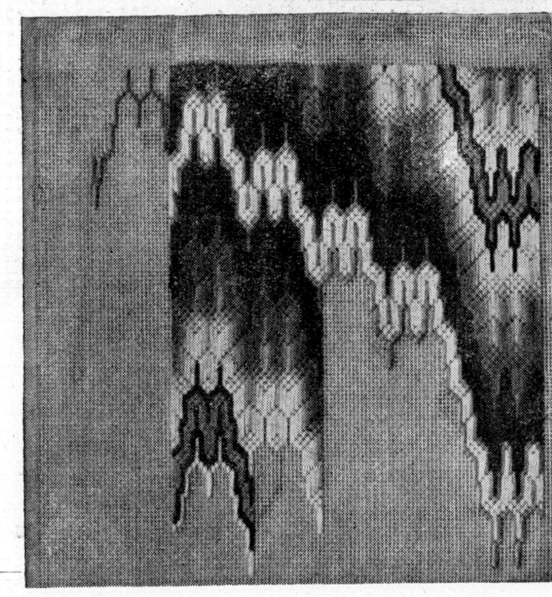

Here are some excellent designs to copy, the general working of which can easily be seen from the photographs. In Nos. 6 and 7 the design is outlined first before being filled in. With the exception of No. 5 these designs are reproduced by kind permission of the Victoria and Albert Museum.

AN ATTRACTIVE BLOTTER

Fig. 8.

FOLLOW THE SIMPLE CHART FOR WORKING

Fig. 9.

ABOVE—THE WORKING OF THE STITCH WHICH IS DONE IN ZIG-ZAG ROWS

Fig. 10.

A FLORENTINE BAG

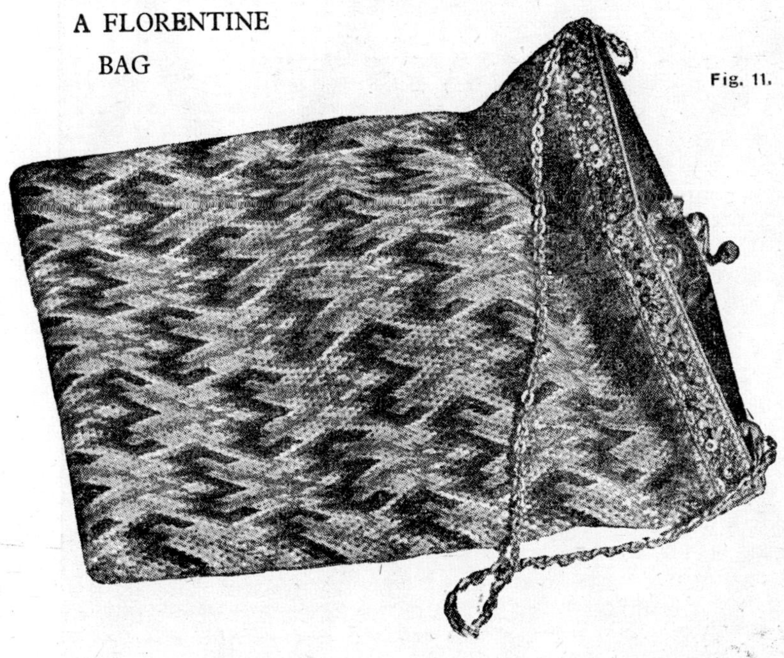

Fig. 11.

the illustration. Repeat from * * twice more. Going upwards, work two blocks of two stitches over six threads. Repeat from * as often as required.

Then the next darkest shade of green is worked as described before, and so on until the lightest green is reached. Then work in the reds, starting at the deepest and working down to the lightest, then the row of white. Now start again with the deepest green and repeat for as many designs as required. This is quite a simple pattern and most effective. It could be worked equally well in silk on finer canvas. Care must be taken to count the first row accurately. When finished, work the horizontal stitch in silk the same colour across the top of each block.

Fig. 14 is worked in blocks of three upright stitches, starting the next block halfway up the last. This pattern can be worked in small vandykes. Starting at the bottom left-hand corner in light brown silk or wool, working upwards for three blocks * downwards for two, upwards for two. Repeat from * as often as required. The next row is in dark brown, the next in light and so on. Across each block work a horizontal stitch. The first row in light brown, the second in dark brown and so on alternately.

Fig. 15 is worked horizontally in vandykes on single thread canvas. Starting at the bottom right-hand corner, work in blocks of two stitches over five horizontal threads in dark red. The next block of stitches is started three threads to the left and one higher. Repeat once more. Now start three threads to the right and one higher, working over five threads of canvas as before, then three threads to the right and one higher again. Repeat for length required.

Start the next row in bright red and work in the same way. Then work one row in green and one in white. Now repeat starting with dark red. Across the end of each block work a stitch in gold silk.

Fig. 16 is worked horizontally over two threads of canvas in two shades of pink wool. The centre of the deeper pink

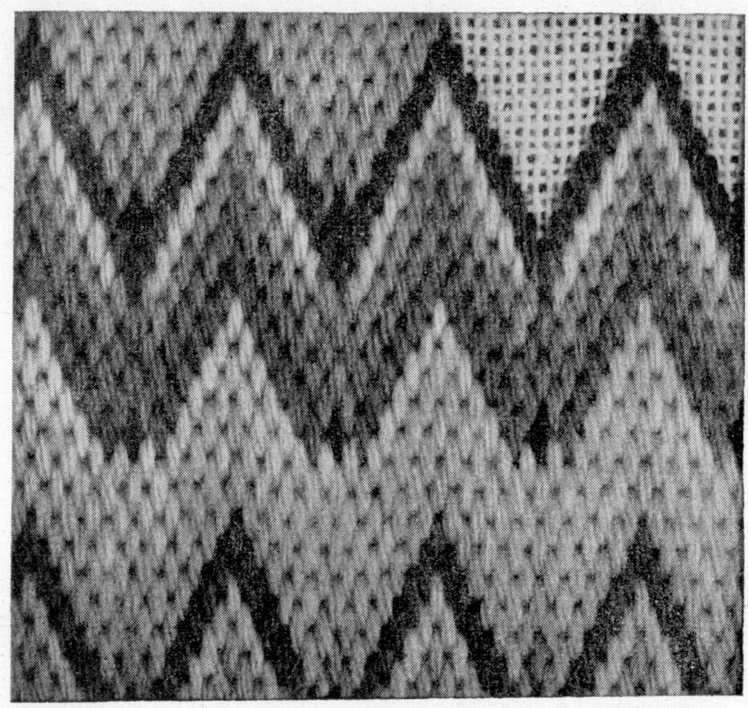

Above, Fig. 12, and below, Fig. 13.

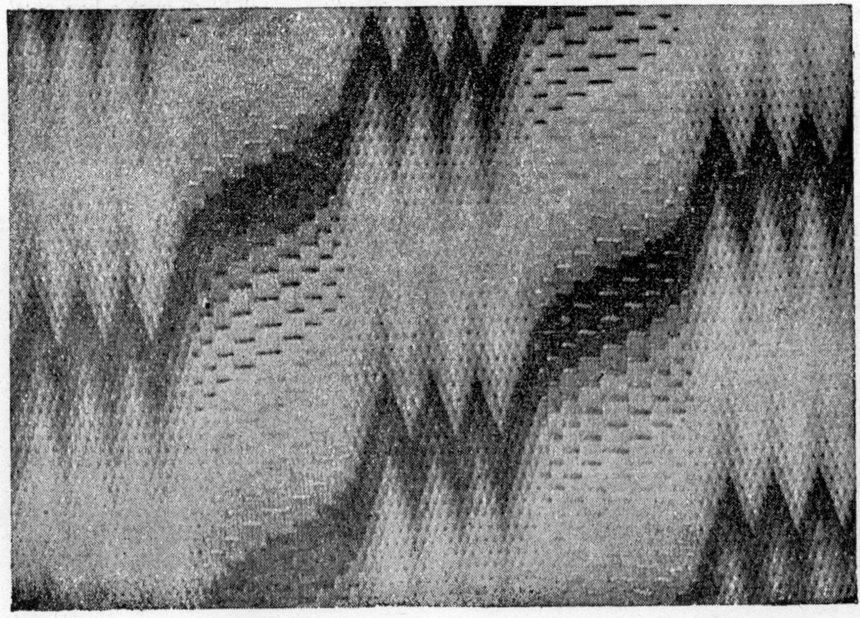

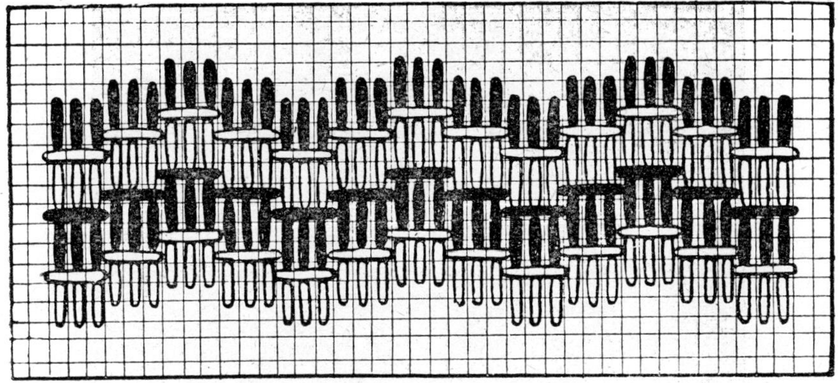

Fig. 14.

diamond shapes is in gold, and of the paler shade, white. The pattern can be clearly followed from the chart.

Fig. 17 is worked on single thread canvas in green, brown and white wools. Starting at the point A in dark green, work one upright stitch over four threads, then one hole to the right (still on the same line) work one upright stitch over two threads, then one hole to the right and on the same line, work another upright stitch over two threads, then one hole to the right and on the same line, work one upright stitch over four threads.

Now with brown wool work one upright stitch over two threads above the green stitch at the point. One hole to the right on the same line, work another upright stitch over two threads, one hole to the right on the same line one upright stitch over four threads, one hole to the right on the same line, work one upright stitch over two threads, then one hole to the right on the same line, work one upright stitch over two threads.

With the white wool, work one upright stitch over two threads above the brown stitch at the point. One hole to the right on the same line; work one upright stitch over two threads, one hole to the right on the same line, work one upright stitch over four threads, one hole to the right on the same line, work one upright stitch over two threads, one hole to the right on the same line, work one upright stitch over two threads.

Now start again with green and work one upright stitch over four threads above the white stitch at point A and continue as before. For the other side, work in the same way only to the left instead of the right as is clearly shown in the chart.

Fig. 18 is worked in wool. The diamonds are black through the centre, pink at either side and white at either end. The alternate diamonds are black through the centre, fawn on either side, and white at either end.

Start working at A in black wool as seen on the chart.

1st row.—Work one upright stitch over three threads of canvas, then * one hole to the right and one thread lower down, work one upright stitch over three threads of canvas, one hole to the right and one thread higher up, work one upright stitch over three threads of canvas. Repeat from * five times. **2nd row** is the same as the first and worked in black. **3rd row.**—Start at C with pink wool, work one upright stitch over three threads of canvas. * One hole to the right and one thread higher up work one stitch over three threads. One hole to the right and one thread lower down, work one stitch over three threads. Repeat from * four times.

4th row.—Start at D, work one upright stitch over three threads of canvas. * miss one hole, work one upright stitch over three threads of canvas. Repeat from * twice more. **5th row.**—Start at E with white

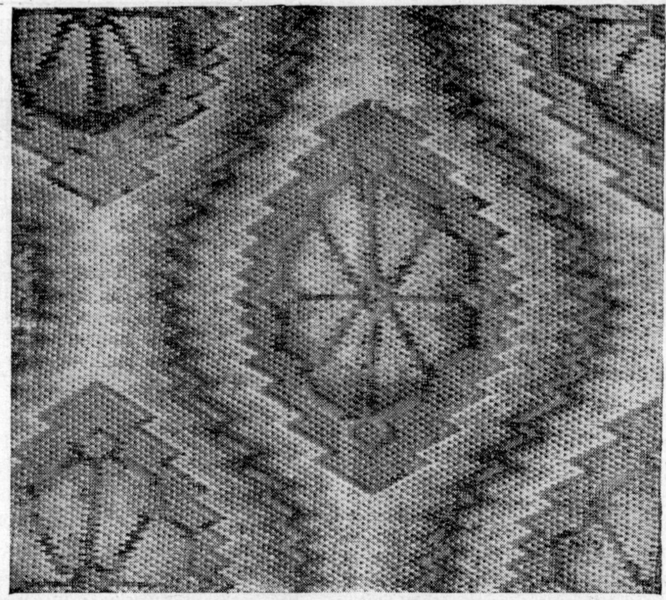

An interesting specimen of Florentine work from the Victoria and Albert Museum. The canvas threads are left unworked to form part of the pattern.

TWO HISTORIC PIECES OF FLORENTINE WORK

Another Museum piece, described on page 226.

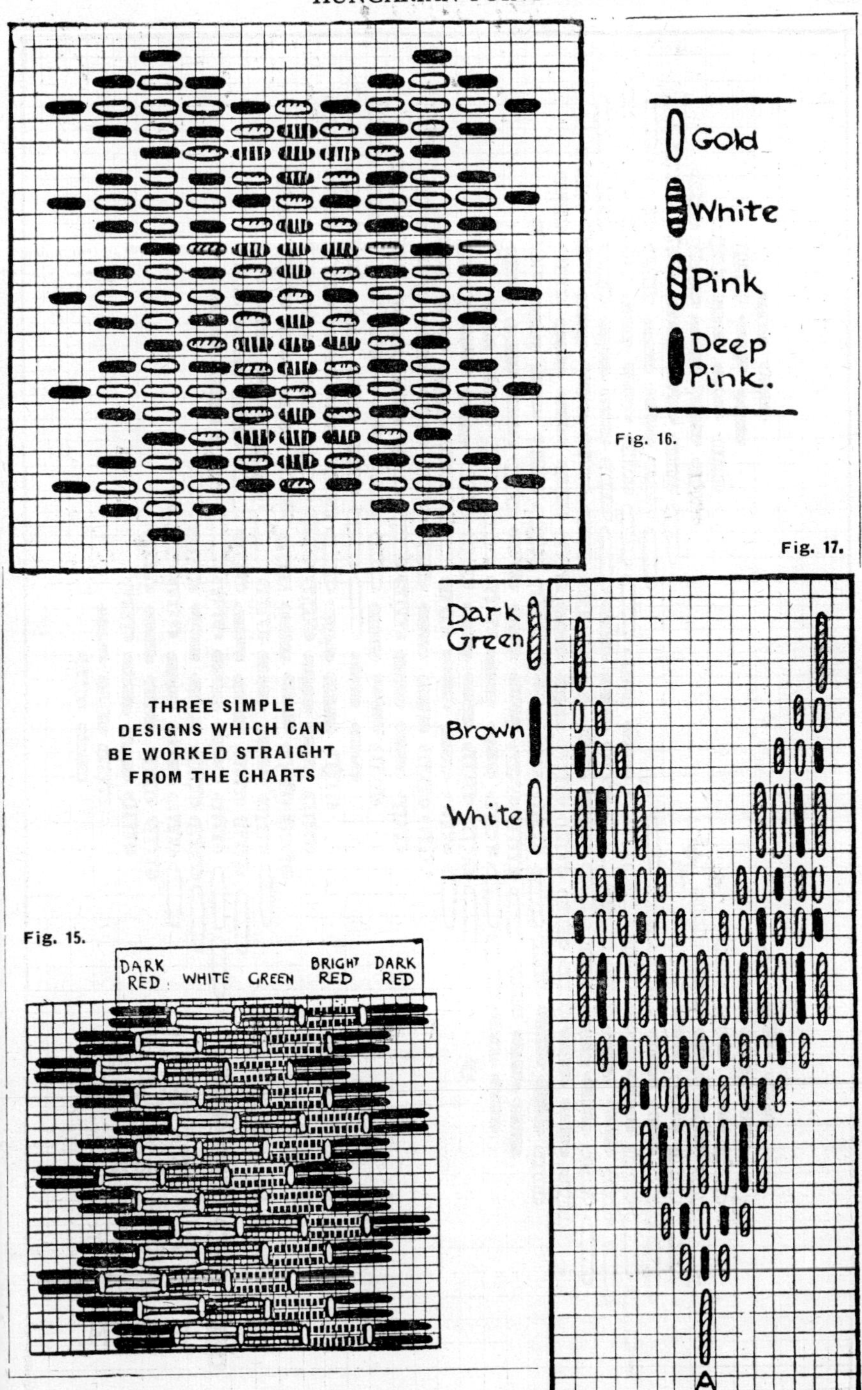

Fig. 16.

Fig. 17.

THREE SIMPLE DESIGNS WHICH CAN BE WORKED STRAIGHT FROM THE CHARTS

Fig. 15.

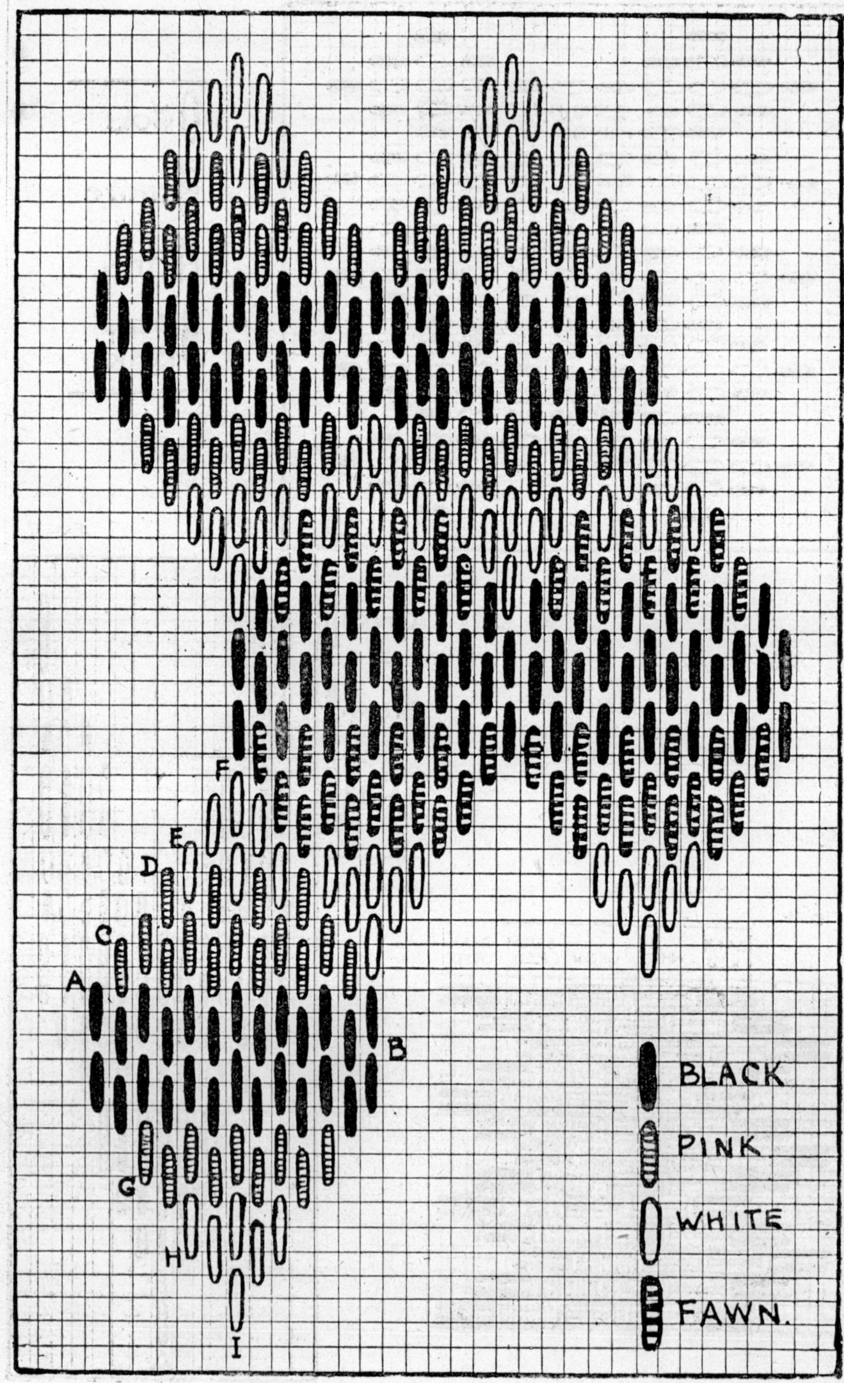

Fig. 18

GAY DESIGNS IN FLORENTINE STITCH ON A MOROCCAN MAT

By kind permission of the Victoria and Albert Museum.

wool and work one upright stitch over three threads of canvas. * One hole to the right and two holes higher up, work one upright stitch over three threads, one hole to the right and two holes lower down, work one upright stitch over three threads of canvas. Repeat once from *.

6th row.—Work one upright stitch in the centre at F over three threads of canvas. **7th row.**—Start at G with pink wool, work one upright stitch over three threads. * One hole to the right and one thread lower down, work one stitch over three threads of canvas, one hole to the right, and one thread higher up, work one stitch over three threads of canvas. Repeat from * three times. **8th row.**—Start at H with white wool and work one stitch over three threads of canvas. * One hole to the right and one thread lower down, work one stitch over three threads of canvas, one hole to the right and one thread higher up work one stitch over three threads of canvas. Repeat from * once more. **9th row.**—Work one upright stitch over three threads of canvas at I, thus completing the diamond. Work the diamonds alternately as will be clearly seen from the chart for the length required.

The lower design on page 222 is a very old piece of Florentine work. The diamonds are in alternate rows of large and small.

For the large ones, three rows of beige are worked over two threads of canvas, then three rows of biscuit, two rows of a very pale blue, and the centre is filled in with a deeper blue. There is one row in black as an outline, then two rows of a yellowy green and four rows of olive. Then the row of smaller diamonds begins. The smaller ones have the one row of black outline, then two rows of biscuit, two rows of a reddy pink, three rows of salmon pink, and the centre is a very small diamond consisting of about eight stitches in all, in white.

These two sets of colouring are used throughout. In the smaller row the diamonds are of alternate shades. The illustration clearly shows the gradation of colours. In the centre of this piece the date (1718) and the initials no longer visible, were worked in afterwards.

INITIALS

Embroidered initials are more often used than any other form of fancy stitchery, as their purpose is useful as well as decorative. Daintily worked on lingerie they make it attractively personal, or simply and practically worked in cross stitch or satin stitch they make a neat method of identification.

Initials may be worked in innumerable ways, a few of the most popular and commonly used being given here.

Cross-stitch Initial.—This is probably one of the most frequently used, as it is quick and clear for marking household linen and blankets. For linen, all sized initials are used according to the article, but generally they are small and clear. To work these, a fast dye in stranded cotton is best. If it is possible to work straight on to the article, it is better to do so. But in some cases it is not possible to count the threads, so tack on a fine piece of canvas, in the position required, and work over that, always keeping the crosses in the same direction. For blankets, the larger cross-stitched initial is best. Fig. 2 is worked in the way described above and is produced in actual size—$\frac{3}{4}$ inches; letters of this style are easily drawn on graph-paper.

Initials worked in Chain stitch are also simple to work and good for marking heavy materials. The outline only can be worked, or else the initial entirely filled in with chain stitch—both being equally good.

INITIALS WORKED ON LINEN

These are embroidered in white and are usually worked in satin stitch which can be varied in many ways. For these a padding cotton is needed, or if it is only a small initial two different thicknesses of mercerised embroidery cotton, the fineness depending upon the work.

Padded Initials.—The simplest method of working an initial is to pad it well first. For the padding, split stitch round the edges of the letter just inside the outline. Still

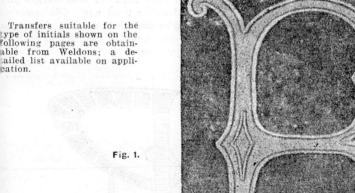

Transfers suitable for the type of initials shown on the following pages are obtainable from Weldons; a detailed list available on application.

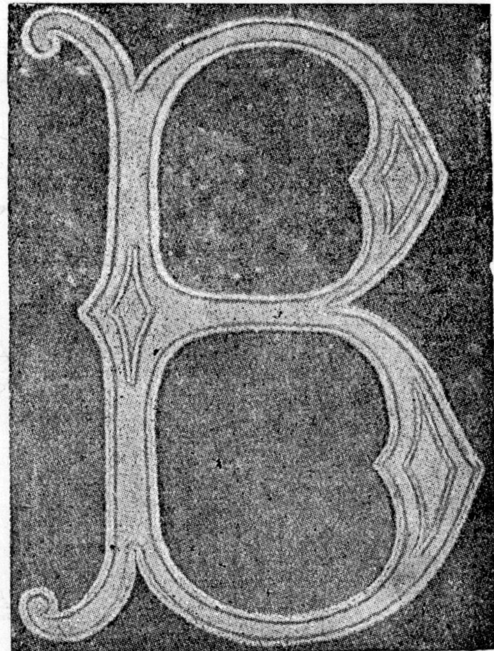

Fig. 1.

A bold initial seven inches high worked in appliqué which is especially suitable for a baby's cot cover.

keeping the shape of the letter, fill up inside the outline with larger split stitches fairly close together. If the initial is small, do two more rows in the centre, just enough to raise it a little, but if the space is large, more padding must be done.

Work the initial in finer cotton in satin-stitch, being careful to keep the shape, and always working from right to left (Fig. 8).

Fig. 3 is padded in the same way as Fig. 8. Work from the top left-hand corner in satin stitch or trailing stitch, which is similar to overcast stitch, except that it is worked over two or three loose trailing threads. This is necessary as the thin part of the "C" is not padded. The eyelet hole between the two halves of the "C" is worked as in Broderie Anglaise (which see). In Fig. 4 the outline of the "T" is worked in satin stitch. The centre is filled with well-padded spots at even distances. Care must be taken to keep these round, and not to let them touch the satin-stitch edges.

Another method of working is shown in Fig. 5. The edges are satin stitched and padded in the usual way. The centre is worked in seed stitch, which is simply two small stitches worked one over the other in irregular rows.

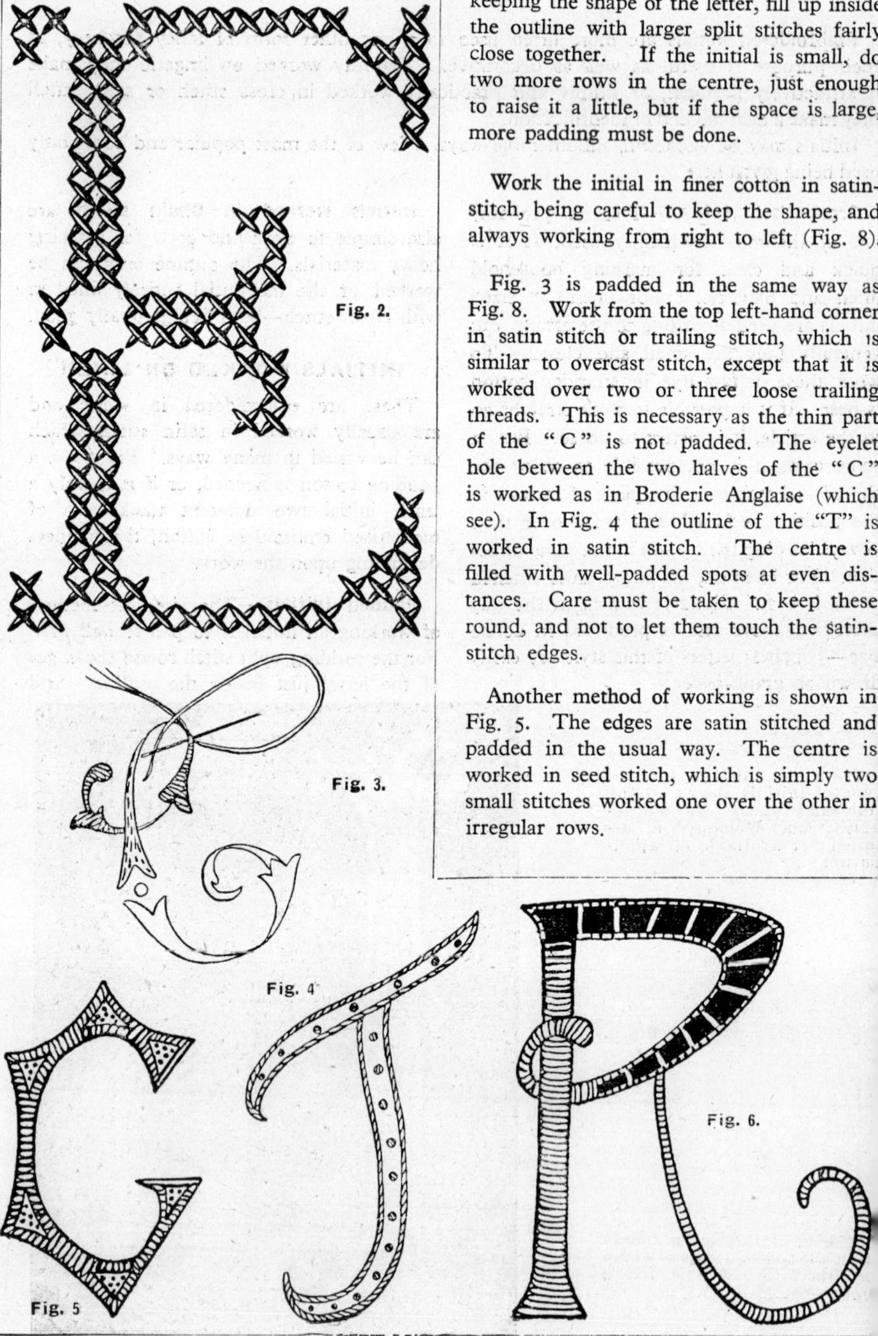

Fig. 2.

Fig. 3.

Fig. 4

Fig. 5

Fig. 6.

A more elaborate initial is shown in Fig. 7, which combines satin stitch, seeding and raised spots and would look well on such articles of household linen as sheets, pillow cases, towels, etc. The illustration shows clearly how it is worked.

Fig. 6 is worked in ladder stitch and satin stitch and makes a striking and unusual initial. For details of working ladder-stitch, see Broderie Anglaise.

A variation of satin stitch is shown in the working of the "U" in Fig. 11, which is worked in satin stitch with a division down the centre. This is padded in two halves. The satin stitch is taken down into the centre. The eyelet holes are worked last in the usual way.

A Richelieu background for an initial is effective. The edges are button-holed in the usual way. The bars are worked from the edge to the letter, with picots breaking the lines. The centre can be filled with any of the fillings above mentioned, but in Fig. 9 raised dots in satin stitch were used. This method of working is very attractive.

Another variation is to pad the initial well before starting. Fig. 15 (taken from the White Work sampler) shows a

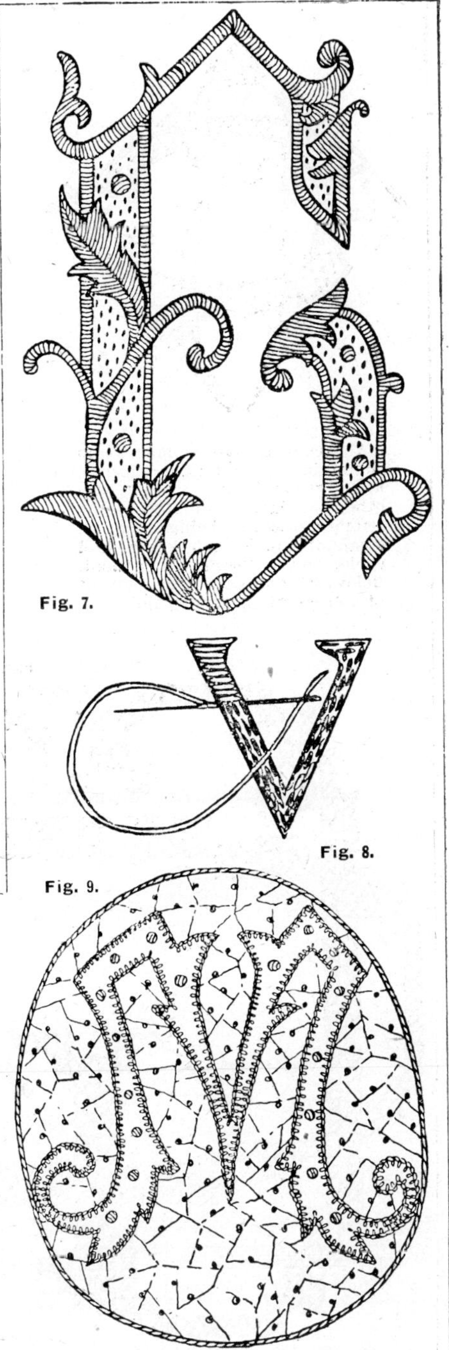

Fig. 7.

Fig. 8.

Fig. 9.

Fig. 11.

Fig. 10.

MONOGRAMS

Fig. 12.

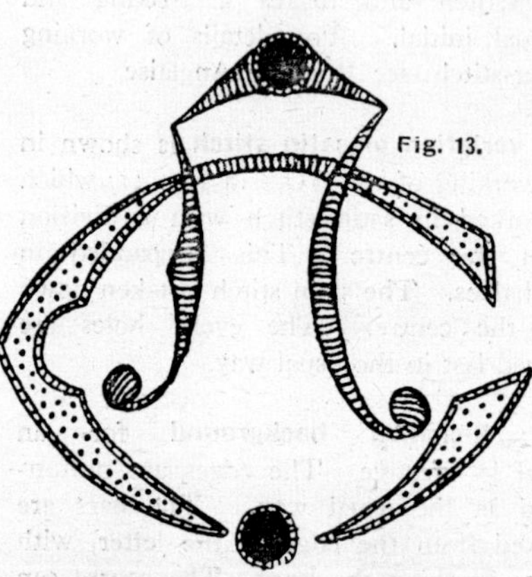

Fig. 13.

Above—an attractive monogram combining satin stitch, trailing, and French knots. Right, another variation of the same stitches, seeding being used instead of the French knots, and eyelet holes being introduced. Below, a decorative arrangement of a cross stitch monogram.

Fig. 14.

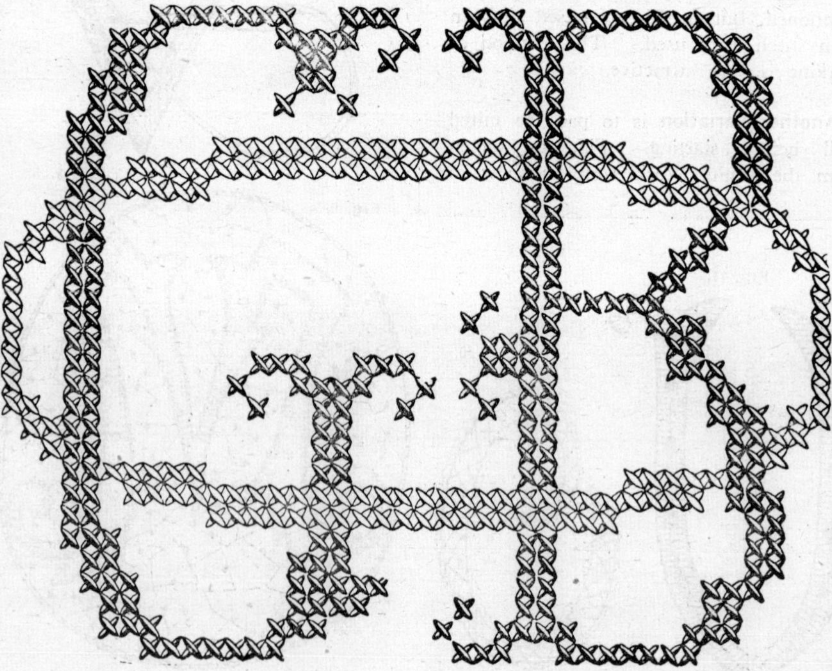

monogram with "M.A.C." The two long arms of the "A" are worked in satin stitch with three loose threads which are taken over and under the satin stitch as it is worked. This is very effective when finished and is simple to do. In the wider parts of the "C" the threads are drawn, then overcast and filled in with a fancy filling.

Fig. 10 is worked entirely in crossed back stitch, the wrong side of the back stitch being the side seen in the illustration. The outline is finished in stem stitch.

An Appliqué Initial is shown in Fig. 1. The initial is first traced on to the material to be applied, then the edges cut out, leaving about an eighth of an inch beyond the outline. Tack into position, trim the edges slightly and hem it down as invisibly as possible with thread to match. The edge is then worked in satin stitch over a fine cord, which gives the slightly raised effect.

Fig. 15.—Raised satin stitch and a drawn thread filling make this unusual monogram, which is taken from the sampler in the White Work chapter.

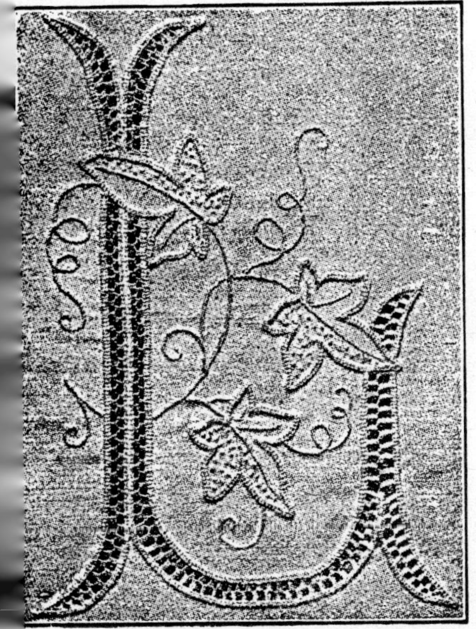

Fig. 16.—Open buttonhole filling is used for this letter L. The detail is shown in Fig. 17. The leaves are worked in buttonhole stitch and seeding and the stalks stem stitch.

Open buttonhole filling is used for the letter L in Fig. 16. Work the buttonholed filling in two rows down the L as seen in the illustration. To work this filling first outline the L with running stitches, then, beginning at the top, take the thread into the left edge, secure it there and buttonhole half-way back. Secure the thread in the right edge and buttonhole half-way back, and so on, backwards and forwards until the space is filled in. The outlines are then buttonholed, with the purl edge inwards. Down the centre of the L is worked double buttonhole stitch. When this is done the material is cut away from underneath. The leaves are in buttonhole stitch with seeding down one side. Stem stitch is used for the stalks.

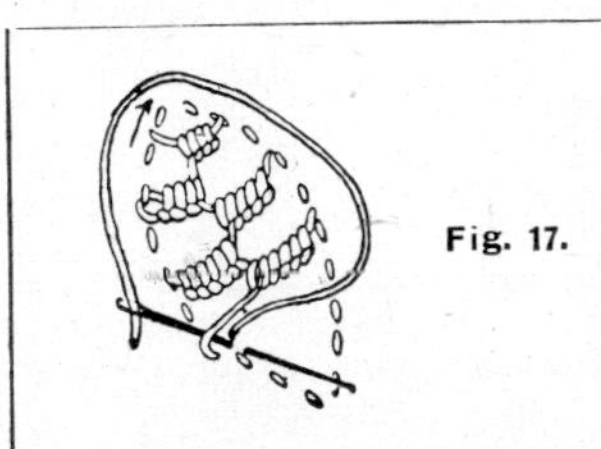

Fig. 17.

MONOGRAMS

There are two ways of arranging letters for monograms from ordinary alaphabet transfers:

Method 1.—Cut out from the transfer sheet each letter separately, allowing only a narrow margin round the ink. Lay the letters on a piece of paper, wax side downwards, so that the letters are the right way round and decide which portions shall overlap which, and interlace the letters. Turn the arranged monogram over and paste down on paper, ink side uppermost, and iron off in the usual way.

Method 2.—Iron off one letter on the material first, arrange the other in position and iron off. When this method is used care must be taken in the working to get the interlacing right as far as possible, one portion being over and the next under. When three letters are employed, iron off the surname initial first, then arrange the other two. It should be easy to see through the transfer paper the letter which has already been transferred.

For the monogram in Fig. 12, trail round the outline of the letter " G ", the centre of which fill in with small French knots. The " R " is worked in satin stitch.

In **Fig. 13** trail round the outline of the letter " C ", and fill in the centre with seeding. The wider part of the " A " is worked in satin stitch, padded well first. The rest is trailed. Work the eyelet holes in the usual way.

IVORY EMBROIDERY

This is a variety of embroidery upon canvas, one of the first advantages of which, is that it requires far less care in counting the threads than does the ordinary work on this material. Another advantage is, that it embraces a far greater range of designs, as it is not necessary to work geometric patterns set in squares, triangles, stars or cross-shapes.

The work is known as Ivory embroidery, from the fact of its being entirely worked in white, at least, as far as the fillings are concerned.

Canvas ready to work, with outlines only can be bought and the worker can put in any fillings. Silk and mercerised threads are used in preference to cotton, and Filoselle is the most useful, as it is already split and can be used either coarse or fine according to the part of the pattern it is used for.

For less expensive work, white or the palest shade of ivory flax thread can be used, but the effect given by the silk will be found more satisfactory on the whole, as it is softer.

A Japanese gold thread makes a good outline for this work, and shows up well against the white fillings. Coloured Filoselles also make good outlines. Ordinary outline stitch is often used, the number of threads over which the stitches are carried varying with the quality of the canvas.

The make of canvas used is "Single thread," or "Tammy cloth." The fillings must always be put in before the outlines, as these will help to cover any slight irregularities there may be at the edges of the work. Use a good-sized long-eyed needle with a blunt point. Tapestry needles will be found most convenient.

Care must be taken not to split any of the threads of the canvas in making a stitch. Never use a knot in the thread and always take a fresh needleful directly the silk shows any signs of wear.

As a general rule, the smaller and more delicate fillings are suitable for the finer and more elaborate portions of the patterns, but this rule is subject to exceptions.

This work is suitable for tea-cloths, table centres, book covers, work bags, blotters, etc.

Simple Fillings of Straight Stitches.—This is almost the simplest filling it is possible to have, for it consists merely of straight stitches arranged in horizontal rows, those of one row alternating with those of the next. Each stitch is upright in direction and is taken over two threads of canvas only. A variation may be made by working the stitches horizontally instead of vertically and by placing them in pairs instead of singly. When a large space is to be filled the stitches may be taken over a greater number of threads. In Fig. 1 the stitch is taken over two threads only, but may be taken over four, six or even eight, where space will allow. One thread of canvas only must be left between each stitch or the stitches in the next row will not fit in sufficiently closely.

Simple Filling in Diagonal Stitches is equally easy (Fig. 2). The stitches are taken diagonally over two threads instead of straight. The stitches in the second row also alternate with those of the first. These fillings are especially useful when a small and intricate space is to be covered, as there is little difficulty in managing the stitches neatly when they approach the edge of the design. With a stitch requiring many threads there may not be sufficient space to work the whole pattern.

Striped Fillings are useful when there are broad, open spaces sufficiently roomy to allow the fillings to be arranged in the form of stripes. The first stripe consists of a row of vertical stitches, each taken over three threads of canvas and with two threads left between each stitch. Below this is a row of stitches slanting upwards from right to left, each carried over two threads, so that they are rather smaller than those in the preceding row. These stitches are placed as closely as the canvas will allow (Figs. 3 and 4). In Fig. 4 the two lines of stitches are similar but their arrangement is reversed, the longer ones—those over three

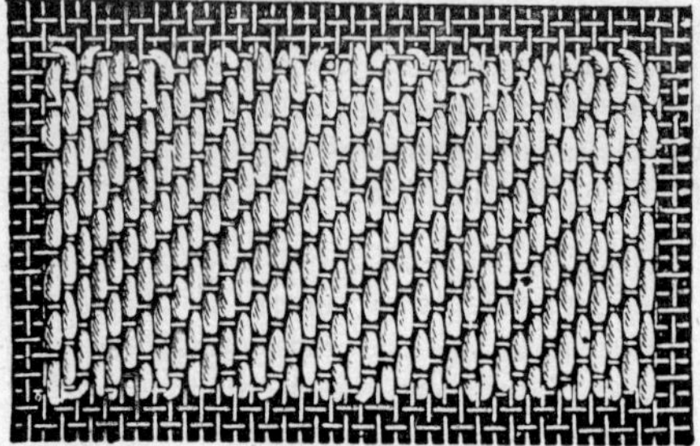

Fig. 1.—SIMPLE FILLING OF STRAIGHT STITCHES

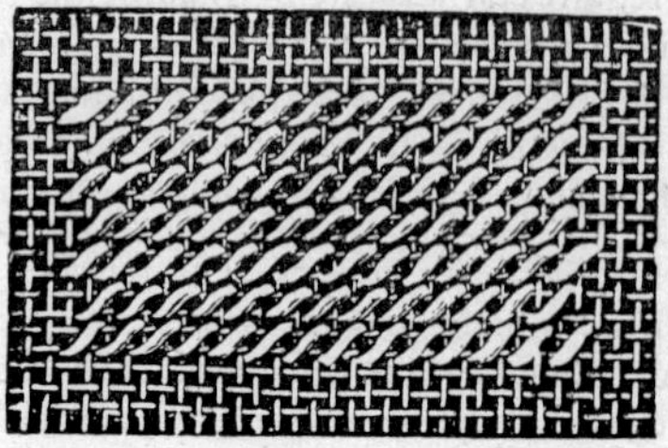

Fig. 2.—SIMPLE FILLING OF DIAGONAL STITCHES

threads—being slanting, the smaller ones over two threads being straight. The slanting stitches are the same as those used in working one half of a cross-stitch.

Simple Darned Fillings.—(Figs. 5, 6 and 7.)—Fig. 5 consists of straight lines of stitches, and is, in fact, simple darning, each stitch being carried over three threads of the material. The needle then passes under one thread, over three, under one, and so on. In the next line the thread that is picked up is the middle one of the three that were passed over in the preceding line. The stitches are placed as closely together as the meshes of the canvas will permit. This stitch allows a considerable amount of variation, and may be worked with the stitches running horizontally or vertically as shown in Figs. 6 and 7. These two details should be noticed, showing how necessary it is to shorten the stitches in order to fit them into the space that is to be covered by them. It will be seen that in places it is not possible to take longer stitches over more than two or even one thread of canvas. Any imperfections thus caused by the curves of the design will be covered by the row of outline stitch or gold thread, which will afterwards be carried round it.

Vandyke Darnings. (Figs. 8 and 9.)—Fig. 9 is more complicated than those given before as the stitches are arranged to form a waved or vandyked pattern. The stitches are all the same length, each passing over three threads of canvas and under one. For six lines the single thread is picked up just one thread below the single one that was picked up in the preceding line. In the next six lines the single thread is always one mesh above that which was picked up before; then it is below again for six lines, then above and so on.

Fig. 8 is similar, but here the broad lines are arranged to alternate with similar, but

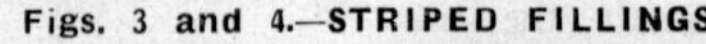

Figs. 3 and 4.—STRIPED FILLINGS

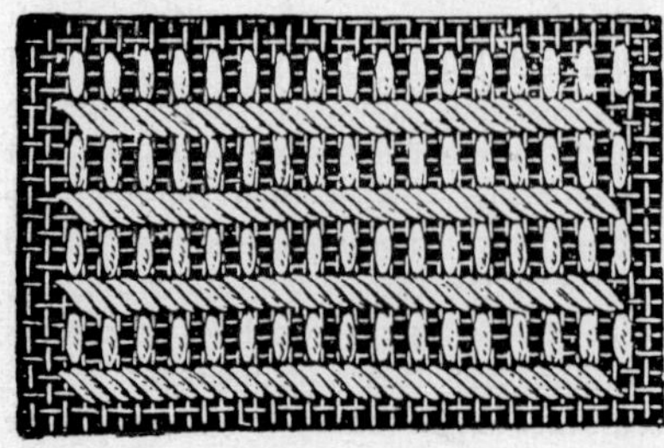

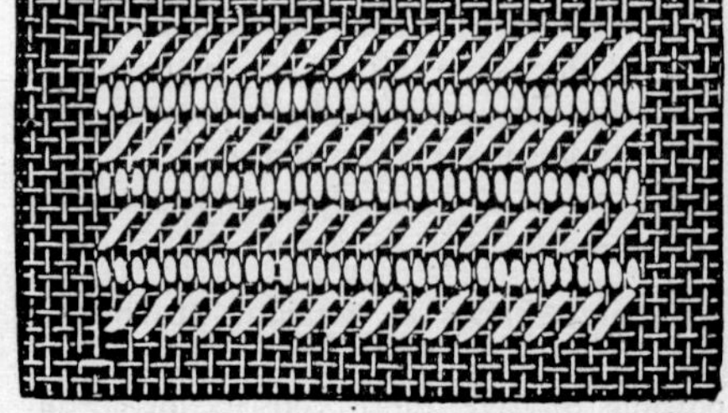

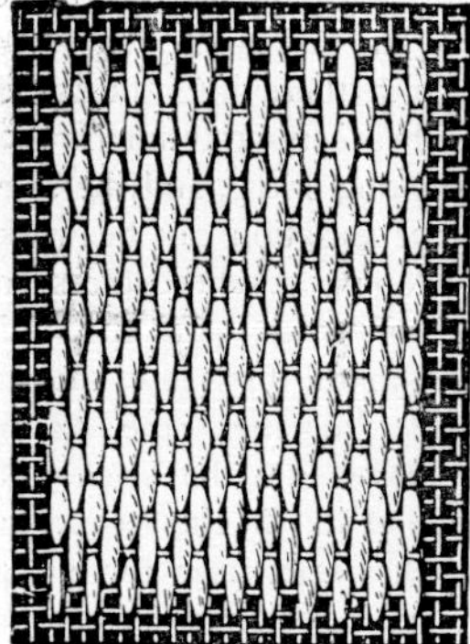

Fig. 5.—SIMPLE DARNED FILLING

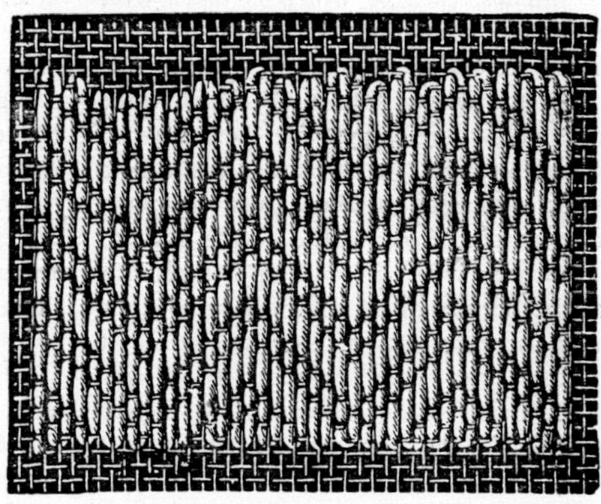

Fig. 8.—DOUBLE VANDYKE DARNING

narrower ones. Take the needle over three, * under one, over one, under one, over three. Repeat from * down the line. In the next line the two stitches which are taken under one thread only of the canvas must be just one thread lower than those of the preceding line. Work thus for eight lines, then work eight in which the two small stitches are one thread higher than those in the preceding line, and when eight lines are finished in this way, work again with the single stitches sloping downwards.

Turkish Stitch Filling.—This arrangement of strokes goes by various names and is half cross-stitch and back stitch. Fig. 10 not only shows how effective it is, but how easily it can be repeated as required. It requires two rows, first a row of

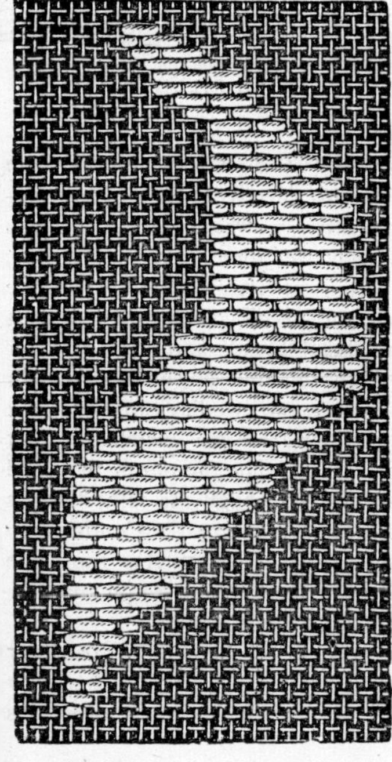

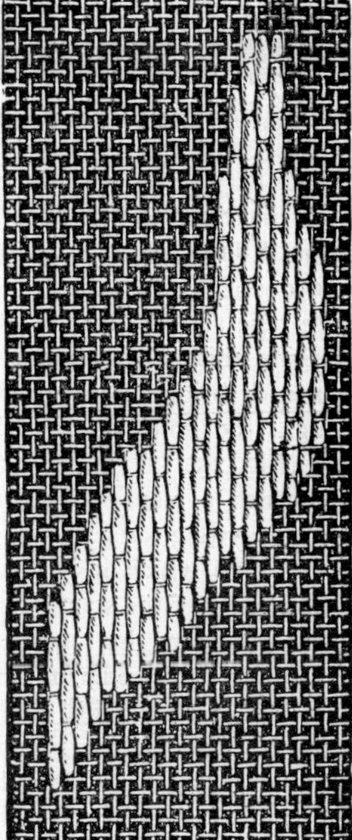

Right: Fig. 6.—VERTICAL DARNED FILLING

Left: Fig. 7. HORIZONTAL DARNED FILLING

back stitches, each of which is taken over three threads of canvas. The second row is rather more complicated. Bring the needle up from the wrong side of the work, three threads below one of the holes between two back stitches, and put it back into the hole between two back stitches, thus making a vertical stitch. * Bring the needle back to the right side where it came up before, that is, at the bottom of this vertical stitch, pass it over three threads diagonally, putting it into the next hole between two back stitches, bring it out three threads lower down. Make the vertical stitch, and repeat from *. Then repeat the first row and continue to work for the space required.

hole. This completes the four corners of the star. Count three threads down from the outer end of the last stitch and work a straight stitch from there into the middle. Make four of these straight stitches, one between each slanting stitch, and the star is finished. Another variation can be worked by taking the sloping stitches across four threads instead of three. In the filling illustrated above, in the first row, the stars are worked close together, the slanting stitches of one fitting into the holes of the stars on each side of it. In the second row, the diagonal stitches start from the straight stitches of the stars above, thus causing them to alternate.

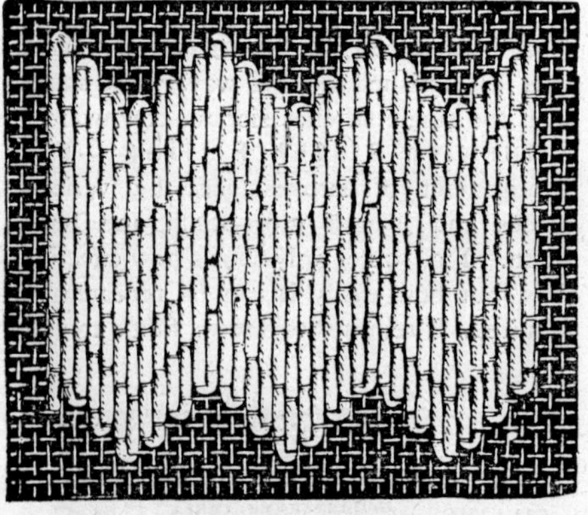

Fig. 9.—VANDYKE DARNING

Fig. 10.—TURKISH FILLING STITCH

Figs. 11 and 12 require no explanation as the diagrams shown here are very clear.

Star Filling is a little troublesome to work, owing to the difficulty of keeping the centre hole slightly open. The best way of managing this, is to begin each star at the outer end, bringing the needle downwards through the middle in completing each stitch (Fig. 13).

To work a star: Bring the needle up from the wrong side making sure that the hole through which it is now passing is to be the middle of the star. Count six threads horizontally from the lower end of the first stitch, bring the needle up and pass it over three threads diagonally, passing it through the centre hole again. Count six threads from the beginning of the last stitch and work another slanting stitch into the centre

Lattice and Cross-stitch Fillings are among the most effective in Ivory Embroidery. The lattice is worked first. Make a slanting stitch over three threads of canvas, sloping it from the left upwards towards the right, pass the needle down three threads and along three threads and make another slanting stitch, this time upwards from right to left, putting the needle into the same hole at the top through which the last stitch was drawn. The bottom of the third stitch also passes through the same hole as the bottom of the second. Continue to work a series of diagonal stitches thus, one to the left and another to the right until a sufficient number are worked.

Work a second set below these, also over three threads and arrange them so that their upper ends pass through the same hole as the lower ends of the first set. In this way a series of tiny squares is formed. The third row of stitches is worked exactly like the first and the fourth like the second. The tiny squares are partially filled with a small cross-stitch which is carried over the two middle threads of the square. All the crosses must be crossed in the same direction. Fig. 14 shows the finished effect.

Lattice and Star Filling.—As in the preceding pattern the lattice is worked first and a portion of it without stars is shown in the lower part of Fig. 15. The stitches are straight instead of slanting, and it is easiest to work in rows across the design. Begin by working a row of back stitches horizontally along the canvas and taking each stitch over three threads. For the second row work a series of vertical stitches also over three threads. Each of these stitches must start from one of the holes between two of the back stitches of the preceding row. These two rows are alternated, thus forming a series of tiny squares all over the ground.

The stars are then put in. Choose a place where four squares meet, count one thread diagonally in either square, bring the needle up from the wrong side and pass it down through the hole where the four straight stitches meet, make one of these slanting stitches in every square passing one end through the same hole, then pass to another place where four squares meet and work four more slanting stitches. Proceed in this way until all the squares are thus filled in. This pattern is particularly easy to work though it looks difficult when finished.

Fig. 11.—ARROWHEAD STITCH

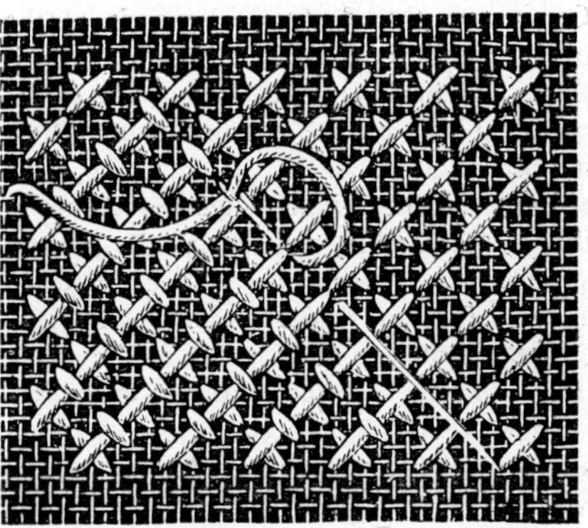

Fig. 12. CROSS AND BACK STITCH

Brick and Cross-stitch Filling.—It will be easier to work the bricks first in this filling than to work both the crosses and bricks together. For each brick, work three horizontal stitches side by side over four threads of canvas, miss four horizontal threads and make another brick in the same way. In the second row the bricks come between instead of directly under those first worked. Each stitch therefore covers two of the threads covered by a brick in the preceding row and two of those covered by the next brick. Miss four threads between each cluster of stitches as before. When all are worked fill these spaces by one large cross-stitch, each stitch of which passes through one of the corner holes of the brick which surrounds the space it is filling (Fig. 16). Finish the cross-stitch by working one vertical stitch over the two middle horizontal threads of the space. This vertical stitch is carried over the large cross-stitch and keeps its somewhat loose threads in order.

Fancy Brick Filling is made up of clusters exactly like those in the preceding pattern, but they are put close together instead of being divided by four threads. One end of the stitches in each cluster passes through the same hole as that of the corresponding stitch in the preceding

Fig. 13.—STAR FILLING

cluster. When one row of bricks is finished make a vertical stitch across each, thus: Count two threads from the ends of the brick, draw the needle through, pass it across the brick and put it into the corresponding hole on the opposite side. Draw it closely and the stitch will have the effect of tying the long stitches slightly together in the middle. The bricks in the second alternate with those of the first, as described above. Fig. 17 shows the finished effect.

Laid Filling.—The space to be filled must first be covered entirely with long stitches of silk, all placed in one direction and worked as closely together as the meshes of canvas will allow. Special care must be taken not to draw these stitches so tightly that they pucker the canvas in the slightest degree. When the whole design is covered, a similar set of stitches must be carried in the opposite direction across those already worked, but instead of being placed close together three threads of canvas must be left between each. As each one is worked, it must be caught down at intervals with a stitch running in the same direction as those first laid. But this is taken only over three threads, and the horizontal stitch over which it is carried must be kept straight exactly between these two threads (Fig. 18). As the canvas on the right side is entirely covered by the first set of stitches, it will be found that the position of the others is best ascertained by looking occasionally at the wrong side. In the second row, these stitches come exactly between those of the first.

Fig 14. LATTICE AND CROSS-STITCH FILLING

Fishbone Filling is a very close filling, therefore it must be sparingly used, or it will give a heavy appearance to the work. It consists simply of lines of slanting stitches,

Fig. 15.—LATTICE AND STAR FILLING

which fit in quite closely one beside the other. To work it, bring the needle up from the wrong side, make a stitch in a diagonal direction over three threads of canvas towards the left, bring the needle back to the hole exactly below that from which the first stitch is started, make another stitch across three threads, putting it into the hole exactly below that in which the first stitch was finished. Continue to work these slanting stitches one below the other until the line is long enough. Begin again at the top of the line, and work a similar set of stitches from left to right. One end of each of these stitches must pass through the same hole as the corresponding stitch in the first line. The third line is worked exactly like the first; the fourth is like the second.

Continue the work until there are a sufficient number of lines (Fig. 19).

Knotted and Slant Stitch.—This, again, is a double stitch, worked in two rows, one backwards and one forwards. Bring the needle up from the wrong side of the work. * count two threads towards the right and six upwards, put the needle into the wrong side and bring it back exactly six threads below where it went in. Repeat from * all along. In returning, after making the last slanting stitch, bring the needle out four threads instead of six below where it went in, make a half cross-stitch from right to left slanting upwards, over two threads of canvas as well as over the long slanting stitch. Work one of these stitches over each

Fig. 16 CROSS AND BRICK STITCH FILLING

of the long stitches, then work the second row in exactly the same way. Between each row of long stitches work a row of back stitches, each of which fits into one of the holes through which the long stitches were passed, this giving additional firmness and closeness to the work. Fig. 20 shows the stitch finished.

Algerian Cross-stitch is something between cross-stitch and herringbone stitch. It can be used for a filling, one row below another, or in a straight line for stems. To work it, * after bringing the needle up from the wrong side, count three threads along and three down, put in the needle and bring it up again on the same line of canvas three threads further to the left. Count three threads up, six along, put in the needle and bring it out again three

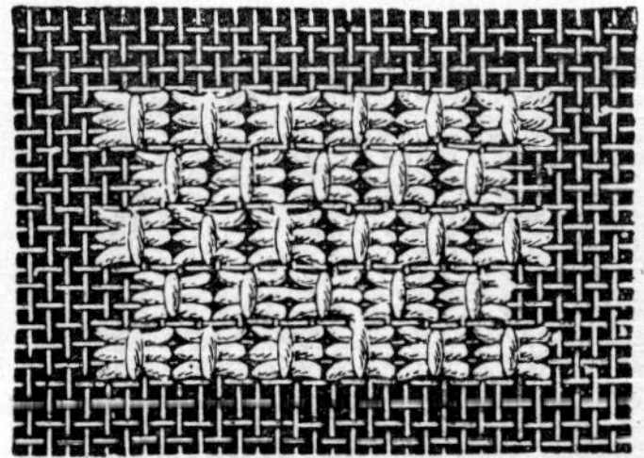

Fig. 17.—FANCY BRICK FILLING

threads to the left as before. Repeat from *. In Fig. 21 the needle is shown making one of the stitches under three threads of the canvas.

Single Buttonhole Stitch is similar to a filling much used by lace workers, and is very simple as it consists only of single button-hole stitches. To work it bring the needle up from the wrong side, hold the silk down beneath the thumb of the left hand, count two threads towards the right of the hole at which the needle came up, put in the needle and bring it out over the silk exactly three threads below where it went in, * count two threads along and three threads up. Put in the needle and bring it out again exactly three threads below where it went in. Repeat from * thus making a series of buttonhole stitches. At the end of the row after making these stitches, put the needle back to the wrong side just where it came out, passing over the cotton, bring it out in a line with and exactly in the middle of, the last buttonhole stitch

Fig. 18.—LAID FILLING

Left: Fig. 19. FISHBONE FILLING

Right: Fig. 21.—ALGERIAN CROSS-STITCH

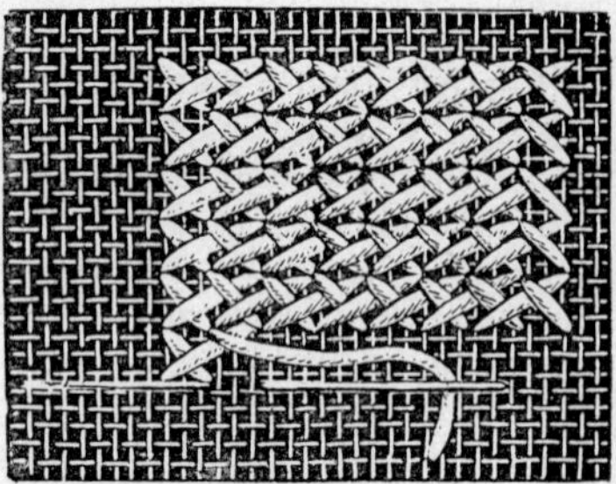

Fig. 22—SINGLE BUTTON-HOLE STITCH

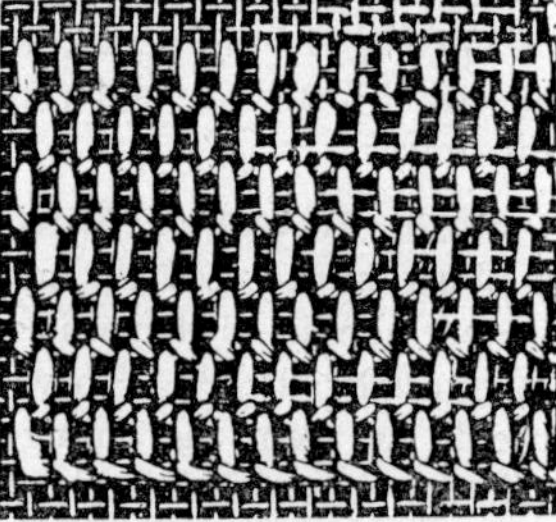

Fig. 20—KNOTTED AND SLANT STITCH

Fig. 23.—TRIPLE BUTTONHOLE STITCH

Fig. 24.—LINK STITCH WORKED AS A STRAIGHT STITCH

Fig. 25.—RING STITCH FILLING

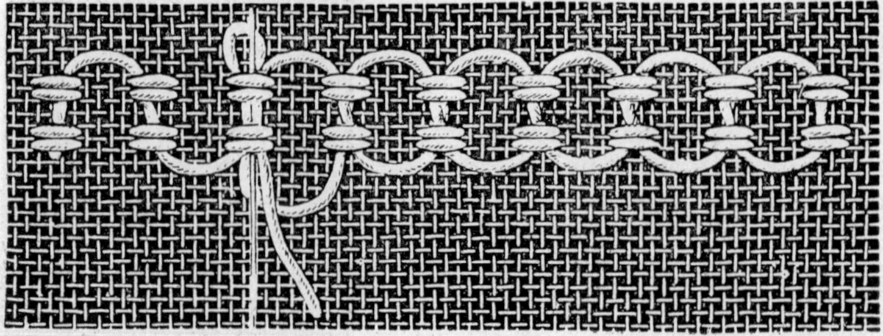

and work back in the same way as the first row, but putting each stitch between those of the preceding line (Fig. 22).

Triple Buttonhole Stitch is worked in exactly the same way as single buttonhole, except that the stitches are worked in groups of three instead of singly. In the first row, work three buttonhole stitches close together, miss three threads, work another group of three. The second row is exactly the same but the triple buttonhole stitches are worked into the spaces left between those of the preceding row. The whole effect is of a close network over the surface of the material (Fig. 23).

Link Stitch Filling is rather complicated, but when fully understood, is most effective for covering large spaces. It consists first of a powdering of straight stitches over the canvas. These are arranged in pairs, which are vertical and horizontal in alternate rows. They are shown in the lower part of Fig. 26.

For the first row which consists of vertical stitches, work two of these upright stitches side by side and over three threads of canvas in height, miss five threads and work another pair of upright stitches. Continue thus all along.

For the second row, leave two threads below the first row, work a pair of horizontal stitches over three threads. These three threads must be the middle of the five that were previously left between each pair of these horizontal stitches. The third row again is like the first, and the fourth like the second. When a sufficient number of stitches is made (the filling must finish with a row of vertical stitches) take a fresh needleful of silk and begin at the pair of stitches marked 1 in this diagram.

```
1     2     3     4     5     6
   7     8     9    10    11
12    13    14    15    16    17
   18    19    20    21    22
23    24    25    26    27    28
```

Pass the needle under 1 (remember that these numbers refer to the pairs of stitches and that the needle is not taken through the canvas) under 7, 13, 8, 3, 9, 15, 10, 5, 11, 17, 6, 11, 16, 10, 4, 9, 14, 8, 2, 7, 12. On reaching the twelfth group of stitches pass the needle down to the wrong side of the canvas, under the stitches and bring it up again one thread further on. This is done so that a fresh start may be made for the links, then bring the needle back under 12, 18, 24, 19, 14, 20, 26, 21, 16, 22, 28, 17, 22, 27, 21, 15, 20, 25, 19, 13, 18, 23. Start again from here, as before, for the next set of links. Be careful to leave the silk loose rather than tight, so as not to pucker the canvas. The needle in Fig. 26 is passing through one of the groups of horizontal and one of the groups of vertical stitches. The stitch as described here is rather large and bold, but when once the general principal is mastered, the worker will see how to arrange the stitches so as to make it more delicate.

Ring stitch is not unlike link-stitch, but it is worked in a bolder and far coarser manner. It looks well used just above the hem of a tea-cloth. In working it four short stitches are needed to support the rings. Use six strands of Filoselle upon a medium weight canvas, and make two horizontal stitches below the other, over four threads, then miss three threads, and work two more horizontal stitches below the others and over the same number of meshes. Miss four threads and work four more short stitches on a level with the first four. Continue thus until there are enough of these. Then take a long needleful of Filoselle, using the entire thickness (12 strands) pass the needle, eye foremost, up under the first two pairs of stitches, down under the second pair, up under the third pair. When the needle has been threaded under all, return in the same way, being careful to draw the thread equally tight between each set of stitches. Fig. 25 shows the stitch in progress.

Link stitch Worked as a Straight Stitch is useful as a heading to borders and bands of Ivory Embroidery. The general principle of working is easily understood. The short stitches are made first. With canvas of medium-sized meshes it is best to use four threads of Filoselle. Make a

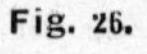
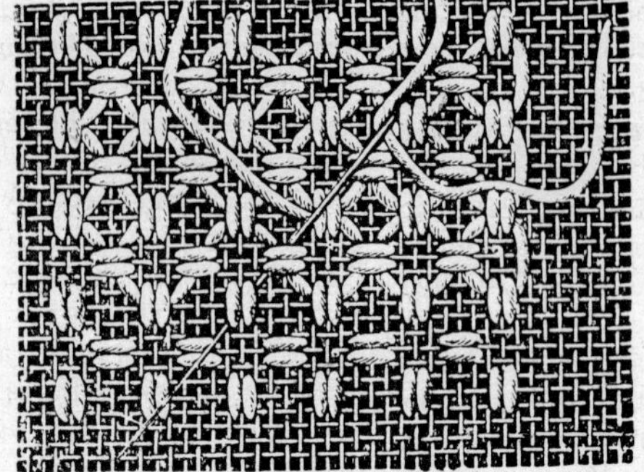

Fig. 26. LINK STITCH FILLING

horizontal stitch over two threads, miss two threads, make a horizontal stitch on a level with the first one. Continue until a sufficient number of these stitches are made. Then take a long needleful of four or six strands of Filoselle, pass the needle downwards under the first short stitch, upwards through the second, downwards through the third and so on until the end of the line is reached. Work back the same way, but reverse the direction of the needle, so that it passes downward under those stitches that it passed through on an upward direction previously. Great dexterity will be needed at first in drawing up this thread equally between each short stitch and in getting it, on the return journey, to set as loosely as it did on the first journey. This can only be gained by practice, but the effect of the stitch is so good that it is worth a little trouble. Fig. 24 shows the stitch being worked. It is a good plan to slip the needle under the stitches with the eye foremost, as when using a bodkin, as shown in Fig. 24. It is less likely to catch in the threads of the Filoselle or canvas than when used in the ordinary way.

Open Fillings of Drawn Threads.—It is first necessary to define the limits of the space required with buttonhole stitches, in order to prevent the threads of canvas, which have to be drawn away as the work proceeds, from unravelling further. In Fig. 27 these buttonhole stitches have been taken over three lines of canvas, and two lines only are missed between each stitch. Two threads of canvas are then removed in each direction across the space, by cutting them at the edge of the buttonhole border. This divides the canvas into a series of tiny squares of two threads each, and the pairs of threads between these are overcast with stout coloured cotton or flax as follows: Join the end of the cotton to the buttonholing on the wrong side, and make a series of slanting stitches over the pairs of threads between each tiny square. When the end

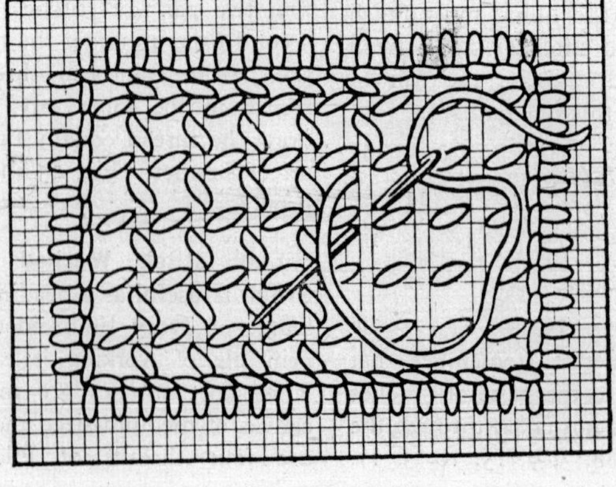

Fig. 27. OPEN FILLING OF DRAWN THREADS

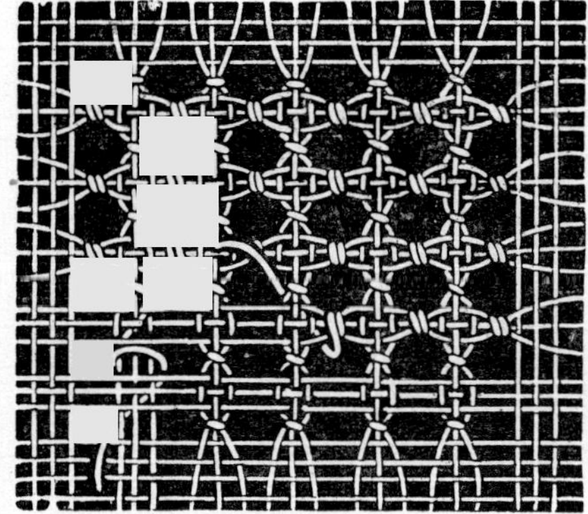

Fig. 28.—SINGLE AND DOUBLE OVERCAST STITCH

In such fillings as these, there is no need to draw the cotton up tightly, as a sufficiently open work appearance is gained by drawing out the threads of the canvas.

Open Filling, Single and Double Overcast Stitch shows the stitches taken in two directions across the canvas. It is advisable to begin with those in a vertical row as shown in the lower part of Fig. 28. When the needle is ready make an upright stitch across three horizontal lines of canvas. Draw it up tightly, bring the needle along three threads and down three threads at the back of the work and make a second upright stitch. Continue thus until the end of the row is reached. Then bring the needle down on the wrong side six threads below the top of the last stitch. Make an upright stitch over the three last of these six threads and exactly below the last stitch of the preceding row. Continue as before, working back in the opposite direction to that taken in the first row. Fasten off the thread when a sufficient quantity is done. Now turn the work, so that that which was the side is now at the top, and work a series of upright stitches as before, but arrange them in pairs instead of singly. Let them set evenly side by side and be careful to draw them all up to the same degree of tightness. These double stitches look well if they are a different colour to the single ones.

Fig. 29.—EASY OPEN FILLING

of the first row is reached, work back along the second in the opposite direction, making the stitches so that they set exactly under those of the first row and slant in the same way. When the whole of the overcasting is finished in this direction turn the work, so that what was the top before is now the side, and make a similar set of half cross-stitches over the pairs of threads that are yet uncovered. In the illustration, the needle is seen making one of the stitches in the return row which slant downwards from left to right. The cotton is taken at the back of the work diagonally across the little squares and so, on the wrong side, a series of cross-stitches should be formed if the work has been done correctly.

Fig. 30.—OPEN FILLING

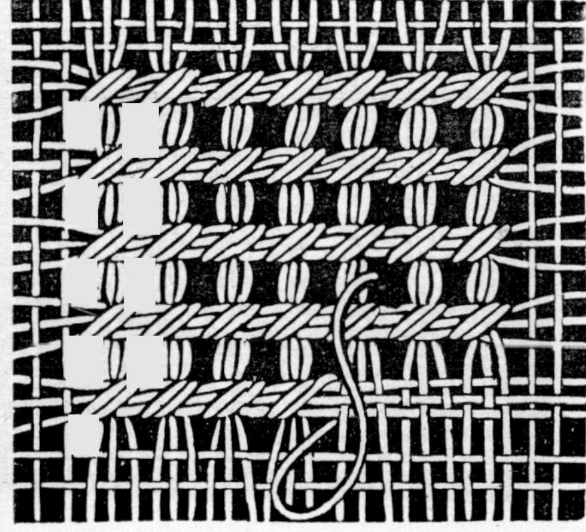

The pattern forms a series of small squares over the canvas, and as the threads of this are drawn very closely together, the filling is nearly as open as though some of the threads of the material had been removed altogether. If any additional ornament be needed, a tiny spot of coloured silk may be added in the middle of each solid square, by working a slanting stitch across the centre thread of the three which form the square.

A border may be made by working about five rows of these open squares and edging them on each side with a row of vandykes made by taking straight stitches over two, three, four, five, four and three horizontal lines of the canvas.

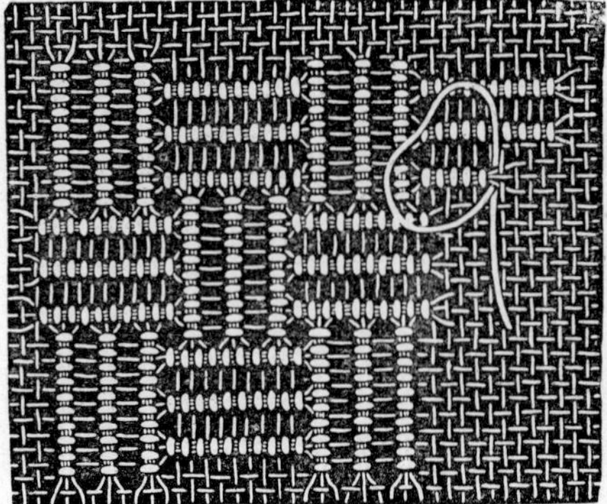

Fig. 31.—BASKET PATTERN

Fig. 32. DESIGN FOR A D'OYLEY

Easy Open Filling.—Open fillings form a distinct feature in the best kind of Ivory Embroidery, while they are simple to work, they require a little attention in pulling up the stitches evenly, so that all the holes are made the same size. Such fillings should be worked with crochet cotton, silk twist or something similar that will stand a pull and not wear rough or snap during the process of the work.

The filling given here is carried over a small number of lines only, and it will be found very useful for narrow spaces, being worked in two rows. Bring the needle up and make an upright back stitch over three horizontal lines of canvas. Draw the thread tight, * then make a half cross-stitch over a square of three threads, that is, count three lengthwise threads on a line with the bottom of the back stitch and three horizontal threads, and put the needle through to the wrong side. Bring it out three threads below where it went in, then make a back stitch over these three threads which draw up tightly. Repeat from * until the end of the row is reached and pass the needle down so that it is in the right position for making the first back stitch in the next row. In passing from row to row it is almost impossible to avoid making a

Fig. 33.—CHENILLE AND EYELET

long stitch on the wrong side, but if the worker arranges this stitch at the outer edge of the design, its appearance between the meshes on the right side can easily be hidden by the gold thread or silk couching used for the outline. (Fig. 29).

Open Filling.—To work this stitch, start at the top left-hand end of the canvas and pass the needle diagonally over a square of three lines of the material, thus making a slanting stitch like a half cross-stitch, and bringing the needle back through the hole from which it started. Draw the thread up tightly and make a second stitch into the same hole as the first one, arranging it so that it does not overlap the other, but sets exactly at the side of it. This time, however, bring the needle out three threads below the upper part of the stitches, thus getting it into position for making a second pair.

When the end of the row is reached and the last pair of stitches made, bring the needle out as if another pair were to be worked but this time take the needle downwards diagonally over a square of three threads, thus making a stitch exactly below the last one of the preceding row. Make a second stitch by the side of the first one, as before, and pass the needle up three threads instead of down, thus getting it into position for the next pair of stitches. It is a great advantage to be able to make the stitches in a reverse direction in this manner especially in the open fillings, where it is not always easy to join a fresh needleful neatly. For this reason, too, it is advisable to use as long a needleful as can conveniently be managed when a good sized space can be filled. Fig. 30 shows open filling in the working.

Open Work Basket Pattern.—Few backgrounds are more effective than this one. As it requires considerable space it is suitable for covering a large surface. It is better worked on a rather loosely woven canvas, which is not so easily puckered by the tightness of the stitches. Use either coloured thread or ordinary cream cotton of a strong twisted make such as will withstand a sharp pull. Crochet twist is good and can be bought to match the canvas exactly. The pattern looks well, too, if the vertical bars are worked with coloured cotton and the horizontal bars with cream.

Begin the pattern at the upper left-hand corner of the space to be filled. Fasten the thread at the back across three vertical lines of the canvas and tie it, by running the end and by making ten stitches over three vertical threads of canvas, exactly underneath one another, drawing each stitch up quite tight. This finishes one bar. Work two more in exactly the same way, keeping the stitches quite even and all equally tight. After making the last stitch of the third bar, pass the needle down three threads of the canvas and make a stitch in an upright direction over three horizontal threads just one thread beyond the last of the three overcast by the last bar made.

Make ten of these upright stitches, working in a straight line from right to left and placing them exactly below those threads crossed by the vertical bars. When the end of the bar is reached bring the needle down three threads and make a second horizontal bar, exactly below the first one, this time working from left to right. Then make a second horizontal bar, exactly below the first one, this time working from left to right. Then make a third from right to left. This finishes the second group of bars and leaves the needle ready to make the third group exactly like the first. Work this, then repeat the second group and continue until the limit of the space to be filled is reached. Then begin again at the top of the work, make a group of horizontal bars exactly by the side of the first set of vertical bars. Below this work three vertical bars and continue thus, alternating the bars, until the end of the space is again reached. The third row again is like the first. (Fig. 31).

When beginning a new needleful, or when passing from point to point in the work, the needle must be run in as much as possible through the stitches on the wrong side. Sometimes this pattern is worked over two threads instead of three, but never over more than three, or the canvas becomes drawn out of shape. The length of the bars may be varied but they should always contain an even number of stitches.

Fine Work for a Dessert D'oyley.—This is a mixture of drawn thread work and fine, but close, silk embroidery. It is often worked on a frame. It is as well to work the narrow band of short stitches all round the square before drawing out any of the threads. Those shown at the sides of Fig. 32 are carried over two threads of canvas and are worked with white silk. At the corners the space left by the joining of the two sets of stitches is filled by one small stitch.

The openwork centre is arranged by removing four threads of canvas and leaving four threads in each direction. There should be an uneven number of solid squares and an even number of open squares thus made. Work an eyelet hole with white silk in the middle of each of the solid squares taking each stitch over two threads of the canvas. Now thread a large-eyed needle with green tinsel passing and made a *point d'Esprit* (see Chapter on Drawn Thread Work) stitch in one of the open squares. This is done simply by working a loose button hole stitch round the innermost of the remaining threads of canvas, then a second similar stitch on the next thread, and so on until four such have been made and the space is filled with a small open square from which spring four small loops. Run the passing into the work on the wrong side. Three colours of tinsel were used in the original—red, yellow, and green, arranged alternately. A loop of gold passing must now be placed under the straight stitch of each of the eyelet holes. The strands of these loops lie flat upon the work with the threads of the canvas that were left undrawn. Care must be taken in going from point to point on the wrong side to keep the threads as much as possible against the closer parts of the pattern so as not to interfere with the regularity of the network.

The closely embroidered border is taken round the D'oyley beyond the narrow straight band. Begin in the corner hole and with white silk, work a short upright stitch over two threads, then one over three, four, five, six, five, four, three, two, one and so continue to form a row of small triangles or vandykes, with a straight edge at the bottom fitting into the same holes as the small straight stitches in the narrow border first worked. A second row of vandykes is made next, the longest stitches of which fit into the longest stitches in the preceding set. The straight edge formed by these stitches sets towards the outside of the work and a series of small squares is thus formed between each vandyke. These are filled in with stitches worked with a double strand of passing, the three colours being used alternately. If the pattern has been correctly followed, the stitches forming these squares should be taken over two, four, six, eight, ten, eight, six, four and two threads of canvas and should fit at each end into the holes already occupied by the stitches forming the vandykes. As seen in the illustration the vandykes fit exactly and naturally one into the other at the corners.

The d'oyley should now be invisibly hemmed all round with white silk, the canvas being turned down quite straight and so arranged that it just meets the upper edge of the embroidery. These d'oyleys are very fascinating to work.

Chenille and Eyelet Pattern is suitable as a grounding for broad spaces, such as those provided by a tea-cloth. The introduction of chenille, either silk or wool is a novel feature in Ivory Embroidery. The eyelet holes should be worked first. Use strong twisted cotton and fasten it by tying it strongly at the back after making a stitch slanting upwards from right to left over a square of three threads. Cut off the shorter end of cotton to neaten it, and with the other length make an upright stitch over two threads just three threads further to the right than the first stitch and passing through the same hole at the bottom. Now bring the needle up three threads further to the right than the top of the last stitch and make a slanting stitch into the same hole as the bottom of the preceding stitch. Make a straight stitch three threads lower, and a slanting stitch three threads lower

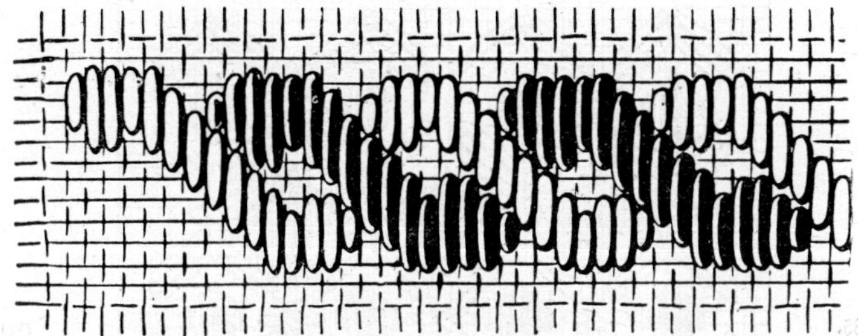

Fig. 34.—TWIST PATTERN

again. Then a straight stitch further to the left by three threads and a slanting stitch three threads further still, all to go into the same hole. Finish the eyelet hole thus made with a horizontal stitch three threads above the last made stitch, run the thread in and out at the back of the work until, if the needleful is long enough, it is in the right position for beginning the next eyelet hole. The eyelet holes are joined one to another at the corners where the slanting stitches pass through the same holes. The space between the eyelet holes in a horizontal and vertical direction is filled with seven upright stitches of chenille, each carried over six horizontal threads of canvas (Fig. 33).

This pattern may be varied in several ways. The chenille may be dispensed with and its place taken by ivory cotton or coloured Filoselle, or the ground may be closely covered with eyelet holes without any solid filling. Three or five rows of the pattern make an excellent border or insertion, with a little vandyked edging on each side. A pretty and uncommon powdering consists of a star composed of a group either of five eyelet holes, one forming the centre and with the corners of chenille, or of five spots of chenille with the eyelet holes as corners. Care must be taken not to carry any of the threads across the wrong side so as to spoil the open effect of any of the eyelet holes.

Twist Pattern.—Two colours are required for this pattern, but as both are worked in the same way, no difficulty need be experienced. It is a good plan to employ not only two colours but two kinds of threads as in Fig. 34, where old gold Filoselle is used with ivory cotton. This pattern is useful for working in stripes down the edges of an insertion or along the top edge of a border.

Begin with the ivory cotton and * work a horizontal stitch over two threads of canvas, below this work two horizontal stitches over four threads, arranging them so that they project one thread at each end beyond the short stitch. Now make a horizontal stitch over three threads, the right-hand end of it being on a level with that of the two preceding stitches. Below this work a stitch over four threads as before, then six similar stitches, each one thread further to the left than the one preceding it. Work a stitch over three threads, its left-hand end on a level with that of the stitch immediately before it. Now make two stitches over four threads and finally one stitch over two threads like that with which the scroll was begun. In starting the second ivory scroll, bring the needle down one thread and four threads towards the right, reckoning from the short stitch with which the last scroll finished, then repeat from *.

The coloured part of the twist is worked in precisely the same way, the first stitch being placed on a line with the fourth of the seven stitches that were taken over four threads, the last stitch being on the left-hand side of the fourth stitch of the slanting line of the seven in the next ivory scroll. The pattern is soon learnt and, as very little counting is involved, can be worked by a beginner.

Fig. 35. QUILTING PATTERN

Quilting Pattern is a useful pattern as it is easily adapted for large or small pieces of work. It is particularly good as a border for a baby's pram cover.

Begin at the top left-hand corner and work downwards using ivory cotton. Bring up the needle, count five horizontal threads and four vertical threads, make a long slanting stitch downwards from right to left. Make two more of the stitches by the side of the first one. Bring the needle out at the hole at the bottom of the last stitch, count four vertical threads towards the right and five horizontal threads, make a long stitch slanting downwards from left to right. Work two more of these stitches besides this one towards the left, their upper ends passing through the same holes as the lower ends of the stitches above them. Make the next of these zig-zags exactly like the first one, but two threads below the bottom of it and continue working them until the stripe is long enough.

Then begin again at the top of the work two threads further to the right than the third stitch of the first zig-zag. This time make three stitches sloping downwards to the right like those of the second half of the zig-zags in the first row, and below them put three stitches like those of the first half of the first set of zig-zags. The third stripe is just like the first, ten threads of canvas being missed between the upper ends of the zig-zags and two between the first and second zig-zags as before.

When all the zig-zag stripes are made, fill the diamond-shaped spaces with coloured Filoselle, making horizontal stitches over two, four, six, eight, six, four, and two threads for the larger spaces, and over two, four, six, four, two for the smaller ones. The zig-zags are connected with ornamental cross-stitches of white Filoselle. Fill the larger gaps, where two threads were missed between the zig-zags with a straight cross-stitch over light threads horizontally and six threads vertically holding it down in the middle with an ordinary cross-stitch over two threads. The other spaces are filled in the same way, but being smaller, the cross-stitch is taken over fewer threads (Fig. 35).

LAID WORK

Laid work is chiefly used for large flat surfaces when economy in time and material has to be studied, as it is quickly worked, and no materials are wasted, all the work being on the surface.

Designs should be bold, important and large. Bold conventional designs are good, as they lend themselves to this work. Laid work is often used to good advantage for backgrounds, as it is quickly done and the colours are easily blended.

Materials required.—A firm background is best. Good quality linen, twill, heavy silk materials, or furnishing satin are all suitable; lighter materials should be backed with linen to give them weight. An embroidery frame should be used to keep the threads taut while working as it makes it much easier and quicker to do.

Stitches Used.—The threads are laid across the surface and these must be carefully secured with surface stitches, which vary according to the materials used. **For wool.**—Feather stitch, split stitch, back stitch, couching, simple crosses and a variety of cross bar fillings are used. **For silk**—two threads laid at equal intervals and caught with small stitches in regular spacings.

Threads may be laid at right angles to form cross bars or lines of split stitch radiating with the growth or following the direction of the outline.

Laid work should be outlined. As it is not very serviceable a raised outline such as a cord helps to protect the work. Of the various outlines that may be used, cord, couching, split stitch, stem stitch or Japanese gold thread are the most usual.

Laid work is a good thing for a beginner,

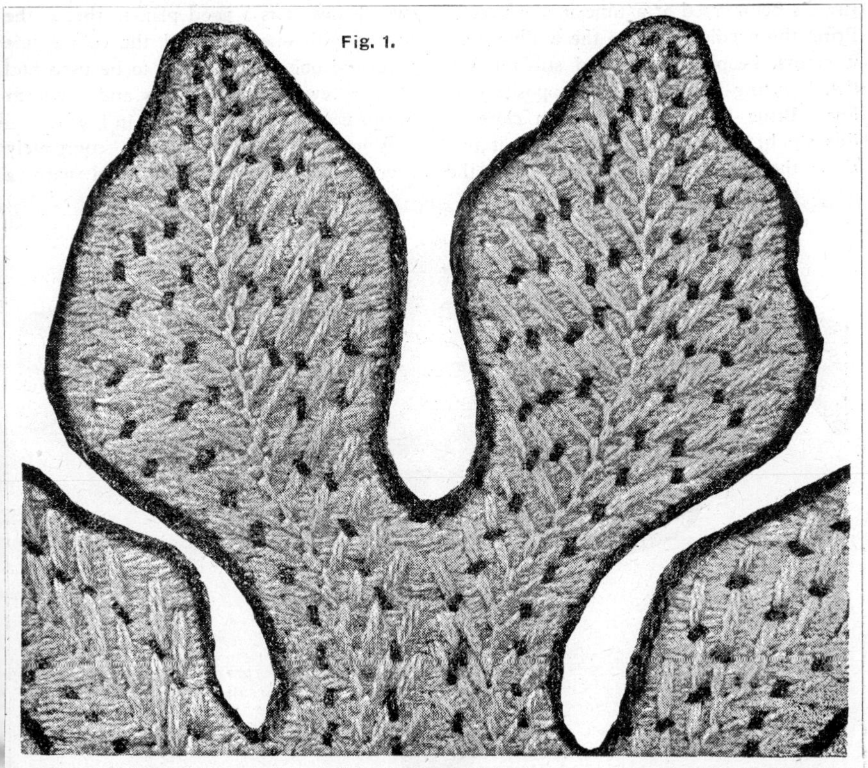

Fig. 1.

who has never used a frame before, as it is simple and is good practice for working with both hands.

Wool should be used by a beginner, two strands being used at a time in the needle. Bring the needle up on to the outline, take it across, keeping the thread straight and flat, inserting it again on the opposite outline. Bring the needle up again close to this stitch, take it across and insert it just above the first stitch, always seeing that the threads lie perfectly flat. Continue backwards and forwards in this way until enough of this shade has been used. In order not to make a hard line between the two shades, it is a good plan to thread the needle with one strand of the colour just used and one of the colour to be used and work a few rows backwards and forwards in this way. This can be seen in Fig. 1.

When the space has been completely covered tie these threads down with a

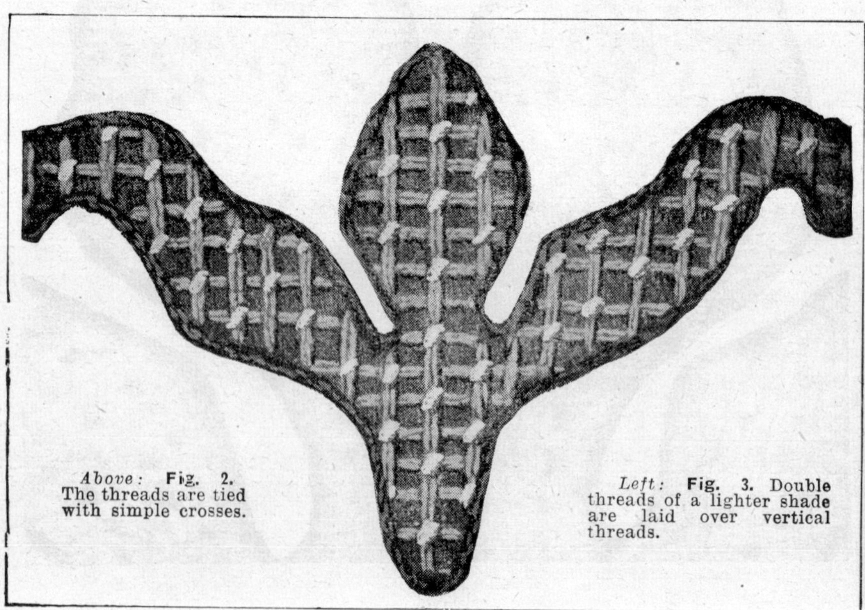

Above: **Fig. 2.** The threads are tied with simple crosses.

Left: **Fig. 3.** Double threads of a lighter shade are laid over vertical threads.

feather stitch worked in one thread of each colour. These threads are again caught down with little stitches the same colour as the outline of the design. The design is outlined in split stitch. Great care must be taken to leave no loose threads.

Fig. 2 is worked in the same way, for the laying of the threads. These are tied with simple crosses, all going in the same direction. These again are stitched through the centre with a small stitch the same colour as the outline which is again in split stitch. The vein through the centre is in two colours. Fly stitch with little coloured tips is quite useful to fill in any spaces not already covered.

In Fig. 3 the threads are not laid across but downwards, these are afterwards tied down with threads going across and down in a lighter shade, two threads of wool being used in the needle. After this a small stitch is taken alternately in a lighter shade as can be seen quite clearly from the diagram.

Figs. 4 and 5 show the laid threads in Filoselle and tied down in two methods of split stitch. In Fig. 5 it will also be noticed that the darker part of green is tied down in basket stitch and at the base, the laid threads are tied down with threads laid at equal intervals and caught down with small stitches in regular spacings. Both are outlined with a silk cord.

In Fig. 6 the fruits are worked in various shades in Filo floss. These are tied down with one thread laid at equal intervals and caught down with small stitches in regular spacings. It will be noticed that the green

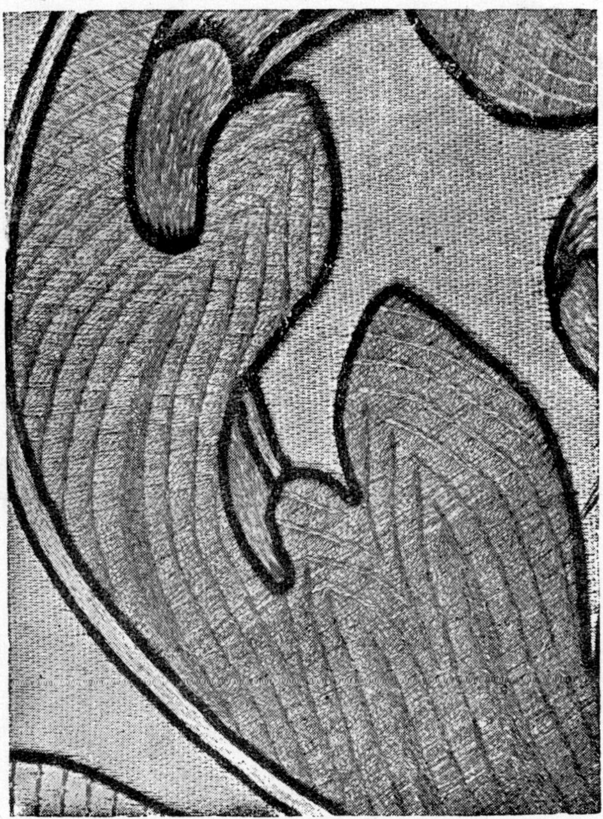

Fig. 4. SPLIT STITCH

THREE WAYS OF LAYING THREADS

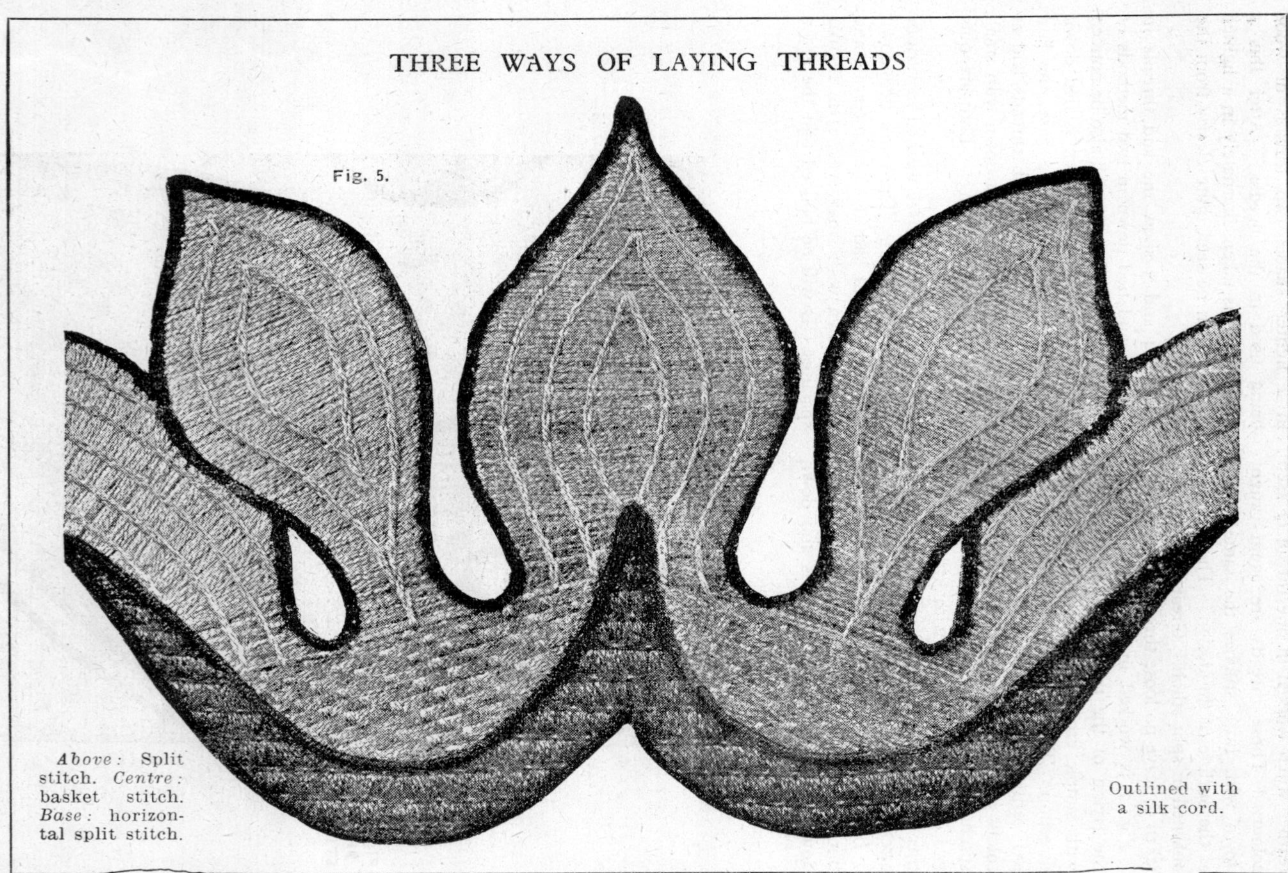

Fig. 5.

Above: Split stitch. *Centre*: basket stitch. *Base*: horizontal split stitch.

Outlined with a silk cord.

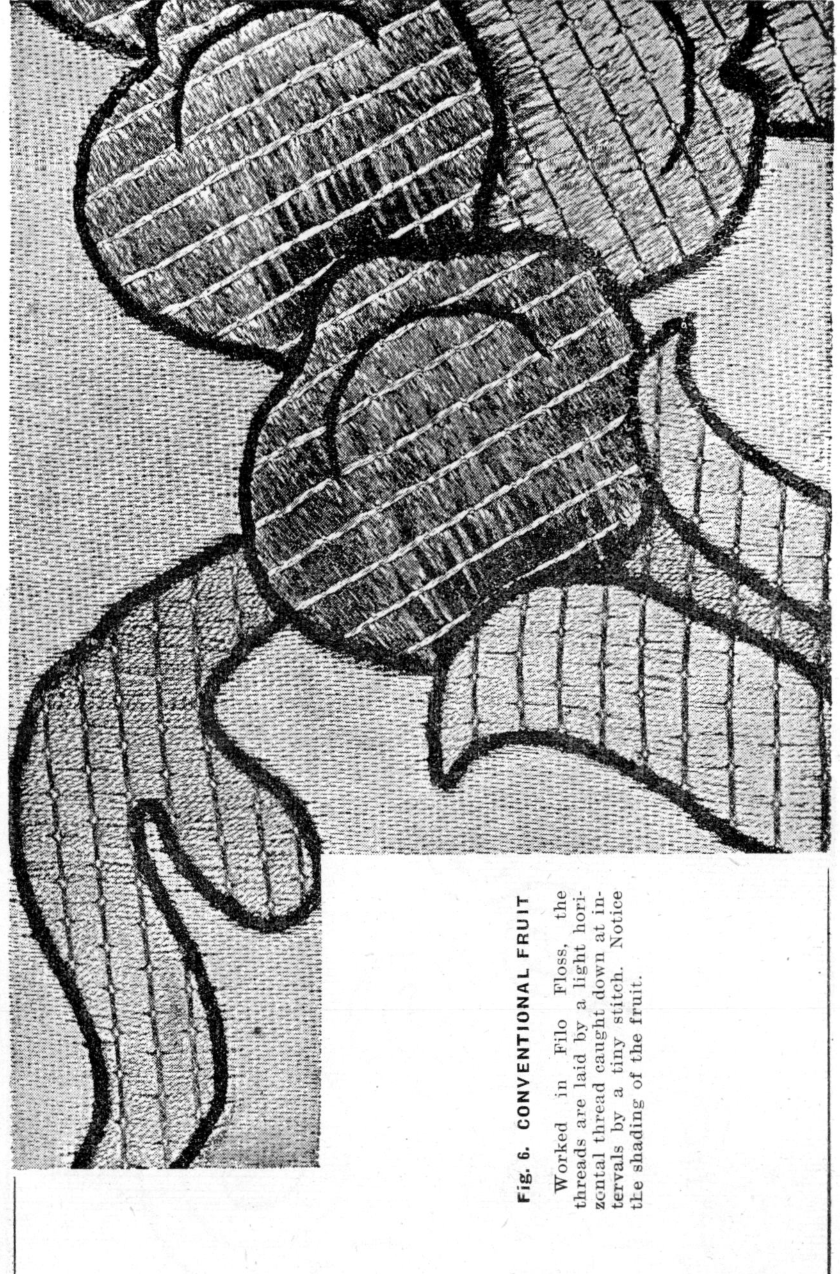

Fig. 6. CONVENTIONAL FRUIT

Worked in Filo Floss, the threads are laid by a light horizontal thread caught down at intervals by a tiny stitch. Notice the shading of the fruit.

in the leaf is shaded differently in the laid work. These threads are tied down like those of the fruits. It is all outlined with a silk cord.

The flower in Fig. 7 is worked entirely in floss silk—the diagram showing how the colours are shaded before being tied down.

Scroll Couching is another method of tying down threads in laid work. It is quite simple and effective when done. Tying the laid threads down in scroll form is another simple way, though no design is traced on the threads. There are many ways of varying these scrolls (Fig. 8).

Laid work has great possibilities and affords great scope to the artist.

Fig. 7.

Fig. 8. SCROLL COUCHING

Reproduced by courtesy of the Victoria and Albert Museum.

BEAUTIFUL SPECIMEN OF SILK LAID WORK

The specimen of silk laid work on the previous page is an excellent example of the combination of laid work and silk shading, and makes a good design for a cushion.

As can be seen in the illustration the background is of a light shade and is entirely laid, the leaves and stems are also laid, whereas the flowers and birds are in silk shading which makes an effective contrast. This piece was lent by courtesy of the Victoria and Albert Museum.

MOUNTMELLICK WORK

Mountmellick work derives its name from the town in Ireland where it first originated. It was started by a lady of the Society of Friends, who taught it to the peasants there as a means of earning a living for them. This work is still done and to this day benefits the poor.

This type of white work differs from others, in as much as there are no drawn or open spaces. The idea of the work is to arrange it so that the majority of stitches lie on the surface with very little thread showing on the wrong side.

This embroidery is quickly worked as it is bold, and it has great charm if the stitches are chosen carefully. The chief attraction of this work is that floral designs can be made to look very realistic.

Mountmellick work is usually finished off with a heavy buttonhole border or knitted fringe.

Designs.—As this work should look as real as possible, very few conventional designs are used. Rugged flowers and fruit are really best as they show up to advantage, though of course, any flower or fruit can be used.

The one thing to remember in designing for Mountmellick work is that the border should be bold and strong, as the work is heavy and requires something to balance it. As the embroidery is raised and in consequence thick and heavy, it requires a strong, firm material. Mountmellick work will repay all the time and labour spent on it, as it is rich in appearance and once the stitches have been mastered, not difficult. This type of embroidery washes well and remains good until the end.

Materials required.—Two thicknesses of cotton are used, one for the embroidery, the other for padding. The materials used are rather coarse, therefore the cottons should be chosen accordingly. A ground of white jean, drill or strong linen can be used.

Crewel needles should be used with large enough eyes to take the cotton easily.

White material and cotton are used for this work.

STITCHES USED

Gordian Knot Stitch is not unlike the Cable stitch in appearance. It is used for stems and outlines, but the link is smaller than in Cable. It may be worked with the material held straight towards the worker or from right to left. The former method is shown in Fig. 1.

Bring the needle up to the right side in the place to start, hold the cotton under the left thumb, pass the needle from right to left under the cotton so held, and with a gentle movement of the thumb push the cotton upwards under the point of the needle. Turn the cotton upwards, reverse the position of the needle from left to right. Insert it horizontally to take up a thread or two of the material in the place where the knot is to be formed, i.e. an $\frac{1}{8}$ of an

Fig. 1.—GORDIAN KNOT STITCH

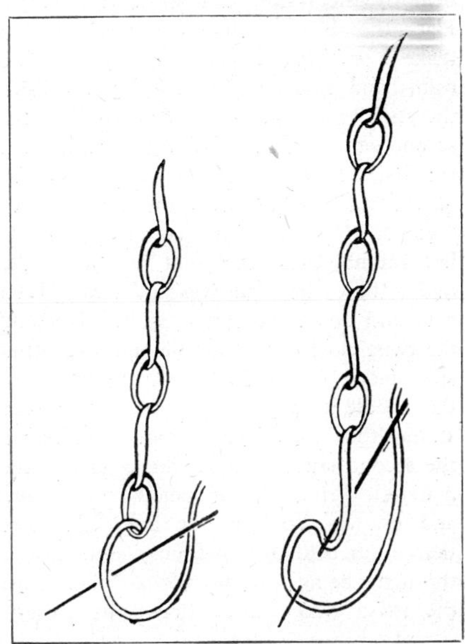

inch below where the cotton was brought out. Turn the cotton downwards under the point of the needle (the position shown in the diagram) and draw it carefully through. There is one long stitch and one knot stitch. All succeeding knots are formed in the same way, at equal distances to each other. It is quickly worked once it has been mastered.

Thorn stitch is a combination of coral stitch and french knots and is useful for stems of medium width and also for the

Fig. 2.—THORN STITCH

outlining of leaves and petals. Two parallel lines should first be drawn the width required for the thorn stitch. Bring the needle out at the top, midway between the two lines, hold the cotton under the left thumb, insert the needle, taking up five or six threads of the material straight on the line towards the left-hand side, and pass the point of the needle over the cotton held by the thumb and draw it through. Place the thumb again on the cotton and make a similar stitch on the line on the right-hand side, and draw through. Both the stitches are set perpendicularly, but the second stitch must be slightly lower than the first. A strand of cotton on the surface of the material connects the two stitches together. Keeping the cotton under the left thumb, pass the point of the needle under the cotton and over and under, then over and under the cotton again. Keeping the twist close on the needle and the cotton still under the thumb, turn the point of the needle upwards and take it over the strand that runs across from the first to the second stitch. Insert the needle in the material, bring it out below the strand and midway between the lines and over the cotton held by the thumb and draw it through, being careful not to disarrange the twist, which when drawn up closely, forms a knot. Continue working like this so that a stem or thorn stitch is produced as seen in Fig. 2.

Bullion stitch resembles a raised roll of twisted cotton lying on the surface of the material. Insert the needle in the material in the position you wish the stitch to lie, taking from $\frac{1}{4}$ to $\frac{1}{2}$ an inch of material on the needle, according to the length of stitch required, then bring the point well out where the cotton already is and, with the needle held in this position, wind the cotton round the point ten or twelve times. Wind the cotton with the right hand, keeping the twist from falling off by pressure of the left thumb. Then draw the needle through the material and through the twists of cotton, turn the cotton towards the top of the stitch and pull it until the stitch lies in position,

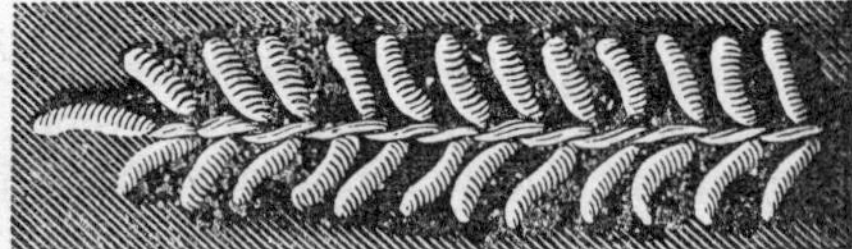

Fig. 3.—BULLION STITCH

with the twisted cotton in a close roll upon it. Insert the needle again at the top of the bullion stitch, and bring it out where the next bullion stitch is to begin. In Fig. 3 the bullion stitches are worked as if branching right and left from a central veining. The vein is worked in afterwards.

Feather stitch and Bullion as seen in Fig. 4 has one side of the stem worked in feather stitch and the other in bullion stitch.

Double Bullion stitch consists of two bullion stitches worked close together, then a space, then two more bullion stitches and so on, corresponding pairs of stitches being worked on the opposite side of the central veining. This stitch is used for working ears of barley and occasionally for filling in centres of flowers (Fig. 5).

Bullion stitch applied to a Leaf.—This stitch is used instead of satin stitch for a leaf and is most useful. In Fig. 6 the stitches are taken across the leaf from side to side and thus vary in length, more

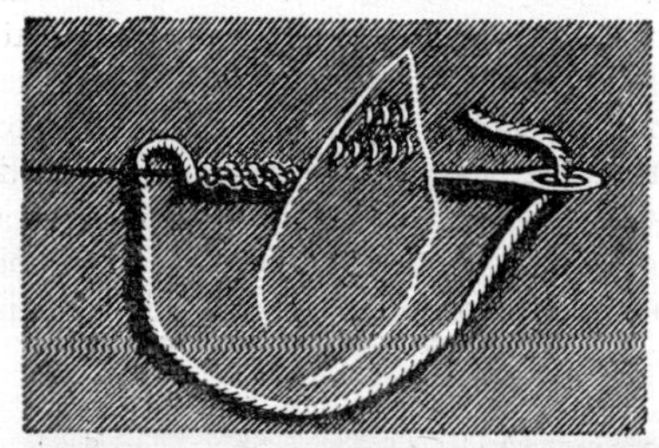

Fig. 6.—BULLION STITCH APPLIED TO A LEAF

twists of cotton being required across the centre than at the tip and base.

Flake stitch is a variety of satin stitch wherein the stitches seem blended one into the other. The outer row of flake stitches is worked first, doing one long and one

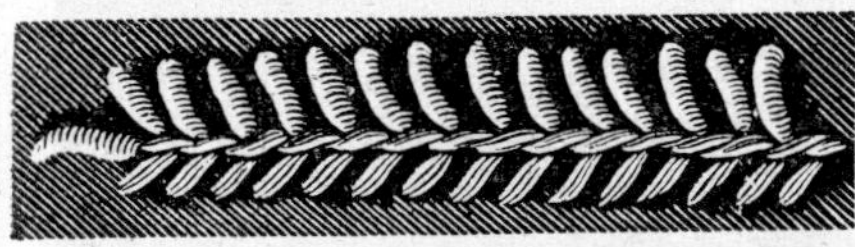

Fig. 4.—FEATHER STITCH AND BULLION

short stitch alternately. In the second row fill in the spaces, making the stitches longer than those of the first row, keeping them long and short alternately. In the third row fill in the spaces left in the second, making the stitches longer than the previous ones and so on until the centre line is reached. This must be kept as the vein of the leaf. Care must be taken to keep the work very smooth to avoid a ridgy appearance (Fig. 7).

A Fern Leaf in Buttonhole stitch makes a very light leaf and is easy to work. The stem is worked in stem stitch. The fronds consist of a series of buttonholed loops worked in the same way as those used for dresses. The buttonhole stitches all lie in the same direction and to do this the bottom of the leaf must always be held towards the worker.

Beginning at the top right-hand side, bring the needle out close to the centre vein, where the first stitch is to be started. Insert the needle in the material about ¼ of an inch to the right, bring it out in the same place as it was first inserted and draw it through. Work two more stitches in the same way. On these three threads the buttonhole stitches are worked. Work them as neatly and evenly as possible. When the loop is competely covered, pass the needle to the back of the material at the top of the loop and bring it out at the side of the centre vein, ready to work another bar a little below the one just completed. Continue like this down the right-hand side until the bottom is reached

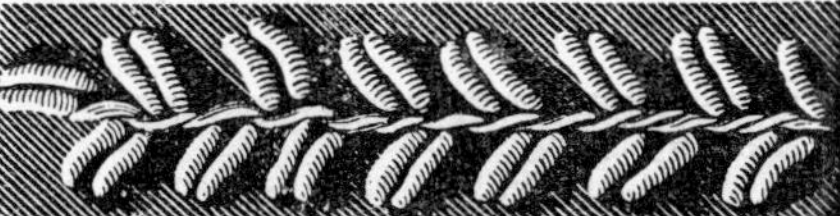

Fig. 5.—DOUBLE BULLION

and then fasten off. Then start at the top of the stem and make a buttonhole loop pointing upwards. Then continue down the left side, making loops to correspond with those on the right, but this time bringing the needle up at the end of the loop furthest away from the vein and inserting it in the material close to the vein, so as to keep the uniformity of the loops (Fig. 8).

Thorn stitch, Trellis and French Knots.—The surface of the material within the thorn stitch outline is decorated by a trellis work of threads taken across the leaf

Fig. 7.—WORKING A LEAF IN FLAKE STITCH

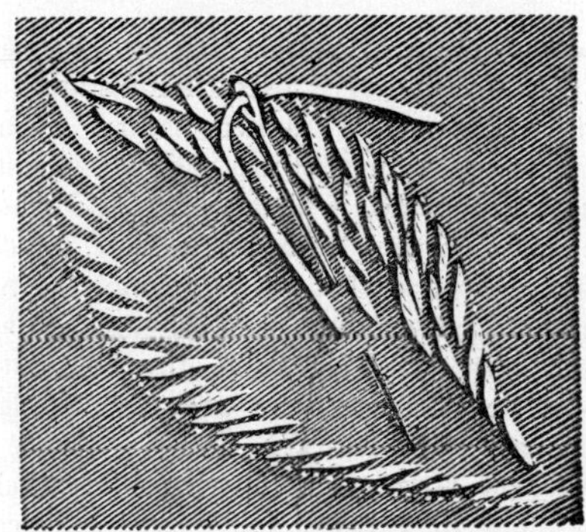

slanting vertically from side to side, three threads in one direction and two in the other. In the places where these threads cross each other, little groups of four french knots are dotted together, working one knot in each corner of the trellis. This leaf is bold in style and useful for large pieces of work (Fig. 9).

Begin by outlining the leaf in a fairly strong cotton. This gives a firmness to the edges. Beginning at the left side of a leaf, bring the needle up to make a satin stitch across the leaf and catch this long satin stitch down in the middle with a short back-stitch. Continue these satin stitches until the entire leaf is covered, catching

Right:

Fig. 8.—FERN LEAF WORKED IN BUTTON HOLE STITCH

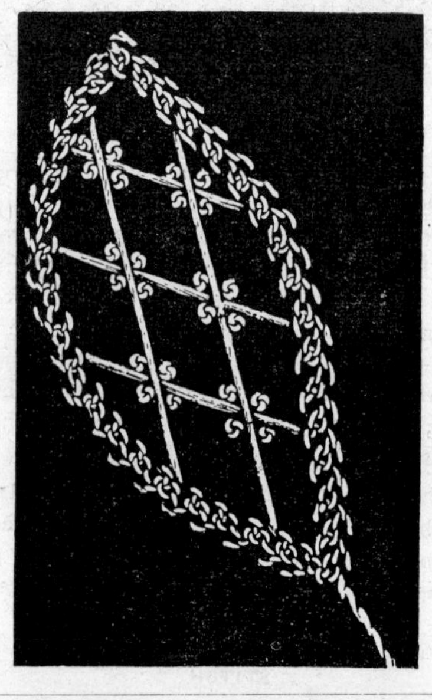

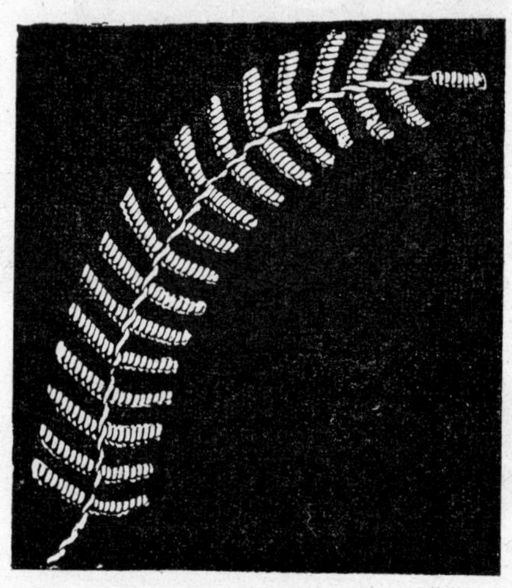

Left:

Fig. 9.—LEAF WORKED IN THORN STITCH TRELLIS AND FRENCH KNOTS

Solid Work of Spot stitch and French Knots.—This leaf is useful for working in with leaves of a lighter nature. The outline is in stem stitch and within this the entire surface is filled with spot stitches interspersed here and there with french knots. Spot stitches are very simple, being formed by working two or three small back stitches one over the other, but care must be taken to keep them at regular distances as seen in Fig. 10.

Faggot stitch is a most effective stitch for filling in leaves or fairly large surfaces. each one down in its centre. When finished, this row of back stitches looks like a vein. When working faggot stitch, it must be remembered that the thicker the cotton used the more effective it is, as it has a heavier, more handsome appearance. In every case the satin stitches must lie close together to look even (Fig. 11).

Leaf with Ornamental Filling.—The outline of this leaf is in stem stitch. The filling is begun by inserting the needle first on the right and then on the left-hand side of the leaf, taking up each time a small piece of material below the stem stitch outline. These stitches themselves are invisible, as they appear only on the wrong side of the material, but from each stitch a strand of cotton is carried across the surface of the leaf, and if the stitches are all the same size these strands of cotton will lie at regular intervals one from another enough (about 2 inches). The serrated edges of the leaf are worked in buttonhole stitch with a little space between the teeth of the stitches. Work the first angular piece at the top of the leaf close to the feather stitch, turn the feather stitch sideways and work a series of small detached curved streaks of buttonhole stitch on the

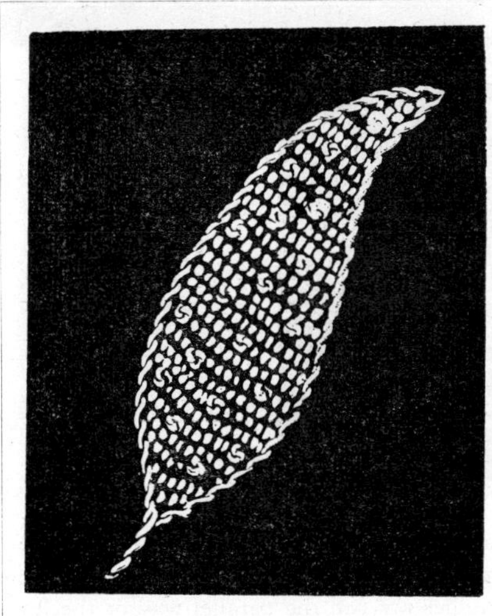

Left:

Fig. 10.—A LEAF IN SOLID WORK OF SPOT STITCH AND FRENCH KNOTS

Right:

Fig. 11.—A SPRAY WORKED IN FAGGOT STITCH

vertically across the leaf as seen in Fig. 12. Now work a line of cross-stitches straight down the centre, working one cross-stitch in the middle of each of the squares between the strands, then a french knot on each side of each cross-stitch. This will fill in the space still left between the cross-stitches and the outline. This completes the leaf.

A Broad Palmate Leaf Deeply Serrated, suitable for a large piece of work. The centre vein is first worked in closely set feather stitch. Begin with a narrow peak at the top widening to nearly $\frac{3}{8}$ of an inch, at which width it is kept until it is long right side of the leaf, not too near the feather stitch, but at the distance shown in Fig. 13. Take the last curved streak (which ends at the base of the feather stitch) further on to the left of the leaf in corresponding shape to that worked on the left side. Turning the material in the hand so as to hold it conveniently, continue working this side to correspond with the side already worked. There should be enough space between the curved streaks of buttonhole stitch and the feather stitch to take two rows of medium-sized french knots.

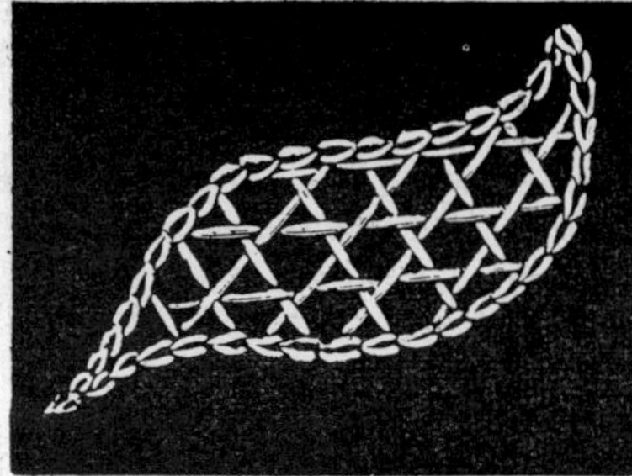

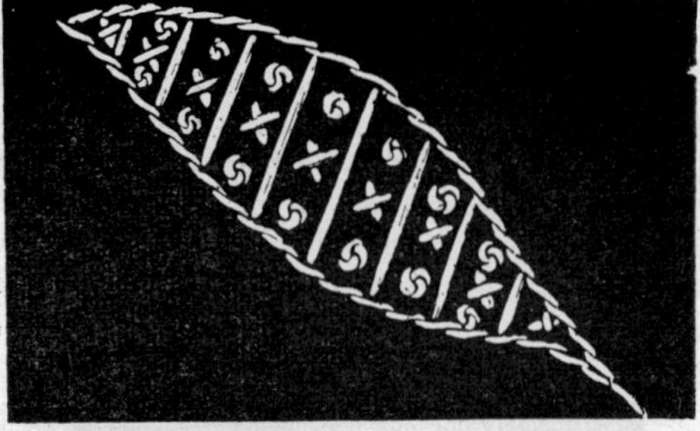

Fig. 14.
BRUSSELS NET STITCH

Fig. 12.
ORNAMENTAL FILLING

Fig. 13.

DEEPLY SERRATED PALMATE LEAF

A Leaf filled with Brussels Net stitch is outlined in simple chain stitch and the interior open-work in imitation of Brussels net. This is done by taking long stitches from one side of the leaf to the other in an oblique direction. Across these work other long stitches slanting in the opposite direction and so arranged that the two sets of stitches form a series of meshes of open diamond net work. Then three long stitches are run the parallel way of the leaf, in darning fashion, passing the needle alternately over and under the net-like threads of the open diamonds and the leaf will appear as in Fig. 14.

Leaf filled with Double Brussels Net

Right:

Fig. 15.—DOUBLE BRUSSELS NET STITCH

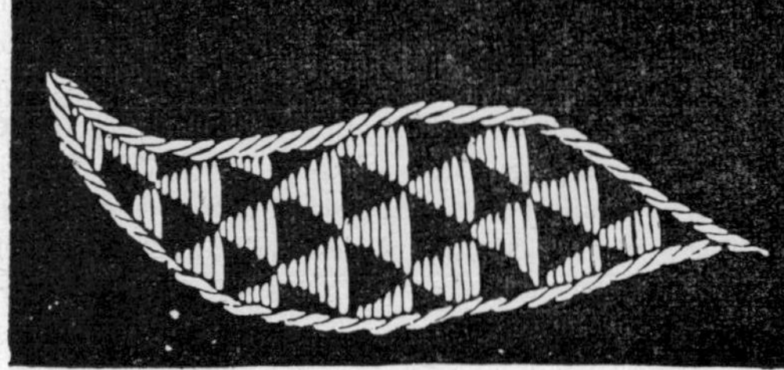

Left:

Fig. 16.
PYRAMID STITCH

stitch has the outline worked in cable-plait-stitch.

To work, trace two parallel lines about a quarter of an inch apart and, working from left to right, bring up the needle on the lower tracing line, holding the cotton down under the left thumb. Pass the needle from right to left under the cotton and draw the cotton under the thumb into a small loop. Put the point of the needle under this, raising the loop to the top tracing line. Insert the needle bringing the point out straight on the bottom tracing-line. Release the loop under the thumb and draw it round the *top* of the needle and through. Every stitch is formed in the same way, and the result produces a raised thick plait on the right side of the material and a series of small perpendicular stitches on the wrong side. When the outline is completed, work backwards and forwards across the narrow way of the leaf, taking a stitch first on the right-hand side, then on the left close against the outline, in such a way that though the stitches themselves being taken through the material do not show, a strand of cotton from stitch to stitch is taken across from side to side at intervals of about $\frac{1}{8}$ of an inch apart. Then the oblique lines of threads are put in as described in the above example. Finish by darning two stitches the long way of the leaf through the network of threads, in such a way as to cross the first set of threads in the exact centre of two lines of diamonds. Secure these in position by working the first half of a cross-stitch as shown in Fig. 15.

Leaf filled with Pyramid stitch.—The outline is worked in stem stitch, and the centre is entirely filled in, in what is known to lace workers as "pyramid stitch.' Begin near the base of the leaf and take the first satin stitch straight across the leaf to form the bottom of the first pyramid, then each successive stitch above this is a trifle shorter, until the top is reached after six or eight stitches. Here a very small stitch, no longer than a dot stitch, is required to complete the pyramid. As can be seen from Fig. 16, there are triangular-shaped space of material visible between the worked pyramids.

Leaf worked in Point de Sorrento.—The outline is worked in two rows of stem stitch, while the centre is filled with a network of buttonhole stitches worked in pairs. This is done in rows backwards and forwards. In the first row work the buttonhole stitches close together, then leave a small space, work two more stitches and so on. In the following rows, after beginning by steadying the turn of the row into the material close against the outline, each pair of buttonhole stitches will be formed along the thread that extends along the space between the buttonhole stitches of the preceding row, and thus the pairs of buttonhole stitches in every row alternate with each other as seen in Fig. 38.

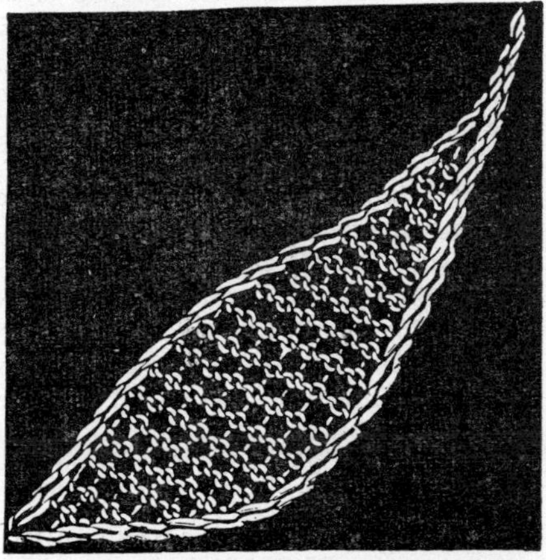

Fig. 17.—A VARIATION POINT DE SORRENTO

Leaf Edged with Indented Overcasting.—Work the centre vein by couching down a single thread of cotton. Pad thickly the margin that is to be covered with overcasting and then work in stitches of alternate lengths. The first stitch must cover the padding and keep it in the required position. The second stitch is level with the first at the vein of the leaf, but projects considerably further outside beyond the padding. These two stitches are repeated as seen in Fig. 18.

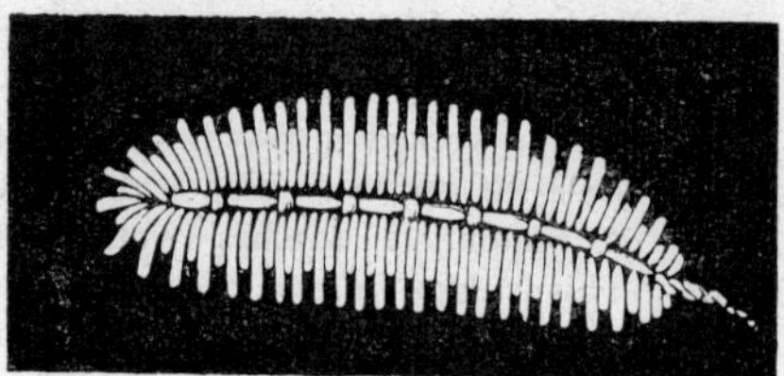

Fig. 18. INDENTED OVERCASTING

Leaf Ornamented with Bullion stitch and Bars of Cable Plait.—The outline of this stitch is worked in small close button-hole stitches. Then four bars of cable plait are worked horizontally across the leaf as in Fig. 19. Between these bars are ornamental bullion stitches, extending vertically from bar to bar. Thus one bullion stitch reaches from the top-most bar to nearly the tip of the leaf. In the next space there are two bullion stitches, in the next three, in the next four, while in the lower space at the base of the leaf there are only two.

Twisted Threads and Point de Reprise.—The outline is in stem stitch, then six bars in Point de Reprise are worked across the leaf. Begin by forming four long stitches close together that are smooth and even like long satin stitches. These stitches should not appear on the back of the work as they are taken backwards and forwards only on the top of the work. With the needle on the right side of the work, take it over the first two of the long threads and under the second two and draw it through. Turn the needle the reverse way and pass it over the two threads and under the two threads and draw it through. Continue thus over and under until the bar is covered with stitches, taking care the needle does not go through the material. Work the other bars in the same way. The next stitch to be worked is the middle twisted one. Bring the needle up to the front of the material close to the point of the leaf, take a small running stitch in the material in the centre of the leaf below the first bar of the Point de Reprise, a similar stitch under the second bars and so on, until the base is reached. Pass the needle to the back of the material and bring it up again to the front within a thread or two of the same place. A single thread of cotton will now be seen running the whole length of the leaf down the centre, hidden only by the bars of the Point de Reprise. Pass the needle four times under and over the first part of the thread which will make a twisted stitch. Pass the needle under the bar and three or four times over the next part of the thread, then continue

Fig. 20. TWISTED THREADS AND POINT DE REPRISE

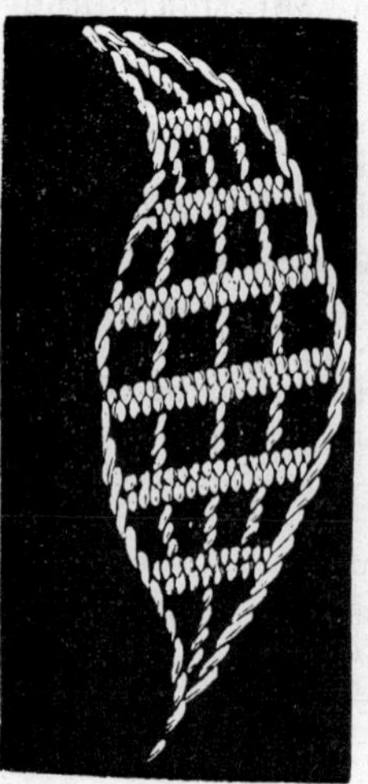

Fig. 19. BULLION STITCH AND BARS OF CABLE PLAIT

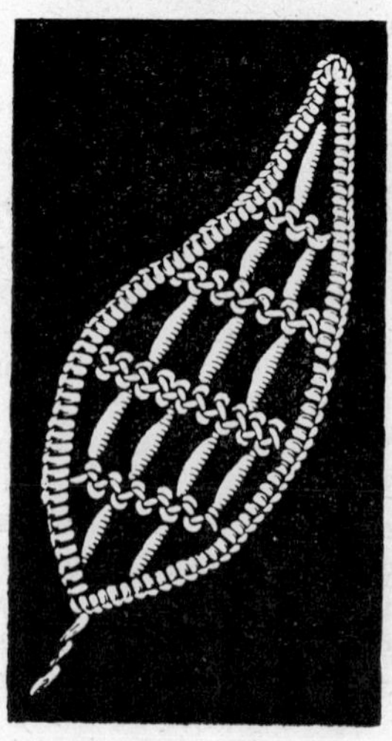

Fig. 21.—DAISY LOOP STITCH

the twisted stitch in the same way up to the point of the leaf. Make two more twisted stitches one on each side of the centre, but reaching in length only from the first to the last bar of the Point de Reprise. The finished leaf is shown in Fig. 20.

Leaf in Daisy Loop stitch.—This is a graceful leaf if worked smoothly. Hold the work in position to work from left to right. Beginning at the base of the leaf, bring the needle to the front on the line of the vein and draw it through. Then, with the cotton held under the left thumb, as if about to buttonhole, insert the needle in the same place from which it was just drawn through and bring it forward upon the outline, passing over the cotton held by the thumb and draw it through. This makes a loop similar to chain stitch loop. Insert the needle outside this loop to the back of the material and bring it out on the vein ready for another daisy stitch and draw it through in this way making a small stitch over the tip of the daisy loop stitch, which besides being ornamental, serves to hold the loop in place. Every successive daisy loop stitch is worked in the same way. They are placed close together and lengthen considerably as the leaf widens. See Fig. 21. After the daisy loop stitches are completed, the vein is worked in stem stitch, which is continued for the stem, too.

Leaf Worked in Spike stitch is begun at the tip or the base, whichever is preferred. Bring the needle to the front of the material on the outline nearest to you. Insert it in the opposite outline and bring it up a little distance within the outline from which it was started, and draw it through. Insert the needle a little distance within the opposite outline and bring it up on the outline nearest to you. Continue like this, alternating with a long and short stitch, keeping them a small space apart. All the stitches will be considerably longer in the centre of the leaf than at either end. The actual length depends on the width of the leaf, but all the long stitches must be on a level with each other. The same applies to the short stitches. This gives the jagged appearance shown in Fig. 22. A line of neat back stitching is taken down

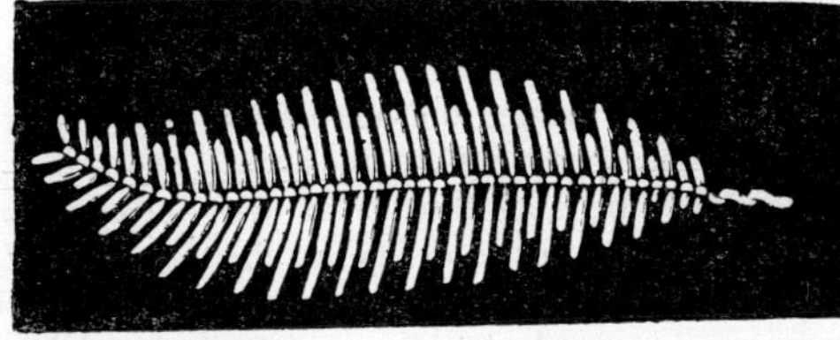

Fig. 22.—SPIKE STITCH

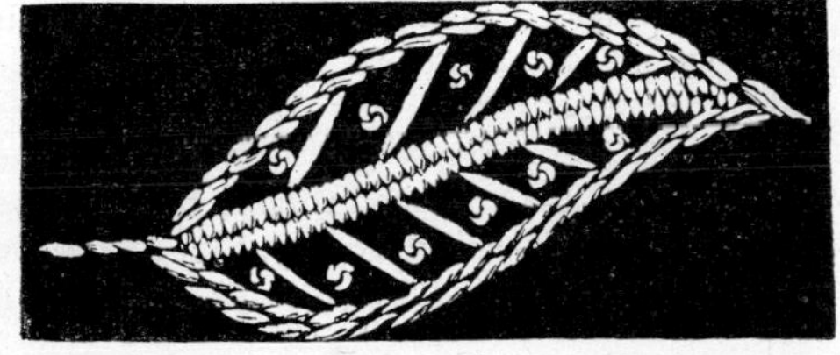

Left:

Fig. 23.—MID-RIB OF POINT DE REPRISE

the centre of the leaf, one back stitch to each spike stitch. This, while forming the vein, serves to steady the spike stitches and adds considerably to the appearance of the leaf.

Leaf with the Vein in Point de Reprise.—The outline is worked in two rows of stem stitch one close to the other. Next the centre vein is worked. Work four threads of cotton on the surface of the material, reaching from the top to the bottom of the leaf, taking the needle to the back only at these points, to avoid making corresponding long threads on the wrong side. Then, with the needle on the right side, work over the first two threads and under the second two and draw through. Then reverse the needle and pass it over the two threads just passed under, and under the two passed over and draw it through. Continue darning in this way for the length of the vein. Then work four or five spikes at regular intervals on each side of the vein, slanting upwards towards the outline, then work one french knot in the centre of each space between the spike stitches. This can be clearly seen from Fig. 23.

Long Narrow Leaf in Buttonhole and Spike stitch.—The main part of the leaf consists of two rows of close, evenly set buttonhole stitches, with the loops of the stitches lying on the outline of the leaf. The severity of this outline is relieved by an edging of spike stitches. Down the vein, where the buttonhole stitches meet, is worked a line of back stitching consisting of one short and one long stitch alternately. See Fig. 24.

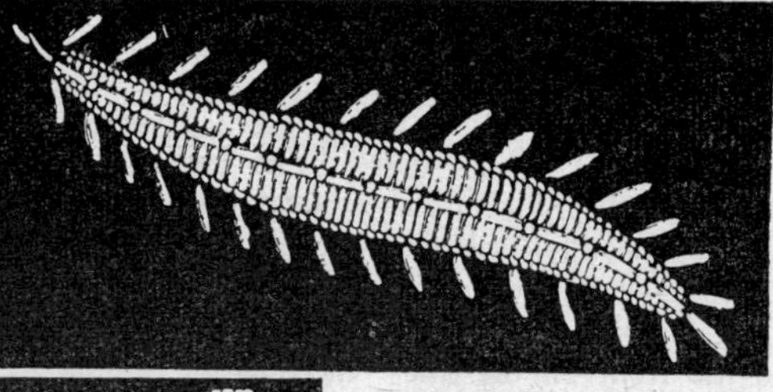

Fig. 24. BUTTON-HOLE STITCH AND SPIKE STITCH

Fig. 25.—LEAF WITH SAW TOOTH OUTLINE

Fig. 26.—OVERCAST AND SPIKE STITCH

Leaf with Saw tooth Outline is produced by working alternately two tall and two short buttonhole stitches in what is known as saw tooth buttonholing. The indentations made by the teeth of the stitches are arranged to point towards the interior, the even loop stitches being on the outline. Down the centre of the leaf a line of open feather stitch is worked (Fig. 25).

Leaf Overcast and Spike stitch.—The outline is worked in raised overcasting worked in a vertical direction. The outside has a border of spike stitches. The centre vein is in feather stitching (Fig. 26).

Leaf with Scalloped Outline.—The outline consists of smooth flat buttonholing scalloped on the outside of the leaf. If a raised buttonhole is preferred it may be padded first. A row of cable plait down the centre marks the vein (Fig. 27).

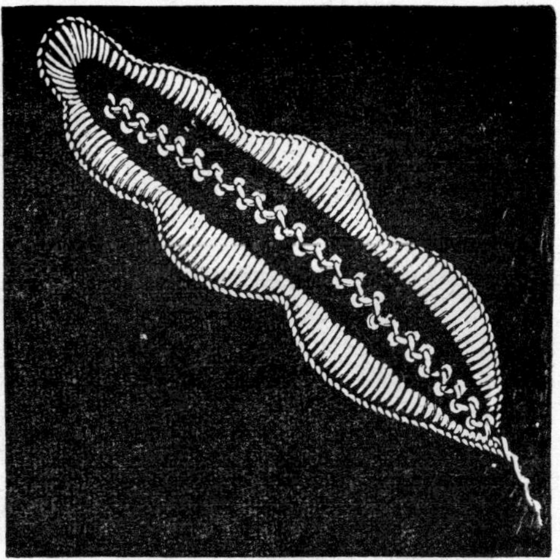

Fig. 27.—LEAF WITH SCALLOPED OUTLINE

A Light Leaf.—This is worked partly in feather stitch and partly in stem-stitch, as seen in Fig. 28. Work a row of french knots down the centre and a row round the outside. This finishes the leaf.

Leaf with Cable plait Veining.—This is very suitable for large pieces of work as it is quickly worked. The outline is also in stem stitch except at the top, where it changes to cable plait to harmonise with the veins which branch out from the centre vein. It is advisable to start the cable plait narrow by the vein, widening towards the outline (Fig. 29).

Leaf in Satin stitch and Back stitch.—This leaf is worked in stem stitch, satin stitch, back stitch and couching. The outline is couched with a thread of cotton two sizes coarser than that used for the embroidery. Work the centre vein in stem stitch. After this, the V-shaped bars are worked as in Fig. 30 in straight satin stitch. The space left is now filled in with back stitching in the same direction as the bars. Small stitches are taken which, although taking longer to work, make the leaf worth while when finished.

Fig. 28.—A LIGHT LEAF

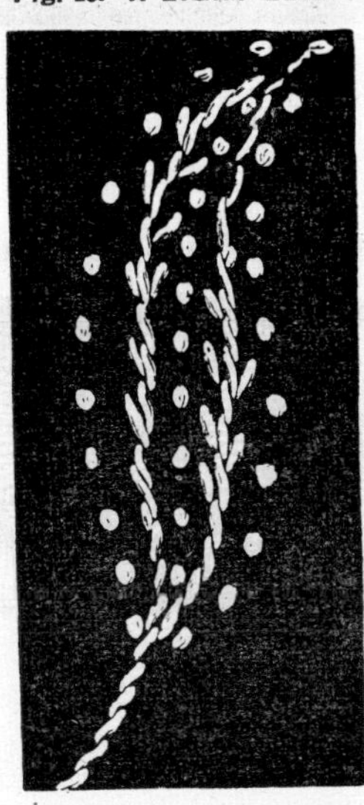

Leaf with Couched Outline.—Four or five threads are used for the couching of this outline. This is held in position at regular intervals by the small stitch worked in one thread as seen in Fig. 31. The V-shaped veins being already traced on the work, six threads of cotton run lengthways perpendicularly up the leaf, three on each side of the centre vein in the position shown in the diagram. These lines followed the shape of the leaf, and are held in position by taking short stitches into the material below the V-shaped veins. They are now changed into twisted threads by passing the needle round each in such a way that the second thread is twisted over the first. The working of the twisted bars and Point de Reprise for the veins has already been fully explained in the working directions for Fig. 20. The vein is in stem stitch.

Leaf Worked in Raised Picot.—The

Fig. 31.
LEAF WITH COUCHED OUTLINE (right)

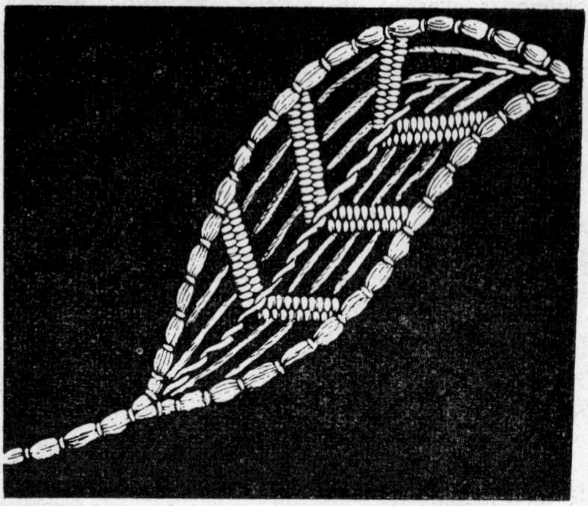

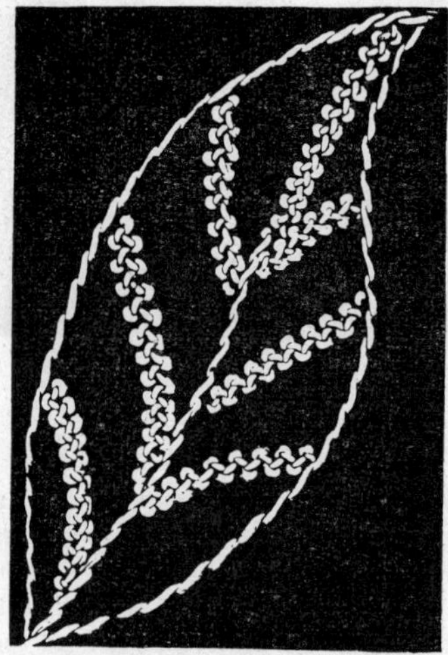

Fig. 29.—LEAF WITH CABLE PLAIT VEINING

Fig. 30.—SATIN STITCH AND BACK STITCH

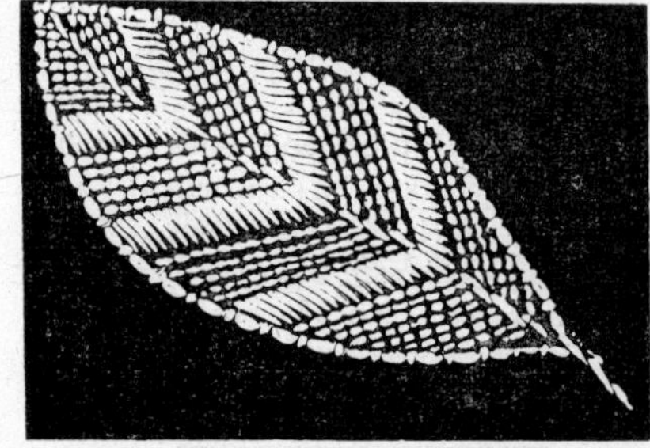

Fig. 32. RAISED PICOTS (below)

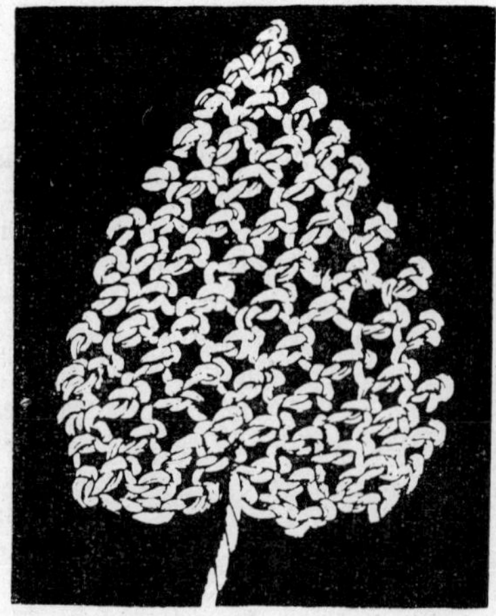

Fig. 33. WIDE BUTTONHOLE EDGE

raised picots which compose this leaf are worked like a french knot except that a small running stitch is used to connect the picots, thus entirely changing the character of the embroidery. Begin working at the top of the leaf, bring up the needle a few threads below the tip of the leaf and bring it out in the same place from which it came, pass the needle under the cotton held by the thumb and draw it through, being careful not to disarrange the twist which is now on top of the needle. Pass the needle below the picot just formed, to the back of the work and bring it up just within the outline on the right-hand side, a little lower down the leaf and make another picot as just described. When this is done pass the needle to the back below the picot and bring it up in the picot again, make a short running stitch on the surface, take about two threads of material on the needle and the needle is now in position to work a picot close to the outline on the left-hand side to correspond with the one just worked. The running stitch extends across the leaf between these two picots. This is the first row.

Take the needle across the back of the material to the left-hand side of the leaf ready to work the second row. Make the first picot and running stitch—as above. The second picot will have to be made in the centre of the leaf and must be worked on the running stitch of the previous row, taking the needle through the fabric as before. Finish this picot with a running-stitch and make a third picot by the outline on the left-hand side of the leaf. Thus three picots and two running stitches make up the second row. Continue with every row in the same way from right to left, increasing one picot and one running stitch every two rows as the leaf widens. Finish with a short stem stitched stem as seen in Fig. 32.

Fig. 34.—TURRET BUTTONHOLING

Two Useful Buttonhole Edgings.—Fig. 33 shows a buttonhole edging which takes a little more time, but is very suitable for Mountmellick work as it is not too light. These scallops are about an inch in height and $\frac{1}{4}$ of an inch wide, the narrow part forming the edge. It is worked like ordinary buttonhole stitch starting at the bottom and working up to the top.

Turret Buttonholing and how to mitre the corners:—This has to be worked with the greatest accuracy to look even. It is helpful to make a stencil plate as a guide with which to trace the outside of the buttonholing. The lower edge of the cardboard will be straight to start with, and from it at regular intervals cut a piece out. To do this draw a series of perpendicular lines $2\frac{1}{2}$ inches up from the edge, the first line to be $2\frac{1}{4}$ inches from the side, and the next $1\frac{1}{2}$ inches from that. Repeat the lines with these alternate spacings as far as the width of the cardboard will allow. Now draw a short line across the top of all the narrowest spaces at the distance of $2\frac{1}{2}$ inches above the edge of the cardboard. These narrow spaces are all cut out to give the shapes of the turrets. Put the cardboard in position and outline the turrets for the loop side of the buttonhole stitches, moving it forward as required; $\frac{3}{8}$ of an inch above this draw another outline whereby the teeth of the buttonhole stitches may be kept level. Then draw a short slanting line from point to point across the angles of the corners to denote the direction of the stitches when mitring the corners. The buttonhole stitch is worked in the usual way, $\frac{3}{8}$ of an inch everywhere except at the corners, where each stitch becomes shorter and shorter following the slanting line until the extreme point of the corner is reached, when they gradually lengthen again in the same proportion. The teeth of the stitches should meet in angular fashion as seen in Fig. 34. When all the buttonholing is complete the material is cut away along the edge.

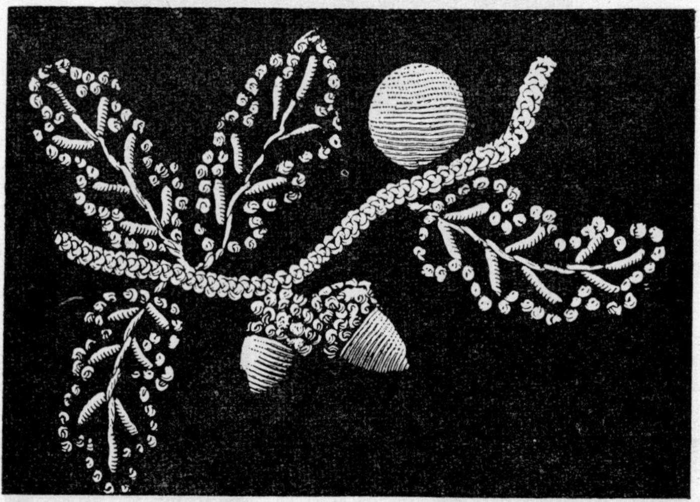

Fig. 35.—BRANCH OF OAK, WITH OAK APPLE AND ACORNS

SIMPLE SPRAYS

Branch of Oak with Oak Apple and Acorns.—The branch is worked in cable plait stitch already described. The oak leaves have rugged edges worked in french knots, with the centre vein in stem stitch on either side of which bullion stitches are worked at intervals to resemble veins. The oak apple is worked in thickly raised satin stitch. The acorns are especially natural, the cup being worked in french knots close together, while the nut, which has the part nearest to the cup raised, is

worked in satin stitch, which gradually narrows and flattens as it reaches the tip (Fig. 35).

A Spray of Chrysanthemums.—The stems, as shown in Fig. 37, are worked entirely in fine overcast stitch. The leaf at the bottom right hand side of the stem is worked in two sections, the upper section is in close evenly worked satin stitch over a slightly padded foundation. The under section is made up of a series of bullion knots in the form of spikes extending from the centre vein to the outline of the leaf. The upper division of the next leaf is in elongated trellis stitch; the centre vein is in stem stitch, the lower part outlined in a narrow buttonhole stitch. The space between is filled in with french knots graduating in size. Work the petals of the full-blown flower in slightly raised satin stitch, and fill in the centre in french knots. The leaf above is worked with a row of spike stitches, each spike stitch having a french knot on it. The lower section is entirely in french knots. The three buds are worked in the same way as the flower, having a base of french knots. The leaf at the top of the stem is outlined in stem stitch like the centre vein, and is then filled in with diamond stitch worked evenly and held in place by a small stitch confining the cross threads of each diamond. The small leaf on the left-hand side is outlined in two rows of stem stitch with five raised spots in satin stitch down the centre. The next leaf has one section worked in thickly raised satin stitch graduating with the shape of the leaf. The other half is worked with rows of small loops of buttonhole stitches worked on a thread of cotton as if making loops used on dresses. The next leaf is simply outlined in cable plait stitch, and the veins are in stem stitch. The small leaf is in satin stitch with a stem stitch vein. The lower leaf is in two sections, one half being filled in indented satin stitch, the other half outlined in stem stitch filled in in rows of small back stitches.

Fig. 37.—A SPRAY OF CHRYSANTHEMUMS

Designs for Borders which can also be adapted for other purposes. The entire depth of the design in Fig. 38 is 6 inches, the two narrow insertions being 1 inch, so that the scroll fills the other 5 inches. After tracing on the design, work two rows of cable plait stitch along the two narrow borders. These narrow borders are filled in with long stitches taken in diamond fashion across and across the space. A french knot is worked in the centre of these and a straight stitch passes over the crossed threads as shown in Fig. 38.

For the scroll, the outline of every leaf, flower and lobe is worked with a laid thread which is couched with a satin stitch taken across it at regular intervals. The petals of the flowers are embroidered, two of them with closely worked Indian filling and four of them with buttonhole filling known as Point de Sorrento. Looking at the diagram it will be noticed that the buttonhole stitches are placed in parallel lines, two stitches close together, a small space, then two more stitches. Details of the working have aready been given. Certain leaves on the outside of the scroll are worked in brick couching which is very simple. Long stitches are taken lengthways of the leaf. These must lie straight and flat and close together, with smaller stitches in the curves of the leaf, filling the leaf completely with a surface of smooth threads. Then other long stitches are taken across the leaf diagonally, not close together, but with a reasonable space between each stitch. These latter stitches are then held in place by dot stitches alternating, as shown in the illustration, in each successive row. A small leaf is completely filled in with french knots, and another in buttonhole loops. The lobes are filled with diamond filling of crossed thread, held in place by small straight stitches wherever the threads of the diamonds cross.

Fig. 42 requires no explanation for working, for when the diagram is carefully studied one can see that the greater part is worked in raised satin stitch and buttonhole stitch. Part of the buttonhole stitch is worked over loose threads. The other stitches used in this border have already been described.

A Conventional Flower shown in Fig. 39 is reproduced the actual size of working.

Fig. 38.—ANTIQUE BORDER

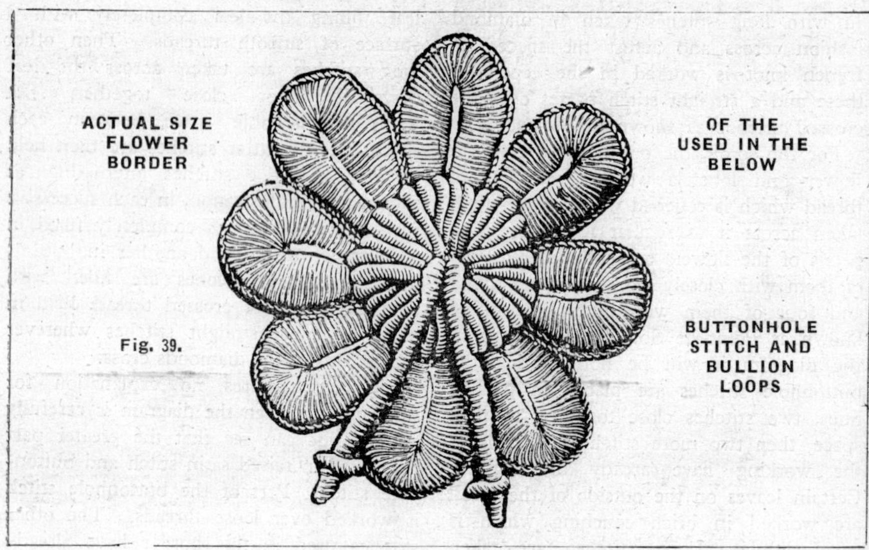

Fig. 39.

It consists entirely of close, firm embroidery surrounded by leaves of an open nature, which makes a good contrast. Two sizes of cotton are required, the coarser being only used for the two very long stamens and for padding. Trace the flower exactly to the size and shape shown in the diagram, drawing a short, straight line down the centre of each of the eight petals, a circle to denote the circumference to which the corona may extend and a dot to mark the exact centre. Begin by padding the interior of the corona, which is done by darning round and round in a circle, making the stitches lie as much as possible on the front of the material, and on one another until raised sufficiently. Pad each of the petals separately in horse-shoe shape, leaving the line down the centre of each quite clear. When the padding is finished,

Fig. 40.—A FLOWER TREATED CONVENTIONALLY

Fig. 41.—WIDE INSERTION

work the petals in wide buttonhole stitch which can be seen from the illustration. The corona consists of a circle of bullion loops. Most of these start from the dot in the centre, but some will have to be worked in the coarser cotton. Bring the needle up at the end of the stamen and insert the needle, which must be a long one, in the centre of the flower and bring it out in the same point as before. Keep it in this position, while the cotton is wound 30 or 40 times round the point of the needle, then, holding the twist firmly, draw the needle through and pull the twist upwards to the centre of the flower without disarranging it. The stamen is then finished. The other stamen is worked in the same way. The tip of each stamen has a small bullion knot horizontally worked. See the diagram. The stem below is worked in a double row of cable-plait, the centre of which is filled in with french knots.

Fig. 42.—A CONVENTIONAL BORDER

Fig. 43.

COAT OF ARMS EMBROIDERED IN MOUNTMELLICK WORK

Fig. 40 shows this flower used in a border. Two thicknesses of thread are used as before. Both flowers are worked in highly raised embroidery and are of the same shape and size. The corona and stamens are worked in the same way, but the petals are more open. These petals are padded close against the outline and then buttonholed. The space between is filled in with diamond trellis. The blossoms are outlinel in chain stitch, showing the eight sections, a french knot occupies the centre of the blossom and four pairs of bullion stitches are worked from the centre. See Fig. 40. A few french knots are then worked on the surface. The stems are wide throughout and worked on both sides in cable plait with french knots at intervals down the centre. Most of the leaves have been described before, the method used for them being clearly seen in the diagram. Two simple leaves that have not been mentioned before are the following: Outline the leaf in stem-stitch, fill the centre with herringbone filling and round the outside work a border of french knots. The other has the outline down one side in chain stitch, then a row of french knots, the centre vein in stem stitch from which a series of daisy loop stitches extend to the right.

Fig. 41 shows a very handsome border comprising a number of stitches already described. It measures 6½ inches in depth. The experienced worker can now tell by looking at the diagram the fillings which have been used. This design can be repeated for the length required.

Coats of Arms are quite a good subject for this work. It is not always possible to work all the details, but it depends on the skill of the worker. Coats of arms may either be worked straight on to the article or may be applied afterwards. The outline in either case should be worked in buttonhole stitching over one or two threads of coarser cotton to raise the stitching well above the level of the foundation. This can be seen from Fig. 43. The quarterings can be defined with stem-stitch, chain-stitch, or cable-stitch, the rest of the stitches being left to the worker.

The Design of Griffins in Fig. 44 requires little explanation as the stitches can be followed from the diagram. Though this is a more elaborate piece, it will be found quite easy and interesting to work. All the stitches used have been described earlier in this chapter.

A Knitted Fringe.—This may be worked in either single or double cotton. Single cotton was used for Fig. 45, but if a thicker fringe is preferred, use the cotton double, that is, wound on two separate balls and knitted from the two together. A pair of No. 11 or 12 knitting needles are required, also a bone netting mesh from $1\frac{1}{2}$ to 2 inches wide to determine the depth of the fringe. A strip of very thick card-board will serve just as well.

Begin by casting on seven stitches. **1st row.**—Insert the needle in the first stitch in the usual way, take the mesh and hold it between the thumb and first finger of the left hand close up to the work, pass the cotton first along the back and then up the front of the mesh and round the point of the right-hand needle, and knit off the

Fig. 44.—DESIGN OF GRIFFINS

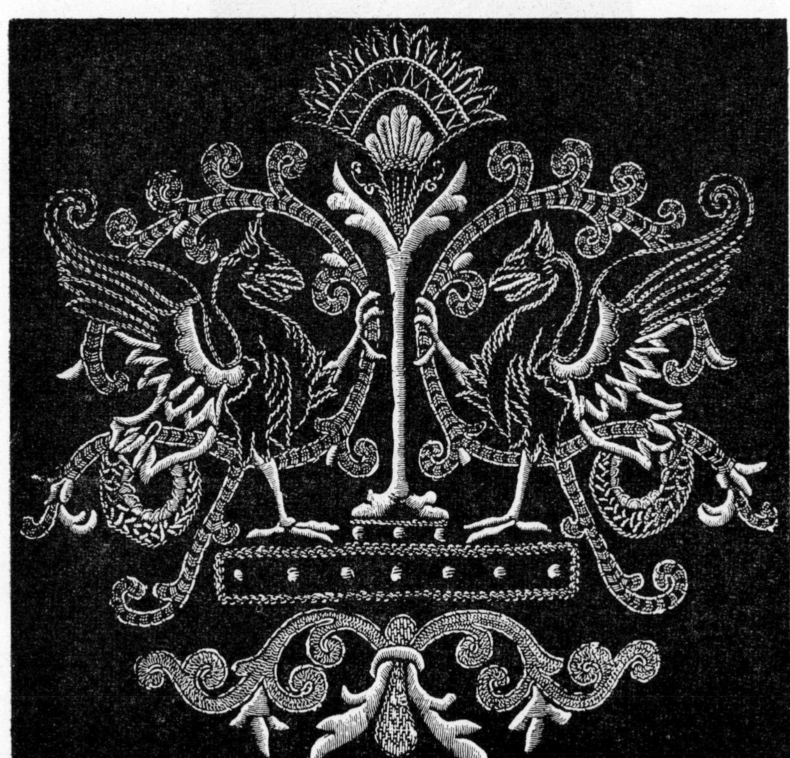

stitch, keeping it close to the mesh on which the loop of the fringe is wound, knit the next stitch plain, make 1, knit 2 together, make 1, knit 2 together, knit 1. **2nd row.**—Slip the first stitch, knit 6. Repeat these two rows alternately for the length required. When the mesh is full of loops, those at the end are slipped off to make room for more. A twist is given to each loop by putting in a knitting needle and twisting the strands of cotton tightly one over the other, then drawing the pin out so that the fringe appears as in the diagram.

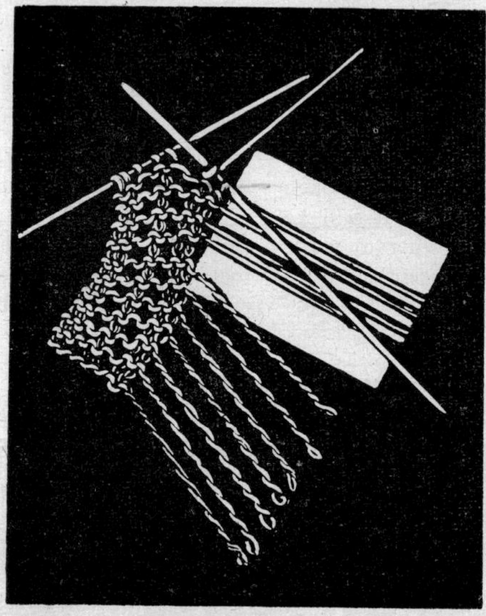

Fig. 45. A KNITTED FRINGE

NEEDLEWEAVING

Needleweaving is a very old craft, many early pieces having been found in Egyptian tombs. It is also known as woven hemstitching and is used for narrow borders on linen. It is a stronger variety of drawn thread work, as the threads left are afterwards worked over backwards and forwards in bright colours to form patterns.

Designs for this work are of a geometrical type using as a foundation the diamond or square. The pattern should be worked out carefully on graph paper and arranged in borders of zig-zags or diagonal lines which can be used for chairbacks, runners, towel ends, curtains, divan covers, etc.

The pattern can be arranged in repeating motifs or to fill a certain space. Long vertical lines should not be used, as they leave gaps which look ugly and are difficult to manage when working in several colours: Only when one colour is used, may a long vertical line be used, as the thread can be kept tighter and the gaps and long lines add much to the beauty of the design.

The planning of the design depends much upon the purpose to which the work is put when finished. When a deep border is being planned, it is advisable to try to leave two or three weft threads at intervals throughout as these help to strengthen the work, and are hardly noticeable. When this is done the weaving can be worked in strips which are much easier to manage.

Initials and monograms can also be worked to advantage in needleweaving and look effective if used in the middle of a border on a towel.

Materials required.—Most loosely woven materials are suitable for this work as the threads can be drawn easily. Coarse linen, art canvas, huckaback, linen crash and handwoven fabrics are amongst those used. The thread used for the weaving is usually a little coarser than the threads withdrawn and is generally silk or wool. A blunt-pointed needle is used for this work. Bright colours are nearly always chosen for needleweaving as they show up better, though one colour only is often used for household linen.

To work needleweaving is quite simple once the weaving backwards and forwards from group to group, and the changing from colour to colour, have been mastered. This only requires a little practice. Simple patterns should be used by beginners, gradually working up to the more elaborate later.

Before starting to work one must be sure of the design as the threads are drawn accordingly. Having decided on this, cut the threads in the middle of the border and unravel them, first to the right, then to the left, taking care not to break them. These threads are not cut, as in drawn thread-work, but are woven back wherever possible, as this makes a tidier and firmer edge. In this work the threads are never drawn right across the work, a narrow border being left at either side. When the edge of the border is reached a needle is threaded with each thread in turn and woven carefully back at either end into the material as shown in Fig. 1. This also shows the threads ready to be darned in and those not yet drawn. At the other end of the border the threads are already darned back. This method does not look

Fig. 1.—DARNING BACK THE DRAWN THREADS

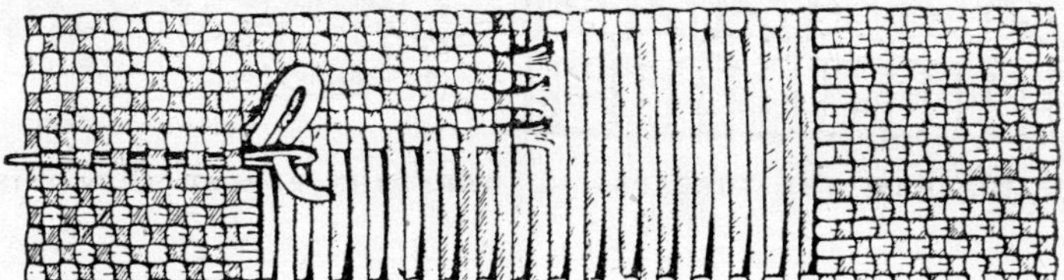

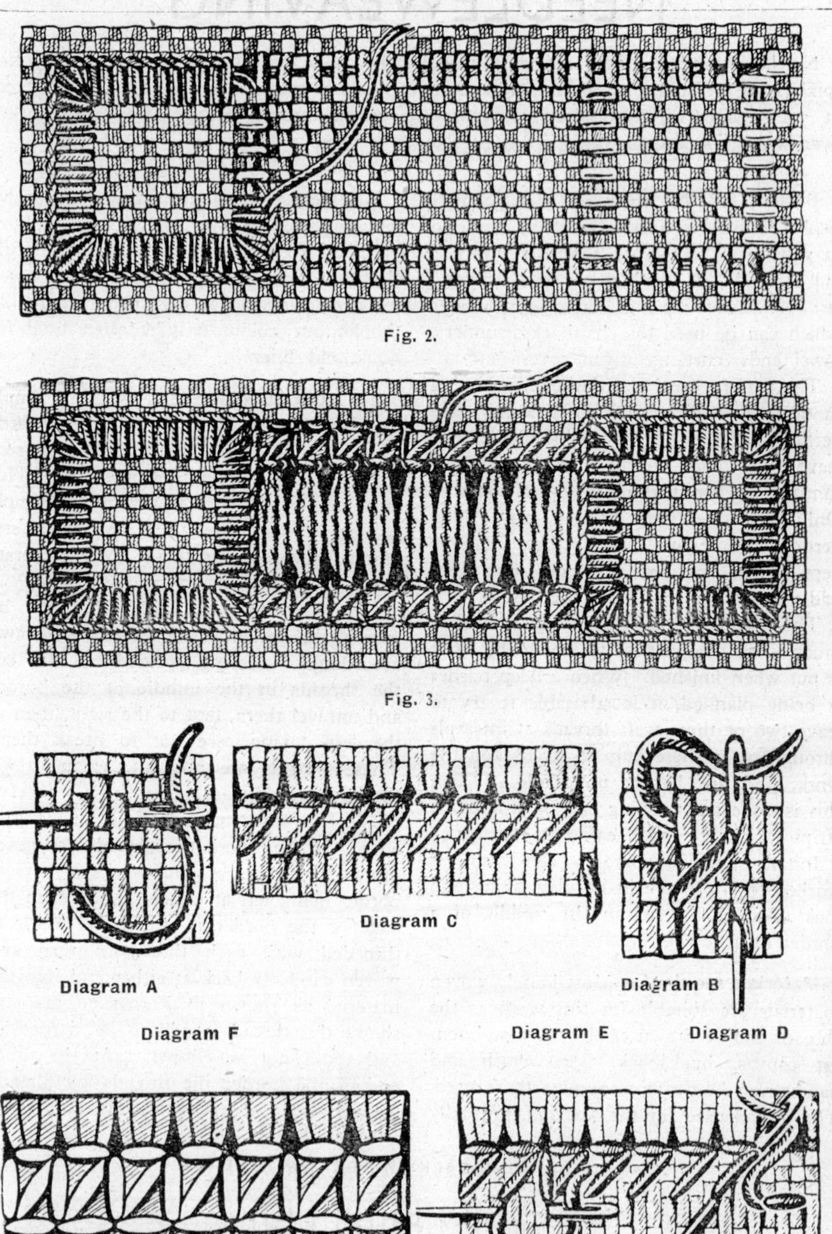

HOW TO DRAW THE THREADS AND WORK THE BORDER SHOWN IN Fig. 3.

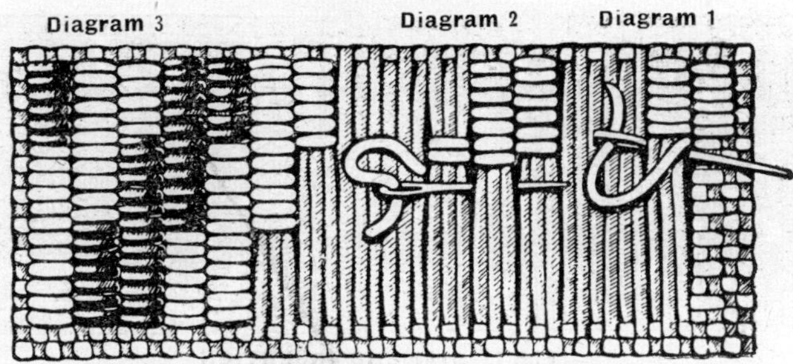

Fig. 4.—HOW THE WEAVING IS DONE

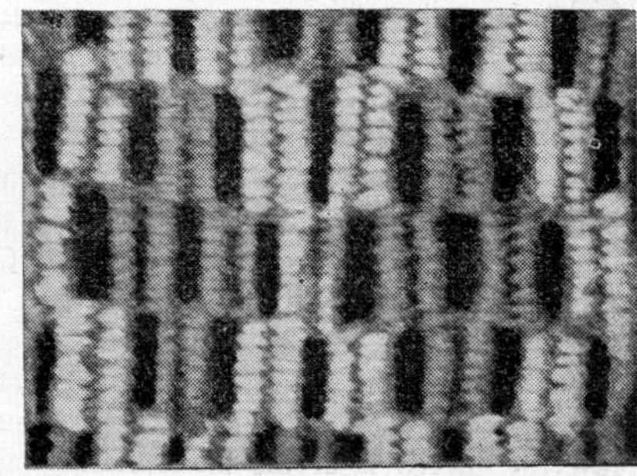

Fig. 6.—A SIMPLE BORDER IN TWO COLOURS, WITH BELOW, A CHART FOR WORKING

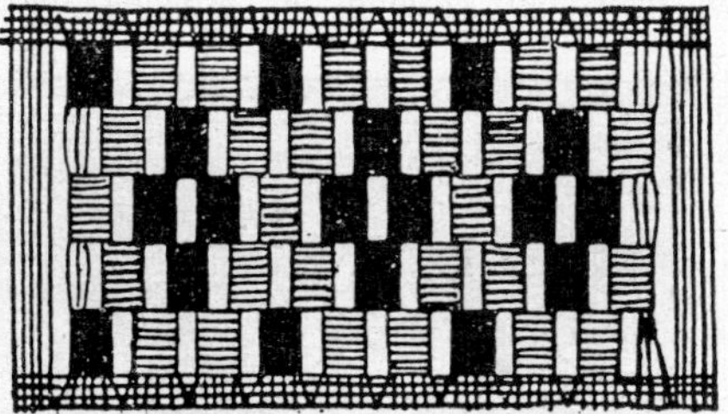

as clumsy as might be imagined, as, when the edge is worked over it, the woven threads are not seen at all.

Another method of preparing the work, after having decided on the border to be worked, is to cut a thread in the middle of each side, the depth the border is required. Draw these threads out until they meet at the corners, then weave them back, as above. This is done for all four sides. To complete the square at either corner, draw the fifteenth thread out, cutting it in the middle and weave back as before (see Fig. 2). Having done this, run a thread round the inside of the square and buttonhole all round, bringing the needle out in the thread which has just been drawn, and keeping the buttonhole on the outside edge as seen in the illustration. Both squares having been buttonholed, the threads are now ready to be drawn. Leave three threads at either edge before drawing the remainder. A drawn-thread stitch then

Fig. 5.—ANOTHER SIMPLE INSERTION

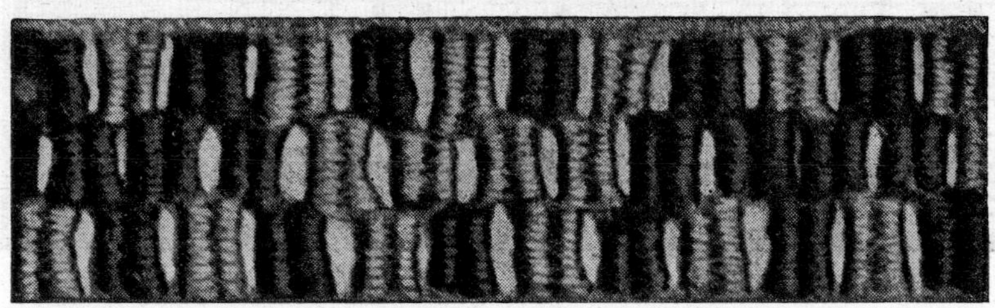

Fig. 7.—DIAMOND INSERTION

divides the threads into clusters as seen in Fig. 3.

If the simple stitch (shown in Diagram C) only is used it can be worked from the wrong side as well. If this is done the stitch is very much straighter when finished.

To work this stitch, run the thread along the back of the buttonhole stitch and bring the needle out on the left-hand side below the three undrawn threads, insert the needle underneath three threads of the upper row as shown in Diagram A, bringing the needle out at the edge of the buttonhole-stitch, then pass over the three threads and insert the needle vertically, bringing it out below the three threads as shown in Diagram B. Continue in this way for the length required. The finished working of the single stitch is shown in Diagram C. It is worked as shown in Fig. 3 when a second stitch is worked along the border.

For the border in Fig. 3 work the first row as described above. For the second row the thread is at the lower right-hand corner. First insert the needle into the

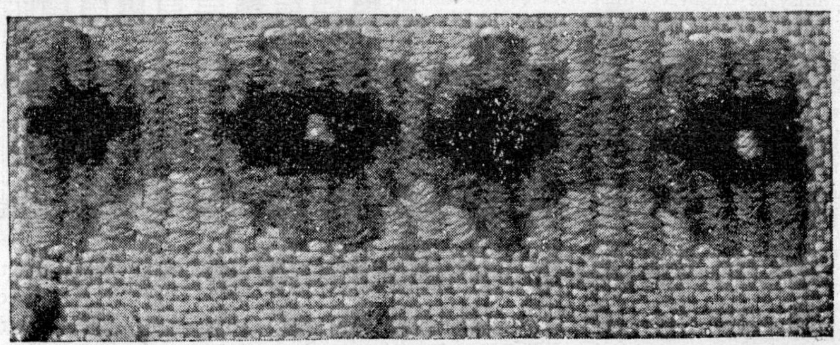

Fig. 8.—AN INSERTION ON COARSE LINEN

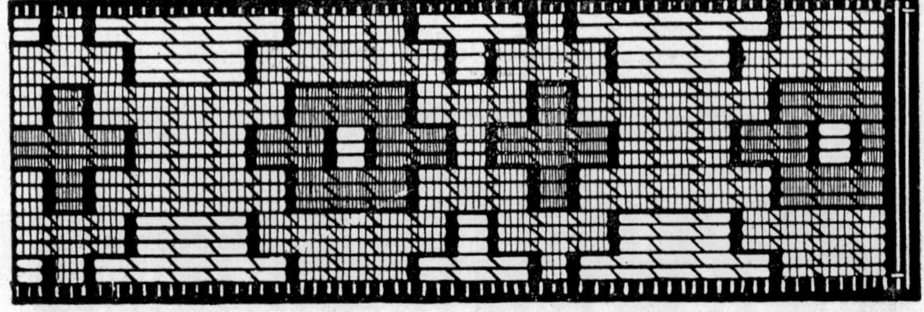

upper row and bring it out three threads to the left in the lower row as shown in Diagram D. Then pass over three threads to the right and insert the needle horizontally and bring it out three threads to the left as shown in Diagram E. Continue from D for the length required. Fig. F shows the stitch completed. The border is now ready for the weaving. Elaborate corners may be worked in place of the squares. These can be filled in with embroidery or fancy drawn-thread work, according to the use to which the work is being put.

A frame is a great help (though it is not essential) as the work must be kept firm without dragging the threads. The weaving must be kept as neat on the wrong side as the right, and all threads can be fastened off when the work is finished. Begin by running the unknotted thread an inch or two above the first block of weaving, leaving enough length to be undone later and fastened off as seen in Fig. 8. The needle is brought out between the material and the first group of three threads and a stitch is taken over two threads of the material, then out and over the first group of three threads and back again under the group of threads into the material. This is continued until a block a third of the depth is worked (Fig. 4, Diagram 1). When this is done the second block is started over the first and second group of

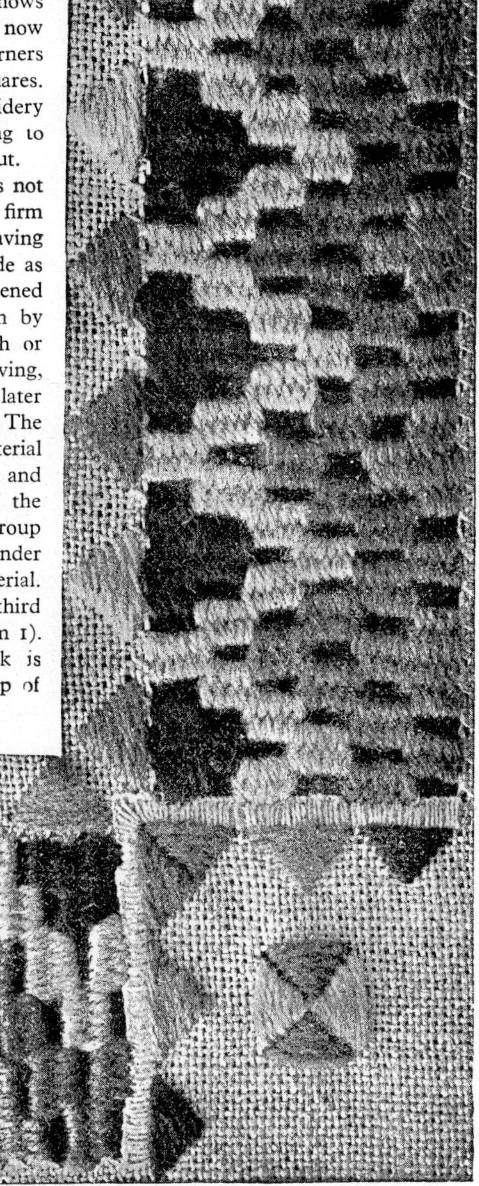

Fig. 9. A GAY AND COLOURFUL BORDER

threads and continued over and under alternately as before for another third of the depth of the border (Diagram 2). The third block is then worked in the same way over the second and third groups of threads. This is done until the border is filled.

The last group being finished, run the thread into the material for an inch or two and leave it until it is next required. Starting at the top again, work with the other colour in like manner. When this block is finished undo the running stitches made in the first group, thread the needle and pass the thread right up the three blocks, so that it cannot be seen, then pass it along the back and bring it out between the fifth and sixth group of stitches in readiness for the next stitch. Two needles, one for each colour can be used if preferred.

Diagram 3 shows the alternate finished groups and the position of the last row of stitches. Each block must be tight and firm. This is done by pushing the threads well up together when the needle comes up between the two groups of threads and in

HERE IS THE CHART FOR WORKING THE DESIGN ON THE FOLLOWING PAGE

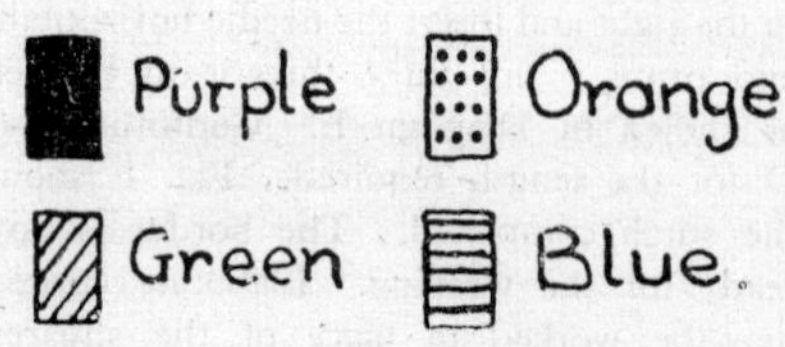

THE CHART FOR WORKING THE DESIGN ON THE PREVIOUS PAGE

taking care in passing from one group to another that the right thread is always above the left as this helps to keep the right tension throughout the work.

When all the needleweaving is finished, there is still part of the edge of the material showing (see Diagram 1, Fig. 4). This is worked in overcasting in the correct colour for the next group of weaving. In Diagram 3, Fig. 4, it can clearly be seen, the first group is in black and the lower one in red. This makes a neat finish to the work. It must also be remembered that this overcasting is taken over two threads of the material and not three as in the groups of threads. This is because the material does not give and pull together like the groups of threads, and when finished they both look the same size.

If the weaving has been worked in a frame it can be taken out and the ends

finished off by hand. To do this, unpick the ends left in the material, thread them in a needle and pass them invisibly inside the blocks. This completes the border.

In working a more advanced design it is advisable to start the weaving from the centre and work towards the left and then to the right to make sure the pattern comes exactly in the centre. This applies especially to monograms.

Designs for Beginner and Expert:—

For Fig. 5, fifteen threads are drawn and the work is prepared as previously described. It is worked in two shades of wool. For each block the darning is passed to and fro over three and under three threads, each block being six stitches deep and each new block taking three stitches from the previous block and three from the new. The method of working the colours can be followed from the illustration.

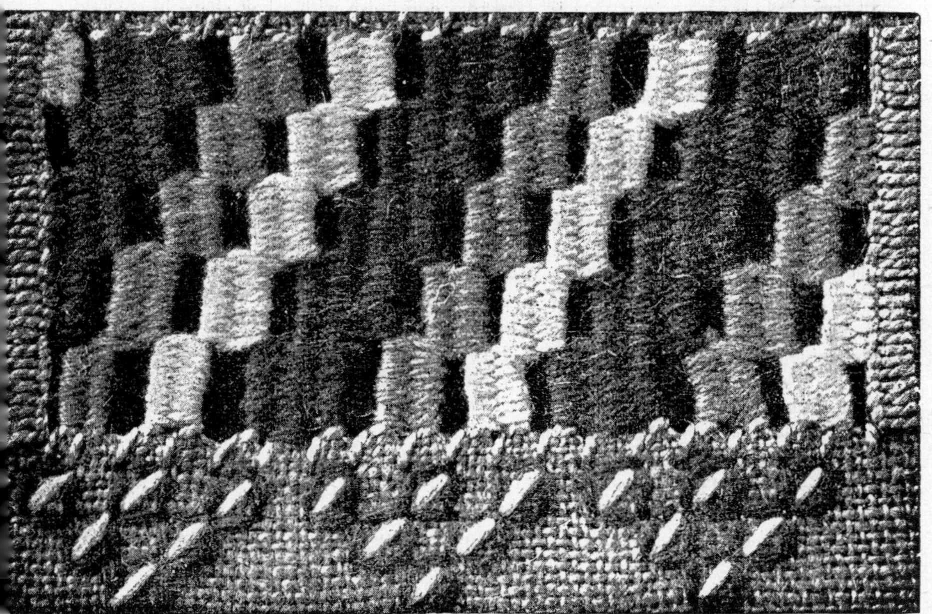

Fig. 10.—A BRIGHT BORDER ON COARSE LINEN

When the weaving is done in one colour only, it can be pulled fairly tightly to form small gaps between the group to make the pattern show up well. When the weaving is worked in several colours this is not necessary.

When the work is finished lay it on a very thick, soft ironing pad to press. Use a damp cloth and a moderately hot iron. This requires careful pressing as needle-weaving should never be flattened out, but should always keep its rounded appearance.

For Fig. 6 draw out twenty-five threads, and work each block on six of the remaining threads, darning to and fro sixteen times in all for each block.

Begin at one edge and darn five blocks in a diagonal line across to the outer edge, each new block should be darned on three threads from the previous block and three new ones. Now work two blocks diagonally from the centre block on each side of the line so that a cross is formed and work a similar cross on each set of eighteen threads to the end. Between the crosses

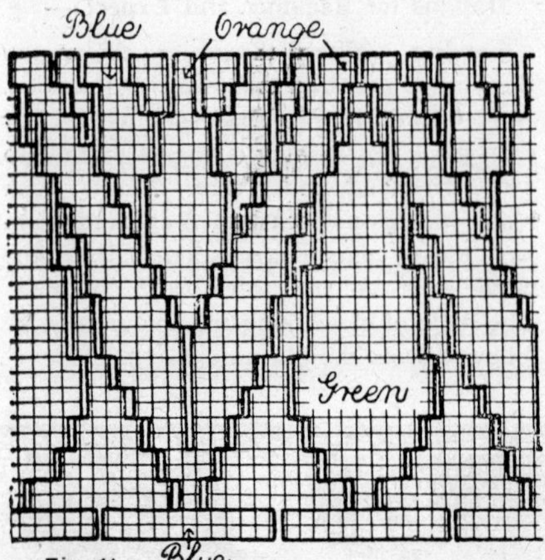

Fig. 11.

work four blocks in diamond shape with a contrasting shade, also one block between the arms of the cross. This makes quite a good border for a towel.

For Fig. 7 use an imitation Russian linen crash in an oatmeal shade. The darning should be done in bright emerald, cherry and blue wool. For this border draw thirty threads. Begin at the centre and with emerald wool darn backwards and forwards eight times in all over the centre thirty-two threads, passing alternately over and under four threads. Then leave four of these threads at each end so that the work goes over twenty-four threads only and darn on these for the same depth, then work over sixteen threads only, then over eight at the centre. Now increase four threads at each end, after each eight rows of darning so that the shape seen in the illustration is formed.

On either side of this, darn in little blocks over eight threads with cherry, then make a diamond shape on each side with blue, beginning over eight threads and increasing to thirty-two at the centre. Continue the border in this way to the end and finish with a half shape in emerald.

Fig. 8 is worked on handwoven material, with fourteen threads drawn. It is worked over groups of three threads and the arrangement can be clearly followed from the illustration and chart.

For Fig. 9 use a coarse linen. The border measures $1\frac{3}{4}$ inches in width, for which draw thirty-eight threads. The darning is done on groups of four threads which are first separated as shown in Diagrams A, B and C of Fig. 3 with a thread from the material. The darning is done in wools in green, orange, blue and purple.

Begin with the blue wool, and working from the chart, first darn over and under four blocks for six stitches in depth. Next, take the two centre blocks immediately above and darn under and over for six stitches in depth. Leave two sets of

Fig. 11.—LOTUS FLOWER BORDER

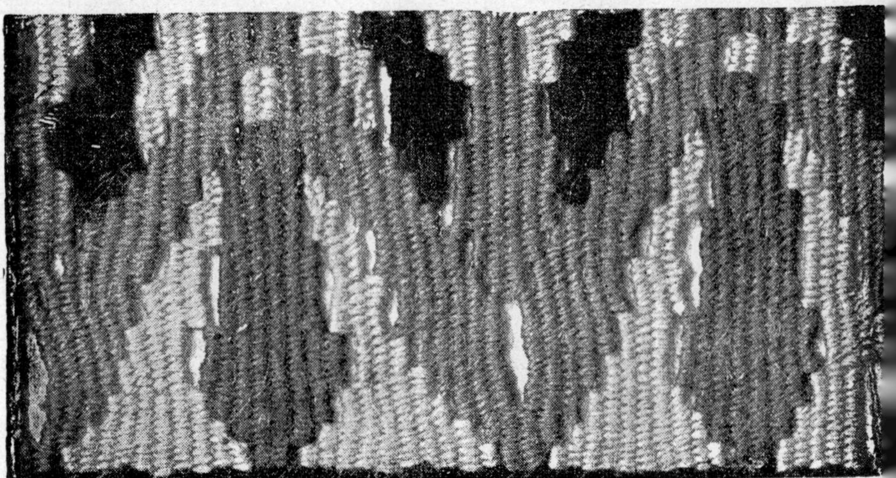

threads and work another blue pattern as before. Continue this for the whole length of the border and then work the purple border on the opposite side of the band in the same way, seeing that the single purple block comes immediately above the unworked threads on the blue border, thus making the border patterns alternate.

the design with alternating colours, having the width of fifteen threads at the base of each. The corner angle is first buttonholed (see illustration) and then three sets at each side of the triangles are worked, two in orange and two in green. Work these to form a square, having a base of twelve threads at each side.

Fig. 12.—SQUARE MOTIF FOR CUSHIONS.

The rest of the weaving is quite simply followed from the chart and the actual piece of work illustrated in Fig. 9. The orange wool is above the blue and the green above the purple.

A border in needleweaving is often finished off with a fancy stitch to break the hard line. An example of this is shown in Fig. 9. For this simple border work satin stitch triangles on the inside edge of

Fig. 10 is worked on a very coarse art canvas in wool. The design measures 2¼ inches. Draw thirty-five threads of canvas and separate these in groups of four as shown in Diagrams A, B and C, Fig. 3, only work this on the wrong side instead of the right, using Sylko to match the canvas. At each end where the threads have been cut, buttonhole closely over five threads of the canvas. Work from the chart.

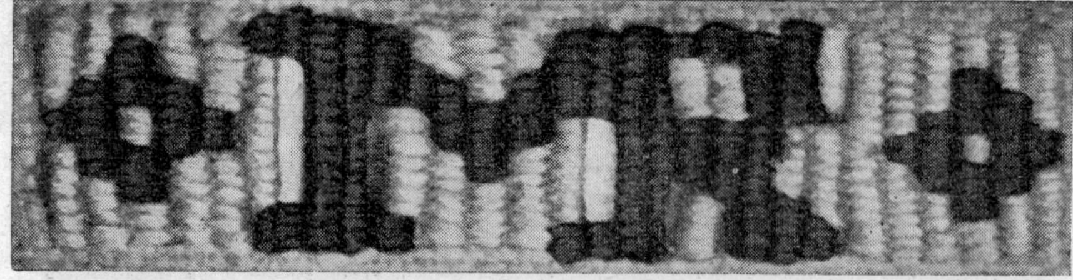

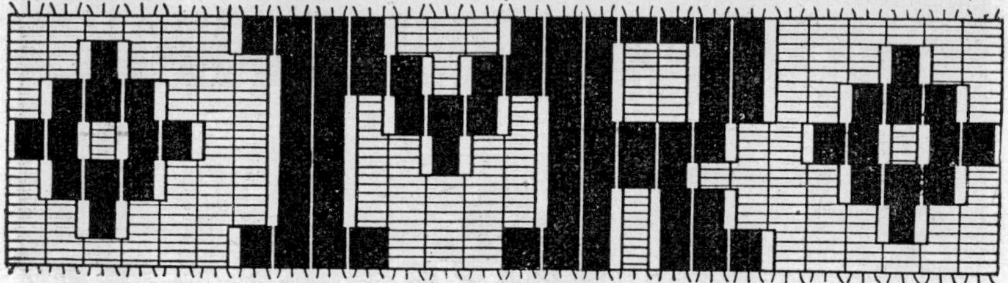

Fig. 14. MONOGRAM IN NEEDLEWEAVING

Fig. 15.—INITIAL FOR MARKING FACE TOWELS

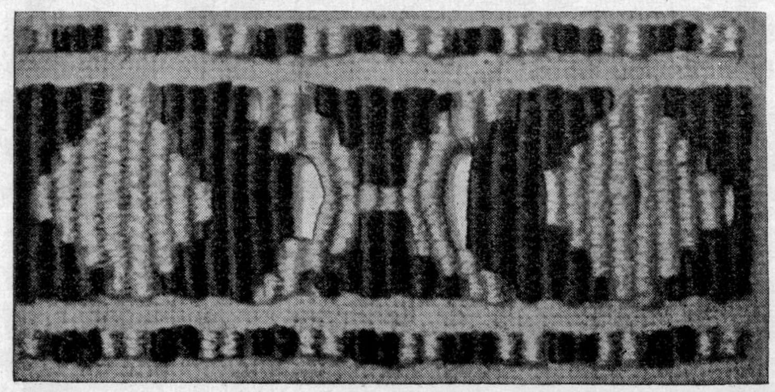

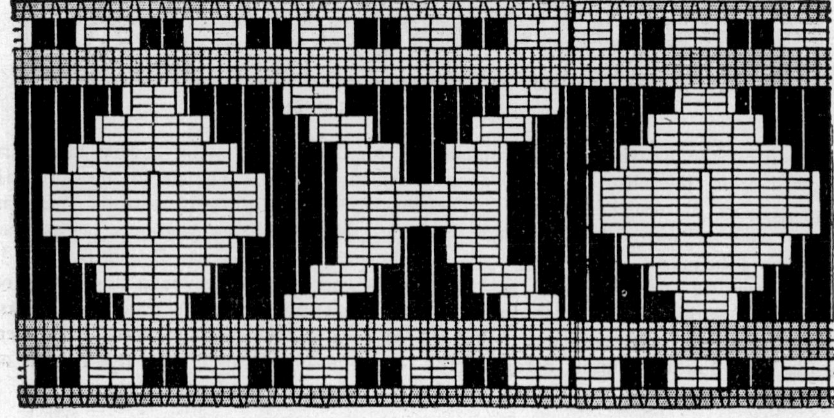

Begin with the brown wool, and taking two groups of four threads, darn under and over them for eight threads in depth. Now take the next group of four to the right and working on these and the second four of the last group, darn in the same way. Repeat this until you have five brown patterns running diagonally to the top edge of the drawn band. Repeat this with the orange wool. With the green, work diagonally as before, but over three instead of two groups of four threads. These three colours complete one whole pattern which is repeated along the whole length of the band.

The design below the weaving is built up of small single stitch squares, each side the depth of four canvas threads, with an orange single stitch diagonally across each. They are arranged in a triangle the base measuring twenty canvas threads across.

The Lotus border in Fig. 11 is an effective and unusual design which measures $3\frac{1}{2}$ inches wide.

The original was worked on art canvas and darned in coloured wools. Orange and royal blue flowers interspersed with jade green bands, the water from which the flowers grow being indicated by a royal blue line. The background of the design was worked with wool to match the ground colour.

The pattern can be followed from the

Fig. 12.

CHART FOR BORDER OF SQUARE MOTIF

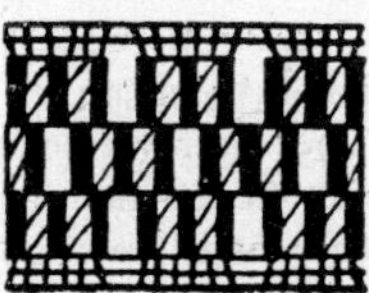

chart given, each block being darned backwards and forwards on two threads, eight times in all. Each square represents two canvas threads and two double (backward and forward rows). Orange is used for the side and centre petals of the flowers and the royal blue for the petals which come between.

For a narrower design use a finer linen and 2 or 3-ply wool instead of 4-ply.

In Fig. 12 is shown a design for a cushion worked on coarse linen in wool. The square itself measures about 6 inches and about $8\frac{1}{2}$ inches when the border is worked all round. It is advisable to work this design in a frame, though it is not absolutely necessary.

Mark the centre of your material and round this draw a 6-inch square. Very carefully cut along two parallel sides of the square, keeping exactly between two threads, then draw out the cut threads and whip along the cut edges to prevent fraying. Then darn in the pattern from the chart, going over four and under four threads backwards and forwards eight times in all for each block. Use deep rose for the centre and deep blue for each section from the points of the centre and paler rose for the sections which come between the blue shapes. Outline the diamond shape now formed with a double row of lighter blue blocks, across each corner work two rows of paler rose block and fill in the rest of the space with deep rose.

In cases where the work comes to the cut edges of the square, the darning must be worked into the edge of the material, as seen in the illustration and chart.

Work satin stitch along the top and bottom of the design over the first four threads of material, using blue where rows of blue blocks meet the background, deep rose at the corners and pale rose between.

Fill in with satin stitch in the same way, the spaces between the darning down the sides of the square.

The narrow border is then worked. Leave about half an inch all round the square and draw out the threads to the depth of an inch along each side. Hemstitch with a thread of the material along both sides of the border, taking up three threads with each stitch and buttonhole stitch along the cut edge of the corners. Darn in the groups of threads in pattern (see chart) with the lighter blue.

At the corners attach the thread to the inner corner of the space and carry it to the opposite corner, and twice to each buttonholed edge at equal spaces catching it back each time over the laid thread to the first corner (see illustration). Darn backwards and forwards eight times on all these twisted bars, taking the thread at either side over the last group of threads in the insertion, in the space between the last two blocks, thus forming a fan-shaped motif in the darning.

The monogram M R is worked on hand-woven material. For this fourteen threads were drawn and darned back at either end into the material. The original was worked in green and black. If the chart is used it will be quite easy to follow. Weave in green backwards and forwards over eighteen threads in groups of three for six rows, then over two groups of three threads, then one, miss one block, then over one group of three, then two, then six groups of three. Now with the black bring the thread out, nine threads along and work over three threads, then work over nine threads. Work over the last group of three threads to the right and the one missed out in the green for six rows. Then move one block to the left and work over three groups for six rows, then over one group in the centre. Pass the wool behind and work the centre blocks which are started four blocks from the edge, which leaves one block in the centre which is filled in with green. Now work with the green again starting at the bottom and working upwards. Work over four groups of three stitches for six rows then, moving one block to the left, work over four groups of three stitches for six rows. The next row is worked over two blocks in the centre of the four, then the next row over two blocks, starting one further to the right, the next is over three blocks, one more to the right.

For the monogram—work over seven groups of three threads for six rows, then over two for twelve rows. Now one to the left, work the next row over five groups, one more to the left, the next row is worked over four groups. Then the next row is worked under the first of the four groups in the previous row and one to the right, then the next row below this and one more to the right.

Miss one group then work over three for one row, starting the next row above the first, work over two groups for one row. Pass the wool up behind two groups and bring the wool out, work over four groups to the left for six rows. The next row is above this and is worked over three groups. Pass the wool behind and bring it out two rows further down and work over three groups to the left. The next row is over one group in the centre of these three. Then pass the wool up two rows and work over four groups to the left; the next row is started above this one, and is worked over four groups, still one more to the left.

Starting at the bottom of the border with black, miss three groups from the last black and weave over four groups to the left for six rows. Then one group to the left, weave backwards and forwards over six threads for eight rows. This completes the monogram. The threads left are filled in with green. A diamond is worked the other side, too, but this can be clearly followed from the chart and illustration.

Fig. 15 is a good initial for a towel which has the fancy border on either side. The original was worked on linen. Three threads were drawn for the narrow border, four threads were left, twenty-four were drawn, four left, and three drawn. The design can be followed clearly with the help of the chart.

NEEDLEWORK-TAPESTRY

Needlework-tapestry is the art of stitching with needle and thread upon canvas in such a way that the ground is entirely covered and the effect of tapestry is obtained.

As the word "tapestry" really applies to the woven article, many people refer to needlework-tapestry by the stitch in which it is worked, such as petit point, gros point or cross-stitch.

There is no limit to the articles which can be made in this form of needlework, chair seats, hangings, pictures, small furnishings, handbags and carpets being the most popular.

Materials required.—Canvas according to the design to be worked; a good smooth thimble that will not fray the wool; a sharp pair of scissors to cut off the ends of thread and knots made in starting (thread or wool should never be broken); needles of the best possible quality (the correct kind, blunt-pointed and not too long, are shown in Fig. 2. For general use No. 22 is a good size, but the choice must depend entirely upon the mesh of the canvas and the wool to be used. On no account must the needle push the canvas threads apart, nor should there be difficulty in pulling the needle through. When working on gauze use a very fine crewel needle.)

When using silks it is advisable to wind each skein on a small piece of cardboard and number it clearly. This saves muddles, especially if several shades of the same colour are in use, and it also prevents waste, as the thread can be cut the required length.

A holder as shown in Fig. 1 is useful for wools of different shades, as it prevents them from getting tangled.

On the next page are shown strands in actual size of the most usual kinds of wools, silks and cottons used for needlework-tapestry.

(*a*) **Tapestry wool.**

(*b*) **Crewel wool.**—A fine two-ply wool, used two or more thicknesses at a time according to the work in hand.

(*c*) **French Tapestry wool.**

(*d*) **A very fine crewel wool** used mostly for working faces.

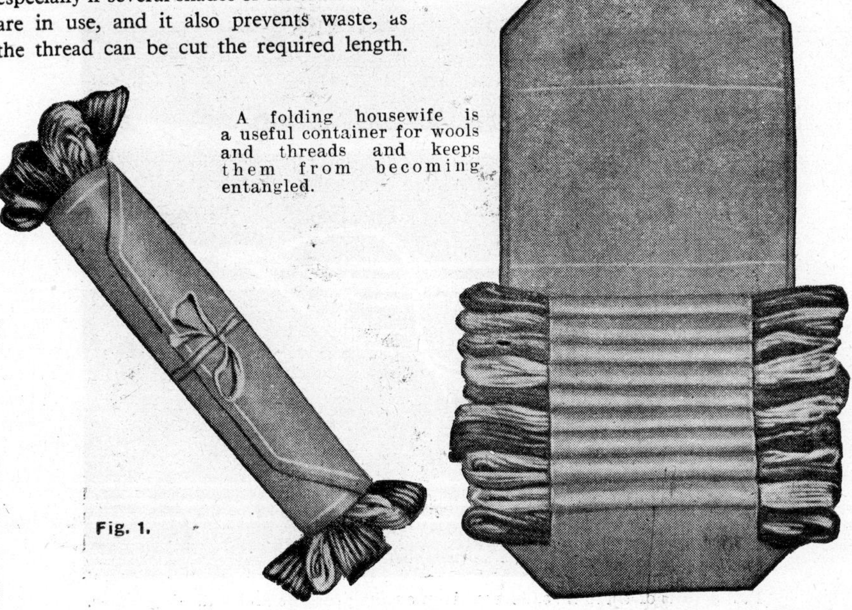

A folding housewife is a useful container for wools and threads and keeps them from becoming entangled.

Fig. 1.

WOOLS AND THREADS

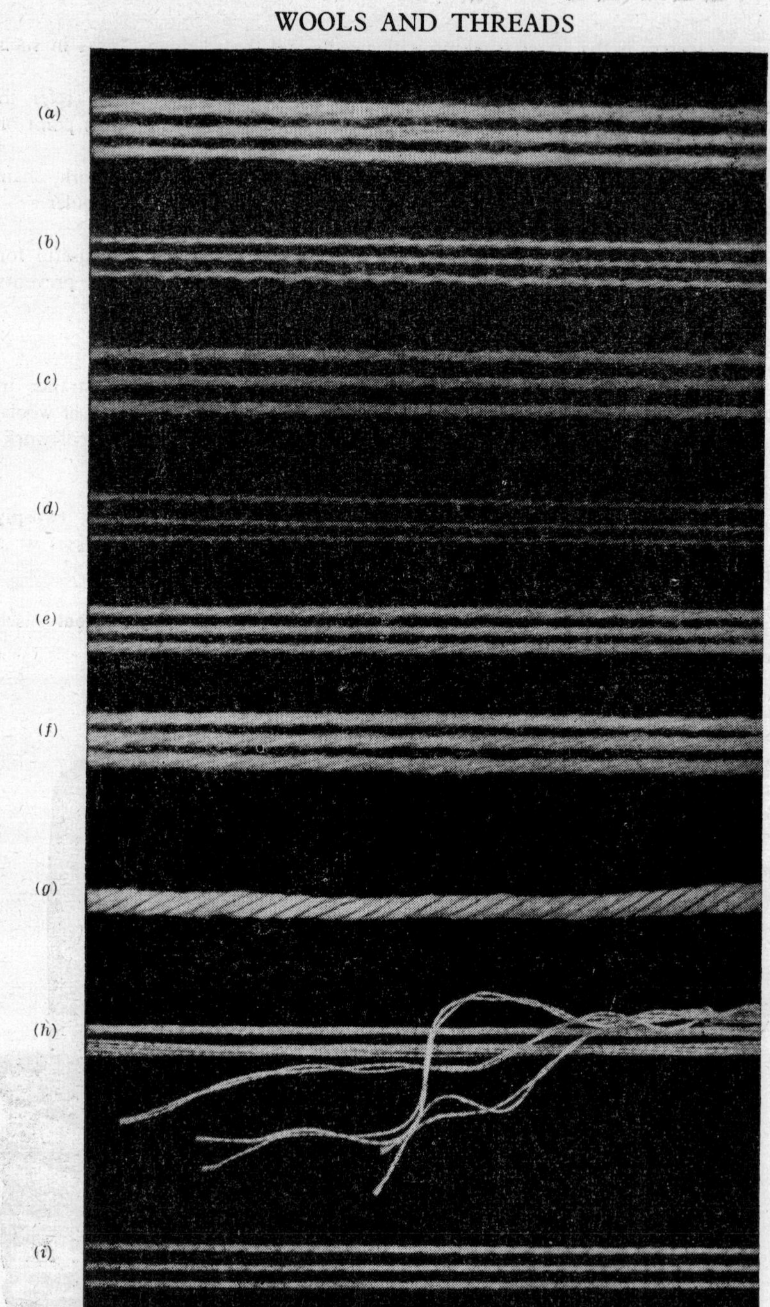

Full details of these threads are given on the previous and following pages.

(j)

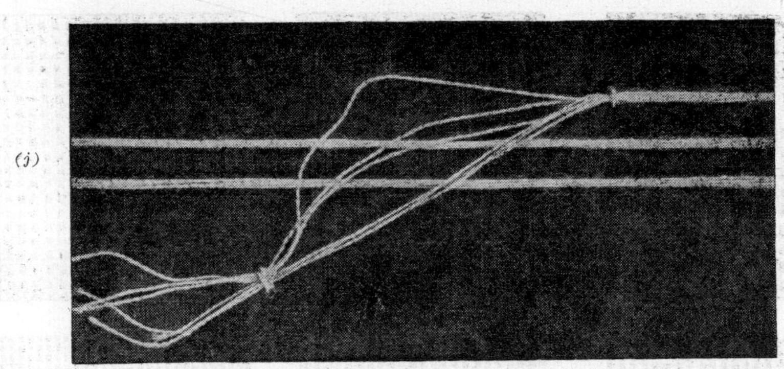

Here and on the opposite page are different wools, silks and mercerised thread that can be used for tapestry work. Full details are given below.

These wools are obtainable in a vast range of colours and shades. When shading, the greater the number of shades used the better the effect.

(*e*) **Embroidery wool** is sometimes used for modern work and pictures.

(*f*) **Thick embroidery wool** is used on very coarse canvas.

(*g*) **Very thick 4-ply wool** which is worked on a special coarse canvas for chair seats, stool tops, rugs, etc.

Mercerised cotton is excellent for working needlework-tapestry and the stranded varieties are the best for general purposes. These can be used as many strands at a time as required, according to the mesh of the canvas. The cottons can be used entirely throughout a piece of work or in conjunction with wool or silk. Sometimes when a design is worked in silk the background is carried out in mercerised cotton. Wide ranges of colours are obtainable in the **mercerised stranded cottons** (*h*) and excellent antique shades are included.

(*i*) is a **twisted mercerised cotton** suitable for canvas work.

Silks are often introduced into designs either for working separate parts of the design or else to give relief and highlights to the parts worked in wool. Designs are also worked entirely in silk.

The kind most often used is (*j*) **Filoselle.** This is a stranded silk which can be used as many strands at a time as required. It has the dull sheen of pure silk and it wears well.

As for quantity, it is safe to estimate that in working a chair seat with a fairly small design and with colours evenly distributed, one skein of each shade is enough for the pattern.

N.B.—It is important to buy all the background wool at once and advisable to purchase slightly more than may be needed, as it is difficult to match the wool

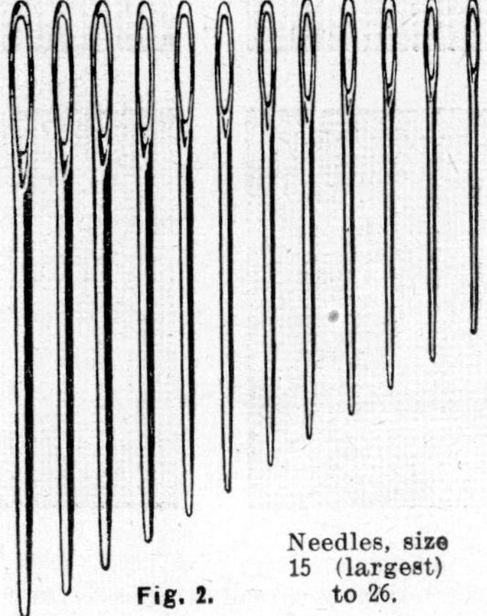

Fig. 2. Needles, size 15 (largest) to 26.

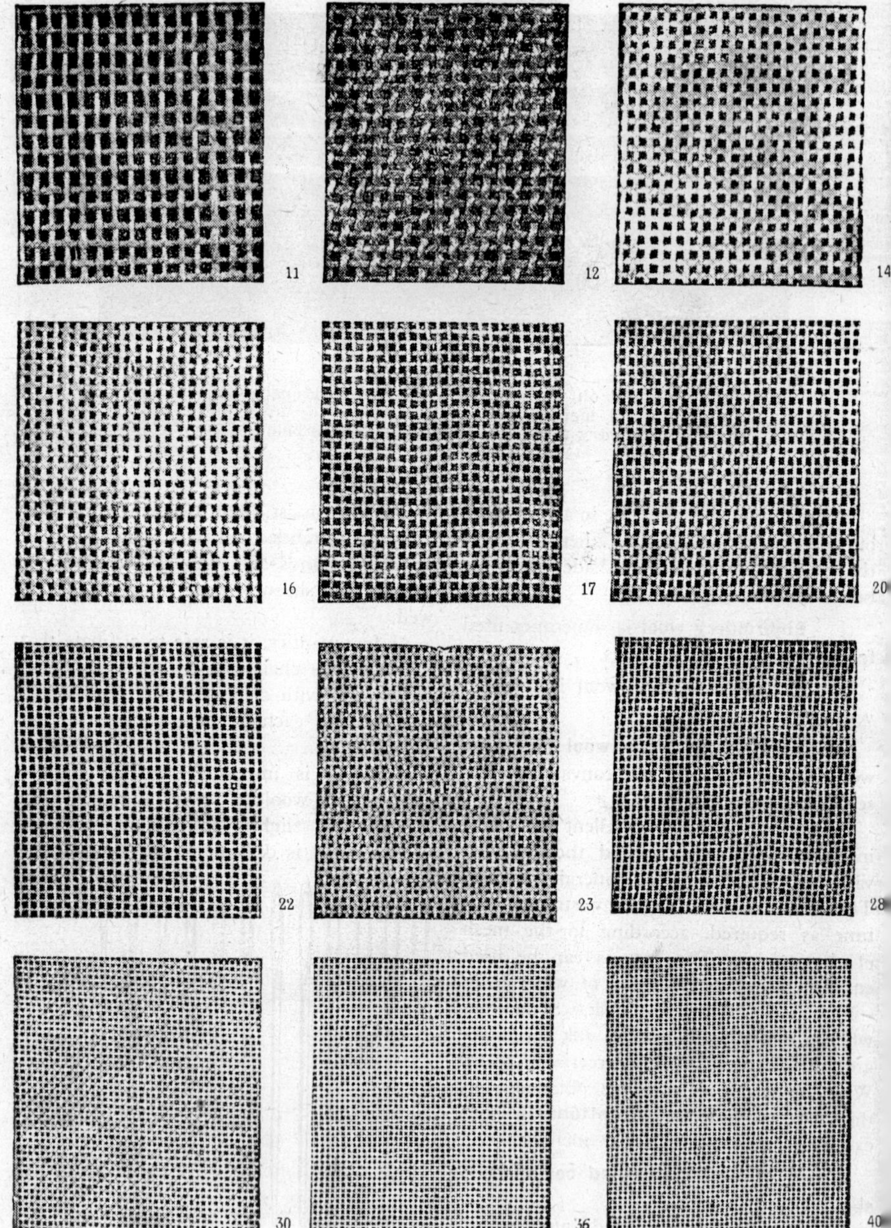

Fig. 3.

Single thread canvases.—The figures on the right of each specimen denote the number of threads to the inch. (Actual Size.)

Fig. 4.

Double thread canvases.—The figures on the right of each specimen denote the number of threads to the inch. (Actual Size.)

exactly again, and even a slight variation in shade will show on a large flat surface.

The choice of wool or thread.—It is most important to choose a thread of the right thickness for the canvas to be used. If the thread is too heavy for the canvas it will push the mesh out of place and the finished work will be puckered and clumsy in effect. If the wool is too thin, the mesh will show through on the right side. In some cases where the thread is too thin for the canvas the meshes can be filled up by laying a "tramé" thread under the stitches.

Canvases.—In the early days needlework-tapestry was done on a loosely woven material like coarse linen. Later, canvas was specially woven, and as time went on machine-woven canvases were produced.

The range of canvases varies from the finest of 40 threads to the inch, to the coarsest with only 5. (See Figs. 3 and 4.) Gauze is only used for fine work, and no background is worked on it.

The introduction of the double thread canvas is comparatively recent. The object of this is to allow more space in the holes through which the thread or wool passes than in those which it merely passes over. Also as the threads are arranged in pairs, it is easier to distinguish which to take up when working.

A single thread canvas is always used for petit point. When this stitch is combined with others and a double thread canvas is chosen, the canvas must be "pricked," that is, the meshes opened with a needle or pin to form a single thread canvas for the parts to be worked in petit point.

Gros point, cross-stitch and other stitches can be worked on single or double canvas, the choice resting entirely on the worker.

Hungarian point work is always done on a single thread canvas, special ones being sold for the purpose.

The best quality canvases are known as "polished thread." The threads of such a canvas are nicely rounded and quite distinct one from the other. The canvas is silky to the touch. Most canvases are made in white, or antique shade which varies from pale buff to écru.

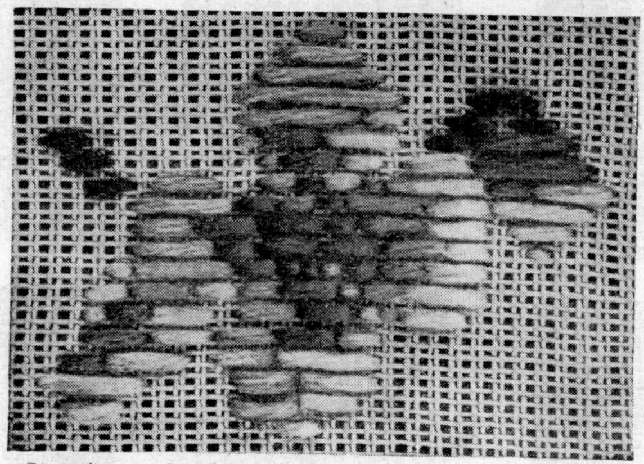

Fig. 5.

Sometimes a design is indicated on the canvas by means of a coloured tramé thread. The tapestry is worked over these threads and the canvas below.

The most usual widths of canvas are 24 and 27 inches. There are also 18-inch and 36-inch widths, and others not so much in general use including sizes up to 54-inch.

Methods of working.—Canvases can be bought ready designed in colours for working. These canvases are either hand painted or stencilled, giving a guide to the correct shading.

Another form in which prepared canvases are to be had is that known as "tramé" or trammed. (See Fig. 5). In these the whole design is laid out in long stitches in the colours in which it is to be worked.

These stitches lie between two threads of the canvas and are afterwards covered by the stitches, usually half cross-stitch or gros point. Such canvases do much to simplify the working, as it is then only a matter of stitching over the laid threads with wool of the same colour.

A third method of working, and one that is popular on account of the great accuracy obtainable, is following the pattern from a chart. In such charts the pattern and colours are indicated by signs, a key being given. Each sign represents one stitch on the canvas.

Fig. 6 shows how to begin a new thread. A long length should be left so that it is held securely by the stitches worked over it.

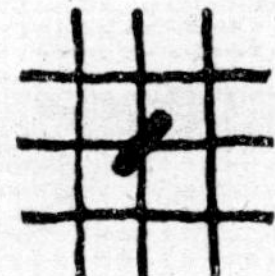

On the left is a diagram showing a single stitch, and below, a diagram showing method of working petit point.

Fig. 6.

Fig. 7.

Fig. 8.

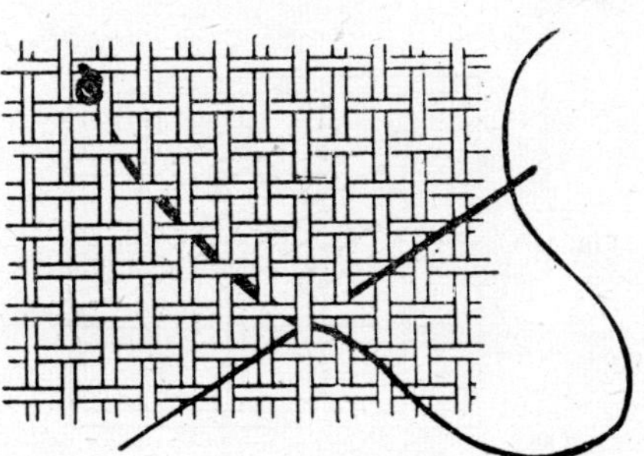

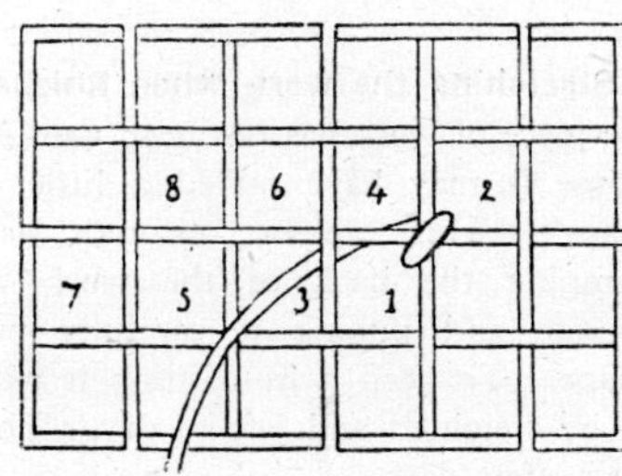

A fourth method of working consists of following the pattern from a started section of the design as in Florentine or Hungarian Point needlework-tapestry. These patterns can be done entirely by counting and are usually of the all-over variety of conventional design.

How to work in a Frame.—It is advisable, when working in a frame, to weight the corners, as the canvas has a tendency to pull out of shape. When possible mount the work in a frame that can be adjusted as the work proceeds. The correct method when using a frame is to have one hand on top and one below. Thus the needle is sent straight down through the canvas and received on the other side by the hand underneath and can be sent straight up again. This adds greatly to the speed and regularity of the work. Two thimbles should be used, one on each hand.

The ordinary square frame, if it has no stand, can be rested against a table with a lead weight on the frame to keep it steady, or placed between the backs of two chairs so that both hands are freed for working. With a tambour frame only one hand can be used for working unless the frame has a stand.

How to begin working.—When starting to work or when beginning a new thread, make a knot at the end of the thread, take the thread down a short distance and a little above where the first stitch is to be worked and in some place that will afterwards be covered by stitchery. Now bring the thread up where required to begin the first stitch as shown in the diagram. The result is a long stitch on the back which will be covered by the stitches. Just before the knot is reached it can be cut off. By this method the back of the work is kept tidy and there is no danger of the thread becoming loose.

To finish off the thread, take it to the back and run it in and out of the canvas where it will afterwards be covered by the stitches. Another way is to run the thread in the back of the stitches already worked.

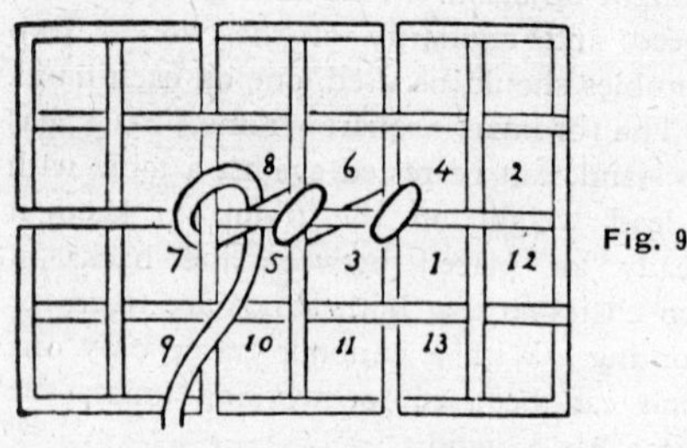

Fig. 9.

DIAGRAM FOR TURNING

Stitches used.—The most frequently used stitches are petit point or gros point, or a combination of the two, or cross-stitch. Gobelin in its many variations, though sometimes used for whole pieces, is more often seen in backgrounds.

Petit point or Tent Stitch.—Consists of single stitches slanting upwards from left to right over one cross of canvas. (Fig. 7.) The working of petit point is demonstrated in Fig. 8. Bring the thread up through 1, take it down at 2; this gives the first stitch. For the second stitch bring the needle up at 3, and take it down at 4. For the third stitch, up at 5 and take it down at 6. For the fourth stitch bring it up at 7 and take it down at 8, and so on for as many stitches as required.

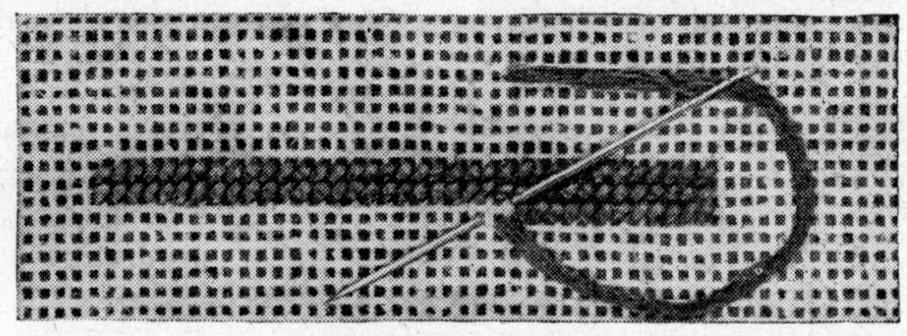

Fig. 10.

PETIT POINT

Stretching the work when finished.—If the piece of work has not been worked on a frame it may have pulled a little out of shape. This can be restored easily by damping the back of the work with a sponge and pulling it carefully back to shape. To keep it in position it will have to be weighted and left to dry. This will take a few days.

Another method of stretching is to place several sheets of dampened blotting-paper on a board and lay the tapestry face upwards over this. Pin the work to the board with drawing-pins placed closely along the edges, gradually drawing the work back to its original shape as the pinning proceeds. If the work has become badly misshapen it will not be possible to get it square the first time, but it should be left covered with a clean cloth for several hours, or overnight, and then the next day pulled a little more into shape. This procedure may have to be repeated several times. In any case the work should be left for a day or two to stretch and then, when removed from the board, it will have regained its original shape.

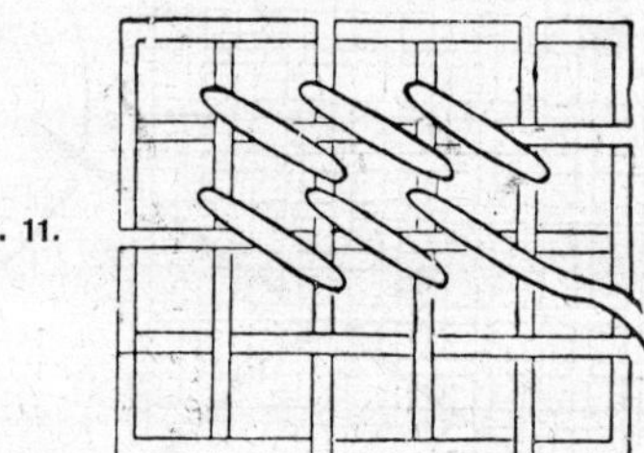

Fig. 11.

REVERSE SIDE OF PETIT POINT

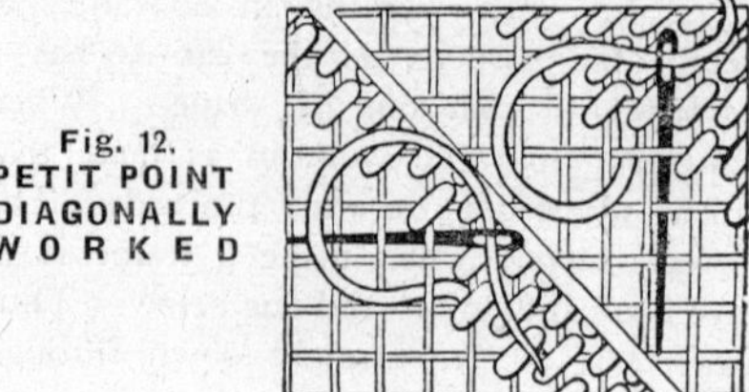

Fig. 12.
PETIT POINT DIAGONALLY WORKED

When the end of the row is reached, the work is done in a contrary direction for the second row, and to reach the point of starting, the needle should be brought up through 5 (this has formed a short upright stitch on the back between 8 and 5) and then is taken down at 9, up at 3, down at 10, up at 1, down at 11, up at 12, and down at 13 (Fig. 9). The third row is worked in the same way as the first, and to bring the needle into starting position it should be brought up below 13. These two rows are repeated as required. It will be found that the back of the work has a succession of long stitches slanting over two threads in width and one in height, while the stitches on the front go diagonally over one thread in width and one in height.

Fig. 13.

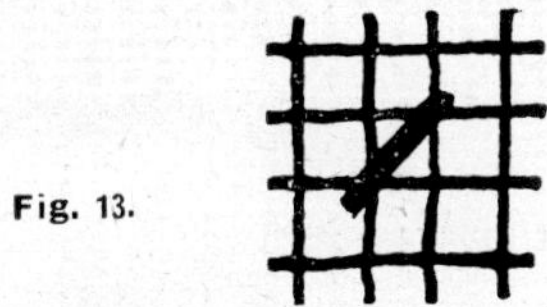

GROS POINT ON SINGLE THREAD CANVAS

Fig. 14.

GROS POINT

Fig. 15.

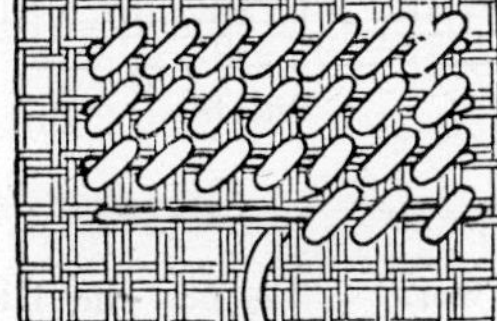

GROS POINT OVER A TRAMÉ THREAD

The design is worked in the way described before, but each section of the design, such as a leaf or flower, is worked separately.

In working tent stitch in several shades it is as well to work the different shades in together which necessitates having several needles with different shades of silk. This is quite easy when working on a frame and is also considerably quicker.

Another method is just to outline the shape with whatever shades come at the edge, then work in the next shade and so on until the shape is completed.

Provided the pieces of colour are not too isolated the thread can be carried from one part to the next without breaking off, and when working with several colours it is advisable to leave the colour not in use hanging in front of the work until required. This saves constantly breaking off and joining on.

When working a large plain surface, such as a background or a sky, petit point is done in diagonal rows, fitted one into the

Fig. 16.
GROS POINT ON DOUBLE THREAD CANVAS

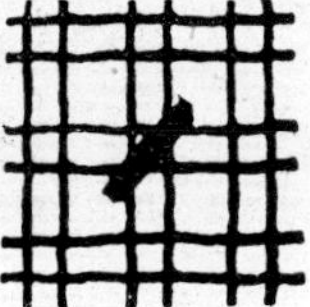

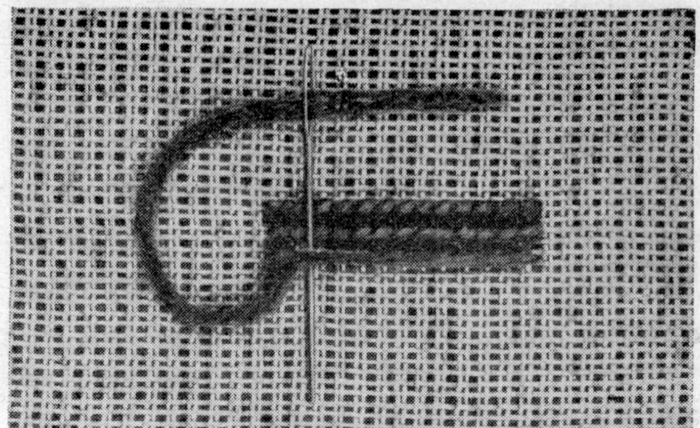

Half cross-stitch worked over a tramé thread from left to right. Follow the order shown by the numbers in Fig. 19 when working.

Fig. 17.

next as in Fig. 12 This work should be started at the top right-hand corner of the space to be filled.

Petit point, worked this way, gives a more even appearance to the finished work. (Fig. 12.)

As petit point is the finest stitch used in needlework-tapestry, it is used for detailed and much shaded work, or for the more delicate parts of a design, such as the faces in figure work.

Gros Point, as its name implies, is a larger edition of petit point, and the two stitches are used together extensively. A great deal of work, of course, is done in gros point alone, and it is a favourite for chair seats. (Figs. 13, 14 and 16).

Sometimes these stitches are worked over a laid (tramé) thread. This is done when the stitches do not sufficiently cover the canvas, or to give a slightly raised effect to the work. To put the laid thread in position the thread is brought up at the left-hand end of the space to be covered and taken down at the right-hand end. It thus lies along between the two threads of the canvas that will be covered by the gros point. It is usual to put in each little

Fig. 18.

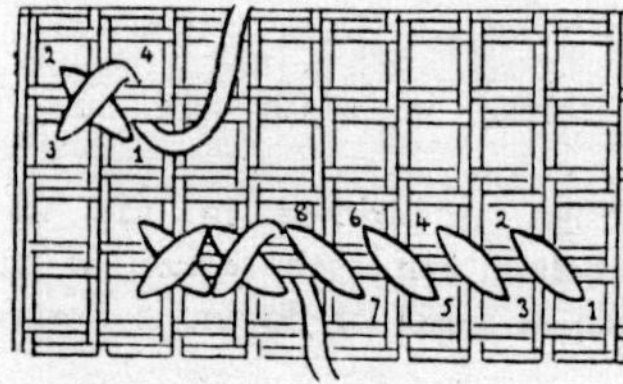

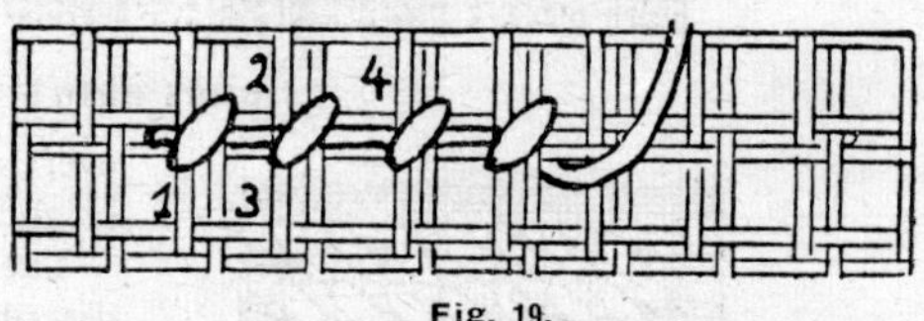

Fig. 19.

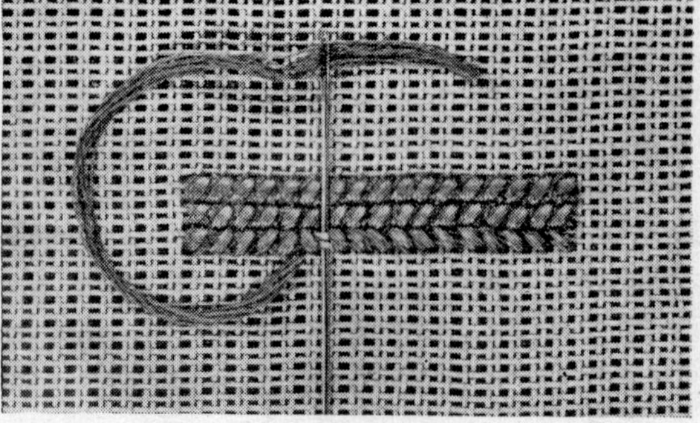

Cross-stitch can be worked so that half the stitch is formed across the row, and then is crossed by working backwards. The crosses must all be formed in the same order—i.e. the upper thread must keep the same direction throughout.

Fig. 20.

piece immediately before covering with the gros point stitches, as then the one thread can be used throughout. However, if the laid thread is required as a guide to the placing of the colours, as is often the case, the whole of the tramé grounding is done first.

Each little section, is, of course, done with the colour that will be used for the gros point.

Half Cross-stitch.—This gives the same effect on the front as gros point, but short upright stitches are formed at the back. The work is begun at the left-hand side instead of the right, the needle being brought up at 1, down at 2, up at 3, down at 4, and so on to the end (Fig. 19). This stitch is usually done over a laid thread

stitch as you go along, as this gives a better appearance to the work (see top of Fig. 18). In working backgrounds, however, you can work half the stitches along a row and then return crossing them. To work a row of cross-stitch, bring the thread up at 1, down at 2, up at 3, down at 4, up at 5, down at 6, up at 7, and so on, returning in contrary direction, thus crossing the stitches (Fig. 18).

Cross-stitch was introduced for tapestry at a much later date than petit or gros point.

Gobelin Stitch.—Is worked in the same way as petit and gros point, but the stitches slant over one thread in width and two in height (Fig. 22). The stitches can also be worked upright as shown in Fig. 21.

Encroaching Gobelin—is another varia-

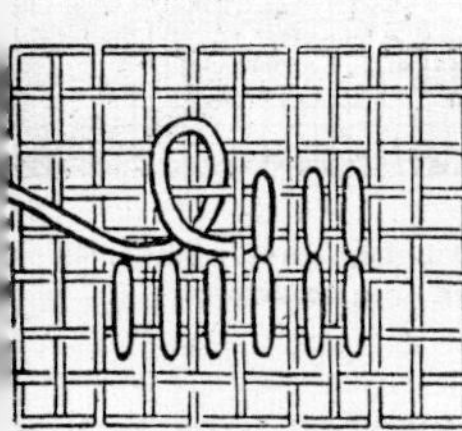

Fig. 21.

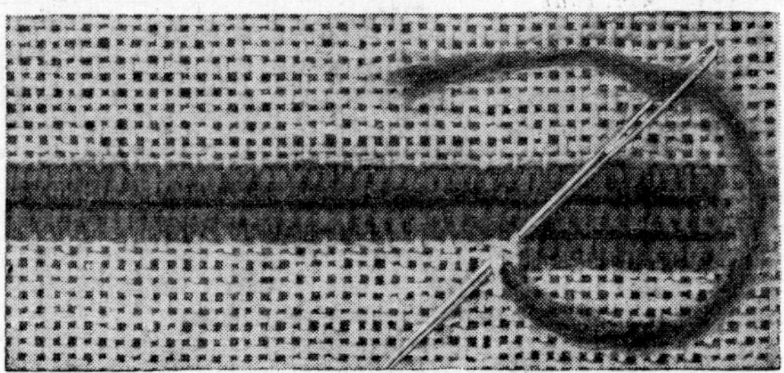

Fig. 22.

GOBELIN STITCH

vhich is brought up at the right-hand end of the space where the stitches are to come and taken down at the left-hand end, and then the stitches worked over it as just described. Much of the tramé work which is now sold is intended to be worked in this stitch.

Cross-stitch.—In working cross-stitch care must be taken that all the crosses have the top stitch in the same direction. Sometimes these slant from left to right, but it is advisable to make the slant from right to left, in the same way as the petit and gros point stitches, and this is even more important if the cross-stitch is being used in conjunction with the other stitches. Cross-stitch varies from petit and gros point stitches in that the stitches on the back are upright and not slanting. When working cross-stitch it is advisable to cross each

tion which is useful for filling in large spaces. It is worked by taking oblique stitches over five vertical and one horizontal thread. Between each stitch leave one thread of canvas. For the second row, start four threads lower down, taking the last thread of the previous row thus making five in all, which forms the encroaching stitch.

Plaited Gobelin is another variety of encroaching Gobelin stitch and is worked backwards and forwards, the slant of the stitches varying in each row. This intercrossing makes an effective background.

Gobelin stitch is usually worked over single thread canvas, though double thread may be used.

When working Backgrounds it is a good idea to use two very close shades, working a needleful of one and then a needleful of the other without keeping any

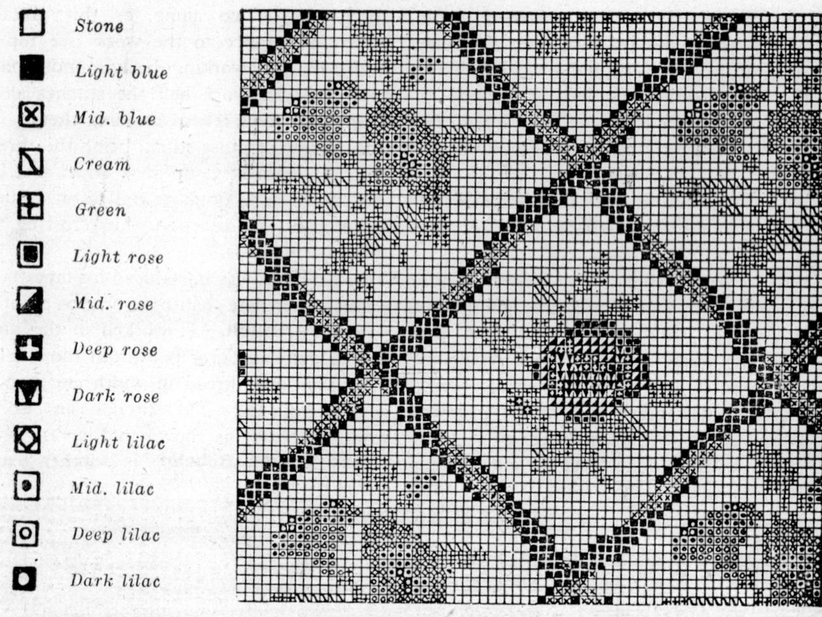

Fig. 24. Above is a simple chart for a beginner. The ribboned trellis can be extended to any size.

Fig. 25.

A realistic floral spray which gives great scope for artistic shading. It is worked entirely in petit point.

definite formation in the placing of the shades. This gives a slightly irregular and faded appearance to the work, which is good when an antique effect is required as for example, when working a seat for a period chair.

Another way of working a background is to work two shades together in the needle. This gives a mottled effect which suits some types of work.

A Simple Chart for the Beginner (Fig. 24) is for a petit point stool-top or handbag, the design being repeated as often as required. The ribboned trellis is worked in two shades of blue, the roses and convolvulus in pinks and lilac as shown in the key to the chart. Black, as a background is always good as it throws up the colours well. It can be worked either in silk or wool. This design could be worked equally well in gros point or cross-stitch. Fig. 25 gives a good idea of light and shade in the working of petit point.

Dinner Mats (Fig. 26) in petit point of an early English design are worked in dull blues, rose, yellow-green and gold on a background the colour of mellow parchment. The curves are accentuated by working the edging on each in the darkest shade of the colour it encloses. In places this has been reversed. The large plain scrolls are worked in two shades, the deeper being on the edge. The smaller, more foliated parts are graduated in shade, which makes a pleasing contrast.

Six strands of silk are used throughout. These mats are practical as they are thick enough to protect a polished table and can be washed easily by drawing them through cold water.

Gauze is also used for petit point and is most effective though it is very fine. The shading shows up well. The piece in Fig. 27 has 1600 stitches to the square inch. For this, gauze with 40 stitches to the inch was used. The material is very slightly stiff and about the same weight as muslin. The threads are set apart as in canvas; each stitch is worked over one crossing of the threads with one strand of filoselle. The background can be left unworked.

As gauze work is so fine it is trying for the eyes, but if a magnifying glass is used, it simplifies the work.

Petit point is also used in Church

DINNER MATS

Fig. 26.

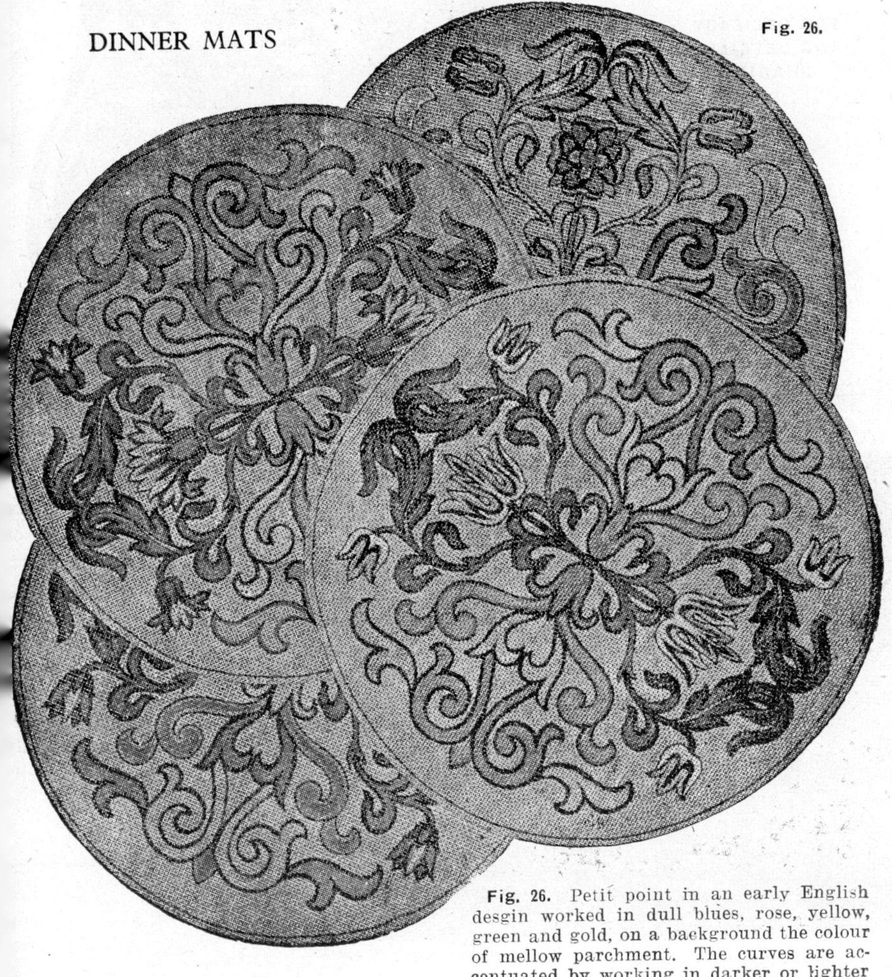

Fig. 26. Petit point in an early English desgin worked in dull blues, rose, yellow, green and gold, on a background the colour of mellow parchment. The curves are accentuated by working in darker or lighter shades, and the scrolls are in two shades.

embroidery for vestments, etc. The design shown in Fig. 40 is worked on canvas with 28 threads to the inch, in two threads of filoselle. The colourings are—for the chalice, four shades of gold, white for the host with rays in grey, the grapes in three shades of mauve, the deepest shade being used nearly always on the outside. The leaves are in three shades of green with two shades of a reddy brown for the stalks and veins. The ears of wheat are in two shades of maize with leaves in two shades of yellowy green. The background is of a dull saxe colour.

Fig. 29 shows a typical Cluny Flower design, which is worked in gros point. This design may be repeated as often as required or each spray worked separately. There are about 128 stitches in the width and height of the section shown here.

PETIT POINT ON GAUZE

FOR DELICACY AND DETAILED SHADING

Fig. 27. A Viennese handbag worked in petit point on gauze.

Fig. 28. The roses in this charming spray worked on gauze vary in shade from shell pink to old rose.

The favourite sprays used in Cluny tapestries. The background is rust the rose two shades of red, the cowslips two shades of yellow, the large flower two shades of purple and the leaves in five shades of green. **Fig. 29.**

So if it is worked on double thread canvas with 11 holes to the inch, it measures about 11½ inches square. It is worked in tapestry wool in three shades each of blue, pink, gold, mauve and three ranges of green. Brown is used for some of the stems. Cluny tapestries are usually worked on a reddish-brown background. This design can also be worked in petit point.

Fig. 30 shows a beautiful flower bunch worked in petit point. There are 290 stitches across the design and 282 in depth; worked on canvas with 16 threads to the inch, the bunch is about 18 inches across. It may be embroidered with wool, filoselle or stranded cottons—a list of the shades required is supplied with the chart, Weldons Design No. W.18, price 2s. 6d., post free

Fig. 30. A lovely flower design on double thread canvas with about sixteen holes to the inch.

from Weldons Ltd., 30 Southampton Street, Strand, London, W.C.2.

A chart for an all-over design that would be very suitable for chair-seats, stools, etc., is shown in Fig. 31. The lions are in 3 shades of red, the fleur-de-lis in 2 shades of gold, and the trellis dividing lines in the lighter gold. The lion motif can be repeated in every diamond or placed in alternate diamonds.

Background is effective in a neutral shade such as fawn, or for variation, fawn in the diamonds in which the lions appear and brown in the alternate diamonds.

Chinese Chippendale.—The Chinese influence can be traced in many kinds of needlework—Chippendale, the furniture designer, chose it for many of his chair seats. The piece in Fig. 32 gives an idea of the detail found in work from the East. It is all beautifully shaded. This piece is worked on canvas, 16 stitches to the inch, and is worked in crewel wool, using two strands at a time. For the background two shades of one colour were worked in the needle at the same time.

Tapestry Pictures are always popular. Fig. 33 is a good example, and could easily be worked in cross-stitch. Many old-fashioned pictures can be adapted, the

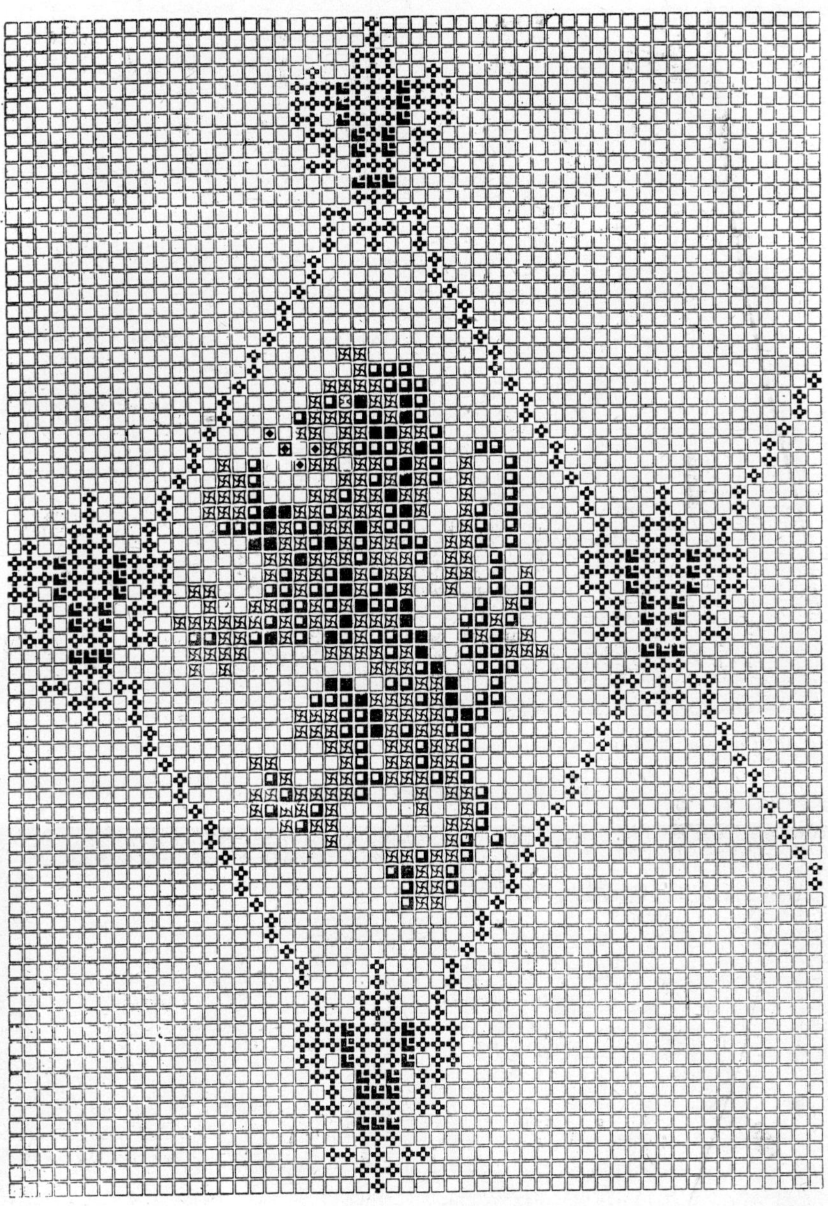

Gold
Gold, Deep
Deep Red
Mid Red
Light Red
Flame
White
Fawn in lion diamonds, Brown in other diamonds

Fig. 31.—Chart for an all-over repeating pattern. To be worked in petit or gros point. The trellis design of diamond shapes and Fleur-de-Lis is extended to the edge of the canvas, and the lions can be worked in every diamond or alternate ones.

Fig. 32. Chinese Chippendale Chair-seat. Design from Weldons Chart No. W.210, price 2s. 6d., post free.

Fig. 33. A needlework-tapestry picture.

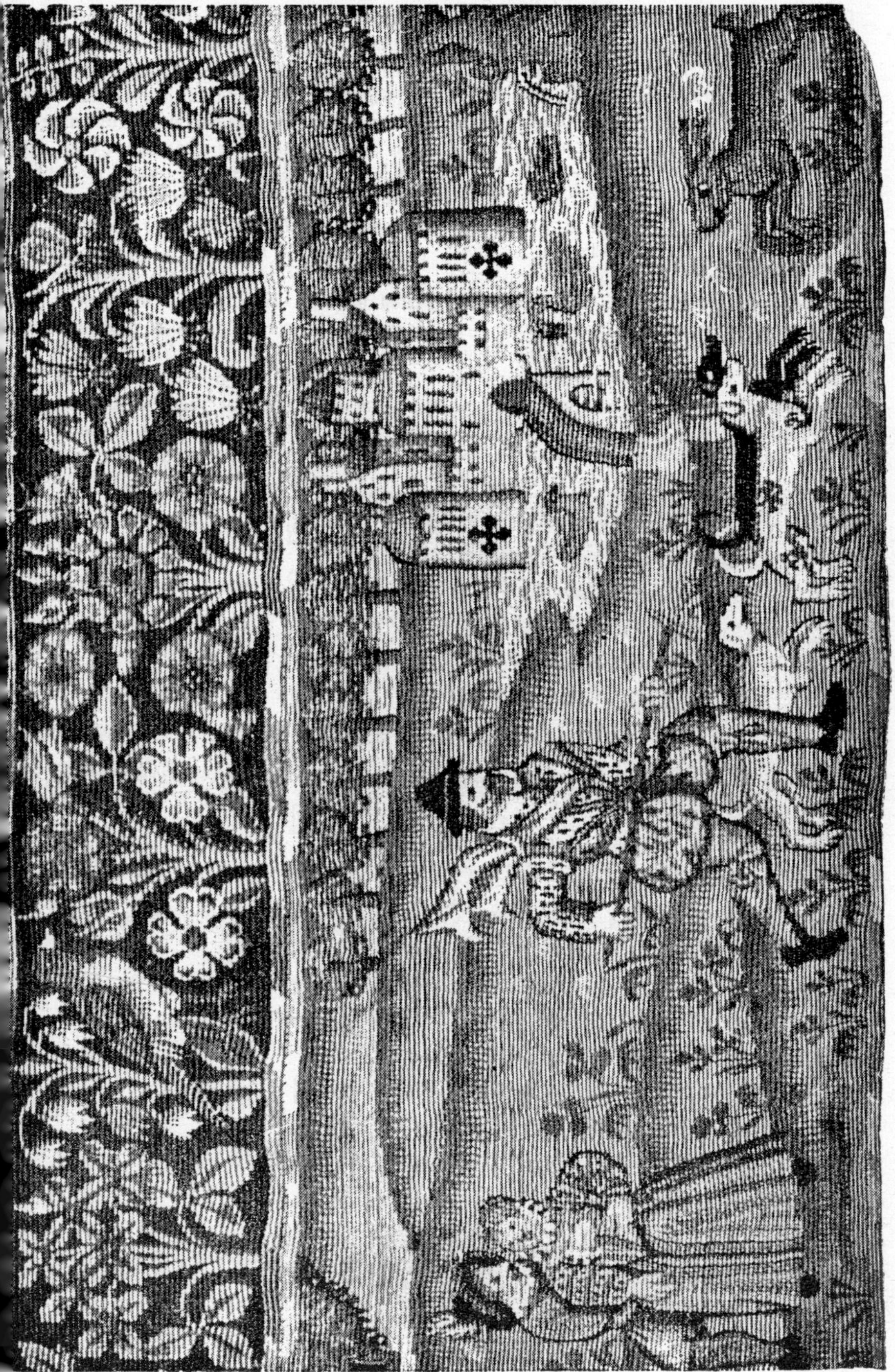

Fig. 34.—A WOVEN TAPESTRY

ideal examples, of course, being those that resemble the old tapestries.

Gobelin Tapestry is a revival on a small scale of ancient tapestry work and is named after the celebrated Gobelins in Paris. Like true Gobelin, it is worked from the back in filoselle or single Berlin wool.

Gobelin work in silk is very beautiful owing to the variety of shades and stitches. Beginners should choose wool, with bold patterns until the details have been mastered. It is worked from counted patterns. A strong wooden embroidery frame, with webbing up both sides is needed for wool work, while a smaller one also with webbing is sufficient for silk.

The frame being ready, cords are carried backwards and forwards from one piece of webbing to the other in parallel lines. The cords are made of fine whipcord. These take the place of canvas and bear the stitches, therefore it is most important to the work that they are arranged at even distances, close together and tightly stretched. The number of lines must be the same as required for the pattern. Very fine twine is used for silk tapestry. Detached flower sprays as for cross-stitch on linen can be used and are quite simple to work. In copying patterns with a good deal of background the one shade is carried straight up the work, but designs of various colours are not so easy. For these it is necessary to thread several needles with shades of colour, secure them in and work them in

Fig. 36.

THE OWL AND CHART FOR WORKING

Fig. 37.—CHART FOR WORKING THE OWL ON THE OPPOSITE PAGE

Fig. 38.—An elaborate and well-balanced coat of arms, showing the combination of helmet, torse, shield, mantling and motto ribbon.

in their places, taking the wool along the work where it is not required, putting it in and making a stitch, then carrying it on again until the top of the frame is reached. It can be easily seen that each shade of colour increases the difficulty of working, therefore it is advisable to start with very few.

When silk Gobelin is worked, the silk need not be threaded. Sufficient for one line should be wound on a thin card and passed through the cord and the loop so made. In this way the silk keeps fresher.

Having prepared the frame as already explained start working from the bottom left-hand side of the frame. Thread a wool needle with the background colour, tie it on to the first cord, bringing the wool, up over the cord. Put the needle in over and under the second cord, bring it out, forming a loop on that cord with the wool, so that the returning wool crosses over the wool coming from the bottom cord. These two loops count as one stitch and must always be drawn up evenly and close together. The next stitch is made on the third line in the same way and so on until every line of cord has a stitch upon it and the top of the frame is reached. The wool is then fastened off and another line started from the bottom close to the first one. The appearance on the right side (the work being done on the wrong side) resembles the tight loops seen in carpets. Silk Gobelin is worked the same as wool, the difference being in the fineness of the pattern produced.

Another way of imitating Gobelin tapestry with silk is only practical for small articles. It is worked on the right side and the stitches are taken over fine knitting needles, which are eventually withdrawn. If the needles are too big, they leave clumsy loops.

The patterns are the same as before, the needles taking the place of the cords. A silk or satin foundation is stitched on the frame and the needles are attached to this close together with strong tacking threads. **To work:** Bring the embroidery silk

Fig. 39. This chair seat, reproduced by kind permission of the Victoria and Albert Museum, is worked in silk and wool in petit point and cross-stitch. The cross-stitch makes a good frame for the finer tent-stitch.

L

Fig. 40.

from the back of the material, pass it over the knitting needle and return it to the back, pass it over the needle again, close to the first place to complete the stitch. If two or three stitches of the same colour come close together on the same line they can be worked at once, but the tendency of the work should always be upward, from the bottom line to the top, and but little deviation from this rule allowed. The material being the ground, only the pattern is worked. When the pattern is finished paste over the back with embroidery paste, leave the knitting needles in position until thoroughly dry, then pull them out. If the design is an arabesque the work can be enriched with a line of gold thread couched round the outline.

Heraldry lends itself to working in needlework-tapestry, and a few examples are given here.

The owl—age-old symbol of wisdom—is frequently used in heraldry, particularly as the crest of school and college coat of arms. On page 311 is a working chart for the owl. Worked in half cross-stitch on double thread canvas with 10 holes to the inch, the design would measure 12 inches deep by 9 inches wide, including the torse. One skein of wool in each colour in the key to the chart is required, the amount for the background depending on area to be covered.

A design can be copied from a print or coloured illustration, and can then be painted on to the most suitable kind of canvas ready for working. For those who wish to draw out the design for themselves it is helpful to make a chart on squared paper first.

Heraldic tapestry can be worked in petit-point or other stitches, or a combination of stitches according to the detail of the design. A double thread canvas with 10 holes to the inch is a good size to choose for general purposes, and to make the chart correspond with this, it should be drawn on graph paper with 10 squares to the inch.

The crest is drawn first—25 to 4[illegible] squares high or long, according to its shape. Then draw the details of the shield which are called "charges."

The helmet is super-imposed, and may cover, or partly cover, any part of the charges at the top of the shield. Outline the helmet before working in the details, such as high-lights, etc.

The torse on which the crest stands is really part of the mantling, and takes its colours from the two principal colours of the shield. When the shield is divided into several compartments, the colours for the torse and mantling are taken from the first compartment only. If working from an uncoloured print, the directions of shading lines indicate the colours: Horizontal—royal blue; perpendicular—pillar box red; shaded with dots—gold; shaded with cross-hatching—black; shaded diagonally—green; unshaded—silver. The torse is always in six equal divisions.

The mantling is in one colour lined with another, and at least five shades of both colours should be used in working, to avoid flatness.

The ribbon to carry the motto may be worked in grey, shaded to show the curves.

The ground colour of the whole work depends on personal choice, but if the colours of the arms permit it, royal blue is extremely effective, and most distinctive.

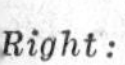

Right:

The Arms of Cambridge University.

HERALDIC ARMS IN CROSS-STITCH

Worked by St. John Rumsey, Esq.

Above:

The Arms of Queen's College, Cambridge.

Above:

The Arms of Magdalen College, Oxford.

BRIEF GUIDE TO PERIOD DESIGNS

As most of the designs used in Tapestry work are period designs, a few examples of standard typical designs and the type of furniture for which they are most suited, together with brief notes, are given here, in the hope that they may help the reader in her search for appropriate designs.

Tudor. (1509-1558.)—Chief designs were small motifs, coats of arms, floral subjects appliquéd to velvet coverings and cushions on hard oak furniture.

Elizabethan. (1558-1603.)—Worked in petit-point, for wall hangings, bed curtains, valances, and cushions; designs were usually a central panel, often with figures dressed in the costume of the day, enclosed by strap work known as the garter. The garter was sometimes divided again into separate panels, each with a filling. A tree bearing fruit was a favourite subject for smaller panels, and birds and beasts were used. Later in this century Hungarian Point became popular.

Jacobean. (1603-1625.)—Large conventional designs worked with wool on twill. The contemporary French designs (Louis XIII) were heavier, and even more ornate.

Stuart. (1625-1649.)—Pictorial pieces were popular, Biblical subjects often being depicted with figures dressed in costume of the time. Others show King Charles, his Queen and palaces. The drawing was quaint and simple. Small pieces of petit point were appliquéd to velvet. Walnut furniture just becoming popular.

William and Mary. (1689-1702.)—The high-backed chairs of this period afforded excellent display for the pictorial subjects and large flowering designs chosen. The Oriental influence is strongly marked. The contemporary French designs—Louis XIV —were rather more delicate.

Queen Anne. (1702-1714.)—The most popular type of design was a large bunch, basket or urn of flowers, in natural colours. The background was usually dark to throw up the design. The winged arm-chair also displayed exquisite needlework and here designs were composed of rather conventional flowers and foliage which more or less covered the whole space.

Georgian Period. (1714-1830.)—Mahogany furniture now used, so designs became heavier. Chinese influence still strong. Floral pattern, still used, and pictorial panels surrounded by flowers, foliage and scroll work.

Chippendale. (1760.)—Formal designs, often with a centre panel with tree-like form and birds surrounded by a flowing pattern of conventional flowers and leaves. Chippendale frequently used Gothic style of design for the needlework covering his chairs.

Hepplewhite, another designer, who lived in the eighteenth century. His furniture was of a lighter style, and needlework and brocade were used to cover chair seats. Designs were light in treatment and generally showed stripes with bands of flowers and ribbons, daintily worked on a light ground.

Sheraton (1751-1806) worked mostly in satin-wood and there was a definite Gothic influence in his designs. The ground was usually divided into sections by dainty arches and each space was filled with a simply drawn flower.

Victorian. (1837-1901.)—The introduction of the embroidery on canvas known as Berlin work came now. Floral and pictorial designs were popular, and numerous articles were embellished with needlework-tapestry.

TUDOR

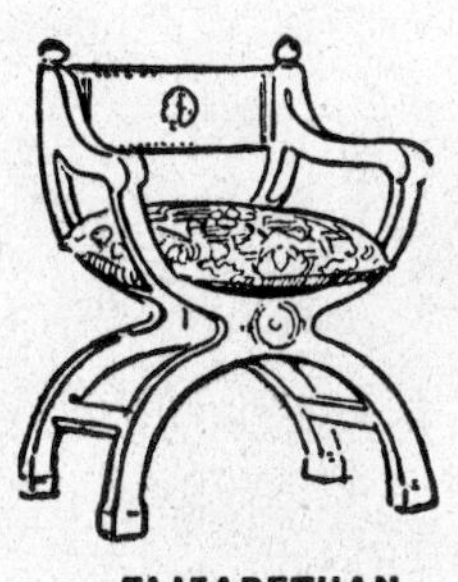

ELIZABETHAN

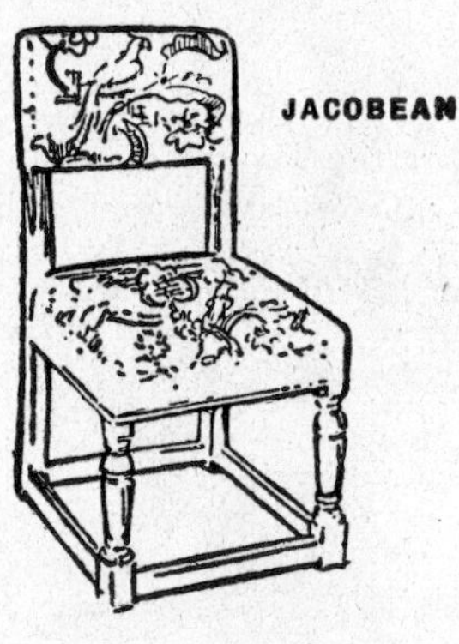

JACOBEAN

STUART

WILLIAM and MARY

QUEEN ANNE

GEORGIAN
CHIPPENDALE
HEPPLEWHITE

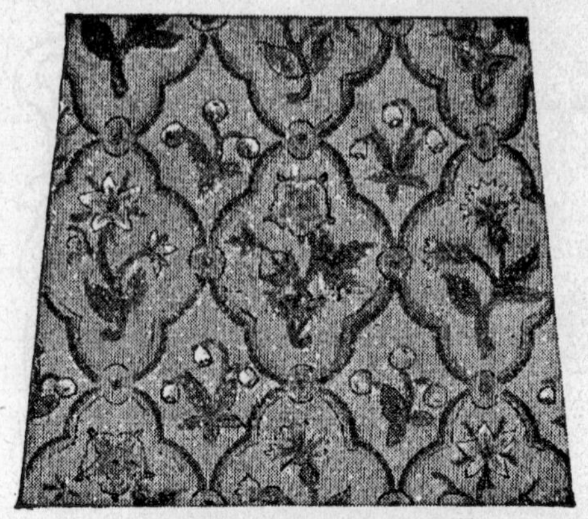

SHERATON

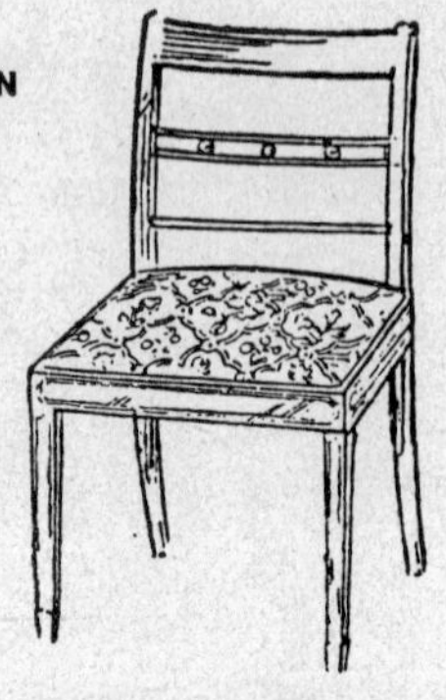

VICTORIAN

NET EMBROIDERY

For all work of this kind use only the best quality net. To test it, push a stiletto, such as is used for Broderie Anglaise, through a mesh, and if it stretches without tearing the net, the quality is good.

For net embroidery, use fine lace thread, mercerised cotton, embroidery cotton, twist or silk. Use a needle with a blunt point, and for large mesh net, use a long needle, so that several threads can be picked up simultaneously, using a fairly long thread to avoid too many joins. A fresh thread is worked in by running it into the last three or four holes of the worked row and cutting the ends off short. The net is worked lengthwise. This must be borne in mind when buying.

An agreeable feature of net embroidery is that in most cases no tracing is necessary, the pattern being counted by following the holes of the net. If, however, the embroidery is worked according to a line tracing, the drawing is transferred with Indian ink to glazed calico or white tracing linen, and the net is then tacked on to this on the straight, the whole being backed with a piece of linen or calico to make it firm for working. The net should be secured to the tracing, all round the pattern. The method of working a pattern is clearly shown in Fig. 1. The pattern is worked in running stitch, along the lines of the drawing, and therefore the working thread can be carried over one or more holes of the net ground according to the requirements.

In net work a distinction is made between open work on net. The patterns are worked with embroidery thread in darning stitch according to two different methods, either by following the rows of holes or by threading through the net in lines following a traced pattern.

The work is generally done without using a foundation but when fine net is used it may be tacked, on the straight, on to a dark waxed cloth or glazed linen foundation. The threads are run through by taking the needle alternately under and over the thread of the net (Fig. 2).

The edges to be cut are outlined with running stitches, then secured either by making buttonhole stitches over a running thread and then cutting off the edges sharply (Fig. 3) or by working round the scalloped border with double crochet after the net is cut and turned in.

In this kind of embroidery, all kinds of fancy stitches, which are mostly carried out in finer thread than the outlines, are used for filling individual figures. By combining fine lace thread for the fillings and mercerised or embroidery cotton or silk for the outlines, attractive shaded effects are obtained. Fig. 5 shows various effective filling stitches which may easily be copied.

In working **eyelet holes** (Fig. 4) first outline by running a thread round them, care being taken to do this inside the tracing so that the hole is not made too large. The net is enlarged with a stiletto and the edges are worked round with overcast stitch. In the case of large round or oval eyelet holes, outline them two or three times, cutting away the net as required (usually two

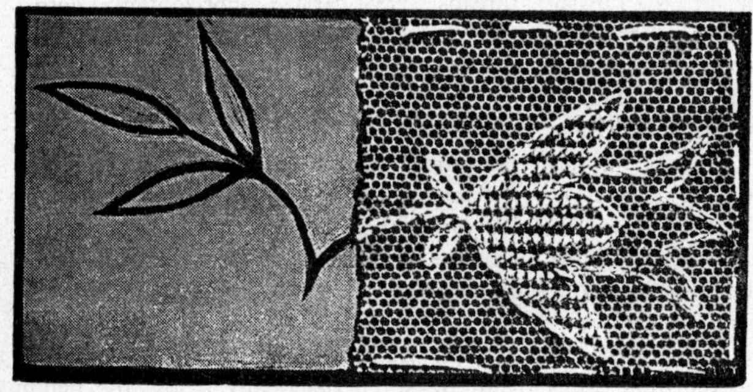

Fig. 1.

When a design is worked over a line tracing the drawing is done in Indian ink on glazed calico and the net is tacked over this.

threads are sufficient) and turning in the edges as in Broderie Anglaise.

For **cord stitch** (Fig. 10) after the outlines of the pattern have been run in, overcast the loose running thread with small stitches, to obtain the cordlike appearance.

Knot stitch filling (Fig. 9) is a useful pattern either for decorating the net ground or for filling flowers as shown here. It is worked either in French knots or with darning stitch over one mesh.

ing threads have to be run through. As net fabric is formed by three layers of thread, two obliquely intersecting and the third connecting the threads horizontally, this is easily seen from the small cross formed by the threads of the fabric. The underlying thread gives the first direction.

Begin by running the first layer of threads through the second or third row of holes beyond the cut edges, and when taking the thread across the actual hole, cut away,

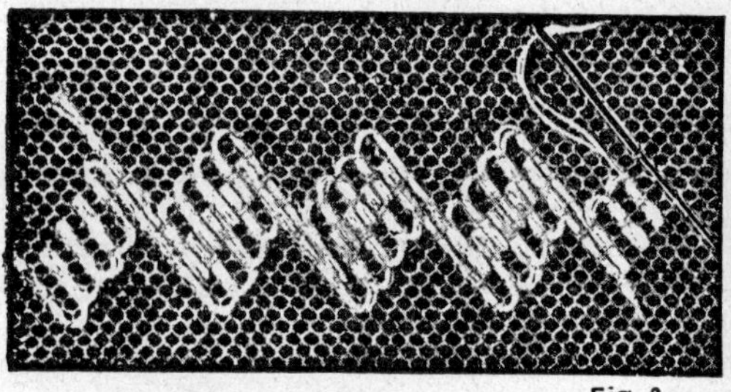

Fig. 2.

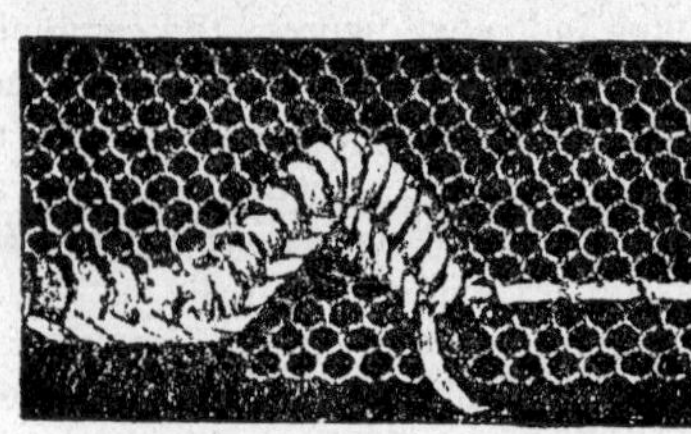

Fig. 3.

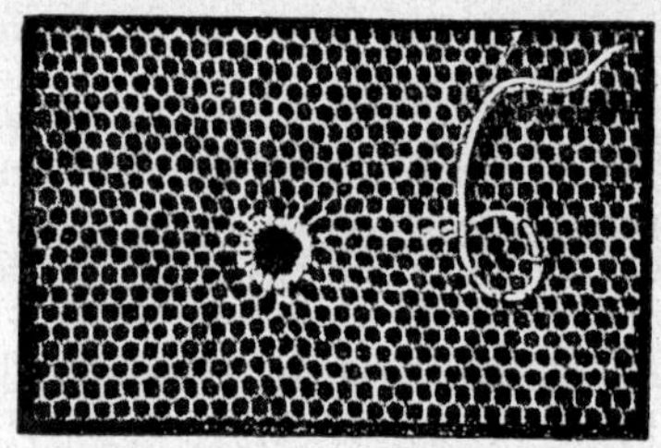

Fig. 4.

Chain stitch and Buttonhole stitch (Fig. 8) are useful for line fillings, such as in Figs. 6 and 7 and may be successfully substituted for the run stitch in either case. They are worked in the usual manner over one or more meshes of the net.

Figs. 11 and 12 show a fancy filling stitch, formed by working loop stitches diagonally across the net on the wrong side.

To darn holes in net, the fabric is tacked on to glazed or tracing linen or stiff paper, and a piece extending to about the fifth or sixth row of holes beyond the edges of the defective part is cut away, preferably following the line of the holes. Now see in which direction the first slant-

catch it into the net several holes away from the cut edge, so that this edge will not ravel (Fig. 14). Repeat this process in the reverse way as Fig. 15. The connecting threads are carried horizontally across these ground threads to strengthen the darn. Start overcasting from the third or fourth row of net foundation at the point where the new threads begin, working over each mesh as seen in Fig. 16 and tightening the sewing thread to give shape to the hole. To work the next row, turn the work so that the thread may again be overcast from right to left.

The insertion in Fig. 13 is an easy piece of work for the beginner. It is worked in running stitch diagonally across the net in

A simple flower worked in counted holes and right, Star pattern filling for which two or three stitches are taken over each hole.

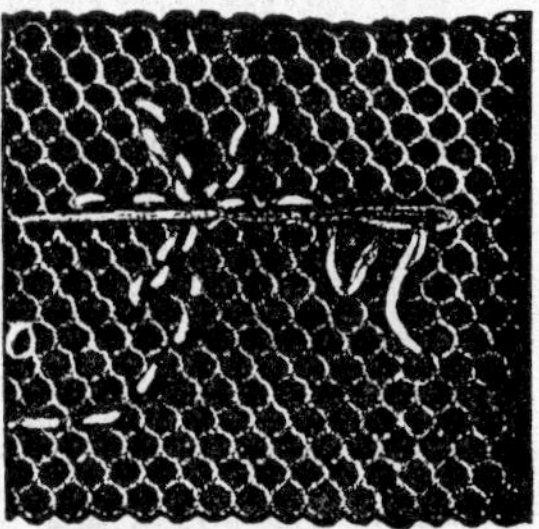

Above, close running in the same row of holes, each alternate bar of net being caught up. Below, a filling pattern worked to and fro in horizontal bars.

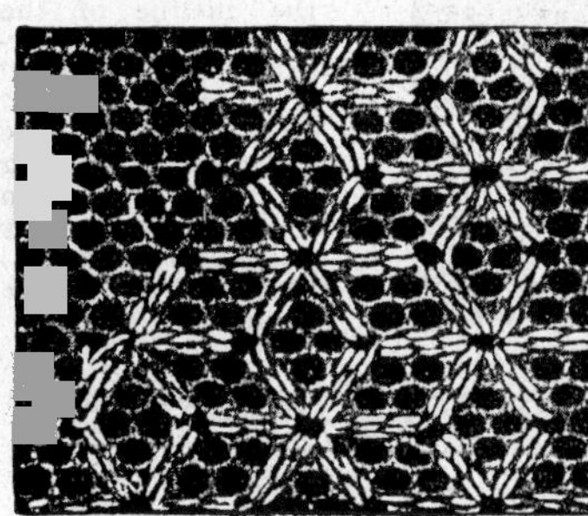

Fig. 5.

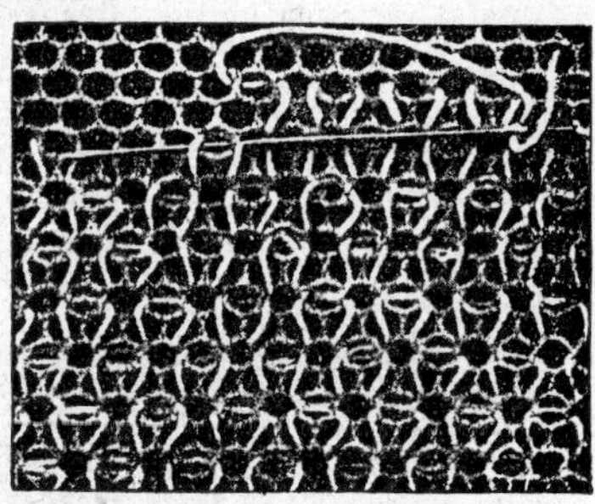

Above, a simple star filling. There are three lines of stitches to each point, each line filling alternate holes, so that each hole is covered.

Left, lattice filling, worked in two rows of holes each being covered by two stitches. Below, a large dot pattern worked obliquely across three, five and three holes.

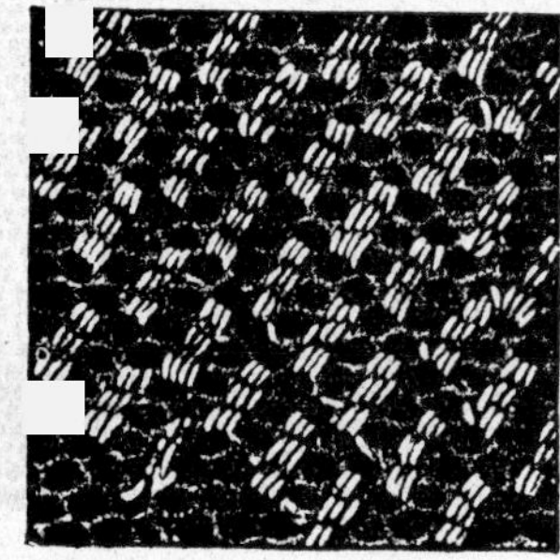

Left, a very simple bar filling worked in slanting rows, with three rows of stitching to each hole.

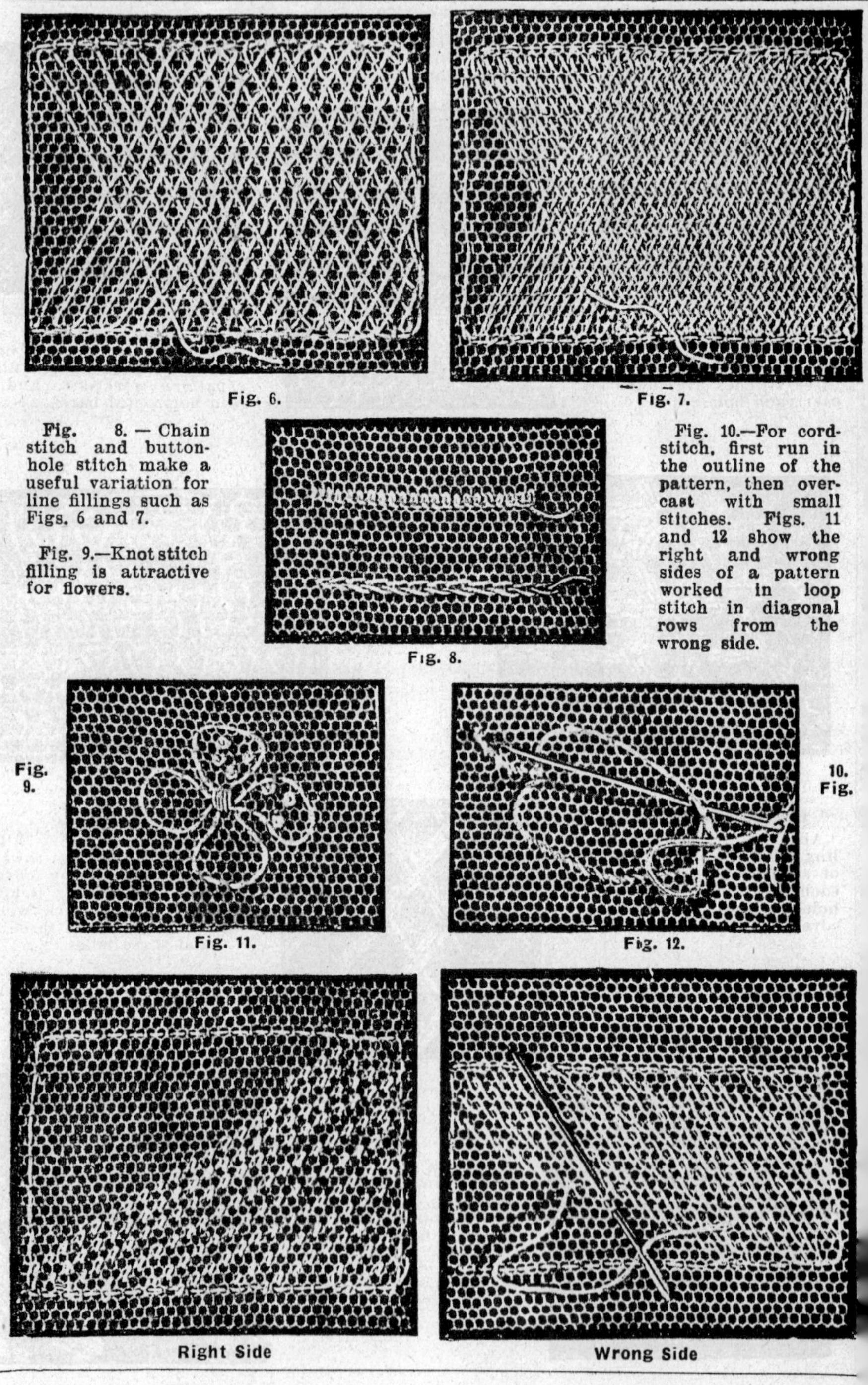

Fig. 6.

Fig. 7.

Fig. 8. — Chain stitch and button-hole stitch make a useful variation for line fillings such as Figs. 6 and 7.

Fig. 9.—Knot stitch filling is attractive for flowers.

Fig. 8.

Fig. 10.—For cord-stitch, first run in the outline of the pattern, then over-cast with small stitches. Figs. 11 and 12 show the right and wrong sides of a pattern worked in loop stitch in diagonal rows from the wrong side.

Fig. 9.

10. Fig.

Fig. 11.

Fig. 12.

Right Side

Wrong Side

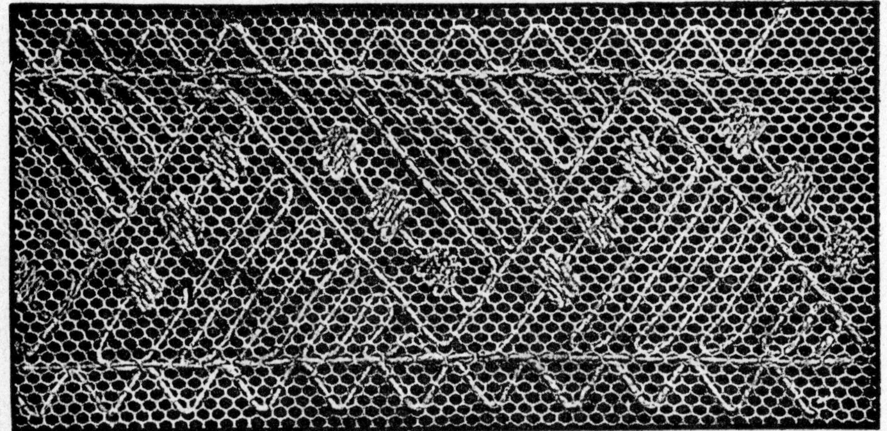

Fig. 13.

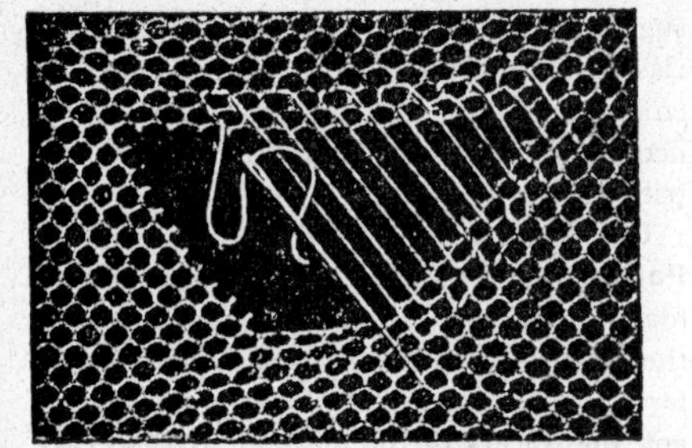

Fig. 14.

Fig. 15.

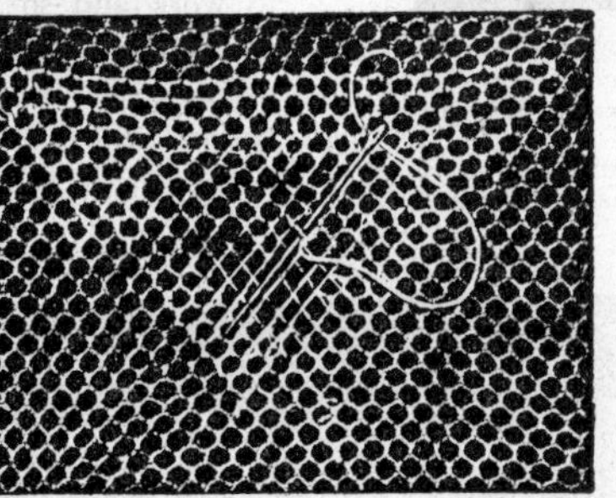

Fig. 16.

triangular forms, which have a filling of run-stitch lines and small darned squares. A vandyke on either side beyond the straight lines forms the border. It is worked on a coarse-mesh ground, and a thread of medium size is used throughout.

The attractive designs in Figs. 17, 18 and 19 need very little explanation. The illustrations are clear enough for the worker to find no difficulty in counting the mesh or following the pattern. They are all in run-stitch and with the exception of the centre one in Fig. 19, each pattern with thread of one size only.

The Star designs in Fig. 20 may be used in a great variety of ways. Applied simply, or combined to form edgings, insertions, or spot patterns, they are always attractive. The stars are worked on a foundation of fine net. For the three small

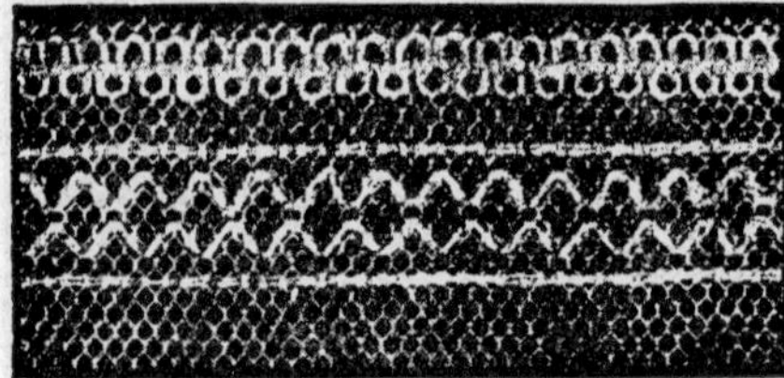

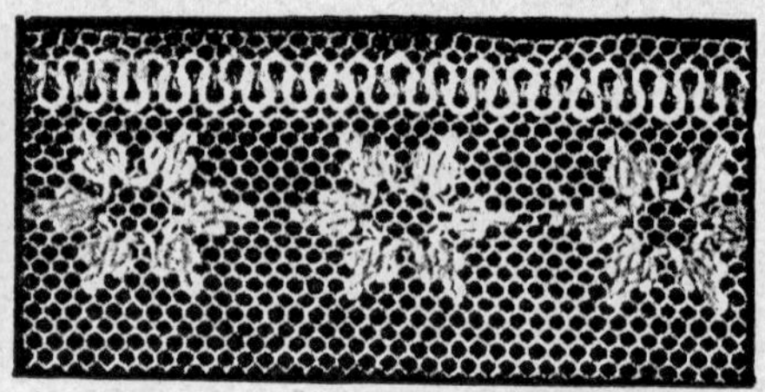

The four designs in Fig. 17 are excellent for edgings and insertions. They are all in run stitch in the same sized thread.

Fig. 17.

Fig. 19 shows three more delightful insertions worked in run stitch. The Greek Bird insertion in the centre is worked in two thicknesses of thread.

patterns only one sized thread is used for working, but the large one is embroidered in various sized threads, using finer towards the outside and round the centre.

The insertion in Fig. 23 with its three rows of running stitches in waved lines, suggestive of a key pattern, can also be classed among the simpler patterns for net embroidery, and no further description is necessary as the illustration shows the pattern clearly.

Oblong and Square Cloth in Counted Patterns.—Net forms an ideal background for embroidery. The fragile appearance of the material, which is very durable, goes far to enhance the skill of the needlewoman and the tracery of the design. It is so easy to work and so quickly done that an all-over pattern may be attempted. A good example of this is shown in Fig. 21. These cloths are made on good washing net

Fig. 19.

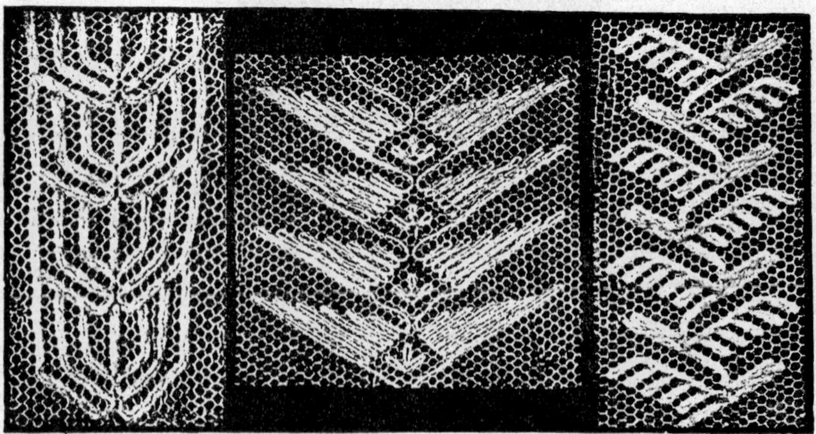

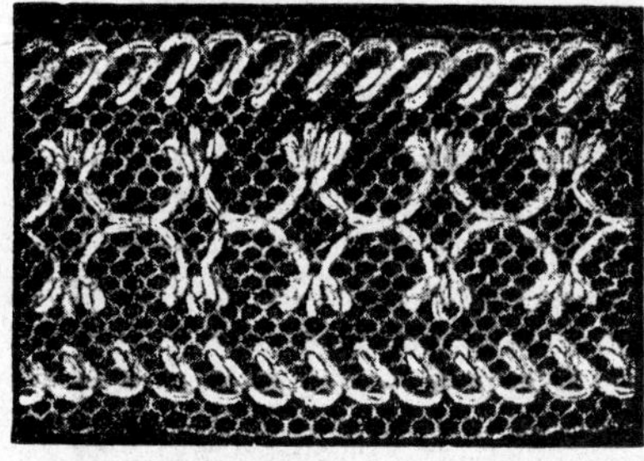

Fig. 18.

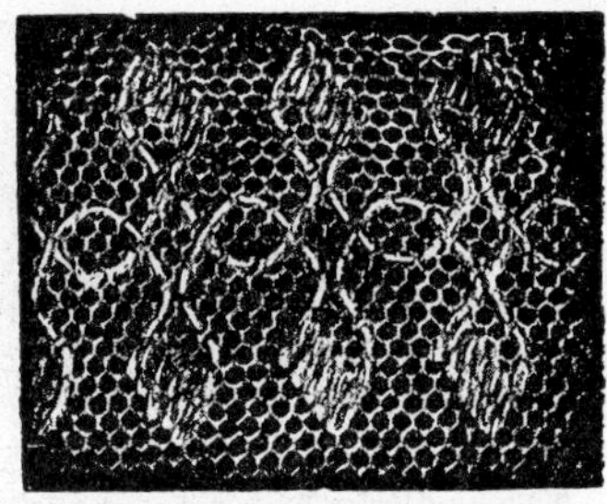

worked with stranded embroidery cotton, mercerised cotton or coarse lace thread.

The illustrated section, Fig. 22, shows the method of working. The design is composed of a border with a diagonal trellis pattern in the centre. There are six double repeats of the border design along each of the long sides of the oblong cloth and the square cloth has three. The different appearance of the pattern at the end is due to the stitches following the same direction of the mesh ground throughout the pattern. The trellis is done in single rows of run stitch and the same stitch is used to secure the hems which finish off the edge.

A Vandyked Insertion.—The insertion (Fig. 24) is embroidered on fine net in threads of varying thickness, which produce a beautiful shaded effect. The pattern can either be traced on to tracing linen or the threads counted. The thickest thread is used at the edges, then graduated threads for the filling-in, the finest being at the top next to the outline. This insertion is

The two designs in Fig. 18 are both suitable for edgings and insertions and are worked in run stitch.

These four star designs can be used in a great many ways. The small stars are worked in one size thread, and the large star in varying sizes.

Fig. 20.

An oblong and square cloth worked entirely in counted patterns. The foundation is washing net and the design is worked in stranded embroidery cotton.

Fig. 21.

particularly adaptable for trimming runners, tray-cloths and curtains.

A Table Centre.—(Fig. 25.) It is about 12 inches square, and is intended to be worked over a tracing on fine washing net with mercerised thread. The method of working is clearly shown in the illustration of the enlarged section from which it will be seen that the flowers are closely filled in with running stitches showing their shape, and have an overcast hole in the centre, as have also the dainty leaves. Holes giving the effect of small berries adorn all the tendrils, and the stems and all the out-

Fig. 22.

A portion of the cloth showing how it is worked. The insertion is particularly adaptable for trimming all kinds of articles.

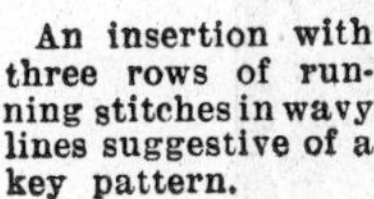

An insertion with three rows of running stitches in wavy lines suggestive of a key pattern.

Fig. 23.

lines are double run with a thicker thread. The outer edge of the cloth is finished with buttonholed scallops, padded first with double running stitch lines (Fig. 26).

Lace Edging shown in Fig. 28 has a border consisting of a close row of holes and two rows of running stitches. The design should be marked off on to tracing linen. The sprays of flowers are worked at intervals in run stitch and the work is carried out in fine soft thread. The lace is useful as a trimming, and if not worked too wide, would make a border for a fine linen or linen lawn handkerchief.

Wide Lace.—This lace (Fig. 27) is made of medium-sized mesh washing net and is suitable for trimming. The net should be cut about as wide again as is shown and the upper part left plain.

Appliqué on Net is effective and easy to do. The materials required for the stag design in Fig. 31 are: a good washing net of a fairly fine mesh, some white organdie and pale blue Filoselle.

First of all transfer the design on to the organdie, then tack it over the net in the required position. This done, tack the whole piece on to some dark waxed cloth.

Outline the stag in a close-running stitch then overcast all round in two strands of blue Filoselle, very close together. This gives a slightly raised effect. When the

Fig. 24.—A dainty lace edging which is worked over a design on tracing linen to form vandykes.

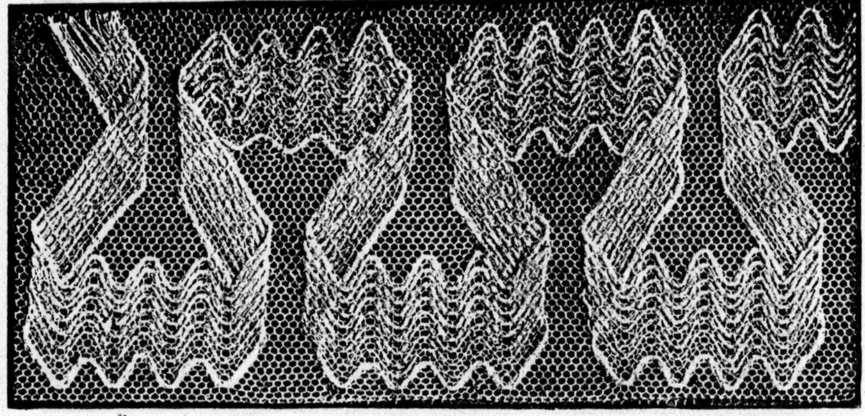

Fig. 25.

A table centre in an extremely delicate design. It is about 12 inches square and is intended to be worked over a tracing in fine washing net with mercerised thread. Below is an enlarged section showing the flowers closely filled in with run stitch.

Fig. 26.

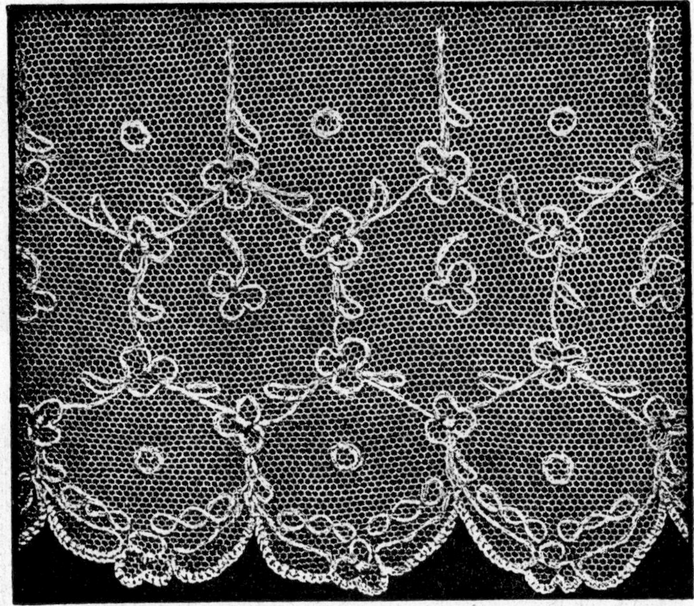

Fig. 27.

stag is completed, then the organdie may be cut close to the edges making the stag stand out well against the net background.

Continue with the flower border in the same manner. The illustration shows the edge of the border being worked.

This is extremely simple to do and most effective when worked. It can be used for tea-cloths, lingerie, table centres, etc.

Braid Insertion on Net is another way of embroidering, for which a very coarse net is the best. For this work bold designs are

Fig. 28.

A dainty lace edging which is worked over tracing linen. The lace is useful for innumerable trimming purposes.

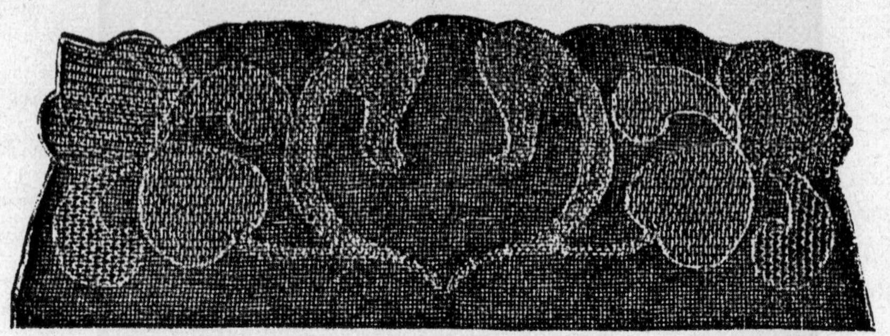

Fig. 29.

Diagram 2.

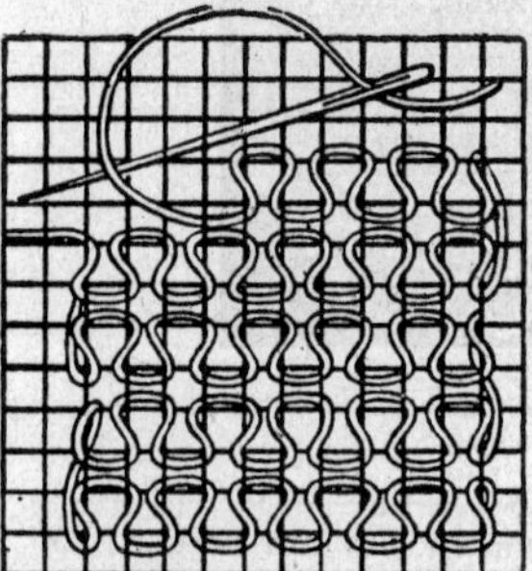

Diagram 1.

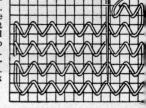

This lovely iris design is particularly suitable for a cheval set. Two fillings are used—the simple zig-zag shown on the right (worked from right to left) and that shown on left which is also worked from right to left. Below.—Braid can be used as an alternative for silk in some designs. Curves are not as easy to work as points.

Fig. 30.

always used. It can be made for any article where one would want to introduce a definite colour or colours. For this purpose use a fine braid.

In working with braid more trouble must be taken, as it is not as easy as cotton, as the braid is likely to twist. But if after taking every stitch the braid is flattened out, it should be quite easy. After the first few stitches it will progress quickly.

Fig. 31. A lovely example of appliqué on net in white with pale blue stitchery. The stag is outlined in close running stitch and then overcast.

For the insertion in Fig. 30 the diamonds in the centre are worked in satin stitch in braid of a different colour to the edging. Many conventional designs can be adapted for this work.

An Iris Cheval Set.

For this piece of needlerun lace in Fig. 29 ½ a yard of 54-inch-wide curtain net with 13 meshes to the inch, 6 skeins of stranded cotton to match, a length of waxed linen large enough to take the design (about 50 inches by 18 inches) are required. The large mat measures about 23½ inches long by 15 inches, and the two smaller ones are 16 inches by 11 inches.

Trace off your design on to the waxed linen. Tack the net firmly and evenly over the designs, leaving good margins round the edges.

Using three strands of cotton in the needle, darn in the whole of the outline, taking the cotton in and out of each mesh whenever possible; it will be necessary to miss an odd mesh here and there to keep the line round a curve.

Knots should never be used as they spoil the look of the work. Each thread should be darned a short distance into the last stitches, both to begin and finish the thread.

The leaves are worked in straight darning stitch backwards and forwards. Simple darned lace stitches are used for filling in the flowers for which clear working diagrams are given here. Only two strands of cotton are required for these stitches and a long row should first be worked across the widest part of the space to be filled. This sets the pattern. The other rows must then be worked on either side of it, stopping as they reach the outline. Care should be taken to finish each thread at the outline, so that it can be darned in without causing a join in the filling.

When the design is finished, cut through the tacking stitches very carefully, and remove the waxed linen. This can be used again. Press the work on the wrong side with a cool iron. Clip the edges at the corners and turn them under. Run them down with a double thread, then finally buttonhole the edges of all three mats and cut away the surplus net close to the stitching with a pair of sharp scissors.

The diagram for the filling for the three lower petals of the iris shows clearly the working of the stitch, which is worked from right to left. Starting at the lower edge of the right-hand side, pass the needle under two bars and one mesh. Bring the cotton up slantwise over two bars and one mesh, putting the needle in one bar back. Repeat the first stitch, then take the cotton down slantwise over two bars and one mesh, putting the needle in one bar back. Repeat these four stitches in a straight row. Next row turn the work and come back, making the bottom stitch of the top row lie side by side in the same mesh with the top stitch of the bottom row.

Diagram I shows the filling for the upper petals. The simplicity of this zig-zag lace filling stitch is clearly shown. Start from the right and work towards the left.

NETTING

This is an ancient art, the earliest chronicles of its existence being on some of the Egyptian monuments where figures were depicted wearing tunics of netting, the loops of which were gaily embroidered in coloured silks or gold and silver threads.

Netting nowadays nearly always serves a useful purpose as each stitch being independent and distinct in itself, there is never any fear of unravelling, and it will stand the hardest wear.

Plain net is often elaborated by darning designs in the meshes with cotton.

Material required: a special netting needle is required, which is split at both ends, and must be easily pliable, a round spool or mesh stick (Fig. 1), the thickness of which regulates the size of the mesh, and a weighted cushion or sewing vice. The working thread is wound on the netting needle as shown in Fig. 1. No more thread should be wound on than the size of the mesh to be woven allows, so that the needle can easily be passed through.

The spool may be made of wood, bone or metal, and must be the same thickness throughout up to the points. Its circumference makes a mesh twice its own size when working.

Steel knitting needles can also be used for spools. A No. 14 needle is equivalent to a flat spool measuring $\frac{1}{8}$ of an inch wide. A No. 7 knitting needle is equivalent to a flat spool $\frac{1}{4}$ of an inch wide.

Crochet and knitting cotton are used for netting—also hemp and flax string. Whip cord is an excellent material. Macramé thread is used for hammocks, tennis nets, shopping bags, and a finer macramé thread is used for ordinary netting.

The netting is begun by tying a strong thread into a loop. This is then fastened to the cushion with a pin (Fig. 3) or slung round the pin of the sewing vice (Fig. 1). The working thread is then knotted to this loop. The work is done from left to right and at the end of each row is turned, the spool drawn out, and a new row begun by replacing the spool into position. To form the meshes (Fig. 6) the spool is held horizontally between the thumb and forefinger of the left hand. It should be noticed that the spool always remains in the same position and must be kept close to each completed row of meshes. The working thread (Fig. 6) from the netting needle is now brought with the right hand over the spool and up behind the third and fourth fingers of the left hand, then upwards behind the spool (Fig. 7), being held firmly in a slanting direction, towards the left over the meshes, with the thumb (Fig. 6). The thread is then brought down again behind the spool, round behind the little finger. The needle is thrust through the loop on the fingers (Fig. 7) and behind the spool from below through the next free loop of thread. The thread must now be drawn to a loop round the spool by releasing the thread held by the thumb and withdrawing the third and fourth fingers from the thread

Fig. 1.—IMPLEMENTS USED FOR NETTING

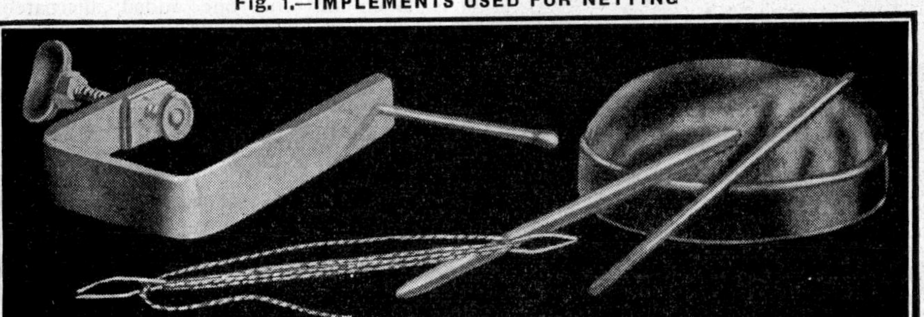

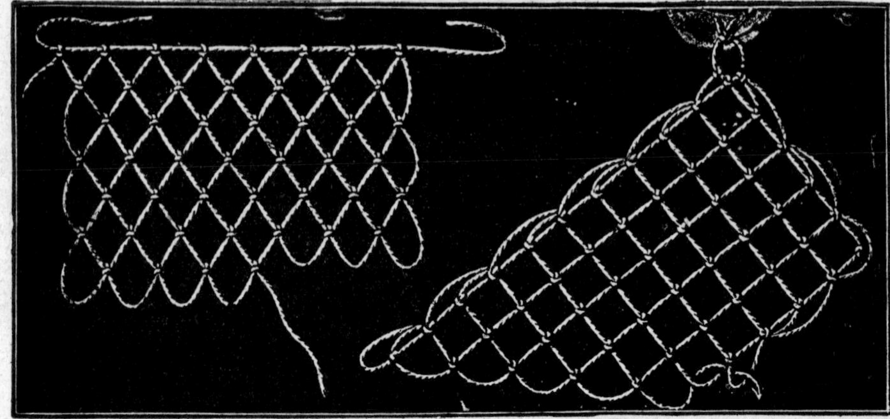

Fig. 2. Fig. 3.

Fig. 4.

Fig. 5.

round them (Fig. 8), the thread being slowly tightened and only held by the little finger until the loop is quite closed. The mesh is now complete and the following meshes are formed in the same way.

There is a difference in the making of plain and diagonal net. In **plain** net, which is the more common, the meshes are parallel with the borders. The work is begun in the same way, whether it is intended to make a strip or square, with a loop of strong thread as in Fig. 6. Two meshes are made to begin with and at the end of each row one mesh is added by making two meshes in the last loop (Fig. 5).

For netting a square, when the desired size is reached, a mesh is taken off at the end of each row in the same way by taking up two meshes together (Fig. 4).

In netting a strip, on the other hand, as soon as the required number of meshes is reached, at the end of each row one mesh is taken off and one added alternately (Fig. 3). In this way the same number of meshes is always maintained. When the desired length of net is made it is finished off in the same way as the square. In order that the work may not get out of shape in working large pieces, it is gathered together after a certain length is reached by a thread passed through the meshes. It is then hung up by this new loop.

In making **diagonal** net the required number of meshes is cast on (Fig. 2). The

HOW THE MESHES ARE FORMED

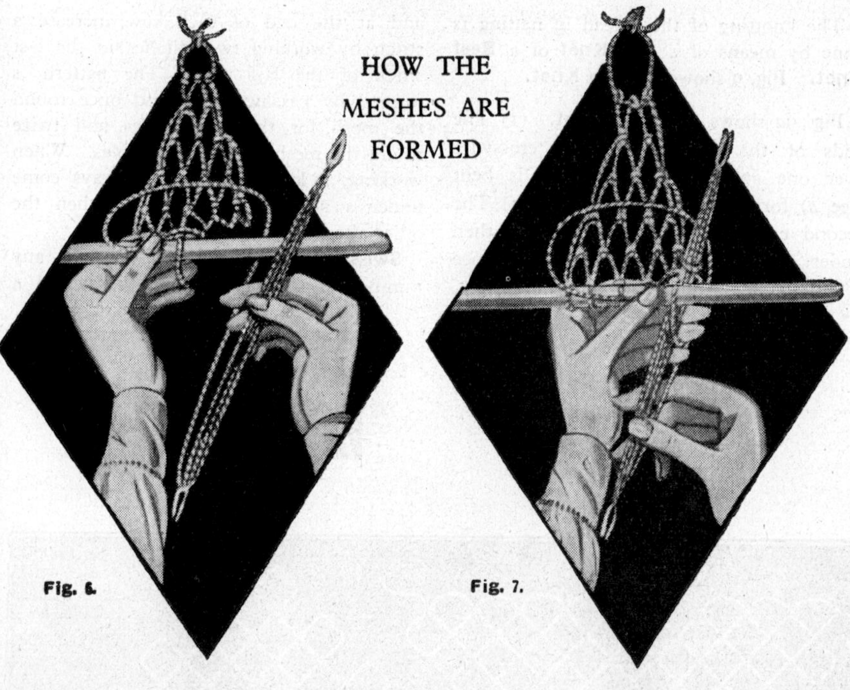

Fig. 6.

Fig. 7.

work is carried to and fro without increasing or decreasing.

To make a square with loops on its outer edge (Figs. 10 and 11) the work is begun by casting on the required number of meshes in the middle of the square at the letter "a" (Fig. 10). Then each row is decreased by leaving the last loop empty. In turning the work, the knot will consequently be made in the last loop but one of the preceding row. In order to make the second half of the square (Fig. 11), begin again at the first row (which forms the middle) and after knotting on the new thread at *b* continue as described above.

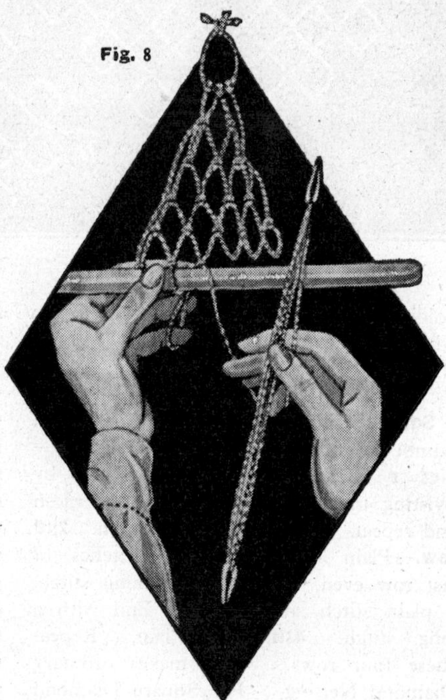

Fig. 8

Figs. 6, 7, and 8 show the three easy stages in making a mesh in netting

The knotting of the thread in netting is done by means of a **Slip Knot** or a **Reef Knot.** Fig. 9 shows the **Slip Knot.**

Fig. 9*a* shows the **Reef Knot.** (1) The ends of the threads are laid crosswise over one another, and one end is bent (see *a*) forwards over the other. (2) The second end is taken backwards and then under (see *a*). (3) *a* is twisted once round *b* and the knot is drawn tight, holding both ends and both threads firmly while drawing.

Fig. 9.—SLIP-KNOT

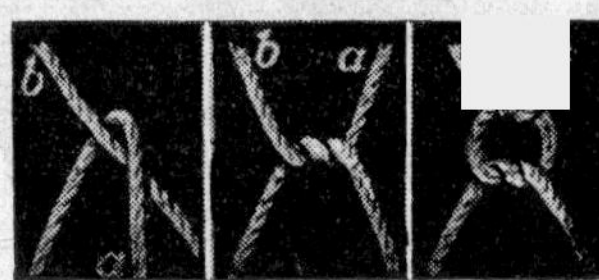

Fig. 9a.—REEF KNOT

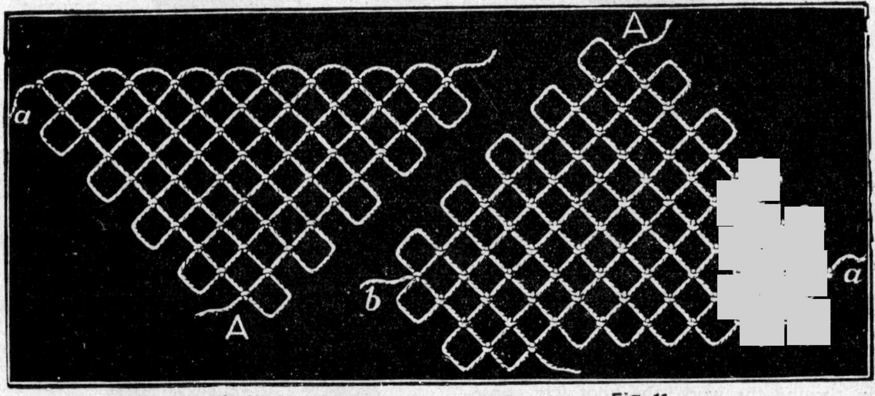

Fig. 10. Fig. 11.

DESIGNS IN NETTING

Square Diamond Netting.—An uneven number of stitches is required. **1st row.**—Net 1 stitch, make 1 long stitch by twisting the thread twice round the mesh and repeat. End with a plain stitch. **2nd row.**—Plain netting, making stitches of last row even. **3rd row.**—1 long stitch, 1 plain stitch, and repeat. End with a long stitch. **4th row.**—Plain. Repeat these four rows. This makes ordinary Diamond Netting. For Square Diamond Netting put on two stitches for the corner and at the end of each row increase a stitch by working two stitches in the last stitch of the last row. The pattern is formed by passing the thread once round the mesh for the small holes and twice round the mesh for the large holes. When working, a long stitch must always come under a short stitch, first one, then the other alternately (Fig. 12).

Swiss Diamond Netting.—Put on any number of stitches divisible by 5, and 4 stitches over at the end to make the edges correspond with each other.

1st row.—Work 4 plain stitches, * work 1 long stitch by passing the thread twice round the spool (twist the thread once round the spool before encircling the loops round the fingers. The rest of the stitch is made by drawing up the knot), work 4 plain stitches and repeat from * to the end of the row. **2nd row.**—1 long stitch, 3 plain stitches, * 1 long stitch into the centre of long stitch of last row, 1 long stitch into the next plain stitch, 3 plain stitches and repeat from *. **3rd row.**—1 long stitch, 2 plain stitches, * 1 long stitch into the next long stitch, 1 plain into the next long stitch,

1 long stitch into the next plain stitch, 2 plain stitches and repeat from * and end with 1 long stitch. **4th row.**—1 plain stitch, 1 long stitch, 1 plain stitch, 1 long stitch, * 2 plain stitches, 1 long stitch, 1 plain stitch, 1 long stitch and repeat from *. **5th row.**—1 plain stitch, 2 long stitches, * 3 plain, 2 long and repeat from * and end with 1 plain stitch. **6th row.**—2 plain stitches, 1 long stitch, * 4 plain, 1 long, and repeat from * and end with 1 plain stitch. **7th row.**—1 plain stitch, 2 long stitches, * 3 plain, 2 long and repeat from * and end with 1 plain stitch. **8th row.**—1 plain stitch, 1 long stitch, 1 plain stitch, 1 long stitch, * 2 plain, 1 long, 1 plain, 1 long and repeat from *. **9th row.**—1 long stitch, 2 plain stitches, 1 long stitch, * 1 plain, 1 long, 2 plain, 1 long and repeat from*. **10th row.**—1 long stitch, 3 plain stitches, * 2 long, 3 plain, repeat from *. This completes one pattern. Repeat from the first row. (Fig. 13).

Round Netting much resembles plain netting in appearance and in the way of working, but by a trifling difference in the method of passing the needle through the loop, the stitches are a little twisted, and a closer and more round looking stitch is produced. It may be started with any number of stitches. The spool is withdrawn and placed in position for working

Fig. 13.—SWISS DIAMOND

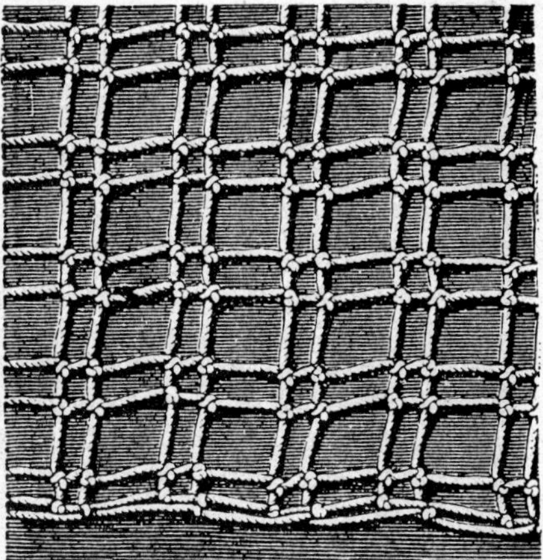

Fig. 12.—SQUARE DIAMOND

the second row. Form the loop on the fingers in the usual way and pass the needle upwards through the loop, encircling the third and second fingers and between the spool and the forefinger, but not taking up the netted stitch of the last row. Retain the position of the thumb and fingers and loop while the needle is drawn so far up as to bring the thread from it close under the little finger. Turn the needle round, and insert it through the stitch of the preceding row downwards over the spool, the thread being to the right of the needle. Draw it through, and let the loops slip one by one from the fingers, and draw the knot in firmly. Continue with every stitch in the same way (Fig. 14).

Looped Netting.—Put on as many stitches as required for the width of the work. **1st row.**—Thread twice round the spool, net for one stitch, and with the thread once round the mesh net two more stitches in the same place. Repeat this in every loop to the end of the row. Every row is the same, inserting the needle under the long loop of the last row, and missing the two short loops. This makes a light lacy-looking pattern (Fig. 15).

Spiked Netting.—Start with an uneven number of stitches. **1st row.**—Plain netting. **2nd row.**—Work 4 stitches in the first loop and 1 stitch into the next loop. 4 stitches in the next, and 1 stitch in the next and

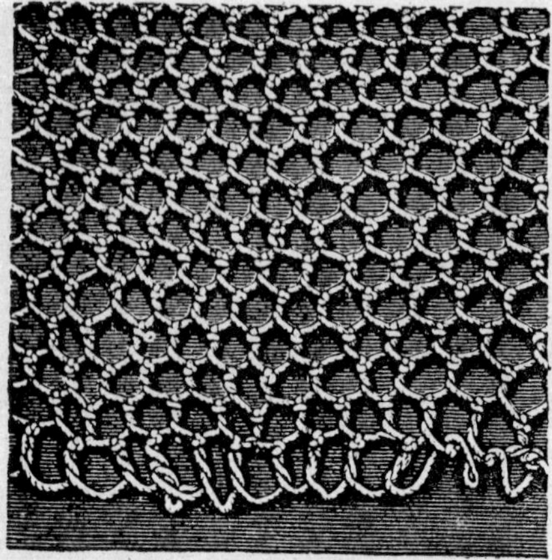

Fig. 14.—ROUND NETTING

so on alternately, and end with 4 stitches in the last loop of the row. **3rd row.**—Plain netting, gathering together the groups of increased stitches as one. **4th row.**—I plain stitch in the first loop and a spike of 4 stitches in the next loop and repeat. The spike stitches are to come between the groups of spike stitches in the second row. **5th row.**—Plain, gathering the 4 spike stitches together as one. Repeat the pattern for the second row (Fig. 16).

Leaf Netting.—Start with any number of stitches divisible by 4, and allow 2 stitches over at the end to fit the pattern in.

Fig 16.—SPIKED NETTING

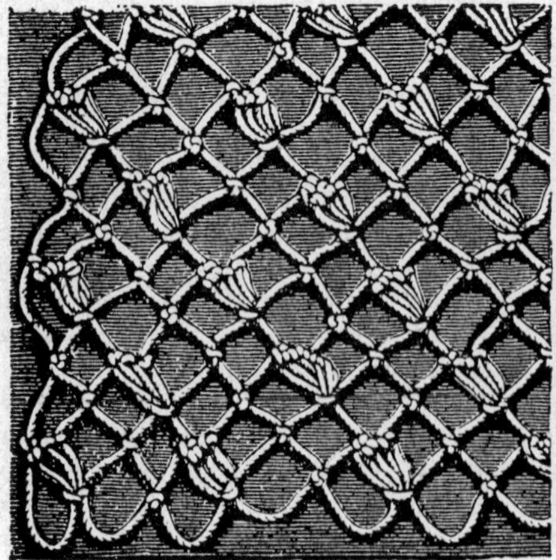

Net two plain rows. **3rd row.**—Net 3 stitches in the first loop, 3 in the next, * 2 consecutive stitches plain, 3 in the next loop, and 3 in the next and repeat from *. **4th row.**—Gather together on the needle the first 5 loops of the last row, picking them up in rotation from left to right. These are the increased stitches of the last row and they form the leaf. Knot them together as one stitch, net 3 consecutive stitches plain, and repeat, ending with a leaf, and I plain stitch. **5th row.**—Plain netting. **6th row.**—Plain. **7th row.**—Net the first 2 loops plain, * do 3 stitches in the next loop, 3 in the next, then 2 stitches plain, and repeat from *. **8th row.**—Net

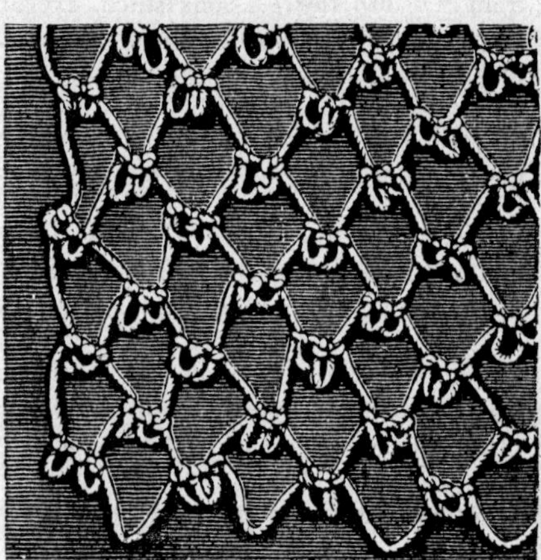

Fig. 15.—LOOPED NETTING

2 stitches plain to begin, * pick up the next 5 loops on the needle and knot them together as I stitch, net 3 consecutive stitches plain, repeat from * to the end of the row, where there will be 2 stitches to net instead of 3. The leaves in this row are formed in intermediate position between those already done. **9th row.**—Plain netting. **10th row.**—Plain. Repeat from the third row for the length required and finish after the sixth row. Count the stitches in the plain row after every leaf, to make sure that none have been increased or diminished (Fig. 17).

Grecian Net or Rose Netting.—Two spools of different size are necessary for this pattern. For the smaller the equivalent of a No. 9 knitting needle is needed and a flat bone mesh measuring about $\frac{1}{3}$ of an inch wide. An even number of stitches are necessary. **1st row.**—Plain netting with the large spool. **2nd row.**—With the small mesh draw the first loop of the previous row upwards through the second loop of the same row, and net a stitch in it. Then look through the first loop, the upper part of which is now secured in the knot just formed and notice a portion of the second loop crossing along just below. Draw this part of the second loop up through the opening under the knot and net a stitch in it. Entwine every two loops together in this

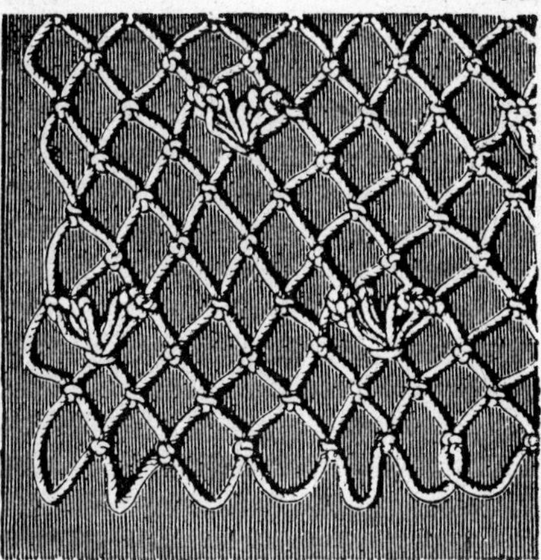

Fig. 17.—LEAF NETTING

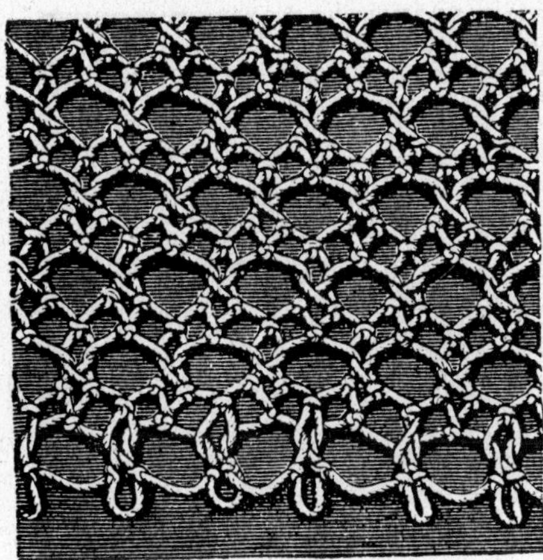

Fig. 18.—GRECIAN NETTING

way to the end of the row. **3rd row.**—Plain netting with the large mesh. **4th row.**—With the small spool—net a plain stitch in the first loop of the previous row, then draw the second loop upwards through the third loop, and net a stitch in it and next bring the second loop up through the little opening under the knot, net a stitch in it and continue. Finish with a plain stitch at the end of the row. **5th row.**—Plain netting with the large spool. Repeat from the second row. The pattern is complete on the termination of the third row (Fig. 18).

Another form of Grecian netting is simply to continue the 1st and 2nd rows, by which means the large holes are produced one over the other in a straight line.

Mosaic Netting or French Ground Net.—Start with an even number of stitches. **1st row.**—Net the first loop in the ordinary way, make the next stitch a long stitch by twisting the thread twice round the mesh (to do this twist the thread once round the mesh before encircling the thread round the fingers. The other twist is given in process of drawing up the knot), continue 1 plain stitch and 1 long stitch to the end of the row. **2nd row.**—Plain netting. The stitches of the last row being

Fig. 19.—MOSAIC NETTING

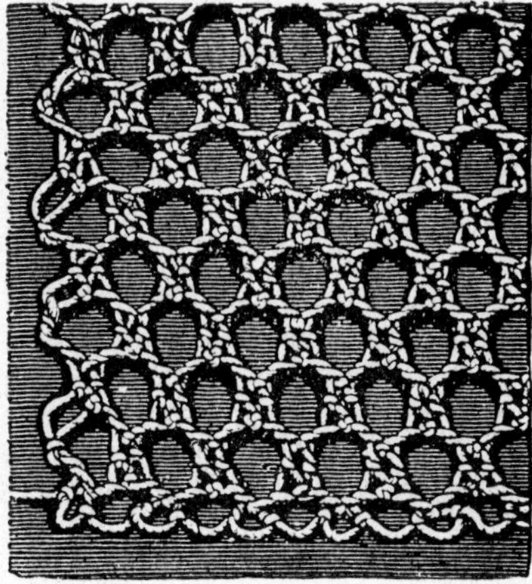

VALENCIENNES AND SPIDER NETTING

Fig. 20.

Fig. 21.

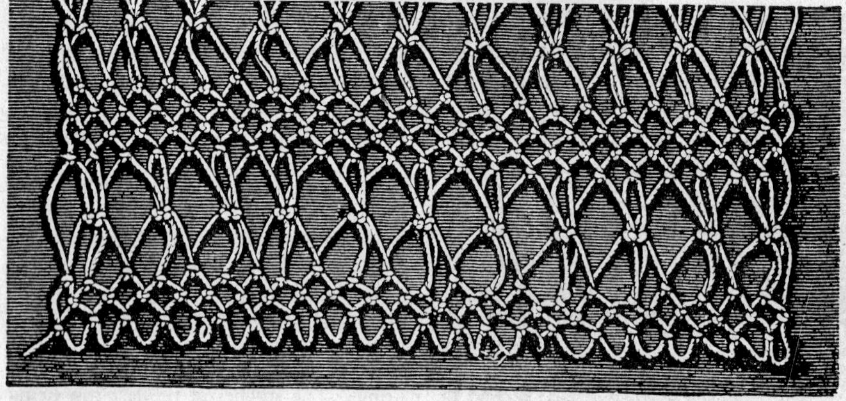

uneven in length. The stitches in this row will also be uneven. **3rd row.**—Work alternately 1 long stitch and 1 plain stitch in this way. Draw the first loop of the last row upwards through the first long loop of the first row and net a long stitch in it. The pressure coming from this action causes the second loop of the last row to come partially up in the same place. Draw it up a little more prominently and net a plain stitch in it and proceed to the end of the row. **4th row.**—Plain netting. **5th row.**—Begin with 1 plain stitch in the first loop of the last row, continue one long stitch and one plain stitch alternately, drawing the loops of the 4th row up through the long loops of the 3rd row, in the same way as instructed for the working of the 3rd row. End the row with 1 long stitch in the last loop. **6th row.**—Plain netting. Repeat from the third row (Fig. 19).

Valenciennes Netting.—Put on any number of stitches divisible by four. Work two rows plain netting. **3rd row.**—Net two stitches plain, * thread over the spool (not round the finger) and insert the needle in the work below the knot immediately underneath in the last row but one, and draw the needle and thread through. Do this twice more, then there will be three loose loops (not stitches) on the spool. Then pass the thread round the spool and fingers in the usual way. Knot a plain stitch in each of the next 4 consecutive loops of the last row and repeat from *. The row will end in two plain stitches. **4th row.**—1 plain stitch, * gather 4 loops together on the needle and knot them as

I stitch, net 3 consecutive stitches plain and repeat from *. There will be two plain stitches to net at the end of the row. **5th row.**—Plain netting. **6th row.**—Plain netting. **7th row.**—Net 4 plain stitches to begin, then * below the knot immediately underneath, and in the last row but one make a group of loose loops as instructed in the 3rd row, knot a plain stitch in each of the next four consecutive loops of the last row and repeat from *. **8th row.**—Plain netting. **9th row.**—Plain netting and repeat from the 3rd row for the length required (Fig. 20).

Spider Netting.—Two spools are required for this, a No. 12 knitting needle and a No. 3 or a flat bone mesh measuring ½ an inch in width. Start with an even number of stitches and work 3 rows of plain netting with the smallest spool. **4th row.**—With large spool, net I stitch in each loop of the last row. **5th row.**—Also with a large spool, take up the second loop and net a stitch, then the first loop and net a stitch next to the fourth loop and then the third loop and so on. Alternately making a stitch forward and a stitch backward to the end of the row and so crossing the stitches as shown in Fig. 21. Now work 3 rows of plain netting with the smallest spool and repeat the pattern for the 4th row.

Bunch Netting.—Spools of three different sizes, No. 14, No. 10 and No. 7, are needed. Begin with any number of stitches divisible by 3 and allow two stitches over at the end of the row to fit the pattern in nicely. **1st row.**—Plain netting on spool No. 10. **2nd row.**—Same. **3rd row.**—

Fig. 22.

BUTTERFLY AND BUNCH NETTING

Fig. 23.

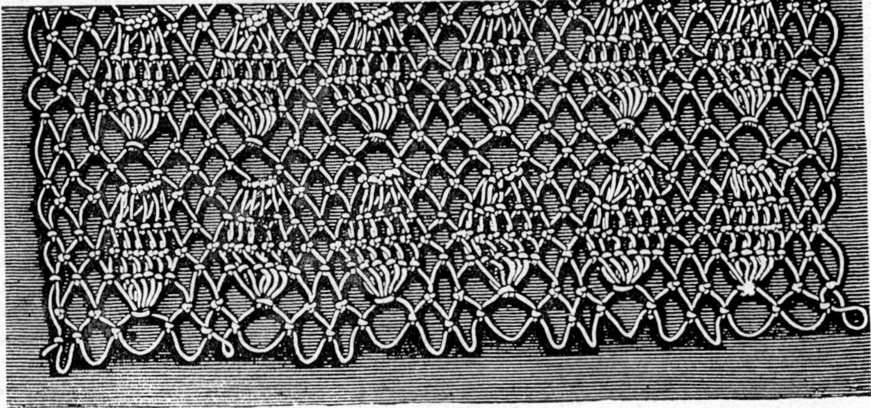

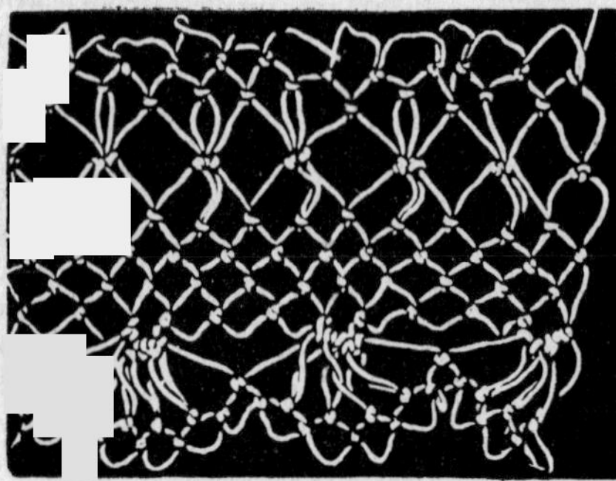

Fig. 24.—BEE BORDER

With the largest spool, net 2 stitches plain, net 5 stitches in the next loop and repeat, ending with 2 plain stitches. **4th row.**—With the smallest spool, net 1 stitch in every loop of the preceding row. **5th row.**—Plain netting with the smallest spool. **6th row.**—Plain netting with the largest spool. **7th row.**—With spool No. 10, net plain the two first loops of the last row, * take up the five next loops, all on the needle and net them together as 1 stitch (these are the 5 loops which were increased before). Net the next 2 consecutive loops plain and repeat from *. **8th row.**—Plain netting with the same spool. Repeat the pattern from the 3rd row (Fig. 23).

Butterfly Border.—Crochet cotton No. 8 and spools No. 14, No. 11, No. 9, No. 8 and No. 5 are required. Place on the foundation with No. 11 spool any number of stitches divisible by 3, and net 1 plain row. **2nd row.**—With No. 8 spool, net 1 stitch in the first loop, 3 stitches in the next loop and 3 stitches in the next loop and repeat to the end. **3rd row.**—With No. 9 spool, net the 6 first loops together as 1 stitch, net 1 plain stitch in the next loop and repeat. **4th row.**—With No. 8 spool, net 3 stitches in every loop of the last row. **5th row.**—With No. 9 spool, net the 3 first loops together, * then net the 5 increased loops together, net 1 plain stitch in the next loop and repeat from *, 3 loops remain to be taken together at the end of the row, and the leaves in this row come immediately between the leaves that were drawn up in the 3rd row. **6th row.**—Same as the 4th. **7th row.**—Same as the 5th. **8th row.**—With No. 5 spool, net 7 stitches in every loop of the last row. **9th row.**—With No. 8 spool, draw each group of 7 stitches together in 1 stitch. **10th row.**—With No. 5 spool, net 11 stitches in the first loop, * insert the needle from left to right through the next two loops and draw it through, cotton over the mesh, and net 11 stitches in the next loop and repeat from *. **11th row.**—With spool No. 14, net 1 stitch in each of the 10 loops forming the scallops, net 1 stitch in the two intermediate loops taken together. **12th row.**—With the same spool, net 1 stitch in each loop of the last row (Fig. 23).

Bee Border.—Use crochet cotton No. 8, and spools numbers 12, 10, 6 and 4. Put on as many stitches as the length required. **1st row.**—With No. 10 spool, plain netting. **2nd row.**—The same. **3rd row.**—With No. 6 spool, work 1 stitch in each loop. **4th row.**—With the same spool, take up 2 loops together and net them as 1 stitch, net another stitch in the same place. Net 4 rows plain with the No. 10 spool. **9th row.**—With No. 4 spool, net 5 stitches in 1 loop, miss 3 loops and repeat. **10th row.**—With No. 12 spool, net 1 stitch in each loop of the last row. **11th row.**—The same. This completes the border (Fig. 24).

The Five Lace Edgings, shown in Fig. 25, are worked in rows lengthwise, with fine linen thread, over fine mesh sticks and spools of various thicknesses. Fine knitting needles can easily be used instead of the former.

The first row in every case is worked over a thread, which should be of the length that the lace should be when finished. The first narrow edging is begun with 2 rows of plain net ground made over a fine knitting needle. **3rd row.**—Plain netting over a spool of medium thickness. **4th row.**—Over the knitting needle, knotting 2 loops of the previous row together and working a long loop into these, which is made by taking the thread once or twice round the spool. **5th row.**—In each long loop and make 5 loops over the spool. **6th and 7th rows.**—As the 1st and 2nd rows. In the 6th row the thread is drawn through and a knot is made, taking together the fifth loop of one group and the first loop of the following group of meshes, as well as the connecting thread which lies between.

The Second Edging is begun in the same way as the first, but a wide spool is used in the 3rd row. **4th row.**—A medium spool and 2 loops of the preceding row are crossed (Fig. 28). **5th row.**—Continue with the same spool and work 5 loops into the mesh between the crossed loops, then make a knot on to the connecting thread, at the same time tightening the thread sharply so as to make the loop a little shorter. **6th and 7th rows.**—As the 1st edging, but in the 6th row connect loops 1 and 5.

The Third Edging can be worked any width desired. The first 2 rows worked over a knitting needle as described for the first edging. **3rd row.**—4 plain loops, 1 long loop repeat to the end of the row. **4th row.**—3 plain loops, take out the needle and work into the long loop of the preceding row, the next loop knotted to equal length and continuing, repeat. Finish each point by decreasing. Work a final row with thicker thread.

The Fourth Edging is worked in the same way as the second up to the 3rd row. **4th row.**—Plain loops over a knitting needle, taking up each time 2 loops of the preceding row. **5th row.**—As 4th row, but work twice into each loop of preceding row.

The Fifth Lace is worked in the same way as the third, but in the increasing triangle 2 loops are netted into each loop of the preceding row as Fig. 27.

Fig. 25.—FIVE LACE EDGINGS

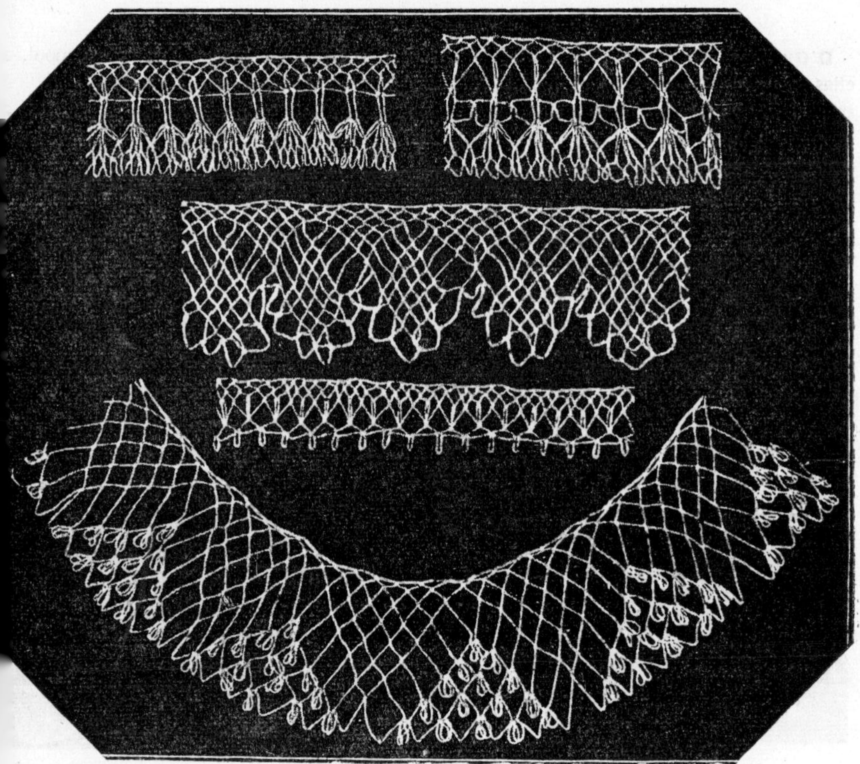

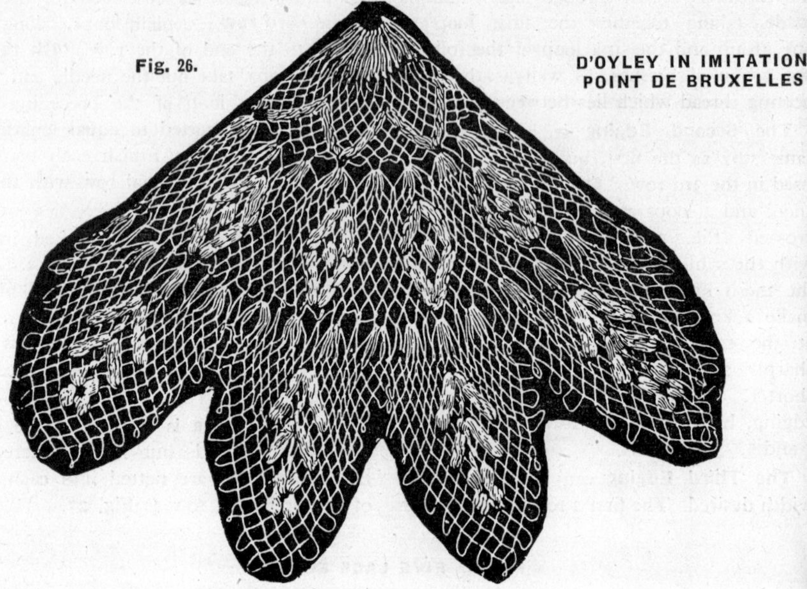

Fig. 26. D'OYLEY IN IMITATION POINT DE BRUXELLES

D'Oyley in Imitation Point de Bruxelles.—No. 30 sewing cotton is used, a skein of white flourishing thread and spools No. 16, 14, 12, 10, 7 and 1. Start with the flourishing thread by winding 56 loops round the No. 1 spool, draw a thread of cotton in them and join them in a circle. Join on the sewing cotton and with No. 7 spool, net a stitch in each of the 56 loops of the circle. Now net 6 plain rounds with No. 16 spool and 2 plain rounds with No. 14 spool.

11th round.—With No. 7 spool, net 5 stitches in one loop of the last round, miss the next loop and repeat. There should be 28 groups of 5 stitches on the round. Net 6 plain rounds with No. 14 spool, 4 plain rounds with No. 12 spool.

22nd round.—With No. 1 spool, net 4 stitches in the 1st loop of the last round, net 1 stitch by taking up the next 2 loops together and repeat. Net single loops instead of two together four times in the course of the round, so as to make 45 groups of 4 stitches with 1 plain stitch between each group. Net 2 plain rounds with No. 12 spool.

For the **Points or Scallops**—use No. 12 spool. Net 17 stitches, turn the work, net 16 stitches, turn the work, net 15 stitches, and so on until brought to a point of 1 stitch only. Here break off

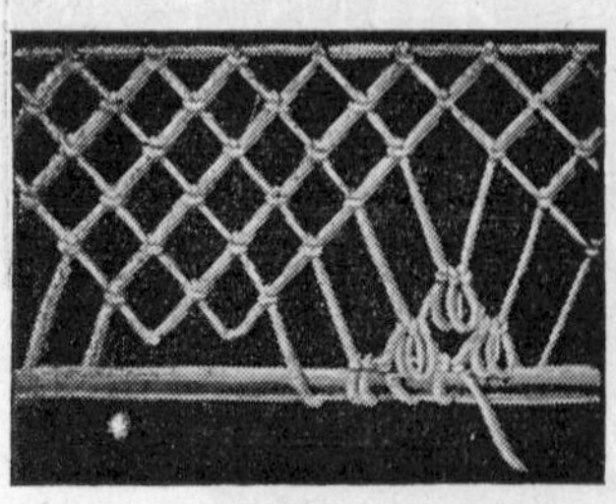

Fig. 27.

Fig.28.

Tie the cotton in the next loop of the twenty-fourth round, and work a similar scallop, and continue until you get 14 scallops in the round. With flourishing thread darn the pattern as shown in Fig. 26.

A Netted Table Centre is begun in the at each row and unless it is perfectly made it will upset the evenness of the work. A spool ½ an inch wide is now used, and two loops of the 1st row are taken up together each time, care being taken that the loops come down evenly. Make the last knot of the row next to the first knot, then with-

Fig. 29.

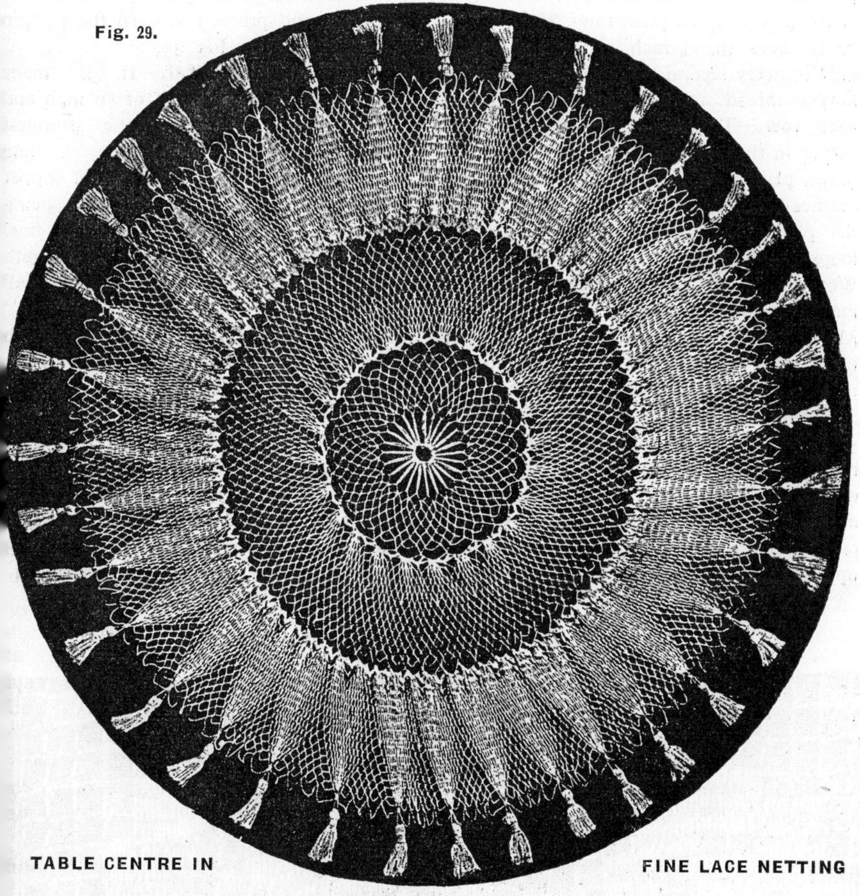

TABLE CENTRE IN FINE LACE NETTING

entre. Cast on 48 loops to a foundation hread over a $1\frac{1}{4}$-inch spool. The foundation thread is then knotted, a loop is made nd this is attached to the cushion for the ork to be continued. A netting knot is nen made without the spool, in the first oop. This must be made very carefully o that the thread shall be neither longer or shorter than the loop. This is repeated out a spool make a knot on to the middle of the first loop as a link to the third row. **3rd row.**—2 knots in each loop. Six plain rows. **10th row.**—Work on a $\frac{5}{8}$-inch spool and miss every alternate loop. **11th row.**—(A pattern row which is worked with double thread) in the first loop make 3 knots over ½-inch spool, in each following loop 6 knots, and at the end of the row 3 more knots in the first loop. **12th row.**—Take up 3 loops (6 threads) each time together in the corners, and between them, in the single threads, make a knot so that each group has again 6 loops. Four plain rows. **17th row.**—Take up the 5th and 6th loops together each time, care being taken that the mesh always comes in the middle of the group. Seven plain rows. **25th row.**—Work over the $\frac{5}{8}$-inch spool with knots only in every second loop. **26th row.**—With double thread work 7 loops in each loop. **27th row.**—Take up 3 double loops together in the corners over the $\frac{1}{2}$-inch spool. Seven plain rows. **35th row.**—Take up 2 meshes together exactly under each group. Six plain rows. **42nd row.**—Take up 6 loops exactly under each group. **43rd row.**—Work over the $\frac{5}{8}$-inch spool, take up 2 meshes together and make 2 loops on them. Make 1 knot in every alternate loop 4 times, and repeat these 2 movements all round. Finish with tassels as Fig. 29.

Darned Netting for Window Curtains.—With No. 8 knitting cotton, and a flat bone mesh $\frac{1}{4}$ inch wide, begin as for square netting, and increase a stitch at the end of every row until the width required for the curtain is reached, then decrease by taking up two loops together on the shortest side of the netting, and still increase on the longest side. These two operations take place at the end of alternate rows, so that the same number of stitches is kept on the spool until the netting is the length required, when decrease at the end of every row to shape the corner. Then the foundation finished, stretch it out, damp and iron if necessary, and proceed to darn the pattern as clearly shown in Fig. 30.

Child's Fishing Net.—It is made with two flat bone spools $\frac{1}{4}$ of an inch and $\frac{3}{8}$ of an inch wide, and the strongest crochet cotton in two colours; a long bamboo cane and about 24 inches of copper wire. The ends of the wire after being run through the loops made in the final round of netting, are pushed into the pith of the cane, and held in place by a small brass ring.

Begin by netting the small square which forms the bottom of the fishing net. Tie a loop in white cotton. In this loop, using red cotton in the netting needle and $\frac{1}{4}$-inch spool, net 7 stitches. When the 7 stitches are worked withdraw the spool, turn the work so that it may be worked from left to right. Continue in rows of 7 stitches backwards and forwards, until in all 13 rows are worked, making an almost per-

Fig. 30.—DARNED NETTING

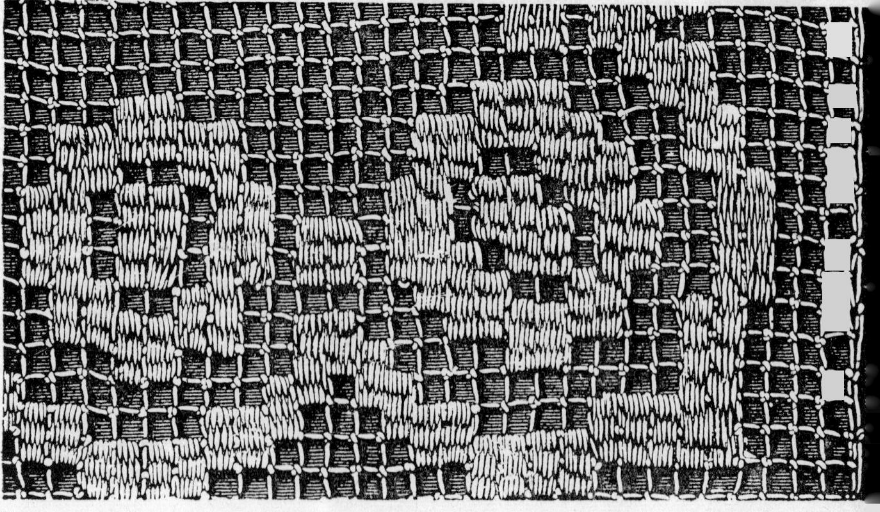

CHILD'S FISHING NET

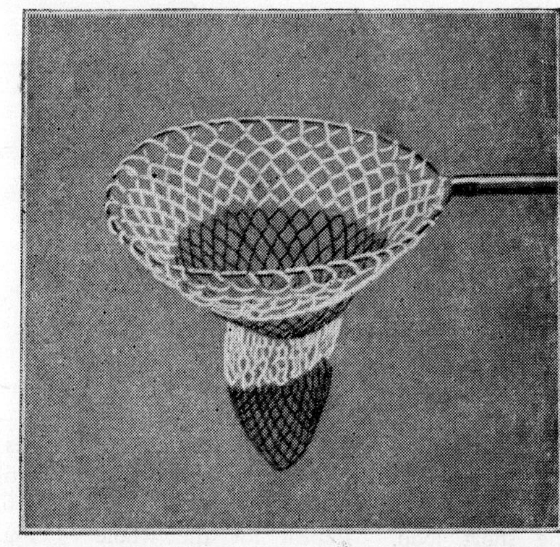

Fig. 31.

'ect square. Keep the working cotton in ts place while the loop on which the 1st ow of stitches were made, is cut. Draw t right away from the line of knots. These nots must now be either untied or picked ut with a pin, when they will disappear nd the stitches will look like ordinary oops, similar to those in the last row of etting.

Pass a piece of cotton through the middle f the square piece of netting and attach t to the cushion. Continue netting from he corner where you left off. Still using a -inch spool and red cotton, work entirely ound the square, doing 1 stitch in each oop along the four sides and 2 stitches in ach corner loop. Do 1 plain round with o increase whatever. Break off the red otton and join evenly round. Join on vhite cotton and net 5 plain rounds and reak off. With red cotton do 4 plain ounds, 1 round in which 1 stitch is ncreased 4 times at regular intervals, more plain round, break off red and oin evenly. Take the white cotton and he $\frac{3}{8}$-inch spool, and net 4 plain rounds. Thread the needle with red and white ottons and, using both cottons together, et 2 plain rounds and fasten off. This nishes the netting. Fix the wire through s already described (Fig. 31).

A Hammock is made of a straight piece f netting 2 yards long by $1\frac{1}{2}$ yards wide. This netting is worked in rows backwards and forwards, with coarse string on a 2-inch wide wooden spool. Instead of the ordinary knot, the "Fisherman's Knot" is used, to save fraying the string and rubbing the fingers. The hammock may be brightened by drawing slips of coloured cloth under the knot in process of tying them. When the piece of netting is finished slip a long round bar of wood into the meshes at the end of the netting which is to be the top of the hammock. The ends of the bar then rest on the branch of the tree. Run some thicker string through the edge stitches round the other three sides of the netting, drawing it in a little tightly. Secure it round. Then with loops of string passed under this at the two corners of the netting suspend the hammock in its place.

Star Netting.—To work as a border—use crochet cotton No. 8, a round spool half an inch in circumference, and a steel netting needle. Work the first three rows in plain netting. **4th row.**—Net the first and second loops in plain netting, pass the cotton twice round the spool, so as to make a loop twice the length of the first. (This long and short loop is shown in row marked **d.**) Repeat the two loops alternately to the end of the row. **5th row.**—Pass the cotton round the spool and the needle over and under the long loop on the preceding row, net a loop,

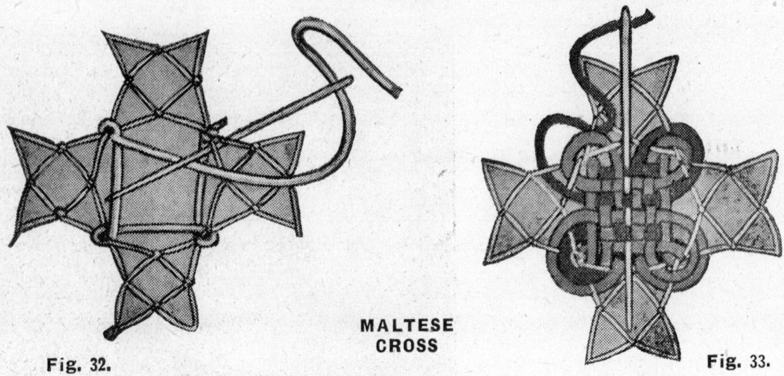
Fig. 32. **MALTESE CROSS** Fig. 33.

pass the cotton again over the spool and the needle over and under the same long stitch on the preceding row and net into the short loop. Repeat for the whole row (the Figures 1, 2 and 3 show the loops formed in this row). **6th row.**—Repeat the 4th row, make the short loop between the figures 1 and 2 and the long between the figures 2 and 3 in Fig. 34. This means that the row begins with a long loop. **7th row.**—as 5th row. **8th row.**—as the 4th. Figs. 32, 36 and 37 show different ways of working over the net. Linen thread No. 80 is used. Fig. 37 shows a large darned star carried across four of the open spaces left in the star netting. To work it, thread a needle with cotton and take it backwards and forwards four times across one of the large spaces, always ending in one of the small stars. Repeat this filling, to form the four arms of the star.

Fig. 33 shows how one of these large spaces can be filled with a thick stitch. For this, loop the needle into the four corners of the square (Fig. 32) and continue these loops, darning each thread in and out as shown in Fig. 33 until the open space is completely filled.

The same stitch can be worked to form a Maltese cross as in Figs. 35 and 36, by looping the thread all round the outside line of the Maltese cross as an outline, then working the second line over the first and darning the two together as shown in Fig. 36.

Netted and Darned Insertion.—Fig. 38

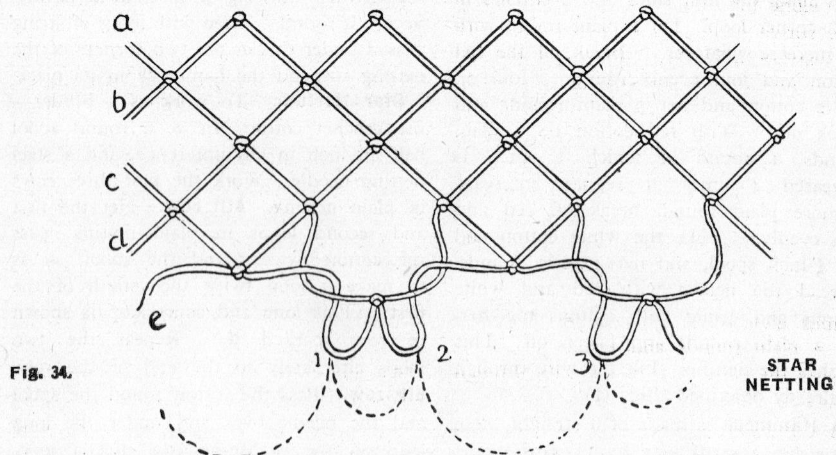

Fig. 34. **STAR NETTING**

STAR NETTING—AND AN ELABORATE DARNED INSERTION

Fig. 38 shows an elaborate insertion which would look very gay worked in bright colours, or if worked in cream, would be a most effective contrast to heavy, coloured fabric.

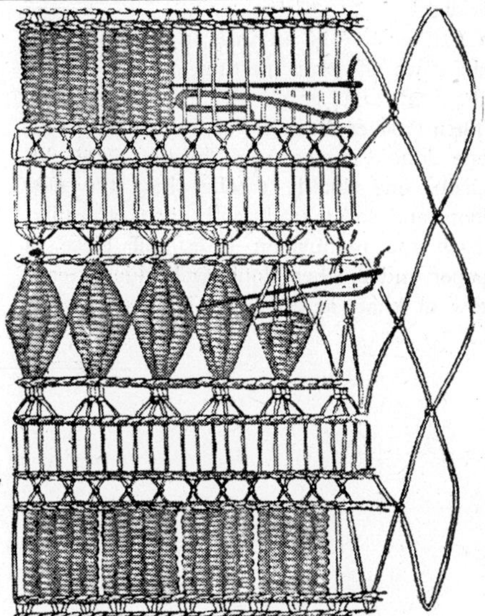

Fig. 38.

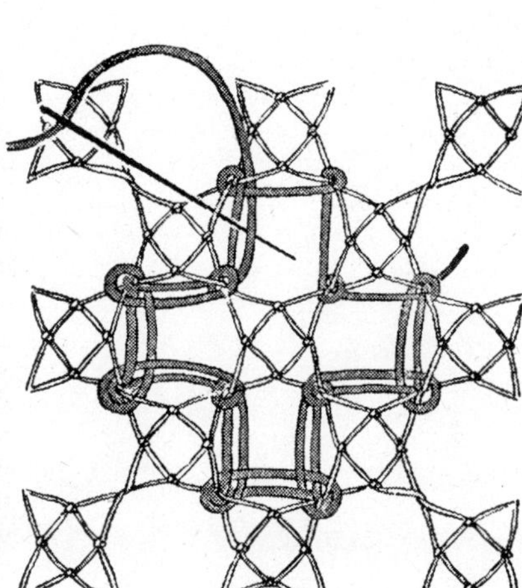

Fig. 36.

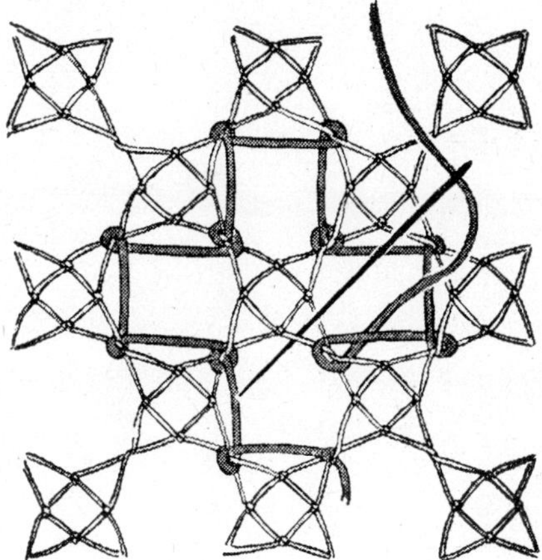

Fig. 35.

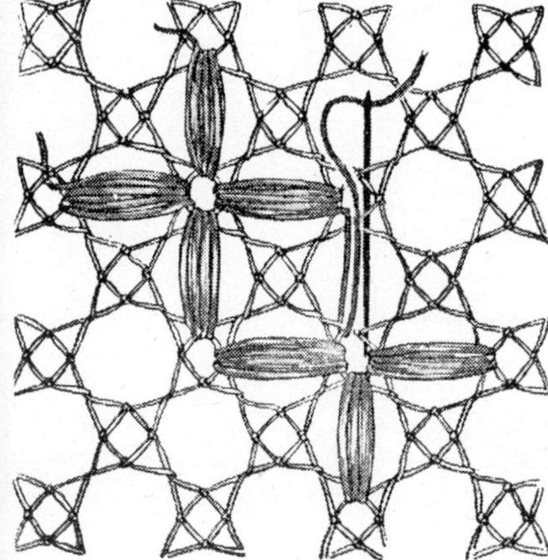

Fig. 37.

Here are two ways of darning star netting. Figs. 35 and 36 show a lighter form of the Maltese Cross than Fig. 33. Fig. 37 shows another cross which is very simply worked

is worked in crochet cotton No. 40 and a flat mesh ¾ of an inch in width. Net six rows of plain netting for the length required and starch the netting slightly. Then crochet the edges of the netting with: one double crochet into the first loop, one chain, one double crochet into the next loop, and so on until both edges are alike. Tack the netting on to a stiff piece of paper and crochet along each side of each row of knots as above. Then darn with fine cotton the pattern shown in Fig. 38 upon the meshes. Darn in and out of five threads for the outside piece of the pattern, knot two threads together for the next piece, knot four threads together for the next piece. For the middle, knot the two centre threads of the four threads together and then darn them. Draw the ends together in the darning and expand the middle so as to form the cone shape in the pattern.

OLD ENGLISH CREWEL EMBROIDERY

The word "Crewel" is said to be derived from the Anglo-Saxon "Cleow," afterwards changed to "Clew" (a ball of thread) and subsequently called Crueli or Krewel, old German Kleuel. During the seventeenth and eighteenth centuries there was a great vogue for hangings, bedspreads, large curtains, etc., embroidered in wools on linen twills. This was also known as Stuart or Jacobean work. The designs were large and usually formed of a central tree-like growth rising from uneven ground roughly indicated, on which were sometimes seen various animals; from the main trunk grew large foliated branches which curved and flowered to fill the required spaces.

Many of these designs were influenced by the work brought from the East by the intrepid travellers who were then establishing trade with foreign countries. As this contact with the ouside world increased, so the designs became more exotic, until the patterns lightened and developed into the more delicate embroideries seen in the Queen Anne period.

Many of these old-time pieces are well worth studying, and they can often be seen in ancestral halls, old castles, museums, and in exhibitions of past-day needlework.

Designs.—These consist chiefly of somewhat unnatural-looking leaves not unlike the acanthus leaf, and flower-like forms, with the introduction of quaint almost grotesque-looking animals and birds, such as lions, deer, squirrels, rabbits, peacocks, parrots, birds of paradise, etc. These may be relics of the symbolism of beasts, as the deer is supposed to stand as a type of the human soul pursued on its way through life by evil, represented by other queer beasts, including even grubs and snails.

The legend of the "Tree of Life" played a great part in influencing the designs. Later, the Queen Anne designs were mostly made up of small flowers and sprays.

Materials required.—The best and most suitable materials should always be chosen for the type of work one is about to start. Wools are used on linen, both the twill and plain weave.

Twill linen is known as Kirriemuir linen or Kirriemuir twill, and can be bought in white or cream, and varies in width.

Most of the old pieces of work were done on a cotton or linen twill, these twills making the most suitable background for this type of work. An unbleached or natural-coloured linen of good quality, the weave of which has to be close and firm, is sometimes used.

Crewel wools are used on both woollen and linen backgrounds. These wools are sold by weight. The colours in any good make of this type of wool are perfectly reliable, and wash extraordinarily well.

There is the ordinary crewel wool, and fine and coarse wool. In some of the old pieces a wool with a twist was used and looked very effective. This wool tends to produce a hard appearance, and in the hands of the inexperienced worker the embroidery may be rendered tight and severe-looking and thus spoil the work.

Special crewel needles should always be used, and these are short with wide eyes which do not fret the wool. Only short lengths of wool should be used in the needle at a time—half the length of the skein being about the maximum, as otherwise the progress of the work is hindered, and long lengths are wasteful as they split and fray before they are used up.

The work is best done in an embroidery frame.

Colours used.—In the old pieces of work green of different shades was the predominating colour, though blue and brown were not very far behind. Terra-cotta, dull rose and yellow were also used. Some pieces of work were carried out entirely in several shades of one colour.

Stitches used.—Some of the stitches most commonly used are: long and short

TWO ENLARGED LEAVES FROM THE PIECE SHOWN IN FIG. 2

The stitches used are coral stitch, stem, running, single chain.

17TH CENTURY PIECE IN WOOL ON COTTON AND LINEN TWILL

Reproduced by courtesy of the Victoria and Albert Museum.

Fig. 2.

split, stem, braid, chain, link, coral, herringbone, buttonhole, satin, feather stitch—block shading, laid and couched work with a variety of couched fillings. French knots and bullion knots, seeding and daisy stitch are also used.

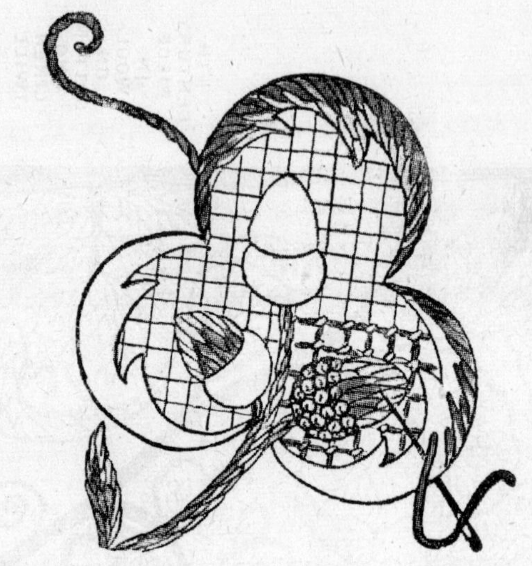

Fig. 1. A SIMPLE LEAF WITH AN EASY TRELLIS FILLING

Fig. 1 shows a simple leaf with an easy trellis filling. The leaf is edged with long and short stitch. The filling has long stitches of wool laid from side to side across the trellis lines and held down where they cross with a stitch of a contrasting colour. The acorns are in long and short stitch with cups in French knots.

Fig. 2 is a mid-seventeenth-century piece worked on cotton and linen twill weave in blue wools. The stems are in close herringbone stitch and the veins in coral stitch. The leaves are outlined in stem stitch and have two rows on either side worked in single chain, running stitch or cross stitch. On some leaves a straight stitch is taken on either side, whereas on other leaves there are three stitches to form an arrow. The centre one is a little longer than the other two which come from either side and slant into the centre. This stitch is much used on the outside of leaves and can be clearly seen from the illustration.

Fig. 3 is a beautiful mid-seventeenth-

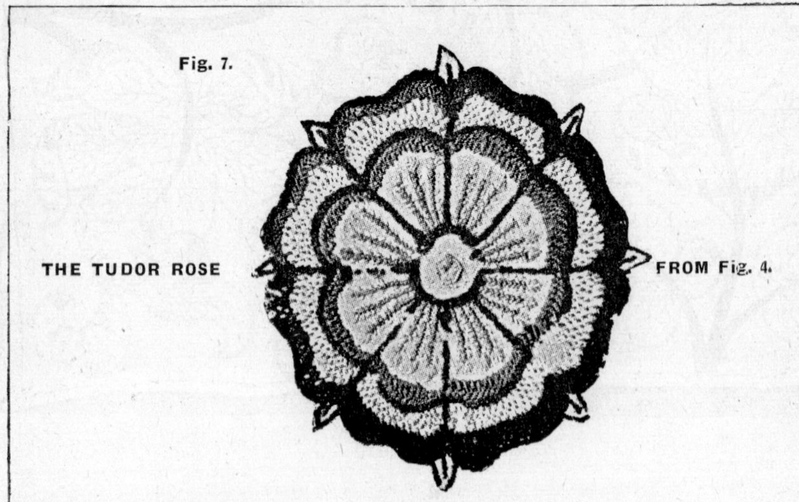

Fig. 7.

THE TUDOR ROSE FROM Fig. 4.

g. 3. *From the Victoria and Albert Museum*

Fig. 4. *From the Victoria and Albert Muse[um]*

Fig. 5.

TWO ENLARGED SECTIONS FROM THE SPECIMEN OPPOSITE

From the Victoria and Albert Museum

Fig. 6.

Fig. 8. A SEVENTEENTH-CENTURY CURTAIN

Worked in wool on linen and cotton in long and short, split, chain and satin stitch with laid and couched filling.

Fig. 3A.

The lower section of the curtain illustrated on the opposite page. Reproduced by courtesy of the Victoria and Albert Museum.

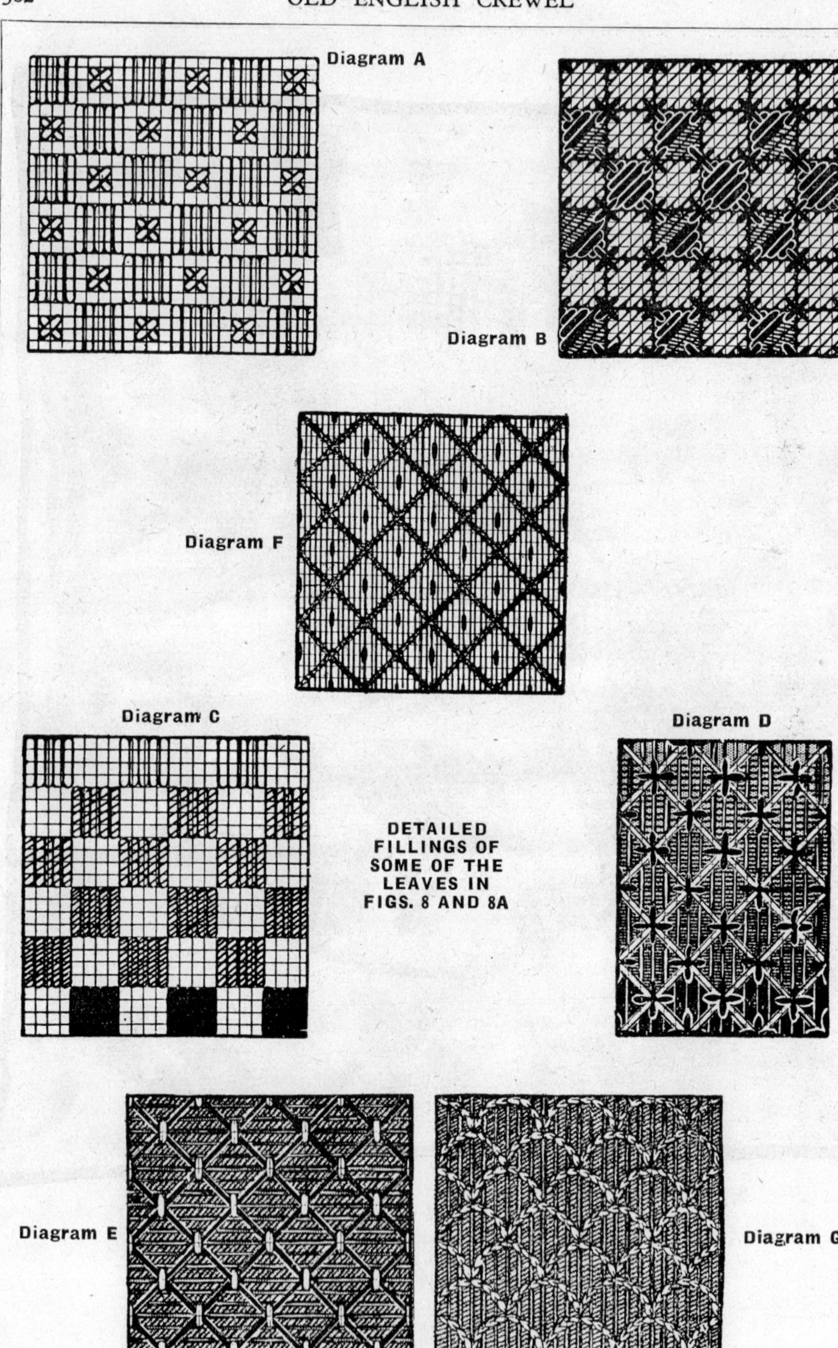

DETAILED FILLINGS OF SOME OF THE LEAVES IN FIGS. 8 AND 8A

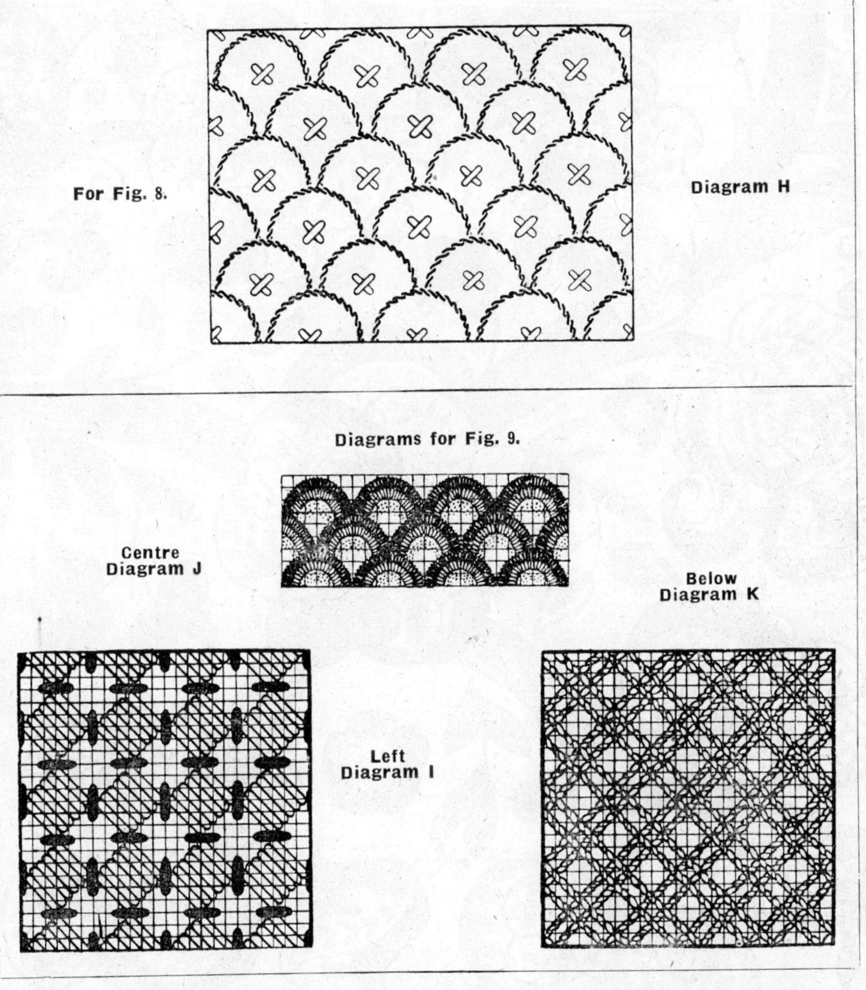

century piece worked on cotton and linen twill weave in wool in shades of greens, yellows and blues. The shading can clearly be seen from the illustration. The coral veinings can be seen worked quite clearly over the shading in chain stitch. The thick stems are herringboned and the leaves are worked in chain stitch, double coral and long and short stitch.

Fig. 4 is part of a curtain belonging to the middle of the seventeenth century. It is wool embroidery on cotton and linen, worked in twisted embroidery wool in herringbone, chain, coral, long and short, feather, buttonhole, satin, stem, braid and link stitch with speckling.

Fig. 5 shows an effective way of working feather stitch, long and short, stem, chain, link, braid and satin stitch.

Fig. 6 is worked in coral, buttonhole, stem and chain stitch.

Fig. 7 shows the Tudor rose worked in herringbone, chain, buttonhole, coral, stem stitch and speckling.

Figs. 8 and 8a show a curtain of the second half of the seventeenth century worked in wool on linen and cotton in long and short, split, chain and satin stitch,

Fig. 9. *From the Victoria and Albert Museum*

17th-CENTURY BED CURTAIN

Worked in dark blue in stem, braid, satin, long and short and link stitch.

Fig. 10. *From the Victoria and Albert Museum*

Fig. 11. *By courtesy of the Victoria and Albert Museum*

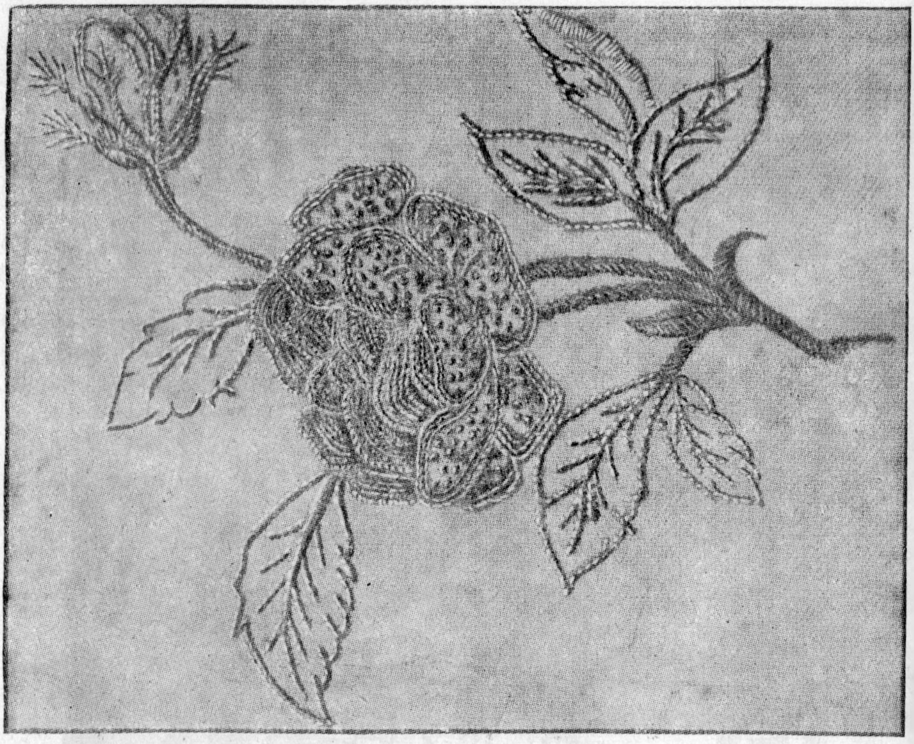

Fig. 14

Fig. 15.

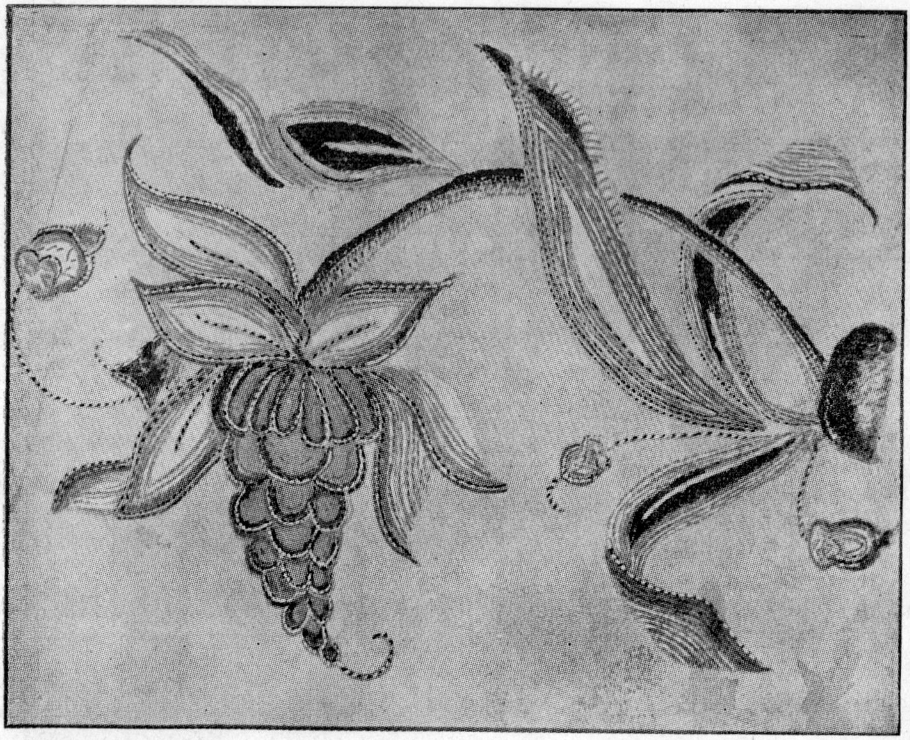

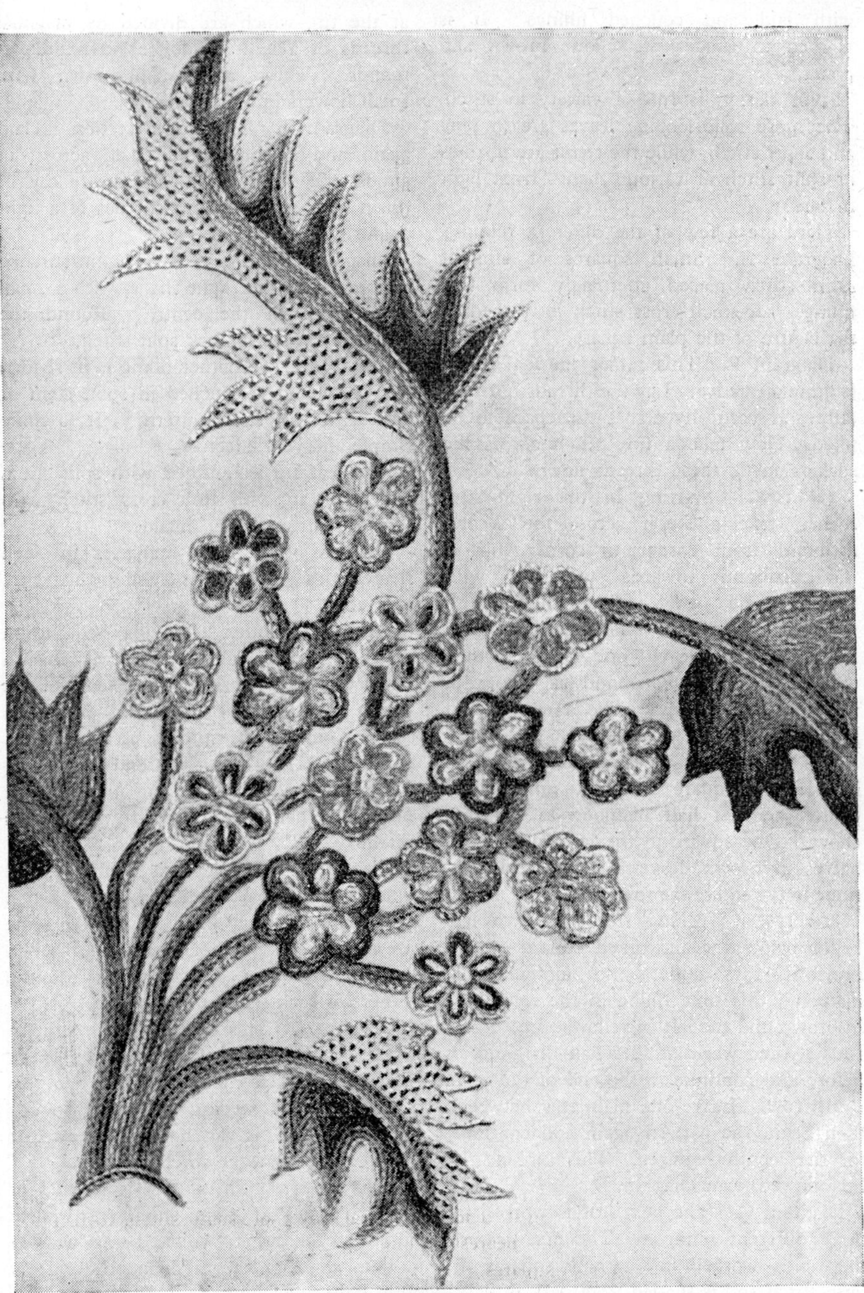

Fig. 18. *From the Victoria and Albert Museum*

with laid and couched fillings. It is worked in shades of yellow, brown and green.

This design is full of variety in stitch. The more solid-looking leaves are in long and short stitch, while the stems are in rows of split stitch of various shades from light to dark.

Here are a few of the different fillings: Diagram A. Small squares of straight satin stitch placed alternately form this filling. A small cross stitch is worked in the centre of the plain square.

Diagram B. This rather unusual filling is quite attractive. Lay the threads horizontally and vertically across the space to be filled. Now take a tiny stitch across the corners to tie these threads down.

1st row. Starting in the right-hand corner, take a stitch across the second diamond from corner to corner, fill in the diamond towards the left with brown, and the other half with yellow. Working horizontally from right to left, leave one square, then work another half diamond as before in the next square, then leave a square and repeat for the length required.

2nd row. Still working from right to left, leave a square unworked immediately below the first half diamond in the row above. One square to the left, fill in both halves in brown, leave a square and continue to the end of the row.

3rd row. Working from right to left begin below the unworked square of the previous row and work another half diamond, this time filling in the right half in brown and the left in yellow. Leave one square, then work another half diamond as before and continue to the end of the row.

4th row. Leave one plain row between, then begin the pattern again and continue for the length required. This can clearly be followed from Diagram B.

Diagram C. The next leaf is worked in three different fillings. The one nearest the tip is worked in alternate squares in satin stitch and is shaded from dark to light at the tip.

Diagram D. The next section is laid in four different shades from dark to light at the tip, which are divided by diagonal threads of a light shade between the diamonds. These are caught down with small flowers in a dark colour.

Diagram E. The upper section is laid again and diagonal lines taken across, in almost the same shade. These are caught down with small upright stitches of a light colour.

Diagram F. These small satin-stitched diamonds are in a light shade, with a small dark stitch in the centre. Round the outside is a line in dark split stitch.

Diagram G. Another filling is in shaded laid work and is couched in split, stem or back stitch in shell pattern. It is quite simple and very effective.

The leaf tip is outlined with split stitch and filled in with tiny cross stitch with arrow points round the outside.

Diagram H. This filling is in shell shapes with a small cross stitch in the centre of each.

Fig. 9 is another charming bed-curtain of the second half of the seventeenth century. It is worked in twisted wool in shades of dark blue on cotton and linen twill. Some of the stitches used are stem, braid, satin, long and short and link stitch. The stems are in rows of stem stitch worked close together and outlined with braid stitch.

Diagram. I. For this filling small squares are worked diagonally at equal distances from each other, leaving the same size unworked square between each. When this is done lines are darned across the corners of each square.

Diagram J. This filling is quite light in appearance and has two rows worked in different coloured chain stitch. When this is done a little seeding is worked in the open space. This can be done in two or three shades in satin stitch.

Diagram K. This filling is worked in diagonal rows of stem stitch, two fairly close to each other, which, being worked in both directions form diamonds. It is quite light and effective.

Fig. 10 is a late seventeenth-century curtain worked in wool on cotton and linen. Some of the stitches used are long

Fig. 19. Reproduced by kind permission of the Victoria and Albert Museum

and short, satin, stem stitch with laid and couched work and also French knots.

The hillocks are worked in block shading, starting with the lightest colour at the top and working down to the darkest. Over this are worked the animals and butterflies and flowers which are so typical of this work.

Fig. 11 shows a late seventeenth-century English bed-curtain in a very handsome design. It is worked in twisted wool on cotton and linen twill weave. Amongst the scrolls will be seen many exotic parrots, birds and butterflies, whilst on the hillocks elephants, monkeys and birds can be clearly seen. The stitches used are mostly brick stitch, French knots, stem stitch and bullion knots.

Flowers have always played a popular part in embroidery, and this can be seen in the Queen Anne designs, when they were worked in groups of flowers and leaves in fine wools and were beautifully shaded. Some of the following examples should help to give an idea of how the embroidery gradually altered. It will be noticed too how the Chinese designs became fashionable and began to influence the work.

Fig. 12, which dates from the beginning of the eighteenth century, shows a nice group of flowers and leaves worked in long and short stitch, stem stitch, French knots, satin and split stitch and herringbone.

Figs. 13 and 14 are also early eighteenth century, other good examples. This time they are worked in satin and stem stitch with French knots and speckling, chain,

Fig. 20A.—Enlarged Section of Border on opposite page.

Fig. 20. *By kind permission of the Victoria and Albert Museum*

Fig. 21. *Reproduced by kind permission of the Victoria and Albert Museum*

This beautiful cover in wools worked throughout in chain stitch on a quilted ground.

and coral stitch. The colouring is shades of old rose wool, and the foundation fabric linen and cotton twill weave.

Figs. 15, 16, 17, show some exotic flowers of the end of the seventeenth century worked in bright-coloured wools on linen. These are beautifully worked and shaded, the whole being done in chain stitch.

Fig. 18, an early eighteenth-century piece, is worked in fine wool entirely in chain stitch except for the filling of speckling in the leaves and the flower centres. The large leaves are still used in this design.

Fig. 19 shows a very handsome valance of the first half of the eighteenth century worked in beautiful shades of wool on a cotton and linen ground. It is worked entirely in long and short and stem stitch.

Fig. 20 is another good design which has an elaborate border. It is worked in wool on cotton and linen twill in satin, stem and long and short stitch. Bunches of flowers are worked throughout and are beautifully shaded.

Fig. 21. This piece of work is in wool on linen worked throughout in chain stitch. The whole design is given and also a separate section. The background is quilted all over in back stitch in yellow silk, but the centre piece and corners are not quilted.

It can be seen in this section how the flowers and fruit are arranged over the leaves.

There is a border all round the design in four rows of chain stitch, each row a different shade of brown wool.

This unusual piece of late seventeenth century work (Fig. 22) is worked in wool on cotton and linen twill weave. It is in two shades only, greeny blue for the stalks and branches and an old rose for the berries. The heavy stalks are worked in herringbone with the curly tips in stem stitch. The thin berries are in plaited knots.

Fig. 21A.

AN ENLARGED CORNER FROM THE COVER ON THE OPPOSITE PAGE

Fig. 22. *By kind permission of the Victoria and Albert Museum*

AN UNUSUAL HANGING FROM THE LATE 17th CENTURY

PATCHWORK

Patchwork is the art of making designs by joining small pieces of odd materials together, such as pieces of silk, satin or chintz, into a handsome piece of needlework. Its manipulation requires both patience and neatness and also calls into play both the reasoning and artistic faculties, as the designs chiefly depend for their beauty upon the taste displayed in the arrangement, and selection of the shades of colour used to make them.

Patchwork patterns are mostly copied from old Mosaics or Parquet designs and also from geometrical figures. Coats of Arms and pictures containing large figures can also be worked.

Materials required.—The first thing to remember when choosing materials for patchwork is *never* to mix washable and unwashable fabrics.

Patchwork can be done entirely in silk, satin or velvet, or silk and velvet together, or satin and velvet, but not silk and satin mixed with velvet. Cotton and silk materials should never be used in the same piece of work. Fancy silks and ribbons with designs of spots, checks and stripes may be used together to advantage by being mixed with plain materials. Linens and prints, cloth and flannel and leather can also be used. Several shades of the one colour linen is most effective. It must be remembered that the best effects are obtained by keeping the same kinds of material together.

Colour has to be carefully studied as a bright patch in the wrong place would spoil the whole design. The shades should be evenly distributed, to make the most of the work.

If fancy stitches are used to ornament the patchwork they should be worked in a neutral shade which tones with the background.

Designs for Patchwork are necessarily geometrical—squares, diamonds, hexagons, octagons, lozenges, triangles, etc., are used —and much patience and ingenuity can be exercised in rendering them more or less elaborate and in selecting suitable colours for certain shaped pieces. It is a good idea to try several effects with the pieces before deciding on a design. Variety in shape is also needed for success, although it is not advisable to have too many circles or squares, and preference should be given to triangular pieces, angles of all kinds, ovals, lozenge shapes, diamond and curious shaped pieces. Stars and crescents may be dotted here and there to good effect.

To work.—Having decided on the design, cut out the key patterns in stiff cardboard, being especially careful to have each strictly accurate. From these trace the shapes on stiff brown or white paper. Cut these out exactly the same size, or the work will not lie smoothly when the sections are joined together. Several thicknesses of paper can be cut out at once. In cutting the material allow an extra $\frac{3}{8}$ inch all round for the turnings. Having cut the material shapes, tack them on to the paper ones, turning the edges over $\frac{3}{8}$ inch on the wrong side. When a number of sections are thus prepared, arrange them edge to edge, according to the pattern, and overcast together on the wrong side, as if working an ordinary seam—making close, neat stitches, and using sufficiently strong sewing silk. When the work is finished the tacking threads are withdrawn and the papers taken out. When removing the papers always begin from the centre as all irregularities can be smoothed out towards the edges. The work is then laid on an ironing blanket wrong side upwards and the seams pressed smooth with a warm iron.

Decorative stitching on the front is a matter of taste, but feather stitch and herring-bone are the most popular, though any outline stitch may be used.

All patchwork is finished with a lining, and in some cases an interlining is also used. This depends on the article made. Patchwork is sometimes quilted by working a running stitch round the outline of each patch.

Dutch Tile Pattern is very simple. The sections for working are only two in number, the octagon and the square. If more than two colours are used, the octagonal pieces are varied, but four of the same colour are kept in a block. The squares should all be alike, with the exception of the one placed in the centre of a block, and that may be any colour in harmony with the

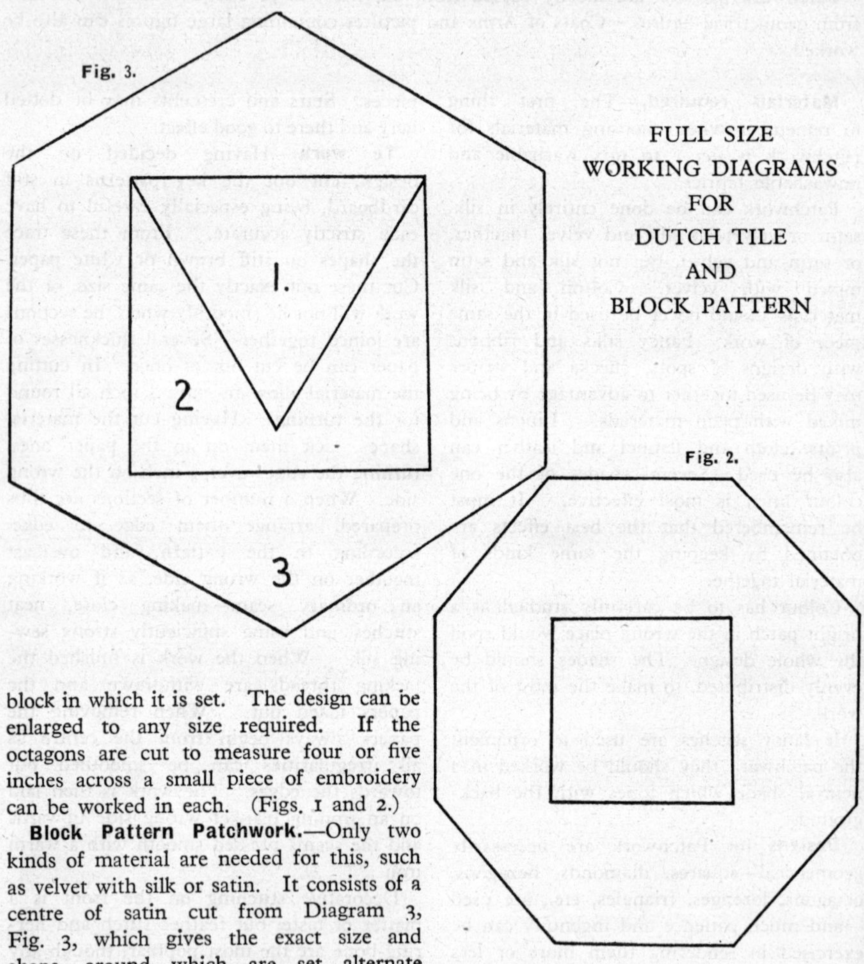

block in which it is set. The design can be enlarged to any size required. If the octagons are cut to measure four or five inches across a small piece of embroidery can be worked in each. (Figs. 1 and 2.)

Block Pattern Patchwork.—Only two kinds of material are needed for this, such as velvet with silk or satin. It consists of a centre of satin cut from Diagram 3, Fig. 3, which gives the exact size and shape, around which are set alternate smaller blocks and triangles, cut from Diagrams 1 and 2. These pieces must be lined with paper and neatly sewn together on the wrong side and when the work is finished the paper is pulled out. Fig. 4 shows the finished design.

Star Patchwork.—This shows an effective arrangement with two materials such as velvet and silk, each white star consisting of eight diamond pieces cut from Fig. 5, Diagram 2, these being divided by velvet squares cut from Diagrams 1 and 3. Paper is tacked on to each piece as before. (Fig. 6.)

Minton Pattern is a kind of mosaic pattern made with patches of four different shapes and forming a combination of squares, crosses, cubes, lozenges or blocks. These should be uniform in colour throughout the piece of work, the blocks being of some light neutral shade, the lozenges black, the blocks and the squares bright

Fig. 4.

BLOCK PATTERN

colours. The square in the centre of each block may be either lighter or darker in shade than the block itself and should be finished with a wheel or other device. The crosses are composed of five squares joined together, a dark square being in the centre (Figs. 7 and 8).

Belmont Pattern consists of squares, lozenges and blocks; the lozenges must be the same colour throughout as they form a kind of framework to the other part of the design. If a deep rich colouring is used for the blocks, the lozenges must be bright in tone to make a good contrast, or vice versa. The square in the centre of the four blocks is embroidered with a wheel, and each of the small blocks has a spray of leaves worked on it. The points of the blocks fit into the angles of the lozenges and the intermediate space is filled with a square patch of neutral colouring cut from the same square used for the embroidered centre of the four blocks (Figs. 9 to 12).

Kaleidoscope Patchwork, I.—Like the figures in a Kaleidoscope, this pattern may be viewed from various centres with an ever varying change in appearance. It is perfectly geometric in design and the sections are of three shapes only—small squares, triangular-shaped pieces and elongated diamonds. The arrangement of the pieces will be seen from Fig. 13. Only three colours should be used, the darkest for the triangular sections, four of which are allotted to each square, these in turn being surrounded by four diamonds.

Kaleidoscope Patchwork, II.—This pattern can be worked in silk, satin or

Fig. 1.—DUTCH TILE PATTERN

Fig. 6.

STAR PATTERN AND DIAGRAMS FOR WORKING

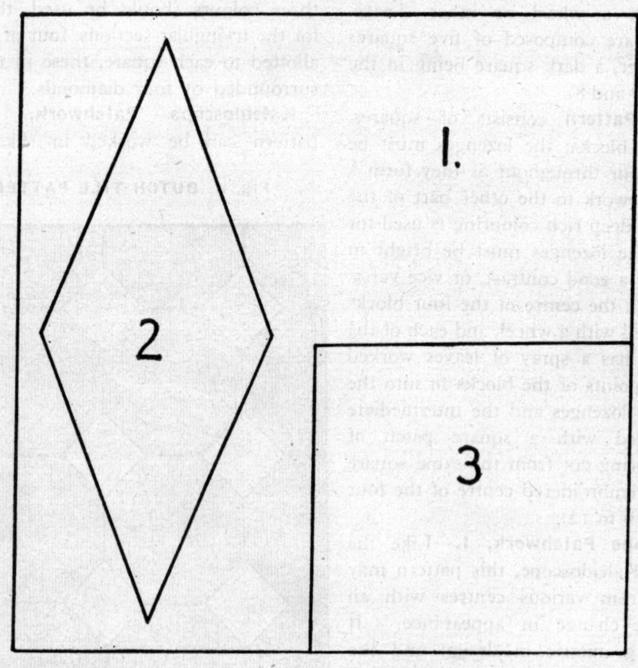

Fig. 5

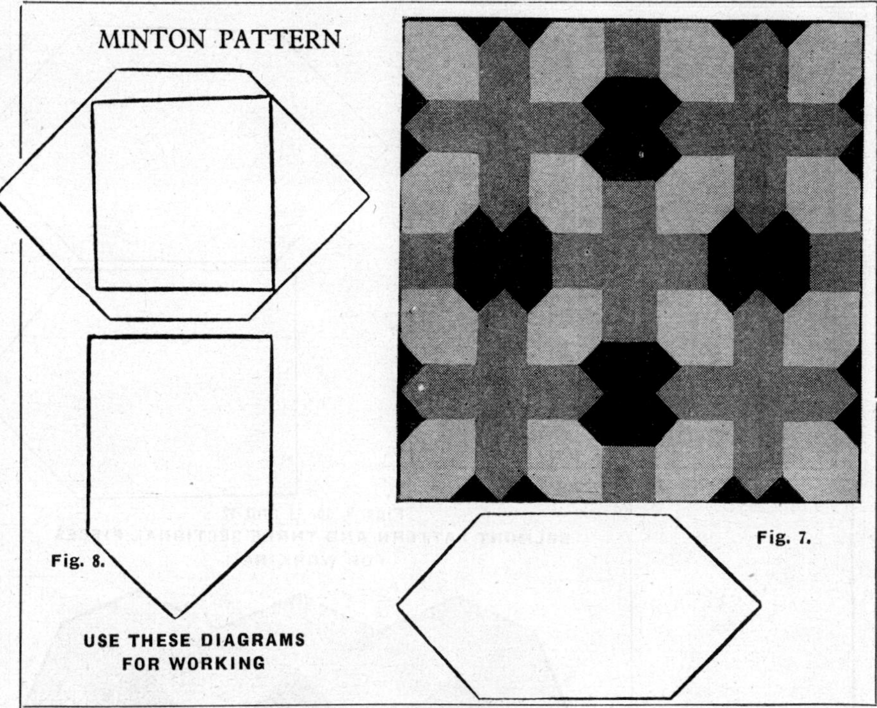

velvet, or one of these materials in three strongly contrasting tints. With Fig. 14 is shown the exact size and shape of the three pieces required to form this design. Six sections of the size and shape of piece No. 1 are necessary to form the star, and six squares like piece No. 3 for joining the star, the corner or point of each square joining to the point of the star, then, dividing these squares are six diamond-shaped pieces cut from piece No. 2. The joining of these pieces produces an almost circular shape. A similar number of No. 1 stars and No. 3 squares are joined in the same way. To these, however, only five diamond-shaped pieces like No. 2 are sewn, one of the diamonds from the previous section being joined at its loose edges to the squares having no diamond piece attached. The next figure is made in the same way, but with only four diamond pieces attached, the loose edges of the two diamond pieces attached to the figures being joined to the squares. The latter process is repeated throughout until the patchwork is the size required (Fig. 14).

Embroidered Kaleidoscope Patchwork. (Fig. 15.)—Two materials only are required for this design, the stars being of silk or satin and the blocks of velvet. The diagram gives the correct size for cutting the material, and by varying the arrangement of these pieces several good designs may be obtained. Omitting the square piece also makes an effective patchwork. The arrangement of Fig. 16, which gives the three different pieces required (1, 2 and 3), can easily be copied. Tack a piece of paper to each and then sew them together on the inside. Any embroidery design can be used.

Brunswick Design is suitable for a large piece of work as it is bold and clear. It may be worked in any kind of material. Four different shaped pieces are required, the full working size being shown in Fig. 18. Begin by making a number of six-pointed stars, each having a hexagon in the centre which may either be darker or lighter in

Figs. 9, 10, 11 and 12
BELMONT PATTERN AND THREE SECTIONAL PIECES FOR WORKING

Fig. 13.

KALEIDOSCOPE PATCHWORK 1 AND PATTERNS FOR WORKING

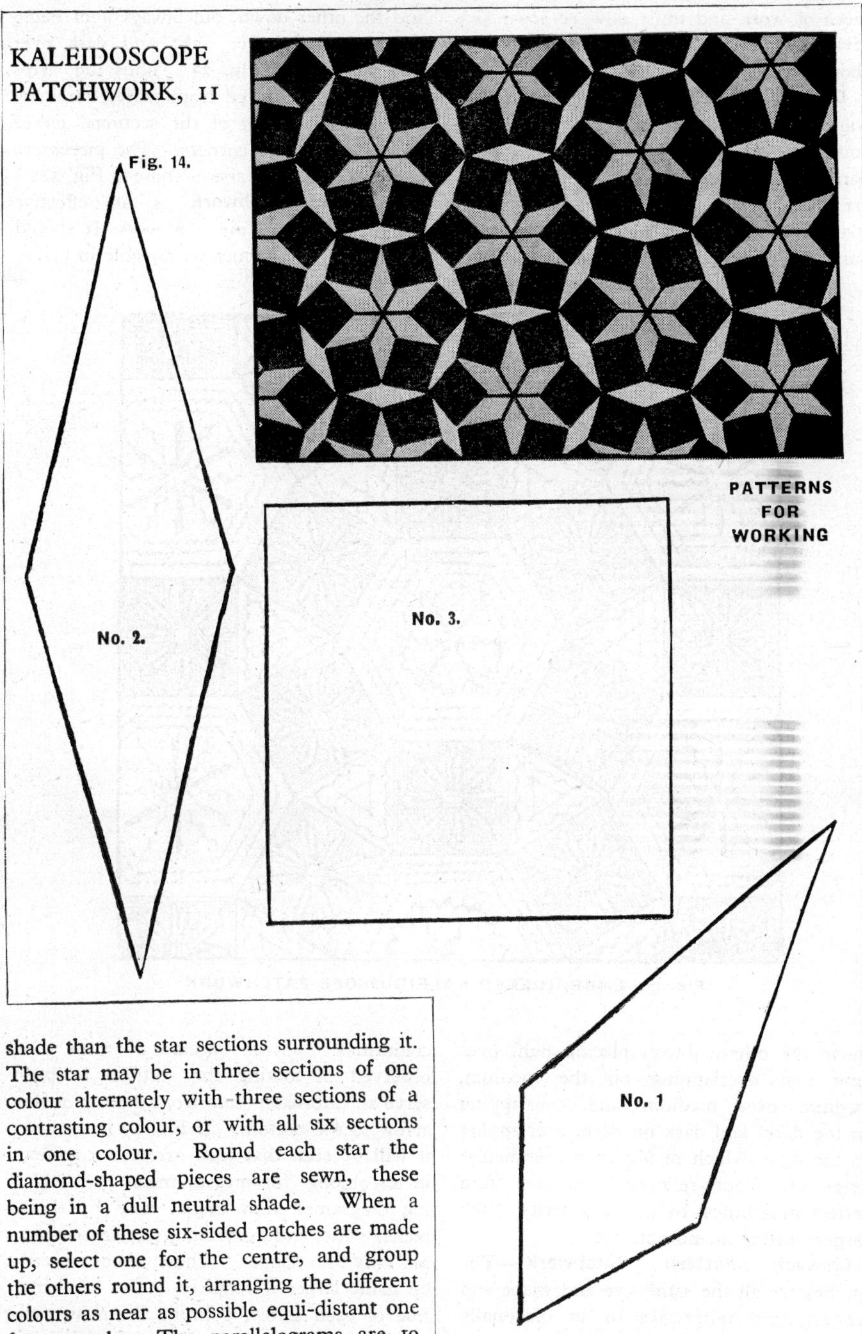

shade than the star sections surrounding it. The star may be in three sections of one colour alternately with three sections of a contrasting colour, or with all six sections in one colour. Round each star the diamond-shaped pieces are sewn, these being in a dull neutral shade. When a number of these six-sided patches are made up, select one for the centre, and group the others round it, arranging the different colours as near as possible equi-distant one from another. The parallelograms are to be self-coloured throughout the entire piece of work and must now be sewn as a dividing line between the star sections as shown in Fig. 17.

Diagonal Patchwork is worked in three colours. The sections are all the same size and shape as can be seen from the accompanying diagram (Fig. 22). The patches are first joined end ways in diagonal stripes in regular rotation of light, medium, dark and then strips are further joined one above the other, always placing light over light and overlapping on the medium, medium over medium and overlapping on the dark, and dark on dark, overlapping on the light, which results in perpendicular strips of colour relieved, however, from perfect straightness by the irregularity of the corners jutting in and out.

Chevron Pattern Patchwork.—The patches are all the same size and shape and are arranged mitreways to sit diagonally in a chevron vandyke, light and dark alternately. One colour slants upwards, and the other down, but always light being perpendicularly over light and dark over dark as seen in Fig. 23. Thus the strips of colour are relieved from perfect straightness by the jutting of the sectional pieces in and out of the corners. The pieces are the same shape and size as those in Fig. 22.

Japanese Patchwork is an effective design for a large piece of work. It should be carried out as much as possible in bright colourings. Great accuracy must be observed in joining the sections to preserve an unbroken seam from the top of the arrow to the bottom. If Fig. 19 is studied, it will be seen that each arrow is confined in an oblong (for measurements see working diagrams), four inches long by three inches wide, and containing sixteen sections but only four shapes. These, of course, can be made larger if required. The left-hand side of each arrow, pointing down as well as up, is to be shaded with the darkest colour, except for the band, where the

Fig. 15.—EMBROIDERED KALEIDOSCOPE PATCHWORK

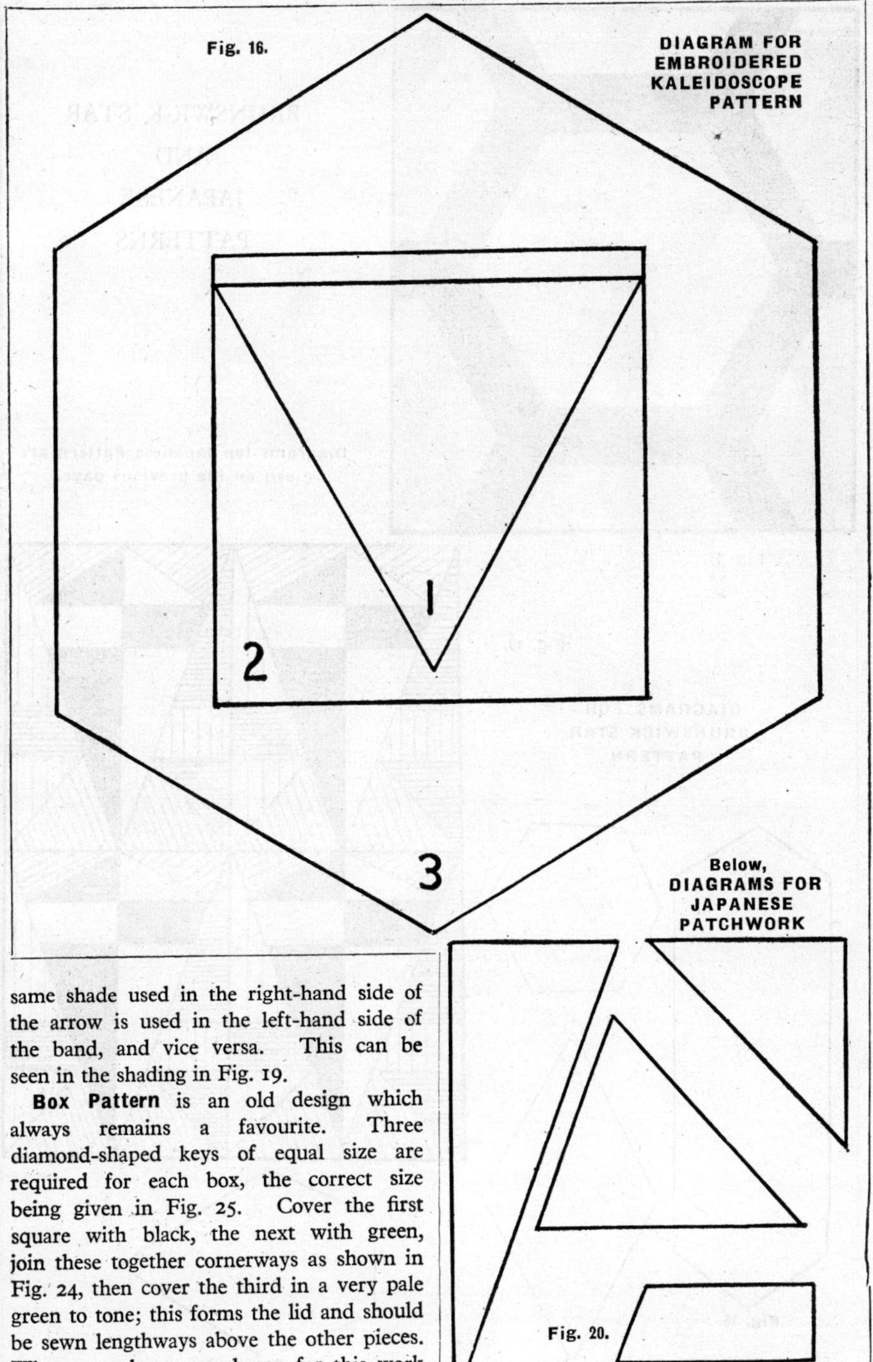

Fig. 16.

Fig. 20.

same shade used in the right-hand side of the arrow is used in the left-hand side of the band, and vice versa. This can be seen in the shading in Fig. 19.

Box Pattern is an old design which always remains a favourite. Three diamond-shaped keys of equal size are required for each box, the correct size being given in Fig. 25. Cover the first square with black, the next with green, join these together cornerways as shown in Fig. 24, then cover the third in a very pale green to tone; this forms the lid and should be sewn lengthways above the other pieces. Whatever colours are chosen for this work

Fig. 17.

BRUNSWICK STAR AND JAPANESE PATTERNS

Diagrams for Japanese Pattern are given on the previous page.

Fig. 19.

DIAGRAMS FOR BRUNSWICK STAR PATTERN

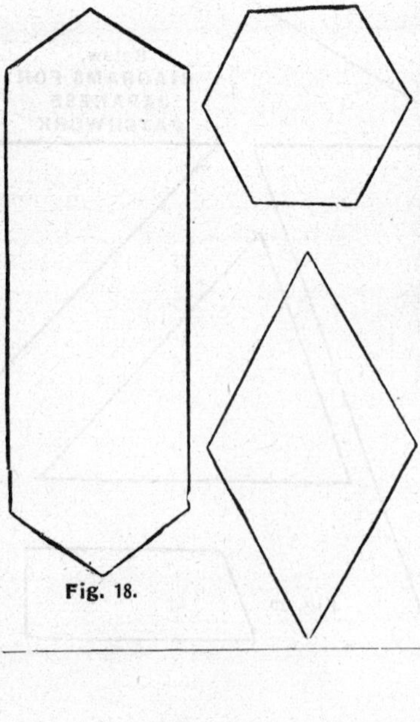

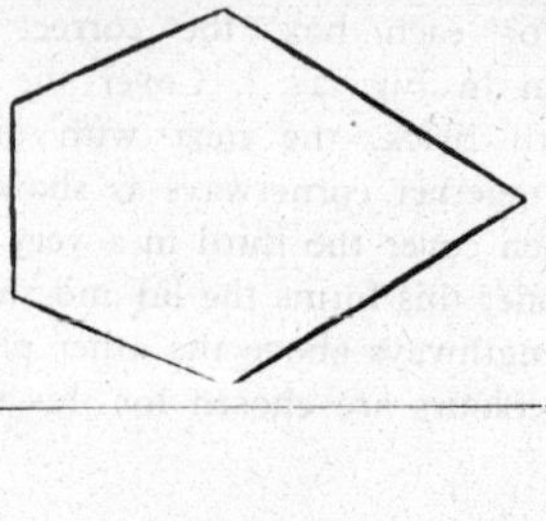

Fig. 18.

Fig. 21.

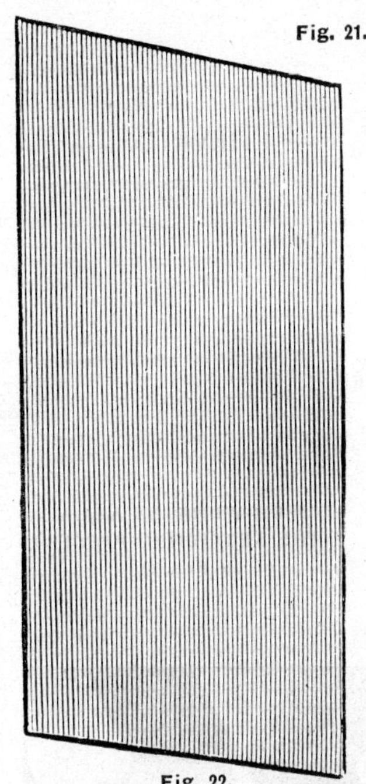

Fig. 22.

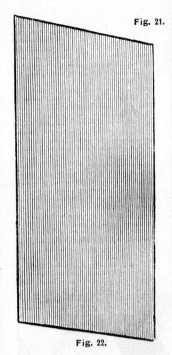

DIAGONAL PATTERN—WITH FULL-SIZE SECTIONAL PIECE

care must be taken that the piece covered with black, which represents the shadow, should always be placed on the left-hand side of the box pattern. The raised appearance of the block depends on this.

By making the two side pieces of the box deeper than the lid a cube will be produced. An elongated box can be made by cutting the right-hand piece in a perfect square and the lid and left-hand piece in longer diamonds. The lightest colour this time will be the square and the darkest the lid.

Trellis Pattern is very simple and looks effective. Only two shapes are required as shown in Fig. 26. These are the correct working size, the deep shade being confined to the square pieces, for which black is most suitable as the background. The trellis may either be two shades of the same colour, or of two contrasting colours, the darkest always being placed on the left-hand side of the squares (Fig. 27).

Cellular Pattern.—This pattern gives a good effect of light and shade and, as will be seen from Fig. 28, has the appearance of being made up of a number of hollow squares surmounted by a trellis of raised bars. There are four sectional shapes which can be cut by Fig. 29. Black is best used for the square that represents the shadow at the bottom of the cell. This is the larger of the two in the diagrams. The small square must be the same colour as the long narrow bars, which it really supplements by helping to continue the bars in vertical direction right and left over the surface of the pattern. As these bars and small squares represent the light, they must be light in colour. The side blocks should be in two shades of one colour. They are arranged with thin shorter sides fitting against the two topmost sides of the square, as seen in Fig. 28. The darkest shade on the left-hand side, the lightest on the right, the slanting points meeting together at the top. Begin by making up a number of the black squares with their two side pieces complete, then make the narrow bars and the small

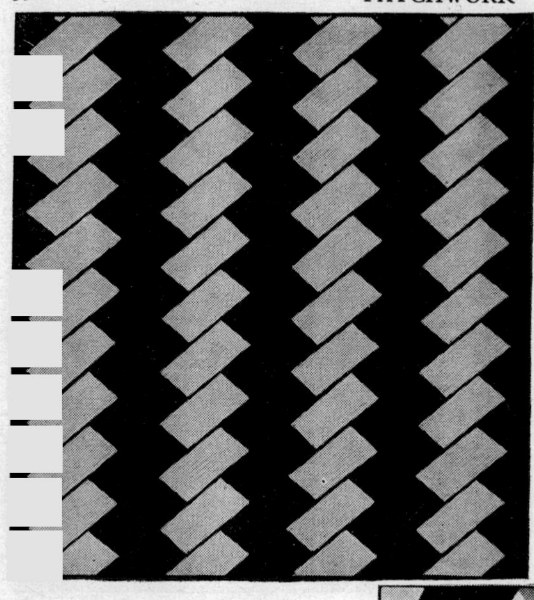

CHEVRON PATTERN

Fig. 23.

FOR WORKING USE THE SECTIONAL PIECE IN Fig. 22.

BOX PATTERN

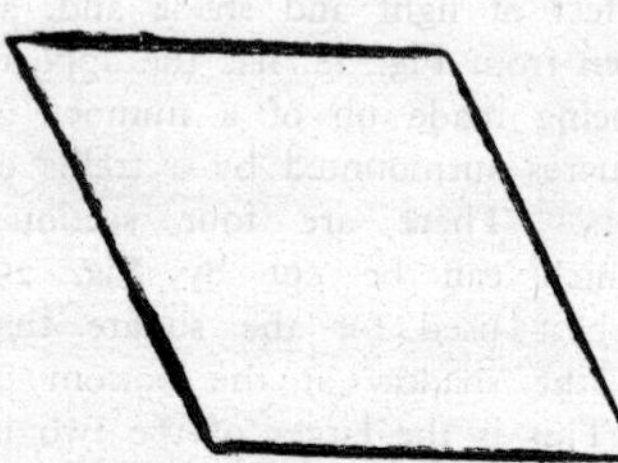

Fig. 25.

SECTIONAL PIECE FOR WORKING

Fig. 24.

squares seen in the illustration. When sufficient has been done, take out the papers and all the tacking threads, press the seams flat and line the work.

Twist Patchwork is suitable for large pieces of work. The diagram consists of an octagon, a square and a narrow parallel bar having one end cut straight and the other end sloped to a point, and this bar, which apparently interlaces itself as it twists and twines round the octagons and squares, gives an air of great originality to the pattern. The actual size of the pieces can be seen in Fig. 30. Three colours should be used, such as shades of red for the octagons, green for the squares and black for the parallel bars, but if a variety of colours is preferred in the work, they may be used provided any one colour does not predominate. The parallel bars on the other hand must be the same colour throughout, for these run in unbroken

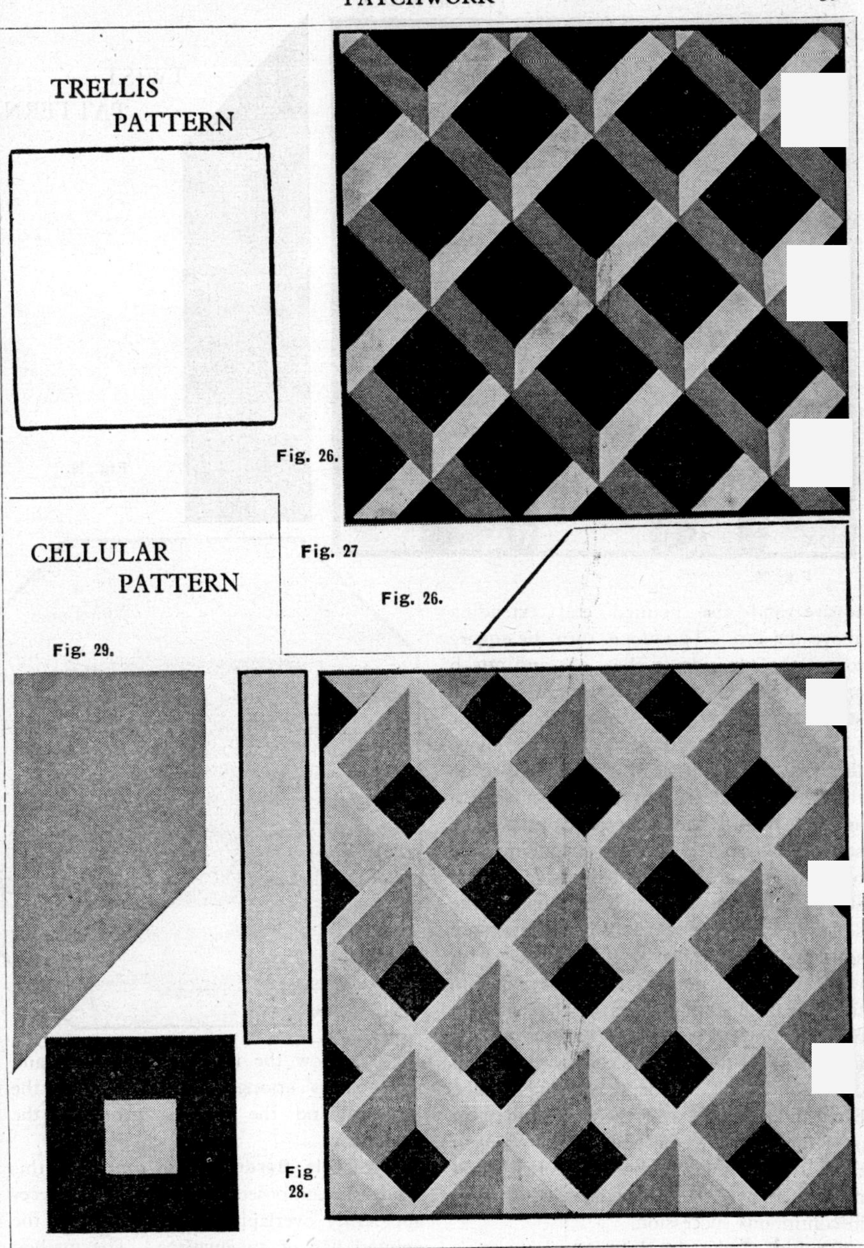

twists both horizontally and perpendicularly over the entire surface of the work. It is a good plan to use velvet for the bars and either silk or satin for the other two sections, the reason for this being that the pile of the velvet will stand up a little upon the surface of the work and will make the bars appear raised and distinct. First, sew a parallel bar upon the right-hand side of a square, the shortest side of the bar next to the square, the straight end level with the bottom of the

Fig. 29.

Fig. 30.

square and the pointed end extending above the top. This done, turn the square to get the top side to the right and attach another bar in the same way, fitting the straight end level with the bottom of the square and the pointed end extending above the top. This done, turn the square so that the top side is to the right and attach another bar in the same way, fitting the straight end of this to the extending side of the first bar, the pointed end of which still extends out. Join two more bars to the square in the same way. When a few more squares are similarly surrounded with parallel bars, arrange for the octagons to fit against the other sides of the bars, an octagon between every two squares. The four short sides of the octagon will fit closely against the four sloped ends of the bars, and the points of the bars, appearing as if folded below the ends of the adjacent bars, will carry on the idea of a twist running between the octagons and squares in continuous succession.

Double Twisted Hexagon is just a slightly different arrangement of the twist pattern. A hexagon figure is used, with long narrow bar-shaped patches that apparently interlace with each other round the hexagons. It will clearly be seen from

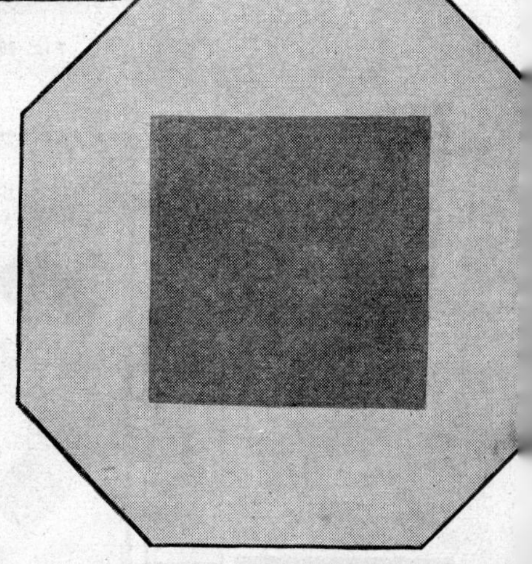

Fig. 31, how the interlacing is done, and the colours arranged. The size of the hexagon and the bars is given in the diagram.

A Simple Border.—The centre of this border is composed of a number of pieces apparently overlapping each other like the pointed flap of an envelope. The method of working is to cut a number of sectional papers the shape of the pointed diagram given for working the Trellis pattern, but making them double that width by carrying on the point further to the left. Cover

DOUBLE TWISTED HEXAGON

Fig. 31.

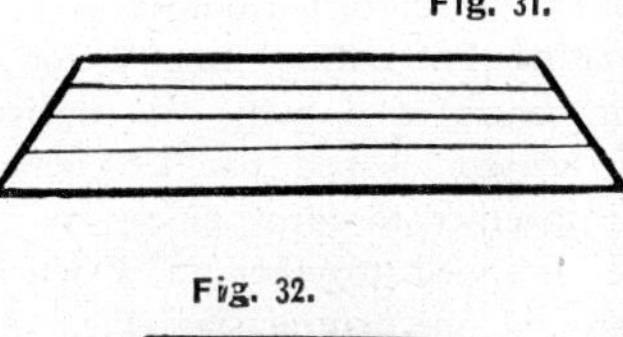

Fig. 32.

these diagram papers with silk scraps in the usual way, and sew two sections together pointways on, as shown in the illustration of the Trellis pattern, these may be both one colour, or one section a dark and the other a light shade of the same colour. If the latter let all the dark-shaded silks come on the lower side of the border. Having a number of sections ready, join one within the other as in Fig. 34, and embroider a few fancy stitches on the tip of each. Fill in the spaces on each side with triangular-shaped patches of a neutral colour. Then arrange the corner pieces. When this is done, sew two long strips of material, about half an inch in width, on each side of the border, mitreing them to fit the corners.

Another Border which could be used on a cloth is quite simple to work, as it consists only of five sectional pieces, two squares, two triangles and the pyramid point, which is used only in the inner part of the pattern, to form a kind of insertion by itself. This may not be necessary if the border is wide enough. The border shown in Fig. 36 worked by the accompanying diagrams, is $6\frac{1}{2}$ inches deep.

The straight strips, two of which run parallel on each side of the border, are $\frac{3}{8}$ inch in width, and if it is not possible to have long lengths, then short lengths joined together are just as good. These bands are mitred at the corners. The arrangement of the sectional pieces can be seen in the illustration. The squares are set in diamond fashion and may be all one shade of a bright colour, or the large squares one colour and the small another, according to the amount of material in hand. A small triangle of some light neutral shade is fitted against two opposite sides of the small squares and a large triangle of a darker shade on each of the other two sides, stretching along the side of the adjoining small triangle. The five sections thus form a parallelogram. A large triangle is set angleways against each side of the large square. The fancy stitches that are embroidered with Filoselles upon all the squares and upon one corner of all the large triangles may be worked either before or after the patches are sewn together. The bands are added when a good length of pattern is done. Then the pyramid points are put on the inner side of the border and overlap the material of which the cloth is made.

A more advanced Border suitable for a quilt or cloth is composed of seven sectional pieces, making the border 8 inches deep when completed. Fig. 40 shows the actual size of the patches. The stars in the central insertion are formed by joining together eight of the No. 1 diamond-shaped sections (having previously cut these in paper and covered them with silk). The squares (No. 2) are placed cornerways between two stars and the triangles (No. 3) fit into the spaces left between the points. These two shapes being of some neutral shade. No. 4 triangle occupies the space directly above and below the No. 2 square, and should be a darker shade of the same colour. Nos. 5, 6 and 7 are used in the diamond-block insertion, Square No. 5 being of a bright cheerful shade. Triangle No. 6, which is set angleways against each side of the square, should be a lighter shade of the same colour. Triangle No. 7 should be of black silk or velvet to give an effective contrast, as well as to distinguish the insertions one from the other. The outer insertion consists simply of triangles No. 7 made up in two rather light contrasting shades of colour, and arranged to fit angleways one to the other, with the straight side of the lightest shade placed flush against the black triangles of the diamond-block insertion. Fig. 39 shows the completed border.

Indian Pine Pattern is suitable for a cushion or centre of a quilt. It consists mostly of hexagon-shaped patches, which are joined together to form pines, six of which are arranged together in a wheel revolving round one central star (Fig. 38). The hexagon used is given in Fig. 32, for Double Twisted Hexagon pattern. The size can be varied according to the article to be made. The sections are cut in paper and covered with material in the usual way. Begin in the centre of the design and make the star by grouping six hexagons in bright coloured material round one hexagon of the same colour, but of a lighter shade. The star, thus made, is heavily embroidered in fancy stitches to make it stand out well against the pines. The pines may be two colours, grouped as shown by the shading in the illustration, or each pine may be a different colour. Again, each individual pine may be entirely one shade of colour, or in graduated shades, dark at the root and lighter in the centre and lightest of all at the top. There are fourteen hexagons in each pine, which are joined together in this way. Sew two hexagons side by side for the first row, sew three hexagons in a row above the two

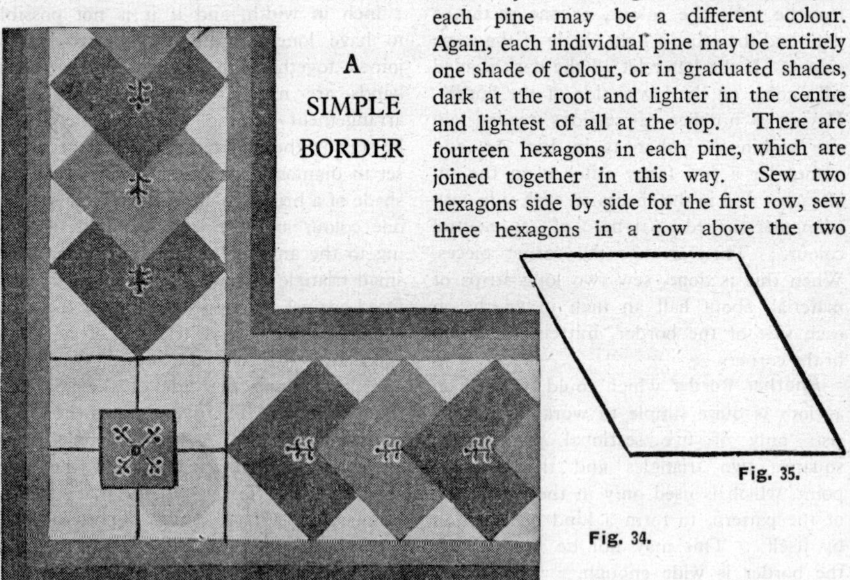

A SIMPLE BORDER

Fig. 35.

Fig. 34.

hexagons then another three in a row slanting a little to the right, another level with the last and one hexagon above the two, and finally one hexagon slanting to the right, another level with the last, and one hexagon bending downwards to the right. The last four hexagons form the head or curve of the pine. Make up five more pines exactly the same shape as the first. Then sew all six pines round the central star and join the sides to each other, as in the illustration. It will be noticed that spaces are left between the pines themselves. The pattern sections are now taken out and the patchwork is laid upon a large circular piece of material, to which it is applied or neatly hemmed down.

The size of the sectional pieces used for the border will greatly depend on the size of material used for the ground of the pine pattern. The border begins with a circle of black bar-like sections each about half an inch or $\frac{3}{8}$ inch wide and of sufficient length for ten bars to fit along one-quarter of a circle. Then a circle of bright-coloured pyramid points is arranged, each section being just long enough at the base to lie flush against the black sections. Then taper off gradually to a point. Three triangular-shaped pieces of some soft neutral shade are fitted in the spaces between the pyramid points. The design is then completed by another circle of black bar-like sections the same width as those of the previous circle but, of course, rather longer, so as still to keep ten bars in one quarter of the circle.

Star Pattern which is particularly suitable for a six-sided cushion in patch-work, which, if it is carried out by the

Fig. 37.

Fig. 36.

A USEFUL BORDER

diagrams in Fig. 42, will measure 18 inches across from side to side. The method of joining the pieces will be clearly seen in Fig. 41 and therefore needs very little explanation. Silk, satin or velvet scraps would be the most suitable, the arrangement of colours depending on the individual. Diagram 1 represents the long central point of the star, and is worked in two separate pieces, the one light and the other dark. Diagram 2 forms the outside tip of the central point. Diagrams 3 and 4 are used to make up the small points of the star. Diagram 5 is the neutral tinted section that fills up the space between the star and the beginning of the border. The border consists first of a ribbon band either black velvet or something dark in colour, which is $\frac{7}{8}$ inch wide and mitred at the corners in true hexagon shape. Then comes the line of lozenge-shaped pieces, Diagram 6, with its spaces, Diagram 7. Then two narrow ribbon bands, one black the other light coloured. Diagram 8 is used for working the zig-zag scroll and Diagram 9 is the intermediate section represented as black in the illustration. Then come four ribbon bands,

Fig. 38.

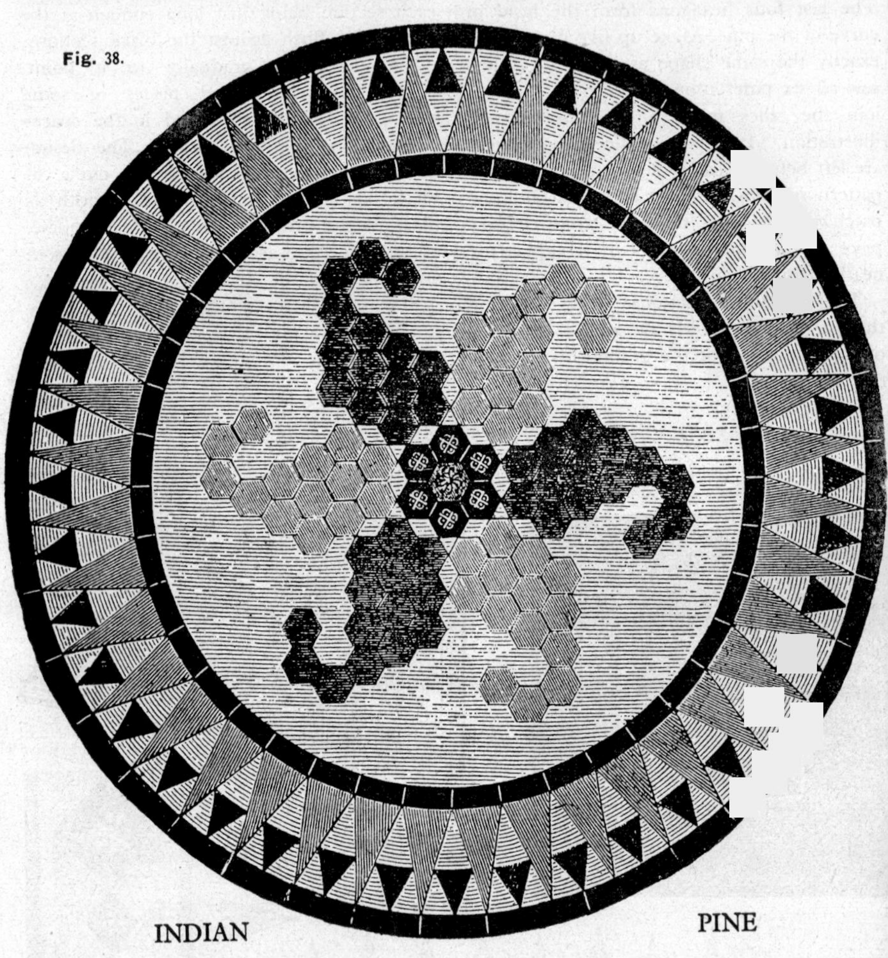

INDIAN PINE

two light and two dark which finish the pattern.

Crazy or Puzzle Patchwork consists of all odd sizes and shapes of material placed together for the best effect. It is very useful for using up all odd ends of material. When all the pieces are cut into shape, place them over a lining to form a design, but instead of stitching two pieces together as in ordinary patchwork, lay one over the other and turn under the edges of the top piece and run it to the bottom one. When all the pieces are in position and have been run to the lining and each other, work round the edge of each patch in bright-coloured Filoselle in Herringbone. Fig. 44 shows a design for this work.

American or Canadian Patchwork.—This is known in Canada as log-house quilting and differs from ordinary patchwork in that the sections are cut in strips, and instead of being sewn, are run one upon the other from the central square, and turned down so that no stitches are visible. The strips are all the same width but vary in length, being longer as they get further from the centre of the pattern. One-half of the design is carried out in light shades,

Fig. 40.

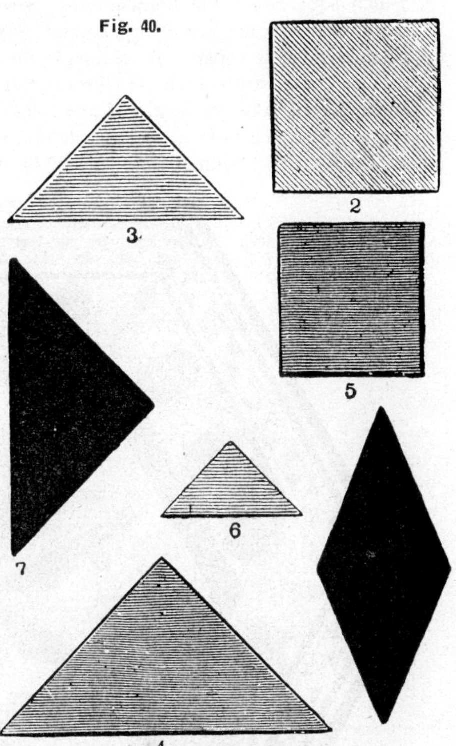

A MORE ADVANCED BORDER

Fig. 39.

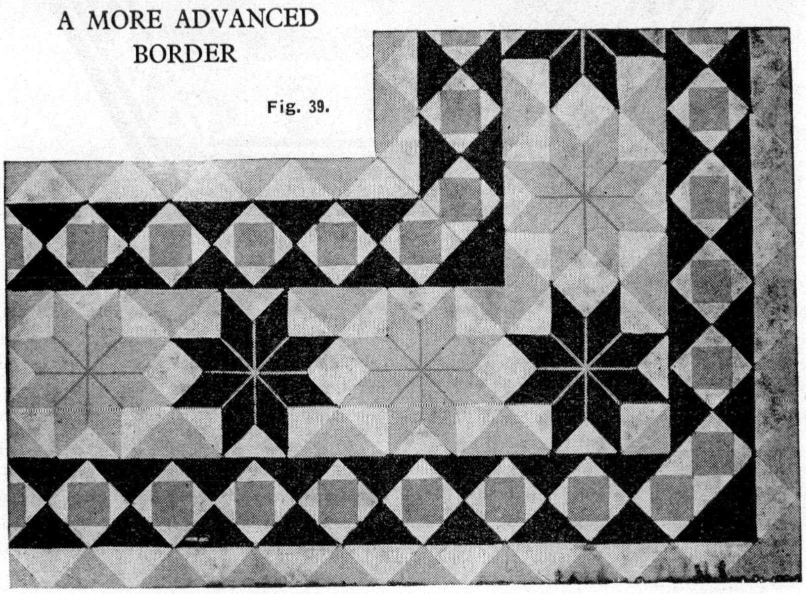

the other half in dark. Cut a number of 7-inch squares for the foundation. Next some pale cream or light-coloured silk patches 1¼-inch square are required, then coloured silk strips each 1¼ inches wide and in seven different shades of one colour. For instance, the tiny square, in pale cream and the strips shading from the lightest pink to deep rich crimson, two strips of each of the seven shades and two strips of black. They should be as long as possible to begin with, for as the work progresses the surplus quantity can be cut away.

Place the cream square exactly in the centre of the foundation and tack it on evenly. Take the first strip (the lightest shade) and placing one edge of it on the edge of the silk square, run both together on to the lining a ¼ inch from the edge, and cut off whatever portion of the strip remains beyond the piece required to cover the end of the square, turn this strip over and press it flat with the thumb. In the same way run a similar strip along the left side of the little square and turn over the end of the strip first joined on. Turn this over and press it down. Take the fifth strip (the third from the darkest) and run it to the left of the back strip, keeping it over the square, and well to the end of the light strip last put on. Turn this over and press it down. Run the same shade along the remaining side of the central square and over both ends of the strips already sewn on and press this down. The result is a perfect square, two sides light and two sides dark. Use the second lightest shade

Fig. 41.

STAR PATTERN

SHT INLAID PATCHWORK *Reproduced by permission of the Victoria and Albert Museum.*

Fig. 42.

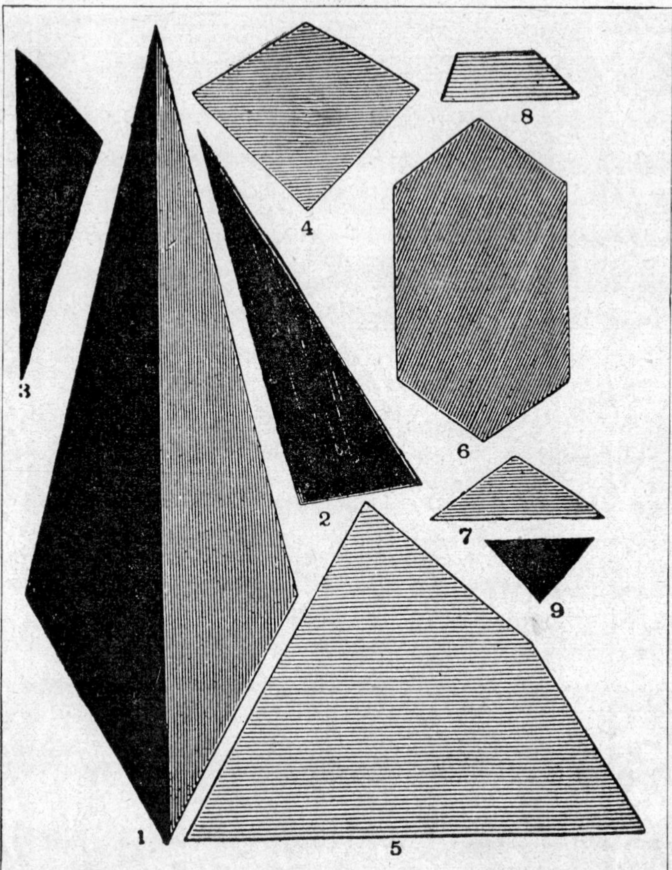

SECTIONAL PIECES FOR WORKING THE STAR PATTERN

and run along the side to the left of the last piece (that is on the same side of the square as the first strip was run) the same shade to the left of that again. Then run the sixth shade to the left of that and the same to the left of that again, this makes another complete square. Take the third lightest shade and run along each of the two sides to the left of the last added. Then add the seventh shade (the darkest) and one on the two sides to the left again and another square is finished. Next use the fourth shade along two sides, and then back on the other two sides. This finishes one square completely. Make three more exactly the same. Then stitch the four squares together, making the light shades meet each other in the centre. It will give the effect of a bright diamond being placed upon a dark square. This will be seen from Fig. 43.

Leather Patchwork.—Leather scraps can be used for patchwork and differ in one thing only from ordinary patchwork. That is, that the pieces are glued to the background instead of being stitched together. The same patterns can be used, and the method of cutting out the sections is the same. Table-mats, folding screens, etc., can be made in this way.

To work.—Find a suitable design which lends itself to leather. Then draw

A QUILT *Reproduced by permission of the Victoria and Albert Museum.*

Fig. 43.

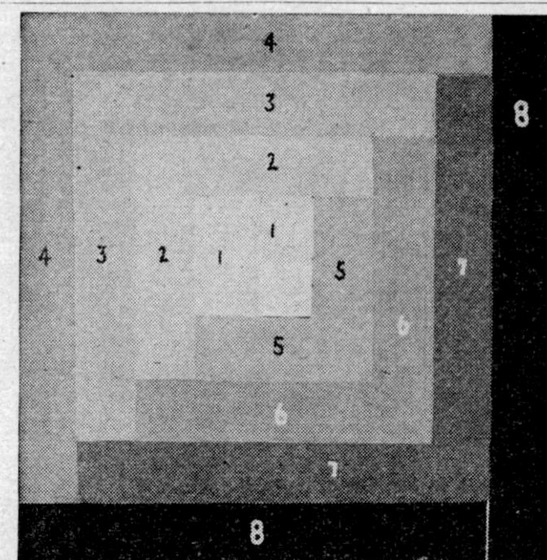

AMERICAN LOG PATCHWORK

Fig. 44.—CRAZY PATCHWORK

A WELL-PLANNED DESIGN MADE FROM COTTON PRINT PIECES

Fig. 45.

By courtesy of the Victoria and Albert Museum.

the pattern accurately on to a piece of millboard and mark the colour of the leather intended for each space. Arrange the pieces in order upon the table, heat some common glue (that is, free from impurities and of equal constituency) and spread it on the back of the leather, which is put on the marked space on the millboard. Work quickly, but be careful that every point is glued down, and see that they are accurately arranged with no spaces between. Keep the millboard in a warm place until the glue has quite dried. The wrong side of the millboard can then be covered with silk or felt according to the article made. The edges can then be gilded or stained.

Inlaid Appliqué or Patchwork is worth noting. It is mostly made at Resht, and is used for carpets, covers, etc. It is patchwork combined with embroidery. The colourings are very bright. The patches are in small intricate patterns cut out in cloth. Besides conventional designs, animals, birds and flowers are used as can be seen on page 399. The pieces are stitched down with chain-stitch and in some cases several rows cover each piece, these rows sometimes being worked in different colours.

PUNCH WORK

Punch stitch is sometimes known as drawn fabric stitch and must not be confused with drawn thread work, as the threads are not withdrawn. This kind of work is to be seen in English embroideries of the seventeenth and eighteenth centuries as well as in present day work. It is more quickly done than drawn thread work and can be worked in small spaces.

In the seventeenth and eighteenth centuries much was done to develop this work in Germany, Denmark and Flanders. This type of work is also to be found in the work of the Greek Islands and in Indian embroideries.

Designs. This work is used chiefly for fillings and backgrounds. Bold designs are best, with clear unbroken outlines and very little detail.

Punch stitch is used very extensively in lingerie for joining lace to material and for appliqué, and is particularly useful on a satin garment when the piece to be appliquéd is on the reverse side. Two coloured materials can also be appliquéd in this way.

When planning a design, bear in mind whether it is to be worked horizontally or diagonally, as this makes a difference.

Materials Required. A coarse, loosely woven linen should be used as the threads are more easily counted. For the finer work a fine linen or linen lawn is used, also satin, or crêpe-de-chine. The working thread should be a little finer than the material and is usually the same colour. A linen thread is used in the coarser work and fine cotton on fine linen or linen lawn.

When working on coarse linen a special needle is used. It is made in several sizes and is fairly thick, being round at the top and becoming three sided one-third of the way down (see Fig. 1). This needle is a great help in dividing the threads and prevents them from splitting. A fine needle is used to fasten off the thread. An embroidery frame can be used as it speeds up the work and prevents it from stretching out of shape.

For the finer work an ordinary coarse needle is used, but care must be taken that the needle is not too large as it would then split the threads. This type of punch work is best worked in the hand.

It is sometimes a help in coarse punch work to use smocking paper for the background, as this saves counting the threads.

To work. The design is first outlined, then the material between the outlines is punched with holes, simply by pushing the thread apart at equal distances in straight lines. Pierce about every fourth thread—the number depending on the coarseness of the material. The work must not be pulled at all and too coarse a thread must not be used.

The thread is tied to the eye of the needle to prevent the thread from slipping through the large eye. An alternative is to pierce the end of the thread with the needle and pull through.

The work is done from right to left and left to right alternately. Starting at the top right-hand corner, bring the needle out again and insert it four threads above, bring the needle out again at the first point, inserting it again at the second, making sure that the thread is tightly pulled each time. Bring the needle out four threads to the left and four down, then insert the needle again four threads directly above, bring it out again at the third point and insert it at the last. Continue like this, taking two upright stitches over four threads, and leaving four threads between each time.

At the end of the first row, work a row in like manner back again, starting four threads lower down, and working from left to right, bring the needle up 4 threads

Fig. 1.—A PUNCH NEEDLE

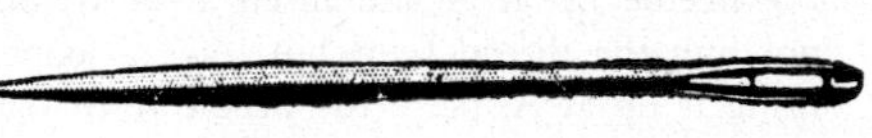

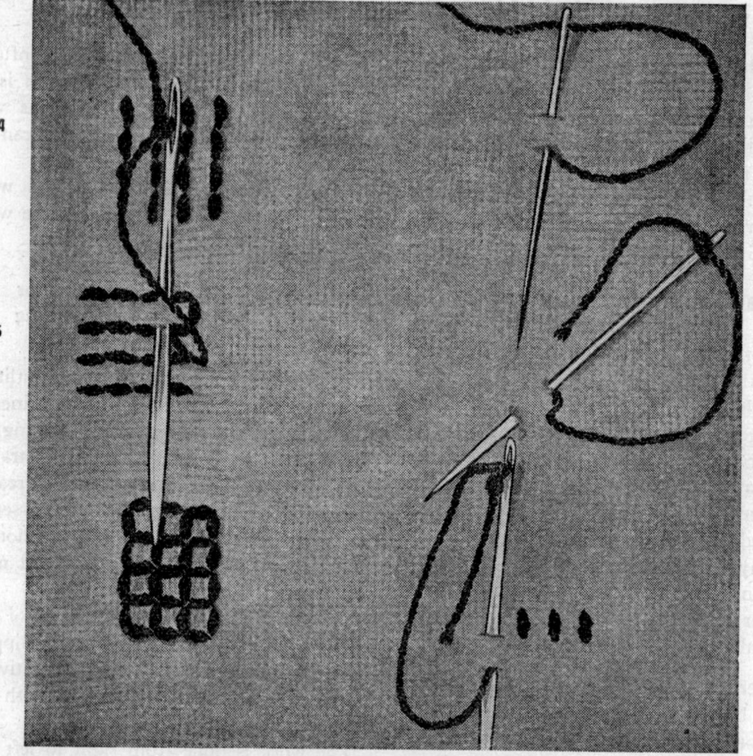

Fig. 2.—SIMPLE PUNCH STITCH
See also diagram on opposite page

below the bottom of the stitch in the previous row, inserting it in the row above as seen in diagram 3, above.

When the space to be filled is covered in this direction, turn the work so that the top row comes down the left-hand side and repeat the stitch as before, to complete the square, working in the holes made in the previous row.

When the punch work is completed the design is padded and worked in satin stitch. Fig. 3 shows a piece completed.

Another method of working this stitch in coarse material is similar to that described above, except that the stitch is knotted. This is done in the following way: Bring the needle up at A and insert it at B (do not pull the thread tight but leave a loop), bring it up at A, place the needle from the back through the loop and draw the thread up tightly. Insert the needle again at B and bring it out at C and continue as before, until the desired space is filled. The working can be clearly seen from the diagrams in Fig. 4. This method should be worked in a frame. The effect is more even and better if the stitches are kept in rows, but this is not always possible.

For a transparent material such as fine linen, linen lawn or muslin, the diagonal stitch is more suitable as the working thread is hardly seen on either side and therefore does not spoil the transparence of the material.

Take a piece of linen lawn and pencil on to it dots at equal distances in squares where the stitches are to be taken. If smocking paper is used, this should be put

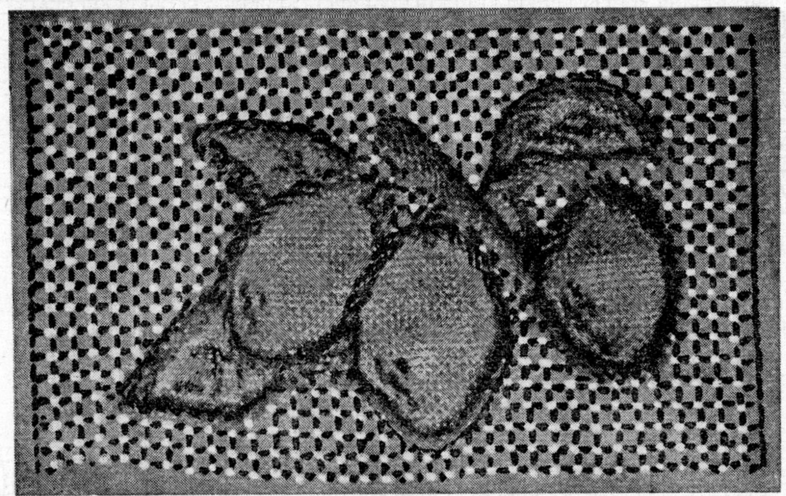

Fig. 3.—PUNCH STITCH ROUND A SIMPLE DESIGN

Fig. 4.—KNOTTED PUNCH STITCH

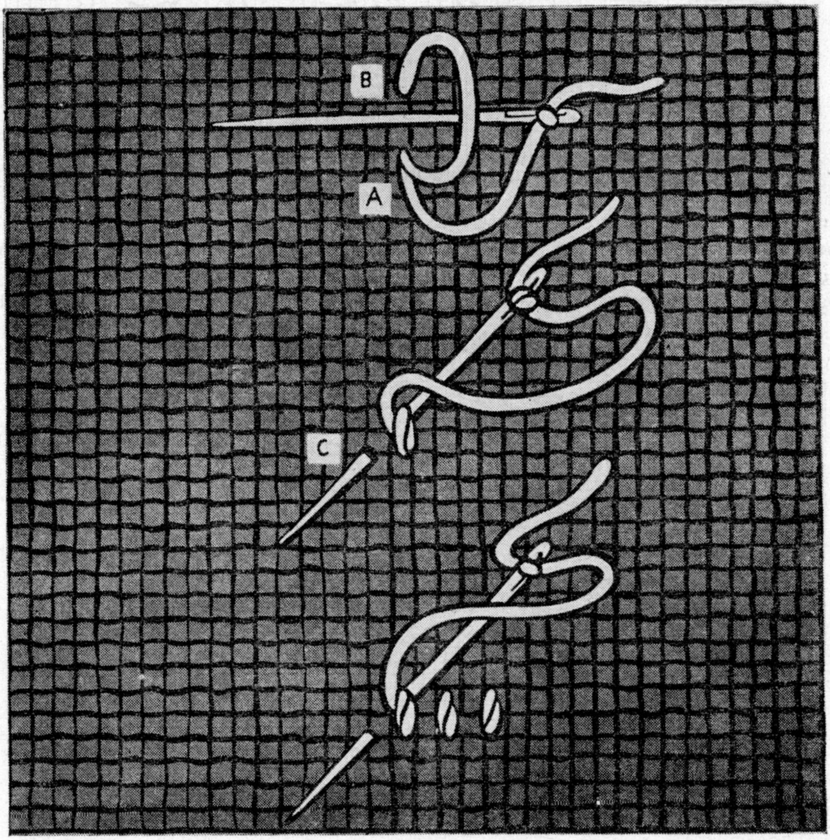

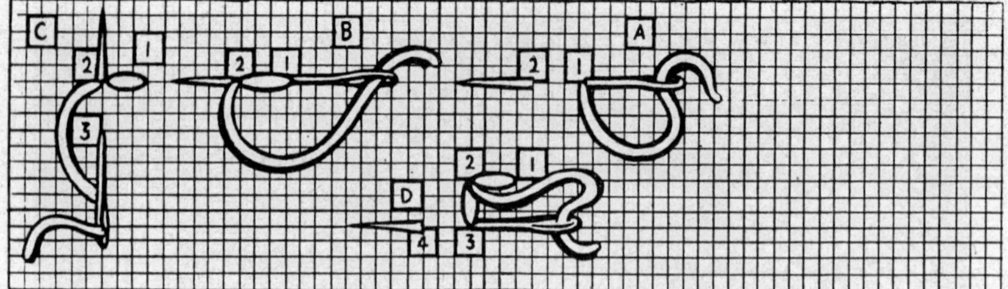

Fig. 5.—THE BEGINNING OF SLANTING PUNCH STITCH

on the wrong side. This, however, is not advisable, as the spots are apt to show when the work is finished.

Tie the thread in the needle (either a fine lace thread or fine cotton can be used), and continue repeating this for the length required. Draw the thread tightly after each stitch as this, together with the large needle, makes the holes (see Fig. 5).

In working the downward line only two

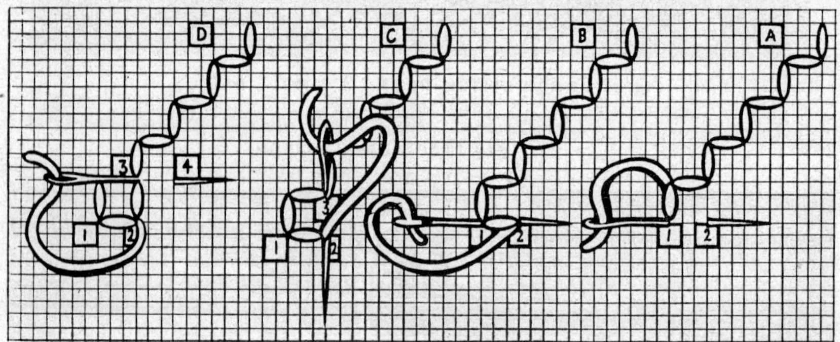

Fig. 6.—SLANTING PUNCH STITCH—cont.

and begin on a downward line. Insert the needle at 1 and out at 2, then in again at 1 and out at 2. Insert the needle at 3 and out at 2, insert it again at 3 and out at 4, sides of the square are worked, the other two sides being worked in the upward line. This completes the square.

To begin the upward line insert the

Fig. 7.—PUNCH STITCH FOR LINGERIE

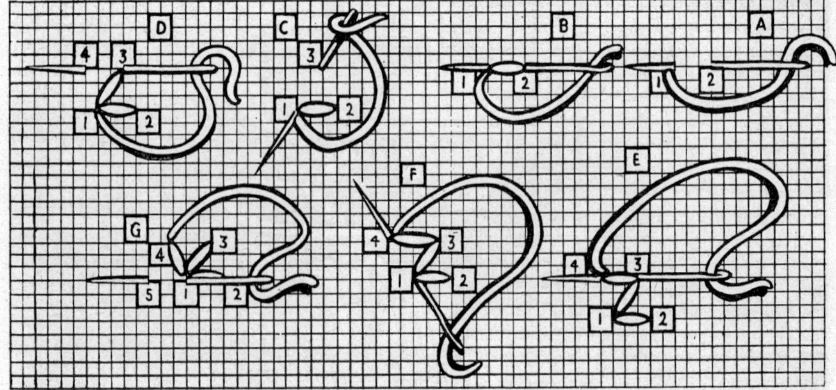

INDIAN PUNCH WORK

An exquisite design in fine white work with punch stitch used for the drawn thread centres. It is worked on superfine Indian muslin. A small strip of border is reproduced on the next page.

Fig. 8.

A LOVELY DESIGN FROM THE VICTORIA AND ALBERT MUSEUM

A BORDER FROM THE INDIAN WORK

needle at 1 and bring it out at 2, then in at 1 again and out at 2. Insert the needle at 3 and bring it out again at 2. Insert the needle at 3 and out at 4 and continue repeating this for the length required. The working of the stitch can be clearly followed

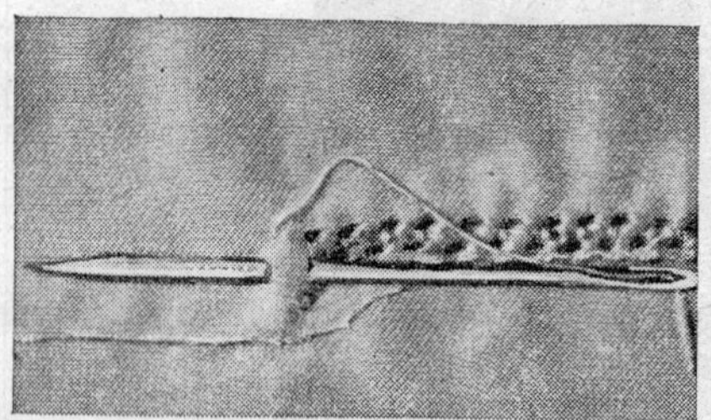

RIGHT SIDE

Fig. 9.
PUNCH STITCH USED TO JOIN A SEAM

WRONG SIDE

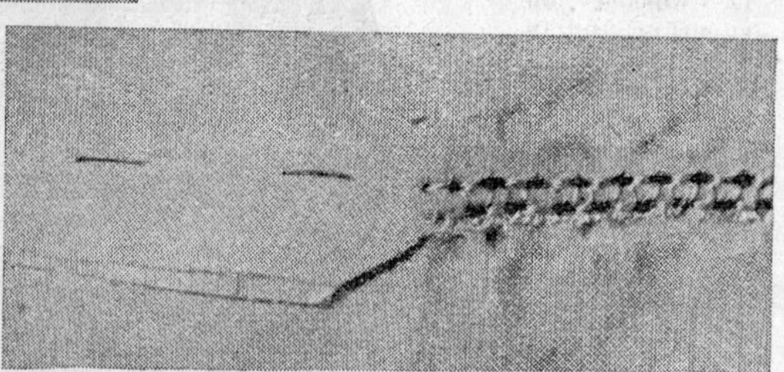

if the diagrams in Figs. 5 and 6 are used. The threads are finished off at the beginning and end by being run, wherever possible, into the surrounding border. For this a small needle is used.

Fig. 8 is a specimen of Indian work. It shows the large piece in the centre motif worked in punch stitch and also the centres in the border design.

Punch stitch on lingerie is not worked in quite the same way. It is usually worked in straight or waved lines instead of hem-stitching. As the threads are not drawn, the stitch can be worked along the warp and weft of the material and can therefore be worked in circles. It is quite quickly worked and is very strong and effective. It is used to join two seams together, to appliqué two pieces of material or to join a piece of lace and material together.

It is worked from right to left and forms a series of back stitches in small triangles. Pulling the thread tightly after each stitch helps to accentuate the holes and gives the appearance of small triangles. By this means the working thread is hardly noticeable. The designs are usually drawn on the material in pencil, as it shows least when the work is finished.

Fig. 10.—LACE JOINED BY PUNCH STITCH

WRONG SIDE

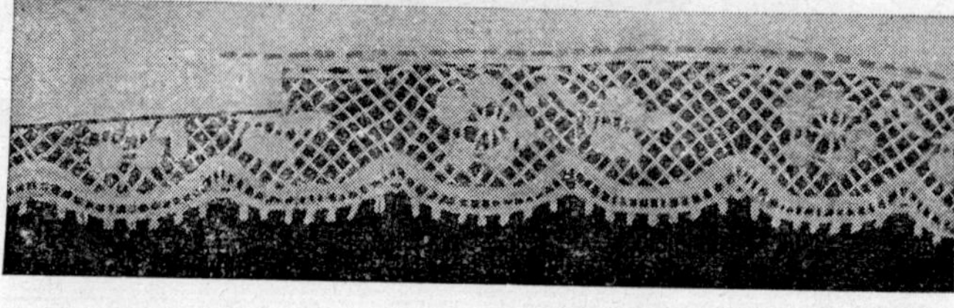

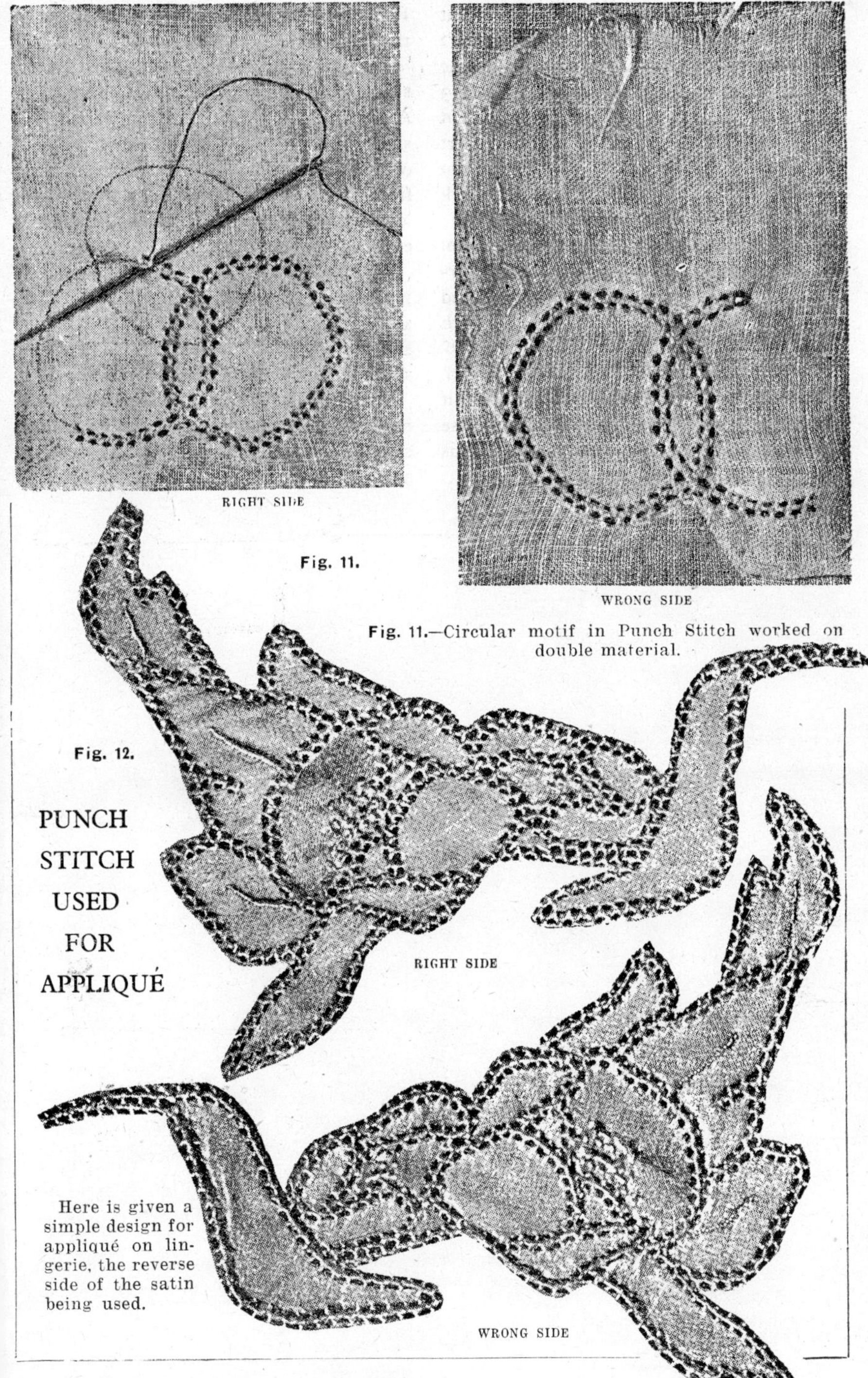

Fig. 11.

Fig. 11.—Circular motif in Punch Stitch worked on double material.

Fig. 12.

PUNCH STITCH USED FOR APPLIQUÉ

Here is given a simple design for appliqué on lingerie, the reverse side of the satin being used.

Bring the needle out at 1 and insert it at 2 and out again at 1. Insert it again at 2 and bring it out at 1. Insert the needle at 3 and out at 1. Insert the needle at 3 and out at 4, then in again at 3 and out at 4 and in at 1 and out at 4 again. Insert the needle at 1 and out at 5. Now repeat in this order for the length required. Fig. 7 shows the working diagrams.

When punch stitch is used **to join a seam** the two edges of the material should overlap about half an inch, then a tacking thread should be taken down the centre. Punch stitch is then worked through both thicknesses of material over the tacking thread. When the work is completed and after it has been pressed, the material is cut close up to the punch stitch on both sides. This makes a neat seam and is very strong.

Fig. 9 shows the preparing and joining of the material.

Fig. 10 shows **lace joined with punch stitch** and the material cut away afterwards. A small circular motif in punch stitch is shown in Fig. 11. When the work has been completed the surplus material is cut away from the back. This has been done at the lower left-hand corner to show the finished effect.

Fig. 12 shows a piece of appliqué using reversible fabric (which in this case was satin) with the shiny side for the ground and the crêpe for the appliqué The punch stitch was worked in Filo Floss.

Lace motifs and lace insertion can also be let in with punch stitch. In both these cases the lace is tacked on to the material and cut away after it has been pressed.

QUILTING

Quilting is an ancient craft which has been practised for many centuries in Europe and in Oriental countries, especially India, Persia and Turkestan and many parts of Africa.

The world "quilt" means a stuffed sack, mattress or cushion which came from the Latin word "culcita".

Quilting still survives in certain districts in northern England and South Wales, where it has been handed down from generation to generation.

One of the oldest and best-known examples of quilting is a beautiful Sicilian Quilt, which depicts a series of scenes from the life of Tristan. But although ornamental quilting was practised in Europe it never reached the same minuteness and beauty of design that distinguishes Oriental quilting. The patience and skill of these workers is reflected in their work.

Quilting reached its height of popularity in England in the seventeenth and eighteenth centuries when quilted suits, doublets and breeches and quilted petticoats were worn. Large coverlets were also among the many things made in quilting

Quilting is used for warmth and many articles such as cot-covers, dressing-gowns, etc., are often made. It is worked in lines of stitches, through three layers of material, one above the other, the middle one being of soft padding.

Quilting designs are fairly simple, the idea being to hold the three layers of material firmly together, which means that the design should cover the entire surface.

Many designs used are handed down from generation to generation. Each area has its own special type, which is varied in the working by the individual embroiderer. These designs are not drawn on to the material, but are clearly visualised by the worker, who first divides the work in halves and quarters which are marked either by a thread or chalk mark.

Quilters often use as guides templates that have been handed down to them for generations. They are often made of wood or metal, but cardboard or stiff paper can be used. When using a template as a guide the worker traces round the edge with the point of a needle. These templates are of different shapes which are seldom used together in any one piece of work. Squares and diamonds are much used in backgrounds, the diamond shaped checks being called "gamboised." The shapes of the various templates used for the Museum specimens in this chapter are easily recognisable.

Materials used.—Silk and satin work up well in quilting, though a fine linen and cotton are good. Good quality materials should always be used. Professional quilters use sheep's wool which has been washed and carded, so as to remove the grease which is contained in raw wool, and which would otherwise spoil the work. Cotton-wool, domette and flannel can also be used. The threads used depend on the material quilted, but silk should always be used on silk fabrics, and cotton, linen or mercerised silk for linens and cottons.

Most colours can be used for quilting, though very often a light shade works up the best. If the work is to be reversible, two colours may be used. The thread used for working should match the material on the right side, though a contrast is sometimes chosen.

To work.—For large pieces of work it is best to use a frame. When a large quilt is being worked it is as well to roll up part of it on one end of the frame, just leaving a quarter or a third to work at. Before putting the material into the frame it has to be tacked together in the following way: Place the bottom layer flat on the table, then immediately above that the

A Sicilian coverlet which is one of the earliest known specimens of quilting. It is worked on a linen ground in linen thread in backstitch. Running stitches in rows are used for the background. The figures and border are padded more than the background, which makes them stand out well. By courtesy of the Victoria and Albert Museum.

padding and finally the top layer. Tack all three well together. Plenty of tacking is the secret of good quilting for although it may be tedious, it is essential to prevent the materials from slipping out of place when being worked.

Always start the tacking from the centre constantly smoothing out the material as you work. Tack horizontally over the surface.

Having marked the centre, the border and corners as already described, the work is ready to put in the frame. Roll under the part not required. Mark out a small part of the design at a time with the help of a template. This remains on long enough to work and leaves no mark when finished.

Should a transfer be used instead, it is advisable to put it on the wrong side if the work is to be done in running stitch as the marks would show when the work is finished. If back stitch or chain stitch is used, then it can be put lightly on

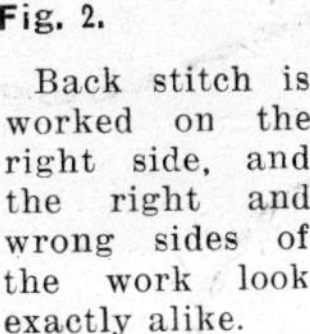

Fig. 2.

Back stitch is worked on the right side, and the right and wrong sides of the work look exactly alike.

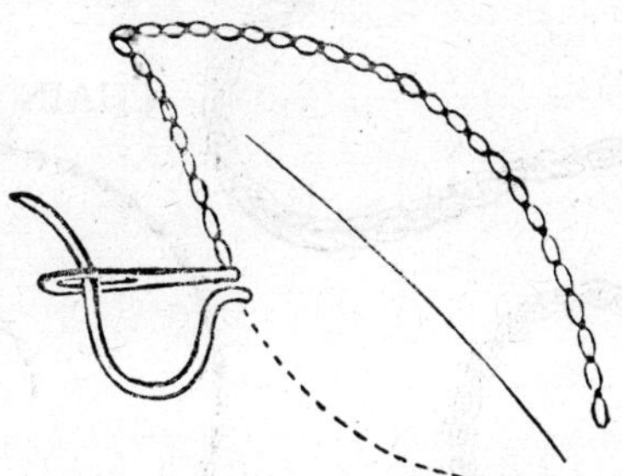

to the right side as it is covered in the working.

Stitches used.—Running, back stitch and chain stitch are most often used, although sometimes stem stitch is seen. It is considered better to use the same stitch throughout one piece of work, although this is not always possible. Fig. 3 shows running stitch being worked from the wrong side, and from the right side. Fig. 2 shows back stitch which is the same both on wrong and right sides. Fig. 4 shows chain stitch, which can be worked from either the right or the wrong side according to choice. The reverse side is similar to back stitch.

Stem stitch is worked on the wrong side, the appearance of the front being similar to back stitch. *N.B.*—Always remember that each stitch must be made through all three layers of material in two distinct movements, one downwards, and the other upwards, *not* all in one movement as in all other kinds of needlework. A good quilter is said to prick her finger with every stitch she takes!

When quilting on a frame, one hand should be above and the other beneath. To start, make a knot, put the needle in from the underneath and bring it out on top, pulling it firmly but gently so that the knot slips through the material and the padding where it remains secure. To finish off, make a single back stitch and run the thread in through the padding. Cut the end further along.

When the quilting is finished it is

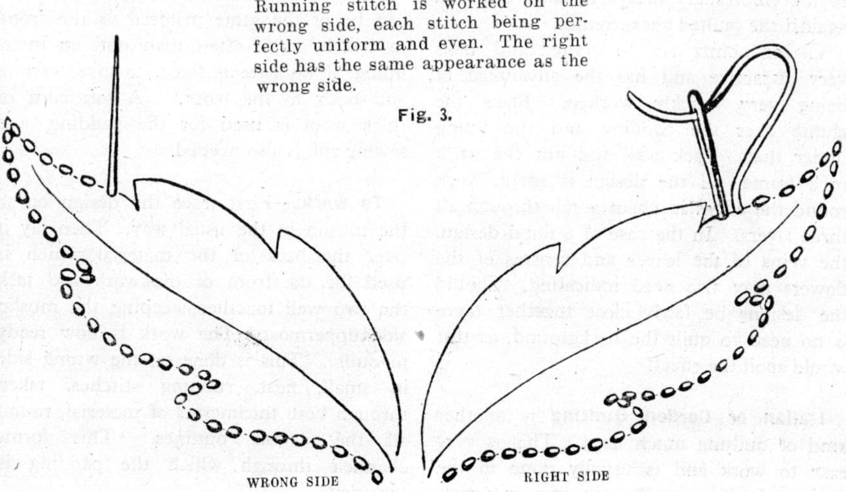

Running stitch is worked on the wrong side, each stitch being perfectly uniform and even. The right side has the same appearance as the wrong side.

Fig. 3.

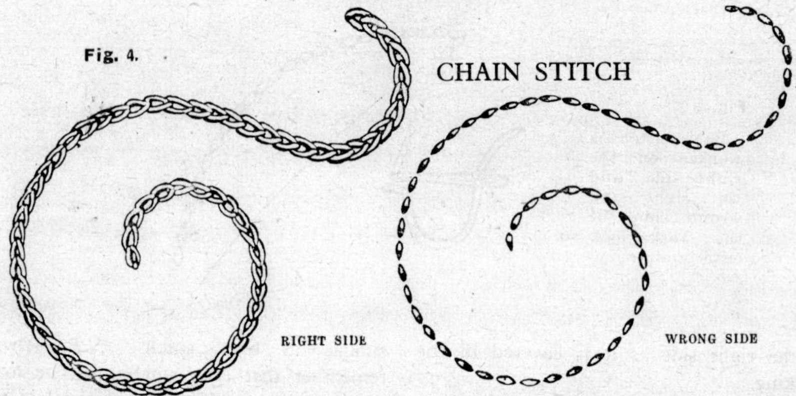

removed from the frame, all the tacking taken out and the edges neatened. There are many ways of finishing off quilting, each depending on the type of article being made. The most usual way is to turn in the edges and slip stitch them together.

Embroidery can quite often be effectively combined with quilting. The design is embroidered on the top layer only, and when this is finished it is placed over the domette and lining and all three thicknesses are tacked well together. If it is a large piece use a frame and back stitch round the design, through all three thicknesses as before. A diamond or square background is very effective, as can be seen from Fig. 6. Working round the outline of the embroidery makes it stand out well against the quilted background.

Glazed chintz can be quilted and looks very attractive and has the advantage of being very quickly worked. Place the chintz over the padding and the lining under that. Tack well and put the work in a frame. If the design is small, work round the edges in chain stitch through all three layers. In the case of a floral design, the veins of the leaves and centres of the flowers may also need indicating. Should the designs be fairly close together there is no need to quilt the background, as this would spoil the effect.

Italian or Corded Quilting is another kind of quilting much used. This is very easy to work and is usually done in the hand. It is worked over two materials only, as no interlining is used. It is worked entirely in two rows of outline through which a cord or thick wool is inserted to produce the raised effect.

Designs for Italian Quilting are made up of double outlines, and traced on to the material as for ordinary embroidery. A template is never used for this work. Floral designs, scrolls and interlaced patterns are very suitable and a great number of designs can be adapted.

Materials required.—Silk and satin are most frequently used in this work, though a fine linen and organdie are also suitable. A coarse muslin of loose weave is used for the second layer, and a lining for the work can be of the same material as the front, to which, more often than not, an interlining of domette is fixed, to give warmth and body to the work. A soft cord or thick wool is used for the padding, and sewing silk is also needed.

To work.—First trace the design on to the muslin in the usual way. Then lay it over the back of the material which is used for the front of the work and tack the two well together, keeping the muslin side uppermost. The work is now ready to quilt: This is done on the wrong side in small, neat, running stitches, taken through both thicknesses of material, round all the double outlines. This forms channels through which the padding is threaded.

Fig. 5.

Simple backstitching is used for this good example which is worked on a coarser linen with a thicker thread. Reproduced by kind permission of the Victoria and Albert Museum.

Fig. 6. *By courtesy of the Victoria and Albert Museum*

A handsome design made from the "feather" template, which can be arranged to form several different designs. Diamond quilting is used for the background. It is worked in running stitch in self-coloured thread.

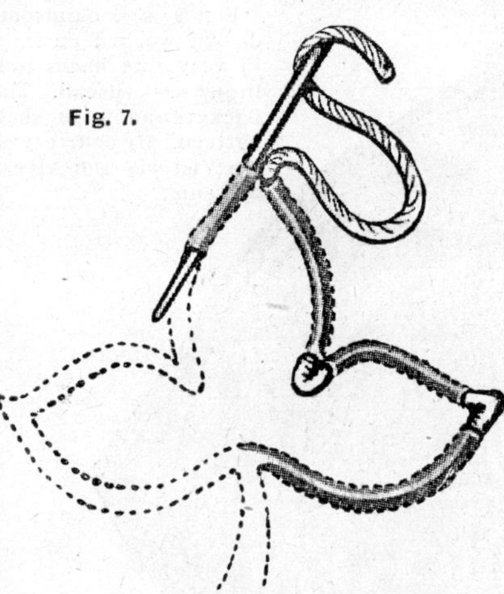

For Italian quilting a padding thread is used. A loop should be left at each corner and the needle should be brought out at each curve and reinserted in the same hole.

The padding is done from the wrong side. Thread the wool or cord through a large-eyed blunt needle and insert it from the wrong side, between the two layers of material, keeping it to the channels just made by the running stitches, until the whole design is completed. Sufficient padding should be put in so that the design stands out well on the front. The effect is completely lost if the padding is too thin. At any definite angle or curve the needle is brought out and inserted again in the same hole as shown in Fig. 7. At a decided angle, as at the tips of petals, leave the wool a little loose to form a loop as seen in Fig. 7. This is to prevent the padding from shrinking when it is washed or from pulling round the corners. When a wider space has to be filled in, two or three rows of padding are worked backwards and forwards until the space is well filled in. These stitches are never seen on the right side. When starting and finishing a thread of wool, replace the muslin over it and take a few stitches through the muslin and wool to keep it in position.

Italian quilting can also be worked from the right side. This time the design is traced on to the silk—not the muslin. The work is prepared in exactly the same way as before, only instead of running it on the wrong side, it is back stitched on the right. When that is done, continue as before.

By using a thin transparent crêpe de Chine or organdie one may get very charming effects. Prepare the work in the usual way. The padding is done in very brilliant coloured wools, so that it shows through on the right side in very much lighter colours. The wools should be fast dyes so that when the work is washed the colours do not run.

It is advisable to put an interlining of domette between the muslin and the lining in such articles as dressing-gowns, cot-covers, etc. It can be stitched to the lining before it is joined to the work. Should the space be large it is as well to work the eyelet-holes at intervals on the

Trapunto quilting worked with cotton wadding, so that it pads the whole shape evenly.

MONOGRAMMED MEDALLION

Fig. 9 is a handsome design worked entirely in very fine backstitch in a silk thread. The background is in shell pattern. By courtesy of the Victoria and Albert Museum.

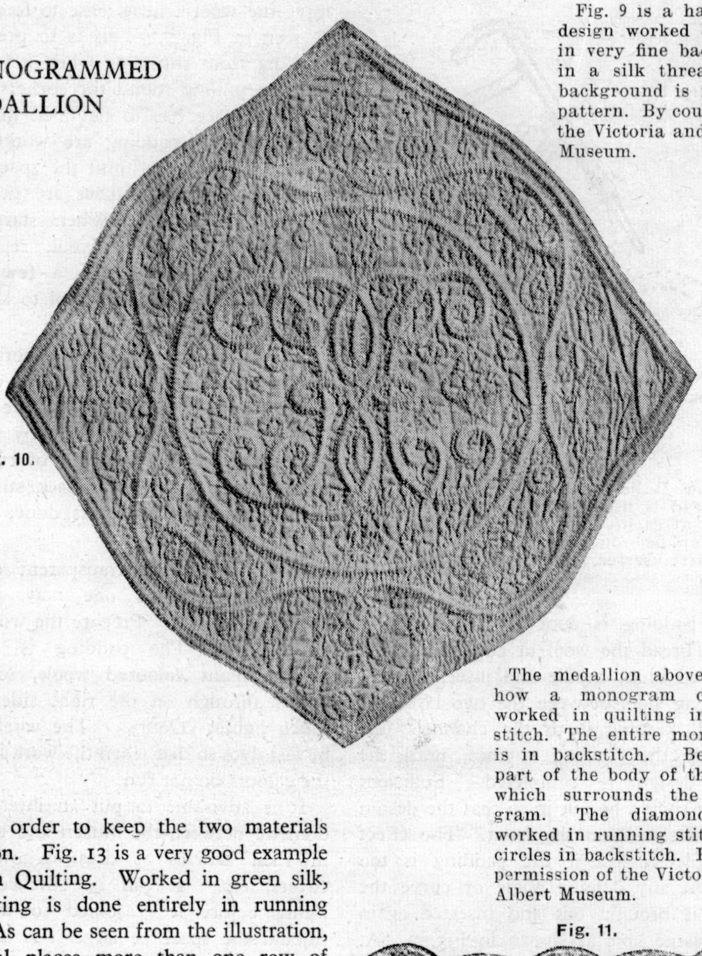

Fig. 10.

The medallion above shows how a monogram can be worked in quilting in backstitch. The entire monogram is in backstitch. Below, is part of the body of the quilt which surrounds the monogram. The diamonds are worked in running stitch, the circles in backstitch. By kind permission of the Victoria and Albert Museum.

Fig. 11.

lining in order to keep the two materials in position. Fig. 13 is a very good example of Italian Quilting. Worked in green silk, the quilting is done entirely in running stitch. As can be seen from the illustration, in several places more than one row of padding is required. This design is particularly suitable for a dressing-gown.

Trapunto quilting is a kind of quilting which is worked through two materials (a silk and muslin) from the back. It differs from the Italian Quilting in that it is worked in single outline only. For this work the padding used is a cotton wadding, which is drawn through the muslin from the back with the aid of a steel crochet hook. Each leaf or petal is filled in entirely. Large designs are unsuitable as they are difficult to pad evenly. Each part of the design is padded separately (see Fig. 8). The chief difficulty in this is to keep the padding smooth and even.

Fig. 9.

By courtesy of the Victoria and Albert Museum

Several stitches are combined in this design. Back stitch and running stitch can easily be distinguished. The flower fillings are in French knots and punched stitch. By courtesy of the Victoria and Albert Museum.

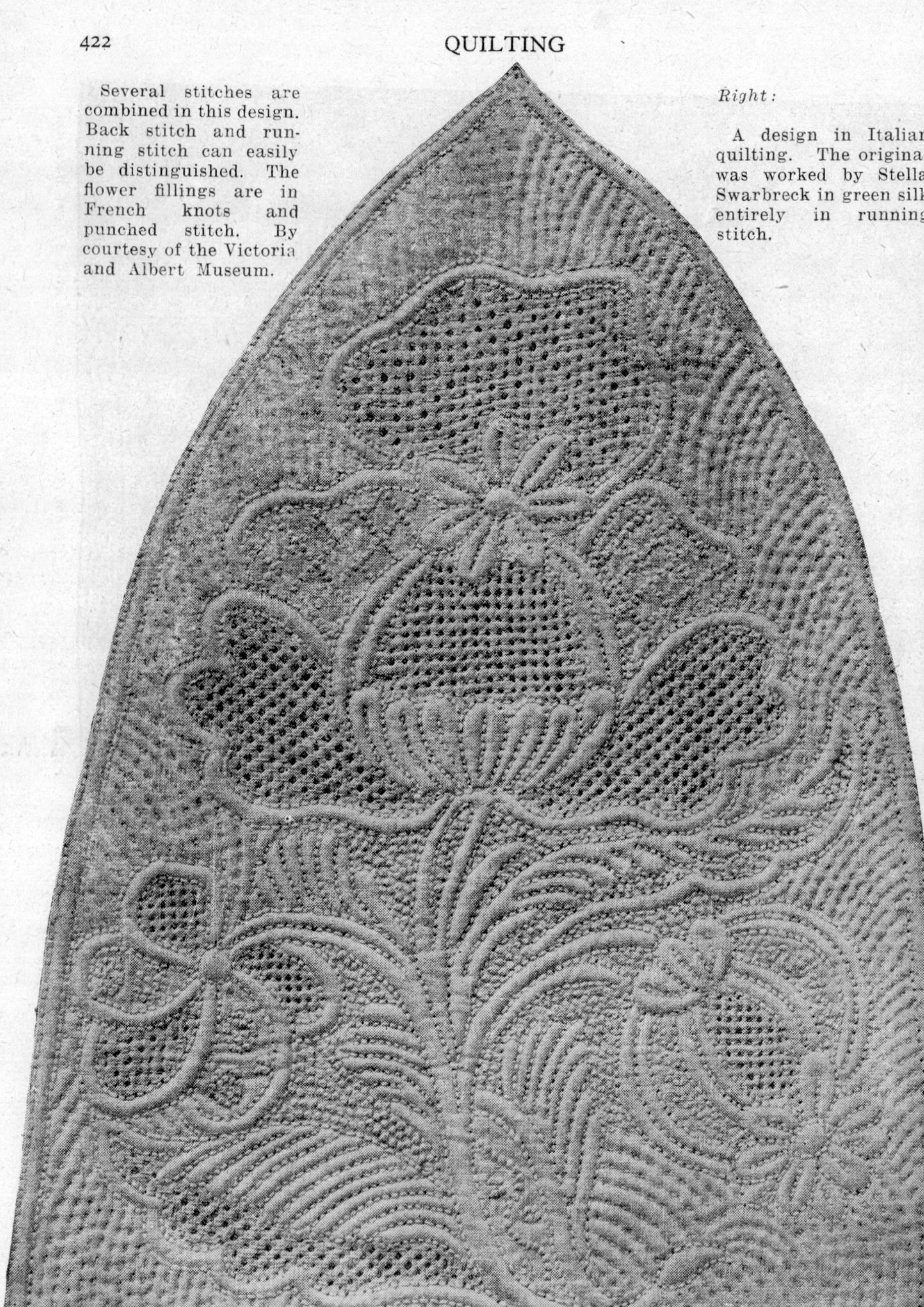

Right:

A design in Italian quilting. The original was worked by Stella Swarbreck in green silk entirely in running stitch.

Fig. 13.

By courtesy of the Victoria and Albert Museum.

Fig. 14.

A simple design in ordinary running stitch on a very fine linen with cotton to match.

Shadow Quilting. In this kind of quilting the design is first worked on a backing of linen or winceyette, using fine wool in fairly strong colours. Then organdie muslin in the same colour as the background is laid over the embroidery, and the two materials quilted together in running stitch or back stitch along the outlines of the design. A filling stitch such as long and short or satin-stitch should be used for the embroidery, as it must clearly define and pad the pattern which will later show in shadow effect through the muslin. Alternatively, felt shapes can be used instead of the embroidery.

RETICELLA OR CUT LINEN WORK

In the fifteenth century much of this work was done, as can be seen from exquisite specimens in the South Kensington Museum. Now, with the revival of all kinds of needlework, Reticella or Cut Linen Work is being worked much, both here and in Italy. For articles intended both for personal and household use it is a most beautiful and lasting form of decoration.

This needlework is suitable for working on blouses, children's frocks, afternoon tea-cloths, sheets and lingerie, as it not only affords a welcome change from ordinary embroidery, but it is effective and durable.

Cut work includes all forms of embroidery where portions of the design or the background between the design are cut away. For the ornamentation of large objects the design is made proportionately bolder and more prominent. The patterns are often joined together, edge to edge, similar to the old-fashioned laces, or in other cases, they are connected where necessary by closely buttonhole-stitched bars. This form of cut embroidery is known as Renaissance work, having been revived during that period.

Materials Required.—Rather firm linen of good quality with a round thread, not too closely woven and American cloth or *toile cirée* on which to tack the work. Suitable working threads are linen threads and embroidery cottons. The best work is done with a coiled thread rather than a flat one.

Reticella really has a likeness to the Danish hedebo but differs in several minor points. Square-shaped, circular and semi-circular openings in the material are general, which are filled in with buttonhole stitchery worked in circles, wheels, pyramids, loops and cross bars. The needlework is extremely symmetrical, as it consists chiefly of square or diamond-shaped openings cut to the required size in the material. Transfer designs are unnecessary.

The buttonholed or whipped edge (Figs. 1 and 2) of a motif forms the foundation or starting-point from which bar threads are laid across (Figs. 3 and 4) and thickened by whipping, darning or working them over in buttonhole stitch or loops; or loop bars can be made and buttonholed over, with or without picots added (see working diagrams 5, 6 and 7). From these again may spring closely worked buttonholed pyramids (diagrams 8, 9 and 10 respectively). These form a great feature of the work, and introduce much beauty and variety into it.

Method of Working.—To prepare a square or other shaped opening for working, first outline the dimensions of the square, which may vary in size from half an inch to two, three or four inches, taking care that the square is perfectly true. Run a thread all along the marked outline, then with a sharp pair of scissors cut it across from each corner to the exact centre. Fold the cut portions under the wrong side, then either overcast the folded edges or

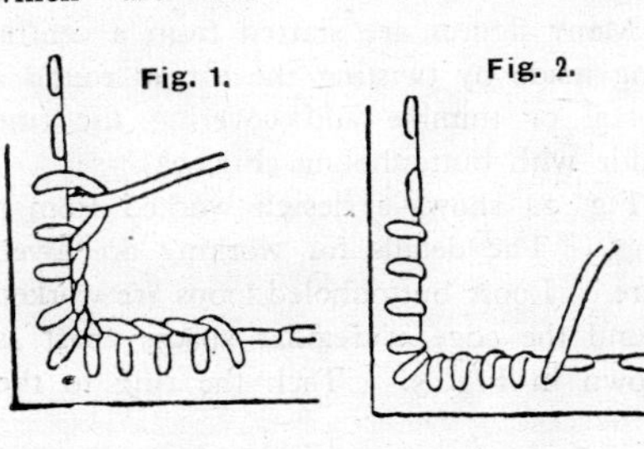

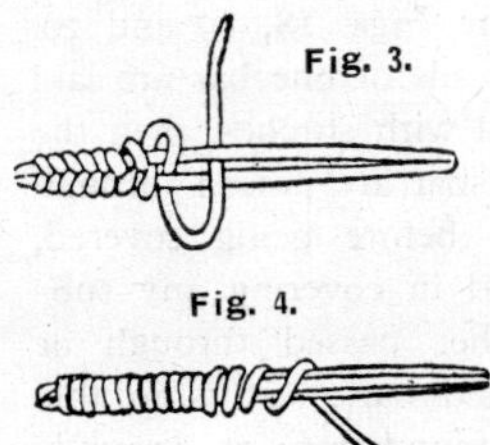

Here are shown two ways of finishing the edge—overcasting and buttonholing, also two kinds of bar — overcast and laced or woven bar.

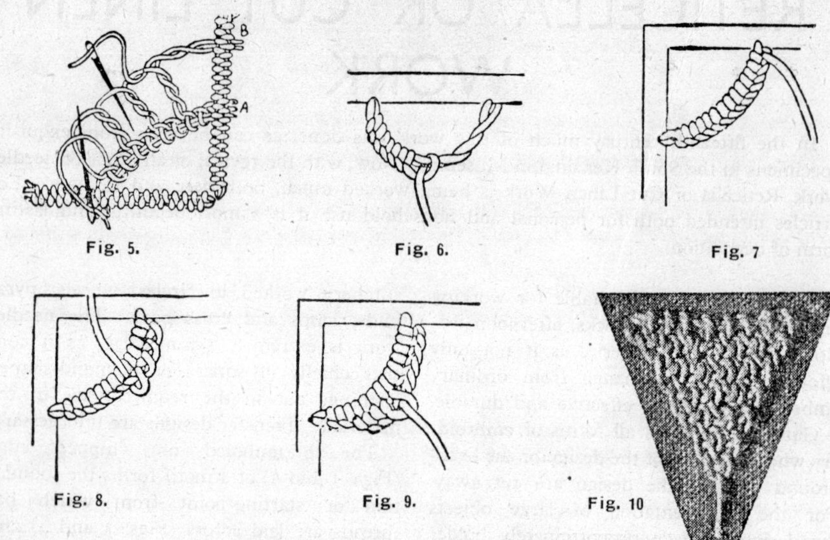

Fig. 5. Fig. 6. Fig. 7

Fig. 8. Fig. 9. Fig. 10

buttonhole all round, as shown in Figs. 1 and 2.

This done, tack the work firmly and evenly on to a piece of American cloth, or *toile cirée,* by a row of tacking, a ¼ inch or a little more beyond the inner edge of the square. This method keeps the work in position, and bars, pyramids, circles, or other figures that are going to be worked in the square will not sag or be uneven.

Circular Openings should be prepared in the same way, but several cuts radiating from the centre will be necessary in order to fold back the edges of the material to form an exact circle. Now the square or circle may be filled in, in any way the worker may select, or as the various designs suggest.

Bars often form a cross or are arranged like the spokes of a wheel, or other symmetrical figure, as in Figs. 18, 19 and 20. The foundation threads of one bar are laid and entirely covered with stitches, then the threads for the crossbar are passed through this completed bar before being covered, and the thread used in covering any subsequent bar is either passed through or behind the completed bar. It is in this way that a firm foundation or groundwork is made ready for other ornamental parts such as pryamids and loops.

To Work a Pyramid.—(*a*) Work a buttonhole bar for the foundation as in Fig. 8, or (*b*) work a row of buttonhole stitches on an existing overcast bar, Fig. 17. (Fig. 18 shows the corner completed), or (*c*) buttonhole into an existing row of the buttonhole stitches on the margin of the opening or some other part of the design, Fig. 20. Then turn, and missing the last buttonhole stitch just worked, oversew back to the start (Fig. 8). Turn, and again missing the last stitch worked (Fig. 9), buttonhole stitch back and continue in this manner until one stitch remains which joins to an already selected part of the design. Each buttonhole row contains the same number of stitches as the last oversewn one, but one stitch less than the previous buttonhole row.

Many figures are started from a central ring made by twisting the thread round a pencil or thimble and covering the ring made with buttonholing (Fig. 23).

Fig. 24 shows a design worked from a ring. The details for working are given here. Loose buttonholed loops are worked round the edge at regular spaces apart as shown in Fig. 5. Tack the ring to the

American cloth in the exact centre of the square pace, and work the connecting parts as required. See Fig. 24.

After the square or circle is filled in, cut the tacking threads and remove the American cloth. The superfluous pieces of linen turned under at the back of the work must be cut away close to the worked edge.

Fig. 26 shows a corner design and the method of working open button-hole spaces and pyramids. Fig. 27 shows how to work the edge.

To Join a Thread.—Do not make a knot, but work the end of the thread in with the stitching. Work from one part to another by oversewing through the buttonhole edge, or slipping the needle and thread invisibly through the back of the stitches. The work is done from left to right.

A favourite combination, particularly in Italy, is cut work with squares made of hand-made filet lace, a style that makes lovely bedspreads.

Diamond-Centre Cushion in Reticella Work.—This handsome cushion cover is worked in embroidery cotton on a fine white linen foundation. The Reticella squares and diamonds are ornamented with embroidery in stem, satin and eyelet-hole stitchery, and around the whole a handsome border is worked entirely with the needle. An enlarged section is given in Fig. 22a. This border measures $1\frac{1}{8}$ inches wide and is suitable for ornamenting tea-cloths, or it may be worked in silk on shantung to great advantage.

Prepare the openings in the usual manner and buttonhole the edges. First the foundation bars are laid and overcast (see Fig. 16 for working). Start in the top left-hand corner. Then the broad and narrow loop bars are worked (Fig. 6), the former having two and the latter one buttonhole and picot row, and lastly the ovals on the overcast bar. To do this join the thread on the back of the loop bar and bring it out at the point where the loop bar edge rests on the overcast bar, and buttonhole down the bar to the other end, placing the stitches just sufficiently apart to allow those which are still to be worked on the other side to lie easily between them. Oversew

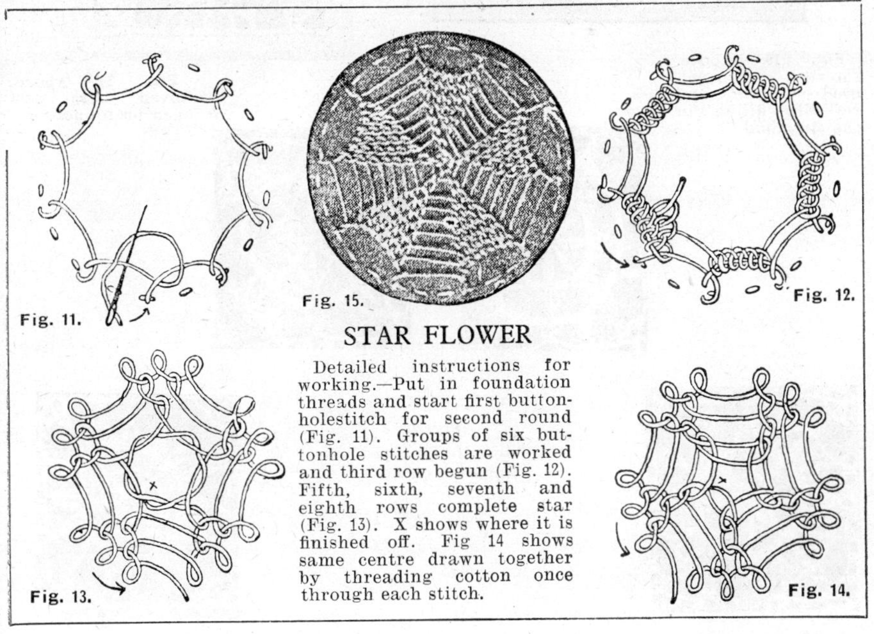

Fig. 11. Fig. 15. Fig. 12.

STAR FLOWER

Detailed instructions for working.—Put in foundation threads and start first buttonholestitch for second round (Fig. 11). Groups of six buttonhole stitches are worked and third row begun (Fig. 12). Fifth, sixth, seventh and eighth rows complete star (Fig. 13). X shows where it is finished off. Fig 14 shows same centre drawn together by threading cotton once through each stitch.

Fig. 13. Fig. 14.

back to the start (see Fig. 8) then, missing the first stitch, turn and buttonhole down this oversewn edge, making a picot halfway and leaving the last stitch unworked. Pass the needle through this stitch and also through the edge of the loop bar and then proceed to fill the other side of the bar in the same manner to complete the oval. Fig. 22 shows the completed cushion.

Fig. 16.

Fig. 17.

Fig. 18.

Fig. 19. — Above, showing embroidered outline and reticella filling in the diamond.

Fig. 20. — Above. woven bars and open buttonholing.

Fig. 21.
Shows four useful fillings for corners.

Fig. 22.—Above is a handsome cushion, worked in reticella filling, and below is an enlarged section of the border with a diagram for working.

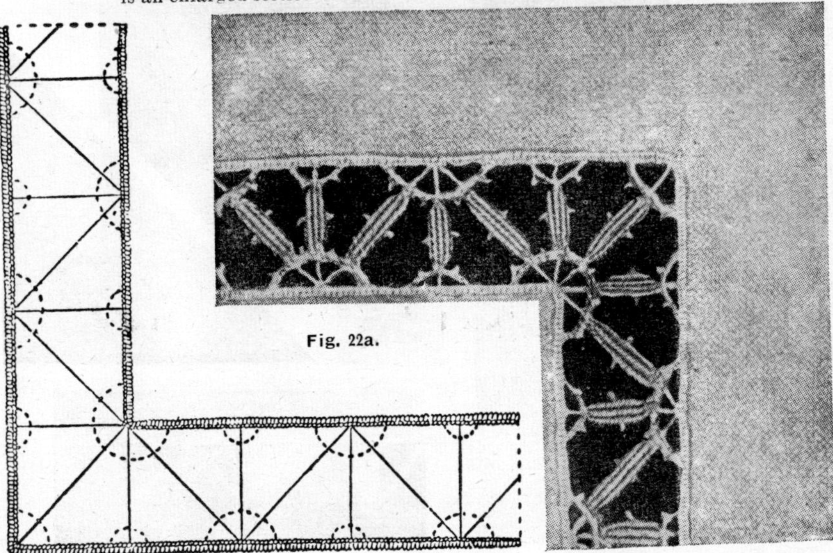

Fig. 22a.

AN EXQUISITE CORNER OF RETICELLA FILLINGS

Reproduced by courtesy of the Victoria and Albert Museum.

Left, Fig. 25, showing a useful corner easily worked.

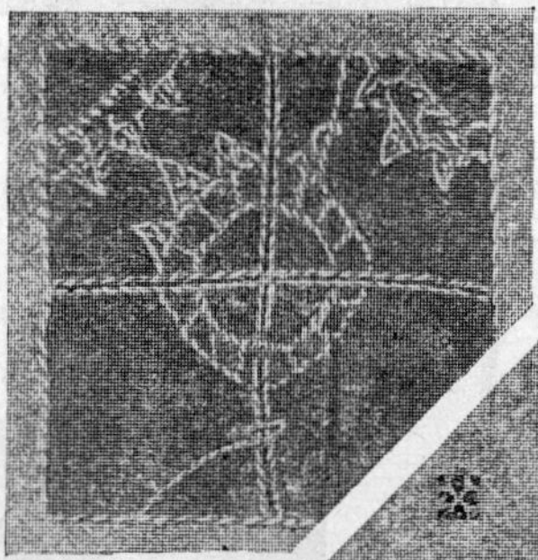

Fig. 23.

Fig. 26.

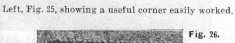

Fig. 24.

Fig. 27.

A BEAUTIFUL PIECE OF RETICELLA EMBROIDERY.

An enlarged section of the corner on page 430.

RIBBON WORK

Ribbon work is many years old and was originally used for embroidering dresses. Narrow ribbons are the easiest to work, although fairly wide shaded ribbons are often used.

Materials for Ribbon Work.—In choosing material it is best to choose one of firm texture such as linen, serge, Roman satin, *moiré* velours, bengaline, and any silk or material that is sufficiently closely woven to bear the strain of pulling the ribbon through. Ribbon embroidery is frequently introduced into work on open-meshed net, also for outlining the designs in lace insertions.

The narrow ribbons are about $\frac{1}{8}$ inch wide and some are shaded, e.g. pale green to dark green, pale blue toned to darker blue with a purple edge on the dark side. Although the special ribbons originally used for this work can rarely be bought today, ordinary ribbon could be used, providing it is of the thin silk variety.

Cotton is sometimes required for the padding and is generally sold in skeins. Silks for outlining the stalks, either Filoselle, Filo floss, twisted embroidery or some coarser kinds of silk are used. Chenille, which can be bought in many shades now, is also useful—embroidery and chenille needles are wanted for this work.

Ribbon embroidery is always easier to work in a frame if one is accustomed to it, but it is quite possible to work in the hand. There are many excellent designs to be had, either ready printed on the material for working, or in the form of transfers to be ironed on the material chosen.

Methods of Working.—There are innumerable ways, depending on the design worked. For all small flowers or leaves (this applies equally to the narrow, crinkled, and wide ribbons) a length of ribbon about 12 inches to 18 inches long is cut off, threaded in a chenille needle sufficiently large to take the ribbon easily, and a knot made in the end, just as one does with silk, to keep it from drawing through the fabric.

No piercer is required to perforate the material, for if the needle is large enough the ribbons draw through easily.

The needle is put "up" from the back of the material and the ribbon pulled through. The ribbon is then held down under the thumb of the left hand to prevent twisting, while the needle is again inserted at the distance required to make the stitch (still keeping the ribbon under the left thumb) and pulled through to the back. The ribbon length is not cut off, after making the stitch, unless only one stitch is required, but it is used as long as necessary. When ready to fasten off, the needle is inserted to the wrong side, the ribbon knotted close to the material and then cut off close to the knot.

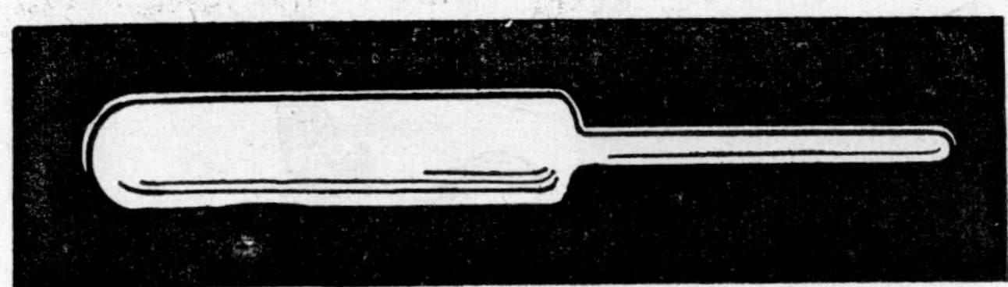

Fig. 1.—A malore made of steel or ivory is sometimes used for holding down the ribbon to prevent its twisting.

In making a stitch great care must be taken, first not to let the ribbon twist, secondly, not to pull the ribbon too tightly through, but to leave it slightly loose on the surface, just as a flower petal would look if thrown on to the material.

If a frame is used for working, some people like a "malore" which is the flat

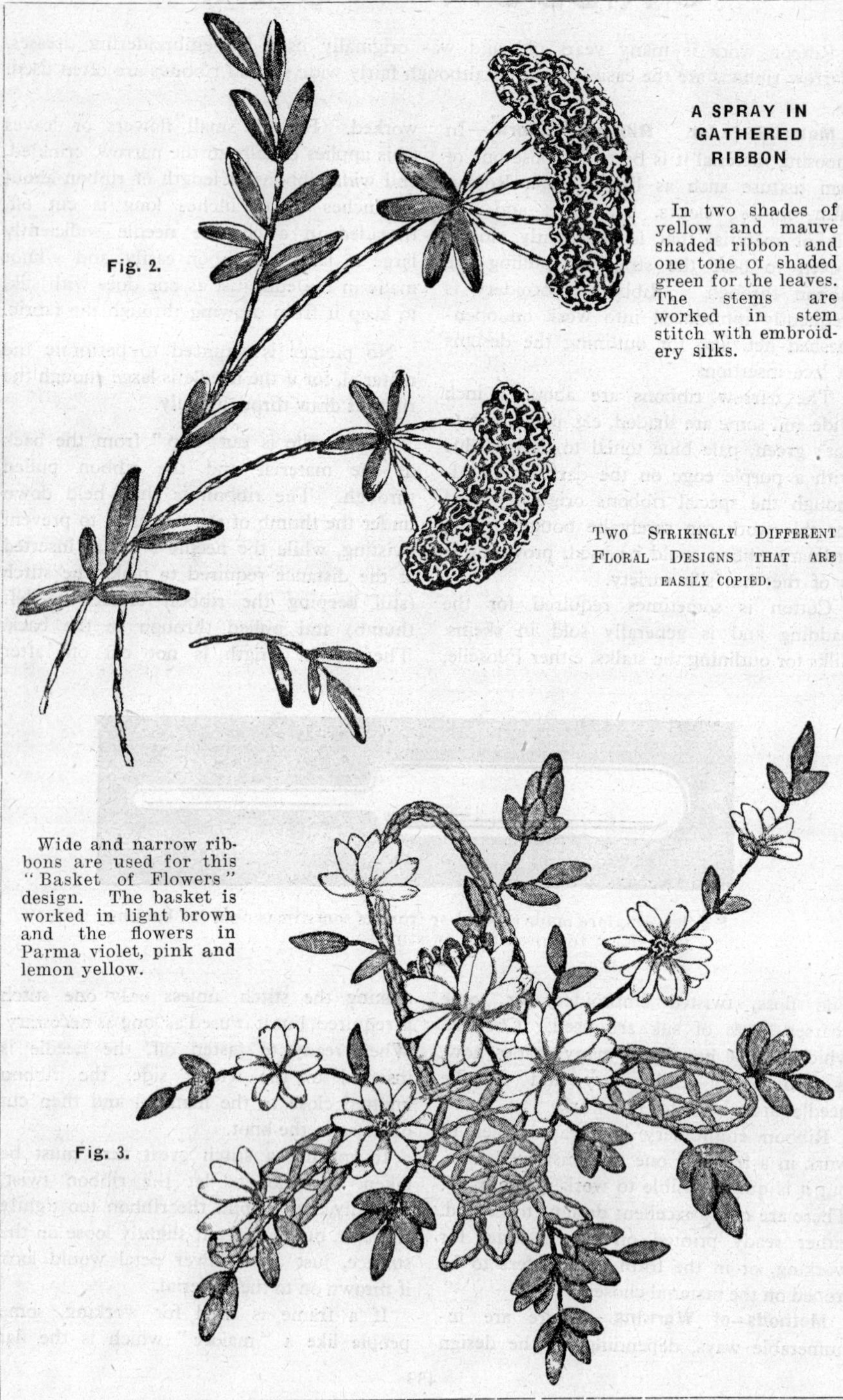

A SPRAY IN GATHERED RIBBON

In two shades of yellow and mauve shaded ribbon and one tone of shaded green for the leaves. The stems are worked in stem stitch with embroidery silks.

TWO STRIKINGLY DIFFERENT FLORAL DESIGNS THAT ARE EASILY COPIED.

Wide and narrow ribbons are used for this "Basket of Flowers" design. The basket is worked in light brown and the flowers in Parma violet, pink and lemon yellow.

steel or ivory instrument illustrated in Fig. 1 for holding down the ribbon to prevent it twisting, as the thumb is rather awkward on such a flat surface. A small pair of scissors, closed, is nearly as convenient. Either is used in the same way as the thumb, when working in the hand, to keep the ribbon stitch flat while the needleful is being drawn through.

Where an extreme surface is to be covered with wide ribbon, the stitches are taken lengthwise side by side, like satin-stitch in embroidery, only, of course, on a larger scale. If left like this the appearance would be a number of long stitches which would never keep in place, so after covering the design in ribbon stitches, with an embroidery needle threaded with silk to match the ribbon, take a number of tiny stitches at both the extreme edges of each of the ribbon stitches to secure them in position invisibly to the material ground. The ribbon between the two slip stitched edges is left slightly loose and full, so that when finished, the surface covered by the ribbon stitches presents almost a "fluted" appearance.

Sometimes both the narrow and the wide ribbons are first gathered along one edge with silk, then drawn up and sewn on by the gathered edge to the material to form rosettes or flowers. After sewing on sufficient for the gathered ribbon to cover the flower design, the ends of the ribbon are threaded in a needle and taken through to the back to make it neat. Crinkled ribbon is not satisfactory for gathering.

A Spray in Gathered Narrow Ribbon.—A most effective way is shown in Fig. 2 of using narrow ribbon after it has been gathered. *Materials required:* Two shades of yellow and mauve shaded ribbon for the flowers, and silk to match.

One tone of shaded green ribbon for the leaves.

To work the flowers: Take a piece of the lighter shade of mauve ribbon, and with a thread of silk to match, run along and gather one edge of the ribbon, then draw it up, and proceed to sew the gathered edge of the little "frill" on the outside line of the flower, taking this shade all round. Now take the second and deeper shade of mauve ribbon and gather up in the same manner, sew it on close to the first shade round and round towards the centre, until the whole flower is filled in. The yellow flower, in two shades, is worked in the same way, but can be varied by putting the darker shade outside and making the centre light. The leaves are worked as described before —one stitch for each leaf.

Basket Worked in Wide and Narrow Ribbons.—This is an excellent design for the ends of a table runner. The basket is worked in two shades of narrow shaded light brown ribbon, the handle, outlines and lines going across the basket being in the darker shade, and the cross bars between the lines in the lighter. The handle is worked in couching style, done by laying down one thread of the darker ribbon and fastening it across with a stitch of darker brown twisted floss. The stitches are taken across at intervals in slightly slanting directions (see illustration). A line of stem stitch in brown silk is put on either side of the ribbon, and the handle is complete. The basket itself is made by first working the cross bars between the horizontal lines. These consist of one stitch up and one stitch down. All these are worked in the lighter shade of brown. For the horizontal bars take the darker shade of ribbon and lay it down in the same way as the handle, tacking the stitches across with brown silk but instead of slanting the stitches, work them straight across the ribbon. This couching is used for all outlines.

The flowers are worked in three shades of Parma violet, pink, and lemon-yellow wide ribbons. The buds are worked with just two stitches taken from the stalk outwards (as explained before) in the colours of the flowers they belong to. Each calyx is made with three stitches of green ribbon. Before working in the ribbon, the flower petals are raised or padded underneath with a stitch of padding cotton. The large flower in the centre of the basket is worked in this way. First the five back petals are worked in the darkest shade of violet, the stitches being taken from the centre outwards. The petals on either side are in the second shade, which is distinct mauve, the centre petals being in the very lightest shade. The stamens are worked with one stitch of yellow Filoselle (taking three strands in the needle at a time) and making a French knot at the end of each stamen. The yellow flower is mauve, and one of palest green. In the pink flower the petals are worked as usual from the centre outwards, one stitch for each. Between each ribbon petal is a long stitch of pale pink twisted floss silk. The centres are made by gathering the ribbons up to form rosettes, one of the pink flowers having a bright yellow ribbon centre and

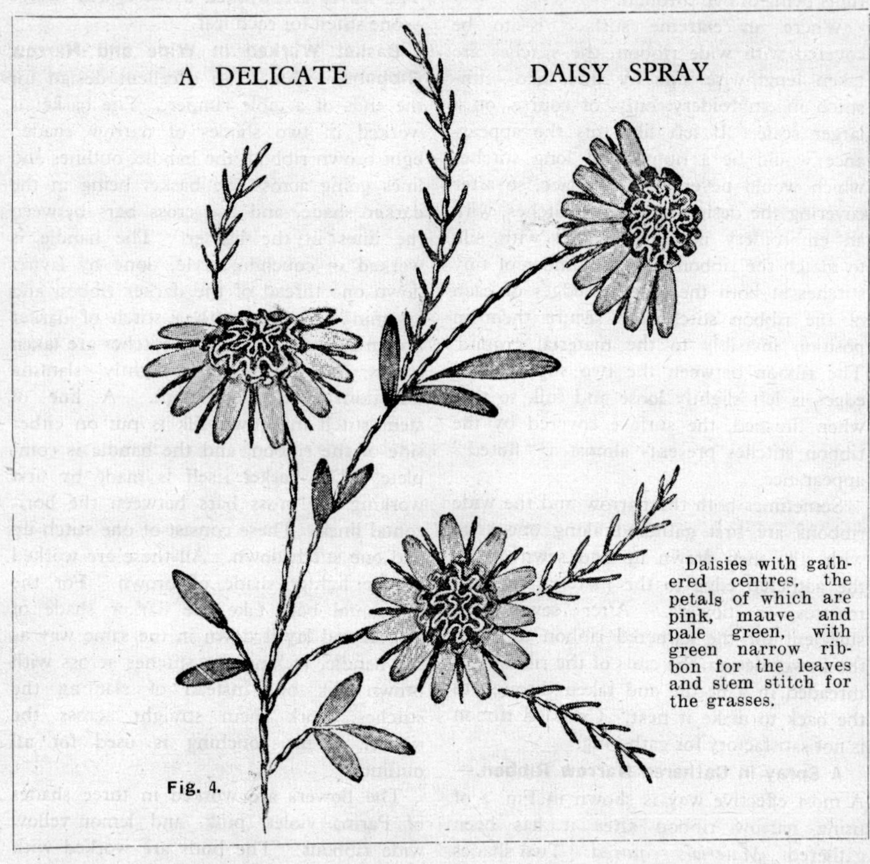

Daisies with gathered centres, the petals of which are pink, mauve and pale green, with green narrow ribbon for the leaves and stem stitch for the grasses.

Fig. 4.

worked in three shades and in the same way, with stamens of bright orange silk. The smaller flowers are worked in shades of flesh pink and have French knots in pale green silk as centres. The leaves are each worked with one stitch of ribbon and two shades only are used. The stalks are stem-stitched in yellow-green Filoselle.

Daisies with Gathered Centres—The petals of these are in one tone of shaded pink ribbon, one shade of pale the other a brownish one. The mauve daisy is done in the same way, only half the petals are mauve, and the other half pale green. A stitch of mauve twisted silk is taken between each petal and the centre is bright yellow gathered ribbon. The leaves are formed by one stitch of shaded green narrow ribbon and the stalks are stem stitch in one shade of green floss. The grass between the daisies is also in green floss silk and is worked in fine stem stitch. This spray could be used for almost any purpose, the colouring depending on the colours of the background.

Butterfly Worked in Wide Ribbon.—This can be worked in a variety of colours for many purposes. For book covers, handkerchief and glove sachets, and covering boxes it would be most effective. A screen panel showing a flight of butterflies would be charming.

The butterfly could be worked on pale green silk, with the large wings in wide ribbon shaded from pale yellow through across the tail, one stitch down the centre of the back, and two French knots for the eyes.

For the wings, take a thread of yellow shaded ribbon, and, starting at the side of the body, and at the top and widest part of the wing, bring the ribbon through, and then with another needle threaded with yellow silk, tack down the red edge of the ribbon on the outline of the wing. Put the ribbon through the outside edge of the wing, and proceed like this four more times, till the whole wing is covered. The red

GAY AND COLOURFUL IN WIDE RIBBON

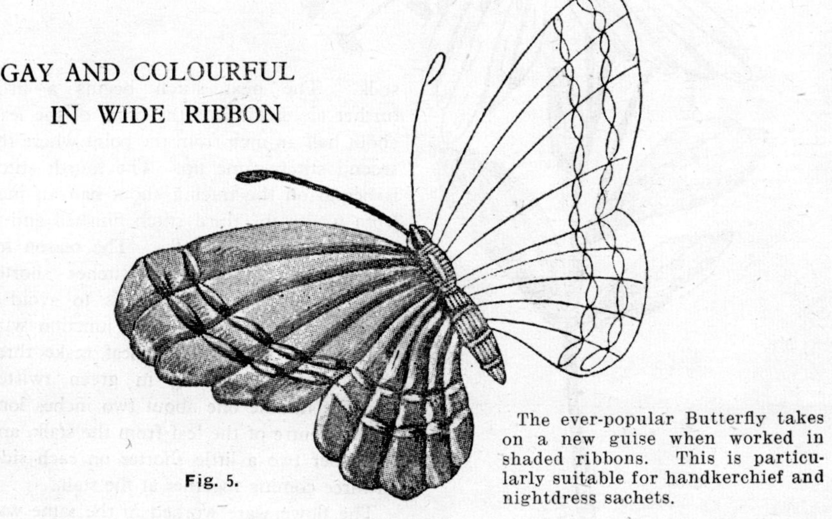

Fig. 5.

The ever-popular Butterfly takes on a new guise when worked in shaded ribbons. This is particularly suitable for handkerchief and nightdress sachets.

orange to red. The lines across the large wings are in narrow shaded yellow ribbon. The body is in a medium tone of fawn twisted silk touched up with black. First, the body must be padded. With a thread of padding cotton work across from the end of the tail to where it joins the body, then take two or three stitches from the head in the direction of the tail to pad the body. The head is not padded. With a thread of fawn silk work in satin stitches, being careful to cover the padding completely. The body and head are both worked across in satin stitch and the fawn silk is used for the antennæ, which are stem stitched, and the ends worked a little thicker. Next, with a thread of black silk make four bars edge of the ribbon must, in each stitch, be uppermost and must very slightly overlap the yellow edge of the previous stitch. Next with the narrow red ribbon make one stitch across each division, about half an inch from the outside edge of the wing. (Do not draw these stitches too tightly or they will flatten down the wide ribbon stitches.) Make a second row of narrow ribbon stitches exactly similar about half an inch nearer the body. The under wing is worked in the same way only in rose-red, with yellow narrow ribbon stitches across it. The wings on the other side are worked similarly.

Tiger Lily Spray is a bold and handsome design for a firescreen. It is worked on

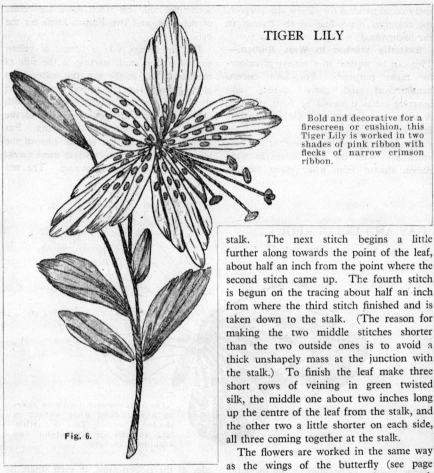

Fig. 6.

TIGER LILY

Bold and decorative for a firescreen or cushion, this Tiger Lily is worked in two shades of pink ribbon with flecks of narrow crimson ribbon.

pale pink ribbed silk, the lily being in two shades of shaded pink wide ribbon, and the leaves in green shaded from palest to dark green. The largest leaf (see illustration) serves as an example for the mode of working. It is made with four long stitches of ribbon.

Begin with the leaf on the lower edge and bring the needle through at the stalk, sew the edge of the ribbon down (with another needle threaded with one thread of green Filoselle) along the traced line. Put the ribbon back again, and bring up the next stitch at the point of the leaf, sew down the ribbon to overlap the stitch before, to about three quarters of the way back, towards the stalk. The next stitch begins a little further along towards the point of the leaf, about half an inch from the point where the second stitch came up. The fourth stitch is begun on the tracing about half an inch from where the third stitch finished and is taken down to the stalk. (The reason for making the two middle stitches shorter than the two outside ones is to avoid a thick unshapely mass at the junction with the stalk.) To finish the leaf make three short rows of veining in green twisted silk, the middle one about two inches long up the centre of the leaf from the stalk, and the other two a little shorter on each side, all three coming together at the stalk.

The flowers are worked in the same way as the wings of the butterfly (see page 437). There are two wide ribbons used, one shaded from light to dark pink, the other from pink through white to pale green. This last is used for the two lower petals, and the first for the three upper ones. In this flower a great deal depends on the way the ribbon is used and which edge is uppermost. Starting at the right lower petal take a needleful of the greeny pink ribbon and begin by putting the needle up in the centre of the flower, and sew down the green edge of the ribbon about three-quarters of the way along the lower edge of the petal. Put the ribbon back and begin the next stitch about half an inch further along towards the point. Now sew down the green edge again over the pink edge of the stitch before, so that hardly any pink shows. Put the ribbon back about an inch from the centre. Begin the third stitch about half an inch nearer the centre than the second finished stitch, and take it to the point of the petal, again keeping the green edge uppermost.

The appearance of this petal is now more green than pink. Now put the needle through quite close to the point where the last stitch finished, and still keeping the ribbon with the green edge uppermost, fill up the outer half of the petal in the same manner, making the length of stitches to correspond with those in the first half. The pink edge should be the one outside in the last stitch, which makes the top half of the petal appear more pink than green, and the whole looking as if it were shaded from pink at the upper edge down to green at the lower. If the ribbon is allowed to twist the whole effect will be spoiled. All the petals are worked in the same way, whether they are in pink and green or just pink. In the pink shaded ribbon the palest edge is kept to the top of the petal. The little dark marks on each petal are made by short stitches in narrow shaded crimson ribbon. These stitches are less than a quarter of an inch long, and are worked at intervals in the direction from the point to the centre of the petal.

The tops of the stamens, of which there are four, are worked in two stitches of plain yellow narrow ribbon in the direction shown in illustration. The pistil in the centre is composed of three stitches of the same yellow ribbon, making a short trefoil. This and the stamens are all touched up with two stitches of dark brown twisted silk, and the stamens are worked in two threads of bright green Filoselle. The stalks of the flower are worked in satin stitch with a middle shade of green twisted silk. The stitches in the stalks are worked in a slightly sloping direction, and not quite straight across, as it gives them a better appearance. One stitch of shaded green narrow ribbon forms each leaf.

Californian Poppy.—The ground is pale green *moiré,* the poppies shaded from palest yellow through pink to a reddish orange, with touches of mauve introduced. The

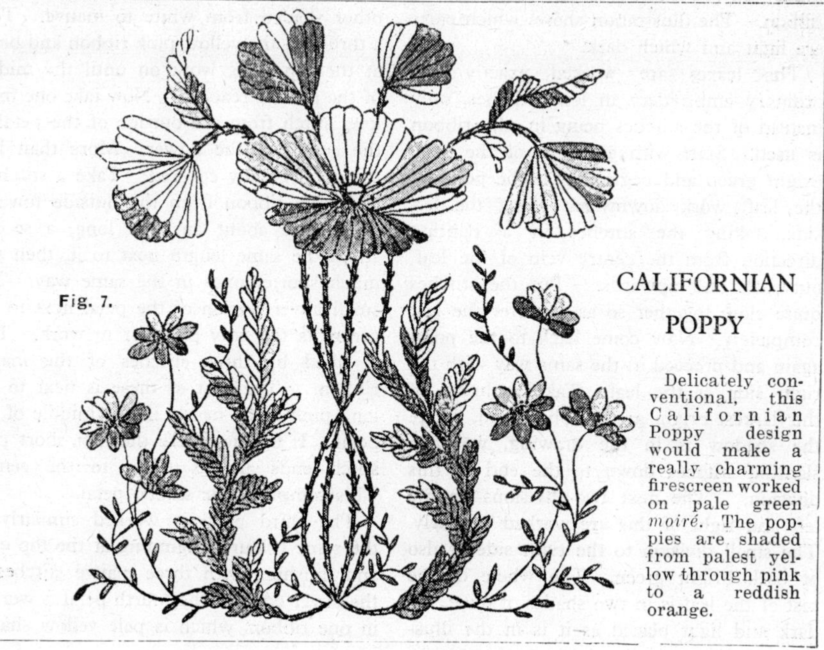

Fig. 7.

CALIFORNIAN POPPY

Delicately conventional, this Californian Poppy design would make a really charming firescreen worked on pale green *moiré*. The poppies are shaded from palest yellow through pink to a reddish orange.

centre of the flower is green silk. Some of the leaves are clear bright green, others olive. The large daisies at the base are in shades of pink and red ribbon with yellow silk centres. The thick poppy stalks are in ribbon with the little hairs on either side worked in green silk.

The daisy leaves have one long ribbon stitch each in olive shaded ribbon, their stalks being of stem stitch in a darker olive twisted silk. The flowers are not padded and each petal is formed of two stitches. Three shades of wide ribbon are used, the palest a dull pink, the middle brighter pink, the darkest, red. Each flower is in two shades. The bud in the middle and darkest shades, the half-open flower in the lightest and middle shade, and the full-blown one in the middle and darkest. The flower centres in thick twisted gold silk are made with a row of French knots for the upper half, and a row of short vertical stitches finished at the base with a line of stem stitch for the lower half.

The poppy leaves: Take the leaf to the right, which begins half-way down the design and finishes at the base. The three top divisions are in bright green ribbon. The illustration shows which parts are light and which dark.

The leaves are worked exactly like ordinary embroidery in long stitches, only instead of the stitches being in silk, ribbon is used. Start with a thread of the pale, bright green and beginning at the point of the leaf, work downwards along the left side, taking the stitches in a slanting direction from the centre vein of the leaf, outwards and upwards. Put the stitches quite close together so as to cover the leaf completely. Now come back to the point again and proceed in the same way with the right side of the leaf. Take a thread of the darkest bright green ribbon, and, where the shadow is in the drawing, work in slanting stitches down to the end of this division. The next two divisions on the left and right of this are worked similarly. The small division to the right side is also of dark bright green. The whole of the rest of the leaf is in two shades of olive, the dark and light placed as it is in the illustration. With a thread of dark green twisted silk vein the leaves in stem stitch.

The two middle stalks of the poppies are in dark olive ribbon and are made with slanting stitches taken from left to right close together. Little stitches in the dark green twisted silk are made all up the stem on either side to suggest the hairs on the poppy stalk. The other stalks are in the same stitch but in dark green ribbon in which the leaves at the top, close to the buds, are also worked. For the centre poppy, number the petals, the middle top one being No. 1, the right-hand No. 2, the left No. 3, and the lowest No. 4. Petal No. 1 is worked exactly like the butterfly's wing, mentioned previously. The whole petal is worked in one ribbon, shaded from cream to pale yellow. Begin at the right edge of the petal and work towards the middle of it, and on to the left edge. All the stitches are taken down to the centre of the flower, none are left short as in the butterfly's wing, but as they come towards the centre they must overlap slightly to make the petal the correct shape.

Petal No. 2 is worked with two ribbons, one shaded from pale yellow to pink, the other shaded from white to mauve. Take a thread of the yellow-pink ribbon and begin at the top edge, work on until the middle of the petal is reached. Now take one more long stitch from the outside of the petal to the centre of the flower. More than half the petal is now covered. Take a stitch of the same ribbon from the outside towards the centre about an inch long, a second stitch the same length next to it, then two much shorter ones in the same way. The small lower section of the petal next to the centre is the only part left to work. This is filled by three stitches of the mauve ribbon. The first of these is next to the long pink stitch nearly in the middle of the petal. It begins where the first short pink stitch ends and is taken to the centre. This completes the second petal.

The third petal is worked similarly in the same colours, beginning at the top edge and finishing with three mauve stitches at the lower edge. The fourth petal is worked in one ribbon, which is pale yellow shaded to reddish orange. Begin at the right side and take most of the stitches to the centre of the flower, with a few stitches only three-quarters of the way, to keep the shape of the petal. The centre of the flower is worked in two shades of green twisted silk. First work the top half of the centre in light green by putting a few horizontal stitches across these in the opposite direction like satin stitch. Now do the lower half in exactly the same way. Take a thread of dark green silk and make three stitches across the top half of the middle and then outline the whole of the centre in stem-stitch in the same colour. The stamens are made by putting stitches about half an inch to an inch long, like rays from the centre, and working a French knot at the end of each. This completes the wide-open flower.

The two half-open flowers are worked in exactly the same way as the petals of the centre one, but the colours are different. The flower to the right of the centre has three stitches of the yellowy pink ribbon at the top edge. Next come four stitches of the mauve, two long stitches of the cream to yellow, and five short stitches of the same at the edge of the flower, the rest being in mauve. The left-hand flower has, first, four stitches of the cream to yellow at the top edge, the centre mauve, and the cream to yellow ribbon for the other side. This flower has a petal as if coming from the back and this is made by short stitches of the yellowy pink ribbon. The two buds are worked the same way, that on the right having the centre in the yellowy pink ribbon, with mauve on either side. The left hand has a mauve middle with the yellowy pink ribbon on each side. This completes the design.

SPRING BLOSSOMS

An example of China Ribbon Embroidery that is well over a hundred years old. Worked on black satin in pink, white, amber, blue and crimson it makes a strikingly vivid design.

Fig. 8.

China Ribbon Embroidery.—Ancient designs in this kind of work were floral and of the Renaissance style. The most suitable patterns are those that introduce flowers of the forget-me-not size, small roses and bluebells.

The design given here is over a hundred years old. The foundation in the original was black satin. The spray to the top left-hand corner was formed of pink and white ribbons, the large flower of amber-shaded ribbon, with buds of a darker shade, and the small bunch of flowers beneath it, were blue with yellow centres. The rose was formed of crimson ribbon closely gathered and run on to the background in circles, so that the overlapping edges of the ribbon stood out from the material in a thick round mass. The two petalled flowers above it were rose colour and the four petal flowers beneath were pink with white centres, and the leaves throughout were of shaded green ribbon. All the stems, rose thorns, and other parts too fine for the ribbon, were worked in rich green silk.

RICHELIEU EMBROIDERY

Richelieu embroidery has existed for many hundreds of years and was at the height of its popularity in about the seventeenth century. Italy was the country where it was most extensively practised.

Originally this form of embroidery came into the class of linen work, and consisted simply of large designs outlined in buttonhole stitch, with the background cut away. The designs or motifs most used originally were scrolls, conventional flowers and leaves, and later, animals and birds such as the griffin and eagle.

Richelieu embroidery was most generally used in what at first appear to be two entirely different spheres—the peasantry and the clergy. But this is accounted for by the fact that the peasants were the craftsmen and devoted a great deal of their time and skill to making and embroidering vestments for the clergy.

This is one of the most effective and easily worked embroideries. It is strong and washes well and is usually worked on linen, but may be used for lingerie worked on crêpe de Chine.

It is used for dresses, handkerchiefs, household linen, cushions, bedspreads, curtains, all of which may be decorated with this stitchery in a suitable degree of coarseness or fineness.

Threads for working should be chosen according to the material used. Linen thread and mercerised twisted embroidery thread can be used on linen. Broriche is good for crêpe de Chine. The size of the needle depends on the coarseness of the thread, as both must be drawn easily through the material. A sharp pair of scissors is also necessary.

The Stitch used in Richelieu is principally buttonhole stitch, which requires practice to gain the perfect evenness which is the chief beauty of this work. The buttonholing should always be worked with the purl edge as the outside edge. When working this stitch place the stitches so that they lie side by side and perfectly evenly. Also, the thread should not be pulled too tightly. Always work from left to right.

Where no bars are included in the pattern the embroidery starts by first outlining the design with running stitches (Fig. 1), for which a somewhat stronger thread may be used.

Bars, when they occur, should always be worked first. Run a few stitches along the outline, take one or more threads across and finish the bar either by overcasting or buttonholing it, as shown in Figs. 2 and 3. Where the bars are to cover large spaces, two, four or six threads should be taken across according to the thickness required, and then darned (Fig. 4).

Fig. 1.
OUTLINING THE DESIGN

Fig. 2.
TWISTED BARS

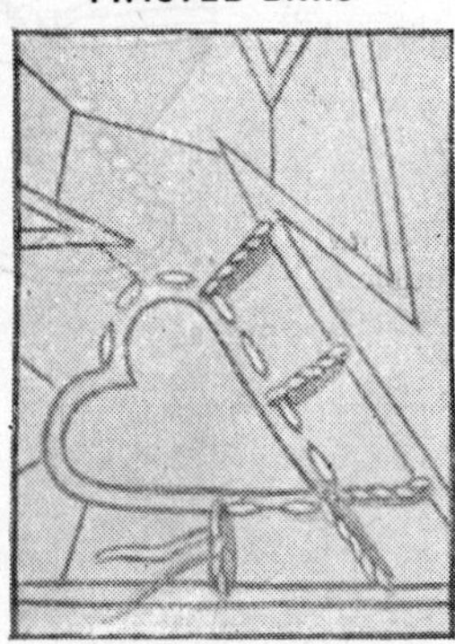

Fig. 3.
BUTTONHOLING A BAR

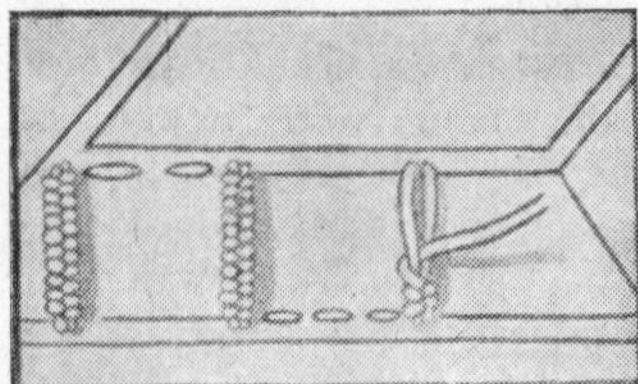

Fig. 4. DARNING A BAR

Fig. 6. TWISTED BARS WITH SPIDERS

Fig. 5.—THREEFOLD OR BRANCHED BAR

To Work a Branched Buttonhole Bar (Fig. 5) proceed as follows: Draw a thread rather loosely across from one edge to the other, buttonhole half of it, then carry a thread over to the opposite edge and buttonhole stitch back to starting-point.

To Work Twisted Bars with Spiders. See Fig. 6.

Picot Bars give an attractive finish as shown in Figs. 7, 8 and 9.

To work Fig. 7 catch down a short loop of thread with a pin and continue buttonholing. Remove the pin when the bar is complete.

For a Buttonholed Picot (Fig. 8) form a loop round the tightly held auxiliary thread "A," work two or three buttonhole stitches round this and bring the thread from the point of the solid little picot back to the bar. Remove the auxiliary thread.

To make a Double Picot as shown in Fig. 9, the thread is twisted round a pin to form a double loop, then the buttonholing is continued.

Bullion Picot is another variation. Fig. 10 shows clearly the method of working.

In buttonholing some of the longer bars, picots help to break the line. When the middle of the bar is reached, pass the needle up through the last buttonhole stitch made to about two-thirds of its length, holding the needle in place with the right thumb, and with the left hand, twist the thread ten times over and round the needle from left to right, pushing the twists towards the eye of the needle, but still keeping the right thumb on them. Draw the needle through with the left hand until the thread can be felt pulling under the thumb. Then remove thumb and draw the needle through.

Fig. 10.

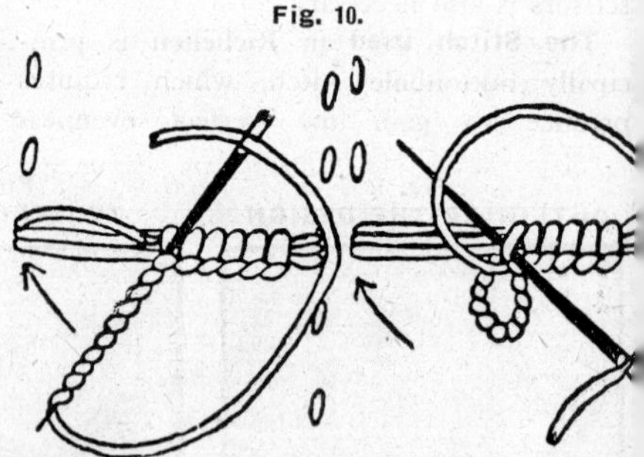

On the right are bullion bars in the making and below three kinds of picots—simple, auxiliary and double.

Fig. 7.

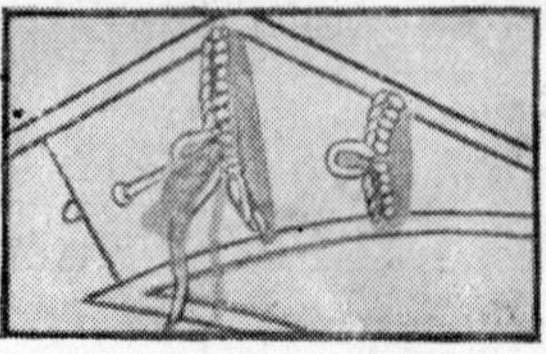

Fig. 8.

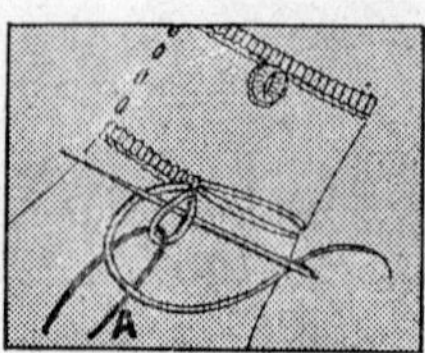

Fig. 9.

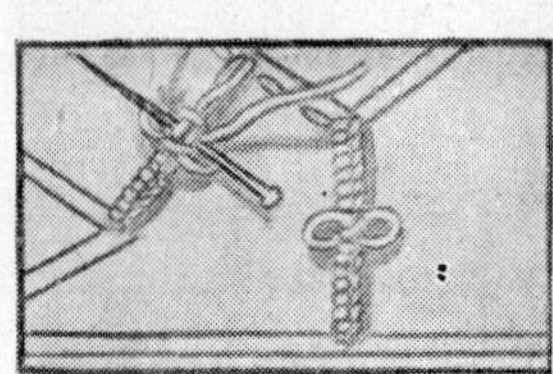

Pass the needle up from below through the last buttonhole stitch, draw it through and continue straightforward buttonholing to the end of the bar.

Crossbars and Branched Bars.—Figs. 11-15 show the stages of working. Lay three threads across from A to B starting at A. Fill a fourth of the bar threads with buttonhole stitches and make a picot as already described then work on to the centre and lay branch threads to C (Fig. 11). Buttonhole back to the centre (making a picot half-way), pass the thread under three bar threads, and, inserting the needle in the material under the stitch at D, lay three bar threads from D to the centre (Fig. 12). Buttonhole back to the centre, making a picot half-way (Fig. 13), pass the needle under the bar thread of A-B, drawing it up between the last buttonhole stitch worked on them and the thread which was first laid from the centre to C, as seen clearly in Fig. 13.

Then insert the needle in the opposite direction under the three threads of A-B, but above the thread which passed from the buttonholing of C under the centre of D. Draw it up between the bar threads A-B and the last buttonhole stitch made when buttonholing from D back to the centre, as seen in Fig. 14. Then buttonhole and picot over the three remaining bar threads back to the starting-point (Fig. 15). To do this the buttonhole stitches must be worked from left to right, and for the picot the thread must be passed under and twisted from right to left on the needle or the work will not look uniform with the rest.

Branched bars consisting of three, five or even six "spokes" are laid and worked in the same way.

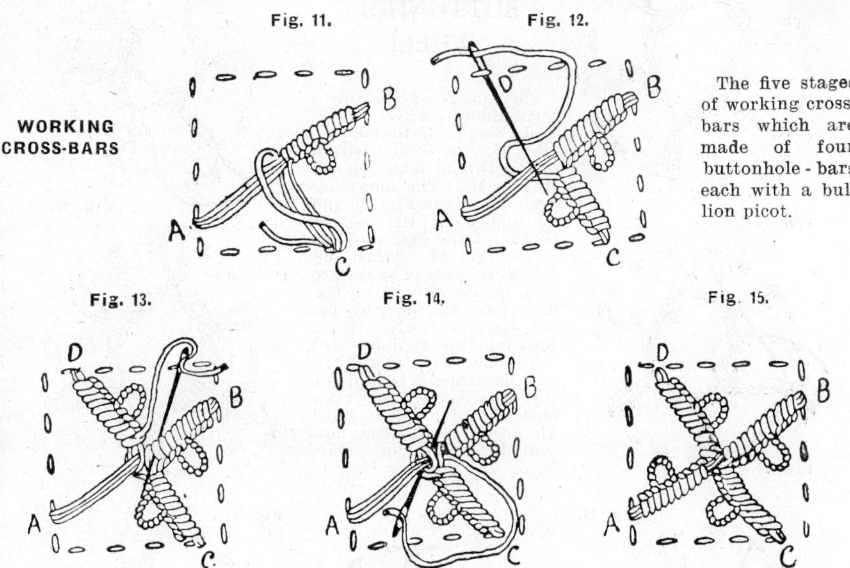

WORKING CROSS-BARS

The five stages of working cross-bars which are made of four buttonhole-bars each with a bullion picot.

A Buttonhole-wheel. — Figs. 16-25 show clearly how this is worked. The arrow on each of these diagrams shows the starting-point. This is useful as a centre filling for flowers. Two more fillings are shown in Figs. 26-29 and also in Figs. 30-35.

If durability is wanted, the buttonholed bar is stronger than the twisted bar. After all the bars have been made, the design should be outlined with one or two rows of running stitches, and where the outlines are far apart or a more raised effect is wanted, extra padding should be added

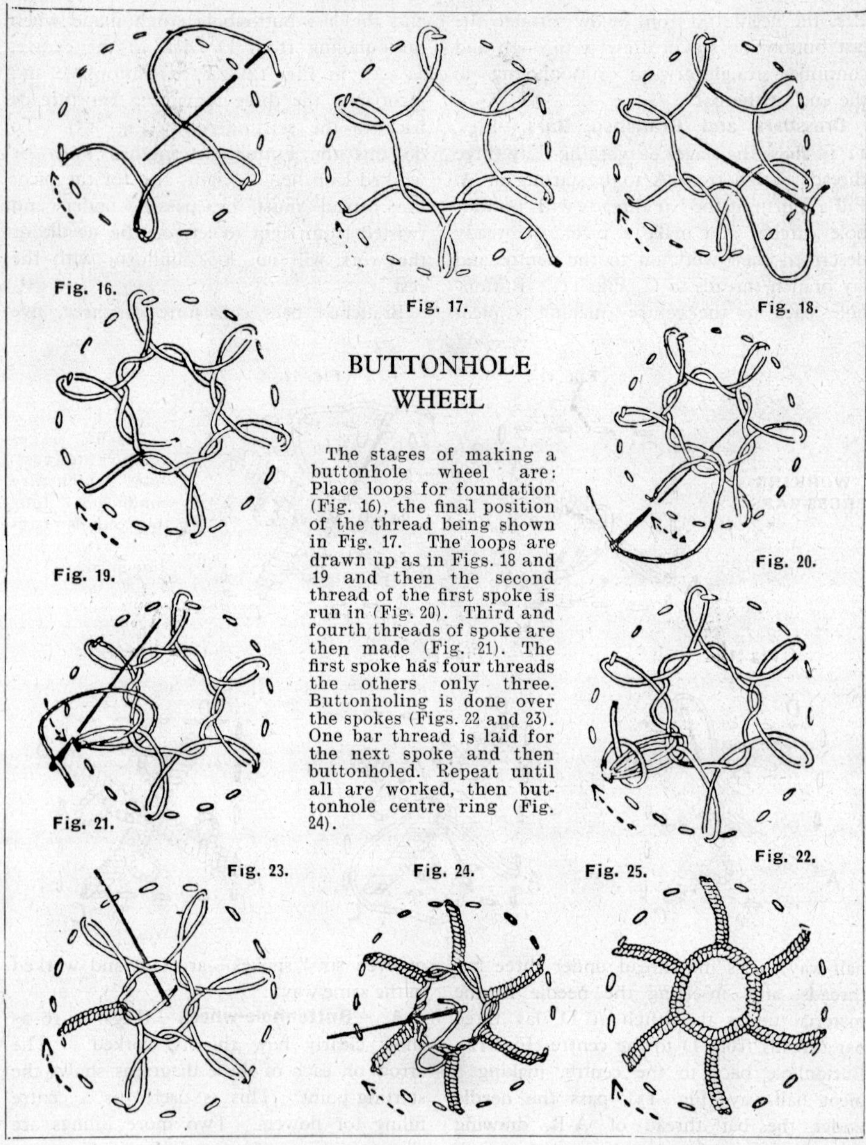

BUTTONHOLE WHEEL

The stages of making a buttonhole wheel are: Place loops for foundation (Fig. 16), the final position of the thread being shown in Fig. 17. The loops are drawn up as in Figs. 18 and 19 and then the second thread of the first spoke is run in (Fig. 20). Third and fourth threads of spoke are then made (Fig. 21). The first spoke has four threads the others only three. Buttonholing is done over the spokes (Figs. 22 and 23). One bar thread is laid for the next spoke and then buttonholed. Repeat until all are worked, then buttonhole centre ring (Fig. 24).

with chain stitches, care being taken not to pucker the material. Finally, all the outlining should be closely worked with buttonhole stitches, purl edge outwards, to make the material edges quite secure.

When all the embroidery is finished, the ground material can be cut away from the pattern. Cut carefully along the edges, avoiding any injury to the bars.

Work that has puckered during embroidery should be carefully stretched by pinning it on to a damp cloth, taking care to keep the work the correct shape.

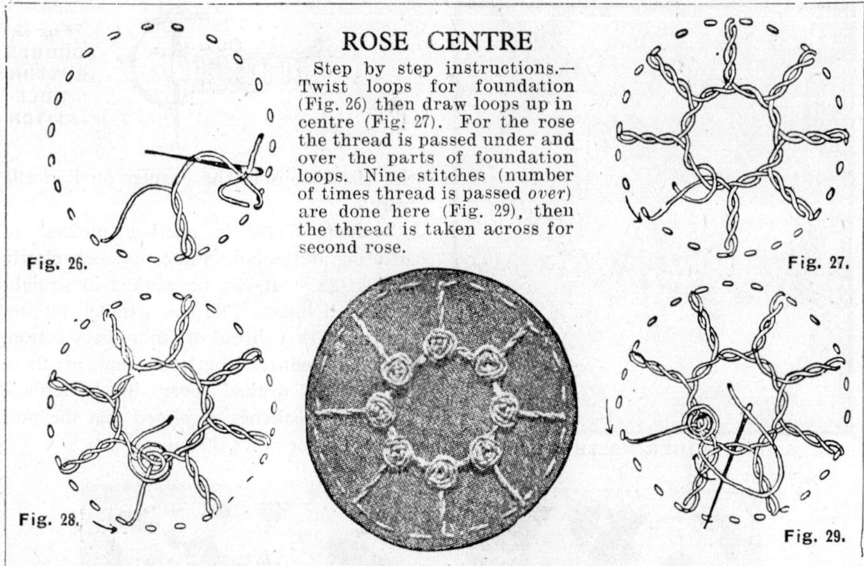

ROSE CENTRE

Step by step instructions.—Twist loops for foundation (Fig. 26) then draw loops up in centre (Fig. 27). For the rose the thread is passed under and over the parts of foundation loops. Nine stitches (number of times thread is passed *over*) are done here (Fig. 29), then the thread is taken across for second rose.

Fig. 26. **Fig. 27.** **Fig. 28.** **Fig. 29.**

Another damp cloth should then be laid on top of the work and left until dry.

Figs. 36 and 37 show the embroidering of the outline and the finished work with the ground partly cut away.

A Pomegranate d'Oyley in modern Richelieu work (Fig. 40). This d'oyley measures 6 inches across, and shows another use for buttonholing—double buttonhole stitchery (see the fruit

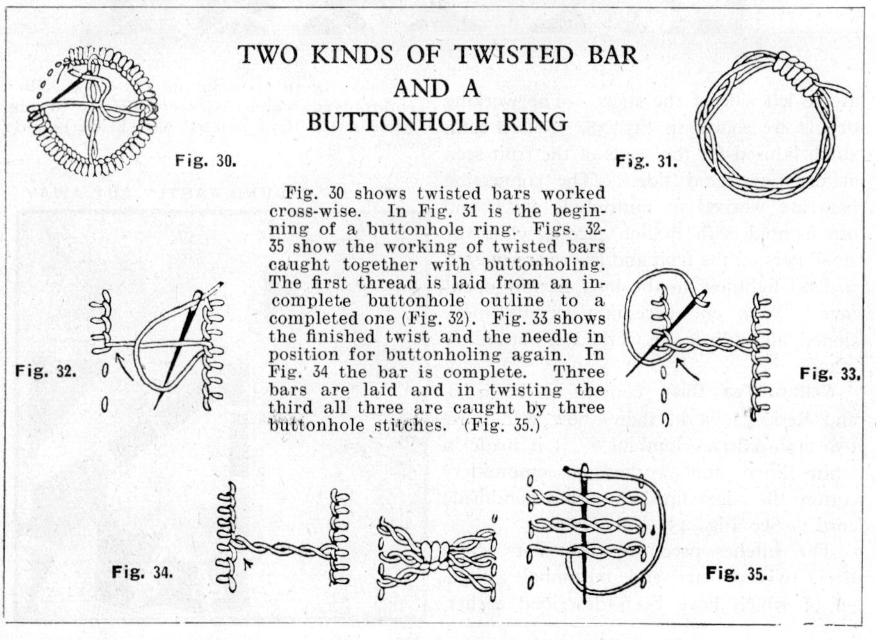

TWO KINDS OF TWISTED BAR AND A BUTTONHOLE RING

Fig. 30. **Fig. 31.**

Fig. 30 shows twisted bars worked cross-wise. In Fig. 31 is the beginning of a buttonhole ring. Figs. 32-35 show the working of twisted bars caught together with buttonholing. The first thread is laid from an incomplete buttonhole outline to a completed one (Fig. 32). Fig. 33 shows the finished twist and the needle in position for buttonholing again. In Fig. 34 the bar is complete. Three bars are laid and in twisting the third all three are caught by three buttonhole stitches. (Fig. 35.)

Fig. 32. **Fig. 33.** **Fig. 34.** **Fig. 35.**

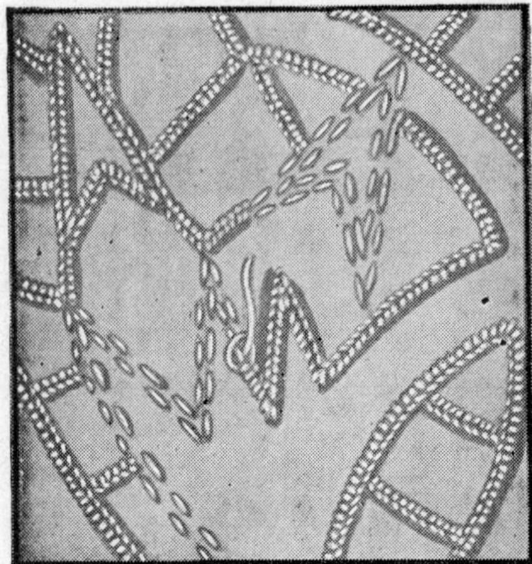

Fig. 36. EMBROIDERING THE OUTLINES

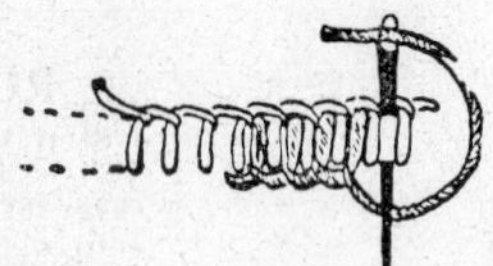

Fig. 38. DOUBLE BUTTON-HOLE STITCH

See also details in the chapter on Reticella work.

Ladder Work is another method of adapting buttonhole stitch, as seen clearly in Fig. 42. It can be worked in straight or curved lines. The two parallel outlines are run with a thread of embroidery cotton, then the entire length of one of these threads is worked over in buttonhole stitch, with stitches so placed that the purl edge faces the other thread.

Fig. 39.

Above, is an excellent design in Richelieu embroidery which is very simple to embroider, the light twisted bars being quickly worked.

at the left side of the stalk). The working details are shown in Fig. 38. Raised satin stitch is used for the seeds of the fruit seen at the right-hand side. The connecting bars are worked in buttonhole stitch and ornamented with bullion picots, while the small bars on the fruit and leaves are twisted to lend lightness to the long narrow openings. With one exception already mentioned, all outlines are worked in buttonhole stitch.

Griffin Tea Cosy combining Richelieu and Reticella work, shows how well those two embroideries combine. It is made in white linen and worked in embroidery cotton, the edges finished with a handmade cord. (See Fig. 45).

The stitches used are picot bars, cross bars, twisted bars and buttonhole stitch, all of which have been described earlier.

Fig. 37.—GROUND PARTLY CUT AWAY

Buttonhole the other thread for ¼ inch making the purl edge face the first line of stitches worked. Lay three bar threads across for the first rung as shown in Fig. 42, but do not twist them. Simply catch them into a stitch exactly opposite the last one made, on a second line of buttonhole stitches being worked.

Buttonhole over these threads (not catching the linen) back to the second side. Pass the needle up through the last stitch worked before the rung was started (see illustration). Again work along the second side of the ladder for ¼ inch and work another rung as before. Continue working until the ladder is complete.

The long lines at each side are worked into the linen but not the rungs or bars. Cut away the material underneath the rungs quite close to the buttonholed edges or sides.

The Uses of Ladder Work.—Seams which would otherwise be unsightly may be joined in this way, or an extra fold of material may be added to a child's sleeve or skirt to lengthen it. It forms a decoration round a tray cloth in either straight or curved lines.

The size of the thread, the width of the ladder and the distance between the rungs should be decided according to the material chosen, and the purpose for which it is to be used.

Fig. 40.

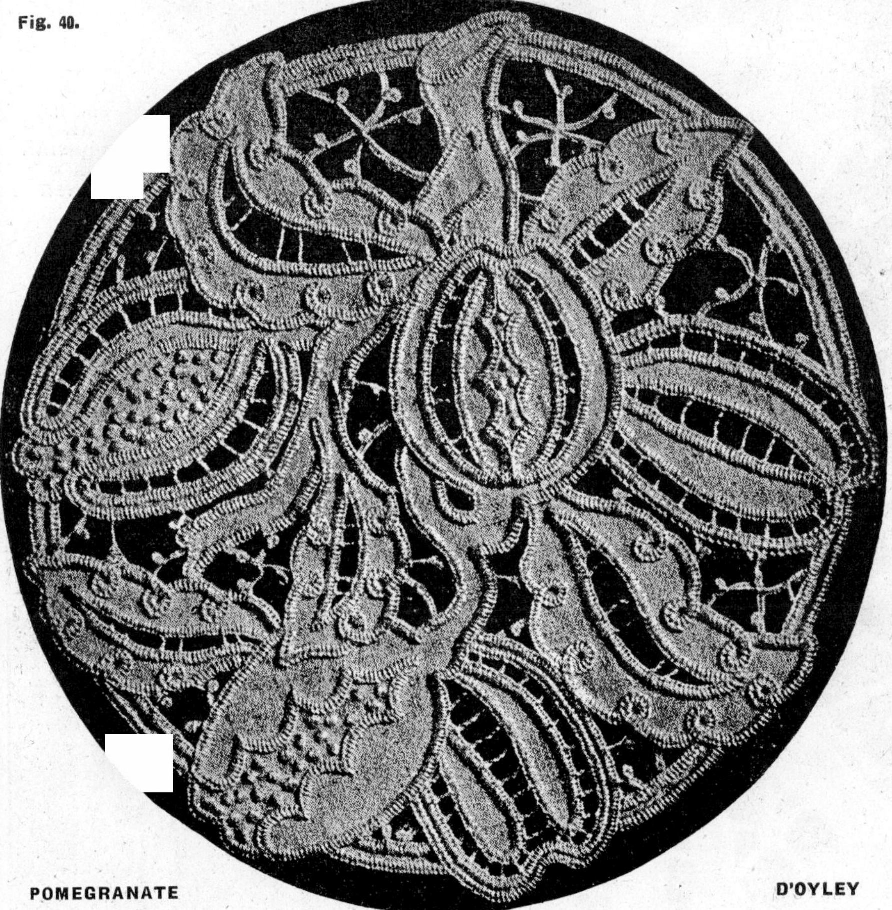

POMEGRANATE D'OYLEY

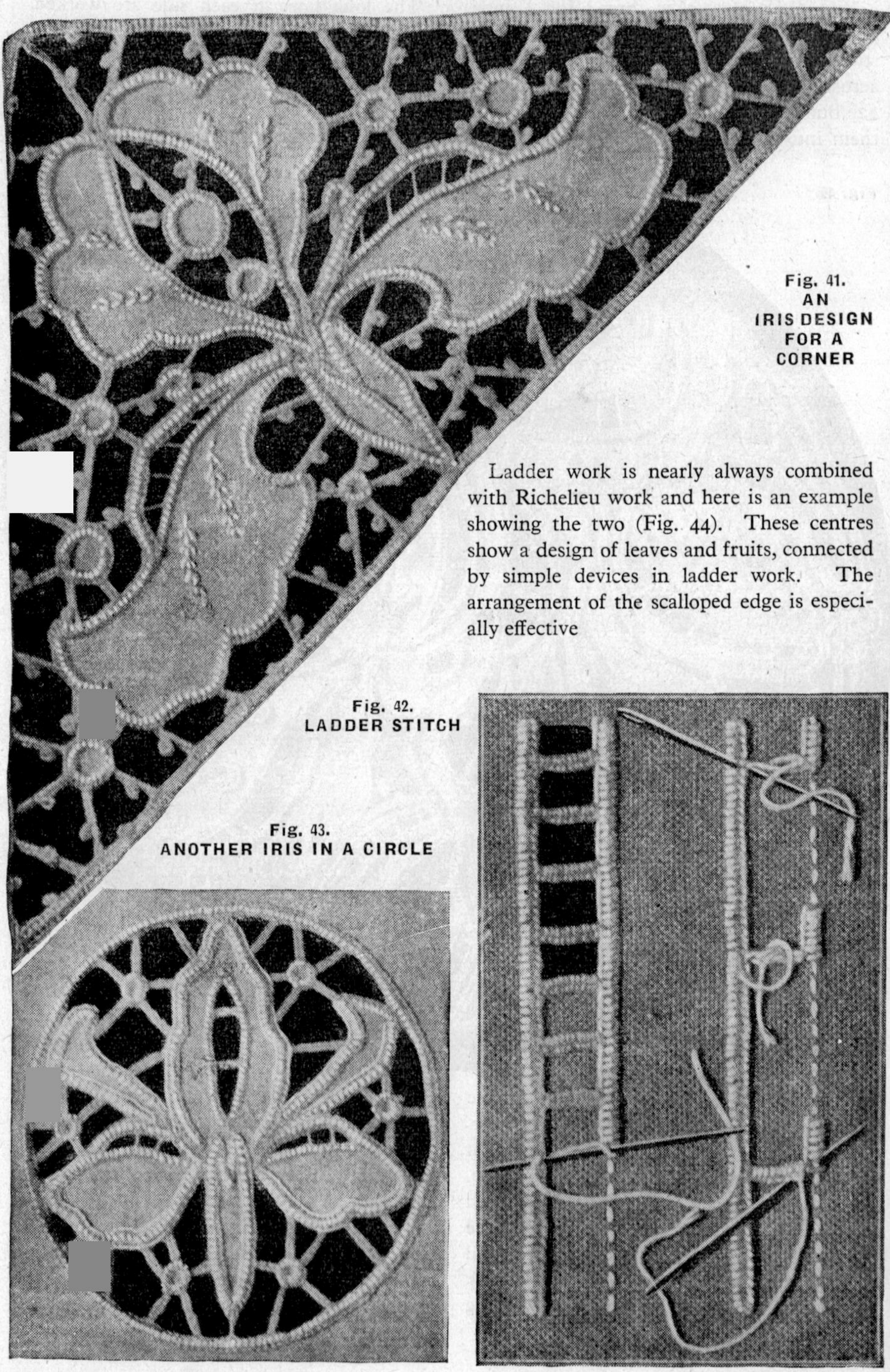

Fig. 41.
AN
IRIS DESIGN
FOR A
CORNER

Ladder work is nearly always combined with Richelieu work and here is an example showing the two (Fig. 44). These centres show a design of leaves and fruits, connected by simple devices in ladder work. The arrangement of the scalloped edge is especially effective

Fig. 42.
LADDER STITCH

Fig. 43.
ANOTHER IRIS IN A CIRCLE

Fig. 44.—Ladder work is at its best in these designs, the dainty tracery of bars making an effective, lace-like background to the design.

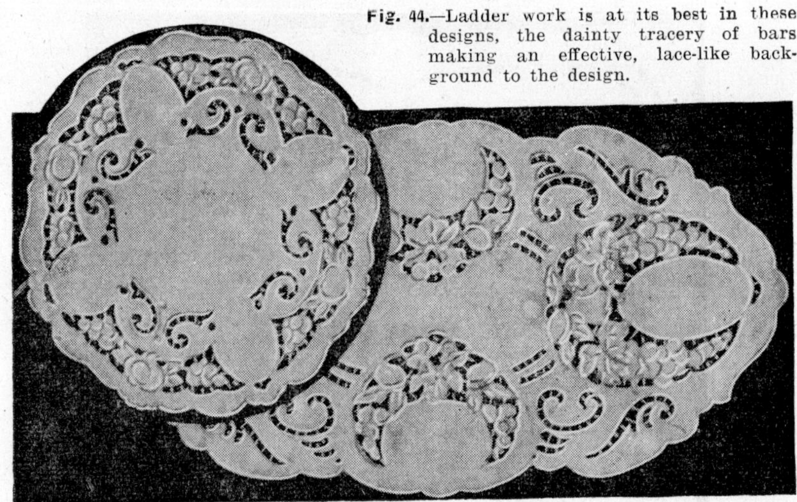

Fig. 46 shows a cloth with a Richelieu centre and ladder-work border. This elaborate design shows a clever arrangement of many buttonholed bars forming

Fig. 45.

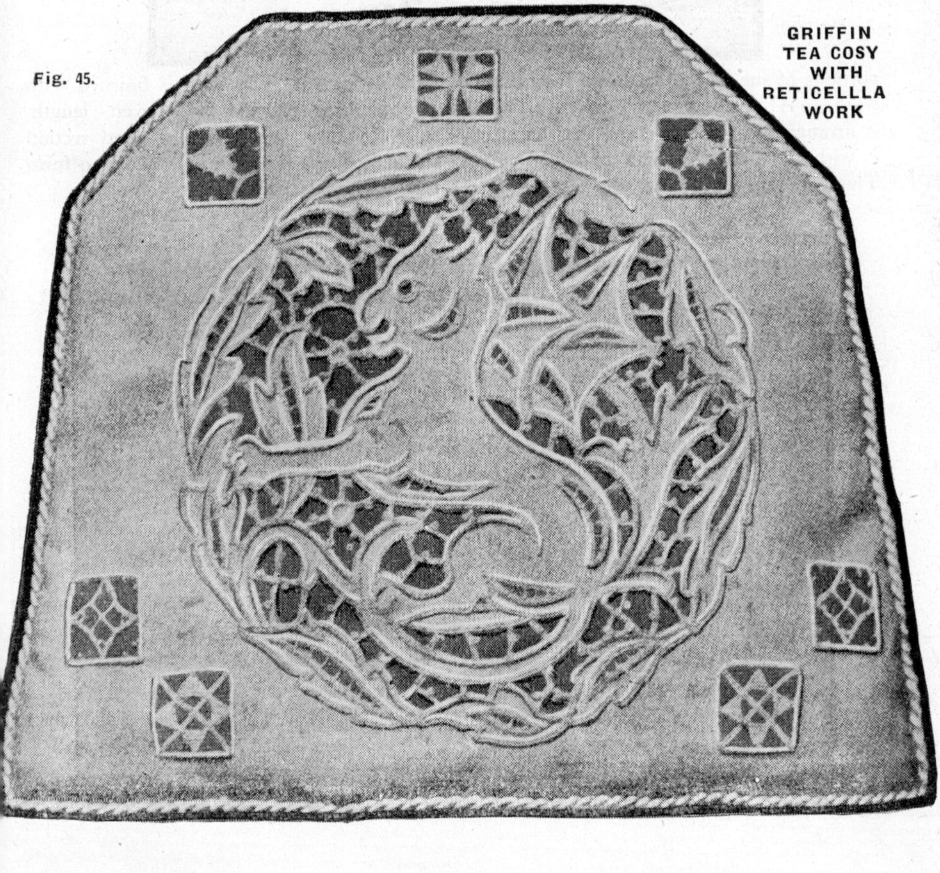

GRIFFIN TEA COSY WITH RETICELLLA WORK

Fig. 46.

portions of the design and also the groundwork. A scroll pattern in satin stitch is arranged round the centre and connects it with the border design in ladder work. The bars in this border are worked with double picots. The cloth is finished with buttonholed scallops of uneven length. Fig. 47 shows an enlarged worked section of the centre. The centre would also form a handsome design for a cushion.

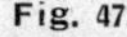

Fig. 47.

SHIRRING or ITALIAN SMOCKING

The peasants of Italy have always been extremely clever with their needles. Italian smocking, or Pattern shirring as it is often called, is a variety of smocking, in which the pattern is made in the preliminary gatherings, which are worked quite closely together and complete the design.

No transfer is needed for this work, but charts, showing the arrangement of the stitches, are used for the designs.

The gathering threads may be of the same colour as the material or of a contrasting shade. Material in narrow stripes of about $\frac{1}{8}$ of an inch wide is easier for a beginner as the stitches can then be regulated by the width of each stripe. Silk or muslin are the best materials to use.

Diamond and vandyke shapes must form the basis of all shirring designs, as it is technically impossible to make any other than those composed entirely of lines, either straight or slanting. The gathering is done in rows from right to left across the material, every two rows with one piece of thread. Thread a needle with a piece of thread twice the length of the design. Start on the right side of the material, at the right-hand top corner of the place where the band of shirring is to be worked. Make a line of small, even running stitches across to the top left-hand corner of the band, leaving one half of thread at the right side. Unthread the needle, rethread it with the other end and insert the needle directly under, and about $\frac{1}{8}$ of an inch below the point where it first entered the material. Then work a line of longer running stitches, each about $\frac{1}{8}$ of an inch long, across to the left-hand side again.

With another thread work a third line of gathering 1/16 inch below, picking up every alternate pleat. Work a 4th across as the 2nd, and repeat the 3rd and 4th rows to the end of the work, leaving the required number of pleats to form the pattern, as shown by the vertical lines in the charts.

The stitches in the last row (after the pattern has been completed) should be the same length as those in the first row, in order to regulate the fullness. As each two rows

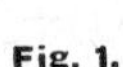

Fig. 1.

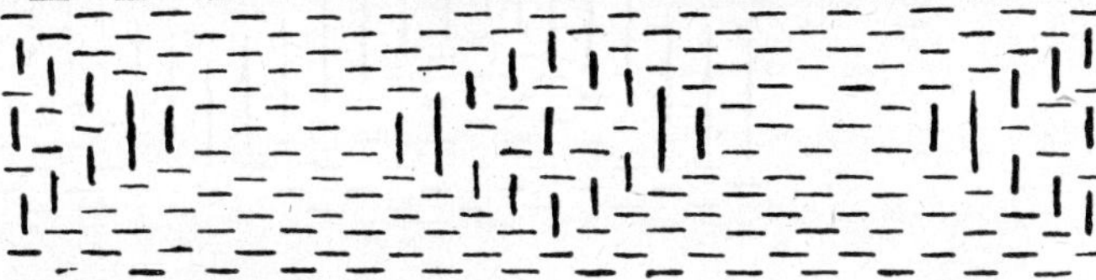

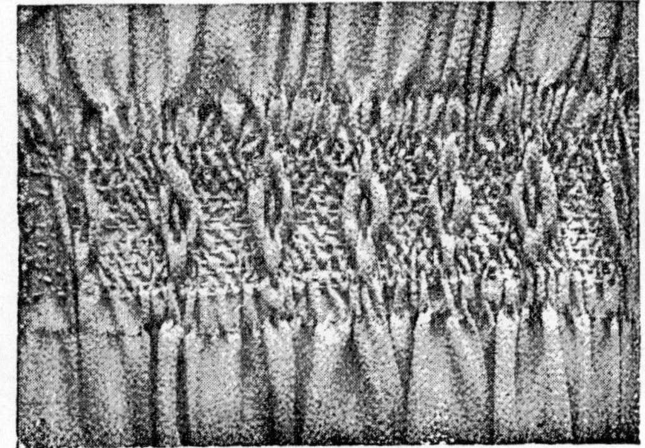

SIMPLE DIAMOND SHIRRING

This is a simple little pattern which would be particularly charming on a child's dress. The chart above shows clearly the arrangement of the stitches, the pattern being repeated any number of times.

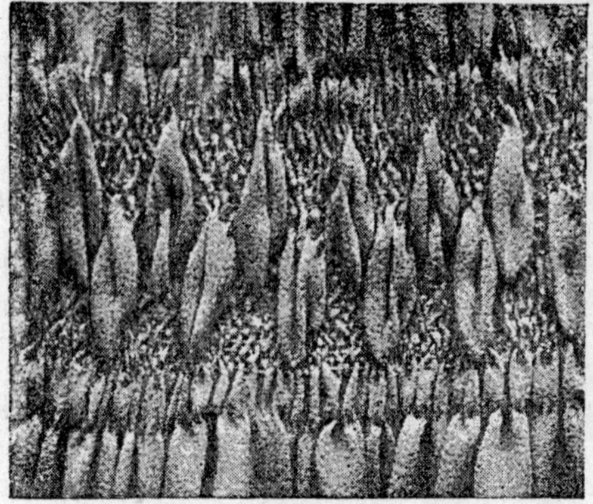

Fig. 2.—Above, is a good design, which stands out clearly. Below are charts for this and the design on the opposite page.

are completed, draw up the gathers and stroke the pleats, then release the thread. Then work the next two rows. Take the thread to the back of the work as each row is completed and, where necessary, make a half-stitch to bring the ends of the rows even. When all the gatherings are finished, draw up the thread, hold all the ends in a row along each end of the band, and overcast them to the material. Twisted embroidery silk, Filo floss or Filoselle are most suitable to use on silk, and washing cotton or cotton fabrics.

Simple Diamond Shirring, as seen in Fig. 1, is quite a simple pattern and makes a charming finish to a child's frock. The

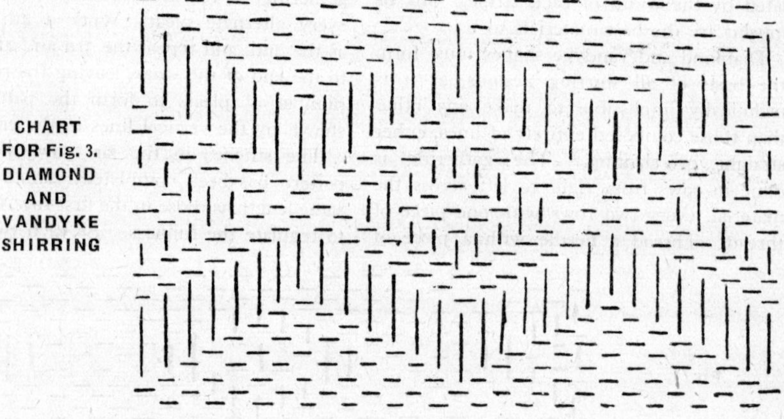

CHART FOR Fig. 3. DIAMOND AND VANDYKE SHIRRING

CHART FOR Fig. 2.—DOUBLE DIAMOND SHIRRING

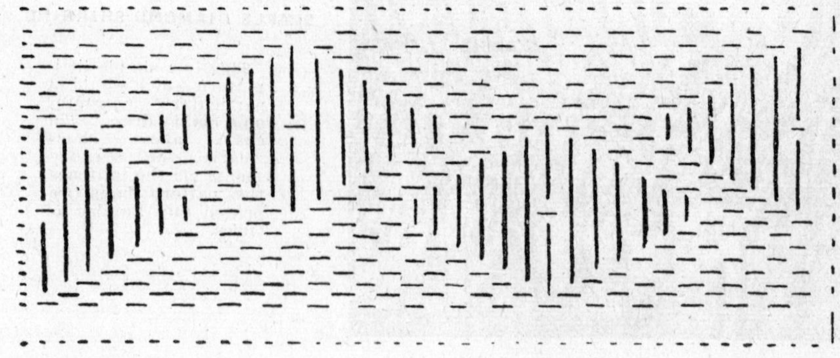

chart shows clearly the arrangement of the stitches and the pattern can be repeated any number of times, should a deeper band be required.

Double Diamond Shirring.—In this

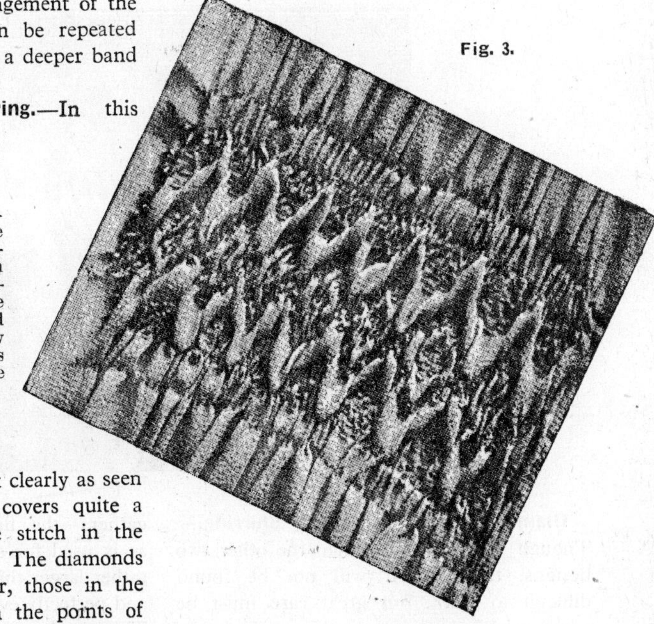

Fig. 3.

On the right is Diamond and Vandyke shirring—a more elaborate pattern for which a chart is given opposite. Below is a piece of shirring on spotted muslin, showing how the gathered portion is sewn to a plain bodice or yoke.

design the pattern stands out clearly as seen in Fig. 2. Each diamond covers quite a large space, with only one stitch in the centre to break the surface. The diamonds are grouped closely together, those in the 2nd row fitting in between the points of those in the 1st row.

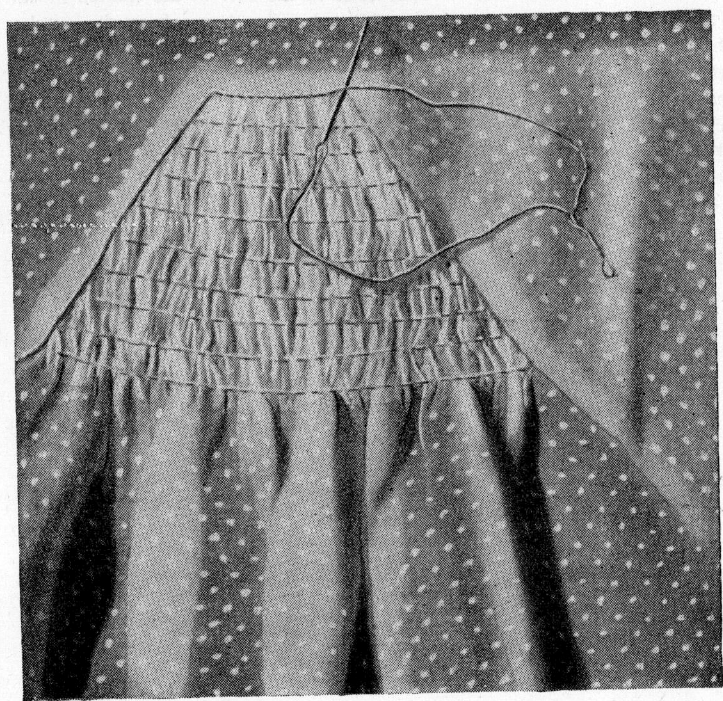

Fig. 4.

Simple shirring worked on a drawn thread voile.

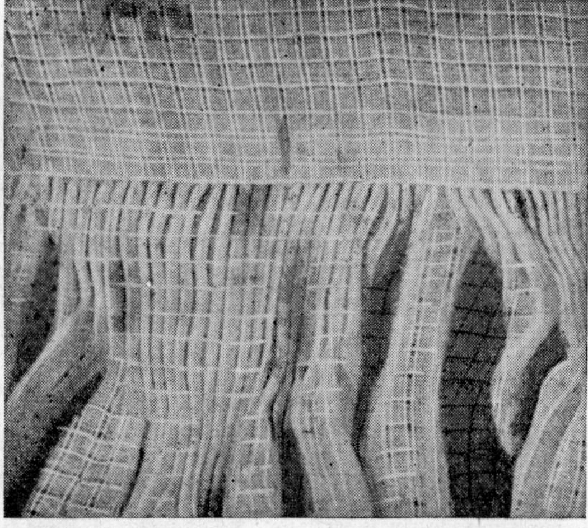

Fig. 5.

Diamond and Vandyke Shirring.—Though more elaborate than the other two designs, this pattern will not be found difficult to work, but great care must be taken in this, as in the others, to keep the gatherings even, or the whole effect will be marred when the threads are drawn up. The pattern should start and end with a complete vandyke, as in this way it is much easier to manipulate the turns at the right-hand end of the work. (Fig. 3).

Simple Shirring is a simplified version of the work described above and is more suitable for patterned materials than smocking.

There are two ways of running the gathers—the first, an even-stroked gather as is used for smocking, the stitches being rather larger than ordinary running stitches, and perfectly even one row below the other. This can be done by using a fine smocking paper, or in the case of the spotted muslin or checked voile shown here the stitches can be kept straight by the pattern (Fig. 5).

The second method of working does not require to be so exact—the lines of thread must run absolutely parallel, but the running stitches need only be approximately the same length. These, when drawn up, give a rougher but quite as decorative a surface. As shown in Fig. 4 the shirring is being set into a yoke with overcast stitch.

SILK SHADING

Silk shading is the art of painting with a needle. A well-known authority on art tells us that " there are no colours so pure as those of clouds and flowers ", so it is not surprising that flowers have always played a prominent part from the earliest embroideries. The art of shading, which really means the art of making shadows by carefully graduating the shades and at the same time keeping them in perspective, is explained here.

The whole idea of silk shading is to make the object look as life-like as possible. Painting with the needle is much harder than with the brush, therefore perspective must be carefully studied, otherwise a flat and uninteresting appearance will be gained. One thing to remember is that the part which projects most towards the worker under ordinary conditions, catches most light, and therefore is worked in the lightest shade of all. This is known as the high light. Shading is used to bring out firmness and distance, both of which are implied by the word "perspective".

Some people are quite satisfied, at first, to graduate the shades and to work the lights and darks without any definite scheme and are then surprised at the flat appearance obtained. Naturally the work does not stand out as it would have done had the rules of perspective been observed.

It is important to remember that before attempting to embroider a flower, special notice should be taken of the characteristics of that particular plant. Take every advantage of the shades and the varieties of colour, and aim at the good effect achieved by carefully placing the light and shade and keeping a good stitch direction. For instance, a leaf may appear to be only one shade to the casual observer, but if it is closely studied, it will be seen that the leaf is not entirely flat, but that the edges turn up or down slightly and in so doing the shade is changed and most likely a shadow cast. The centre may be slightly rounded and the highest part will catch the light. Do not be afraid of mixing shades as the result will be far more effective than if only one range of shades is used.

Materials required.—A very firm silk or satin makes a good background for silk shading. A fine linen can also be used, but whatever material is chosen it should be remembered that it must be without dressing, and firm. A dull material usually gives the best results.

Filo floss is one of the best silks to use as it can be bought in such wide ranges of colour and is stranded and soft.

It is a help when working a flower to have a real one, but this is not always possible. If one can study the growth and the blending of the colours it is so much easier. If this is not possible a good coloured print is a help.

Ordinary embroidery needles should be used with a large enough eye to avoid fraying the silk.

An ordinary embroidery frame is really necessary, but when working a small spray a tambour frame can be used. Two thimbles are also useful as they speed up the work. These should not be rough in any way as they will catch in the silk and spoil the effect of the work.

Stitches Used.—For the natural or soft blending of colours use long and short edge, coming up from the inside and going down on the outline. After the first row has been worked, bring the needle up about half-way through the stitches just made. All the stitches are of equal length, but alternate in position, so that they appear long and short.

There are one or two examples on the next page showing the outside edge or long and short, and the split edge. In the leaf the outside edge is used, but for the orange and the bird a split edge is used, so that there is a soft line round the curves. For a turnover, work the stitches in exactly the reverse way from the flat.

For a beginner it is quite a good plan to get the direction of the stitch for the turnover of the leaf or petal by tracing the shape on to the piece of tracing paper, then drawing in the direction of the stitches.

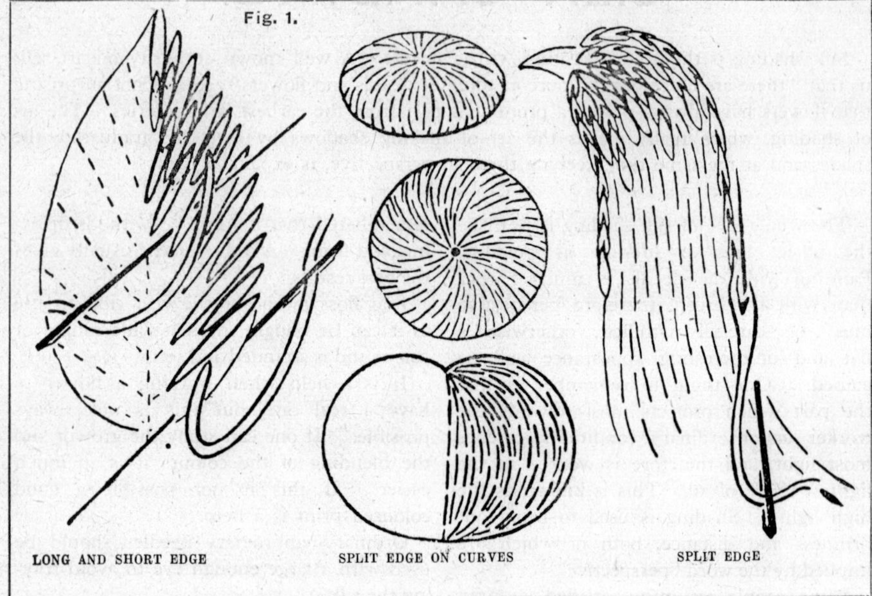

Turn back the turnover portion and the direction the stitches are to take will show through.

The first row is most important in determining the curve of the stitch. Before beginning to work, pencil in the direction. After this is done work a long and short edge, then split stitch down these pencil lines to ensure a good direction. Always insert the needle in a perpendicular position and drive it down straight (this is most important).

When working long and short stitch for shading, care should be taken never to have any hard lines. The colours must be carefully blended.

It must be remembered that any prominent part of a flower casts a shadow on the rest, the size and depth of the shadow depending on the distance between the two parts and also on the direction of the light.

When working the part under the turnover of a leaf or petal, work in dark shades, with the turnover itself in light. It is sometimes a help to work a split stitch round the edge of the turnover with a long and short edge over this.

If the general characteristics of a flower are well studied before working, it will be found much easier; the joints of the flowers and leaves must be carefully studied, as it is very important to work them the right way—the way in which they grow from the stem.

It is a good plan if silk shading has not been done before, to begin by working in wools as they are easier. Fig. 3 is a very simple leaf, with a long and short edge. The upper side is shaded in three shades of

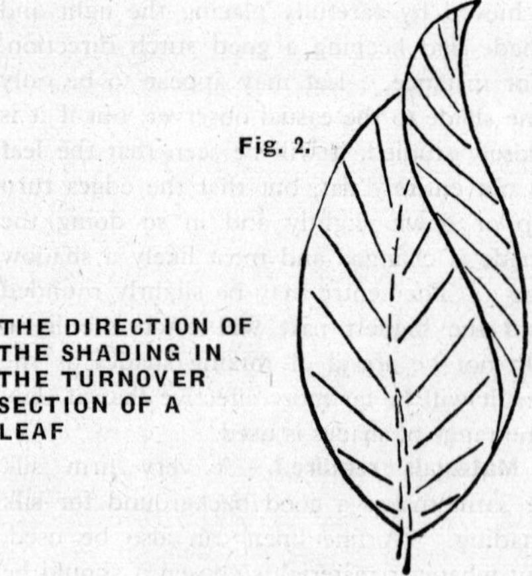

THE DIRECTION OF THE SHADING IN THE TURNOVER SECTION OF A LEAF

green gradually darkening towards the centre vein. The other half is in two shades, the lighter near the vein. The back of the leaf is in a darker shade and the centre vein is in split stitch in two shades.

In Fig. 4 the way the iris bud grows is clearly shown in the direction the stitches take, and the light and shade gives the rounded appearance necessary to make them look life-like.

Fig. 5 shows a petal and some rose leaves. These show how the turnover is worked and the colours blended. In Fig. 6 the working of a poppy petal is shown, also a poppy leaf which is worked in green in three shades from one range of colour. The roundness of the poppy-head which is also worked in green, is shown by the shading.

All these specimens were worked in wools.

In the pomegranate shown in Fig. 7 it can be seen clearly how to work in the high light in order to give the rounded effect. For this, great care must be taken with the shading. A split edge is worked so that there is no hard line.

The direction the stitches are to take can be seen pencilled in ready for working in the flower above the iris. The upper petal of the iris is already worked, the back petal having been worked first as can be seen from Fig. 8. This is worked in Filo floss.

It is a good idea to keep several different needles threaded with each shade of silk, as this saves time. Knots are never made in silk shading. To begin and end a thread make two small stitches in the material. These are eventually worked over, so do not show.

IRIS BUD

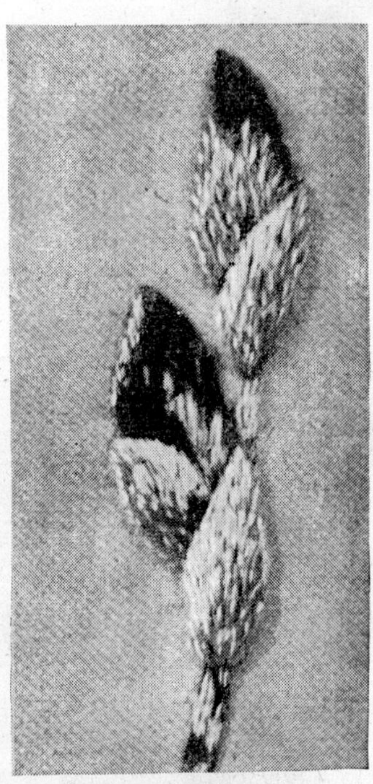

Fig. 4.

A SIMPLE LEAF

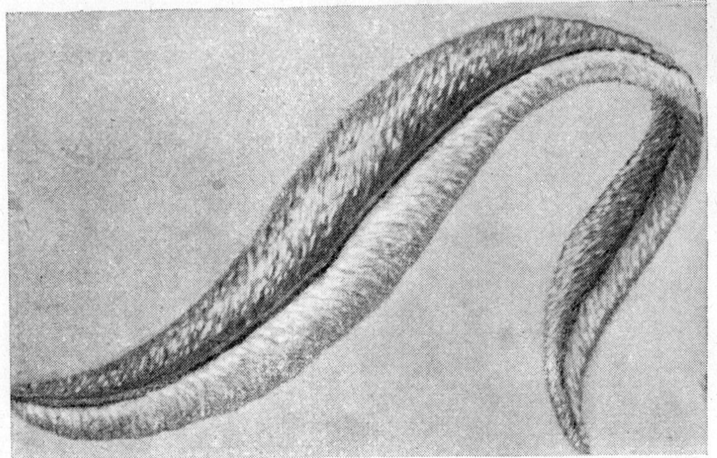

Fig. 3.

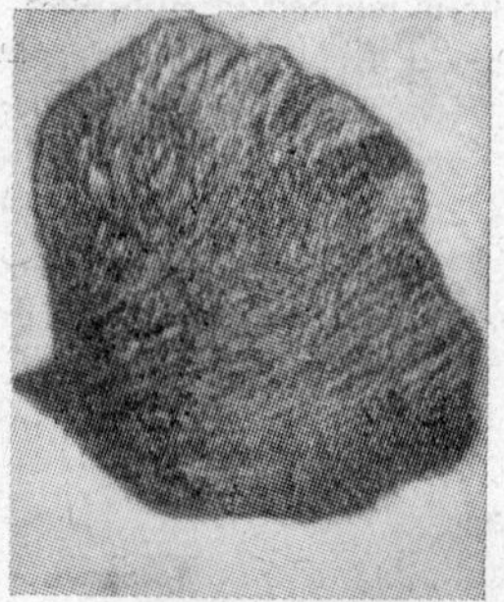

Fig. 6.—A POPPY PETAL LEAF AND POPPY-HEAD

SOME TYPICAL LEAVES AND PETALS

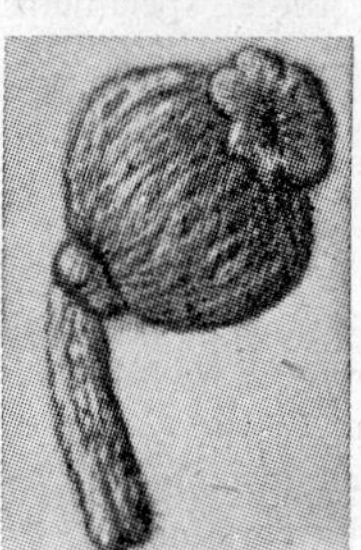

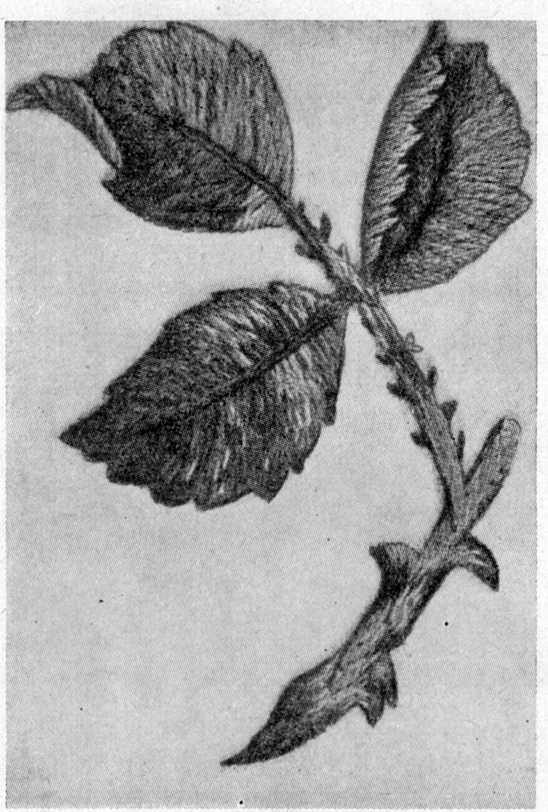

Fig. 5.—ROSE LEAVES (left) **AND A PETAL** (below).

A POMEGRANATE

Fig. 7.

AN IRIS WITH A CONVOLVULUS UNWORKED TO SHOW THE PENCILLED DIRECTION LINES

Fig. 8.

Fig. 9.—A STITCHERY FIGURE

The thread can also be fastened off by running in and out at the back of the part already worked, but this is not often done when working in a frame as the first method is quicker and better.

To keep the skeins of silk from rubbing it is a good plan to wind them on to a card as shown in the Introductory Chapter. The number of the shade should be written on each card and the cards kept neatly in a box,

Reproduced by kind permission of the Master of Campion Hall, Oxford.

A REALLY LOVELY SILK SHADED PANEL

Fig. 10.—A FACE WHICH GIVES SOME IDEA OF THE SHADING

arranged in shades of one colour, and standing so that the silk shows. This method makes it easy to find the required shade.

In large pieces of work begin working at the top of the design, covering each completed section with tissue paper as the work proceeds downwards. This protects the work from rubbing.

Block Shading is another method used, but with quite a different effect. This is worked in rows of satin stitches, each one going down through the ends of the previous row. These stitches must be kept absolutely even. Block shading can be worked in one colour or in several colours, and if well worked can be most effective.

Tapestry Shading is worked in straight, perpendicular stitches irrespective of the shape, which is indicated by the shading or the use of an outline.

Stitchery Figures.—Silk shading is once again used, the stitch always being kept in the one direction. Filo floss is used and finest silk for the faces. This is usually split in half to get it finer still. For stitchery figures it is always advisable to use a very good, firm linen, but this must be very fine as there are so many stitches put in a small space. The shadows are again depicted with light and shade carefully blended. In Fig. 9 the folds on the cloak are shown by the high lights in a lighter shade. The arm beneath the cloak is shown by shadows and by the stitchery being worked in a definite line.

The veil is worked in lighter shades of blue, the inner part of the fold being in a deeper shade to give the depth.

The hands are worked in flesh shades of fine silk which is split as for the face. The nails and fingers are outlined when the hands are finished, in fine silk a shade deeper. A very neat split stitch is used for this.

Faces and hands are difficult, so it is advisable to practise on a spare piece of linen. It would be as well to start with the cheek, in this instance, to get used to working with fine silk, as it is quite a large space. (Fig. 10).

The object is to blend the colours so that no stitches show. A long and short stitch is worked all the time. The nose is always difficult to work. In this case a high light had to be kept on the edge. The underside of the face is in shadow and must therefore be darker. The eyebrows are worked in afterwards and so is the mouth.

As faces take a great deal of working, it is advisable when finished to cover them to prevent rubbing. The same applies to the dress, as rubbing ruins the work. In Fig. 9 can be seen the depth given to the folds by working the shading correctly.

SMOCKING

The art of smocking is supposed to be of ancient origin though little is really known of it until the thirteenth century, at which period it was usual for women and girls to wear loose garments called " smocs " or " smickets ", the name being derived from the Anglo-Saxon word " Smoce ", signifying a " Garment to creep into ".

These smocs were made of fine linen, richly ornamented with embroidery in gold and colours, and that they retained their distinctive name, though probably changing somewhat in character and material, is evidenced from the fact that when in the reigh of Queen Anne a fair was held annually in the neighbourhood now known as Mayfair, smock races figured largely among the amusements, and young girls competed attired in their smocks, the prize being a new embroidered lace smock for each successful competitor.

Later, smocking was known or its association with the loose, coarse garb adopted as an outdoor dress by countrymen, farm labourers and shepherds. These smock-frocks, as they were called, were usually made of jean or strong holland. The bodices and sleeves were stitched in wonderfully quaint and elaborate devices, and the skirt left loose and hanging.

Materials used.—Materials that are not too thick are most suitable for smocking—crêpe de Chine, voile, linen, muslin, georgette, flannel, etc. Broriche, twisted embroidery, Filoselle and stranded cottons are the most commonly used threads.

Sewing cotton or Sylko is used for the gathering, except on delicate materials, when pure sewing silk is used, as it does not mark the fabric.

Smocking is most effective worked in several shades of one colour, or even in several colours, and makes a charming trimming for children's frocks, blouses and lingerie.

Smocking has to be carefully prepared as the whole beauty depends on the evenness and regularity of the gatherings. Three times the amount of material should be allowed to the width of smocking required. As it is difficult to keep the lines straight and the spaces even, it is advisable to use a transfer. Iron on the wrong side of the material as many rows of the transfer as are necessary for the design to be worked. Start with a large knot and secure the thread firmly with a back stitch; run in and out at every dot, leaving the thread hanging at the end of the row. For the next and all successive rows be sure and start immediately under the last row. This is most important or it will throw all the smocking out and will look most untidy. Fig. 1 shows clearly the running being worked.

When all the rows have been run, draw the threads up tightly together and knot them. Begin with the first two, twist them together and knot them, then take the next

Fig. 1.—PREPARING THE WORK

Fig. 2.—THE PLEATS IN POSITION

two, twist them in with these and so on until they are all twisted. Should the smocking be deep, knot the threads at intervals. Knot them all together and if necessary twist them round a pin to secure them more. Stroke the gathers so that they lie evenly. Fig. 2 shows the work ready to be smocked. Turn the work on the right side, and the rows of tacking will be a guide for keeping the smocking straight.

Fig. 3 shows how to iron off the dots for a rounded area, such as a yoke or neckline, the paper being neatly cut into equal-sized slits mid-way between the rows of dots as required, so that the lower part spreads out as much as is necessary to cover the area.

When the smocking is completed take out the gathering thread allowing the work to expand. Pin it out to the desired size, right side down on a thick ironing blanket. Press very lightly on the back with a moderately hot iron; do not allow the iron to rest on the material as this would flatten the pleats. A slightly damp cloth can be placed under the iron if necessary.

In smocking the needle should always be put in absolutely straight, otherwise the stitches soon look untidy and uneven. The thread must always be drawn through to even tightness. Smocking is always worked from left to right, with one or two exceptions.

It is as well to start smocking with two straight lines of stitching to keep it in place. A stitch frequently used for this is **outline stitch** which is similar to that used in embroidery, the difference being that a pleat is taken up each time.

Bring the needle up on the left side of a pleat, make a stitch over the pleat to secure

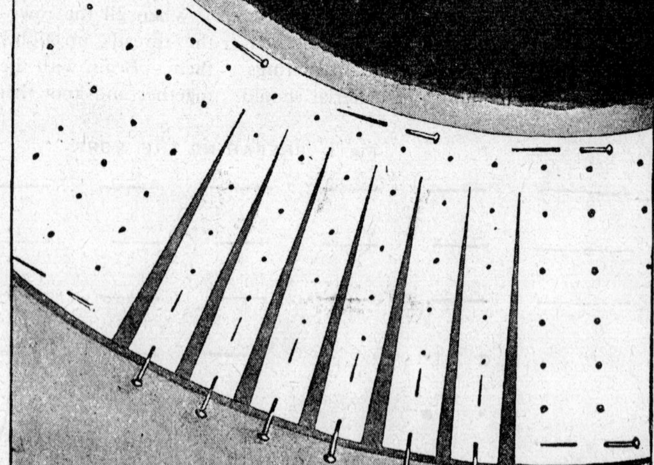

Fig. 3. LAYING OUT AND CUTTING THE TRANSFER FOR A ROUND CORNER

it firmly before starting, then pick up the top of the next pleat to the right, keeping the needle absolutely straight. Draw the stitch up and continue to the end in same way, taking up every pleat in turn, keeping the line perfectly straight, and using the tacking thread as a guide. A second row can be worked immediately underneath, if liked. (Fig. 5).

Cable Stitch is used a great deal as an alternative for outline stitch when starting a piece of work. For this stitch every pleat is picked up in turn, as in outline stitch, and the needle is kept absolutely straight. Keep along a gathering thread as a guide and work as in outline stitch, only keep the thread over and under the needle alternately. This forms the cable as shown in Fig. 5.

Double Cable Stitch is worked in the same way as single cable. The rows are worked side by side, starting in the same stitch. This forms a chain when finished, as shown in Fig. 5. An attractive pattern can be formed by working several rows of cable one below the other.

Outline Stitch worked in Vandykes.—Stitches worked in vandykes (or points) are a great feature of smocking.

Instead of making the stitches in a straight row, as previously explained, work each a little higher than the last, up to the gathering thread above, then work each a little lower than the last, down to the gathering thread on which the work was started, and continue thus until sufficient vandykes are worked. (Fig. 6).

Several rows of this stitch, fitted one into the next, are most effective. The vandykes can also be reversed to form diamonds, as will be seen in Fig. 7.

Honeycomb Stitch. — Some people always refer to smocking as "Honeycombing," but this is not technically

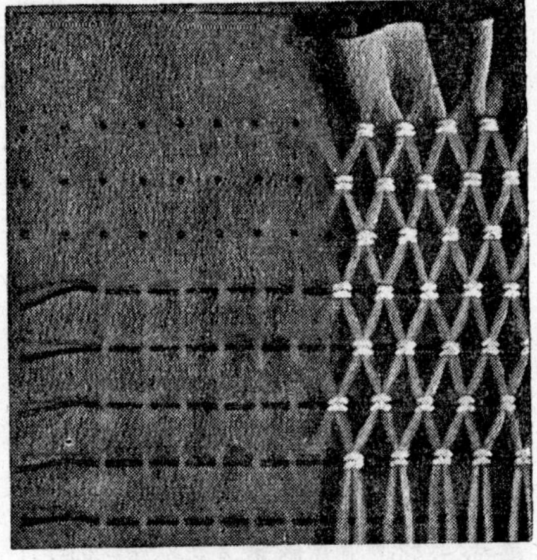

Fig. 4.—HONEYCOMB STITCH

Below, Fig. 5, shows diagrammatically the working of Outline Stitch, Cable Stitch, and Double Cable. On the right, Fig. 6, is shown the working of outline stitch in vandykes, which can be varied to form diamonds as in Fig. 7.

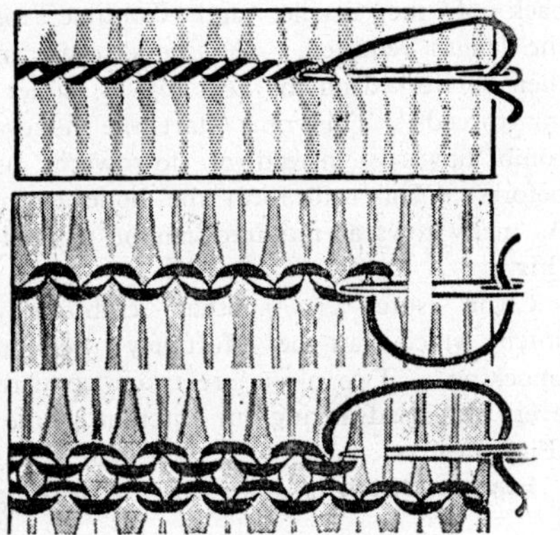

Fig. 6.

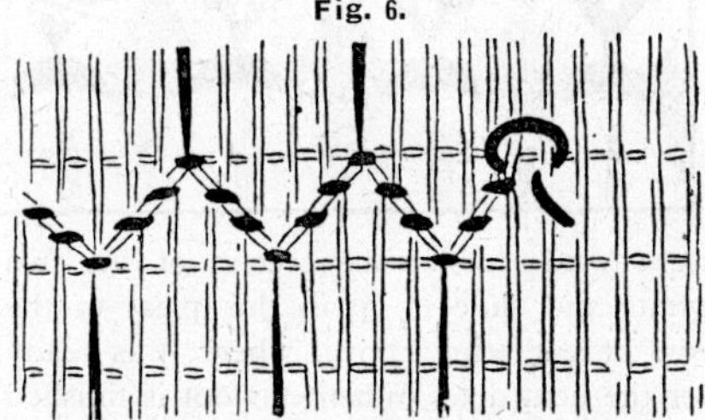

Fig. 7.

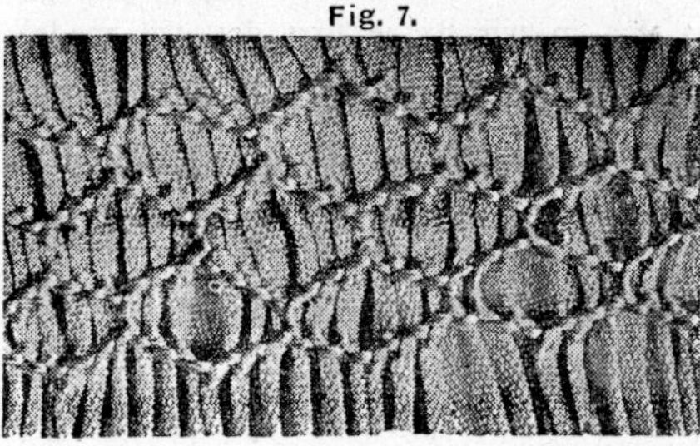

correct. Honeycomb stitch is a favourite smocking stitch and as its name implies gives a honeycomb effect to the surface. It can be worked in bands or in points.

The work is done in rows, two rows of dots being worked in each. A row of gathering is required for each of the two rows of dots in depth.

Start at the top left-hand side and take a stitch through the top of two pleats, bringing the needle out just below where it first came up. Take it down through the right-hand side of the second of the two pleats and slide it up in this pleat to the row of gathering above, where it is ready for the next dot. When this dot is finished slide it down to the same row of gatherings as that in which the first dot was made. Continue up and down to the end of the row. (Fig. 9).

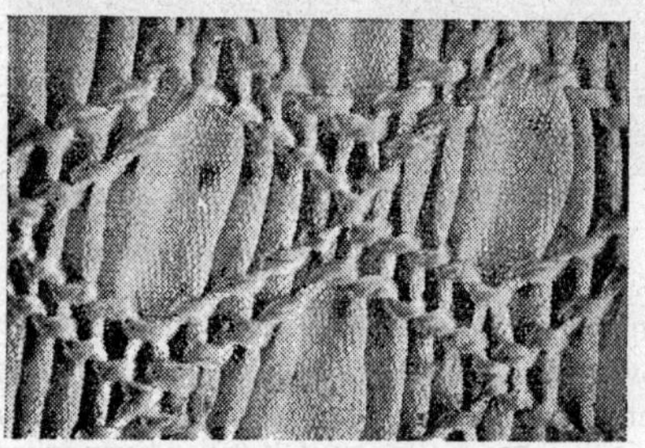

Fig. 9.—HONEYCOMB STITCH

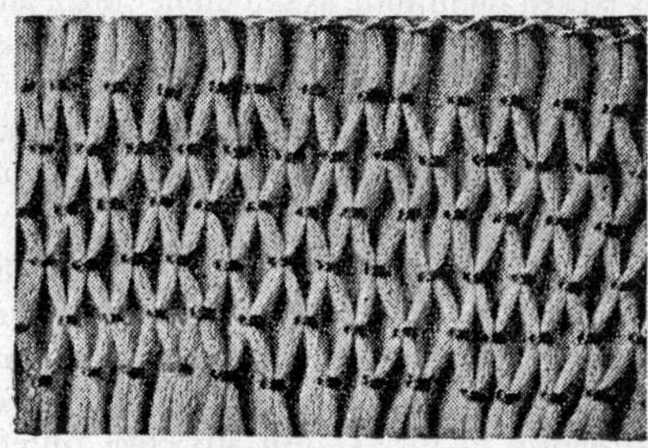

Fig. 8.—OUTLINE IN DOUBLE VANDYKES

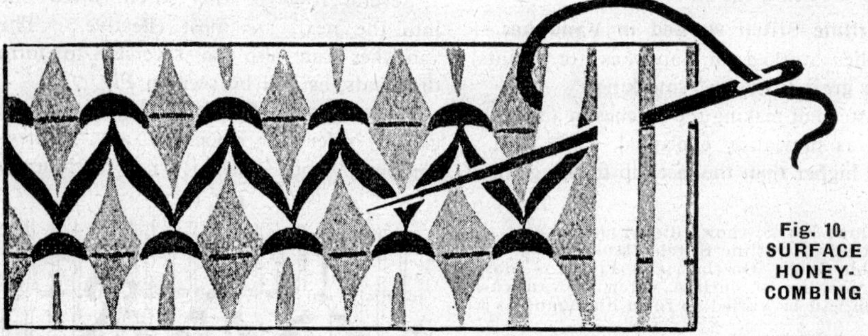

Fig. 10. SURFACE HONEYCOMBING

In working points or diamonds, each point must be made separately, graduating the rows off by working a dot less at each end.

Surface Honeycombing is very effective and simple to work. Start as for ordinary honeycomb at the top left-hand side, take a stitch through the top of the first two pleats, and instead of bringing the needle just below where it first came up, take it out between the two pleats, take it down to the next row of gathering threads, take a stitch over the same pleat as above, the silk being on the surface. Now take a second stitch through the next pleat; bring the needle up between the two and then taking the same pleat in the top row of gathering threads, keep the thread at the back of the needle, and continue for the length required. A second row can then be worked on the next row of gathering threads. This time start the honeycomb upwards instead of downwards as before. This will form the honeycomb. As many rows as required can be worked. (Fig. 10).

Chain stitch is another embroidery stitch which can be effectively used in smocking. Two pleats are taken up with every stitch, advancing one stitch at a time. (Fig. 11).

Feather Stitch is quite easy to work as

Fig. 11.

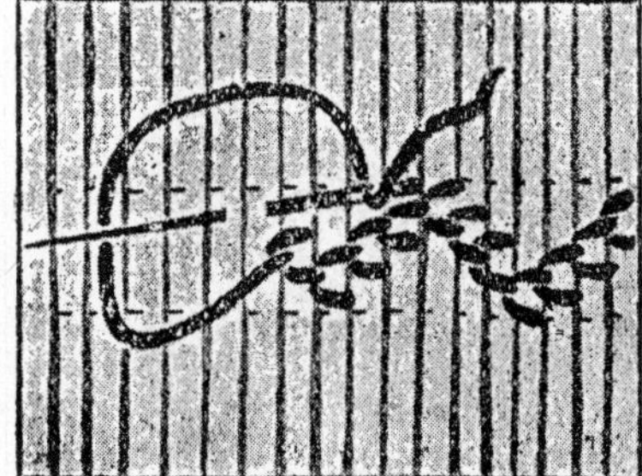
Fig. 12.

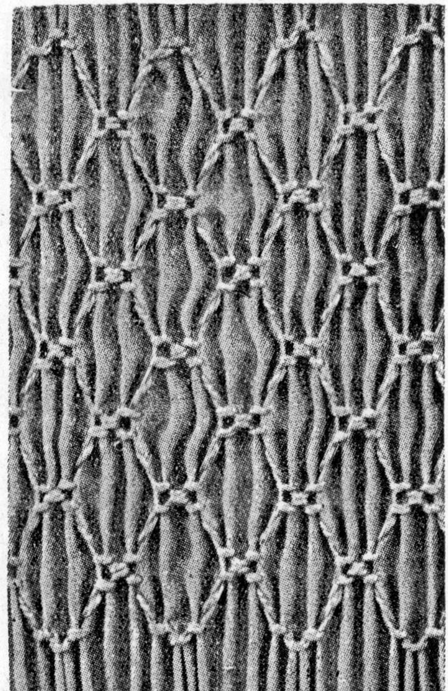
Fig. 13.

Fig. 14.

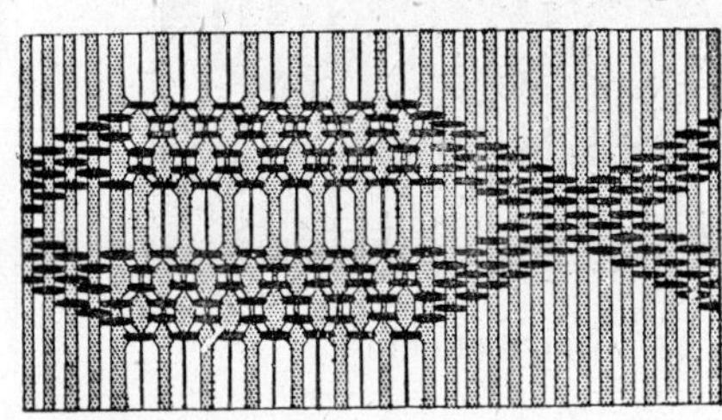

Fig. 15.

it is exactly the same as that used in ordinary needlework. It is worked the same way, from right to left. One pleat should be taken up with each stitch as clearly shown in Fig. 12. A diamond pattern can be evolved by working two rows of feather stitch, so that the top points of the second row touch the lower points of the first row.

Another useful stitch which can be worked in two colours is **outline and cable stitch combined.** Fig. 15 is worked in red and green. Start with the red silk in the needle and work 11 outline stitches so that they slant gradually down to the next row of gatherings, then work 11 stitches in single cable in a straight line, then 11 outline stitches slanting up to the top row of gatherings, then 11 cables in a straight line along the gatherings, and so on, for as many patterns as required. Now with the green, work 11 rows in outline close to the red, then 11 cable, then 11 outline, and so on until the end of the row. Now with the red again, work 11 stitches in outline close up to the green, then 11 cable, 11 outline, and so on. This completes one half.

The second half is worked in like manner, as seen from the illustration, except that where the outline stitches cross, they go under the first worked. This stitch, though simple, needs slightly more care in the working.

Fig. 16 shows a little heavier design

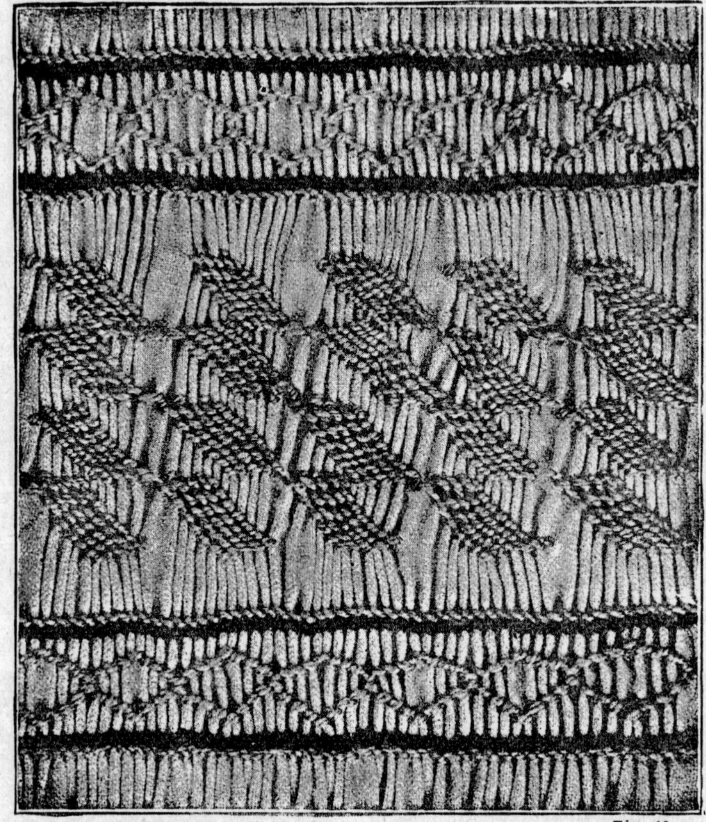

Fig. 16.

A DESIGN FOR A SMOCK OF CHILD'S FROCK

which is quite effective. Eleven rows of gathering are required. This pattern can be worked effectively in two colours.

On the 1st, 3rd, 9th and 11th threads work 2 rows of outline stitch, one in each colour, and between these bands at the top and bottom of the work arrange two rows of outline stitch in vandykes (5 stitches up and 5 stitches down) to form diamonds. Between each pair of the centre five rows of gathering the little blocks of outline stitch are worked as follows: Start on the 4th thread and work outline stitch slantwise downwards (7 stitches) to the 5th thread. Work the next row back close to this, up to the 4th row and continue thus until 5 rows in all are worked to complete the block. Continue straight on to make the second block between the next two gathering threads, this starting on the 12th pleat. Next make the 3rd block in the 3rd row and then the 4th block in the 4th row. Work blocks in slanting rows for the length required, and fill in the necessary blocks at the beginning and end to complete the band.

Fig. 18 is a band of smocking worked on a child's frock. Nine rows of gathering are required. The original was worked in green Broriche on a heavy pale pink crêpe de Chine. Two rows of double cable are worked on the 1st two rows of gathering and also on the 8th and 9th rows. On the 5th row of gathering threads start the

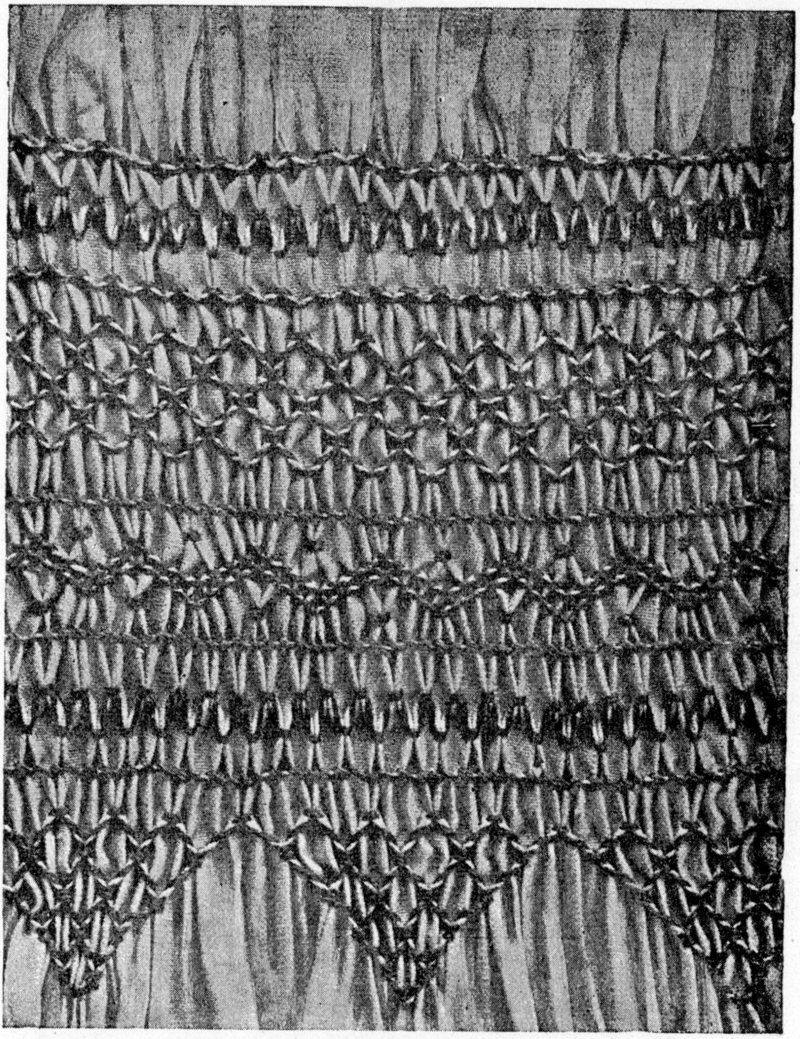

Fig. 17.—A CHARMING COMBINATION OF STITCHES

Fig. 18.

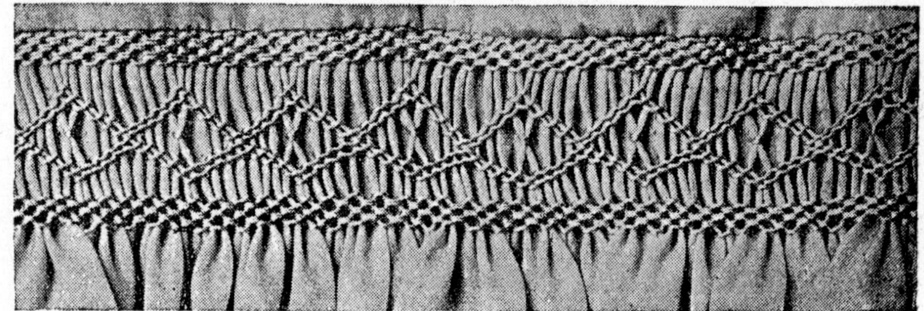

Fig. 19.

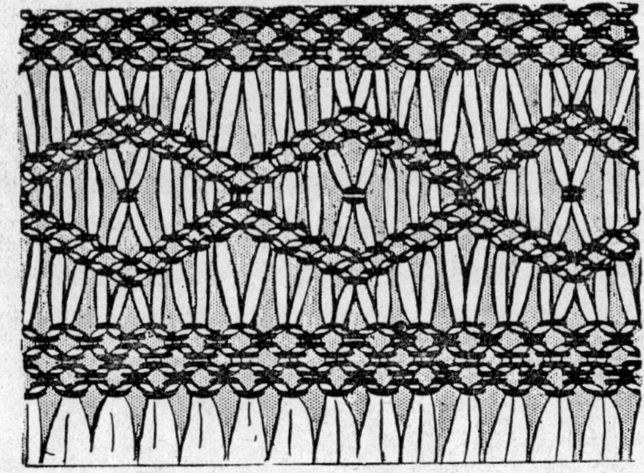

THE DIAGRAM FOR THE BAND OF SMOCKING IN Fig. 18.

vandykes, work on six pleats slanting downwards and so continue to the end of the row. Start the 2nd row inside the last one and work 5 stitches up and down as before. Now work the other 2 rows of vandykes; in the centre of the diamonds work over 2 pleats together with 2 or 3 slightly pulled satin stitches. This is very simple, yet attractive when finished.

For Fig. 17 iron off 13 rows of dots. On the 1st and 3rd threads work a line of cable stitch in green and blue respectively. On 6th, 8th and 10th rows, work a row of outline stitch, green, blue, green respectively. Between the 1st and 3rd, and 8th and 10th rows, work a line of honeycomb-stitch, with red, carrying the thread on the top of the work. Between the 3rd and 6th threads, work 4 lines of vandykes in honeycomb formation, each 2 stitches up and 2 stitches down. Between the 6th and 8th threads work 2 lines of outline stitch in vandykes, 4 stitches up and 4 down. In the centre of each vandyke, take 2 pleats together, with 2 or 3 tightly pulled satin stitches. Over 11th, 12th and 13th rows, work 5 rows of vandykes in the same way as the band between the 4th and 6th threads, but arranging them to form points as seen in the illustration.

TAMBOUR WORK

This embroidery is of Eastern origin, and was worked in China, Persia, India and Turkey long before it became known in England. Until the middle of last century, Tambour work was not known in Europe, except in Turkey and the Levant, but at that time it was introduced into Saxony and Switzerland where it was worked only on white muslin and cambric with white thread, and was used for trimmings. The peasants of these countries soon excelled in the embroidery, and their Tambour work was not only bought on the Continent, but large quantities were shipped to the East.

For many years this work was only done on crêpe de Chine, muslin and fine cambric as the worker considered it necessary to be able to see the left hand working under the material to form the tambour stitch correctly. Later it was found unnecessary; embroideries with gold thread and coloured silks on fine cloth and other thick materials were tried and found to be successful.

Materials required are:—a frame, a tambour hook, embroidery cottons or silks, gold thread known as Passing, and muslin, cambric, crêpe de Chine or satin.

The old tambour frames were made of two hoops shaped like the top of a drum, and made either of iron or wood. These hoops were covered with velvet to fit closely

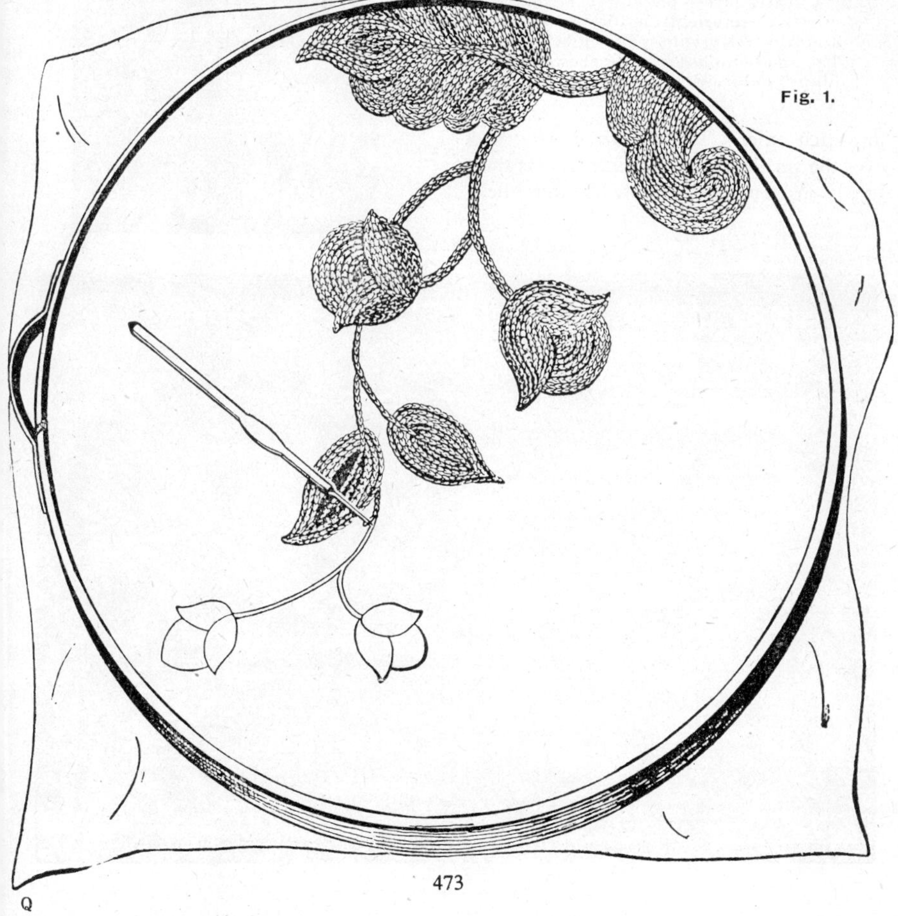

Fig. 1.

cannot become slack. The round frames are still used for muslin and crêpe, but for other materials ordinary embroidery frames are used.

To Work Tambour Stitch.—A tambour needle, which resembles a crochet needle, except that it is not quite so hooked at the tip, is used. Frame the material and attach the thread to the under side. With the right hand put the tambour needle through to the back of the frame at the beginning of the traced lines. Hold the thread in the left hand under the line, catch hold of the thread with the hook, and

A really lovely piece of Tambour work on cambric, from the Victoria and Albert Museum is shown below. The smaller photographs show the fillings enlarged.

into each other. The material is stretched over the smaller hoop, the larger one is then fitted on top, and the work thus held

Fig. 2.

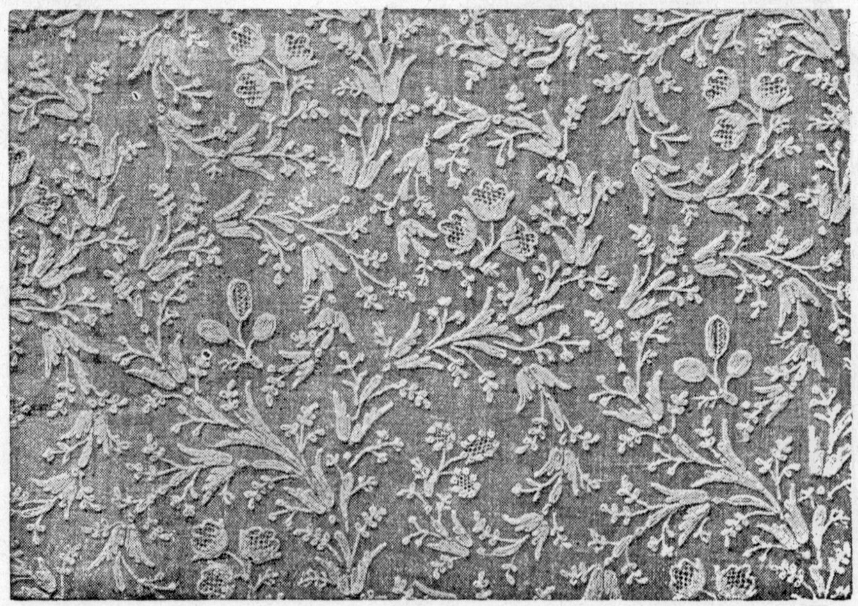

bring it through to the front of the work as a loop. Only allow enough thread to come through to make the loop, which is kept on the hook. Put the hook again through the material to the back of the frame, one-tenth of an inch beyond the first insertion. Let it take up the thread there, and pull it up as a loop to the front, and let the first made loop slide over the second and down upon the traced line. See that the loops that make the outline are the same distance apart and that the thread making them is always evenly stitched. On the right side a continuous chain-stitch will have been formed so designs with continuous scroll-like lines are most suitable for this work. (Fig. 1).

When working on muslin, cambric or net, trace the design on the material, frame it in a tambour frame, then work in tambour or chain stitch with embroidery cotton. This cotton should be coarser than the threads of the material, otherwise it will not stand out.

When working on thicker material, just

Below, Tambour work on net—a delicate piece of work, also from the Victoria and Albert Museum. The Tambour stitch is also used for edging the net appliqué. Above, another motif from the design on the previous page.

trace the design on the material, then frame in an embroidery frame. Work over in tambour or chain stitch the outline of every leaf, flower or petal with embroidery silk of a matching colour. To fill in, work a straight line of tambour or chain stitch down the centre of the leaf or petal, and then lines of chain stitch from the outline to the centre. For the stalks, work two or three rows according to their thickness. For geometrical patterns, the outlines need only be indicated by the two lines of tambour stitch worked close together. These lines should be in two shades of one colour, the darkest outside, or with an outline of gold or silver thread in the inside of bright silk.

The work shown in the bottom photograph on the previous page looks like fine lace when finished. The design is net appliquéd on net, which is first tacked, then stitched round the edge in tambour stitch. The edge is worked with a little coarser thread in the same stitch.

VENETIAN EMBROIDERY

Venetian Embroidery takes its name from Venetian lace, owing to a certain similarity in its general appearance. In the former the linen represents the needle-made groundwork of the latter.

Outlines are worked in high relief, and are carried out in buttonhole stitch. Connecting buttonhole bars are with or without picots, and the linen grounds are generally ornamented with filling stitches, raised dots and open holes worked in buttonhole in relief, and are adorned with picots.

The design given here (Fig. 8) is a portion of a collar shown in the actual size. It gives a good idea of the striking individuality of this kind of embroidery.

Materials for Working.—Linen, the threads of which can be easily counted, is the most suitable foundation material. Embroidery cotton, ordinary padding cotton and embroidery scissors, also a piece of *toile cirée,* are all that is required.

This Venetian collar is worked on soft green linen in embroidery cotton. A fine thread is used for all the work, except the running and padding where a coarser thread is used.

Directions for Working.—Outline the entire design in small running stitches, then tack the work right side up, on to the *toile cirée.* Work in the buttonhole bars and filling stitches, raised dots, lace stitches (see the centre leaves in the Venetian collar) also the holes, etc. Then proceed to pad the outlines. This is an important part of the embroidery, and on its careful execution much of the regularity of the finished work depends. Where the outlines are single, four or five strands of padding cotton will be sufficient and more strands should be added (graduating up to sixteen or even twenty) for the broader parts. The padding threads should be caught down at short intervals with a very fine embroidery thread (see the detail of the stitch in Fig. 9).

When completed, buttonhole over the entire padded outline, making the purl edge of the buttonholing lie towards the buttonhole bars, and afterwards cut away the material under these purl edges.

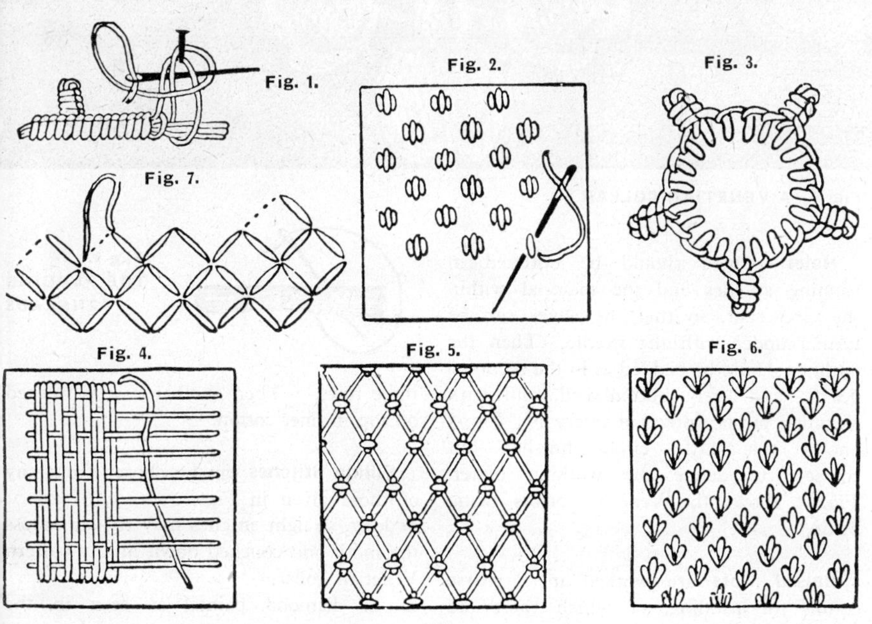

Fig. 8.—A VENETIAN COLLAR

Holes.—These should be outlined in running stitches and the material within the circle cut, so that the edges can be turned under with the needle. Then the outlines should be padded as in the sectional design, and lastly buttonholed, and with Venetian picots worked at intervals. Fig. 3 shows this little circle finished—but coarsely to define the working better. Fig. 1 shows the Venetian picots being made.

Raised Dots are worked in a coarse cotton for padding, of which there are

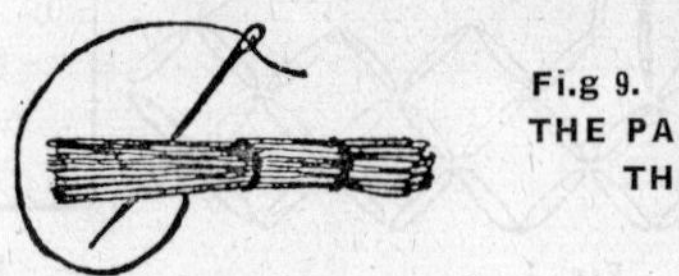

Fi.g 9. THE PADDING THREADS

three rows. Then another row is worked on top in finer cotton.

Filling Stitches can be chosen from any of those given in Figs. 2, 4, 5, 6 and 7; or long, straight stitches may be laid across the motif and couched down in any pattern Venetian collar.
or in diamond points, as seen in the

WHITE WORK

White Embroidery, so called from its being worked on white material in white mercerised cottons, came from the East. It gave the first idea of lace and may be looked upon as the mother of all lace work.

For a long time in Europe it was only worked in convents for Church purposes, but later on it spread and the natives of Saxony were the first to become expert at it.

It is usually best to work white work in a frame. Satin stitch is a stitch most frequently used in this kind of work, and although it looks very easy, it requires a great deal of practice to make it perfect. When the art of padding is mastered, one of the greatest difficulties is overcome.

When padding for raised satin stitch, it must be remembered that it is most important to keep the shape. Another point to remember is that the last row of padding stitches is worked in the opposite direction to the final row of satin stitch. This applies mostly when the padding consists of laid threads and it is not worked in curves.

The padding is worked in coarser cotton than that in which the satin stitch is worked. Start padding with a few running stitches, but never with a knot. For curved lines, the padding is done in split or chain stitch, always keeping the shape. The length of stitch used depends entirely on the size of the curves. Very little material is taken up each time so that the greater part of the stitch is on the surface. Further rows of padding are worked over the first. The last row of padding should be even, so that the satin stitch lies smoothly. The satin stitch should be worked closely and the thread pulled evenly each time, so that the stitch lies evenly over the laid thread and shows the shape.

Another method of padding used for curves is to work the first row as before, take several threads of padding cotton and lay them over the centre of the padding then work over them in satin stitch.

Trailing is another stitch used in white work. It is used for outlining shapes that are afterwards to be drawn or are to have fillings in the middle, or as a vein through the centre of leaves. Trailing is worked over several loose threads of padding cotton, according to the thickness required.

The trailing thread must always be held tightly in order to keep a firm edge. It is worked in ordinary overcast stitch, the stitches being kept close together and even. Very little material must be taken up with each stitch, as this helps to give it the rounded look which is necessary. Care must be taken to keep the shape at the points.

When the threads are drawn inside a trailed shape, the edge will be quite firm and the material will not pull away. On no account must threads be drawn on both sides of a trailing thread. Trailing needs practice to keep even and is best worked on an embroidery frame.

Fig. 1 shows the various methods of satin stitch and trailing just explained above. When satin stitch is combined with drawn thread fillings in a design, the satin stitch is worked first.

How to work some of the filling stitches in Fig. 1.

(A) Work a stitch diagonally from left to right over four threads, then work three other stitches each side over one thread less each time. This forms a square. Work this stitch in diagonal rows leaving a plain square in between. From each corner of the square work a stitch into the centre, pulling it slightly in order to make a little hole in the middle.

(B) is worked in raised satin stitch with eyelet holes.

(C) is worked in seeding stitch, which consists of two back stitches worked one on top of the other, scattered unevenly over the spaces to be filled.

(D) is worked over laid threads, which gives the raised appearance. Start by

Fig. 1.

FLOWERS and FRUIT

A fine example of White Work, containing a variety of fillings, the most important of which are given here with clear diagrams. This spray is taken from the sampler shown in the chapter on Drawn Thread Work. It was originally used as decoration for a tray, being covered with glass.

Worked by Mary A. Caraman.

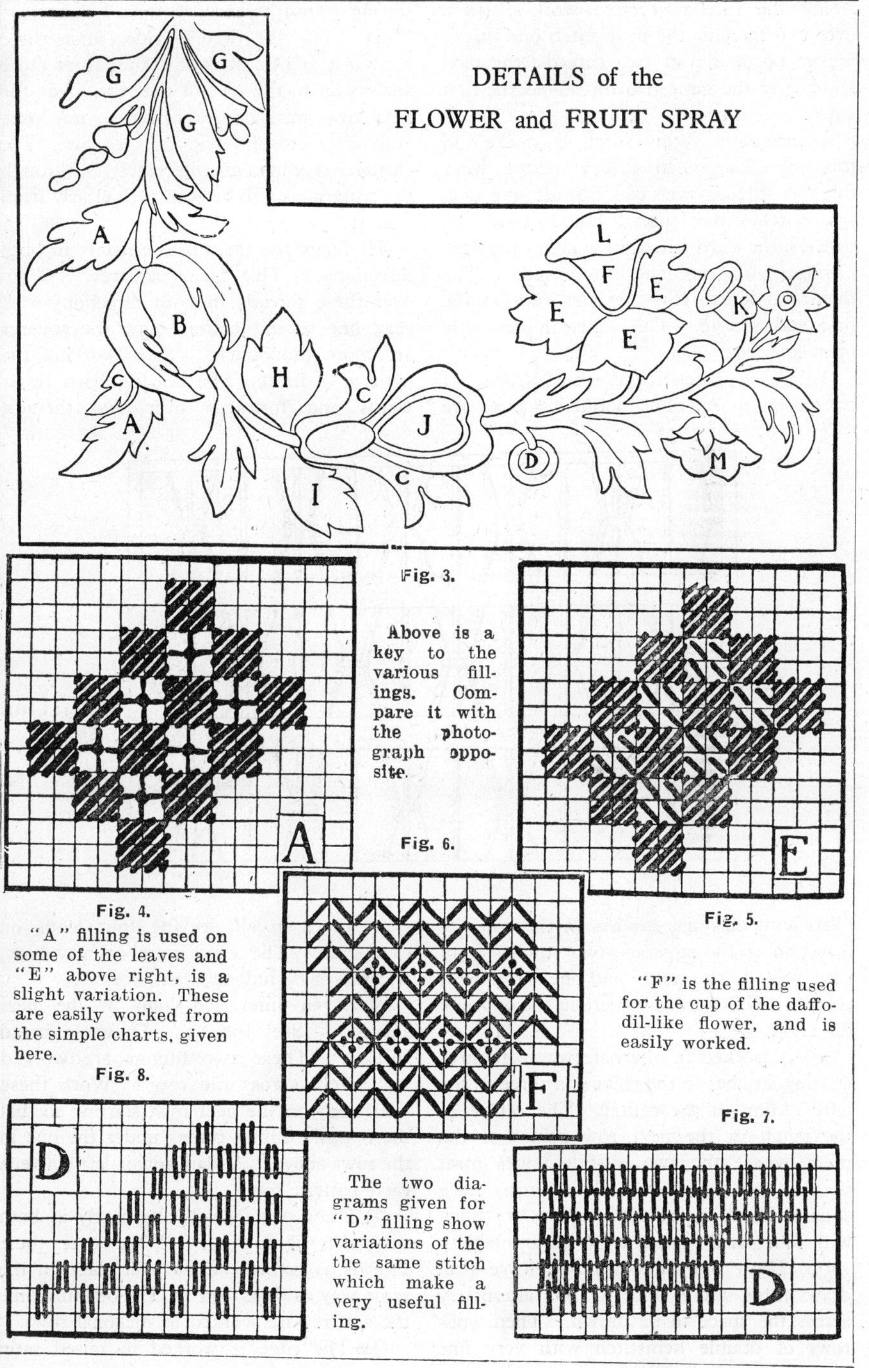

Fig. 3.

Above is a key to the various fillings. Compare it with the photograph opposite.

Fig. 6.

Fig. 4.

"A" filling is used on some of the leaves and "E" above right, is a slight variation. These are easily worked from the simple charts, given here.

Fig. 5.

"F" is the filling used for the cup of the daffodil-like flower, and is easily worked.

Fig. 8.

Fig. 7.

The two diagrams given for "D" filling show variations of the the same stitch which make a very useful filling.

laying the threads evenly, work a stitch over two threads, the next stitch one thread higher up, and over two threads, the next stitch over the same two threads as the first stitch and so on.

A variation of this stitch is worked in this way: Lay the threads as before, work the two stitches over two threads, the next two stitches one thread higher over two threads, the third stitch the same as the first. Continue for the length required. The third and fourth rows are the same as the first and second. This stitch leaves little open squares.

(E) is worked in diagonal rows of squares as in A. The unfilled squares are filled with diagonal stitches in the opposite direction to the squares—two stitches from each point to the centre and one across each corner. This forms a square in the opposite direction.

(F) is worked in alternate rows, in three starting stitches to the right and three to the left, joining in the centre. The centre of the stitch in the next row comes at the point where the two outside edges meet in the previous row. This forms little squares between the rows which are filled with four small French knots close together.

(G) Draw out three threads, leave two, draw three more and so on, alternately across the space to be drawn. Then work rows of double hemstitch with very fine sewing cotton, taking one thread each time. Work from the wrong side, knot three clusters together, miss one, knot three more and so on to the end of the row. For the next row, miss one, knot three, miss one and so on to the end of the row. The clusters have to come alternately all through the pattern, as will be seen very clearly from Fig. 1.

(H) Draw the threads alternately in both directions. This forms squares. Whip over these threads in both directions with very fine sewing cotton—now the squares are more pronounced. Start working the pattern. In the first square, darn backwards and forwards over two threads, eight times in all, leaving four loops on each bar. The exact number may vary, and has to be judged when working.

Work an interlaced loop in the next square. (See Fig. 34, Drawn Thread Work.) These two fillings are worked alternately across the row. Work these alternately on the next row, starting so that the opposite filling comes under the one in the rows above. A plain row is left between each pattern row.

(I) Draw two threads alternately in both directions as in (L). Whip over these threads as before. Darn over these in the same way as described in (H), but this time the squares are worked in diagonal rows.

(J) The edge is worked in raised satin

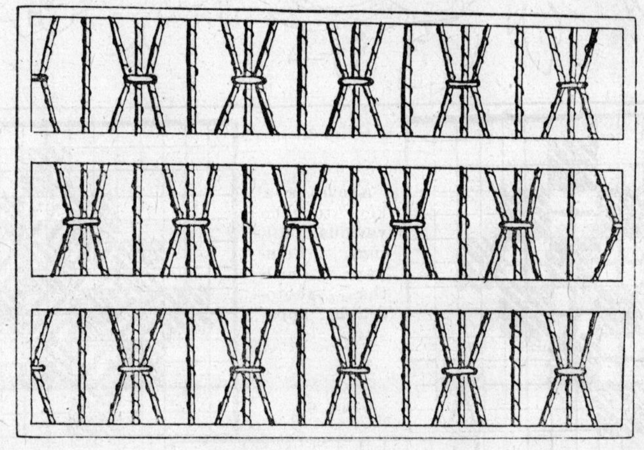

Fig. 9. "G" FILLING

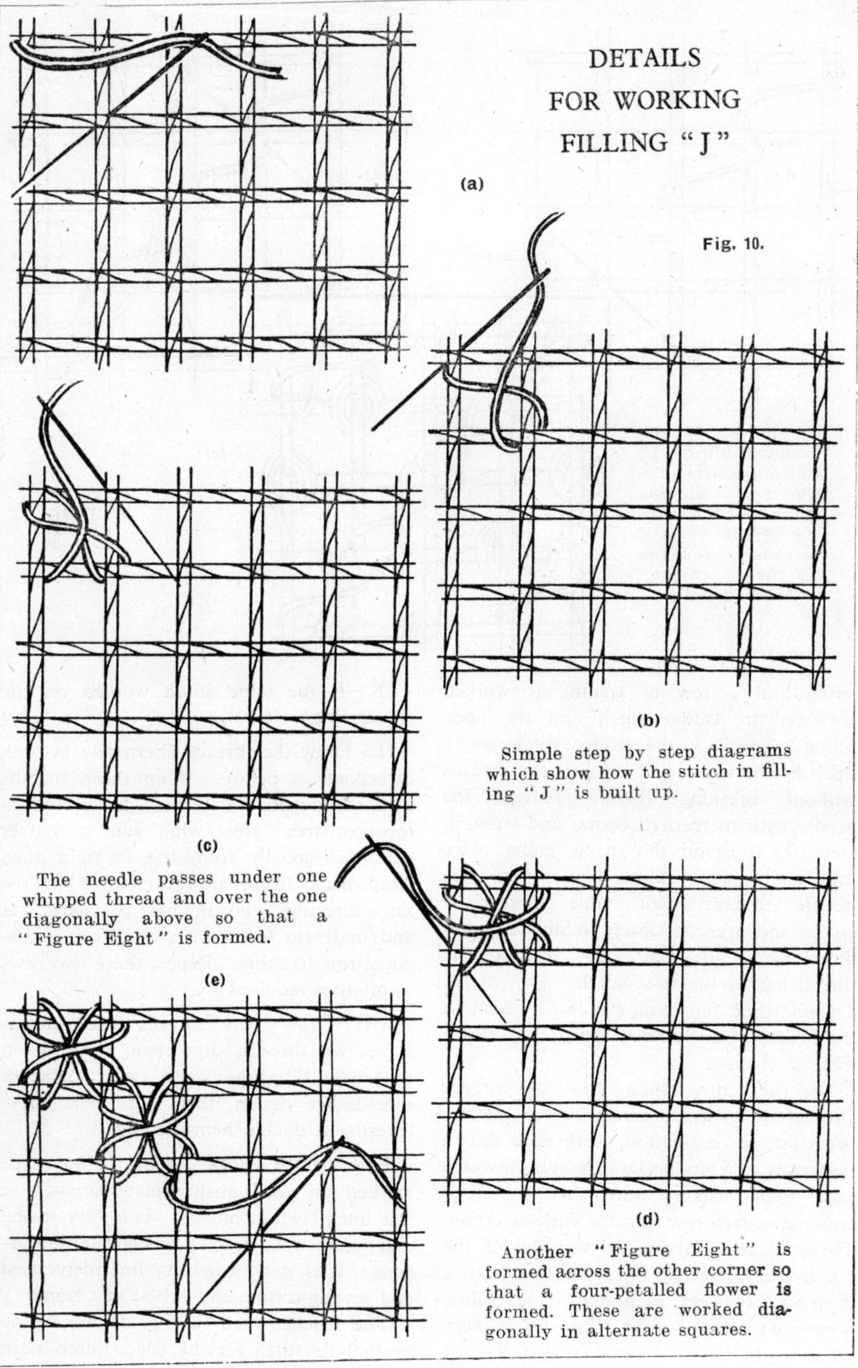

Simple step by step diagrams which show how the stitch in filling "J" is built up.

The needle passes under one whipped thread and over the one diagonally above so that a "Figure Eight" is formed.

Another "Figure Eight" is formed across the other corner so that a four-petalled flower is formed. These are worked diagonally in alternate squares.

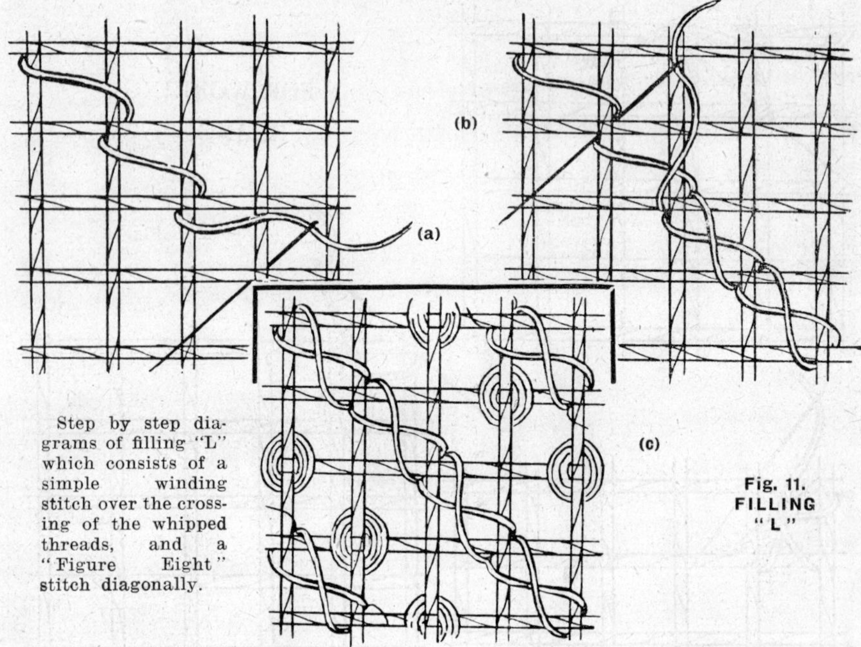

Step by step diagrams of filling "L" which consists of a simple winding stitch over the crossing of the whipped threads, and a "Figure Eight" stitch diagonally.

Fig. 11. FILLING "L"

stitch and a row of trailing is worked between the ladder stitch and the open filling. To work the ladder stitch use a thick needle which will separate the threads without breaking them. Thread the needle with mercerised cotton and work in stem stitch round the shape, going twice into each hole. Then take a very fine needle threaded with fine mercerised cotton and overcast closely in small stitches down each side—one side covering the thread left by the stem stitch. This makes a good stitch for veining a leaf as seen in the completed sampler in the Drawn Thread chapter.

For the centre filling draw two threads alternately in both directions as before. With fine sewing cotton, work each square separately. Whip backwards and forwards each time, making sure that the final crossing in each row is in the same direction. These diagrams show the working of the stitch quite clearly. Leave one square unworked between each row. This filling is worked on the right side and is very quick to do.

(K) is the same stitch worked on the wrong side.

(L) Draw the threads alternately in both directions as before. Whip those threads in both directions, with very fine cotton, to form squares. Now whip with a coarser cotton diagonally from left to right then whip back again, always crossing in the same direction. For the next row darn over and under to form a circle. Work a diagonal row like this. Repeat these two rows as often as required.

(M) Draw two threads horizontally, leave two threads, draw two, continue in the one direction only until sufficient threads are drawn, then work over these threads in double hemstitching.

Fine white work should always be worked on good quality material such as fine linen lawn or muslin. It is very strong and wears well, despite its delicate appearance. It is worked in very fine mercerised and sewing cotton, and is best in a frame.

The stitches used in Fig. 12 are a fine buttonhole stitch for the edge, raised satin

Fig. 12.—A DELICATE PIECE OF FINE WHITE WORK

stitch and trailing. Very fine seeding is used to fill up the flower petals and some of the leaves. Small eyelet holes form the centres for the half-daisies round the border, and ladder stitch is worked through the centre of the trailed shapes. These stitches are worked in the same way as in coarse white work.

The drawn thread centres are worked in punched stitch, for the working of which see the chapter on Punch Work. In Fig. 13 the squares are afterwards recrossed alternately with fine cotton. This makes a slight variation to the filling, as will be seen from the illustration.

If fine white work is worked on linen lawn, the spaces to be filled can first be trailed round, then drawn, as for coarse white work, being, of course, on a finer scale.

The example of white work in Fig. 14 on fine linen lawn gives plenty of variety in stitching.

Padded satin stitch is used in the greater part of the design for the wider parts of the stems, and for each petal of the large flower. These are worked in two rows, both from the outside and going down the centre, forming one row towards the centre.

Satin stitch is also used for the outside of

Fig. 13.—AN ALTERNATIVE FILLING

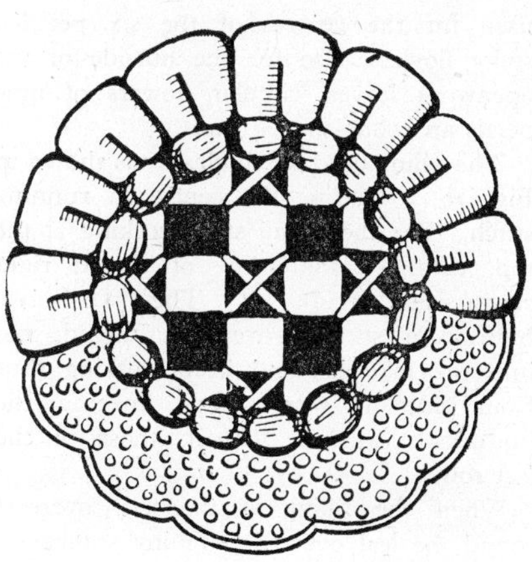

Fig. 14.

An example of Fine White Work showing the fineness and delicacy of the stitchery.

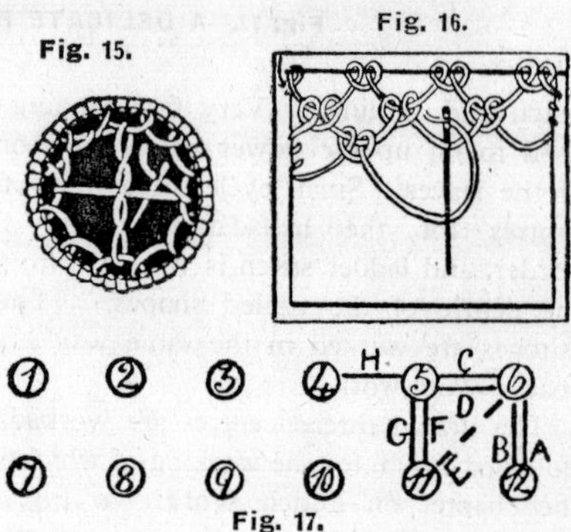

Fig. 15.

Fig. 16.

Fig. 17.

the calyx of the large flower, the centre being filled in with seeding. The calyx of the lower and smaller flower is worked entirely in satin stitch, while the circles at the base of the petals are alternately satin stitch and overcast eyelets. Satin stitch is used for the centres of the six petalled spiky flowers, also for the outside of the openwork leaves, circular flowers of nine petals and cone-shaped buds.

The filling used for th eleaves is shown in Fig. 16. Outline the centre in running stitch. For the filling start working at the top, taking a short line of thread right across and secure it. Then take two buttonhole stitches over the thread, not into the material, and keep working thus from side to side, always making the buttonhole stitches between those of the last row.

When the filling is finished, overcast round the leaf over the running stitches.

The stems are worked over three strands of cotton and overcast as explained earlier in this chapter. The spiky flowers and the petalled flower are worked in the same stitch, an eyelet hole being worked in the centre of each of the first flowers and seeding in the centres of the latter. Fig. 18 gives a leaf enlarged which shows clearly the method of working.

The centres of the round flowers are first of all run round with the purl edge inside, then a second row of loose buttonhole stitches are worked into every third and fourth stitch. Then take the thread across and secure it in the opposite side; twist back and slip stitch along the loose thread and make another twisted bar as shown in Fig. 15. Cut away the material from under the purl edges, and fill in the space between the satin stitch and buttonhole with seeding. Fig. 19 shows clearly the completed flower.

The centres of the two large flowers are filled in with punch work, the working of which is quite easy to follow, with the help of the chart given here (Fig. 17).

To work this stitch a large needle is used (a small carpet needle is sometimes used). The needle must be large enough to divide the threads without breaking them. Thread the needle, leaving an inch or two of thread, which is afterwards darned in with an ordinary needle. Bring the needle and thread up at dot 12, take the thread (A) up and put the needle through to the back at 6, drawing the thread closely to make the bind. Bring

An exquisite design beautifully worked. Particularly lovely are the varied fillings in the scroll-like border. A really beautiful specimen of Swiss White Work from the Victoria and Albert Museum.

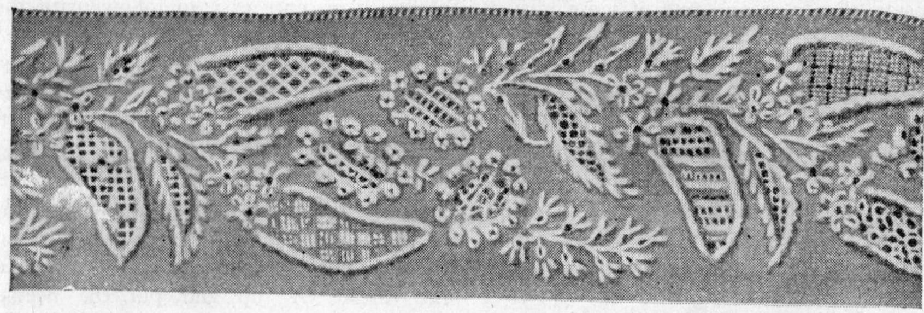

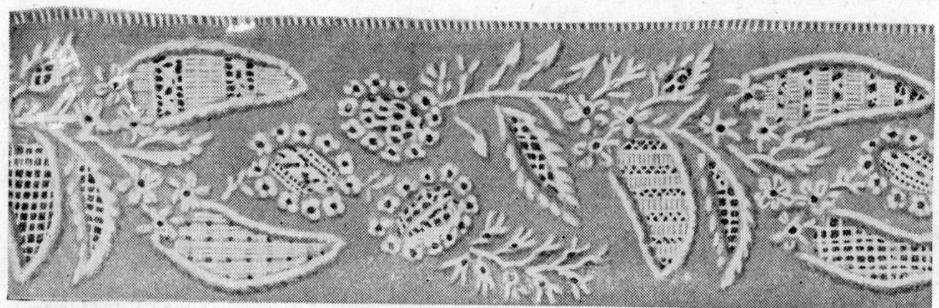

Fig. 20. Delicate fillings of great variety make these panels a masterpiece of stitchery. Few of the fillings are identical, each one varying slightly. Originally they were used to decorate a man's dress shirt.

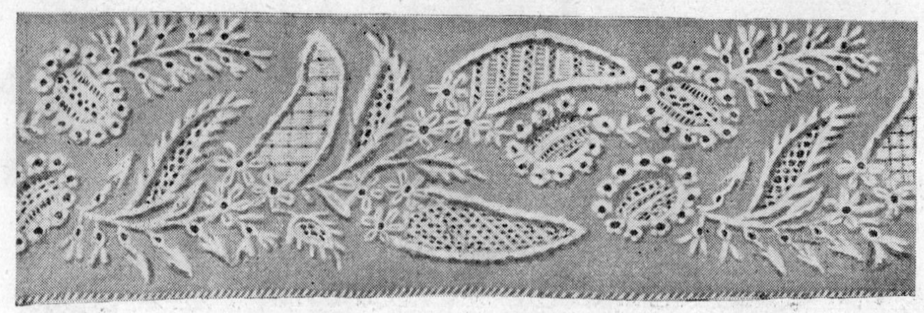

Fig. 18.

The filling used for the leaves. The centre is outlined in running stitch.

Fig. 19.

An enlarged blossom showing open buttonholed centre, with seed dots and satinstitch petals.

the thread up again at 12 (B), in again at 6, drawing the needle up through 5, back (C) through 6 and up through 5 (D), through 6 again and up through 11 (the broken line E shows the direction of the thread passed at the back of the work (F), in at 5, up through 11 (G), in at 5 again, and up through 4 (H), back in 5 again and continue working thus to the end of the row. After making the second bar of the last stitch, bring the needle up at the first dot in the same way, only slightly reversing the movements made in the previous row. Work to and fro in this way until the whole centre is filled.

Work the shadow eyelets in the same way as described in the chapter on Broderie Anglaise

BLOCK SHADOW WORK

This dainty work is extremely effective for embroidering muslin, and is most useful for voile blouses, collars, afternoon tea-cloths and handkerchiefs. It can also be worked on thin crêpe de Chine for lingerie.

The stitchery may be carried out with white or coloured silk or thread as preferred, and is worked on the wrong side, the right side showing the squares, diamonds or other shapes outlined with back stitches, the white or coloured thread showing through the shapes.

The squares which form the designs measure $\frac{1}{4}$ inch in size, and before starting to work, the squares should be measured and drawn out on a piece of stiff paper, and the outline inked in. The muslin can be laid over and the design lightly traced on to the wrong side in pencil.

The fundamental stitch used in block shadow work and herring-boning crossed at right angles. Below a simple arrangement of blocks that is most effective. Fig. 23 shows the stitch used when a large area is worked, and on the extreme right, Indian shadow stitch.

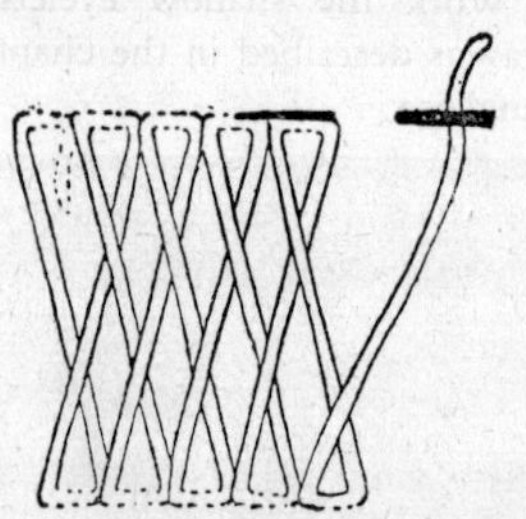

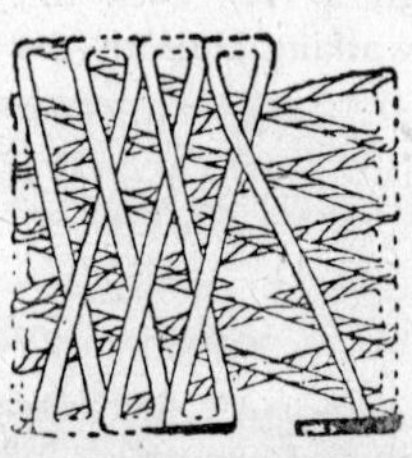

Fig. 21.

Fig. 22.

WRONG SIDE

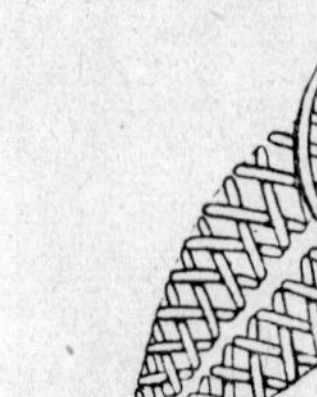

RIGHT SIDE

INDIAN SHADOW STITCH

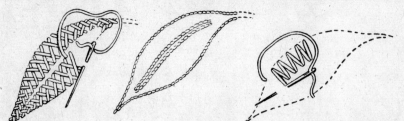

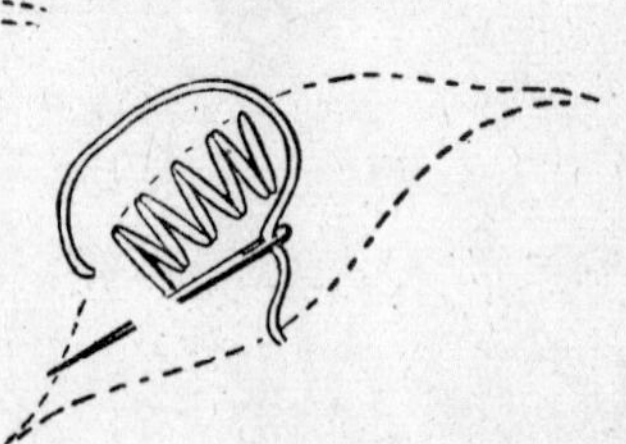

Fig. 23.

Fig. 24.

Another arangement of blocks—this time to form diamonds. The herringboning is often worked in gay colours, so that the shadow appears in delicate tints.

Fig. 21 shows how the stitch is worked. It is a close herringbone stitch which is first worked in one direction and then a second row is worked across it, thus forming on the right side, back stitches on the four sides of the square. Each stitch should be taken half the length of a stitch in advance of the previous one.

Many designs may be arranged. Bands of shadow are effective, in which case the stitches should be taken in the short direction only and not crossed.

When working large spaces in block shadow work it is sometimes necessary to work it in two halves (i.e. for leaves), in which case the top of the leaf is worked right across in the usual way and as the wide part is reached, it is divided. The

Fig. 25.

A charmingly dainty spray of wistaria, which, when worked on organdie, makes a delightfully feminine cosy and tray-cloth.

dividing line in the centre makes a double row of backstitching which serves as a vein and saves its being put in afterwards. Fig. 25 shows a wistaria spray in shadow work. For a cloth, $1\frac{1}{8}$ yards of white organdie were used and $1\frac{1}{4}$ yards of mauve for the hem. If a good quality organdie is chosen, then it will wash and wear well.

Trace the design through in pencil on to the wrong side, with the exception of any small markings which are afterwards added in backstitch on the right side. It is worked in stranded cotton. Use three strands in the needle throughout. Simple herringbone is worked across each petal, leaf or stem, each stitch being taken in where the last one came out, so that a perfect backstitch is formed on the right side.

Care should be taken that the crossing stitches lie as they fall, even if they overlap. This is especially the case when working a circle or deep curve. Do not pull the work or cause it to pucker in any way.

This design was worked in colour which looks well through the white. Four shades of mauve were used, one of green, and one of brown. Add single lines for the stems and veins in backstitch afterwards. In this design the leaves are not large enough to split as explained above. When the work is finished add the false hem of mauve organdie, which can be stitched on with rows of backstitch, or joined together with fagotting.

There is another method of shadow work which is sometimes known as **Indian shadow work.** In this the stitches do not cross on the back, but zigzag from side to side instead, and the effect is very similar. Very little material is picked up each time otherwise the shadowy effect is soon lost. The stitches still touch in order to make the backstitch effect on the right side.

Fig. 23 shows the working quite clearly.

Below—An enlarged section of the block shadow work on the opposite page, lent by the Victoria and Albert Museum. Another section appears on page 489, showing the combination of drawn thread fillings and block shadow work.

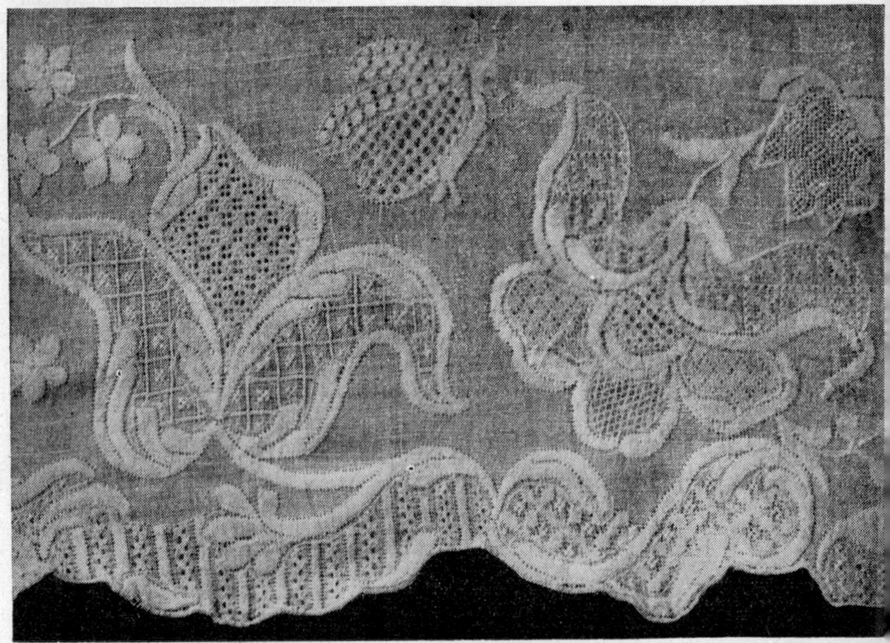

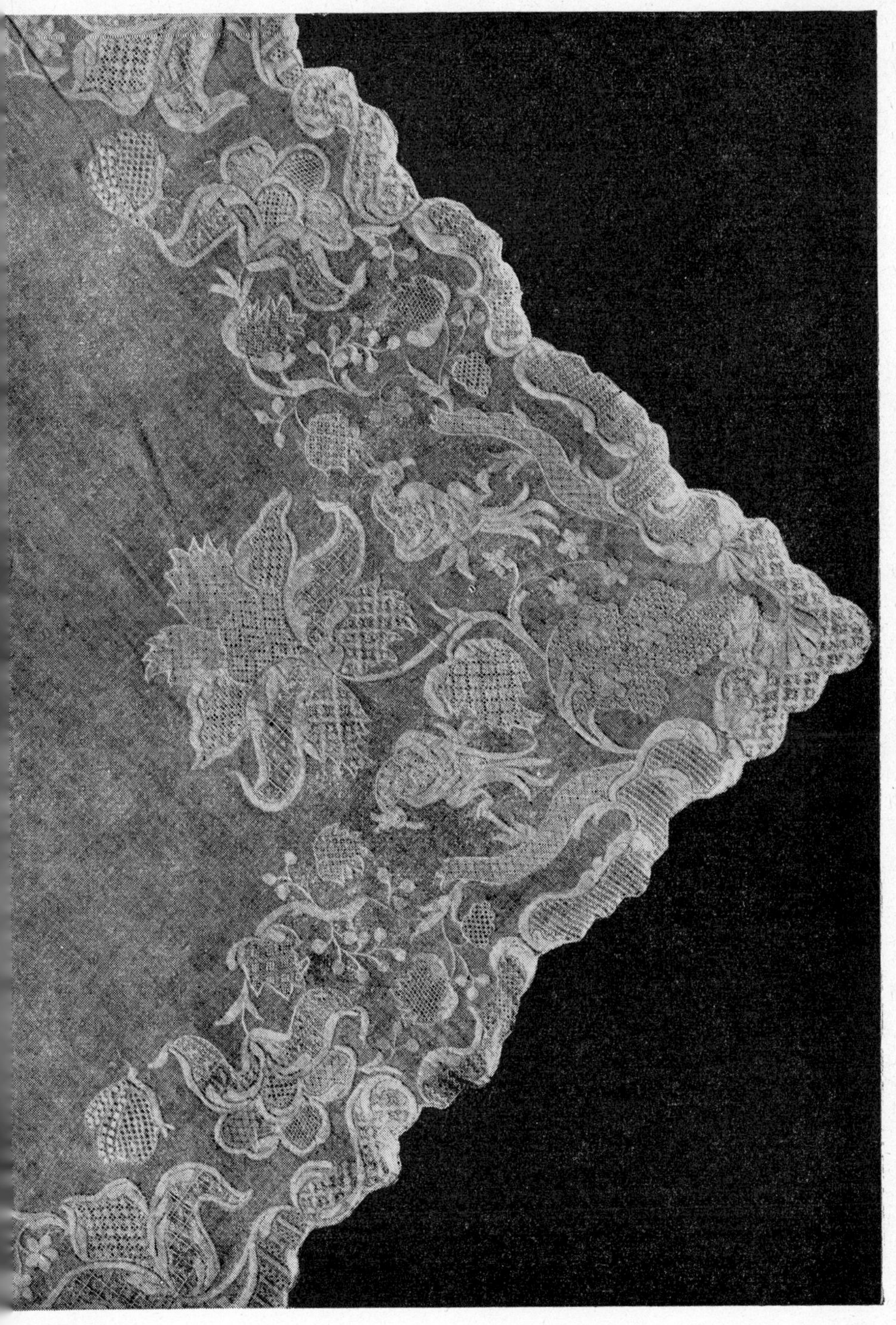

PLAIN SEWING
DRESSMAKING
MACHINING
AND
MENDING

BOOK II

DRESSMAKING. TAILORING.
PRESSING. MACHINING.
MACHINE ATTACHMENTS.
MENDING. DARNING.

Essential Equipment for the Sewing Room

1. A large, firm table or clean floor for the cutting-out surface, covered with a sheet or paper so that the shears slip along easily.

2. Long-bladed cutting-out shears and small sharp scissors for trimming edges and cutting threads. A pair of buttonhole scissors are also useful for cutting buttonholes correctly.

3. Tape measure and yard stick for measuring the hem.

4. A box or two of good sharp steel pins. Non-steel pins mark the fabrics.

5. A good well-oiled and cleaned sewing machine of reputable make, equipped with attachments.

6. Black and white cotton, tacking thread, and silk and cotton to match the garment being sewn. If the exact shade is unobtainable get the shade darker, as thread always works up lighter.

7. A thimble which is smooth and even so that it does not catch or pull delicate fabrics.

8. Good steel needles of all sizes. Thread several with tacking thread and silk, so that you always have some ready to hand and do not have to keep stopping to thread a needle.

9. A heavy pressing iron—preferably a tailor's goose—and an ironing board, sleeve board, pressing cloth and tailor's cushions.

10. A dressmaker's model of your own size, or a foundation pattern that fits you exactly.

11. Most important of all, a paper pattern in the correct size and good materials of the right widths.

12. If doing a great deal of handsewing sit up to a table, with feet straight in front—not crossed. See that the table is the right height, so that the hands can rest comfortably on it.

Fabrics--and their Characteristics

● **WOOL**—
fabrics are usually bulky and suitable for garments that are not too full. The material should be shrunk before use. To do this, snip the selvedges, damp a length of muslin, lay smoothly over the material, roll both up tightly, leave for a few hours then unroll and hang up to dry. Press away any crease-lines before making up. Most woollen fabrics are sold in double width (54 inches) with the right side folded inwards on the bale. (The crease thus made often helps in distinguishing the right side.) Fabrics with a nap—a hairy surface—should be cut so that the nap lies the same way throughout the garment —from top to bottom. Wool crêpe, and tweeds are sewn with cotton, and fabrics with a sheen, such as broadcloth, with silk. All wool is apt to sag, so hang up the garment for a day or two before turning up the hem, and stretch the seams slightly when sewing.

● **COTTON**—
materials are usually sold in single width (36 inches) and are wound singly on the bales with the right side uppermost or folded with right side inside. Always sew with cotton thread. These fabrics are the easiest to handle, except for cotton voiles and organdies.

● **LINEN**—
sold in single width like cottons, is inclined to shrink when washed, so it is advisable to allow leeway when making a garment. Use cotton for sewing. Linen looks its best when made into simple tailored styles.

● **SILKS**—
need fine sewing, fine needles and fine silk thread and careful and innumerable tackings, as the seams are apt to come out of place easily.

● **VELVET**—
is one of the trickiest fabrics to deal with. The pile should always lie upwards —i.e. should lie flat and shining when stroked from the bottom upwards. For Panne velvet, the reverse applies. Cut out in single material, for when velvet is laid double with nap on nap, it pulls slightly out of line, so that the cutting is not accurate. Use silk for sewing.

● **ARTIFICIAL SILKS**—
are treated in the same way as silks. As they fray easily seams should be well finished. Warm irons only should be used for pressing as heat rots the fabric.

Cutting Out--

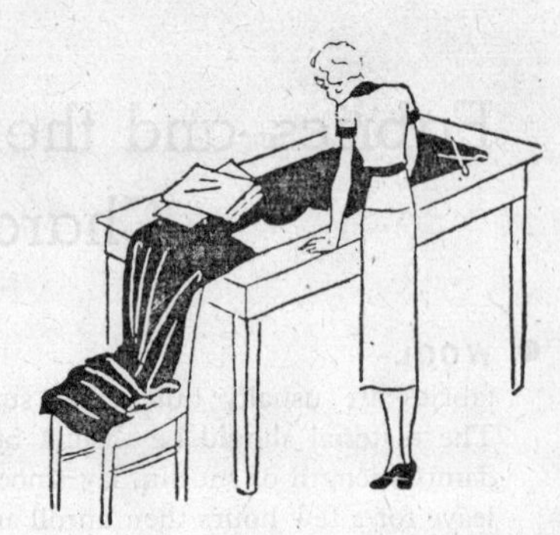

First, make sure that every instruction given in the pattern is clear to you, and that you understand the significance of every notch and perforation.

Before attempting to cut out, straighten the edges of the material by snipping the selvedge and tearing across. If using taffeta or georgette, or any material liable to fray, draw out a woof or horizontal thread, and use that as the cutting line. Should the material be creased, press before laying on the pattern. Remember that all woollen fabrics must be shrunk first. (See previous page.)

Pin the pattern carefully on to the material, following the chart given with each pattern, for the width of material you are using. Do not spare the pins and place each piece carefully, paying especial attention to the perforations indicating the correct grain of the fabric. Pin on all pieces before cutting out.

Velvets should never be cut double, so, to simplify the cutting out, make a duplicate pattern in paper, and place on to the fabric in reverse. This is less likely to cause mistakes than using the same pattern-piece twice. Fabrics with a sheen or nap need especial care as the nap must lie the same way throughout the garment. Stripes, plaids and patterns must be carefully matched at all horizontal and vertical seams and flowered sprays should always "grow" upwards. (See illustrations below.)

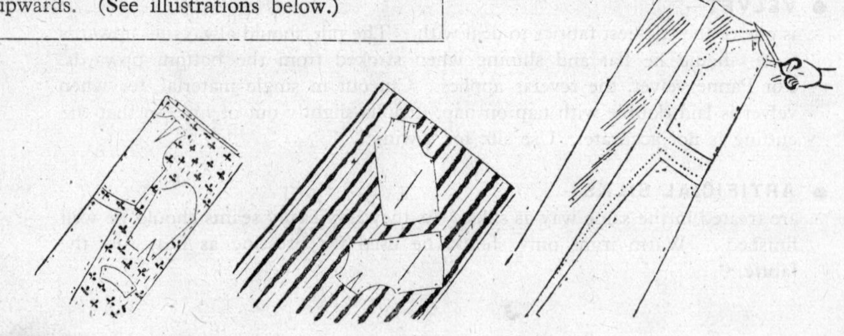

and Preparing for Sewing

The cutting-out surface should be smooth so that the scissors slip along easily. If the floor is used, a sheet should be laid down, and if the table, see that the material does not pull, but rests easily on a chair.

The pattern is now ready for cutting out—use long, smooth cuts with sharp shears. A professional cutter uses the middle of the blades and not the tips of the scissors. Avoid raising the material while cutting, by resting the left hand on the material. If there is no seam allowance, remember to leave an extra half-inch all round (see bottom illustration on opposite page). If turnings are allowed, cut out close to pattern edges.

Before removing the pattern mark all notches, pleats and perforations. If the material is thick the notches and sewing line can be marked with ordinary or tailors' tacks (which see). Another method, especially suitable for dark fabrics is to mark one side heavily with tailor's chalk, then lay the two pieces together, press hard with the fist or flat of the hand, and then strengthen the faint lines of chalk that are thus left on each piece. For thin materials and cottons with a firm weave, a tracing wheel can be used (see illustrations, left).

Mark the centre back and front of the skirt and bodice with long tacking threads. This is a great help when making up and trying on.

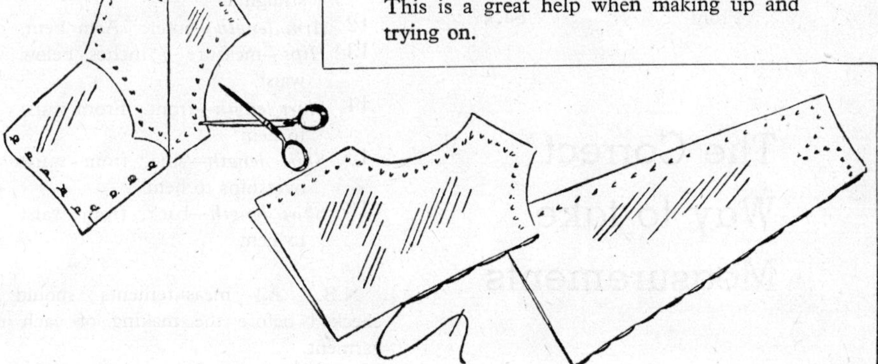

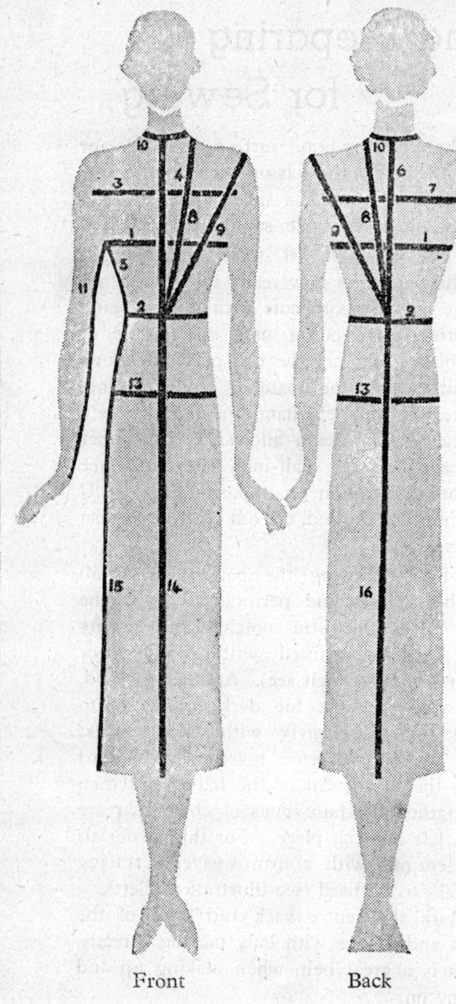

Front Back

Keep this Chart for your own Measurements

1 *Bust*—under the arms, along the back and loosely over widest part of bust.

2 *Waist*—tie tape round, and allow to fall into proper waist-line. Measure tape.

3 *Front Chest*—across front from armpit to armpit.

4 *Front length*—from neck to waist. Large busts need extra length.

5 *Side length*—from underarm to waist.

6 *Back length*—from neck to waist.

7 *Back width*—from armpit to armpit.

8 *Shoulder height*—from waist to shoulder and back shoulder to back waist.

9 *Shoulder height*—from waist to shoulder end, and back to waist.

10 *Neck*—round neck.

11 *Arm length*—inner. Arm straight.

12 *Arm length*—outer. Arm bent.

13 *Hips*—measure 7 inches below waist.

14 *Skirt length*—front. From waist to hem.

15 *Skirt length*—side, from waist over hips to hem.

16 *Skirt length*—back, from waist to hem.

The Correct Way to take Measurements

N.B. All measurements should be checked before the making of each new garment.

Trying on the Pattern

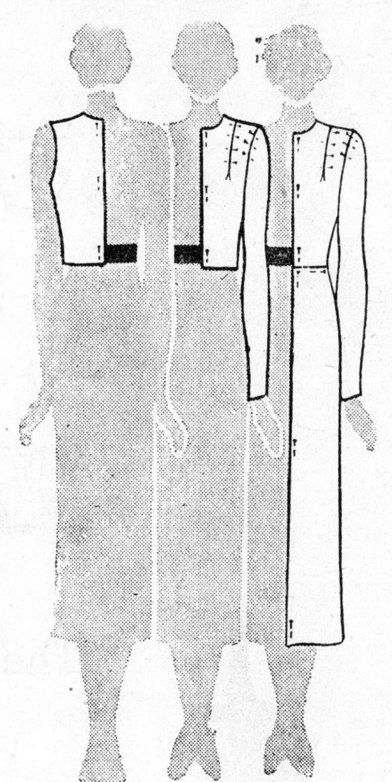

The trying-on of the pattern is most important as it may affect the whole fit of the dress. Dress patterns should be tried on over a slip, and coat patterns over a dress, to get an accurate fit. If you have a dressmaker's model or foundation pattern the pattern can be tried on over these, and all alterations marked. Great care must be taken when pinning that the pattern does not tear. The three drawings above show you how the pattern is pinned on to the figure. Allowance must, of course, be made for the difference between the hang of paper and that of material.

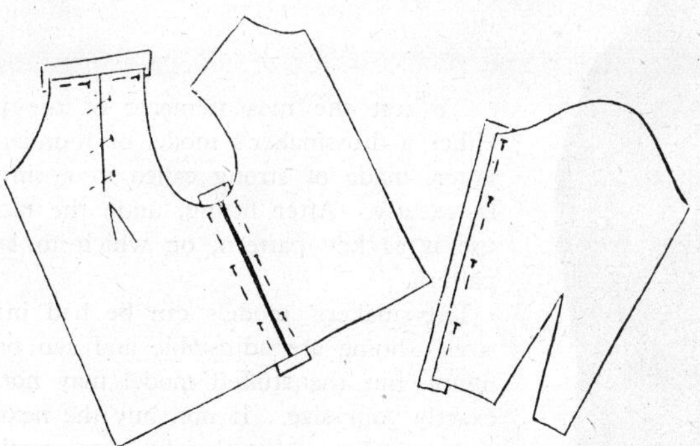

Pin the pattern together over paper strips.

The drawings above show how the patterns are pinned together, so that they can be easily manipulated if no seam allowance is made. The pattern edges should just touch, and a strip of paper should be pinned under the joins. If there is a turning allowance, and this is usually the case, the edges should be pinned together, leaving the turnings on the outside when trying on.

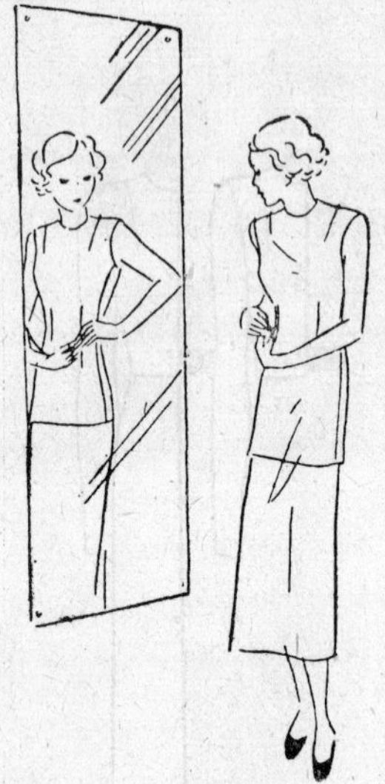

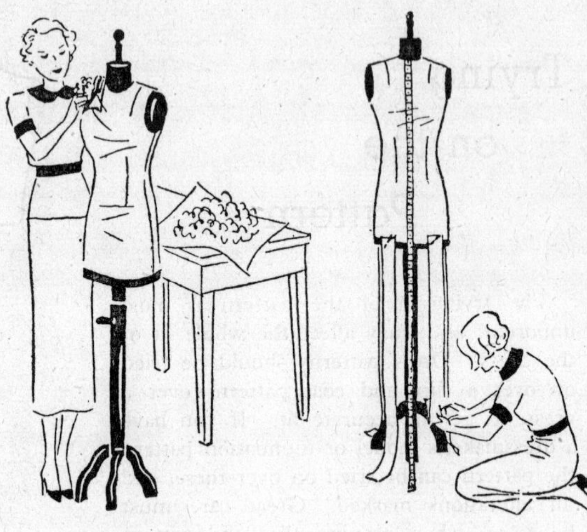

The Dressmaker's Model and Foundation Pattern

To test the measurements of the paper pattern use either a dressmaker's model or foundation pattern. The latter, made of strong calico in a simple design should fit exactly. After fitting, undo the tacking threads, and use it as key pattern, on which to lay the new paper pattern.

Dressmakers' models can be had in many forms and sizes. Some are adjustable and can be made to fit any figure, but the stuffed model may not be obtainable in exactly your size. If not, buy the next size smaller, and make a calico jacket that fits you exactly, and place it on the model, leaving the shoulder seams open. Stuff with kapok so that the jacket is firm and even all round. Any slight defects in your figure, such as sloping or round shoulders should be reproduced as nearly as possible in the model, so that you will have some idea of how the finished garment will hang. When the stuffing is completed, close the shoulder seams. The white circles on the left, indicate where careful stuffing is needed. Skirt lengths can be gauged by cutting strips of material the correct length and pinning them on to the model.

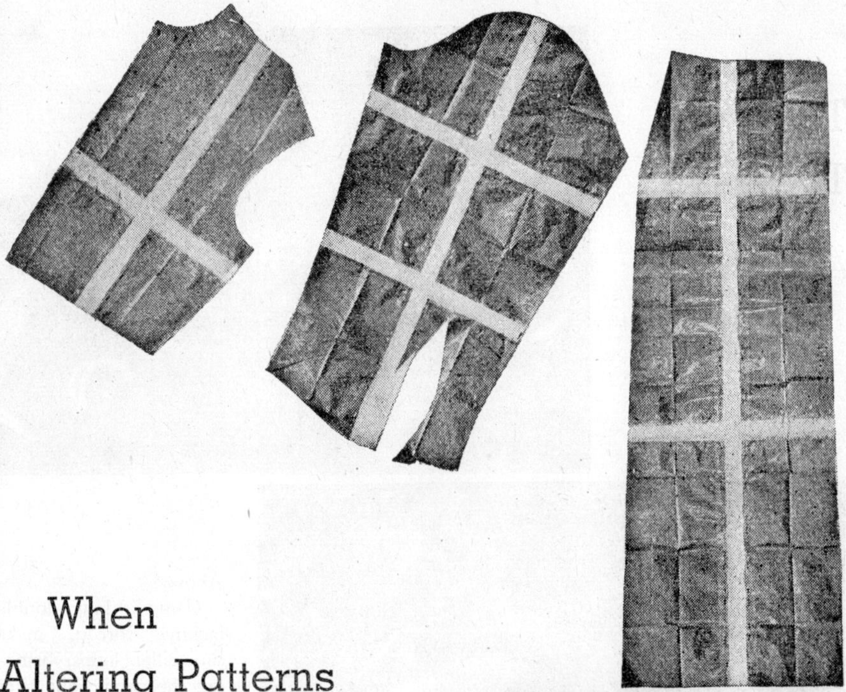

When Altering Patterns to Fit

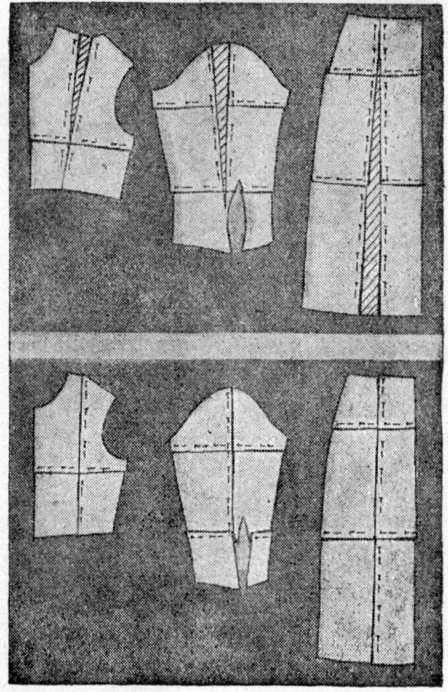

Although paper patterns are made in several sizes, they may want altering slightly, as all figures vary a little.

The balance of the garment must, however, be preserved. It is always better to make small alterations in two places, than one large alteration, as these are not so likely to upset the shape of the garment.

To enlarge a portion of a pattern, cut through in the places shown in the diagram above, separate the pieces, and pin or stick on to strips of paper the correct width. Keep the shape of all curves.

To reduce pleat the pattern in the correct places, again paying special attention to the curves. The top photograph shows a pattern that has been widened and lengthened, and the right-hand diagram, a pattern that has been widened and shortened, and also a pattern that has been narrowed and shortened.

Tailor's Tacks--

Are used for Marking

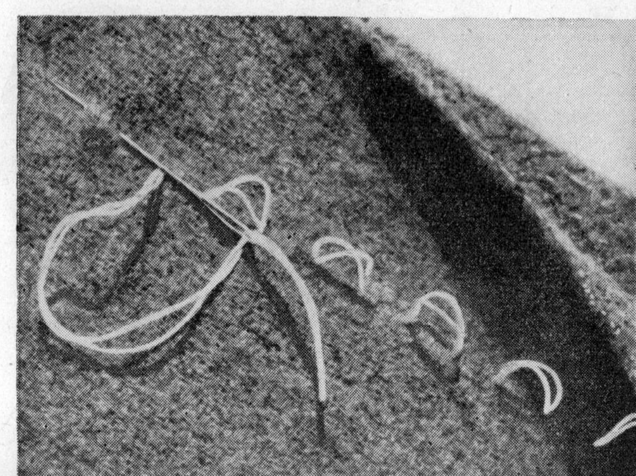

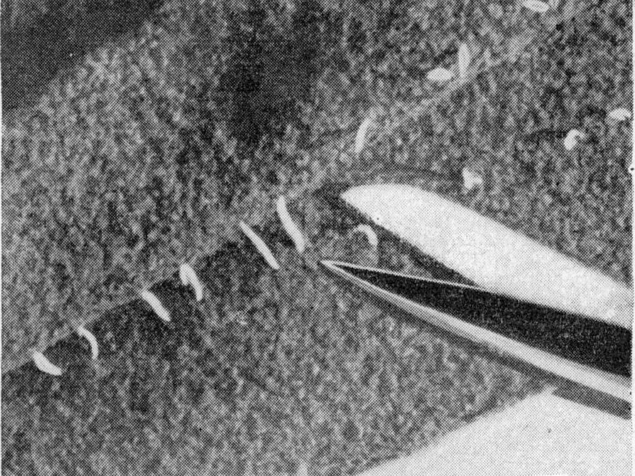

Above:

Using a long double tacking thread, make caterpillar loops, bringing the needle out after every stitch. To cut, pull the material gently apart, and snip in the middle of each thread.

Right:

Ordinary tacking or basting stitches may be any length up to one inch, but they should be smaller and nearer together on curves and scallops. Thread of a contrasting colour should always be used.

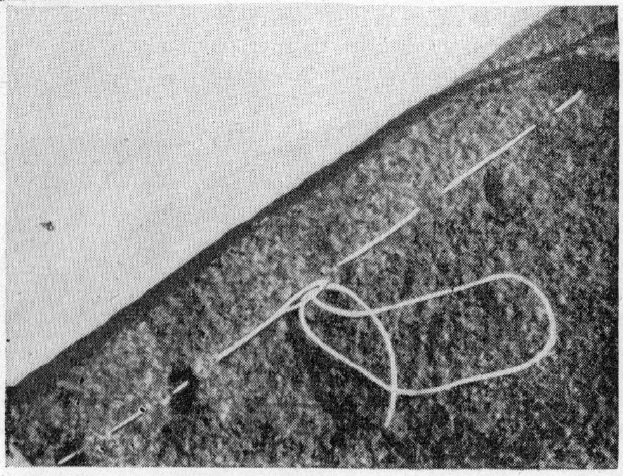

Using the tailor's tacks as a sewing guide and matching all notches carefully, tack two pieces of material together with right sides facing, for an ordinary seam.

Tacking and Slip-Basting

When two pieces of material have to be joined as shown in the sketch, the top piece should be turned in, tacked and pressed first, before being tacked to the under piece. A similar method of joining two pieces, which is known as slip-basting, is shown below

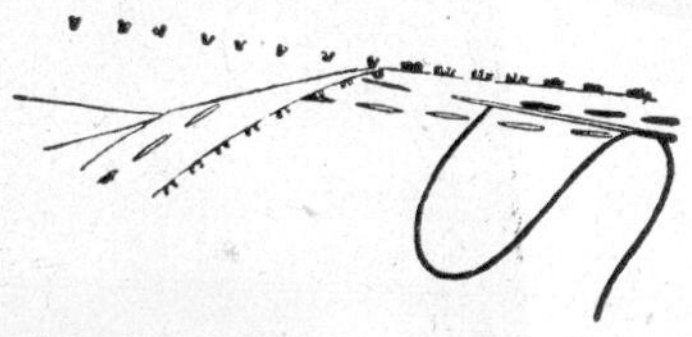

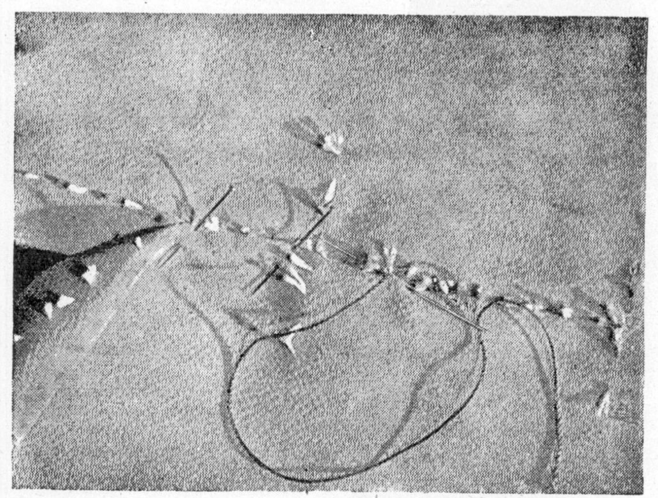

Slip-basting is used for joining so that weave and pattern are matched exactly. First pin in place, the pins being removed only when reached by the tacking. The needle takes up bottom and top fabrics alternately.

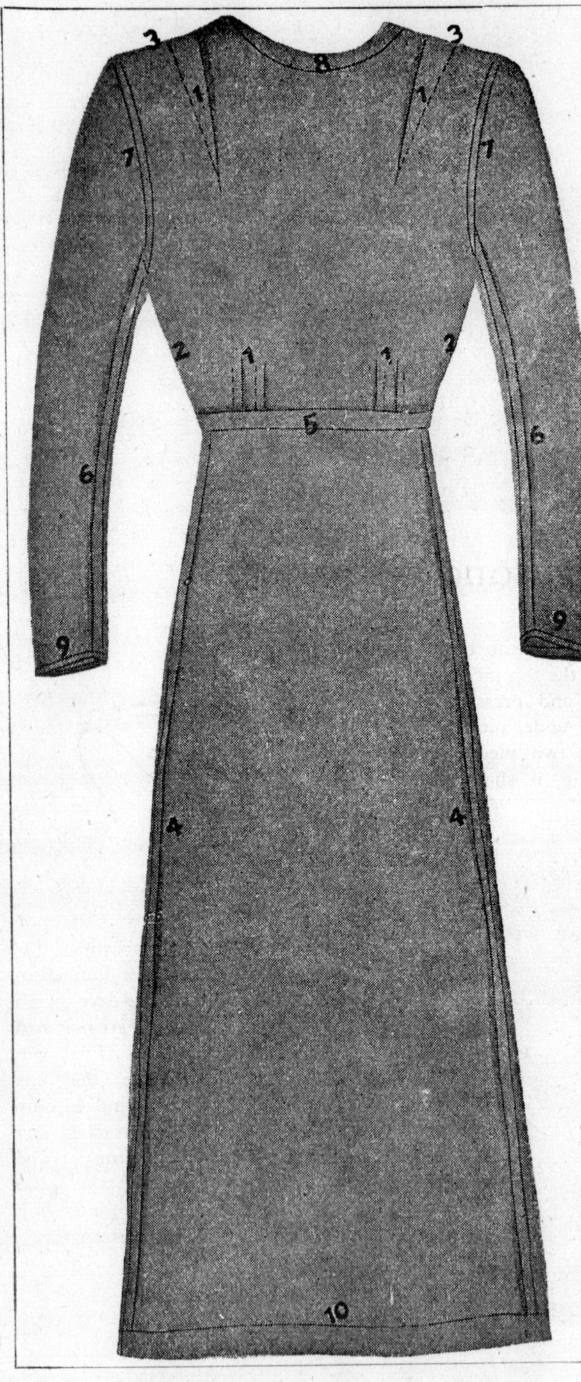

The sequences for making-up on the opposite page naturally have to be altered for jackets and complicated garments. Especially important is the frequent pressing, which has to be done after every seam is sewn All embroidery should be worked before the garment is made up, unless the design crosses the seams, in which case it is better done afterwards.

Follow this order for Making Up a Dress

The Sequence for Sewing a Dress

1. Put in darts at back, front and side. Draw out tacking threads and press.
2. Machine side seams, draw out tacking threads, and press. Any fastenings can be left until last.
3. Machine shoulder seams, draw out tacking threads, and press.
4. Machine shirt seams, pull out tacking threads, and press.
5. Join skirt and bodice, remove tacking threads, and press.
6. Machine sleeve seams, remove tacking threads and press.
7. Put in sleeves, press and finish off.
8. Finish off neck.
9. Finish the wristbands.
10. Turn up the hem, press all seams again, put on trimmings, and press finally.

The Sequence for Sewing a Coat

1. Machine darts at front, trim and press, shrinking material at the points.
2. Machine underarm and shoulder seams, and finish them if coat is to be unlined. Press.
3. Cut canvas or linen interfacing, and tack to wrong side. Join to coat and outer edge of under collar. Press.
4. Join under collar and coat—snip seam turnings and press open.
5. Make bound buttonholes.
6. Join coat facing to collar.
7. Join collar and facing to coat fronts and under-collar.
8. Turn facing and collar to inside, tack into position.
9. Turn up hem.
10. Make pockets.
11. Cut out and fix in lining.

Points to Watch–

Beginners often fit too well—a well-fitted garment should make you appear to have a perfect figure, so learn to know your faults and try to disguise them. Wear the foundation clothes that you will wear when the garment is finished.

1. Fullness at the shoulder seam and armhole can be remedied by undoing the seam and taking up more material back and front. The shoulder darts may also need deepening slightly.

2. To remedy underarm puckers unpick the shoulder seams, darts and side seams. Fit the darts first, then the shoulder and side seams, and the armhole last.

3. Straight shoulders need more material taking up in the shoulder seam. If the neckline is thus made too small, recut later.

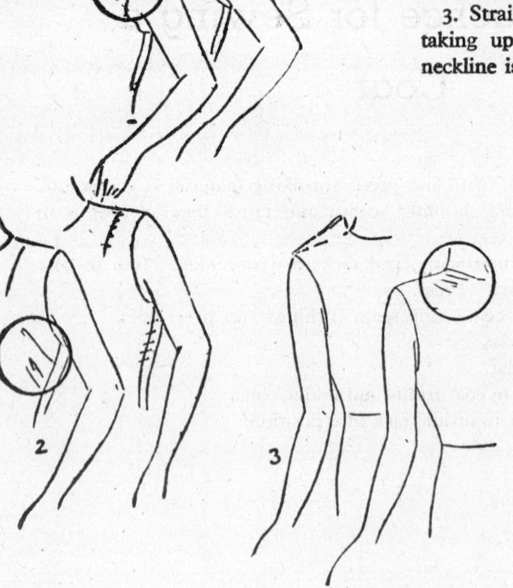

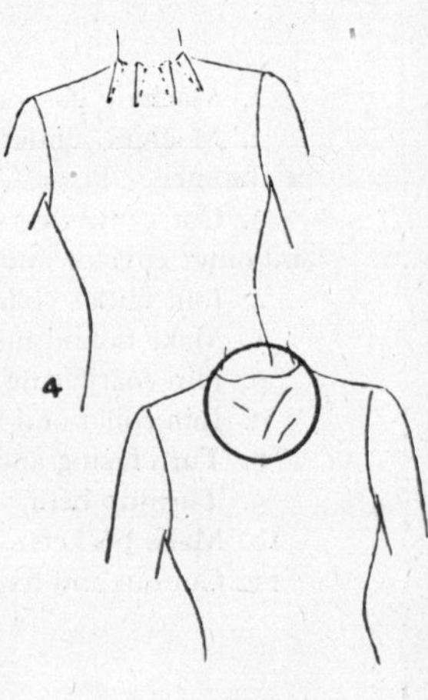

–When Trying On

4. Round shoulders need small sun-ray darts at the neckline. Make one large dart when fitting and divide it later. For very round shoulders, put a dart at the back of the underarm seam close to the armhole.

5. Fullness at the waist is often caused by a sway back. In a one-piece garment put in a narrow tuck at the waist from side seam to side seam. Otherwise raise the skirt at the waist.

6. When the back hangs away from the figure, put a dart about 4 or 5 inches from the centre line. In one-piece garments this can be carried to the same distance below the waist.

7. When the bust is very full, tiny darts under the arm as well as the shoulder make a better fit. If necessary, put darts at the waist. The position of these darts varies according to your figure.

8. For skirts that drop at the back, lift at the back waistline. This is also effective for skirts that cling too closely to the figure.

9. For one-piece garments, fit the waist first, and smooth away all fullness towards the neck, and afterwards down to the hem.

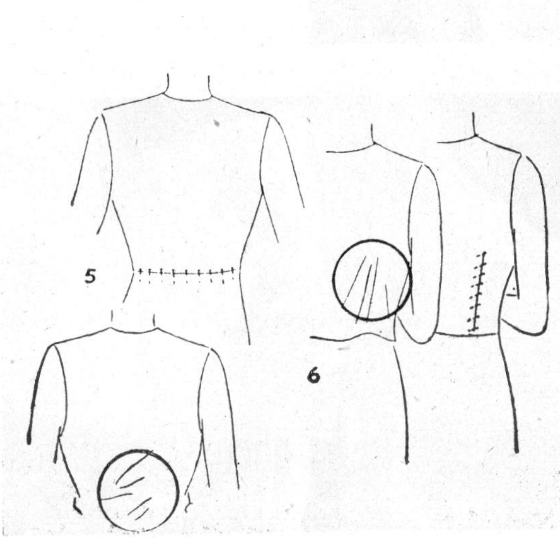

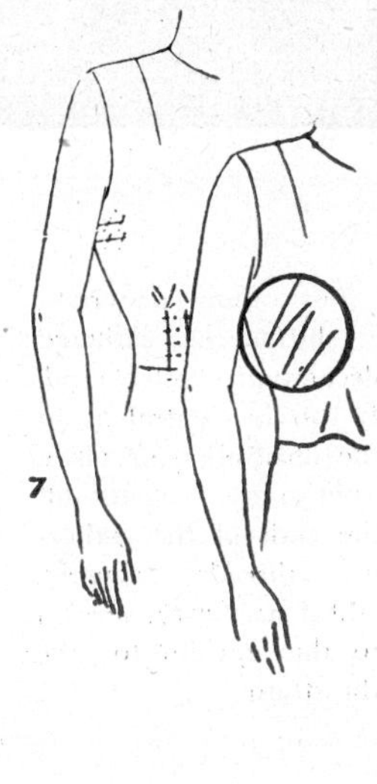

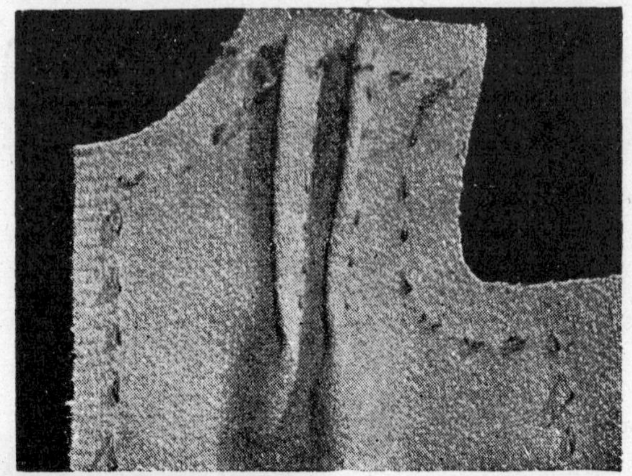

Before tacking up shoulder seams, sew in one or two tapered darts in the front on the wrong side, if pattern allows for them. They should taper gradually, so that there are no gathers at the bottom.

Shoulder–

Below:
Another alternative for thin fabrics is to have narrow, parallel tucks on the right side, which can be either machined or handsewn

For thin materials, a shirred or gathered decoration is often used. It can be central as in the illustration or taken right across. Fasten off the ends of the gathering threads securely, and if necessary, sew on to thin muslin to take the strain.

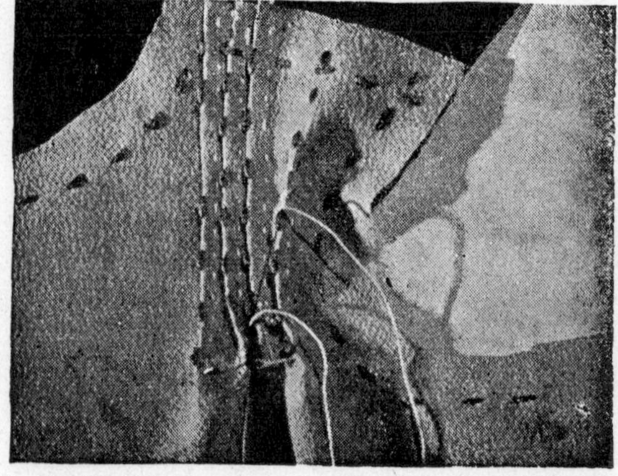

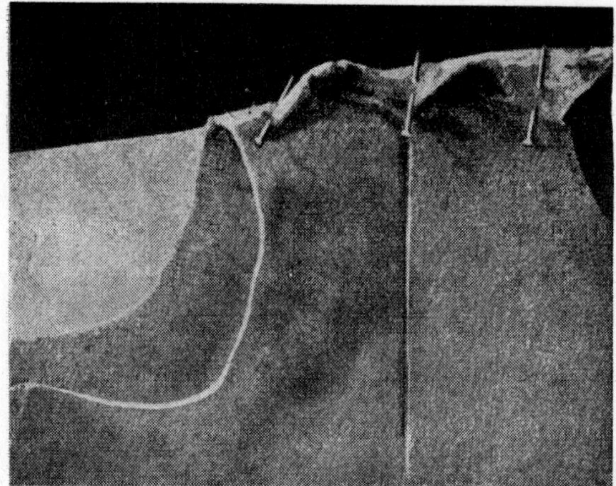

When the dart has been sewn and pressed, pin the ends of the shoulder seam together at neck and arm edges, then ease in any extra fullness so that no pleats form.

–Darts and Seams

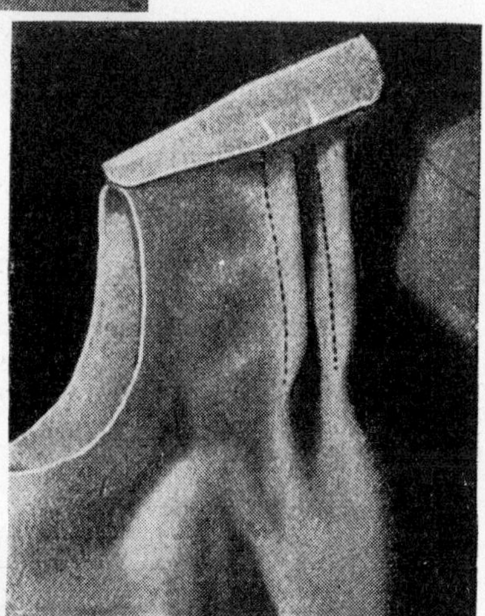

Two more ways of finishing off shoulder seams and darts are shown here. The darts are left uncut and pressed either flat or to one side.

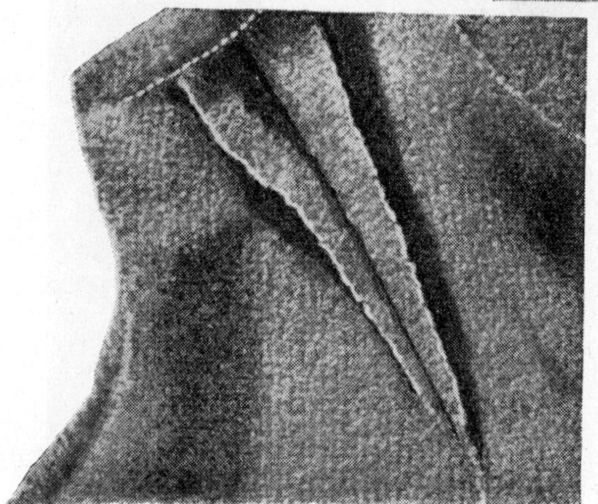

In thick material, when one dart only is made, it should be cut and pressed open before the shoulder seam is machined.

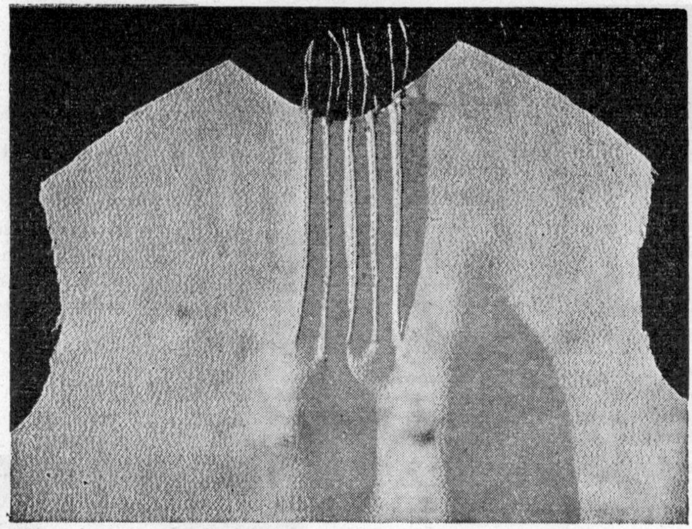

Tucks at the Back give a Better Fit

For shoulder fullness with high shoulder blades the narrow parallel tapered tucks shown above are the best. The tucks are made on the wrong side, the thread ends being well fastened off. Slightly round shoulders and full backs need tapered tucks (below). When fittting, pin one large tuck, and then divide into four or five smaller tucks later. Any fullness at the base can be shrunk away.

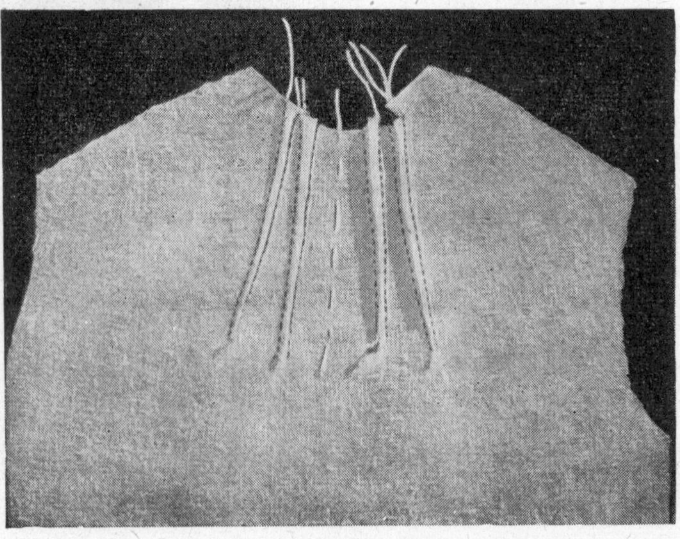

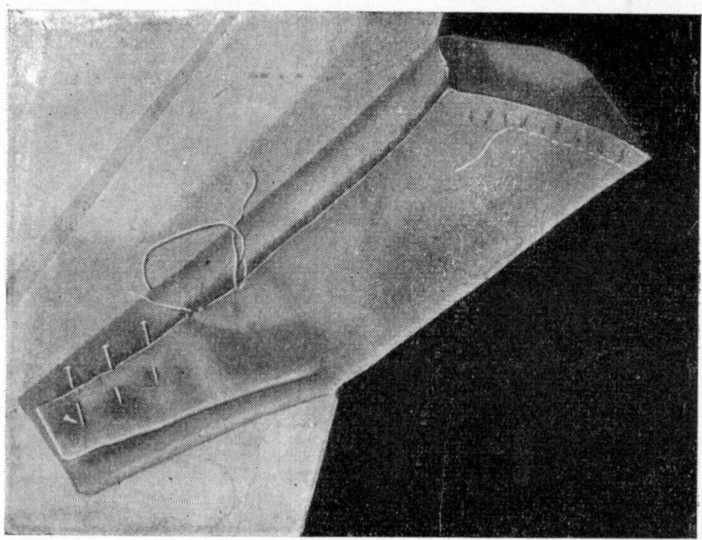

Making up a Fitted Sleeve

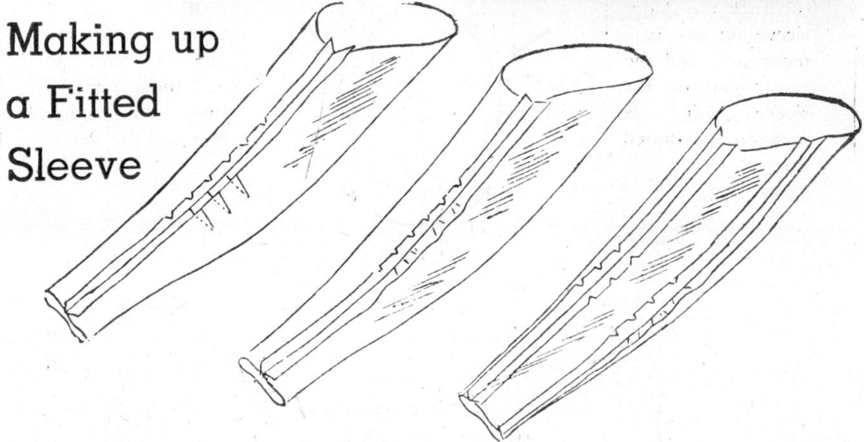

Before tacking up a two-piece sleeve (right-hand sketch) place the upper sleeve flat on the table with under portion upon it, the two front edges exactly level, and pin them together.

Keep the sleeve flat on the table with the front seam away from you. Bring the back edge over to meet the back edge of the under sleeve. Pin from top to elbow, then from wrist to elbow. The space of the upper sleeve will be found too large to fit the space of the under sleeve, and the extra fullness must be gathered to fit.

In a one-piece darted sleeve with second seam from elbow to wrist, the outer seam must be tapered gradually at the elbow end (see photograph). Notice the position of the pins, the slip-tacking and the gathering threads round the armhole.

When sleeves are trimmed, fix trimmings before sewing up. Before neatening, snip the edges of the seams at the curves to allow the material to lie flat. The drawing above shows two kinds of elbow fullness—almost imperceptible gathers and small tapered darts. Neaten the seams by overcasting.

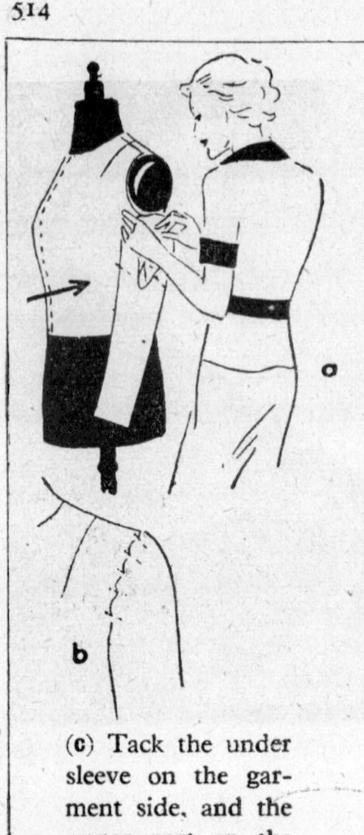

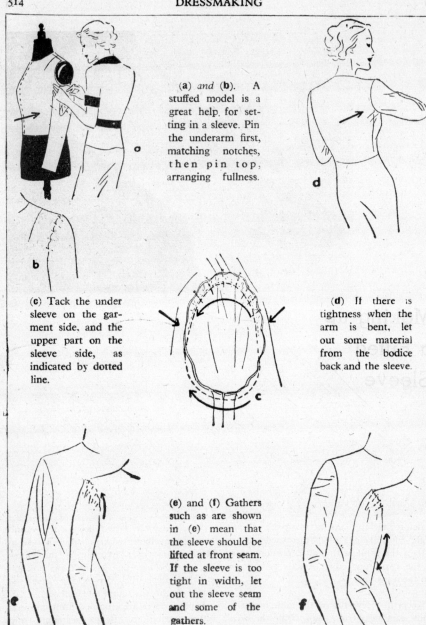

(**a**) *and* (**b**). A stuffed model is a great help for setting in a sleeve. Pin the underarm first, matching notches, then pin top, arranging fullness.

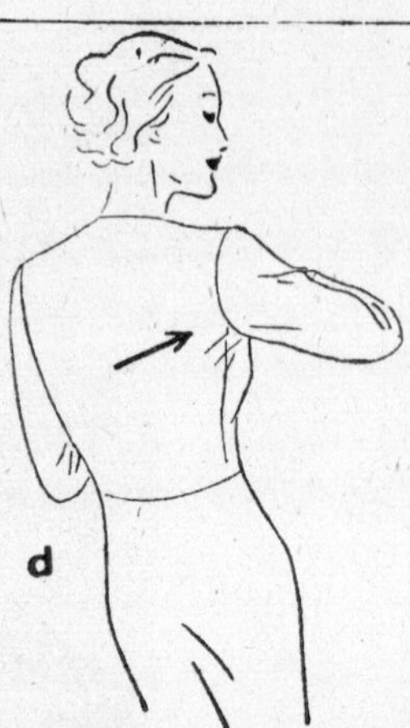

(**c**) Tack the under sleeve on the garment side, and the upper part on the sleeve side, as indicated by dotted line.

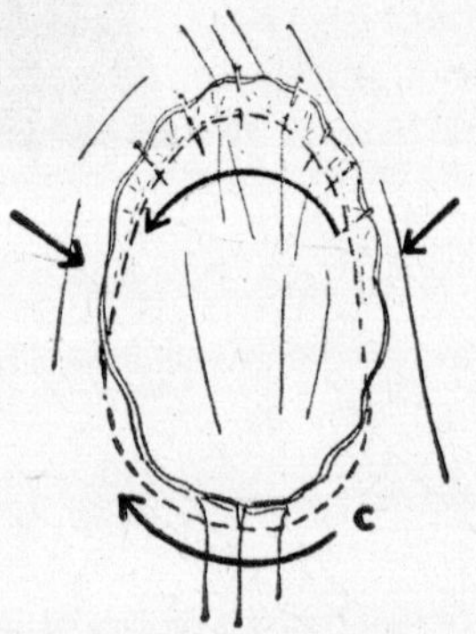

(**d**) If there is tightness when the arm is bent, let out some material from the bodice back and the sleeve.

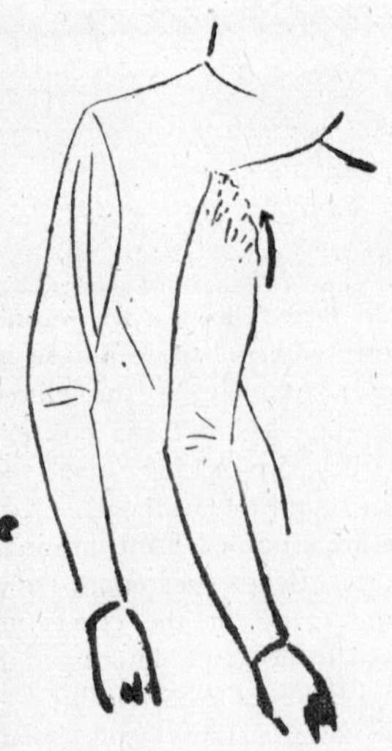

(**e**) and (**f**) Gathers such as are shown in (**e**) mean that the sleeve should be lifted at front seam. If the sleeve is too tight in width, let out the sleeve seam and some of the gathers.

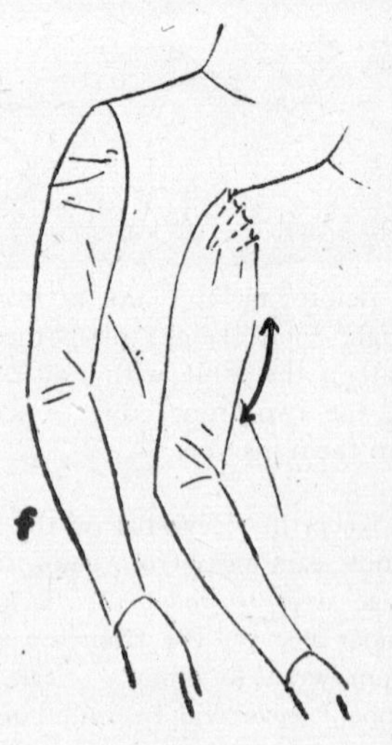

Setting in and Fitting the Sleeves

Before setting in a sleeve run one or two gathering threads round the top to ease the fullness when setting in. To test which is the right and which the left sleeve, lay both flat on the table, seams inwards. The cutaway part of the underarm is the front. To set in a sleeve, hold the bodice wrong side towards you, and put the right hand through the armhole to bring up the sleeve, right side out, and pin front seam of sleeve into position marked in armhole.

Pin round under part of the armhole up to the back. Place the back-notch in sleeve to corresponding notch in the back armhole. Distribute easing evenly over top of sleeves, placing pins about 1 inch apart, pointing downwards. Tack round the under-part of sleeve and fasten off. Begin again at the front, inside armhole and tack in the direction of the arrows in (**c**)

The sleeve is now ready for trying on. Put a tacking thread in the top centre of the sleeve along the vertical grain, and cross it at right angles with another thread. This helps in determining whether the sleeve hangs quite straight. Bend the arm as in (**d**), and if there is any tightness, let out some material from the back of the bodice and the sleeve seams. (**e**) Folds that fall towards the front, show that the sleeve should be set further back. (**f**) If the sleeve is too tight, let out the seams and some of the fullness from the gathers.

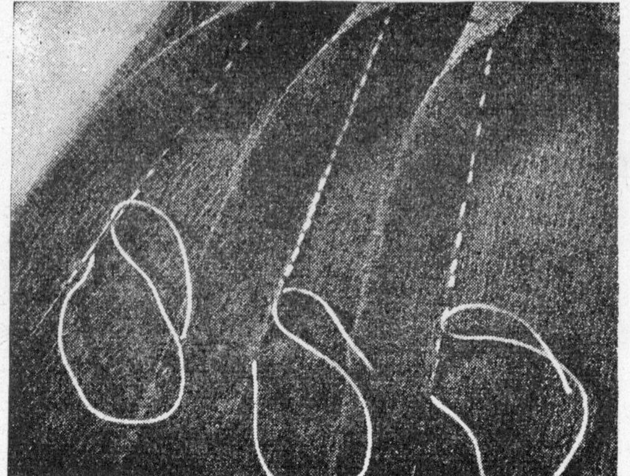

1.

On the left is running stitch, in the centre, back stitch, and on the right, a seam worked in running stitch with an occasional back stitch to secure it.

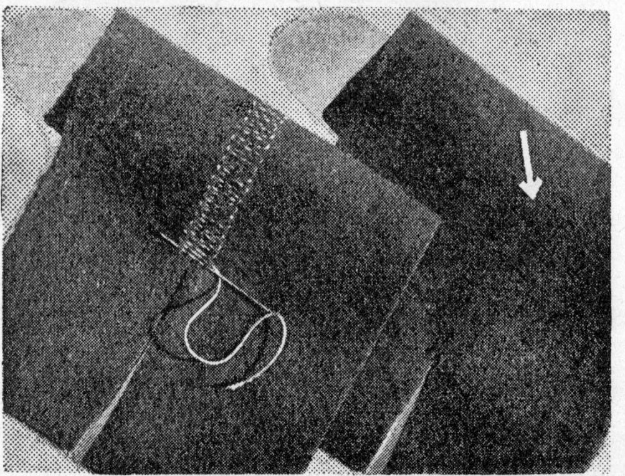

2.

3.

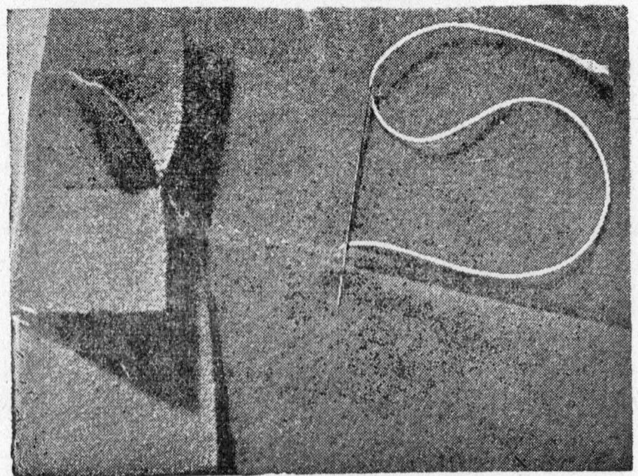

Above, a darned seam. The arrow shows the right side with no stitches visible. Right, an invisible seam in thin material. Any visible stitches can be covered by scratching the pile slightly with the needle point.

Hand Sewn Seams

1. Back stitch and running stitch are the foundation of all handsewing. Running stitch, worked with a fine needle, should be close and even, the needle being passed in and out of the material several times before the thread is drawn up. Back stitch is much more secure, and is worked from right to left, the needle being brought out after every stitch, a short distance from the last stitch worked and then taken back to be reinserted next to that stitch. The finished seam should resemble machine stitching, being absolutely even, with no space between the stitches. Running and back stitch need practice and care to reach the standard of fineness and evenness necessary for neat sewing.

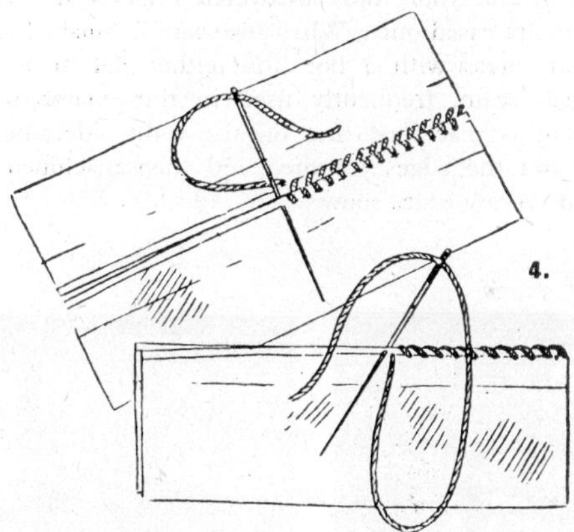

2. A darned seam should be invisible on the right side of thick wool fabric. The two edges do not overlap, but are held together over the fingers of the left hand. Tiny darning stitches worked backwards and forwards across the join on the wrong side, keep the edges securely together. The stitches must not show on the right side. 3. Thin material with a pile can be first machined and then neatly and closely darned on the right side as shown in the photograph. 4. Overcasting can be worked either from left to right or right to left. The stitches should be evenly spaced and the slant kept even. A quick way to overcast thin fabrics is to take two or three stitches before drawing up the thread. An alternative to overcasting is done with the material held as for a darned seam, the stitches being arranged alternately on each side (see top sketch).

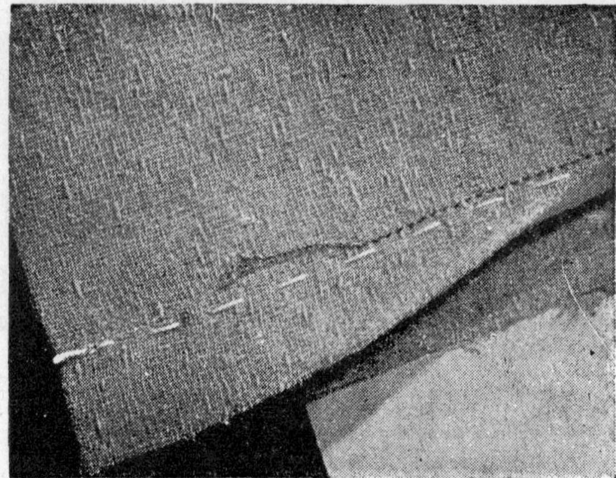

Plain Seams–

1.

Do not machine on the tacking line, but just inside it, so that the tacking threads can be drawn out easily. Leave a long thread after machining, and before fastening off, run your thimble-covered finger down the machining, so that any puckers are eased out When the seam is finished and the tacking threads drawn out, press with a hot iron, either flat or to one side (**2**). (**3**) shows a french seam, frequently used in thin material that is liable to fray. The seam is machined first on the right side, then the tacking threads removed and the edges trimmed and then machined again on the wrong side, so that no raw edges show.

2.

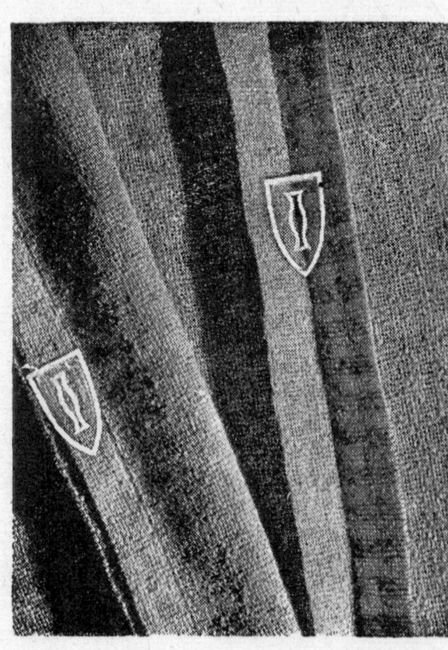

3.

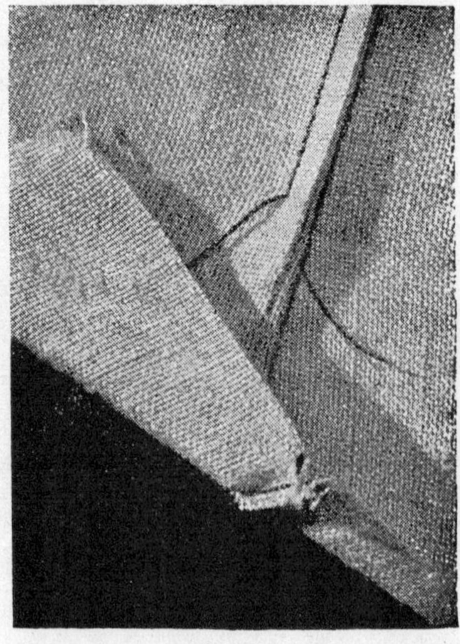

–and How They are Neatened

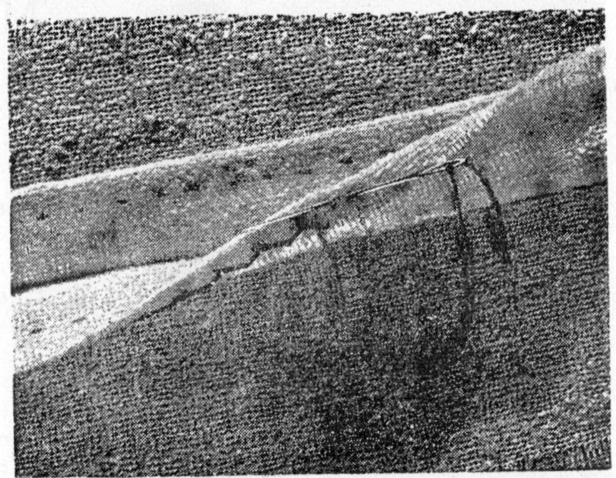

The way in which a seam is finished on the wrong side is the true test of good workmanship. Many a piece of otherwise fine sewing has been ruined by inadequate and untidy seam finishing. A seam that has fairly wide turnings and is in light-weight material that will not fray, can be turned under and neatly herringboned on the under side. Do not draw the stitching up too tightly. Another way for flat-pressed seams in material that will not fray, is to turn under once and machine down each side. For a seam that is pressed to one side, the edges can be turned inwards and slip stitched together, so that they lie flat.

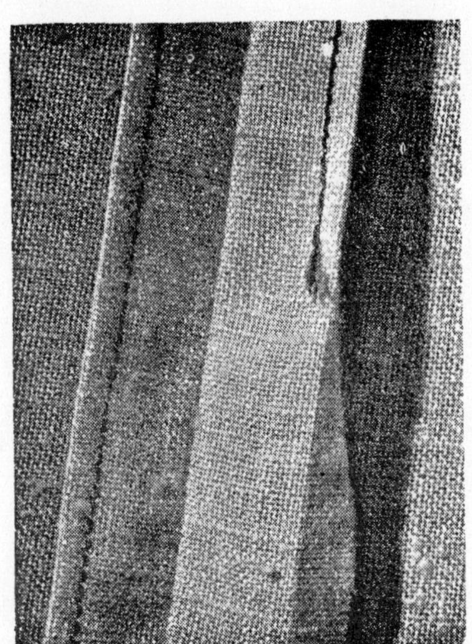

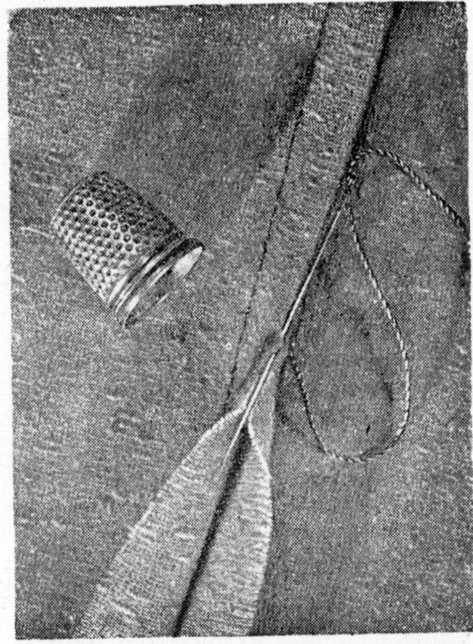

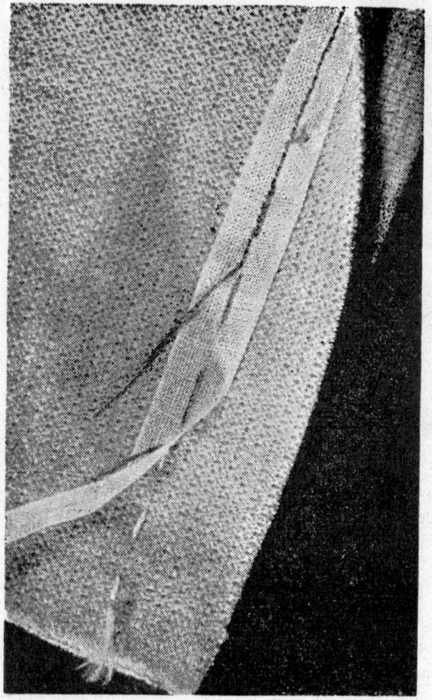

More Seams–

Some materials such as stockinette stretch out of shape while being machined. To keep the line, a strip of narrow tape should be tacked on to the wrong side and placed directly under the presser foot of the sewing-machine. Take care not to force or stretch the material while guiding. For neatening seams of this kind, the most effective way is to herringbone them flat to the material, as they are liable to roll over. The stitches should not show on the right side.

Thin cottons and georgettes fray easily, and the seam should be tightly rolled back and overcast with fine stitches in silk.

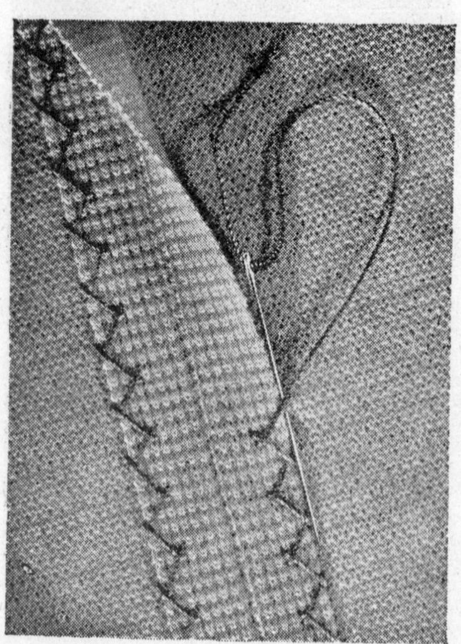

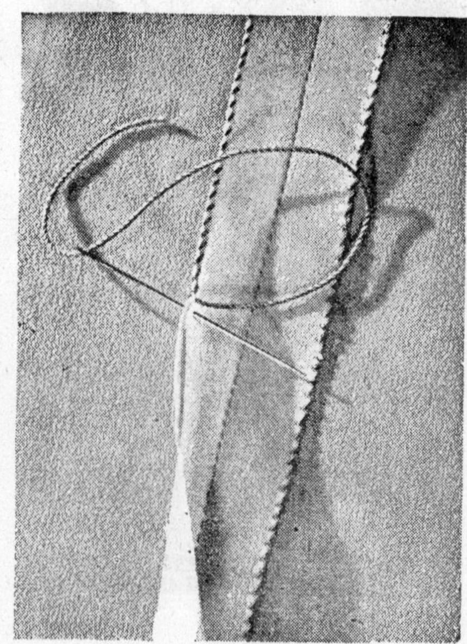

–and Ways of Neatening

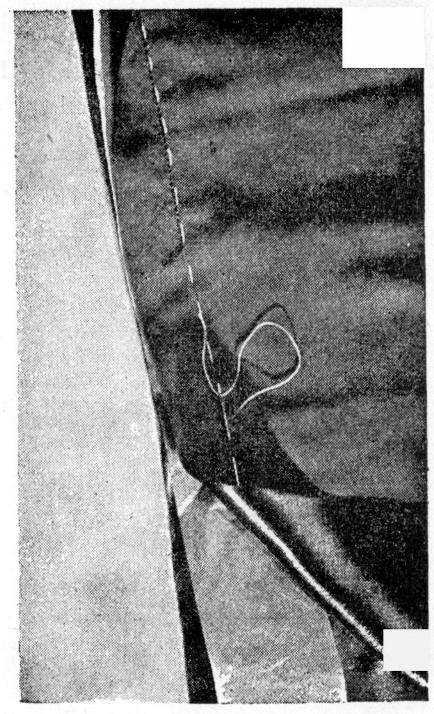

Silk or panne velvet rubs out of position when placed nap on nap, so a strip of paper should be placed between the seam and gently pulled away after machining. Always machine the way of the nap.

A seam that can be neatened at the same time with only one machining, is shown below. Leave an unequal allowance, so that one side will wrap well over the other. If there is a selvedge, the top edge need not be turned under. Careful tacking is absolutely necessary.

Narrow binding can be used for finishing a seam in thick material. It should be machined first, and then turned under by hand.

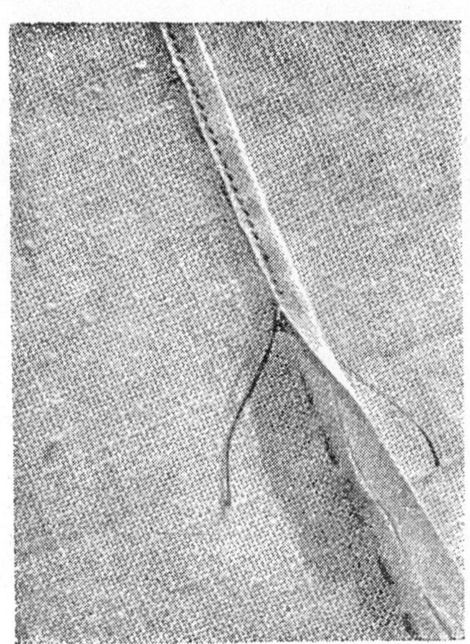

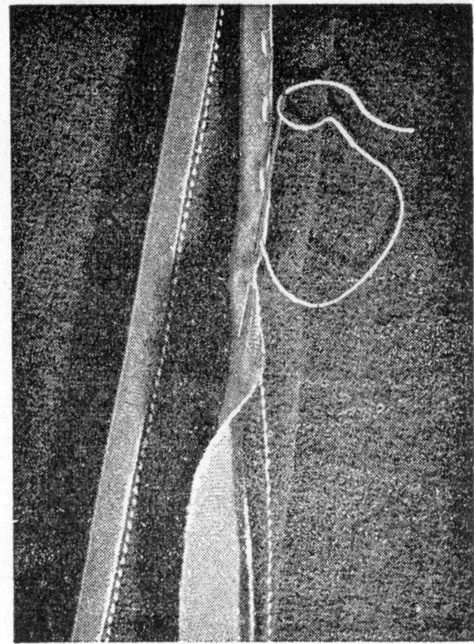

Neatening Seams in Thick Material

Blanket stitch (worked downwards towards the edge of the material, the thread loop being kept under the needle) makes an effective finish for nearly all thick materials. It is both neat and secure. It should be worked in silk to tone, the stitches being kept slack rather than tight (a). Buttonhole stitch, worked from the edge downwards as seen in the photograph on the opposite page, can also be used. Plain overcasting is another alternative, the stitches being kept loose and even. A curved seam should first be snipped, before being either overcast or button holed. The finishes shown here are especially suitable for skirts, woollen dresses and tailored or unlined coats.

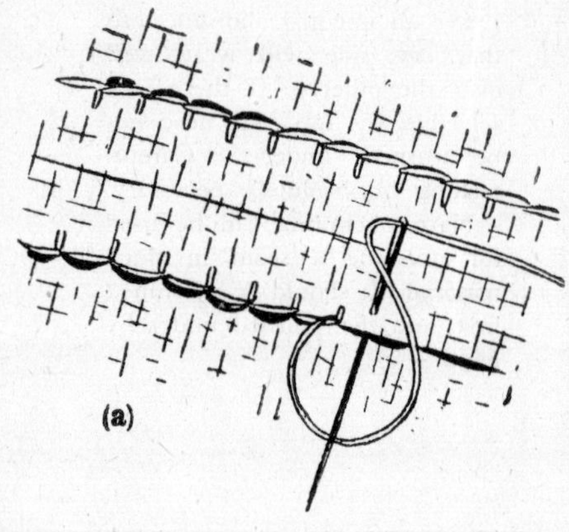

(a)

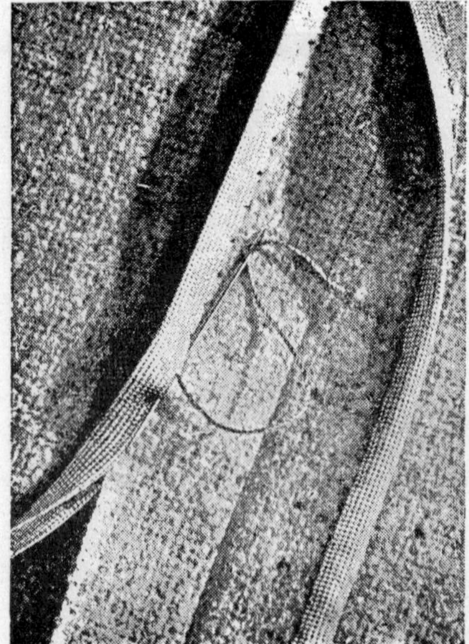

A narrow turning, secured by neat running stitches with an occasional back stitch to secure it, can also be used. This has the advantage of being easily worked.

Sometimes a coat is lined with material of the same weave instead of silk (see the top photograph on the opposite page). This means that the seams must be particularly well finished off. Turn the edges inwards, and slip stitch them together.

When the seams are finished, they should be pressed with a hot iron, each side being first pressed separately, i.e. lay each side of the finished seam on the ironing board, and press the stitching before ironing the seam as a whole.

Right, a coat seam lined with material of the same thickness. Notice how the edges are neatened. Below—a curved seam snipped and overcast

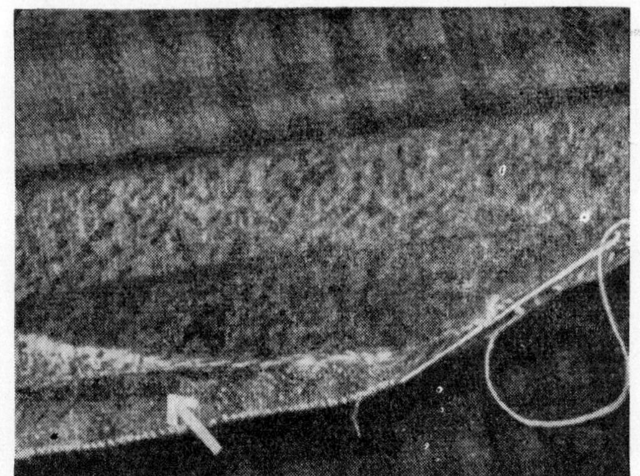

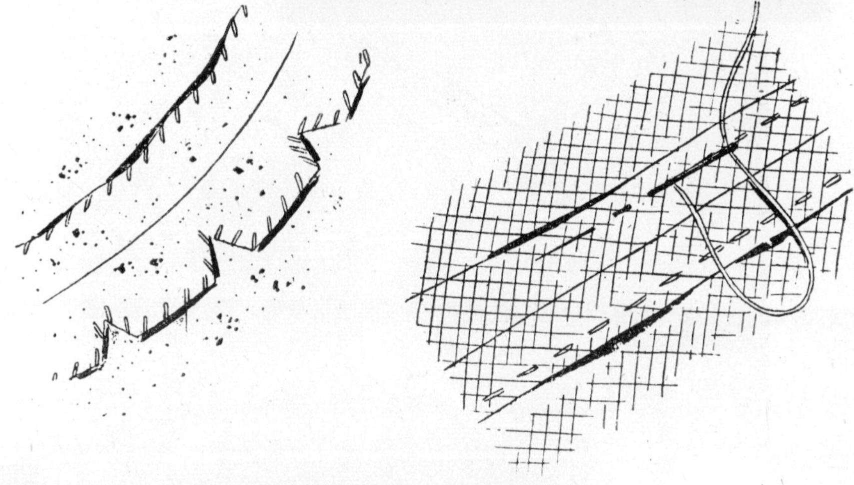

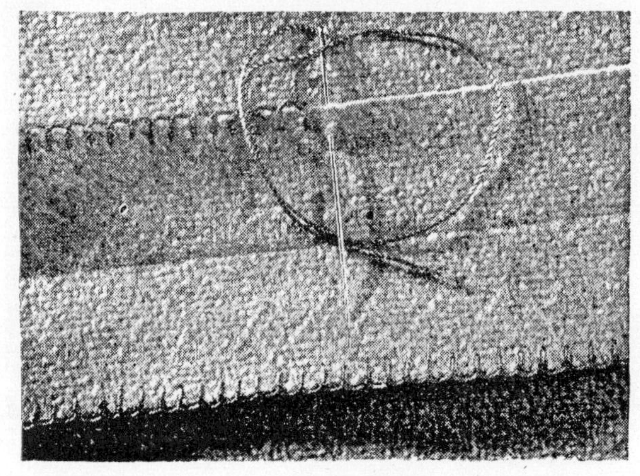

Buttonhole stitch (left) worked downwards from the edge. Above, a turned-in edge secured by running stitch with an occasional back stitch.

Slot Seams

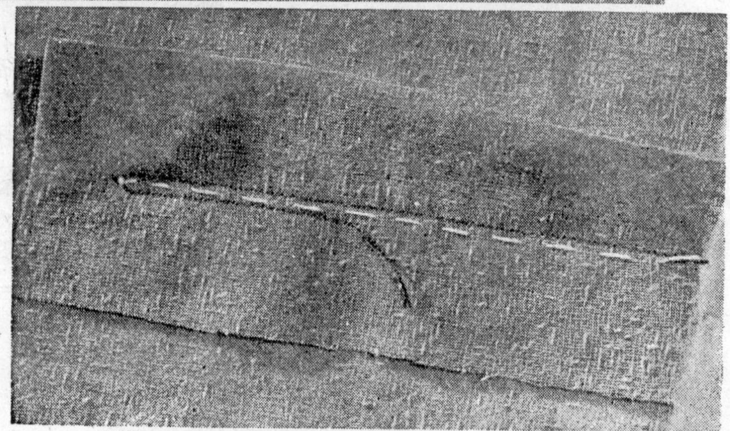

Follow the order shown in the photographs for a slot seam, which is suitable for any non-transparent fabric.

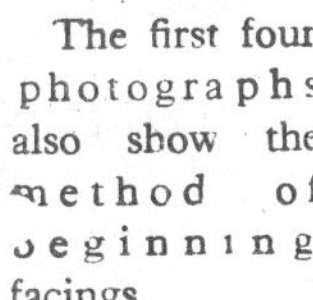

The first four photographs also show the method of beginning facings.

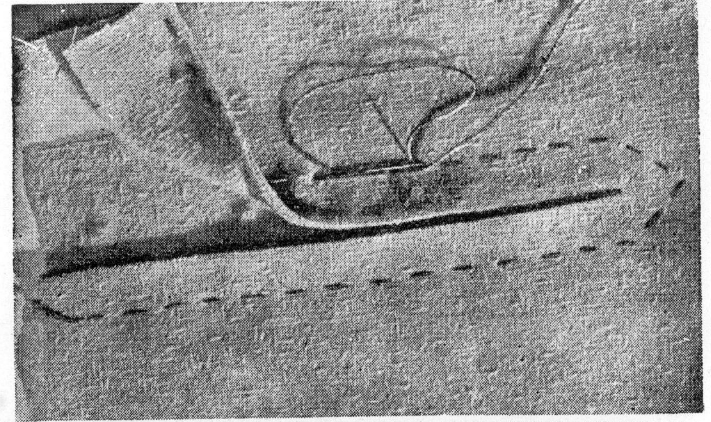

Hems in Thin Fabrics

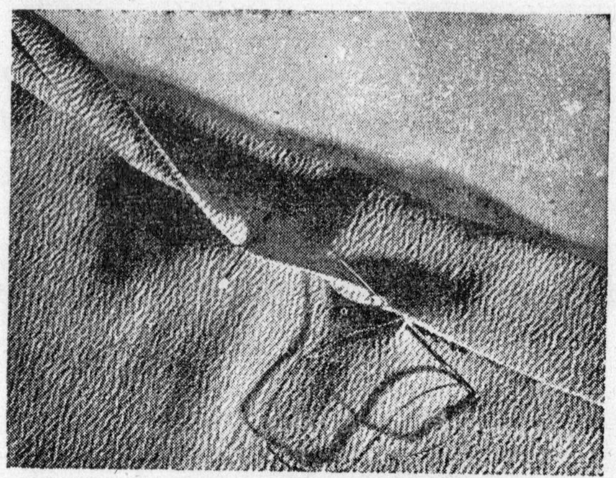

(a)

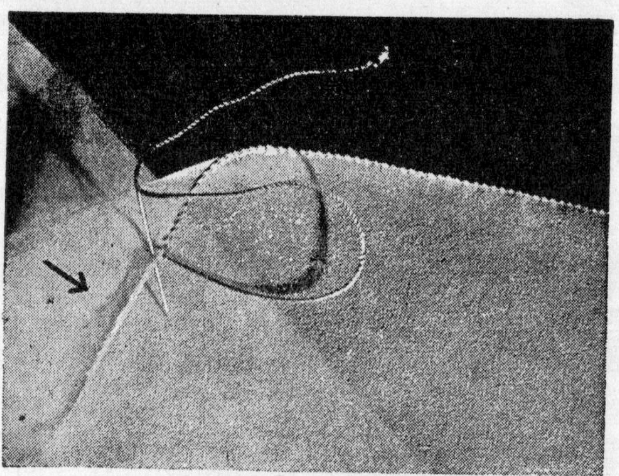

(b)

(c)

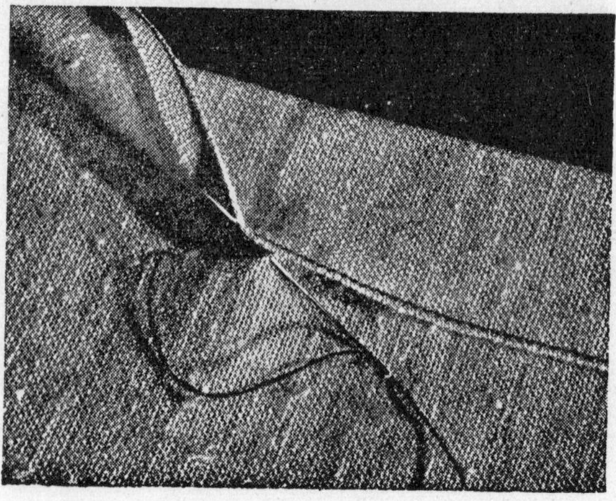

(**a**) Turn in the material once, and press. Then turn over again and hem, the needle taking up one or two threads only. Stitches should be slack and invisible. (**b**) For georgette and delicate weaves use a rolled hem. Small, even overcasting in silk, secures the material which is rolled towards the wrong side. (**c**) With springy material, instead of just pressing the first turn, machine it near the edge.

False Hems

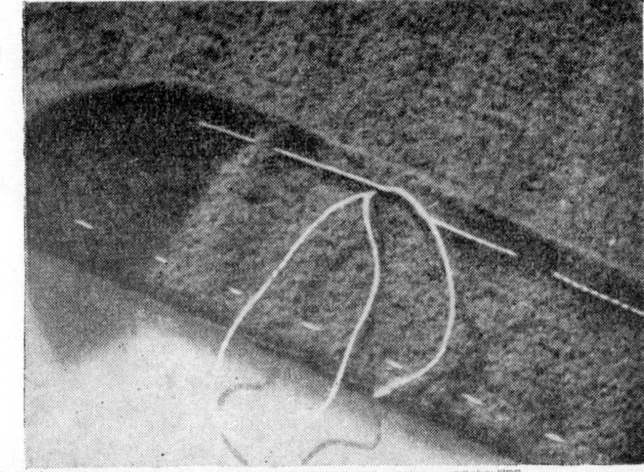

(d)

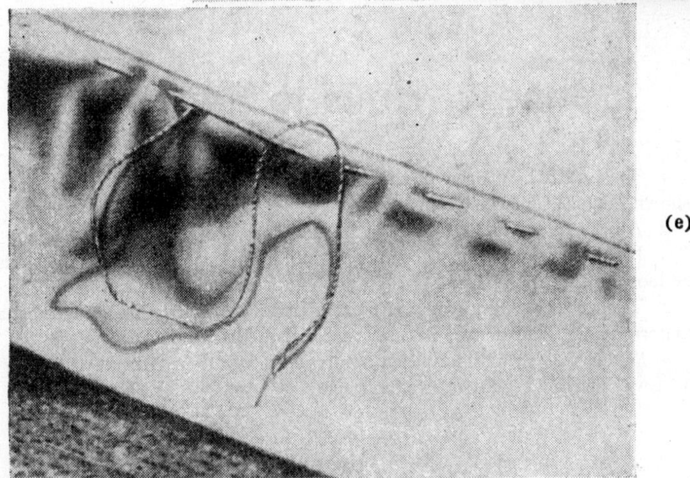

(e)

(f)

Machine two edges together, turn, tack together as shown in the photographs and press, before tacking down the upper part. Hem invisibly by hand. If lining is used, the bottom seam should be pressed so that it does not show on the right side.

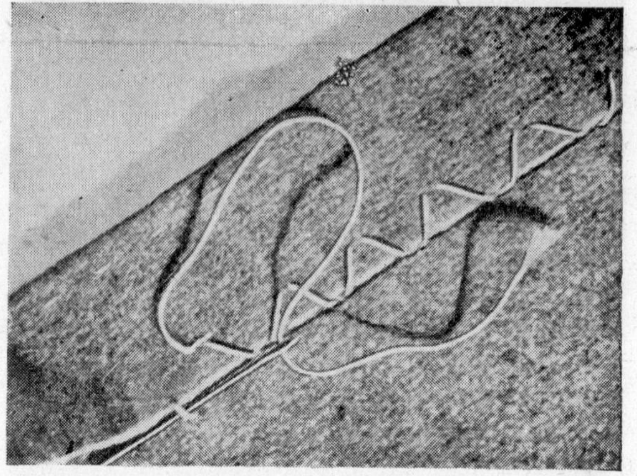

When coats are lined, the hem need only be roughly finished. Use herring boning as illustrated.

General Hints to Remember

1. To ensure an even hem, make a cardboard gauge similar to that shown for bias binding (see page 532).

2. Any cross seams that come inside the hem should be pressed open.

3. No matter what method of hemming is chosen, the stitches should be loose so that there is no pimply drawn appearance on the right side.

4. The general ruling for width is: narrow hems for thin and transparent material, and wide hems for thick materials, skirts and coats.

5. When making children's garments, a tuck put just inside the hem is a neat way of allowing for future lengthening.

An alternative for a lined coat is to pink the edge, and catch-stitch the hem in position.

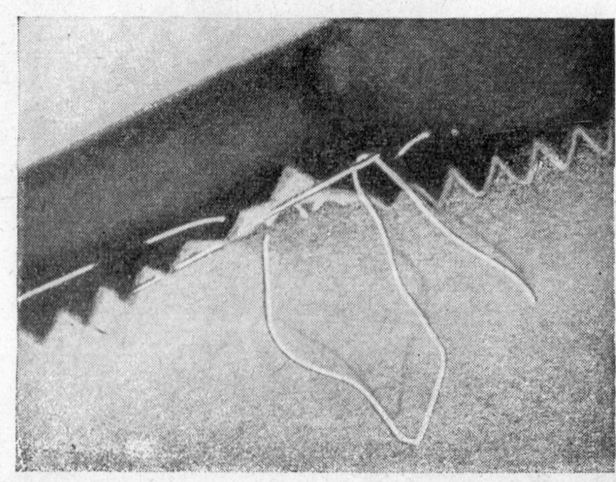

Curved Hems

Curved hems need especial care. They should first be pinned as above, and then tacked so that tiny pleats are formed. These should be carefully pressed with a hot iron and damp cloth, from the edge inwards. This will also help to shrink away some of the fullness. Tack the edge carefully and hem with long, loose stitches. Circular skirts should be hung for about forty-eight hours before turning up the hem.

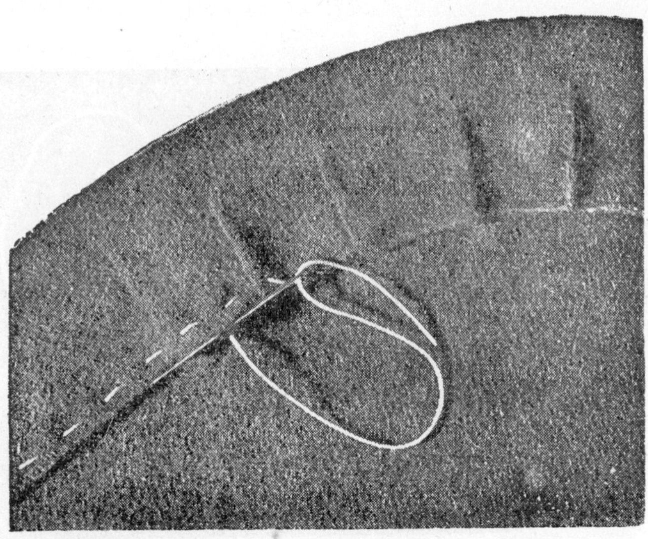

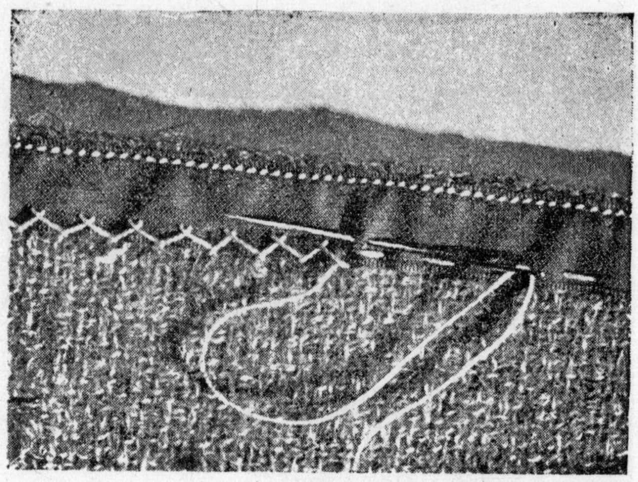

Binding Used for Hems

(a)

Braid binding can be used for neatening hems. After machining the raw edge to the binding, tack in position and press. Then herringbone, catching one or two threads only.

Use bias binding for finishing an unlined coat as shown on the opposite page. Sew first, as shown in (**c**), pulling the binding slightly while tacking. Then turn in and back stitch through from the right side (**d**) or hem (**e**) before catchstitching to the fabric. A Concertina hem (**f**) is sometimes used, and is made with wider bias binding, which is pressed with an inwards fold, before hemming down.

(b)

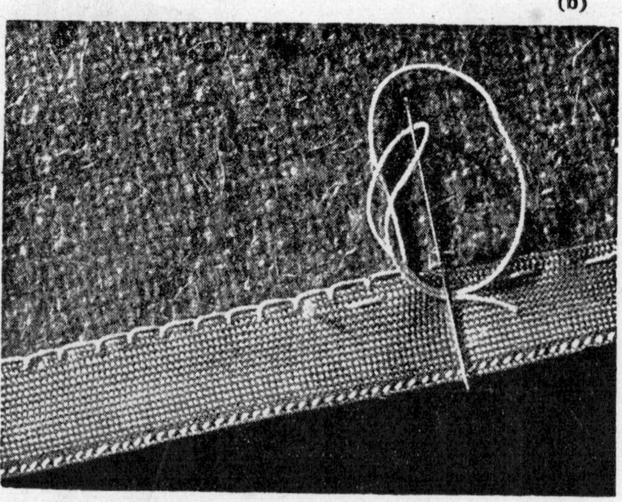

Buttonholing can be used as an alternative to herringboning for neatening braid-finished seams.

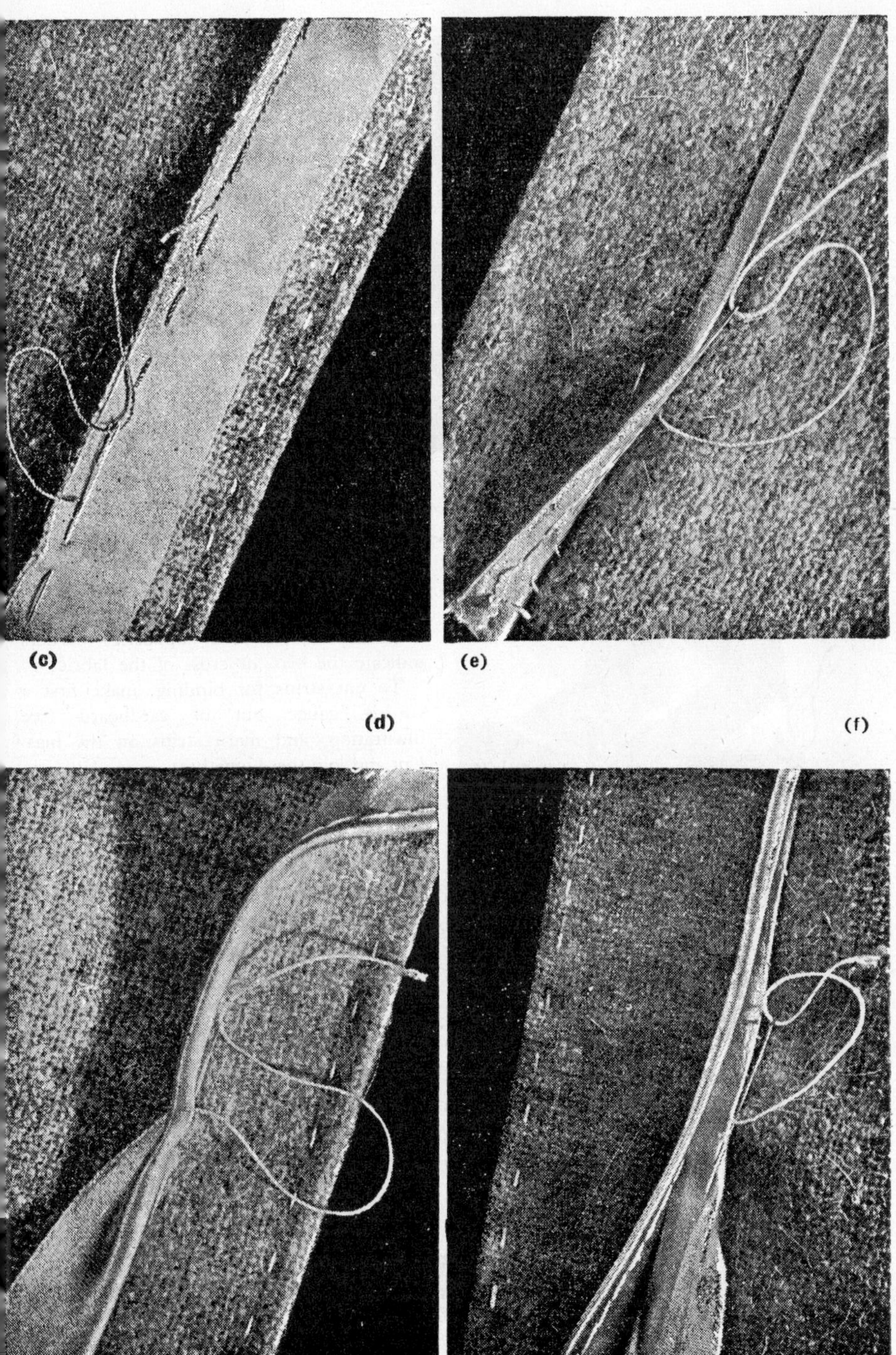

(c) (e)

(d) (f)

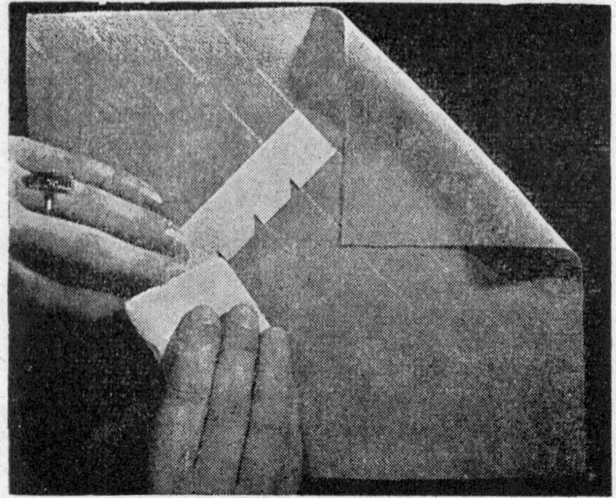

Bias Binding and Piping

To get the true bias of a fabric, cut an exact square, the edges of which are absolutely parallel with the weave. The diagonal lines from opposite corners indicate the bias, or cross of the fabric.

To cut strips for binding, make first a cutting gauge out of cardboard (see illustration) and mark strips on the bias. Cut and join these together.

Pin together as in the photograph on the left, and machine. If there are several strips to be joined, they can be run together. Trim the edges as shown below. Care must be taken to see that the right side of the binding matches the right side each time, as it is very easy to go wrong.

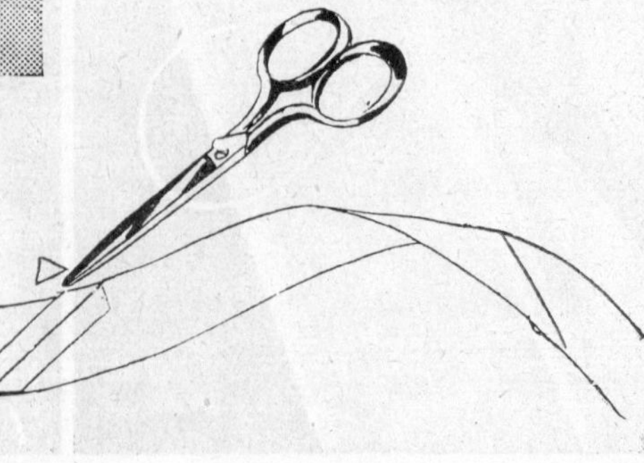

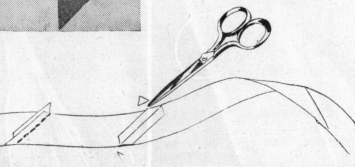

A flat piping is sometimes made out of strips of bias binding, which are folded, and tacked flatly on to the under strip of material. The upper material is then laid over it so that a narrow edge is left showing.

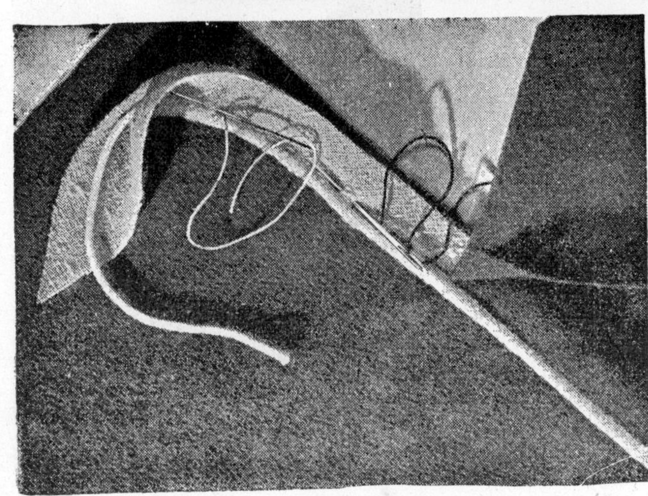

Piping made out of narrow woollen cord is often covered by bias binding. Tack the binding tightly round the cord, then stitch securely. Sew the upper piece of material to the bias binding so that it comes right up to the cord

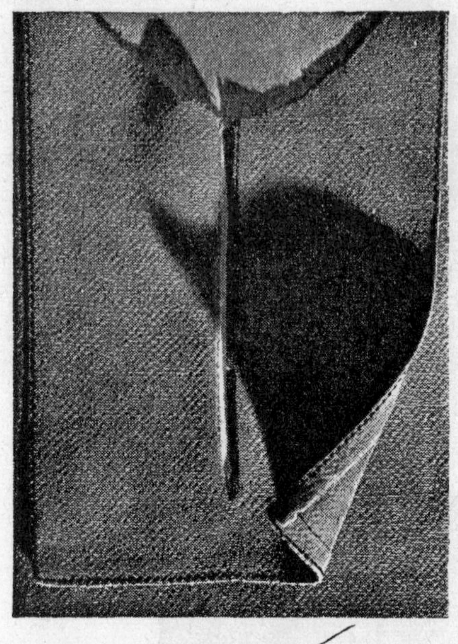

Front Facings

The pictorial instructions given previously for making a slot seam apply equally well for facings. The same procedure is followed except that the facing should be wide enough to reach to the shoulder seam. The edges are turned in (photograph on left) and caught lightly at the corners so that there is no pull on the right side. Complete with one or more buttons and loops. For a facing that has to carry fasteners (see lower photograph) a strip cut on the cross is sewn on to the right side (lower sketch). Machine down one side, the point, and a quarter of the way up the second side. The under strip is cut on the straight and bound in the usual way.

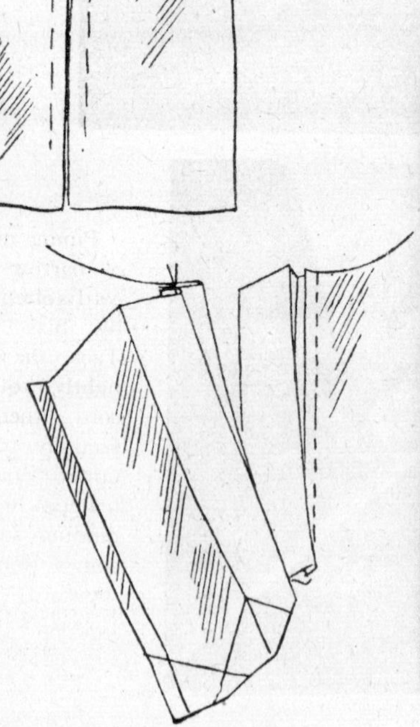

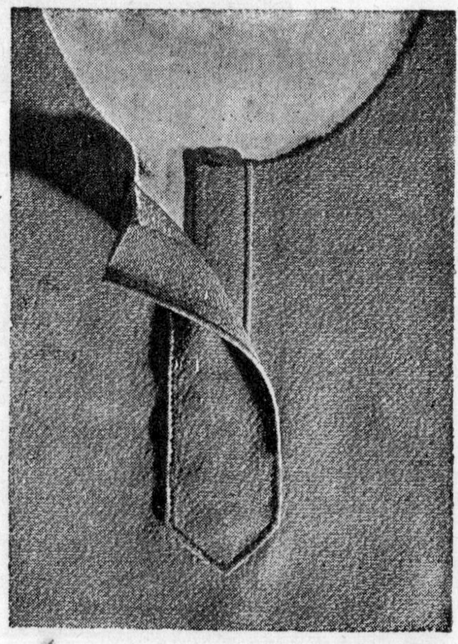

Bound Necklines

Cut square necks by the paper pattern so that the way of the grain is the same as that of the garment. Sew first on the right side then turn and press, snipping the corners (see arrow) so that they lie flat. The ends can be turned in and handsewn or machined as in the photograph.

The pattern can be cut in pieces and joined at corners as shown in (b) and (c).

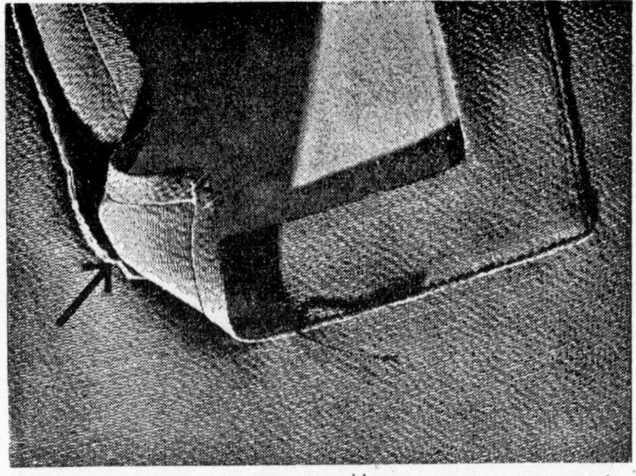

(a)

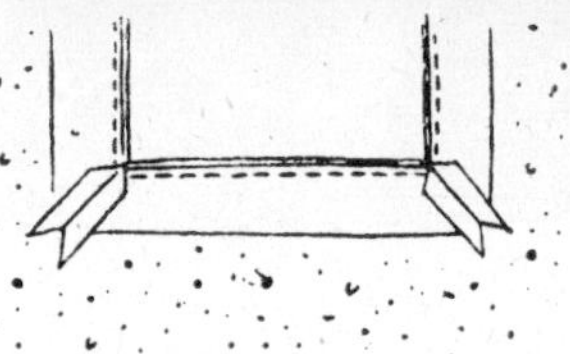

(b)

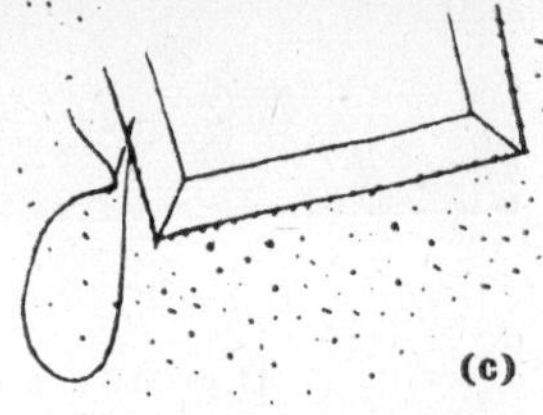

(c)

Use bias-binding for pointed or V necks. Machine from centre back to front, break off and start at back again.

Join the strips as indicated by arrow and press. Turn in invisibly as in photograph.

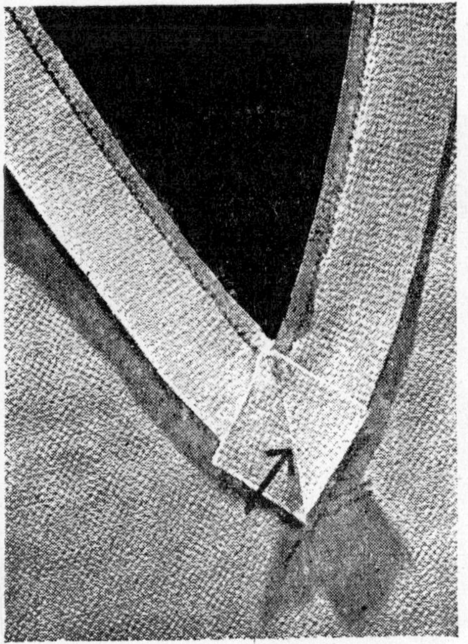

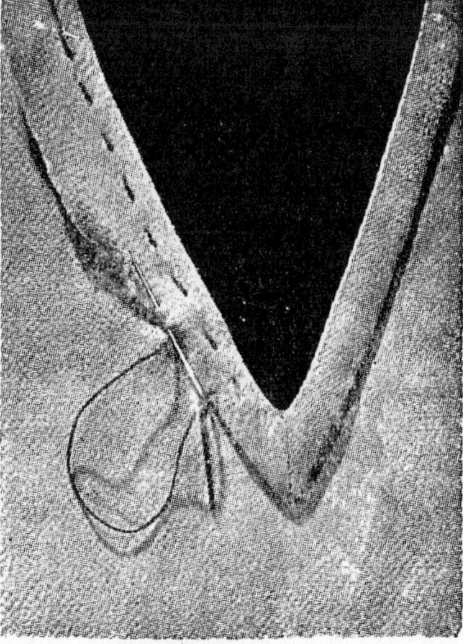

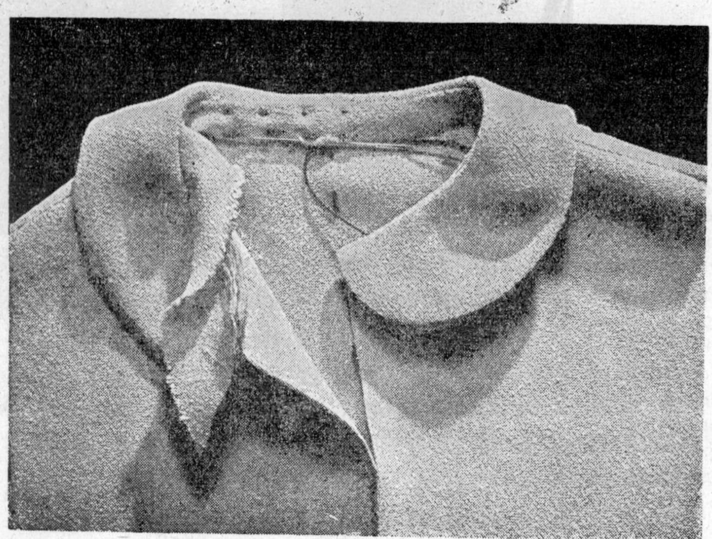

(a)

Dressmaker's collars can be lined or unlined. When the collar is of single material tack the inner edge to the garment neck, and tack a bias strip of the same material over the collar, and machine. Snip the turnings so that the seam lies flat, and bring the bias-binding over and hem.

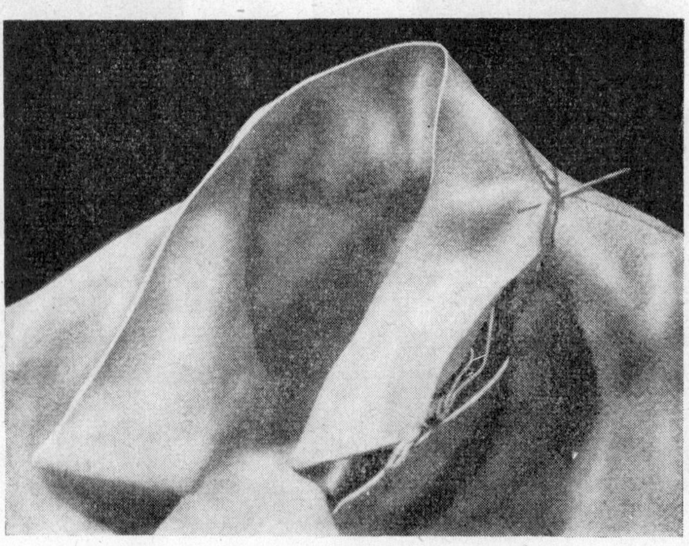

(b)

Collars

(c)

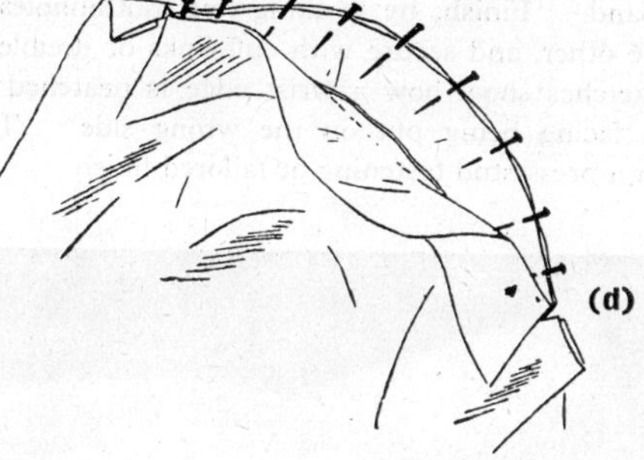

(d)

The lined collars shown on these two pages are made in double material, (**b**) being cut on the straight and the others on the cross.

N.B. There is no definite rule for cutting, but a collar cut absolutely straight with no shape, should be cut on the bias.

In (**d**) the inner edge of the collar is pinned and tacked to the wrong side of the garment, the centre of the collar matching the centre back exactly. Machine and snip the edges to allow the seam to lie flat. Now secure the outside edge of the collar to the right side of the garment with slack, invisible hemming (**b**) to cover the machine stitching. As there are four thicknesses along this seam, press particularly well with a hot iron and a damp cloth

An alternative way of attaching a collar is to use a bias strip of material, which is stitched as in (**a**) and then hemmed on to the wrong side of the garment.

Detachable collars should be finished with a strip of bias binding (**c**) In this case the neck edge of the garment is also bound.

Stand-up collars are first sewn on to the right side of the garment and then hemmed on the wrong side

Cuffs

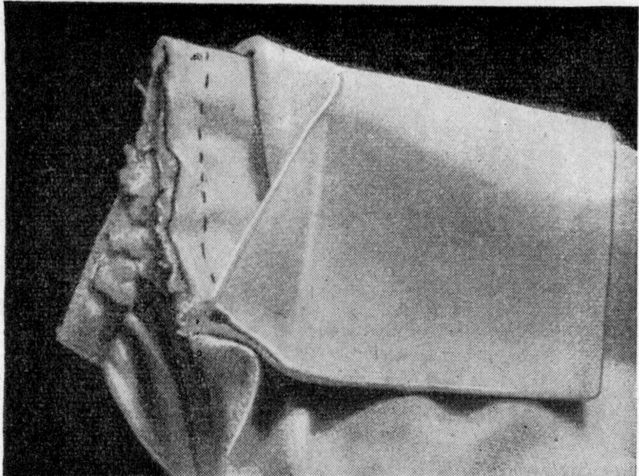

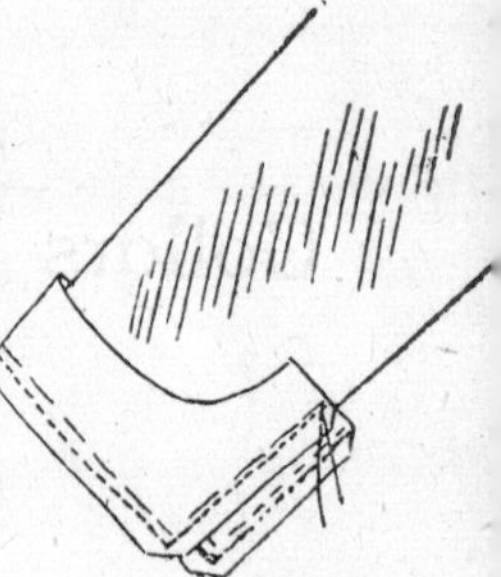

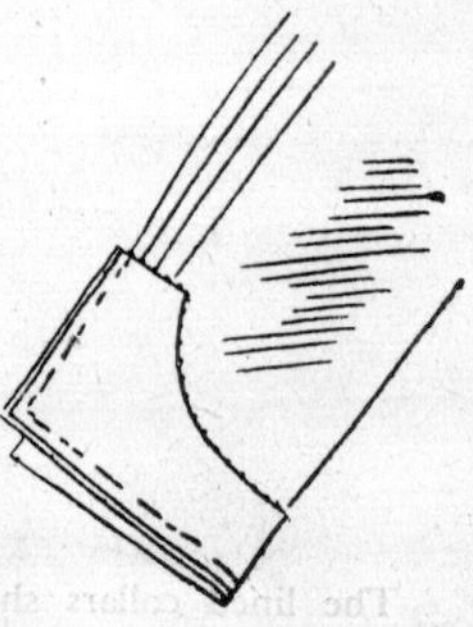

The width of the cuff varies according to the thickness of material and the type of garment. The one shown here is about 4 inches wide and is most suitable for blouses, overalls and shirts. First run a double gathering thread round the wristband. Then machine round three sides of the cuff, turn right side out, and machine the under side of the cuff to the wristband. Remove tacking threads, and secure the other side of the cuff to the under or wrong side of wristband. Finish, by working four buttonholes one on top of the other, and secure with cuff-links or double button. The sketches show how a wrist edge is neatened without a cuff, a facing being put on the wrong side. This also allows for a press-stud fastening or tailored finish.

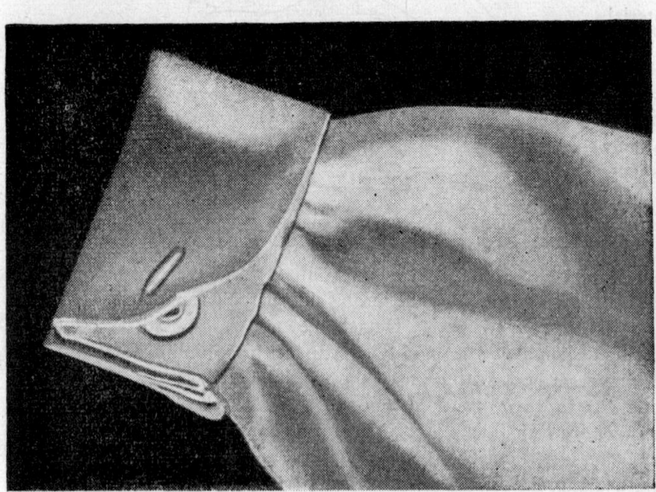

Finishing a Close-fitting Sleeve

The correct wrist finish is important in a close-fitting sleeve. As a sleeve is about $\frac{1}{4}$ to $\frac{1}{2}$ inch shorter when worn, this must always be allowed for. The photographs below show the wrong and right side of a placket opening secured by press studs. The dart is opened, and turned back or bound. The whole placket should be as inconspicuous as possible. If the placket will not overlap flatly, fancy buttons, similar to those shown in the photograph on the right, can be used with buttonhole loops. Full instructions for making these are given in this chapter.

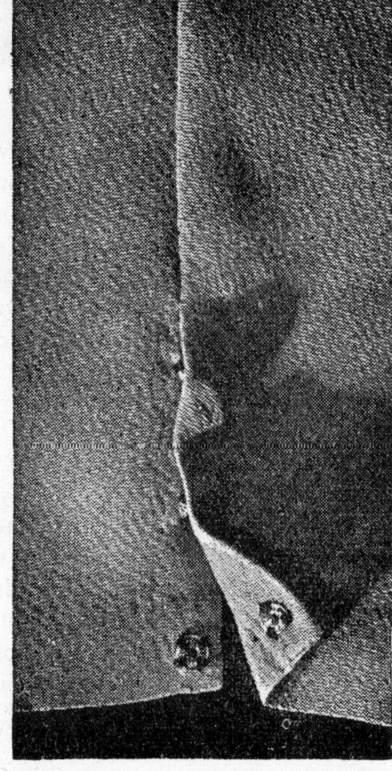

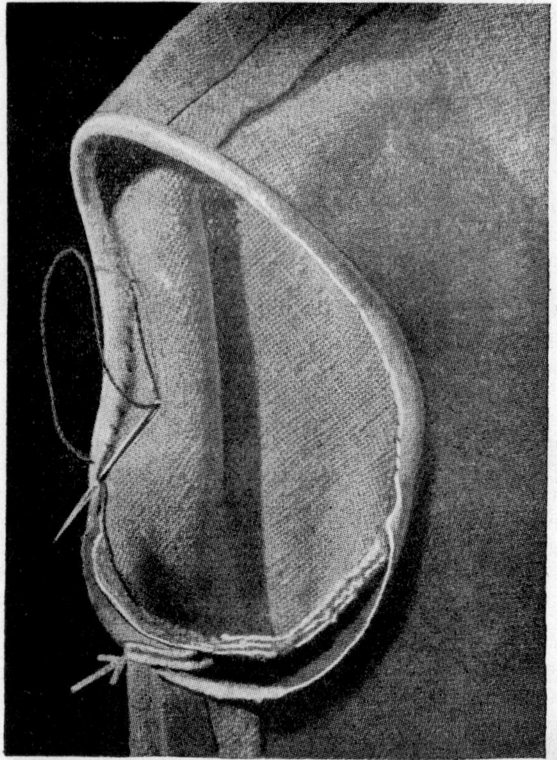

More Sleeves

Armholes can either be neatened by overcasting or by bias binding as in the photograph. Note the position of the join in the binding, indicated by the arrow.

A puff sleeve should be cut twice the width of an ordinary, close-fitting sleeve, and should have at least two rows of gathering threads round the armhole, as well as two rows round the lower edge. The fullness should be even, with slightly more gathers at the top than under the arm. When setting in, the machine stitching should come between the two rows of gathering.

A Raglan sleeve (bottom right, on the opposite page) is made to fit by a dart down the centre, as shown in the sketch at the top of the page. The shoulder seams are sewn before the sleeve is joined. These can either be pressed flat and overcast, or sewn as in the photograph, when they are pressed double into the armhole.

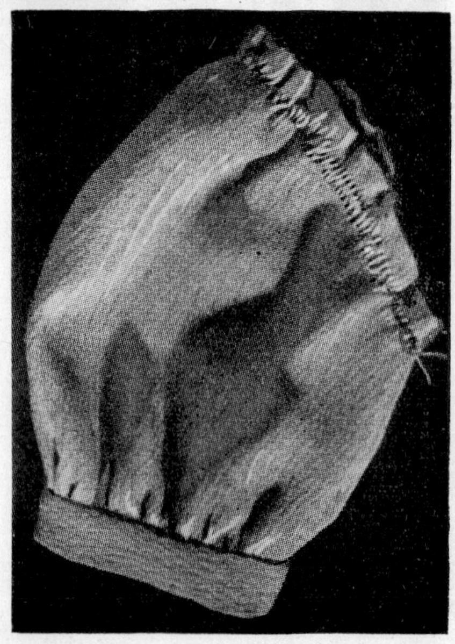

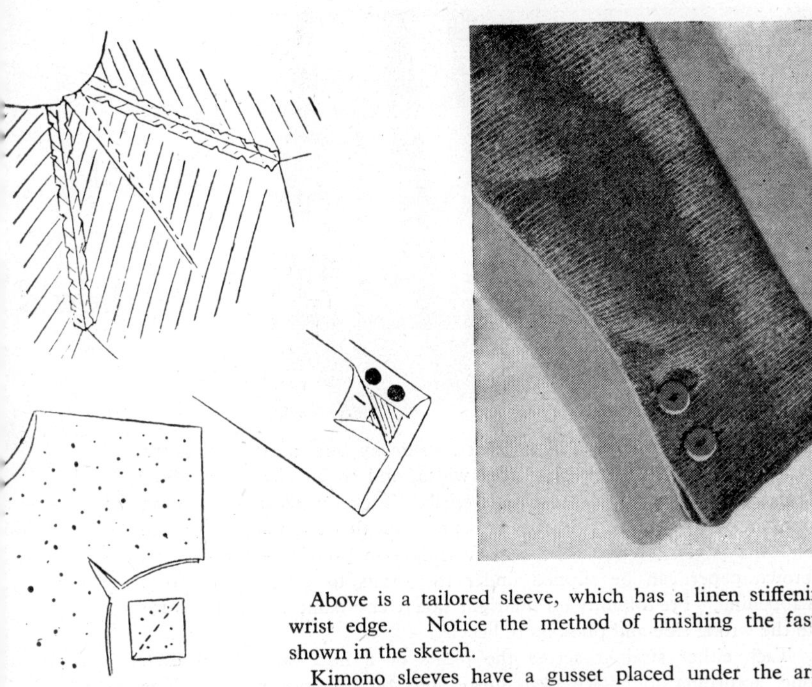

Above is a tailored sleeve, which has a linen stiffening at the wrist edge. Notice the method of finishing the fastening as shown in the sketch.

Kimono sleeves have a gusset placed under the arm. This should be slightly larger than the slit. Taper the side seams, where the slit comes, but do not press the gusset seams open.

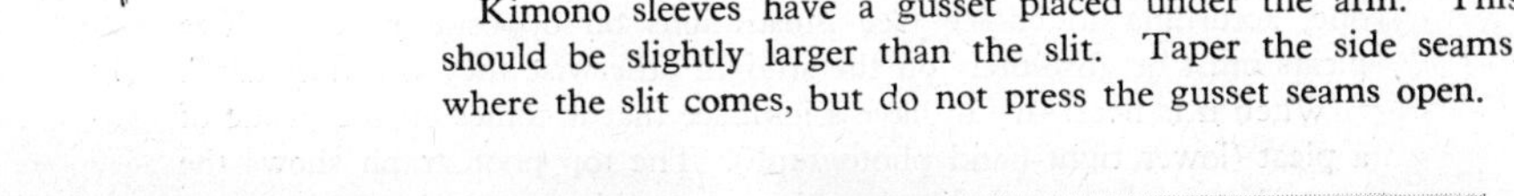

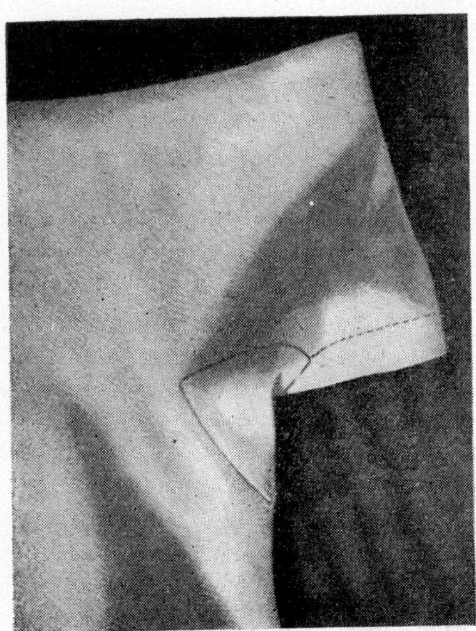

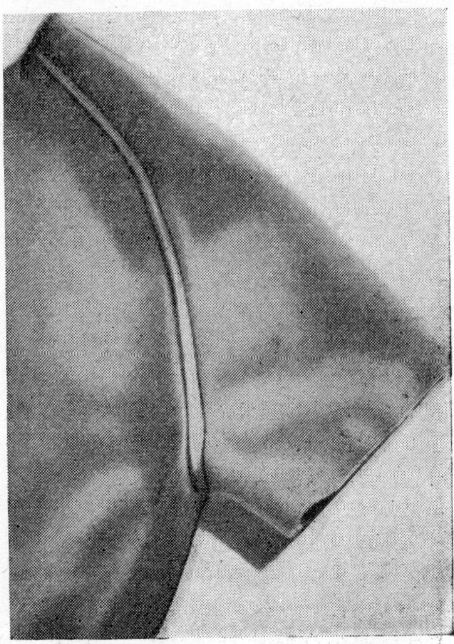

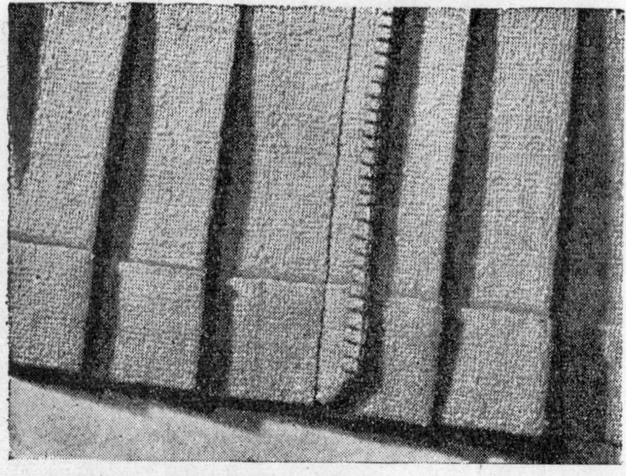

The Art of Making Pleats

For pleats of the same depth that lie side by side, measure first the width of the pleat then twice that width, and so on along the whole length. Mark with pins or tailor's chalk. Tack the pleats in position or pin on the ironing board and press in the creases lightly (see opposite page). There should be no ridges in pressing—if necessary, brown paper can be slipped under the pleats to prevent this from happening. Press lightly on the right side over a damp cloth, then turn to the wrong side and press more heavily.

Tack either straight across the pleats or a little way down each one, according to choice (see illustrations on opposite page). The pleats must be absolutely on the straight otherwise they will not " sit ".

When it is necessary to have a join, see that it comes on the inside of a pleat (lower right-hand photograph). The top photograph shows the seam, hem and pleats finished on the wrong side.

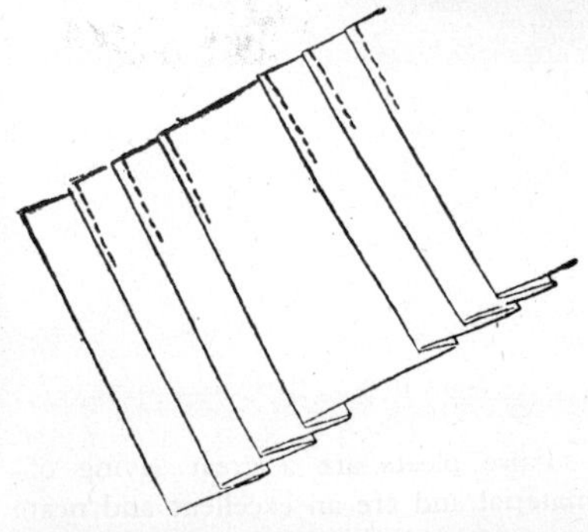

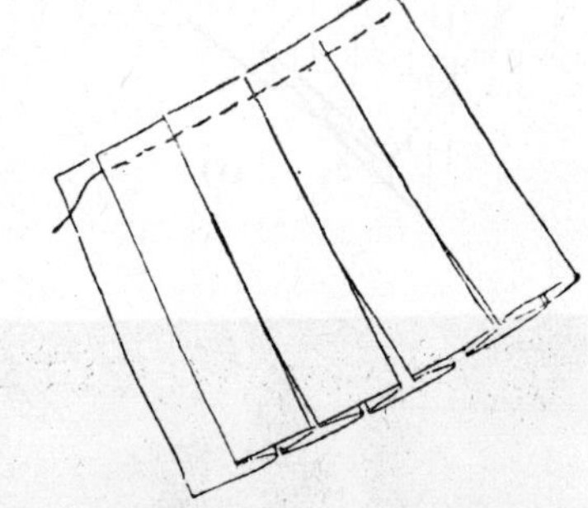

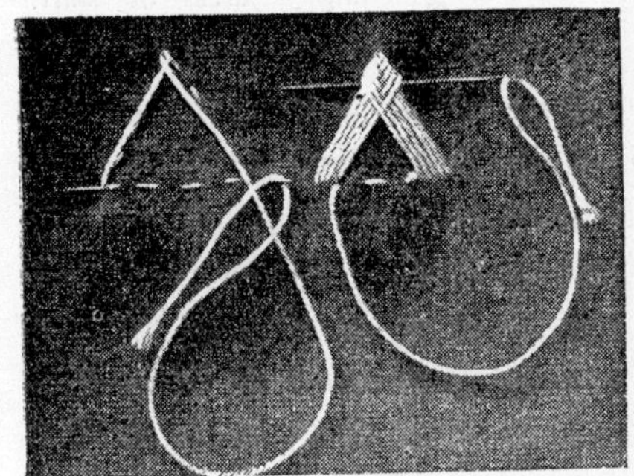

For the arrowhead, a backing of a three-cornered piece of tailor's canvas or linen is necessary. It is worked in silk, and used to keep the pleat in position. Outline first with a running thread, and then work as shown in the photograph.

False Pleats

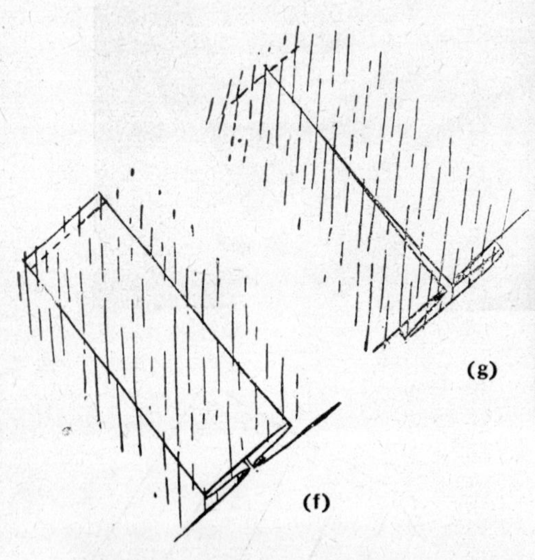

(g)

(f)

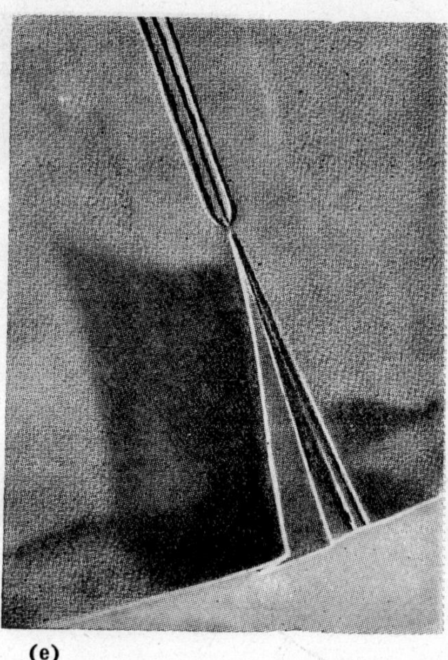

(e)

(h)

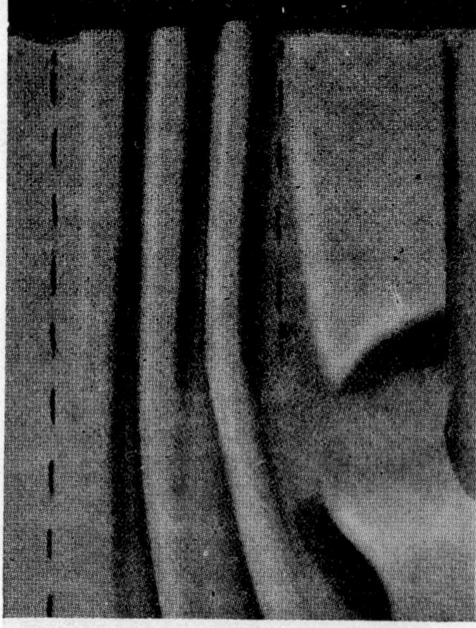

False pleats are a great saving of material and are an excellent and neat way of widening a dress or skirt. (**e**) Shows an inset pleat, arranged in fan pleats. These need careful arranging on the wrong side, with special attention to the weave of the fabric, which should be kept absolutely on the straight. Notice the slot seam finish. (**f**) and (**g**) show the most commonly used form of false pleat, the wrong side (**f**) and the right (**g**).

Cartridge pleats are often used in thin, soft material. The top piece should be well finished, all seams being joined, before the pleats are started. Accurate marking is essential. They are laid from left to right and each pleat is finished completely before another is begun. They do not need pressing.

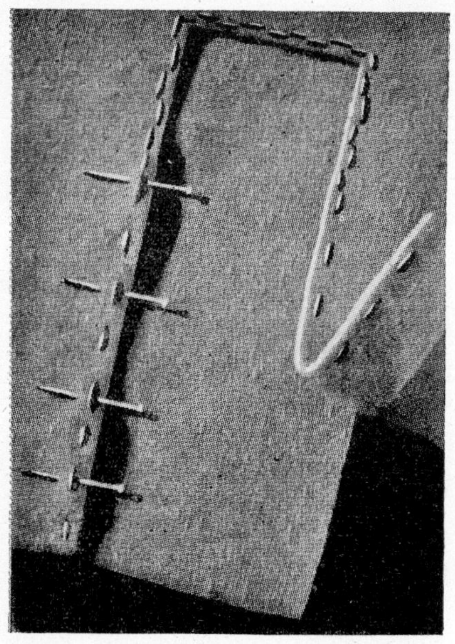

(a)

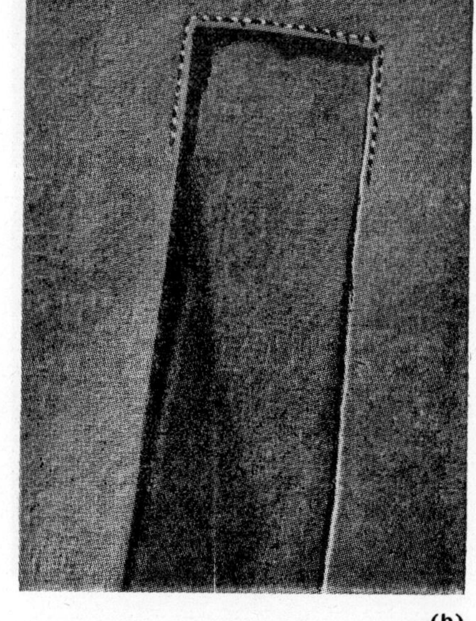

(b)

An inset pleat (**a**) and (**b**) has the joins hidden. Turn back the top edges before pinning and tacking to the inset piece. Machine along the top and a little way down each side on the right side and press.

For (**c**) and (**d**) the applied piece is placed over the slit in the fabric, and the edges are sewn together. Overcast the edges on the wrong side. Press well on the right side before machining.

(c)

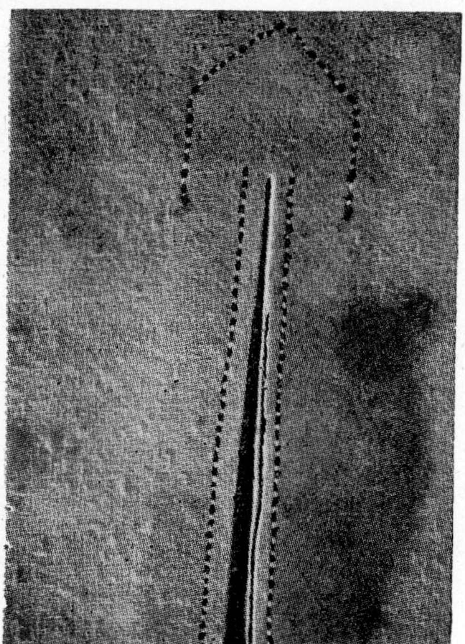

(d)

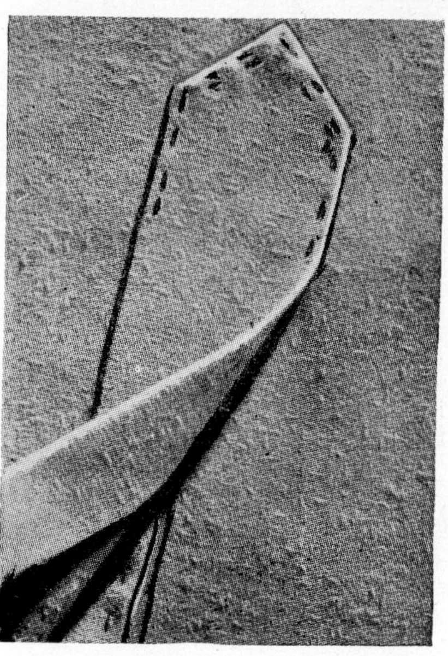

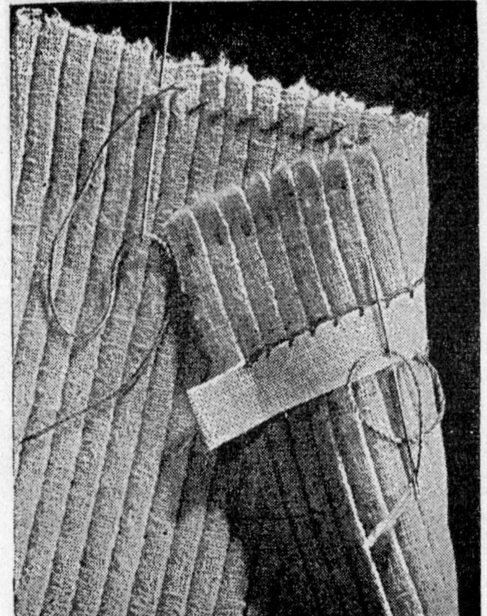

Sun-ray Pleats

To secure pleats that are done at the pleaters, put a line of stitching on the right side to secure each pleat (see top needle), or sew a strip of tape to the back and secure with blanket or buttonhole stitch.

(a)

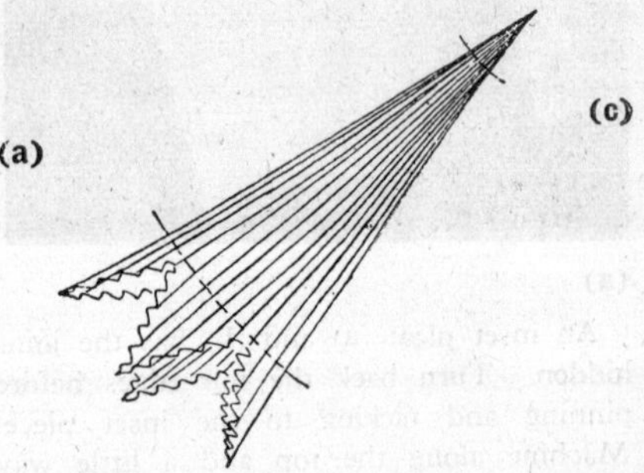

(c)

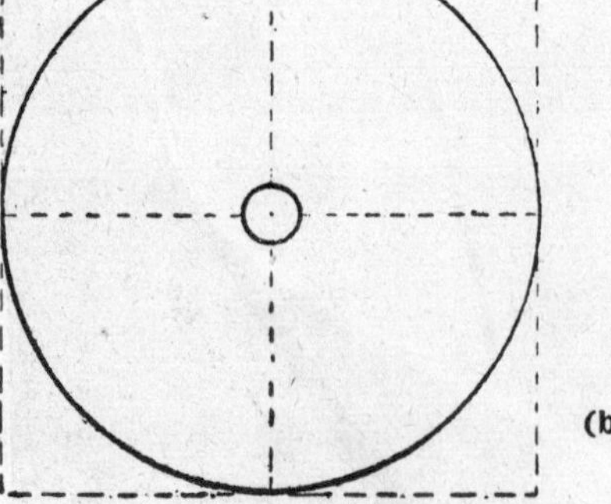

(b)

To cut a sun-ray pleated skirt, a full circle of material is needed. To make this, join four square pieces of fabric, as in (**b**) and draw the circle in tailor's chalk. The seams should be tacked, but must not be finished until the pleating has been done, so that they can be placed on the inside of a pleat. The small circle in the centre of (**b**) should be about 6 inches in diameter.

Before turning up the hem, the skirt should hang at least forty-eight hours. Then trim, as shown in (**c**), and turn in. The top of the skirt should be finished entirely before turning up the hem

Fringes

For the fringe in photograph (**a**) the silk is first wound evenly on a card the width of the finished fringe. Then cut along the top edge of the card. There will now be several uniform lengths of silk. Each fringe thread is double length and is threaded through the material and knotted as shown in the photograph. For a tassel (**c**) wind on to the card, knot, cut the edges, and bind near the top with more silk.

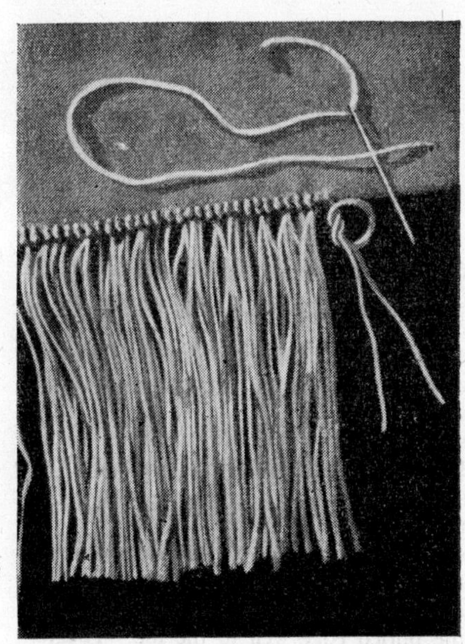

(a)

(b)

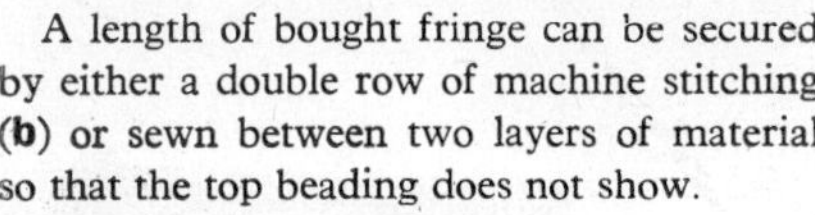

A length of bought fringe can be secured by either a double row of machine stitching (**b**) or sewn between two layers of material so that the top beading does not show.

(c)

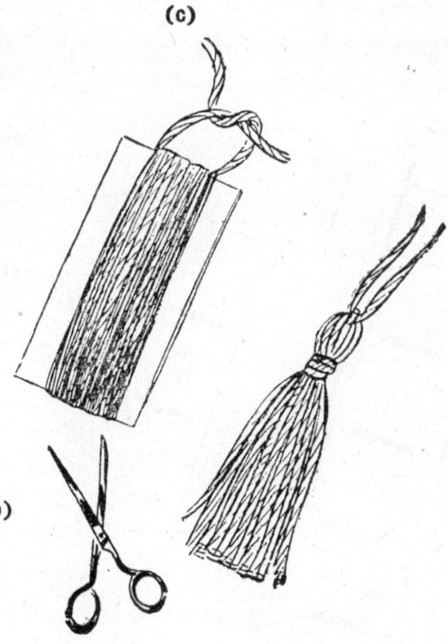

Buttonholes

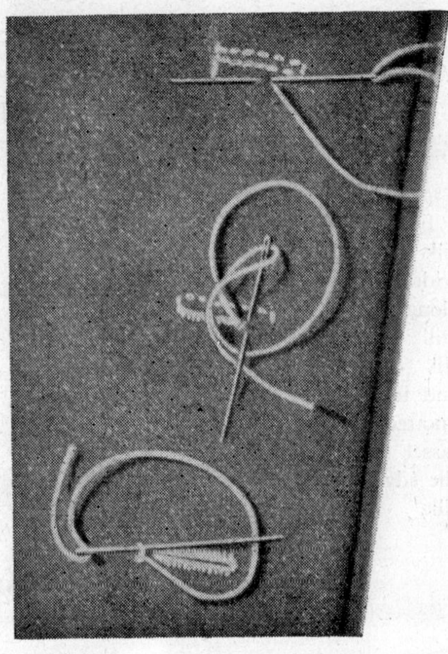

(a)

(**a**) shows simple worked buttonholes in two or three layers of fabric. First mark the position, by laying the button on the fabric. Put a needle through the button centre to mark the position of the rounded end of the buttonhole. Measure the width of the button from this end, inwards, and mark with tailor's chalk. Back stitch or machine round this line before slitting. Buttonhole from left to right round the slit, and finish with an overcast bar. For tailor's buttonholes (**c**) first overcast the slit and enlarge the rounded end slightly. Lay a length of the waxed buttonhole silk along the edge and work over this, keeping the purled edge well to the top. Diagram (**b**) shows a row of simple buttonholes, worked over a canvas interlining. When working one buttonhole only, insert a small piece of lining for the backing.

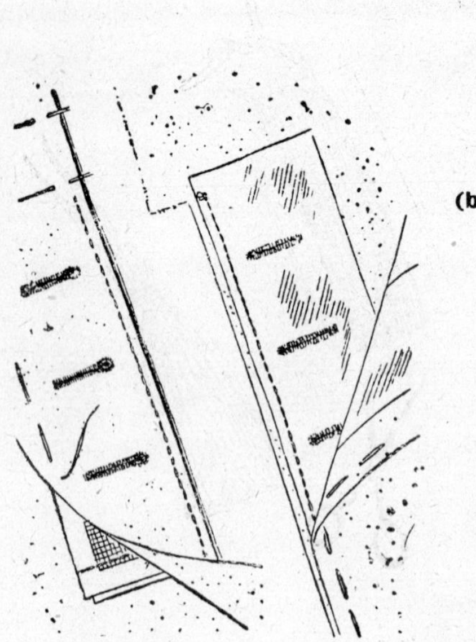

(b)

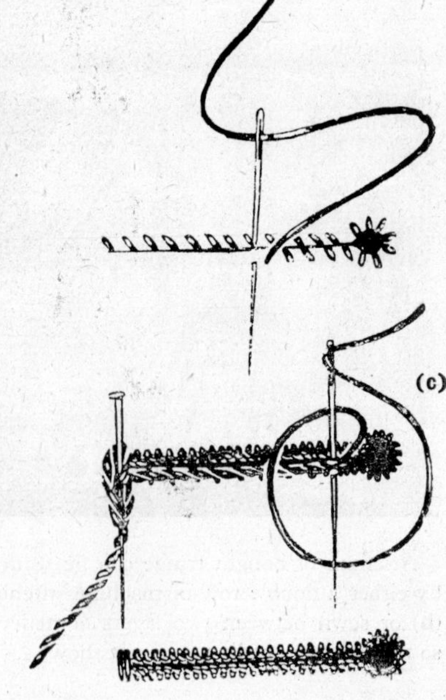

(c)

(e)

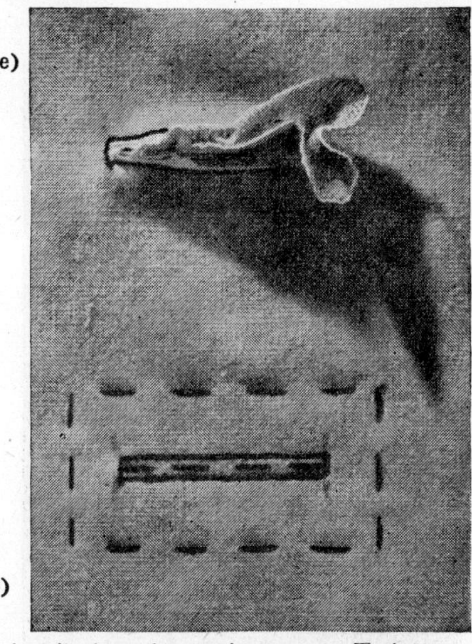

(d)

For bound buttonholes mark as described on the previous page. Tack on to the right side, over the marking, a bias-cut rectangle of fabric (**d**). Machine round (**e**), and pull the material through to the wrong side. On the right side, secure the binding by neat back stitches (**g**) and tack the buttonholes together until ready for wear. The finishing of the buttonhole is shown on next page. (**f**) Shows a bound buttonhole in braid.

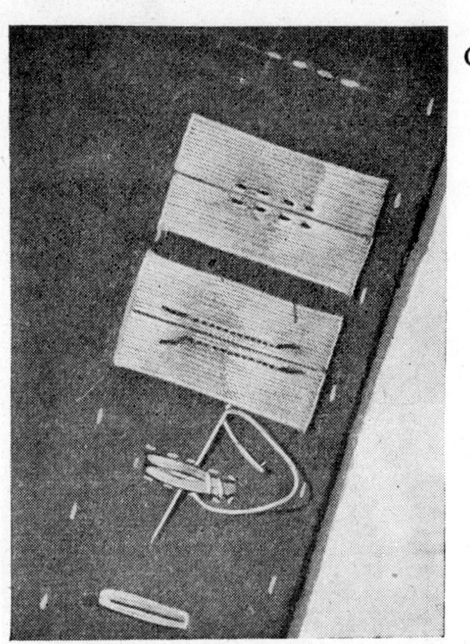

(f)

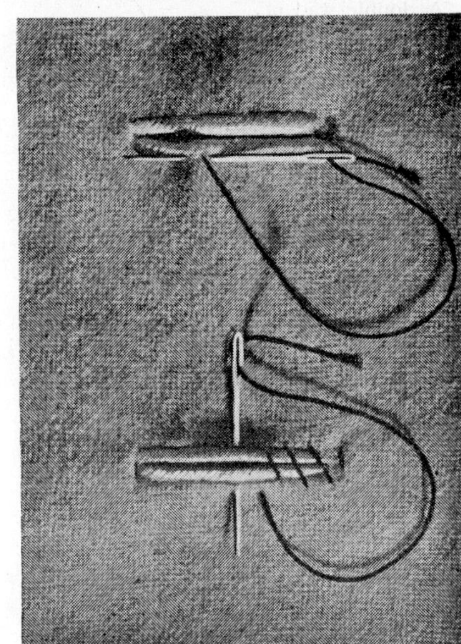

(g)

Sewing on Buttons

Finish the buttonholes by herringboning to the stiffening, and mark the position of the slit on the facing, and hem neatly to the buttonhole.

When sewing buttons on to thin fabrics, a smaller button or double wad of fabric should be sewn on to the back to relieve the strain on the material. Use buttonhole silk or strong twine for sewing.

A double wad of fabric is used here, and a small button in the photograph on the right.

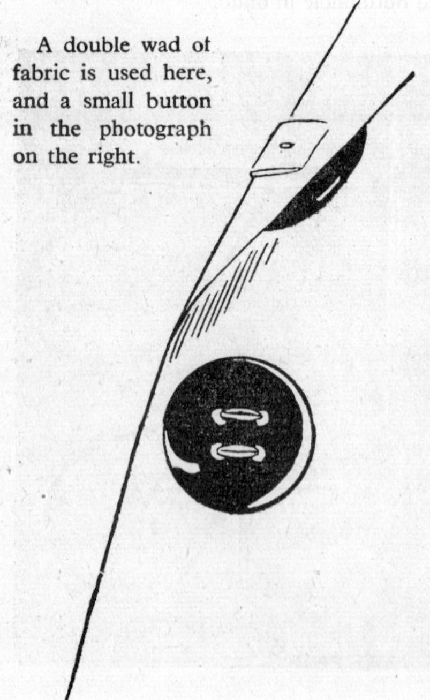

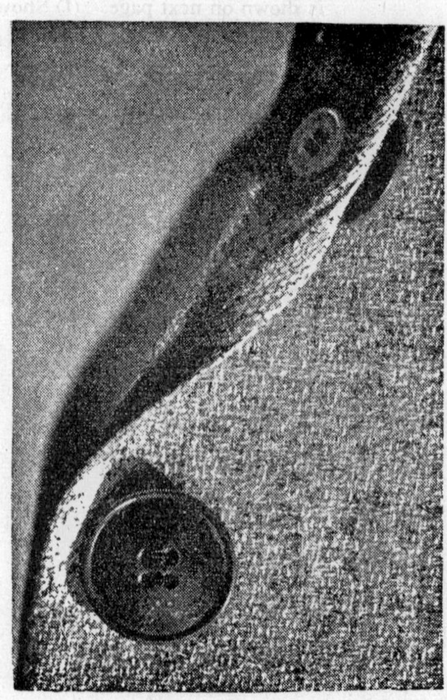

Coat Buttons

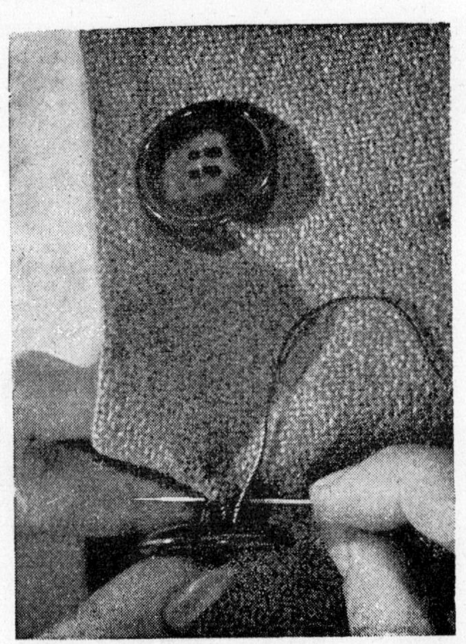

Buttons sewn on to a coat should not be pulled tight, but should have a shank made by winding the buttonhole silk round and round the connecting threads, so that the button lies easily when the thick layer of the material is fastened under it. Sometimes with large two-holed buttons a neat, narrow strip of fabric can be used, as can be seen in the photograph below. This is forced through the facing with a stiletto, and finished on the wrong side as shown in the sketch below.

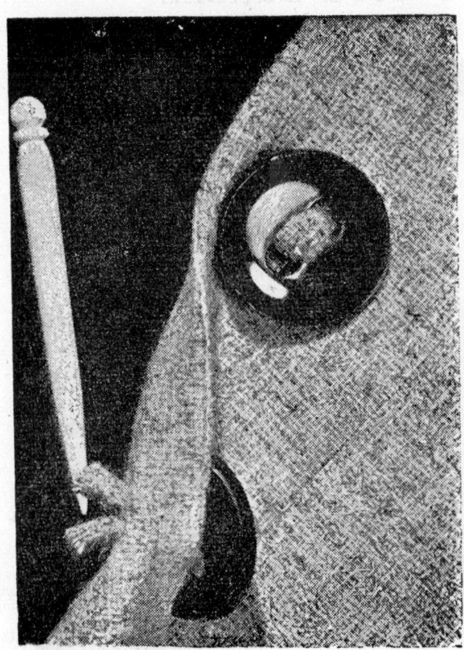

Link and Covered Buttons

Slide Fasteners–

—make an attractive finish and can be had in most lengths and colours

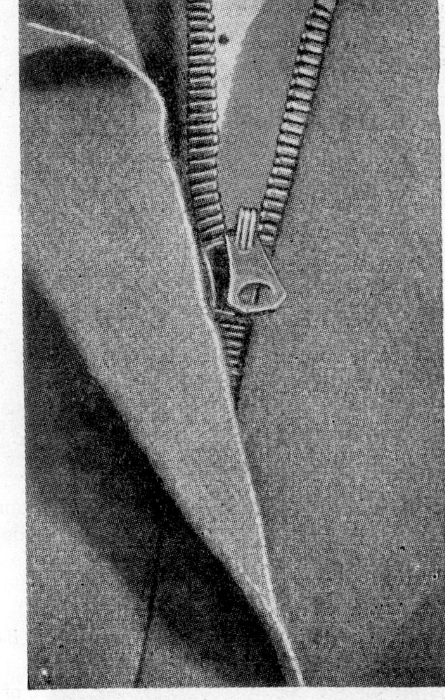

Link buttons can be joined either by thick silk, which is passed through the holes five or six times, the shank being then buttonholed over, or by a neat strip of fabric, on to which the buttons are sewn in the normal way (see previous page).

To cover wooden buttons, cut out a circle of fabric considerably larger than the button, and turn in the edge, at the same time running in a gathering thread. Slip this over the button, draw up tightly and fasten off well.

Slide fasteners should be kept closed while being sewn on. The fabric should be eased slightly, and the stitching kept at least a quarter of an inch away from the metal.

One way of sewing on this kind of fastener is between two layers of fabric, so that only the metal is visible. Start at the top and work downwards when sewing. Another way is to fix the fastener into a slot seam, so that it is partially covered. A third way, covering the fastener entirely, is illustrated above.

Buttonhole Loops in Silk and Fabric

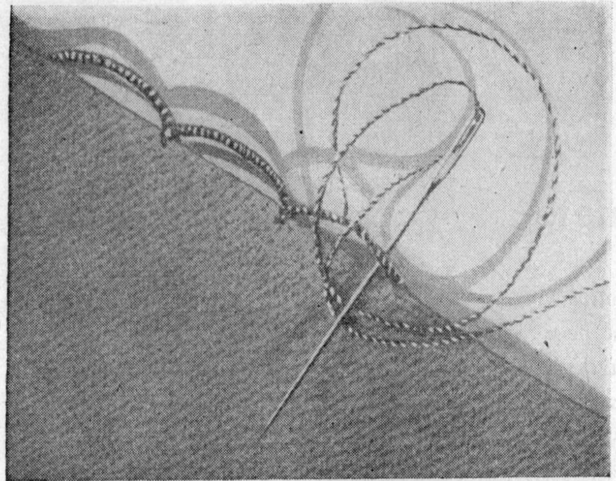

Worked loops are often used. Close buttonholing is worked over two strands of silk, the purl edge being kept to the inside

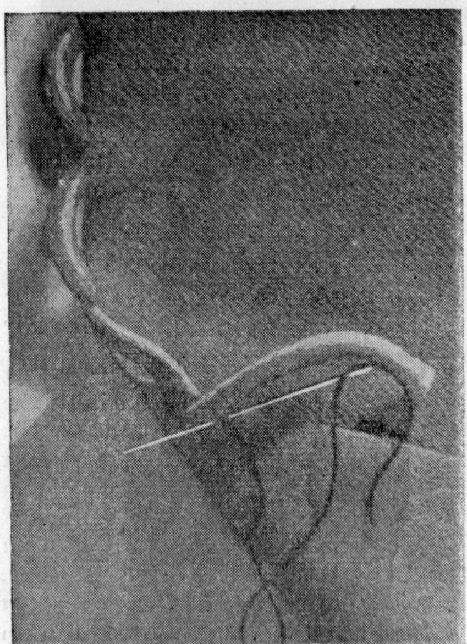

When more than one loop is needed in thin material, a long rolled strip is prepared, and caught down securely at the correct intervals to give the appearance of separate loops.

Below:

Single loops can be made of a fine roll of bias-cut fabric, which is pushed into the seam with a stiletto and secured as invisibly as possible on the wrong side.

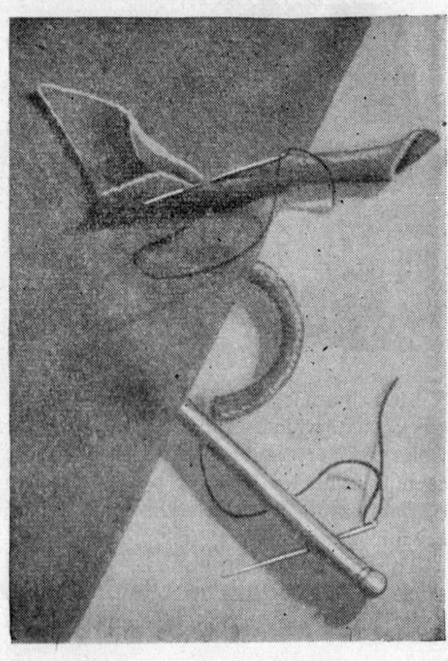

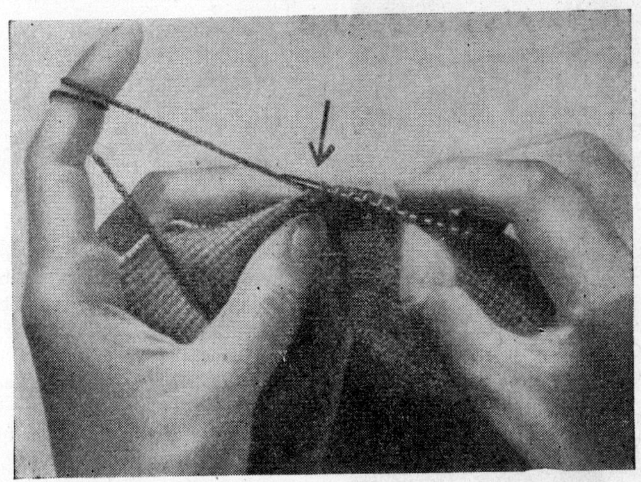

A Novel Knitted Finish to a Fabric Jumper

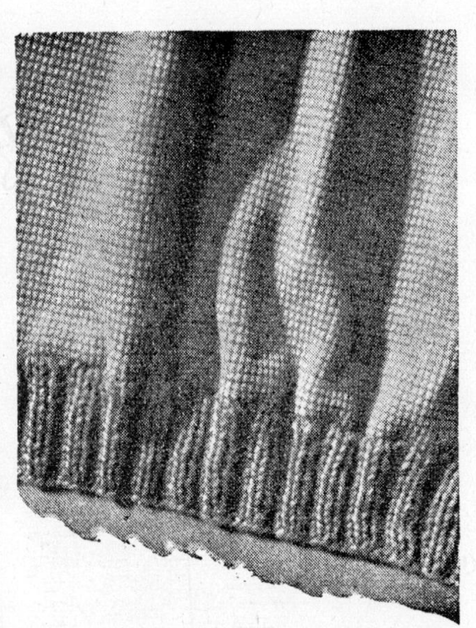

A length of knitted ribbing added to a thick material is an effective way of lengthening. The material must be fairly wide, as the knitting will draw it in. If the material is open enough, the first row of stitches is caught straight up on to the needle, otherwise a crochet hook is used. The needle should be inserted into the folded material from the front through to the back, the stitches being an even distance apart. The knitted band should not be too wide, otherwise it will look too much like an added piece.

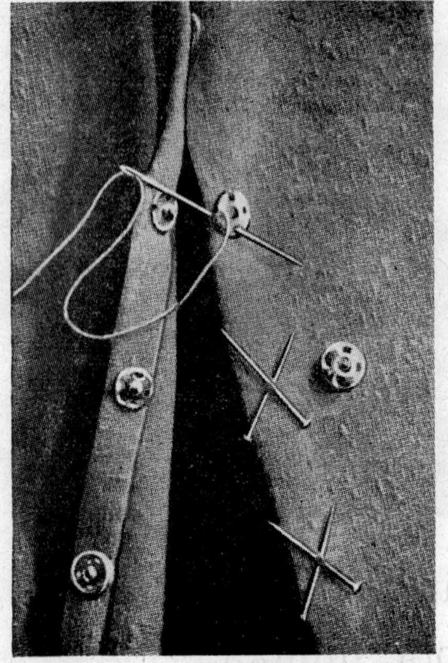

Fastenings–
Press-Studs

Press-studs should be sewn on double material. To make this possible, without catching the top layer of fabric, slip a strip of binding or lining in the placket hem. Sew the upper or stud part of the press-stud on first, in the places marked after trying on the garment. Next, mark the position of the second half with either tailor's chalk or crossed pins. The two parts must be exactly opposite each other. (**c**) shows the extra strip of lining inserted, and (**b**) the bar, worked as shown on the opposite page, which is added to prevent the placket tearing at the bottom.

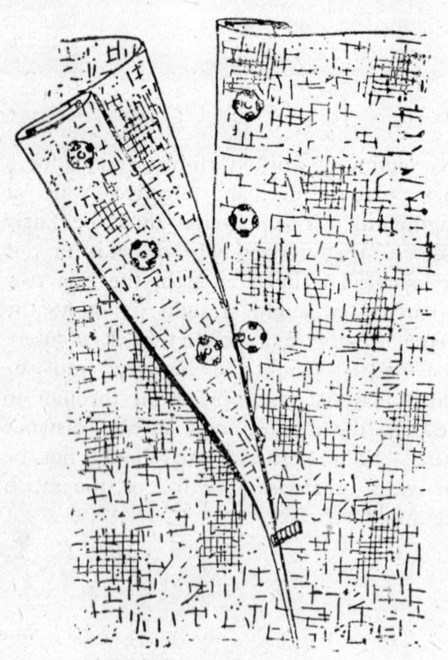

(b)

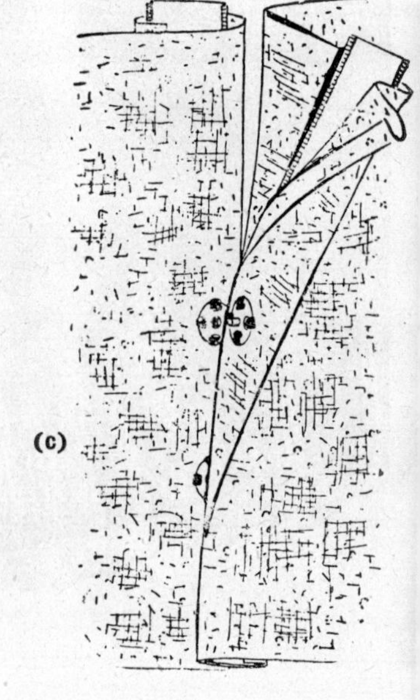

(c)

Hooks and Eyes

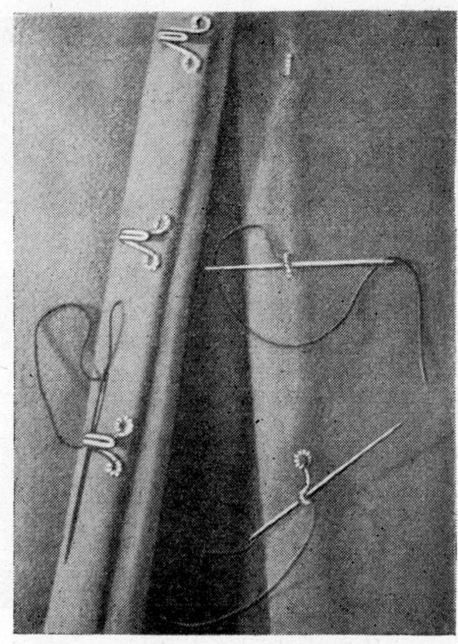

Hooks and eyes should be opened wider before sewing on. Again sew on double material, and arrange so as not to overlap the placket edge. Should this be unavoidable, buttonhole over the bars in silk to match the garment.

Hooks and eyes may be sewn with all the hooks down the same side, but to make the fastening doubly secure, sew alternately as shown below left

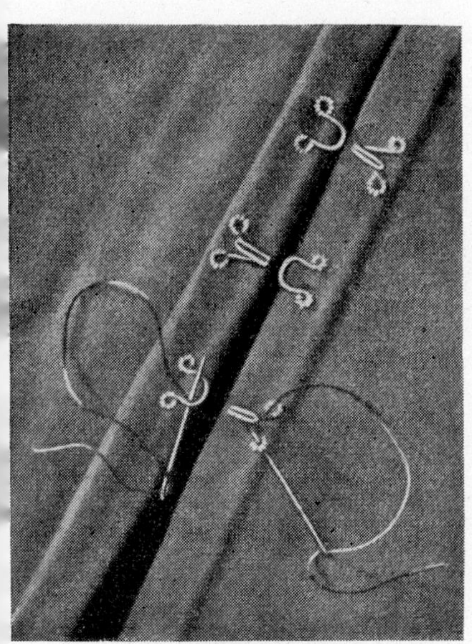

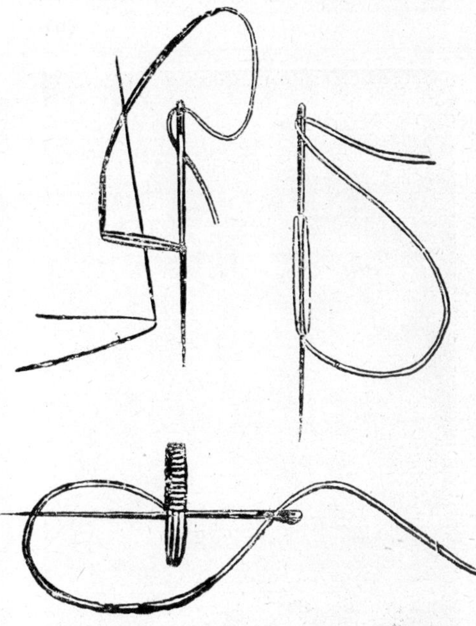

(a)

Pockets

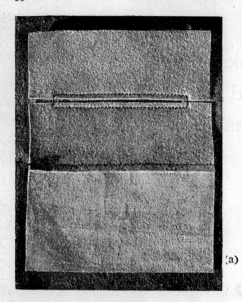

Horizontal slot pockets are made in very much the same way as bound buttonholes. The position of the pocket as given in the pattern should have been marked at the time of cutting out. Check this position by trying on. Mark the width of the slot and tack two pieces of bias-cut fabric on each side of this. Machine round the slot, and cut. Pull the two patches through to the wrong side, and bringing the top piece over on to the bottom, join as in (**c**), finishing the trimmed edges by buttonholing or overcasting. The right side (**b**) should be finished with two worked bars at either end.

The vertical welted pocket shown in the photographs on the opposite page is made similarly, except that the welt is stitched in with the upper part of the pocket (**d**).

The sketches show how to make a horizontal flap pocket (pocket concealed), and there is a photograph of the finished pocket (j) on page 561.

(b)

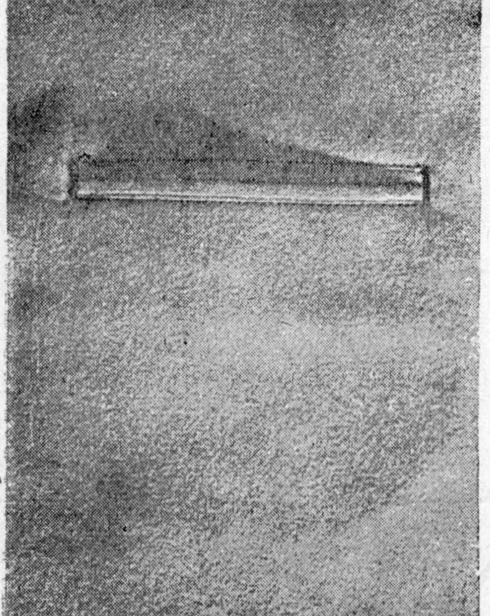

(c)

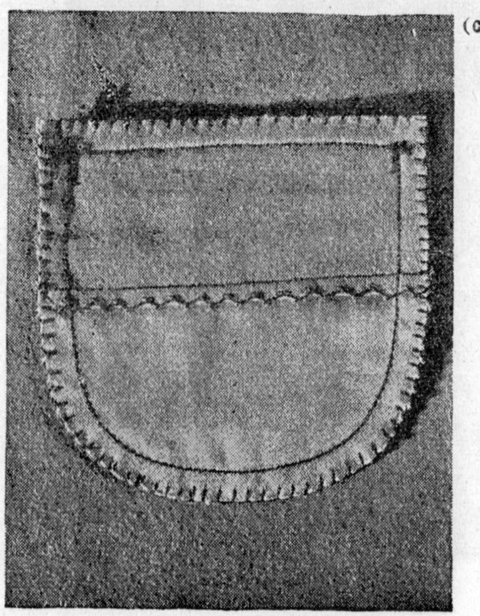

Flap Pockets

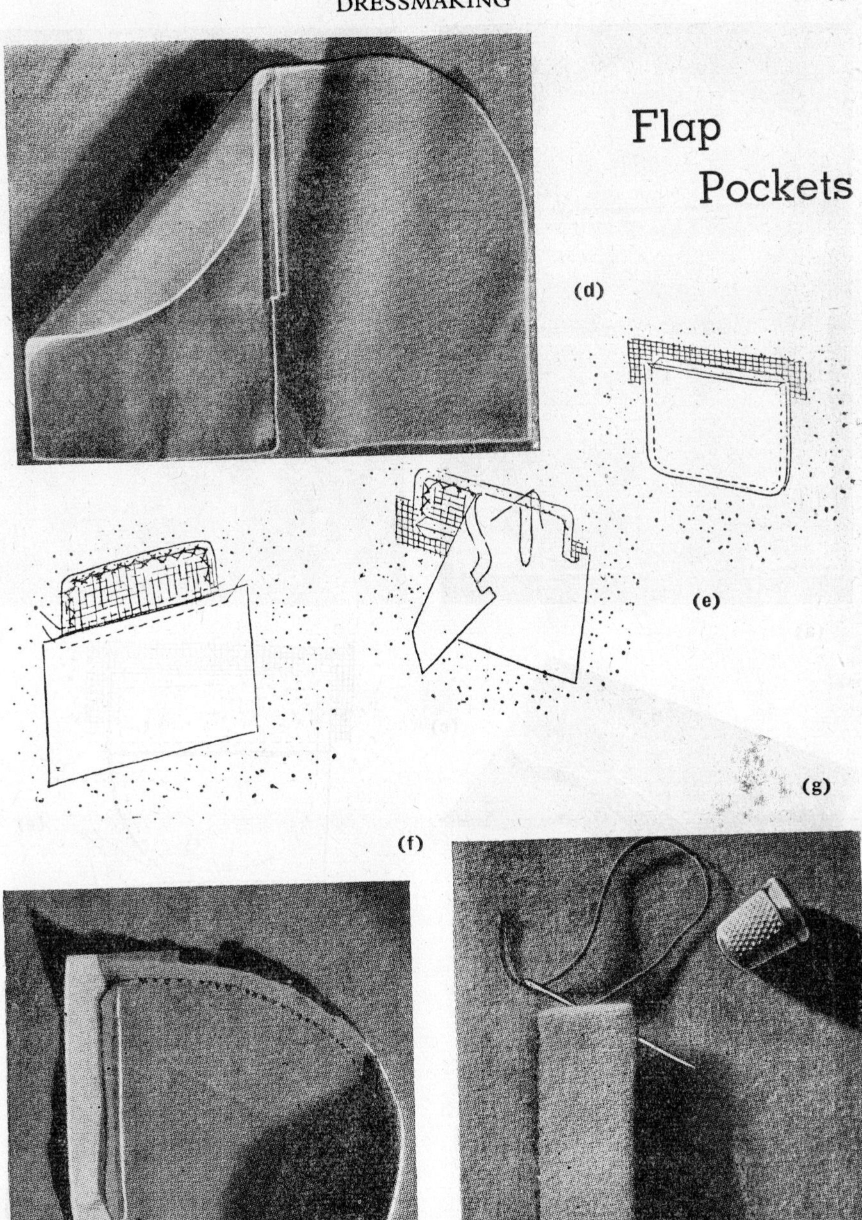

(d)

(e)

(f)

(g)

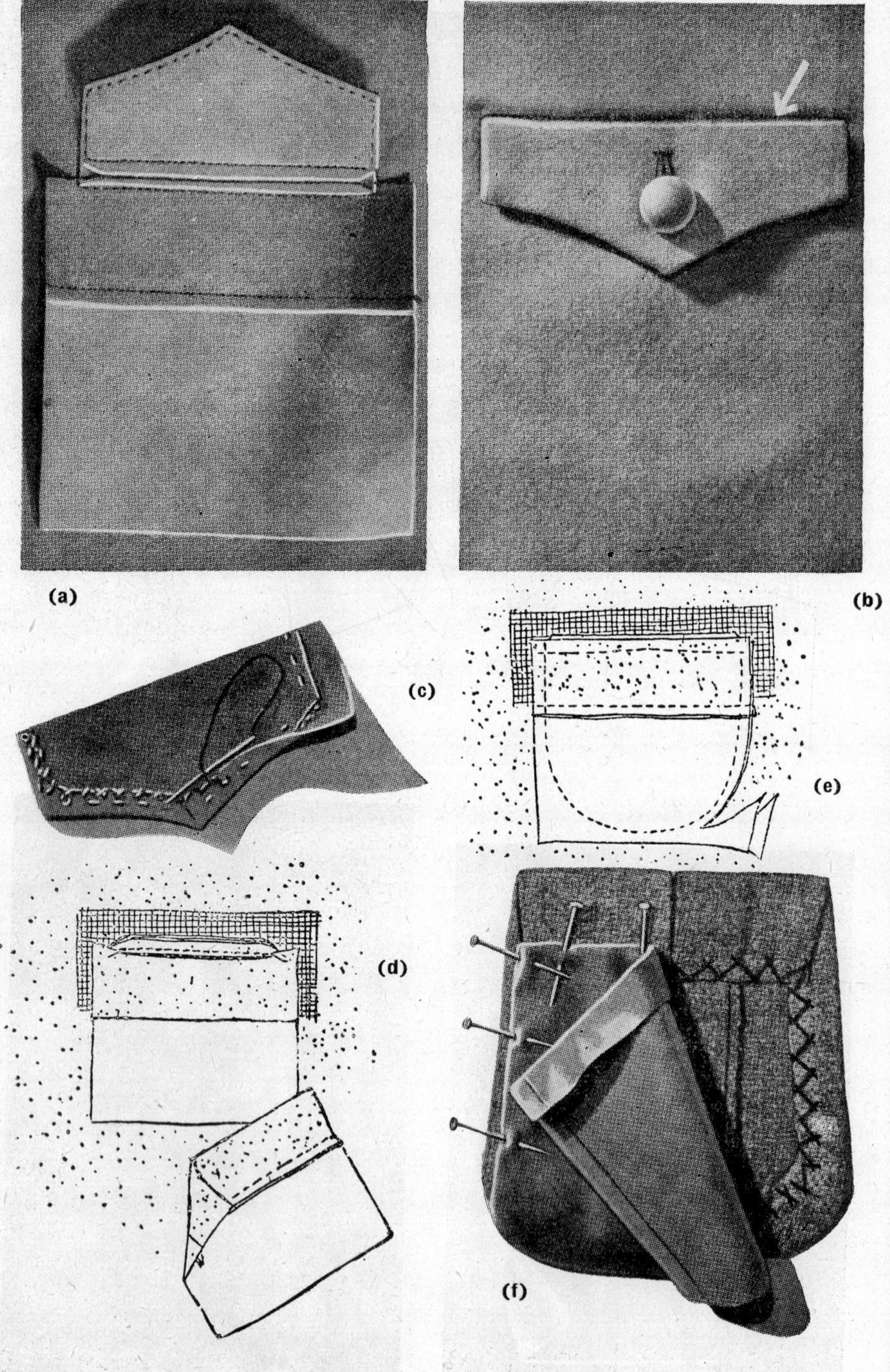
(a)
(b)
(c)
(e)
(d)
(f)

More Pockets

(g)

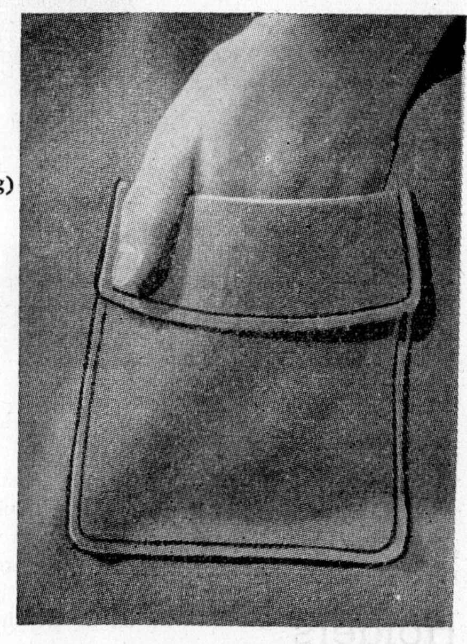

The horizontal flap pocket on the left is made in the same way as shown on the previous pages. The pointed flap is cut and made as in (**c**), the interlining being of stiff canvas. The sketches (**d**) and (**e**) show the working of the pocket. If a buttonhole is required in the flap, it should be made before joining on to the garment. The arrow at (**b**) shows the flap carefully pressed and finished with button and buttonhole. (**g**) is a simple patch pocket, and (**f**) shows the making of another kind of applied pocket, which has to be well lined. (**h**) is a Norfolk-jacket pocket, and (**j**) shows one with a horizontal flap.

(h)

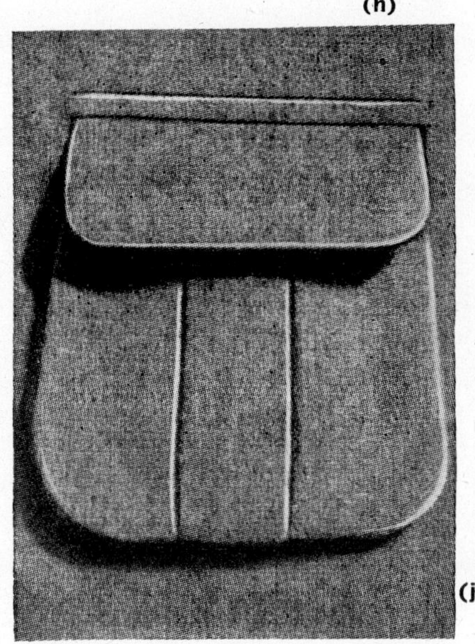

(j)

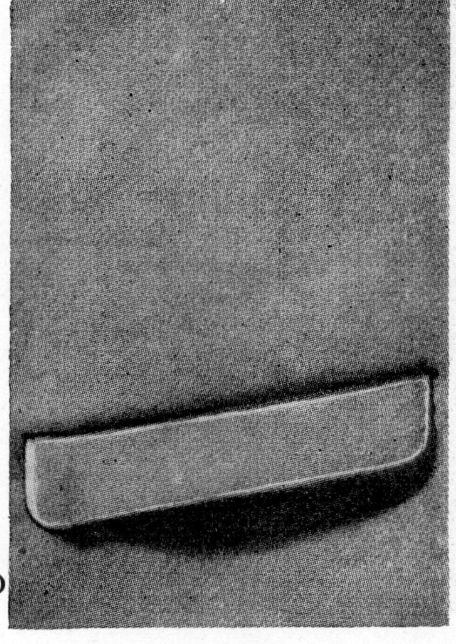

Two Finishing Touches—

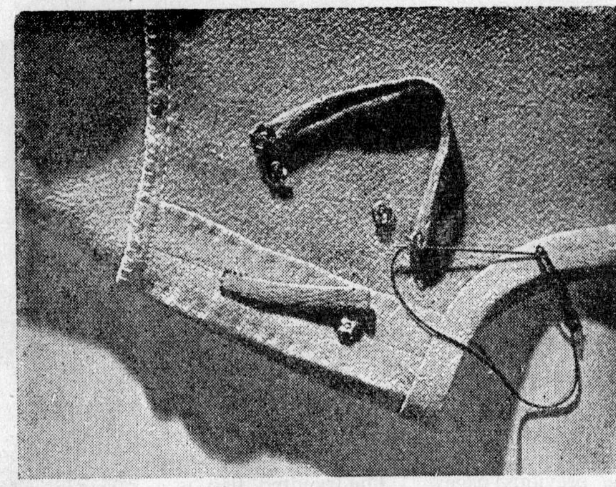

Lingerie Strap Holders

Lingerie strap holders attached to the shoulder seam prevent shoulder straps from slipping into view. These are made from narrow strips of bias-cut fabric. The two straps are made together, the press-studs being sewn to each end before the straps are cut in the centre. Sew on to the shoulder seam so that the press-studs are on the inside near the neck.

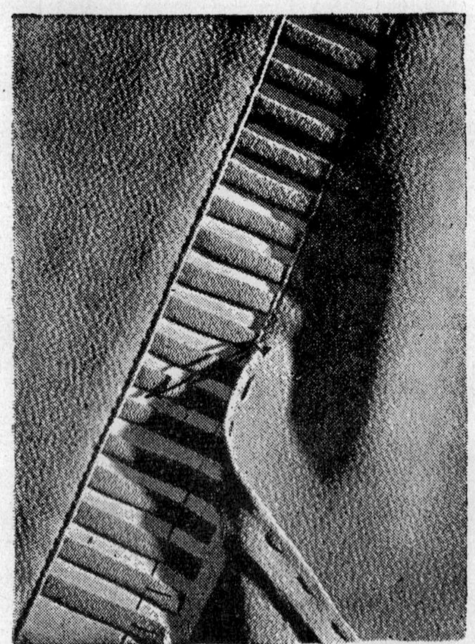

Ladder Insertion

Ladder insertion is sometimes used as a decoration. The bars are made out of bias-cut strips of material. Pin them at even distances apart on to a piece of stiff paper. Machine the material on to the strips, being careful to keep the insertion the same width all the way down. Careful and frequent tacking is absolutely necessary. This is not an easy task for the beginner.

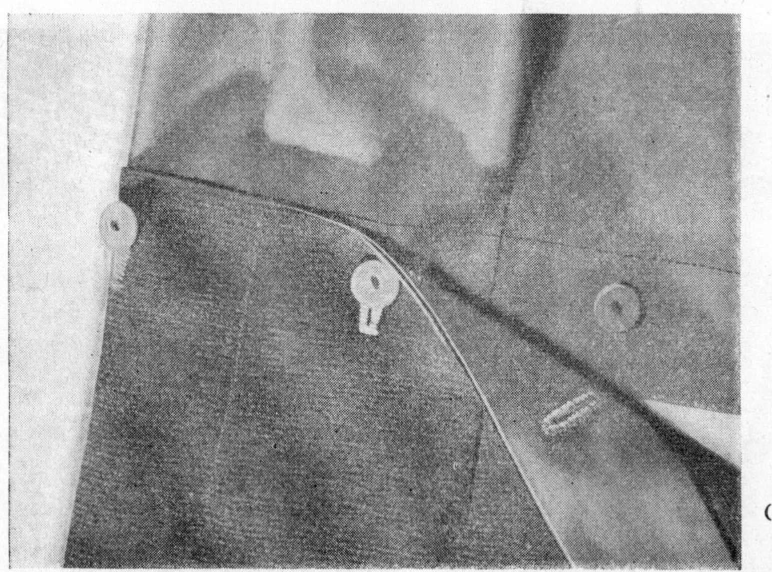

(a)

Skirt Bands and Fastenings

The side press-stud and fastening of a skirt or bodice needs a seam allowance of at least ½ inch so that the upper and lower edges are wide enough to take the fastenings. The edges are bound. The press-studs should be sewn on double material without coming through to the right side. See also sketches (e) overleaf. A buttonholed bar secures the base. Above is a detachable skirt, which is fastened to a top by flat buttons.

(b)

(c)

(a)

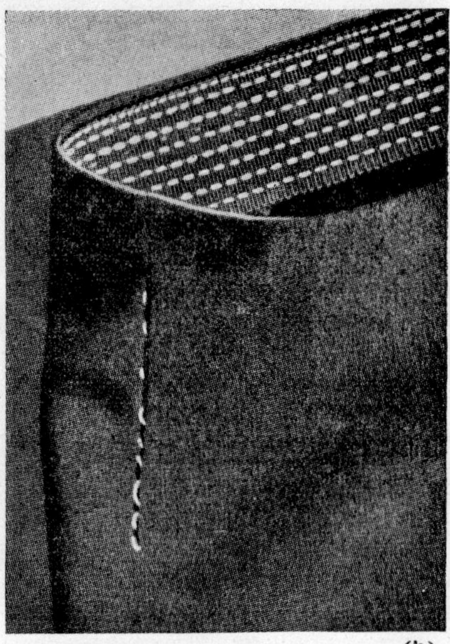

(b)

Skirts and Plackets

(c)

Another kind of placket is shown at (**a**). This is absolutely invisible from the right side. The placket is lined with tailor's canvas, and the side seam has to be pressed open.

(**b**) Darts at the waist can either be machined down or tacked and then pressed, the tacking threads being afterwards removed so that the dart will give with any strenuous movement.

(**c**) Shows a neat way of securing the pleats at the top so that they do not sag. Notice the neat buttonhole finish to the seam.

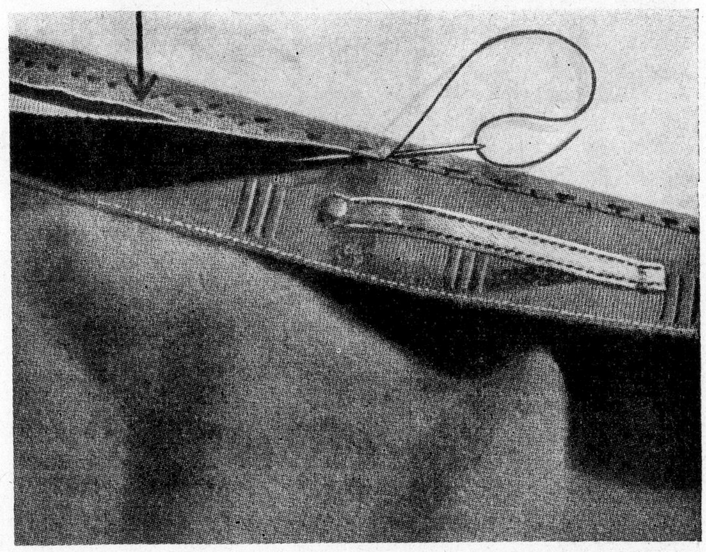
(d)

The correct hang of a skirt depends on the way the band is attached. After trying on, pin the skirt to the band, easing on any fullness evenly, and sew on by hand (**d**). If the band is sewn under the turning, as in (**f**), a strip of binding or narrow braid should be added afterwards. Sew narrow horizontal bands on to the skirt-band for hanging up.

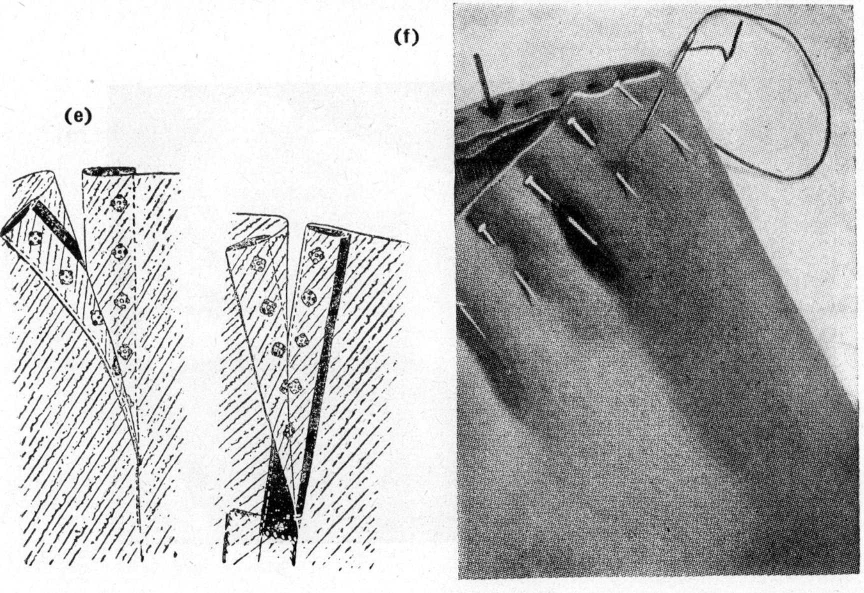
(e) (f)

Belts

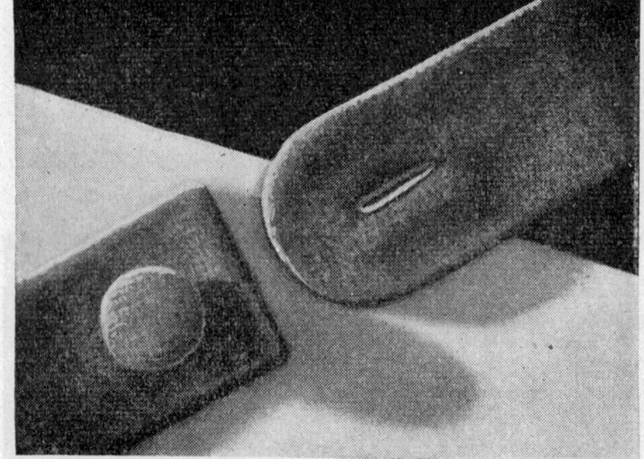

(a)

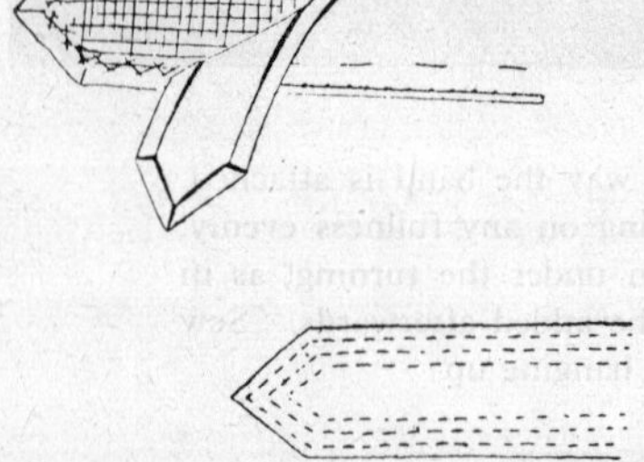

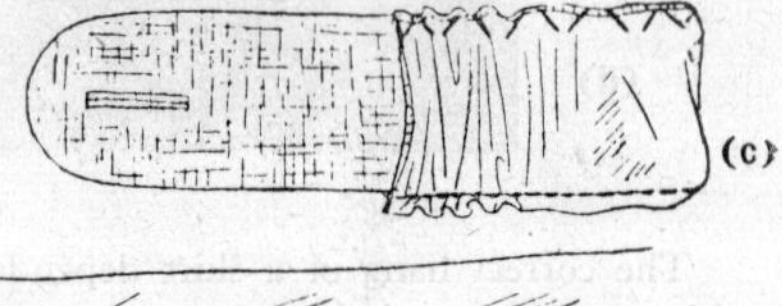

(c)

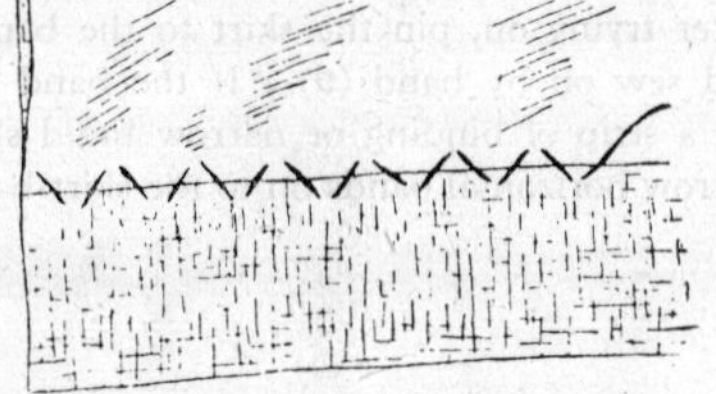

(b)

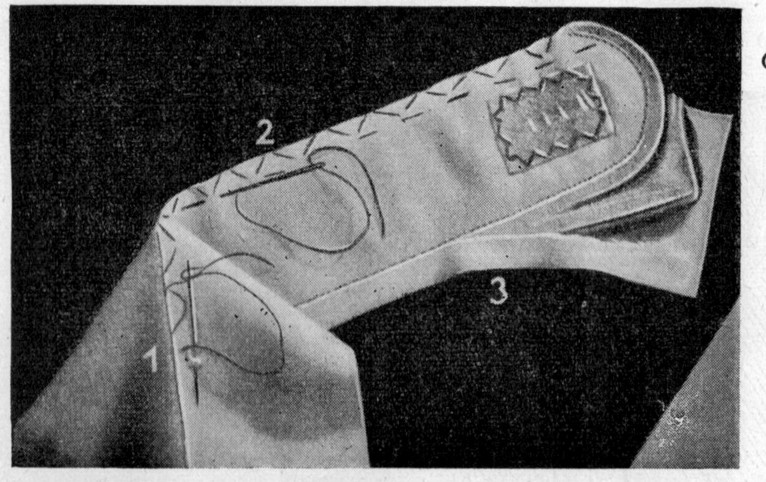

(d)

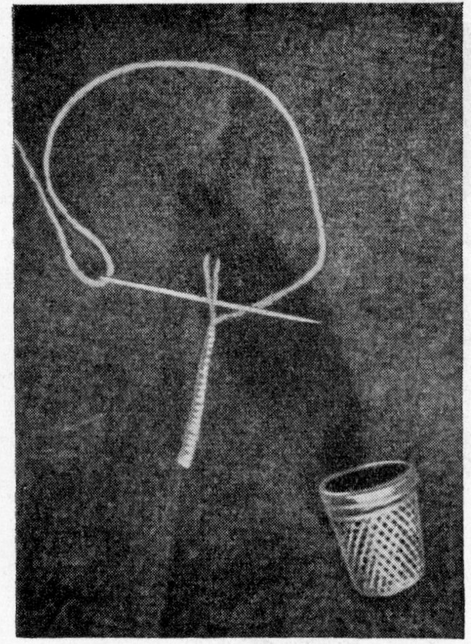

(e)

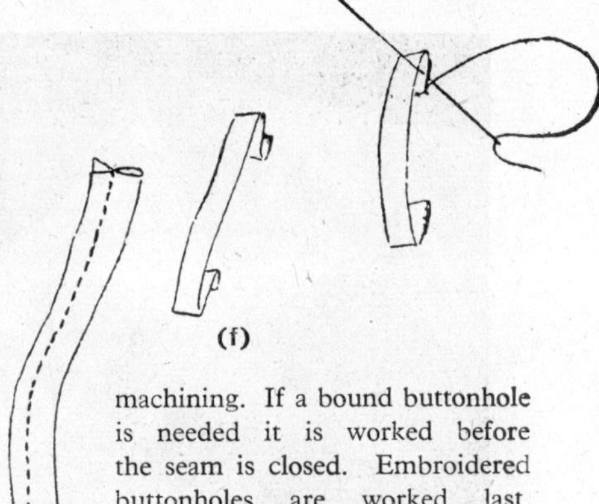
(f)

Coat belts are usually made ot double material cut on the straight. In thick material a lining of tailor's canvas or stiff linen is unnecessary, unless the belt is abnormally wide, but thinner materials need a stiffening. A thin lining, the width of the finished belt, should be herringboned on the fold (1), then tacked through three layers (2), and machined round remaining edges. The seam is trimmed close to the machining. If a bound buttonhole is needed it is worked before the seam is closed. Embroidered buttonholes are worked last. The belt is now pulled through to the right side (**c**) and is pressed. If a belt is to be particularly strong, use a stiffer canvas.

After trying on and marking the exact length, finish the ends, and sew on the covered button. If a buckle is used (**h**) the belt is made longer, and small holes are pierced at the opposite end and overcast or buttonholed with silk.

(**b**) Shows a pointed belt, machined in rows for decoration.

Slots are fixed to the side seams of the garment to hold the belt in position. If the bodice is joined to the skirt, the belt usually hides the seam. These bars can either be buttonholed over two or three strands of silk (**e**), or made from bias-cut strips of fabric (**f**).

(h)

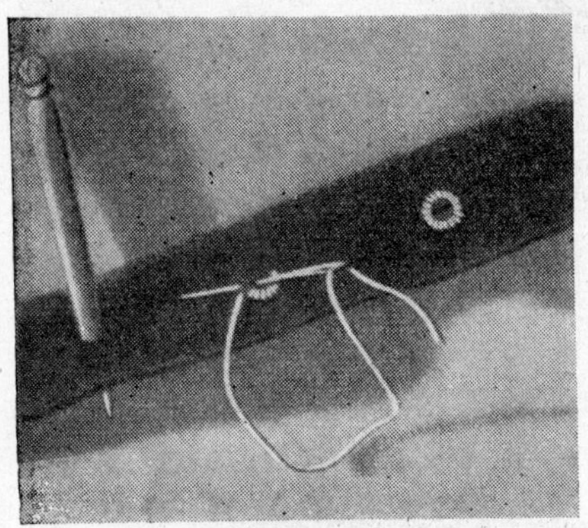
(g)

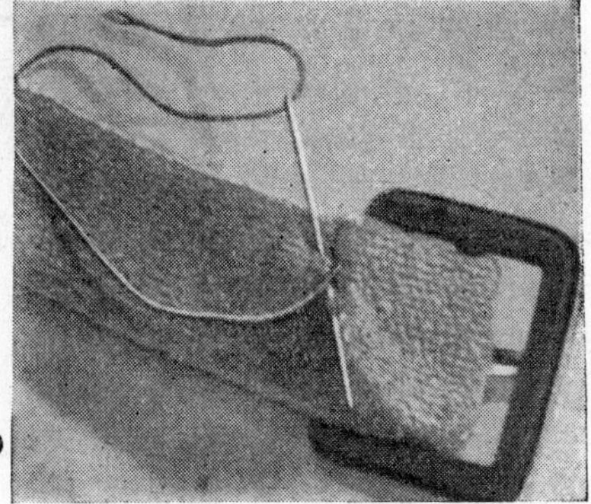

Pointed Edging

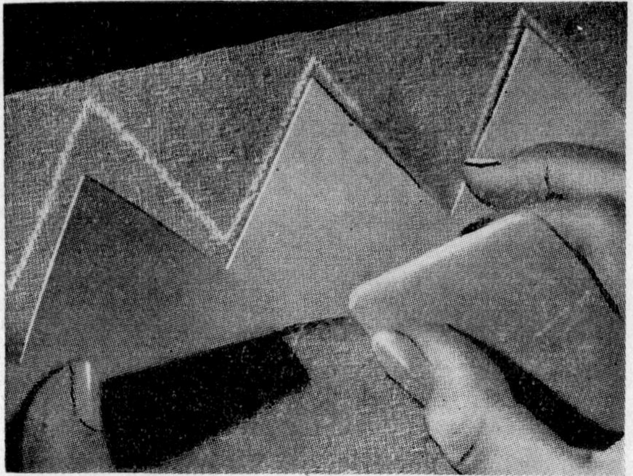

First make a cardboard pattern as shown in the sketch, and mark the position of the scallops with tailor's chalk on the wrong side of the material. A second strip of fabric is then laid on the right side, and the two thicknesses joined together by tacking along the chalked line After machining, turn on to the right side and tack along the edges before pressing.

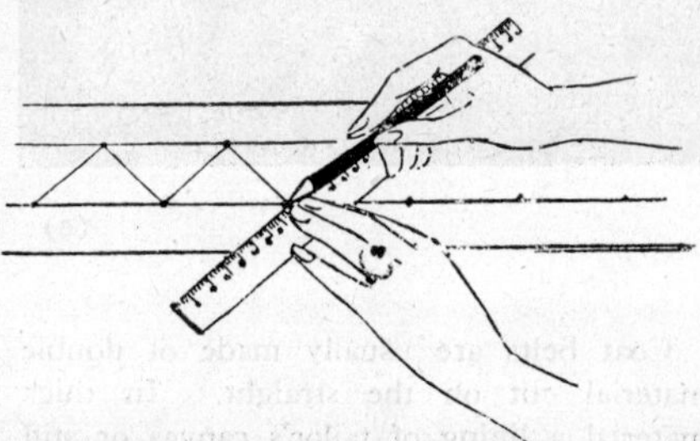

When trimming the scallops, snip the points as shown by the arrows. Pull them out on the right side, with the point of a needle.

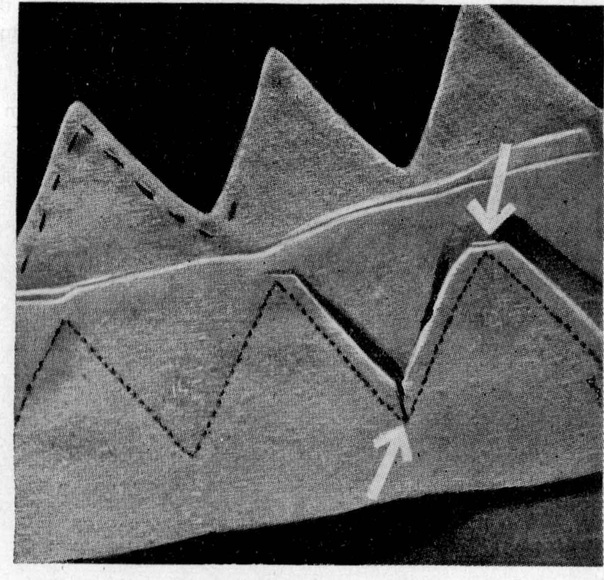

Scallops

Again a cardboard pattern is necessary, this time the scallops being drawn round a coin of the appropriate size. Thick material should have a thin lining to keep the scallops as flat as possible. When the seam is being trimmed, a slit down into the point (see arrow below) will keep the sharp outline

Trim the edge to within about ¼ inch of the machine stitching before turning on to the right side. After turning, tack the edges down flat, press with a hot iron and damp cloth, remove the tacking threads and press again

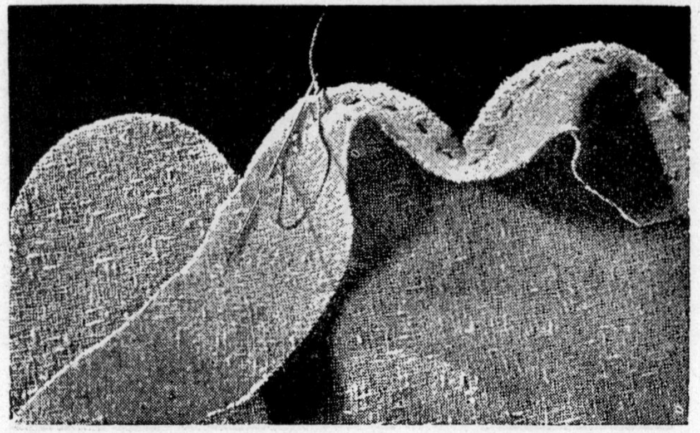

Bound

(a)

Bias strips of material can be used for binding scallops. The outlines should be cut first, and the binding tacked on. Ease the binding while sewing, and arrange all joins so that they come at the points.

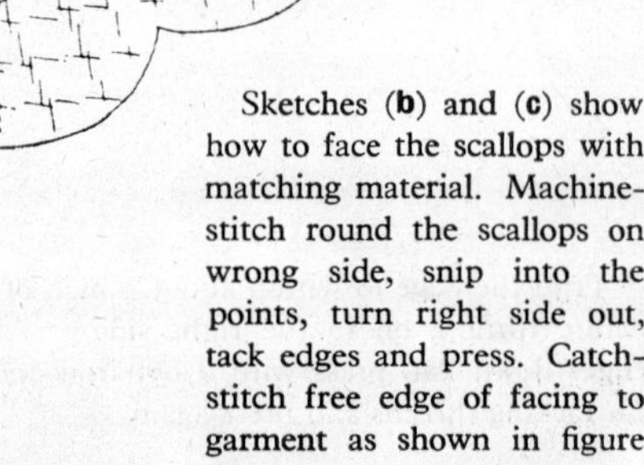

(b)

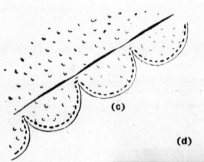

(c)

Sketches (**b**) and (**c**) show how to face the scallops with matching material. Machine-stitch round the scallops on wrong side, snip into the points, turn right side out, tack edges and press. Catch-stitch free edge of facing to garment as shown in figure (**b**).

(d)

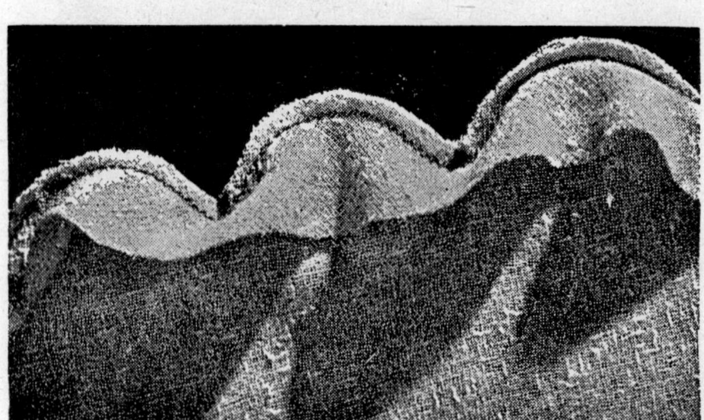

Scallops

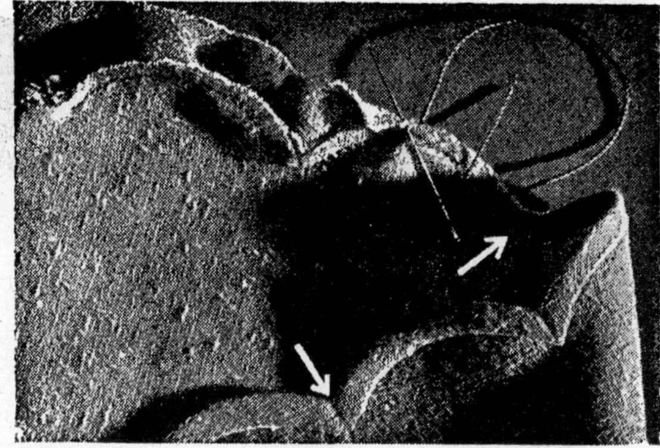

(e)

When turning the binding on to the wrong side, stitch along the line of machining so that the stitches are not visible on the right side. The corners should be creased downwards and then lightly stitched (see arrow).

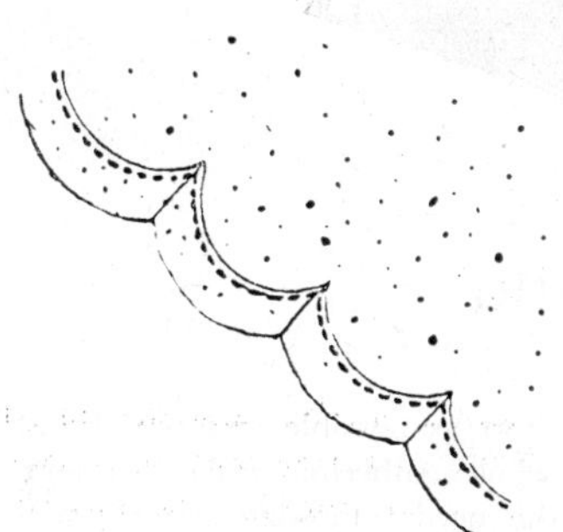

(f)

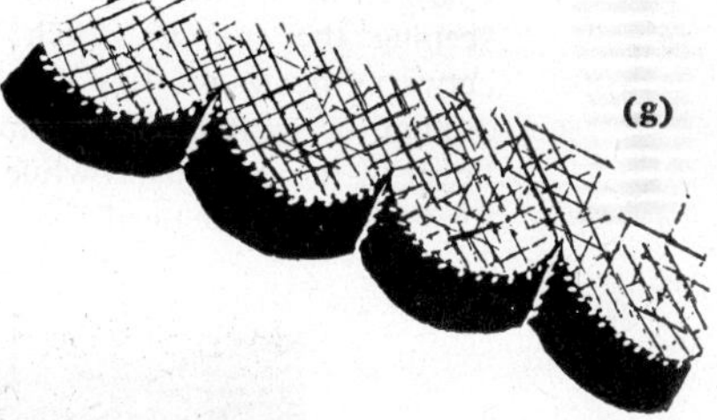

(g)

The binding can be turned right back so that only a very narrow strip is visible from the right side. In (**h**) the binding is machined double and then turned back on to the wrong side. (**f**) and (**g**) show two ways of finishing scallops that are bound on the right side as trimming.

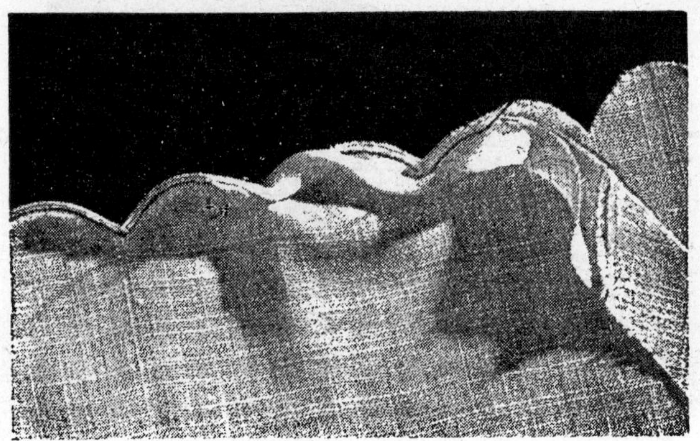

(h)

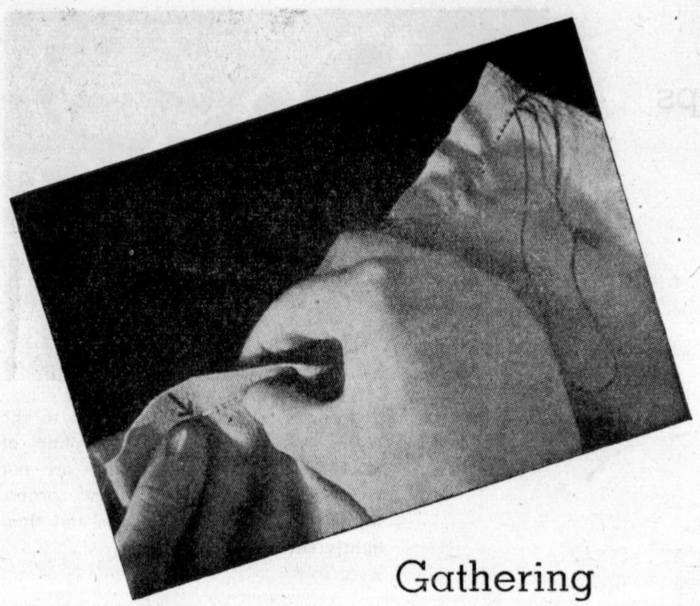

Gathering

For gathering, the needle should be as short as possible and the thread strong and long enough to complete the whole gathering without a join. Begin with a knot and back stitch, run the needle through the material keeping the running stitch as fine as possible and holding the material between the thumb and fingers of both hands. Pin the beginning on to a cushion or something firm and hold the needle between the thumb and first finger of the right hand while the left hand works the material backwards and forwards on to the needle.

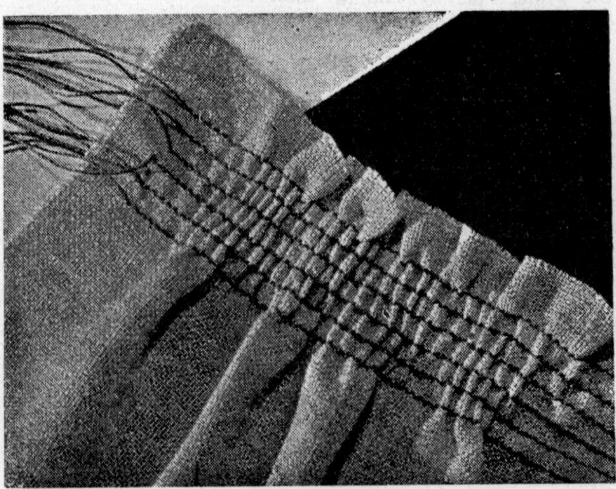

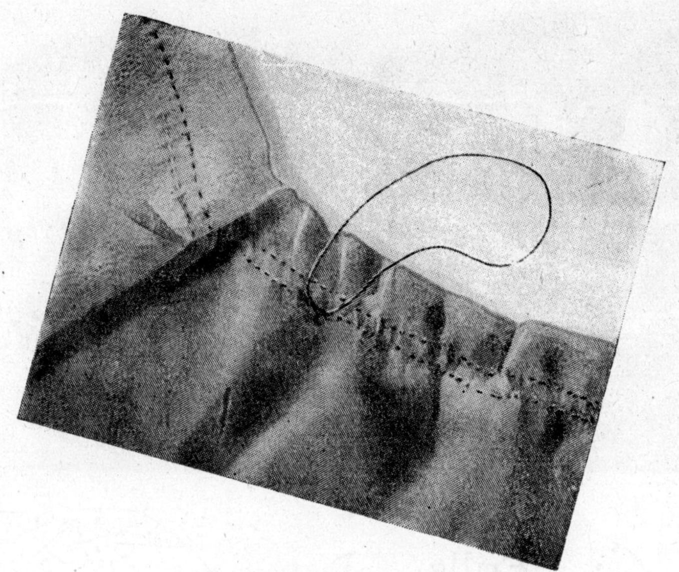

The thread should not be drawn through until the end of the gathering is reached. If the area to be gathered is particularly long, it is permissible to draw the thread up halfway across and put the needle in afresh. Long ends should be left until the gathers are drawn up to the correct length, when they are taken through to the wrong side and finished off neatly.

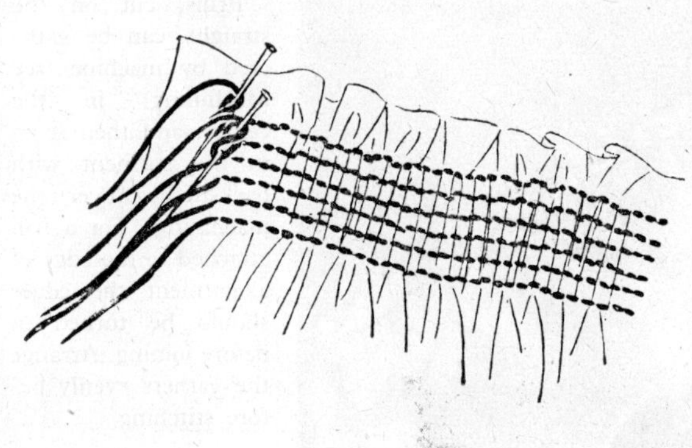

At least a double row of gathering threads is necessary to make the fullness hang evenly. If joined on to a straight piece of fabric, the joining seam should be between the two lines of gathers. Several rows of gathers can be done on the machine quickly and easily. (See photograph opposite.)

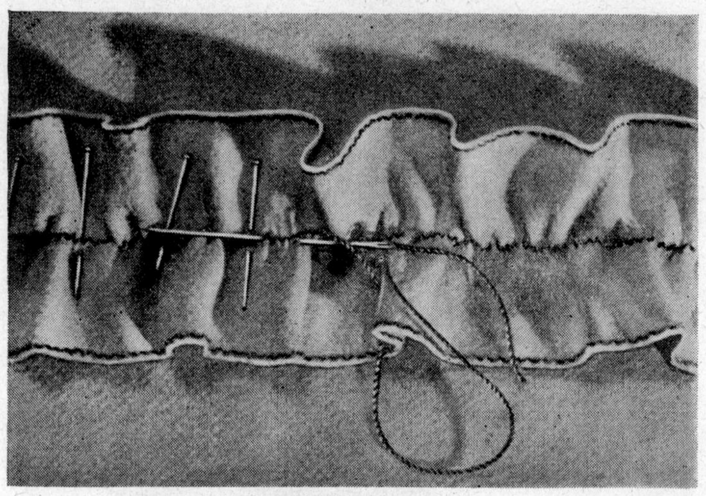

Frills and Flounces

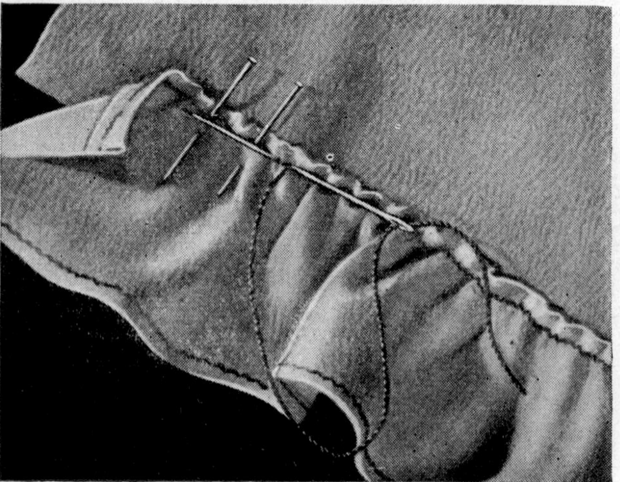

Frills, cut on the straight, can be gathered by machine (see Machining) in the centre, and then sewn to the garment with backstitches over the machining. For a frill attached to the edge of a garment the edges should be turned in before joining. Arrange the gathers evenly before stitching.

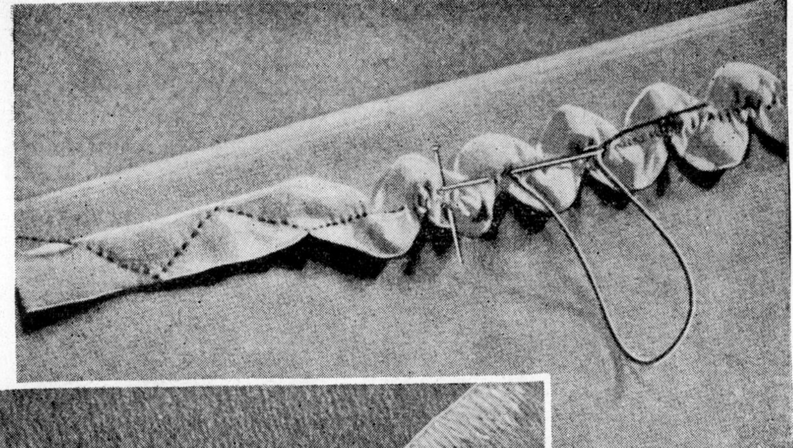

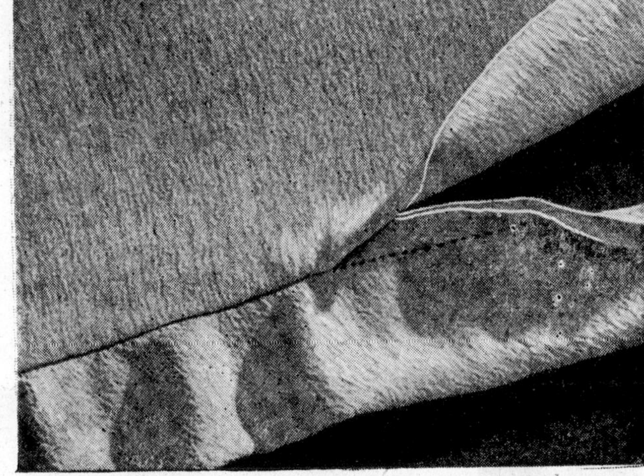

Zig-zag frills are worked from a straight strip of bias-cut fabric, which is gathered in zig-zags, the line being straightened when joined to the fabric. A double, bias-cut flare falls softly and gracefully. The flare is joined by running and back stitch and sewn to the garment by hand. The fold is pressed lightly.

Flares in single material are cut out in the form of circles or semi-circles (see opposite page) and afterwards opened out and joined together. The hem can be machined or picot-edged. Join to the garment by machine, being careful not to stretch the inner edge.

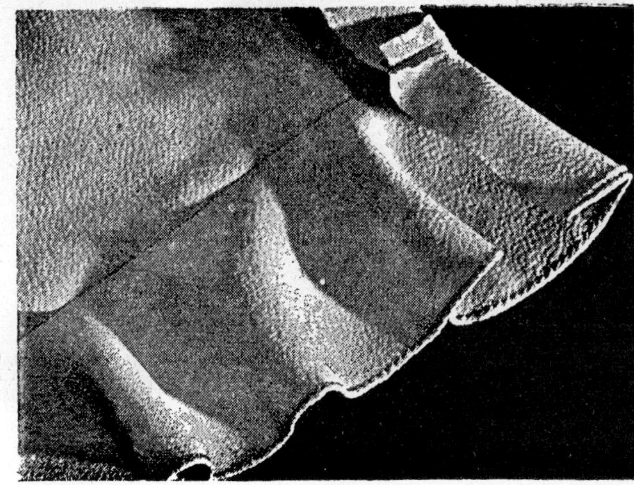

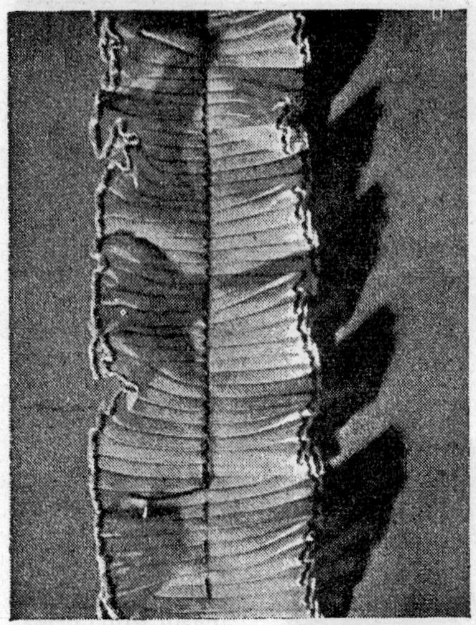

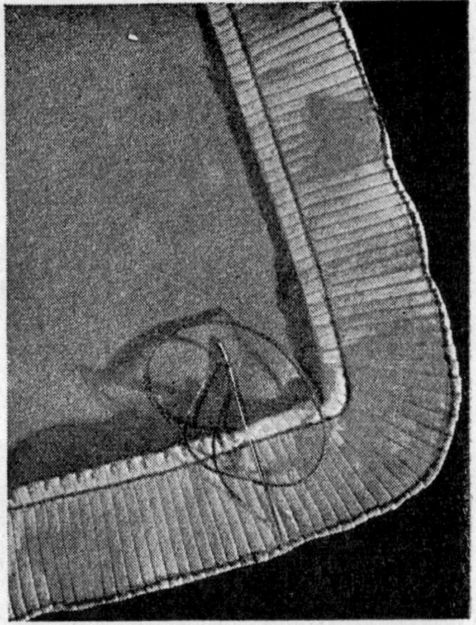

Pleated frills, particularly suitable for thin fabrics, consist of material three times their finished length. The machined edge can be done before or after the pleating, but if done afterwards, the effect is more fluffy. The pleats can be machined down the centre or along the edge, according to the position on the garment. If joined to the edge the frill can either be bound in thin material (below, right) or overcast with buttonholing (top, right).

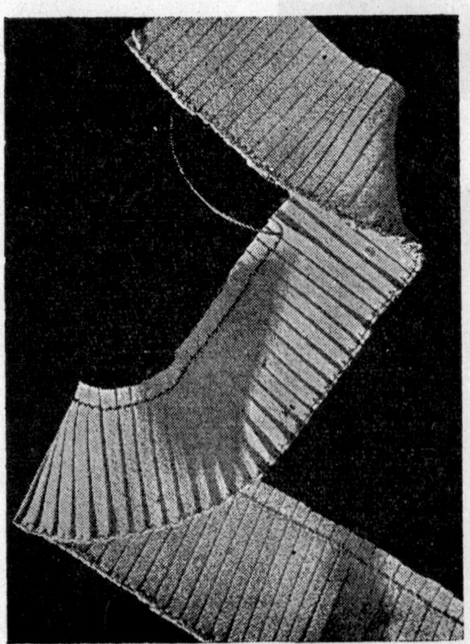

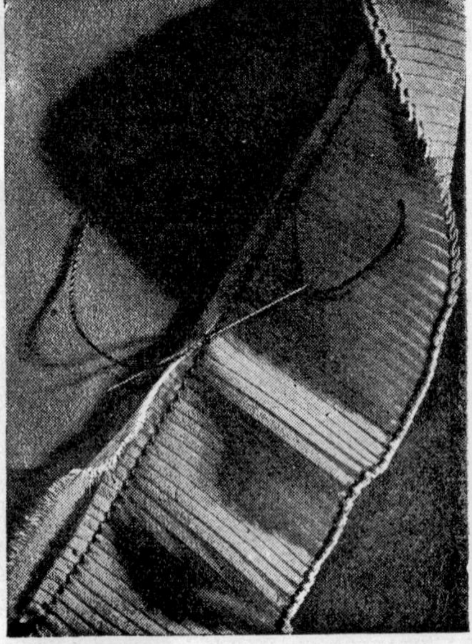

Pleated Frills and Ruching

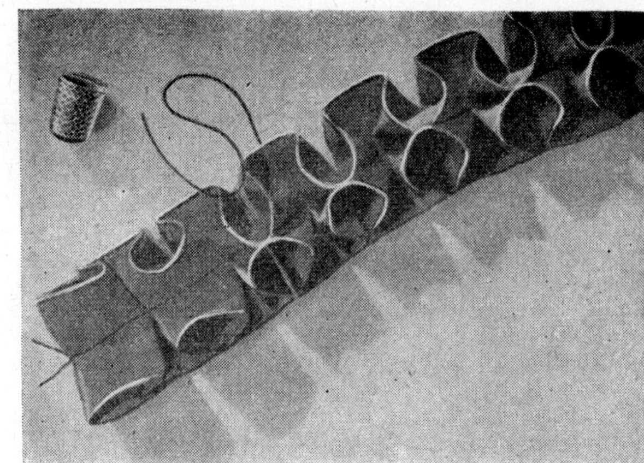

The Toby frill above, cut on the straight, takes three times its length in material. Machine into box pleats, the centres of which are caught up, afterwards. Tulle frills need three to four times their length in material. Single or double box pleats can be made according to the fullness needed.

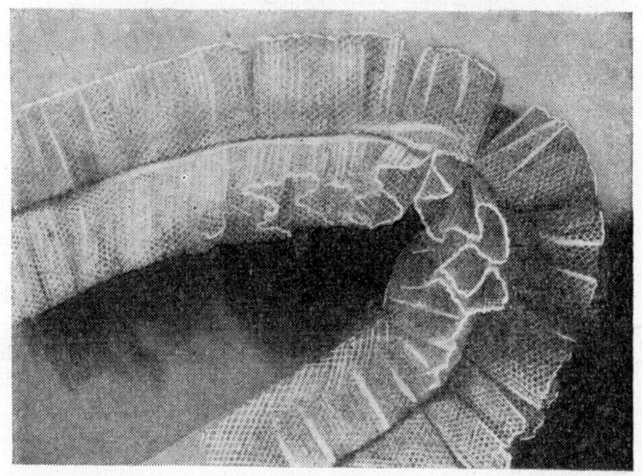

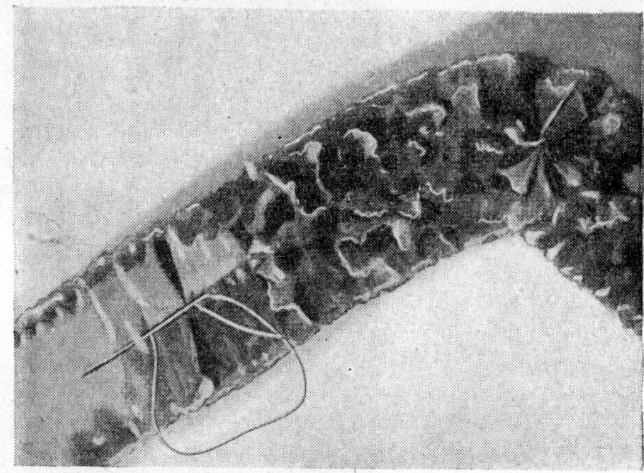

On the right is rose ruching made in frayed taffeta cut on the bias. The taffeta is box-pleated by hand and the centre of each pleat is then caught up and joined to the centre of its neighbour, so that a circular rose is formed

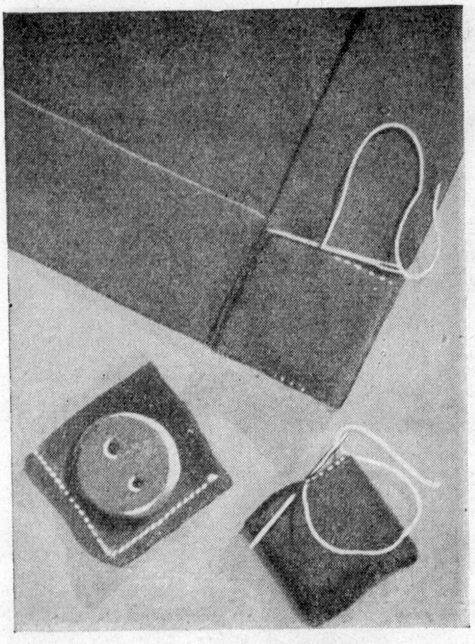

Lead Weights

These are sometimes used for keeping down corners and ends of garments. They can only be placed where there is a firm hold on the material, and where the seams are not likely to tear.

The weights are not sewn in the seams, but are encased in small bags (see photograph) and stitched on to the wrong side of the corner. The bag should not fit the weight too closely as the lead will soon wear through. Weights that are to be put on a seam can be covered by two circles of material, as shown below. Sew round the edge of the weight and herringbone the two edges of material together.

Slots for Draw Threads

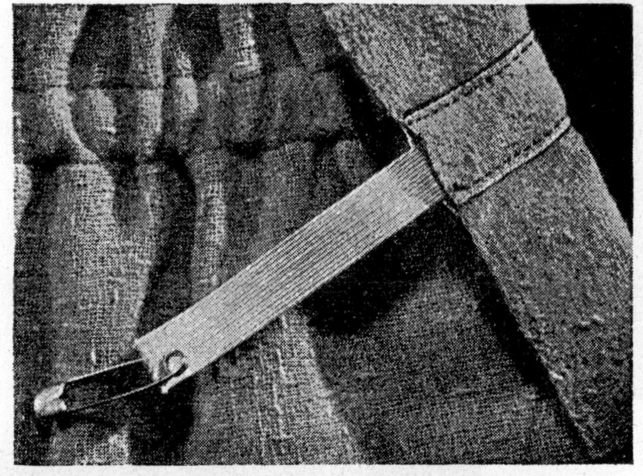

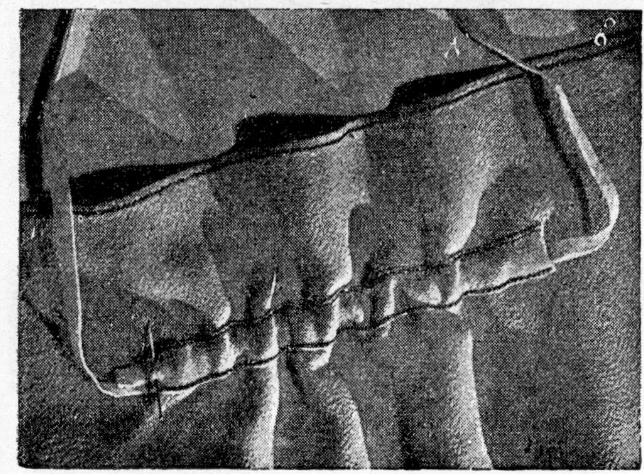

A casing of the same material, cut on the straight, is usually made for a draw thread (see top photograph). Elastic or tape can be used. In the bottom photograph the casing is on the right side and is stitched in a different colour to make it more decorative.

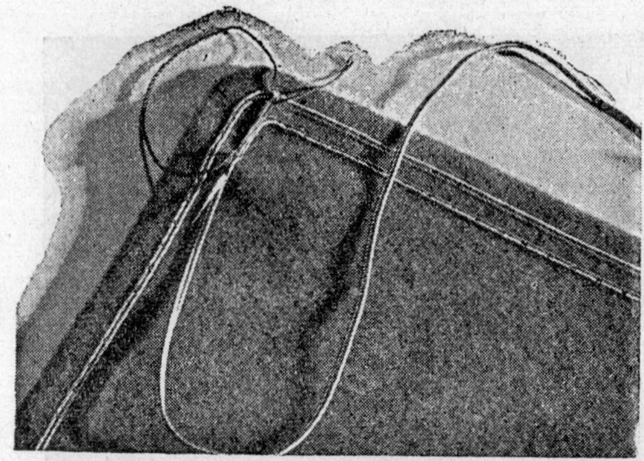

Soutache braid is sometimes used to decorate and neaten a seam. It should be sewn flat, the centre rib making the sewing line. If coiled patterns are made, the braid can be sewn so that it stands up on its end.

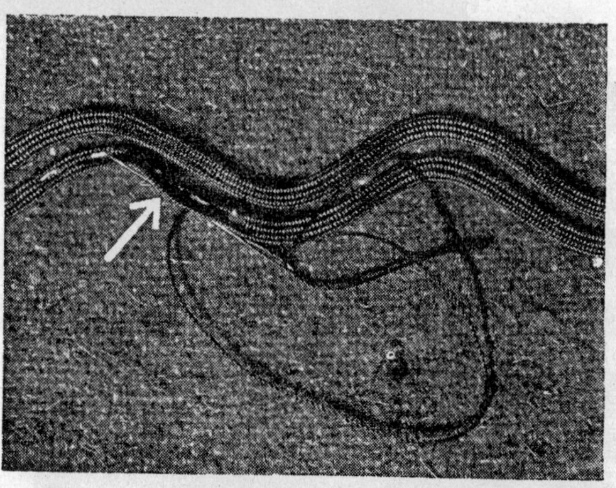

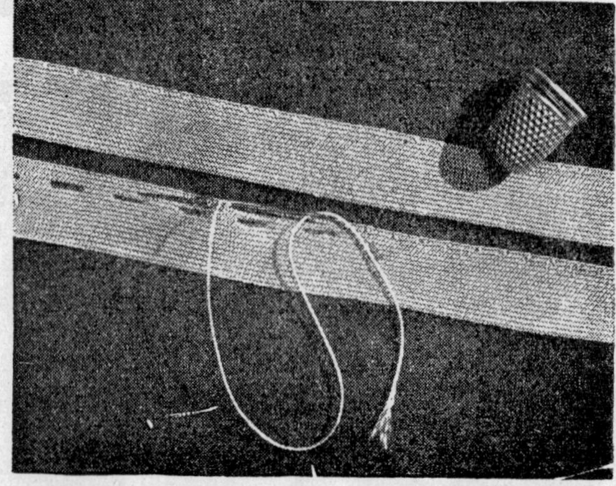

Narrow silk braid is often used for decoration. It should first be tacked, and each side should be invisibly slip stitched, the stitches being closer together on the inside of a curve.

Braid Trimming

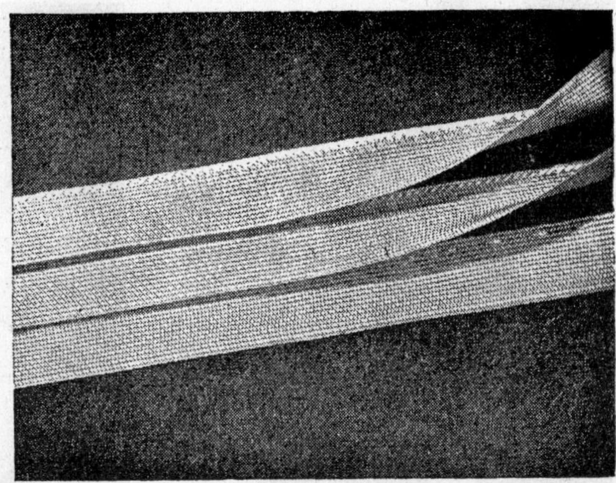

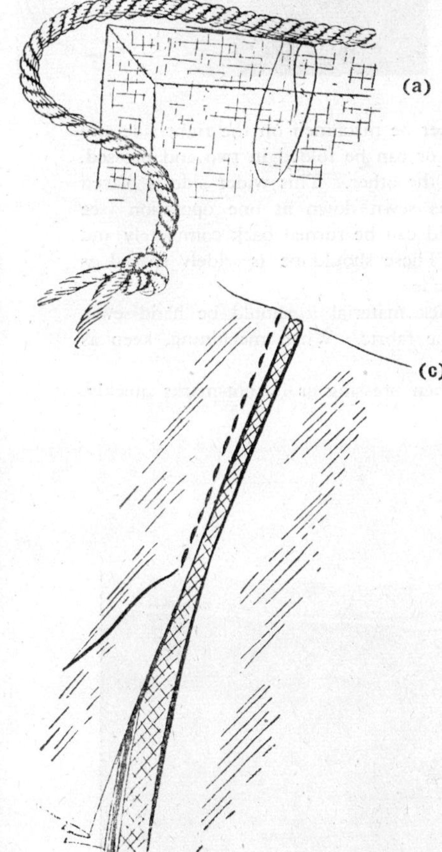

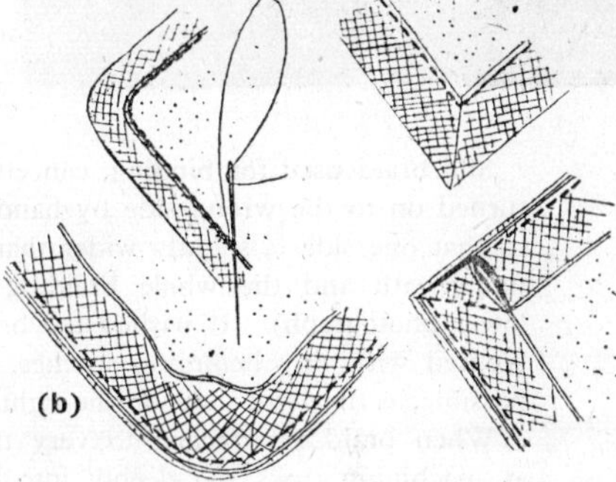

Cord is often used as an edging, and is sewn by invisible stitches along the folded edge of the article (see **a**). Tie a knot at the ends to prevent them from becoming unravelled.

Flat silk braid is very often used as a trimming. When placed in parallel rows the stitches should be done by hand, the tiny, evenly spaced stitches being as invisible as possible. If sewn to overlap the top edge may be machined, and the lower edge left free to cover the stitching.

When binding with braid, ease slightly round curves, so that the braid lies flat when turned over. At sharp corners, take up the surplus braid with a cross-wise seam (**b**) then snip the edges before turning over. Sometimes braid is let into a seam like piping for trimming (**c**)

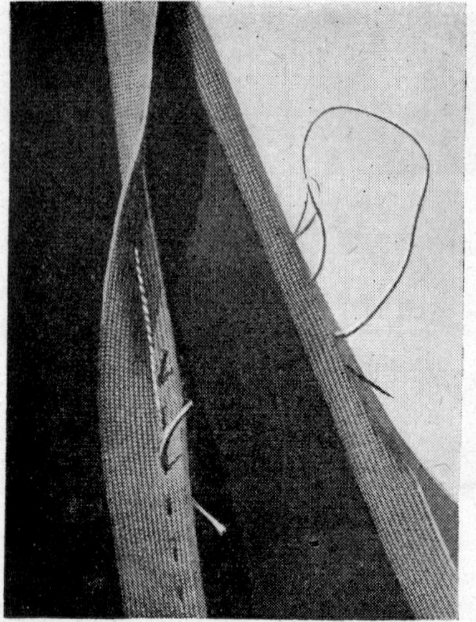

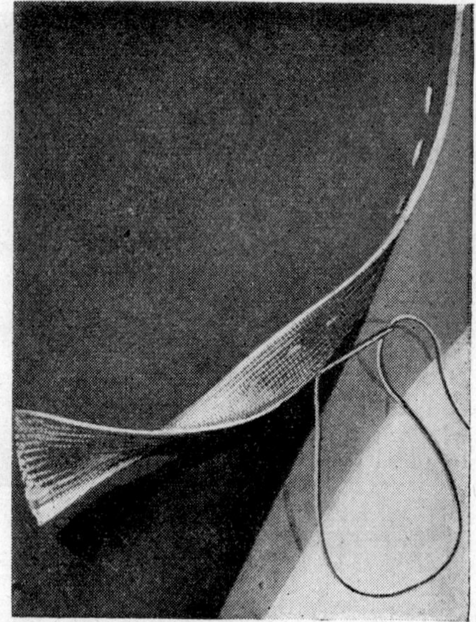

Silk braid used for binding, can either be machined on the right side and turned on to the wrong side by hand, or can be folded in two and pressed, so that one side is slightly wider than the other. This wider side is placed underneath and the whole braiding is sewn down at one operation (see lower photograph). If wished the braid can be turned back completely and secured with tiny hemming stitches. These should be as widely spaced as possible, as they will show on the right side.

When braid is attached to very thick material it should be hand-sewn, as machining sinks too deeply into the fabric. When machining, keep as near the edge as possible.

Braid should never be dampened when pressing as it spot-marks quickly.

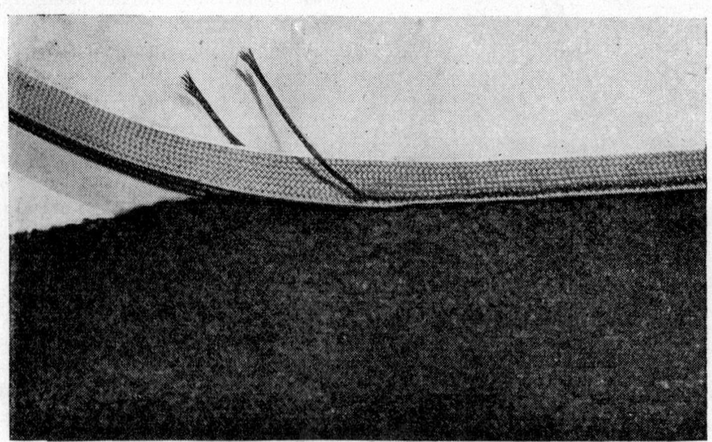

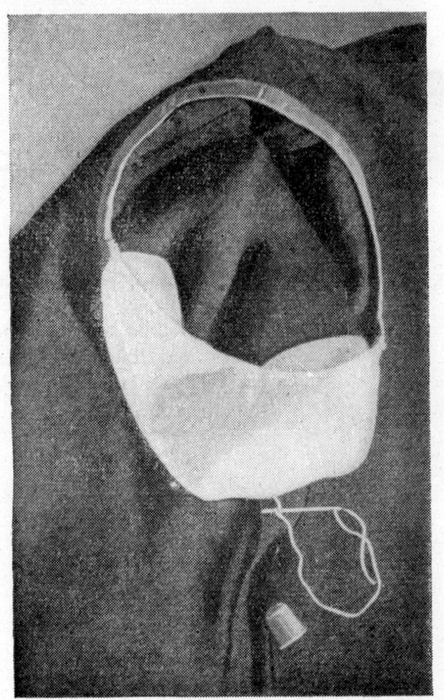

Dress Shields

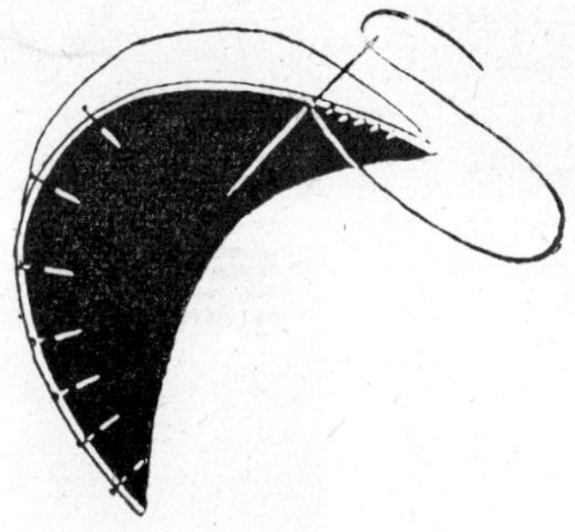

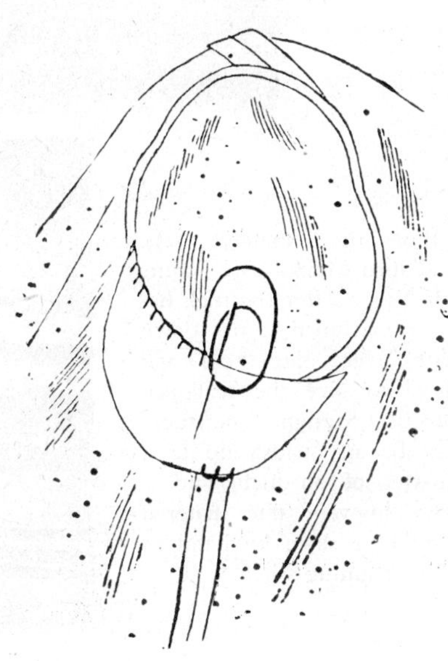

Dress shields can be bought in several sizes and colours. They should be soft and thin, so that they do not make the garment appear bulky.

Sew them in so that the main part of the shield lies towards the front, with only a little to the back of the side seam. A double shield should be caught at the edges only, the loose ends being caught by an overcast bar.

For very short sleeves or sleeveless dresses there are special half-shields, which should be buttonholed into the armhole (see lower drawing). For coats and jackets, in which the shield will be conspicuous, line it with thin silk to match the coat lining.

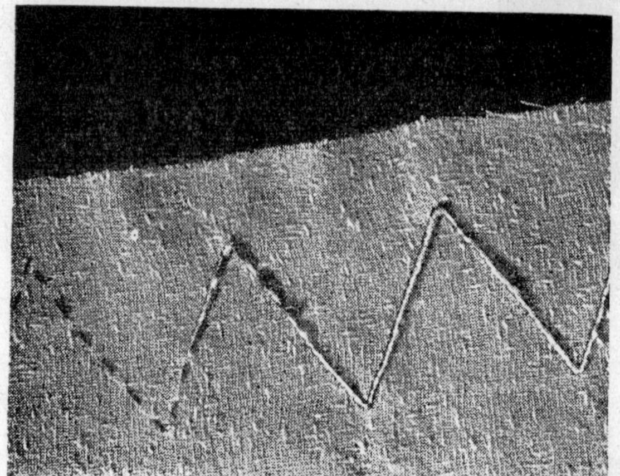

Tucks and Piping

Very fine pin tucks shaped in either curves or zig-zags are difficult to do. They should first be tacked along the marked lines, and then machined a needle's breadth from the edge.

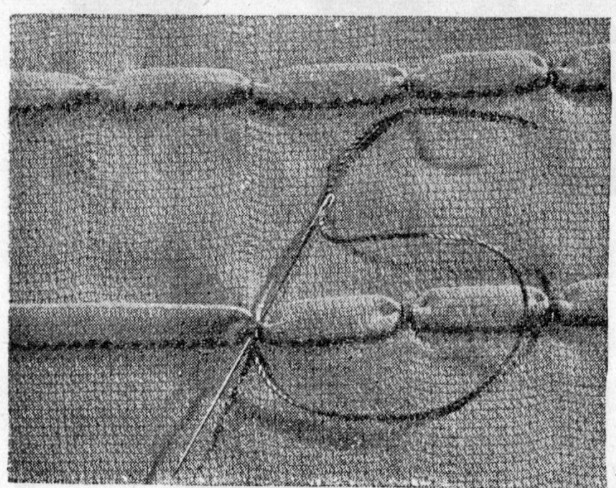

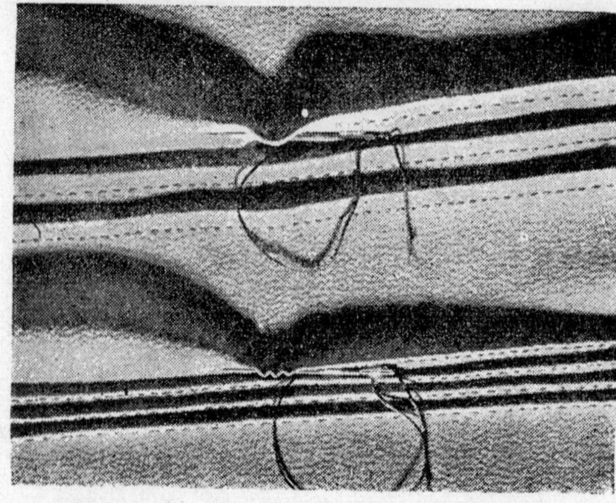

For thin material, the scalloped tucks are quite effective. After the tuck has been machined, catch down with overcasting here and there to give the scalloped effect. Straight pin-tucks can be any width up to a quarter of an inch, and if done in very fine material should be sewn by hand in a fine running stitch.

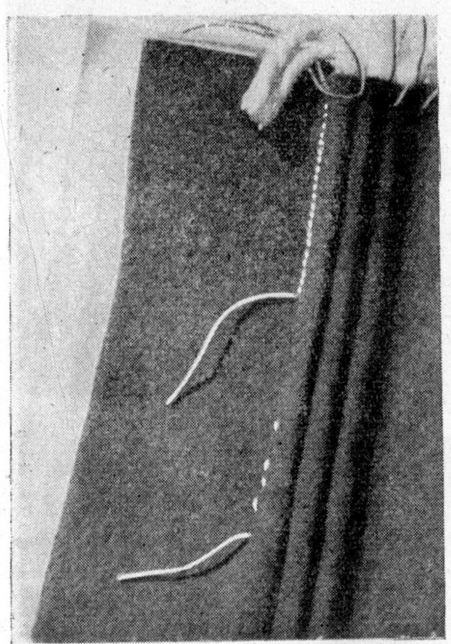

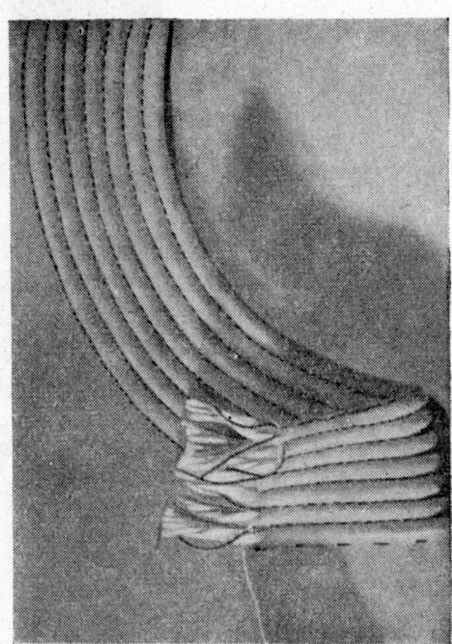

Soft woollen cord is used for piping. The most usual way of padding material with this cord is to tack the cord in position between the double thickness of material, and then machine down each row, as close to the padding as the presser foot will allow. Very careful tacking is necessary to keep the lines absolutely even and parallel.

Curves, as above, need especial care as they are more difficult to keep even.

When very thick material is piped, a thinner material is used for the backing to prevent bulkiness. Each row of piping must be finished completely before a new row is begun.

Gathers are sometimes done over piping, the gathering thread being run very close to the piping.

See also chapter on Upholstery.

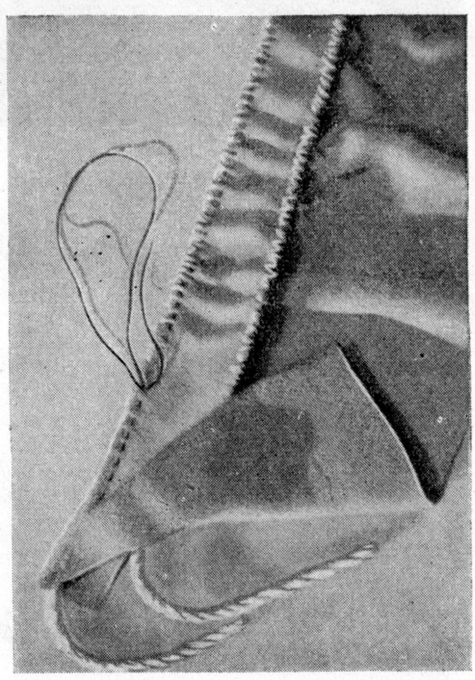

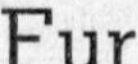

Fur

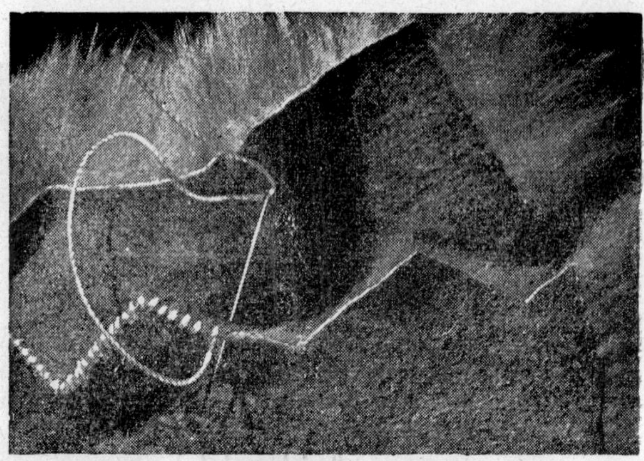

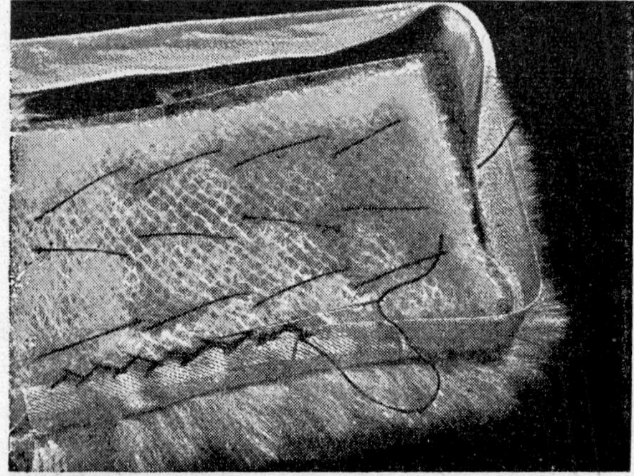

Damp the skin before sewing and cutting, with a soft sponge, and then nail the skin on to a board, hairy side down, stretching it slightly. The skin must dry naturally in the air, otherwise it will be hard. On the dried, stretched skin draw out the part to be cut. If more than one piece is cut join carefully with an eye to colour and fur. For cutting use a sharp razor blade, and avoid cutting the hairs. The seams are overcast with strong thread or silk.

Fur needs a between lining of cotton wool, domette, etc., according to the purpose of the collar. The lining is secured with large herring-bone stitches, and finished with a silk lining if separate, or stitched to the tailor's canvas of the collar of a coat.

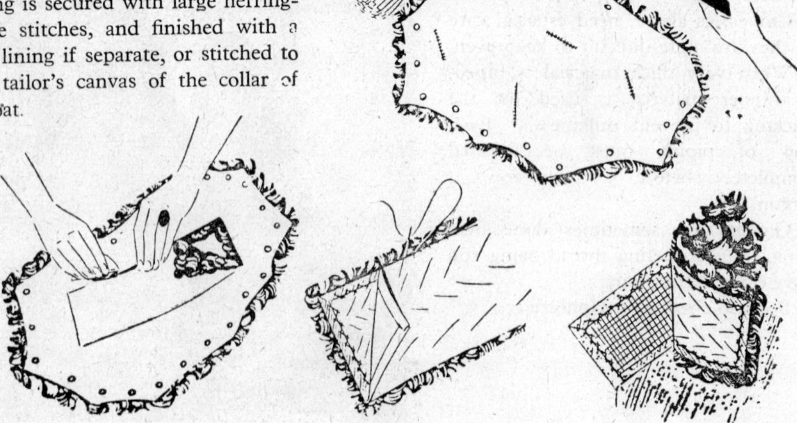

Joining Lace

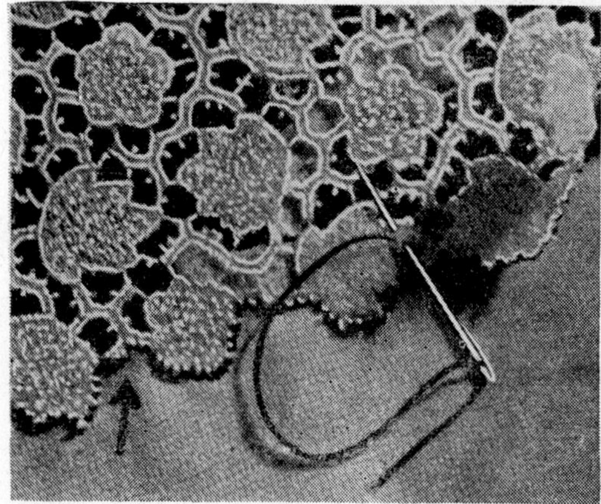

Some laces have such thick, fine weaves that the cut edges do not need securing. Delicate laces on a fine net background are apt to roll over unless secured immediately. If the pattern is followed as shown in the illustrations, the edges should be neatly and closely overcast, so that each lace thread is caught.

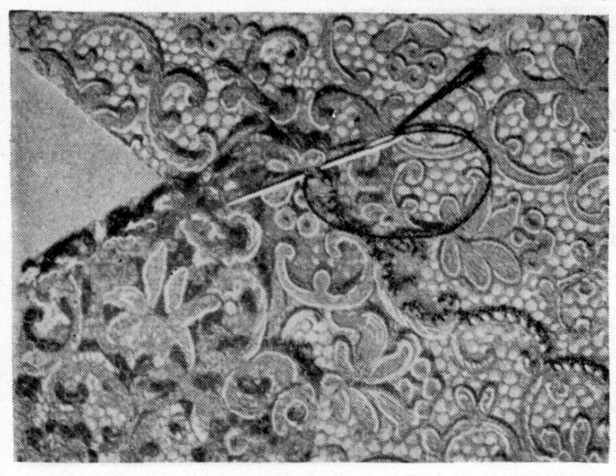

When lace is overcast on to fabric, the fabric should be cut away underneath (see arrow). When two pieces of lace are joined, the lace is again overcast round the pattern. If silk of the same shade is used for stitching, the joins should be almost invisible.

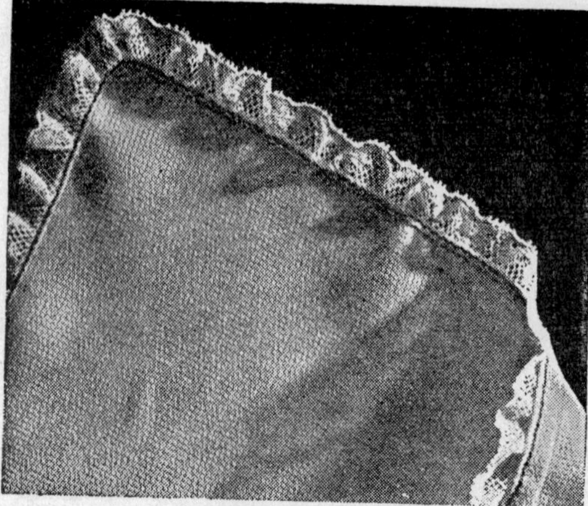

How to Sew Lace

Narrow lace edgings need neat and careful sewing, and they can either be machined (which see) or done by hand, according to the daintiness of the garment or article to which it is intended to be sewn.

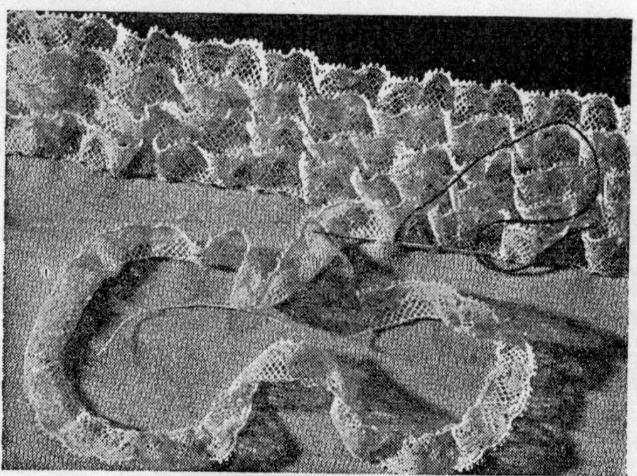

Lace frills are sewn by hand, so that each layer of lace covers the stitching of the previous row. Very narrow silk or georgette bias binding should be used for lace that unravels. It should be first machined (under tissue paper so that the lace threads do not catch in the presser foot). The binding should not be more than an eighth to quarter of an inch wide.

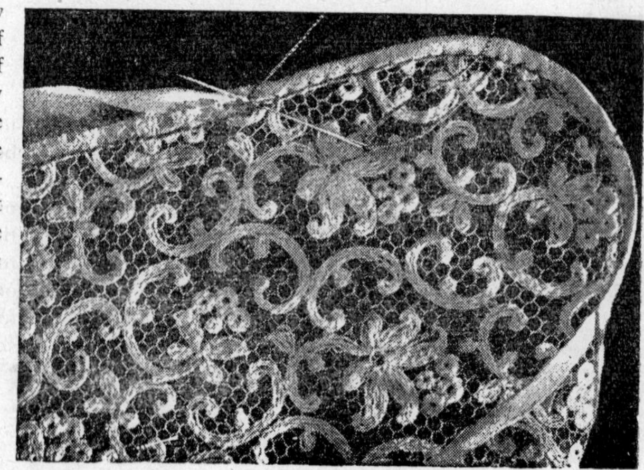

Bows

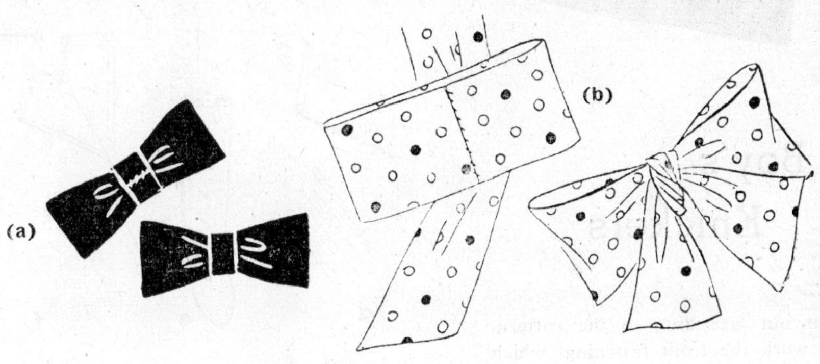

A decorative plait can be made out of neat double strips of bias-cut material. Pin four or more pieces side by side on to a board or table, and plait carefully, leaving each curve fairly loose, so that the plait will lie flat when finished. As the plaiting takes up one-third to one-half the length, allow extra length. Secure the ends well when finished.

Bows can be made in one or two pieces If made all in one piece, it is sometimes difficult to get them to lie flat. Small, stiff, velvet bows (**a**) are made in two pieces The first strip is joined as at (**b**), and the central shaft covers this join, and is sewn neatly at the back.

Large, floppy bows are made in the same way, except that the central piece is longer, and is tied at the back, so that the long ends lie flat.

For Artist's bows each piece is cut separately. The petal pieces are neatly gathered at the end, and looped up, the loose ends being gathered at one end only. All the gathered ends are joined together, flatly, and the central piece laid in gathers over the join and sewn at the back.

Special safety-pins can be bought, to sew on to the back of bows. These are quite invisible and secure.

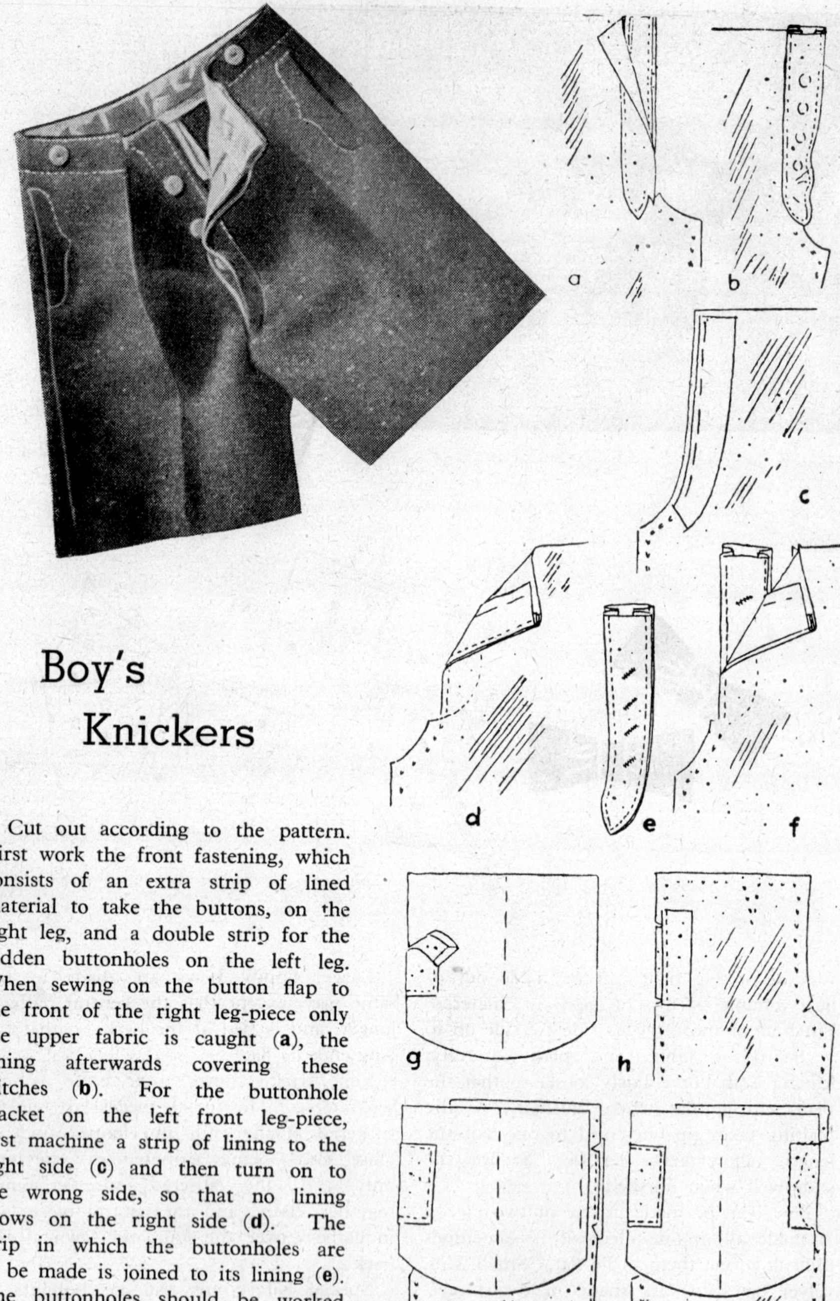

Boy's Knickers

Cut out according to the pattern. First work the front fastening, which consists of an extra strip of lined material to take the buttons, on the right leg, and a double strip for the hidden buttonholes on the left leg. When sewing on the button flap to the front of the right leg-piece only the upper fabric is caught (**a**), the lining afterwards covering these stitches (**b**). For the buttonhole placket on the left front leg-piece, first machine a strip of lining to the right side (**c**) and then turn on to the wrong side, so that no lining shows on the right side (**d**). The strip in which the buttonholes are to be made is joined to its lining (**e**). The buttonholes should be worked on the slant, being deeper in front.

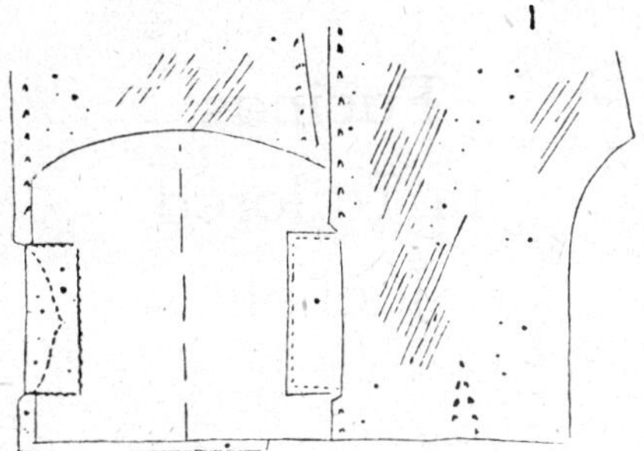

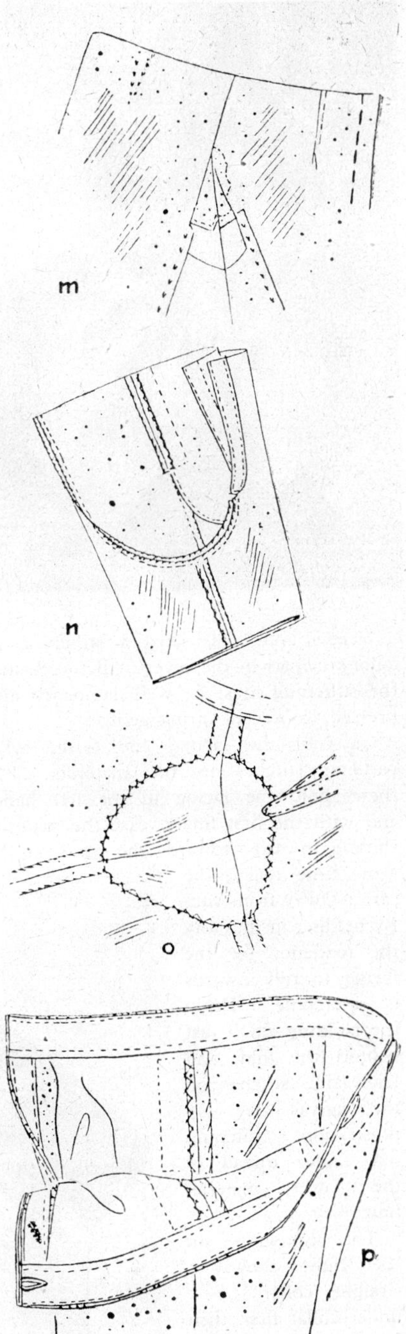

The finished strip is now joined to the leg-piece as at (**f**).

The side pockets are made out of strong calico. The side opening is strengthened by a band of the trouser fabric (**g**). Another strengthening strip being added to the right side of the trouser (**h**). The pocket is then tacked in position (**i**) and the strengthening on the trouser turned over to the wrong side and neatly hemmed to the pocket (**k**). The strengthening on the pocket is then fastened to the wrong side of the back leg-piece (**l**). The pocket is then folded in half and the back and front leg-pieces joined, the opening of the pocket being left free (**m**). Now join the other side seams and the centre (**n**). The whole can be lined, or if preferred a lining can be placed in the centre only. The back should be deeper than the front (**o**). Herringbone the lining to the fabric.

Darts at the back and small pleats at the front take up any fullness at the waist. Finish the upper edge with a strong bias strip of calico. Finish all the seams on the inside (**p**).

If braces are to be worn, buttons should be sewn on to either the right or wrong side, and if a belt is preferred, strong bands of the materials should be sewn, vertically, at the side seams.

Press thoroughly with the crease down the front and back.

Facings in Tailored Jackets

Jackets and coats need a stiffening of tailor's canvas in the revers. Before using, the stiffening must be well dampened and pressed, to prevent shrinkage later.

Cut out the facing, and fasten with padding stitches to the material. For these, hold the facing in the left hand, and with the first finger, ease the material slightly inwards, towards the hand, at the same time easing the canvas away from you. By holding in this way the tendency for the facing to roll inwards is overcome. Begin the padding stitch just behind the fold, and take large stitches on the canvas (see top illustration) catching one under thread of the lower material only.

The photograph on the right shows a straight collar. Sew under collar first, then slip-stitch collar to facing carefully, using tiniest stitches possible. Another collar is in three parts, the under collar and stiffening (cut on the cross and with a central seam) and the upper collar which is cut on the straight and is seamless. The under collar and stiffening are catch-stitched together. The position of these stitches is shown by the upper diagram.

A stand-up collar should be eased in slightly when stitching, so that it sits better, and a turn-down collar should be pulled gently at the edge, to lie flat. The under collar should be turned in, hemmed to the outer edge of the garment. On the inside the stiffening should be herringboned down before the upper part of the collar is sewn on.

The upper part is sometimes sewn with

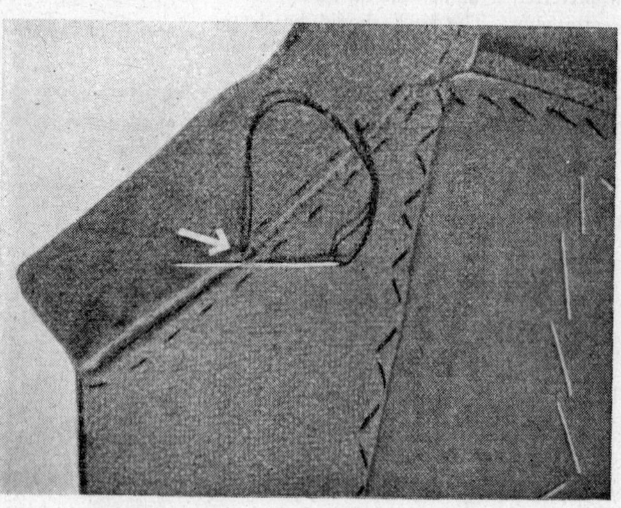

the seam allowance left on the outside. This is afterwards fastened down with herringboning so that the edges are flat after pressing and the edges do not show through.

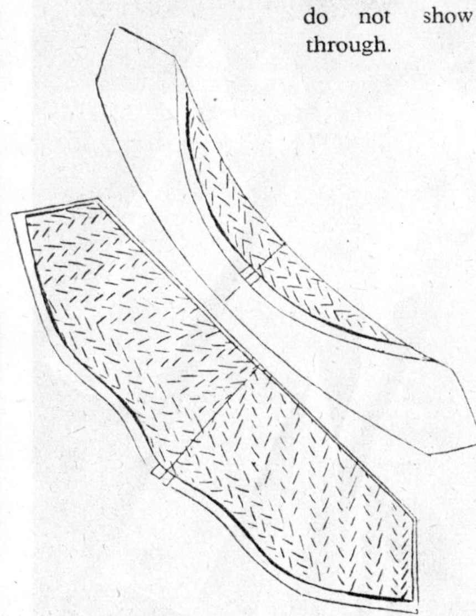

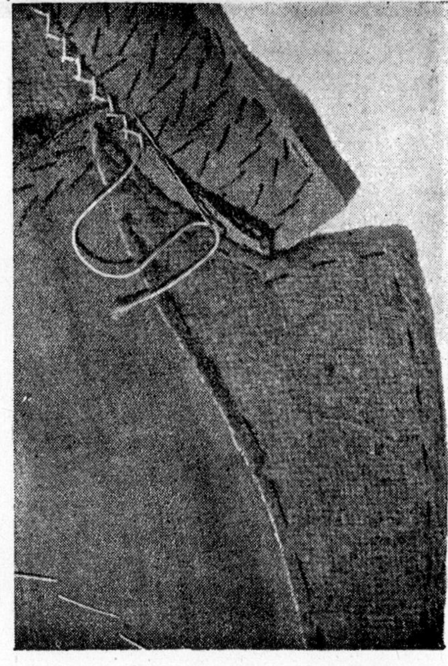

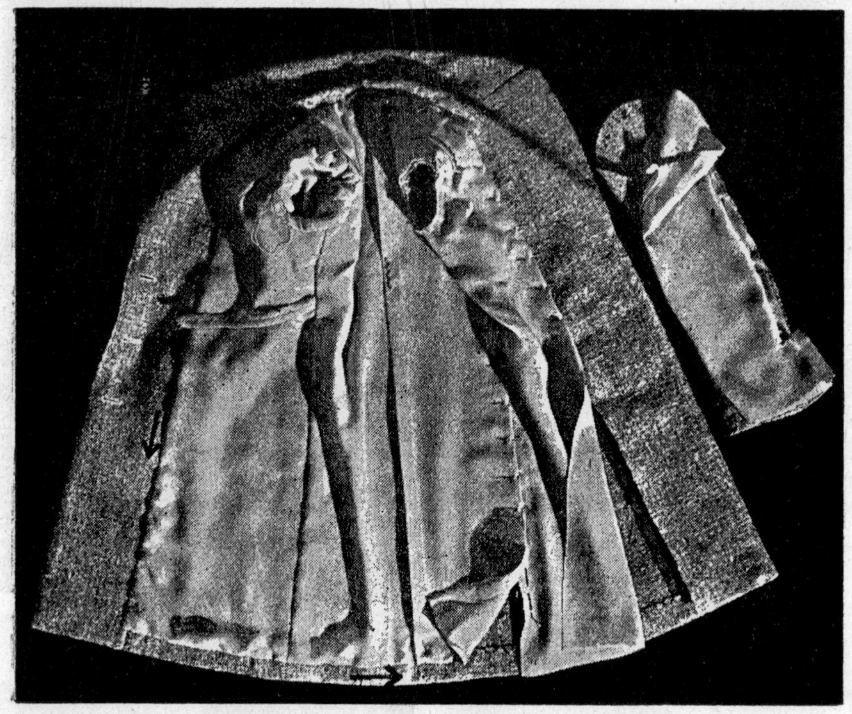

Lining a Coat

The ideal lining for durability should be a mixture of artificial silk and wool, the colour toning with the coat, unless a definite contrast is wanted.

The lining should never be cut smaller than the coat, but should have plenty of fullness, which is afterwards taken up in a large fold at the centre back. Machine the inner seams of the lining before sewing in.

The lining should be fitted before the sleeves are put in the coat. A dressmaker's model simplifies fitting considerably. After pinning to the model, the coat should be spread out on a large table for sewing.

First tack the front side and shoulder seams to the corresponding seams of the coat. Tack the fullness fold into position. These seams can be left pinned until the sleeves have been inserted.

The sleeve lining seam should be machined and then tacked along the wrist to keep it in position. The armhole edge is not secured until the sleeve is finished entirely. It then covers the armhole seam and is hemmed to the main coat lining.

When sewing in the lining, use loose stitches and begin at the shoulder seam, and work round the outside edge in the direction of the arrow. Leave plenty of fullness along the bottom, so that the lining hangs loosely over the hem when finished (see drawing of dressmaker's model).

One or two lengths of flat ribbon or lining should be sewn into the side

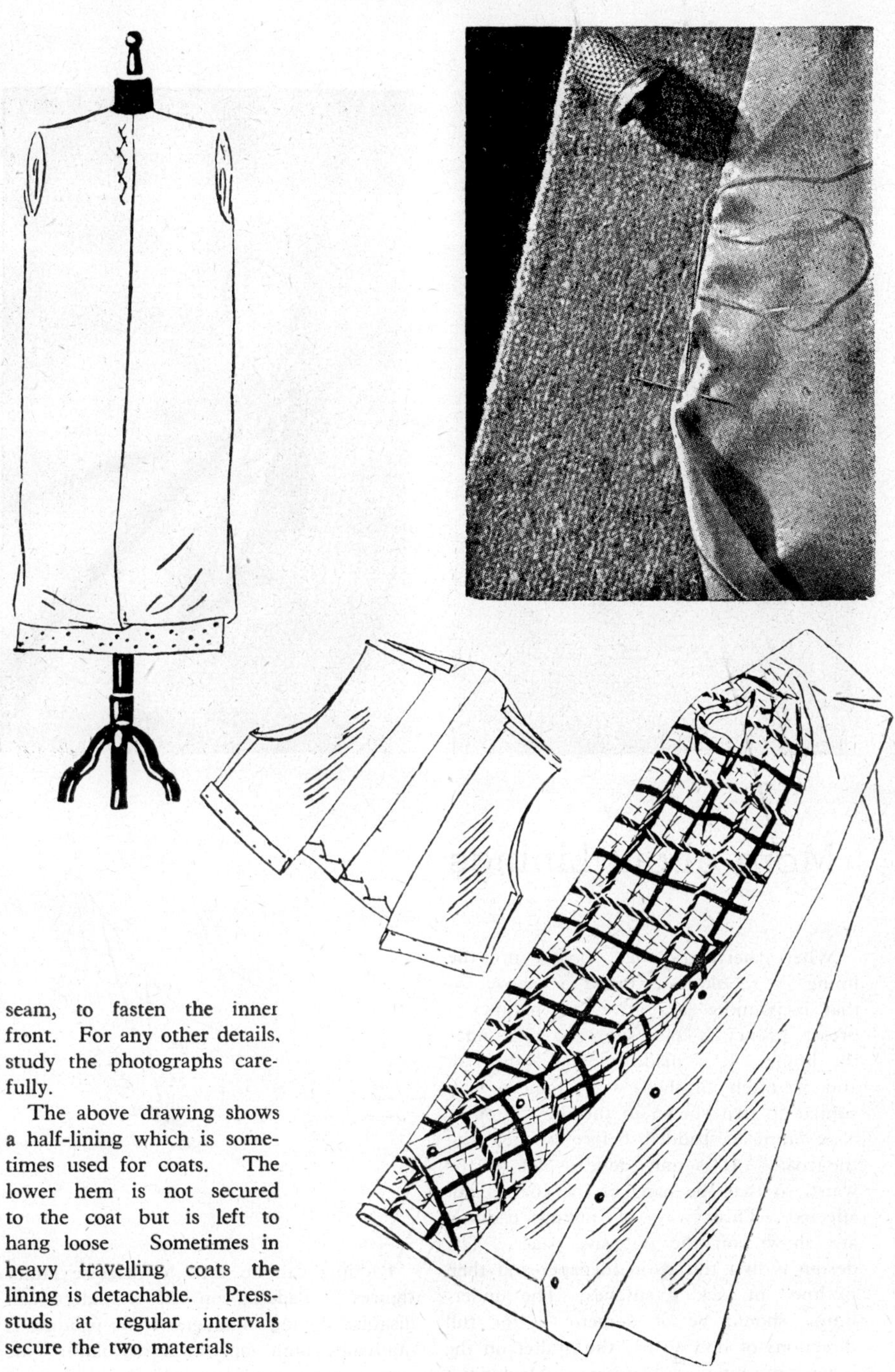

seam, to fasten the inner front. For any other details, study the photographs carefully.

The above drawing shows a half-lining which is sometimes used for coats. The lower hem is not secured to the coat but is left to hang loose Sometimes in heavy travelling coats the lining is detachable. Press-studs at regular intervals secure the two materials

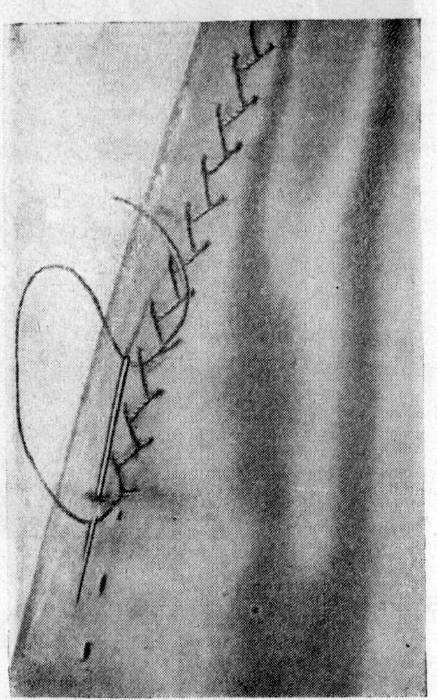

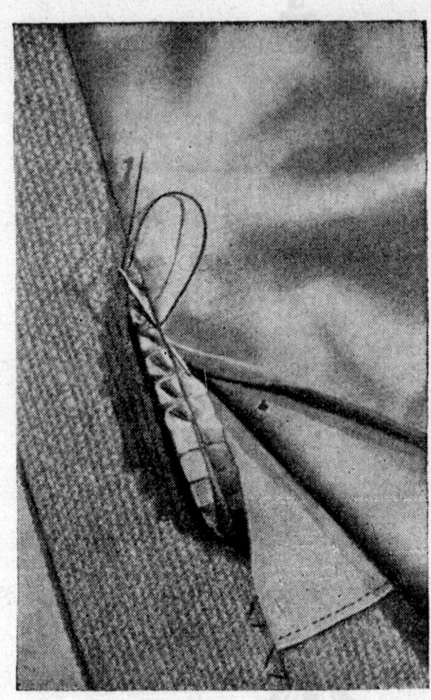

More about Linings

When herringboning shows in the lining, it should be worked as above, so that it is more decorative. Sometimes a breast pocket is put sideways on under the lining. It is made of single material, and is often finished with a neat frill, similar to that shown in the illustration.

A lining is padded before sewing into the coat. It is only done as far as the waist, so that the hang of the coat is not affected. Three ways of quilting padding are shown on the opposite page. The design is first traced on to paper and then outlined in tacking stitches. The under-lining should be of domette. For full directions of how to use the quilter on the sewing machine, see chapter on Machining.

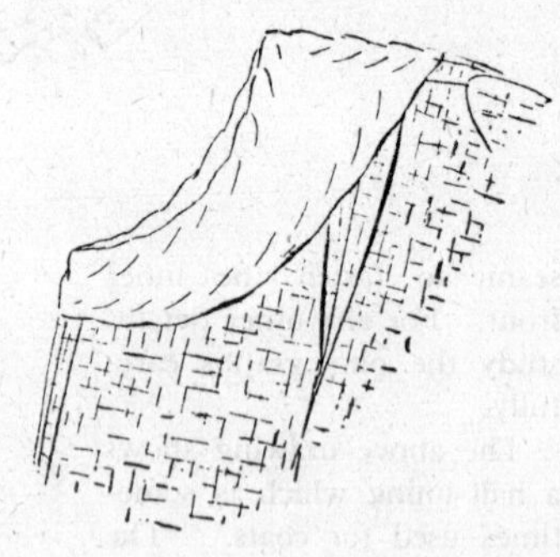

Padding can be used to disguise faulty figures. Padding on the shoulders will disguise sloping shoulders The padding is gradually built up, layer by layer, the edges being pulled out to lie flat.

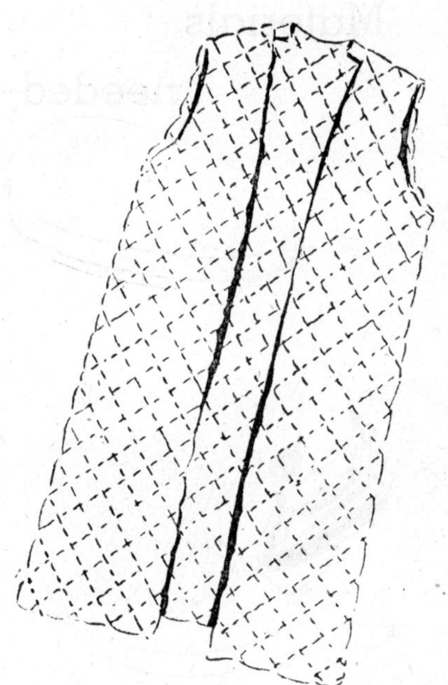

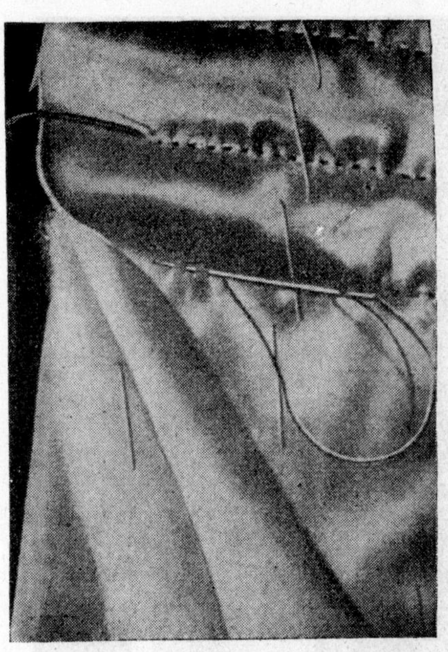

Padded Linings

1

Materials needed—

5

6

7

An iron—as heavy as possible. A tailor's goose is ideal.

1. An ironing board, with a pointed end and a detachable cover that can easily be removed for washing. The pattern of this can easily be followed from the illustration.

2. A sleeve board also with a detachable cover. The sleeve to be pressed is slipped over this, the widest part towards the top.

3. Two tailor's cushions, one large and one small, for pressing facings and awkward curves (**5, 6, 7**). These can be made out of tailor's canvas padded with wadding and covered with fabric.

4. A pressing cloth of linen or some

for Pressing

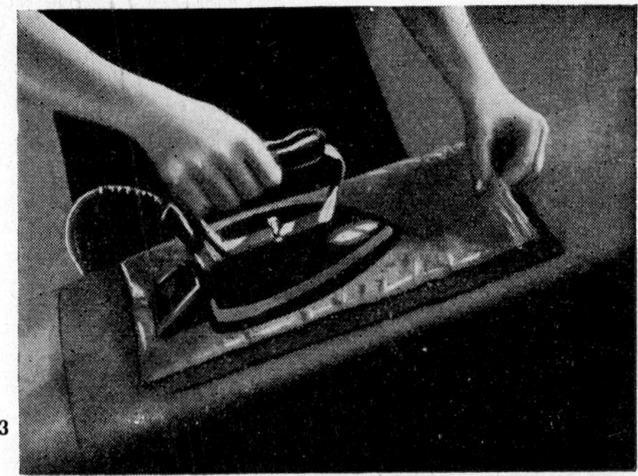
3

soft fabric that does not leave any hairs or fluff. Several thicknesses may be needed, so the cloth should be fairly large. Professionals use a heavy unbleached cotton drill, but muslin that has been well washed can be used.

5. A small mop made out of ribbons or white material tied together in the form of a tassel, is useful for damping seams when shrinking. A sponge may be used if preferred.

For pressing velvet a needle board is sometimes used. The velvet is placed face downwards on this so that the pile is not pressed flat.

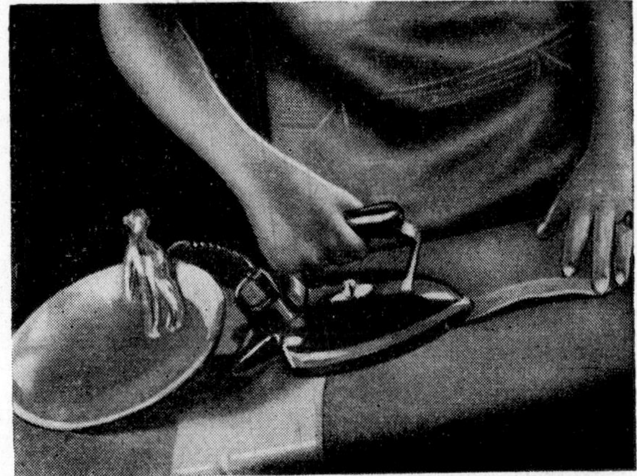
4

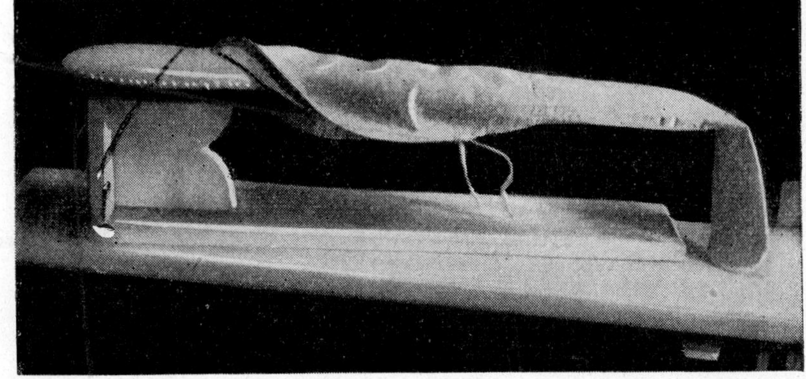

Pressing Velvet

—needs Special Care and Tactics

Any finger-marks that have been made while sewing should be steamed out. Hold the velvet over a pan or kettle of boiling water, and allow the steam to permeate into the fabric. This will raise the pile again. Should the pile be stubborn a second person should brush it up lightly while it is held over the steam.

Seams should not be pressed flat in the normal way. Stand the hot iron upright and pass the fabric over the flat surface. An alternative way is for one person to hold the velvet, while another presses the seam lightly. Small velvet pads under the fingers prevent finger-marks

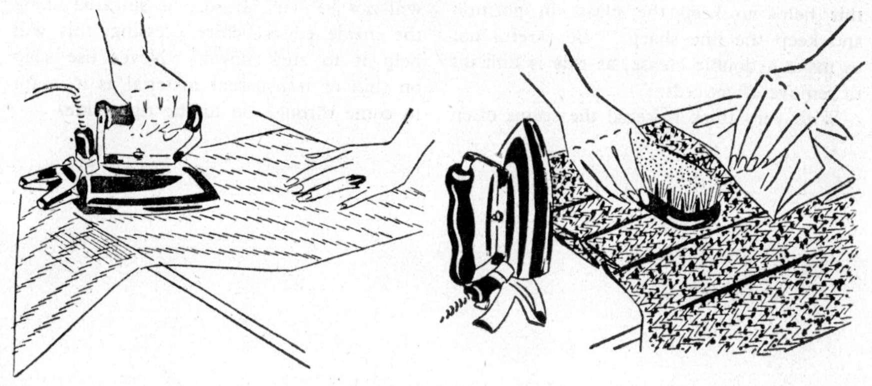

More about Pressing

Good and frequent pressing is absolutely essential to make a garment look tailored. Every seam and every join, dart or gather should be pressed as soon as it is finished, and then the whole garment pressed again before putting away.

Some points to remember:

Always press with the grain of the fabric.

Always test the fabric under a damp cloth before pressing any part of the garment. Some fabrics go limp, and some, especially those with a metallic thread, will not stand any great heat at all. Less heat is needed for silk and artificial silk than for wool. Use a warm, damp pressing cloth for wool, and a dry cloth placed between the damp cloth and the iron for silk or artificial silk. On no account must a hot iron touch artificial silk.

Press every seam that crosses another just before stitching the second, so that all seams lie the same way. It is very easy to make the mistake of pressing the seam allowance in the wrong direction occasionally.

In pressing, the object is to steam the material rather than iron out the creases.

For seams, lay the pressing cloth on the seam, dampen with the cloth-mop and press. Lift the cloth quickly to allow the steam to escape.

Use the tailor's cushions for shrinking fullness away on curves, sleeves and all awkward places. Use the point of the iron when working on the curved surface.

If any pressing has to be done on the right side care should be taken to prevent shine. If the pressing cloth is lifted quickly and then the fabric brushed with a soft brush, this should be prevented.

Another way to prevent this is to place a thick layer of material under the pressing cloth, as can be seen in illustration 3 in the previous pages.

Care must be taken when pressing bias binding and any material cut on the cross, not to stretch it out of shape.

Pleats should be pressed first on the wrong side, then on the right. Use a warm iron and a damp cloth, folded double when necessary.

Sometimes when the iron has just been removed the warm dampness makes the pleats spring out of position again. If a clothes brush is pressed quickly over the pleats when the iron has been removed, this helps to keep the pleats in position and keep the line sharp. Be careful not to make a double crease, as this is difficult to remove afterwards.

With very thick material the seams often will not lie flat. If soap is smeared along the inside edges before pressing, this will help it to stick down. Never use soap on thin or transparent material as it is apt to come through on to the right side.

MACHINING

In the following hints and instructions it is assumed that the reader is already familiar with her own sewing machine and its component parts, and that she has studied the Instruction Book that is given with every machine, with regard to care and oiling. These are as vitally important to the good working of a sewing machine as they are to the safety of a car or plane.

The first essential when preparing for sewing is to make absolutely certain that the thread and needle correspond with the material to be sewn. The following simplified chart will help you.

Size of Needle.	*Class of Work to be Sewn.*	*Sizes of Cotton, Linen or Silk.*
9.	Very thin silk, muslin, cambric, light-weight delicate fabrics.	100-150 cotton 30 silk
11.	Fine calicoes, linens, shirtings, fine silk goods, etc.	80-100 cotton 24-30 silk
14.	Shirtings, sheetings, bleached calicoes, silk and general domestic goods, light woollen goods and all classes of general work.	60-80 cotton 20 silk
16.	All kinds of heavy calicoes, drill, woollen goods, etc.	40-60 cotton 16-18 silk
18.	Tickings, woollen goods, trousers, boys' clothing, corsets, cloaks, mantles, etc.	30-40 cotton 60-80 linen
19.	Heavy woollens, tickings, bags, heavy coats, trousers, and heavy clothing generally.	24-30 cotton 60-80 linen
21.	Bags, coarse cloths, heavy goods.	40-60 linen

The tensions must also be adjusted to suit various materials. There are two tensions, the upper and the lower. The former controls the thread from the needle, while the latter controls the thread from the shuttle or bobbin-case.

For ordinary stitching, the tension on the upper and under threads should be equal and just sufficiently strong to lock both threads in the centre of the work. Fine materials require a light tension and heavy materials more tension to produce a perfect stitch.

Bobbins must be wound evenly if they are to work properly in the machine. In winding them see that the thread is placed smoothly and evenly. A correctly wound bobbin will prevent uneven stitching. Never wind thread on to a partly wound bobbin, as it usually makes it uneven and may cause trouble in the bobbin-case.

Sewing a Seam.—The edge of the garment to be stitched should be placed just far enough under the presser foot to allow the first stitch to be taken in the material. Do not place the material so that the first stitch misses the material, as this causes the thread to become entangled in the lower mechanism.

When finishing a seam, never sew beyond the end of the material, and do not attempt to release the material from the machine until the take-up lever is at the highest point. Remove the material by pulling it back and to the left, and sever the threads. Always leave 3 or 4 inches of thread to prevent its being pulled through the needle when beginning the next seam.

N.B.—Always keep the bulk of the material to the left of the presser foot. This allows greater freedom of feeding than when the garment is allowed to pass under the arm of the machine.

Bias seams should be stitched with the bias instead of against it. e.g. When sewing two bias seams on a skirt, start at the bottom of the garment and work up. This prevents the seam from stretching. The tensions should be sufficiently loose to prevent puckering of the seams.

When sewing a straight edge to a bias edge, place the bias piece against the feed. This allows the feed to take care of the possible stretching of the bias and permits the operator to guide the stitching from the warp or lengthwise threads of the material.

An invaluable help when sewing seams, is the cloth guide, which is included in the equipment of all Singer machines. This ensures that all seams are sewn perfectly straight, with no wavering. The guide is fastened to the machine by means of the thumb screw, and can be adjusted to various distances from the needle (Fig. 1).

SOME COMMON CAUSES OF MACHINE TROUBLES

Causes of upper thread breaking.—Machine incorrectly threaded.
Tensions too tight.
Needle bent or having blunt point.
Needle too fine for size of thread and material to be sewn.
Burr on needle hole in throat plate (caused by needle striking plate).
Burr on slot in presser foot (caused by sewing over pins or breaking needle).
Needle incorrectly set.
Take-up spring bent or broken.
Tension discs work so that thread works in a groove.

Causes of lower thread breaking.—Tension too tight.
Thread wound unevenly on bobbin or bobbin wound too full.
Spring or bobbin case being worn.

To avoid breaking needle.—Do not sew heavy seams with too fine a needle.
Use correct size of needle for thread and material to be sewn.
See that presser foot or attachments are securely fastened to presser bar and that needle in its descent is central in the hole of the attachment and throat plate.
Do not attempt to pull or remove the material until the needle is above the work; otherwise the needle may become bent and strike the throat plate when restarting to sew.
Do not leave pins in material after tacking.

Causes of missing stitches.—Needle not accurately set in needle bar or being blunt or bent.

Causes of stitches looping.—Tension being too loose.
Upper and lower threading incorrect.
Sometimes caused by placing of bobbin case or shuttle so that threads pull from wrong side of bobbin or by bobbin being wound too full.

Causes of Machine not feeding correctly.—Pressure on work being too light for material.
Tensions may be too tight.
Feed dog may be worn. (This may be determined by running the finger over the teeth.) If they are not sharp they should be replaced.
The stitch regulator screw may have been adjusted too far, thus making the feed inoperative.

Causes of Machine working heavily.—If machine works hard after standing, probably needs a general cleaning.

The belt may be too tight thus putting excessive pressure on the bearing. The belt should be just long enough to grip the balance wheel without slipping.

The bobbin winder may have been inadvertently snapped down into operative position, thus putting pressure on the balance wheel. If so, release winder by pressing lever located behind the bobbin spindle.

Causes of puckered seams.—Stitch too long for material being sewn.

Tension too tight.

Causes of noisy treadle.—Screws on which treadle is pivoted probably need tightening. Release one of the screws by giving the nut a turn or two with the wrench, then place a screwdriver in the slot of the screw and advance the nut and test the treadle. If still noisy, repeat the operation at the other side.

Ornamental Stitching can be done in several ways. By winding the bobbin with heavy embroidery silk and using plain sewing silk in the needle, all kinds of decorations can be made. The under tension is entirely released for this. The silk should pull perfectly free from the bobbin. The stitching is then done as for plain sewing with the right side of the material down. If desired, a silk of contrasting colour may be used on top to show between the stitches. Thread the machine in the usual way and pull the under thread before starting to stitch. The length of stitch will vary the effect of this trimming and the upper tension may also be adjusted slightly to make the stitches stand up and appear loose. About ten stitches to the inch makes an attractive decoration for woollen materials (Figs. 2 and 3).

Tacking can be done on the machine by setting the tension for the largest pos-

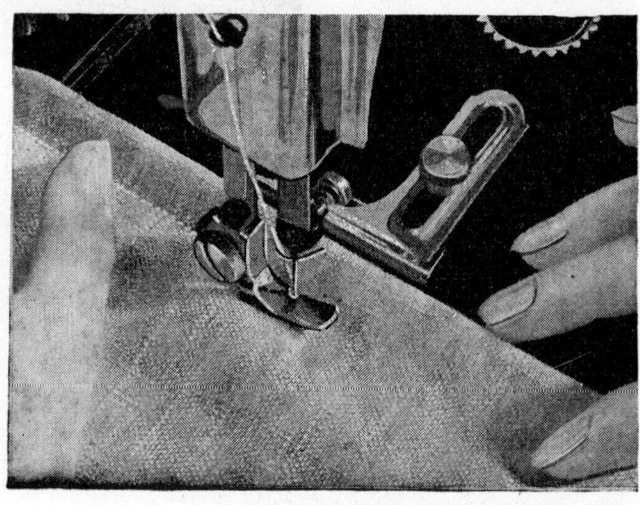

Fig. 1. The Cloth Guide which is supplied with every machine is an invaluable help for straight machining, either for seams or hems. The width is adjusted by loosening the screw and sliding the guide to the correct position, then tightening the screw again.

sible stitches, and allowing plenty of thread at the beginning and end of the seam. Use the cloth guide to keep an even seam allowance.

ATTACHMENTS

A few attachments are given with nearly every machine, and the following hints are based on the seven attachments that are given with Singer sewing machines.

The Binder.—This attachment folds and guides the binding, and by a simple adjustment, the stitching can be regulated to come close to the edge of the binding.

Bias Binding.—The bias cutting-gauge which costs very little from any Singer shop, is useful for cutting bias strips for use with the Binder attachment. Binding should be cut about $\frac{7}{8}$ inch wide, if the material contains dressing, and about 1 inch wide for soft materials. In Fig. 5 the letter F shows the position at which to set the blue spring or indicator at the end for facings, B for binding, and C for cording or piping. The blue spring, when set at B, will cut material about $\frac{7}{8}$ inch wide. The gauge has to be fitted to the pointed end of the scissors, and the material is inserted up to the blue spring when cutting.

One yard of material, 36 inches wide, is enough for about 30 yards of bias strips $\frac{7}{8}$ inch wide. Cut the strips, lay the two diagonal ends and stitch them together. The stitching should be as close as possible

Fig. 2 and 3.—Ornamental stitching done by machine can be very effective. For Fig. 3 very fine silk braid was used, and for Fig. 2 a thick contrasting silk.

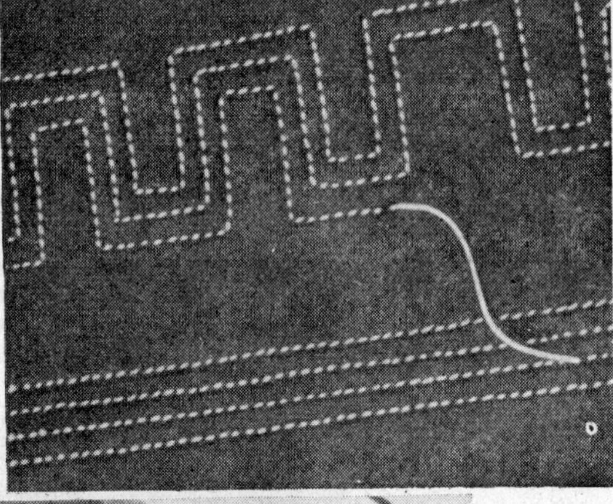

Fig. 2.

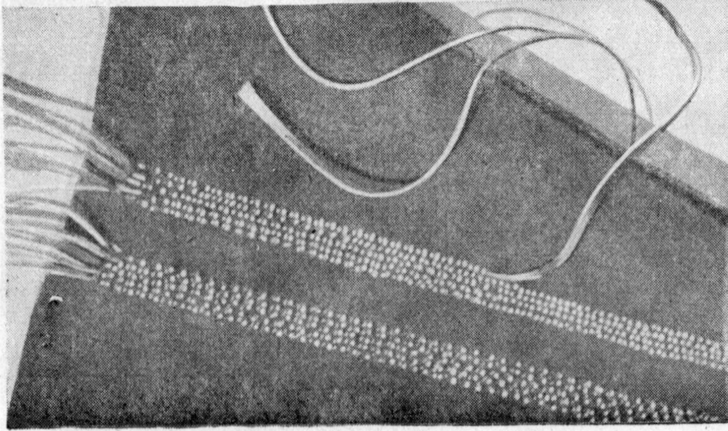

Fig. 3.

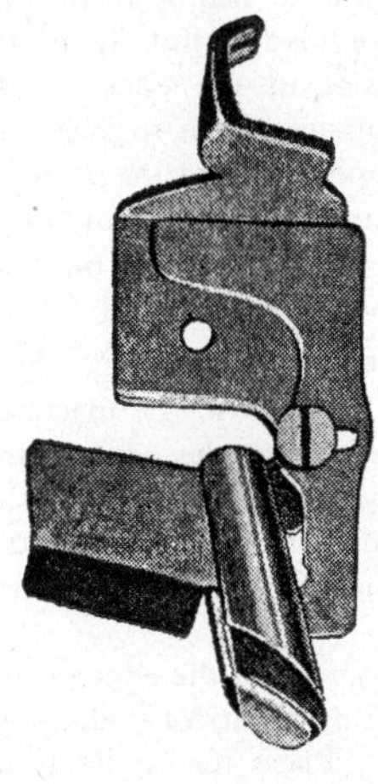

Fig. 4. — The Binder, which automatically folds and guides the binding. Folded binding or braid that only needs turning in once is inserted in the outside slot only.

Fig. 5.—The Bias cutting gauge is useful for cutting bias strips. The grooved edge is clamped on to a pair of scissors and the material slipped under the spring, so that the edge rests against the adjustable blue spring.

so that the seam passes through the Binder freely. When the strips are straightened out, the edges are exactly even. It is advisable to press the seams open and if the strips are not to be used immediately they should be wound on a piece of card to keep them from stretching.

The strips are now ready for the Binder attachment which is fitted instead of the presser bar. See that the needle passes through the centre of the needle-hole in the attachment.

To insert the binding, fold it in the centre and cut to a point. Insert the pointed end into the binder scroll, until it comes out at the lower end. Now place the edge of the material to be bound between the scroll of the Binder and pass it and the binding under the presser foot of the Binder, then lower the presser bar and start to sew. As the binding passes through the scroll the edges are turned in.

Folded binding should be inserted in the outside slot of the Binder. The Binder is adjusted and operated in the same manner as when using unfolded binding. Half-inch braid or ribbon may be used in the same way.

N.B.—Binding that is inserted in the outside slot of the Binder will be turned only once so that it is absolutely necessary to have finished edges when using binding in this slot.

The edge of the material to be bound should be held well within the centre slot of the scroll. If the material is allowed to slip away from the scroll when near the needle, the edge will not be caught in the binding. With a little practice it is quite easy to hold the edge in the scroll.

Various materials and conditions require different adjustments of the Binder to bring the stitching close to the edge. A wider adjustment of the Binder is required when binding curves than is necessary when binding a straight edge.

When the material is turned in the proper direction, push up enough binding on the top and under sides to allow for turning the corner. This needs a little practice. If the binding is not caught on the under side at the corner, it may be fastened down with a few stitches by hand.

Binding plackets.—First fold the material in a straight line, and placing the

Fig. 6.—The Binder at work, showing how the binding is folded and fed under the presser foot so that it is machined correctly.

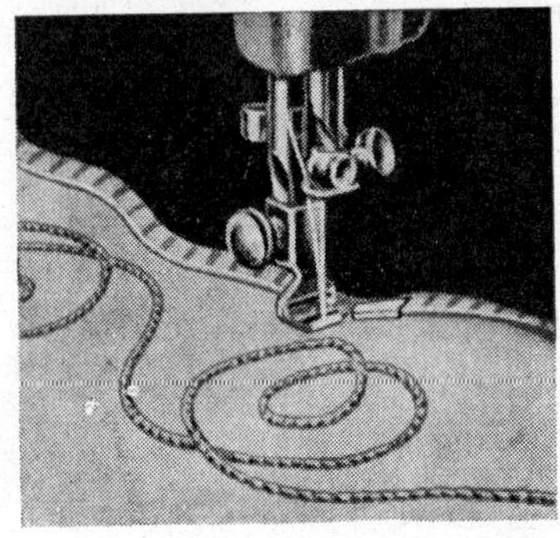

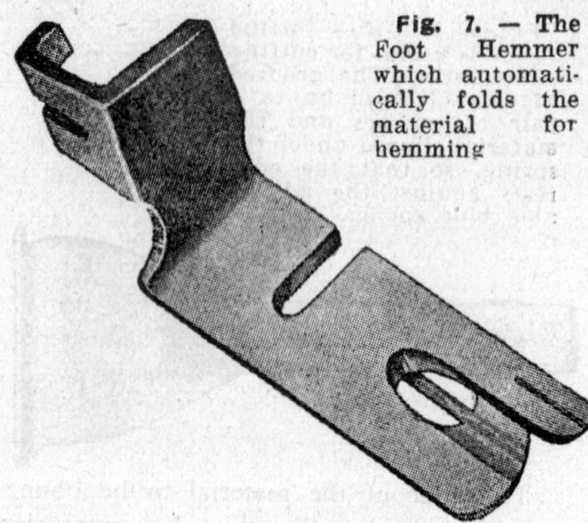

Fig. 7. — The Foot Hemmer which automatically folds the material for hemming

fullness in a flat fold on the under side of the material. Insert the edge of the placket in the Binder and stitch the binding on in the usual way. Run the machine slowly as the point is reached and take care that too much material is not allowed to feed into the Binder. As soon as the point of the placket is reached, fold the material to the other side of the slit and bind to the end.

Bound scallops.—The point at the top of the scallop is bound in exactly the same way as the placket. Practise the binding of a small single scallop first before attempting to bind a row of scallops. If the material is soft and liable to stretch, add a row of stitching close to the edge of the scallop before starting to bind the edge.

Bound buttonholes can also be made with the Binder and are made similarly to the placket. Cut a slot in the edge of the material to the depth you wish to make the buttonhole and shape it. Fold the material in the same manner as when binding a placket. Trim off the edge of the binding, and bind the edge with the Binder.

The Foot Hemmer.—Fit according to the instructions issued with the machine. The starting of the hem at the edge of the material is of great importance. If the hem is not started at the edge, and the material is pulled bias, a perfect hem cannot be made.

Fold over about $\frac{1}{16}$ inch of the edge of the material at the starting-point for a distance of about one inch. Place the material in the Hemmer at a point just beyond the fold. Draw the material towards you through the Hemmer, at the same time making the second fold at the very edge. Continue to draw the material through the Hemmer until the edge is just under the needle. Place the upper and lower threads together under the Hemmer foot and assist the starting of the hem by slightly pulling the threads from the back after the first stitch has been made (Fig. 8).

When making a hem, the same width must be kept in the Hemmer at all times. Guide the material with the thumb and forefinger of the right hand, so that the

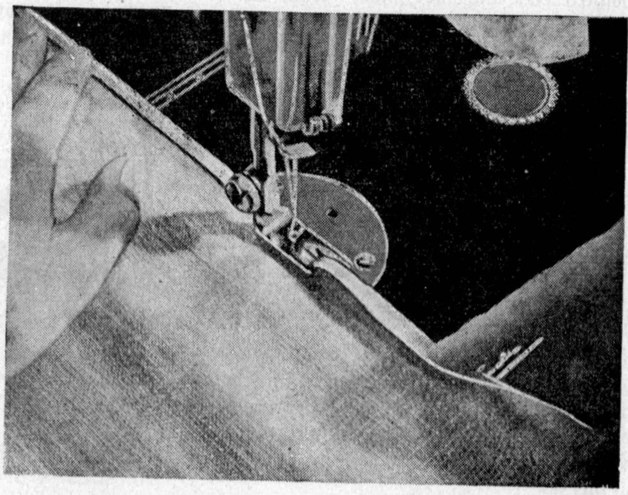

Fig. 8. The material should be loosely folded over when feeding the Hemmer. Always allow a deeper fold, never a narrower, as the material is apt to slip out of position in the Hemmer.

edges lies flat over the top of the Hemmer, and start to sew, taking care to keep the Hemmer curl just full. Should the edge begin to run out, move the hand to the right; should too much material run in, move to the left.

A seam can be hemmed, and is especially suitable for underwear or any garment where a straight seam is used and where a small double seam would be suitable.

When using this seam the garment must be first fitted and the edge of the material trimmed, allowing for about ⅛ inch seam. The two edges are placed together and inserted in the Hemmer in the same manner as a single hem. If the material is bulky, the edge of the upper piece of material may be placed about ⅛ inch in from the edge of the lower piece (Fig. 10).

The free edge of a hemmed seam may be stitched flat to the garment if desired. First open the work out flat, then place the hem in the scroll of the Hemmer, which acts as a guide, holding the edge of the hem in position while it is being stitched. If the seam is stitched flat to the garment one row of stitching is visible on the right side. The hemmed seam may be used on muslin, lawn, organdie, or other materials that need a fine seam.

Hemming and sewing on lace.—Start the hem in the usual way, and, with

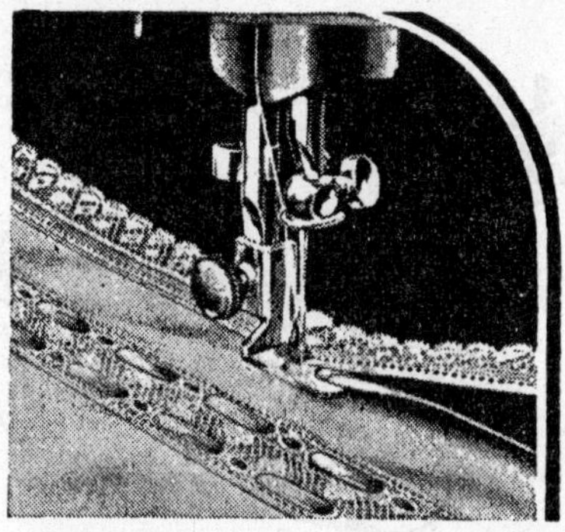

Fig. 9.—Lace can be sewn on at the same time as the hem is turned. The lace is guided with the left hand, the hem with the right.

the needle holding the hem in position, raise the presser bar sufficiently to allow the edge of the lace to be slipped in under the Foot Hemmer. Lower the bar, turn the balance wheel and catch the edge of the lace with the needle. Guide the hem with the right hand and the lace with the left. Care should be taken not to stretch the lace as it is being fed into the Hemmer.

It is not practical to sew gathered lace on with the Foot Hemmer as the gathers catch in the Hemmer slot.

Another way of applying lace, so that the stitching of the hem is invisible is to start the hem in the usual way, slipping the

Fig. 10.—A hemmed seam lies flat. First machine the single edges together, then trim, and with the foot hemmer hem the longer side on to the other.

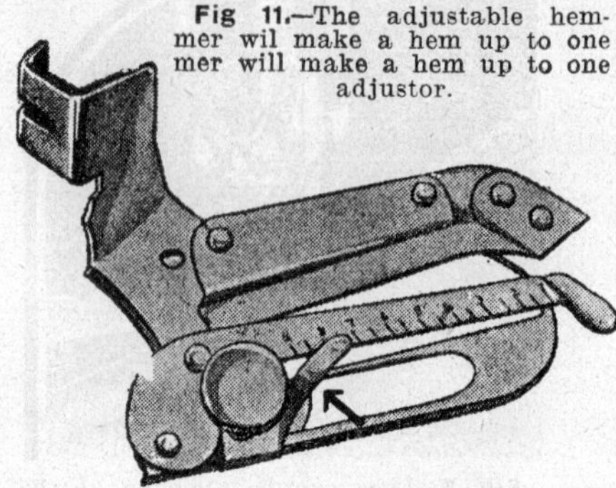

Fig 11.—The adjustable hemmer wil make a hem up to one mer will make a hem up to one adjustor.

lace in from the left as you would the second piece of material when making a seam.

When hemming fine materials such as georgette or crêpe de Chine with the Foot Hemmer, the material will not feed through properly and the stitch will be very much shorter than when sewing with the presser foot on the same material.

To overcome this difficulty and to assist in holding soft materials so that they will be turned properly with the Foot Hemmer, insert a piece of paper under the material between the feed and the foot of the Hemmer and allow it to feed through with the material. Strips of thin paper or the edges of newspapers are very convenient for stitching. Never use tissue paper as this will be difficult to pull away from the material.

A curved or bias edge may be hemmed with the Foot Hemmer by inserting paper under the Hemmer. The paper takes up the fullness in the material and, with a little care in guiding, a curve, such as would be used on men's shirts or the edge of an apron, may be perfectly hemmed.

The Adjustable Hemmer is part of the set of attachments supplied with most family machines. This Hemmer will make a hem of any width up to one inch (Fig. 11).

Remove the presser foot and attach the Hemmer to the presser bar, taking care that the needle descends in the centre of the needle-hole after you tighten the thumb screw. To insert the material fold over the edge at the end of the material to be hemmed, as instructed for starting a hem with the Foot Hemmer. Place the material in the Hemmer under the scale and draw it backwards and forwards until the hem is formed.

You will then be able to determine the width and to fold over the end of the hem for the second turning. Draw the material back until the end comes directly under the needle.

If unused to this attachment, practise on striped material, and when you are able to match each stripe exactly you are prepared for hemming a garment properly.

When hemming soft material, liable to stretch, a piece of paper slipped under the Hemmer, next to the feed, is a great help. This will prevent the material from stretching and will assist in turning the hem.

Hems can be prepared for hand sewing by setting the Hemmer for the desired width, and running the material through the Hemmer without threading the needle. The holes made by the needle soften the linen and make it more pliable for hand work. Hemstitching can also be prepared in this way.

To make a hem over an inch wide, loosen the thumb screw and draw the slide to the right as far as it will go, then turn this part toward you. Fold and crease down a hem of the desired width, pass the fold under the extension at the right of the Hemmer, insert the edge of the material into the folder, and stitch. The Hemmer will turn the edge and stitch it flat, but the

Fig. 12.—The adjustable hemmer can be altered to make a wide hem by loosening the thumb screw and turning the slide away from the hem.

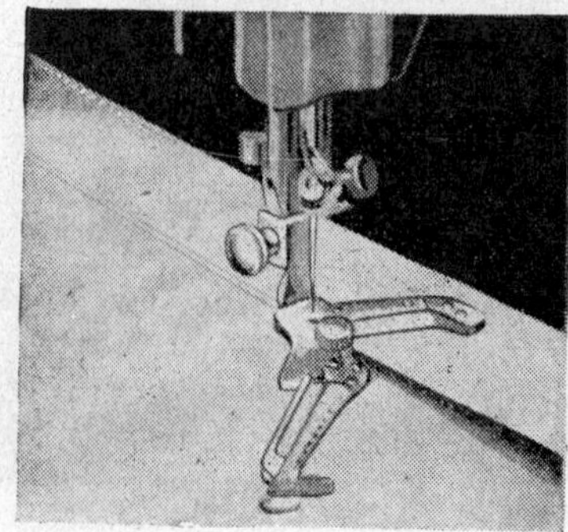

operator must keep the crease for the width of the hem even as the machine sews. Hems may be applied to sheets or similar articles in this way (Fig. 12).

The Tucker.—Fit as directed in Instruction Book.

As the Tucker is rather a complicated-looking instrument, here are some details of the various parts:

The Tuck Guide, which is adjustable and may be set for any desired width of tuck.

The Tuck Scale, containing figures which indicate different widths of tucks. The tuck scale also acts as a smoothing blade keeping the tucks of uniform width.

it passes between the grooved and spur blades.

The adjustment of the Scales on the Tucker, determines the width of the tucks and the space between them. Adjustment for width of tuck is made by loosening the tuck guide adjusting screw, which allows you to move the tuck guide to the desired figure on the tuck scale. The tuck guide should be set just over the figure you wish to use. The adjusting screw should always be well tightened.

The figures on the tuck scale indicate the width of tuck in eighths of an inch, the marks between figures being sixteenths.

To adjust for the width of space between

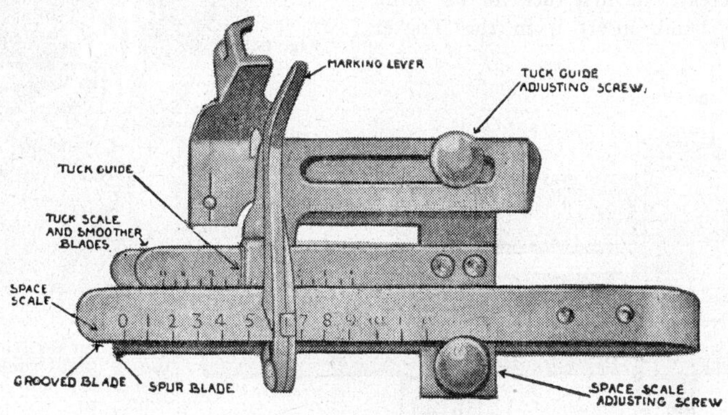

Fig. 13

THE TUCKER

The Tuck Guide Adjusting Screw, by means of which the tuck guide may be set at any point on the tuck scale.

The Space Scale, contains figures on the upper blade which indicate the width of the space between tucks. The middle or grooved blade contains a groove into which the material is pressed by the spur at the end of the lower or spur blade, thus marking the goods for the folding of the next tuck.

The Space Scale Adjusting Screw, by means of which the space scale may be set at any desired point.

The Marking Lever, which presses on the grooved blade, marks the material as

the tucks, loosen the space scale until the desired figure is directly in line with the centre of the needle-hole. You will find a line in front and behind the needle-hole to indicate the centre.

Before starting to sew, tighten the screw well to prevent the scale shifting when the Tucker is in operation.

The marks on the space scale are double the width of those on the tuck scale, so that when both scales are set at the same figure, blind tucks without spaces between them are made.

To make spaces between tucks, first set the tuck scale, then move the space scale to the same number and as much further to the left as you wish to have space. Each number on the space scale represents one-quarter of an inch and each mark between numbers, one-eighth of an inch.

Here is a table that may assist you in setting the Tucker.

	Tuck guide	Space guide
$\frac{1}{8}''$ tucks with no space	1	1
$\frac{1}{8}''$ " " $\frac{1}{8}''$ "	1	$1\frac{1}{2}$
$\frac{1}{4}''$ " " no "	2	2
$\frac{1}{4}''$ " " $\frac{1}{4}''$ "	2	3
$\frac{1}{2}''$ " " no "	4	4
$\frac{1}{2}''$ " " $\frac{1}{2}''$ "	4	6
$1''$ " " no "	8	8

When inserting the material to be tucked, fold and crease the first tuck for its entire length by hand, insert it in the Tucker

Fig. 14.

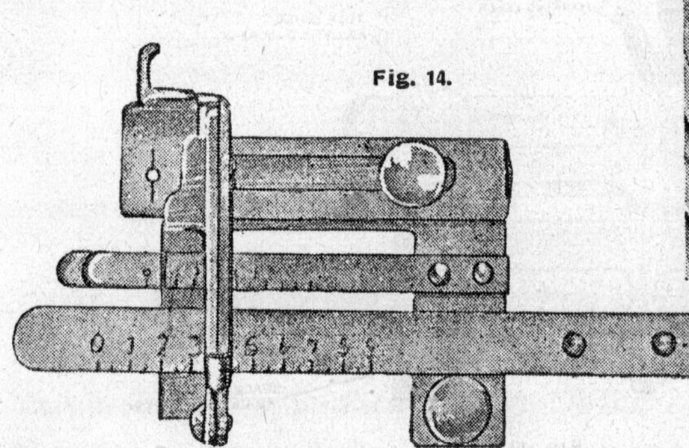

from the left, placing it between the grooved blade and the spur blade of the space scale, and between the two blades of the tuck scale. Care should be taken to see that the material is placed far enough in the Tucker to feed against the tuck guide. Draw the material toward you until the edge is directly under the needle. Lower the presser bar and sew. The Tucker is now making the mark for the next tuck.

Fold the material at the crease and, with its plain side uppermost, proceed as before. When making the last tuck, raise the marking lever so that it does not press on the double flat spring. While it is in this position no crease for a succeeding tuck can be made in the material.

Silks and taffetas can be tucked as easily as cotton materials, but soft materials such as chiffon and crêpe de Chine, are harder to crease, but may be tucked successfully if a piece of paper is slipped under the Tucker. It is absolutely essential that the tensions be adjusted before starting to tuck fine materials as a tight tension will pucker the material and cause the thread to break when the tuck is pressed.

When making fine tucks use thread of the proper size to suit the material to be tucked. A fine needle, fine thread and a fine stitch are the secrets of attractive tucking.

Fig. 15.

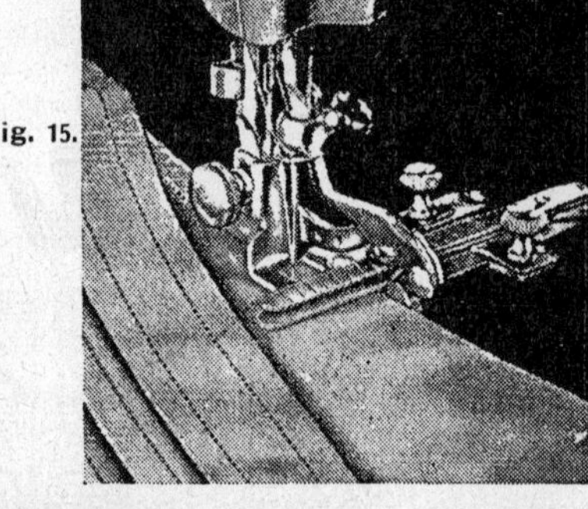

The Tucker set for making ¼ inch tucks with no space between and on the right, in operation, making the tucks with a space between them.

For cross tucking, first decide on the combination of tuck and space you wish to use, and set the Tucker accordingly. Tuck the entire piece of material lengthwise, then crosswise over the tucks. To prevent the material from becoming bias as it is tucked, it is as well to press the tucks with an iron before the cross tucks are made.

Another form of tucking is to tuck the material lengthwise and then bias across the tucks.

A Ruffler is used for making ruffles, frills and pleats (Fig. 16).

The essential parts of the Ruffler are:

The Foot—the part by which the Ruffler is attached to the presser bar.

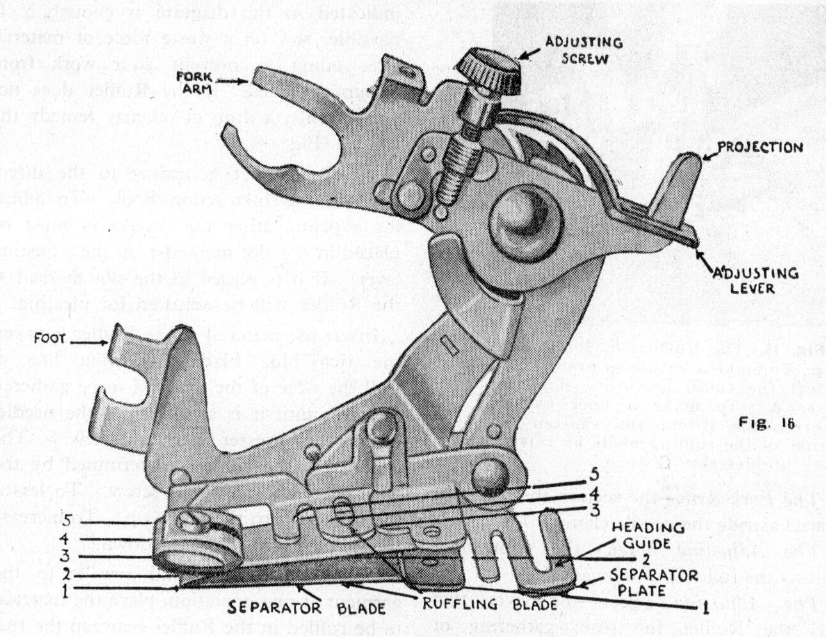
ADJUSTING SCREW
FORK ARM
PROJECTION
ADJUSTING LEVER
FOOT
Fig. 16
5
4
3
5
4
3
2
1
HEADING GUIDE
2
SEPARATOR PLATE
SEPARATOR BLADE
RUFFLING BLADE
1

THE RUFFLER

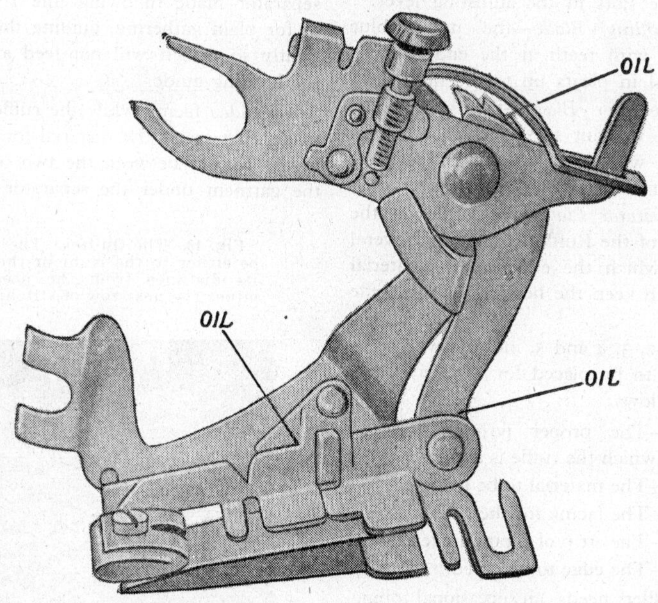
OIL
OIL
OIL
Fig. 17

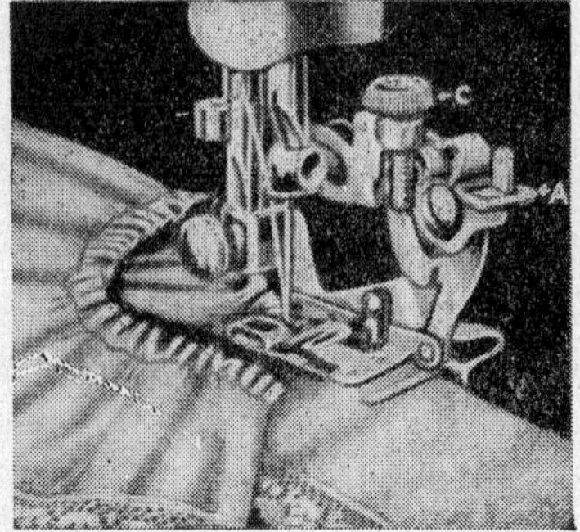

Fig. 18.—The Ruffler set for gathering. To make a gather at every stitch insert the small post into slot 1 of lever A. To make a finer gather, shorten the stitch, and shorten the stroke of the ruffling blade by raising the thumb-screw C.

The Fork Arm—the section that must be placed astride the needle clamp.

The Adjusting Screw—the screw that adjusts the fullness of the gather.

The Adjusting Lever—the lever that sets the Ruffler for plain gathering or pleating.

The Projection—that part that projects through the slots in the adjusting lever.

The Ruffling Blade—the upper blue steel blade with teeth at the end to push the material in pleats up to the needle.

The Separator Blade—the lower blue stele blade without teeth, which prevents steel blade without teeth, which prevents into contact with the teeth on the feed dog.

The Separator Plate—the guide on the under side of the Ruffler, containing several slots into which the edge of the material is slipped to keep the heading of the ruffle even.

Lines 1, 2, 3, 4 and 5, indicate where the material is to be placed for various operations, as follows:

Line 1.—The proper position for the material to which the ruffle is applied.

Line 2.—The material to be gathered.

Line 3.—The facing for the ruffle.

Line 4.—The strip of piping material.

Line 5.—The edge to be piped.

The Ruffler needs an occasional oiling of all working parts to prevent them from sticking. A drop of oil at each point indicated in the diagram is enough. If possible, sew on a waste piece of material after oiling to prevent your work from becoming soiled. If the Ruffler does not pleat evenly, a drop of oil may remedy the trouble (Fig. 17).

Fit the Ruffler according to the directions in the Instruction Book. To adjust for a plain gather the projection must be placed in the slot marked 1 on the adjusting lever. If it is placed in the slot marked 5, the Ruffler will be adjusted for pleating.

Insert the material in the Ruffler between the two blue blades following line 2. Pull the edge of the material to be gathered forward until it is slightly past the needle, lower the presser bar and sew. The fullness of the ruffle is determined by the position of the adjusting screw. To lessen the fullness turn the screw up. To increase the fullness turn the screw down.

To make a ruffle and sew it to the garment at one operation, place the material to be ruffled in the Ruffler between the two blue blades and insert the garment to which it is to be attached under the separator blade following line 1. Proceed as for plain gathering, guiding the material lightly so that it will not feed away from the heading guide.

To add a facing while the ruffle is being made, first insert the material for the ruffle in the Ruffler between the two blades and the garment under the separator blade, as

Fig. 19.—The Quilter. The Guide can be either to the right or the left, and its distance from the needle determines the next row of stitching.

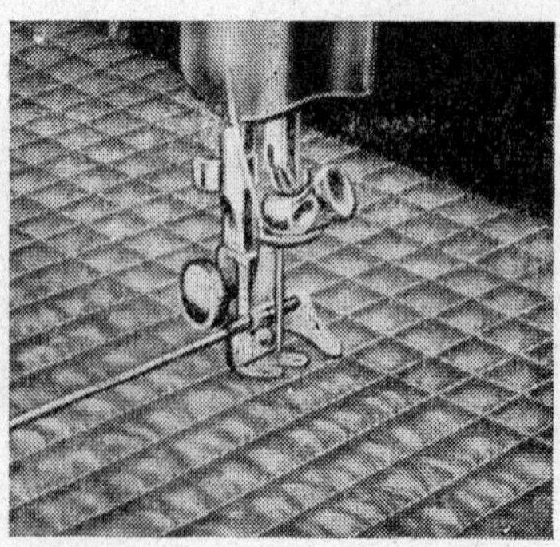

directed for sewing the ruffle on the garment in one operation. Place the material for the facing in the Ruffler following line 3. The facing may be of straight or bias material. If the facing is to be on the right side of the garment, place the garment and the ruffle so that their wrong sides are together. If the facing is to be on the wrong side of the garment place the right sides together.

To apply rows of ruffles, place the work under the Ruffler and the material in the guide when following line 2, but place the edge of the ruffle between the blades and to the right of the needle the desired distance, up to one inch, and guide it as the machine sews.

The edges of the ruffles may be hemmed with the foot hemmer or picot-edged on a special attachment.

For **pleating** the Ruffler may be adjusted by placing the projection in the slot, marked 5, in the adjusting lever. The adjusting screw on the Ruffler will make a pleat about $\frac{1}{8}$ inch wide. To make the pleats further apart, lengthen the stitch on the sewing machine. To make them closer together, shorten the stitch.

Any material that contains dressing, such as lawn, organdie or taffeta may be successfully pleated with the Ruffler. Softer material will not lie flat unless well pressed.

For pleats in groups, lift the adjusting lever and place it on top of the projection at the point indicated by the star on the adjusting lever. This should be done at the points where there are to be spaces between the pleats.

The Ruffler will then stop and plain stitching will be made until the lever is again adjusted so that the projection comes up through the slot 5. The sewing machine must be run slowly and the pleats counted. e.g. When making pleats in groups of five with 1-inch spaces between the groups, run the machine until the fifth pleat has been made, then adjust the Ruffler to stop pleating and stitch plain for 1 inch.

For **shirring**—remove the lower blued blade from the Ruffler by loosening the small screw at the side of the Ruffler, then attach the latter to the presser bar. Place the material between the blued blade and the shirring plate, lower the presser bar and proceed as for ruffling.

Shirring may be done with a loose upper tension when it is desired to slide the gathers on the thread to fit a certain space. Embroidery silk may be used in the bobbin and a very ornamental stitch will be visible along the rows of shirring.

The Quilter—is attached to the machine instead of the presser foot. The Guide can be used at either the right or left of the needle, and the distance of the guide from the needle determines the width between the rows of stitching. Slide the wires into the holder prepared for it on the foot and set it to the width required, then lower the foot on to the material.

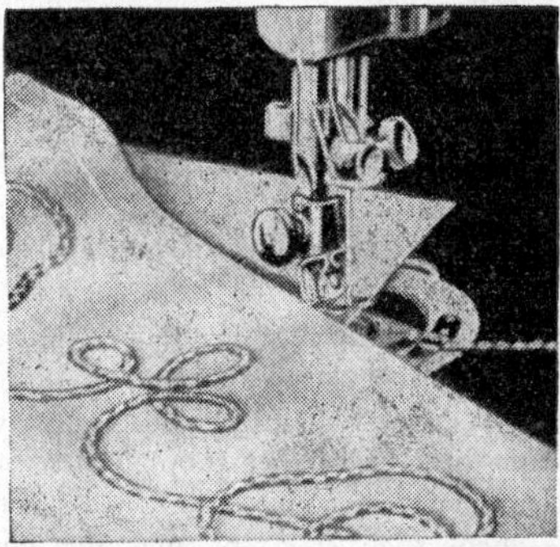

Fig. 20.—The Underbraider works from the wrong side. A medium length stitch should be used, but a shorter stitch is sometimes necessary on a curve.

For the first row of stitching, let the Quilter guide follow the edge of the material, a straight crease, or a line, as preferred. The succeeding rows are made straight and at a uniform distance by keeping the previous row of stitching steadily under the guide.

The Underbraider.—For this, fit the quilter foot without the movable bar, unless it is wished to apply braid in parallel rows when the bar may be left to act as a guide.

Any braid that will fit the Underbraider tube and be stitched through the centre may be used in the Underbraider It is sometimes necessary to force the braid under the spring by pulling it, or to lift the spring with the screwdriver. The braid should be well under the foot before starting to sew.

Braiding designs may be copied with the machine by taking several thicknesses of paper and pinning it to the design to be copied. The perforated pattern is then pinned to the material to be braided and torn away when the braiding is finished.

The design to be braided must be applied to the wrong side of the garment. For most braiding a medium length of stitch should be used, but when braiding small curves it is sometimes necessary to use a shorter stitch and to run the machine slowly in order to follow the curves.

A braiding design should always be started where it is convenient to pull the braid through to the under side. A good starting point is usually on an inside curve or at the end of a scroll, but this can be determined best from the design to be braided. The braid should always pull freely from the roll, and require no guiding except to see that it does not turn over as it feeds into the braider tube. When braiding a square corner, sew until the corner is reached, then stop the machine with the needle in the braid, raise the presser bar and turn the material, using the needle as a pivot. Then lower the presser bar, and start again.

When the braiding is finished make a small hole with a stiletto or with scissors at each end of the design and pull the ends of braid through to the underside of the material. Fasten the ends with a hand sewing needle.

To braid on net or fine material it is necessary to have the design stamped on paper, and if the material is difficult to stitch when using a single thickness, it is a good plan to slip a piece of paper under the quilter foot also.

Darning.—The special fittings necessary for this are a darning or embroidery hoop, a small plate to cover the feed, and a little spring presser to hold the material in position while the needle is on its upward course.

To ensure a soft, smooth finish, it is essential that a fine needle and fine mercerised cotton should be used. Ordinary cotton however fine, results in a rather stiffer, heavier darn. As the feed of the machine is covered by the feed cover plate, the movement of the work and the length of stitch must be controlled by the operator moving the darning hoop. A slow movement of the hand will give a short stitch and a quick movement, a longer one. Hold the hoop with both hands, and with a steady continuous movement, work backwards and forwards across the hoop, keeping the lines of stitches an equal distance apart and running $\frac{1}{4}$ inch beyond the edge of the hole and working in the same direction as the weft of fine threads of the material.

After the stitching has been completed one way, turn the hoop round and continue in a similar manner across the first line of stitching. These second lines of stitching should be close together and run parallel with the warp or thicker threads of the material. Take this stitch in about $\frac{1}{2}$ inch beyond the hole, thus covering the first lines of thread entirely. This will strengthen the material round the hole without giving a heavy darn. When finished the darn should be either round or oval in shape, thus avoiding too much strain on one thread. If the material is sheer, leave a loose darn by moving the hoop far enough to make a long stitch.

MENDING

There is just as much of an art in mending and darning linen and household articles neatly and efficiently as there is in the more elaborate forms of needlework. There are innumerable methods of mending different articles, the main ones being given here.

Table Linen.—Quite often some of the tiny holes that appear in linen are caused by a tiny insect which attacks cotton and linen just as the moth attacks woollen goods. A simple precaution against this is to keep moth balls, naphthalene or lavender in the linen cupboard. Another excellent and historical cure is a dried apple or orange stuck porcupine-wise with cloves.

Before mending or darning table linen, any glazed or starched surface should be damped to soften it. All mending should be done before the article is sent to the laundry.

Fig. 1.—A strengthening darn for linen that is wearing thin is run in lengthways. Fig. 2 shows an ideal square darn. Note the long loops at the end and the depth of the darning in the sound part of the linen.

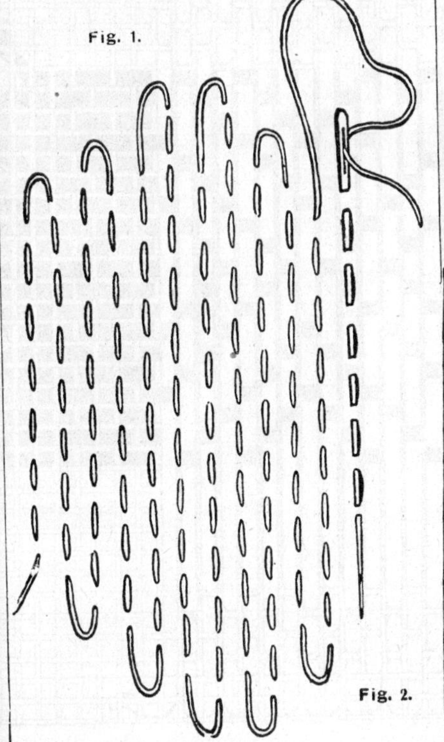

Fig. 1.

Darning.—Small holes, and threadbare parts that do not need patches are quite adequately mended by darning. The most suitable thread to use is that of which the material itself is woven. This can be obtained by undoing one of the hems, ripping it, and ravelling one or two rows. The hem should then be remade. If, for some reason, this is impracticable, a fine linen thread should be used to tone exactly with the material. For linen, a simple Tambour frame should be used, the wrong side of the material being uppermost. Use the special long darning needle.

A square darn.—For this a fine thread should be run in, starting about half an inch from the weak edge of the hole. Run the thread in lengthwise, exactly parallel to the lengthwise threads of the weave, over one cross-thread of the fabric, under the next, over the next, and so on, leaving the thread slack, and a small loop at each turn to allow for shrinkage and the tightening of the threads by the cross-threads. When the threadbare portion or the hole has been entirely covered by lengthwise threads, the horizontal threads are run in, taking up one lengthwise thread and dropping one, alternately. The finished

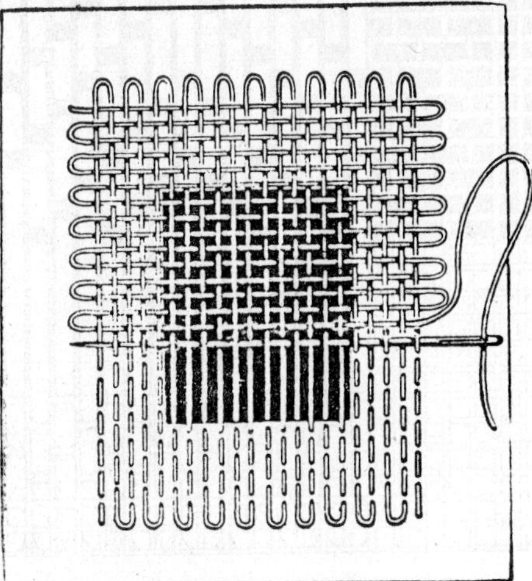

Fig. 2.

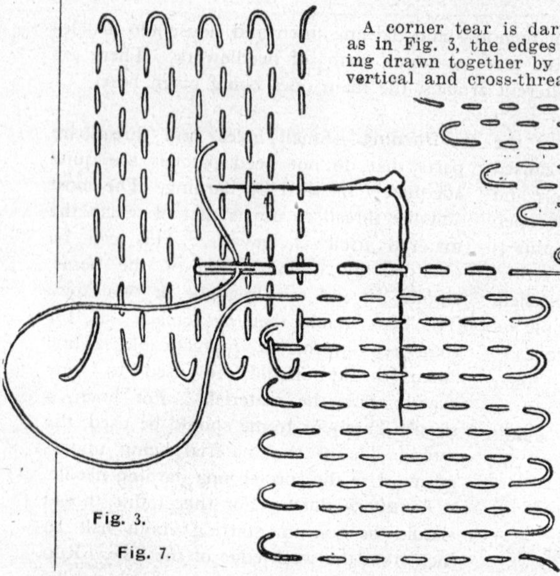

A corner tear is darned as in Fig. 3, the edges being drawn together by the vertical and cross-threads.

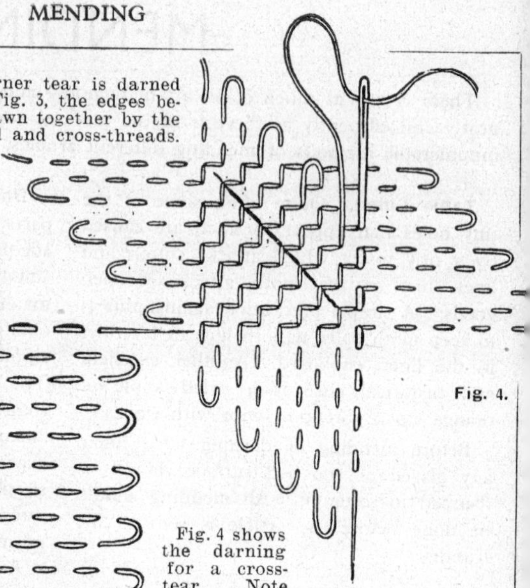

Fig. 4.

Fig. 4 shows the darning for a cross-tear. Note the formation where they cross.

Fig. 3.

Fig. 7.

effect should resemble the weave as nearly as possible (Fig. 2).

A twill darn differs slightly from the ordinary darn, in that it has to resemble the twill weave of the fabric for which it is used. The lengthwise threads are run in in much the same way as above, except that instead of taking up every alternate woven thread, every second or third is taken up, according to the pattern of the twill. When the cross-threads are run in, the same pattern is kept, the thread that is taken up advancing one stitch in the same direction in each row, so that there is a diagonal line of threads showing when the darn is finished.

A tear, especially a three-cornered tear, is usually the result of catching a garment

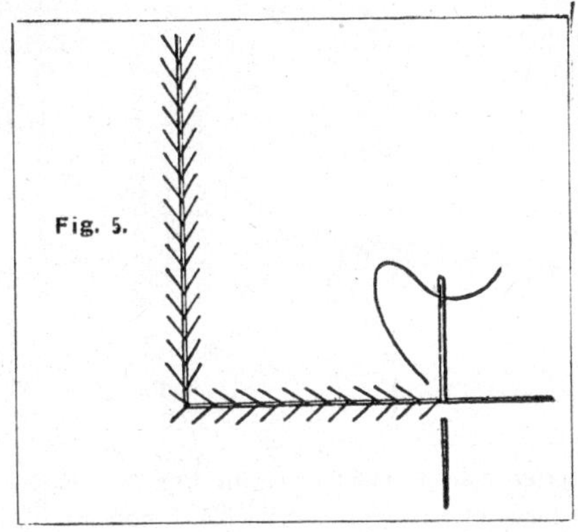

on a nail or sharp object. Sometimes the best way is to draw the edges together by fishboning as in Fig. 5. Another, and

Above, a clean-cut cross tear can be joined together by "fish-boning." Below, and on the opposite page, is a damask darn which is used for patterned damask. The design varies to match the material. It must be remembered that the working of the right side is the exact opposite

Fig. 8.

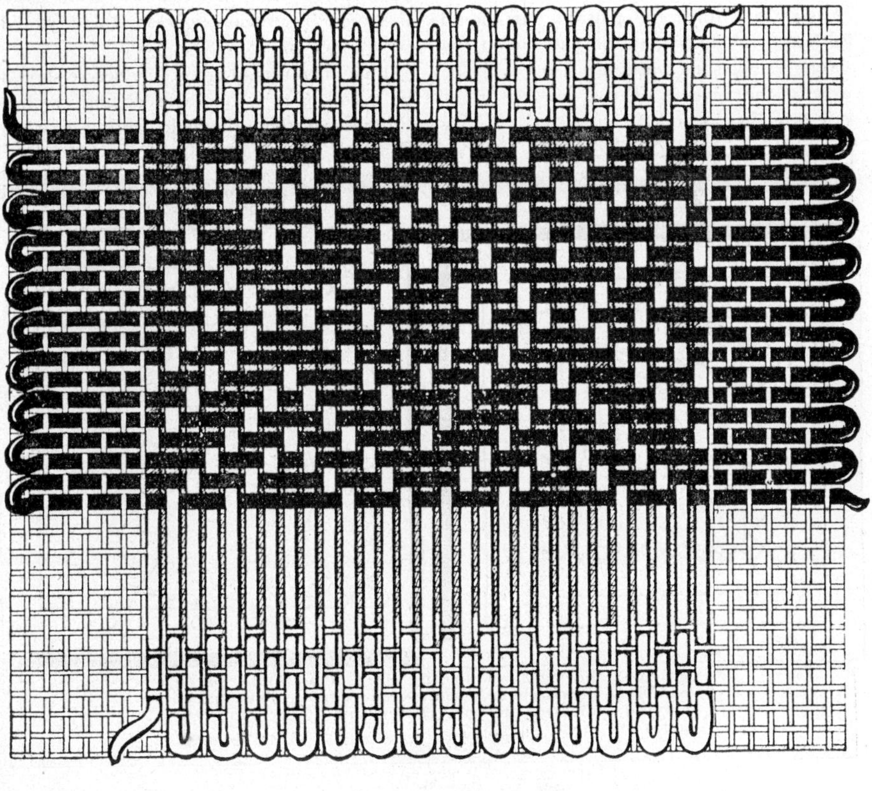

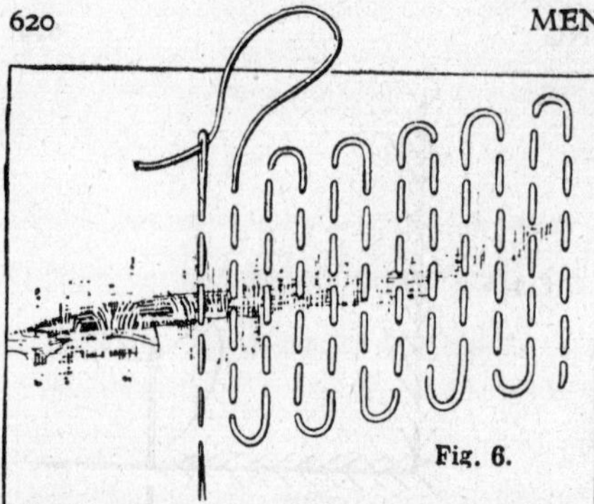

better way, is to darn as in Fig. 6. Tack a piece of paper on the back for working.

A cross-cut darn should be done as in Fig. 4. A piece of paper should be tacked under the darn first, or the edges could be roughly fishboned together.

A damask darn is more complicated than the ordinary darn, as it should be worked to resemble as closely as possible the weave of the cloth. The darn is begun in exactly the same way as before, but the cross-threads form the pattern. It should be borne in mind that the pattern on the wrong side, or working side, will be exactly the reverse of that on the right side (see Figs. 7 and 8).

Invisible or fine drawn darning is usually worked on a straight cut or gash. The edges are tacked in position, and a fine thread darned neatly criss-cross over the tear. See Fig. 6. Some people use hair, which has been specially treated to remove all grease, as it is stronger and almost invisible.

Frayed edges of table linen, caused by laundering and hard wear, usually have to be cut away and rehemmed. Should this make the article too narrow, a false hem of the same kind of material, washed and "faded" to match, should be faggotted on to the article.

For darning by machine see the chapter on MACHINING.

Patches are used when a rent or tear is too large for darning. The ideal material for a patch is a piece taken from another part of the garment to be mended or a piece that has been in use some time and is as mature and weathered as that to be patched. If new material has to be used, it should be previously washed and should be thinner in texture.

Fine linen thread and a fine needle should be used. Cut a square or oblong patch a little larger than the hole, and tack it on

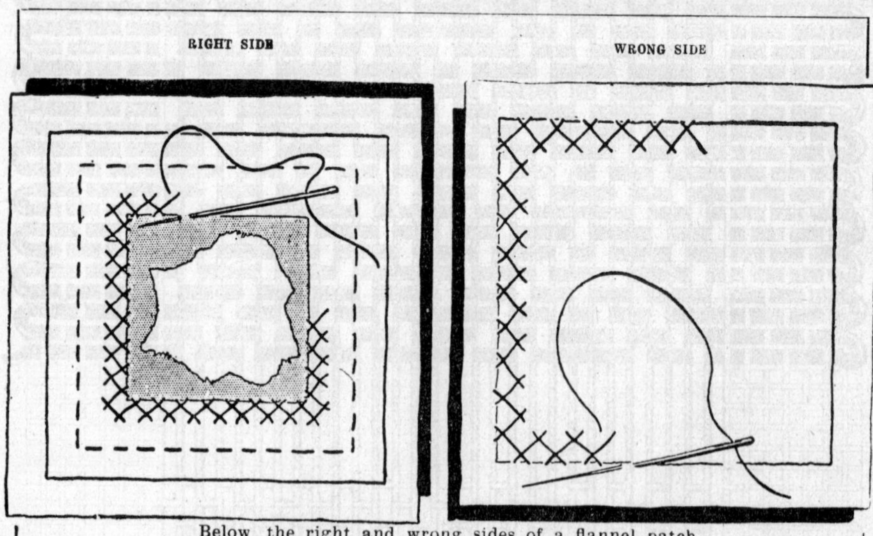

Below the right and wrong sides of a flannel patch which is herringboned round the edges The shaded portion indicates the part that is cut away before the edges are sewn.

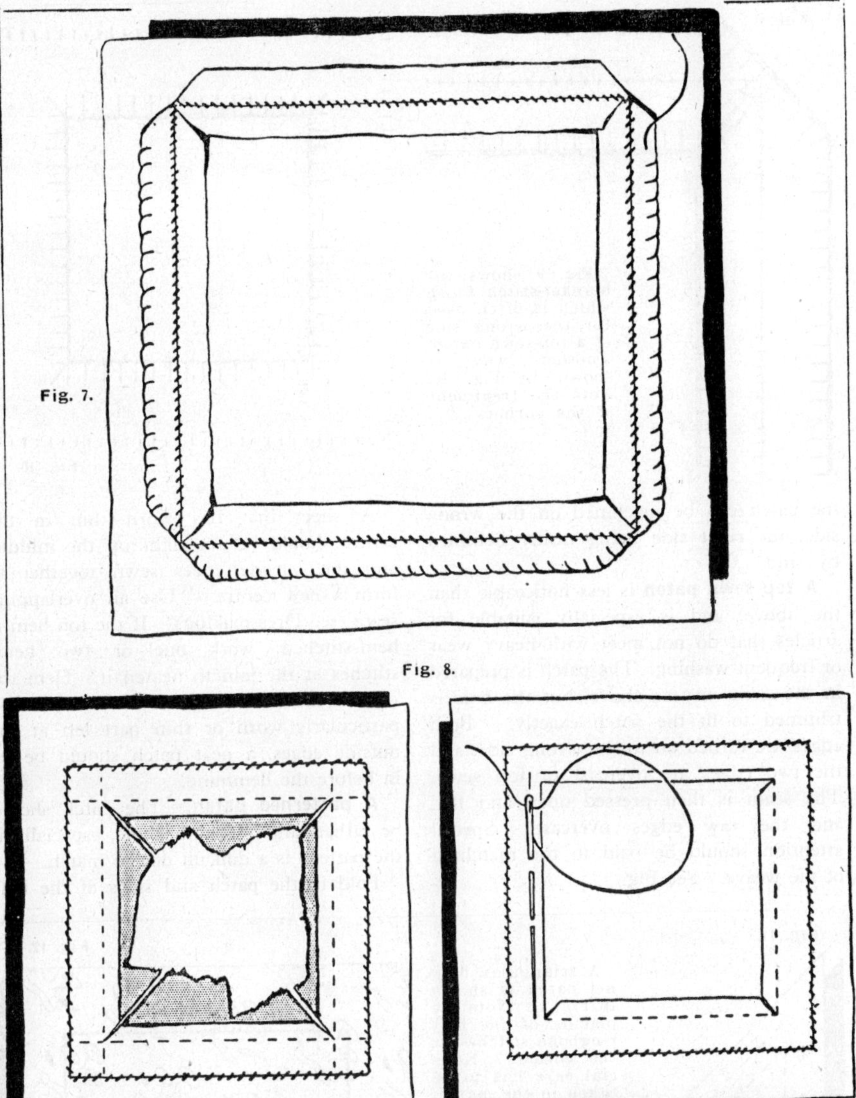

Fig. 7 shows a top-sewn patch. Note the method of finishing the edges and the cut-away corners. Fig. 8 shows the two stages of cutting away a patch. The shaded portion shows the part to be cut away and the illustration on the right how the edges are turned in and tacked down.

to the wrong side of the material, with the edges turned neatly inward. Hem the patch, and turn the material on to the right side and trim the hole so that it forms a neat square a little smaller than the patch. The edges of this are turned in, the corners being snipped so that they fit neatly. The edges are hemmed on this side. If preferred,

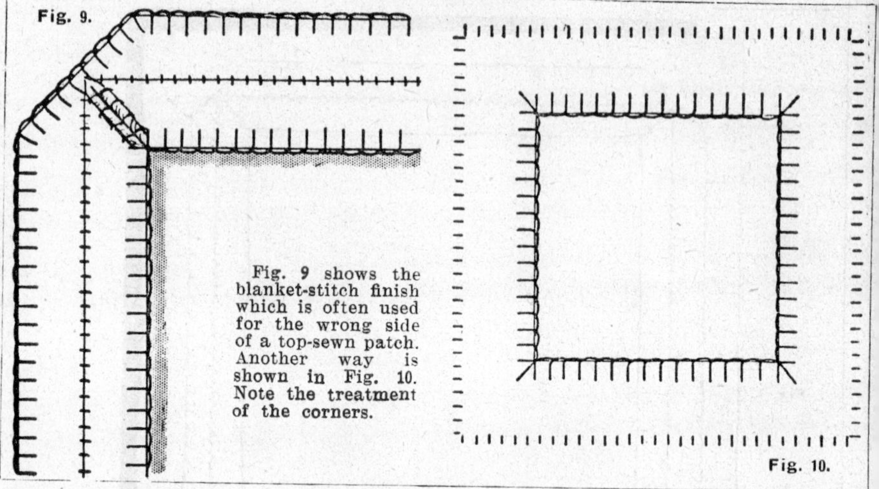

Fig. 9 shows the blanket-stitch finish which is often used for the wrong side of a top-sewn patch. Another way is shown in Fig. 10. Note the treatment of the corners.

the patch can be machined on the wrong side, the right side being neatly hemmed by hand.

A top sewn patch is less noticeable than the above, and is especially suitable for articles that do not meet with heavy wear or frequent washing. The patch is prepared in the same way as above, but the hole is trimmed to fit the patch exactly. Both edges are turned on to the wrong side, and the two edges are overcast or top sewn. The seam is then pressed open and flat, and the raw edges overcast. Special attention should be paid to the matching of the weave. See Fig. 7.

A sheet that has worn thin in the centre should be cut right up the middle, and the outside edges sewn together to form a new centre. Use an overlapping seam (see Dressmaking). If the top hem is hem-stitched, work one or two hem-stitches at the join to neaten it. Hem the outside edges. If there should be any particularly worn or thin part left at the outside edges, a neat patch should be let in before the hemming.

A patterned patch.—The patch should be rather larger than the hole, especially if the pattern is a difficult one to match.

Fold in the patch and sides of the hole

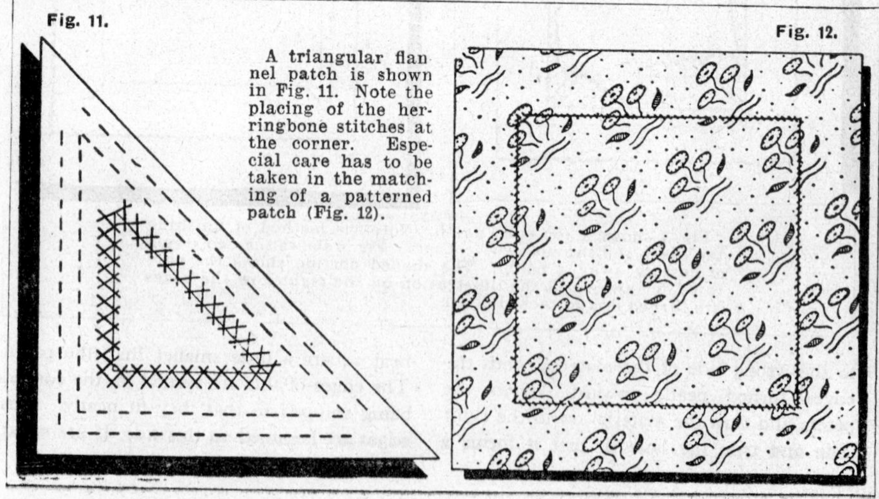

A triangular flannel patch is shown in Fig. 11. Note the placing of the herringbone stitches at the corner. Especial care has to be taken in the matching of a patterned patch (Fig. 12).

When grafting a patch on to knitting, the stitches should resemble the stitch as nearly as possible. These diagrams show how to regulate the stitch for stocking-web, ribbed and plain knitting.

and put the patch in the right side of the garment over the hole, exactly matching the pattern on both sides. Pin in position and turn under the horizontal sides, keeping the corners sharp. Should the pattern not be absolutely parallel with the threads, match the pattern rather than the threads.

Sew neatly all round the right side. On the wrong side cut away the damaged material and edges of the patch. The usual method of finishing off is to use blanket-stitch. Buttonhole-stitch should never be used, as it leaves a hard ridge along the edges. If done carefully, the stitch should not show on the right side. Keep the thread slack and put a diagonal stitch at the corners.

Another way of finishing the wrong side of a top-sewn patch is to mitre the corners of the patch and cut away the corners of the garment (see Fig. 9), and press the seam flat, overcasting the two edges separately.

A Flannel patch is apt to be bulky, so the edges are not turned in. The patch is pressed on to the wrong side, tacked and then herringboned. The stitches should catch through the two thicknesses of material at the top and the patch only at the bottom. On the right side the hole is trimmed and again herringboned loosely.

A Triangular Flannel Patch.—Quite often a hole is more conveniently mended by a triangular shaped patch. To cut the patch, two sides must be absolutely parallel with the grain of the material and the third side on the true bias. It is stitched in exactly the same way as a square patch, the

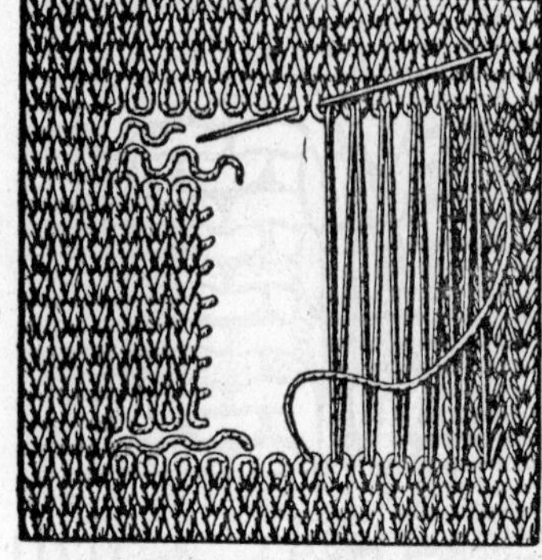

Fig. 16.

SWISS DARNING

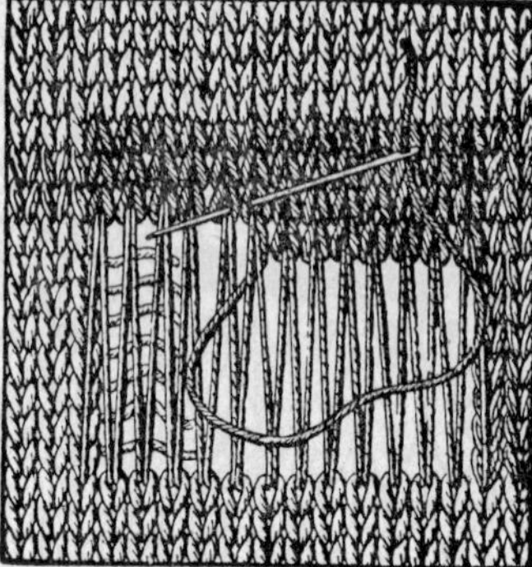

Fig. 18.

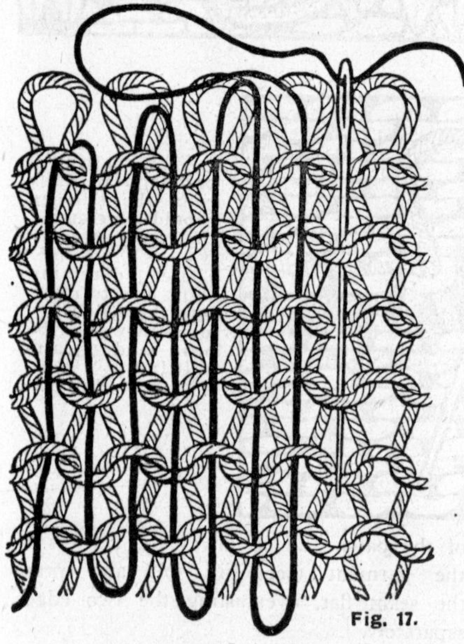

Fig. 17.

Fig. 17.—Strengthening weak stocking-web, and Fig. 18—Scotch darning which is worked in blanket-stitch from left to right over single cross-threads.

warp or vertical side being sewn first and the bias side last.

Fine drawing or invisible darning on heavy fabrics with a nap, such as blanket cloth, should be done with very fine silk. For a straight tear the edges are tacked into position, and then darned neatly criss-cross over the two edges from the wrong side. As little as possible of the material should be taken up, so that it is quite invisible on the right side. Should any stitches show through, the nap should be scratched gently over them with the point of a needle.

Machine-knitted fabrics such as stockinette that have to be patched, are treated in this way: The patch of the same material is not turned in, but is placed on the right side, the edges being neatly herringboned. On the wrong side the hole is trimmed and herringboned again, this time the top part of the herringboning being the only part that will show through on the right side.

Hand-knitted garments that need patching should have a fresh piece knitted, which is grafted on. Cut out the damaged section, exactly even, the long way of the stocking web. Then pull out the threads at the top and bottom of the

STRENGTHENING A BOY'S KNICKERS

Fig. 19.

Fig. 20.

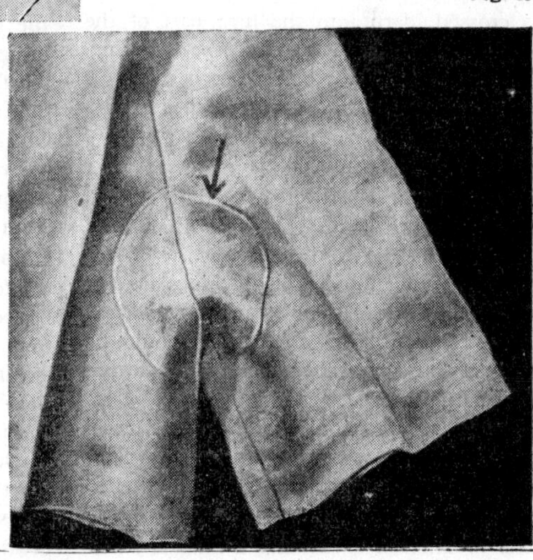

The seat of young boy's trousers frequently needs mending or reinforcing. Above, the position of the patch is outlined with tacking threads, then the patch cut, and pinned in position. On the right is the finished patch. It can either be hemmed by hand, or, if wished, machined to withstand hard wear.

square so that the loops are left perfectly free and open. The piece to be inserted should be treated in the same way, and should be slightly wider than the hole so that the edges can be turned in and sewn in the ordinary way. Hold the two pieces in position with the finger and thumb of the left hand, so that the loops left after unravelling show clearly and are alternate to one another. Bring the needle, threaded with the same wool or thread, through the sound part of the garment and then pass it through the first loop of the garment, pointing the needle to the left, then through the first and second loops of the patch, drawing the thread gently so as not to disarrange the loops. Insert the needle again through the first loop, taking with it the second loop. Draw the thread gently through. Pass the needle through the second loop of the patch last taken up, take with it the loop next to it, and continue this until the end of the row is reached. Fasten off securely and work the bottom row in the same way.

Swiss Darning is another way of mending knitted garments, to imitate stocking-web with needle and thread.

Lengthwise threads should be run in the usual way as for darning, and then, working over a darner or mushroom, insert the needle, threaded with wool or silk of the same ply and colour, at the left-hand side, securing it in the firm part of the garment, and darning in and out until the hole is reached. Now insert the needle between the first and second lengthwise threads bringing it out under the first thread, then pass it between the second and third threads, bringing it out between the first and second, and insert it again between the third and fourth threads bringing it out between the third and second. Continue thus until the last lengthwise thread is reached, always keeping the needle pointing to the left. When the last thread is crossed, darn into the firm part of the garment, turn and reverse the working. Continue until the whole space is filled.

Stockings that are wearing thin at the heels can be strengthened by running a thin thread of the same colour up and down each stocking-web rib. There is no need to work across as well unless the stocking is very old and worn. When darning woollen socks or stockings do not use cotton as it is apt to tear the wool.

Seams that have come apart should be overcast on the wrong side, with sewing silk or lisle thread.

Holes in the toes or heels should be darned over a darner or mushroom on the right side in the way described for table linen.

Scotch Darning.—For a large hole in the heel or knee of a stocking a blanket-stitch darn may be used. Secure the darning thread well in the sound part of the stocking, then run in one horizontal thread from right to left, taking it well into the stocking. Work back over this thread in blanket-stitch, catching the loops of the top row and taking the needle under the cross thread. When the row is finished, run into the side of the hole and take another horizontal thread across. Always work the blanket-stitch from left to right and take up the purl of the previous row's stitches with the new cross thread.

For hand-made socks or stockings a heel that is very badly worn can be remodelled entirely. (See Knitting chapter.)

Ladders can be caught up with a very fine crochet hook (there are special hooks for the purpose). Insert the hook between the first and second bars of the ladder, bringing it out through the loop and under the first bar. Thus, the first bar is pulled through the loop to form a new loop, which in its turn has the second bar passed through it. Care must be taken not to split the fine threads, and to finish off securely.

Boys' trousers can be strengthened in the following way: Unpick the centre seam between the legs, and the seams leading up to it. Indicate the size of the patch with tacking threads (see arrow). The patch should then be cut to fit, allowing ample turnings. Pin and tack into place. The patch is sewn in and the damaged parts are then cut away on the wrong side, the edges trimmed, and all seams closed again. Press carefully. If properly done, a patch of this kind is hardly noticeable.

KNITTING

BOOK III

PLAIN KNITTING
FANCY KNITTING
SOCKS AND STOCKINGS
FAIR ISLE JUMPERS
LACES AND INSERTIONS

KNITTING

Next to plain sewing, knitting is the most useful form of needlework, and it is claimed that it was one of the earliest known domestic arts. Various media are employed, from wool in every texture, to knitting silk, cotton or mercerised thread.

Knitting needles are plain, rounded bars of steel, bone, wood, celluloid or various compositions, of varying degrees of thickness, from ½ inch and ooooo, to 24 Knitting can be done on two, three or four needles. That worked on two needles is sometimes called " flat web " and is used for knitted garments which are sewn together, whilst that done on four needles forms a round.

Plain Knitting Stitches.

Casting On.—All knitting is begun from a single loop on the needle, made by holding wool between thumb and first finger of left hand, the "tag" hanging down in the palm. With right hand twist wool round into a ring (Fig. 2) held in position with the left thumb. Let the wool from the ball pass over the tag-end keeping the ball on the right. Pull the wool from the ball up through the ring (Fig. 3) then let the ring gradually slide up this wool and so form a loop. Pass this loop on to a needle.

Hold the needle with the loop in the left hand, take the second needle in the right hand, holding it between the thumb and first finger, exactly as when holding a pen, the wool being over the first finger, under the second and third fingers and over the fourth finger. Pass the point of the needle from front to back through the upper thread of the loop on the left-hand needle, when the left needle will be on top (Fig. 4).

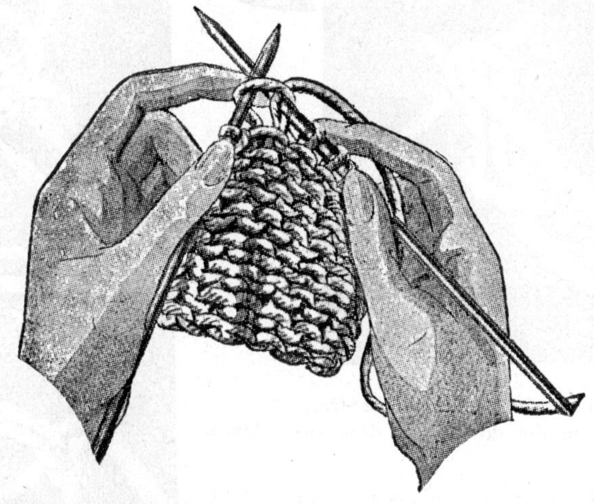

N.B.—The German method of holding the needles and wool varies slightly, and is considered by some people to be the quickest way of knitting. Hold the hands over the needles, which are held between the first finger and thumb of each hand, with the thread over the first, second and third fingers of the left hand, and held tightly between the little and third finger. Put the right needle through the stitch, but at the back instead of the front, open the stitch out, twist the needle round the thread stretched on the left fingers, draw it through the stitch, with a movement of the left

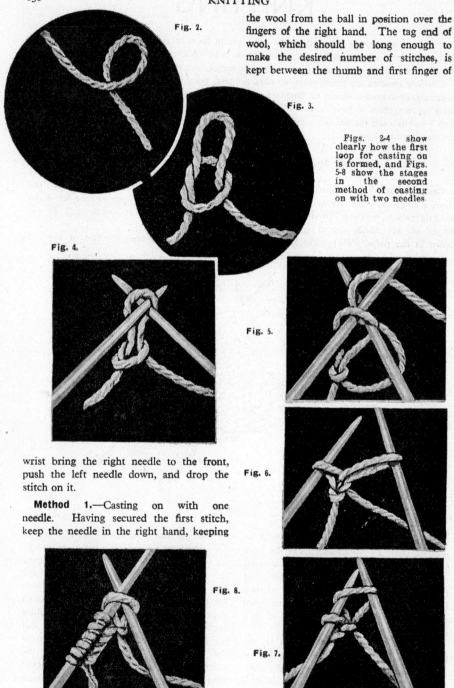

the wool from the ball in position over the fingers of the right hand. The tag end of wool, which should be long enough to make the desired number of stitches, is kept between the thumb and first finger of

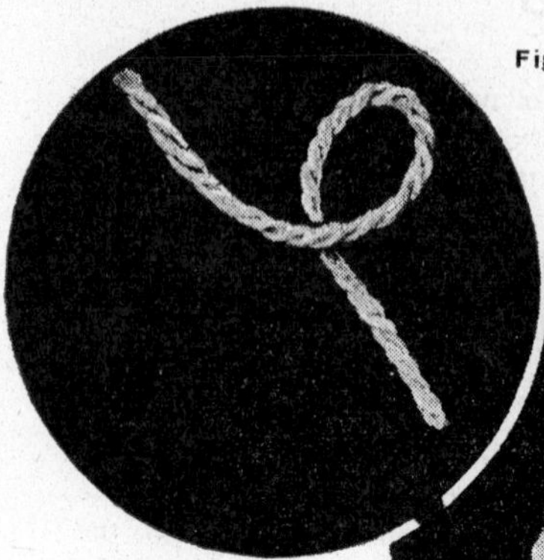

Fig. 2.

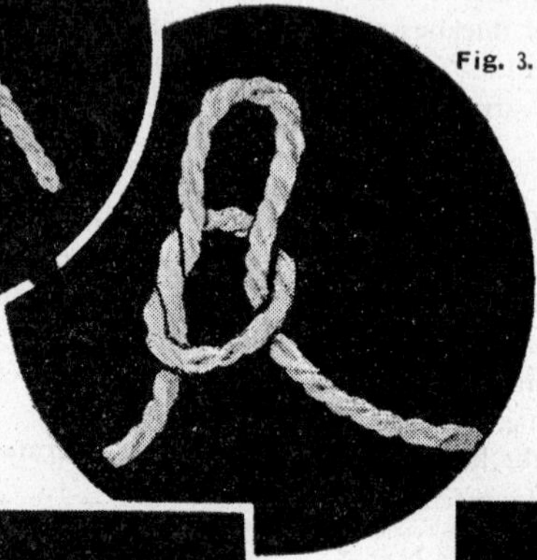

Fig. 3.

Figs. 2-4 show clearly how the first loop for casting on is formed, and Figs. 5-8 show the stages in the second method of casting on with two needles

Fig. 4.

Fig. 5.

Fig. 6.

wrist bring the right needle to the front, push the left needle down, and drop the stitch on it.

Method 1.—Casting on with one needle. Having secured the first stitch, keep the needle in the right hand, keeping

Fig. 8.

Fig. 7.

the left hand and this wool must now be passed over the thumb from left to right, then under the thumb from right to left and again over, thus completely encircling the thumb. Place the point of the needle from front to back, under the two top rows of this ring, pass the wool from the ball, over the point of the needle, guide the needle with this wool on it through the ring and draw the stitch thus made, up against the needle. At the same time release the ring drawing up the wool to complete the stitch. Each is an inch or more long (Fig. 6), then put the point of the left-hand needle into this loop. Slip out the right-hand needle, and so add a new stitch to the left-hand needle, gently pulling it up close to the needle (Fig. 7). Continue like this until the specified number of stitches are all on the left-hand needle (Fig. 8).

Plain Knitting or Garter Stitch.—Begin by casting on the required number of stitches, then take the needle with the cast-on stitches and hold it in the left hand,

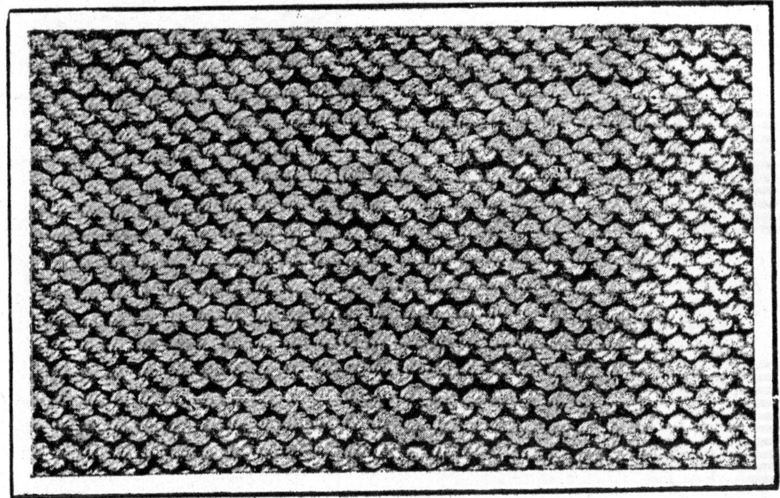

Fig 9.—Plain knitting or Garter stitch is the easiest stitch of all, and is exactly the same on right and wrong sides. It is one of the principal basic stitches in patterns.

following stitch is made in the same way. With this method of casting-on, it is not necessary to knit into the backs of the stitches for the first row.

Method 2.—Casting on with two needles (Fig. 5) is not quite so firm but is generally used for fine work. With the single loop on the needle, start by bringing the wool up at the back of both needles, then over the point of the right-hand one, drawing it upwards through the loop on the left-hand needle. There is now the original stitch on that needle and the new stitch on the right-hand needle. Pull the stitch on the right-hand needle out until it with its point between the thumb and first finger. Take the other needle between thumb and first finger of the right hand (Fig. 1). Then insert the point of the needle from left to right through the first stitch on the left-hand needle. With the first finger of the right hand, pass the wool round the point of the right-hand needle (first under, then over) keeping the wool always at the back of the work, draw the wool on the needle through the stitch to the front of the knitting, slip the old stitch off the left-hand needle, and keep the new stitch on the right-hand needle. Continue in this way until all stitches are worked.

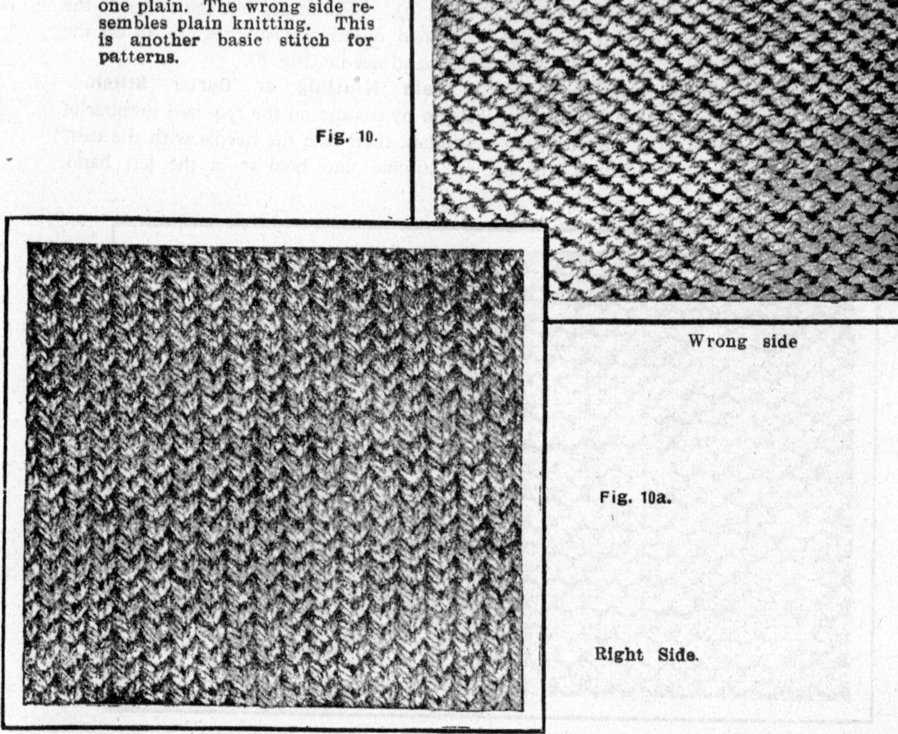

Stocking-stitch, or stocking-web as it is often called, consists of one row of purl and one plain. The wrong side resembles plain knitting. This is another basic stitch for patterns.

Fig. 10.

Wrong side

Fig. 10a.

Right Side.

Now reverse the needles, hold them as at first and continue to work each row in exactly the same way for the length required (Fig. 9).

Stocking-stitch.—(Fig. 10.) Cast on the number of stitches required and, holding the needles as previously described, knit one plain row. The second row is purl. Hold the needles as before, the full needle in the left hand and the spare needle in the right (for this row always keep the wool in fron tof the work), pass the point of the right-hand needle under the wool and insert it from right to left, through the first stitch bringing the needle in front of the left needle. With the first finger of the right hand, pass the wool over the point, then under the needle to the front again. Then draw the wool on the needle through the stitch to the back of the work, slip the old stitch off the left-hand needle and keep the new stitch on the right-hand needle. Continue in this way until all stitches are worked off. Repeat these two rows (1 plain, 1 purl) for the length required.

Ribbed Knitting.—(Fig. 11.) This is done on any number of stitches, divisible by the number of stitches in the rib, and is worked by knitting first plain and then purl, in twos or fours, as desired. This type of knitting is chiefly used for cuffs, neck-bands, and welting for stockings and jumpers. It is particularly elastic so that while fitting closely, it will stretch to almost any size.

To Increase.—This is simply done

Fig. 11.—Ribbed Knitting. The width of the rib can be varied according to the article being knitted. The usual combination for welts is either two plain, two purl, or one plain, one purl.

by knitting two stitches into one, i.e. by knitting into the back as well as the front of the stitch, before slipping off the needle. Another very neat way is to knit a stitch into the loop just below the next stitch to be knitted on the left-hand needle (Figs. 12 and 14).

To Decrease.—Stitches in knitting can be decreased either by knitting two stitches together, or purling two stitches together, as the case may be (Fig. 13). Another way is to slip one stitch, knit the next, then pass the slipped stitch over. To slip a stitch, simply take the stitch from the left-hand needle to the right-hand needle, without knitting it.

To make a stitch—in open knitting patterns: i.e. in plain knitting, pass the thread to the front of the work through the pins and back again over the pins. In purl knitting when the thread is already at the front of the work, pass it over the needle and right round it, so that it comes to the front again. This makes a new stitch when knitted off in the next row.

Double Knitting.—Work is begun by casting on an even number of stitches. Bring the wool to the front and slip purlwise, pass the wool to the back and knit the next stitch, plain. Bring the wool to the front and slip the next stitch purlwise. Pass the wool to the back and knit the following stitch plain. Repeat in this way, alternately slipping one stitch and knitting one stitch to the end of the row. Repeat for the length required. The stitch which was slipped in one row, must always be knitted in the next. (Fig. 15).

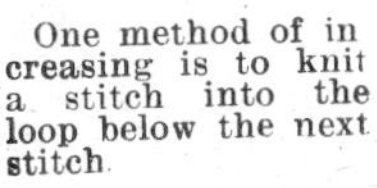

One method of increasing is to knit a stitch into the loop below the next stitch.

Fig. 12.

Grafting.—This is the method of neatly joining together two pieces of knitting and is much used for the shoulders of jumpers, etc. When leaving stitches for grafting, do not break the wool off close to the last stitch, but leave a long end. Thread this into a wool needle and place the two needles containing stitches together, right side outside, holding the work so that the end of the wool is at the right-hand end of the back needle (Diagram A).

Pass the wool needle through the first loop of the front needle, purlwise (Diagram B), but do not slip the loop off the knitting needle. Pass the needle through first loop of the back needle as if about to knit but do not slip loop off (Diagram C). Slip off the first loop as if for plain knitting in the front row, but keep the loop on the wool needle until the next loop is worked Pass the needle through the second loop as if for purling, but do not slip the loop off the knitting needle (Diagram D). In the back row, slip off the first loops as for purling, keeping on the wool needle, pass through the second loop as for knitting, but do not slip the loop off the knitting needle Repeat until all the loops are worked off. Fasten off.

One way of decreasing is to knit or purl two stitches together.

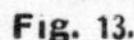

Fig. 13.

Another way of decreasing is to slip one stitch, knit the next, and then pass the slipped stitch over the knitted one

Another way of increasing, by knitting twice into one stitch.

Fig. 14.

Casting Off.—Knit the first two stitches then pass the left-hand needle from left to right through the first stitch and pull the stitch over the second one and off the right-hand needle Now knit the next stitch and take the second one over this and off the needle in the same way as the first stitch. Continue thus until only one stitch remains, break off the wool and slip

HOW TWO PIECES OF KNITTING ARE GRAFTED TOGETHER

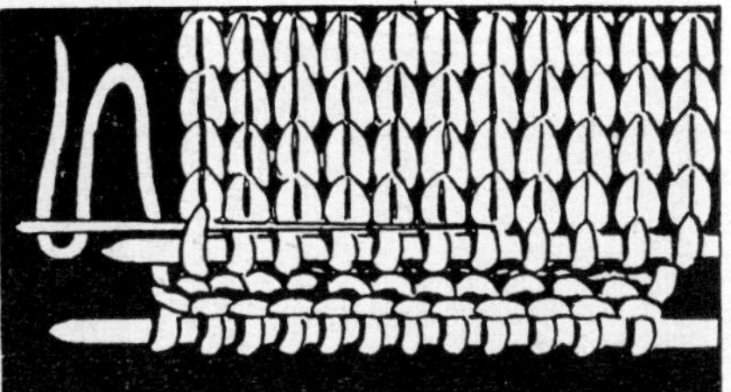

Diagram A

When leaving stitches for grafting, do not break the wool off close to the last stitch, but leave a long end. Thread this into a wool needle and place the two needles containing stitches together right side outside, holding the work so that the end of the wool is at the right-hand end of the back needle.

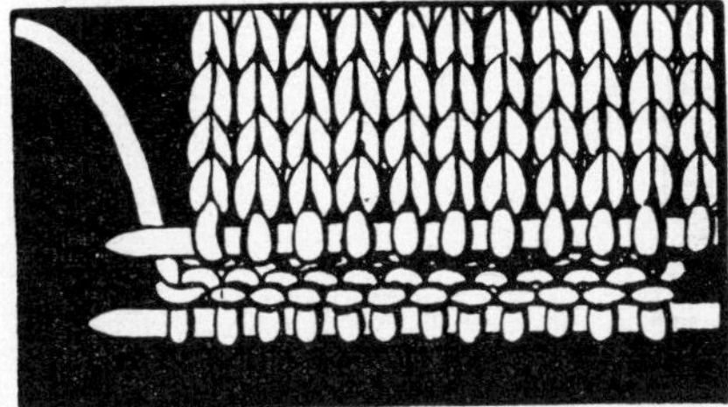

Diagram B

Pass the needle through the first loop of the front needle, purl-wise, but do not slip the loops off the knitting needle. (Diagram C.) Pass the needle through the first loop of the back needle as if about to knit, but do not slip the loop off

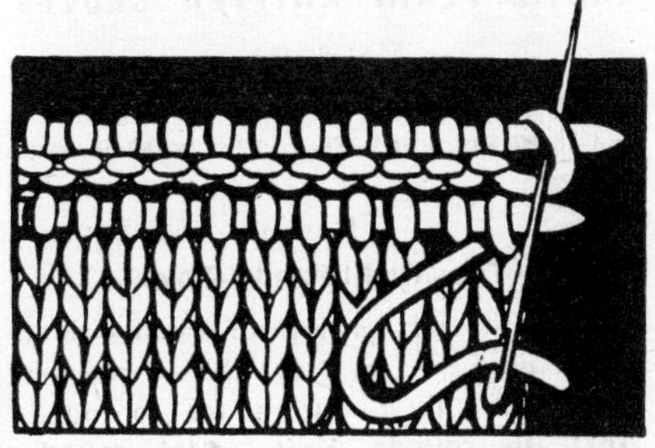

Diagram C

Slip off the first loop as if for plain knitting in the front row, but keep the loop on the wool needle until the next loop is worked. Pass the needle through the second loop as if for purling, but do not slip the loop off the knitting needle.

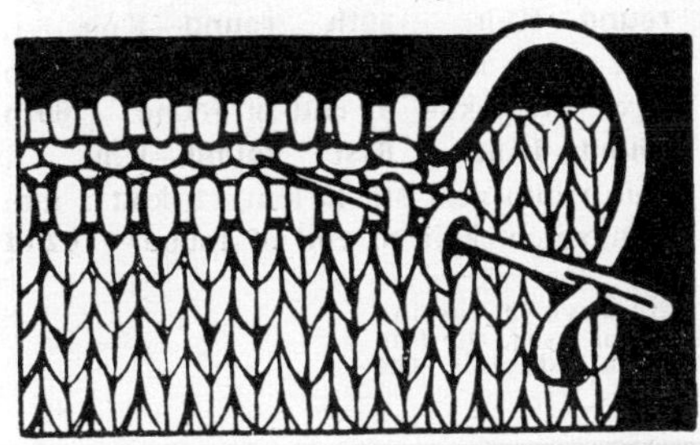

Diagram D

the end through the last stitch, which is now slipped off the needle and the end drawn tight. Another method is to knit the first two stitches together, slip the stitch on the right-hand needle on to the left one, then knit this stitch together with the third one on the right-hand needle. Continue thus until only one stitch remains. Break off the wool. Fig. 16

Stitches accidentally dropped should be picked up at once, or the whole piece of work may be spoilt. They can be detected at once, by the loop forming the stitch running down the whole length of the work. If it is impossible to pick this up neatly, unravel the work, place the loop in its right position on the needle once more and proceed to re-knit.

One of the features of good knitting is its evenness, which may be obtained by working steadily, whether quickly or slowly. Usually a quick worker knits more evenly than a slow one

Always finish a row before putting the knitting down, for if left in the middle, the stitches will stretch.

Double knitting is done by alternately slipping a stitch and knitting a stitch. The stitch slipped in one row must always be knitted in the next.

Fig. 15.

LADY'S PLAIN KNITTED GLOVES

MATERIALS:

3 oz. of 3-ply wool.
4 knitting pins No. 13 (pointed each end).

Fig. 17.

The Right-hand Glove.

Begin at cuff, casting 52 stitches on to three needles (18, 16, 18). Knit in ribbing of knit 2, purl 2, for 40 rounds **Next 10 rounds**—Knit. **51st round**—Here increasings for thumb commence—knit 1, knit 2 into next stitch, knit 2, knit 2 into next stitch, knit to end of round. **52nd round**—Knit. **53rd round**—Knit 1, knit 2 into next stitch, knit 4, knit 2 into next stitch, knit to end of round. **54th round**—Knit. **55th round**—Knit 1, knit 2 into next stitch, knit 6, knit 2 into next stitch, knit to end of round. **56th round**—Knit. **57th round**—Knit 1, knit 2 into next stitch, knit 8, knit 2 into next stitch, knit to end of round. **58th round**—Knit. **59th round**—Knit 1, knit 2 into next stitch, knit 10, knit 2 into next stitch, knit to end of round. **60th round**—Knit. **61st round**—Knit 1, knit 2 into next stitch, knit 12, knit 2 into next stitch, knit to end of round **62nd**

Fig. 16.—There are two ways of casting off stitches, but whichever is used, the tension of the knitting should remain the same

round—Knit. **63rd round**—Knit 1, knit 2 into next stitch, knit 14, knit 2 into next stitch, knit to end of round. **64th round**—Knit. **65th round**—Knit 1, knit 2 into next stitch, knit 16, knit 2 into next stitch, knit to end of round. **66th round**—Knit. **67th round**—Knit 2, slip next 18 stitches on to a piece of wool for thumb, cast on 4, knit to end of round. **Next 21 rounds**—Knit. Here divide for fingers. **1st round for First finger**—Knit 8, slip all but the last 8 stitches on to a piece of wool, leaving last 8 stitches on needle, cast on 3, for inside of finger. Divide stitches thus: (6, 7, 6). Knit in plain rounds for length required. **Next 2 rounds.**— * Knit 1, knit 2 together, repeat from * until 1 remains knit 1. **Next round.**—Each needle, knit 1, knit 2 together (6 stitches). Break off wool, leaving end, thread into darner and take off all stitches from needles, draw up tightly and sew on wrong side. **The Second finger.**—Take 7 stitches from wool each side on to 2 needles, with another needle, pick up 3 stitches at base of first finger, cast on 3 stitches for inside of finger. Divide stitches thus: (7, 6, 7). Join on wool. Knit in plain rounds for length required.

Next round.— * Knit 1, knit 2 together, repeat from * until 2 remain, knit 2 together. **Next round.**— * Knit 2 together, knit 1, repeat from * until 1 remains, knit 1. **Next round.**—Each needle, knit 1, knit 2 together (6 stitches). Finish as for first finger. **The Third finger.**—Take 6 stitches from wool each side, pick up 3 stitches at base of second finger, cast on 3 stitches for inside of finger. Divide stitches thus: (6, 6, 6). Knit in plain rounds for length required. **Next round.**—Each needle, knit 1, knit 2 together, knit 1, knit 2 together. **Next round.**—Each needle, knit 2, knit 2 together. **Next round.**—Each needle, knit 1, knit 2 together (6 stitches). Finish as for first finger. **The Fourth finger.**—Slip remaining 12 stitches from wool on to 2 needles, pick up 3 stitches at base of third finger. Divide stitches thus: (5, 5, 5). Knit in plain rounds for length required

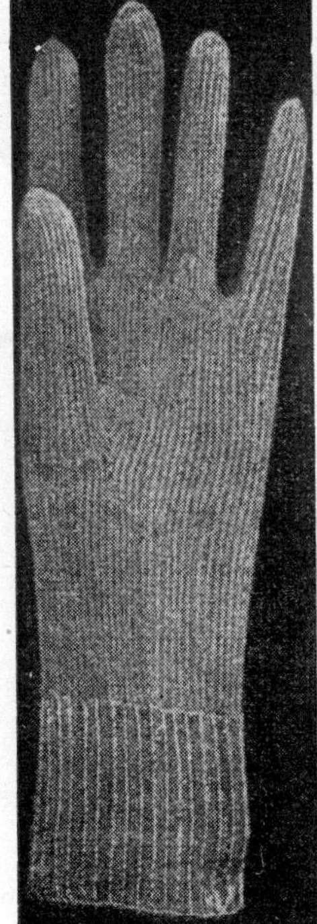

A lady's glove—a standard pattern for which is given here.

Fig. 17

Next round.—Each needle, knit 2 together, knit 1, knit 2 together. **Next round.**—Each needle, knit 2 together, knit 1 (6 stitches). Finish as for first finger. **The Thumb.**—Divide the 18 stitches on to 2 needles, with 3rd needle pick up 4 stitches at base. Divide stitches thus: (7, 8, 7). Knit in plain rounds for length required. **Next round.**— * Knit 1, knit 2 together, repeat from * until 1 remains, knit 1. **Next round.**—Each needle, knit 2 together, knit 1, knit 2 together. **Next round.**—Each needle, knit 2 together, knit 1 (6 stitches). Finish as for first finger.

The Left-hand Glove.

Knit as directed for right-hand glove, but making thumb towards end of last needle, instead of commencement of first, working the 51st round thus: knit until 5 remain, knit 2 into next stitch, knit 2, knit 2 into next stitch, knit 1. Continue working in this way until all increasings

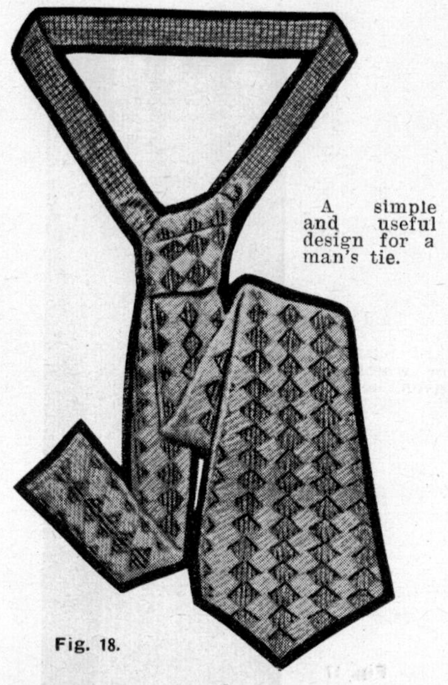
A simple and useful design for a man's tie.

Fig. 18.

are finished. Finish as for right-hand glove. Press under a damp cloth with a hot iron.

A KNITTED TIE.

For the tie in Fig. 18, needles No. 17 should be used. Do not slip the first stitch of any row. Begin at lower edge of narrow end. Cast on 41 stitches. Knit 1 row plain, knitting into back of every stitch. **1st pattern row.**—Purl 1, * knit 9, purl 1, repeat from * to end. **2nd pattern row.**—Knit 2, purl 7, * knit 3, purl 7, repeat from * until 2 remain, knit 2. **3rd pattern row.**—Purl 3, knit 5, * purl 5, knit 5, repeat from * until 3 remain, purl 3. **4th pattern row.**—Knit 4, purl 3, * knit 7, purl 3, repeat from * until 4 remain, knit 4. **5th pattern row.**—Purl 5, knit 1, * purl 9, knit 1, repeat from * until 5 remain, purl 5. **6th pattern row.**—As 4th row. **7th pattern row.**—As 3rd row. **8th pattern row.**—As 2nd row These 8 rows form 1 pattern. Repeat last 8 rows 11 times more. * **97th row.**—Knit 2 together, work in pattern until 2 remain, knit 2 together Work 7 more rows without decrease to complete pattern (N.B. Care must be taken when decreasing and increasing to keep pattern over pattern.) Repeat from * 9 times more. (21 stitches.) Now work in stocking-web (1 row plain and 1 row purl) for 14 inches. ** Now work from 1st to 7th rows inclusive. **Next row.**—Knit 2 into first stitch (by knitting into back as well as front of stitch before slipping it off needle). Work in pattern until 1 remains, knit 2 into last stitch. Repeat from ** 9 times more. (41 stitches.) *** Work 15 rows in pattern. **Next row.**—Knit 2 into first stitch, work in pattern until 1 remains, knit 2 into last stitch. Repeat from *** 14 times. (71 stitches.) Now decrease for point by knitting 2 together at beginning and end of every row until all stitches are worked off, care being taken to keep pattern over pattern. Press well under a damp cloth with a hot iron. Beginning 8 stitches from point, sew edges together then press well, making seam down centre back

SOCKS AND STOCKINGS.

To join into a round.—(Fig. 19.) Cast the required number of stitches on the three needles. The end of the third needle with the ball of wool attached to it, is placed to the beginning of the first needle, beside the tag end of wool, making a triangle. Arrange all the cast-on stitches evenly on their respective needles without twisting. Insert the fourth needle into the first cast-on stitch, beside the tag end of wool on the first needle, and knit all the stitches from the first needle on to the empty needle. Care must be taken to pull the first stitch particularly tight, to avoid a gap.

The welt is usually knitted in a rib of either 2 plain and 2 purl, or 1 plain and 1 purl (Fig. 20).

Seam stitch down back of leg.—This is marked by working one purl stitch in the plain portion above the welt. This is only required when socks and stockings are to be decreased to shape for the ankle.

Decreasings on a plain stocking.—(Fig. 21.) Decreasings are always worked one on each side of the seam stitch. Knit one stitch past seam stitch, knit the next two stitches together, then knit plain to

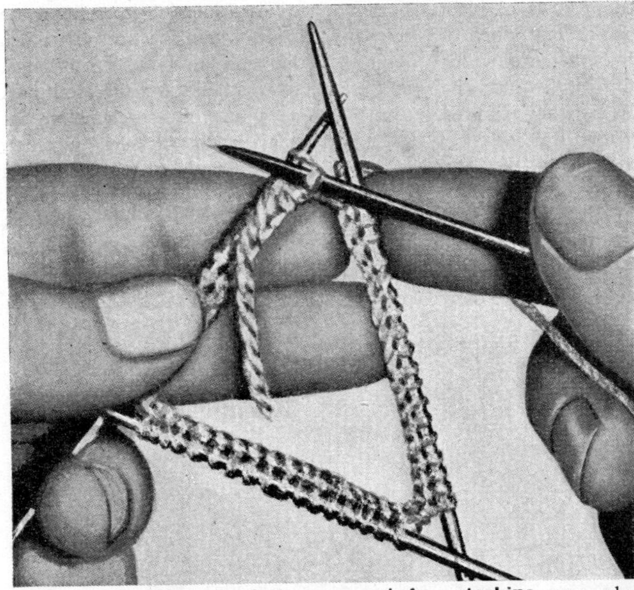

Fig. 19.

The position of the needle when joining a round. The stitch that is just being worked should be pulled particularly tight to prevent the needles from straining apart.

within three stitches, of the seam stitch, knit the next two stitches together, knit 1, then purl the seam stitch. Plain rounds are worked between each decreasing, the number varying according to the size and style of sock or stocking.

Decreasings at the back of a ribbed stocking are always worked one each side of a purl rib. Continue until the ribbing becomes even again.

The Heel Flap.—About half the number of stitches used for the ankle are required, and should be placed evenly each side of a seam-stitch, or at the back of the sock.

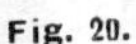

Fig. 20.

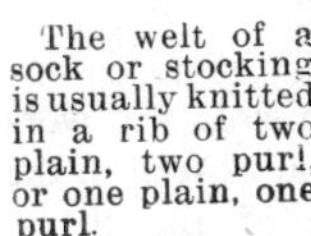

The welt of a sock or stocking is usually knitted in a rib of two plain, two purl, or one plain, one purl.

The heel flap is worked in rows of plain and purl, always slipping the first stitch of each row. The length of flap should be a little over a third of the width round the ankle. When the flap is the required length, the heel is ready for turning.

To Turn a Heel—Method 1.—(Fig. 22.) The stitches are divided by three, and any odd stitch left over, should be counted in the centre group. For the first row, knit first group and to within one stitch of second group, knit the next two stitches together, purl one, and turn. A small gap will now be seen at each side, where the work is turned. Knit to within one stitch before this gap, knit the next two stitches together, knit one, turn. Purl to within one stitch before the gap, purl the next two stitches together, purl one. Continue thus until all stitches each side of the gusset are worked.

Picking up Stitches at side of heel Flap.—(Fig. 24.) When the heel is turned, stitches are picked up each side in preparation for the foot. To do this, knit

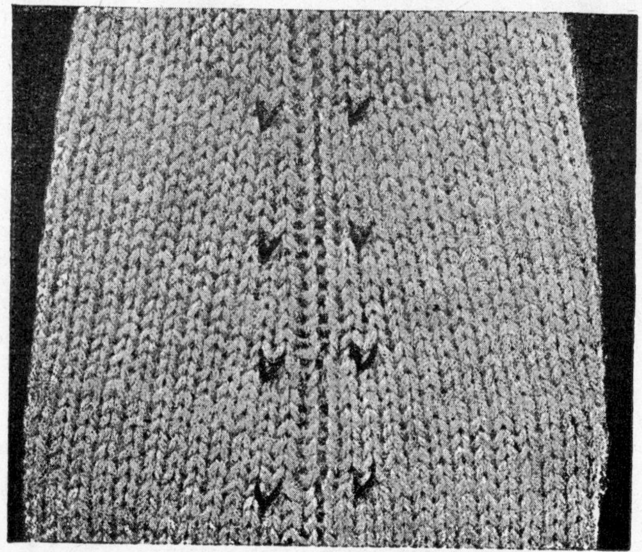

Fig. 21. The decreasings in a plain sock or stocking are shown here, each place where a stitch has been decreased being marked by a piece of coloured cotton.

and turn. Purl the centre group all but one stitch, knit the next two stitches together, and turn. Continue in this way until all stitches each side have been worked off and only the centre group remains.

Method 2.—(Fig. 23.) Here the stitches are divided by two, and for the first row, knit to one stitch past the centre or centre stitch, according to whether an even or uneven number of stitches are in heel flap, knit next two stitches together, knit one, turn. Purl to one stitch past the centre, purl the next two stitches together, the heel stitches then hold the work with the heel flap in position as seen in the illustration. Along side of the flap, where stitches were slipped, tiny loops are seen. Insert the needle, holding the heel stitches into the first of these loops, pass the wool over the point of the same needle, and draw through, thus forming a stitch on the needle. Repeat this with every loop down the side of the flap With a second needle, knit all the front stitches; with the third needle pick up the stitches along the other side of heel flap, in the same way as along

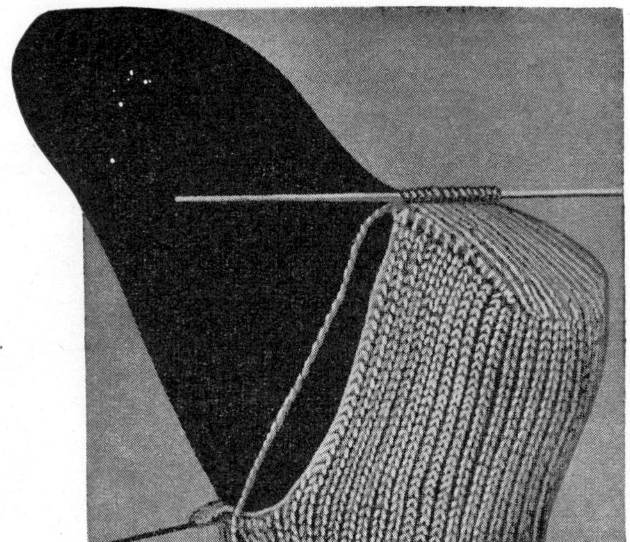

Fig. 22.

Fig. 22 shows one method of turning a heel which gives a square gusset. Fig. 23 below shows the second method which forms the pointed gusset.

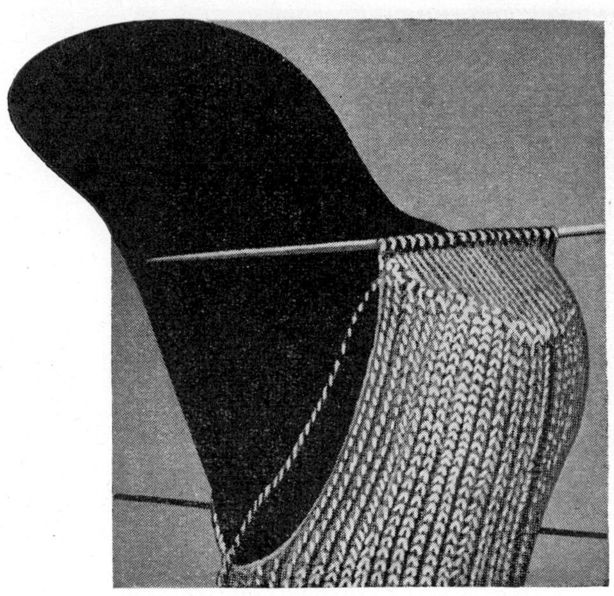

Fig. 23.

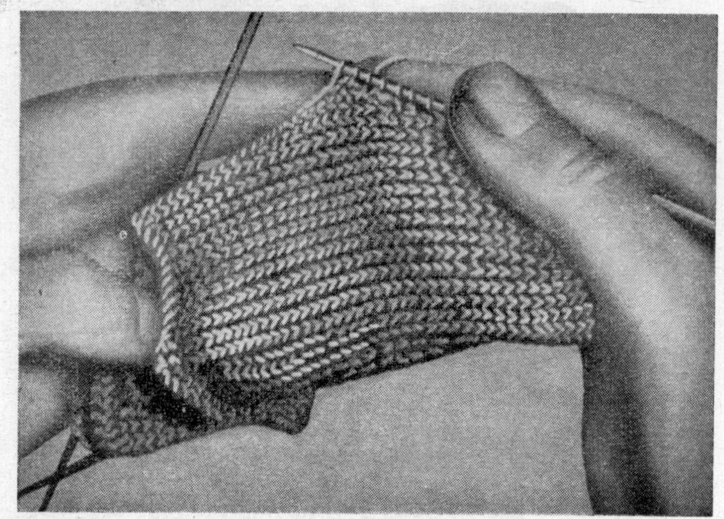

Fig. 24. PICKING UP STITCHES AT SIDE OF HEEL FLAP

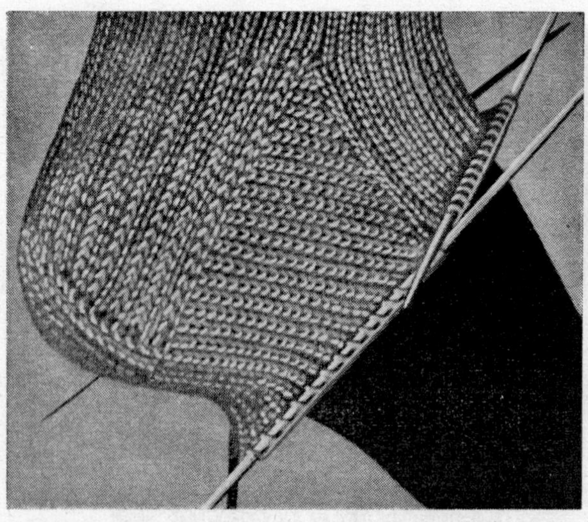

Fig. 25. INSTEP SHAPING

Fig. 26.

A KNEECAP

the first side, and knit half the number of gusset stitches from the first to the third needle.

Instep shaping.—Knit two stitches together at the end of the first needle, and beginning of the third needle, in each alternate round, until the number of stitches is the same as round the ankle. or the first and third needle together equal the second needle. If it is necessary to decrease only a few stitches it is advisable to knit two rounds between each decreasing (Fig. 25).

How to Strengthen a Heel.—When the stitches are divided at the ankle an even number must be used for the heel flap which, instead of being knitted in rows of plain and purl is worked as follows: Beginning in an outside row, * slip one, knit one, repeat from * to end. **Next row.**—Slip one, purl to end. Repeat these two rows until the flap is the required length. If desired the strengthening can be continued until the heel is turned and the picking up of the stitches down the side of the heel flap is started or can be discontinued when the flap is finished.

Another way of strengthening is to knit a strand of machine twist of the same shade, in with the wool.

The Toes.—(1) Oval. This style is popular (Fig. 29). The number of stitches on the first and third needles should equal those on the second needle. To begin shaping: **1st round.**—First needle, knit to within three stitches of the end, knit 2 together, knit 1. Second needle, knit 1, knit 2 together, knit to within 3 of end, knit 2 together, knit 1.

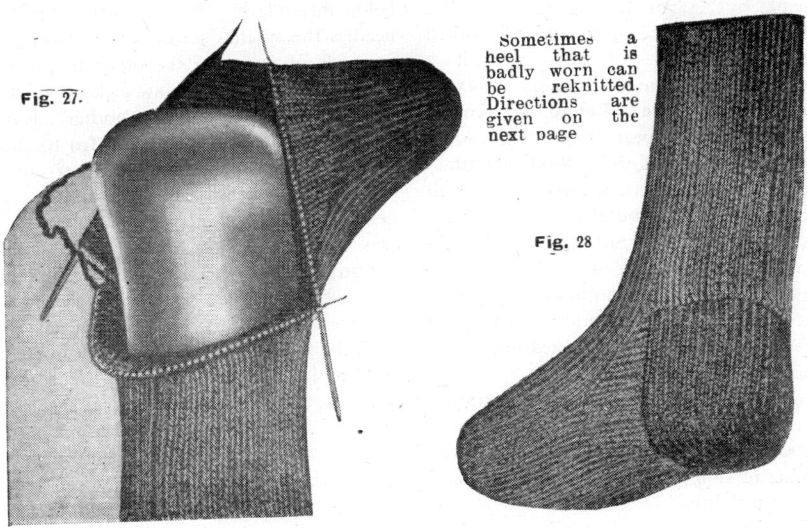

Fig. 27.

Sometimes a heel that is badly worn can be reknitted. Directions are given on the next page

Fig. 28

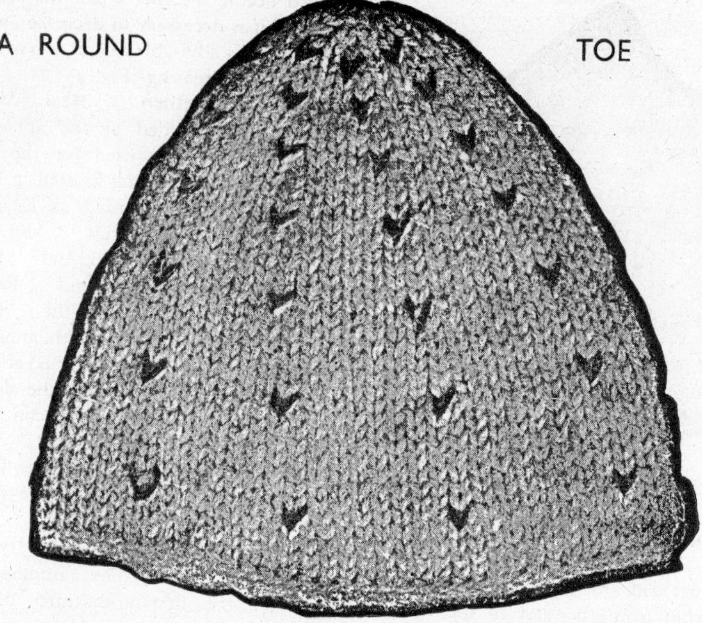

Third needle, knit 1, knit 2 together, knit to end. **Next round.**—Knit. Repeat these two rounds until between 16 and 20 stitches are left. Then knit stitches from first needle to third and graft stitches together.

Round Toe.—(Above.) There must be on the needles a number of stitches divisible by 7, 8 or 9. E.g. in a stocking with 63 stitches, the toe would be worked thus: **1st round.**— * Knit 7, knit 2 together, repeat from * all round. **Next 7 rounds.**—Knit. **Next Round.**— * Knit 6. knit 2 together, repeat from * all round. **Next 6 rounds.**—Knit. **Next round.**— * Knit 5, knit 2 together, repeat from * all round. **Next 5 rounds.**—Knit. Continue in this way, knitting a stitch less between each decrease in each decreased round, and working that number of rounds between each decrease round, as when you knit 5 stitches between decreasings, knit 5 rounds.

Continue in this way until 2 are knitted together all round, and when the remaining stitches can be divided equally and grafted together or slipped on to a piece of wool and drawn up tightly

How to Knit a New Heel into Sock or Stocking.—Wool to match the sock in colour and thickness should be used, and four steel needles which will give a similar tension in knitting to that of sock or stocking. Unravel the worn heel, being careful not to unpick a single stitch of the leg below instep level. Pick up on two knitting needles the stitches across sole of foot from one side of instep to the other to prevent them from dropping. Now pick up stitches for the heel flap on to another needle. Join on wool and work to and fro for heel flap thus: Knit to within last stitch of heel needle, slip one stitch off the side needle, on to heel needle, and knit these two together. Turn and purl to within last stitch on heel needle, and as before slip one off from side needle and take 2 together. Do this at end of each row until the heel flap is long enough. Count the stitches left at the centre of the sole of the sock, put them on one needle, then turn the heel by the same method used in the original knitting. There should then be left on the heel needle as many stitches as were counted on the sole. Hold the two

HOW TO GRAFT THE TOES OF A SOCK OR STOCKING

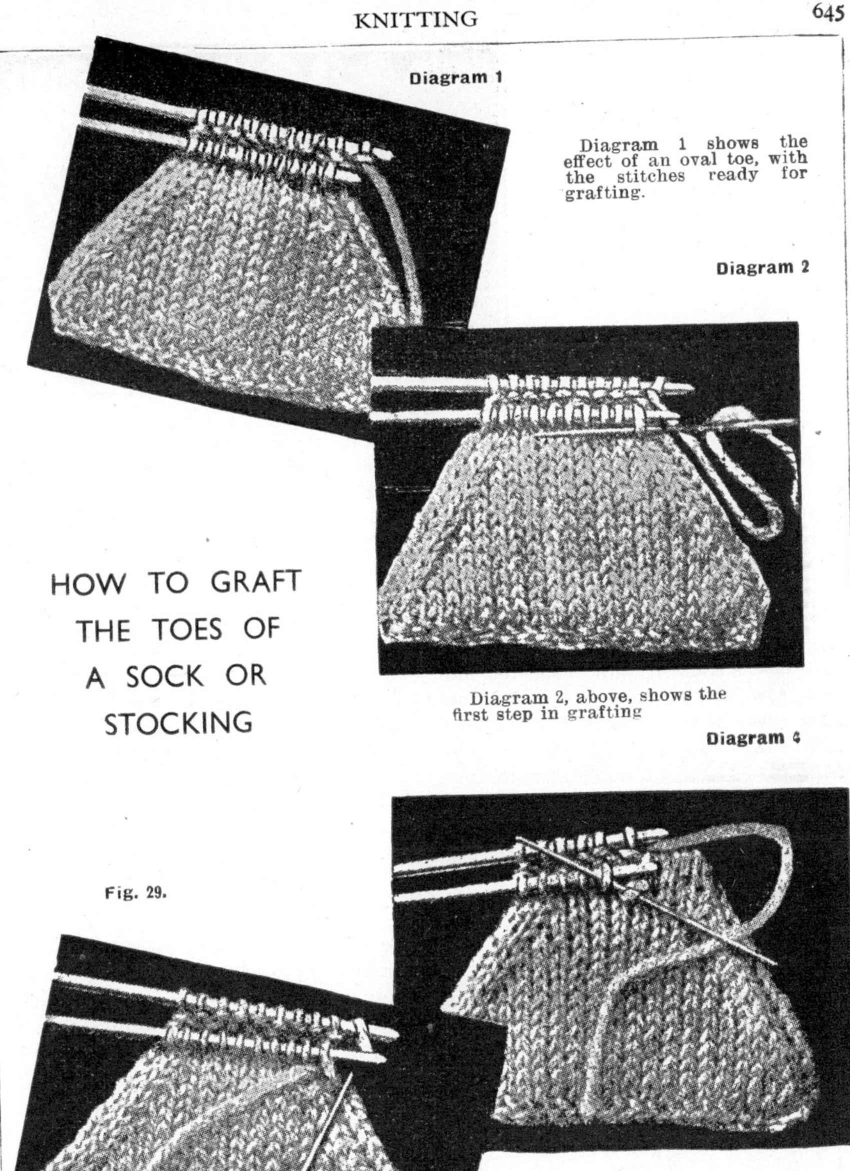

Diagram 1

Diagram 1 shows the effect of an oval toe, with the stitches ready for grafting.

Diagram 2

Diagram 2, above, shows the first step in grafting

Diagram 4

Fig. 29.

Diagram 3, left, shows the second step in grafting; and Diagram 4, above, the stitching half grafted.

Diagram 3

ARROWHEAD PATTERN

Fig. 30.

needles together and take a wool needle and graft the heel and foot together. All ends of wool, both old and new, must be darned in neatly and securely, especially near the instep, and at the end of the grafting.

A Kneecap.—(Fig. 26.) Cast on 72 stitches, knit in ribbing of knit 2, purl 2, for 18 rows. **19th row.**—Knit 2, purl 2, alternately 10 times, turn, knit 8, turn. **21st row.**—Knit 9, turn, knit 10, turn. **23rd row.**—Knit 11, turn, knit 12, turn. **25th row.**—Knit 13, turn, knit 14, turn. **27th row.**—Knit 15, turn, knit 16, turn. **29th row.**—Knit 17, turn, knit 18, turn. **31st row.**—Knit 19, turn, knit 20, turn. Continue to work thus, knitting one more stitch each end until there are 36 plain stitches in the centre, and 18 rib stitches at each end. **49th row.**—Knit 33, knit 2 together, knit 1, turn, knit 32, knit 2 together, knit 1, turn. **51st row.**—Knit 31, knit 2 together, knit 1, turn. Continue to knit thus, decreasing at each end of plain stitches, in centre until there are only 8 plain stitches left. Pick up and knit 14 stitches along side of plain stitches, knit remaining stitches in rib. **Next row.**—Knit 2, purl 2 alternately to end of plain stitches, then pick up and knit 14 stitches along other side of plain stitches (72), knit ribbing of knit 2, purl 2, for 17 rows. Cast off. Fold in half and join edges together.

FANCY KNITTING STITCHES.

Arrowhead Pattern.—(Fig. 30.) Begin by casting on a number of stitches divisible by 8 with 1 over. **1st row.**—Knit 3, * knit 2 together, make 1, knit 6, repeat from * until 6 remain, knit 2 together, make 1, knit 4. **2nd row.**—Purl. **3rd row.**—Knit 2, * knit 2 together,

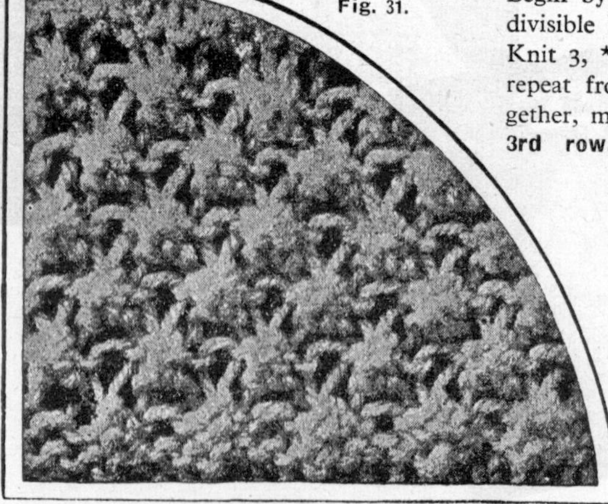

Fig. 31.

BLACKBERRY STITCH

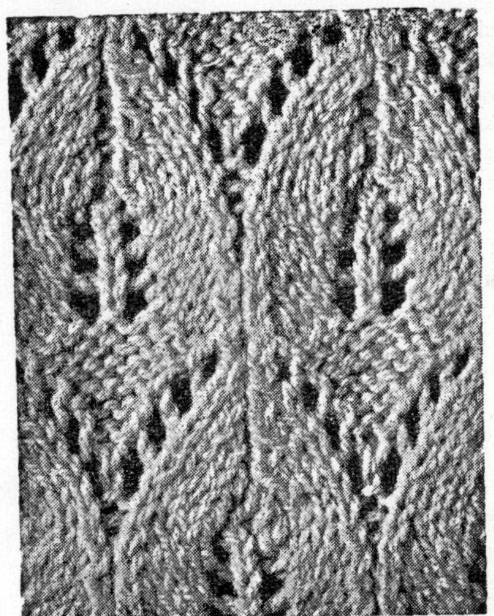

Fig. 32. CHURCH WINDOW DESIGN

make 1, knit 1, make 1, slip 1, knit 1, pass slipped stitch over, knit 3, repeat from * until 7 remain, knit 2 together, make 1, knit 1, make 1, slip 1, knit 1, pass slipped stitch over, knit 2. **4th row.**—Purl. **5th row.**—Knit 1, * knit 2 together, make 1, knit 1, make 1, knit 2 together, make 1, slip 1, knit 1, pass slipped stitch over, knit 1, repeat from * to end. **6th row.**—Purl. **7th row.**—Knit 7, * knit 2 together, make 1, knit 6, repeat from * until 2 remain, knit 2. **8th row.**—Purl. **9th row.**—Knit 6, * knit 2 together, make 1, knit 1, make 1, slip 1, knit 1, pass slipped stitch over, knit 3, repeat from * until 3 remain, knit 3. **10th row.**—Purl. **11th row.**—Knit 5, * knit 2 together, make 1, knit 1, make 1, knit 2 together, make 1, slip 1, knit 1, pass slipped stitch over, knit 1, repeat from * until 4 remain, knit 4. **12th row.**—Purl. Repeat these 12 rows for length required.

Blackberry Stitch.—(Fig. 31.) Cast on any number of stitches divisible by 4, with 6 over. These 6 stitches are for the border—3 at each edge. **1st row.**—Knit 3, * then knit 1 and purl 1, and knit 1 into the next stitch (thus making 3 stitches), pass the wool to the front of the work and purl the next 3 stitches together, pass the wool to the back of the work repeat from * until 3 remain, knit 3. **2nd row.**—Purl. **3rd row.**—Knit 3, * purl the next 3 stitches together, then knit 1 and purl 1 and knit 1 into the next stitch, repeat from * until 3 remain, knit 3. **4th row.**—Purl. Repeat these 4 rows for length required.

Cable Stitch.—(Fig. 33.) Cast on any number of stitches divisible by 11 with 1 over. **1st row.**—Knit 1, * purl 2, knit 6, purl 2, knit 1, repeat from * to end. **2nd row.**—Knit 3, * purl 6, knit 5, repeat from * until 9 remain, purl 6, knit 3. Repeat these 2 rows once. **5th row.**—Knit 1, * purl 2, slip the next 3 stitches on to spare needle, place them in front of the work, knit the next 3 stitches, place the needle containing the 3 slipped stitches to back of work, and knit these 3 stitches (the

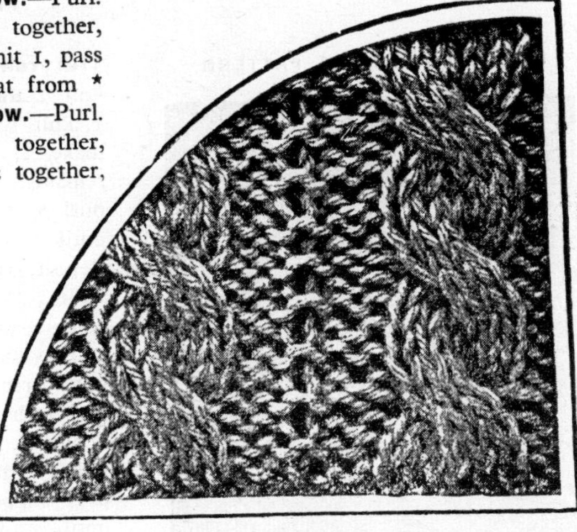

Fig. 33.

last 6 stitches form the cable pattern), purl 2, knit 1, repeat from * to end. **6th row.**—As 2nd row. Repeat these 6 rows as desired.

Church Window Design.—(Fig. 32.) Cast on any number of stitches divisible by 12 with 3 over. **1st row.**—Knit 1, * purl 1, thread back, slip 1, knit 1, pass slipped stitch over, knit 3, make 1, knit 1, make 1, knit 3, knit 2 together, repeat from * until 2 remain, purl 1, knit 1. **2nd row.**—Knit 2, * purl 11, knit 1, repeat from * until 1 remains, knit 1. Repeat these 2 rows 3 times.

9th row.—Knit 1, * purl 1, make 1, knit 3, knit 2 together, purl 1, thread back, slip 1, knit 1, pass slipped stitch over, knit 3, make 1, repeat from * until 2 remain, purl 1, knit 1. **10th row.**—Knit 2, * purl 5, knit 1, repeat from * until 1 remains, knit 1. **11th row.**—Knit 1, purl 2, * make 1, knit 2, slip 1, knit 1, pass slipped stitch over, purl 1, knit 2 together, knit 2, make 1, purl 3, repeat from * until 11 remain, make 1, knit 2, slip 1, knit 1, pass slipped stitch over, purl 1, knit 2 together, make 1, purl 2, knit 1. **12th row.**—Knit 3, * purl 4, knit 1, purl 4, knit 3, repeat from * to end. **13th row.**—Knit 1, purl 3, * make 1, knit 1, slip 1, knit 1, pass slipped stitch over, purl 1, knit 2 together, knit 1, make 1, purl 5, repeat from * until 11 remain, make 1, knit 1, slip 1, knit 1, pass slipped stitch over, purl 1, knit 2 together, knit 1, make 1, purl 3, knit 1. **14th row.**—Knit 4, * purl 3, knit 1, purl 3, knit 5, repeat from * until 11 remain, purl 3, knit 1, purl 3, knit 4. **15th row.**—Knit 1, purl 4, * make 1, slip 1, knit 1, pass slipped stitch over, purl 1, knit 2 together, make 1, purl 7, repeat from * until 10 remain, make 1, slip 1, knit 1, pass slipped stitch over, purl 1, knit 2 together, make 1, purl 4, knit 1. **16th row.**—Knit 5, * purl 2, knit 1, purl 2, knit 7, repeat from * until 10 remain, purl 2, knit 1, purl 2, knit 5.

Fig. 35. DOUBLE MOSS STITCH

Fig. 34. CRISS-CROSS PATTERN

17th row.—Knit 2, * make 1, knit 3, knit 2 together, purl 1, thread back, slip 1, knit 1, pass slipped stitch over, knit 3, make 1, knit 1, repeat from * until 1 remains, knit 1. **18th row.**—Knit 1, purl 6, * knit 1, purl 11, repeat from * until 8 remain, knit 1, purl 6, knit 1. Repeat last 2 rows 3 times. **25th row.**—Knit 1, * purl 1, knit 2 together, knit 3, make 1, purl 1, make 1, knit 3, slip 1, knit 1, pass slipped stitch over, repeat from * until 2 remain, purl 1, knit 1. **26th row.**—As 10th row. **27th row.**—Knit 1, * purl 1, knit 2 together, knit 2, make 1, purl 3, make 1, knit 2, slip 1, knit 1, pass slipped stitch over, repeat from * until 2 remain, purl 1, knit 1. **28th**

row.—Knit 2, * purl 4, knit 3, purl 4, knit 1, repeat from * until 1 remains, knit 1. **29th row.**—Knit 1, * purl 1, knit 2 together, knit 1, make 1, purl 5, make 1, knit 1, slip 1, knit 1, pass slipped stitch over, repeat from * until 2 remain, purl 1, knit 1. **30th row.**—Knit 2, * purl 3, knit 5, purl 3, knit 1, repeat from * until 1 remains, knit 1. **31st row.**—Knit 1, * purl 1, knit 2 together, make 1, purl 7, make 1, slip 1, knit 1, pass slipped stitch over, repeat from * until 2 remain, purl 1, knit 1. **32nd row.**—Knit 2, * purl 2, knit 7, purl 2, knit 1, repeat from * until 1 remains, knit 1. Repeat these 32 rows for length required.

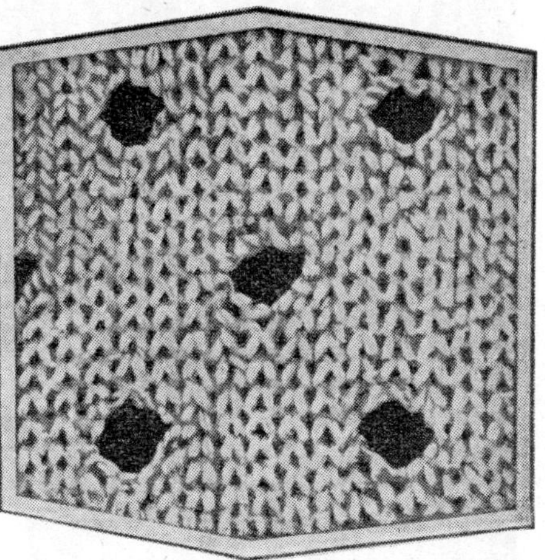

Fig. 37. EYELET HOLE PATTERN

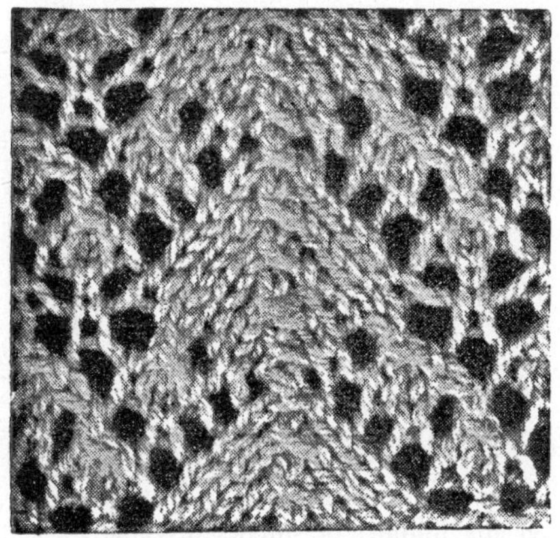

Fig. 36. FAN PATTERN

Criss-cross Pattern.—(Fig. 34.) Cast on any number of stitches divisible by 4, with 2 over. **1st row.**—Slip 1, * make 1, purl 1, repeat from * until 2 remain, make 1, knit 2. **2nd row.**—Slip 1, knit 1, * drop the strand from previous row, slip 1, and repeat this 4 times so that there are four long stitches on the right needle, pass the two first over the two last, then pass all four over to the left needle and knit them, repeat from * to end. **3rd row.**—Slip 1, purl until 1 remains, knit 1. **4th row.**—Slip 1, knit to the end. **5th row.**—As 3rd row. **6th row.**—As 4th row.

Repeat these 6 rows for length required.

Double Moss stitch.—(Fig. 35.) Cast on an even number of stitches. If the number is divisible by 4, work as follows: **1st row.**—Knit 2, purl 2 alternately to end. **2nd row.**—Purl 2, knit 2 alternately to end. Repeat these rows for length required. Should the number of stitches be divisible by 2 only, and not 4, work each row thus: Knit 2, then purl 2, knit 2, alternately to end.

Eyelet Hole Pattern.—(Fig. 37.) Cast on a number of stitches divisible by 8, with 4 over. Knit 4 rows of stocking-stitch. **5th row.**—Knit 4, * knit 2 together, make 1, knit 2 together, knit 4, repeat from * to end. **6th row.**—Purl 5, * then knit 1, and purl 1 into the made stitch (by knitting and purling into stitch before slipping it off needle), purl 6, repeat from * until 6 remain, knit 1, and purl 1 into the made stitch, purl 5. Knit 4 rows stocking-stitch. **11th row.**— * Knit 2 together, make 1, knit 2 together, knit 4, repeat from * until 4 remain, knit 2 together, make 1, knit 2 together. **12th row.**—Purl 1, * knit 1, and purl 1 into made stitch, purl 6, repeat from * until 2 remain, knit 1, and purl 1 into made stitch, purl 1. Repeat these 12 rows for length required.

Fig. 38. FEATHER STITCH

Fig. 39. FERN PATTERN

Fig. 40. LADDER STITCH

Fan Pattern.—(Fig. 36.) Cast on any number of stitches divisible by 12 with 2 over. **1st row.**—Knit 2, * make 1, knit 4, slip 1, knit 2 together, pass slipped stitch over, knit 4, make 1, knit 1, repeat from * to end. **2nd row.**—and all even-numbered rows—Knit 1, purl until 1 remains, knit 1. **3rd row.**—Knit 3, * make 1, knit 3, slip 1, knit 2 together, pass slipped stitch over, knit 3, make 1, knit 3, repeat from * until 11 remain, make 1, knit 3, slip 1, knit 2 together, pass slipped stitch over, knit 3, make 1, knit 2. **5th row.**—Knit 1, knit 2 together, * make 1, knit 1, make 1, knit 2, slip 1, knit 2 together, pass slipped stitch over, knit 2, make 1, knit 1, make 1, slip 1, knit 2 together, pass slipped stitch over, repeat from * until 11 remain, make 1, knit 1, make 1, knit 2, slip 1, knit 2 together, pass slipped stitch over, knit 2, make 1, knit 3. **7th row.**—Knit 1, * make 1, slip 1, knit 1, pass slipped stitch over, knit 2, make 1, knit 1, slip 1, knit 2 together, pass slipped stitch over, knit 1, make 1, knit 3, repeat from * until 1 remains, knit 1. **9th row.**—Knit 2, * make 1, slip 1, knit 2 together, pass slipped stitch over, make 1, knit 1, repeat from * to end. **10th row.**—As 2nd row. Repeat these 10 rows for length required

Feather Stitch.—(Fig. 38.) Cast on any number of stitches divisible by 12. Knit 1 row, purl 1 row. **1st row.**—Knit 2 together, knit 2 together, * make 1, knit 1 alternately 4 times, then knit 2 together, 4 times, repeat from * until 8 remain, then make 1, knit 1 alternately 4 times, knit 2 together, knit 2 together. **2nd row.**—Purl. **3rd row.**—Knit. **4th row.**—Purl. Repeat these 4 rows for length required

Fern Pattern.—(Fig. 39.) Cast on any number of stitches divisible by 22 with 10 over. **1st row.**—Knit 5, * make 1, knit 2 together, knit 2 together, knit 6, make 1, purl 2, make 1, knit 7, knit 2 together, knit 1, repeat from * until 5 remain, make 1, knit 2 together, knit 3. **2nd row.**—and all even numbered rows—

Knit 3, purl 2, * make 1, purl 2 together, purl 8, knit 2, purl 10, repeat from * until 5 remain, make 1, purl 2 together, knit 3. **3rd row.**—Knit 5, * make 1, knit 2 together, knit 2 together, knit 5, make 1, knit 1, purl 2, knit 1, make 1, knit 6, knit 2 together, knit 1, repeat from * until 5 remain, make 1, knit 2 together, knit 3. **5th row.**—Knit 5, * make 1, knit 2 together, knit 2 together, knit 4, make 1, knit 2, purl 2, knit 2, make 1, knit 5, knit 2 together, knit 1, repeat from * until 5 remain, make 1, knit 2 together, knit 3. **7th row.**—Knit 5, * make 1, knit 2 together, knit 2 together, knit 3, make 1, knit 3, purl 2, knit 3, make 1, knit 4, knit 2 together, knit 1, repeat from * until 5 remain, make 1, knit 2 together, knit 3. **9th row.**—Knit 5, * make 1, knit 2 together, knit 2 together, knit 2, make 1, knit 2, knit 2 together, make 1, purl 2, make 1, knit 2 together, knit 2, make 1, knit 3, knit 2 together, knit 1, repeat from * until 5 remain, make 1, knit 2 together, knit 3. **11th row.**—Knit 5, * make 1, knit 2 together, knit 2 together, knit 1, make 1, knit 3, knit 2 together, make 1, purl 2, make 1, knit 2 together, knit 3, make 1, knit 2, knit 2 together, knit 1, repeat from * until 5 remain, make 1, knit 2 together, knit 3. **13th row.**—Knit 5, * make 1, knit 2 together, knit 2 together, make 1, knit 4, knit 2 together, make 1, purl 2, make 1, knit 2 together, knit 4, make 1, knit 1, knit 2 together, knit 1, repeat from * until 5 remain, make 1, knit 2 together, knit 3. **15th row.**—Knit 5, * make 1, knit 3 together, make 1, knit 5, knit 2 together, make 1, purl 2, make 1, knit 2 together, knit 5, make 1, knit 2 together, knit 1, repeat from * until 5 remain, make 1, knit 2 together, knit 3. **16th row.**—As 2nd row. Repeat from 3rd row for length required.

Ladder Stitch.—(Fig. 40.) Cast on any number of stitches divisible by 20 with 17 over. **1st row.**—Knit 2 together, knit 6, * make 1, knit 1, make 1, knit 6, knit 2 together, make 1, knit 3 together, make 1, knit 2 together, knit 6, repeat from * until 10 remain, make 1, knit 3

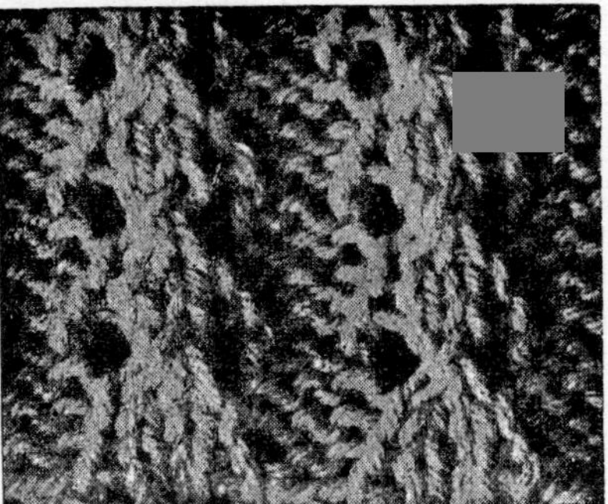

Fig. 41. LEMON PATTERN

Fig. 42. NORWEGIAN FIR PATTERN

Fig. 43. MOSS STITCH

Fig. 44 shows the right and wrong side of Ringwood stitch, and Fig. 45, Scallop stitch, Fig. 47, Zig-zag stitch, and Fig. 46, Ridged Feather stitch.

Figs. 44 and 44a

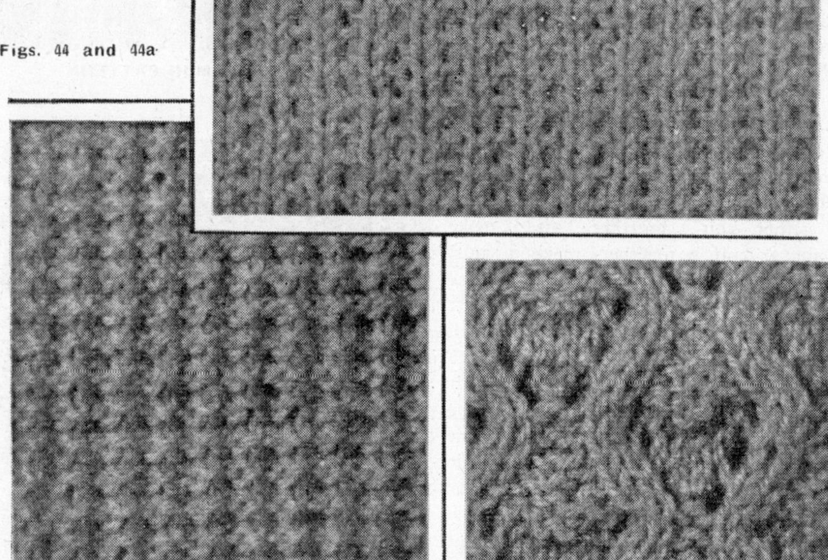

Fig. 45.

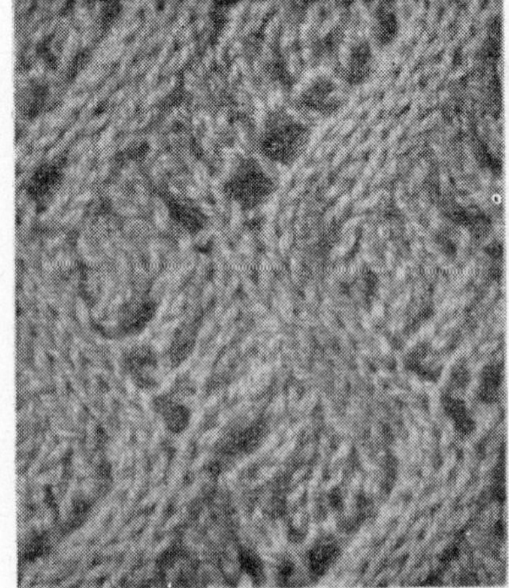

Fig. 47

Fig.46.

together, make 1, knit 6, knit 2 together **2nd row.**—Purl. Repeat these two rows for length required.

Lemon Pattern.—(Fig. 41.) Cast on any number of stitches divisible by 6, with 3 over. **1st row.**—Purl 3, then knit 3, purl 3, alternately to end. **2nd row.**—Knit 3, then purl 3, knit 3, alternately to end. Repeat these 2 rows once. ** **5th row.**—Purl 3, * make 1, knit 3 together, make 1, purl 3, repeat from * to end. Repeat 2nd, 1st and 2nd rows respectively once. Repeat from ** for length required.

Moss Stitch.—(Fig. 43.) Any number of stitches can be used for this pattern. Each row should always be begun with the same stitch as the previous row finished with, e.g. if an uneven number of stitches are cast on, work as follows: knit 1, then purl 1, knit 1, alternately to end of row. Repeat this row for length required. If an even number of stitches are cast on work thus: **1st row.**—Knit 1, purl 1, alternately to end. **2nd row.**—Purl 1, knit 1, alternately to end. Repeat these 2 rows for length required

Norwegian Fir Pattern.—(Fig. 42.) Cast on any number of stitches divisible by 12, with 2 over. **1st row.**—Slip 1, purl 3, * knit 3, make 1, knit 3, purl 6, repeat from * until 10 remain, knit 3, make 1, knit 3, purl 3, knit 1. **2nd row.**—Slip 1, knit 3, * purl 7, knit 6, repeat from * until 11 remain, purl 7, knit 4. **3rd row.**—Slip 1, purl 2, * knit 2 together, knit 2, make 1, knit 1, make 1, knit 2, slip 1, knit 1, pass the slipped stitch over, purl 4, repeat from * until 12 remain, knit 2 together, knit 2, make 1, knit 1, make 1, knit 2, slip 1, knit 1, pass slipped stitch over, purl 2, knit 1. **4th row.**—Slip 1, knit 2, * purl 9, knit 4, repeat from * until 12 remain, purl 9, knit 3. **5th row.**—Slip 1, purl 1, * knit 2 together, knit 2, make 1, knit 3, make 1, knit 2, slip 1, knit 1, pass slipped stitch over, purl 2, repeat from * until 13 remain, knit 2 together, knit 2, make 1, knit 3, make 1, knit 2, slip 1, knit 1, pass slipped stitch over, purl 1, knit 1. **6th row.**—Slip 1, knit 1, * purl 11, knit 2, repeat from * to end. **7th row.**—Slip 1, * knit 2 together, knit 2, make 1, knit 5, make 1, knit 2, slip 1, knit 1, pass slipped stitch over, repeat from * until 14 remain, knit 2 together, knit 2, make 1, knit 5, make 1, knit 2, slip 1, knit 1, pass slipped stitch over, knit 1. **8th row.**—Slip 1, purl until 1 remains, knit 1. **9th row.**—Slip 1, purl 3, * knit 3, make 1, knit 2, knit 2 together, purl 6, repeat from * until 11 remain, knit 3, make 1, knit 2, knit 2 together, purl 3, knit 1. Repeat from 2nd row for length required.

Ridged Feather Stitch.—(Fig. 46.) Cast on any number of stitches divisible by 12, with 4 over. Knit 1 row, purl 1 row. **1st row.**—Knit 2, * purl 2 together, purl 2 together, then make 1, knit 1, alternately 4 times, purl 2 together, purl 2 together, repeat from * until 2 remain, knit 2. **2nd row.**—Purl. **3rd row.**—Knit. **4th row.**—Purl. Repeat these 4 rows for length required.

Ringwood Stitch.—(Figs. 44 and 44a.) Cast on any number of stitches divisible by 2. **1st row.**—Knit. **2nd row.**—Knit 1, purl 1, alternately to end of row. Repeat these two rows for length required.

Scallop Stitch.—(Fig. 45.) Cast on any number of stitches divisible by 12, with 6 over. **1st row.**—Slip 1, knit 1, * knit 2, make 1, knit 1, make 1, knit 2, purl 7, repeat from * until 4 remain, knit 4. **2nd row.**—Slip 1, knit 1, purl 2, * knit 2, slip 1, knit 2 together, pass slipped stitch over, knit 2, purl 7, repeat from * until 2 remain, knit 2. **3rd row.**—Slip 1, knit 1, * knit 2, make 1, knit 3, make 1, knit 2, purl 5, repeat from * until 4 remain, knit 4. **4th row.**—Slip 1, knit 1, purl 2, * knit 1, slip 1, knit 2 together, pass slipped stitch over, knit 1, purl 9, repeat from * until 2 remain, knit 2. **5th row.**—Slip 1, knit 1, * knit 2, make 1, knit 5, make 1, knit 2, purl 3, repeat from * until 4 remain, knit 4. **6th row.**—Slip 1, knit 1, purl 2, * slip 1, knit 2 together, pass slipped stitch over, purl 11, repeat from * until 2 remain, knit 2. **7th row.**—

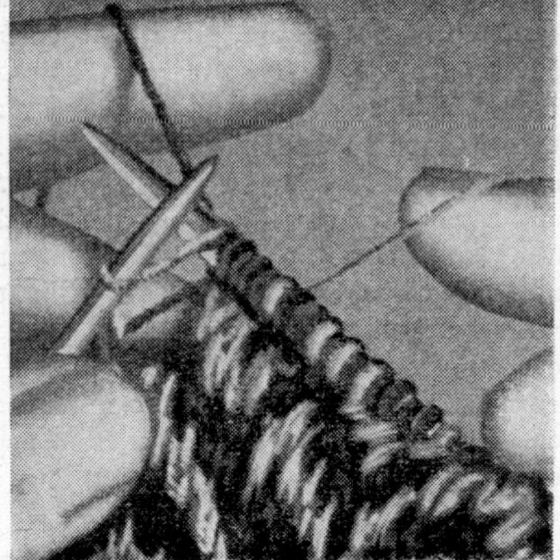

Fig. 48.

Fig. 49.

KNITTING WITH TWO COLOURS

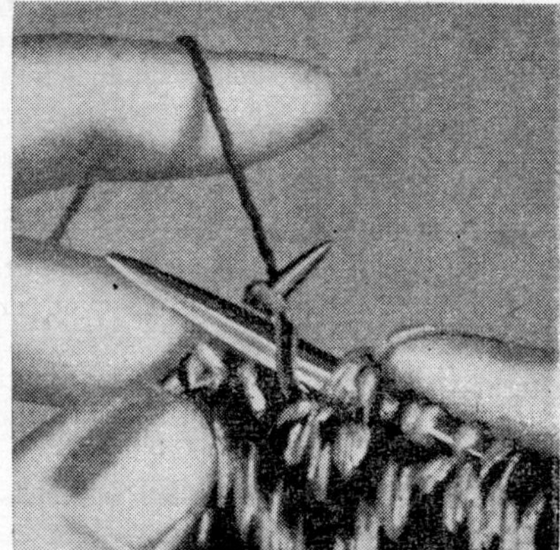

Fig. 50.

The top three figures show how the wool is held when knitting with two colours, and below, two-colour effects which are easy to work

Fig. 51.

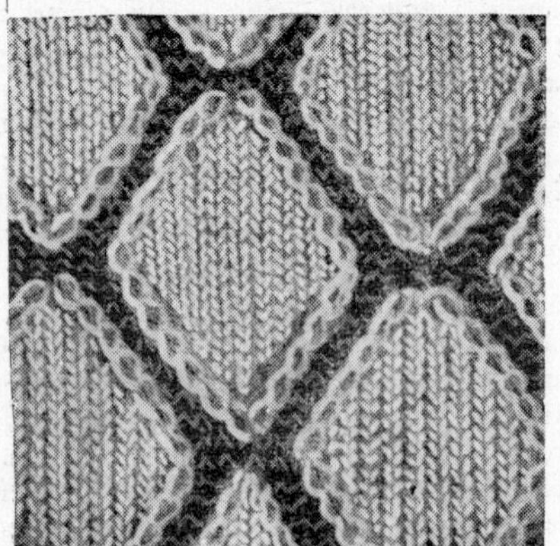

Fig. 52.

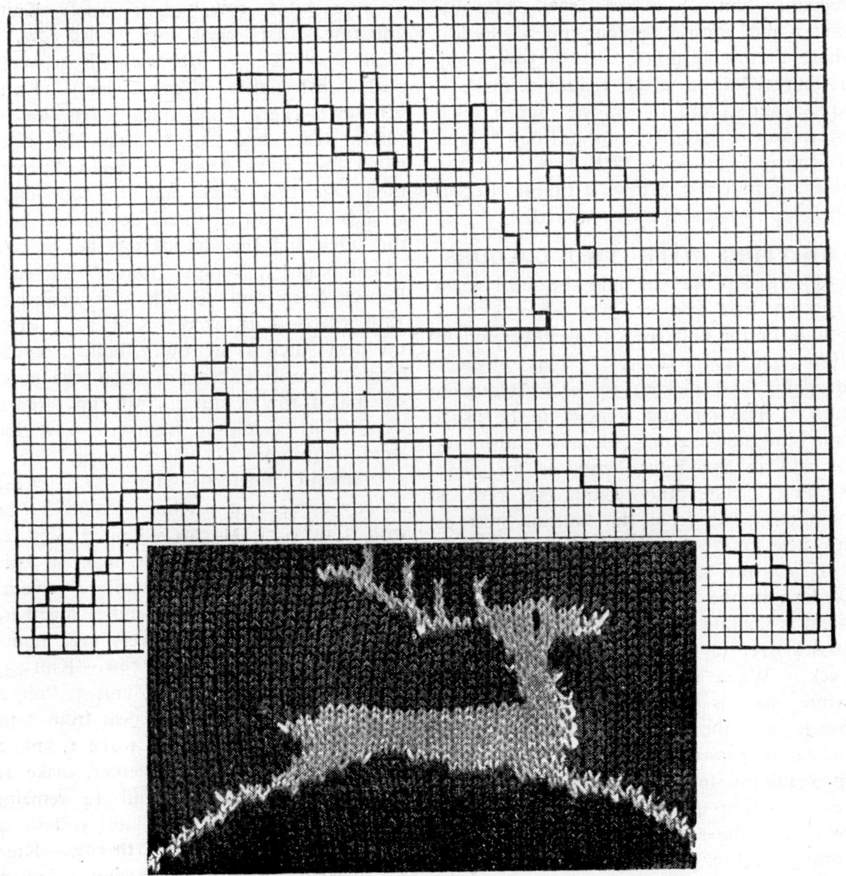

Several charming and effective motifs can be worked with the help of a chart made on graph paper. The small photograph shows the errors to be avoided in knitting these motifs: (a) straggly and uneven stitches and (b) distortion of shape by knitting too tightly.

Slip I, knit I, * knit 2, purl 7, knit 2, make I, knit I, make I, repeat from * until 4 remain, knit 4. **8th row.**—Slip I, knit I, * purl 7, knit 2, slip I, knit 2 together, pass slipped stitch over, knit 2, repeat from * until 4 remain, purl 2, knit 2. **9th row.**—Slip I, knit I, * knit 2, purl 5, knit 2, make I, knit 3, make I, repeat from * until 4 remain, knit 4. **10th row.**—Slip I, knit I, * purl 9, knit I, slip I, knit 2 together, pass slipped stitch over, knit I, repeat from * until 4 remain, purl 2, knit 2. **11th row.**—Slip I, knit I, * knit 2, purl 3, knit 2, make I, knit 5, make I, repeat from * until 4 remain, knit 4. **12th row.**—Slip I, knit I, * purl II, slip I, knit 2 together, pass slipped stitch over, repeat from * until 4 remain, purl 2, knit 2. Repeat from Ist row for length required.

Zig-zag Pattern.—(Fig. 47.) Cast on any number of stitches divisible by 9, plus 6. **1st row.**—Slip I, knit I, * knit 2, slip I, knit I, pass slipped stitch over, knit 2 together, knit 2, make I, knit I, make I, repeat from * until 4 remain, knit 4. **2nd row.**—Slip 1, knit 1, purl until 2 remain, knit 2. Repeat these 2 rows 4 times. **11th row.**—Slip 1, knit 1, knit 2, make 1, knit 1, make 1, knit 2, slip 1, knit 1, pass the slipped stitch over, knit 2 together, repeat from * until 4 remain, knit 4. **12th row.**—As 2nd row. Repeat last 2 rows 4 times. Repeat these 20 rows for length required.

KNITTING WITH TWO COLOURS

The easiest way to hold the wool when working Fair Isle or Jazz patterns in a round, or for knit rows is as illustrated in Figs. 48, 49 and 50. This obviates dropping and picking up each colour in turn. The knitting is held in the usual way and one colour (white for instance) is held in the right hand, as for plain knitting. The other colour (say red), is held out away from the knitting, just as it is held for crochet. (Fig 48.)

If a white stitch is to be worked, this is done in the usual way, and as the left hand is holding out the red wool the white passes over it and thus strands it at the back. When a red stitch is required, the white wool is still retained in the right hand, and the point of the right-hand needle is passed through the next stitch in readiness for knitting, then over the red wool (Fig. 49), and under it from right to left, at the same time pulling the wool through. (Fig. 50.)

This method does not weave the wools, but merely strands them. For weaving, work as follows: Hold the colour to be woven in the left hand as shown, then work as just described, but at every alternate stitch, or every second or third, if preferred, pass the point of the right-hand needle through the stitch, then under red wool, pass white wool over point of right-hand needle, then draw it through stitch allowing red wool to slip off. The colour to be woven must always be held in the left hand. When weaving a purl row, the wools are held in the same way, and one stitch is worked under and one over the wool.

Brick Pattern.—(Fig 52.) Cast on any number of stitches divisible by 4 with 3 over. **1st row.**—(dark wool) Knit. **2nd row.**—(dark wool) Purl. **3rd row.**—(light wool) Knit. **4th row.**—(light wool) purl. **5th row.**—(light wool) Knit. **6th row.**—(light wool) purl. **7th row.**—(dark wool) knit 3, * drop the next stitch four rows down, to the dark row; then take this stitch and the four light strands up on to left-hand needle and knit the stitch and the strands together as one stitch, knit 3, repeat from * to end. Repeat from 2nd to 6th row inclusive. **13th row.**—(dark wool) Knit 1, * drop the next stitch as in row 7, knit 3, repeat from * until 2 remain, drop the next stitch as in row 7, knit 1. **14th row.**—(dark wool) Purl. Repeat from 3rd row for length required.

Diamond Pattern.—(Fig. 51.) Cast on any number of stitches divisible by 14 with 3 over. **1st row.**—Knit 1, knit 2, together, * make 1, knit 11, make 1, knit 3 together, repeat from * until 14 remain, make 1, knit 11, make 1, knit 2 together, knit 1. **2nd row.**—and every even numbered row.—Purl. **3rd row.**—Knit 3, * make 1, knit 2 together, knit 7, knit 2 together, make 1, knit 3, repeat from * to end. **5th row.**—Knit 4, * make 1, knit 2 together, knit 5, knit 2 together, make 1, knit 5, repeat from * until 14 remain, make 1, knit 2 together, knit 5, knit 2 together, make 1, knit 4. **7th row.**—Knit 5, * make 1, knit 2 together, knit 3, knit 2 together, make 1, knit 7, repeat from * until 12 remain, make 1, knit 2 together, make 1, knit 3, knit 2 together, knit 5. **9th row.**—Knit 6, * make 1, knit 2 together, knit 1, knit 2 together, make 1, knit 9, repeat from * until 11 remain, make 1, knit 2 together, knit 1, knit 2 together, make 1, knit 6. **11th row.**—Knit 7, * make 1, knit 3 together, make 1, knit 11, repeat from * until 10 remain, make 1, knit 3 together, make 1, knit 7. **13th row.**—Knit 5, * knit 2 together, make 1, knit 3, make 1, knit 2 together, knit 7, repeat from * until 12 remain, knit 2 together, make 1, knit 3, make 1, knit 2 together, knit 5. **15th row.**—Knit 4, knit 2 together, * make 1, knit 5, make 1, knit 2 together, knit 5, knit 2

A FAIR ISLE PULL-OVER

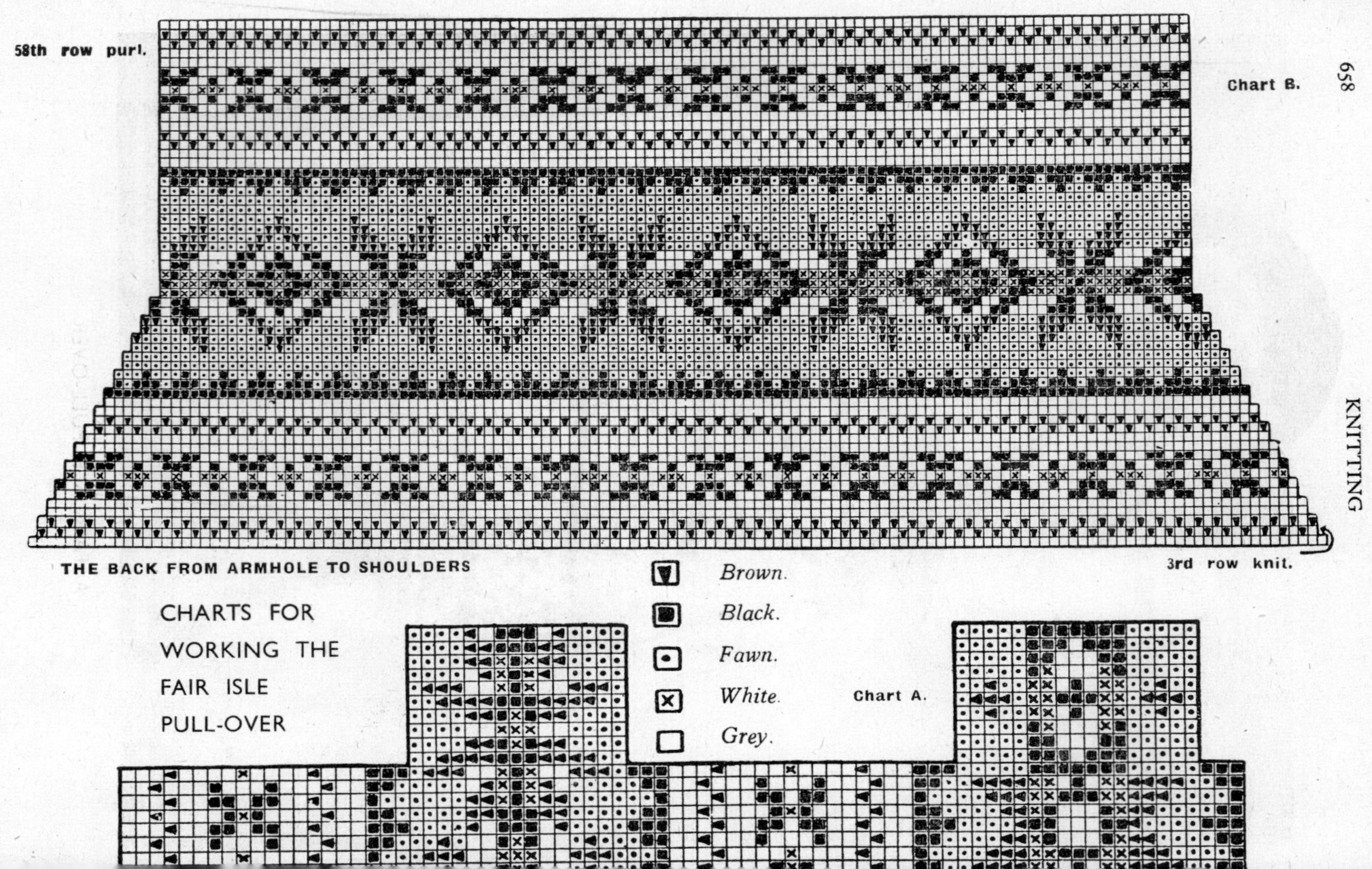
58th row purl.
Chart B.
3rd row knit.
THE BACK FROM ARMHOLE TO SHOULDERS
Brown.
Black.
Fawn.
White.
Grey.
Chart A.
CHARTS FOR WORKING THE FAIR ISLE PULL-OVER

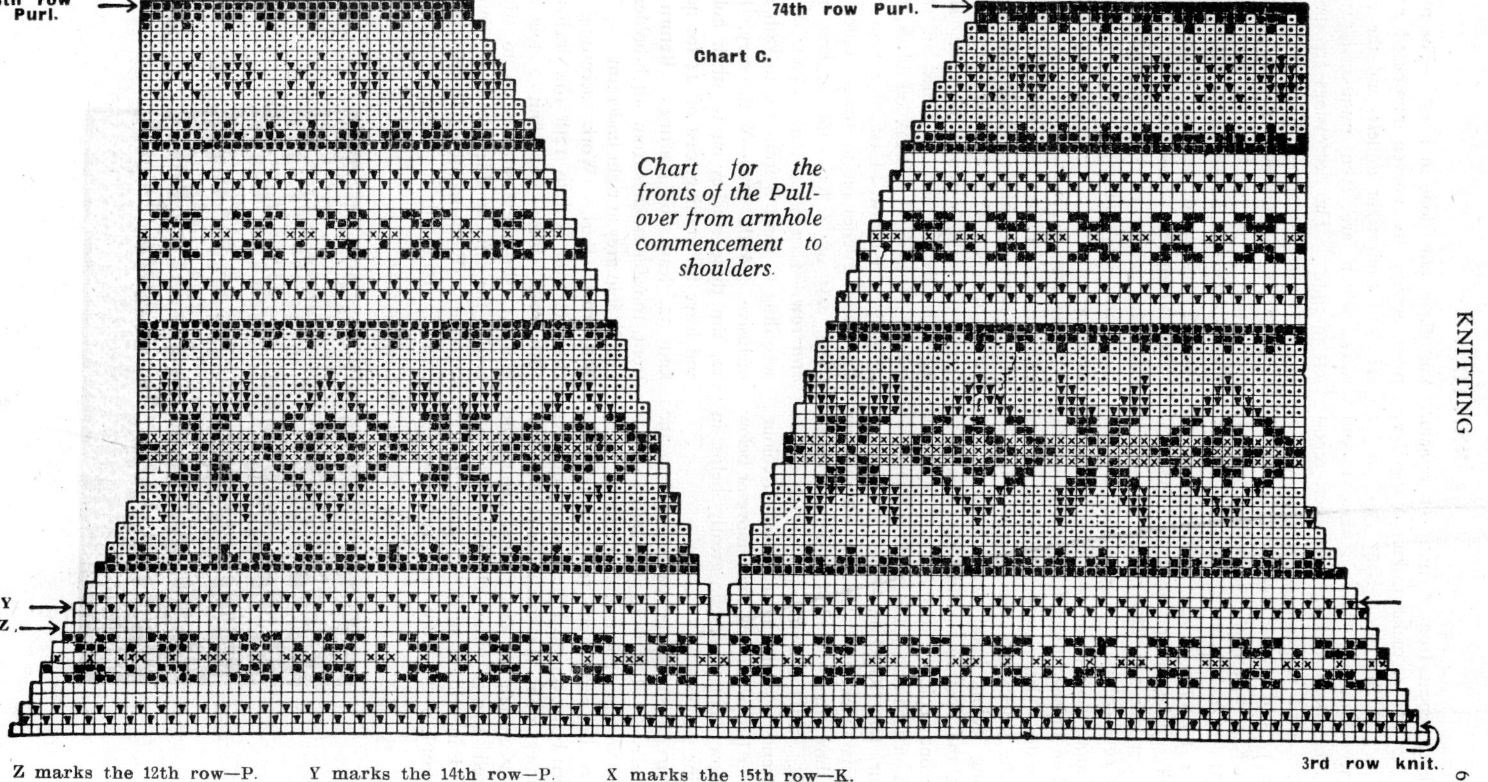

Chart C.

Chart for the fronts of the Pull-over from armhole commencement to shoulders.

Z marks the 12th row—P. Y marks the 14th row—P. X marks the 15th row—K.

together, repeat from * until 11 remain, make 1, knit 5, make 1, knit 2 together, knit 4. **17th row.**—Knit 3, knit 2 together, * make 1, knit 7, make 1, knit 2 together, knit 3, knit 2 together, repeat from * until 12 remain, make 1, knit 7, make 1, knit 2 together, knit 3. **19th row.**—Knit 2, knit 2 together, * make 1, knit 9, make 1, knit 2 together, knit 1, knit 2 together, repeat from * until 13 remain, make 1, knit 9, make 1, knit 2 together, knit 2. **21st row.**—As 1st row. **22nd row.**—Purl. Repeat from 1st row for length required.

When finished press the work on wrong side under a damp cloth with a warm iron. For the embroidery use thread of a contrasting colour, and work chain stitch along the openwork diamonds, then with a second colour work a row of chain stitch on each side of the first row.

Fair Isle Knitting.—On the previous pages is an example of a Fair Isle pullover that shows the method of working from the charts. In the charts given, each square represents a stitch, and each sign a colour. A ruler laid across the chart above or below the row being worked, greatly helps in keeping the place.

Chart A shows the patterns up to the armholes. The work is done in rounds as far as this point and the chart must always be read from right to left, the pattern being repeated the required number of times to fit the stitches in the round. The beginning of each round should be marked by a piece of coloured wool knitted in with a stitch. Charts B and C complete the front and back and the knitting is now done in rows. The plain rows, which are uneven numbered rows are read from right to left, and the purl rows, which are even numbered, from left to right. The decreasings are shown by the steps at the edge of the chart.

Materials Required.—4 oz. 3-ply grey wool, 2 oz. each fawn and black, 1 oz. each white and brown. 4 No. 9 pins pointed at each end. 2 stitch holders.

Measurements.—Shoulder to lower edge, 24 inches; round chest, 38 inches; underarm, 14½ inches; across shoulder, 4½ inches.

Using grey, begin at lower edge, casting 288 stitches on to three needles (96, 96 96). Knit in ribbing of knit 1, purl 1, for 23 rounds. Work according to chart A from 24th to 101st round inclusive. Here work is divided and continued in rows instead of rounds. Break off black, join on grey. **1st row.**—Cast off 4, knit 136, slip these stitches on to stitch holder for front, cast off 8 for armhole, knit 140. **2nd row.**—Cast off 4, purl to end. Work according to chart B from 3rd to 58th row inclusive. **59th row.**—With grey, knit 32, slip these stitches on to stitch holder and leave for grafting, cast off 44 for neck, knit 32, leave for grafting. Return to front, transfer stitches from stitch-holder to needle, join grey at right underarm. **2nd row.**—Purl. Work according to chart C from 3rd to 12th row inclusive. **13th row.**—With grey, knit 2 together, knit 61, slip these stitches on to stitch-holder for left shoulder, knit 61, knit 2 together. Work according to left side of chart C from 14th to 74th row inclusive.

Fig. 55 SQUARE INSERTION

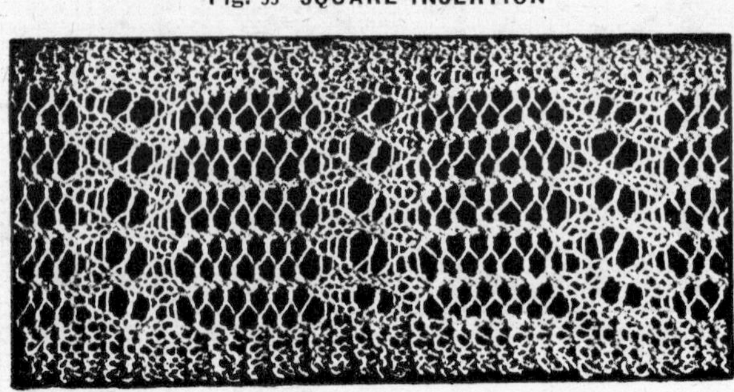

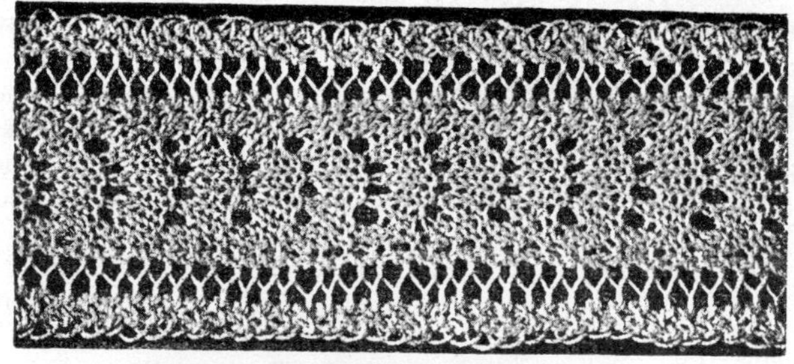

Fig. 56.

SHELL INSERTION AND ELAINE EDGING

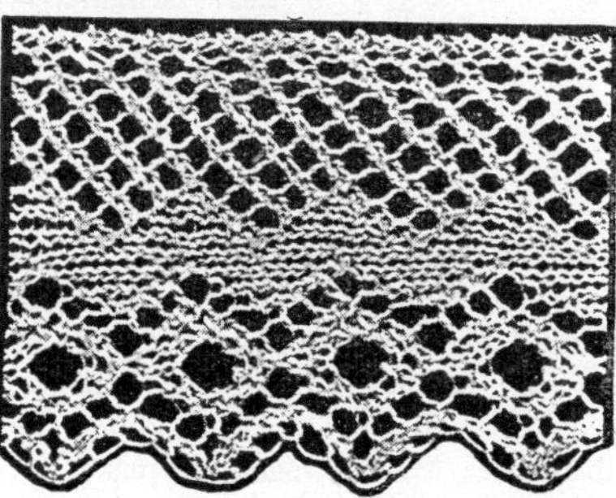

Fig. 57.

Leave stitches for grafting. Return to left shoulder, transfer stitches from stitch-holder to needle, join on grey and brown at centre front.

14th row.—Purl 2 together brown, then purl 1 grey, 1 brown alternately to end. Work according to right side of chart C from 15th to 74th row inclusive. Graft shoulders together.

The Neckband.—Using grey wool, cast on 50 stitches. Knit in ribbing of knit 1, purl 1, for 10 rows. **11th row.**—Knit 1, purl 1, alternately 6 times, slip these stitches on to a piece of wool, cast off 26, knit 1, purl 1, alternately for 6 times. * Knit in ribbing of knit 1, purl 1, for 8 inches, ending last row at inside of neck. **Next row.**—Knit 2 together, knit in rib to end. **Next row.**—Knit in rib until 2 remain, knit 2 together. Repeat last 2 rows until all stitches are worked off.* Return to the 12 stitches on wool, and transfer to needle, join wool at neck edge. Repeat from * to *.

The Armhole Bands.—(both alike). Using grey wool and 3 needles, pick up and knit 170 stitches, round armhole. Divide stitches thus: 56, 58, 56 Knit in ribbing of knit 1, purl 1, for 7 rounds. Cast off. Pin out to measurements given and press well on wrong side under a damp cloth with a hot iron. Sew in neckband, and join shaped ends together to form V.

KNITTED LACES AND INSERTIONS

Regularity in working is the greatest necessity in making lace. Good quality crochet cotton and fine steel needles are used.

Square Insertion.—(Fig. 55.) This is worked with No. 20 cotton and needles, No. 18. Cast on 17 stitches. **1st row.**—Slip 1, knit 3, then make 1 and knit 2 together 5 times, knit 3. **2nd row.**—Slip 1, knit 3, purl 10, knit 3. **3rd row.**—Slip 1, knit 16. **4th row.**—Slip 1, knit 3, purl 10, knit 3. **5th row.**—Slip 1, knit 16. Next **13 rows.**—Slip 1, knit 3, then make 1, and knit 2 together for 5 times, knit 3. **19th row.**—Slip 1, knit 16. **20th row.**—Slip 1, knit 3, purl 10, knit 3. Repeat the last 2 rows once. **23rd row.**—Slip 1, knit 3, then make 1 and knit 2 together 5 times, knit 3. **24th row.**—Slip 1, knit 3, purl 10, knit 3.

Repeat from 1st row for the length required.

Fig. 58.—A USEFUL NARROW LACE INSERTION

Shell Insertion.—(Fig. 56.) No. 20 crochet cotton and No. 18 or 19 needles are needed.

Cast on 19 stitches: here make 1, knit 2 together, knit 4, purl 7, knit 6. **1st pattern row.**—Make 1, knit 2 together, knit 1, make 1, knit 2 together, knit 2 together, knit 5, slip 1, knit 1, pass slipped stitch over, knit 1, make 1, knit 2 together, knit 2. (17 stitches now on needle.) **2nd row.**—A raised ridge is formed on right side of the work in this row. Make 1, knit 2 together, knit 1, make 1, knit 2 together, knit 8, make 1, knit 2 together, knit 2. **3rd row.**—"Holes" forming the shell. Make 1, knit 2 together, knit 1, make 1, knit 2 together, knit 2, make 1, and knit 1 alternately 3 times, make 1, knit 3, make 1, knit 2 together, knit 2. (21 stitches.) **4th row.**—Make 1, knit 2 together, knit 1, make 1, knit 2 together, knit 1, purl 9, knit 2, make 1, knit 2 together, knit 2. **5th row.**—Make 1, knit 2 together, knit 1, make 1, knit 2 together, knit 2 together, knit 7, slip 1, knit 1, pass slipped stitch over, knit 1, make 1, knit 2 together, knit 2. (19 stitches.) **6th row.**—Make 1, knit 2 together, knit 1, make 1, knit 2 together, knit 1, purl 7, knit 2, make 1, knit 2 together, knit 2. Repeat from the 1st pattern row for length required.

Leaf Edging.—(Fig. 60.) Cast on 9 stitches and work 1 plain row. **2nd row.**—Knit 4, make 1, knit 2 together, make 1, knit 2 together, make 1, knit 1. **3rd and every alternate row.**—Plain. **4th row.**—Knit 5, make 1, knit 2 together, make 1, knit 2 together, make 1, knit 1. **6th row.**—Knit 6, make 1, knit 2 together, make 1, knit 2 together, make 1, knit 1. **8th row.**—Knit 7, make 1, knit 2 together, make 1, knit 2 together, make 1, knit 1. **10th row.**—Knit 8, make 1, knit 2 together, make 1, knit 2 together, make 1, knit 1. **12th row.**—Knit 9, make 1, knit 2 together, make 1, knit 2 together, make 1, knit 1. **13th row.**—Cast off 6, knit 8, leaving 9 stitches on needle. Repeat from 2nd row for length required.

Elaine Edging.—(Fig. 57.) Materials: Crochet Cotton, No. 70, and steel knitting

Fig. 59.

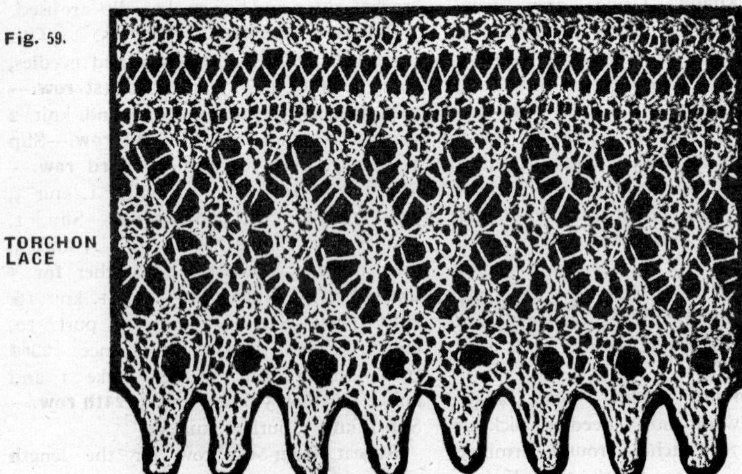

TORCHON LACE

pins, No. 18, will make the edging about $1\frac{1}{2}$ inches wide.

Cast on 20 stitches—**1st row.**—Slip 1, knit 1, then make 1, knit 2 together, alternately 4 times, purl 3, knit 2 together, make 1, knit 3, make 1, knit 2. **2nd row.**—Make 1, knit 2 together, knit 19. **3rd row.**—Slip 1, knit 2, then make 1, knit 2 together, alternately 3 times, purl 3, knit 2 together, make 1, knit 5, make 1, knit 2. **4th row.**—Make 1, knit 2 together, knit 20. **5th row.**—Slip 1, knit 1, then make 1, knit 2 together, alternately 3 times, purl 3, knit 2 together, make 1, knit 2 together, knit 2 together, make 3, knit 2 together, knit 1, make 1, knit 2. **6th row.**—Make 1, knit 2 together, knit 4, purl 1, knit 16. **7th row.**—Slip 1, knit 2, then make 1, knit 2 together, alternately 3 times, purl 3, knit 1, make 1, knit 2 together, knit 3, knit 2 together, make 1, knit 2 together, knit 1. **8th row.**—As 4th row. **9th row.**—Slip 1, knit 1, then make 1, knit 2 together, alternately 4 times, purl 3, knit 1, make 1, knit 2 together, knit 1, knit 2 together, make 1, knit 2 together, knit 1. **10th row.**—As 2nd row. **11th row.**—Slip 1, knit 2, then make 1, knit 2 together, alternately 4 times, purl 3, knit 1, make 1, slip 1, knit 2 together, pass slipped stitch over, make 1, knit 2 together, knit 1 **12th row.**—Make 1, knit 2 together, knit 18. Repeat from 1st row for length required. Press edging under a damp cloth with a hot iron.

LEAF EDGING

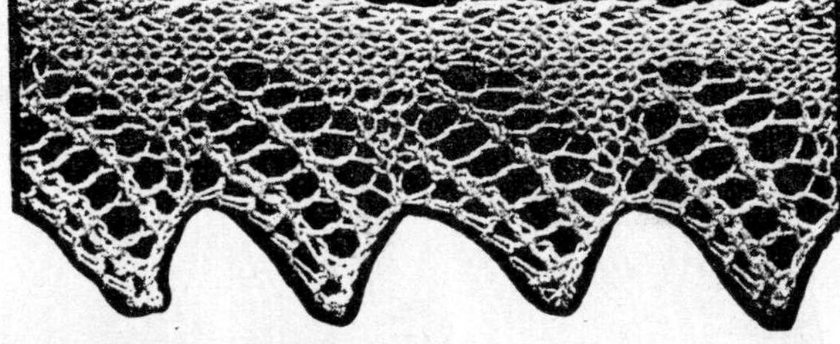

Fig. 60.

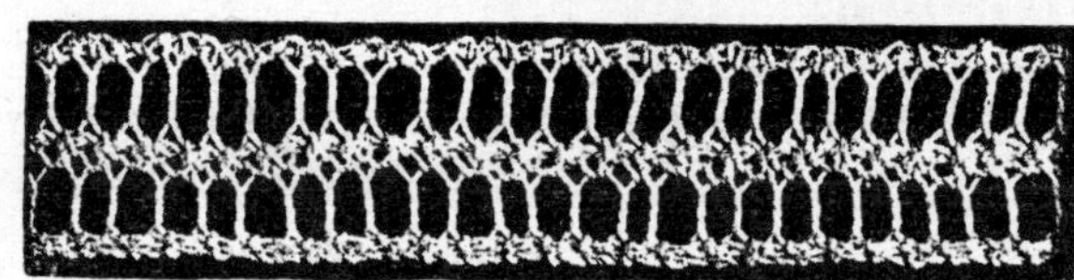

Fig. 61.

DOUBLE BEADING

Useful Narrow Insertion.—For the lace in Fig. 58 cast on 9 stitches and knit one row plain. **1st pattern row.**—Slip 1, knit 2, make 1, knit 2 together, knit 1, make 2, knit 1, make 2, knit 2. **2nd row.**—Cast off 2 stitches, purl 3, knit 1, purl 1, knit 2, make 1, knit 2 together, knit 1. **3rd row.**—Slip 1, knit 2, make 1, knit 2 together, knit 1, knit 2 together, make 2, knit 1, make 2, knit 2 together. **4th row.**—Slip 1, knit 1, purl 3, knit 1, purl 3, knit 1, purl 2, knit 2, make 1, knit 2 together, knit 1. **5th row.**—Slip 1, knit 2, make 1, knit 2 together, knit 1, knit 2 together, knit 3, knit 2 together. **6th row.**—Cast off 2 stitches, purl 3, knit 2, make 1, knit 2 together, knit 1. Repeat from the beginning of the 1st pattern row for length required.

Torchon Lace.—(Fig. 59.) Cast on 20 stitches. **1st row.**—Slip 1, knit 2, make 1, knit 2 together, knit 2, make 1, knit 2 together, knit 5, knit 2 together, make 1, knit 3, knit 2 in last stitch. **2nd row.**—Knit 6, make 1, slip 1, knit 1, pass slipped stitch over, knit 3, knit 2 together, make 1, knit 4, make 1, knit 2 together, knit 2 **3rd row.**—Slip 1, knit 2, make 1, knit 2 together, knit 4,

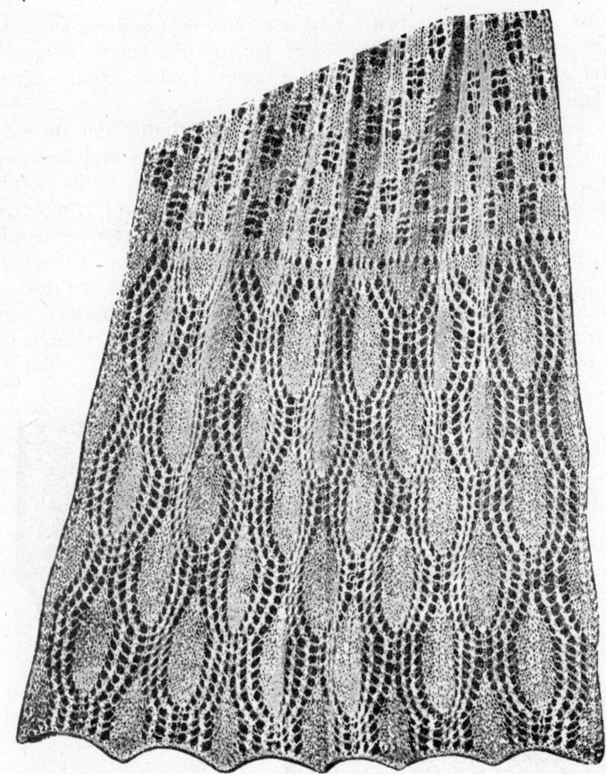

Fig. 62.

A COSY SCARF

from the first row for the length required.

Double Beading.—(Fig. 61.) Cast on 8 stitches. **1st row.**—Knit 2 together, make 2, knit 2 together, knit 1, make 2, knit 2 together, knit 1. **2nd row.**—Slip 1, knit 2, purl 1, knit 2 together, knit 1, purl 1, knit 1. Repeat from 1st row for length required.

make 1, slip 1, knit 1, pass slipped stitch over, knit 1, knit 2 together, make 1, knit 6, knit 2 into last stitch. **4th row.**—Knit 9, make 1, slip 1, knit 2 together, pass slipped stitch over, make 1, knit 6, make 1, knit 2 together, knit 2. **5th row.**—Slip 1, knit 2, make 1, knit 2 together, knit 4, knit 2 together, make 1, knit 1, make 1, knit 2 together, knit 4, make 2, knit 3, knit 2 into last stitch. **6th row.**—Knit 6, purl 1, knit 3, knit 2 together, make 1, knit 3, make 1, slip 1, knit 1, pass slipped stitch over, knit 4, make 1, knit 2 together, knit 2. **7th row.**—Slip 1, knit 2, make 1, knit 2 together, knit 2, knit 2 together, make 1, knit 5, make 1, slip 1, knit 1, pass slipped stitch over, knit 9. **8th row.**—Cast off 5, knit 2, knit 2 together, make 1, knit 7, make 1, slip 1, knit 1, pass slipped stitch over, knit 2, make 1, knit 2 together, knit 2. (20 stitches on the needle.) Repeat

A COSY SCARF

Materials required.—4 oz. Fine Shetland wool. Knitting needles No. 8.

Cast on 118 stitches. **1st row.**—Knit. **2nd row.**—Knit 2, purl until 2 remain, knit 2. **3rd row.**—Knit 2, * slip 1, knit 1, pass slipped stitch over, knit 3, make 1, slip 1, knit 1, pass slipped stitch over, make 1, slip 1, knit 1, pass slipped stitch over, make 1, knit 1, make 1, knit 2 together, make 1, knit 2 together, make 1, knit 3, knit 2 together, repeat from * 5 times, knit 2. **4th row.**—As 2nd row. Repeat last 2 rows 3 times. **11th row.**—Knit 2, * slip 1, knit 1, pass slipped stitch over, knit 2, make 1, knit 2 together, make 1, knit 2 together, make 1, knit 3, make 1, slip 1, knit 1, pass slipped stitch over, make 1, slip 1, knit 1, pass slipped stitch over, make 1, knit 2, knit 2 together, repeat from * 5 times, knit 2. **12th row.**—

As 2nd row. **13th row.**—Knit 2, * slip 1, knit 1, pass slipped stitch over, knit 1, make 1, knit 2 together, make 1, knit 2 together, make 1, knit 5, make 1, slip 1, knit 1, pass slipped stitch over, make 1, slip 1, knit 1, pass slipped stitch over, make 1, knit 1, knit 2 together, repeat from * 5 times, knit 2. **14th row.**—As 2nd row. **15th row.**—Knit 2, * slip 1, knit 1, pass slipped stitch over, make 1, knit 2 together, make 1, knit 2 together, make 1, knit 7, make 1, slip 1, knit 1, pass slipped stitch over, make 1, slip 1, knit 1, pass slipped stitch over, make 1, knit 2 together, repeat from * 5 times, knit 2. **16th row.**—As 2nd row. **17th row.**—Knit 3, * make 1, knit 2 together, make 1, knit 2 together, make 1, knit 3, knit 2 together, knit 4, make 1, slip 1, knit 1, pass slipped stitch over, make 1, slip 1, knit 1, pass slipped stitch over, make 1 **, slip 1, knit 1, pass slipped stitch over, repeat from * 4 times, then from * to **, knit 3. **18th row.**—As 2nd row. **19th row.**—Knit 3, * make 1, knit 2 together, make 1, knit 2 together, make 1, knit 3, knit 2 together, slip 1, knit 1, pass slipped stitch over, knit 3, make 1, slip 1, knit 1, pass slipped stitch over, make 1, slip 1, knit 1, pass slipped stitch over, make 1, knit 1, repeat from * 5 times, knit 2. **20th row.**—As 2nd row. Repeat last 2 rows 3 times. **27th row.**—Knit 4, * make 1, slip 1, knit 1, pass slipped stitch over, make 1, slip 1, knit 1, pass slipped stitch over, make 1, knit 2, knit 2 together, slip 1, knit 1, pass slipped stitch over, knit 2, make 1, knit 2 together, make 1, knit 2 together, make 1, knit 3, repeat from * 5 times, knit 1. **28th row.**—As 2nd row. **29th row.**—Knit 5, * make 1, slip 1, knit 1, pass slipped stitch over, make 1, slip 1, knit 1, pass slipped stitch over, make 1, knit 1, knit 2 together, slip 1, knit 1, pass slipped stitch over, knit 1. make 1, knit 2 together, make 1, knit 2 together, make 1, knit 5, repeat from * to end. **30th row.**—As 2nd row. **31st row.**—Knit 6, * make 1, slip 1, knit 1, pass slipped stitch over, make 1, slip 1, knit 1, pass slipped stitch over, make 1, knit 2 together, slip 1, knit 1, pass slipped stitch over, make 1, knit 2 together, make 1, knit 2 together, make 1 **, knit 7, repeat from * 4 times, then from * to **, knit 6. **32nd row.**—As 2nd row. **33rd row.**—Knit 2, slip 1, knit 1, pass slipped stitch over, knit 3, * make 1, slip 1, knit 1, pass slipped stitch over, make 1, slip 1, knit 1, pass slipped stitch over, make 1, slip 1, knit 1, pass slipped stitch over, make 1, knit 2 together, make 1, knit 2 together, make 1, knit 3, knit 2 together **, knit 4, repeat from * 4 times, then from * to **, knit 2. **34th row.**—As 2nd row. Repeat from 3rd to 34th row inclusive twice. **99th row.**—Knit. **100th row.**—As 2nd row. **101st row.**—Knit 2, then make 1, knit 2 together, alternately 57 times, knit 2. **102nd row.**—As 2nd row. **103rd row.**—Knit 12, * knit 2 together, knit 21, repeat from * 3 times, knit 2 together, knit 12 (113 stitches). **104th row.**—As 2nd row. *****105th row.**—Knit 6, knit 2 together, * make 1, knit 1, make 1, slip 1, knit 1, pass slipped stitch over, knit 3, knit 2 together, repeat from * until 9 remain, make 1, knit 1, make 1, slip 1, knit 1, pass slipped stitch over, knit 6. **106th row.**—Knit 2, purl 4, * knit 5, purl 3, repeat from * until 3 remain, purl 1, knit 2. Repeat last two rows three times. **113th row.**—Knit 2, knit 2 together, * make 1, knit 1, make 1, slip 1, knit 1, pass slipped stitch over, knit 3, knit 2 together, repeat from * until 5 remain, make 1, knit 1, make 1, slip 1, knit 1, pass slipped stitch over, knit 2. **114th row.**—Knit 7, * purl 3, knit 5, repeat from * until 2 remain, knit 2. Repeat last 2 rows 3 times ***. Repeat from *** to *** 21 times. Repeat from 105th to 114th row inclusive, then repeat 113th and 114th rows twice. **471st row.**—As 113th row. Leave these stitches for grafting. For the border on the other end, work as directed until 103rd row is completed. Graft stitches together. (For grafting, see Fig. 29.) Pin out and press well on wrong side under a damp cloth with a hot iron.

EIGHT-POINTED STAR D'OYLEY

Materials required: No. 16 crochet

cotton and five No. 16 steel knitting needles.

Begin in centre of the d'oyley with 2 stitches on each of four needles. Knit two rounds plain. **1st pattern round.**—Make 1, knit 1, make 1, knit 1 and repeat to end of round. **2nd and every alternate round.**—Plain. **3rd round.**—Make 1, knit 2 and repeat to end of round. **5th round.**—Make 1, knit 3 and repeat. **7th round.**—Make 1, knit 4 and repeat. **9th round.**—Make 1, knit 5 and repeat **11th round.**—Make 1, knit 6 and repeat. **13th round.**—Make 1, knit 7 and repeat. **15th round.**—Make 1 and knit 8 and repeat. There are now 18 stitches on each of four needles, making 72 stitches in the round. **17th round.**—Make 1, knit 1, make 1, knit 2 together, knit 6 and repeat to the end of round. **19th round.**—Make 1, knit 3, make 1, knit 2 together, knit 5 and repeat. **21st round.**—Make 1, knit 5, make 1, knit 2 together, knit 4 and repeat. **23rd round.**

D'Oyley. Eight-Pointed Star.

—Make 1, knit 7, make 1, knit 2 together, knit 3 and repeat. **25th round.**—Make 1, knit 9, make 1, knit 2 together, knit 2 and repeat. **27th round.**—Make 1, knit 11, make 1, knit 2 together, knit 1 and to the end of round. **33rd round.**—Make 1, knit 1, purl 1, knit 1, make 1, knit 2 together, knit 12 and repeat. This row begins the moss-stitch knitting which comes between each point of the star.

D'Oyley, in Dahlia Pattern.

repeat. **29th round.**—Make 1, knit 13, make 1, knit 2 together and repeat. The end of the first division of the star is now reached. There should be 32 stitches on each needle, making 128 stitches in the round. **31st round.**—Make 1, knit 1, make 1, knit 2 together, knit 13 and repeat

34th round.—Instead of knitting plain, introduce moss-stitch over the moss-stitch of the previous row and thus: knit 1, purl 1, knit 1, purl 1, knit 14 and repeat. **35th round.**—Make 1, knit 2, purl 1, knit 2, make 1, knit 2 together knit 11 and repeat. **36th round.**—Knit 2, purl 1, knit 1, purl 1, knit 14, and repeat. **37th round.**—Make 1, knit 1, purl 1 and knit 1 alternately 3 times, make 1, knit 2 together, knit 10 and repeat. **38th round.**—Knit 1 and purl 1 alternately 4 times, knit 12 and repeat. **39th round.**—Make 1, knit 2, purl 1, knit 1, purl 1, knit 1, purl 1, knit 2, make 1, knit 2 together, knit 9 and repeat.

40th round.—Knit 2, purl 1 and knit 1 alternately 3 times, purl 1, knit 12 and repeat. **41st round.**—Make 1, knit 1, purl 1 and knit 1 alternately 5 times, make 1, knit 2 together, knit 8 and repeat. **42nd round.**—Knit 1, purl 1 alternately 6 times, knit 10 and repeat. **43rd round.**—Make 1, knit 2, purl 1 and knit 1 alternately 4 times, purl 1, knit 2, make 1, knit 2 together, knit 7 and repeat. **44th round.**—Knit 2, purl 1 and knit 1 alternately 5 times, purl 1, knit 10 and repeat. **45th round.**—Make 1, knit 1, purl 1 and knit 1 alternately 7 times, make 1, knit 2 together, knit 6 and repeat. **46th round.**—Knit 1 and purl 1 alternately 8 times, knit 8 and repeat. **47th round.**—Make 1, knit 2, purl 1 and knit 1 alternately 6 times, purl 1, knit 2, make 1, knit 2 together, knit 5 and repeat. **48th round.**—Knit 2, purl 1 and knit 1 alternately 7 times, purl 1, knit 8 and repeat. **49th round.**—Make 1, knit 1, purl 1 and knit 1 alternately 9 times, make 1, knit 2 together, knit 4 and repeat. **50th round.**—Knit 1 and purl 1 alternately 10 times, knit 6 and repeat. **51st round.**—Make 1, knit 2, purl 1 and knit 1 alternately 8 times, purl 1, knit 2, make 1, knit 2 together, knit 3 and repeat. **52nd round.**—Knit 2, purl 1 and knit 1 alternately 9 times, purl 1, knit 6 and repeat. **53rd round.**—Make 1, knit 1, purl 1 and knit 1 alternately 11 times, make 1, knit 2 together, knit 2 and repeat. **54th round.**—Knit 1 and purl 1 alternately 12 times, knit 4 and repeat. **55th round.**—Make 1, knit 2, purl 1 and knit 1 alternately 10 times, purl 1, knit 2, make 1, knit 2 together, knit 1 and repeat. **56th round.**—Knit 2, purl 1 and knit 1 alternately 11 times, purl 1, knit 4 and repeat. **57th round.**—Make 1, knit 1, purl 1 and knit 1 alternately 13 times, make 1, knit 2 together and repeat. **58th round.**—Knit 1 and purl 1 alternately 14 times, knit 2 and repeat until 1 stitch remains on the fourth needle. Transfer this stitch to the beginning of the first needle, and then to make the number of stitches on each needle equal (60) transfer a stitch from the end of each of the other needles on to the adjacent needle in the same way. **59th round.**—Make 1, knit 2 together, knit 1 and purl 1 alternately 13 times, knit 2 and repeat. **60th round.**—Plain, with 60 stitches on each of four pins, making 240 stitches in the round. **61st round.**—Knit 1 in the front and 1 in the back of the first stitch, knit 29, and repeat. This will increase 2 stitches on each needle. **Next 3 rounds.**—Purl. This forms the raised ridge. **65th round.**—Plain, increasing 2 stitches on each needle. **66th round.**—Make 1, knit 2 together and repeat to end of round. **67th round.**—Plain. There should now be 64 stitches on each needle. **Next 3 rounds.**—Purl. Cast-off loosely.

For the **Border.**—Using the same cotton and No. 17 steel needles, cast on 14 stitches. **1st row.**—Slip 1, knit 2, make 1, knit 2 together, knit 1, make 2, knit 2 together, make 2, knit 2 together, make 2, knit 2 together, make 2, knit 2 together. **2nd row.**—Knit 2, purl 1, knit 2, purl 1, knit 2, purl 1, knit 2, purl 1, knit 3, make 1, knit 2 together, knit 1. **3rd row.**—Slip 1, knit 2, make 1, knit 2 together, knit 13. **4th row.**—Knit 15, make 1, knit 2 together, knit 1. **5th row.**—Slip 1, knit 2, make 1, knit 2 together, knit 13. **6th row.**—Cast off 4, knit 11, make 1, knit 2 together, knit 1. Repeat these 6 rows until the border is long enough to go right round the d'oyley. Cast off and sew on to d'oyley.

DAHLIA D'OYLEY

Materials required: No. 16 crochet cotton, and four No. 16 steel needles. Begin in the centre of the d'oyley by casting on 6 stitches, 2 on each of three needles and knit 1 plain round.

1st pattern round.—Make 1, knit 1, make 1, knit 1, repeat to end of round. **2nd and every alternate round.**—Plain.

3rd round.—Make 1, knit 1, make 1, knit 1 and repeat to end of round. There will now be 8 stitches on each needle. **5th round.**—Make 1, knit 3, make 1, knit 1 and repeat to the end of round. **7th round.**—Make 1, knit 5, make 1, knit 1 and repeat. **9th round.**—Make 1, knit 7, make 1, knit 1 and repeat. **11th round.**—Make 1, knit 9, make 1, knit 1 and repeat. **13th round.**—Make 1, knit 11, make 1, knit 1 and repeat. There should now be 28 stitches on each needle, 84 in all. **15th round.**—Make 1, knit 1, make 1, knit 1, make 1, knit 2, knit 2 together, slip 1, knit 1, pass the slipped stitch over, knit 1, knit 2 together, make 1, knit 1, make 1, knit 1, make 1, knit 1, and repeat. **17th round.**—Make 1, knit 2, make 1, knit 3, make 1, knit 3 together, slip 1, knit 2 together, pass the slipped stitch over, make 1, knit 3, make 1, knit 2, make 1, knit 1 and repeat. **19th round.**—Make 1, knit 3, make 1, knit 1, make 1, slip 1, knit 1, pass the slipped stitch over, knit 1, knit 2 together, slip 1, knit 1, pass the slipped stitch over, knit 1, knit 2 together, make 1, knit 1, make 1, knit 3, make 1, knit 1 and repeat. **21st round.**—Make 1, knit 4, make 1, knit 3, make 1, knit 3 together, slip 1, knit 2 together, pass the slipped stitch over, make 1, knit 3, make 1, knit 4, make 1, knit 1 and repeat. **23rd round.**—Make 1, knit 5, make 1, knit 1, make 1, slip 1, knit 1, pass the slipped stitch over, knit 1, knit 2 together, slip 1, knit 1, pass the slipped stitch over, knit 1, knit 2 together, make 1, knit 1, make 1, knit 5, make 1, knit 1 and repeat. **25th round.**—Make 1, knit 6, make 1, knit 3, make 1, knit 3 together, slip 1, knit 2 together, pass the slipped stitch over, make 1, knit 3, make 1, knit 6, make 1, knit 1 and repeat. **27th round.**—Knit 5, knit 2 together, make 1, knit 1, make 1, slip 1, knit 1, pass the slipped stitch over, knit 1, knit 2 together, make 1, slip 1, knit 1, pass the slipped stitch over, knit 1, knit 2 together, make 1, knit 1, make 1, slip 1, knit 1, pass the slipped stitch over, knit 6 and repeat. **29th round.**—Knit 4, knit 2 together, make 1, knit 3, make 1, knit 3 together, make 1, knit 1, make 1, slip 1, knit 2 together, pass the slipped stitch over, make 1, knit 3, make 1, slip 1, knit 1, pass the slipped stitch over, knit 5 and repeat. **31st round.**—Knit 3, knit 2 together, make 1, knit 1, make 1, slip 1, knit 1, pass the slipped stitch over, knit 1, knit 2 together, make 1, knit 3, make 1, slip 1, knit 1, pass the slipped stitch over, knit 1, knit 2 together, make 1, knit 1, make 1, slip 1, knit 1, pass the slipped stitch over, knit 4 and repeat. **33rd round.**—Knit 2, knit 2 together, make 1, knit 3, make 1, knit 3 together, make 1, knit 1, make 1, slip 1, knit 2 together, pass the slipped stitch over, make 1, knit 1, make 1, slip 1, knit 2 together, pass the slipped stitch over, make 1, knit 3, make 1, slip 1, knit 1, pass the slipped stitch over, knit 3 and repeat. **35th round.**—Knit 1, knit 2 together, make 1, knit 1, make 1, slip 1, knit 1, pass the slipped stitch over, knit 1, knit 2 together, make 1, knit 1, make 1, knit 2 together, make 1, knit 1, make 1, knit 2 together, make 1, knit 1, make 1, slip 1, knit 1, pass the slipped stitch over, knit 1, knit 2 together, make 1, knit 1, make 1, slip 1, knit 1, pass the slipped stitch over, knit 2 and repeat. **37th round.**—Knit 2 together, make 1, knit 3, make 1, knit 3 together, make 1, knit 1, make 1, knit 2 together, make 1, knit 1, make 1, slip 1, knit 2 together, pass the slipped stitch over, make 1, knit 1, make 1, knit 2 together, make 1, knit 1, make 1, slip 1, knit 2 together, pass the slipped stitch over, make 1, knit 3, make 1, slip 1, knit 1, pass the slipped stitch over, knit 1 and repeat. **38th round.**—Plain. At the end of the first needle knit off 1 stitch from the second needle, at the end of the second needle knit 1 stitch from the third, and at the end of the third needle knit 1 stitch from the first needle. This brings the top stitches of each alternate dahlia petal close together at the end of each pin. There should now be 60 stitches on each of the three needles, making 180 stitches. **39th round.**—Make 1, knit 1, make 1, slip 1, knit 1, pass the slipped stitch over, knit 1, knit 2 together, make 1, knit 1, make 1, knit 2 together, make 1, knit 1, make 1, slip 1, knit 2 together, pass the slipped stitch over, make 1, knit 1, make 1, slip 1, knit 2 together, pass the slipped stitch over, make 1, knit 1, make 1, knit 2 together, make 1, knit 1, make 1, slip 1, knit 1, pass the slipped stitch over, knit 1, knit 2 together, make 1, knit 1, make 1, slip 1, knit 2 together, pass the slipped stitch over and repeat. **41st round.**—Make 1, knit 2 together 3 times, make 1, knit 1, make 1, knit 2 together, make 1, knit 1, make 1, slip 1, knit 2 together, pass the slipped stitch over, make 1, knit 1, make 1, slip 1, knit 2 together, pass the slipped stitch over, make 1, knit 1, make 1, slip 1, knit 2 together, pass the slipped stitch over, make 1, knit 1, make 1, knit 2 together, make 1, knit 1, make 1, then slip 1, knit 1 and pass the slipped stitch over three times, then make 1, knit 1 and repeat.

43rd round.—Knit 1, knit 3 together, make 1, knit 1, make 1, knit 2 together, * make 1, knit 1, make 1, slip 1, knit 2 together, pass the slipped stitch over, repeat from * 3 times, make 1, knit 1, make 1, knit 2 together, make 1, knit 1, make 1, slip 1, knit 2 together, pass the slipped stitch over, knit 2 and repeat. **45th round.**—Knit 2 together, make 1, knit 1, make 1, knit 2 together, * make 1, knit 1, make 1, slip 1, knit 2 together, pass the slipped stitch over, repeat from * 4 times, make 1, knit 1, make 1, knit 2 together, make 1, knit 1, make 1, slip 1, knit 1, pass the slipped stitch over, knit 1 and repeat. **46th round.**—As 38th round. **47th round.**—Make 1, knit 1, make 1, knit 2 together, * make 1, knit 1, make 1, slip 1, knit 2 together, pass the slipped stitch over, repeat from * 5 times, make 1, knit 1, make 1, knit 2 together, make 1, knit 1, make 1, slip 1, knit 2 together, pass the slipped stitch over and repeat. **48th round.**—Plain. There should now be 72 stitches on each needle, making 216 stitches on the round. **49th row.**—Plain. Increase at intervals 6 times on each of the three needles. **Next 6 rounds.**—Purl to make a raised edge. **56th round.**—Plain. Increase 2 stitches on each needle. There should now be 80 stitches on each needle—240 in the round. **57th round.**—Plain. **58th round.**—Make 1, knit 2 together, repeat to the end of the round. **59th round.**—Plain. **60th round.**—As 58th. **61st round.**—As 59th. **62nd row.**—As 58th. **63rd row.**—59th. **64th round.**—Plain, and increase 4 stitches on each needle. **Next 6 rounds.**—Purl to form a raised edge. **71st round.**—Plain. Cast off loosely.

Edging to match.—Work with the same cotton and No. 17 steel needles. Cast on 9 stitches. **1st row.**—Slip 1, knit 1, make 1, knit 2 together, make 1, knit 1, make 1, knit 1, make 1, knit 1, make 1, knit 2.

2nd row.—Purl 11, knit 2. **3rd row.**—Slip 1, knit 1, make 1, knit 2 together, make 1, knit 3, make 1, knit 1, make 1, knit 3, make 1, knit 2. **4th row.**—Purl 15, knit 2. **5th row.**—Slip 1, knit 1, make 1, knit 2 together, make 1, slip 2, knit 3 together, pass the slipped stitches over, make 1, knit 1, make 1, slip 2, knit 3 together, pass the slipped stitches over, make 1, knit 2. **6th row.**—Cast off 4, purl 7, knit 2. Repeat these six rows until sufficient edging is knitted to go round the d'oyley, and cast off and sew on.

CROCHET HAIRPIN CROCHET AND TATTING

BOOK IV

PLAIN CROCHET
TRICOT CROCHET
IRISH CROCHET
HAIRPIN CROCHET
DESIGNS FOR D'OYLEYS
TATTED LACES AND
EDGINGS etc.

CROCHET

The word crochet is derived from the French *croches*, or *croc*, and old Danish *krooke*—a hook. The work was known on the Continent as early as the sixteenth century, but was worked almost entirely by the nuns. Ireland was the first of the British Isles to take it up, and it reached great perfection there, but England and Scotland, although they knew of it, did not take it up until early in the nineteenth century, when it rapidly became popular. Now, it ranks with knitting as one of the most useful as well as one of the most decorative forms of needlework.

Materials for Crochet Work.—Crochet is carried out with a crochet hook and thread, and to work evenly, these should be properly adapted to one another in size. As crochet cottons and mercerised threads are sometimes numbered differently, thicknesses should be compared carefully if it is desired to substitute one for another. Hooks for wool or silk gauge from 2-16, and for cotton from 00-7½.

The thread used may be of cotton, linen, silk, or wool, and though all the stitches can be effectively worked in wool, cotton crochet usually consists of chain, double crochet, trebles, long trebles, holes, small holes, open meshes, bars, and lacets.

Abbreviations used in Crochet.—It is usual to use certain abbreviations in crochet, in order to lessen the space taken by directions, and here are some of those in most general use:

Chain.—(Abb.: ch.) In order to begin, there must be a loop on the hook, so make it, as shown in Fig 1, and hold the base of the loop where the cotton crosses, between the thumb and finger of left hand. Let the cotton pass over the first and second fingers, under the third, and over the fourth or little finger, allowing it to flow freely from the ball, but having it under perfect control. With hook in the right hand, insert it in the loop, as in Fig. 2, and pull cotton up, releasing the loop, but still holding the tag end to enable the loop to be drawn up close to the hook. Now hold the base of the loop between thumb and finger, and cotton in position over fingers as just stated, when there will be a loop on the hook. * Pass cotton over hook as in Fig. 3, draw through loop on hook, which forms a chain stitch, and repeat from * until length of chain required has been made.

ch., chain.	*l.*, lacet.
s.s., slip-stitch.	*2 d. c. d. tog.*, 2 double crochet drawn together.
d.c., double crochet.	*2 tr. d. tog.*, 2 treble drawn together.
s. tr., short treble.	*p.*, picot.
h. tr., half treble.	*sp.*, space.
tr., treble.	*st.*, stitch.
l. tr., long treble.	*patt.*, pattern.
extra l. tr., extra long treble.	*rep.*, repeat.
d. l. tr., double long treble	*rem.*, remain.
v. l. tr., very long treble.	*alt.*, alternately.
o. m., open mesh.	*dec.*, decrease.
h., hole.	*inc.*, increase.
s. h., small hole.	*S. k.*, Solomon's knot.
b., bar.	*kt.*, knot.
gr., group.	

Method of Working the Elementary Crochet Stitches.—Practically all crochet commences with a length of chain for the foundation.

Keep all the stitches as even as possible, making them of uniform size, and do not work too loosely unless especially directed to do so.

Fig. 1.

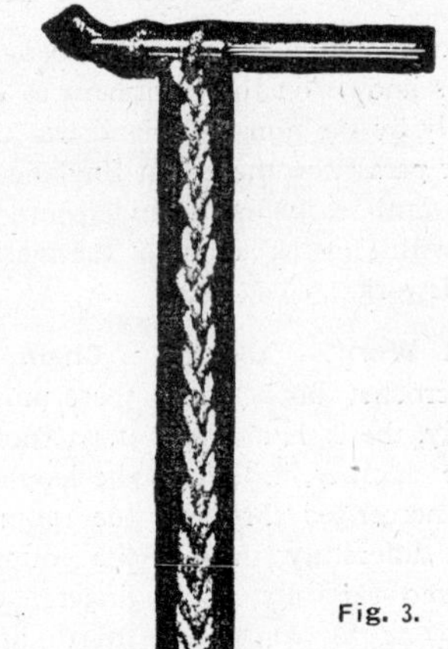

Fig. 3.

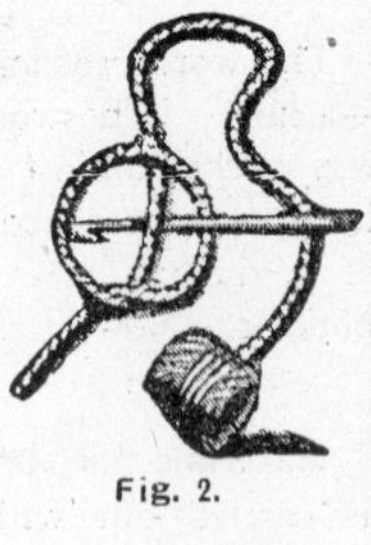

Fig. 2.

HOW TO START A CHAIN

Here are shown the two stages for beginning chain-stitch and length of chain on the hook.

The loops should be just large enough for the hook to pass easily through.

Slip-stitch.—(Abb.: s. s.) This is the next stitch to be learned, and it is used for passing from one part of the work to another, making an almost invisible stitch. With a loop already on the hook, insert hook into first stitch to the left, put the wool over the hook, and draw through the stitch in which the hook was inserted, and through the loop on the hook, thus making one slip-stitch (Fig. 4).

Double Crochet.—(Abb.: d. c.) To work double crochet, there should be a loop already on the hook. * Then insert hook into stitch to the left, wool over hook, draw through this stitch (two loops now on hook), wool over hook, draw through two loops on hook, thus making one double crochet. Repeat from * for the number of times required (Fig. 5.).

2 Double Crochet Drawn Together.—(Abb.: 2 d. c. d. tog.) With a loop already on the hook, insert hook into next stitch, wool over and draw through, insert hook into next stitch, wool over and draw through (3 loops now on hook), wool over, draw through all three loops.

To increase in double crochet, work 2 double crochet into a stitch.

Treble—(Abb.: tr.) To work treble, there should be a loop already on the hook. * Then wool over hook, insert hook into stitch to the left, wool over hook, draw

Fig. 4.—SLIP STITCH

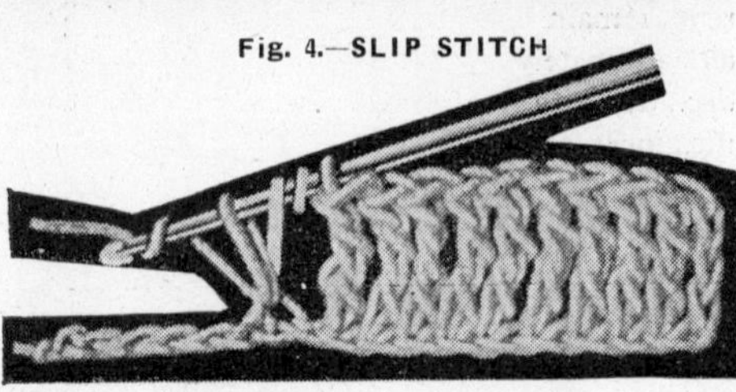

Fig. 7.—LONG TREBLES

Fig. 5.—DOUBLE CROCHET

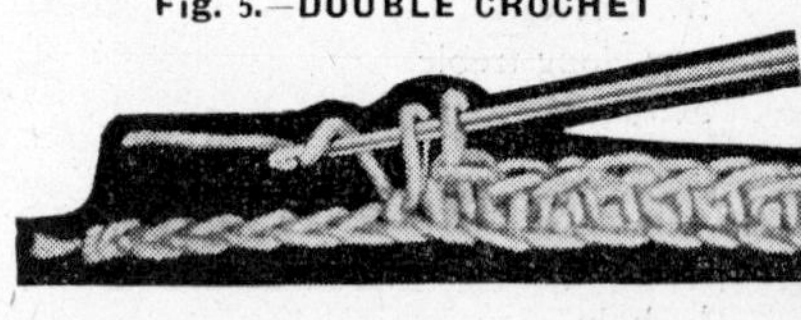

Fig. 6.—TREBLE CROCHET

through this stitch (three loops now on hook), wool over hook, draw through first two loops on hook, wool over hook, draw through two remaining loops, thus making a treble, and repeat from * for the number of times required (Fig. 6).

2 Treble Drawn Together—(Abb.: 2 tr. d. tog.) With a loop on hook, * pass wool over hook, insert hook into next stitch or place required, wool over, draw through, wool over, draw through two loops, repeat from * once more, then wool over, draw through all loops on hook.

3 Treble Drawn Together—(Abb.: 3 tr. d. tog.) Work as for 2 treble drawn together, but repeat from * twice more, instead of once.

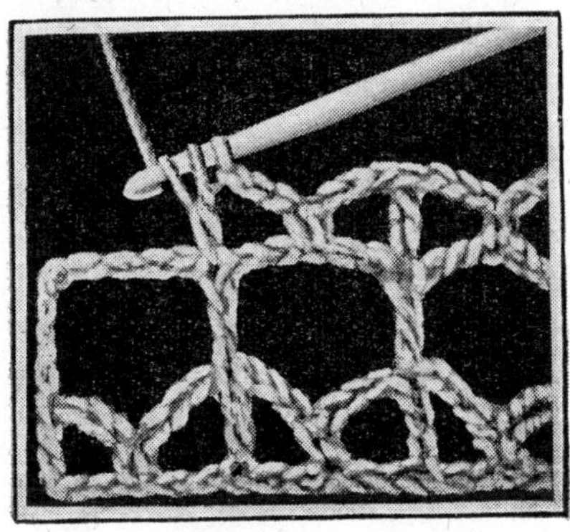

Fig. 9.—A LACET IN PROGRESS

4 Treble Drawn Together.—Work as for 2 treble drawn together, but repeat from * 3 times more, instead of once.

To increase in trebles, work 2 trebles into a stitch.

Short Treble.—(Abb.: s. tr.) With a loop on the hook, * wool over hook, insert hook into a stitch to the left, wool over, draw through this stitch (three loops now on hook), wool over hook, draw through all loops on hook, thus making a short treble. Repeat from * for the number of times required.

Long Treble.—(Abb.: l. tr.) With a loop on the hook, * pass wool twice over the hook, then insert hook into stitch to the left, wool over hook, draw through this stitch (four loops now on hook), wool over hook, draw through two loops on hook, wool over hook, draw through two more loops, wool over hook, draw through remaining two loops, thus making a long treble. Repeat from * for number of times required (Fig. 7).

2 Long Treble Drawn Together.—With a loop already on the hook, * pass wool twice over hook, insert hook into next stitch or place required, wool over, draw through, wool over, draw through two loops, wool over, draw through two more loops, repeat from * once, then wool over, draw through all loops on hook.

3 Long Treble Drawn Together.—Work as for 2 long treble drawn together, but repeat from * twice instead of once.

4 Long Treble Drawn Together.—Work as for 2 long treble drawn together, but repeat from * 3 times instead of once.

Fig. 8.—HOLES

Extra Long Treble.—(Abb.: extra l. tr.) With a loop on hook, pass wool three times over hook, insert hook into place required, wool over hook, draw through this stitch, * wool over, draw through two loops on hook, repeat from * 3 times.

Double Long Treble.—(Abb.: d. l. tr.) With a loop on hook, pass wool four times over hook, insert hook into place required, wool over, draw through this stitch, * wool over, draw through two loops on hook, repeat from * 4 times.

Very Long Treble.—(Abb.: v. l. tr.) With a loop on the hook, pass wool five times over the hook, then insert hook into stitch to left, wool over hook, draw through this stitch, * wool over hook, draw through two loops on hook, repeat from * until only one loop remains on hook, thus making a very long treble.

Lacets.—(Abb.: l.) A lacet consists of

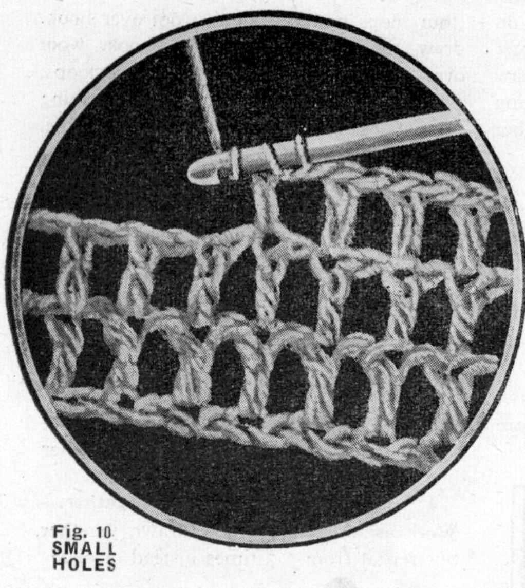

Fig. 10 SMALL HOLES

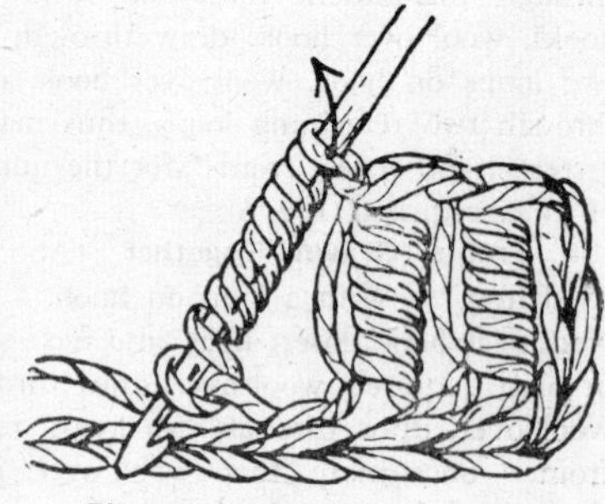

Fig. 11.—BULLION-STITCH

Fig. 12.—LACET AND BAR

3 chain, miss 2 stitches, 1 double crochet into middle stitch of bar, 3 chain, miss 2 stitches, 1 treble into treble at end of bar (Fig. 9).

Holes.—(Abb.: h.) To work holes, first make 1 treble into a stitch, * then make 2 chain, miss 2 stitches, make 1 treble into the third stitch (thus completing a hole) and repeat from * as required (Fig. 8).

Small Holes.—(Abb.: s. h.) For a small hole, first make 1 treble into a stitch, * then make 1 chain, miss 1 stitch, make 1 treble into second stitch, and repeat from * as required (Fig. 10).

Open Mesh.—(Abb.: o. m.) For an open mesh, first work 1 long treble into a stitch, * then make 3 chain, miss 3 stitches, 1 long treble into next stitch, and repeat from * as required

Bars.—(Abb.: b.) A bar comprises 5 chain, miss 5 stitches or a lacet, 1 treble into next stitch. The treble finishing the last hole, bar or lacet before a group of trebles, also counts as the first treble of that group (Fig. 12).

Bullion Stitch.—This stitch is very suitable for ornamenting edges, and is worked by passing the thread eight or ten times loosely over the hook, inserting the hook into a stitch in the previous row, pulling the thread through the stitch, and after passing it over the hook, pulling it through all the loops (Fig. 11).

Picots.—(Abb.: p.) Begin at the required stitch with 1 double crochet, then make 8 chain, insert hook into fifth chain from hook, pass thread over hook, draw through this stitch and loop on hook, then make 3 chain (Fig. 13).

Solomon's Knot.—(Abb.: S. k.)

1st row.—Loop wool on to hook, then * draw out stitch on hook to form about ½ inch loop, wool over hook and draw through loop, insert hook into back thread of loop, wool over, draw through, wool over, draw through both loops on hook (this completes one Solomon's knot), repeat from * for length required.

2nd row.—Miss first three Solomon's knots, then work 1 double crochet into knot (see illustration on next page), 2 Solomon's knots, miss 1 Solomon's knot in previous row, 1 double crochet into knot, repeat from * all along, 2 Solomon's knots, turn.

On the right is Solomon's knot, a useful lacey stitch, and below, picots, which make a simple edging.

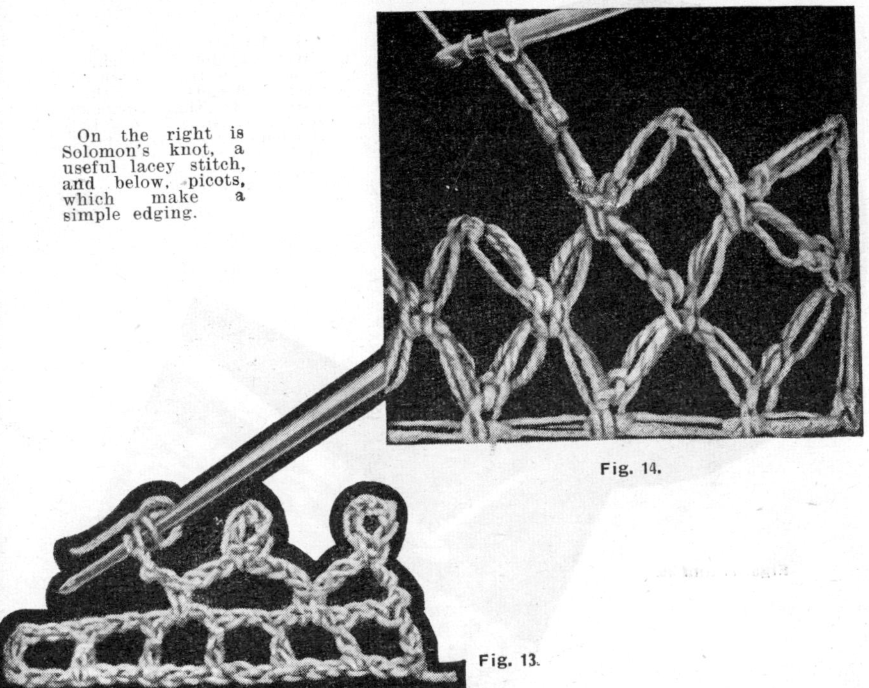

Fig. 14.

Fig. 13.

3rd row.—Miss first three Solomon's knots, then work 1 double crochet into next knot, * 2 Solomon's knots, miss 2 Solomon's knots in previous row, 1 double crochet into knot, repeat from * to end, 2 Solomon's knots, turn. Repeat third row for length required (Fig. 14).

Variations of Double Crochet and Trebles.—Having mastered the basic stitches, of which double crochet and trebles are two of the most used, we now pass on to variations of these two stitches, which go to the formation of quite delightful though definitely simple patterns, as can be seen from the illustrations.

Double Crochet.—Commence with a length of chain.

1st row.—Miss first chain, then work 1 double crochet into every chain, 1 chain, turn.

2nd row.—1 double crochet into every double crochet of previous row, always working into the two top threads of every stitch. Repeat 2nd row.

Ridged Double Crochet.—Begin with a length of chain (Fig. 15).

1st row.—Miss first chain, then 1 double crochet into every chain, 1 chain, turn. **2nd row.**—1 double crochet into every double crochet in previous row, always working into top back thread only of every stitch, 1 chain, turn. Repeat 2nd row.

Double Crochet in a Vandyke Pattern.—Begin with a length of chain divisible by sixteen with two over. **1st row.**—Miss first chain, 2 double crochet drawn together, ** 1 double crochet into each of next 6 stitches, 3 double crochet into next stitch, 6 double crochet, then 3 double crochet drawn together thus: * insert hook into next stitch, draw wool through, repeat from * twice more, wool over, draw through all loops on hook **, repeat from ** to **, working 2 double crochet drawn together at end of row instead of three, 1 chain, turn.

Work into top back thread of every stitch to give a ridged effect.

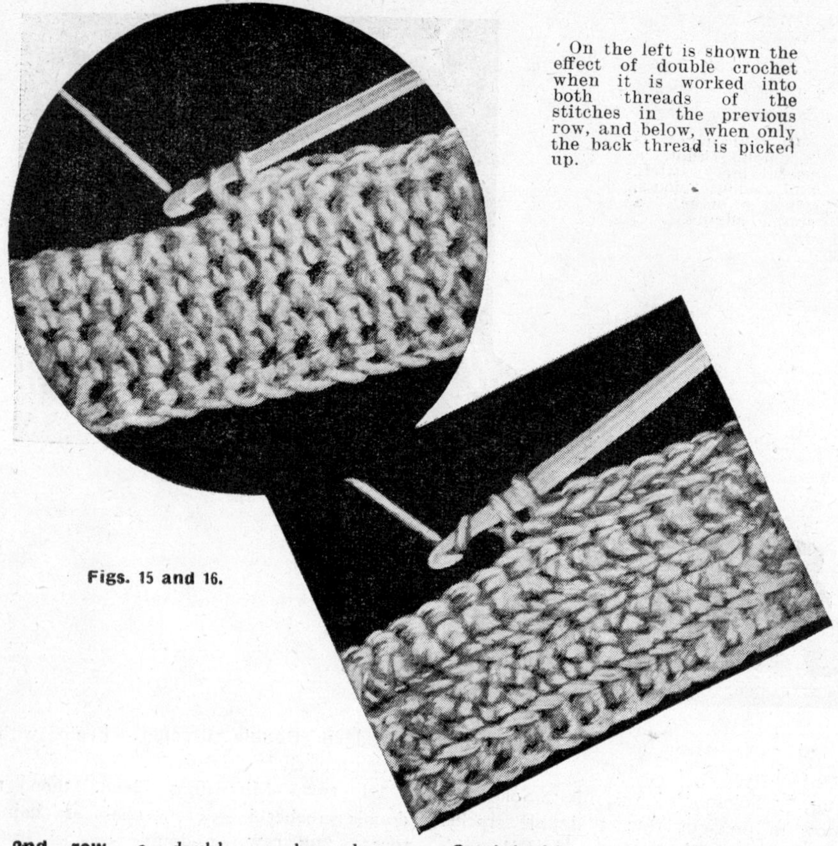

On the left is shown the effect of double crochet when it is worked into both threads of the stitches in the previous row, and below, when only the back thread is picked up.

Figs. 15 and 16.

2nd row.—2 double crochet drawn together, * 6 double crochet, then 3 double crochet into next stitch, 6 double crochet, then 3 double crochet drawn together, repeat from *, working 2 double crochet drawn together at end of row instead of three, 1 chain, turn. Repeat 2nd row for length required (Fig. 24).

Moss Stitch.—Begin with a length of chain divisible by two.

1st row.—Miss first three chain, 1 double crochet into next chain, * 1 chain, miss 1 chain of the foundation, 1 double crochet into next chain, repeat from * to end, 2 chain, turn. **2nd row.**—1 double crochet into first 1 chain space, * 1 chain, 1 double crochet into next space, repeat from * to end, 2 chain, turn. Repeat 2nd row for length required

Semi-double Crochet Pattern.—Begin with a length of chain divisible by two, with one over.

1st row.—Miss first three chain, insert hook into next chain, draw wool through, insert hook into next chain, draw wool through, wool over, draw through all loops on hook at same time, this forms first semi-double crochet, * 1 chain, insert hook into next foundation chain, draw wool through, insert hook into next chain, draw wool through, wool over, draw through all loops on hook at same time, repeat from * to end, 2 chain, turn.

2nd row.—Miss first two chain, then insert hook into first semi-double crochet in previous row, draw wool through, insert hook into next chain, draw wool through, wool over, draw through all loops on hook

Treble can also be worked into both threads of the stitches in the previous row, or into one thread only, which makes the ridged effect.

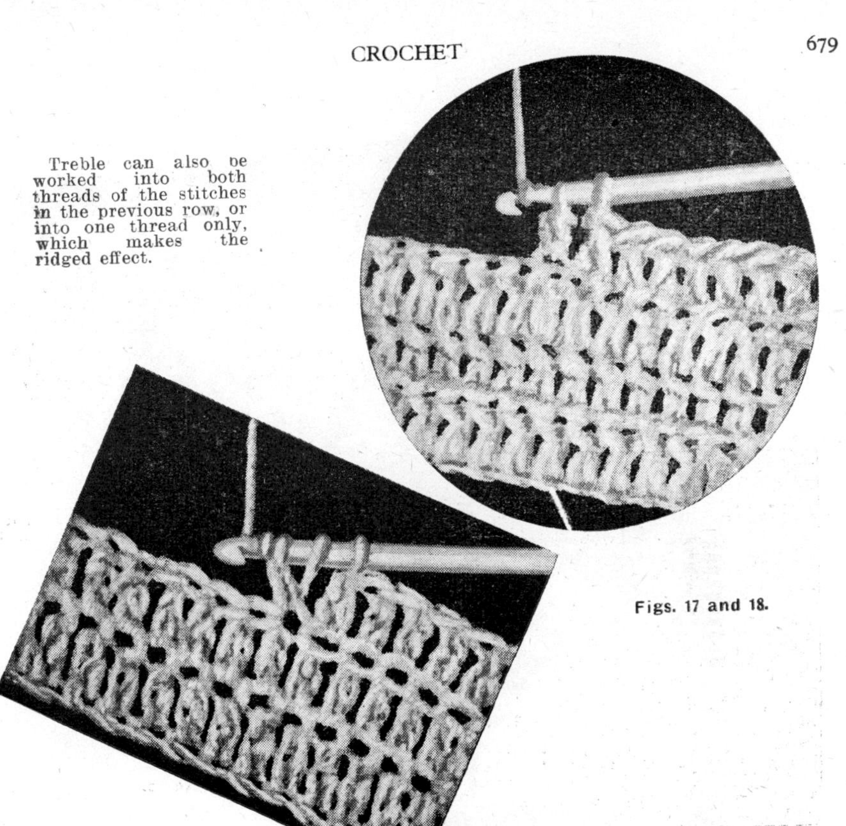

Figs. 17 and 18.

at same time, this forms first semi-double crochet, * 1 chain, then work next semi-double crochet thus: insert hook into next semi-double crochet in previous row, draw wool through, insert hook into next chain, draw wool through, wool over, draw through all loops on hook at same time, repeat from * to end, 2 chain, turn. Repeat 2nd row for length required.

Ridged Treble.—Begin with a length of chain.

1st row.—Miss first three chain, then work 1 treble into every chain, 3 chain, turn. **2nd row.**—Miss first treble, then work 1 treble into every stitch of previous row, always working into top back thread only of every stitch, 3 chain, turn. Repeat 2nd row for length required (Fig. 18).

SOME SIMPLE STITCHES

No. 1.—A very simple stitch. Begin with a length of chain divisible by three and one over (Fig. 19).

1st row.—1 treble into fourth chain from hook, working into both threads of the chain, 1 chain, 1 double crochet into front thread only of same chain, * miss 2 chain, 1 treble into both threads of next chain, 1 chain, 1 double crochet into front thread only of same chain, repeat from * to end, 2 chain, turn.

2nd row.—1 treble into both threads of first treble, 1 chain, 1 double crochet into front thread only of same treble, * 1 treble into both threads of next treble, 1 chain, 1 double crochet into front thread only of same treble, repeat from * to end, 2 chain, turn. Repeat 2nd row for length required.

No. 2. Groups and Double Crochet.—Begin with a length of chain (Fig. 20).

On the right is a very simple stitch, No. 1; and below, No. 2, which consists of rows of groups and double crochet.

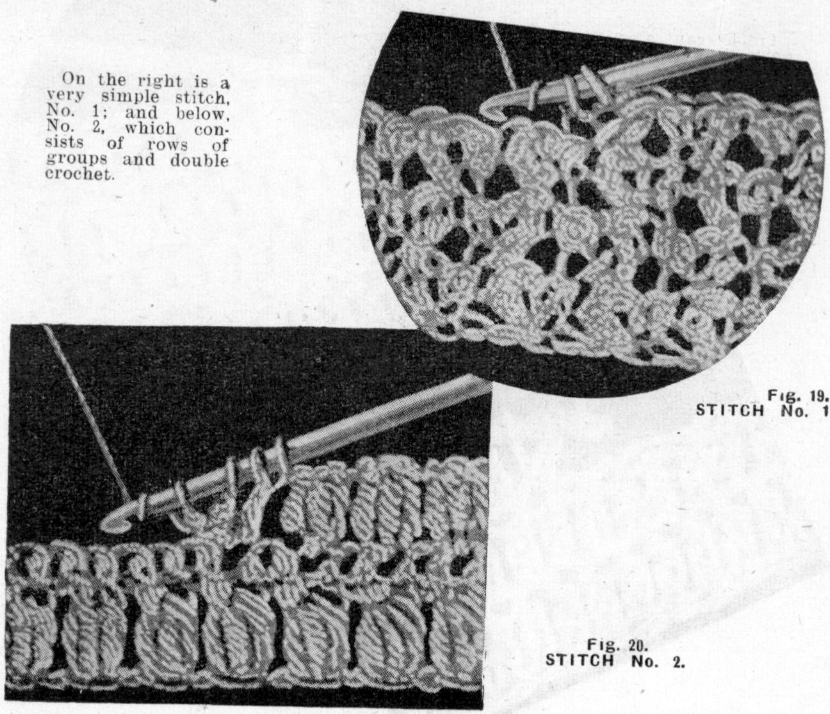

Fig. 19.
STITCH No. 1

Fig. 20.
STITCH No. 2.

1st row.—Miss first three chain, then work one group thus: wool over hook, insert hook into next stitch, draw wool through, wool over, draw through two loops, wool over, insert hook into same place, draw wool through, wool over, draw wool through two loops, wool over, insert hook into same place again, draw wool through, wool over, draw through two loops, wool over, draw through all loops on hook at same time, * 1 chain, miss 1 chain of the foundation, then work one group as already described into next chain, repeat from * to end, 1 chain, turn.

2nd row.—1 double crochet into every stitch, 3 chain, turn.

3rd row.—Miss first double crochet, then work one group into next double crochet, * 1 chain, miss 1 double crochet, then work one group into next double crochet, repeat from * to end, 1 chain, turn. Repeat last two rows for length required.

No. 3. Half Treble.—With a loop

Fig. 21.—STITCH No. 5

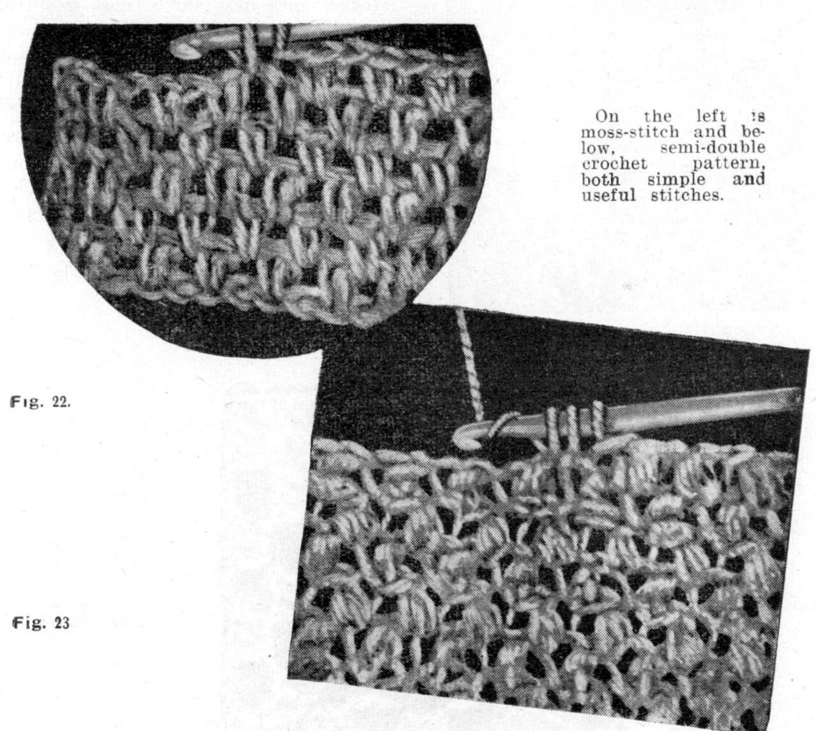

On the left is moss-stitch and below, semi-double crochet pattern, both simple and useful stitches.

Fig. 22.

Fig. 23

already on the hook, * pass wool over the hook, insert into required stitch, draw wool through, wool over, draw through first loop on hook, wool over, draw through all loops on hook at same time, repeat from *

Fig. 24.—DOUBLE CROCHET IN A VANDYKE PATTERN

No. 4.—Begin with a length of chain divisible by three, with two over (Fig. 29).

1st row.—Miss first chain, 1 double crochet, 2 chain, 1 double crochet all into next stitch, * miss 2 stitches, then 1 double crochet, 2 chain, 1 double crochet all into next stitch, repeat from * to end, 1 chain, turn. **2nd row.**—1 double crochet, 2 chain, 1 double crochet all into every two chain space of previous row, 1 chain, turn.

Repeat 2nd row for length required.

No. 5.—Begin with a length of chain divisible by four, with two over (Fig. 21).

1st row.—Miss first chain, 1 double crochet into next, * 1 chain, miss 1 stitch, 1 treble, 1 chain, 1 treble all into next stitch, 1 chain, miss 1 stitch, 1 double crochet into next, repeat from * to end, 4 chain, turn. **2nd row.**—1 treble into

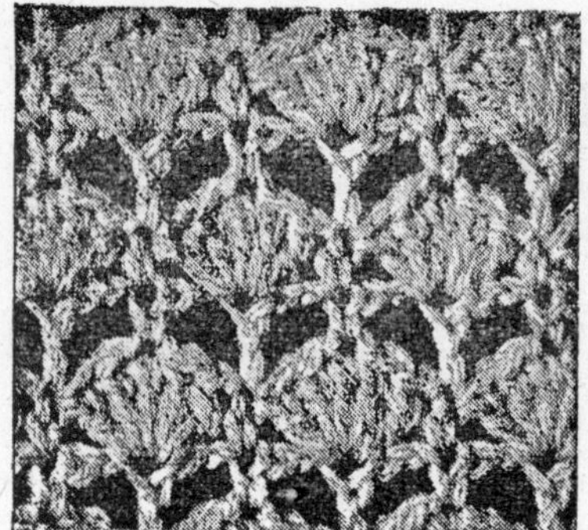

Fig. 25.—STITCH No. 8

into next stitch, * miss 2 stitches, 1 double crochet into next stitch, miss 2 stitches, 2 treble into next stitch, repeat from * to end, 1 chain, turn. **2nd row.**—1 double crochet into first treble, miss 1 treble, then 2 treble into next double crochet, * 1 double crochet into next treble, miss 1 treble, then 2 treble into next double crochet, repeat from * to end, 1 chain, turn. Repeat 2nd row for length required.

No. 7.—Begin with a length of chain divisible by nine, with six over (Fig. 30).

Fig. 26. STITCH No. 10

first double crochet, * 1 chain, 1 double crochet into space between trebles, 1 chain, 1 treble, 1 chain, 1 treble all into next double crochet, repeat from * to end, 1 chain, turn. **3rd row.**—1 double crochet into first space, * 1 chain, 1 treble, 1 chain, 1 treble all into next double crochet, 1 chain, 1 double crochet into next space between trebles, repeat from *, working last double crochet into 4 chain space at end, 4 chain, turn. Repeat last 2 rows for length required.

No. 6.—This gives a lacy effect if slightly stretched and pressed. Begin with a length of chain divisible by six, with five over (Fig. 28).

1st row.—Miss first chain, 1 double crochet into next, miss 2 stitches, 2 treble

Fig. 27.—STITCH No. 9

1st row.—Miss 3 stitches, 1 treble into each of next 3 stitches, * miss 2 stitches, 2 treble, 1 chain, 2 treble all into next stitch, miss 2 stitches, 4 treble, repeat from * to end, 3 chain, turn. **2nd row.**—Miss first treble, 3 treble, then * 2 treble, 1 chain, 2 treble all into 1 chain space between trebles, miss 2 treble, then 4 treble on 4 treble, repeat from * to end, working last treble into chain at end, 3 chain, turn.

Repeat 2nd row for length required.

No. 8.—Begin with a length of chain divisible by six, with two over (Fig. 25).

1st row.—Miss first chain, 1 double crochet into next, * 2 chain, miss 2 stitches, 1 treble into next, 2 chain, miss 2 stitches, 1 double crochet into next, repeat from * to end, 1 chain, turn.

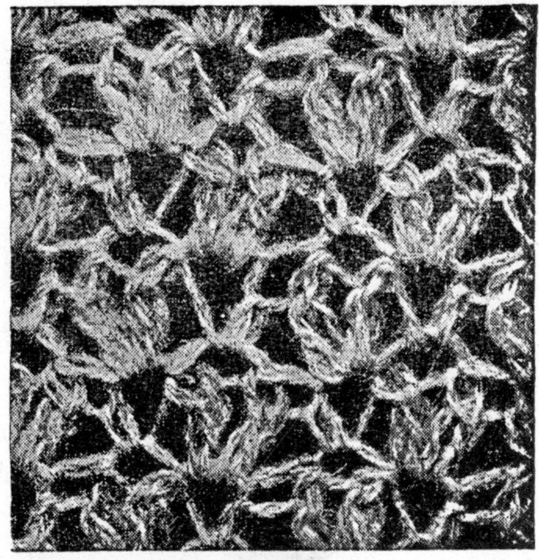

Fig. 28.—STITCH No. 6

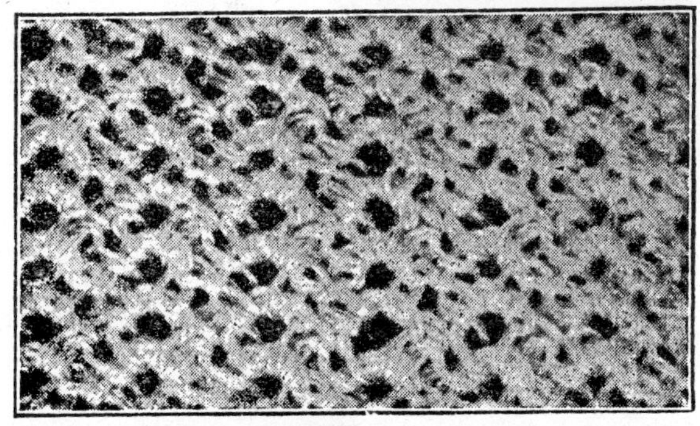

Fig. 29. STITCH No. 4

Fig. 30. No. 7 STITCH

2nd row.—1 double crochet into first double crochet, * 5 treble into next treble, 1 double crochet into next double crochet, repeat from * to end, 5 chain, turn.

3rd row.—1 double crochet into centre treble of group of five, 2 chain, 1 treble into next double crochet, * 2 chain, miss 2 treble of next group, 1 double crochet into next, 2 chain, 1 treble into next double crochet, repeat from * to end, 3 chain, turn.

4th row.—2 treble into first treble, * 1 double crochet into next double crochet, 5 treble into next treble, repeat from *, working 3 treble only into third chain of five at end, 1 chain, turn.

5th row.—1 double crochet into first treble, * 2 chain, 1 treble into next double crochet, 2 chain, miss 2 treble of next group, 1 double crochet into next stitch, repeat from * to end, 1 chain, turn Repeat from beginning of 2nd row for length required

No. 9.—This is slightly stretched and pressed when finished to give a lacy effect. Begin with a length of chain divisible by three (Fig. 27).

1st row.—Miss first three chain, * insert hook into next stitch, draw wool through and keep loop on hook *, repeat from * to * twice more, wool over, draw through all loops on hook, ** 2 ch., now repeat from * to * 3 times, wool over draw through all loops on hook, repeat from ** to end, 3 chain, turn.

2nd row.—Miss the 3 chain just made, *insert hook into next stitch, draw wool through and leave loop on hook *, repeat from * to * twice more, wool over, draw through all loops on hook, ** 2 ch., now repeat from * to * 3 times, wool over, draw through all loops on hook, repeat from ** to end, 3 chain, turn. Repeat 2nd row for length required.

No. 10.—This pattern is begun in the centre and worked round and round. Begin with 4 chain (Fig. 26).

1st round.—2 treble into fourth chain from hook, * 3 chain, 3 treble into same stitch, repeat from * twice more, 3 chain, slip-stitch to top of chain at beginning of round. **2nd round.**—6 chain, 3 treble, 3 chain, 3 treble all into next space, * 3 chain, then 3 treble, 3 chain, 3 treble all into next space, repeat from * once more, 3 chain, 3 treble into next space.

Fig. 31.

On the left is star-stitch, worked in rows from right to left.

Right. Star-stitch worked to make both sides alike.

Fig. 32.

3 chain, 2 treble into same space, slip-stitch to third chain of six at beginning of round. **3rd round.**—3 chain, 2 treble into first space, * 3 chain, 3 treble, 3 chain, 3 treble all into corner space, 3 chain, 3 treble into next space, repeat from * twice more, 3 chain, 3 treble, 3 chain, 3 treble all into next corner space, 3 chain, slip-stitch to top of chain at beginning of round.

4th round.—6 chain, 3 treble into next space, * 3 chain, 3 treble, 3 chain, 3 treble all into next corner space, 3 chain, 3 treble into next space, 3 chain, 3 treble, into next space, repeat from * twice more, 3 chain, 3 treble, 3 chain, 3 treble all into

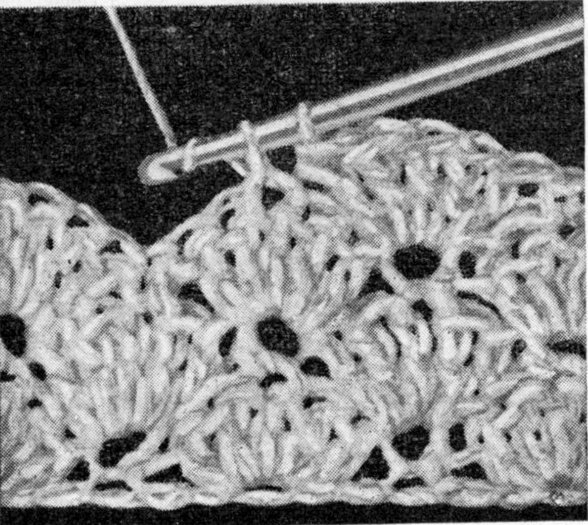

Fig. 33. SCALLOP SHELL PATTERN

next corner space, 3 chain, 2 treble into next space, slip-stitch to third chain of six at beginning of round. Continue thus, working 3 treble into every space, 3 chain between, and when corner spaces are reached, work 3 treble, 3 chain, 3 treble all into these.

Effective Stitches that form Charming Patterns.—

Star Stitch (*worked in rows from right to left*).—Begin with a length of chain divisible by two, with one over (Fig. 31).

1st row.—Miss first chain, * insert hook into next chain, draw wool through * repeat from * to * 4 times (6 loops now on hook), wool over, draw through all loops on hook at same time, ** 1 chain. insert hook into small hole formed by the one chain at top of star just worked, draw wool through, insert hook into back of last loop of same star, draw wool through, insert hook into chain last worked into of the foundation, draw wool through, repeat from * to * twice, wool over, draw through all loops on hook at same time **, repeat from ** to ** until one chain remains, then 1 chain, 1 treble into last chain of the foundation, fasten off.

2nd row.—Slip-stitch into beginning of previous row, 3 chain, miss first chain of these, insert hook into next chain, draw wool through, insert hook into next chain, draw wool through, insert hook into stitch along side of first star in previous row, draw wool through, insert hook into hole of same star, draw wool through, insert hook into stitch along side of next star, draw wool through, wool over, draw through all loops on hook, * 1 chain, insert hook into hole of star just made, draw wool through, insert hook into back of last loop worked of same star, draw wool through, insert hook into same place as last stitch of previous star, draw wool through, insert hook into hole of star in previous row, draw wool through, insert hook into stitch along side of next star, draw wool through, wool over, draw through all loops on hook, repeat from *, and when working the last star, instead of inserting hook into the stitch along side of star, insert hook into treble at end of row, draw wool through, wool over, draw through all loops on hook, 1 chain, 1 treble into same treble again, fasten off.

Star Stitch (*worked in rows backwards and forwards*).—Begin with a length of chain divisible by two, with one over.

1st row.—Miss first chain, * insert hook into next chain, draw wool through *, repeat from * to * 4 times (6 loops now on hook), wool over, draw through all loops on hook at same time, ** 1 chain, insert hook into hole at top of star just made, draw wool through, insert hook into back of last loop of same star, draw wool through, insert hook into chain last worked into of the foundation, draw wool through, repeat from * to * twice, wool over, draw through all loops on hook at same time, repeat from ** until one chain remains, then 1 chain, 1 double crochet into last chain of the foundation, 3 chain, turn.

2nd row.—Miss first chain, insert hook into next chain, draw wool through, insert hook into next chain, draw wool through, insert hook into double crochet, draw wool through, insert hook into hole of next star in previous row, draw wool through, insert hook into stitch along side of same star, draw wool through, wool over, draw through all loops on hook, * 1 chain, insert hook into hole of star just made, draw wool through, insert hook into back of last loop of same star, draw wool through, insert hook into same place as last stitch of previous star, draw wool through, insert hook into hole of next star, draw wool through, insert hook into stitch along side of same star, draw wool through, wool over, draw through all loops on hook, repeat from *, then 1 chain, 1 double crochet into extreme end of row, 3 chain, turn. Repeat 2nd row (Fig. 32).

Scallop Shell Stitch.—Begin with a length of chain divisible by six, with two over.

1st row.—Miss first chain, 1 double crochet into next, * miss 2 chain, 5 treble all into next chain, miss 2 chain, 1 double crochet into next chain, repeat from * to end, 3 chain, turn.

2nd row.—2 treble into first double crochet, * miss next 2 treble, 1 double crochet into next treble, then 5 treble all into next double crochet, repeat from *, working only 3 treble into last double crochet, 1 chain, turn

3rd row.—1 double crochet into first treble, * miss next 2 treble, then 5 treble all into next double crochet, miss next 2 treble, 1 double crochet into next treble, repeat from *, working last double crochet into top of 3 chain here seen, 3 chain, turn. Repeat last two rows for length required (Fig. 33).

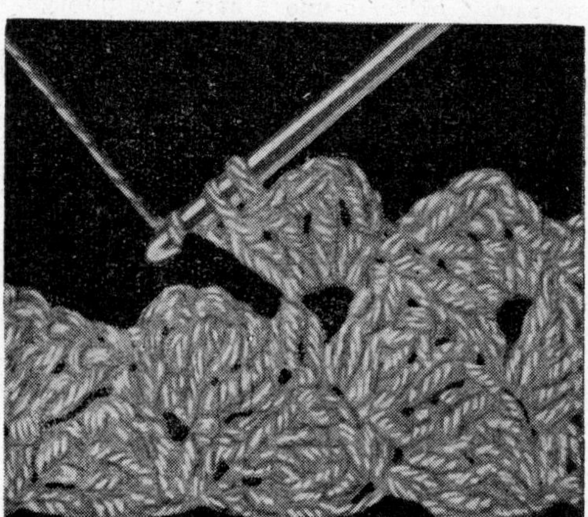

Fig. 34. CRAZY STITCH

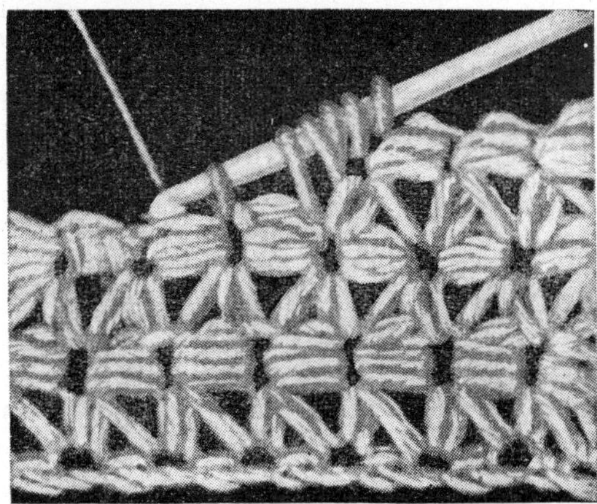

Fig. 35.
DAISY OR
MARGUERITE STITCH

Crazy Stitch.—Begin with a length of chain divisible by four, with two over.

1st row.—Miss first chain, then work 1 double crochet, 2 chain, 3 treble all into the next chain, * miss 3 chain of the foundation, then work 1 double crochet, 2 chain, 3 treble all into the next chain of the foundation, repeat from * to end, 1 chain, turn.

2nd row.—Work 1 double crochet, 2 chain, 3 treble all into the first two chain space, * then work 1 double crochet, 2 chain, 3 treble all into the next two chain space, repeat from the * to end, 1 chain, turn. Repeat 2nd row for length required.

This is a light and dainty stitch, very suitable for shawls, matinee coats and other baby wear and is easily and quickly worked (Fig. 34).

Daisy Stitch.—Begin with a length of chain divisible by two, with one over.

1st row.—Miss first chain, * insert hook into next chain, draw wool through * repeat from * to * 4 times (6 loops now on hook), wool over, draw through all loops on hook, ** 1 chain, insert hook into hole at top of daisy just made, draw through, insert hook into back of last loop of same daisy, draw through, insert hook into chain last worked into of the foundation, draw through, repeat from * to * twice, wool over, draw through all loops on hook at same time, repeat from ** all

Fig. 36.
VARIATION OF
DAISYSTITCH

Fig. 37.—KNOTTED STITCH

along, then 1 chain, 1 double crochet into last foundation chain, 2 chain, turn.

2nd row.—1 double crochet into hole of first daisy, 1 chain and 1 double crochet into hole of every daisy, then 1 double crochet into extreme end of last daisy in previous row, 3 chain, turn.

3rd row.—Miss 1 chain, * insert hook into next chain, draw through, repeat from * once, insert hook into first double crochet, draw through, insert hook into next double crochet, draw through, insert hook into next chain, draw through, wool over, draw through all loops on hook at same time, ** 1 chain, insert hook into hole at top of daisy just made, draw through, insert hook into back of last loop of same daisy, draw through, insert hook into chain already worked into, draw through, insert hook into next double crochet, draw through, insert hook into next chain, draw through, wool over, draw through all loops on hook at same time, repeat from ** all along, then 1 chain, 1 double crochet into stitch last worked into, 2 chain, turn Repeat last two rows.

Another Daisy Stitch.—Begin with a length of chain divisible by two, with one over.

1st row.—Miss first two chain, insert hook into next chain, draw wool through loosely, wool over, insert hook into same chain, draw wool through loosely, miss 1 chain, insert hook into next chain, draw wool through loosely, miss 1 chain, insert hook into next chain, draw wool through loosely (6 loops now on hook), wool over, draw through all loops on hook, * 1 chain, insert hook into small hole just formed by the one chain, draw wool through loosely, wool over, insert hook into same place, draw wool through loosely, insert hook into foundation chain last worked into, draw wool through loosely, miss 1 chain, insert hook into next chain, draw wool through loosely, wool over, draw through all loops on hook, repeat from * to end, 3 chain, turn.

2nd row.—Miss first chain, insert hook into next chain, draw wool through loosely, wool over, insert hook into same place, draw wool through loosely, insert hook into first small hole in previous row, draw wool through loosely, insert hook into next small hole in previous row, draw wool through loosely, wool over, draw through all loops on hook, this completes first daisy, * 1 chain, insert hook into small hole just formed by the one chain, draw wool through, wool over, insert hook into same place, draw through, insert hook into small hole last worked into in previous row, draw wool through **, insert hook into next small hole in previous row, draw wool through, wool over, draw through all loops on hook, this completes another daisy, repeat from * until last daisy is reached, then work thus: Repeat from *

Fig. 38.—Knotted stitch worked in rows backwards and forwards.

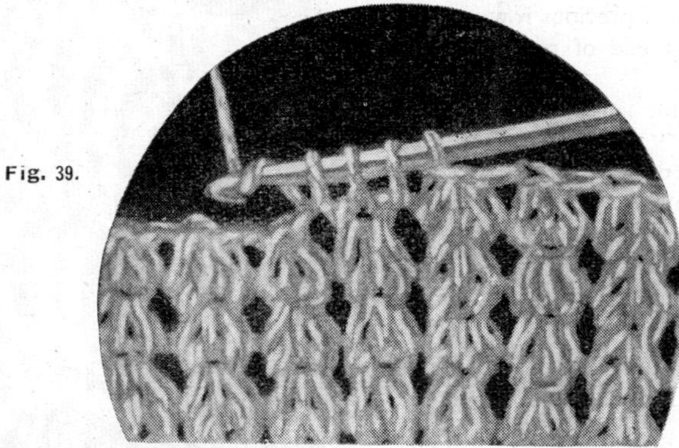

Fig. 39. TRINITY STITCH

to ** once, insert hook into extreme end of row, draw wool through, wool over, draw through all loops on hook, 3 chain, turn. Repeat 2nd row (Fig. 36).

Knotted Stitch.—This stitch is worked in rows from right to left. Begin with a length of chain (Fig. 37).

1st row.—Wool over hook, miss first 2 chain, insert hook into next chain, draw wool through chain and first loop on hook, wool over, draw through the two loops on hook, * wool over, insert hook into next chain, draw wool through chain and first loop on hook, wool over, draw through the two loops on hook, repeat from * to end, fasten off.

2nd row.—Begin at the beginning of previous row. With a loop on the hook, pass wool over hook and insert it into first stitch in previous row, draw wool through stitch and first loop on hook, wool over, draw through two loops on hook, * wool over, insert hook into next stitch, draw wool through stitch and first loop on hook, wool over, draw through two loops on hook, repeat from * to end, fasten off. Repeat 2nd row for length required.

Knotted Stitch (*worked in rows backwards and forwards, both sides of the work being alike*).—Begin with a chain of the length required (Fig. 38).

1st row.—Wool over hook, miss first two chain, insert hook into next chain, draw wool through chain and first loop on hook, wool over, draw through two loops on hook, * 1 knot worked thus: wool over, insert hook into next stitch, draw wool through stitch and first loop on hook, wool over, draw through two loops, repeat from * to end, 2 chain, turn.

Fig. 40. BALL STITCH

2nd row.—Miss first knot, then work 1 knot into every knot of previous row, 1 knot into top of chain at end of row, 2 chain, turn.

Repeat 2nd row for length required

Trinity Stitch (*worked in rows from right to left*).—Begin with a length of chain.

1st row.—Miss first three chain, * insert hook into next chain, draw wool through *, repeat from * to * twice (4 loops now on hook), wool over, draw through all loops on hook at same time, ** 1 chain, insert hook into chain last worked into, draw wool through, repeat from * to * twice, wool over, draw through all loops on hook at same time **, repeat from ** to ** all along, then 1 chain, 1 double crochet into last chain of the foundation, fasten off.

Fig. 41.—WAVY PATTERN

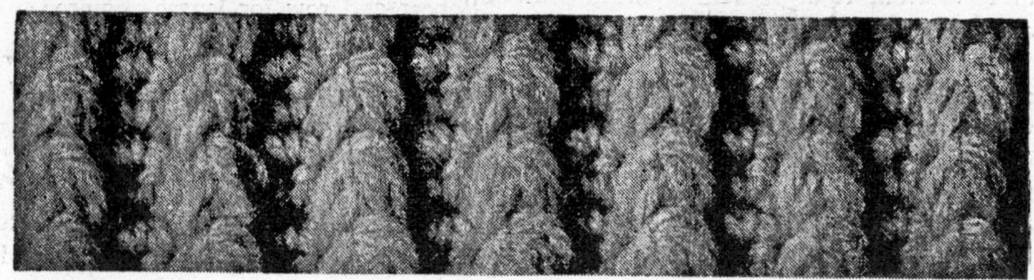

Fig. 42. CABLE STITCH

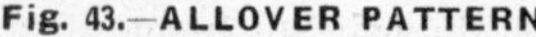

Fig. 43.—ALLOVER PATTERN

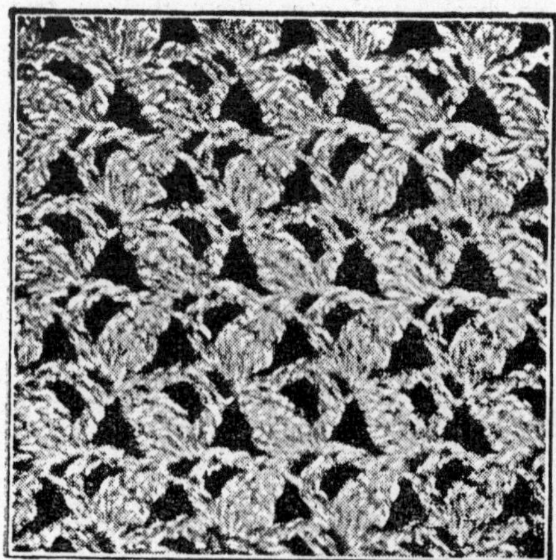

2nd row.—Slip-stitch into top of chain at beginning of previous row, 2 chain, insert hook into small space here seen before first group, draw wool through, insert hook into top of next group in previous row, draw wool through, insert hook into next stitch, draw wool through (4 loops now on hook), wool over, draw through all loops on hook at same time, * 1 chain, insert hook into stitch last worked into, draw wool through, insert hook into top of next group in previous row, draw wool through, insert hook into next stitch, draw wool through, wool over, draw through all loops on hook at same time, repeat from * all along, then 1 chain, 1 double crochet into last stitch again, fasten off. Repeat 2nd row for length required (Fig. 39)

Ball Stitch.—This is worked in rows backwards and forwards, both sides of the work being alike. Commence with a chain the length required.

1st row.—Miss first three chain, then wool over hook, insert hook into next chain, draw wool through loosely, wool over, insert hook into same chain, draw wool through loosely, wool over, insert hook into same chain again, draw wool through loosely (7 loops now on hook), wool over, draw through all loops on hook at same time, * 1 chain, miss 1 chain of the foundation, then work 1 ball-stitch as follows: wool over hook, insert hook into next chain, draw wool through loosely, wool over, insert hook into same chain, draw wool through loosely, wool over, insert hook into same chain again, draw wool through loosely, wool over, draw through all loops on hook at same time, repeat from * to end, 3 chain, turn.

2nd row.—1 ball stitch into space between first and second ball stitches in previous row, * 1 chain, 1 ball stitch into next space, repeat from * to end, 3 chain, turn. Repeat 2nd row for length required (Fig. 40).

Effective Allover Pattern. (Fig. 43)—Begin with a length of chain divisible by four, with seven over.

1st row.—3 treble drawn together into 7th chain from hook, * miss 3 stitches, 1 treble into next stitch, 2 chain, 3 treble drawn together into same stitch, repeat from * until 4 chain remain, then miss 3 stitches, 1 treble into next stitch, 5 chain, turn. **2nd row.**—3 treble drawn together into first treble, * miss 1 space, 1 treble into next treble, 2 chain, 3 treble drawn together into same stitch, repeat from * until space at end is reached, then work 1 treble into this, 5 chain, turn.

Repeat 2nd row for length required

Wavy Pattern. (Fig. 41)—Begin with a length of chain divisible by twelve, with three over.

1st row.—Miss first three chain, 3 treble drawn together, ** 1 chain and 1 long treble into each of next 2 stitches, 1 chain, 1 long treble, 1 chain, 1 long treble all into next stitch, 1 chain and 1 long treble into each of next 2 stitches, 1 chain, then 7 treble drawn together thus: wool over, insert hook into next stitch, draw wool through, wool over, draw through 2 loops, repeat from * 6 times more, wool over, draw through all loops until two remain, wool over, draw through these two loops, repeat from ** until nine stitches remain, 1 chain and 1 long treble into each of next 2 stitches, 1 chain, 1 long treble, 1 chain, 1 long treble all into next stitch, 1 chain and 1 long treble into each of next 2 stitches, 1 chain, 4 treble drawn together, 3 chain, turn. **2nd row.**—1 treble into first space, 1 treble into each of next 11 stitches, * wool over, insert hook into next space, draw wool through, wool over, draw through 2 loops, wool over, insert hook into next space, draw wool through, wool over, draw through 2 loops, wool over, draw through all loops on hook, 1 treble into each of next 11 stitches, repeat from * until one 1 chain space remains, wool over, insert hook into next space, draw wool through, wool over, draw through 2 loops, wool over, insert hook into chain at end, draw wool through, wool over, draw through 2 loops, wool over, draw through all loops on hook, 3 chain, turn.

3rd row.—Miss 3 chain and first stitch of previous row, 3 treble drawn together, * 1 chain and 1 long treble into each of next 2 stitches, 1 chain, 1 long treble, 1 chain, 1 long treble all into next stitch, 1 chain and 1 long treble into each of next 2 stitches, 1 chain, 7 treble drawn together, repeat from *, working 4 treble drawn together at end of row instead of seven, 3 chain, turn.

Repeat last 2 rows for length required.

Cable Stitch. (Fig. 42)—Begin with a chain of the length required.

1st row.—Miss first chain, then 1 double crochet into every stitch, 1 chain, turn. **2nd row.**—1 double crochet into every stitch of previous row, 1 chain, turn.

3rd row.—3 double crochet on 3 double crochet, then wool over hook, insert hook into fourth double crochet of first row, * draw wool through loosely, wool over, insert hook into same place, draw wool through loosely, wool over, insert hook into same place again, draw wool through loosely (7 loops now on hook), wool over, draw through first six loops on hook, wool over, draw through remaining two loops *, miss 1 double crochet of last row, then work 3 double crochet on next 3 double crochet, ** wool over hook, miss next 3 double crochet of first row, insert hook into next double crochet of same row, repeat from * to * once, miss 1 double crochet of last row, 3 double crochet **, repeat from ** to ** to end, 1 chain, turn.

Fig. 44. CROSSED TREBLE

4th row.—As 2nd row. **5th row.**—3 double crochet, * 1 cable worked thus: wool over hook, insert hook under the bunch of raised loops here seen, draw wool through loosely, wool over, insert hook into same place, draw wool through loosely, wool over, insert hook into same place again, draw wool through loosely (7 loops on hook), wool over, draw through first six loops on hook, wool over, draw through remaining two loops, miss 1 double crochet of last row, 3 double crochet, repeat from * to end, 1 chain, turn. Repeat last 2 rows for length required.

Crossed Treble Pattern. (Fig. 44)—Begin with a length of chain divisible by four, with one over.

1st row.—Miss first 4 chain, then ** 1 cross worked thus: pass wool twice over hook, insert hook into next stitch, draw wool through, wool over, draw through 2 loops, wool over, miss 2 stitches, insert hook into next stitch, draw wool through, * wool over, draw through 2 loops, repeat from * 3 times more, thus making 3 treble, then 2 chain, 1 treble into centre of these 3 treble to complete cross, repeat from ** until one stitch of foundation chain remains, 1 long treble into this stitch, 4 chain, turn.

2nd row.—Miss long treble, work 1 cross over every cross of last row, then work 1 long treble into top of chain at end of row, 4 chain, turn.

Repeat 2nd row for length required.

Check Pattern. (Fig. 45)—This is worked with two colours. Using dark, begin with a length of chain divisible by four, with one over.

1st row.—Miss first chain, then 1 double crochet into every stitch, join on light and work 3 chain, turn. When changing from one colour to another, always draw colour next to be used, through last two loops of last stitch of present colour.

2nd row.—With light, miss first double crochet, then work 1 treble into every stitch, 3 chain, turn. **3rd row.**—With light, miss first treble, then 1 treble into every stitch, and draw dark wool through last two loops of last treble, then work 1 chain, turn. **4th row.**—With dark, work 1 double crochet into each of first 2 treble, now miss the two treble rows just worked, also first 2 double crochet of next double crochet row, then work 1 extra long treble into next double crochet of same row, * 1 check as follows: miss 1 treble of previous row, 3 double crochet on next 3 stitches, now miss 3 stitches of last double crochet row worked, 1 extra long treble into next stitch of same row, repeat from * until 2 stitches of previous row remain, miss 1 treble of previous row, 1 treble of previous row, 3 double crochet on next 3 stitches, repeat from * to end, 1 chain, turn. **9th row.**—As 5th row. Repeat from beginning of 2nd row for length required.

Tufted Pattern (Fig. 46)—Begin with a length of chain divisible by six.

1st row.—Miss first chain, 1 double crochet into every stitch, 1 chain, turn.

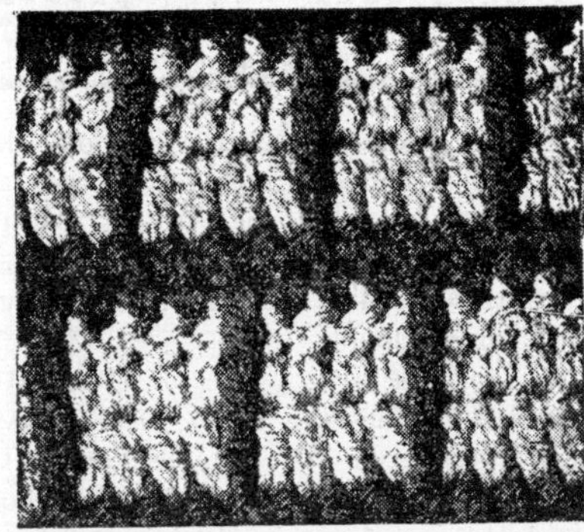

Fig. 45. CHECK PATTERN

Fig. 46. TUFTED PATTERN

1 double crochet into end stitch, 1 chain, turn. **5th row.**—With dark, 1 double crochet into every stitch, then with light, work 3 chain and turn. Repeat 2nd and 3rd rows once.

8th row.—With dark, work 1 extra long treble into first double crochet of last double crochet row worked, miss first treble of previous row, 3 double crochet on next 3 stitches, * miss 3 stitches of last double crochet row worked, 1 extra long treble into next stitch of same row, miss

Always work into top *front* thread of every stitch throughout.

2nd row.—1 double crochet into every stitch of previous row, 1 chain, turn.

3rd row.—2 double crochet, then 4 treble drawn together into top thread of third double crochet of last row but one, miss 1 stitch of last row, 5 double crochet on next 5 stitches, * miss 5 double crochet of last row but one, 4 treble drawn together into top thread of next stitch in same row, miss 1 stitch of last row, 5 double crochet

Fig. 47. LATTICE INSERTION

on next 5 stitches, repeat from *, working 2 double crochet instead of five at end of row, 1 chain, turn.

4th row.—As 2nd row. **5th row.**—5 double crochet, then * 4 treble drawn together into top thread of centre double crochet of five between tufts in last row but one, miss 1 stitch of last row, 5 double crochet on next 5 stitches, repeat from * to end, 1 chain, turn. **6th row.**—As 2nd row. **7th row.**—2 double crochet, * 4 treble drawn together into top thread of centre double crochet of five in last row but one, miss 1 stitch of last row, 5 double crochet on next 5 stitches, repeat from *, working 2 double crochet instead of five at end of row, 1 chain, turn. Repeat from beginning of 4th row for length required.

TWO SIMPLE CROCHET INSERTIONS

Some people prefer to work out their patterns from a chart. For this reason, charts of both these designs have been included, as well as the chart for working the little "Mostyn" Inset, which is illustrated overleaf, and for which complete directions are also given.

The Lattice Insertion.

MATERIALS:

Mercer Crochet Cotton, No. 60.

Steel crochet hook, No. 6.

The insertion should measure about $2\frac{1}{2}$ *inches wide* (see Fig. 47).

For abbreviations see beginning of chapter

Begin with 68 chain.

1st row.—Miss first 7 ch., then 1 tr. into each of next 4 ch., 6 h., 16 tr., 6 h., 4 tr., 1 h., 5 ch., turn. **2nd row.**—4 tr. on 4 tr., 8 h., 4 tr., 1 l., 7 tr., 4 h., 4 tr., 1 h., 5 ch., turn. **3rd row.**—4 tr. on 4 tr., 2 h., 7 tr., 1 l., 1 b., 4 tr., 3 h., 7 tr., 3 h., 4 tr., 1 h., 5 ch., turn.

4th row.—4 tr. on 4 tr., 2 h., 13 tr.,

Chart for working the above insertion.

2 h., 4 tr., 1 l., 1 b., 1 l., 4 tr., 1 h., 4 tr., 1 h., 5 ch., turn. **5th row.**—4 tr. on 4 tr., 1 h., 4 tr., 1 b., 1 l., 1 b., 4 tr., 2 h., 13 tr., 2 h., 4 tr., 1 h., 5 ch., turn.

6th row.—4 tr. on 4 tr., 2 h., 13 tr., 2 h., 4 tr., 1 l., 1 b., 1 l., 4 tr., 1 h., 4 tr., 1 h., 5 ch., turn.

7th row.—4 tr. on 4 tr., 2 h., 7 tr., 1 l., 1 b., 4 tr., 3 h., 7 tr., 3 h., 4 tr., 1 h., 5 ch., turn. **8th row.**—4 tr. on 4 tr., 8 h., 4 tr.,

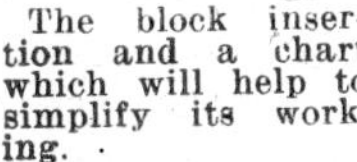

The block insertion and a chart which will help to simplify its working.

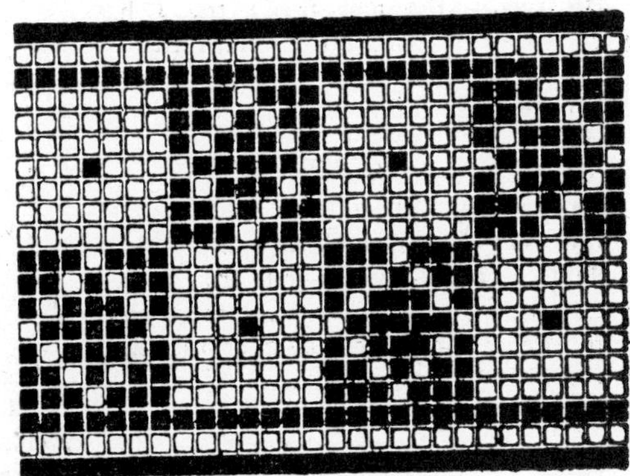

Fig. 48.

1 l., then 2 tr. into first loop of next lacet, 1 tr. on d.c., 2 tr. into next loop of same lacet, 1 tr. on next tr., 4 h., 4 tr., 1 h., 5 ch., turn. **9th row.**—4 tr. on 4 tr., 6 h., 16 tr., 6 h., 4 tr., 1 h., 5 ch., turn.

10th row.—4 tr. on 4 tr., 4 h., 7 tr., 1 l., 4 tr., 8 h., 4 tr., 1 h., 5 ch., turn.

11th row.—4 tr. on 4 tr., 3 h., 7 tr., 3 h., 4 tr., 1 b., 1 l., 7 tr., 2 h., 4 tr., 1 h., 5 ch., turn. **12th row.**—4 tr. on 4 tr., 1 h., 4 tr., 1 l., 1 b., 1 l., 4 tr., 2 h., 13 tr., 2 h., 4 tr., 1 h., 5 ch., turn.

13th row.—4 tr. on 4 tr., 2 h., 13 tr., 2 h., 4 tr., 1 b., 1 l., 1 b., 4 tr., 1 h., 4 tr., 1 h., 5 ch., turn. **14th row.**—4 tr. on 4 tr., 1 h., 4 tr., 1 l., 1 b., 1 l., 4 tr., 2 h., 13 tr., 2 h., 4 tr., 1 h., 5 ch., turn.

15th row.—4 tr. on 4 tr., 3 h., 7 tr., 3 h., 4 tr., 1 b., 1 l., 7 tr., 2 h., 4 tr., 1 h., 5 ch., turn. **16th row.**—4 tr. on 4 tr., 4 h., 7 tr., 1 l., 4 tr., 8 h., 4 tr., 1 h., 5 ch., turn. **17th row.**—4 tr. on 4 tr., 6 h., 16 tr., 6 h., 4 tr., 1 h., 5 ch., turn. Repeat from commencement of 2nd row for length required.

The Block Insertion.

MATERIALS:

Mercer Crochet Cotton, No. 60.

Steel crochet hook, No. 6.

The insertion should measure about $2\frac{1}{4}$ *inches wide* (see Fig. 48).

Begin with 57 chain.

1st row.—Miss first 3 ch., then 1 tr. into each of next 3 ch., 4 h., 4 tr., 3 h., 22 tr., 1 h., 4 tr., 3 ch., turn. **2nd row.**—

Miss first tr., then 1 tr. into each of next 3 tr., 1 h., 22 tr., 2 h., 4 tr., 1 h., 4 tr., 3 h., 4 tr., 3 ch., turn.

3rd row.—Miss first tr., 3 tr., 2 h., 4 tr., 3 h., 4 tr., 1 h., 22 tr., 1 h., 4 tr., 3 ch., turn. **4th row.**—Miss first tr., 3 tr., 1 h., 10 tr., 1 h., 13 tr., 5 h., 4 tr., 1 h., 4 tr., 3 ch., turn.

5th row.—As 3rd row.

6th row.—As 2nd row.

7th row.—Miss first tr., 3 tr., 4 h., 4 tr., 3 h., 22 tr., 1 h., 4 tr., 3 ch., turn.

8th row.—As 7th row.

9th row.—As 2nd row.

10th row.—As 3rd row.

11th row.—As 4th row.

12th row.—As 3rd row.

13th row.—As 2nd row.

Next 2 rows.—Miss first tr., 3 tr., 4 h., 4 tr., 3 h., 22 tr., 1 h., 4 tr., 3 ch., turn. Repeat from beginning of the 2nd row until length required.

The Mostyn Inset.

MATERIALS:

Mercer Crochet Cotton, No. 70.
Steel crochet hook, No. 6½.
Begin with 62 chain.

1st row.—1 tr. into 8th ch. from hook, 18 h., 5 ch., turn.

2nd row.—19 h., 5 ch., turn.

3rd row.—2 h., 4 tr., * 1 h., 4 tr., repeat from * 6 times 2 h., 5 ch., turn.

4th row.—* 3 h., 7 tr., 1 h., 7 tr., repeat from * once, 3 h., 5 ch., turn.

5th row.—2 h., 10 tr., * 1 h., 10 tr., repeat from * twice, 2 h., 5 ch., turn.

6th row.—5 h., 4 tr., 7 h., 4 tr., 5 h., 5 ch., turn. **7th row.**—2 h., 10 tr., * 1 h., 10 tr., repeat from * twice, 2 h., 5 ch., turn. **8th row.**—* 3 h., 7 tr., 1 h., 7 tr., repeat from * once, 3 h., 5 ch., turn **9th row.**—2 h., 4 tr., * 1 h., 4 tr., repeat from * 6 times, 2 h., 5 ch., turn **10th row.**—9 h., 4 tr., 9 h., 5 ch., turn. Now work from 3rd to 9th row inclusive once **18th row.**—19 h., 5 ch., turn. **19th row.**—19 h., then work double crochet all round inset Join and fasten off securely (Fig. 49)

SIMPLE PATTERNS FOR EDGINGS AND INSERTIONS

Crochet laces with matching insertions are always useful.

Also included is a charming Leaf Design insertion, which is exceptionally useful, in that, by merely adding a tiny edging, it forms a delightful lace.

THE MARIE PATTERN

MATERIALS:

Mercer Crochet Cotton, No. 70.
Steel crochet hook, No. 6½.

MEASUREMENTS:

THE INSERTION.—Nearly ½ inch wide.
THE EDGING.—A little over ¾ inch wide (Fig. 50).

For abbreviations see beginning of chapter.

The Insertion.

Begin with 12 chain.

1st row.—Miss 1 ch., 2 d.c., then 4 ch., miss 3 ch., 1 l.tr. into next ch., 4 ch., miss 3 ch., 2 d.c., 8 ch., turn.

2nd row.—1 d.c. into first sp., 1 d.c. on l.tr., 1 d.c. into next sp., 4 ch., 1 l.tr. on d.c. at end, 1 ch., turn.

3rd row.—1 d.c. on l.tr., 1 d.c. into sp., 4 ch., miss 1 d.c., 1 l.tr. on next d.c., 4 ch., 2 d.c. into next sp., 8 ch., turn. Repeat 2nd and 3rd rows until a corner is required.

The Corner

This is begun after the 3rd row of insertion has been worked.

4th row.—1 d.c. into first sp., 1 d.c. on l.tr., 1 d.c. into next sp., 4 ch., 1 l.tr. on d.c. at end, turn. **5th row.**—Miss first sp., then 1 d.l.tr. into 5th ch. of next sp. Fasten off. Work along ends of rows for second side of corner.

The Second Side of Corner.—6th row.—Hold work with d.l.tr. towards left-hand side, then miss last 4 rows worked, 1 d.c. into next row, 1 d.c. into next row, 4 ch., 1 l.tr. into next row, 4 ch., 1 d.c. into top of l.tr. at end of 4th row, 1 d.c. into d.l.tr., 8 ch., turn. Repeat 2nd and 3rd rows of insertion until another corner is required.

The Edging.

Work as for insertion, then add following edging thus: **1st round.**—2 d.c. into sp. before corner, 9 ch., 2 d.c. into sp. after corner, then 5 ch. and 2 d.c. into every sp., and work all corners as first, 5 ch., join. **2nd round.**—S.s. into corner sp., 5 ch., 1 l.tr. into same sp., then 1 ch. and 1 l.tr. 8 times into same sp., 2 ch., 2 d.c. into next sp., 2 ch., * 1 l.tr. into next sp., 1 ch. and 1 l.tr. 5 times into same sp., 2 ch., 2 d.c. into next sp., 2 ch., repeat from *, working 1 l.tr. into each corner sp., 1 ch. and 1 l.tr. 9 times into same sp. Join. **3rd round.**—S.s. into first sp., 1 d.c. into same sp., then 3 ch. and 1 d.c. into each of next 9 sp., 1 d.c. on next d.c., 1 d.c. into next sp., * 3 ch. and 1 d.c. into each of next 6 sp., 1 d.c. on next d.c., 1 d.c. into next sp., repeat from *, working all corners as first. Join and fasten off.

VANDYKE PETAL PATTERN

MATERIALS:

Mercer Crochet Cotton, No. 60.
Steel crochet hook, No. $6\frac{1}{2}$.

MEASUREMENTS:

THE EDGING.—1 inch wide.

THE INSERTION.—$\frac{1}{2}$ inch wide (Fig. 51).

The Edging.

Begin with 23 chain.

1st row.—1 tr. into 8th ch. from hook, miss 2 ch., then 1 tr., 2 ch., 1 tr. all into

CHART FOR INSET ABOVE

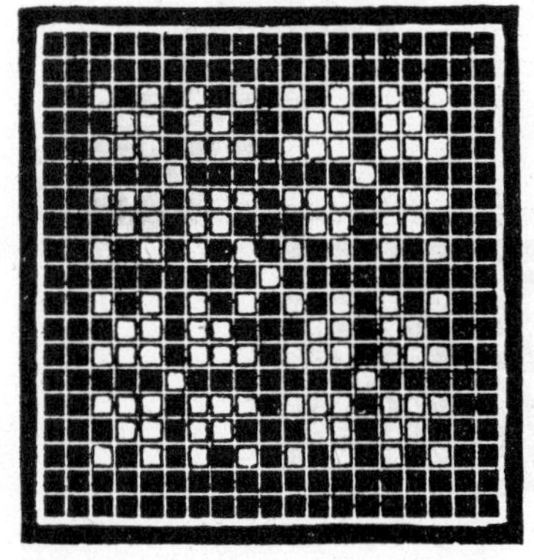

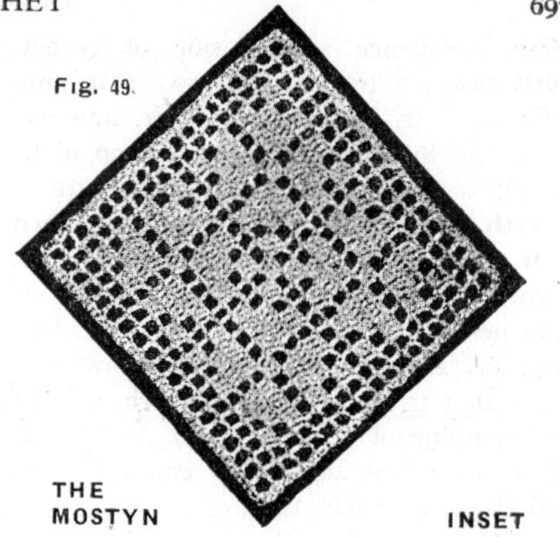

Fig. 49. THE MOSTYN INSET

next ch., miss 2 ch., 1 tr. into next ch., 1 h., 5 ch., miss 5 ch., then 1 tr., 3 ch., 1 tr. all into next ch., 3 ch., turn. **2nd row.**—7 tr. into first sp., 1 tr. into next tr., 7 tr. into next sp., 1 tr. into next tr., 1 h., then 1 tr., 2 ch., 1 tr. all into next sp., miss 1 tr., 1 tr. into next tr., 1 h., 5 ch., turn.

3rd row.—1 h., then 1 tr., 2 ch., 1 tr. all into next sp., miss 1 tr., 1 tr. into next tr., 1 h., 5 ch., miss 7 tr., then 1 tr., 3 ch., 1 tr. all into next tr., 3 ch., turn. Repeat 2nd and 3rd rows until a corner is required.

The Corner.

The First Side.—Work 2nd and 3rd rows of edging.

4th row.—7 tr. into first sp., 1 tr. into next tr., 7 tr. into next sp., 1 tr. into next tr., 1 h., then 1 tr., 2 ch., 1 tr. all into next sp., miss 1 tr., 1 tr. into next tr., 1 ch., turn.

5th row.—S.s. into each of first 2 tr., s.s. into sp., 4 ch., 1 tr. into same sp., miss 1 tr., 1 tr. into next tr., 1 h., 5 ch., miss 7 tr., then 1 tr., 3 ch., 1 tr. all into next tr., 3 ch., turn.

6th row.—7 tr. into first sp., 1 tr. into next tr., 7 tr. into next sp., 1 tr. into next tr., 5 ch., turn.

7th row.—Miss first 8 tr., then 1 tr., 3 ch., 1 tr. all into next tr., 3 ch., turn. **8th row.**—7 tr. into first sp., 1 tr. into next tr., 7 tr. into next sp., 1 d.c. into tr. at end of 6th row, 5 ch., turn.

9th row.—Miss first 7 tr., then 1 tr., 3 ch., 1 tr. all into next tr., 3 ch., turn.

Now commence second side of corner. **10th row.**—7 tr. into first sp., 1 tr. into next tr., 7 tr. into next sp., 1 tr. into d.c. at end of 8th row, 2 ch., s.s. to top of tr. at left, s.s. along next 3 st., 2 ch., turn.

11th row.—1 h., 5 ch., miss 7 tr., then 1 tr., 3 ch., 1 tr. all into next tr., 3 ch., turn. **12th row.**—7 tr. into first sp., 1 tr. into next tr., 7 tr. into next sp., 1 tr. into next tr., 2 ch., 1 tr. into end of s.s. now reached, 1 tr. into base of the 4 ch. worked at beginning of 5th row, 2 ch., s.s. to top of tr. at end of 4th row, 2 ch., 1 tr. into 3rd ch. of 5 at left, turn.

13th row.—Miss h. just made, 1 tr., 2 ch., 1 tr. all into next sp., miss 1 tr., 1 tr. into next tr., 1 h., 5 ch., miss 7 tr., then 1 tr., 3 ch., 1 tr. all into next tr., 3 ch., turn.

14th row.—7 tr. into first sp., 1 tr. into next tr., 7 tr. into next sp., 1 tr. into next tr., 1 h., then 1 tr., 2 ch., 1 tr. all into next sp., miss 1 tr., 1 tr. into top of tr. now reached, 1 h., 5 ch., turn.

15th row.—As 3rd row of edging. Repeat 2nd and 3rd rows of edging until another corner is required.

The Insertion.

Begin with 17 chain

1st row.—1 tr. into 8th ch. from hook, miss 2 ch., then 1 tr., 2 ch., 1 tr. all into next ch., miss 2 ch., 1 tr. into next ch., 1 h., 5 ch., turn.

2nd row.—1 h., then 1 tr., 2 ch., 1 tr. all into next sp., miss 1 tr., 1 tr. into next tr., 1 h., 5 ch., turn. Repeat 2nd row until a corner is required.

The Corner.

The First Side.

3rd row.—1 h., then 1 tr., 2 ch., 1 tr. all into next sp., miss 1 tr., 1 tr. into next tr., 1 ch., turn.

4th row.—S.s. into each of first 2 tr., s.s. into next sp., 4 ch., 1 tr. into same sp., miss 1 tr., 1 tr. into next tr., 1 h., 8 ch., turn.

5th row.—Miss first tr., s.s. into next tr., s.s. along next 3 st., 2 ch., turn.

6th row.—1 tr. into 3rd ch. of 8, 5 ch., turn.

7th row.—1 tr. into last s.s. worked, 1 tr. into base of the 4 ch. worked at

Fig. 50.—THE MARIE EDGING AND INSERTION

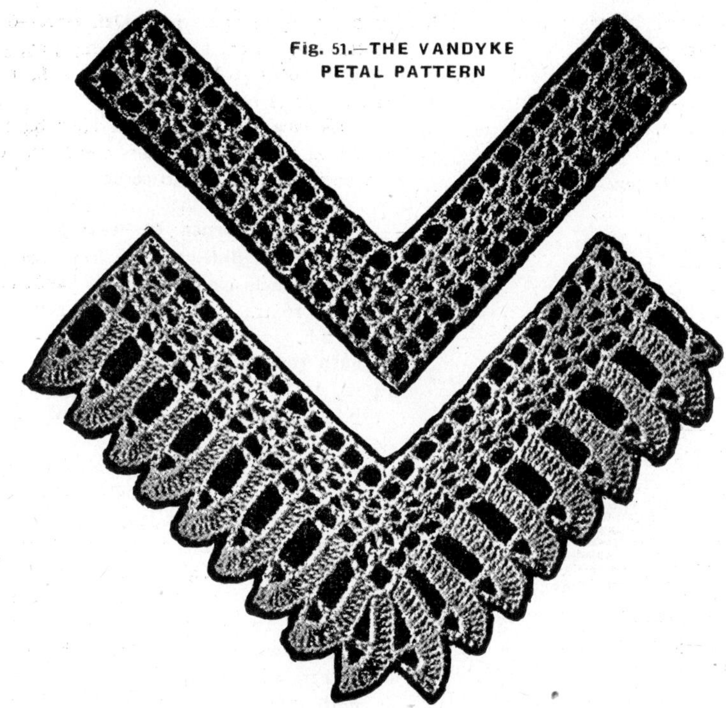
Fig. 51.—THE VANDYKE PETAL PATTERN

beginning of 4th row, 2 ch., s.s. to top of tr. at end of 3rd row, 2 ch., 1 tr. into 3rd ch. of 5 at left, turn.

8th row.—Miss h. just made, then 1 tr. 2 ch., 1 tr. all into next sp., miss 1 tr., 1 tr. into next tr., 1 h., 5 ch., turn.

9th row.—1 h., then 1 tr., 2 ch., 1 tr. all into next sp., miss 1 tr., 1 tr. into top of tr. now reached, 1 h., 5 ch., turn. Repeat 2nd row of insertion until another corner is required.

A LEAF DESIGN

MATERIALS:

Mercer Crochet Cotton, No. 80.
Steel crochet hook, No. 6½.

MEASUREMENTS:

THE INSERTION.—About 2¼ inches wide.

THE LACE.—About 2½ inches width (Fig. 52).

The Insertion

Begin with 71 chain

1st row.—1 tr. into 8th ch. from hook. 4 h., 16 tr., 1 h., 1 b., 1 l., 1 b., 4 tr., 4 h. Always turn with 5 ch. at ends of rows unless otherwise directed. **2nd row.**—4 h., 4 tr., 1 l., 1 b., 1 l., 4 tr., 10 h.

3rd row.—9 h., 4 tr., 1 h., 1 b., 1 l., 1 h., 4 tr., 5 h. **4th row.**—5 h., 4 tr., 1 h., 1 b., 1 l., 1 h., 4 tr., 9 h.

5th row.—8 h., 4 tr., 1 l., 1 b., 1 l., 4 tr., 6 h. **6th row.**—6 h., 4 tr., 1 b., 1 l., 1 b., 4 tr., 8 h. **7th row.**—2 h., 4 tr., 5 h., 4 tr., 1 l., 1 b., 1 h., 4 tr., 7 h.

8th row.—8 h., 4 tr., 1 l., 1 b., 4 tr., 4 h., 7 tr., 2 h. **9th row.**—2 h., 7 tr., 3 h., 4 tr., 1 h., 1 l., 1 h., 4 tr., 2 h., 16 tr., 2 h. **10th row.**—2 h., 7 tr., 1 h., 10 tr., 2 h., 4 tr., 1 b., 1 h., 4 tr., 1 h., 7 tr., 1 h., 4 tr., 2 h. **11th row.**—2 h., 4 tr., 1 h., 10 tr., 1 b., 1 l., 1 h., 13 tr., 1 h., 7 tr., 3 h. **12th row.**—3 h., 10 tr., 2 h., 10 tr., 1 b., 1 h., 10 tr., 2 h., 4 tr., 2 h. **13th row.**—2 h., 7 tr., 2 h., 10 tr., 1 l., 7 tr., 1 h., 13 tr., 4 h.

14th row.—5 h., 13 tr., 1 h., 4 tr., 1 b., 7 tr., 1 h., 13 tr., 2 h.

15th row.—3 h., 13 tr., 1 h., 4 tr., 1 h., 4 tr., 1 h., 13 tr., 6 h.

16th row.—7 h., 16 tr., 1 h., 16 tr., 4 h. **17th row.**—9 h., 4 tr., 12 h.

18th row.—8 h., 13 tr., 1 h., 4 tr., 8 h.

19th row.—7 h., 4 tr., 1 l., 4 tr., 1 h., 10 tr., 7 h. **20th row.**—6 h., 10 tr., 1 h., 7 tr., 1 b., 4 tr., 7 h. **21st row.**—7 h., 4 tr., 1 l., 10 tr., 1 h., 10 tr., 5 h.

22nd row.—4 h., 10 tr., 1 h., 10 tr., 1 h., 1 b., 1 h., 4 tr., 6 h.

23rd row.—6 h., 4 tr., 1 h., 1 l., 1 b., 10 tr., 2 h., 7 tr., 3 h.

24th row.—3 h., 19 tr., 1 h., 4 tr., 1 h., 1 b., 1 l., 4 tr., 5 h.

25th row.—5 h., 4 tr., 1 b., 1 l., 1 b., 4 tr., 3 h., 13 tr., 2 h.

26th row.—9 h., 4 tr., 1 l., 1 b., 1 l., 4 tr., 5 h. **27th row.**—5 h., 4 tr., 1 b., 1 l., 1 b., 1 h., 4 tr., 8 h.

28th row.—8 h., 4 tr., 1 h., 1 l., 1 b., 1 l., 4 tr., 5 h. **29th row.**—6 h., 1 b., 1 l., 1 b., 1 h., 4 tr., 1 h., 4 tr., 6 h.

30th row.—5 h., 7 tr., 1 h., 4 tr., 1 h., 1 l., 1 b., 19 tr., 2 h. **31st row.**—3 h., 7 tr., 1 h., 13 tr., 1 b., 1 h., 4 tr., 1 h., 7 tr., 5 h. **32nd row.**—5 h., 10 tr., 1 b., 1 h., 10 tr., 2 h., 7 tr., 4 h.

33rd row.—5 h., 10 tr., 1 h., 10 tr., 1 l., 10 tr., 5 h. **34th row.**—2 h., 10 tr., 1 h., 7 tr., 1 b., 7 tr., 1 h., 10 tr., 6 h.

35th row.—5 h., 4 tr., 1 h., 10 tr., 1 h., 4 tr., 1 l., 7 tr., 1 h., 7 tr., 3 h.

36th row.—3 h., 10 tr., 1 h., 4 tr., 1 h., 7 tr., 1 h., 7 tr., 1 l., 4 tr., 5 h.

37th row.—5 h., 4 tr., 1 b., 1 h., 7 tr., 1 h., 4 tr., 1 h., 13 tr., 4 h.

38th row.—5 h., 10 tr., 1 h., 10 tr., 1 b., 1 l., 4 tr., 5 h. **39th row.**—6 h., 4 tr., 1 h., 1 l., 1 b., 1 h., 4 tr., 8 h.

40th row.—6 h., 4 tr., 1 h., 4 tr., 1 h., 1 l., 1 b., 1 h., 4 tr., 6 h.

41st row.—7 h., 4 tr., 1 l., 10 tr., 1 h., 4 tr., 1 h., 4 tr., 5h. **42nd row.**—4 h., 4 tr., 1 l., 7 tr., 1 h., 10 tr., 1 h., 4 tr., 7 h. **43rd row.**—8 h., 13 tr., 1 h., 7 tr., 1 b., 4 tr., 4 h. **44th row.**—3 h., 4 tr., 1 h., 1 l., 7 tr., 1 h., 13 tr., 8 h.

45th row.—7 h., 13 tr., 1 h., 7 tr., 1 b., 1 b., 1 h., 4 tr., 3 h.

46th row.—3 h., 4 tr., 1 h., 1 l., 1 b., 7 tr., 1 h., 10 tr., 7 h. **47th row.**—6 h., 7 tr., 2 h., 10 tr., 1 l., 1 b., 1 h., 4 tr., 3 h.

48th row.—3 h., 4 tr., 1 h., 1 l., 1 b., 1 h., 13 tr., 1 h., 4 tr., 6 h.

49th row.—5 h., 16 tr., 1 h., 1 b., 1 l., 1 b., 4 tr., 4 h. This completes one pattern, and now begin corner.

The Corner (3 leaves).

The First Side.—Work from 2nd to 48th row inclusive of insertion. **49th row.**—5 h., 16 tr., 2 h., 4 tr., 1 l., 1 b., 1 l., 4 tr., 2 h.

50th row.—2 h., 4 tr., 1 b., 1 l., 1 b., 4 tr., 12 h. **51st row.**—13 h., 4 tr., 1 h., 1 b., 1 l., 4 tr., 2 h. **52nd row.**—2 h., 4 tr., 1 b., 1 l., 1 h., 4 tr., 13 h.

53rd row.—3 h., 13 tr., 6 h., 4 tr., 1 h., 1 b., 1 l., 4 tr., 2 h. **54th row.**—2 h., 4 tr., 1 b., 1 l., 4 tr., 4 h., 19 tr., 4 h.

55th row.—4 h., 7 tr., 2 h., 10 tr., 3 h., 4 tr., 1 b., 1 l., 4 tr., 2 h.

56th row.—2 h., 4 tr., 1 b., 1 l., 4 tr., 2 h., 10 tr., 1 h., 10 tr., 5 h.

57th row.—6 h., 10 tr., 1 h., 10 tr., 1 h., 4 tr., 1 b., 1 l., 4 tr., 2 h.

58th row.—2 h., 4 tr., 1 b., 1 l., 4 tr., 1 h., 10 tr., 1 h., 10 tr., 6 h.

59th row.—7 h., 10 tr., 1 h., 7 tr., 1 h., 4 tr., 1 b., 1 h., 4 tr., 3 h.

60th row.—3 h., 4 tr., 1 h., 1 l., 4 tr., 1 h., 4 tr., 2 h., 10 tr., 7 h.

61st row.—9 h., 10 tr., 1 h., 4 tr., 1 h., 1 b., 1 h., 4 tr., 3 h.

62nd row.—3 h., 4 tr., 1 h., 1 l., 1 b., 4 tr., 12 h. **63rd row.**—7 h., 16 tr., 1 h., 16 tr., 4 h. **64th row.**—3 h., 13 tr., 1 h., 4 tr., 1 h., 4 tr., 1 h., 13 tr., 6 h.

65th row.—5 h., 13 tr., 1 h., 4 tr., 2 h., 7 tr., 1 h., 13 tr., 2 h.

66th row.—2 h., 7 tr., 2 h., 10 tr., 2 h., 4 tr., 1 h., 13 tr., 5 h.

67th row.—4 h., 13 tr., 1 h., 7 tr., 1 h., 1 l., 7 tr., 2 h., 7 tr., 2 h.

68th row.—2 h., 4 tr., 1 h., 10 tr., 1 h., 1 b., 1 h., 10 tr., 2 h., 10 tr., 3 b.

69th row.—3 h., 7 tr., 1 h., 13 tr., 1 b., 1 l., 1 b., 1 h., 4 tr., 1 h., 4 tr., 2 h.

70th row.—2 h., 7 tr., 1 h., 4 tr., 1 l., 1 b., 1 l., 1 b., 10 tr., 1 h., 7 tr., 2 h.

71st row.—2 h., 19 tr., 1 l., 1 b., 1 l., 1 b., 4 tr., 1 h., 7 tr., 2 h.

72nd row.—2 h., 4 tr., 3 h., 4 tr., 1 h., 1 b., 1 l., 1 h., 4 tr., 8 h.

73rd row.—8 h., 4 tr., 1 h., 1 b., 1 l., 4 tr., 7 h. **74th row.**—8 h., 4 tr., 1 h., 1 l., 1 b., 7 tr., 6 h.

75th row.—5 h., 4 tr., 1 b., 1 l., 1 b., 1 h., 4 tr., 8 h.

76th row.—4 h., 13 tr., 1 b., 1 l., 1 b., 1 l., 1 h., 4 tr., 4 h.

77th row.—3 h., 4 tr., 1 l., 1 b., 1 l., 1 h., 19 tr., 5 h. **78th row.**—5 h., 7 tr., 2 h., 10 tr., 1 b., 1 l., 1 b., 1 h., 4 tr., 8 ch., turn. **79th row.**—Miss first 4 tr. and 1 h., then 1 tr. on next tr., 1 l., 1 b., 1 h., 10 tr., 1 h., 10 tr., 6 h.

80th row.—7 h., 10 tr., 1 h., 10 tr., 1 l., 1 b., 1 l., 8 ch., turn.

81st row.—1 b., 1 l., 1 b., 10 tr., 1 h., 10 tr., 7 h. **82nd row.**—8 h., 10 tr., 1 h., 7 tr., 1 l., 1 b., 6 ch., turn.

83rd row.—1 l., 1 b., 4 tr., 2 h., 10 tr., 8 h. **84th row.**—10 h., 7 tr., 1 h., 4 tr., 1 l., 8 ch., turn. **85th row.**—1 b., 1 h., 10 tr., 10 h. **86th row.**—13 h., 4 tr.

87th row.—1 h., 13 tr., 9 h.

88th row.—7 h., 19 tr., 1 h.

89th row.—1 h., 7 tr., 1 h., 13 tr., 6 h.

90th row.—5 h., 13 tr., 1 h., 10 tr., 1 h.

91st row.—1 h., 10 tr., 1 h., 16 tr., 4 h.

92nd row.—4 h., 10 tr., 2 h., 10 tr., 2 h.

93rd row.—2 h., 16 tr., 1 h., 10 tr., 3 h.

94th row.—3 h., 7 tr., 1 h., 16 tr., 3 h.

95th row.—4 h., 16 tr., 1 h., 4 tr., 3 h.

96th row.—3 h., 13 tr., 7 h.

97th row.—14 h., 10 ch., turn work so that top of trebles are at right-hand side.

The Second Side of Corner.—98th row.—1 tr. into 8th ch. from hook, 2 ch., miss tr. last worked in 97th row, s.s. to top of next tr., s.s. along next 3 st., 2 ch., turn.

99th row.—2 h. **100th row.**—1 h., 2 ch., s.s. to top of next tr. at left, s.s. along next 3 st., 2 ch., turn. Repeat last 2 rows 5 times. **111th row.**—2 h.

112th row.—7 h., 19 tr., 2 ch., miss 2 ch. of 8 at left, s.s. along next 4 ch., 2 ch., turn. **113th row.**—1 h., 4 tr., 1 h., 16 tr., 6 h. **114th row.**—5 h., 16 tr., 1 h., 7 tr., 1 h., 5 ch., s.s. to d.c. of lacet at left, s.s. along next 4 ch., 3 ch., turn. **115th row.**—1 l., 1 h., 10 tr., 1 h., 13 tr., 5 h. **116th row.**—4 h., 13 tr., 2 h., 10 tr., 1 h., 1 b., 3 ch., miss 1 row, 1 d.c. into top of tr. at end of next row, 3 ch., miss 2 ch. of 8 at left, s.s. along next 4 ch., 5 ch., turn.

117th row.—1 b., 1 l., 1 b., 13 tr., 2 h., 7 tr., 4 h. **118th row.**—3 h., 7 tr., 1 h., 16 tr., 1 h., 1 l., 1 b., 1 l., 1 b., 4 tr., 2 ch., s.s. to top of tr. at left, s.s. along next 3 st., 2 ch., turn.

119th row.—2 h., 4 tr., 1 h., 1 b., 1 l., 1 b., 1 l., 16 tr., 1 h., 4 tr., 3 h.

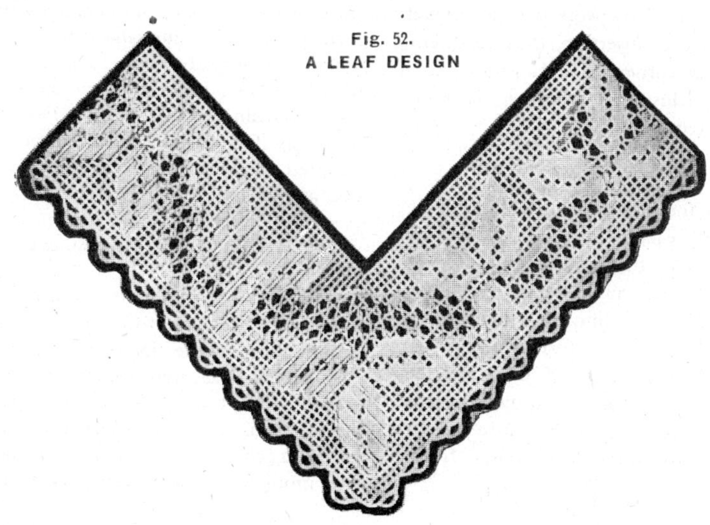

Fig. 52.
A LEAF DESIGN

120th row.—3 h., 16 tr., 1 l., 1 b., 1 l., 1 b., 1 l., 4 tr., 3 h. **121st row.**—4 h., 4 tr., 1 h., 1 l., 1 b., 1 l., 1 h., 4 tr., 1 h., 13 tr., 3 h. Now work from 75th row back to 63rd row inclusive, always working each row backwards.

135th row.—12 h., 4 tr., 1 l., 1 b., 1 h., 4 tr., 3 h. **136th row.**—3 h., 4 tr., 1 h., 1 l., 1 h., 4 tr., 1 h., 10 tr., 9 h.

137th row.—7 h., 10 tr., 2 h., 4 tr., 1 h., 4 tr., 1 b., 1 h., 4 tr., 3 h.

138th row.—3 h., 4 tr., 1 h., 1 l., 4 tr., 1 h., 7 tr., 1 h., 10 tr., 7 h.

139th row.—6 h., 10 tr., 1 h., 10 tr., 1 h., 4 tr., 1 b., 1 l., 4 tr., 2 h.

140th row.—2 h., 4 tr., 1 b., 1 l., 4 tr., 1 h., 10 tr., 1 h., 10 tr., 6 h.

141st row.—5 h., 10 tr., 1 h., 10 tr., 2 h., 4 tr., 1 b., 1 l., 4 tr., 2 h.

142nd row.—2 h., 4 tr., 1 b., 1 l., 1 h., 4 tr., 2 h., 10 tr., 2 h., 7 tr., 4 h.

143rd row.—4 h., 19 tr., 3 h., 4 tr., 1 h., 1 b., 1 l., 4 tr., 2 h.

144th row.—3 h., 4 tr., 1 h., 1 l., 1 b., 4 tr., 5 h., 13 tr., 3 h.

145th row.—11 h., 4 tr., 1 h., 1 l., 1 b., 1 h., 4 tr., 3 h. **146th row.**—4 h., 4 tr., 1 l., 1 b., 1 l., 4 tr., 10 h.

147th row.—10 h., 4 tr., 1 b., 1 l., 1 h., 4 tr., 5 h. **148th row.**—6 h., 7 tr., 1 h., 1 l., 1 h., 4 tr., 9 h.

149th row.—2 h., 4 tr., 5 h., 4 tr., 1 l.,. 1 b., 4 tr., 8 h. Now work from 8th to 49th row inclusive of insertion, thus completing pattern after corner. Work from 2nd to 49th row inclusive of insertion until next corner is required.

The Lace.

Work as for insertion, then add edging: * 2 d.c. into each of next 6 h., 1 d.c. into next h., 7 ch., turn; miss 5 d.c., 1 d.c. into next, 7 ch., miss 5 d.c., 1 d.c. into next, turn; 8 d.c. into first loop, 4 d.c. into next loop, 7 ch., turn; miss 7 d.c., 1 d.c. into next, turn; 8 d.c. into loop just made, 4 d.c. into loop now reached already worked into, 1 d.c. into h. now reached already worked into, repeat from * to end.

WHEEL-PATTERN LACE AND INSERTION

MATERIALS:

Mercer Crochet Cotton, No. 50.

Steel crochet hook, No. $6\frac{1}{2}$.

MEASUREMENTS:

The Lace.—$1\frac{1}{2}$ inches wide (Fig. 53).

The Insertion.—$1\frac{5}{8}$ inches wide

The Lace.

The First Wheel.—Begin with 6 ch. and join into a ring. **1st round.**—12 d.c. into ring, join. **2nd round.**—5 ch., 1 tr. on next d.c., then 2 ch. and 1 tr. on every d.c., 2 ch., join. (12 spaces all round.) **3rd round.**—1 d.c., 3 ch., 1 d.c. all into every sp., join.

4th round.—8 ch., miss first 3 ch. loop, 1 tr. between next 2 d.c., * 5 ch., miss next 3 ch. loop, 1 tr. between next 2 d.c., repeat from * 9 times, 5 ch., s.s. to 3rd ch. of 8 at beginning.

5th round.—1 d.c., 5 tr., 1 d.c. all into every sp., join. Fasten off.

The Second Wheel.—Begin with 6 ch. and join into a ring. Work first 4 rounds as for first wheel. **5th round.**—1 d.c., 3 tr. all into first sp., join to centre tr. of corresponding group on previous wheel, then 2 tr., 1 d.c. all into sp. on present wheel already worked into, 1 d.c., 3 tr. all into next sp., join to centre tr. of corresponding group on previous wheel, then 2 tr., 1 d.c. into same sp. on present wheel that already has 1 d.c. and 3 tr. worked into it, 1 d.c., 5 tr., 1 d.c. all into every remaining sp., join. Fasten off. Work as for second wheel until length required, leaving four groups of treble free at top and lower edges of each wheel as seen in illustration.

The Heading.—Work along one side of wheels thus:

1st row.—1 l.tr. into centre tr. of fourth free group of treble on first wheel, counting from the join of two wheels, * 7 ch., 1 d.c. into centre tr. of next group, 5 ch., 1 d.c. into centre tr. of next group, 7 ch., 1 l.tr. into centre tr. of next group, 2 ch., l.tr. into centre tr. of first free group on next wheel, repeat from *

Fig. 53.

to end. Fasten off. **2nd row.**—Begin again at beginning of previous row, and work 1 tr. into first l.tr., 2 ch., miss 2 st., 1 tr. into next, * 2 ch., miss 2 st., 1 tr. into next, ** 2 ch., 1 tr. on next d.c., 2 ch., miss 2 st., 1 tr. into next, repeat from ** once, 2 ch., miss 2 st., 1 tr. into next, 2 ch., 3 tr. into sp. between l.tr., 2 ch., 1 tr. into second chain after next l.tr., repeat from * to end. Fasten off.

The Insertion.

Work as for the lace, putting the heading along each side of wheels.

A FEW GENERAL HINTS ON CROCHET

Before passing on to other forms of crochet work, it is as well to note a few general hints which will enable you to make the very best of your work, and give it a professional finish.

Articles worked in cotton should always be pinned out to the width given in the measurements, and pressed carefully under a damp cloth, paying particular attention to edgings, points, vandykes, etc., which should be of uniform depth after pressing.

In the case of woollen articles, the pressing depends on the type of stitch used. Double crochet, for instance, requires to be very well pressed, whereas such a stitch as "Crazy Pattern" only needs very light pressing with a moderately warm iron.

All hand-made laces can be washed quite successfully in tepid water in which pure shredded soap has been well dissolved. Sluice up and down and squeeze gently, then rinse in several lots of tepid water. Lay out flat on a clean towel, and when partly dry, pin out to shape on a well-padded board, and press with a warm iron.

Very delicate laces, or those which have been in use for a number of years and are in danger of becoming damaged during the process of ordinary washing, should be washed by the bottle method. For this, fill a perfectly clean and fairly wide-mouthed bottle with very, very soapy, almost cold water, and gently lower the lace into it. Put your hand over the mouth of the bottle, and shake the bottle vigorously. Repeat the process several times, until the lace is quite clean, then rinse in the same way in several lots of tepid water. Naturally, you must not fill the bottle so full that there is no room for the lace to move about with the shaking, or otherwise you will not loosen the dirt from the fine threads.

Sometimes it becomes necessary to join lace, as in the case when a long length is being made in sections by more than one person. This is quite simple to do invisibly in the following way. Finish on a row that will fit correctly to first row of the pattern, then cut the foundation chain between all the stitches, and carefully draw away the cut thread as the stitches are required. Sew lower portion of each treble to top of last row made, passing the needle through the two loops at the base of the treble so that they cannot pull out. Attach in the right position along the row to preserve the pattern, and sew firmly but neatly, using the same thread with which the crochet was worked.

TRICOT CROCHET

Tricot Crochet is simplicity itself to work, and is an excellent medium for the fashioning of a great variety of crochet woolly work—pram covers, cot coverlets, baby rugs, and so on.

The only necessity for this work is that a special tricot hook should be used, which is of uniform thickness from the hook upwards, and which should be longer, if possible, than the width of the work, to allow for all the stitches comfortably.

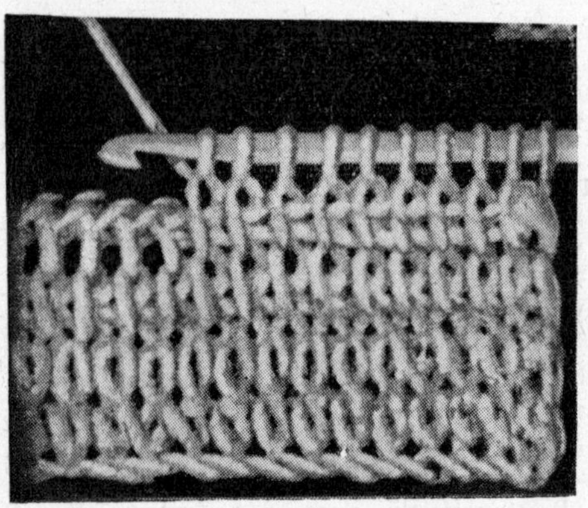

Fig. 54.—PLAIN TRICOT

Plain Tricot.—Each row of tricot really consists of two rows—a forward row and a backward row. Begin with a length of chain. **1st row.**—Forward Row. Miss first chain, insert hook into next chain, draw wool through and keep this loop on hook, * insert hook into next chain, draw wool through and keep this loop also on hook, repeat from * all along, when there should be the same number of loops on hook as the number of foundation chain.

Backward Row. Wool over hook, draw through first loop on hook ** wool over, draw through two loops on hook, repeat from ** to end.

2nd row.—Forward Row. The loop that remains on hook forms the first stitch of the row, therefore insert hook from right to left through second upright stitch in previous row, draw wool through and keep loop on hook, * insert hook from right to left through next upright stitch, draw wool through and keep this loop also on hook, repeat from * to end. Backward Row. Wool over, draw through first loop on hook, ** wool over, draw through two loops on hook, repeat from ** to end. Repeat 2nd row for length required, and finish by working one slip-stitch into each upright stitch of the last row worked (Fig. 54).

To Decrease.—This is always made in a forward row, thus: Insert hook from right to left through two upright stitches and draw wool through both of these at same time.

To Increase.—This is always made in a forward row. To increase at beginning of a row, insert hook from right to left through first upright stitch, draw wool through, then continue along row as for plain tricot. To increase at end of a row, work as forward row for plain tricot until one upright stitch remains, insert hook into stitch between upright stitches, draw wool through, insert hook into last upright stitch, draw wool through, then work backward row as described for plain tricot.

Fancy Tricot.—Begin with a length of chain. **1st row.**—Forward Row. Miss first chain, insert hook into next chain, draw wool through and keep this loop on hook, * insert hook into next chain, draw wool through and keep this loop also on hook, repeat from * to end, when there should be the same number of loops on hook, as the number of foundation chain. Backward Row. Wool over hook, draw through first loop on hook, ** wool over, draw through two loops on hook, repeat from ** to end. It will be seen that there is a row of small horizontal stitches at the back along top of row, and these are the stitches that are worked into in the following rows. **2nd row.**—Forward Row. Insert hook into horizontal stitch at back of second upright stitch in previous row, draw wool through, * insert hook into horizontal stitch at back of next upright stitch, draw wool through, repeat from * to end. Backward Row. Wool over hook, draw through first loop on hook, ** wool over, draw through two loops on hook, repeat from ** to end.

Repeat 2nd row for length required.

Plaited Tricot.—Begin with a length of chain divisible by two. **1st row.**—Work in the same way as described for the first row of plain tricot.

2nd row.—Forward Row. Insert hook from right to left through third upright stitch, draw wool through, insert hook through second upright stitch, draw wool through, * miss one upright stitch, insert hook through next upright stitch, draw wool through, insert hook through the stitch that was missed, draw wool through, repeat from * until one upright stitch remains, insert hook through this stitch, draw wool through. Backward Row. Wool over, draw through first loop on hook, ** wool over, draw through two loops on hook, repeat from ** to end.

Repeat 2nd row for length required, and finish by working one slip-stitch into

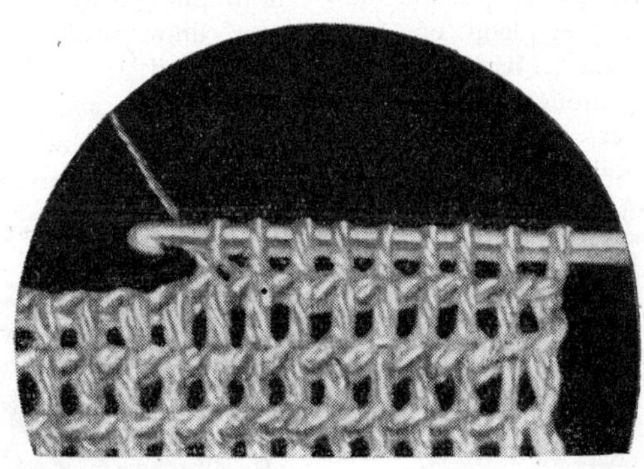

Fig. 55.
FANCY TRICOT

Fig. 56.
TRIPLE TRICOT

Fig. 57.
RIDGED TRICOT

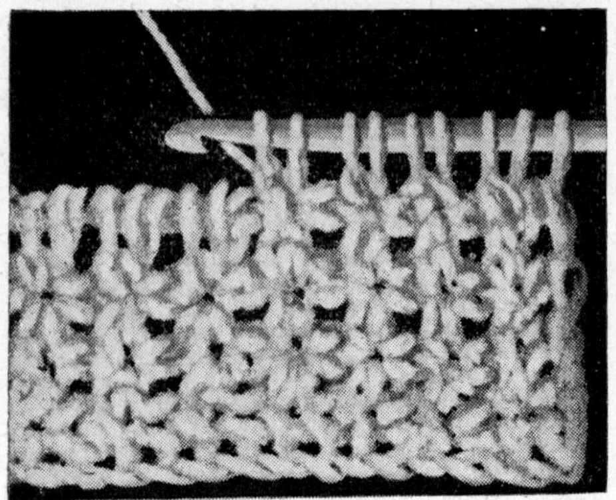

Fig. 58.—PLAITED TRICOT

each upright stitch of the last row worked (Fig. 58).

Ridged Tricot.—Begin with a chain the length required.

1st row.—Forward Row. Miss first chain, * insert hook into next chain, draw wool through and keep loop on hook, repeat from * to end. Backward Row. Wool over, draw through first loop on hook, ** wool over, draw through two loops on hook, repeat from ** to end, do not turn. **2nd row.**—Slip-stitch into each upright stitch of previous row, 1 chain, turn.

3rd row.—Forward Row. Miss first slip-stitch, * insert hook into top back thread of next slip-stitch, draw wool through and keep loop on hook, repeat from * to end. Backward Row. Wool over, draw through first loop on hook, ** wool over, draw through two loops on hook, repeat from ** to end, do not turn. Repeat last 2 rows for length required (Fig. 57).

Shell Pattern Tricot.—Begin with a chain divisible by three, with two over.

1st row.—Forward Row. Miss first chain, * insert hook into next chain, draw wool through and keep loop on hook, repeat from * to end. Backward Row. ** 2 chain, then wool over and draw through 4 loops on hook, repeat from ** until two loops remain on hook, 1 chain, wool over, draw through remaining 2 loops.

2nd row.—Forward Row. Insert hook into the one chain last worked, draw wool through and keep loop on hook, * insert hook into small horizontal stitch at top back of next group of loops, draw wool through and keep loop on hook, insert hook into the first of the two chain worked between loops, draw wool through and keep loop on hook, insert hook into the next chain, draw wool through and keep loop on hook, repeat from * to end. Backward Row. Work as for backward row of first row. Repeat 2nd row for length required (Fig. 59).

Triple Tricot.—Begin with a chain the length required.

1st row.—Forward Row. Miss first three chain, then * wool over, insert hook into next stitch, draw wool through, wool over, draw through one loop on hook, wool over, draw through two loops, repeat from * to end. Backward Row. Wool over, draw through first loop on hook, ** wool over, draw through 2 loops, repeat from ** to end.

2nd row.—Forward Row. 2 chain, miss first stitch of last row, * wool over, insert hook into upright stitch seen at upper

Fig. 59.—SHELL PATTERN

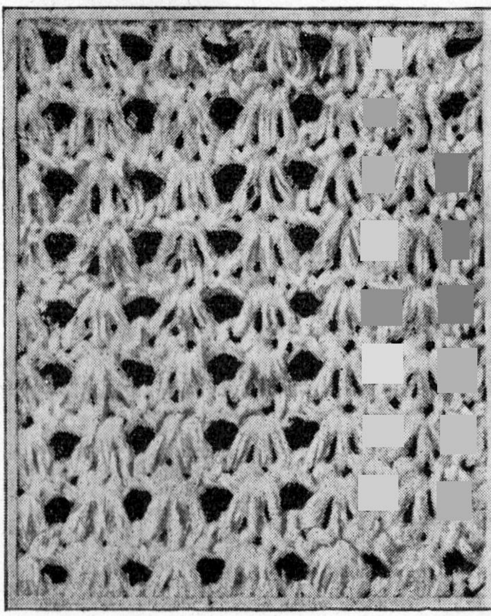

portion of next stitch in previous row, draw wool through, wool over, draw through one loop, wool over, draw through two loops, repeat from * to end. Backward Row. Work as for backward row of first row.

Repeat 2nd row for length required (Fig. 56).

Cellular Blankets are especially easy to crochet with the aid of a particular make of crochet hook known as the Blanket Needle, and a special kind of Blanket Wool, which is obtainable in either summer or winter weight. Blankets made in this way are easily and quickly made and have the added advantage that they can be made in shades to tone with most bedroom furnishing schemes.

MATERIALS:

For a pair of blankets, single bed size, 3 lb. of Blanket Wool, summer weight, or 4 lb. winter weight, will be required.

1 Blanket Needle.

Satin ribbon for binding.

For a blanket, single bed size, begin with 130 to 140 chain.

1st row.—Forward Row. Miss first ch., * insert hook into back stitch of next ch., draw wool through and keep loop on hook, repeat from * to end. Backward Row. Wool over, draw through first loop on hook, ** wool over, draw through 2 loops, repeat from ** to end. **2nd row.**—Forward Row. Insert hook into stitch at back of second upright stitch in previous row, draw wool through and keep loop on hook, * insert hook into stitch at back of next upright stitch, draw wool through and keep loop on hook, repeat from * to end. Backward Row. Work as for backward row in 1st row. Repeat 2nd row for length required. Bind top and bottom of blanket with satin ribbon.

For a blanket, double bed size, begin with 160 to 180 chain, and work in same way as described above.

The Blanket Needle is adjustable to give varying lengths.

IRISH CROCHET

Irish Crochet is certainly the most beautiful of all, and also the most valuable, being eagerly sought after by those who prize hand-made laces. It gives great scope for taste and ingenuity on the part of the worker, and though so elaborate in design, it is quite simple to work, and can be attempted by anyone who is acquainted with ordinary crochet.

It is worked, however, in quite a different fashion from ordinary crochet, the roses, shamrocks, grapes, etc., which are a feature of the work, being made separately from the background, which is worked round them afterwards. The background itself is formed of a network of picots, open spaces or Clones Knots and is called "Filling," and is extremely light and dainty in appearance. Padding is also a feature of Irish Crochet, and enters into many of the motifs.

Baby Irish Lace is much used for trimming babies' and children's garments: it is worked with a very fine thread, and usually consists of small sprigs or motifs which are built up into squares with picot loops, and then joined together, the picoted loops being a special feature of this work. Some delightful examples of this simplest manner of working, are shown in the following pages.

For the more elaborate Irish crochet, various sprigs and motifs are first worked; they are then placed in position, right side downward on a "foundation" of glazed linen or stout paper on which the shape of the article to be made has been traced, and joined together with one or the other different fillings.

Materials for Irish Crochet.—Materials used should be of the very best possible quality, as the type of work is such that it will last practically for ever, and it is well worth putting the best into it. The thread should be very fine, a special cotton for making Irish Lace being obtainable. The finer numbers of ordinary crochet cotton could be used. The finest steel crochet hooks are used, and professional workers prefer those which have a very short steel part fixed into a flat piece of wood. This type is supposed to be extra firm, but most work can be achieved quite well with an ordinary hook.

General Hints on Working Irish Crochet.—As has been explained already, the various motifs making up the design—scrolls, flowers, leaves, etc.—are worked according to the directions, and when finished, they are sewn into position upon the linen upon which the pattern is traced. All spaces are then filled in with a filling.

Single Picots are loops made thus, unless otherwise directed: 1 double crochet into the edge of one of the devices, 5 chain, 1 double crochet or slip-stitch into the third of these chain, 2 chain, 1 double crochet again into the edge of the device.

Loops with Two Picots are worked as follows, unless otherwise directed: 1 double crochet, (8 chain, then 1 double or single crochet into the third of these chain) twice, 2 chain, 1 double crochet into the pattern, and so on.

There may be as many picots in the loops as the worker likes, but one of the rules for making good Irish crochet is to keep all the meshes of the network of the same size, or as nearly so as circumstances will allow.

When the network filling is complete, cut the tacking threads from the back of the linen, taking care not to cut any of the crochet. Then spread the work on a thick ironing cloth, lay a damp cloth over it, and press well with a hot iron on the wrong side.

For large lengths or areas of Irish crochet, which may have become soiled in the making, the professional way of treating it is thus: Remove the lace carefully from the foundation, and wash it by soaking it well in thick soapsuds. Squeeze it several times in the rich lather, but do not rub or wring it. Rinse well, then tack it on the foundation again, and leave it to dry. It should then be slightly gummed before ironing. This is done with a small clean sponge dipped in a solution of white gum arabic.

The edges and picots should be carefully pulled out with a crochet hook before ironing, the pressing to be done as already described.

Padded Rings, as has been previously stated, are also a favourite feature on this type of lace, and to make them a pencil is required, and a good length of padding cotton. The latter is wound round and round the end of the pencil until the ring is of the desired thickness. The cotton is then cut, the ring being slipped off the pencil, and then covered with double or treble crochet. Some workers find it convenient and helpful to overcast the windings slightly with a needleful of very fine cotton, to give a little extra firmness. Others twist the padding cotton round one

Fig. 60.—Two methods of padding rings. The two circles on the left show double crochet being worked round the padding, and those on the right, button hole stitch worked with a needle.

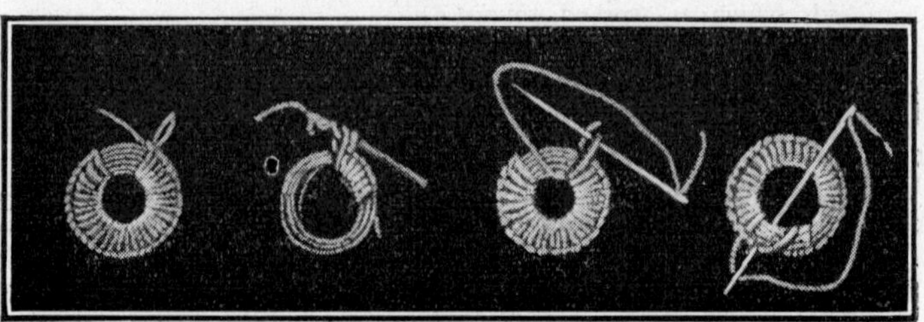

of the fingers of the left hand, and crochet directly over the ring thus made. The making of these rings needs practice, as they are apt to slip and come apart when taken off the pencil, but a little trouble will soon prove to the worker that they are really quite simple to do.

Sometimes the rings are given buttonholed instead of crochet edges; and again, they are sometimes varied with a picot of 4 or 5 chain after every 3 or 6 double crochet stitches.

They can also be so thickly covered that no opening shows in the middle, and in this case they may be used in clusters to form the "grapes" so often seen in Irish crochet.

When a simple circle is made to emphasise the centre of a flower or some other device, it is often added after the lace is completed. Stitches securing it are then taken through from the wrong side to the right with a fine needle, using the same type of thread as has been employed for the rest of the crochet, and holding the circle meanwhile between the thumb and finger of the left hand.

THE MAKING OF IRISH CROCHET MOTIFS

Having outlined the method of making this delightful lace, we will now go on to some of the motifs which are most generally used, and it will well repay the worker to practise them a number of times before atetmpting to insert them into a design. These specimen motifs need not be wasted, however, for they make dainty and unusual insets for house, table, and personal linen of all kinds.

Fig. 61.—THE DAISY

The Daisy is undoubtedly the simplest motif of all, and it is fashioned thus: Begin with 10 ch., and join into a ring. **1st round.**—3 ch., 35 tr. into ring, join. **2nd round.**—6 ch., miss 2 tr., 1 tr. on next, * 3 ch., miss 2 tr., 1 tr. on next, repeat from * all the way round, 3 ch., join. **3rd round.**—1 d.c., 1 tr., 3 l.tr., 1 tr., 1 d.c. all into every space. Join, and fasten off (Fig. 61).

The Wheel is another simple but very dainty motif. Commence with 5 ch. and join into a ring. **1st round.**—8 d.c. into ring, join, and turn. **2nd round.**—7 ch., miss 1 ch., s.s. along 6 ch., turn; 4 d.c., p., 3 d.c. over s.s., then s.s. into last s.s., * 12 ch., turn; s.s. into next d.c. of ring, turn; 4 d.c. p., 3 d.c. into loop, repeat from * 6 times, 6 ch., turn; s.s. to end of bar first worked, turn. **3rd round.**—2 d.c. into first sp., p. and 2 d.c. 3 times into same sp., * 2 d.c. into next sp., p. and 2 d.c. 3 times into same sp., repeat from * all round. Join, and fasten off (Fig. 62)

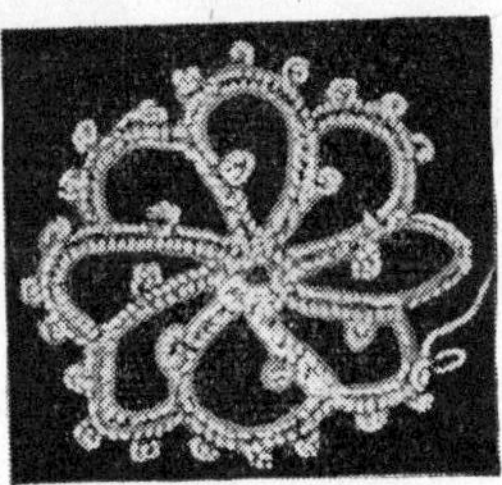

Fig. 62.—THE WHEEL

A Single Rose is extremely popular in Irish crochet, and it is worked as follows: Commence with 12 ch. and join into a ring. **1st round.**—21 d.c. into ring, join. **2nd round.**—* 3 ch., 3 tr. on next 3 d.c., 3 ch., turn; 2 tr. on first tr., 1 tr., 2 tr. on next, 1 tr. into chain at end, 3 ch., turn; miss 1 tr., 4 tr., 2 tr. on next tr., 1 tr. into chain at end, 3 ch., s.s. into same place as last tr., s.s. along end of next row, s.s. into top of tr. now reached, 3 ch., s.s. into d.c. last worked into on ring, s.s. into next d.c., repeat from * 4 times. **3rd round.**—* 3 d.c. into first row of small petal, 3 d.c.

into next row, 4 d.c. into next, 7 d.c. on 7 tr., always working into back thread of each tr., 2 d.c. into first chain of three now reached, 2 d.c. on next 2 ch. of same three, 3 d.c. over s.s., then 3 d.c. on 3 ch. at end of 1st row of petal, s.s. between petals, repeat from * 4 times. Fasten off securely (Fig. 63).

The Bunch of Grapes is a simple motif, ideal for table linen, though it can be used for every other purpose for which Irish crochet is intended.

For a grape, wind thread 30 times round the end of an ordinary pencil, slip off and fill ring with d.c., then join, and fasten off. Make twelve grapes altogether, then sew them together to form a bunch. The stem is made by s.s. into top of bunch, then work over three strands of thread 33 d.c., 3 ch., turn; miss 1 d.c., 4 tr., 3 s.tr., then 1 d.c. into every remaining d.c. Join to top of bunch, then fasten off securely. Cut off padding cotton, and sew ends firmly at back of bunch (Fig. 64).

A Simple Leaf Spray is made thus: For a leaf, begin with 16 ch. Miss 1 ch., 2 d.c. into next, 13 d.c., 3 d.c. into next, 13 d.c. down other side of foundation chain, 1 d.c. into same place as the 2 d.c. at the beginning, join, and turn. Always work into the back thread of every stitch. **Next row.**—13 d.c. on 13 d.c., 1 ch., turn. **Next row.**—13 d.c., 3 d.c. into next stitch, 11 d.c., 1 ch., turn. **Next row.**—12 d.c., 3 d.c. into next stitch, 11 d.c., 1 ch., turn. **Next row.**—12 d.c., 3 d.c. into next stitch, 9 d.c., 1 ch., turn. **Next row.**—10 d.c., 3 d.c. into next stitch, 9 d.c., 1 ch., turn. **Next row.**—10 d.c., 3 d.c. into next stitch, 7 d.c., 1 ch., turn. **Next row.**—8 d.c., 3 d.c. into next stitch, 7 d.c., 1 ch., turn. **Next row.**—8 d.c., 3 d.c. into next stitch, 5 d.c. Fasten off.

Make two more leaves in the same way.

The stem is made by working 30 ch., then joining to the base of a leaf, 8 ch., join to base of another leaf, now work over three strands of thread into the chain, 1 d.c. into every stitch, 1 ch., turn; s.s. into every stitch until opposite first leaf, join to base of third leaf, then s.s. into every remaining d.c. of stem, s.s. into base of leaf now reached. Fasten off securely. Cut off padding cotton, and sew ends firmly at the back (Fig. 65).

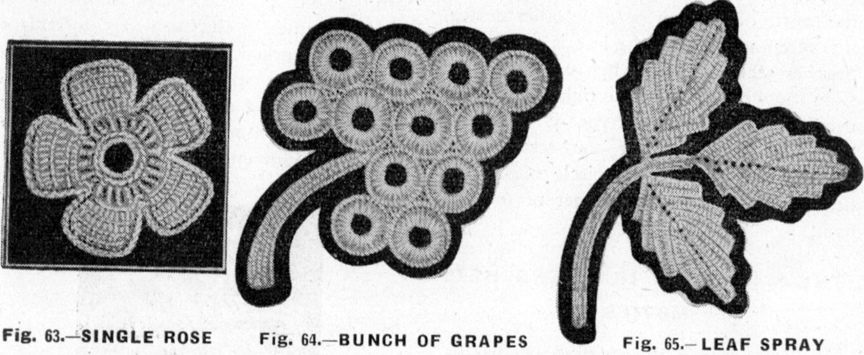

Fig. 63.—SINGLE ROSE Fig. 64.—BUNCH OF GRAPES Fig. 65.—LEAF SPRAY

The Bell Motif is a little more elaborate than those just given, but it is nevertheless quite simple to work. The motif is begun by first making the trefoil (or shamrock) in the centre, in the following way: Work over 5 strands of thread, 2 d.c., 21 tr., 2 d.c., then s.s. to first d.c., still work over padding cotton, 25 d.c. on 25 stitches of leaf, * work 2 d.c., 21 tr., 2 d.c. over padding cotton only, s.s. to first d.c. of this leaf, 25 d.c. over padding cotton on 25 stitches of this leaf, repeat from * once, s.s. into base of centre leaf, also into base of first leaf, s.s. along to centre d.c. of first leaf made.

1st round.—24 ch., 1 d.c. into centre d.c. of second leaf, 20 ch., 1 d.c. into centre d.c. of next leaf, 20 ch., join. **2nd round.**—33 d.c. into first loop, 27 d.c. into next loop, 28 d.c. into next loop, join. **Next row.**—* 3 ch., miss 2 d.c., 1 d.c. on next *, repeat from * to * 3 times, ** 3 ch., miss 1 d.c., 1 d.c. on next **, repeat from * to * once, repeat from ** to ** twice, repeat from * to * twice, repeat from ** to ** 3 times, 4 ch., turn.

Next 4 rows.—1 d.c. into first sp., 4 ch. and 1 d.c. into every space, 4 ch., turn. **Next row.**—As previous row, 1 ch., turn. **Next row.**—1 d.c., 5 tr. into first sp., 1 d.c., 3 tr. into next sp., 2 tr., 1 d.c. 2 tr. all into next sp., 3 tr., 1 d.c. into next sp., 1 d.c., 4 tr. into next sp., * 1 d.c., 2 tr. into next sp., 2 tr., 1 d.c. into next sp., 1 d.c., 5 tr. into next sp., repeat from * once, 1 d.c., 2 tr. into next sp., 2 tr., 1 d.c. into next sp., 4 ch., turn.

Next row.—Miss 3 stitches, 1 d.c. on next, 4 ch., miss 3 stitches, 1 d.c. on next, * 4 ch., miss 2 stitches, 1 d.c. on next, repeat from * twice, 4 ch., miss 3 stitches, 1 d.c. on next, 4 ch., miss 1 tr., 1 d.c. on next, 4 ch., miss 3 stitches, 1 d.c. on next, 4 ch., miss 1 tr., 1 d.c. on next, 4 ch., miss 2 stitches, 1 d.c. on next, 4 ch., 1 d.c. on next d.c., 4 ch., miss 2 stitches, 1 d.c. on next, 4 ch., miss 2 stitches, 1 d.c. on next, 4 ch., miss 3 stitches, 1 d.c. on next, 4 ch., 1 d.c. on next d.c., 4 ch., miss 2 tr., 1 d.c. on next, 4 ch., miss 1 tr., 1 d.c. on next, 1 ch., turn.

Next round.—1 d.c., 2 tr. into first sp., 1 d.c., 3 tr. into next sp., 2 tr., 1 d.c. into next sp., 1 d.c., 5 tr. into next sp., 1 d.c., 1 tr. into next sp., 3 tr., 1 d.c. into next sp., * 1 d.c., 4 tr. into next sp., 1 d.c. into next sp., repeat from * once, 1 d.c., 3 tr. into next sp., 1 tr., 1 d.c. into next sp., 1 d.c., 5 tr., 1 d.c. into next sp., 1 d.c. 2 tr. into next sp., 2 tr., 1 d.c. into next sp., 1 d.c., 4 tr., 1 d.c. into next 2 sp., turn sideways, 2 ch., 1 tr. into end of group now reached, 1 ch. and 1 tr. into next 2 rows, 1 ch., 1 tr., 1 ch., 1 tr. into next row, 1 ch. and 1 tr. into next 3 rows, 1 ch.,

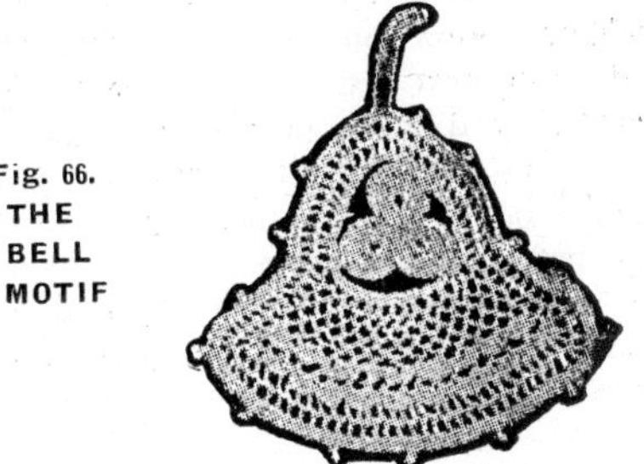

Fig. 66. THE BELL MOTIF

1 tr. on next d.c., ** 1 ch., miss 1 stitch, 1 tr. on next, repeat from ** 26 times, 1 ch. and 1 tr. into next 4 rows, 1 ch., 1 tr., 1 ch., 1 tr. into next row, 1 ch. and 1 tr. into next 3 rows, 1 ch., 1 tr., 1 ch., 1 tr. into end of next row, 1 ch., miss 1 tr. of group, 1 tr. on next, *** 1 ch., miss 1 st., 1 tr. on next ***, repeat from *** to *** twice, 1 ch., miss 2 stitches, 1 tr. on next, repeat from *** to *** 4 times, 1 ch., miss 3 stitches, 1 tr. on next, 1 ch., miss 1 stitch, 1 tr. on next, 1 ch., 1 tr. on stitch, 1 ch., 1 tr. on next d.c., 1 ch., miss 1 stitch, 1 tr. on next, 1 ch. and 1 tr. on next 2 stitches, repeat from *** to *** 7 times, 1 ch., miss 2 stitches, 1 tr. on next, repeat from *** to *** 6 times, 1 ch. and 1 tr. on next 2 stitches, 1 ch., 1 tr. on next d.c., 2 ch., 1 d.c. into next sp., 2 ch., 1 tr. into next sp., 1 ch. and 1 tr. into next 21 sp., 1 ch., 1 tr., 1 ch., 1 tr. into next sp., 1 ch. and 1 tr. into next 2 sp., 1 ch., 1 tr., 1 ch., 1 tr. into next sp., 1 ch. and 1 tr. into next 19 sp., 1 ch. and 1 tr. 3 times into next sp., 1 ch., 1 tr., 1 ch., 1 tr. into next sp., 1 ch. and 1 tr. into next 29 sp., 1 ch., 1 tr., 1 ch., 1 tr. into next sp., 1 ch., 1 tr. into next sp., 1 ch., 1 tr., 1 ch., 1 tr. into next sp., 1 ch., 1 tr. into next sp., 1 ch., 1 d.c. into next sp.

Next round.—Work over padding cotton, 2 d.c. into same sp. last worked into, 2 d.c. into next 5 sp., 1 d.c., p., 2 d.c. into next sp., 2 d.c. into next 7 sp., 1 d.c., p., 2 d.c. into next sp., 2 d.c. into next 4 sp., 1 d.c., p., 2 d.c. into next sp., 2 d.c. into next 2 sp., turn; 24 d.c. over padding cotton only for a stalk, 1 ch., turn; 24 d.c. over padding cotton on 24 d.c., 1 d.c. over padding cotton into sp. last worked into, 2 d.c. into next 7 sp., 1 d.c., p., 2 d.c. into next sp., 2 d.c. into next 5 sp., 1 d.c., p., 2 d.c. into next sp., 2 d.c. into next 8 sp., 1 d.c., p., 2 d.c. into next sp., * 2 d.c. into next 4 sp., 1 d.c. p., 2 d.c. into next sp., repeat from * once, 2 d.c. into next 5 sp., 1 d.c., p., 2 d.c. into next sp., 2 d.c. into next 5 sp., 1 d.c. p., 2 d.c. into next

Fig. 67. A SHAMROCK MOTIF

sp., 2 d.c. into next 6 sp., 1 d.c., p., 2 d.c. into next sp., 2 d.c. into next 6 sp., 1 d.c., p., 2 d.c. into next sp., 2 d.c. into next 2 sp., 1 d.c., p., 2 d.c. into next sp., 2 d.c. into every remaining space. Join, and fasten off. Cut off padding cotton and sew ends firmly at back (Fig 66).

The Shamrock Motif is very lacy and delicate, and for the working of it, a very fine cotton and hook are needed (Fig. 67).

For the Shamrock.—Work over 5 strands of thread, 3 d.c., 29 tr., 3 d.c., then s.s. to first d.c., * 3 d.c., 29 tr., 3 d.c. over padding cotton only, s.s. to first d.c. of this leaf, repeat from * once, then still working over padding cotton, work 35 d.c. on first 35 stitches of first leaf, 35 d.c. on 35 stitches of next leaf, 35 d.c. on 35 stitches of next leaf, join. Cut off padding cotton, and sew ends firmly.

The First Large Leaf.—1st row.—S.s. along first 7 d.c. of first leaf, 5 ch., miss 1 d.c., 1 d.c. on next, 5 ch., miss 1 d.c., 1 d.c. on next, * 5 ch., miss 2 d.c., 1 d.c. on next, repeat from * twice, 5 ch., miss 3 d.c., 1 d.c. on next, 5 ch., miss 3 d.c., 1 d.c. on next, 5 ch., turn.

2nd row.—1 d.c. into first loop, 5 ch. and 1 d.c. into next 5 loops, 5 ch., turn.

Next 2 rows.—As 2nd row.

5th row.—1 d.c. into first loop, 5 ch. and 1 d.c. into next 2 loops, 5 ch., turn, and leave remainder unworked. **6th row.**—1 d.c. into first loop, 5 ch. and 1 d.c. into next 2 loops, 1 ch., turn.

7th row.—S.s. to centre of first loop, 5 ch. and 1 d.c. into next 2 loops, 1 ch., turn. **8th row.**—S.s. to centre of first loop, 5 ch., 1 d.c. into next loop. Fasten off.

Work 1 d.c. into same loop last worked into in 5th row, 5 ch. and 1 d.c. into next 3 loops, 5 ch., turn. **6th row.**—1 d.c. into first loop, 5 ch. and 1 d.c. into next 2 loops, 1 ch., turn. **7th row.**—S.s. to centre of first loop, 5 ch. and 1 d.c. into next 2 loops, 1 ch., turn. **8th row.**—S.s. to centre of first loop, 5 ch., 1 d.c. into next loop. Fasten off.

The Second Large Leaf.—Miss 8 d.c. of second small leaf of shamrock, 1 d.c. on next, * 5 ch., miss 2 d.c., 1 d.c. on next, repeat from * 5 times, 5 ch., turn. Repeat from 2nd row of first large leaf.

The Third Large Leaf.—Miss 8 d.c. of third small leaf of shamrock, 1 d.c. on next, * 5 ch., miss 2 d.c., 1 d.c. on next, repeat from * 5 times, 5 ch., turn. Repeat from 2nd row of first large leaf.

Work all round leaves thus: 1 d.c. into first sp. on first large leaf, 2 ch., 1 tr. into next loop, then 2 ch., 1 tr. into end of

Fig. 68.—OPEN SPACE FILLING

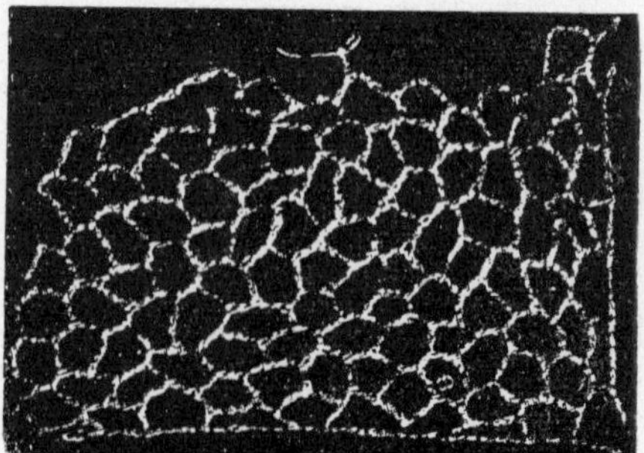

next row, * 2 ch., 1 tr., 1 ch., 1 tr. all into end of next 5 rows *, 2 ch. and 1 tr. 5 times into next loop, ** 2 ch., 1 tr., 1 ch., 1 tr. into next row, 2 ch., 1 tr. into next row, 2 ch., 1 tr. into the dip, 1 d.c. into next loop, 2 ch., 1 tr. into next row, 2 ch., 1 tr., 1 ch., 1 tr. into next row, 2 ch., 1 tr. into next loop, 2 ch., 1 tr. into same loop, 1 ch. and 1 tr. 5 times into same loop **, 2 ch., 1 tr., 1 ch., 1 tr. all into next 4 rows, 2 ch. and 1 tr. into next 3 rows, 2 ch., 7 d.c. on next 7 d.c. of leaf, 8 d.c. on first 8 d.c. of next leaf, 2 ch. and 1 tr. into end of next 2 rows, 2 ch., 1 tr., 1 ch., 1 tr. all into next 2 rows, 2 ch., 1 tr. into next row, 2 ch., 1 tr., 1 ch., 1 tr. all into next 2 rows, 2 ch., 1 tr. into next loop, 1 ch. and 1 tr. 5 times into same loop, 2 ch., 1 tr., 1 ch., 1 tr. into next row, 2 ch., 1 tr. into next, 2 ch., 1 tr. into the dip, 1 d.c. into next loop, 2 ch., 1 tr. into next row, 2 ch., 1 tr., 1 ch., 1 tr. into next row, 2 ch., 1 tr., 1 ch., 1 tr. into next loop, 1 ch. and 1 tr. 6 times into same loop, 2 ch., 1 tr., 1 ch., 1 tr. into next row, 2 ch., 1 tr. into next row, 2 ch., 1 tr., 1 ch., 1 tr. all into next 3 rows, 2 ch. and 1 tr. into next 2 rows, 2 ch., 8 d.c. on next 8 d.c. of leaf, 8 d.c. on first 8 d.c. of next leaf, 2 ch. and 1 tr. into next 2 rows, repeat from * to * once, 2 ch., 1 tr. into next loop, 1 ch. and 1 tr. 5 times into same loop, repeat from ** to ** once, 2 ch., 1 tr., 1 ch., 1 tr. into next row, 2 ch., 1 tr. into next, 2 ch., 1 tr., 1 ch., 1 tr. all into next 3 rows, 2 ch. and 1 tr. into next 2 rows, 2 ch., s.s. along next 3 d.c. of leaf, 2 ch., turn.

2nd row.—1 tr., 2 ch., 1 tr. into first sp., * 2 ch. and 1 tr. into next 2 sp., 2 ch., 1 tr., 2 ch., 1 tr. into next sp., 2 ch. and 1 tr. into next 3 sp., 2 ch., 1 tr., 2 ch., 1 tr. into next sp. *, 2 ch., 1 tr. into next sp., 2 ch., 1 tr., 2 ch., 1 tr. into next sp., repeat from * to * once, 2 ch., 1 tr., 2 ch., 1 tr. into next sp., 2 ch. and 1 tr. into next 3 sp., 2 ch., then 1 d.c. into next 2 sp., ** 2 ch. and 1 tr. into next 2 sp., 2 ch., 1 tr., 2 ch., 1 tr. all into next 2 sp., 2 ch. and 1 tr. into next 2 sp., 2 ch., 1 tr., 2 ch., 1 tr. all into next sp., 2 ch., 1 tr. into next sp. **, 2 ch., 1 tr., 2 ch., 1 tr. into next sp., 2 ch. and 1 tr. into next

Fig. 69.—SINGLE PICOT LOOP FILLING

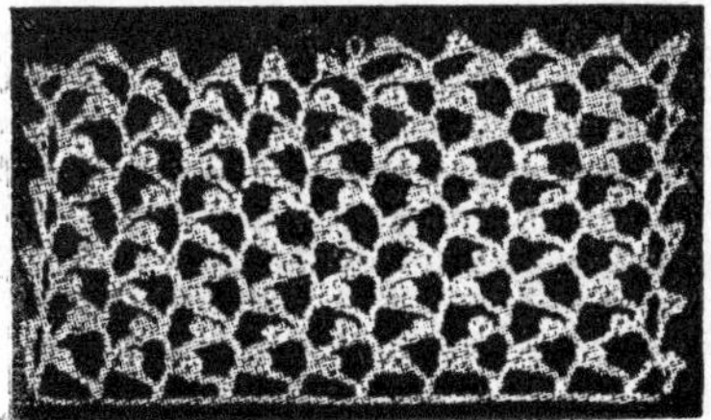

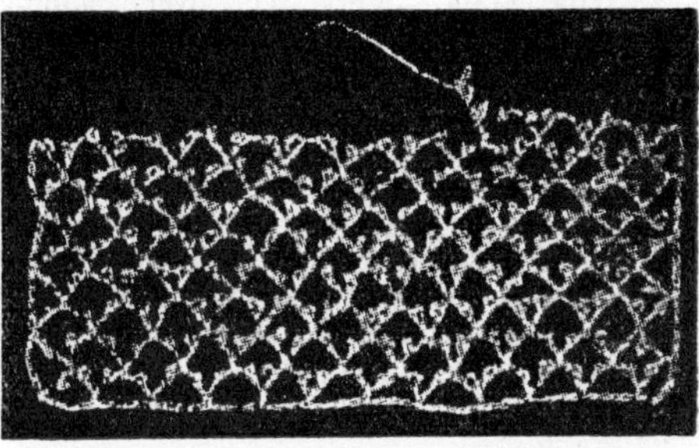

Fig. 70.—DOUBLE PICOT LOOP FILLING

12 sp., 2 ch., miss 2 d.c., 4 d.c., miss 3 d.c., 5 d.c., 2 ch., 1 tr. into next sp., 2 ch., 1 tr., 2 ch., 1 tr. into next sp., repeat from ** to ** once, 2 ch. and 1 tr. into next 4 sp., 2 ch., 1 tr., 2 ch., 1 tr. into next sp., 2 ch. and 1 tr. into next 2 sp., 2 ch., 1 tr., 2 ch., 1 tr. into next sp., 2 ch. and 1 tr. into next 4 sp., 2 ch., 1 d.c. into next 2 sp., 2 ch. and 1 tr. into next 2 sp., 2 ch., 1 tr., 2 ch., 1 tr. all into next 3 sp., 2 ch. and 1 tr. into next 2 sp., 2 ch., 1 tr., 2 ch., 1 tr. into next sp., 2 ch. and 1 tr. into next 12 sp., 2 ch., miss 2 d.c., 4 d.c., miss 3 d.c., 5 d.c., 2 ch. and 1 tr. into next 2 sp., 2 ch., 1 tr., 2 ch., 1 tr. into next sp., 2 ch. and 1 tr. into next 4 sp., 2 ch., 1 tr., 2 ch., 1 tr. into next sp., *** 2 ch., 1 tr. into next sp., 2 ch., 1 tr., 2 ch., 1 tr. into next sp. ***, repeat from *** to *** once, 2 ch. and 1 tr. into next 2 sp., 2 ch., 1 tr., 2 ch., 1 tr. into next sp., 2 ch. and 1 tr. into next 6 sp., 2 ch., 1 d.c. into next 2 sp., 2 ch., 1 tr. into next sp., 2 ch., 1 tr., 2 ch., 1 tr. all into next 3 sp., repeat from *** to *** once, 2 ch. and 1 tr. into next 2 sp., 2 ch., 1 tr., 2 ch., 1 tr. into next sp.,

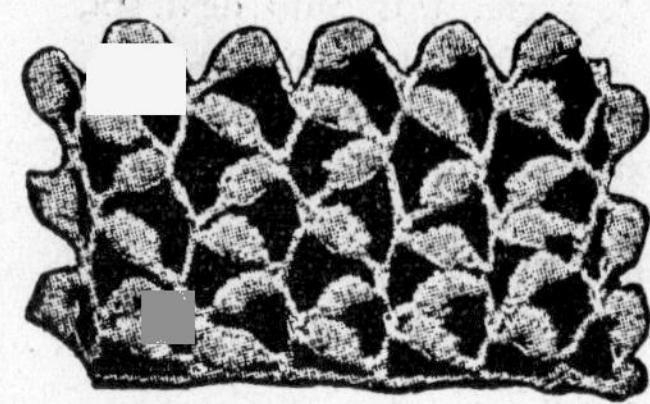

Fig. 71.
CLONES KNOT FILLING

2 ch. and 1 tr. into every remaining sp., 2 ch., s.s. into next stitch on leaf. Fasten off.

The Stalk.—Work d.c. over padding cotton for $1\frac{1}{2}$ inches, 1 ch., turn; 1 d.c. over padding cotton on every d.c. Fasten off securely, cut off padding cotton and sew this end to back of shamrock.

FILLINGS SUITABLE FOR THE BACKGROUND OF IRISH CROCHET

Open Space Filling is the daintiest of all, and it is worked thus: Work 1 tr. into place required, * work number of chain needed, then 1 tr. into place required, and then continue from * (Fig. 68)

Single Picot Loop Filling is worked in the following way: Work 1 d.c. into place required, * 7 ch., 1 d.c. into 5th ch. from hook, 2 ch., 1 d.c. into place required, and now continue from * until entire background is filled (Fig. 69).

Double Picot Loop Filling is worked thus: Work 1 d.c. into place required, * 7 ch., 1 d.c. into 5th ch. from hook, 7 ch., 1 d.c. into 5th ch. from hook, 2 ch., 1 d.c. into place required, and continue from * as desired (Fig. 70).

Clones Knot Filling is just a little more elaborate, but no more difficult to work than those already given.

Work 1 d.c. into place required, * 5 ch., ** thread over, insert hook under chain, thread over, draw through, repeat from ** 9 times, insert hook into second chain

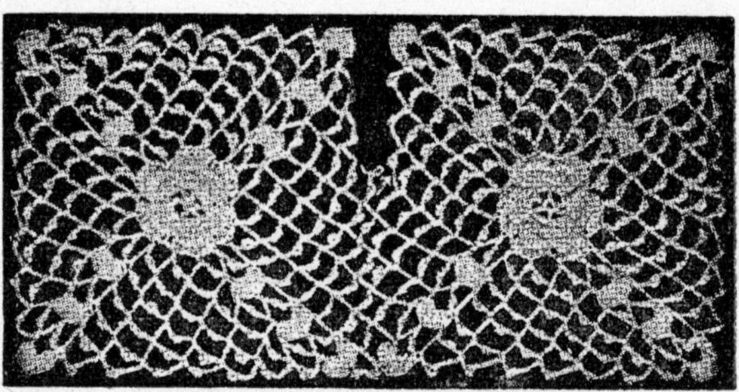

Fig. 72.
JOINING SQUARES TOGETHER WITH SINGLE PICOT LOOPS

Fig. 73.
JOINING SQUARES TOGETHER WITH DOUBLE PICOT LOOPS

made of five, thread over, draw through, thread over, draw through all loops on hook, 4 ch., 1 d.c. into place required, and now continue from * to fill in a complete background.

Joining Squares Together with Picot Loops.—Sometimes it is necessary to join squares of Irish crochet together, and this can be done either with single or double picot loops; according to the type of filling used for the background.

To Join Squares with Single Picot Loops.—Work 1 d.c. into place required on a square, * 1 p. (made as in the square), 1 ch., 1 d.c. into place required on square to be joined, 2 ch., 1 d.c. into place required on first square again, repeat from * until all squares are joined (Fig. 72).

To Join Squares with Double Picot Loops.—Work 1 d.c. into place required on a square, * 1 p. (made as in the square), 1 ch., 1 d.c. into place required on square to be joined, 1 p., 2 ch., 1 d.c. into place required on first square again, and repeat from * until all squares are joined (Fig. 73).

ROSE AND SHAMROCK DESIGN D'OYLEY

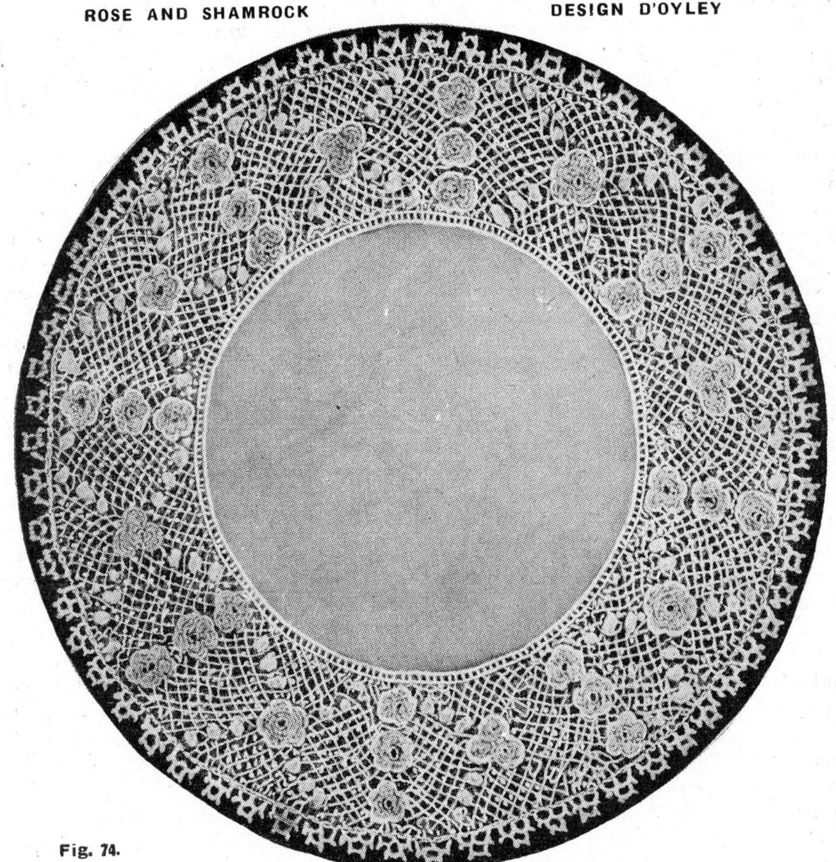

Fig. 74.

D'OYLEYS IN IRISH CROCHET

The Rose and Shamrock Design D'oyley, if worked with Crochet Thread 50, and a steel crochet hook, No. $6\frac{1}{2}$, will give a lace of about 2 inches wide (Fig. 74).

For a Rose Motif.—Begin with 8 chain, join into a ring.

1st round.—15 d.c. into ring, join. **2nd round.**—1 d.c. on 1st d.c., * 3 ch., miss 2 d.c., 1 d.c. on next, repeat from * 3 times, 3 ch., join. **3rd round.**—1 d.c., 5 tr., 1 d.c. into every sp., join. **4th round.** —* 5 ch., s.s. between next 2 petals, repeat from * all round, 5 ch., join. Bend petals forward so that chain is at the back.

5th round.—1 d.c., 7 tr., 1 d.c. into every sp., join. **6th round.**—* 6 ch., s.s. between next 2 petals, repeat from * all round, 6 ch., join.

7th round.—1 d.c., 9 tr., 1 d.c. into every sp., join. **8th round.**—1 picot thus: * 7 ch., 1 d.c. into 5th ch. from hook, then 3 ch., 1 d.c. on 2nd tr. of petal, 1 p., 3 ch., miss 2 tr., 1 d.c. on next, 1 p., 3 ch., miss 2 tr., 1 d.c. on next, repeat from * 3 times, 1 p., 3 ch., 1 d.c. between next 2 petals, 1 p., 3 ch., 1 d.c. on first tr. of petal, 1 p., 3 ch., miss 2 tr., 1 d.c. on next, 1 p., 3 ch., miss 2 tr., 1 d.c. on next, 1 p., 3 ch., 1 d.c. after next p. **9th round.**—1 arch thus: 1 l.tr. after next p., 1 d.c. 7 tr., 1 d.c. under l.tr., 1 p., 3 ch., 1 d.c. into same place as l.tr. (this completes arch), * 1 p., 3 ch., 1 d.c. after next p. *, repeat from * to * twice, 1 arch, repeat from * to * 4 times, 1 arch, repeat from * to * 3 times, 1 arch, repeat from * to * twice.

10th round.—(* 1 p., 3 ch., 1 d.c. on 2nd tr. of arch, 1 p., 3 ch., miss 3 tr., 1 d.c. on next *, ** 1 p., 3 ch., 1 d.c. after next p. **, repeat from ** to ** 3 times, repeat from * to * once, repeat from ** to ** 5 times), repeat whole of directions between brackets once more.

11th round.—(1 arch, * 1 p., 3 ch., 1 d.c. after next p. *, repeat from * to * 4 times, 1 arch), repeat from * to * 6 times, repeat whole of directions between brackets once, repeat from * to * 4 times. **12th round.**—(* 1 p., 3 ch., 1 d.c. on 2nd tr. of arch, 1 p., 3 ch., miss 3 tr., 1 d.c. on next *, ** 1 p., 3 ch., 1 d.c. after next p. **, repeat from ** to ** 5 times, repeat from * to * once, repeat from ** to ** 7 times), repeat whole of directions between brackets once.

13th round.—(1 arch, * 1 p., 3 ch., 1 d.c. after next p. *, repeat from * to * 6 times, 1 arch), repeat from * to * 8 times, repeat whole of directions between brackets once, repeat from * to * 6 times, 1 p., 3 ch., 1 d.c. on 2nd tr. of arch, 1 p., 3 ch., miss 3 tr., s.s. into next. Fasten off. Make four rose motifs altogether.

For a Shamrock Motif.—Always use 4 strands of thread for a padding cord. Work thus: 2 d.c., 16 tr., 2 d.c. over padding cord, s.s. to 1st d.c., then work over padding cord, 1 d.c. into every stitch of leaf, * 2 d.c., 16 tr., 2 d.c. over padding cord only, s.s. to 1st d.c. of this leaf, work over padding cord, 1 d.c. into every stitch of this leaf, repeat from * once, s.s. into base of centre leaf and also into 1st leaf, turn; s.s. along 2 d.c. of last leaf worked, turn; 1 p., 3 ch., 1 d.c. on 2nd d.c. of 1st leaf, ** 8 ch., miss 16 d.c. of same leaf, 1 d.c. on next, 1 p., 3 ch., 1 d.c. on 2nd d.c. of next leaf, repeat from ** once. The loops of 8 chain should be at the back of the shamrock Cut off padding cord and sew ends firmly at back.

1st round.—* 1 p., 3 ch., miss 2 d.c. of leaf, 1 d.c. on next, 1 p., 3 ch., miss 1 d.c., 1 d.c. on next, 1 p., 3 ch., miss 2 d.c., 1 d.c. on next, 1 p., 3 ch., miss 1 d.c., 1 d.c. on next, 1 p., 3 ch., miss 2 d.c., 1 d.c. on next, 1 p., 3 ch., 1 d.c. after next p., repeat from * once, 1 p., 3 ch., miss 2 d.c., 1 d.c. on next, 1 p., 3 ch., miss 2 d.c., 1 d.c. on next, 1 p., 3 ch., miss 3 d.c., 1 d.c. on next, 1 p., 3 ch., miss 2 d.c., 1 d.c. on next, 1 p., 3 ch., 1 d.c. after next p., 1 p., 3 ch., 1 d.c. after next p. **2nd round.**—** 1 arch, * 1 p., 3 ch., 1 d.c. after next p. *, repeat from * to * twice **, repeat from ** to ** once, 1 arch, repeat from * to * 4 times, 1 arch, repeat from * to * 3 times

3rd round.—(* 1 p., 3 ch., 1 d.c. on 2nd tr. of arch, 1 p., 3 ch., miss 3 tr., 1 d.c. on next *, ** 1 p., 3 ch., 1 d.c. after next p. **, repeat from ** to ** 3 times), work whole of directions between brackets once, repeat from * to * once, repeat from ** to ** 5 times, repeat from * to * once, repeat from ** to ** 6 times. **4th round.**—** 1 arch. * 1 p., 3 ch.,

1 d.c. after next p. *, repeat from * to * 4 times **, repeat from ** to ** once. 1 arch, repeat from * to * 6 times, 1 arch. repeat from * to * 5 times.

5th round.—(* 1 p., 3 ch., 1 d.c. on 2nd tr. of arch, 1 p., 3 ch., miss 3 tr., 1 d.c. on next *, ** 1 p., 3 ch., 1 d.c. after next p. **, repeat from ** to ** 5 times), repeat whole of directions between brackets once, repeat from * to * once, repeat from ** to ** 7 times, repeat from * to * once, repeat from ** to ** 8 times. **6th round.**—** 1 arch, * 1 p., 3 ch., 1 d.c. after next p. *, repeat from * to * 6 times **, repeat from ** to ** once, 1 arch, repeat from * to * 8 times, 1 arch, repeat from * to * 7 times, 1 p., 3 ch., 1 d.c. on 2nd tr. of arch. Fasten off.

Make four shamrock motifs altogether.

For the Small Roses.—Begin with 8 chain, join into a ring.

1st round.—6 ch., 1 tr. into ring, 3 ch. and 1 tr. 3 times into ring, 3 ch., join. **2nd round.**—1 d.c., 4 tr., 1 d.c. into every sp., join. **3rd round.**—* 5 ch., s.s. between next 2 petals, repeat from * all round, 5 ch., join. Bend petals forward so that chain is at the back.

4th round.—1 d.c., 6 tr., 1 d.c. into every sp., join. Fasten off.

Make twenty-four small roses altogether.

Mark on linen a circle 8½ inches in diameter. Measure 1½ inches in from edge, and mark another circle. Tack a rose and a shamrock motif alternatively into the 1½ inch space between pencil lines, being careful to place the widest side at outer edge, and leaving a space between the motifs, then tack 3 small roses into each of these spaces between motifs (see illustration). Fill in spaces between motifs and roses with a single picot loop filling, keeping inner and outer edges to pencil lines.

Heading Round Inner Edge.—Work spaces of 1 tr. and 1 ch. all round, join. **2nd round.**—S.s. into 1st sp., 4 ch., 1 tr. into next sp., then 1 ch. and 1 tr. into every sp. Join. **3rd round.**—2 d.c. into every sp. Join. Fasten off.

Edging Round Outer Edge.—Work spaces of 1 tr. and 1 ch. all round outer edge, join. The number of spaces should be divisible by 5. **2nd round.**—* 2 d.c. into next 4 sp., 1 d.c. into next, 6 ch., turn; miss 3 d.c., 1 d.c. on next, 6 ch., miss 3 d.c., 1 d.c. on next, turn; 2 d.c., 1 p., 5 d.c. into 1st sp., 3 d.c. into next, 6 ch., turn; miss 5 d.c., 1 d.c. on next, turn; 2 d.c., 1 p., 5 d.c., 1 p., 2 d.c. all into this loop, 2 d.c., 1 p., 2 d.c. into loop now reached, 1 d.c. into sp. now reached already worked into, repeat from * all round. Join. Fasten off.

THE FLOWER MOTIF D'OYLEY

This is made entirely of crochet, (see Fig. 75), and is worked with a very fine mercer crochet cotton, and a steel crochet hook, No. 7.

For Centre of D'oyley.—Commence in centre with 8 chain and join into a ring. **1st round.**—4 ch., 1 d.c. into ring, 3 ch. and 1 d.c. 3 times into ring, 3 ch., join. **2nd round.**—1 d.c., 5 tr., 1 d.c. into every sp., join. **3rd round.**—* 4 ch., 1 d.c. between next 2 petals, repeat from * all round, 4 ch., join. Bend petals forward so that chain is at the back.

4th round.—1 d.c., 7 tr., 1 d.c. into every sp., join. **5th round.**—* 6 ch., 1 d.c. between next 2 petals, repeat from * all round, 6 ch., join.

6th round.—1 d.c., 10 tr., 1 d.c. into every sp., join. **7th round.**—S.s. along to 4th tr. of 1st petal, * 5 ch., miss 2 tr., 1 d.c. on next *, repeat from * to * once, ** 5 ch., 1 d.c. on 1st tr. of next petal, repeat from * to * 3 times **, repeat from ** to ** 3 times, 5 ch., 1 d.c. on 1st s.s. of 1st petal, 5 ch., join.

8th round.—5 ch., 1 d.c. into 1st sp., 5 ch. and 1 d.c. into next 19 sp.

9th round.—5 ch. and 1 d.c. into next 22 sp., turn; s.s. to centre of last loop, turn.

10th round.—6 ch., 1 d.c. into 5th ch. from hook to form picot, then 1 ch., 1 d.c. into loop that last d.c. was worked into, * 1 gr. thus: 1 l.tr. into next loop, 1 d.c., 5 tr. under this l.tr., 1 p., 1 ch., 1 d.c. into same loop *, ** 1 gr., 1 p., 1 ch., 1 d.c. into next loop **, repeat from * to *

3 times, repeat from ** to ** once, repeat from * to * once, repeat from ** to ** once, repeat from * to * twice, repeat from ** to ** twice, repeat from * to * once, repeat from ** to ** once, 1 l.tr before next p., 1 d.c., 5 tr. under l.tr. 1 p., 1 ch., 1 d.c. after p. of previous round.

1 p., 1 ch., 1 d.c. on 2nd tr. of next gr., repeat from * to * once.

12th round.—1 p., 1 ch., 1 d.c. before next p., miss 2 p., 1 d.c. after p., * 1 l.tr. after next p., 1 d.c., 7 tr. under l.tr., 1 p., 1 ch., 1 d.c. after next p., 1 l.tr. after next p., 1 d.c., 7 tr. under l.tr., 1 p., 1 ch., 1 d.c.

FLOWER MOTIF

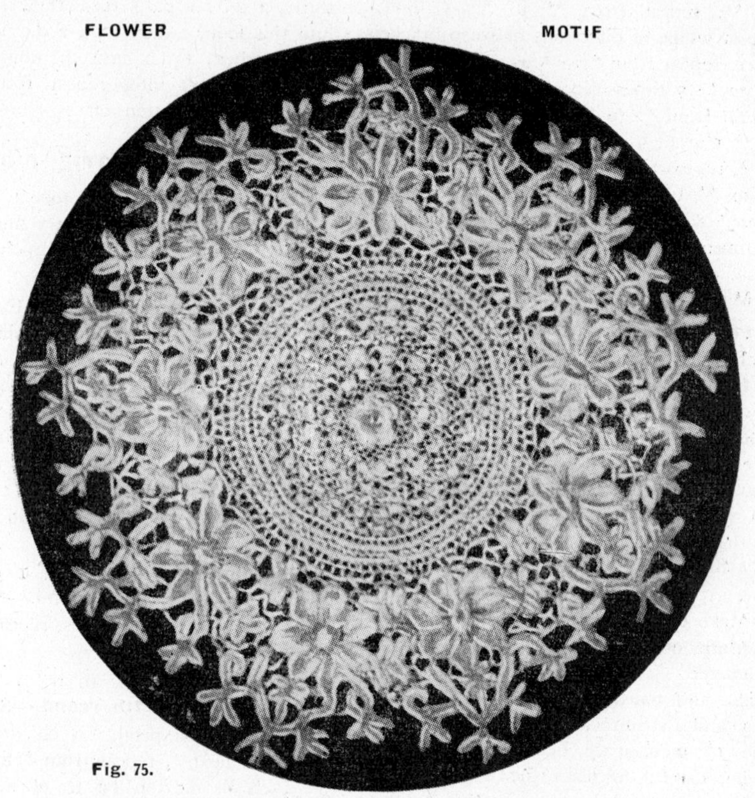

Fig. 75.

11th round.—1 p., 1 ch., 1 d.c. on 2nd tr., * 1 p., 1 ch., 1 d.c. before next p., 1 p., 1 ch., 1 d.c. on 1st tr. of next gr., 1 p., 1 ch., miss 1 tr., 1 d.c. on next *, 1 p., 1 ch., 1 d.c. after next p., 1 p., 1 ch., 1 d.c. on 4th tr. of next gr., repeat from * to * twice, 1 p., 1 ch., 1 d.c. on 2nd tr. of next gr., repeat from * to * twice, 1 p., 1 ch., 1 d.c. on 1st tr. of next gr., 1 p., 1 ch., miss 1 tr., 1 d.c. on next, 1 p., 1 ch., 1 d.c. before next p., 1 p., 1 ch., 1 d.c. on 2nd tr. of next gr., repeat from * to * 3 times, 1 p., 1 ch., 1 d.c. before next p., after next p., 1 l.tr. after next p., 1 d.c., 7 tr. under l.tr., 1 p., 1 ch., 1 d.c. after next p., 1 d.c. after next p., repeat from * 4 times, 1 l.tr. after next p., 1 d.c., 7 tr. under l.tr., 1 p., 1 ch., 1 d.c. after next p.

13th round.—* 3 ch., 1 d.c. on 2nd tr. of gr., 3 ch., miss 3 tr., 1 d.c. on next *, repeat from * to * once, ** 3 ch., 1 d.c. on 2nd tr. of gr., 3 ch., miss 3 tr., 1 d.c. on next, 3 ch., 1 d.c. before p. **, repeat from * to * once, repeat from ** to ** twice, 3 ch., 1 d.c. after p., repeat from ** to ** once (3 ch., 1 d.c. on 1st tr. of gr., 3 ch., miss 2 tr., 1 d.c. on next, 3 ch., miss 2 tr., 1 d.c. on next, 3 ch., 1 d.c. after p.), repeat whole of directions between brackets once more, repeat from ** to ** twice, repeat whole of directions between brackets twice, 3 ch., 1 d.c. on d.c. of gr., 3 ch., miss 1 tr., 1 d.c. on next, 3 ch., miss 1 tr., 1 d.c. on next, 3 ch., miss 2 tr., 1 d.c. on next, 3 ch., 1 d.c. after p., repeat from ** to ** twice.

14th round.—3 ch., 1 d.c. into next loop, * 3 ch., 1 d.c., 3 ch., 1 d.c. into next loop *, 3 ch. and 1 d.c. into next 11 loops, repeat from * to * once, 3 ch. and 1 d.c. into next 7 loops, repeat from * to * once, 3 ch. and 1 d.c. into next 29 loops, repeat from * to * once. **15th round.**—3 ch. and 1 d.c. into next 56 loops, 1 d.c. into next.

16th round.—(* 1 gr., then 1 p., 1 ch., 1 d.c. into next loop, repeat from * 5 times, 1 d.c. into next loop), repeat whole of directions between brackets twice, ** 1 gr., then 1 p., 1 ch., 1 d.c. into next loop, repeat from ** 7 times. **17th round.**—(* 1 p., 1 ch., 1 d.c. on 2nd tr. of gr., 1 p., 1 ch., 1 d.c. before p. *, repeat from * to * once, ** 1 p., 1 ch., 1 d.c. on 1st tr. of gr., 1 p., 1 ch., miss 2 tr., 1 d.c. on next, 1 p., 1 ch., 1 d.c. before p. **), repeat from ** to ** once, repeat whole of directions between brackets once, repeat from * to * once, *** repeat from ** to** once, repeat from * to * 3 times, 1 p., 1 ch., 1 d.c. on 1st tr. of gr., 1 p., 1 ch., miss 2 tr., 1 d.c. on next ***, repeat from * to * once, 1 p., 1 ch., 1 d.c. on 1st tr. of gr., 1 p., 1 ch., miss 2 tr., 1 d.c. on next, repeat from *** to *** once, repeat from ** to ** once, repeat from * to * 5 times, 1 p., 1 ch., miss 2 p., 1 d.c. after p., 1 p., 1 ch., 1 d.c. after next picot.

18th round.—(* 1 l.tr. after next p., 1 d.c., 5 tr. under l.tr., 1 p., 1 ch., 1 d.c. after next p. *, repeat from * to * once, miss 2 p., 1 l.tr. after p., 1 d.c., 5 tr. under l.tr., 1 p., 1 ch., 1 d.c. after next p.), 1 d.c. after next p., repeat whole of directions between brackets once, miss 2 p., 1 l.tr. after p., 1 d.c., 5 tr. under l.tr., 1 p., 1 ch., 1 d.c. after next p., repeat from * to * once, 1 d.c. after next p., repeat from * to * once, 1 d.c. after next p., 1 l.tr. after next p., 1 d.c., 5 tr. under l.tr., miss 2 p., 1 p., 1 ch., 1 d.c. after p., repeat from * to * 3 times, 1 l.tr. after next p., 1 d.c., 5 tr. under l.tr., 1 p., 1 ch., 1 d.c. into same place after p., repeat from * to * 8 times, 1 d.c. after next p., repeat from * to * once, 1 l.tr. after next p., 1 d.c., 5 tr. under l.tr., 1 p., 1 ch., 1 d.c. into same place after p., repeat from * to * twice.

19th round.—3 ch., 1 tr. on 2nd tr. of gr., * 1 ch., miss 1 tr., 1 tr. on next, 1 ch., 1 tr. before p., 1 ch., 1 tr. after p., 1 ch., 1 tr. on 2nd tr. of gr. *, repeat from * to * 12 times, ** 1 ch., 1 tr. before p., 1 ch., 1 tr. after p., 1 ch., 1 tr. on 2nd tr. of gr. **, repeat from * to * 5 times, repeat from ** to ** once, repeat from * to * once, 1 ch., miss 1 tr., 1 tr. on next, 1 ch., 1 tr. before p., 1 ch., 1 tr. on centre tr. of gr., 1 ch., 1 tr. before p., *** 1 ch., 1 tr. on 2nd tr. of gr., 1 ch., miss 1 tr., 1 tr. on next, 1 ch., 1 tr. before p., repeat from *** twice, 1 ch., 1 tr. into next loop.

20th round.—* 1 ch., 1 tr., 1 ch., 1 tr. into next sp. *, 1 ch. and 1 tr. into next 5 sp., repeat from * to * once, 1 ch. and 1 tr. into next 19 sp., repeat from * to * once, 1 ch. and 1 tr. into next 3 sp., repeat from * to * once, 1 ch., 1 tr. into next sp., repeat from * to * once, ** 1 ch. and 1 tr. into next 8 sp., repeat from * to * once **, 1 ch. and 1 tr. into next 3 sp., repeat from * to * twice, repeat from ** to ** once, 1 ch. and 1 tr. into next 12 sp., repeat from * to * once, *** 1 ch. and 1 tr. into next 6 sp., repeat from * to * once ***, repeat from *** to *** once (1 ch. and 1 tr. into next 2 sp., repeat from * to * once), repeat whole of directions between brackets twice more, 1 ch. and 1 tr. into next 2 sp., 1 ch., 1 d.c. into next space. **21st round.**—2 d.c. into next 108 sp., 1 d.c. into next 3 sp., s.s. into d.c. now reached. Fasten off. (220 stitches.)

For a Flower Motif.—1st round.—15 d.c. over padding cotton, s.s. to 1st d.c., turn. **2nd round.**—11 d.c. over padding cotton only, * 1 ch., turn; leave padding cotton, 1 d.c. on 1st d.c., 10 tr. on 10 d.c., 1 d.c. on next d.c. of ring, turn; miss 1 d.c., then 10 tr., 1 d.c., now 1 d.c.

over padding cotton only, turn: miss 1 d.c., 11 d.c. over padding cotton on next 11 stitches, 1 d.c. over padding cotton on next d.c. of ring, turn *; (miss 1 d.c., 6 d.c. over padding cotton on 6 d.c., 11 d.c. over padding cotton only, turn; 6 d.c. over padding cotton on 6 d.c., turn; ** 3 d.c. over padding cotton on 3 d.c., 3 d.c. over padding cotton only, turn; 6 d.c. over padding cotton on 6 d.c., turn **; 6 d.c. over padding cotton only, turn; 6 d.c. over padding cotton on 6 d.c., 1 d.c. over padding cotton between first 2 small leaves made, turn; miss 1 d.c., 3 d.c. over padding cotton on 3 d.c., 3 d.c. over padding cotton only, turn; 6 d.c. over padding cotton on 6 d.c., s.s. into base of 1st small leaf made, leave padding cotton, 1 d.c., 10 tr. on next 11 d.c. now reached, 1 d.c. on next d.c. of ring, turn; miss 1 d.c., 10 tr., 1 d.c., then 1 d.c. into base of small leaves, turn; miss 1 d.c., 11 d.c. over padding cotton on next 11 stitches, 1 d.c. over padding cotton on next d.c. of ring, turn; miss 1 d.c., 6 d.c. over padding cotton on 6 d.c., 5 d.c. over padding cotton only, repeat from * to * once), miss 1 d.c., 6 d.c. over padding cotton on 6 d.c., 5 d.c. over padding cotton only, turn; leave padding cotton, 1 d.c., 10 tr. on 11 d.c., 1 d.c. on next d.c. of ring, turn; miss 1 d.c., 10 tr., 1 d.c., then 6 d.c. over padding cotton only, turn; 6 d.c. over padding cotton on 6 d.c., turn; repeat from ** to ** 3 times, 1 d.c. over padding cotton between 2nd and 3rd small leaves, turn; miss 1 d.c., repeat from ** to ** once, 1 d.c. over padding cotton between first 2 small leaves, 11 d.c. over padding cotton on next 11 stitches down side of petal, 1 d.c. over padding cotton on next d.c. of ring, turn; miss 1 d.c., 6 d.c. over padding cotton on 6 d.c., 10 d.c. over padding cotton only, 1 d.c. over padding cotton into tip of 2nd small leaf, 12 d.c. over padding cotton only, 1 d.c. over padding cotton into tip of next small leaf, 12 d.c. over padding cotton only, 1 d.c. over padding cotton into tip of next small leaf, 14 d.c. over padding cotton only, 1 d.c. over padding cotton into top of free petal, turn; 12 d.c. over padding cotton on 12 d.c., turn; 26 d.c. over padding cotton only, s.s. into base between 16th and 17th d.c., counting from last d.c. worked, turn; miss s.s., 16 d.c. over padding cotton on 16 d.c., turn; *** 9 d.c. over padding cotton only, turn; 9 d.c. over padding cotton on 9 d.c., turn; 2 d.c. over padding cotton on 2 d.c., 7 d.c. over padding cotton

Fig. 76.—MOTIFS PLACED IN POSITION AND FILLINGS BEGUN

only, turn; 9 d.c. over padding cotton on 9 d.c., turn; 2 d.c. over padding cotton on 2 d.c., 7 d.c. over padding cotton only, turn; 9 d.c. over padding cotton on 9 d.c., 1 d.c. over padding cotton between first 2 small leaves ***, 24 d.c. over padding cotton on next 24 d.c. now reached, turn, **** 10 d.c. over padding cotton only, turn; 8 d.c. over padding cotton on 8 d.c., turn; 3 d.c. over padding cotton on 3 d.c., 5 d.c. over padding cotton only, turn; 8 d.c. over padding cotton on 8 d.c., turn; 3 d.c. over padding cotton on 3 d.c., 5 d.c. over padding cotton only, turn; 8 d.c. over padding cotton on 8 d.c., s.s. into base of centre small leaf, 2 d.c. over padding cotton on 2 d.c. left unworked of the 10 ****, 10 d.c. over padding cotton on next 10 d.c., turn; repeat from **** to **** once, 11 d.c. over padding cotton on 11 d.c., turn; 26 d.c. over padding cotton only, s.s. into base between 16th and 17th d.c., counting from last d.c. worked, turn; miss s.s., 4 d.c. over padding cotton on next 4 d.c., 2 ch., join to centre d.c. of 11 worked after last 3 small leaves worked, 2 d.c. over 2 ch., 8 d.c. over padding cotton on next 8 d.c., turn; repeat from *** to *** once, 1 d.c. over padding cotton on next 14 d.c., leave padding cotton, 1 d.c., 10 tr. on next 11 stitches, 1 d.c. on next d.c. of ring, turn; miss 1 d.c., 10 tr., 1 d.c., then 1 d.c. over padding cotton on next d.c., turn; miss 1 d.c., 11 d.c. over padding cotton on 11 d.c., 1 d.c. over padding cotton on next d.c. of ring, turn; repeat whole of directions between brackets once, 20 d.c. over padding cotton only, turn; s.s. into same d.c. last worked into on ring. Fasten off. Cut off padding cotton and sew ends firmly, also sew ring last made over centre of flower. Make 8 more motifs in the same way.

Mark on linen a circle 8 inches in diameter. Tack centre of d'oyley in centre of circle, then make another circle ½ inch from outer edge of centre just tacked on. Tack motifs in position as seen in Fig. 76. Fill in spaces between flower motifs with a single picot loop filling, being careful to keep inner edge to pencil line, and leaving ½ inch space free. Work spaces of 1 tr. and 1 ch. round inner edge of motifs, making 101 spaces altogether. Join.

2nd round.—S.s. into 1st sp., 4 ch., 1 tr. into next s.p., then 1 ch. and 1 tr. into every sp., 1 ch., join. **3rd round.**—* 2 d.c. into next 4 sp., 3 d.c. into next, repeat from * 17 times, 2 d.c. into next 11 sp., join. **4th round.**—1 d.c. on 1st d.c., 1 ch., 1 d.c. on a d.c. of centre of d'oyley, * 1 ch., miss 2 d.c. of 3rd round, 1 d.c. on next, 1 ch., miss 1 d.c. of centre of d'oyley, 1 d.c. on next, 1 ch., miss 1 d.c. of 3rd round, 1 d.c. on next, 1 ch., miss 2 d.c. on centre of d'oyley, 1 d.c. on next, repeat from * all round. Join. Fasten off.

Remove tacking stitches and take completed crochet from linen, then press lightly on the wrong side under a damp cloth with a warm iron.

MORE CROCHET PATTERNS

A Rose Lace worked in Three Colours (Fig. 76).

MATERIALS

Mercer Crochet Cotton, No. 60, in ecru, pink and jade green.
Steel crochet hook, No. 6½.

MEASUREMENT

About 3½ inches wide.

When changing from one colour to another, always pull colour next to be used through last two loops of last treble of colour being used. In some places you will find that the cotton has to be stranded along from one place to another, in this case, always work over it so that it is invisible.

For abbreviations see beginning of chapter.

The Lace.

Using ecru, begin with 75 chain.

1st row.—Miss 3 ch., 15 tr., 1 h.

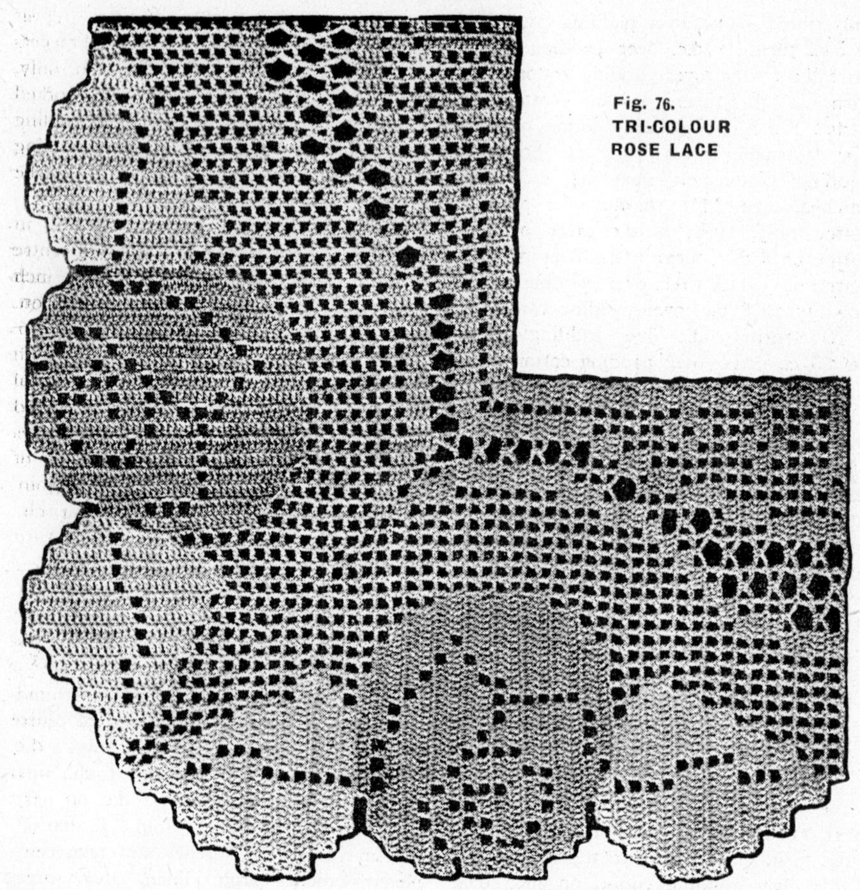

Fig. 76. TRI-COLOUR ROSE LACE

4 tr., 1 h., 4 tr., 1 b., 1 l., 1 b., 4 tr., 8 h., join on green and work 5 ch. with it, then turn. **2nd row.**—Miss 3 ch., 2 tr., leave green, then with ecru, work 1 tr. on next treble, 8 h., 4 tr., 1 l., 1 b., 1 l., 4 tr., 2 h., 4 tr., 4 h., 4 tr. Always turn with 3 ch. at ends of rows unless otherwise directed. **3rd row.**—Miss first tr., 3 tr., 7 h., 4 tr., 1 b., 1 l., 1 b., 4 tr., 7 h., leave ecru, with green, work 6 tr., 7 ch., turn. **4th row.**—Miss 1 ch., s.s. along next 4 ch., miss first tr., 8 tr., leave green, with ecru, work 1 tr. on next tr., 6 h., 4 tr., 1 l., 1 b., 1 l., 4 tr., 7 h., 4 tr. **5th row.**—Miss first tr., 3 tr., 2 h., 4 tr., 4 h., 4 tr., 1 b., 1 l., 1 h., 4 tr., 7 h., leave ecru, with green, work 3 tr., 1 h., 7 tr., 5 ch., turn. **6th row.**—Miss 3 ch., 9 tr., 1 h., 6 tr., leave green, with ecru, work 1 tr. on next tr., 6 h., 4 tr., 1 h., 1 b., 1 l., 1 h., 4 tr., 2 h., 4 tr., 1 h., 10 tr. **7th row.**—Miss first tr., 3 tr., 2 h., 4 tr., 3 h., 4 tr., 1 h., 1 b., 1 l., 1 h., 4 tr., 6 h., leave ecru, with green, work 3 tr., 1 h., 13 tr., 7 ch., turn. **8th row.**—Miss 1 ch., s.s. along next 4 ch., miss first tr., 12 tr., 1 h., 6 tr., leave green, with ecru, work 1 tr. on next tr., 6 h., 4 tr., 1 b., 1 l., 1 h., 4 tr., 6 h., 4 tr. **9th row.**—Miss first tr., 3 tr., 5 h., 4 tr., 1 l., 1 b., 1 h., 4 tr., 7 h., leave ecru, with green, work 6 tr., 1 h., 16 tr.

In the following rows, no notice is taken of the asterisks seen in these rows, until the first side of corner is reached, when you will see that they are then referred to. **10th row.**—* Miss first tr., 12 tr., 1 h.,

9 tr., leave green, with ecru, work 1 tr. on next tr. *, 8 h., 4 tr., 1 l., 1 b., 4 tr., 3 h., 4 tr., 1 h., 4 tr. **11th row.**—Miss first tr., 6 tr., 1 h., 4 tr., 2 h., 4 tr., 1 l., 1 h., 4 tr., 9 h., leave ecru, with green, work 9 tr., 1 h., 13 tr. **12th row.**—* Miss first tr., 12 tr., 1 h., 15 tr., leave green, with ecru, work 1 tr. on next tr. *, 8 h., 4 tr., 1 b., 1 h., 4 tr., 2 h., 4 tr., 1 h., 4 tr. **13th row.**—Miss first tr., 3 tr., 4 h., 4 tr., 2 h., 4 tr., 9 h., leave ecru, with green, work 15 tr., 1 h. 10 tr. **14th row.**—* Miss first tr., 9 tr., 1 h., 12 tr., leave green, with ecru, work 1 tr. on next tr. *, 11 h., 4 tr., 1 l., 4 tr., 3 h., 4 tr. **15th row.**—Miss first tr., 3 tr., 3 h., 4 tr., 1 b., 4 tr., 12 h., * leave ecru, with green, work 9 tr., 1 h., 7 tr., fasten off green, turn *. **16th row.**—* Miss last 6 tr. worked, then with pink, s.s. into next tr., 10 ch., miss 1 ch. of these ten, s.s. along next 7 ch., then 2 tr. into h., 15 more tr., leave pink, with ecru, work 1 tr. on next tr. *, 10 h., 4 tr., 1 l., 1 h., 4 tr., 2 h., 4 tr. **17th row.**—Miss first tr., 3 tr., 2 h., 4 tr., 2 h., 4 tr., 9 h., * leave ecru, with pink, work 15 tr., 3 h., 7 tr., 5 ch., turn *. **18th row.**—* Miss 3 ch., 18 tr., 2 h., 12 tr., leave pink, with ecru, work 1 tr. on next tr. *, 8 h., 4 tr., 1 h., 1 b., 4 tr., 1 h., 4 tr. **19th row.**—Miss first tr., 3 tr., 1 h., 4 tr., 1 l., 7 tr., * 7 h., leave ecru, with pink, work 12 tr., 1 h., 25 tr., 5 ch., turn * **20th row.**—* Miss 3 ch., 6 tr., 2 h., 19 tr., 1 h., 9 tr., leave pink, with ecru, work 1 tr. on next tr. *, 8 h., 4 tr., 1 b., 4 tr., 1 h., 4 tr. **21st row.**—Miss first tr., 3 tr., 1 h., 4 tr., 1 l., 4 tr., 7 h., * leave ecru, with pink, work 9 tr., 1 h., 19 tr., 1 h., 7 tr., 1 h., 4 tr., 1 ch., turn *. **22nd row.**—* S.s. along first 4 tr., 7 ch., miss 1 ch. of these seven, s.s. along next 4 ch., then 2 tr. into next h., 4 tr. on 4 tr., 1 h., 4 tr., 1 h., 19 tr., 1 h., 6 tr., leave pink, with ecru, work 1 tr. on next tr., 7 h., 4 tr., 1 b. *, 4 tr., 1 h., 4 tr. **23rd row.**—Miss first tr., 3 tr., 1 h., 4 tr., * 1 l., 4 tr., 7 h., leave ecru, with pink, work 9 tr., 1 h., 13 tr., 1 h., 4 tr., 3 h., 7 tr. *. **24th row.**—* Miss first tr., 3 tr., 2 h., 4 tr., 1 h., 4 tr., 2 h., 7 tr., 1 h., 12 tr., leave pink, with ecru, work 1 tr. on next tr., 7 h., 4 tr., 1 b., 4 tr., 1 h. *, 4 tr. **25th row.**—Miss first tr., 3 tr., * 1 h., 4 tr., 1 l., 4 tr., 7 h., leave ecru, with pink, work 12 tr., 3 h., 4 tr., 1 h., 4 tr., 1 h., 7 tr., 1 h., 4 tr. *. **26th row.**—* Miss first tr., 3 tr., 1 h., 13 tr., 1 h., 7 tr., 1 h., 15 tr., leave pink, with ecru, work 1 tr. on next tr., 7 h., 4 tr., 1 b. *, 4 tr., 1 h., 4 tr. **27th row.**—Miss first tr., 3 tr., 1 h., 4 tr., 1 l., 4 tr., 7 h., * leave ecru, with pink, work 15 tr., 1 h., 10 tr., 1 h., 7 tr., 1 h., 7 tr., 1 ch., turn **28th row.**—* S.s. along first 4 tr., 3 ch., 6 tr., 3 h., 10 tr., 1 h., 15 tr., leave pink, with ecru, work 1 tr. on next tr. *, 7 h., 4 tr., 1 b., 4 tr., 1 h., 4 tr. **29th row.**—Miss first tr., 3 tr., 1 h., 4 tr., 1 l., 7 tr., * 7 h., leave ecru, with pink, work 12 tr., 1 h., 25 tr., 1 ch., turn *. **30th row.**—* S.s. along first 4 tr., 3 ch., 21 tr., 1 h., 12 tr., leave pink, with ecru, work 1 tr. on next tr. *, 7 h., 4 tr., 1 h., 1 b., 4 tr., 1 h., 4 tr. **31st row.**—Miss first tr., 3 tr., 2 h., 4 tr., 2 h., 4 tr., 8 h., * leave ecru, with pink, work 12 tr., 3 h., 7 tr., join on green, work 9 ch. with it, turn *. **32nd row.**—* Miss 1 ch., s.s. along next 4 ch., miss next 2 ch., then 5 tr. green, leave green, with pink, work 1 tr. on next tr., 1 h., 18 tr., break off pink, with ecru, work 1 tr. on next tr. *, 8 h., 4 tr., 1 l., 1 h., 4 tr., 2 h., 4 tr. **33rd row.**—Miss first tr., 3 tr., 3 h., 4 tr., 1 b., 4 tr., 12 h., * leave ecru, with green, work 9 tr., 1 h., 7 tr., 5 ch., turn *. **34th row.**—* Miss 3 ch., 9 tr., 1 h., 12 tr., leave green, with ecru, work 1 tr. on next tr. *, 11 h., 4 tr., 1 l., 4 tr., 3 h., 4 tr. **35th row.**—Miss first tr., 3 tr., 4 h., 4 tr., 2 h., 4 tr., 9 h., * leave ecru, with green, work 15 tr., 1 h., 10 tr., 5 ch., turn *. **36th row.**—* Miss 3 ch., 12 tr., 1 h., 15 tr., leave green, with ecru, work 1 tr. on next tr. *, 8 h., 4 tr., 1 b., 1 h., 4 tr., 2 h., 4 tr., 1 h., 4 tr. **37th row.**—Miss first tr., 6 tr., 1 h., 4 tr., 2 h., 4 tr., 1 l., 1 h., 4 tr., 8 h., leave ecru, with green, work 9 tr., 1 h., 16 tr. **38th row.**—* Miss first tr., 15 tr., 1 h., 9 tr., leave green, with ecru, work 1 tr. on next tr. *, 7 h., 4 tr., 1 l., 1 b., 4 tr., 3 h., 4 tr., 1 h., 4 tr. **39th row.**—Miss first tr., 3 tr., 5 h., 4 tr., 1 l., 1 b., 1 h., 4 tr., 7 h., * leave

ecru, with green, work 6 tr., 1 h., 16 tr., 1 ch., turn *. **40th row.**—* S.s. along first 4 tr., 3 ch., 12 tr., 1 h., 6 tr., leave green, with ecru, work 1 tr. on next tr. *, 6 h., 4 tr., 1 b., 1 l., 1 h., 4 tr., 6 h., 4 tr. **41st row.**—Miss first tr., 3 tr., 2 h., 4 tr., 3 h., 4 tr., 1 h., 1 b., 1 l., 1 h., 4 tr., 6 h., * leave ecru, with green, work 6 tr., 1 h., 10 tr., 1 ch., turn *. **42nd row.**—* S.s. along first 4 tr., 3 ch., 6 tr., 1 h., 6 tr., leave green, with ecru, work 1 tr. on next tr. *, 6 h., 4 tr., 1 h., 1 b., 1 l., 1 h., 4 tr., 2 h., 4 tr., 1 h., 10 tr. **43rd row.**—Miss first tr., 3 tr., 2 h., 4 tr., 4 h., 4 tr., 1 b., 1 l., 1 h., 4 tr., 7 h., * leave ecru, with green, work 3 tr., 1 h., 7 tr., 1 ch., turn *. **44th row.**—* S.s. along first 4 tr., 3 ch., 8 tr., leave green, with ecru, work 1 tr. on next tr. *, 6 h., 4 tr., 1 l., 1 b., 1 l., 4 tr., 7 h., 4 tr. **45th row.**—Miss first tr., 3 tr., 7 h., 4 tr., 1 b., 1 l., 1 b., 4 tr., 7 h., leave ecru, with green, work 6 tr. **46th row.**—Miss first tr., 2 tr., leave green, with ecru, work 1 tr. on next tr., 8 h., 4 tr., 1 l., 1 b., 1 l., 4 tr., 2 h., 4 tr., 4 h., 4 tr. **47th row.**—Miss first tr., 15 tr., 1 h., 4 tr., 1 h., 4 tr., 1 b., 1 l., 1 b., 4 tr., 8 h., with green, work 5 ch., turn. This completes one pattern.

THE CORNER

The First Side.—Work from 2nd to 23rd row inclusive of lace once. **24th row.**—Work from * to * in 24th row of lace, then 5 ch., turn. **25th row.**—Work from * to * in 25th row of lace. **26th row.**—Work from * to * in 26th row of lace, then 6 ch., turn. **27th row.**—1 d.c. into b., 3 ch., 4 tr. on 4 tr., 3 more tr., 6 h., work from * to * in 27th row of lace. **28th row.**—Work from * to * in 28th row of lace, then 6 h., 4 tr., 1 h., 5 ch., turn. **29th row.**—1 h., 4 tr., work from * to * in 29th row of lace. **30th row.**—Work from * to * in 30th row of lace, then 6 h., 4 tr. **31st row.**—Miss first tr., 3 tr., 7 h., work from * to * in 31st row of lace. **32nd row.**—Work from * to * in 32nd row of lace, then 7 h., 5 ch., turn. **33rd row.**—11 h., work from * to * in 33rd row of lace. **34th row.**—Work from * to * in 34th row of lace, then 8 h., 5 ch., turn. **35th row.**—7 h., work from * to * in 35th row of lace. **36th row.**—Work from * to * in 36th row of lace, then 5 h., 5 ch., turn. **37th row.**—6 h., leave ecru, with green, work 9 tr., 1 h., 16 tr. **38th row.**—Work from * to * in 38th row of lace, then 4 h., 5 ch., turn. **39th row.**—5 h., work from * to * in 39th row of lace. **40th row.**—Work from * to * in 40th row of lace, then 3 h., 5 ch., turn. **41st row.**—4 h., work from * to * in 41st row of lace. **42nd row.**—Work from * to * in 42nd row of lace, 2 h., 5 ch., turn. **43rd row.**—3 h., work from * to * in 43rd row of lace. **44th row.**—Work from * to * in 44th row of lace, then 1 h., 5 ch., turn. **45th row.**—2 h., leave ecru, with green, work 6 tr. **46th row.**—Miss first tr., 2 tr., break off green, with ecru, work 1 tr. on next tr., 1 h., 5 ch., turn. **47th row.**—1 h., 1 ch., turn; s.s. along first 4 stitches, join on green, work 5 ch. with it and turn work so as to commence second side of corner.

The Second Side.—48th row.—Miss 3 ch., 2 tr., leave green, with ecru, work 1 tr. into end of s.s. worked in 47th row, 1 h., 2 ch., s.s. to top of next tr. at left, s.s. along next 3 stitches, 2 ch., turn. **49th row.**—1 h., leave ecru, with green, work 6 tr., 7 ch., turn. **50th row.**—Miss 1 ch., s.s. along 4 ch., miss first tr., 8 tr., leave green, with ecru, work 1 tr. on next stitch, 1 h., 2 ch., s.s. to top of next tr. at left, s.s. along next 3 stitches, 2 ch., turn. **51st row.**—2 h., leave ecru, with green, work 3 tr., 1 h., 7 tr., 5 ch., turn. **52nd row.**—Miss 3 ch., 9 tr., 1 h., 6 tr., leave green, with ecru, work 1 tr. on next tr., 2 h., 2 ch., s.s. to top of next tr. at left, s.s. along next 3 stitches, 2 ch., turn. **53rd row.**—3 h., leave ecru, with green, work 3 tr., 1 h., 13 tr., 7 ch., turn. **54th row.**—Miss 1 ch., s.s. along 4 ch., miss first tr., 12 tr., 1 h., 6 tr., leave green, with ecru, work 1 tr. on next tr., 3 h., 2 ch., s.s. to top of next tr. at left, s.s. along next 3 stitches, 2 ch., turn. **55th row.**—4 h., leave ecru, with green, work 6 tr., 1 h., 16 tr. **56th row.**—Work from * to * in 10th row of lace, 5 h., 2 ch., s.s. to top

Fig. 77. NEEDLE-POINT DESIGN

of next tr. at left, s.s. along next 3 stitches, 2 ch., turn. **57th row.**—6 h., leave ecru with green, work 9 tr., 1 h., 13 tr. **58th row.**—Work from * to * in 12th row of lace, then 5 h., 2 ch., s.s. to top of next tr. at left, s.s. along next 3 stitches, 2 ch., turn. **59th row.**—6 h., leave ecru, with green, work 15 tr., 1 h., 10 tr. **60th row.**—Work from * to * in 14th row of lace, 8 h., 2 ch., s.s. to top of next tr. at left, s.s. along next 3 stiches, 2 ch., turn. **61st row.**—10 h., work from * to * in 15th row of lace. **62nd row.**—Work from * to * in 16th row of lace, then 9 h., 2 ch., s.s. to top of next tr. at left, s.s. along next 3 stitches, 2 ch., turn. **63rd row.**—8 h., work from * to * in 17th row of lace. **64th row.**—Work from * to * in 18th row of lace, 7 h., 4 tr., 2 ch., miss 2 tr. at left, s.s. along next 4 stitches, turn. **65th row.**—3 tr., work from * to * in 19th row of lace. **66th row.**—Work from * to * in 20th row of lace, 7 h., 4 tr., 1 h., 2 ch., 1 tr. into 4th ch. of six at end of lacet now seen, turn. **67th row.**—2 tr. into h., 4 tr. on 4 tr., 6 h., work from * to * in 21st row of lace. **68th row.**—Work from * to * in 22nd row of lace, 2 tr. into end of next row, miss 2 tr. at left, s.s. along next 4 stitches, turn. **69th row.**—3 tr., work from * to * in 23rd row of lace. **70th row.**—Work from * to * in 24th row of lace, 2 tr. into end of next row, miss 2 tr. at left, s.s. to next stitch, 3 ch., turn. **71st row.**—3 tr. on 3 tr., work from * to * in 25th row of lace. Now work from 26th to 47th row inclusive of lace once Work from 2nd to 47th row inclusive of lace until another corner is required.

LACE IN NEEDLEPOINT DESIGN

MATERIALS

Mercer Crochet Cotton, No. 80.
Steel crochet hook, No. $6\frac{1}{2}$.

MEASUREMENT

Nearly 2 inches wide (Fig. 77).
For abbreviations see beginning of chapter.

FOR FIRST MOTIF

1st row.—Commence with 8 ch., then work 1 tr. into 8th ch. from hook, 4 ch. and 1 tr. 3 times into same place, 1 ch., turn.
2nd row.—5 d.c. into every sp., 5 ch., turn.
3rd row.—Miss first 2 d.c., 1 tr. on next d.c., * 2 ch., miss 1 d.c., 1 tr. on next d.c., 2 ch., miss 2 d.c., 1 tr. on next d.c., repeat from * twice, 2 ch., 1 tr. on last d.c., 1 ch., turn.

4th row.—4 d.c. into first sp., * 2 d.c. into next sp., 5 ch., turn; miss 3 d.c., 1 s.s. into next d.c., turn; 6 d.c. into loop just made, 2 d.c. into sp. now reached already worked into, 1 d.c. on next tr., 4 d.c. into next sp., repeat from * twice, 2 d.c. into next sp., 5 ch., turn; miss 3 d.c., 1 s.s. into next d.c., turn; 6 d.c. into loop just made, 2 d.c. into sp. now reached already worked into, 16 ch., turn.

5th row.—1 l. tr. on centre d.c. between first two small arches, * 11 ch., 1 l.tr. on centre d.c. between next two arches, repeat from * once, 11 ch., 1 l.tr. on d.c. at end of row, 1 ch., turn.

6th row.—* 11 d.c. into next sp., 1 ch., turn; miss 1 d.c., 10 d.c., 1 ch., turn; miss 1 d.c., 9 d.c., 1 ch., turn; miss 1 d.c., 8 d.c., 1 ch., turn; miss 1 d.c., 7 d.c., 1 ch., turn; miss 1 d.c., 6 d.c., 1 ch., turn; miss 1 d.c., 5 d.c., 1 ch., turn; miss 1 d.c., 4 d.c., 1 ch., turn; miss 1 d.c., 3 d.c., 1 ch., turn; miss 1 d.c., 2 d.c., 1 ch., turn; miss 1 d.c., 1 d.c. then s.s. down side of this point of double crochet, 1 d.c. into sp. now reached already worked into, repeat from * 3 times, 15 ch., turn.

7th row.—1 d.c. into top of first point, * 9 ch., 1 v.l.tr. into st. between points, 9 ch., 1 d.c. into top of next point, repeat from * twice, 9 ch., 1 v.l.tr. into l.tr. at end of 5th row, 1 ch., turn.

8th row.—* 1 d.c. on v.l.tr., 11 d.c. into sp., 1 d.c. on next d.c., 11 d.c. into next sp., repeat from * 3 times, then 1 d.c. into last sp. again, 7 ch., turn.

9th row.—Miss first 6 d.c., 1 d.c. on next d.c., * 7 ch., miss 5 d.c., 1 d.c. on next d.c., repeat from * to end, 1 ch., turn.

10th row.—* 9 d.c. into next sp., 5 d.c. into next sp., 7 ch., turn; miss 9 d.c., 1 s.s. on next d.c., 1 ch., turn; 4 d.c., 1 p., 4 d.c. all into sp. just made, 4 d.c. into sp. now reached already worked into, repeat from * to end. Fasten off.

** FOR NEXT MOTIF

Work as for first motif until the 9th row has been completed, and turn with 13 ch. instead of 1 ch. at end of 9th row.

10th row.—Join to d.c. last worked on previous motif, s.s. into each of the thirteen chain, 9 d.c. into first sp., 5 d.c. into next sp., 7 ch., turn; miss 9 d.c., 1 s.s. on next d.c., 1 ch., turn; 4 d.c. into sp. just made, 3 ch., join to corresponding picot on previous motif, 2 ch., 1 d.c. into top of d.c. last worked on present motif, 4 d.c. into sp. now reached already worked into, 4 d.c. into next sp. now reached already worked into, and now finish row as usual. Repeat from ** until a corner is required.

To form a corner, work as for first motif until the 9th row has been completed, and turn with 3 ch. instead of 1 ch. at end of 9th row.

10th row.—Join to d.c. last worked on previous motif, 2 ch., 1 s.s. into d.c. worked at end of 9th row on present motif, 9 d.c. into next sp., 5 d.c. into next sp., 7 ch., turn; miss 9 d.c., 1 s.s. on next d.c., 1 ch., turn; 4 d.c. into sp. just made, 3 ch., join to corresponding picot on previous motif, 2 ch., 1 d.c. into top of d.c. last worked on present motif, 4 d.c. into sp. now reached already worked into, 4 d.c. into next sp. now reached already worked into, and now finish row as usual.

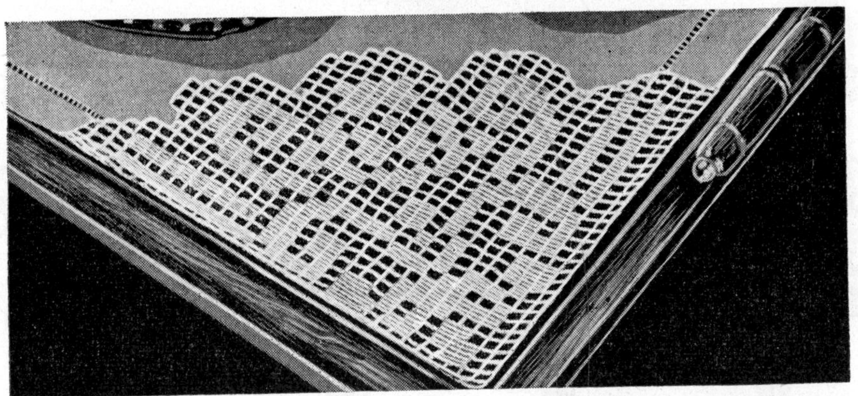

Fig. 78. FILET INSET TRAYCLOTH

The Heading.

1st round.—Work d.c. all round inner edge of motifs, join and fasten off.

2nd round.—Work 1 d.c. into d.c. about $\frac{1}{2}$ an inch from a corner, 10 ch., miss nearly $\frac{1}{4}$ inch, 1 d.c. on d.c., 10 ch., miss $\frac{1}{4}$ inch after corner, 1 d.c. on next d.c., * 10 ch., miss nearly $\frac{1}{4}$ inch, 1 d.c. on next d.c., repeat from *, working all corners as first, join.

3rd round.—S.s. along to centre of first loop, 1 d.c. into same loop, 1 d.c. into corner loop, 1 d.c. into loop after corner, * 4 ch., 1 d.c. into next loop, repeat from *, working all corners as first, join.

4th round.—1 d.c. into every st., join and fasten off.

FILET INSET FOR TRAYCLOTH

MATERIALS

Linen Crochet Thread, No. 35.
Steel crochet hook, No. 6$\frac{1}{2}$.

MEASUREMENTS

About 7$\frac{1}{2}$ inches along each straight side
For abbreviations see beginning of chapter.

THE INSET

Begin with 136 chain.

1st row.—1 l.tr. into 12th ch. from hook, * 3 ch., miss 3 sts., 1 l.tr. into next, repeat from * 30 times. Always turn with 7 ch at end of each row unless otherwise directed. **2nd row.**—1 l.tr. on second l.tr. to form first o.m., 9 more o.m., 9 l.tr., 20 o.m. **3rd row.**—3 o.m., 45 l.tr., 1 o.m., 17 l.tr., 1 o.m., 13 l.tr., 1 o.m., 9 l.tr., 2 o.m., 9 l.tr., 2 o.m. **4th row.**—2 o.m., 13 l.tr., 1 o.m., 5 l.tr., 1 o.m., 5 l.tr., 1 o.m., 9 l.tr., 1 o.m., 5 l.tr., 2 o.m., 9 l.tr., 14 o.m., 1 ch., turn.

5th row.—S.s. along first 5 sts., 7 ch., 1 l.tr. on next l.tr., 1 o.m., 41 l.tr., 1 o.m., 9 l.tr., 1 o.m., 9 l.tr., 4 o.m., 5 l.tr., 1 o.m., 5 l.tr., 1 o.m., 9 l.tr., 3 o.m.

6th row.—5 o.m., 17 l.tr., 4 o.m., 9 l.tr., 1 o.m., 9 l.tr., 12 o.m., 1 ch., turn.

7th row.—S.s. along first 5 sts., 7 ch., 1 l.tr. on next l.tr., 10 o.m., 9 l.tr., 8 o.m., 25 l.tr., 2 o.m.

8th row.—2 o.m., 5 l.tr., 2 o.m., 9 l.tr., 1 o.m., 13 l.tr., 4 o.m., 9 l.tr., 2 o.m., 21 l.tr., 3 o.m., 13 ch., turn.

9th row.—Miss 1 ch., s.s. along next 5 ch., then 3 ch., 1 l.tr. on first l.tr., 2 o.m., 13 l.tr., 2 o.m., 13 l.tr., 1 o.m., 21 l.tr., 3 o.m., 5 l.tr., 1 o.m., 13 l.tr., 3 om.

10th row.—2 o.m., 5 l.tr., 4 o.m., 5 l.tr., 1 o.m., 5 l.tr., 14 o.m., 9 l.tr., 3 o.m.

11th row.—3 o.m., 9 l.tr., 1 o.m., 9 l.tr., 1 o.m., 9 l.tr., 6 o.m., 9 l.tr., 2 o.m., 5 l.tr., 3 o.m., 13 l.tr., 1 o.m.

12th row.—1 o.m., 13 l.tr., 4 o.m., 5 l.tr., 1 o.m., 9 l.tr., 3 o.m., 13 l.tr., 1 o.m., 5 l.tr., 1 o.m., 5 l.tr., 2 o.m., 9 l.tr., 3 o.m., 1 ch., turn.

13th row.—S.s. along first 5 sts., 7 ch., 1 l.tr. on next l.tr., 2 o.m., 17 l.tr., 2 o.m., 9 l.tr., 2 o.m., 9 l.tr., 4 o.m., 5 l.tr., 8 o.m.

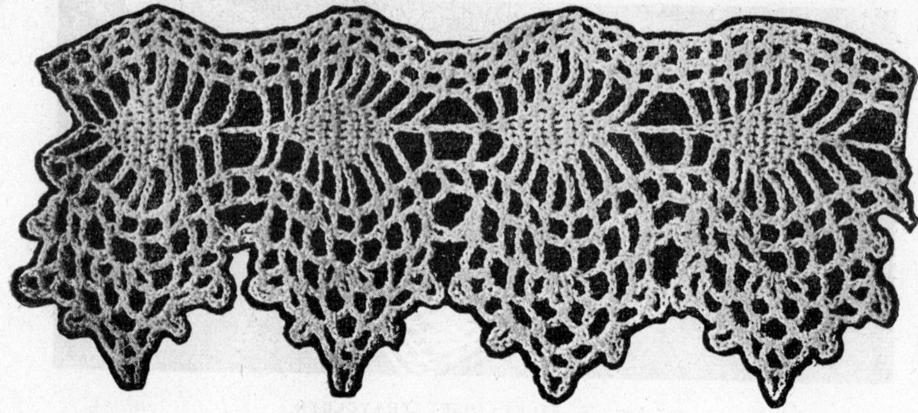

Fig. 79. TORCHON LACE DESIGN

14th row.—2 o.m., 17 l.tr., 2 o.m., 5 l.tr., 3 o.m., 9 l.tr., 1 o.m., 9 l.tr., 1 o.m., 9 l.tr., 7 o.m., 1 ch., turn.

15th row.—S.s. along first 5 sts., 7 ch., 1 l.tr. on next l.tr., 5 o.m., 5 l.tr., 1 o.m., 13 l.tr., 2 o.m., 5 l.tr., 3 o.m., 5 l.tr., 2 o.m., 9 l.tr., 1 o.m., 5 l.tr., 2 o.m. **16th row.**—2 o.m., 5 l.tr., 4 o.m., 9 l.tr., 2 o.m., 5 l.tr., 1 o.m., 9 l.tr., 7 o.m., 10 ch., turn.

17th row.—1 l.tr. on first l.tr., 2 o.m., 9 l.tr., 1 o.m., 5 l.tr., 1 o.m., 9 l.tr., 1 o.m., 5 l.tr., 3 o.m., 25 l.tr., 2 o.m. **18th row.**—3 o.m., 17 l.tr., 1 o.m., 5 l.tr., 2 o.m., 9 l.tr., 1 o.m., 5 l.tr., 3 o.m., 13 l.tr., 2 o.m.

19th row.—3 o.m., 17 l.tr., 2 o.m., 9 l.tr., 1 o.m., 5 l.tr., 1 o.m., 5 l.tr., 5 o.m., 5 l.tr., 2 o.m.

20th row.—2 o.m., 5 l.tr., 1 o.m., 5 l.tr., 2 o.m., * 9 l.tr., 1 o.m., repeat from * twice, 13 l.tr., 4 o.m., 1 ch., turn.

21st row.—S.s. along first 5 sts., 7 ch., 1 l.tr. on next l.tr., 3 o.m., 5 l.tr., 9 o.m., 5 l.tr., 2 o.m., 5 l.tr., 1 o.m., 5 l.tr., 2 o.m

22nd row.—2 o.m., 5 l.tr., 1 o.m., 5 l.tr., 2 o.m., 5 l.tr., 2 o.m., 13 l.tr., 8 o.m., 1 ch., turn.

23rd row.—S.s. along first 5 sts., 7 ch., 1 l.tr. on next l.tr., 2 o.m., 7 ch., 1 s.s. on next l.tr., s.s. along next 4 sts., 7 ch., 1 l.tr. on next l.tr., 1 o.m., 5 l.tr., 1 o.m., 5 l.tr., 1 o.m., 9 l.tr., 2 o.m., 5 l.tr., 1 o.m., 5 l.tr.. 2 o.m.

24th row.—2 o.m., 5 l.tr., 1 o.m., 5 l.tr., 2 o.m., 9 l.tr., 3 o.m., 5 l.tr., 2 o.m.

25th row.—2 o.m., 21 l.tr., 3 o.m., 5 l.tr., 1 o.m, 5 l.tr., 2 o.m.

26th row.—2 o.m., 5 l.tr., 1 o.m., 5 l.tr., 4 o.m., 13 l.tr., 3 o.m., 1 ch., turn.

27th row.—S.s. along first 5 sts., 7 ch., 1 l.tr. on next l.tr., 4 o.m., 7 ch., turn; 4 o.m., 1 ch., turn; s.s along first 5 sts., 7 ch., 1 l.tr. on next l.tr., 1 o.m., 7 ch., miss 3 ch. of next mesh, s.s. into next ch., 7 ch., miss next 3 ch. of same mesh, 1 tr. into top of l.tr. now reached, 1 l.tr. on next l.tr. in 26th row, 3 o.m., 5 l.tr., 1 o.m., 5 l.tr., 2 o.m.

28th row.—2 o.m., 5 l.tr., 1 o.m., 5 l.tr., 2 o.m., 7 ch., turn.

29th row.—2 o.m., 5 l.tr., 1 o.m., 5 l.tr., 2 o.m. **30th row.**—6 o.m., 1 ch., turn. **31st row.**—S.s. along first 5 sts., 7 ch., 1 l.tr. on next l.tr., 4 o.m. **32nd row.**—4 o.m., fasten off. This completes inset.

TORCHON LACE

Materials

Mercer Crochet Cotton, No. 60.
Steel crochet hook, No. $6\frac{1}{2}$.

Measurement

About 2 inches wide (Fig. 79).
For abbreviations see beginning of chapter.

The Lace.—Begin with 24 chain.

1st row.—1 tr. into 8th ch. from hook, 5 ch., miss 5 ch. of foundation, 1 d.c. into next ch., 5 ch., miss 5 ch. of foundation, 1 tr. into next chain, 2 s.h., 4 ch., turn. **2nd row.**—2 s.h. over 2 s.h., 5 ch., 1 d.c. into next loop, 1 d.c. on d.c., 1 d.c. into next loop, 5 ch., 1 tr. on next tr., 1 h., 5 ch., turn. **3rd row.**—1 h., 5 ch., 1 d.c. into next loop, 3 d.c. on 3 d.c., 1 d.c. into next loop, 5 ch., 1 tr. on next tr., 2 s.h., 4 ch., turn. **4th row.**—2 s.h., 5 ch., 1 d.c. into next loop, 5 d.c. on 5 d.c., 1 d.c. into next loop, 5 ch., 1 tr. on next tr., 1 h., 9 ch., turn. **5th row.**—1 tr. on first tr., 1 h., 5 ch., 1 d.c. into next loop, 7 d.c. on 7 d.c., 1 d.c. into next loop, 5 ch., 1 tr. on next tr., 2 s.h., 4 ch., turn. **6th row.**—2 s.h., 5 ch., miss 1 d.c., 7 d.c., 5 ch., 1 tr. on next tr., 1 h., then 5 ch. and 1 d.c. 4 times into 9 ch. loop now reached, 5 ch., miss 1 row along edge, s.s. along end of next row, 5 ch., turn. **7th row.**—1 d.c. into first loop, 5 ch. and 1 d.c. into each of next 4 loops, 5 ch., 1 tr. on next tr., 1 h., 5 ch., miss 1 d.c., 5 d.c., 5 ch., 1 tr., on next tr., 2 s.h., 4 ch., turn. **8th row.**—2 s.h., 5 ch., miss 1 d.c., 3 d.c., 5 ch., 1 tr. on next tr., 1 h., then 5 ch. and 1 d.c. into each of next 6 loops, 5 ch., miss 1 row along edge, s.s. into next st., 1 ch., turn. **9th row.**—2 d.c., 5 ch., 2 d.c. all into first loop, * 3 ch., 1 tr. into next loop, 6 ch., 1 tr. into top of tr. just made, 1 tr. into same loop, 3 ch., 2 d.c., 5 ch., 2 d.c. all into next loop, repeat from * twice, 1 s.s. on next tr., 5 ch., 1 tr. on next tr., 5 ch., miss 1 d.c., 1 d.c. on next d.c., 5 ch., 1 tr. on next tr., 2 s.h., 4 ch., turn. **10th row.**—2 s.h., 5 ch., 1 l.tr. on next d.c., 5 ch., 1 tr. on next tr., 1 h., 5 ch., turn. **11th row.**—1 h., 5 ch., 1 d.c. on l.tr., 5 ch., 1 tr. on next tr., 2 s.h., 4 ch., turn. This completes the first pattern.

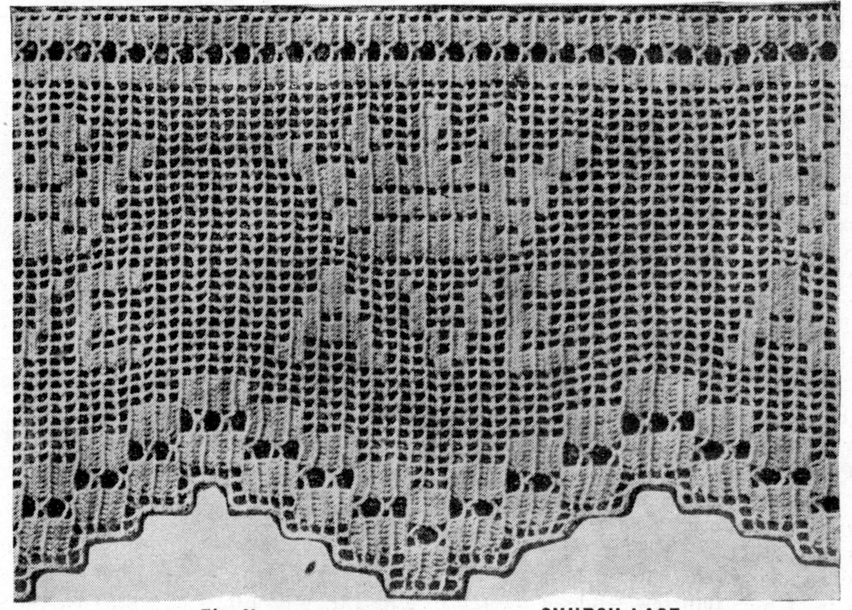

Fig. 80. CHURCH LACE

** Work from 2nd to 8th row inclusive once.

Next row.—2 d.c. into first loop, 2 ch., join to corresponding picot on previous scallop, 2 ch., 2 d.c. into first loop again on present scallop, * 3 ch., 1 tr. into next loop, 6 ch., 1 tr. into top of tr. just made, 1 tr. into same loop, 3 ch., 2 d.c., 5 ch., 2 d.c. all into next loop, repeat from * twice, 1 s.s. on next tr., 5 ch., 1 tr. on next tr., 5 ch., miss 1 d.c., 1 d.c. on next d.c., 5 ch., 1 tr. on next tr., 2 s.h., 4 ch., turn.

Next row.—As 10th row. **Next row.**—As 11th row **. Repeat from ** to ** until length required.

A CHURCH LACE

Materials

Mercer Crochet Cotton, No. 70.

Steel crochet hook, No. 6½.

Measurement

About 5½ inches wide (Fig. 80).

For abbreviations see beginning of chapter.

The Lace.

Begin with 113 chain.

1st row.—Miss first 7 ch., 7 tr., 1 l., 7 tr., 24 h., 4 tr., 1 l., 4 tr., 1 h. Always turn with 5 ch. at ends of rows unless otherwise directed.

2nd row.—1 h., 4 tr., 1 b., 4 tr., 24 h., 7 tr., 1 b., 7 tr., 1 h., 10 ch., turn.

3rd row.—Miss first ch., s.s. along 7 ch., then 2 ch., 7 tr. on 7 tr., 1 l., 7 tr., 24 h., 4 tr., 1 l., 4 tr., 1 h. **4th row.**—1 h., 4 tr., 1 b., 4 tr., 24 h., 7 tr., 1 b., 7 tr., 3 h. **5th row.**—1 h., 7 tr., 1 l., 7 tr., 26 h., 4 tr., 1 l., 4 tr., 1 h.

6th row.—1 h., 4 tr., 1 b., 4 tr., 26 h., 7 tr., 1 b., 7 tr., 1 h., 10 ch., turn.

7th row.—Miss first ch., s.s. along 7 ch., then 2 ch., 7 tr. on 7 tr., 1 l., 7 tr., 4 h., 4 tr., 15 h., 4 tr., 5 h., 4 tr., 1 l., 4 tr., 1 h.

8th row.—1 h., 4 tr., 1 b., 4 tr., 5 h., 7 tr., 12 h., 10 tr., 4 h., 7 tr., 1 b., 7 tr., 3 h. **8th row.**—1 h., 7 tr., 1 l., 7 tr., 8 h., 10 tr., 9 h., 7 tr., 6 h., 4 tr., 1 l., 4 tr., 1 h. **10th row.**—1 h., 4 tr., 1 b., 4 tr., 7 h., 10 tr., 5 h., 10 tr., 1 h., 4 tr., 8 h., 7 tr., 1 b., 7 tr., 1 h., 10 ch., turn.

11th row.—Miss first ch., s.s. along 7 ch., then 2 ch., 7 tr. on 7 tr., 1 l., 7 tr., 8 h., 4 tr., 1 h., 10 tr., 3 h., 7 tr., 1 h., 7 tr., 7 h., 4 tr., 1 l., 4 tr., 1 h.

12th row.—1 h., 4 tr., 1 b., 4 tr., 4 h., 4 tr., 3 h., 4 tr., 1 h., 4 tr., 1 h., 4 tr., 4 h., 10 tr., 8 h., 7 tr., 1 b., 7 tr., 3 h.

13th row.—1 h., 7 tr., 1 l., 7 tr., 8 h., 10 tr., 6 h., 4 tr., 1 h., 13 tr., 1 h., 10 tr., 3 h., 4 tr., 1 l., 4 tr., 1 h. **14th row.**—1 h., 4 tr., 1 b., 4 tr., 4 h., 4 tr., 1 h., 7 tr., 1 b., 7 tr., 1 h., 10 ch., turn.

1 h., 4 tr., 1 h., 7 tr., 8 h., 4 tr., 8 h., 7 tr.,
15th row.—Miss first ch., s.s. along 7 ch., then 2 ch., 7 tr. on 7 tr., 1 l., 7 tr., 17 h., 7 tr., 1 h., 4 tr., 1 h., 7 tr., 6 h., 4 tr., 1 l., 4 tr., 1 h.

16th row.—1 h., 4 tr., 1 b., 4 tr., 7 h., 4 tr., 1 h., 4 tr., 1 h., 7 tr., 2 h., 4 tr., 14 h., 7 tr., 1 b., 7 tr., 3 h.

17th row.—1 h., 7 tr., 1 l., 7 tr., 13 h., 10 tr., 3 h., 7 tr., 1 h., 4 tr., 1 h., 7 tr., 2 h., 4 tr., 3 h., 4 tr., 1 l., 4 tr., 1 h. **18th row.**—1 h., 4 tr., 1 b., 4 tr., 2 h., 19 tr., 1 h., 4 tr., 1 h., 7 tr., 6 h., 7 tr., 11 h., 7 tr., 1 b., 7 tr., 1 h.

19th row.—1 h., 7 tr., 1 l., 7 tr., 10 h., 4 tr., 8 h., 7 tr., 1 h., 4 tr., 1 h., 7 tr., 2 h., 4 tr., 3 h., 4 tr., 1 l., 4 tr., 1 h.

20th row.—1 h., 4 tr., 1 b., 4 tr., 7 h., 4 tr., 1 h., 4 tr., 1 h., 7 tr., 6 h., 7 tr., 9 h., 7 tr., 1 b., 7 tr., 3 h., 1 ch., turn.

21st row.—S.s. along first 2 h., then 5 ch., 7 tr. on 7 tr., 1 l., 7 tr., 11 h., 10 tr., 3 h., 7 tr., 1 h., 4 tr., 1 h., 7 tr., 6 h., 4 tr., 1 l., 4 tr., 1 h.

22nd row.—1 h., 4 tr., 1 b., 4 tr., 4 h., 4 tr., 1 h., 7 tr., 1 h., 4 tr., 1 h., 7 tr., 2 h., 4 tr., 14 h., 7 tr., 1 b., 7 tr., 1 h.

23rd row.—1 h., 7 tr., 1 l., 7 tr., 17 h., 4 tr., 1 h., 13 tr., 1 h., 10 tr., 3 h., 4 tr., 1 l., 4 tr., 1 h.

24th row.—1 h., 4 tr., 1 b., 4 tr., 4 h., 4 tr., 3 h., 4 tr., 1 h., 4 tr., 1 h., 4 tr., 2 h., 22 tr., 6 h., 7 tr., 1 b., 7 tr., 3 h., 1 ch., turn.

25th row.—S.s. along first 2 h., then 5 ch., 7 tr. on 7 tr., 1 l., 7 tr., 6 h., 4 tr., 2 h., 4 tr., 2 h., 4 tr., 3 h., 7 tr., 1 h., 7 tr., 7 h., 4 tr., 1 l., 4 tr., 1 h.

26th row.—1 h., 4 tr., 1 b., 4 tr., 7 h., 10 tr., 5 h., 4 tr., 2 h., 4 tr., 2 h., 4 tr., 6 h., 7 tr., 1 b., 7 tr., 1 h. **27th row.** – 1 h., 7 tr., 1 l., 7 tr., 6 h., 4 tr., 5 h., 4 tr., 7 h., 7 tr., 6 h., 4 tr., 1 l., 4 tr., 1 h.

28th row.—1 h., 4 tr., 1 b., 4 tr., 5 h., 7 tr., 8 h., 4 tr., 5 h., 4 tr., 4 h., 7 tr., 1 b., 7 tr., 3 h., 1 ch., turn. **29th row.**—S.s. along first 2 h., then 5 ch., 7 tr. on 7 tr., 1 l., 7 tr., 20 h., 4 tr., 5 h., 4 tr., 1 l., 4 tr., 1 h. **30th row.**—As 6th row, 5 ch., turn. **31st row.**—As 5th row. **32nd row.**—As 4th row, 1 ch., turn. **33rd row.**—S.s. along first 2 h., then 5 ch., 7 tr. on 7 tr., 1 l., 7 tr., 24 h., 4 tr., 1 l.,

4 tr., 1 h. This completes one pattern. Repeat from beginning of 2nd row until length required. When length of lace has been finished, work double crochet all round the outer edge.

1st round.—12 d.c. into ring, s.s. to first d.c. **2nd round.**—6 ch., miss next d.c., 1 tr. into next, * 3 ch., miss 1 d.c., 1 tr. into next, repeat from * 3 times more, 3 ch., s.s. to third chain of six at beginning

Fig. 81.

THE ROSE AND LEAF D'OYLEY

MATERIALS

Mercer Crochet Cotton, No. 80.
Steel crochet hook, No. $6\frac{1}{2}$.

MEASUREMENT

About $7\frac{1}{2}$ inches in diameter (Fig. 81).

The Centre Rose Motif.

Begin with 6 ch. and join into a ring.

of round. **3rd round.**—1 d.c., 8 tr., 1 d.c. all into every space, s.s. to d.c. at beginning. **4th round.**—* 4 ch., s.s. under next treble in second round, repeat from * all round, 4 ch., join. The chain should be kept at the back of the petals. **5th round.**—As 3rd round. **6th round.**—Work * 2 picot thus: 7 ch., 1 d.c. into fifth ch. from hook, 7 ch., 1 d.c. into fifth ch. from hook (this completes the 2 picots), then 2 ch., 1 d.c. into centre of next petal, 2 picots, 2 ch., 1 d.c. into dip between petals, repeat from * 5 times more. **7th round.**—* 2 picots, 2 ch., 1 d.c. between picots of next loop in previous round, repeat from * 11 times more. **8th round.**—As 7th round, then work 2 picots, 2 ch., 1 s.s. between picots of next loop, fasten off.

For First Leaf.—Commence with 7 chain.

1st row.—Miss first chain, 5 d.c. on next 5 ch., then 3 d.c. into next stitch, now work along opposite side of foundation chain, 5 d.c. over 5 d.c., 1 ch., turn. Always work into top back thread only of every double crochet. **2nd row.**—6 d.c., then 3 d.c. into next stitch, 6 d.c., 1 ch., turn. **3rd row.**—7 d.c., then 3 d.c. into next stitch, 7 d.c., 1 ch., turn. **4th row.**—8 d.c., then 3 d.c. into next stitch, 8 d.c., 1 ch., turn. **5th row.**—9 d.c., then 3 d.c. into next stitch, 9 d.c., 1 ch., turn. **6th row.**—10 d.c., then 3 d.c. into next stitch, 10 d.c., 1 ch., turn. **7th row.**—12 d.c., now work 1 d.c. between picots of a loop on centre motif, then 2 d.c. into d.c. last worked into on leaf, 11 d.c. on next 11 d.c. of leaf, fasten off.

** **For a Wheel.**—Commence with 6 ch., join into a ring.

1st round.—3 ch., then 19 tr. into ring, join. **2nd round.**—1 d.c. into top of chain at beginning of 1st round, * 5 ch., miss 1 tr., 1 d.c. into next, repeat from * 8 times more, 5 ch., s.s. to d.c. at beginning. **3rd round.**—S.s. along to centre of first loop, 1 d.c. into same loop, 6 ch. and 1 d.c. into each of next 2 loops, 3 ch., work 1 d.c. into fourth double crochet from end of last row on previous leaf, 2 ch., 1 d.c. into next loop on wheel, 3 ch., miss next 3 d.c. on leaf 1 d.c. into next d.c., 2 ch., 1 d.c. into next loop on wheel, 6 ch., 1 d.c. into next loop, 3 ch., 1 d.c. between picots of next loop on centre motif, 2 ch., 1 d.c. into next loop on wheel, 6 ch. and 1 d.c. into each of next 3 loops, 6 ch., s.s. to d.c. at beginning. Fasten off securely.

For Next Leaf.—Work as directed for first leaf until the 6th row is completed. **7th row.**—4 d.c., then miss 3 loops on previous wheel, counting from where wheel is joined to leaf, work 1 d.c. into next loop on wheel, 4 d.c. on next 4 d.c. of leaf, 1 d.c. into next loop on wheel, 4 d.c. on next 4 d.c. of leaf, now work 1 d.c. between picots of next loop on centre motif, 2 d.c. into d.c. last worked into on leaf, 11 d.c. on next 11 d.c. of leaf, fasten off ** Repeat from ** to ** 4 times more, then work another wheel and join to first leaf as well to complete round.

Work round outer edge of leaves and wheels thus:

1st round.—1 d.c. into first free loop on a wheel, * 2 picots, 2 ch., 1 d.c. into next loop, 2 picots, 2 ch., 1 d.c. into next loop, 2 picots, 2 ch., 1 tr., into loop that has been joined to leaf, 1 d.c. into end of last row of leaf, 2 picots, 2 ch., miss 3 rows, 1 d.c. into next row, 2 picots, 2 ch., miss 4 rows, 1 d.c. into next row, 2 picots, 2 ch., 1 d.c. into end of leaf, 1 tr. into next loop that has been joined to leaf **, 2 picots, 2 ch., 1 d.c. into next loop on wheel *, repeat from * to* 4 times more, then from first * to ** once, 2 picots, 2 ch., s.s. into d.c. at beginning.

Next 2 rounds.—* 2 picots, 2 ch., 1 d.c. between picots of next loop in previous round, repeat from * 41 times more. **4th round.**—* 2 picots, 2 ch., 1 d.c. between picots of next loop, repeat from * 41 times more, 2 picots, 2 ch., 1 s.s. between picots of next loop, fasten off securely.

The Rose Motifs Round Outer Edge.

For first motif, begin with 6 ch. and join into a ring. **1st and 2nd rounds.**—Work as for 1st and 2nd rounds of centre rose motif. **3rd round.**—1 d.c., 6 tr., 1 d.c. all into every space, join. **4th round.**—As 4th round of centre rose motif. **5th round.**—1 d.c. 6 tr., 1 d.c. all into every space, join. **6th round.**—As 6th round of centre rose motif. **7th round.**—2 picots, 2 ch., 1 d.c. between picots of next loop, * 7 ch., 1 d.c. into fifth ch. from hook, 1 ch., 1 d.c. between picots of next loop on last round of d'oyley, 6 ch., 1 d.c. into fifth ch. from hook, 2 ch., 1 d.c. between picots of next loop on present motif, repeat from * twice more, ** 2 picots, 2 ch., 1 d.c. between picots of next loop, repeat from ** 7 times more, 2 picots, 2 ch., 1 s.s. between picots of next loop, fasten off. For second motif, work as for first, but in 7th round, as well as joining motif to next three loops in last round of d'oyley, join also to two loops of previous motif (i.e. the two free loops immediately next to those joined to d'oyley). Work two more motifs in same way. *** For next motif, work as for second motif, but join to two hoops of d'oyley instead of three.

Work four more motifs as for second motif ***. Repeat from *** to *** once more.

For last motif, work as for first six rounds of first motif. In the 7th round, join as usual to two loops of previous motif and two loops on d'oyley, also to two loops on first motif made to join up the round. Fasten off securely.

Press on wrong side under a damp cloth with a hot iron.

HAIRPIN CROCHET

Fig. 1.—TYPE OF HAIRPIN USED TODAY

The part-name "Hairpin" comes from the hairpin-like tool used to gauge the loops which are a feature of this charming type of crochet work. In fact, originally ordinary hairpins were used, but, as the work became popular, special tools were made for the purpose . . . a range is shown below, reproduced from a Victorian needlework magazine. For a time Hairpin Crochet was not widely worked, and during the late war years the manufacture of the hairpins was discontinued altogether. Recently, however, the work has come into vogue again and now the hairpins are available at most needlework shops. These modern prongs are simple in form (see Fig. 1 above) and are in a range of sizes suitable for modern work. These sizes are $\frac{1}{4}$ in., $\frac{1}{2}$ in., $\frac{3}{4}$ in., 1 in., $1\frac{1}{4}$ in., $1\frac{1}{2}$ in., 2 in. and 3 in. wide, and all are 5 inches long.

Figs. 2 to 6 show the types of Hairpins that were originally used. Fig. 2 is an ordinary hairpin, Fig. 3 a later development with strong steel prongs. Fig. 4 wood or bone type, Figs. 5 and 6 have prongs arranged for working fancy patterns and were sometimes known as "forks".

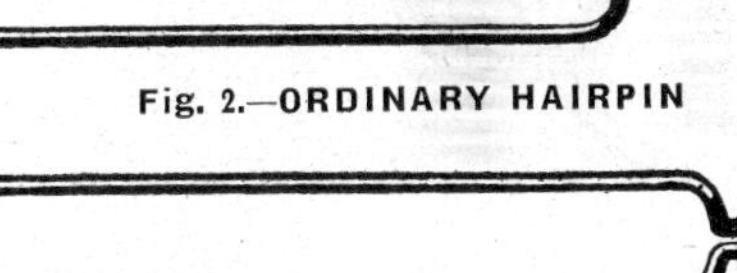

Fig. 2.—ORDINARY HAIRPIN

Fig. 3.—STEEL HAIRPIN

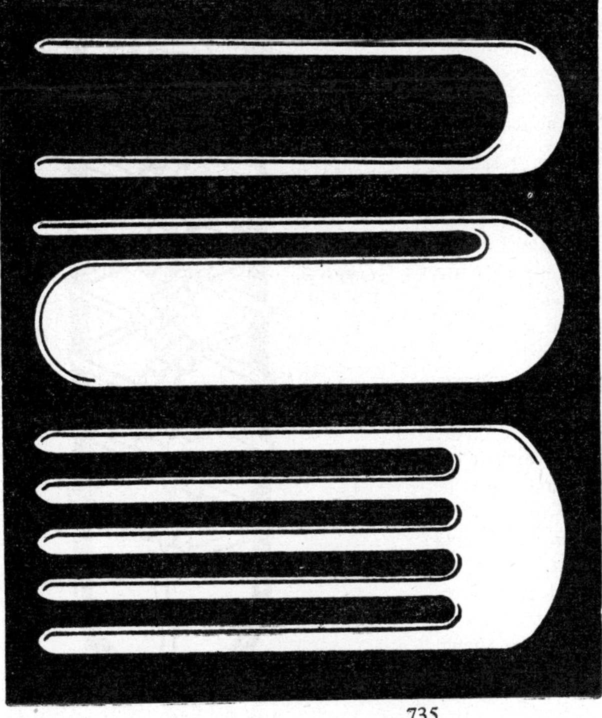

Fig. 4.
HAIRPIN MADE OF WOOD OR BONE

Fig. 5.
FORK OF WOOD OR BONE

Fig. 6.
WIDE FORK OF WOOD OR BONE

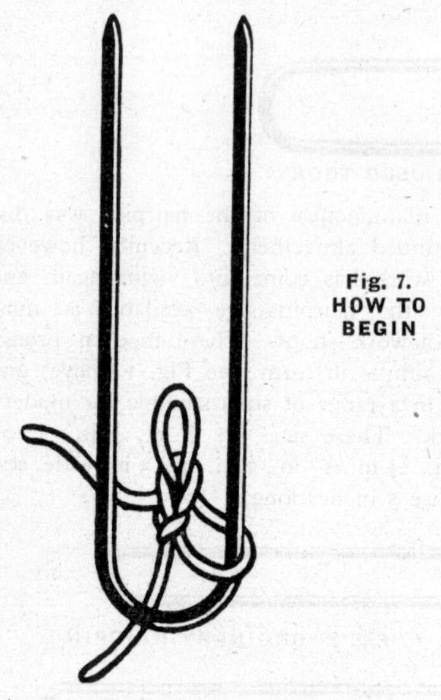

Fig. 7.
HOW TO
BEGIN

The crochet itself is worked with an ordinary crochet hook, of steel or bone according to the fineness or coarseness of the work.

Almost any thread suitable for ordinary crochet can be used; for hairpin crochet lace for trimming house linens, crochet cotton is best, for shawls, scarves and similar articles a lightweight wool.

Method of Starting and Working.—Hold the crochet hook in the right hand and tie a stitch on it as if about to crochet. Take the hairpin in the left hand and hold it flat between the thumb and first finger, with the prong end uppermost and the round part downwards in the palm of the hand. Now slip the tag of cotton between the prongs, by pressure of the thumb upon it, while at the same time passing the working thread over the right-hand prong and carry it between the second and third fingers of the left hand. This is the position for working. Pass the hook round the cotton that is held between the fingers and draw it through the stitch on the needle. This is the first movement and if the hook is now withdrawn there will be a stitch similar to that shown in Fig. 7. The hook is seldom withdrawn. The modern way being to work stitch after stitch continuously, guiding it from side to side with the movement of the hairpin. Now, * bring the hook with its stitch to the front, in such a way that it can be momentarily rested horizontally across the hairpin, and, keeping the hook in front, pass the stem downwards through the space between the prongs, and simultaneously with this movement, turn the hairpin from right to left (that is, turn the prong that hitherto has been nearest to the tip of the finger, over to the left side) and thereby restore the needle to its original position, i.e. the stem in front and the hook at the back. Now pass the hook round the cotton that still is held between the second and third fingers and draw it through the stitch on the needle (as if doing a chain stitch). Insert the hook to take up one top thread of the loop that stands on the left prong and draw the cotton through, then with cotton over the needle, draw through two stitches

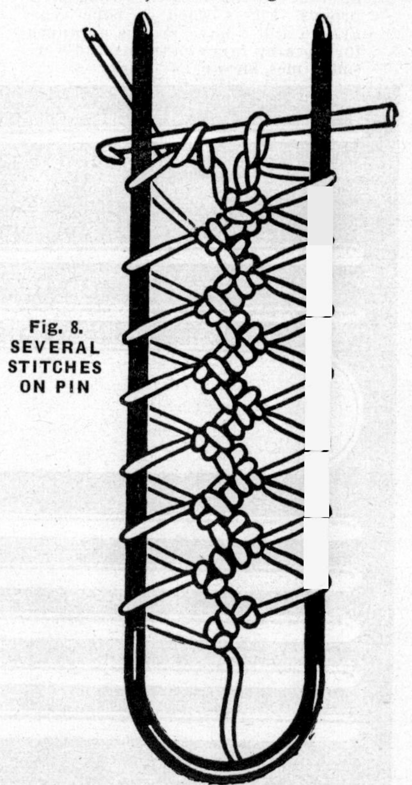

Fig. 8.
SEVERAL
STITCHES
ON PIN

on the needle (like working a double crochet stitch). The action of this is shown in Fig. 8. Repeat from * continuously and you will find that every turn of the hairpin will produce a loop upon the prong, first one prong, then the other, alternately, and after every turn, work first a chain stitch and then a double crochet stitch upon the braid that runs up the centre of the hairpin. Always draw the double crochet stitches tightly. Keep the crochet plait or braid as near as possible in the exact centre of the space between the prongs so that the loops are the same size on either side. Fig. 8 shows clearly hairpin trimming as it appears on the pin in the course of working. As the pin becomes full press the work closely downwards and when there is no room for more, remove the whole lot of the work from the prongs and replace the last three loops on each side in their former position so as to form a firm hold and proceed as before until sufficient length of trimming is made.

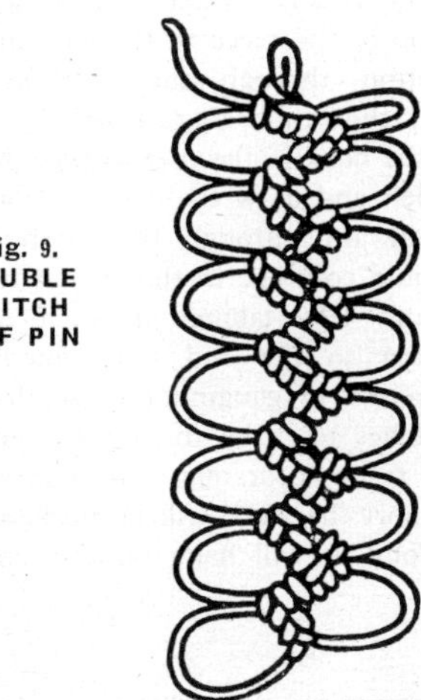

Fig. 9. DOUBLE STITCH OFF PIN

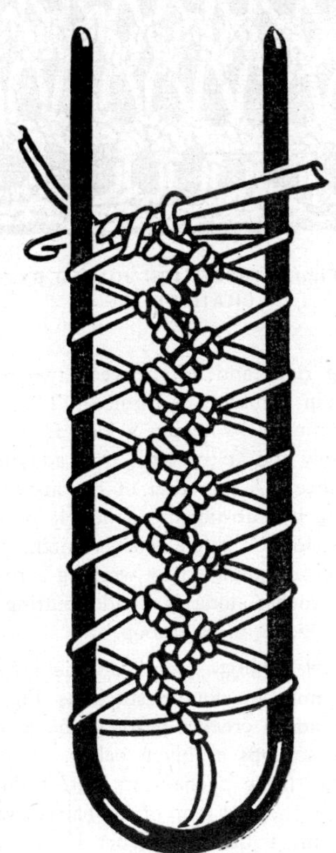

Fig. 10.—A DOUBLE STITCH

Double Stitch.—Fig. 10 shows how double stitch looks on the hairpin and Fig. 9 shows a piece of work completed. Two crochet stitches are worked together in each loop instead of the usual one double crochet. The additional stitch increases the width of the crochet braiding, and also renders it more solid.

Joining together Two Pieces of Work.—This method is the same as that used in connecting two strips in wool crochet. Work a stitch from right to left alternately and so join the strips by forming a series of slip stitches running perpendicularly upwards. In Fig. 11 the slip stitches run perpendicularly between two pieces of hairpin trimming, joining them by drawing together alternately a loop from each piece. The trimming is worked as in Fig. 8. Two pieces of equal length are required. First tie a stitch on the crochet needle, then take up two pieces of trimming and hold them side by side between the thumb and first finger of the left hand. Insert the hook in the first loop of the piece to the right and draw the cotton through the loop, and also through the stitch that is on the needle. Insert the hook in the first loop of the piece to the left, and draw the cotton through the loop and also through the stitch that is on the needle. Insert the hook in the first loop of the piece to the left and draw the cotton through the loop and also through the stitch on the needle and continue in this way, alternately right and left, taking up each loop in succession to the end. Judgment must be exercised in gauging the length of the slip stitches to make them just sufficiently long to reach accurately from loop to loop; if too short the work will be puckered, and if too long, it will hang untidily and look

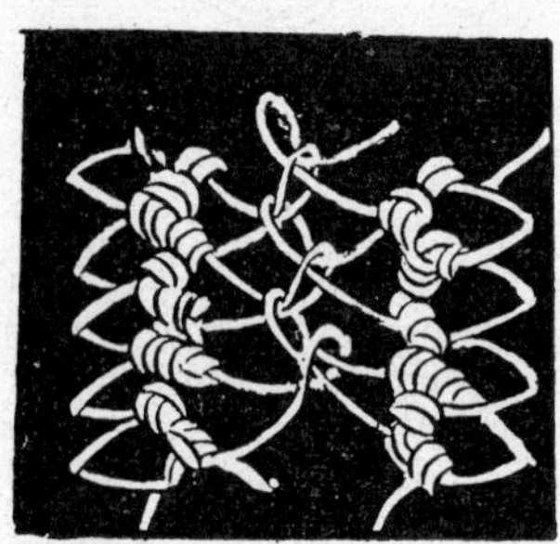

Fig. 11.—METHOD OF JOINING TOGETHER TWO PIECES OF HAIRPIN WORK

stretched. Any number of pieces may be joined in this manner. This is the simplest method of joining.

Insertion joined by chain-stitch—as Fig. 12 is composed of two pieces of hairpin trimming joined together by a zigzag chain-stitch crochet. This is one of the most popular methods of joining.

For the **insertion** (Fig. 12) a fork ¾ inch or 1 inch, coarse crochet cotton and a medium-sized steel crochet hook are needed. Work the hairpin trimming as in Fig. 8 making two pieces of trimming of equal length.

To Join these together: Begin by tying a stitch on the needle, then take up one piece of hairpin trimming, insert the hook in the first loop and draw the cotton through the loop and the stitch that is on the needle, 2 chain. Take the other piece, insert the hook in the first loop and draw the cotton through the loop and through the stitch on the needle (this in crochet work is termed a single crochet stitch). Now keeping the two pieces side by side by pressure of the thumb against the finger of the left hand, and with the cotton held downwards between the second and third fingers of the left hand, * do 2 chain, 1 single crochet in the next loop of the piece to the right, 2 chain, 1 single crochet in the next loop of the piece to the left and repeat from *. In this manner a zigzag of chain

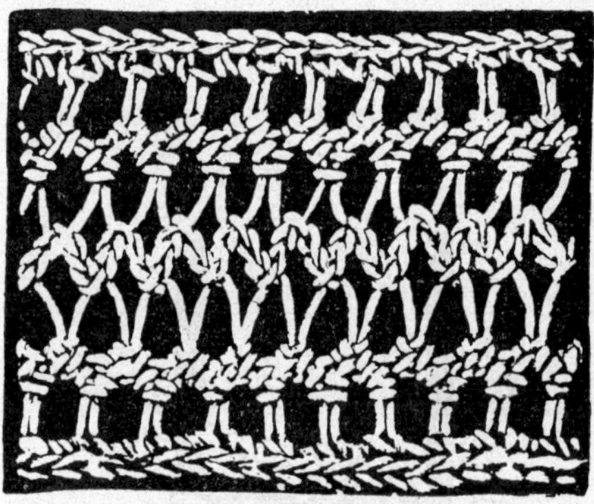

Fig.12.—INSERTION JOINED BY CHAIN-STITCH

running right and left between two pieces of hairpin trimming is formed. This joins the trimmings by taking a loop from each alternately and at the same time adds to its appearance. A variation of the above can be made by substituting a double or even a treble, for the single crochet stitch. The insertion is completed by working a row of double crochet along each side, putting two double crochet in each loop.

Narrow Edging.—Work sufficient length of trimming in double stitch as Fig. 10. To this add a crochet heading and a series of little scallops as given below. For the **Heading**—make 2 chain stitches, 1 double crochet in the first loop of the hairpin work, * 2 chain, 1 double crochet in the next loop, and repeat from * to the end (Fig. 13).

For the Edge. **1st row.**—Work 1 double crochet in the first loop, * 3 chain, 1 double crochet in the next, and repeat from * to the end. Break off the cotton. **2nd row.**—Beginning on the right-hand side: 1 double crochet in the centre stitch of the three chain of the previous row, * 6 chain, 1 single crochet in the fifth chain from the needle, 1 chain, 1 double crochet in the centre stitch of the next three chain of the previous row, and repeat from * to the end. The edging is now ready to use.

The Design for a Shawl is simple. The original was worked in two colours, blue embroidery wool for the forkwork and white fingering for the crochet. Use a steel or wooden fork from $1\frac{3}{4}$ inches to 2 inches wide, and a small bone crochet hook. A warmer shawl may be made by using the wool double for the forkwork and single for the crochet. In this case the fork should be $2\frac{1}{2}$ inches to 3 inches wide. Work hairpin trimming on the fork in the usual manner. The pieces may be about a yard in length, according to the size of the shawl. When several pieces are finished, they can be drawn together.

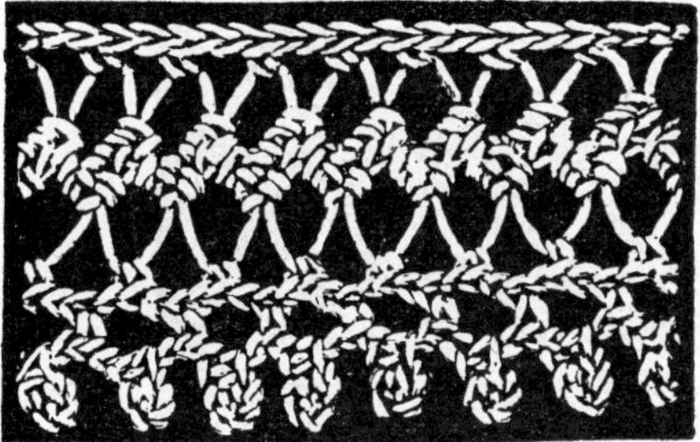

Fig. 13.—NARROW EDGING

On the **first piece** crochet one row thus: Take up every loop of trimming in reverse position, i.e. by inserting the hook in an upward direction, from the back to the front, so as to cause the uppermost thread of every loop, to cross over the under thread, as shown in Fig. 14. Work 1 double crochet in each of the next 3 consecutive loops, * 5 chain, 1 double crochet in each of the next 3 consecutive loops and repeat from * to the end. The loops on the opposite side of this piece must remain unworked for the present. Take the **second piece** and work along one side as just described, then work the other side similarly, but as you work join to the first piece in this manner: 1 double crochet in each of the next 3 consecutive loops, * 2 chain, 1 single crochet in the centre stitch of 5 chain of the previous piece, 2 chain, 1 double crochet in each of the next 3 consecutive loops, and repeat from * to the end. Crochet the third piece and join it by the same process to the second piece and so on with the other pieces of trimming until they are all joined to the size the shawl is required. Then margin the outside edge with a simple line of chain and double crochet, taking separately up, crossways, each stitch of the margin of the first piece, and also the last piece, 1 double crochet in the first loop, * 1 chain, 1 double crochet in the next loop and repeat from *. Along the sides of the trimming 5 chain will be needed instead of one only (Fig. 14).

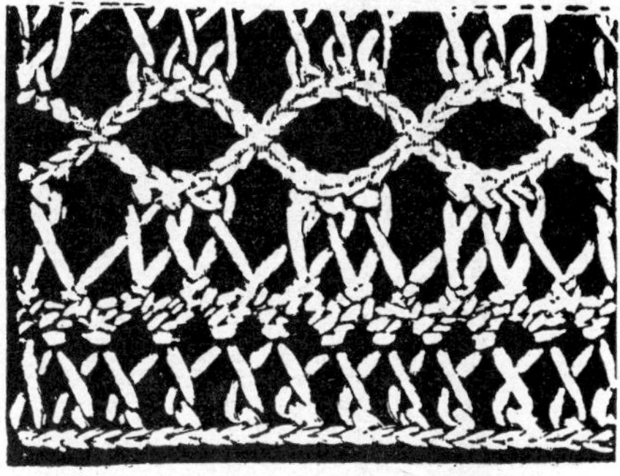

Fig. 14.—A SHEPHERD'S HEY DESIGN

Cluny Lace Insertion is worked with four threads of crochet cotton No. 10. Silk may also be used. A fine steel crochet hook and a strong, large hairpin, are also needed. Make two pieces of hairpin trimming in the ordinary way, both equal in length. Those seen in Fig. 15 run straight along each side of the insertion.

For the crochet—**1st row.**—Work 5

chain, take up one piece of hairpin trimming and insert the hook in the first loop on the left-hand side. Hold the hairpin trimming below the crochet, and proceed from left to right, i.e. in a backward direction. Draw the cotton through the hairpin loop, and also through the stitch of chain that is on the needle (this is practically a single crochet stitch) do 1 single crochet in the fifth stitch of chain (that is the chain-stitch nearest the needle) * 8 chain, 1 single crochet in the sixth chain from the needle, 12 chain, 1 single crochet in the sixth from the needle (a bar of six stitches is thus left between two picots), 3 chain, miss three loops of the hairpin trimming and do one single crochet in the next loop to the right and also one single crochet in the last of the three chain-stitches (that is in the chain stitch nearest the needle), 9 chain, miss one loop, 1 single crochet in the next and also 1 single crochet in the chain stitch nearest to the needle end. Repeat from *. The work is still done from left to right along the trimming and the trimming is kept below the crochet all the time, that is to say, the trimming is nearest the worker and the crochet is above. It will be necessary to curve the hook slightly to the right downwards each time. At the end of the row make ten chain instead of nine.

The **2nd row.**—Take the other piece of trimming and hold it above the crochet you have already worked. Insert the hook in the first loop on the right-hand side and draw the cotton through the loop and through the stitch on the needle in a single crochet, do 1 single crochet in the tenth stitch of chain (the stitch nearest the needle) * 8 chain, 1 single crochet in the sixth chain from the needle, 1 chain and work 1 double crochet, 4 treble and 1 double crochet along the bar of 6 chain stitches, then 7 chain, 1 single crochet in the sixth chain from the needle, 3 chain, miss 3 loops of trimming, 1 single crochet in the next loop and 1 single crochet in the third stitch of the 3 chain, 4 chain, 1 double crochet in the centre stitch of the loop of 9 chain of the previous row, 4 chain, miss one loop of the trimming, 1 single crochet in the next loop and 1 single crochet in the fourth stitch of the 4 chain. Repeat from * to the end. This completes the central portion of the insertion.

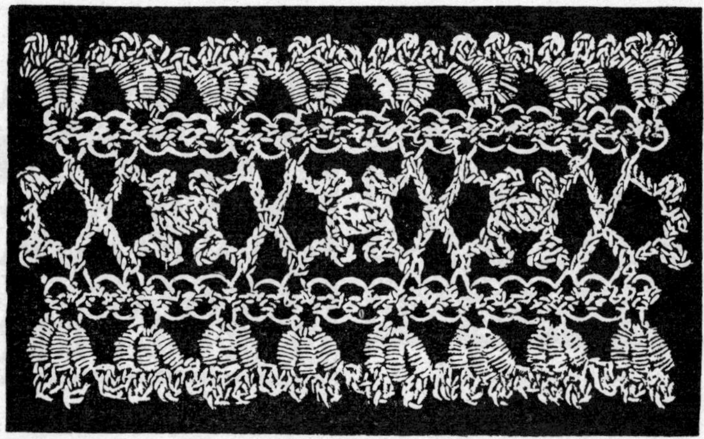

Fig. 15.—CLUNY LACE INSERTION

Heading.—Begin with a stitch tied on the needle and do 4 chain, 1 single crochet in the fourth chain from the needle, 1 rice stitch made thus: cotton 9 times round the needle, insert the hook into the first loop of the hairpin trimming and draw the cotton through. Cotton over the needle and draw through all the stitches on the needle, being careful to keep the roll smooth, 1 picot thus: 4 chain, 1 single crochet in fourth chain from needle; another rice stitch in the same loop with the first, 1 picot, 1 more rice stitch in the same loop, 1 picot, then miss two loops of the hairpin trimming; in the next loop, work a similar group of 3 rice stitches with immediate picots and continue the same to the end. Crochet a similar heading on the opposite side of the insertion.

hairpin, take the hook out and turn the hairpin, which brings * the cotton to the front, put it over the right-hand prong to the back, put the crochet hook into the loop from which it has just been taken and draw the cotton through which makes a fresh loop on the needle. Then do a double crochet which secures the loop and forms a firm centre to the work. Take out the hook and turn the hairpin, then repeat from *.

Along the inside edge, work as follows:—One single crochet in two loops taken

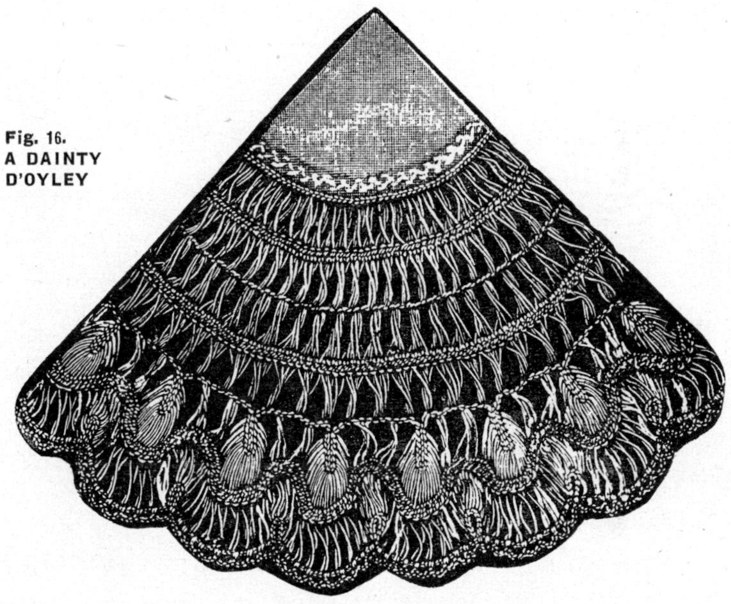

Fig. 16. A DAINTY D'OYLEY

A D'Oyley in hairpin work is dainty as shown in Fig. 16. Materials required: One ball of crochet cotton No. 24, a fine steel crochet hook and a hairpin with prongs about 1¼ inches apart, a small circle of fine linen measuring 3¾ inches in diameter, which must be neatly hemmed all round. Work a piece of hairpin trimming as follows, about 18 inches long and join round:—

To start the hairpin crochet, hold the hairpin in the left hand, the round part downwards. Now make a loop on the crochet hook and twist the cotton round the left prong, drawing it through the loop on the crochet hook from the centre of the

together, 1 chain. Repeat, and sew on to the linen centre. Work another piece of hairpin trimming about ¾ yard long and join round. Join this to the first trimming by working * 1 single crochet and 2 chain into 2 loops taken together in the outer strip, and 1 single crochet and 2 chain into 3 loops taken together into the inner strip and repeat from * all round and fasten off.

Work another length of hairpin trimming about 1½ yards long and fasten off. Join this to the second piece of trimming by working ** 1 single crochet and 2 chain into 3 loops taken together in the outer strip, and 1 single crochet and 2 chain into 2 loops taken together in the inner strip. Repeat from ** once, 1 single crochet and 2 chain into 3 loops taken together of the third piece of trimming, 2 chain and 1 single crochet into each of the next 11 loops of the second piece of trimming. Take out the hook and insert in the fourth stitch and draw the eleventh stitch through it, work 4 more single crochet stitches in the next 4 loops, making 15 single crochet stitches altogether and draw the last stitch through the first, 2 chain and repeat from first ** all round. Join and fasten off.

Along the outside edge—**1st row:** work 1 single crochet and 2 chain into the first nine loops, 1 single crochet into each of the next ten loops, take out the hook and insert it in the first single crochet and draw the 10th stitch through it, 2 chain and repeat.

2nd row.—1 double crochet into the first space of 2 chain, 4 chain and 1 double crochet into each of the next nine spaces of 2 chain and repeat.

TATTING

The French name of "La Frivolité" has been adopted by most European countries, but Italians still call the work "occhi," which means eyes, and Orientals retain the ancient designation of "makouk," which comes from the shuttles with which the work is executed.

The English word, "Tatting," comes from the French word *Tâter,* to touch. The work is composed entirely of three kinds of stitches—single stitches, double stitches and picots—and the *feel* or *touch* of the stitches passing through the fingers is sufficient to tell you, after a little practice, if it is being rightly done. It does not need much thought or counting, and is ideal to pick up in odd moments of leisure.

Tools for Tatting.—A tatting shuttle and an ordinary good-sized steel pin or a fine steel crochet hook, and cotton, are the only real necessities. Some workers keep another little implement, a ring and pin (see Fig. 2) close at hand. The ring is usually placed on the thumb of the left hand, and the tool is used to place under a picot or to draw the cotton through a picoted loop. This is not a real necessity, however, and the fine steel crochet hook can easily be used instead, if the ring seems to get in the way of the worker.

The shuttles used to be made in bone, ivory, pearl and tortoiseshell, and today many are made in plastic; but whichever you may be able to get, look out for the following things: that the points are smooth and even, and that they are set closely together. Some shuttles have brass pins which go through the centre and fasten together the two sides of the implement. These should be fitted in perfectly flat, and this is important, for if these pins protrude, even ever so slightly, they will cause great trouble by catching against the cotton.

The block in the centre of the shuttle acts as a bobbin or a spool on which to wind the cotton, and it should have a round hole in the centre of it, for the end of the cotton to be threaded through in order to keep it taut.

Shuttles are made in two or three sizes, for coarse or fine cotton—the coarser the thread, the larger should be the shuttle. A shuttle 3 to 3½ inches long is the most convenient size for ordinary work.

Tatting Stitches.—The actual working of tatting is fully described farther on in this section, but so that the three main stitches shall be quite clear from the very beginning, study the diagrams on the next page.

Figure 7.—This shows you the first and main stitch — "single" stitch — which closely resembles that made in working buttonholes. These single stitches are worked on a single thread, and this thread can be drawn up to form a loop.

Figure 8.—This shows the "double" stitch, which is the one mostly used in modern tatting. It is really a continuation of the single stitch, and in Figs. 3-5 you will see clearly illustrated the three movements which go to the making of this stitch. Double stitches worked on a single

Fig. 1.—TATTING SHUTTLE.

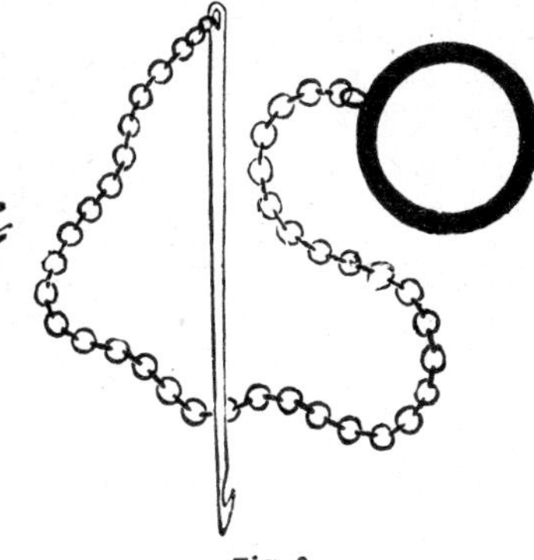

Fig. 2.

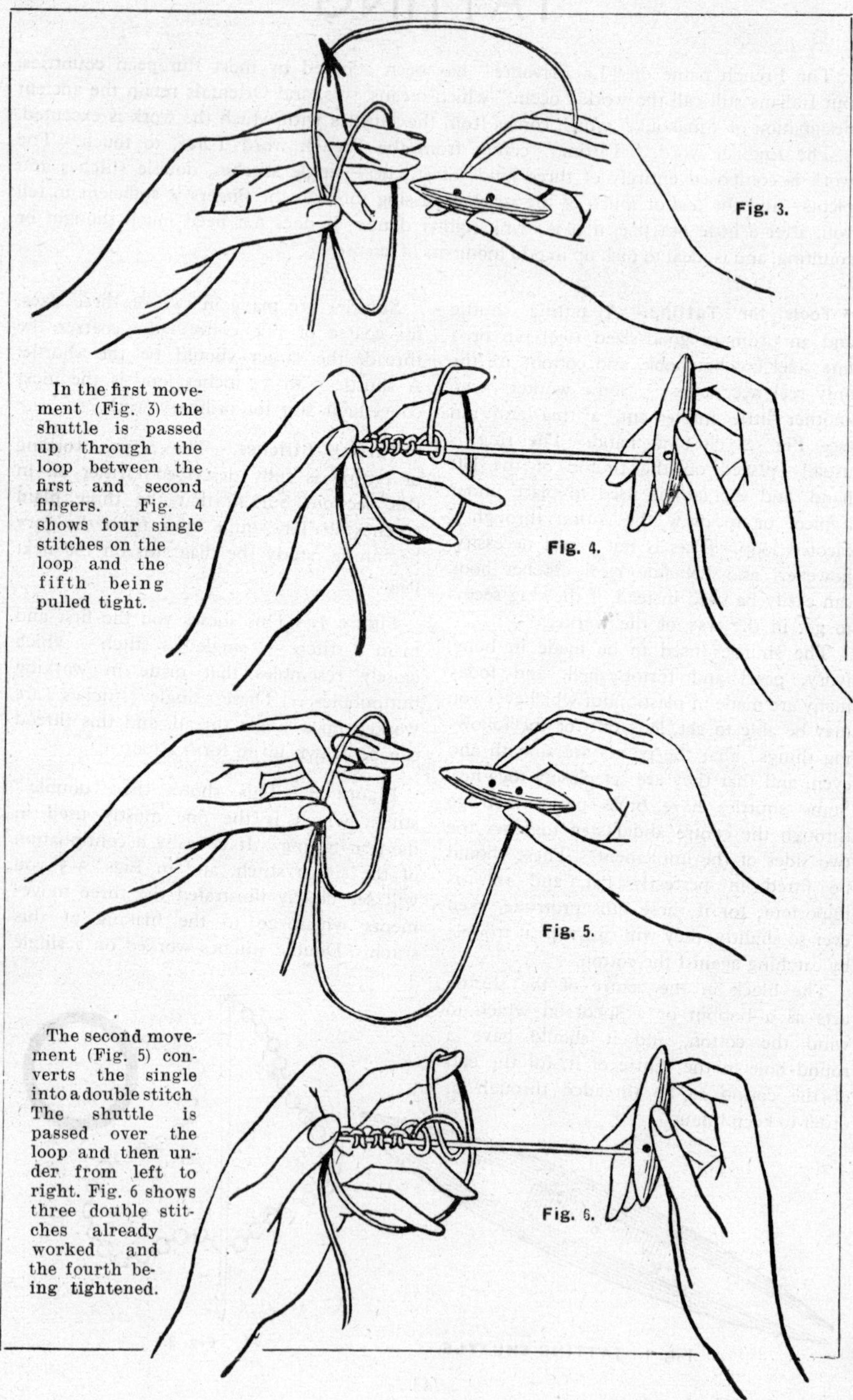

In the first movement (Fig. 3) the shuttle is passed up through the loop between the first and second fingers. Fig. 4 shows four single stitches on the loop and the fifth being pulled tight.

The second movement (Fig. 5) converts the single into a double stitch The shuttle is passed over the loop and then under from left to right. Fig. 6 shows three double stitches already worked and the fourth being tightened.

thread can be drawn up into loops and scallops as for the single stitch.

Ovals can be formed by working twelve double stitches on a loop on the fingers, then withdrawing the loop from the fingers, and drawing it up quite close and firm, the last stitch of the oval touching the first one; * make another loop on the fingers, and begin to work a double stitch, leaving ⅜ of an inch of cotton from the oval just made; do in all 12 double stitches, and again draw up, and continue from * for the length required.

Figure 9.—This shows the working of picots. A picot, or as some workers and textbooks call it, a "purl," is formed by leaving a loop of cotton between the double stitches. The size of this loop of cotton will vary according to the requirements of the

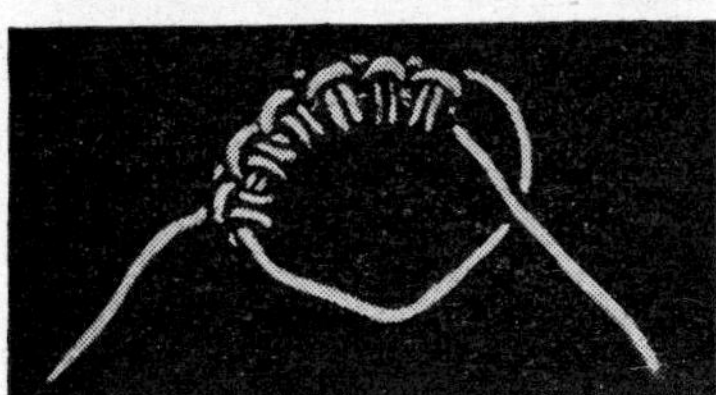

Fig. 8.—Double Stitch.

pattern being worked, and may be regulated by use of the pin, or the eye will usually be a correct guide.

Every picot is quite independent of the stitch before and after it; thus, the example in Fig. 9 is worked—2 double stitches, 1 picot, 2 double, 1 picot, 2 double, 1 picot, 2 double, 1 picot, 2 double, 1 picot, 2 double.

Picots are used to ornament the edges of scalloped lace, and also to connect various parts of the pattern together.

Working Instructions.—The stitch of tatting is formed by two movements. The first movement produces a "single" stitch. (See Fig. 7.) The second, or reverse, movement, twists the thread in a contrary direction, and, together with the first, is termed a "double" stitch. (See Fig. 8.)

The chief difficulty experienced by the beginner is the proper drawing up of the

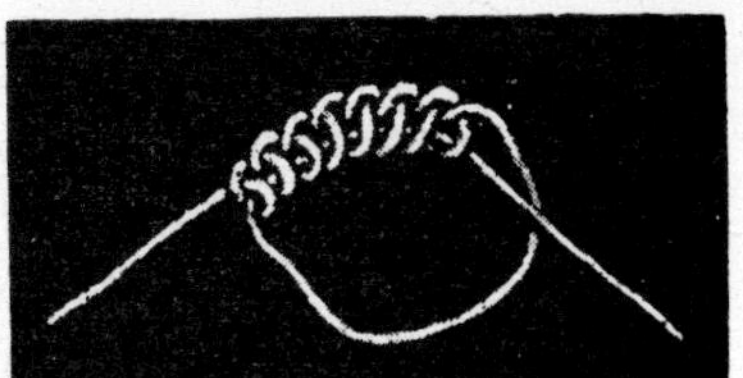

Fig. 7.—Single Stitch.

shuttle thread. To one not accustomed to the work, it would naturally appear that the stitches should be formed by the thread which comes directly from the shuttle: but this is not so. The stitches are actually made by the thread that is looped round the fingers of the left hand. The right hand holds the shuttle, and makes with it the necessary movement to twist the cotton for the formation of the stitch, then the shuttle thread must be extended and drawn up straight with a jerk, and this jerk twists up on the shuttle thread the cotton that is looped round the fingers, and so produces a stitch. The shuttle thread thus runs through the row of stitches worked by the loop thread, and is able to draw up the loop larger, or tighten it, as occasion requires.

Filling the Shuttle.—This is the first step in tatting. To do this, pass the end of the cotton from the reel or skein through the round hole that is bored in the middle of the shuttle, and secure it there by tying a knot; then wind the cotton round and round upon the block in the centre of the shuttle, by passing the cotton between the blades, until the shuttle is full. Do not wind too great a quantity, however, or the pressure may bend the blades and cause them to gape open. Cut off the cotton from the reel, leaving about three-quarters of a yard hanging from the shuttle.

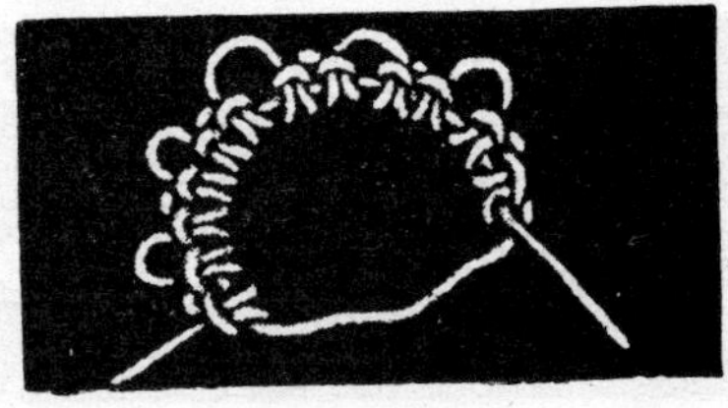

Fig. 9.—Picots.

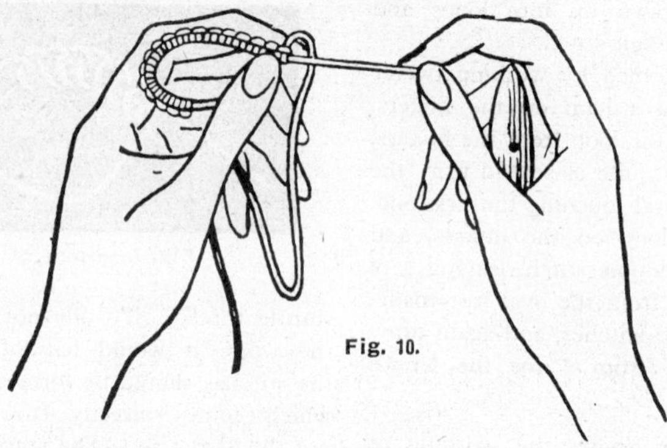

Fig. 10.

The First Movement.—Hold the shuttle between the thumb and first finger of the right hand (see Fig. 3) take the cotton between the thumb and first finger of the left hand, passing round the back of the hand with about 5 inches of the end hanging down against the palm of the hand, bring it round from the back of the hand up between the thumb and forefinger again, letting it hang round the back of the hand by the second knuckle, pass the shuttle from you up through the loop between the first and second fingers, and in front of the shuttle thread (see Fig. 3), where the arrow denotes the direction the shuttle should take. Pull the shuttle up, draw it tight with a jerk to the right, and at the same time raise the second finger of the left hand within the loop to stretch and raise up the loop, and the thread of the loop will form a stitch upon the shuttle thread. This is a "single" stitch, as shown clearly in Fig. 7. Fig. 4 shows four single stitches worked upon the loop, with the hands in the position of pulling tight the shuttle thread to form the fifth single stitch.

The Second Movement.—The second movement is the one which forms the "double" stitch. Commence as for a "single" stitch (Fig. 3). Take the cotton between the thumb and finger of the left hand, passing round the back of the hand, with five inches hanging down against the palm of the hand, bring it round from the back of the hand up between the thumb and forefinger again, and letting it hang round the back of the hand by the second knuckle, pass the shuttle up through the loop, between the first and second fingers, and in front of the shuttle thread. Draw up the shuttle, pull it tight to the right with a jerk, and at the same time raise the second finger of the left hand within the loop to stretch and raise the loop, and the thread of the loop will form a "single" stitch upon the shuttle thread.

Retain the loop upon the fingers, pressing the thumb on the single stitch just made. Now let the shuttle thread hang in front of the loop (Fig. 5), pass the shuttle over the knuckle of the second finger of the left hand, and bring it towards you through the loop, as indicated by the arrow. Draw up the shuttle to the right with a jerk and at the same time raise the loop with the second finger of the left hand, and the thread of the

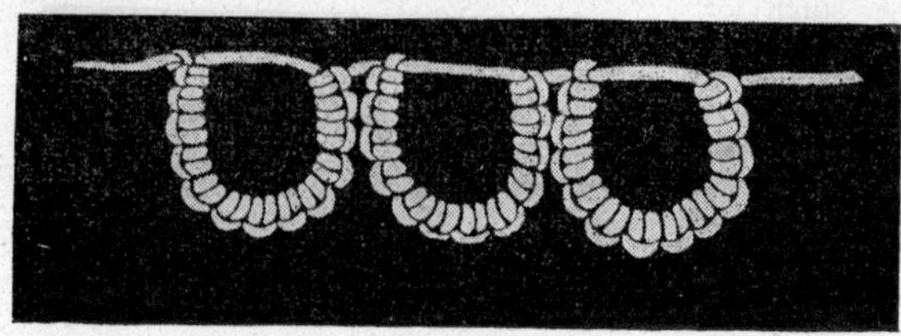

Fig. 11.—Detached scallops of double stitches with twelve double stitches on each loop.

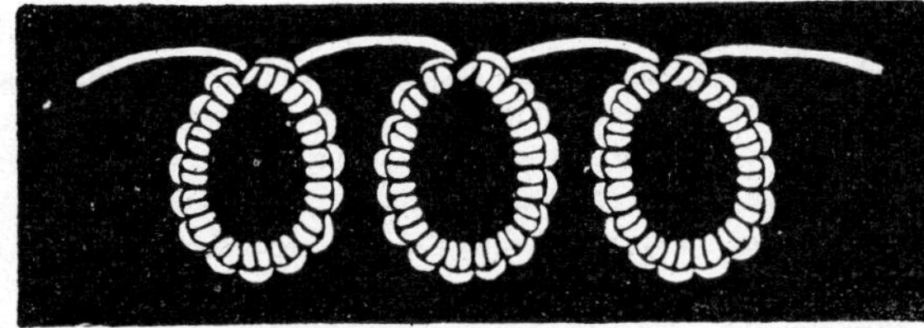

Fig. 12.—Scallops converted into ovals are used a great deal in various medallions and motifs.

loop will form a stitch upon the shuttle thread. Every "double" stitch is made up of these two movements—first movement (Fig. 3), and second movement (Fig. 5).

Figure 6 shows the position of the fingers, shuttle, and cotton, with 3 double stitches worked upon the loop, and the hands in the act of pulling tight the shuttle thread for the completion of the fourth stitch.

As the stitches are formed, they are pushed to the left-hand side of the loop, and held down between the thumb and first finger of the left hand, and the shuttle thread must always run smoothly and easily through the stitches to loosen or tighten them as required. For instance, as the loop gets used up in the formation of stitches, you need to draw the loop thread to the left, to bring more cotton into the loop to replenish the supply, and when you have completed the number of stitches necessary in that particular loop, you slip the shuttle into the palm of the right hand, as in Fig. 6, release the loop from the fingers of the left hand, and draw up the shuttle thread to the right, till the loop is quite closed, and the last stitch is brought to meet the first; the loop is now converted into an oval. Press this oval quite flat and shape nicely, and go on to work another, beginning always with a loop in the same manner

Detached Scallops of Double Stitches.—Make a loop on the fingers with the shuttle thread, and work 12 double stitches as shown in Fig. 10. Slip the fingers out of the loop, and draw the loop up into a semicircle or scallop (see (Fig. 11); make another loop on the fingers with the shuttle thread, and beginning quite close to the last double stitch of the last scallop, work again 12 double stitches, slip the fingers out of the loop, and draw the loop up into another scallop. Repeat this until you are able to do it speedily and easily.

Fig. 14.

Fig. 13.—Josephine knots. **Fig. 14.**—A square medallion worked with two threads. Above, an octagonal medallion.

Fig. 13.

Scallops converted into Ovals.—Make a loop on the fingers with the shuttle thread, and as in the foregoing example work 12 double stitches. Withdraw the fingers from the loop, and draw the loop up quite close and firm in the shape of an oval. The last stitch of the oval should touch the first stitch. * Make another loop on the finger and begin to work a double stitch, leaving $\frac{3}{8}$ of an inch of cotton from the oval just made. Work 12 double stitches, and then draw up again quite close, and continue from * for the length required (see Fig. 12).

Tatting with Two Threads. — Most tatting is done with two threads, and this is achieved in the following manner. Thread your shuttle as usual, and work an oval of 16 double stitches, then draw up. Reverse this oval, that is, turn it over, placing it between the thumb and finger bottom side uppermost, so that the two ends of cotton come at the top, the shuttle thread being still to the right-hand side. Take a second thread—this may be used direct from the reel, or a length of cotton may be wound upon a second shuttle—as most convenient to the worker—place the end of the cotton behind the oval between the thumb and finger of the left hand, and pass a portion of the reel or second shuttle thread in a loop round the fingers, twisting it round the third finger of the left hand to keep the loop steady. ( ) Make with the shuttle the usual movements, and form 8 double stitches with the second thread, which is now the loop thread. When the 8 double stitches are accomplished, again reverse the work, make a loop on the fingers with the shuttle thread, and being very careful to get the first stitch quite close to the stitches worked with the second thread, proceed with another oval. Reverse the work again, take the second thread, loop it round the fingers, securing it by twisting it once or twice round the third finger, and work another straight bar of 8 stitches, and so on.

Another way of tatting with two threads is to wind the cotton upon two shuttles, and keep the cotton on one shuttle for special use as a foundation or shuttle thread, and the cotton on the other shuttle for special use as a loop thread. For working in this manner, it is a good idea to have the shuttles of two different colours.

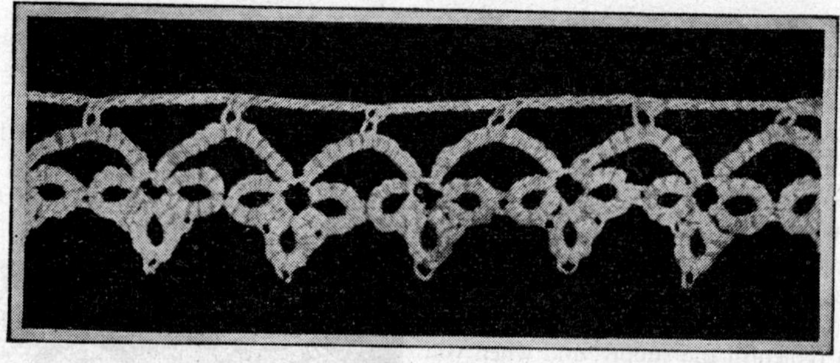

Fig. 15.—Trefoil edging makes a dainty finish for towels, pillow-slips and household linen.

By working this way, the cotton goes farther without knots, but the foundation thread cannot be drawn up like an ordinary loop to form an oval, so first and last stitches of the loop are drawn together and joined by a small loop made like a picot.

Josephine Knots.—These stitches are frequently mentioned in tatting designs, and they consist of small bunches of stitches knotted on the shuttle thread, and are used as an ornament for spaces. To work them, make a loop, work four single stitches, and draw up very closely into a knot.

MEDALLIONS.—Medallions in tatting are very effective as pincushion tops,

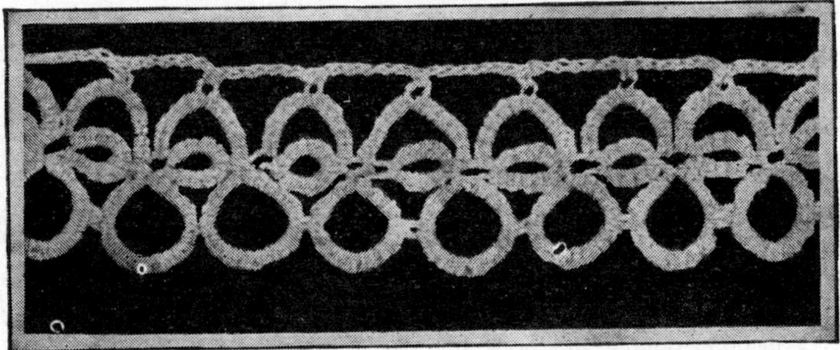

Fig. 16.—A scalloped edging which is easily worked with two threads.

d'oyleys, etc., and joined together make handsome bedspreads, nightdress sachets, and so on. These medallions can be round or square, and can be joined together to make varied geometrical forms.

A Square Medallion.—A square medallion is worked with two threads. Fill the shuttle and make a loop on the fingers with the shuttle thread. Work 8 double stitches, 1 picot, 6 double, 1 picot, 3 double, and draw up. Make another loop close to the first, work 3 double, join to last picot in oval just worked, 2 double and 1 picot alternately six times; 3 double, draw up. Make a loop close, work 3 double, join to last picot in last oval, 6 double, 1 picot, 8 double, and draw up. There is now a corner of three ovals or "leaves", resembling a trefoil. Reverse the work. Take the reel thread and make with it a loop round the fingers and work a bar of 10 double stitches. * Reverse work, make a loop with shuttle thread, work 8 double, join the last picot in last oval, 6 double, 1 picot, 3 double, draw up. Make a loop close, work 3 double, join to last picot in last oval, 2 double and 1 picot alternately six times, 3 double, draw up. Make a loop close, work 3 double, join to last picot in last oval, 6 double, 1 picot, 8 double and draw up. Reverse the work. Take the reel thread and make a loop, work a bar of 10 double stitches. Repeat from *. Join the last leaf of the fourth trefoil to the first leaf of the first trefoil, and when the square is finished, cut the cotton and tie the ends securely in a knot.

When working successive squares, join by the corner picots, or the picots next to

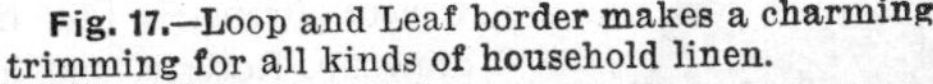

Fig. 17.—Loop and Leaf border makes a charming trimming for all kinds of household linen.

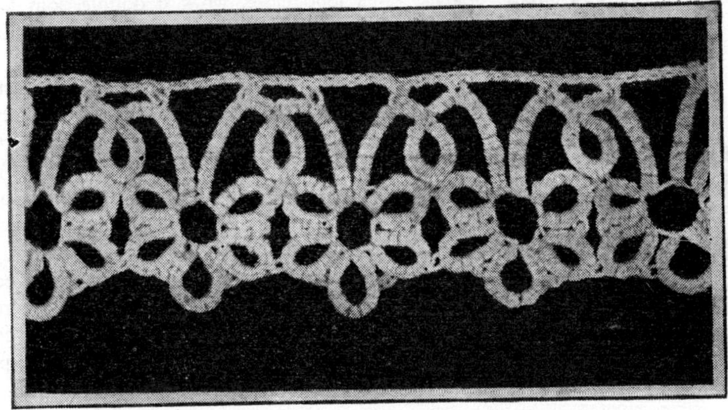

the corner to the corresponding picots in the squares already worked.

An Octagonal Medallion.—This is tatted with the shuttle thread only. Having sufficient cotton wound on the shuttle, begin for a large oval—make a loop on the fingers and work 5 double stitches, 1 picot, 2 double and 1 picot alternately four times, 5 double and draw up. For small oval, reverse the work, make a loop close, work 6 double, 1 picot, 6 double and draw up. Reverse the work for large oval, make a loop close, work 5 double, join to the last picot in the first large oval, 2 double and 1 picot alternately four times, 5 double and draw up. * For another large oval, make a loop, and leaving a sixth of an inch thread between this oval and the last, work 5 double, join to the last oval, 2 double and 1 picot alternately four times, 5 double and draw up. Reverse, and for small oval make a loop close, work 6 double, join to picot in first small oval, 6 double and draw up. Reverse, and for a large oval, make a loop close, work 5 double, join to the last large oval, 2 double and 1 picot alternately four times, 5 double and draw up. Repeat from * twice, and in working last (eighth) large oval, join last picot to first picot of first large oval. This completes the octagon. Join round securely and cut cotton.

Fig. 18.

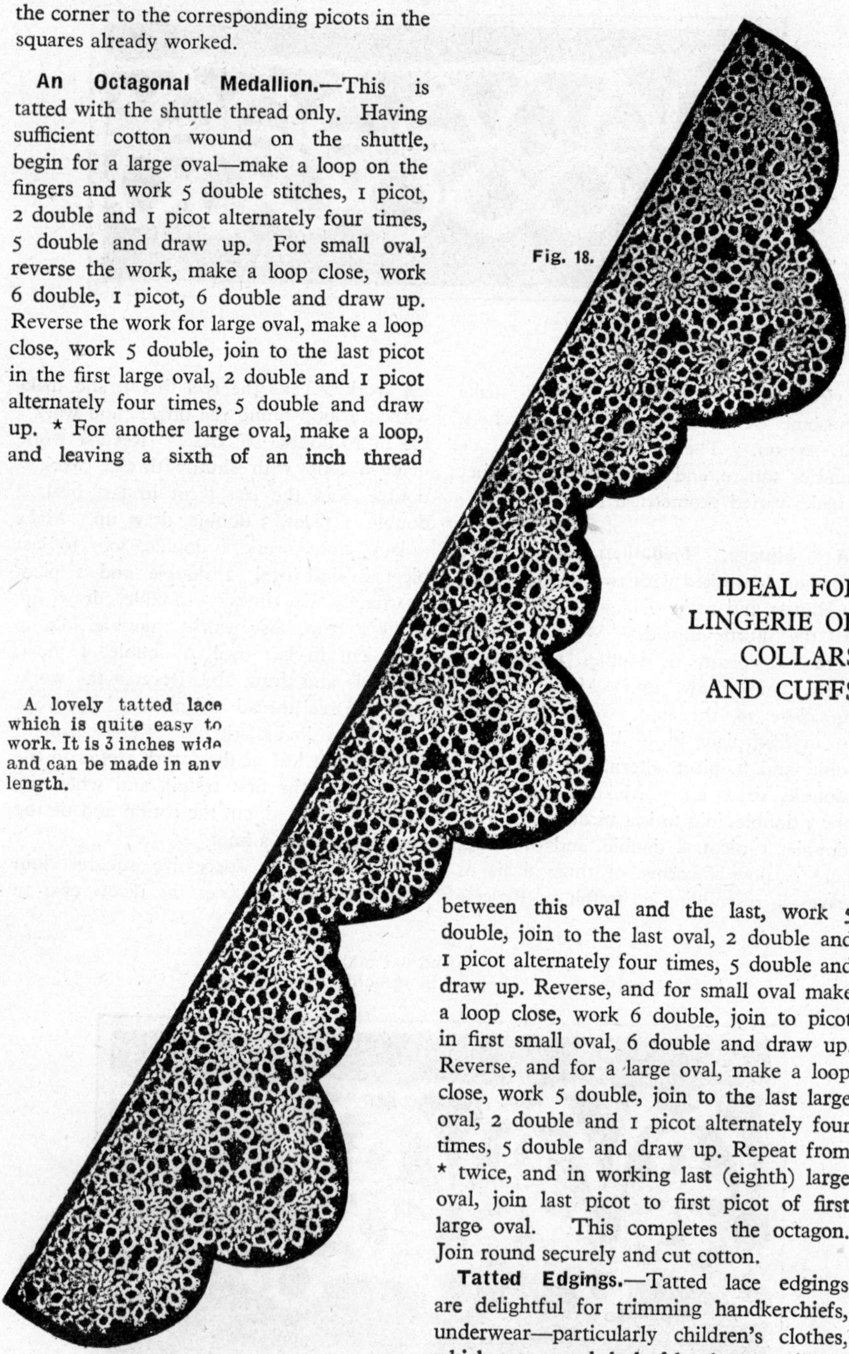

IDEAL FOR LINGERIE OR COLLARS AND CUFFS

A lovely tatted lace which is quite easy to work. It is 3 inches wide and can be made in any length.

Tatted Edgings.—Tatted lace edgings are delightful for trimming handkerchiefs, underwear—particularly children's clothes, which get a good deal of hard wear, pillow-slips, guest towels, tray-cloths and many other varieties of personal, house and table linen.

Trefoil Edging. (Fig. 15.)

MATERIALS:

Crochet Cotton, Nos. 14 and 18.
Steel Crochet hook, No. 4½.
Tatting Shuttle.

Thread the shuttle with No. 14 cotton. Make a loop with the shuttle thread, work 5 double, 1 picot, 3 double, 1 picot, 2 double, draw up; * make a loop close to the last stitch of the oval, do 2 double, join to the last picot of last oval, 3 double, 1 picot, 3 double, 1 picot, 2 double, draw up; make another loop close, do 2 double, join to the last picot of the oval just made, 3 double, 1 picot, 5 double, and draw up; arrange the three leaves of the trefoil in proper form; reverse the work, take a second thread, make a loop, and work 6 double, 1 picot, 6 double; reverse, make a loop with the shuttle thread, with 5 double, join to the last picot of last trefoil, 3 double, 1 picot, 2 double, and draw up.

Repeat from * for length required.

With No. 18 cotton, work a straight line of crochet along the top of the edging, 1 double crochet in the picot of the straight bar of tatting, 8 chain, 1 double crochet in the next picot, and continue.

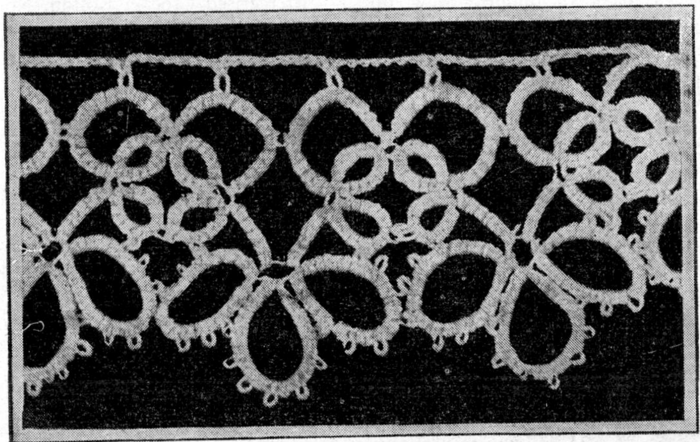

Fig. 19.—An actual size strip of Leaf Edging which makes decorative trimming for table linen.

Scalloped Edging. (Fig. 16.)

MATERIALS:

Mercerised Crochet Cotton, No. 15.
Steel Crochet Hook, No. 4½.
Tatting Shuttle.

Wind the first thread on the shuttle, and use the second thread direct from the reel. Make a loop with the shuttle thread, work 6 double, 1 picot, 12 double, 1 picot, 6 double, draw up. * Reverse the work, take the second thread, make a loop, and do 6 double, 1 picot, 6 double; reverse, make a loop with the shuttle thread, work 6 double, join to thread at the bottom of the large oval, where the second thread is begun, 5 double, and draw up; make another loop with the shuttle thread, work 6 double, join to the last picot in the last large oval, 12 double, 1 picot, 6 double, draw up. Repeat from * for the length required. Crochet along the top for a heading, 1 double crochet in a picot, 4 chain, and repeat. Press on wrong side under a damp cloth with a hot iron when completed.

Loop and Leaf Border.

MATERIALS:

Crochet Cotton, Nos. 16 and 20.
Steel Crochet Hook, No. 4½.
Tatting Shuttle.

Make a loop with the shuttle thread, work 7 double, 1 picot, 7 double, and draw up; reverse the work, and with a second thread work 3 double, 1 picot, 9 double; reverse, make a loop with the shuttle thread, do 7 double, join to the picot of the small oval just done, 3 double, 1 picot, 4 double, draw up; make another loop, do 4 double, join to the picot in the last oval, 3 double, 1 picot, 3 double, 1 picot, 4 double, draw up; * make another loop, do 4 double, join to the picot in the last oval, 8 double, 1 picot, 4 double, draw up; make a loop again, do 4 double, join to the picot in the last oval, 3 double, 1 picot, 3 double, 1 picot, 4 double, draw up: again make a loop, do 4 double, join to picot in last oval, 3 double, 1 picot, 7 double, draw up; these five ovals form a "leaf." Reverse the work, and with the second thread, work 9 double, 1 picot, 3 double; reverse, make a loop with the shuttle thread, do 7 double, join to the picot in the last oval of the leaf, 7 double, draw up; reverse, and with second thread, work 3 double, 1 picot, 9 double; reverse, make a loop with the shuttle thread, do 7 double, join to the picot in the last oval of the last leaf (where join is already made), 3 double, 1 picot, 4 double, draw up; make another loop, do 4 double, join to picot in last oval, 3 double, join to the picot in the last but one oval of last leaf, 3 double, 1 picot, 4 double, and draw up; and continue from * for the length you desire the border to be. For the crochet heading as shown in the illustration, use Cotton No. 20, 1 double crochet in the picot to the right of the top oval, 3 chain, 1 double crochet in the next oval, 4 chain, and so on.

Leaf Edging. (Fig. 19.)

MATERIALS:

Mercerised Crochet Cotton, Nos. 15 and 20.

Steel Crochet Hook, No. 4.

Tatting Shuttle.

Thread the shuttle, and begin by making a loop with the second, or reel thread, work 6 double, 1 picot, 6 double, 1 picot, 6 double; reverse, make a loop with the shuttle thread, do 7 double, 1 picot, 7 double, draw up; make another loop quite close, do 7 double, 1 picot, 2 double, 1 picot, 5 double, draw up; reverse, and with

Fig. 20. A DAINTY EDGING

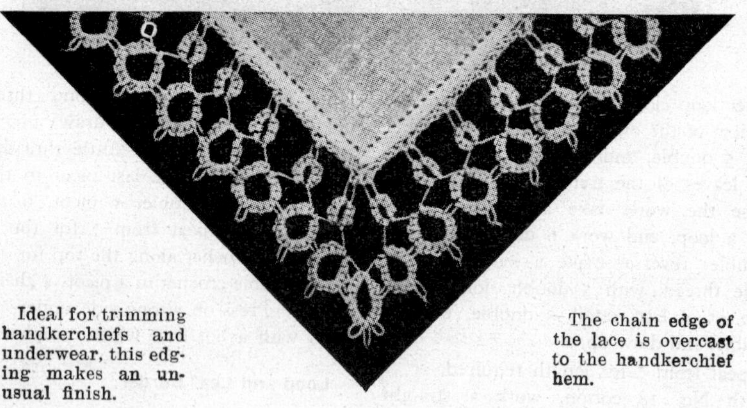

Ideal for trimming handkerchiefs and underwear, this edging makes an unusual finish.

The chain edge of the lace is overcast to the handkerchief hem.

Fig. 21.—A light, exquisitely dainty design for lingerie. The lace is about 2½ inches wide.

the second thread work 6 double; reverse, make a loop with the shuttle thread, do 7 double, join to last picot of last small oval, 3 double, then 1 picot and 3 double alternately five times, 1 picot, 7 double, draw up; * make another loop quite close, do 7 double, join to last picot of large oval, 3 double, then 1 picot and 3 double alternately five times, 1 picot, 7 double, draw up; work another large oval the same as the last; reverse, resume the second thread and work 6 double; reverse, make a loop with the shuttle thread, do 5 double, join to the last picot of the last large oval, 2 double, 1 picot, 7 double, draw up; make another loop quite close, do 7 double, 1 picot, 7 double, draw up; reverse, and with the second thread work 6 double, join to the corresponding picot in the opposite bar, 6 double, 1 picot, 6 double, and join to the picot in the small oval last done; still with the second thread, work 6 double, 1 picot, 6 double, 1 picot, 6 double; reverse, make a loop with the shuttle thread, do 7 double, join to the picot of the opposite oval (where join is already made), 7 double, draw up; make another loop quite close, do 7 double, join into the picot of the small oval opposite, 2 double, 1 picot, 5 double, draw up; reverse, and with the second thread work 6 double, reverse, make a loop with the shuttle thread, do 7 double, join to the last picot of the small oval, 3 double, 1 picot, 3 double, 1 picot, 3 double, join to the middle picot of last large oval, 3 double, 1 picot, 3 double, 1 picot, 3 double, 1 picot, 7 double, draw up; continue from * for the length required, leaving off with the last section of the second thread top bar. With Cotton No. 20 crochet a heading into the picots of the top bar, 8 chain, 1 double crochet; the same all along.

A Lovely Lace for Lingerie Trimming, or for Collar and Cuff Sets. (Fig. 18.)

MATERIALS:

Tatting Cotton, No. 40.
Steel Crochet Hook, No. 4½.
A Tatting Shuttle.

For a Motif—

1st round—12 picot, with 1 stitch between each, draw up.

2nd round—6 double, join first picot, 6 double, draw up; 1 knot (for a knot work 4 double and draw up), 1 oval (for an oval work 4 double, 1 picot, 4 double, 1 picot, 1 double, 1 picot, 1 double, 1 picot, 4 double, 1 picot, 4 double, draw up).

* Work 1 knot, 6 double, join to next picot on first round, 6 double, draw up, 1 oval.

Repeat from * all round, but in place of 1st picot on each oval, join to the last picot on previous oval. Join last oval to first oval. Fasten off.

Make five motifs thus for top of each point required, joining each successive motif at the centre of the 1st oval to centre picot on 8th oval of previous motif, and at centre of second oval to centre picot on

7th oval of previous motif. Every 6th motif is only connected to the previous one by the 2nd oval being joined to the centre picot on 7th oval of previous motif.

In the second row of lace, work 2 motifs for each point required, joining each pair in same way as in first row, also joining 3rd oval of 1st motif to 10th oval of second motif in first row:—Make 2 double, join to same motif in first row, and 5th oval to 12th oval in 3rd motif in first row, and the 6th oval to the 11th oval of same motif in first row.

For the half motif between 1st and 2nd motif in first row:—Make 2 double, join to centre picot on 9th oval of 1st motif, 1 double, 5 picot with 1 double between each, 1 double, join to centre picot on 12th oval of 2nd motif in first row, 2 double, 6 picot, with 1 double between each, 2 double, draw up. Turn, leaving short length of cotton and work 6 double, join to 1st picot, 6 double, draw up. Join to 10th oval of 1st motif in first row, 1 knot, turn work, 4 double, join to 11th oval on 1st motif in first row. 4 double, 1 picot, 1 double, 1 picot, 1 double, 1 picot, 4 double, 1 picot, 4 double, draw up; 1 knot, 6 double, join to next picot on 1st round, 6 double, draw up. Work in this way into next 4 picots on 1st round, but instead of 1st picot on each oval, join to last picot on previous oval. Work 1 knot, 1 oval, joining the last picot on last oval to 10th oval of 2nd motif in first row, 1 knot, join to 11th oval of 2nd motif in first row, 6 double, join to next picot in 1st round, 6 double, draw up, and fasten off. Work a half motif in same way between 1st and last two motifs of each group of five in first row, and each pair of motifs in second row.

For Heading.

Between the 1st two motifs in first row, work thus: 6 double, join between the motifs, 6 double, draw up, 4 double, join to centre picot on 3rd oval of 2nd motif, 4 double, 1 picot, 4 double, 1 picot, 4 double, draw up; 4 double, join to last picot made, 4 double, 1 picot, 4 double, 1 picot, 4 double, draw up; 4 double, join to last picot made, 4 double, 1 picot, 4 double, join to 6th oval of 1st motif, 4 double, draw up. Fasten off. Work in same way between every 2 motifs along top of lace.

For Straightening Edge.

Join to top picot on filling between motifs, 3 knots, 4 double, join to centre picot of next oval of filling, 4 double, join to 1st picot on 4th oval of 2nd motif in first row, 4 double, draw up; 3 knots, 4 double, join to 3rd picot of 4th oval of motif in first row, 4 double, join to 1st picot of 5th oval of same motif, 4 double, draw up; 3 knots, 4 double, join to 3rd picot on same oval, 4 double, join to picot on 1st oval of next filling, 4 double, draw up; 3 knots, join to centre picot of top oval on next filling. Work in this way all along the top of the lace.

A Dainty Tatted Edging. (Fig. 20.)

MATERIALS:

Tatting Cotton, No. 40.
Steel Crochet Hook, No. 4½.
A Tatting Shuttle.

Make 4 double, 1 picot, 4 double, 1 picot, 4 double, 1 picot, 4 double, draw up into loop, and turn. * Leave short length of cotton, and work 4 double, 1 picot, 4 double, draw up and turn, again leaving short length of cotton, 4 double, join to third picot on previous large loop, 4 double, 1 picot, 4 double, 1 picot, 4 double, draw up and turn. Repeat from * until sufficient for one side. Then, for corner, work 4 double; join to last picot on last large loop, 4 double, 1 picot, 1 double, 1 picot, 1 double, 1 picot, 4 double, 1 picot, 4 double, draw up. Repeat from * for next side, but omitting first small loop in first repeat.

Join the thread to picot on one of the small loops, crochet * 4 chain, 1 d.c. into picot on next small loop. Repeat from * to corner, 1 d.c. into picot on next small loop, then work along each side and at each corner in same way.

Rosette Lace. (Fig. 21.)

MATERIALS:

Mercerised Crochet Cotton, No. 30.
Tatting Shuttle.
Steel Crochet Hook, No. 4½.

Fill a shuttle with the cotton, and make a ring of 24 doubles, making a picot (one long and one short alternately) after every 2 doubles. Fasten the thread and cut it. Using two shuttles, or 1 shuttle and another thread straight from the reel or ball, fasten one thread to a short picot, then make * 3 double, 1 picot, then 2 double, 1 picot, four times, 3 doubles. Pass over one long picot of previous round and fasten to next short picot. Repeat from * five times more, but fastening the last picot of previous loop to corresponding stitch in loop being made. Fasten off and cut the thread. Tie the thread to one picot of previous round, * 4 double, 1 picot, 4 double, fasten to next picot, and repeat from * all around (18 loops).

4th Round.—8 double, 1 picot all round, fastening to a picot of previous round after each 8 double.

5th Round.—Form a row of loops, one loop over each bar of previous round, passing the thread through the picot between the bars from behind and bringing it up through the picot below. Each loop is formed of 3 double, 1 picot, 2 double, 1 picot, 2 double, 1 picot, 3 double. Join the medallions with the centre picots on the four corresponding loops at each side.

The Heading.

The four connected loops at each side leave 5 loops free for the top and bottom edges. On to the first picot above the joining, make a long treble, drawing one loop through the next picot, * 3 chain, 1 double crochet into next picot, 3 chain, 1 treble into next picot, taking in the following picot with this stitch*. Repeat from * to * twice more, then 3 chain, 1 double crochet into next picot, 3 chain, 1 long treble into next picot, drawing in following picot with one loop, 3 chain. Repeat from 1st long treble over each motif.

2nd row.—3 double crochet into each space. **3rd row.**—2 chain, 1 treble into every third double crochet.

4th row.—3 double crochet into every space.

SOFT FURNISHINGS
AND
RUGMAKING

BOOK V

LOOSE CHAIR COVERS
LOOSE DIVAN COVERS
CURTAINS AND PELMETS
RENOVATING SOFT FURNISHINGS
CANVAS AND HESSIAN RUGS
KNITTED AND CROCHET RUGS
TAPESTRY AND WOVEN RUGS

SOFT FURNISHINGS

Patterns mentioned in this section are obtainable from Weldons.

MAKING LOOSE COVERS

Well-made loose covers on the three-piece suite and odd chairs in a lounge can easily re-make the colour scheme of a room at small expense. From a practical standpoint, too, loose covers have the double advantage of covering shabby upholstery with old-fashioned lines and making odd pieces of different patterns harmonise beautifully. Again, a new suite provided at once with washable loose covers never has a chance to lose its first freshness owing to wear or grime.

Contrary to popular opinion, there is nothing overwhelmingly difficult about making loose covers at home—and the economy of doing so is great.

Paper Patterns.—For more or less standard chairs and couches of a type that does not readily date, splendid paper patterns with clear cutting and making-up instructions are obtainable. (See sketches and particulars on next page.) Furniture, even of the same shape, varies in size; so before any cutting is done, the pattern pieces should be carefully tested for size by laying them on in their correct positions.

To test accurately on, say, an arm-chair, first divide the chair in half down the inside and outside back, the seat and the seat depth (called the collar): this halving is necessary because, except for sofas, which are unsymmetrical, only half the pattern of these parts is given. The dividing line is easily made by carefully measuring and marking it either with tailor's chalk, pins or a length of fine piping cord pinned on. (Fig. 1.)

The pattern for the inside back, when laid on the chair (Diagram A), should follow the outer and top curve accurately and its inner edge should reach just to the

Above: The popular Fireside Chair, with loose cover on seat and back, cut from Weldons Pattern 396. **Right:** Arm-chair with loose cover from Weldons Pattern 326. Patterns are 2s. 9d. each by post.

dividing line. The depth should be great enough to tuck right down the crevice between the seat and back and this applies also to the seat and inside arm edges which come next to crevices.

If the pattern piece does not reach as far as the half-way line, your chair is wider than the pattern and it must be let out by cutting it vertically in two down its middle and pasting in a slip of paper wide enough to give the extra width required. If the pattern piece is not deep enough, slash and let in, in the same way, horizontally across the part (either above or below the top of the arm) which is too short (see Diagram

Diagram A. The pattern should follow the outer and top curves exactly and the inner edge reach to the half-dividing line.

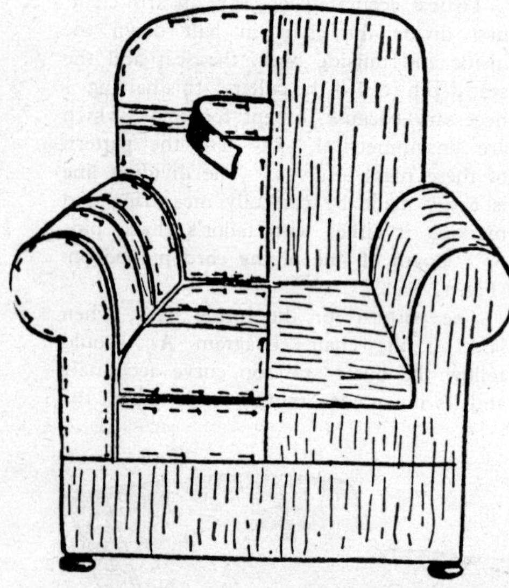

C). A pattern which is too large for the chair should have a tuck pinned in it, instead, in the same position, as in Diagram B. These two diagrams (B and C) also show similar alterations made in the inside arm piece. Other pieces may be adjusted in the same way.

Sometimes the outer curves need slight trimming. But if these differ much from those of your chair, especially on the scroll (front arm thickness) it is advisable to dispense with a pattern and cut your material to shape directly on the chair, as in Figs. 1 to 10. You will need to adopt this plan also for very modern types of furniture or pieces of unusual shape or size.

Cutting Out a Cover Direct in Material. This needs care and accuracy. The following instructions and the clear stage-

Diagram B (below), a pattern that is too large should have small tucks put in and, **Diagram C,** one that is too small should be slashed and a strip of paper pinned on to give the extra width or length.

LOOSE COVER PATTERNS

Sketched here are some of the furniture styles for which Weldons Loose Cover Patterns are available. They are price 2s. 9d. each including postage and packing.

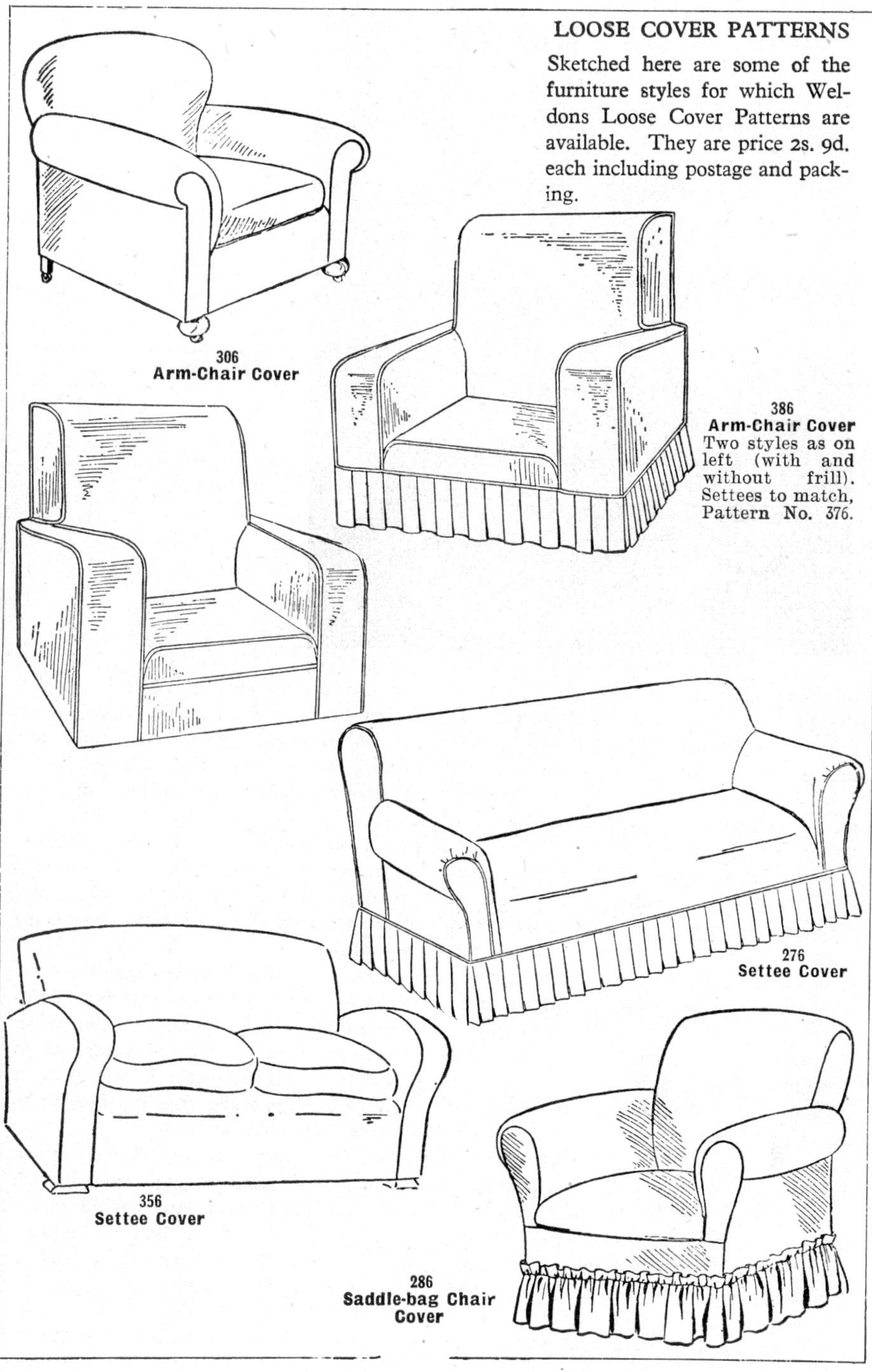

306
Arm-Chair Cover

386
Arm-Chair Cover
Two styles as on left (with and without frill). Settees to match, Pattern No. 376.

276
Settee Cover

356
Settee Cover

286
Saddle-bag Chair Cover

Fig. 1.—Piping cord is used to divide a chair exactly in half. The inside back, arm and seat pieces are placed on the chair, and cut to shape, fitting darts being put at the back and arm corners.

by-stage photographs (Figs. 1 to 10) simplify the work and make it easy to follow successfully. If you really feel unsure of yourself or are using a costly material (though this last is not advisable for a first attempt) you can shape a pattern first in cheap calico.

Before the material can be bought, however, the chair or other piece must be measured to judge the number of yards required. Measure (*a*) from the floor in front, up and along the seat from front to back, up and over the back and down again to the floor behind; (*b*) from the floor at the side, up and over an arm, and right down into the seat crevice.

Double this measurement to allow for the second arm, add to the first measurement, allowing one yard extra for tuck-ins, turnings and piping. Allow additionally for any loose cushion the chair may have and for the frill, if there is one. For a gathered frill, reckon one and a half times the finished length wanted; for a box-pleated frill, two and a half times.

Add all together to get a grand total and buy this number of yards in 30-inch material for a small chair, small couch or old-fashioned sofa, in 46-50-inch material for a large chair (greatest width or depth exceeding 27 inches) or large couch. If you use different widths from these you will waste stuff. For example, for a large chair cover in 30-inch material you must allow nearly double the quantity of 48-inch stuff and your seams may come awkwardly.

Here are some average quantities by which to check your measurements. Arm-chair (small) 5½ to 8 yards, 30 inches wide; arm-chair (large) 5½ to 7½ yards, 46-50 inches wide; couch (small) or sofa, 9 to 12 yards, 30 inches wide; couch (large) 10 to 15 yards, 46-50 inches wide.

Remember that plain and all over printed materials, and small designs, generally, are more economical than large-spaced motifs or bold stripes, which require centring on the back, seat and outside arms and so waste material.

If the cover is to be piped with contrasting, instead of self material (see Fig. 12) deduct half a yard when buying the cover material and get this quantity in contrasting fabric, or use cotton bias tape of which from six to ten yards are needed for an arm-chair. You will also require the same length of medium piping cord; shrink it before use by boiling it.

To cut out the cover, begin by dividing the chair in half as already explained for adjusting a paper pattern. Double your length of material in half, lengthwise, selvedge over selvedge, wrong side out; and place it down the inside back, the fold exactly to the dividing line and with the cut edge a clear inch above the top of the back, for turnings.

If the chair is a small one, as in Fig. 1, and fairly straightly and thinly upholstered, the width of material will probably be sufficient to go round the back thickness as well as across the inside back. In this case allow enough turnings at the top for the material to cover the top thickness similarly and join directly on to the outside back, when this is cut.

Larger pieces or those with definitely shaped thicknesses, must have portions cut separately from either front or back, as in Fig. 5. The same applies to the arms. The larger pieces, however, should always be cut first.

Tuck the material well down between inside back and seat and cut off there with ample turnings. It is most important there should be plenty of spare stuff all round the seat, tucked into its crevices. Pin the cut material to the upholstery to keep it firm, then cut it to the inside back shape, allowing at least 1-inch turnings sticking out. If this piece is folding round the thicknesses as well, dart it neatly to fit at the top outside corner, as in Fig. 1.

Care is needed when fitting the curve between the inside back and inside arm. Tuck well into the crevice here, and fit gradually by short inward slashes, *not* by cutting off material up or down. Be very careful not to slash as far in as the seam line will be.

Next, similarly lay doubled material on the seat and cut and fit this in place. If the chair has a perfectly straight front seat edge, pin an inch-wide tuck along this edge (to be cut open later for a piped seam) and continue the material down the front thickness (collar) of the seam to the bottom edge of the chair frame. Cut off here with a 1-inch turning if a frill is to be added or 2 inches if there is to be no frill. The collar, opened out to single width, is seen clearly in Fig. 6. Note that it extends farther across than the seat piece, on most chairs, so that it will meet the outside arm piece.

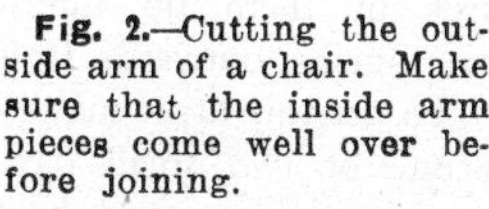

Fig. 2.—Cutting the outside arm of a chair. Make sure that the inside arm pieces come well over before joining.

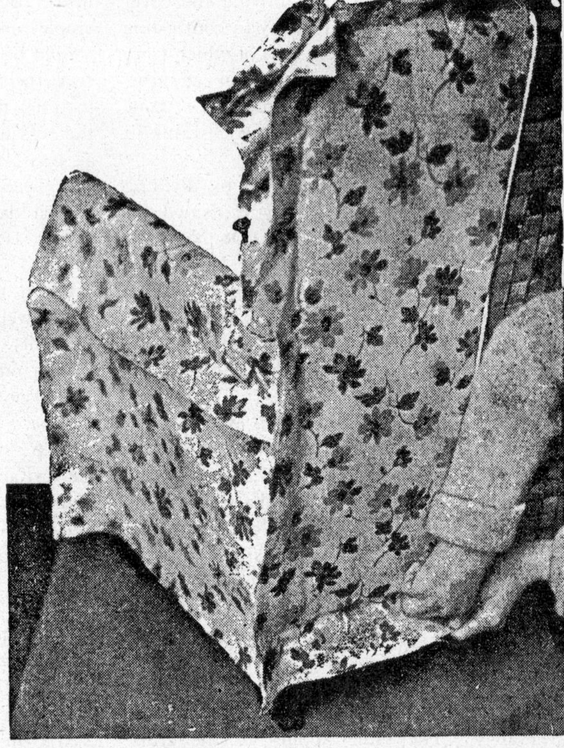

Fig. 3.—Fitting the outside back. Pin the material together along the edges, so that the back fits snugly. Do not make it too tight, as, when the tacking is done, any slight error might make the corners too small. After pinning, trim the edges so that the bottom turning matches the top.

If the front seat edge is curved, cut off the seat piece here with a turning and cut the collar piece quite separately.

Leave each piece as cut on the chair and join succeeding cut portions to it or to each other with pins, so that the whole cover is gradually built up in position.

The inside arm is tackled next. The arm pieces, inside and outside, like dress sleeves, are cut out whole, but a double thickness of stuff is used in order to cut for the two arms at once. Be careful, if the material is printed, that the pattern is the right way up on both thicknesses. To ensure this, two separate widths must often be cut and laid together for shaping—*not* one length folded across the width.

To avoid an ugly and uncomfortable seam across the top of the arm, carry the inside arm piece well over to the outside (see Fig. 2). If the arm rolls outwards, the seam of inside and outside pieces should occur right under the roll. On small chairs a dart similar to that in the inside back is needed at the arm front. Now the cover has reached the stage shown in Fig. 1.

Cut the remaining pieces (outside arm and back and any thickness strips required) in a similar way. Fig. 2 helps you with the outside arm and Fig. 3 with the outside back. Allow the same bottom turnings on these as on the collar. If the arm and back roll outwards fit them up tightly under the roll, not sagging outwards from it to the ground. To get this fit, it may be necessary to pin one or two small darts in the roll edge of inside arm and back pieces, should these extend over without thickness strips between.

This completes the cutting out for a small chair cover. Before continuing with the assembling and making of this, here are additional instructions needed when cutting for a larger chair or couch.

Cutting Out Thickness Pieces. (Large or Much Curved Furniture).—When thickness pieces are used they will consist of (1) front arm thickness (called the scroll, if much shaped, as in Fig. 7): (2) back thickness strips, between the outside arm and outside back. A modern straight-line chair may have, instead of these, one strip which runs upwards up the front arm thickness and along the arm top to the back, and a second which covers the thickness of the back, encircling it from arm-top to arm-top. The positions and shapes of these pieces are clearly shown by the blanks in Fig. 5. Notice that in this case the inside arm and back portions end at the tops of arms and back, instead of being darted over as for the small chair.

Another plan, preferable with some patterns of covering material, is shown in Fig. 4. Straight front thickness strips are cut for the arms and similar ones for the sides of the back thickness, while the material goes straight over the whole of both arm and back, with wide tucks pinned up along both edges to allow for piping being introduced here.

Wing chairs require two additional pieces, inside and outside wing, cut in the same way as arm pieces. Shape carefully by gradual slashing the rather tricky curved seam between the wing and the inside back. (Fig. 8.)

Scrolls are most easily shaped if an oblong of material, considerably larger each way than the scroll, is first cut out roughly and pinned in position. Feeling through it, chalk on it the exact outline of the scroll, then shape to this by gradual cutting and slashing (Fig. 7), leaving a fairly wide turning for safety.

When pinning the scroll piece to the front arm edge, the latter piece may need darting or easing into the scroll to fit snugly.

Assembling a Loose Cover.—When all pieces are cut and in position, satisfactorily fitted, trim off the turnings everywhere to an even $\frac{3}{4}$ inch. It is a helpful plan also to mark the seam lines by running a piece of tailor's chalk along the chair edges, over the pins.

All turnings must now be notched, just as paper patterns are, for identification purposes. To do this, take small scissors (cutting-out shears are too large) and every few inches, at irregular intervals, cut a V out of all thicknesses of turnings along each edge. Take care, of course, to keep the notches well outside the seam lines.

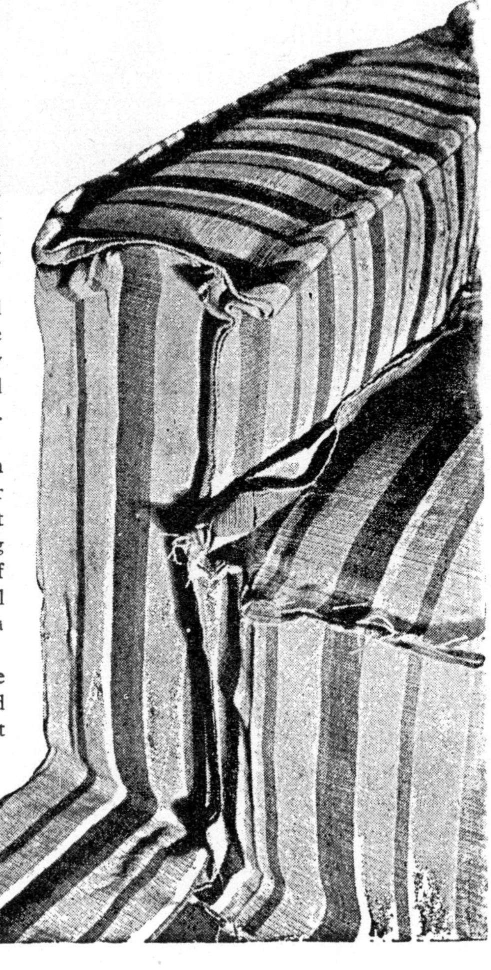

Fig. 4.—Separate pieces (with the stripes running upright if patterned material is used) are cut for the front thicknesses of the arms when these are wide. **Allow a wide turning.**

Fig. 5.—A chair of this type should have separate thickness strips cut for the arm and back portions. Join as in Fig. 4.

TWO DIFFERENT TYPES OF CHAIR

Unpin the doubled half cover completely and repin it as a whole cover in single thickness, carefully matching the notches so that the correct edges come together everywhere. **Try it on the chair, inside**

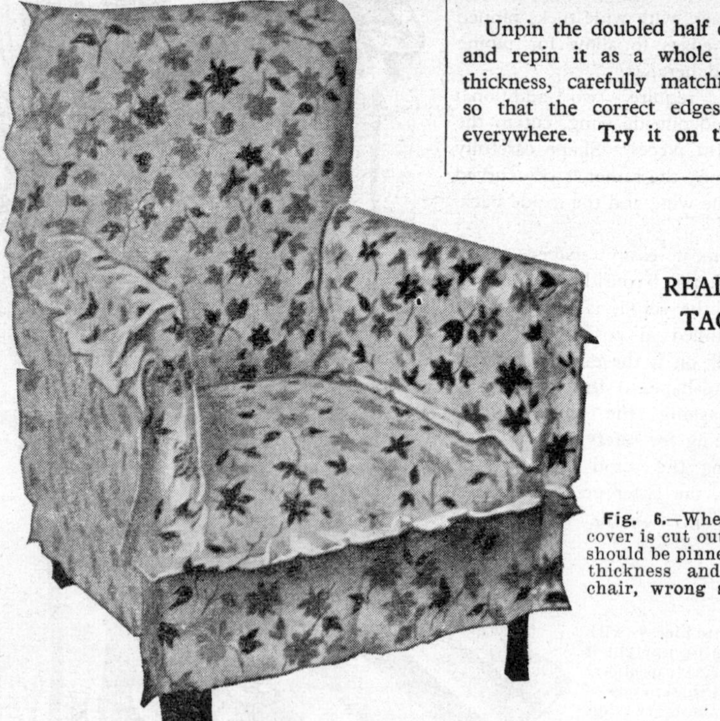

READY FOR TACKING

Fig. 6.—When the whole cover is cut out and fitted, it should be pinned up in single thickness and tried on the chair, **wrong side out.**

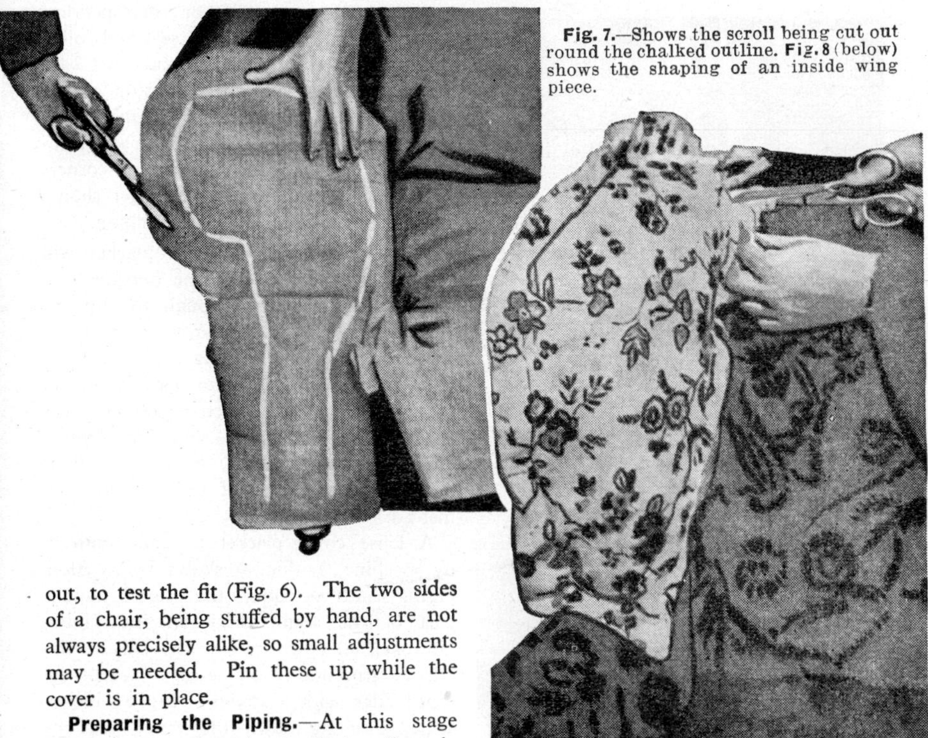

Fig. 7.—Shows the scroll being cut out round the chalked outline. **Fig. 8** (below) shows the shaping of an inside wing piece.

out, to test the fit (Fig. 6). The two sides of a chair, being stuffed by hand, are not always precisely alike, so small adjustments may be needed. Pin these up while the cover is in place.

Preparing the Piping.—At this stage the piping, yards of it, should be all ready for use. As preparing it is hand work, the best plan is to start this job as soon as you buy the materials and get it done in odd moments. Unpiped covers not only look definitely amateurish and home-made, but soon wear out along the edges, if they have no strong-corded finish to take the friction.

Shrink the piping cord by boiling and drying it. For its covering, cut strips on the true bias 1½ inches wide, joining them on the straight thread to the length required. Press out the tiny seams as flat as possible. Double the strips lengthwise over the shrunk cord, and tack them together with matching cotton as close to the cord as possible.

There are two distinct methods of inserting the piping in a loose cover. For the first remove the cover from the chair and unpin its parts. Lay one seam edge flat on the table, right side up, and along it tack the prepared piping, with its edges outwards and lying flush with the material edge and the cord just inside the chalked seam line. Lay over it, and hold with a few pins, the other edge to be seamed. Where angles must be turned or curves followed, slash the piping covering (Fig. 10).

With rather large stitches, overcast together all four raw edges; this serves both as a tacking and a seam finish. Finally, stitch the seam through all thicknesses, close to the cord, which is felt through the upper layer of material as you work.

Bias binding is less than 1½ inches wide. So, if this is used for piping, place the corded edge to the chalk line and use a deeper overcasting stitch to catch in the edges, which will not reach as far as the material edges.

The other method of piping is to leave the cover on the chair, unpin each seam a few inches at a time, insert the piping and tack it in place. This is rather a tiring

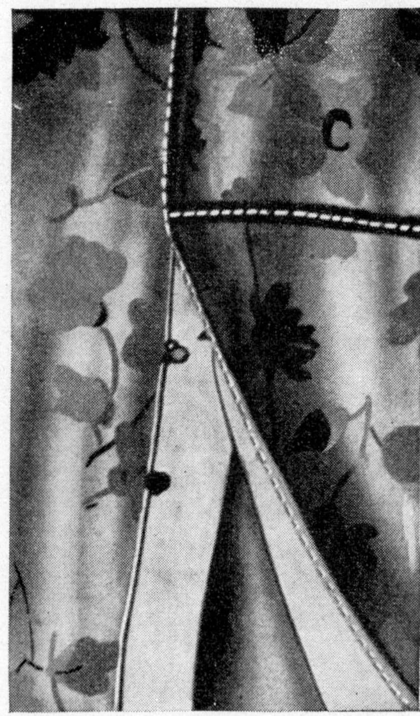

and awkward way of working, but enables you to see exactly how the cover is shaping. In this case, after tacking in the piping everwhere, take off the cover, stitch the seams and overcast their turnings separately afterwards.

Whichever plan is used, start by piping round the front scrolls (or corresponding pieces) and along the join of seat and collar. Then make-up each arm and the back separately and join their outside seams. Finally, stitch the unpiped seams which tuck in between the inside back and arms and all round the seat. Any thick corners into which the machine cannot get should be finished with strong backstitching.

Loose Cover Plackets.—A placket will be needed, down one of the outside back and arm seams, long enough to slip the cover on and off the chair without strain. This usually means leaving the seam open from the arm top down to floor. (On old fashioned "occasional" chairs of Victorian type which have this seam too much curved to take a placket, arrange a straight one down the centre of the outside back instead.)

A loose cover placket is made entirely by machine, as Fig. 9 shows you. After piping and stitching the closed upper part of the seam, carry on the piping unbroken all down, but tack it only to the outside arm side of the seam. Face in the piped edge with a straight strip $2\frac{1}{4}$ inches wide, stitching down the inner edge of this facing, after tacking it, from the right side, so as to make it neater. With a second 3-inch wide strip make a wrap on the outside back edge, by first seaming wrap and edge together with right side of wrap to wrong side of cover and then doubling the wrap over to the right side

Fig. 9.—A loose cover placket (above) and **Fig. 10.** piping being tacked to one seam edge. The other edge is laid over and pinned, the whole being overcast together.

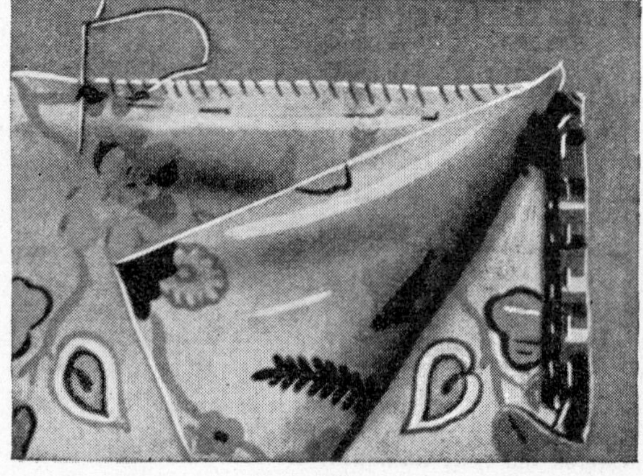

by stitching it down invisibly over the first stitched line.

To close the placket, sew on press studs, with an occasional hook and eye for greater security, at 2-inch intervals.

To complete a frill-less cover, as in Fig. 11, stitch an inch-wide hem, reaching just down to the base of the upholstery, all round the lower edge from placket back to placket. Run a long tape through this, and when the cover is on the chair, pull up its lower edge tightly on the tape, tie at the placket and tuck the ends underneath. If preferred, a short tape may be sewn to the cover where each leg comes, to tie round it and keep the cover from rucking up in wear.

Gathered and Box-Pleated Frills.—On many types of furniture the upholstered frame ends quite high above the ground, and a frill to cover the gap gives more grace and finish. Where there are definite but quite short legs (see Fig. 11), the cover may be finished with or without a frill, as preferred.

Frills may be either gathered or box-pleated, according to taste and the material used. Gathered frills are softer and more gracious, fitting in well with floral patterns and with drawing-room and bedroom furnishings. Box-pleated frills, Fig. 12, have a trim, tailored look which makes them suited to plain, horizontally striped or checked fabrics and to the lounge, dining-room or study.

Fig. 11. — A simple legged chair with contrasting piping, and a close-fitting lower edge.

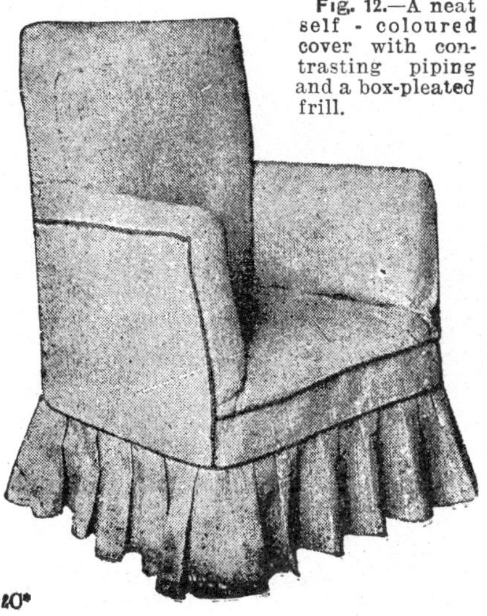

Fig. 12.—A neat self - coloured cover with contrasting piping and a box-pleated frill.

Frills should be cut across the width of the stuff, but may have numerous joins in them. Measure the distance from the bottom of the chair frame to the floor and cut the frill lengths 1 inch deeper than this measurement. For a gathered frill, the strips cut, when joined, should measure one and a half times the distance all round the chair legs; for box-pleated frills, two and a half times this measurement. Turn in and stitch a narrow hem all along the lower edge, arranging for the frill to end about an inch above the floor when joined to the cover.

For a Gathered Frill, mark out the top edge with pins into four equal quarters; similarly mark into quarters the lower edge of the cover. Gather each frill quarter on a separate thread, drawing it up to fit the corresponding section on the cover. Seam the frill to the cover, piping the join. Neatly hem each end of the frill.

For a Box-pleated Frill, mark with pins along both top and bottom edges, beginning an inch from one end, placed—$1\frac{1}{2}$ inches, $\frac{3}{4}$ inch, 3 inches apart. Repeat along length of material. Pin up each 3-inch division as a wide tuck, afterwards opening this out flat as a box pleat so that one edge of it just reaches to the pin, $\frac{3}{4}$ inch away. Pin each pleat, afterwards pressing all in well with a hot iron and damp cloth. Seam the frill to the cover, piping the seam, and hem each end of the frill.

Loose Cushions.—Cut two pieces of material the exact size and shape of the cushion, with added $\frac{1}{2}$-inch turnings on all edges. Cut also a thickness strip to go right round the cushion, with the same turnings added. Seam the strip between the two shaped pieces, piping both seams and leaving one seam open along the lower back edge for inserting the cushion. Afterwards slipstitch the open ends together.

Chesterfields, Settees and Sofas.—Any kind of couch or settee is regarded merely as a larger version of the chairs belonging to it and loose-covered in exactly the same way, using two or more widths for seat and back instead of one. (For differences in estimating the quantity of material required, see beginning of chapter.)

Sofas, of the Victorian kind, are still found in many homes, and with modern loose covers, made at home, look wonderfully modern and comfortable. Patterns for one or two different types may be bought quite cheaply, but if you are cutting out without a pattern the cutting rules already given must be modified. The reason for this is that, as a sofa has not two sides alike, it is impossible to cut for half of it in doubled material.

Instead, cut the whole of each piece in single thickness, using 30-inch material for preference. To avoid joins, place the selvedges along back and front of the long seat, collar, back, inside and outside arms, but vertically when cutting the front and back scrolls. All cutting out should be done with the material laid on the sofa right side uppermost. If the back is roll-shaped, cover it all over with one piece of material, sausage fashion, and gather the foot-end of this tightly under a large self-covered buttonmould. If the back is high and flat, cut for it inside and outside pieces connecting with a narrow top strip, as described for large arm-chairs.

The cover being right side out, pin the various pieces togther, as cut, with lapped seams, which are easily converted during making into plain, wrong-side seams. Lap neighbouring pieces on to the scrolls, rather than the scrolls on to them, as a

A settee pattern, No. 316, price 2s. 9d. by post. The matching chair, Pattern 326, is shown at the beginning of the chapter.

A neat and attractive idea for a divan with tiny box-pleated frill.

better shape is preserved this way. Chalk along the lapped edges as a guide to inserting the piping or do this on the sofa, as explained for chairs.

Sofa backs being sometimes none to well padded, it is a good plan to buy enough stuff to cover also several odd cushions, which may be placed to make the back more comfortable.

Divan Loose Covers.—Divan beds, being wide and flat, are not very decorative in themselves, but a well-made cover of tailored type always lends distinction. To detract from the long horizontal line, and give an impression of more height, the cover should be finished with a box-pleated frill.

As there is no shaping to do, this is a very simple job. Cut an oblong piece for the top, with a collar (depth pieces) running all round just under it and the frill attached to its lower edge. Pipe all seams. If the divan is a very low one, the frill may be joined direct to the top without a collar intervening.

The cover should be completely finished and frilled on all four sides, even if one or more are against a wall, so that it may be turned round occasionally to get even wear or hide stains. No placket is required, as the cover just drops on. A bolster and one or two cushions covered to match are always an improvement.

A plan which often looks effective (and may enable you to use up two remnants, is to make the top of a striped or patterned material, and the collar and frill of a plain one matching its ground colour.

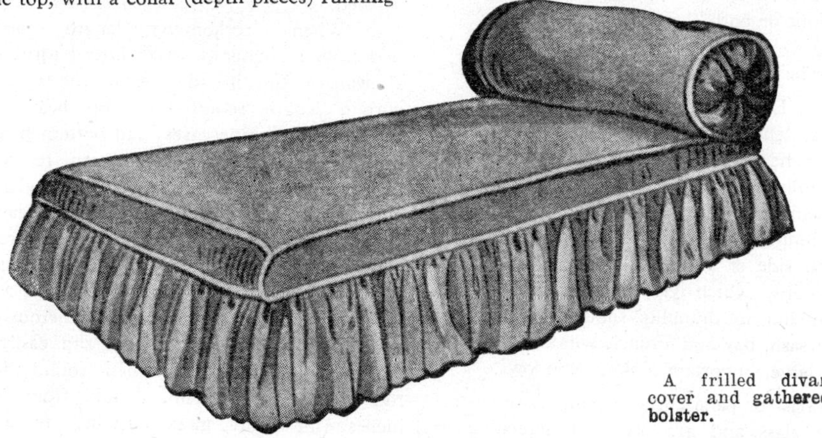

A frilled divan cover and gathered bolster.

Fig. 13.—Lined velvet draw-curtains with a matching pelmet trimmed with fringe and tassels. The all-over glass-curtain is of horizontally striped voile.

CURTAINS

Between loose covers and curtains there should be some definite link, so it is wise never to get the one new without considering its effect on the other. To have them matching may be too overpowering, especially in patterned material, but they should harmonise in texture or colour or both.

The following may be helpful:

(1) Draw curtains may be of sill or floor length (the latter actually end about 2 inches above the floor, for reasons of cleanliness). Sill curtains are suited to casement or other small or shallow windows, including the small ones often found on each side of a French door. Floor-length curtains, which give weight and dignity and shut out draughts, should be chosen for tall sash, bay and French windows, and for all large, important-looking windows.

Glass or pane curtains hang close against the glass and are used for screening or softening purposes. They hang right across the window, either from top to bottom, as in Fig. 13, or across the lower half. In order not to block out too much light, they should be of transparent or semi-transparent materials. In almost all cases they should end just above the sill or enough below it (at first) to allow for shrinkage when washed.

(2) When reckoning length and quantities of material, make liberal turning allowances, for, in addition to the actual curtain length required, a top heading, top casing (in some cases) and bottom hem must be allowed for. In addition, reckon for washable curtains (especially net glass curtains) a shrinkage allowance of at least 1 inch per yard of length. For a heading allow double its height, plus ½ inch turning; thus, an inch-wide heading requires 2½ inches allowance. For a casing generously wide, into which the rod will slip easily, reckon double the measurement round the rod. For a bottom hem, all told, from 1½ inches (for short glass curtains) to 4½

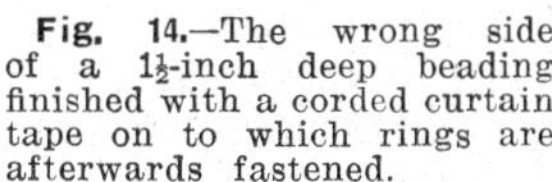

Fig. 14.—The wrong side of a $1\frac{1}{2}$-inch deep beading finished with a corded curtain tape on to which rings are afterwards fastened.

inches; the longer and heavier the curtain, the deeper its hem should be.

The hems of transparent curtains should be made 3-ply (that is, with the first raw-edge turning the full depth of the hem) as otherwise the narrow turn shows through against the light and gives an ugly effect.

Any shrinkage allowance may either be left in the curtain, making this hang too long until washed, put into an extra deep hem for letting down after laundering or, in suitable materials, be hand-run as a temporary tuck just above the hem, where it will add a touch of decoration until let down.

(3) Before buying the material, the curtain width necessary must also be considered. Measure the curtain rod or other fitment (not the actual window width, which is often less) and allow one and a half times this measurement in curtain width. The only exception is very soft, thin material, such as voile or a flimsy artificial silk, when from one and three-quarters to twice the rod width gives the best results.

(4) If a half-width has to be added to a complete width to give the required fullness, join the half-width on the outside of each curtain with a flat-fell seam, which is flat, strong and inconspicuous. In such a case, of course, three curtain widths will be required to make a pair of curtains, the third width being halved vertically for joining to the full widths. Remember to allow the necessary turnings on *each* width, not merely on each curtain, when buying the material.

When buying for lined curtains, if more convenient the lining material may be an inch or two narrower and shorter than the curtain fabric. On the latter allow somewhat smaller length allowances than for unlined curtains.

UNLINED CURTAINS

Reckon and write down the length and width (including all allowances) required for each curtain. Straighten one cut edge of the material by carefully pulling a thread or tearing, so that you have an even edge from which to measure. All measuring is best done with a wooden yardstick (also useful for measuring lengths up the windows without climbing on steps) as this will not slip or stretch like a tape measure.

From the straightened edge, measure the curtain length required just inside one selvedge and mark it with a pin. Do the same just inside the other selvedge. Then check the length before cutting by measuring back from each pin to the even edge. If correct, fold over the material from pin to pin across the width and cut evenly with sharp cutting-out shears.

When the material has good selvedges they will form the side edges of the curtain and need no finishing. But if the selvedges are badly coloured, not coloured at all or are tighter than the fabric, they must be concealed and narrow side hems used. If width is ample, they may be cut off. If not, slash them *slantwise* every inch or two (this gives stretch to the tight edges) before folding them into side hems. Join the cut edge of a half-width to a whole width, if more than one is used, so that both side edges will have selvedges. When a curtain takes two widths, selvedges, if bad, should be cut off before the widths are joined.

Any width joining being done, finish the curtain top, taking care that a pattern with a definite up and down will hang the right way up. Curtain tops may be finished in three ways: (*a*) plain; (*b*) with a heading (Fig. 14); (*c*) with a heading and casing.

(*a*) **A plain finish** is used in conjunction with a pelmet or valance, which will hang down and conceal the curtain top, when this is not gathered directly on to a rod, but suspended with hooks on to rings or a " railway " fitting. Allow a 1-inch turning, folding this down singly to the wrong side. Stitch down on the wrong side, over its raw edge, a length of corded and pocketed curtain tape, which should be cut 1 inch longer than the curtain width. This tape is very cheap and may be bought to match curtains of almost any colour. Stitch it down along both edges, so that the raw edge of the material is concealed between the two lines of stitching, and take care not to stitch through the cords anywhere.

Fold in the raw edge of the tape at each end, so that it does not project beyond the curtain edge. When the curtains are hung pull up the cords to the (drawn-across) width required and knot them together. They may be loosened for laundering, so that the curtain will iron flat.

(*b*) **A heading** is used to give a finish to a curtain top which has no pelmet or valance frill or ends half-way up the window, as do many glass curtains. Mark with a few pins the actual top of the curtain, then mark above this the depth of the heading—say 1 inch. Fold down singly to the wrong side all material above the upper marking, and hold the edge as described under (*a*) with corded curtain tape. (Fig. 14.) The upper edge of this should come exactly along the lower pin marking.

(*c*) **A heading with a casing below it** is used for thin glass curtains run directly on a rod or wire spring or for heavier curtains, without pelmet or valance frill, if they are hung in the same way. Mark the actual curtain top with pins as described under (*b*) and above it the casing width, with the heading depth above this again. Fold down singly to the wrong side all material above this. If turning allowances have been reckoned as explained previously, this turning should end about ½ inch below the lowest pin marking. Stitch through both thicknesses right across the curtain, the heading depth below the fold, to form the heading. Then fold in the raw edge to the depth required for the casing and stitch again at this level to hold it in place. Run the rod or wire spring directly through the casing, frilling the curtain into fullness as you go.

When the curtain top is finished in one of the ways given above, turn up and stitch a hem along its lower edge to finish the curtain. Before stitching the second hem, measure this curtain against its fellow to make sure both are just the same length.

LINED CURTAINS

Most draw curtains, except those of purely casement type, are improved by being lined. The extra layer of material makes them hang and wear better, and gives greater screening and draught-breaking powers. Also, curtains varying in pattern and hue to suit the colour schemes of different rooms will give a uniform effect from outside if all are lined alike. The larger the draperies and the more expensive their material the more essential a lining is.

Quite a cheap fabric will make a good lining. Unbleached calico costs little and wears well for light country curtains which have little to soil them; other good materials for the purpose are casement cloth or cotton jaspé. Joins (plain seams pressed open) are easily made, should the lining be narrower than the curtain fabric.

Cut out both curtains and lining as explained for unlined curtains, but allow rather smaller turnings and cut the linings a little smaller each way than the curtains. Any joins required to obtain the necessary width, in either curtains or linings, should be made in each quite separately. Use plain (not flat-fell) seams, pressed open, one turning each way, on a table or ironing board only thinly padded.

Spread a curtain out perfectly flat and unwrinkled, wrong side uppermost, on a large table. Over it spread, equally flat and right side uppermost, its lining, centring this so that the curtain shows equal turnings beyond the lining on each side, and comparing top with bottom. Fold back vertically one-third of the lining width in a straight downward line, but leaving the curtain portion beneath quite undisturbed. Now lock the curtain and lining together all down the lining fold.

To lock, simply catch fold and single curtain thickness together with a tiny buttonhole stitch in cotton which matches the curtain exactly and so will be practically invisible on the right side. (Fig. 15.) Space the buttonhole stitches very wide apart—one every 4 inches except on velvet, which requires locking every 2 inches. Fold back a similar third from the other side edge of the lining and lock this in the same way.

Fig 15.—The lining is folded back vertically and locked to the curtain with long loose buttonhole stitches.

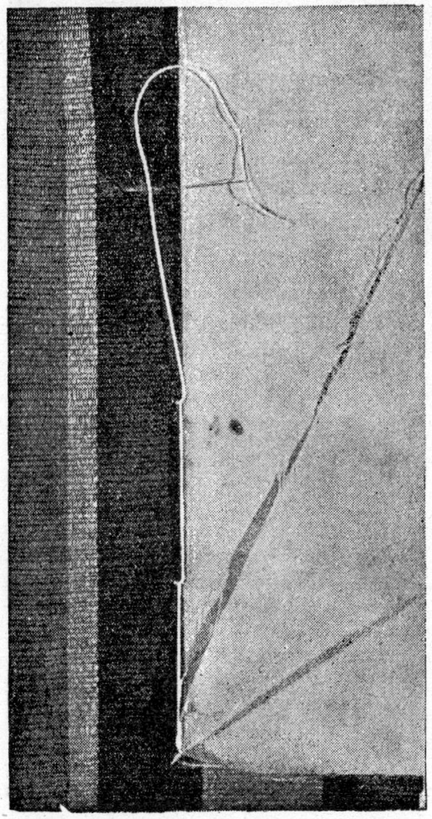

Locking holds curtain and lining smoothly and securely together, so that they will hang in the same folds and never "bag" in a wind. Should the curtain be more than one width wide, three lockings instead of two are needed. In this case, first fold the lining over in half and lock here, before doing the two lockings already described. Lockings should end both top and bottom before the turning allowances are reached.

Fold in wide single turnings down each side edge of the curtain and press these down. Fold in and press similar lining turnings which do not reach within ½-inch of the curtain edges. Slip stitch the two folds together, using a much longer "slip" between the stitches than in dressmaking.

At the top, finish the curtain with or without a heading, as for the corresponding unlined draperies. If there is a heading, shorten the lining to come only to its lower edge; if a plain finish, fold down curtain and lining together under the corded tape.

Finish the bottom by turning up and slip stitching, as for the sides, making the lining at least an inch shorter than the curtain, which must have a deep fold (at least 1½ inches).

TRIMMINGS FOR CURTAINS

For casement curtains, bound edges are often attractive, particularly a plain binding on a printed fabric or a patterned binding on a plain one. A contrasting binding also serves to introduce a second colour note, or it may finish a raw edge neatly, where bathroom curtains of rubber fabric are bound with checked bias tape. To bind curtains, double a straight or bias binding lengthwise, with the curtain raw edge

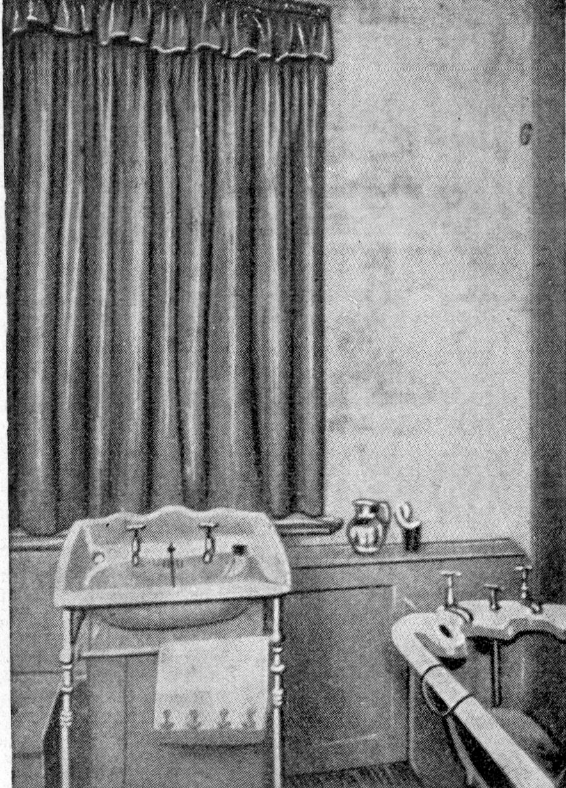

For bathrooms, kitchens and sculleries where there is much steam and heat, curtains of plastic in colours and patterns are always attractive and serviceable.

Fig. 16.

between the two thicknesses, and stitch both sides on at once.

Fringe is quite often suitable for an edging for heavy, handsome curtains. A short looped fringe is used and sewn on by hand or machine.

Hand embroidery may be a decorative trimming. Border designs may be darned in bright-coloured wools along the hems of net glass curtains, in and out of the mesh, and look practically the same on both sides.

Frilled edges are a soft, pretty finish for muslin, voile or organdie curtains. The frills should be 2 inches wide, made up as for gathered valances with the gathered edge seamed to the curtain edge.

VALANCE FRILLS AND PELMETS

Where ceilings are low, curtains may look best merely finished with a top heading of their own. But in high rooms or those which have space above the window tops, either a pelmet or a valance frill is needed to link the separated curtains together, and, with them, to form a complete frame round the windows. A pelmet or valance is particularly necessary for bays or where several windows are set close enough together to be curtained as a whole.

Valance frills have a graceful informality which suits casement and other small windows; also low French doors with a little casement on either hand. Valances are easy to make and easy to wash. They should always match the curtains. There are two types of valance frill, the gathered and the box-pleated. They correspond with gathered and box-pleated frills for loose covers and have much the same advantages.

Gathered valances (Fig. 16), are the quicker of the two to make, take less

A simple yet decorative pelmet which is cut straight, and is trimmed with braid stitched on in scallops.

An attractive decoration with a shaped pelmet and a curtain that can either be looped back in Regency style or left to hang straight. In the circle is another form of pelmet, which is scalloped and finished with braid or galon.

TWO DISTINCTIVE CURTAIN ARRANGEMENTS

material and are preferable for all narrow frills finishing 6 inches or less in depth. Never use this method for deep valances or in a dignified room. Cut out and hem as described for gathered loose-cover frills given earlier, but finish the top edges with corded curtain tape as for unlined curtains.

Box-pleated valances are half-way in effect between the "cottagey"-looking gathered frill and the formal, dignified pelmet. They give a semi-tailored look and in a low room their straight vertical lines add an appearance of greater height. They look best if between 6 and 10 inches in depth when finished. Cut out, hem and pleat just as explained previously for box-pleated loose cover frills, except that if the depth exceeds 8 inches the pleating measurements should be 2, 1 and 4 inches, instead of those given. Finish the top edge as for unlined curtains with plain or corded curtain tape stretched across the wrong side of the pleats. If corded tape is used, the cord, of course, will not be drawn up.

According to the fitment at the window, both types of valance frill may be either suspended from a front pelmet rod or rail fixed a few inches in front of the curtain rod or rail, or they may be fastened with tacks or drawing-pins to the front edge of a narrow wooden pelmet board.

Pelmets which are shaped, lined and stiffened, give a gracious dignity and finish to large, important windows, and accord well with floor-length curtains. A pelmet usually matches the draw curtains when these are of plain material: when they are patterned, it may be of plain fabric matching the predominant curtain colour and perhaps have an appliqué motif from the pattern.

Very simple strip pelmets, which are unlined and really nothing but valance frills devoid of fullness, are sometimes seen. They are quite effective in narrow widths across narrow spaces, but should not be used elsewhere. As, being unstiffened, they tend to sag and collect dust, they should always be made of washable material, or of coloured American cloth.

Properly lined and stiffened pelmets are nearly always far preferable.

Windows vary so much in size and **proportions** that it is best to cut one's own pelmet pattern to fit one's window exactly. There are many possible shapes, some much curved and quite elaborate. A simple squared design with drop ends, however, as in Diagram 1, is always in good taste and suits most modern rooms. It may be cut very easily without any knowledge of drawing, as all the outlines are ruled.

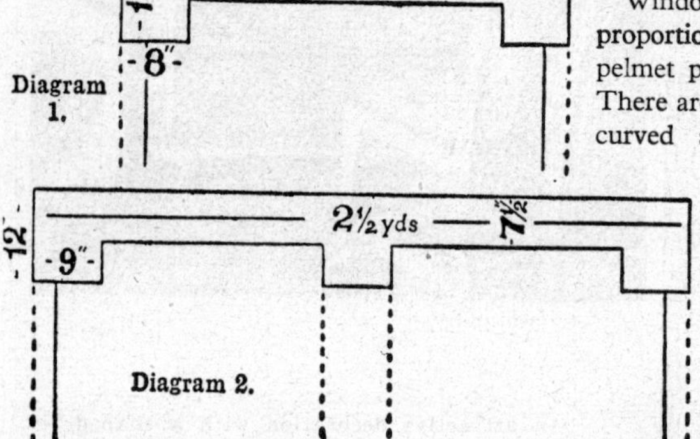

A diagram showing how a straight pelmet with drop ends is cut. **Diagram 2** shows the arrangement when the pelmet stretches over two casement windows.

Diagram 1 shows a pelmet pattern this shape, 1½ yards wide. This is front width only. Actually, a pelmet is not merely stretched across the window, but turns the corners and covers also the sides of the narrow pelmet board to which it is fixed. To cover this return, as it is called, the pattern as shown in the diagram must be extended each end by the depth of the particular pelmet board in question—usually 3 to 4 inches.

It is really simplest to rule and cut out this pattern as it is (using a roll of kitchen

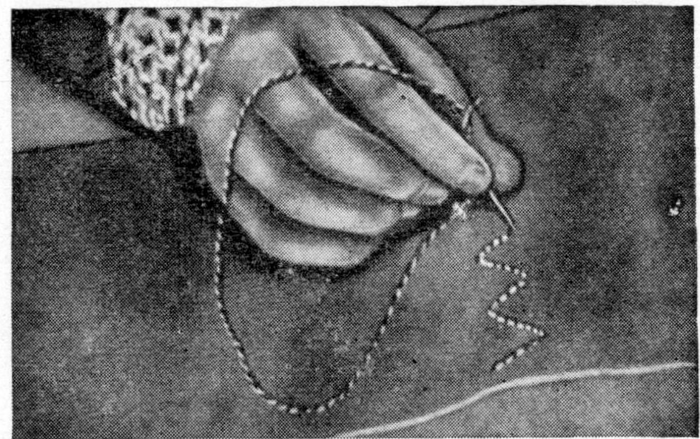

Fig. 17.—To join buckram, overlap the edges about one inch and stab stitch them together in zigzags.

paper and a yardstick for ruling the lines) and then, if necessary, to reduce or enlarge the pattern to fit a particular window. This is easier than making the alterations before cutting.

To make the pelmet smaller, fold over and pin enough of the narrow centre part to get the required width only.

To increase the width, cut the pattern vertically down the centre and paste in an added strip, wide enough to give the additional width desired.

To cut a pelmet for a pair of windows set close together; remember that these are treated as one unit (see Diagram 2) and need a continuous frame. In this case, cut down the centre of the pelmet pattern, and insert between the halves a rectangle the same depth as the drop ends and wide enough to cover the space between the windows.

The pelmet depth may need altering if your windows are much taller or lower than the average. A good guide to the correct depth is that the pelmet should be $1\frac{1}{2}$ inches deep for every foot of curtain depth, if the curtains are sill-length; or if they extend to the floor, the pelmet at its deepest point should be one-sixth of the distance from the floor to the top of

Fig. 18.—After dampening the buckram edges, press the turnings of material down on to them to make them stick.

Fig. 19.—The corners of the material should be slashed and neatly folded in before pressing.

the window. As modern ideas favour the utmost light and air, however, pelmets are usually kept rather on the shallow side.

Depth is altered by cutting a strip off the top of the pattern or pasting an additional strip on.

A pelmet consists of three thicknesses, the outside ornamental fabric or surface, the stiffening of buckram and the lining. For the up-to-date and quick method of making pelmets, which is described below, yellow-brown upholstery buckram, 36 inches wide, is the *only* stiffening which can be used.

As pelmets are long but seldom more than half the width of the fabric in width, the most economical plan is to make two from the same materials, laying them side by side in the width. If only one is wanted, buy material, lining and buckram only half as long (plus turnings) as the pelmet width. Divide in half down the width and make joins at the centre front. Well pressed, these will not be noticeable when the pelmet is hung.

The making of a pelmet is easily followed from the following hints, which show the fashioning of the slightly arched pelmet. Stitch and press any centre-front seams before cutting out. Joins on the buckram must be made by hand, by overlapping the two halves 1 inch (take care the top edge forms a perfectly straight continuous line) and stab stitching them together with a large zigzag back stitch. (Fig. 17.)

Cut the surface fabric with 2-inch turnings, and then the lining with 1-inch turnings and the buckram without turnings. As the paper pattern cannot be pinned to the stiff buckram, the latter should first be fastened down to the table with drawing pins or fine upholstery skewers. The pattern is fastened down to it in the same way and outlined round in pencil. Unfasten pattern and buckram and cut out the latter along the pencil lines.

Much work is saved by the surface material being stuck (not sewn) to the interlining, the glue with which the buckram is stiffened acting as the adhesive.

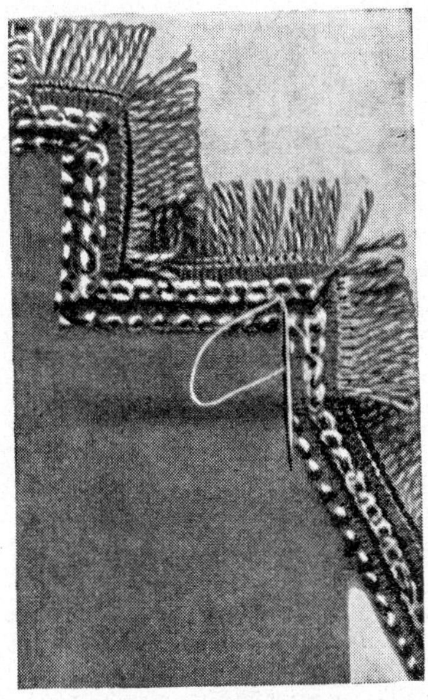

Spread the cut-out surface, perfectly smooth, wrong side uppermost, on a large table. Centre the cut-out interlining over it and secure in place with skewers or drawing pins. Have ready a hot iron and a wet sponge. Rapidly damp the buckram edges all round to a depth of 2 inches. Immediately fold over them and iron down the 2-inch turnings of the surface. (Fig. 18.) The heat and damp will bring out the glue in the buckram and stick the turnings firmly. Fig. 19 shows how they must be slashed and folded in at corners to lie neat and flat.

Lay the lining, right side uppermost, over the buckram. Fold in its turnings so that it is a little smaller all round than the interlining and slip stitch them down to the stuck surface turnings (Fig. 21), using the long upholstery slip stitch mentioned previously.

Trim the side and lower edges with a silk pelmet fringe, sewing it on by hand with running stitch through the surface material only, not the buckram. Run along twice, along both upper and lower edges of the braid part of the fringe, as in Fig. 20. Mitre the fringe neatly to turn corners and ease it a little along any curve. The pelmet is now complete.

Sometimes rather deep pelmets are additionally trimmed with braid sewn on in a pattern. This must be done *before* the lining is added. After ironing down the surface on to the buckram, rule out on the buckram side with tailor's chalk where the line or lines of trimming are to come. Tack through with stab stitches so that a guide line of tacking appears on the surface. Sew down the braid (which should match the fringe) along this line, as described above for the fringe. Then add the lining and fringe.

To hang a pelmet, fasten it with drawing

Above:

Fig. 20.—Fringe is sewn through the upper braid portion. **Fig. 21.**—On the wrong side the lining is secured to the curtain by long slip-stitches.

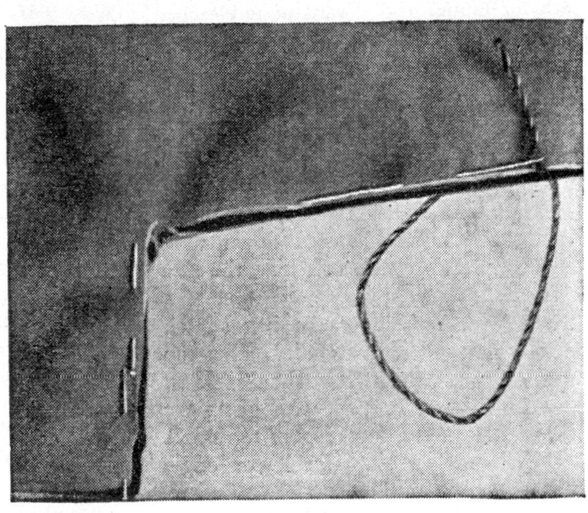

Fig. 21.

pins or tacks to the front thickness of a pelmet board. Begin by securing its exact centre-front to the centre-front of the board, then stretch it tautly both ways, carrying it round the board width to meet the wall at each side.

MAKING A BOX POUFFE

A strong wooden packing-case, from the local oilshop or grocer, may be fashioned into a handsome and useful piece of furniture at very small expense. Neatly lined inside and with the lid upholstered to form a seat, it makes a comfortable fireside or dressing-table stool, while the inside storage space, in a small home, is most useful for spare bedding, shoes, hats or left-overs of dressmaking and home furnishing materials.

The best size for the packing-case is approximately 18 inches long, 15 inches wide and 12 inches deep, or somewhere near these dimensions. For real strength, the wood of the box should be at least $\frac{3}{8}$ inch thick ($\frac{1}{2}$ inch is better). It should have an unbroken lid; failing this, cut one to fit in strong plywood. Rub the rough wood smooth everywhere, both inside and out, with glass-paper.

A box of approximately the size given will require for outer covering about $1\frac{1}{2}$ yards of 30-inch material such as cretonne, poplin or cotton jaspé, and a little less (say $1\frac{1}{4}$ yards) of 27-inch coloured American cloth for lining; also $\frac{1}{2}$ yard of unbleached calico and about $\frac{1}{2}$ lb. of stuffing, which may be either kapok or flock.

Line the inside of the box neatly with American cloth, cutting sides 3 inches deeper than the box, so that they will extend over the thickness of the wood at the top and on to the bottom of the box; a separate inside bottom piece, with turnings folded in and fastened down with matching drawing-pins, will hide the side edges here.

Round the outside of the box stretch the outer covering material. The top edges of this, which you should fasten down every inch or two with gilt chair pins, will cover the turned-over top edges of the lining. Finish the lower edges similarly at floor level.

Line the inside lid with American cloth, bringing the edges of this over to the top side, where the padding will conceal them. From tacks knocked in the lid edges at each corner and the middle of each side, stretch criss-cross loops of string, all at the same tension and slack enough to take a 2-inch depth of stuffing under them. Fill all the space between them and the lid with kapok or flock, first picked over between the fingers and then packed in as tightly as possible. Use more than $\frac{1}{2}$ lb. if required to make an absolutely firm padding, well finished at the rims and corners.

Over this stretch a large oblong of unbleached calico, holding it down by driving in small tacks. The calico is concealed by an outer cover matching the outside of the box. Draw this smoothly and tautly down all round to the thickness of the lid, where the raw edge must be turned in and held with closely set chair pins. Pleat the surplus material tidily at each corner.

It is best to have box and lid separated while this work is being done. Now hinge them together and fix a length of fine chain or a strap of material inside from one box side to the lid, to keep the latter from falling right back when opened. If liked, screw on a fastening for the lid and two ring handles by which the box pouffe may be lifted easily.

SOFT FURNISHING REPAIRS AND RENOVATIONS

Loose covers may wear through at particular points where there is much rub or cigarettes may burn holes in them. Such weak spots may be patched, and when neatly done, in patterned materials at least, will hardly show if the pattern is carefully matched. When making the new cover, cut a good-sized oblong of the same material from left-over pieces and stitch one edge of this in with the seam joining the inside back and seat—on the wrong side, of course. In wear, this invisible piece will tuck down in the crevice out of the way; but it will be washed with the cover. Consequently, later you can cut from it a patch which has laundered exactly the same tint.

Sometimes, especially at small corner fireplaces, a chair must stand so close to the hearth that in time the collar portion nearest the fire gets scorched to rotting-away point. Here again, a matching patch may be inserted. Better still, either when making the new cover or repairing it, make the susceptible portion double, so that when the top layer goes it may be cut away to reveal the good one beneath.

The centre top of the inside back and the tops of the arms of a loose cover always soil long before the rest. So it is a real economy when cover-making to buy a little extra stuff and from it to make a chair-back and arm pieces which may be laid on and washed whenever required. Match the pattern neatly and they will not in any way spoil the look of the cover.

Curtains are difficult to repair, as any mends show up against the light, but they may be renovated or converted in various ways. The part at the top, which receives the most soil and fading from the window being most often open here, is usually the first to wear out. If the material is otherwise good, cut off the top foot or so, make a fresh top finish and the curtains will give good service at smaller windows elsewhere. They may be similarly reduced in width, for use at narrower windows, if the outside edges have faded more than the rest, as often happens.

When a shrinkage allowance has not been made for glass curtains and these are too short after laundering, add a double hem of contrasting, non-transparent material; or unpick the top heading and casing to lengthen the curtain, and add a new one of matching or contrasting fabric. In both cases the effect may be very pretty, not in any way suggesting a repair.

If heavy long curtains of such a material as velours or chenille are too short when transferred to a new home, the best remedy is to add a deep matching silk fringe along the bottom edge, rather than a contrasting hem.

Eiderdowns are not cheap to buy, so ways of lengthening their life are always welcome. Corners, which on silk eiderdowns usually wear first, exposing the white lining beneath, may be patched, all four alike, with a contrasting material. Cut this to stretch in a broad strip diagonally across the eiderdown border, fitting it at both inner and outer angles, and hem it down neatly.

A down quilt border, when worn, often "leaks" feathers through the seam and so gets thin and limp before its time. To plump it out, extra feathers may be added from another eiderdown or pillow too old for further use. Carefully open the seam at the edge of the border a few inches, without letting feathers escape. Have the new feathers ready in a stout paper bag or pillow ticking. Tack the edges of this securely to the quilt opening, pleating up the larger to fit the smaller. Then, by

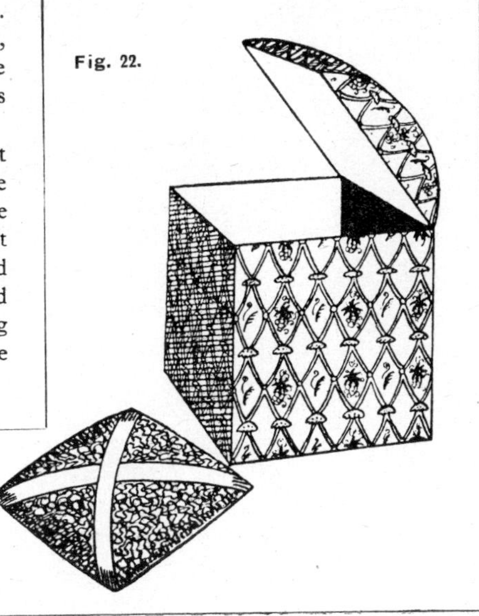

Fig. 22.

A BOX POUFFE

feel, coax and push the feathers through from bag to eiderdown. In this way there is no risk of their being scattered about the room.

Remove the bag, sew up the eiderdown opening closely and distribute the new feathers evenly all round the border by tapping them along with the side of your hand. To prevent further leakage through the weakened seam, put the quilt in your machine; slowly and carefully stitch round through all thicknesses just inside the faulty seam, taking care not to pucker the underside while doing so.

RUGMAKING

Hand-made rugs provide a fascinating and useful hobby. They can be made in several different ways, all of which are quite simple and fascinating to work. Here are shown a few of the different methods.

How to make your own designs for working.—Here are some simple designs that can be adapted to any desired scale. Working on canvas, with the larger composite squares already outlined by the blue thread, any of these patterns can be easily modified.

A sheet of draughtsman's paper, a mapping or other finely-pointed pen, and a small paint-brush are required. To keep the paper straight it should be fastened at the corners with drawing-pins on to a drawing-board or other flat piece of wood. This allows you to tilt the paper towards you, and makes the drawing much easier.

Having an idea of the design required, dot along the lines of the small squares of the paper. If the idea is vague, a pencil can first be used. When a pleasing and proportionate design has been evolved the dotted lines are thickly outlined, and filled in with a paint brush, as shown clearly in Fig. 1.

The designs shown here (Figs. 2, 3, 4 and 5) can be made larger or smaller as required, but they must be worked to scale, that is to say, that the number of strands and meshes utilised by the design must be increased proportionately if the design is enlarged, and decreased in the same way if a smaller pattern is required.

The diamond design, with the fine small squares in the centre worked in a different colour, would make an attractive border. So would the key pattern. The diamonds could be used for the corners of a rug only, or could be grouped together in the centre forming one large diamond. Quite a modern effect is obtained if the double zig-zag design is used, each zig-zag in a different colour.

When finished, the design may be drawn on the canvas or worked from the home-made chart. It should be remembered that the larger squares on the draughtsman's paper are equal to $2\frac{1}{2}$ square inches on medium canvas. Fig. 5 shows another border which is a little more advanced.

Different makes of wool should never be used for one rug. Whether it is a plain rug, or one with a border or design, the same make of wool must be used throughout, in order to keep the thickness of the pile even.

Cable-type wools are the thickest of all rug wools, and if desired can be worked only on alternate ridges of the canvas.

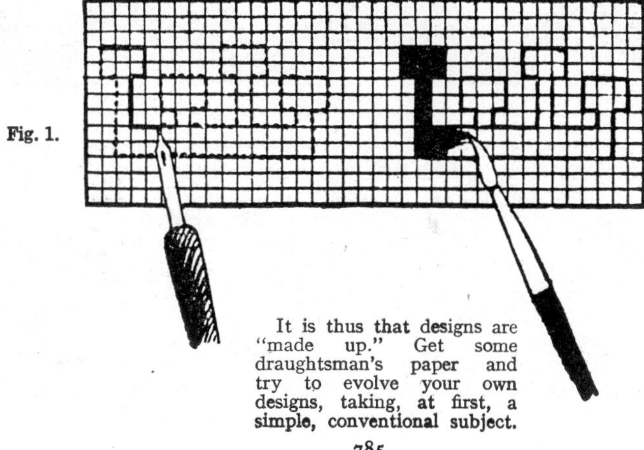

Fig. 1.

It is thus that designs are "made up." Get some draughtsman's paper and try to evolve your own designs, taking, at first, a simple, conventional subject.

SIMPLE DESIGNS TO COPY

These easily worked designs can be quickly copied. Innumerable similar designs can be made up, using the method shown on the previous page.

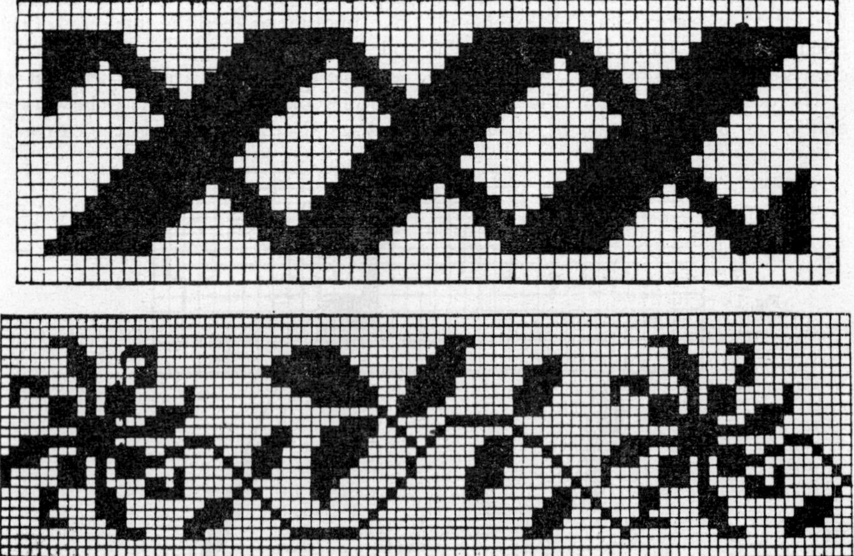

Figs. 2 to 5.

Materials required.—Rug canvas or hessian is used. The canvas may be plain or divided with a coloured thread in squares of eight holes. The latter is a help if a design is attempted. Canvas is obtainable in several different widths, 12, 14, 18, 22, 27, 30, 36, 40, 45 and 48 inches being the most usual. Each has a standard number of holes, and most charts have a corresponding number of spaces in width, so that when the design is worked it fills exactly the width of the canvas. With a sharp pair of scissors, a strong steel or bone crochet hook, a rug hook, a rug needle, a pair of knitting needles, a pencil and a wooden gauge, most rugs can be made.

For ease in working the canvas should be put on a table and held in place by a weight which helps to resist the pull when making the knots. The end of the rug which has been turned up should be nearest the worker. Start working over double canvas for a few rows, working from left to right, the finished portion falling on your knees. To prevent the bits of fluff sticking to your clothes, cover your knees with a cloth.

Most people in making a rug turn the canvas under on to the wrong side. This leaves an untidy ridge. If the canvas is turned up on to the right side, and then worked through the double canvas it is much neater, as no ridge is left. As the pile is thick, it does not show through on the right side.

Another point to remember is that it is better to even off the pile as one goes along, and not leave it until the end, when the rug is finished. If this is done each time before putting it away, it becomes far less tedious. The fluff which collects in the working should also be brushed off with the hand each time, always keeping it in the same direction. This gives a much better finish to a rug.

Hand-tufted rugs are made by knotting short lengths of wool into a specially made canvas. The knotting is done with a hook, and various kinds of wool are used, the 6-fold or ply being the most usual. Other kinds include 2- and 4-ply wool, cable-type wool and thrums—these are pieces left over from carpet making, and can be bought very cheaply either in plain colours or mixed.

When buying rug wool it is advisable to obtain the whole quantity required at one time to ensure that the dye is the same shade throughout; it seldom comes up twice exactly the same.

The life of the rug depends upon the canvas, so it is worth while getting the best and strongest quality.

Always work the whole of the rug in the same direction, as this makes the pile lie evenly; if stitches are put in in various ways, there will be ridges in the finished work, and where the two sets of knots meet, the pile will be inclined to open and show a space.

For a long pile rug, the wool must be wound evenly and fairly tightly on the gauge and then cut along the grooved side with sharp scissors or a knife. A rug gauge is of the simplest construction—just an inch wide piece of wood grooved along one side (see Fig 6 overleaf); the groove allows the scissor point to be passed along under the wound wool for cutting it into separate pieces. There is also obtainable a patent rug-wool cutter—The Patwin—that is very speedy in use.

Patterned rugs can be worked from charts, each square of which counts as one stitch in the rug, or the canvas can be bought with the design ready stencilled in colours so that you have only to fill in each part with the colour indicated.

Before starting a rug turn up the canvas as described earlier in this chapter. If working from a chart, it is advisable to turn the canvas to a blue line, and on stencilled canvas, to the beginning of the pattern.

When within two inches of the end of the design, turn up the end of the canvas and work the last few rows through the double thickness as at the beginning.

The following stitch makes a good finish for the selvedge edges. With the

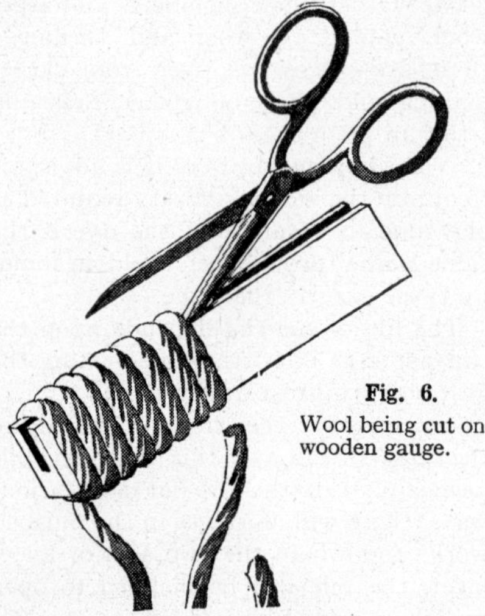

Fig. 6. Wool being cut on wooden gauge.

wrong side of the rug towards you, work over the selvedge into the first row of holes from left to right. Put the threaded needle in the first hole, and bring it towards you, leaving an end of wool which is darned in later. Work forwards from the first hole to the third hole, then from the second to the fourth, and from the third to the fifth and so on. A stitch similar to a large cross-stitch is formed as will be seen in Fig. 7.

The ground colour or the one predominant at the edge should be used. The end of the rug can be left plain or the edges overcast.

Rugs which are not rectangular must have the edges neatened with webbing sold for this purpose. The canvas is cut to within about two inches of the rug. This is turned under and faced with webbing which is sewn on with carpet thread.

Some prefer to line the rug with hessian or adhesive backing, but this is not necessary unless the rug is to be laid on an uneven floor.

Long-pile Rug-hook method.—The tufts are knotted on to the double threads running across the width of the canvas between the lengthway threads. **To make a tuft, pass the hook under the** double threads of the canvas where the knot is required, pushing it right through until the latch is past the threads of the canvas, and open. Take a piece of wool, fold it in half with the ends exactly together, and catch the looped end on to the hook (Fig. 8). Draw the hook back under the threads of the canvas. The catch will automatically close, thus holding the wool firmly and preventing the hook from catching on the canvas. Still hold the ends of the wool between the thumb and index finger of the left hand and draw the loop through about one-third the length of the doubled wool (Fig. 9). Still holding the wool, push the hook back through the loop until past the latch so that the latch again opens; this is clearly shown in Fig. 10; pass the hook round the two ends of the wool which are held in the fingers, ready to draw the ends through the loop, as shown in Fig. 11. Now leave go of the ends of the wool: if the fingers are placed on the looped end it helps with the last movement which completes the knot (Fig. 12). Draw the hook back through the loop, bringing the ends of wool with it and pull the ends tight when the tuft is complete as shown in Fig. 12. Although the making of the tufts is described here in four stages to make it quite clear for beginners, it is really the simplest operation, and with very little practice the four stages become one, worked with lightning rapidity.

Fig. 7. Binding the Edge.

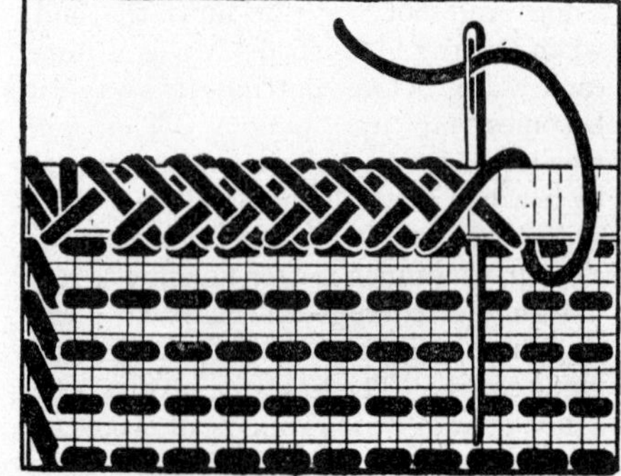

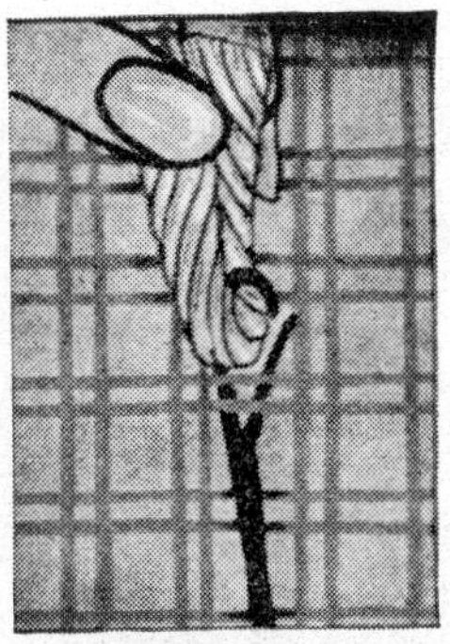

Fig. 8.

Push hook under two threads of the canvas, and catch the loop of wool on the hook.

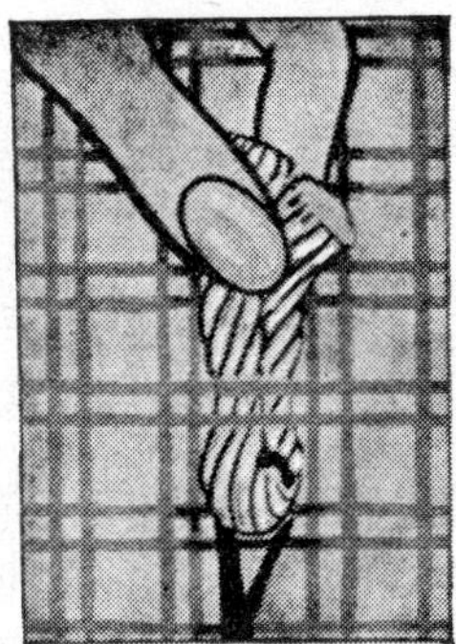

Fig. 9.

With the hook draw the wool under the threads of the canvas.

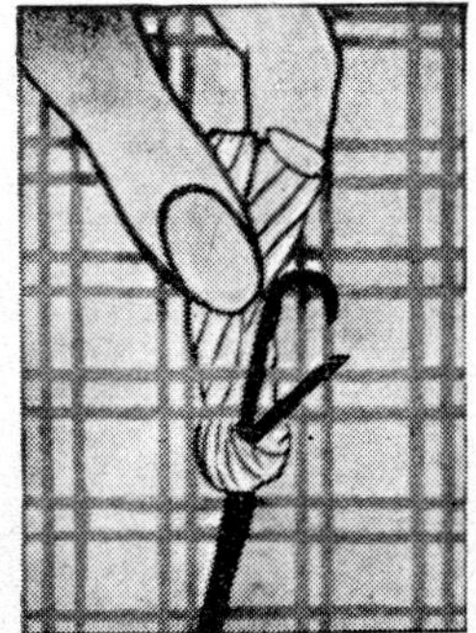

Fig. 10.

Push the hook and latchet back through the loop.

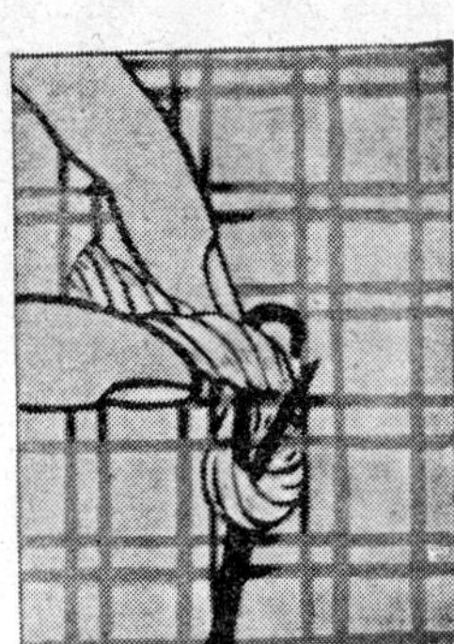

Fig. 11.

Catch hook round the ends of the wool, drawing the ends through the loop.

Fig. 12.

Tighten the knot by pulling the ends of the tuft.

Here are one or two designs for the rug-hook method. Fig. 13 shows a very simple yet attractive rug for the beginner, the chart for which is given in Fig. 15. Two yards of 36-inch wide rug canvas are needed. The rug can be made in any two shades, black and white being recommended for smartness. It takes 8 lbs. of black wool and 2½ lbs. of white to complete the rug. A rug-hook is also necessary. It is worked in the hook method just described and when finished measures 36 inches by 60 inches, the spare inches at either end being used for turnings.

The rug in Fig. 14 is very simple to work. It measures 36 inches across and is worked in chestnut and beige with the curved lines in black. The pile is deep and silky, as cable-type wool is used; this works up quickly for the knots are made in every other space instead of in each one. If the chart (page 794) is studied it will be quite easy to see how the stitches are arranged. When using the plain canvas, fold it in half, get the exact centre of one side and start working from there. Trim off the spare canvas neatly, leaving sufficient for turnings, which are tacked down and neatened with binding. Materials needed are; 1¼ yards of 36-inch canvas, 2¾ lbs. each of chestnut and beige wool, and ¾ lb. of black; a rug-hook and a wooden gauge measuring approximately 1¾ inches wide.

For the more advanced worker the Persian rug in Fig. 16 is interesting to work. For this more elaborately patterned style a stencilled or hand-painted canvas

Fig. 13. An attractive rug in modern design. Chart on page 791.

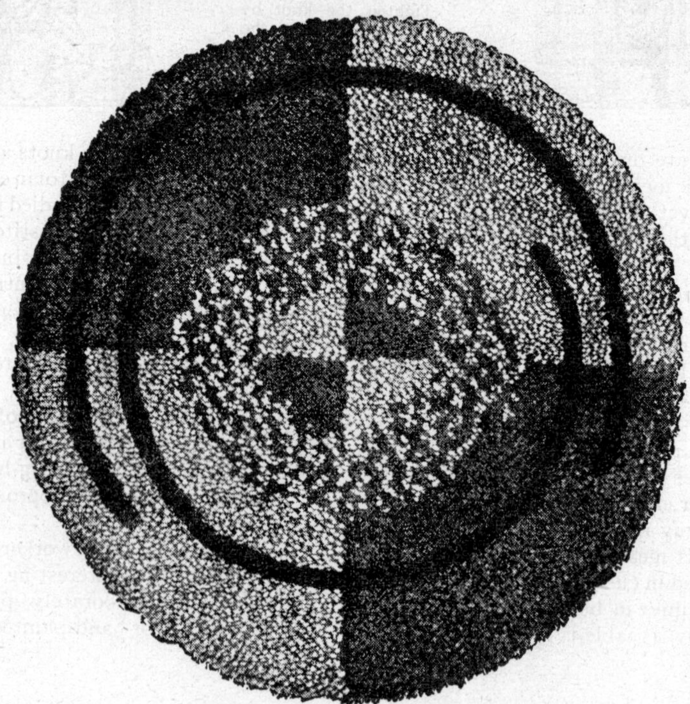

Fig. 14. Rug in cable-type wool. Chart on page 794.

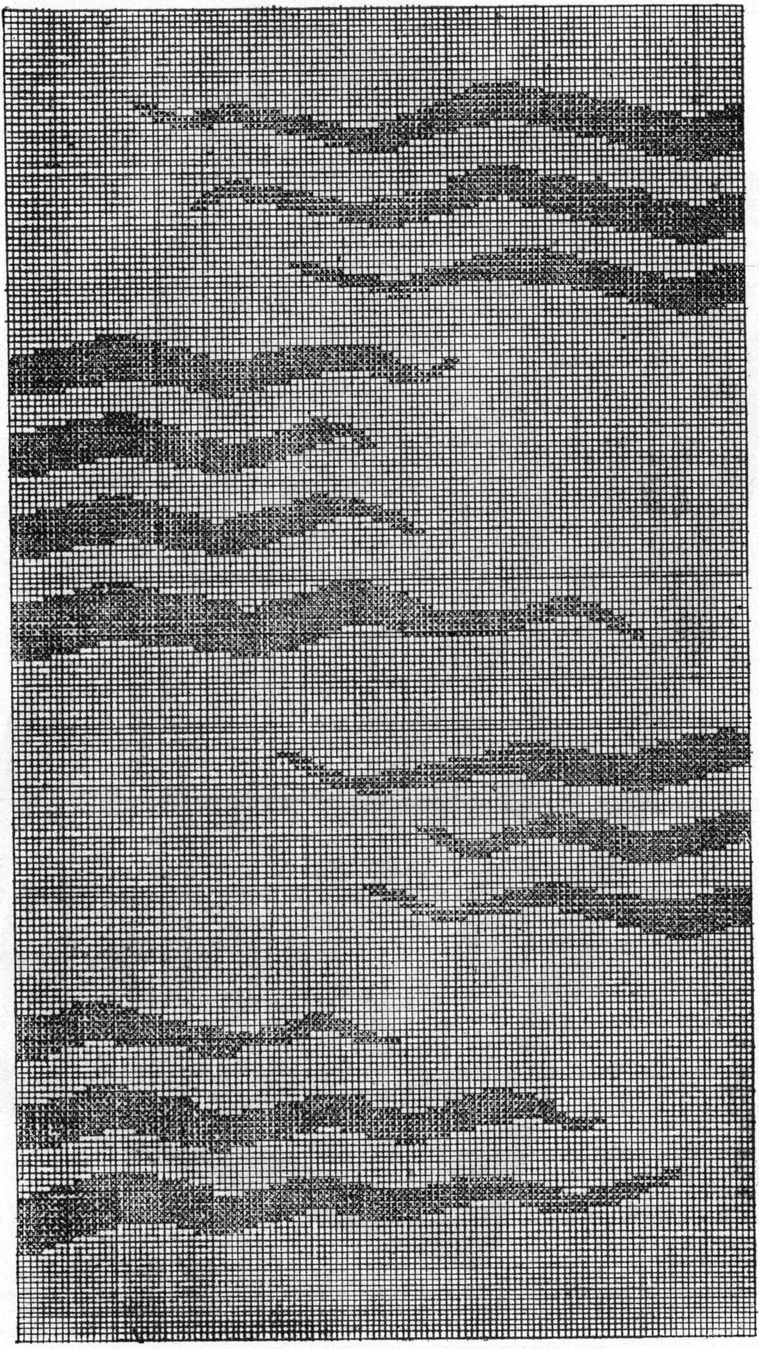

Fig. 15. Chart for the Modern Rug at the top of facing page.

FOR THE LOUNGE

Fig. 16.

"KHORASAN"— AN ORIENTAL DESIGN

A handsome rug ideal in design and colouring for the lounge or dining-room. In blue and red with a touch of yellow, brown and green, it will harmonise with almost any colour scheme.

is needed. The original rug took $3\frac{1}{2}$ lbs. of deep blue, $2\frac{3}{4}$ lbs. sand colour, $2\frac{1}{4}$ lbs. Oriental red, $\frac{3}{4}$ lb. each of apple green and maize yellow, $\frac{1}{2}$ lb. each of dark brown and azure blue. The rug measured 36 inches by 63 inches when finished and was worked by the hook method.

The amusing nursery rug (Fig. 17) is quite simple to make. The background is divided into sections of bright blue and cherry and the animals and ark are in greys and yellow. The size is 47 inches in diameter. Materials needed are: 3 lbs. of blue wool, 3 lbs. of cherry, $\frac{1}{4}$ lb. of grey, 1 lb. of light grey and 14 oz. of yellow and $1\frac{1}{2}$ yards of 54-inch rug canvas.

The Spring-type rug maker can be used in place of a hook. The wool is cut in even lengths as before. One of these lengths is folded in half. The ends, exactly level, are held in the left hand to form a loop. The rug hook is held in the right hand, the loop of the wool passed over it and the hook pushed through a hole in the canvas bringing it out in the hole immediately above. The spring of the hook is then pressed down, and the two cut ends evenly placed between the catch, while the spring is released, then the whole drawn back and a tight knot made. This stitch finished, the next is worked in the same way, and so on until the end of the row. With this method, too, the work must always follow the same direction.

In making a rug in this method, it is as well to bend the canvas a little, or to fold it along the row, so that the hook can easily be passed under the two threads of the canvas. Fig. 18 shows the stitch in the working. The same method can be followed using a coarse crochet hook instead of a spring hook.

FIG. 17. FOR THE NURSERY.

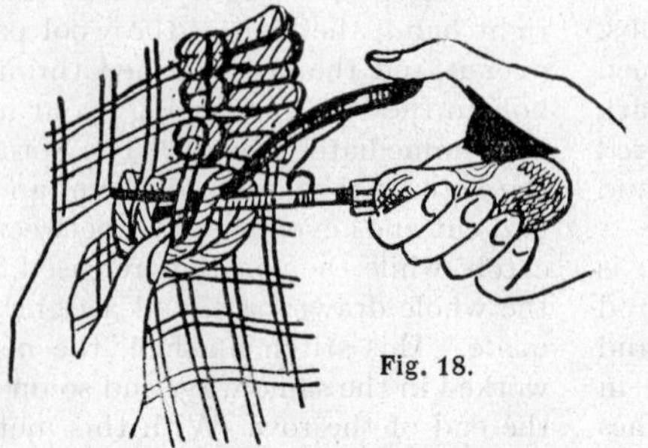

Fig. 18.

Left. The Spring-type Rugmaker can be used instead of a hook for making long-pile rugs.

Below. Chart for the circular rug illustrated on page 790. In this pattern alternate holes are left unworked as shown by the blank squares of the chart.

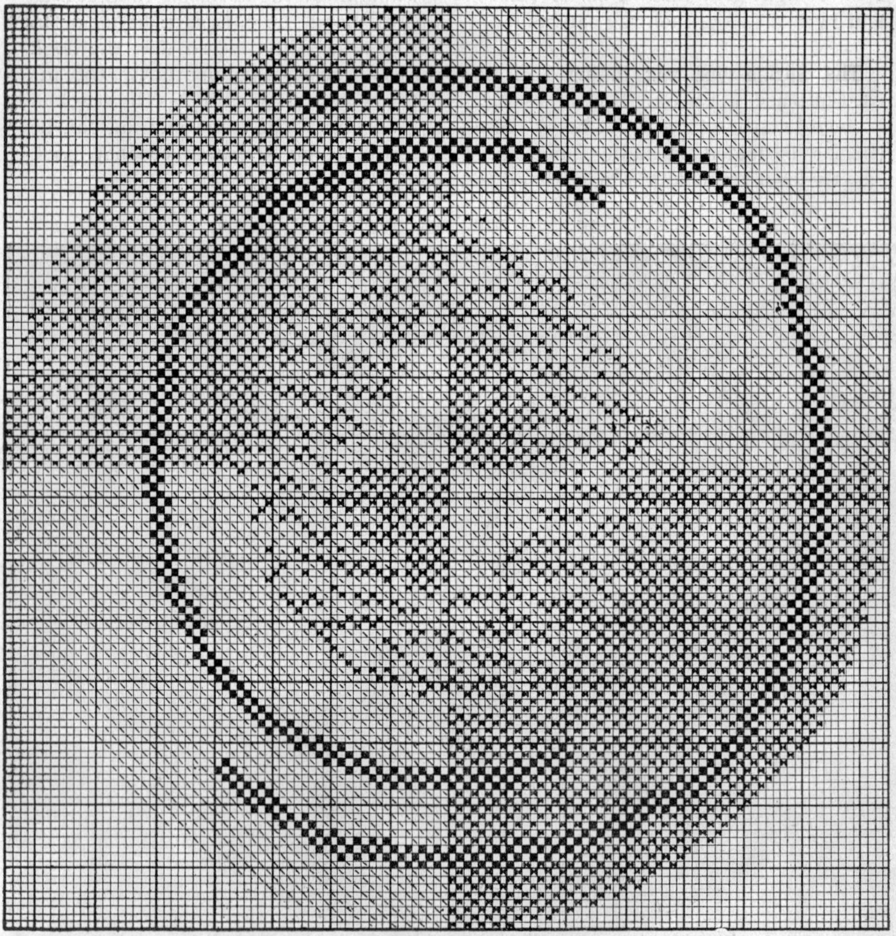

Black Chestnut Beige

Fig. 19.

CHEVRON DESIGN for a DOORMAT

Here is an attractive modern design for slip-mats for use at each door in a hall. The pattern is worked from the chart below and colouring can be chosen to fit in with any scheme. Notice how the chevrons and stars are effectively shadowed with a darker shade. The mat illustrated was worked in long-pile tufting, using 6-ply rug wool; the finished rug measured 14 inches wide by 30 inches long.

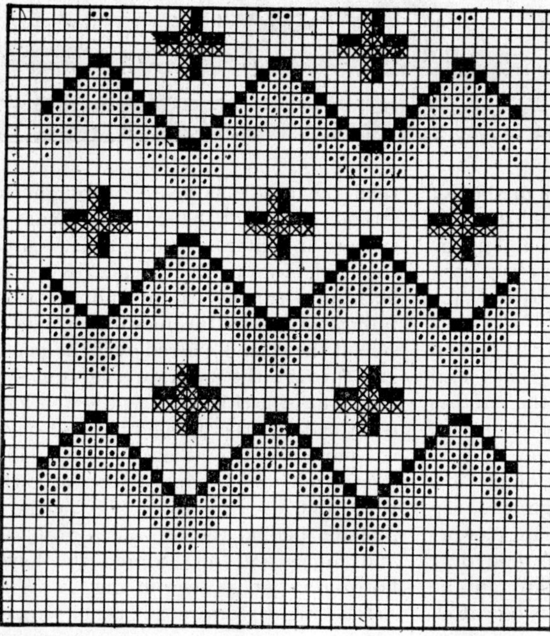

To make the mat allow 1 yard of 14-inch rug canvas, and of 6-ply rug wool, 1½ lbs. for background, ½ lb. for the chevrons, ¼ lb. for stars, and ¼ lb. of dark grey or any suitable colour for the shadows.

Chart for the Chevron Doormat illustrated above. Work in rows across the narrow way of the canvas starting from the base of the chart. When all the charted rows are completed, work the chevrons in reverse for the second half of the mat.

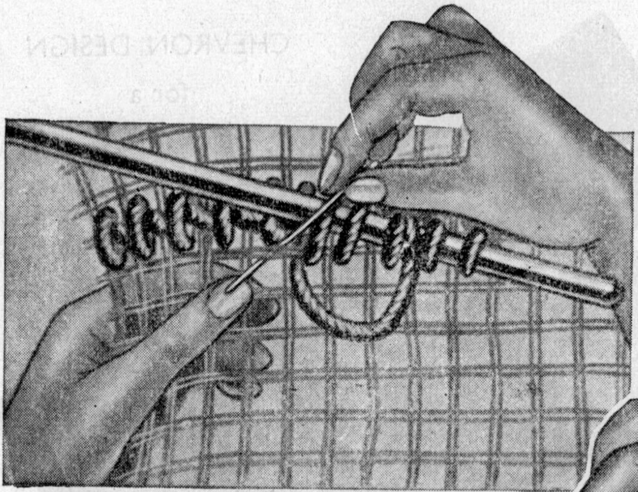

Fig. 21.

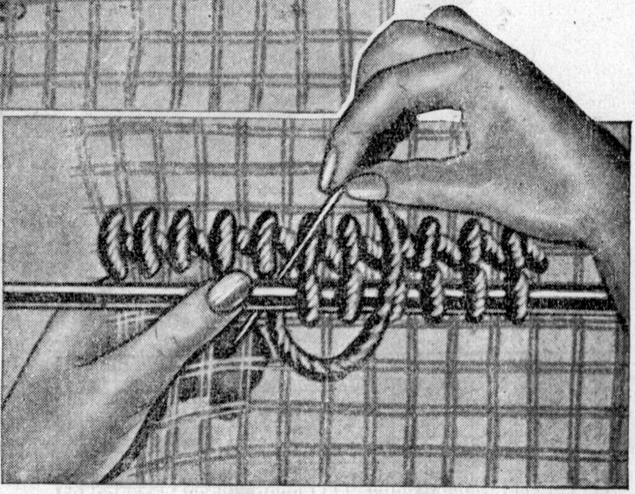

Fig. 20.

RUG MAKING WITH A NEEDLE

Loops are formed over a pencil or any thick round gauge to obtain a close even pile. The illustrations show the working in two stages.

Another quick and effective method of rugmaking in which the loops are made over a pencil or any thicker round gauge is illustrated above. Ordinary rug canvas is used, a rug needle with blunt point, and rug wool.

For Figs. 20 and 21, showing the pencil in its two positions, Berlin wool was used in order that the working of the stitches might be shown more clearly than with the thicker rug wool.

In starting the stitching, a long length of wool is threaded through the rug needle and the end fastened by passing the needle through the mesh and over the strand of canvas and through the mesh on the other side. This is repeated, then the needle is passed through the strands of wool at the back of the canvas two or three times. Having thus secured the end, the pencil is laid over the horizontal canvas strand and the wool brought through the mesh on the near side of the strand, passed over the pencil and through the mesh directly opposite on the far side (Fig. 20). So the first loop is formed and the needle is passed on to the next mesh, by making a little sideway stitch, which not only forwards the work, but also secures it. The needle is inserted behind the top horizontal bar, and comes out from behind the lower horizontal bar, as seen in Fig. 21. This stitch is tightly drawn, the pencil slipped

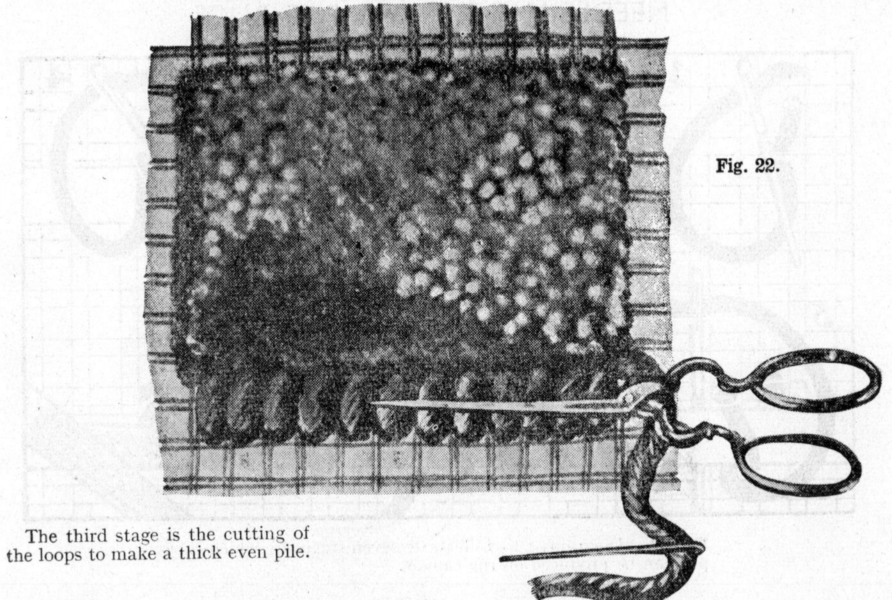

The third stage is the cutting of the loops to make a thick even pile.

back into its position over the strand and the wool passed over it again. This is repeated until the length of wool is finished, taking care that the last stitch is one beneath the pencil, and that the end is secured at the back of the canvas. A fresh length of wool is then taken and the same directions followed. It is best to work all rows from right to left in this method.

Using a pencil produces a short pile when the wool is cut. For a longer pile a larger gauge should be used, this method being equally good for long or short pile. When the work is actually being done with rug wool the rows come very closely together as the work proceeds, as can be seen from Fig. 22. It is easier to keep the pile even if the cutting is done each time the work is put away, but care must be taken not to cut within at least a row of the work still to be done.

If a pattern is worked, this can be done before the background, or worked in with it. The latter is usually the best method.

When the rug is finished, a strong lining of hessian, black linen or brown holland can be put at the back of the rug.

This type of rug is excellent for the method described on these pages.

NEEDLE-MADE SHORT PILE RUGS

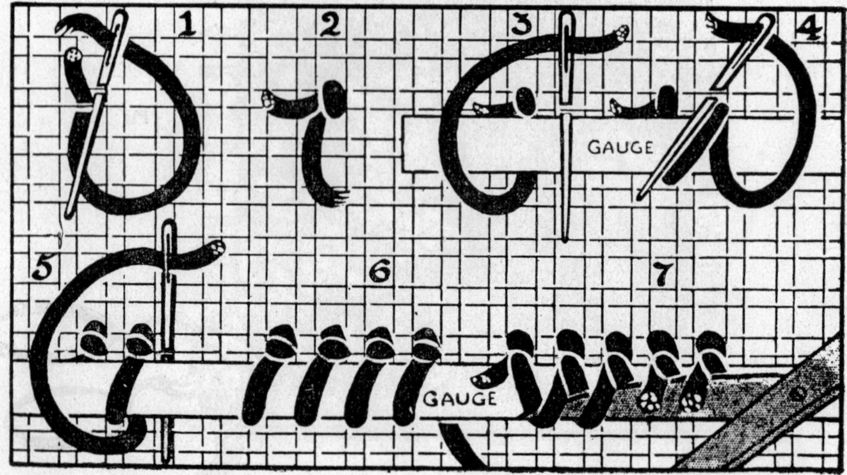

Fig. 23. Diagrams 1 to 7 illustrate seven stages by which short pile can be produced on rug canvas.

Short Pile Method.—By using this method the same effect is obtained as in the hook rugs, but as its name implies, this system gives a short pile, and therefore uses less wool—only about two-thirds the quantities quoted for the long pile. The way in which these rugs are worked is quite different. The idea of this method is, by continually using convenient lengths of wool, to make a number of even loops knotted on to the canvas.

A short pile gauge, scissors and short pile needles are required. The needles are not unlike packing needles, being about 2¾ inches long with a very large eye. One needle should be used for each colour in the design. The gauges are made of wood about ⅜ inch wide and 8 inches long.

To work:—Lay the canvas on the table and hold it in position with a weight so that the row to be worked lies exactly along the edge.

Thread one of the needles with a length of wool and beginning on the first row of the pattern (allowing about 2 inches of canvas for turning), work from left to right of the double weft (width-ways) threads of canvas. Inserting the needle in the lower thread of the first mesh, draw the wool through, and leave the free end the length of the width of the gauge. Holding the free end firm with the thumb of the left hand, insert the needle into the upper thread, so that the wool lies to the right of the needle, drawing the wool through to form a knot (Fig. 23/1 and 2).

Lay the gauge on the canvas, the upper part resting against the knot, pass the thread under and over the gauge, insert the needle in the lower thread of the next mesh, so that the wool lies to the left of the needle (Fig. 23/3), draw it through and insert the needle into the upper thread of the same mesh so that the wool then lies to the right of the needle (Fig. 23/4) and draw the wool through. The completion of these two stitches by pulling them tight makes a secure knot, from the left-hand side of which, when cut, come two ends forming one square of the design (Fig. 23/5). Repeat along the row (Fig. 23/6), working the various colours into the design as required.

When the thread is finished or the colour in the design changes, cut the end of the wool in use so that it is the same length as the width of the gauge. Thread the needle with the new length of wool and begin in the same way as at the start.

The rows are longer than the gauge, so that the latter must be moved along at intervals. When this is necessary, first cut the completed loops evenly with a pair of scissors (Fig. 23/7).

It is essential that the ends are cut exactly the same length as this saves unnecessary work in the finishing. When the rug is finished rub thoroughly with the hand across the surface so that any loose fluff is worked out, then clip lightly with a pair of sharp scissors to obtain an even surface. Turn back and sew the edges of the canvas and bind with a strong webbing about three inches wide.

Fig. 24 is quite a good example of the short pile method. For this rug 1 lb. 12 oz. of stone, 7 oz. dark brown, 12 oz. green and 13 oz. dull yellow are required, also needle and short pile gauge. It is worked exactly as just described.

Choice of Rug Designs.—For the methods described on this and the previous pages, all of which worked on ordinary rug canvas, almost any design can be used. Patterns can be prepared as detailed at the beginning of the chapter, or the canvas may be bought with a design ready stencilled on it—a wide variety is obtainable at most needlework shops for rugs of all sizes, and for both the rectangular and favourite semi-circular shape like the one illustrated below.

The usual proportions for a semi-circular rug are 54 inches long by 30 inches wide, for rectangular rugs 54 inches by 27 inches or 72 inches by 36 inches.

ATTRACTIVE RUG FOR THE SITTING-ROOM

made by the short pile method.

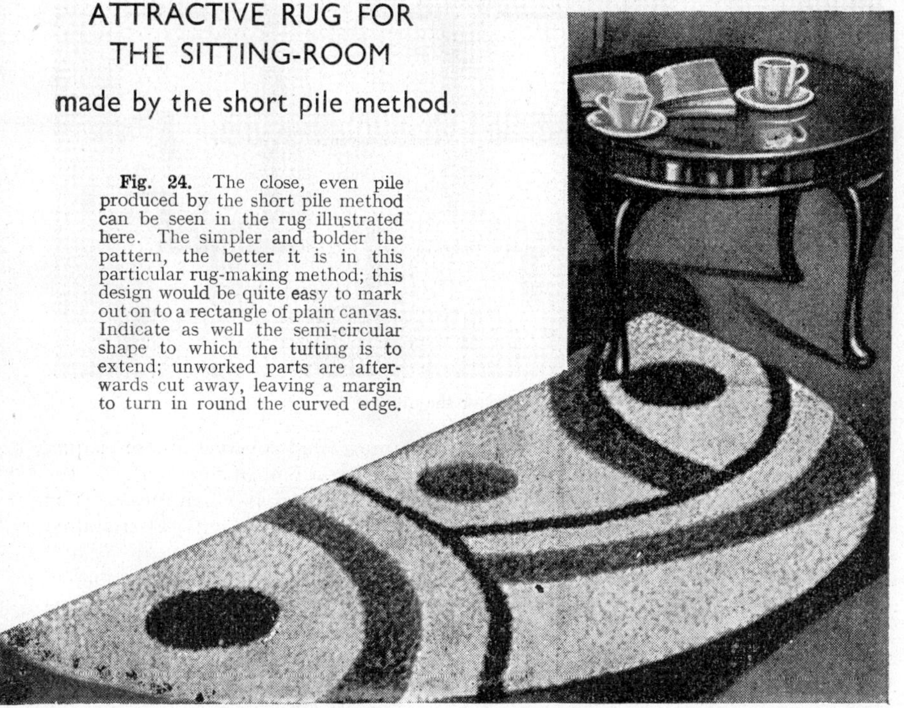

Fig. 24. The close, even pile produced by the short pile method can be seen in the rug illustrated here. The simpler and bolder the pattern, the better it is in this particular rug-making method; this design would be quite easy to mark out on to a rectangle of plain canvas. Indicate as well the semi-circular shape to which the tufting is to extend; unworked parts are afterwards cut away, leaving a margin to turn in round the curved edge.

When all rows in the chart have been completed, repeat from last row back to first for second half of rug, so that the "shadow" falls on the right-hand side throughout.

A BEAUTIFUL CHINESE RUG

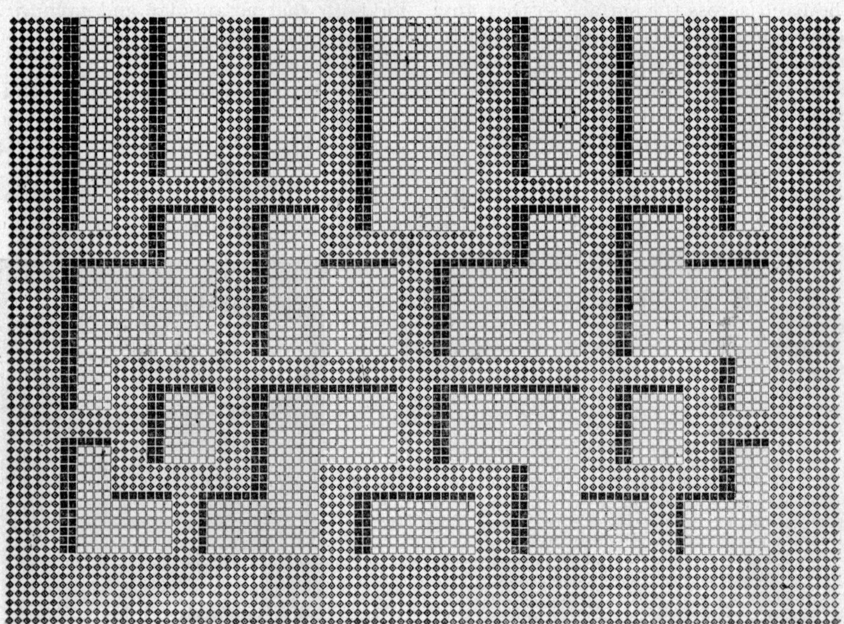

Fig. 25. Chart for the Chinese rug.

Traditional Chinese patterning lends elegance to the rug illustrated above. This is the perfect design for a hall, for a small sitting-room, or a bedroom. The simple colouring can be worked out to suit any colour scheme, as the design is merely in one colour attractively "shadowed" with a deeper shade, on a neutral background. The original rug had a warm beige ground, and, for the patterning, that lovely Cinhese-lacquer red that has a hint of rust.

To make the rug, which measures 27 inches by 40 inches, materials required are $1\frac{1}{4}$ yards of 27-inch wide canvas, and best quality 6-ply rug wool in the following quantities: background, 2 lbs.; pattern, $3\frac{3}{4}$ lbs.; shadow, $\frac{3}{4}$ lb.

The rug is made by the long-pile method as described on pages 788 and 789.

RUGS IN CROSS-STITCH

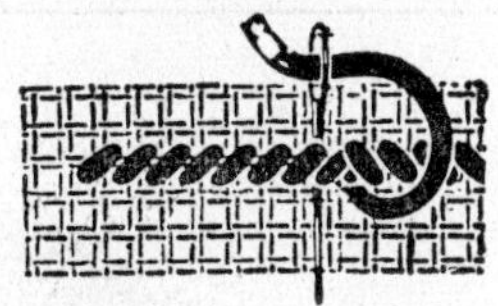

Fig. 26. Cross-stitch.

Cross-stitch rugs are another variety which are very useful, and which at the same time can look most attractive. They are very suitable for the nursery, kitchen or bathroom as they are easy to wash.

A cross-stitch rug is made on ordinary canvas and 6-ply rug wool is the best to use. The wool is used in lengths threaded in a specially large blunt needle with a very big eye. Any rug design can be used for this method, working from charts on stencilled canvases.

The working of cross-stitch is very simple and is clearly shown in Fig. 26. Bring the threaded needle up through a hole and draw it through until two inches of wool are left at the back. The end is held down by the stitches, the same being done with the end when the needleful of wool is finished, and each time a new thread is started. Now make a stitch slanting upwards to the right by taking the needle down in the next row of holes to the right, one row above where the needle first came out. Bring the needle up in the hole immediately below the one it has just gone into. This makes a short stitch on the back, and when repeated to the end of the row, the result is a succession of neat upright stitches on the back. The work is sometimes finished at this stage which is known as half cross-stitch. A good effect is obtained when a rug is worked entirely in this method.

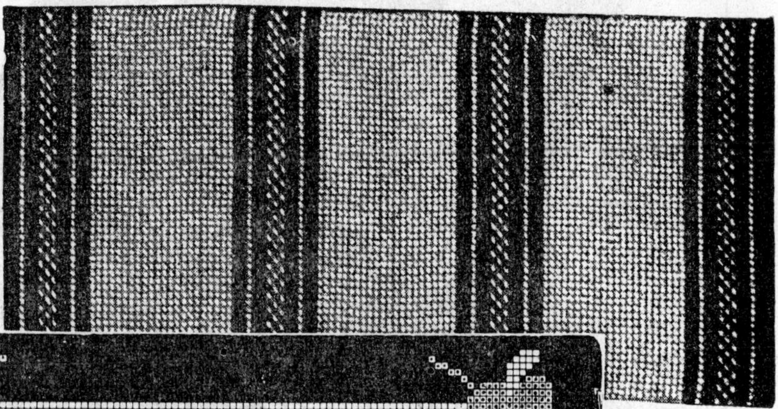

Fig. 27. Small rug worked in cross-stitch. The pattern could be copied from this illustration.

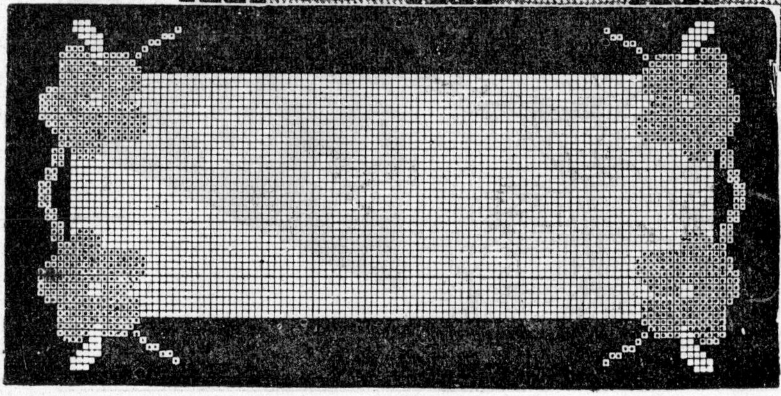

Fig. 28. Chart of a simple design suitable for cross-stitch.

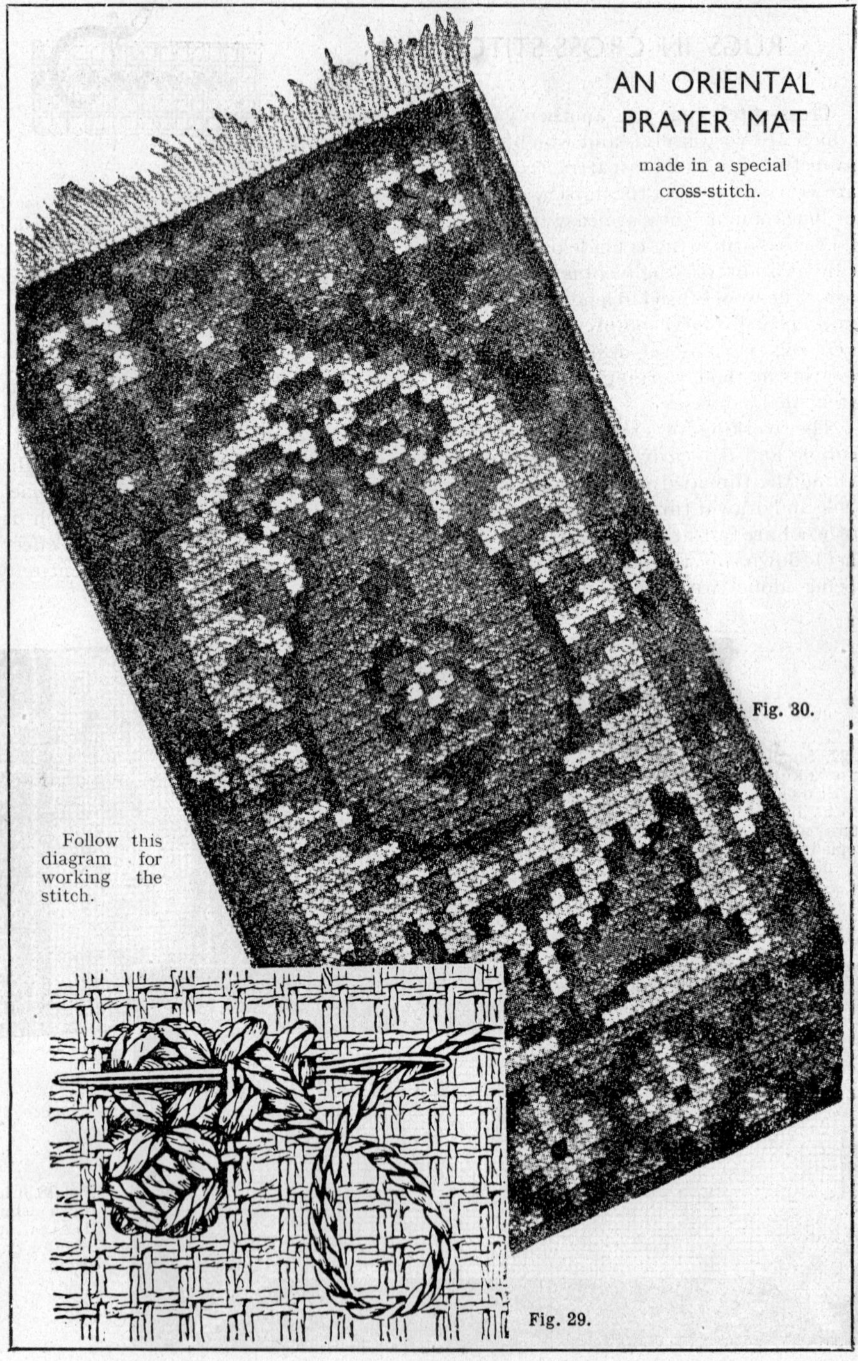

AN ORIENTAL PRAYER MAT

made in a special cross-stitch.

Fig. 30.

Follow this diagram for working the stitch.

Fig. 29.

To cross the stitch, however, the procedure is repeated in the contrary direction over the row just worked, which means that each stitch is covered with another so that complete crosses are formed. It is most important that all the stitches throughout the rug should cross in the same direction.

When working a rug with straight edges, it is best to count out the number of squares needed, and to turn in, working the first rows through double canvas. With a shaped rug, work the pattern first, then turn the canvas edges on to the wrong side when the cross-stitch is complete, and face with webbing. Care must be taken not to pull the canvas out of shape when working in any of the needle methods. This can be avoided by keeping the tension loose and pressing the rug from time to time on the wrong side under a damp cloth. A final press with a damp cloth must be given to the finished rug.

Should the canvas show at all along the turned-in edge, whip over with the wool, making one stitch in each hole. Do this right round, then come back in the opposite direction, working across and over the stitches made in the first journey.

Another variation of cross-stitch is shown in Fig. 29. A rug worked in this method is seen in Fig. 30.

The basic cross is made over four double threads of canvas in width and height, then a small stitch is made at each corner, crossing each arm, so that the one completed square of colour has almost the effect of four crosses. Large rug needles are needed. These rugs are usually worked in 2-ply wool which is used double throughout, but sometimes 4-ply is used and then it is worked singly. Ordinary rug canvas is used as the base for this rug. Fig. 29 shows the working of the stitch.

In the chart (Fig. 31) every square represents one large cross. The pattern makes a rug 18 inches wide by 32 inches long. Finish the edge of the canvas by whipping over and over with wool.

Fig. 31. The Chart for the Oriental Design on the opposite page. Each square represents one of the cross-stitches shown in Fig. 29.

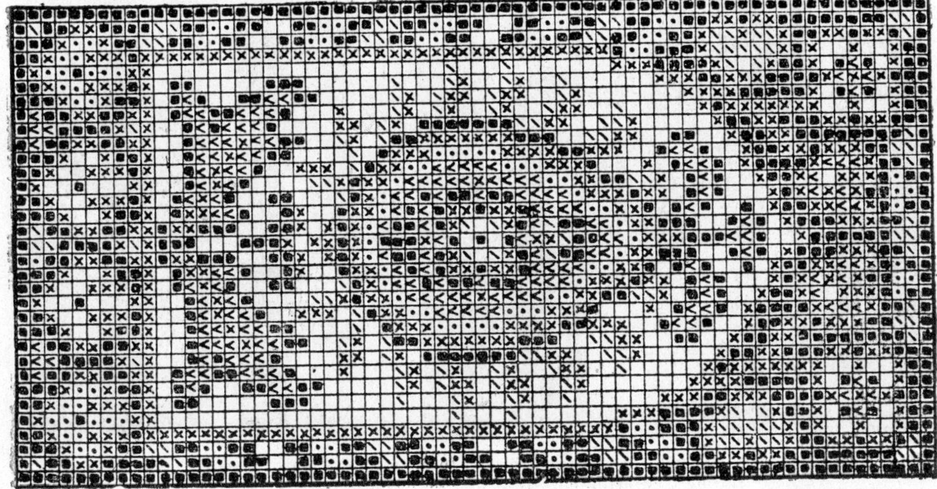

PATTERN in PILE—GROUND in CROSS-STITCH

Long-pile tufting combined with cross-stitch which gives a flat surface gives an interesting texture contrast. The effect is modern, and accords well with the new furnishing fabrics, which often have the pattern indicated by change of texture rather than change of colour.

Below is shown a very simple design for this method, composed of stripes of tufting in three shades used in turn, on a cross-stitch background worked with one colour only; the ends are fringed with the background colour. The width the stripes are made would depend on the size of the finished rug—for the average 27-inch wide hearth-rug about four rows of tufting interspersed by eight rows of cross-stitch would be suitable.

Work the cross-stitch stripes first, then fill in the tufting which is worked as described on pages 788 and 789. Finish ends by knotting in lengths of wool to make a fringe.

The Hiawatha rug on the facing page has the design in red, brown and off-white on a dusky fawn background bordered with thick off-white fringe. The pattern is tufted on a flat cross-stitch background in the same way as the striped rug below. Of 6-ply rug wool, 2 lbs. of the background colour are needed, also ½ lb. each red and off-white and ¼ lb. brown. Allow 1½ yards of 27-inch plain rug canvas, for a rug size 27 inches by about 50 inches, including the fringe.

Cut 192 10-inch pieces of off-white for fringe, then cut rest of white, red and brown wool into pieces of even length by winding the wool on a standard-width rug gauge and cutting along one side; following the charts on facing page, tuft three diamonds across centre of canvas with six of the other motifs each side 12 holes away. Fill in background with crosses, one over every double crossing of the canvas, using conveniently long strands of wool and a rug needle. Ten rows beyond pattern, turn under rest of canvas, leaving one pair of threads projecting, along which work the fringe. Back rug with hessian.

Fig. 32. The raised stripes of this rug are worked in long-pile tufting, contrasting effectively with the flat cross-stitch background.

Fig. 33. The Hiawatha Rug. This pattern is worked in long-pile tufting, in red, brown and off-white on a flat cross-stitch background in dusky fawn. The fringed ends are also in off-white.

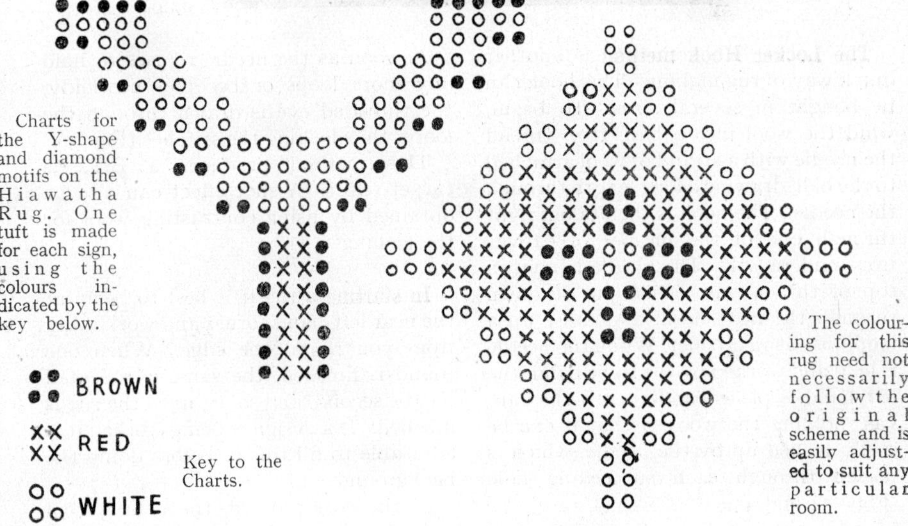

Charts for the Y-shape and diamond motifs on the Hiawatha Rug. One tuft is made for each sign, using the colours indicated by the key below.

Key to the Charts.

The colouring for this rug need not necessarily follow the original scheme and is easily adjusted to suit any particular room.

THE LOCKER HOOK METHOD

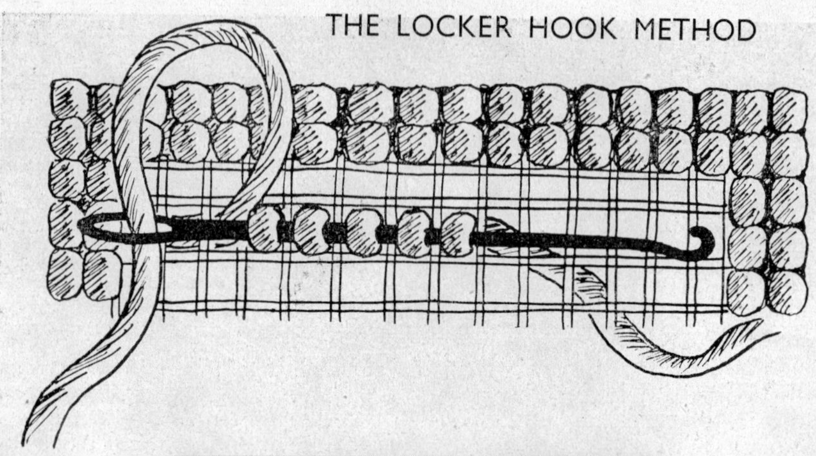

Fig. 34. The diagram above shows at a glance how the Locker Hook operates.

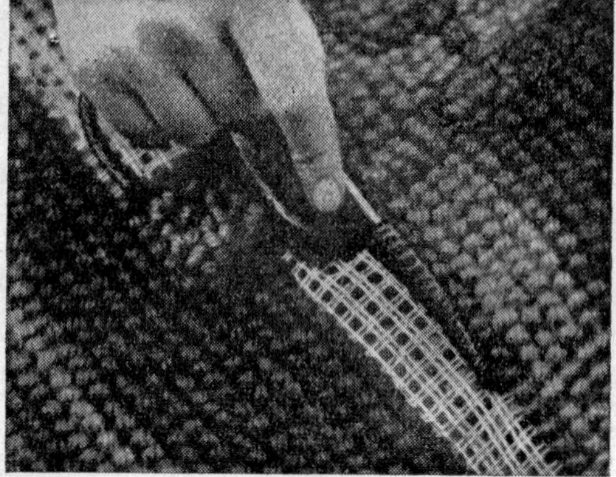

Fig. 35. In this photograph a row of loops has been picked up ready to be "locked" as in Fig. 36. The hook is drawn through the loops, carrying with it the threads that "locks" the loops to the canvas.

The Locker Hook method is another quick way of rug making. This hook can be bought in several sizes. To begin, wind the wool into a ball, then thread the needle with a strand of wool attached to the ball, drawing a long length through the needle. The hook is then taken right through one of the meshes of canvas from underneath. The needle is now on top of the canvas. Then put it down through the next mesh and draw up a loop, just as in crochet. While the needle is held and worked by the right hand; the left hand is placed underneath the canvas, holding the wool so that it can be easily picked up by the needle, which is placed through each succeeding hole (Figs. 34 and 35).

As soon as the needle refuses to hold any more loops or becomes unwieldy, the threaded eye is drawn through the loops, thus locking the stitches (Fig. 36).

This method produces a Brussels carpet effect. A shot effect can also be obtained by using contrasting wool for the locking.

In starting a rug it is best to begin at the near left-hand corner and work away from you round the edge. When one round is finished, the same is repeated for the second, and so on, until the rug is finished. If a design is being worked it is advisable to fill this in before doing the background.

As the work proceeds the locking wool

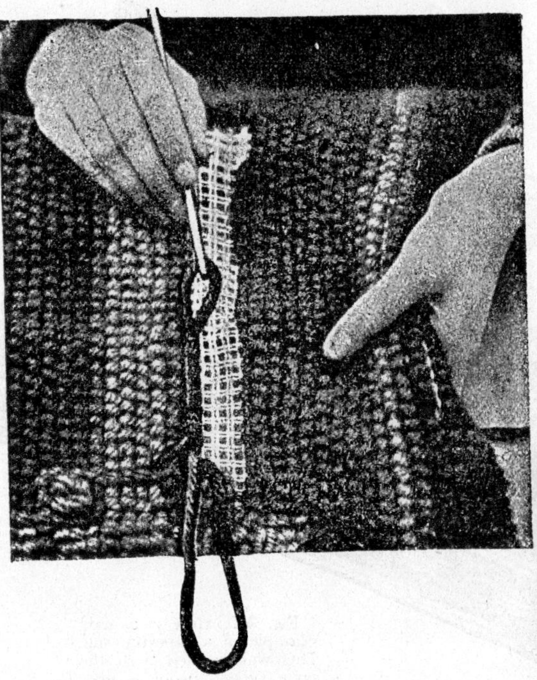

Fig. 36. Here the Locker Hook had been drawn through the loops; the thread is pulled still further through until the lower loop in the illustration disappears.

Fig. 37. The pattern in the chart below is suited ideally for the Locker Hook method and makes an average-size slip mat.

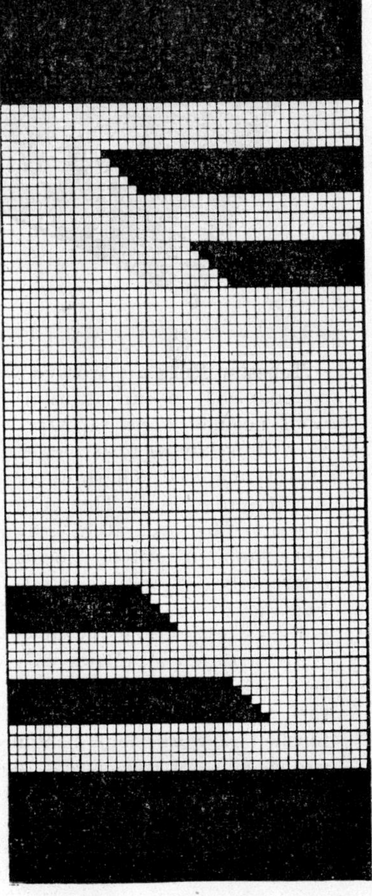

becomes used up. Another long strand is then cut from a ball of the same colour; this is stitched to the end of the used locking wool. If the wool is joined in this way, all knots are avoided, and there is nothing to interfere with the smoothness and evenness of the work when finished.

It is quite a good idea to make a border of one colour and then introduce it into the centre by using it for the locking thread.

Approximately a ¼ lb. of wool covers a square foot of rug canvas with this method. Considerable saving can be made when working with thick wool by using fine wool for the locking of the loops.

TAPESTRY RUGS

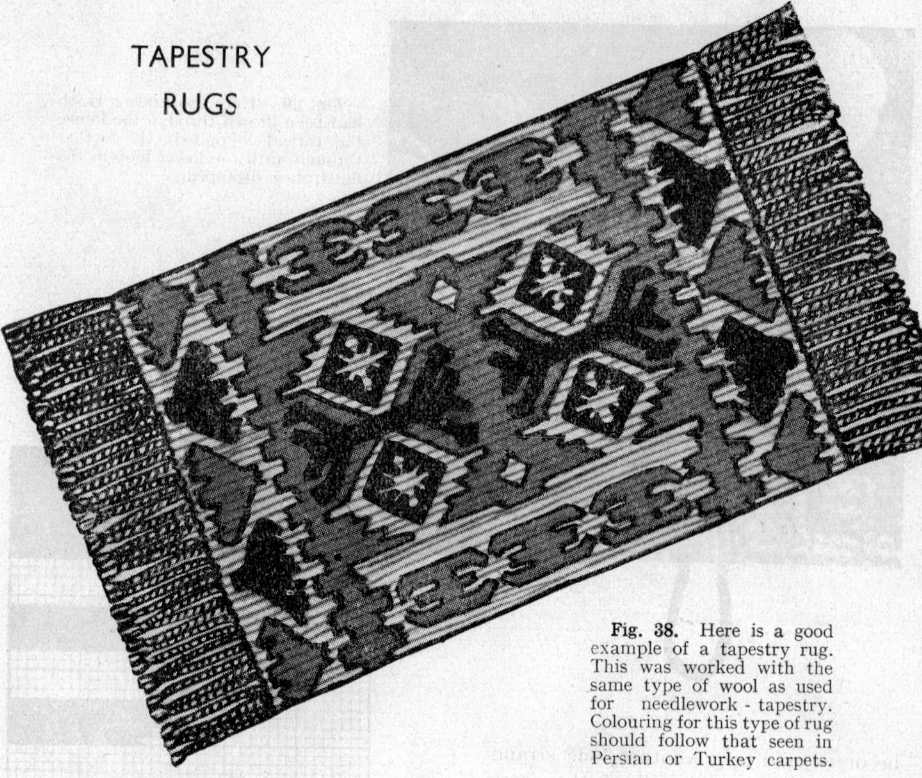

Fig. 38. Here is a good example of a tapestry rug. This was worked with the same type of wool as used for needlework - tapestry. Colouring for this type of rug should follow that seen in Persian or Turkey carpets.

Tapestry Rugs are worked with wool on coarse Java canvas using ordinary wool needles. The tapestry stitch is worked in slanting rows over two squares of the material length-ways and one square crossways. The pattern must therefore be accurately planned out. The rows of stitches being worked alternately up and down are seen in Figs. 39 and 40. Figs. 41 and 42 show how to work slanting outlines.

To carry out a pattern, first work all the outlines of the design (Fig. 43) and then proceed with the filling. When finished the work should be ironed on the wrong side. Large pieces should be worked in a frame, and when finished the wrong side should be damped slightly and left until dry before removing from the frame. In order to stiffen the work, add a weak solution of gum arabic to the water before damping. The rugs can be lined with hessian.

The rug in Fig. 38 measures 40 inches in length without the fringe and 25 inches in width. The woollen fringes, which are knotted on, are 4 inches long. Work on coarse canvas with rug wool, beginning as usual with the outlines. When the work is finished damp as previously described. A design of Persian or Turkish origin should be chosen as these patternings are usually geometric in form. A design from a carpet could be adapted successfully for smaller rugs to use at hearth and door. Also it is possible to adapt squared charted patterns to this method if each V of stitches is counted as one square of the pattern.

TAPESTRY STITCH

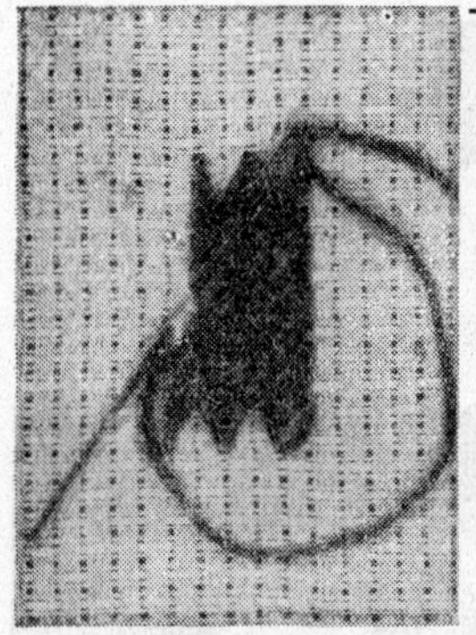

Fig. 39.

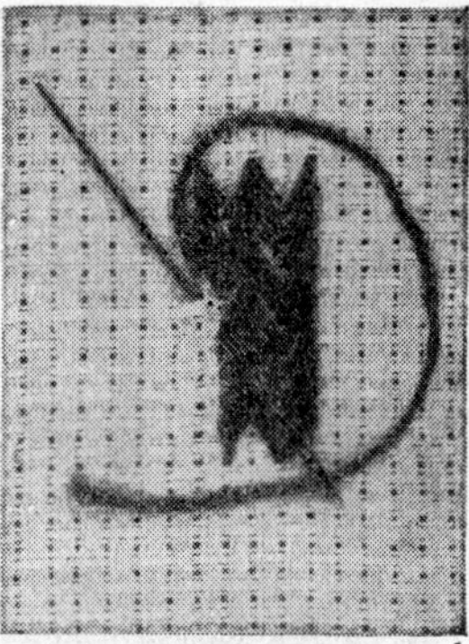

Fig. 40.

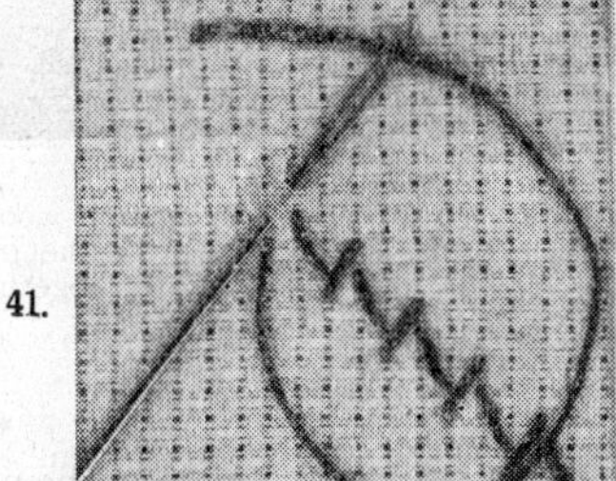

Fig. 41.

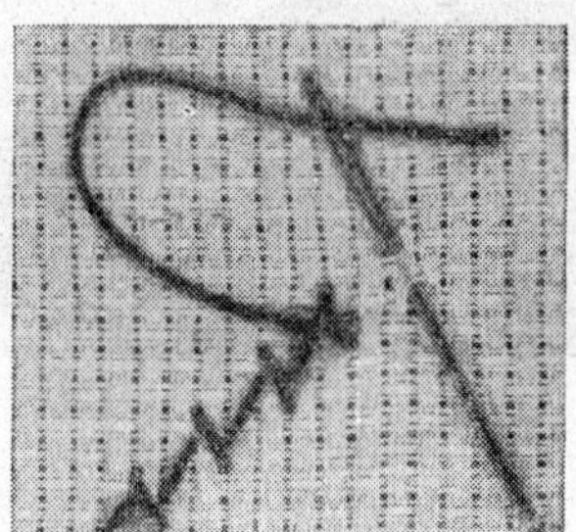

Fig. 42.

Fig. 43.

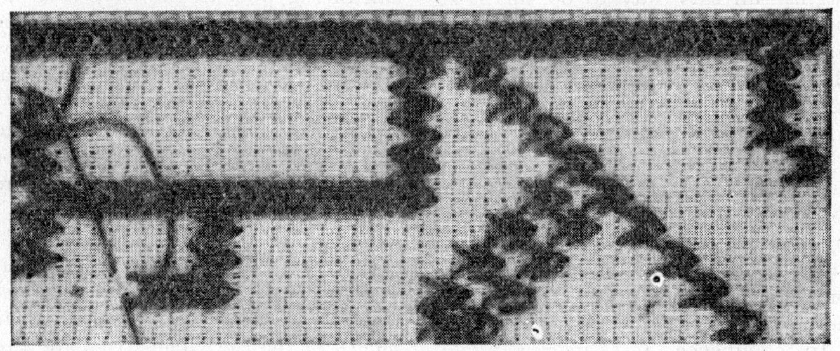

Fig. 39 shows the first row of tapestry-stitch worked upwards, and Fig. 40 the second, worked downwards. Figs, 41 and 42 show lines being worked upwards diagonally to the right and left. Fig. 43 shows the pattern outlined before the background is filled in,

Note These stitches were worked with fine thread in order to show the detail clearly; when actually making a rug use tapestry wool of a thickness that will cover the canvas well.

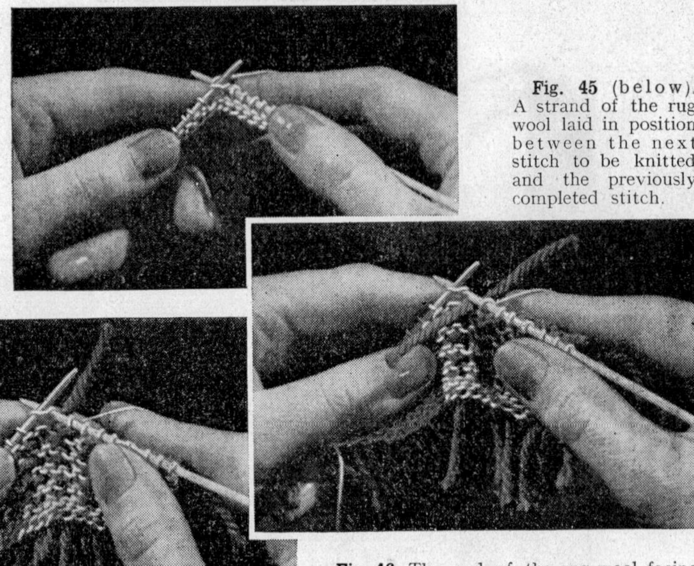

Fig. 44. Showing how the knitting is commenced for the start of the rug, using the knitting cotton only.

Fig. 45 (below). A strand of the rug wool laid in position between the next stitch to be knitted and the previously completed stitch.

Fig. 46. The end of the rug wool facing the worker has been taken to the pile side, so that the two ends stand up together.

Knitted or Smyrna Rugs have a knitted foundation worked on long steel needles with strong knitting cotton, and into this foundation are worked cut lengths of 6-ply rug wool to form the pile. The wool should be cut into 2½-inch lengths—an easy way to do this is to wind it round a 1¼-inch strip of stiff cardboard, then cut the wool along one edge only. When making patterned rugs from a chart, count each knitted-in piece of rug wool as one square of the design.

Using No. 13 knitting needles, a tension of four stitches to the inch is produced, so that for a 12-inch wide slip-mat 48 stitches are cast on, plus one stitch, as an uneven number is required; for every extra inch needed cast on four more stitches.

To commence a 12-inch slip-mat, cast on 49 stitches with the cotton and knit two rows plain (Fig. 44).

3rd row—(wrong side)—Knit 1, * place a length of rug wool between the needles, centralising it as in Fig. 45, then carry cotton over back half of rug wool and knit the next stitch. Now take front half of rug wool to the back (Fig. 46), carry cotton over this half and knit next stitch; repeat from * to end of row.

4th row—Knit plain. Repeat the last two rows till work measures about 30 inches, knit one more row with cotton and cast off. Trim the ends of the pile evenly, and if necessary pass a hot iron over the back of the rug.

For wider rugs the knitting can be done in conveniently wide strips (three 12-inch wide strips for a 36-inch wide rug); each strip can extend the full length of the rug. The strips are afterwards sewn together with the cotton.

CROCHET RUGS

Crochet Rugs have the advantage of not needing a canvas foundation. These rugs are reversible, and are excellent for bathrooms, nurseries or sun porches.

The stitch is simple, as ordinary double crochet is worked throughout, always passing the hook under both loops of the stitch in the previous row (Fig. 47). This gives extra firmness to the rug and also makes it reversible.

In working these rugs it is advisable to work them in small sections which can afterwards be joined with strong wax thread; this makes it easier to work, for if it is a large rug it is inclined to become very heavy. These rugs are made with ordinary rug wool.

The edges should always be kept straight, otherwise they will not join well. It is a help to make two chain stitches to turn at the end of each row, then miss the first stitch in the next row. At the end of the row make one into the turning chain of the previous row. This makes up for the stitch which was missed.

Here is a circular crochet rug made all in one piece which is very easy for beginners (Fig. 48). Seven hanks each of red, jade, brown and fawn, and five hanks of yellow wool are needed, also a bone crochet hook, No. 2.

Using fawn start in the centre with 4 chain; join into ring with slip-stitch.

1st round.—Work 2 double crochet into each of the 4 chain. Continue working double crochet round and round, increasing as many stitches as required in each round to keep the work flat (to increase, work 2 double crochet into a stitch). Use one hank of each colour until about a third of the rug is done (roughly 12 inches across). After that work two rounds in each colour alternately until the rug is finished. Press the rug well under a damp cloth.

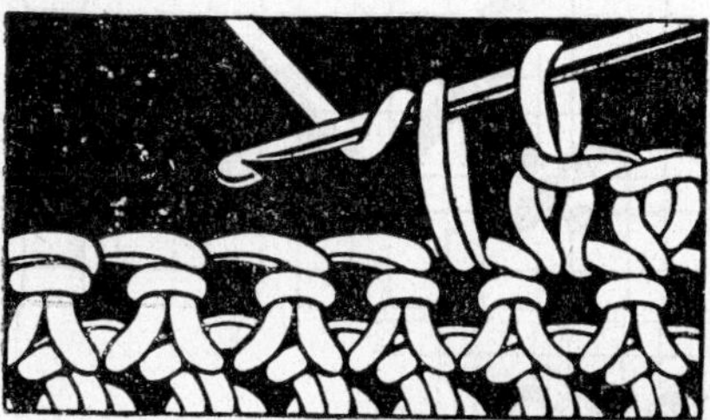

Fig. 47. This diagram shows how the double crochet is worked. each new stitch passing under both of the loops of a stitch in the previous row.

Fig. 48. A circular rug crocheted in bands of five colours, Full instructions for making this rug are given above; colours can be adjusted to suit any scheme

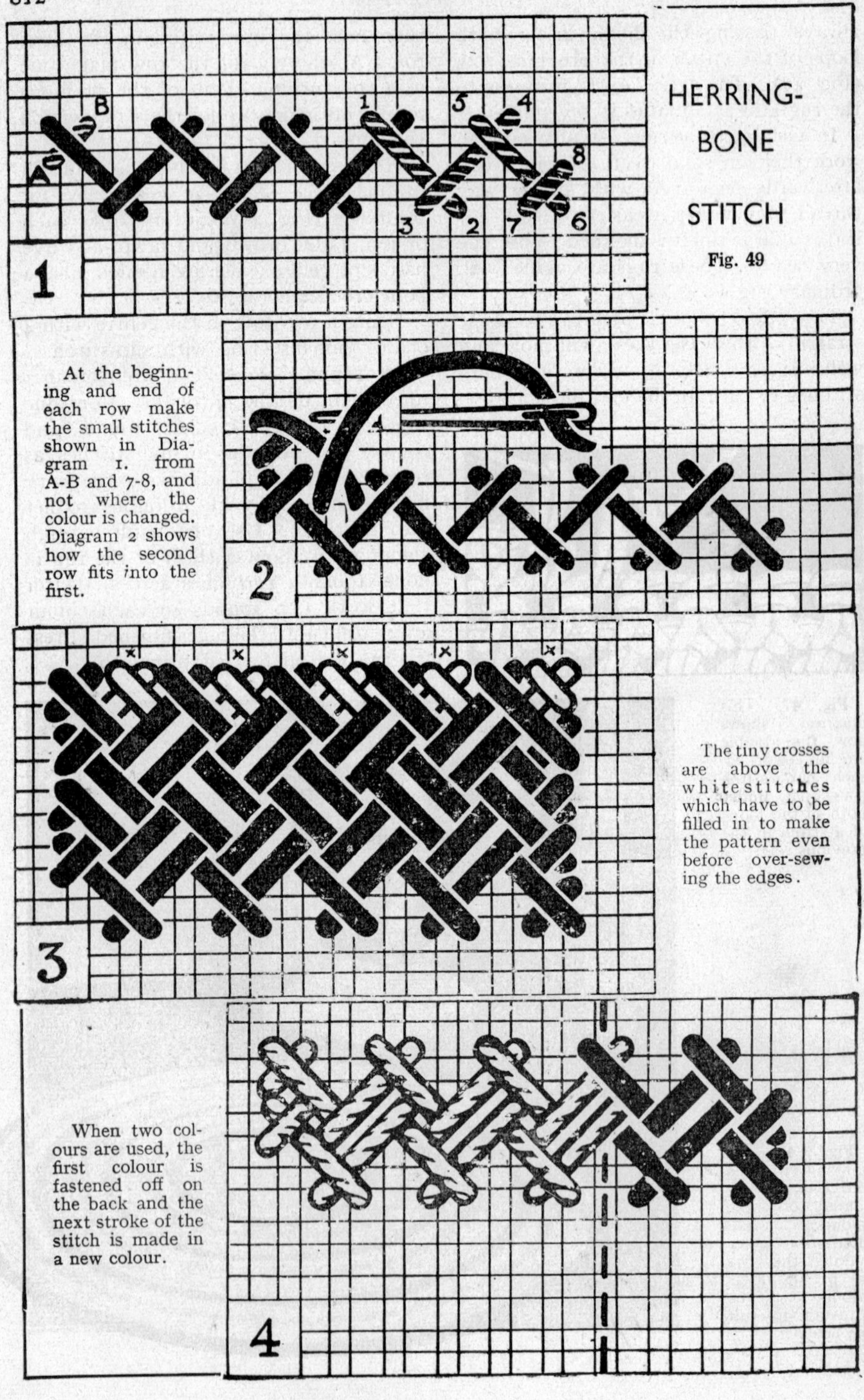

HERRING-BONE STITCH

Fig. 49

At the beginning and end of each row make the small stitches shown in Diagram 1. from A-B and 7-8, and not where the colour is changed. Diagram 2 shows how the second row fits *into* the first.

The tiny crosses are above the white stitches which have to be filled in to make the pattern even before over-sewing the edges.

When two colours are used, the first colour is fastened off on the back and the next stroke of the stitch is made in a new colour.

HERRINGBONE STITCH METHOD

Herringbone makes a pleasing rug which looks exactly like basket work when finished. It is worked in rows of stitches backwards and forwards across the canvas at right angles at the selvedges, and is quite easy to do.

To work the Stitch.—Make the small stitches shown in Diagram 1, Fig. 49, from A to B and from 7 to 8 at the beginning and end of each row, and not when changing the colour. For the second row turn the work upside-down and work back along the row. Diagram 2 shows how the stitches fit in with the previous row. When the first and last rows are worked there are spaces left between the herringbone stitches. These have to be filled in with small cross-stitches, the cross of which must be in the same direction as that of the herring-bone (Diagram 3). The changing of the different colour wool is shown in Diagram 4. Fasten off the first colour at the back and make the next part of the stitch in the new colour. If a geometrical design is being worked, the changing of the colour should be kept in line.

RUGS ON HESSIAN

Rugs on Hessian are the quickest and easiest rugs made. The base of the rug is a piece of hessian upon which the design is traced. The work is most often done with a 6-ply wool, though finer wools are also used. The wool is wound into balls before starting the work. The wool is worked into the hessian with a special little tool, known as a rug-maker or needle, the action of which is to take the wool through the hessian, and then withdraw it again, leaving a loop on the other side. A succession of these loops when cut forms the pile of the rug.

There are several kinds of rug-makers. For those shown overleaf the wool is threaded down the hollow inside and the needle is worked with the right hand, while the hessian is held with the left. The wool is not cut into lengths, but feeds direct from the ball wound in the usual way.

To work the rug, hold the hessian with the design uppermost, and starting near the middle of the mat, work away from you in straight rows, or following the design. Place the needle, eye down, and point on the hessian, then push the needle through right up to the hilt,

Fig. 50. A rug made on hessian by the method illustrated in Figs. 51 to 54 overleaf

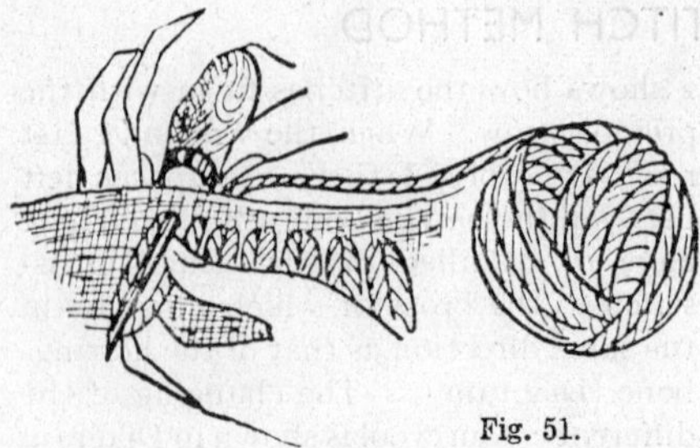

Fig. 51.

Pull the end of the first stitch through to the back; after that pull the needle back and push it in again about four threads farther on (Figs. 51 and 52). Do not lift the point of the needle right off the material as to do so slightly alters the length of the pile. At the end of the row turn the work and cut through the row of loops with sharp scissors, as shown in Fig. 53.

Fig. 52.

Figs. 51 and 52 show the method of working on hessian. The needle is held eye downwards and pushed through to the hilt, then withdrawn and the needle re-inserted 3 or 4 threads ahead of the last stitch.

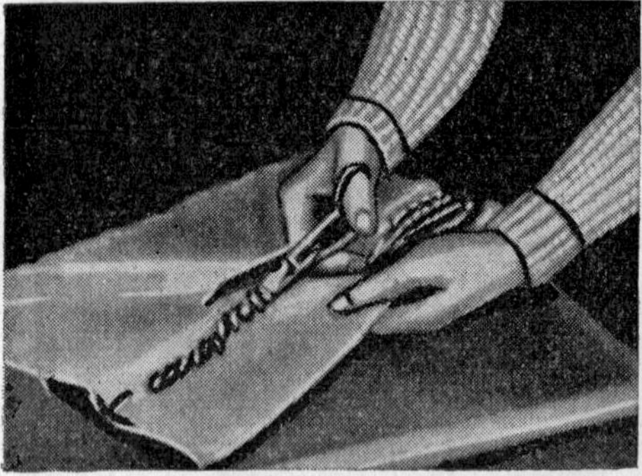

Fig. 54.
Brush over the back of the work with thick starch before the hessian backing is stitched in place.

When the work is finished, go over it and replace any stitches which mayhave been pulled out, then back the rug with fine black hessian or linen. Even a few days' wear will intermix the cut ends in such a way as to make them quite firm, but if any doubt remains on this point, a thick starch can be made and rubbed into the back of the mat before the backing is stitched on (Fig. 54), or an adhesive backing which sinks into the back of the rug can be ironed on.

Points to Remember.—See that the first stitch of each row is pulled right through and that the wool runs freely through the needle. Cut each row as it is finished or you may stick the needle into a loop and pull it out. Practise a few rows before starting the actual mat, to get an even movement and test the length of pile as most needles have a gauge to set this.

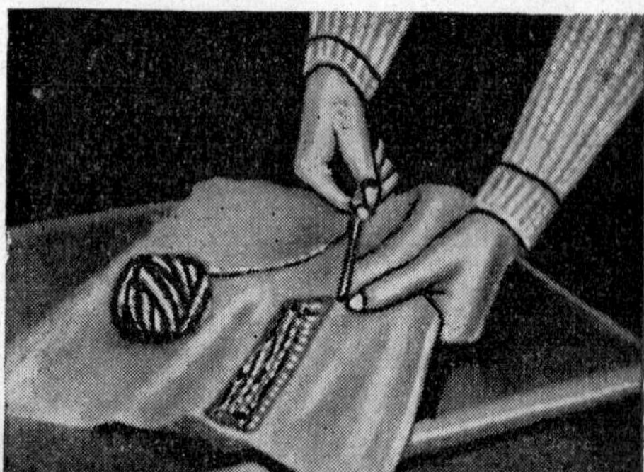

Fig. 53.
At the end of each row the work is turned over and the loops cut through before the next row is begun.

There is another hessian style in which the pile, instead of being one height over the whole surface, is a little shorter along the outlines of the pattern, thus bringing the design into relief (Fig. 56).

Tightly twisted 2-ply rug wool is used, three strands together (Fig. 55), which produces a firm pile as necessary to avoid the pattern-outline grooves treading out in wear.

The actual working is as for the ordinary hessian method except that the outlines of the pattern, and of the background meeting the pattern, are worked first and the pile of these rows is afterwards shaved down lower than the rest of the rug: alternatively the groove rows can be *worked* shorter than the rest by using a needle that is adjustable, to produce various lengths of loops; some needles have screw-on points—one for short pile and one for long.

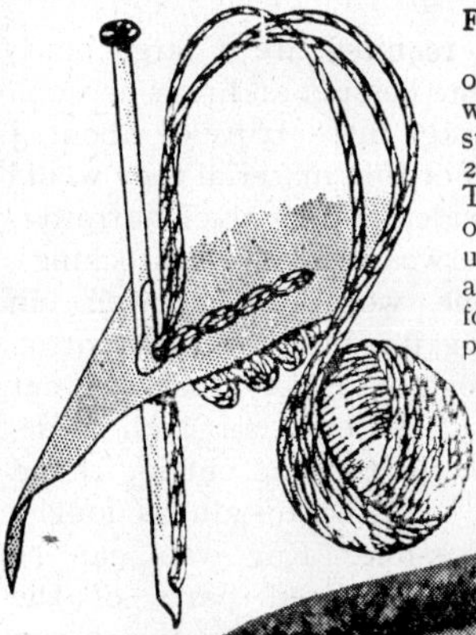

Fig. 55. Working on hessian with three strands of 2-ply wool, The loops on the underside are cut to form the pile.

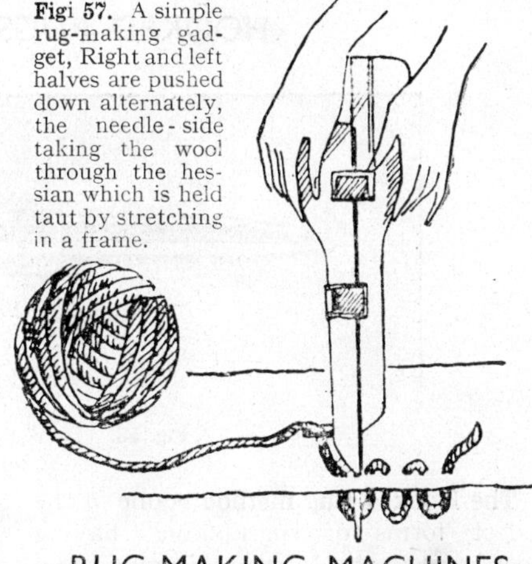

Figi 57. A simple rug-making gadget, Right and left halves are pushed down alternately, the needle-side taking the wool through the hessian which is held taut by stretching in a frame.

RUG-MAKING MACHINES

Various types of rug machines have been invented for making rugs on hessian. These produce loops like those made by the hand-prodded type of needle in Figs. 51 and 55, but aim at speedier working. Types range from simple gadgets like the one illustrated above, to a model that screws on to the edge of a table and is foot-operated below. Full instructions for use are supplied with each machine.

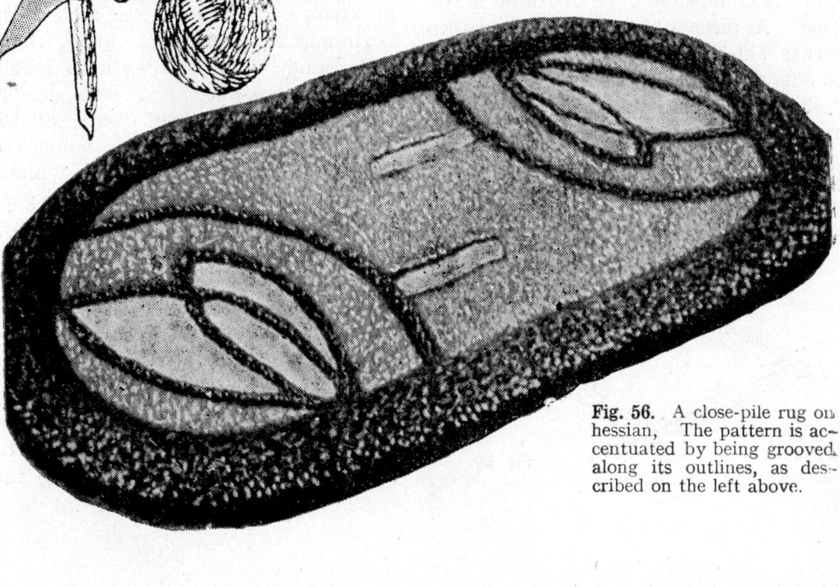

Fig. 56. A close-pile rug on hessian, The pattern is accentuated by being grooved along its outlines, as described on the left above.

HOOKED RUGS ON HESSIAN

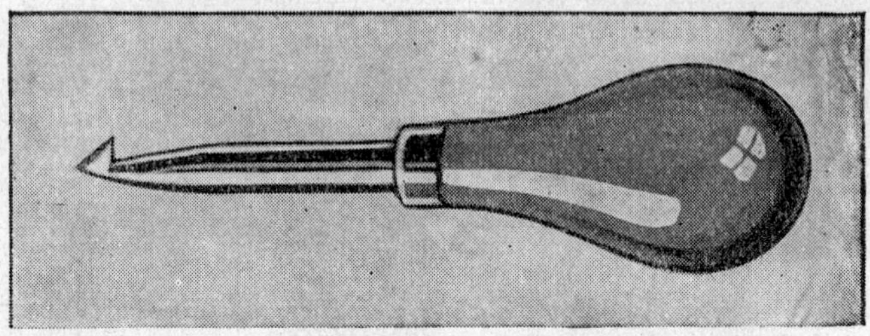

Fig. 58. Hook for use on hessian.

The Hooked Rug method is one of the oldest forms of rug-making, having been used in the North of England and Scotland for many centuries. The Pilgrim Fathers are believed to have introduced it to America in the seventeenth century, where it has remained popular ever since.

These rugs are made on hessian, mostly out of rags, but wool is also used. A frame is used for working. The American women aim to get the work as fine as possible, as the finer the loops the better the appearance of the rug.

The hessian should be hemmed all round in order to strengthen it, and then should be sewn into a frame at either end. A collapsible type of frame is the best. A piece of webbing is sewn to either side in the usual way. Leave about 18 inches of the work exposed, rolling the remainder round the bottom part of the frame. Then stretch it fairly tight but not too rigid. The hessian is now ready for working. When not in use the frame can be dismantled and the work rolled up and put away.

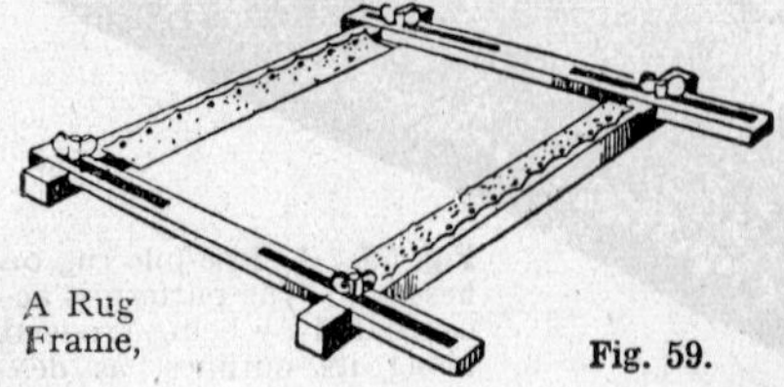

A Rug Frame, **Fig. 59.**

Work done on hessian does not need to be tied or knotted in any way, as hessian is a material that expands when pierced by a tool and contracts by the addition of row after row of loops which firmly bind the material into the foundation and cannot possibly shake out if the rug is properly made.

Materials required are a large hook, a frame, some hessian and rags or wool.

Cut the rags into strips of about ½ inch wide. For thin material they would need to be wider, and for thick narrower. Woven underwear and old silk stockings, dyed to tone, work in very well. In working a rug, it is best not to use cotton and wool together. For stockings, cut in strips of at least an inch wide, beginning at the top and cutting round and round, so as to obtain as long a length as possible. Rug wool can be used for the coloured parts of the design, or rough flannelette, which can be bought in bright colours and black.

If rug wool is used with the rags a good effect can be obtained by cutting the loops and shearing the wool, and then the pile stands out well. If there is not enough material of the same kind to make the background it is a good idea to mix it.

To work.—Place the frame at a convenient height to work naturally and comfortably. Begin by taking a strip of rag in the left hand, holding this underneath the hessian. Now take the hook in the right hand, push it through the hessian and draw up the end of the rag. Working from right to left, take the hook over three or four strands of hessian, then insert the hook again and draw up a loop to about $\frac{1}{4}$ or $\frac{3}{8}$ inch in height and release the hook. Miss three or four strands of hessian, insert the hook and draw up a loop to the same height as before. Continue working in this way until the piece of cloth is used up, always leaving three or four threads of hessian between each loop.

The whole pattern is worked in this way, and when it is finished none of the hessian is visible. The underneath is not like the top, as the material is drawn up close to the hessian. The beginning and ends are brought up on to the top and trimmed down afterwards.

Begin by working the outline. Black is a good colour to use, unless the background is a dark one, as this shows the colours up well. Then fill in the pattern in colour. The background is usually worked up to the edge of the hessian.

In working this, always work from right to left and hook in straight rows, leaving about three threads between the rows of loops.

When this part of the rug is completed, roll round the top part of the frame and continue working on the lower half.

To finish off the edges of the hessian, turn them under in the usual way and face them with a backing.

RAG RUGS (second method)

Rag rugs like the one at the foot of the page have been used for generations in cottage homes, and have a charming old-world look which accords perfectly with antique furniture. Patterns for this style of rug need be very simple, such as a waved border in a dark colour, with centre introducing a mixing of coloured rags.

To make a rug cut oddments of material into $\frac{1}{2}$-inch wide, 2-inch long strips; for the foundation use an old sack or hessian, and pencil on it the size and shape required, also an indication of the pattern. Now work the rag cuttings into the backing as shown in Fig. 60 . . . the nose of the tool is pushed under three or four threads of the material, the end of the rag placed in the jaws of the tool

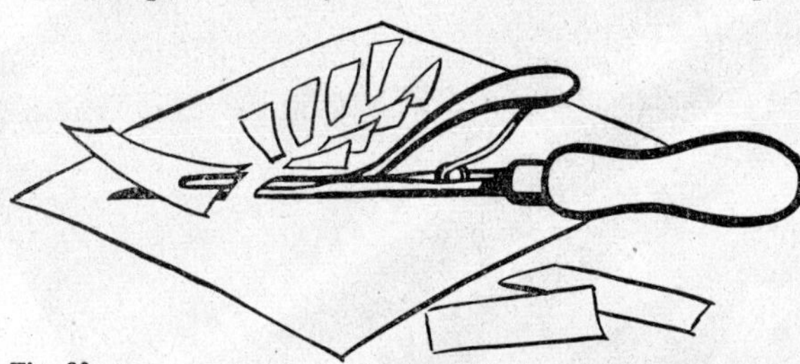

Fig. 60. For rag rugs strips of rag are drawn through the hessian using a jaw-type tool.

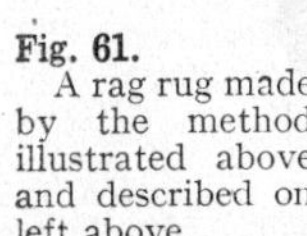

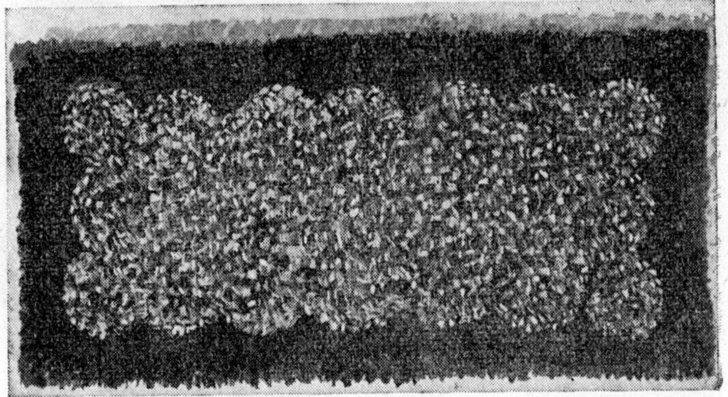

Fig. 61. A rag rug made by the method illustrated above and described on left above.

which open by pressing the lever; th rag is then pulled halfway back throug the material, so that the two ends ar of equal length. This tufting is don closely all over the background an results in a shaggy pile.

When the tufting is finished hem th edges of the foundation on the back o the rug.

1.
2.
3.

WOVEN RUGS

Very beautiful rugs. with either a flat surface as in the rug below, or introducing pile, can be woven on hand-weaving looms. Instructions for use are supplied with the looms.

The sampler on the left shows some of the traditional weaving designs that can be introduced—1, Monk's Belt. 2, Honeycomb. 3, Rose-path.

A rug woven on a small hand-loom. The colours are pastel pinks, beige and blue.

LACE

BOOK VI

AN ILLUSTRATED SUPPLEMENT SHOWING THE MOST IMPORTANT NEEDLE-MADE AND PILLOW LACES

PHOTOGRAPHS BY COURTESY OF THE VICTORIA AND ALBERT MUSEUM

NEEDLEPOINT LACE

The origins of needlepoint lace are to be traced in the cut and drawn linen work which was practised from an early date and which reached a high stage of development in Italy in the sixteenth century. The earliest examples, invariably geometrical in character which dispense altogether with the linen ground, mark the real beginning of needlepoint lace. They appear about the second half of the sixteenth century, a period when some of the first pattern books (Pagani, 1558; Ostaus, 1567; Vecellio, 1592; Franco, 1596; and Parasole, 1600) were published in Venice.

The manner of making needlepoint lace is as follows: The pattern is first drawn upon parchment, which is then stitched to two thicknesses of linen. A skeleton pattern is formed by means of a linen thread laid over the chief outlines, and stitched down through both parchment and linen (A, page 822). To this framework the solid parts of the design and the meshes are attached; the former are known as clothing (Fr. *fond* or *toilé*), and they are always composed of closely worked buttonhole stitches (B, pp. 822 and 824). These parts are united either by ties or bars (*brides*) or by regular meshes (*réseaux*). The ties consist of a few threads buttonholed over, often decorated with small knots (*picots*) and rosettes (*brides picotées et rosacées*) as can be seen in Venetian Rose Point (C, p. 822, and Chasuble, p. 823). The meshes are made by looping the threads or by forming regular hexagons overcast with buttonhole stitch; the two varieties are well shown in *Point d'Alençon* (D, p. 825) and *Point d'Argentan* laces (E, pp. 826 and 827). When the lace is finished, it is released from the parchment by passing a knife between the two thicknesses of linen at the back, and thus cutting the connecting threads. The segments are then skilfully joined together to make a large piece. The outline often has a raised edging (*cordonnet*) the foundation of which is made of one or more thick threads, generally of linen, but sometimes of horsehair as in *Point d'Alençon* (D, p. 825), closely worked over with buttonhole stitches. In such laces as Venetian Rose or Snow Point (C, p. 822), Venetian Gros Point (F, p. 828), and Point de France (G, p. 829), those parts in relief are enriched with rows of minute scallops or picots. Some needlepoint laces have diaper or geometrical fillings (*modes à jours*) both in pattern and along the edge, as in *Point d'Alençon* (D, p. 825), *Point d'Argentan* (E, pp. 826 and 827), and *Point de Venise à réseau* (H, below).

H

Border of needlepoint lace—"Point de venise à réseau," made in Italy in the first half of the eighteenth century.

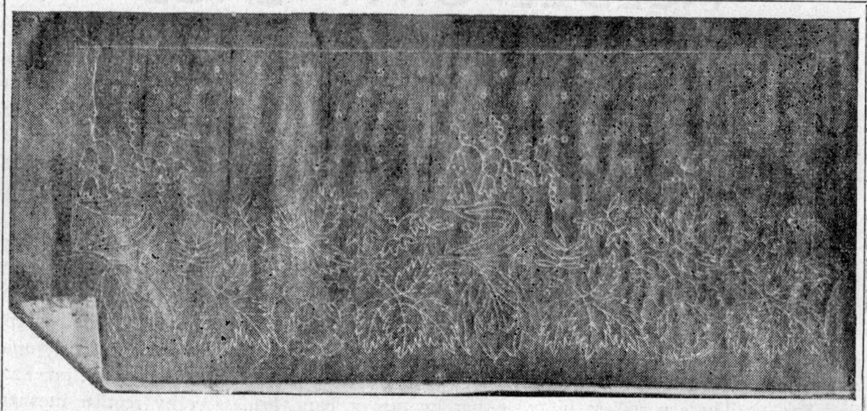

A.—A skeleton pattern.

B.—Imitation of Italian *punto in aria* seventeenth-century lace.

C.—Venetian raised or "rose-point" Venetian lace.

Below: A section of the Chasuble on the next page.

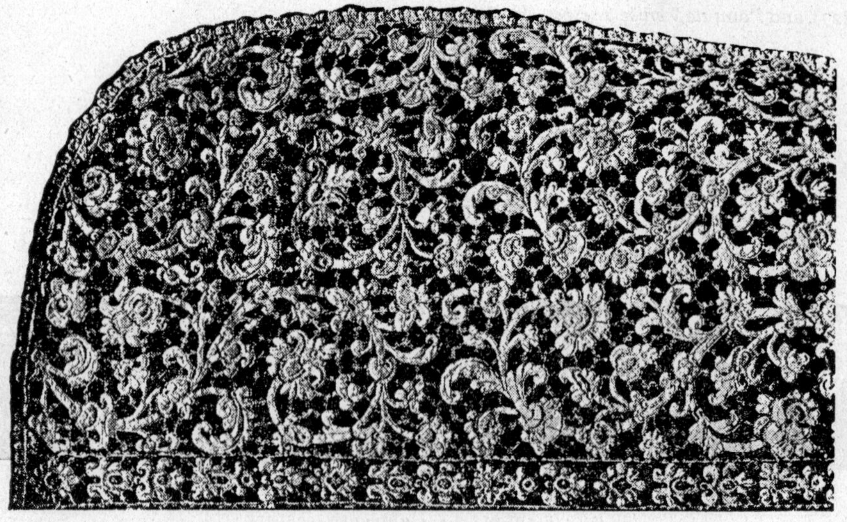

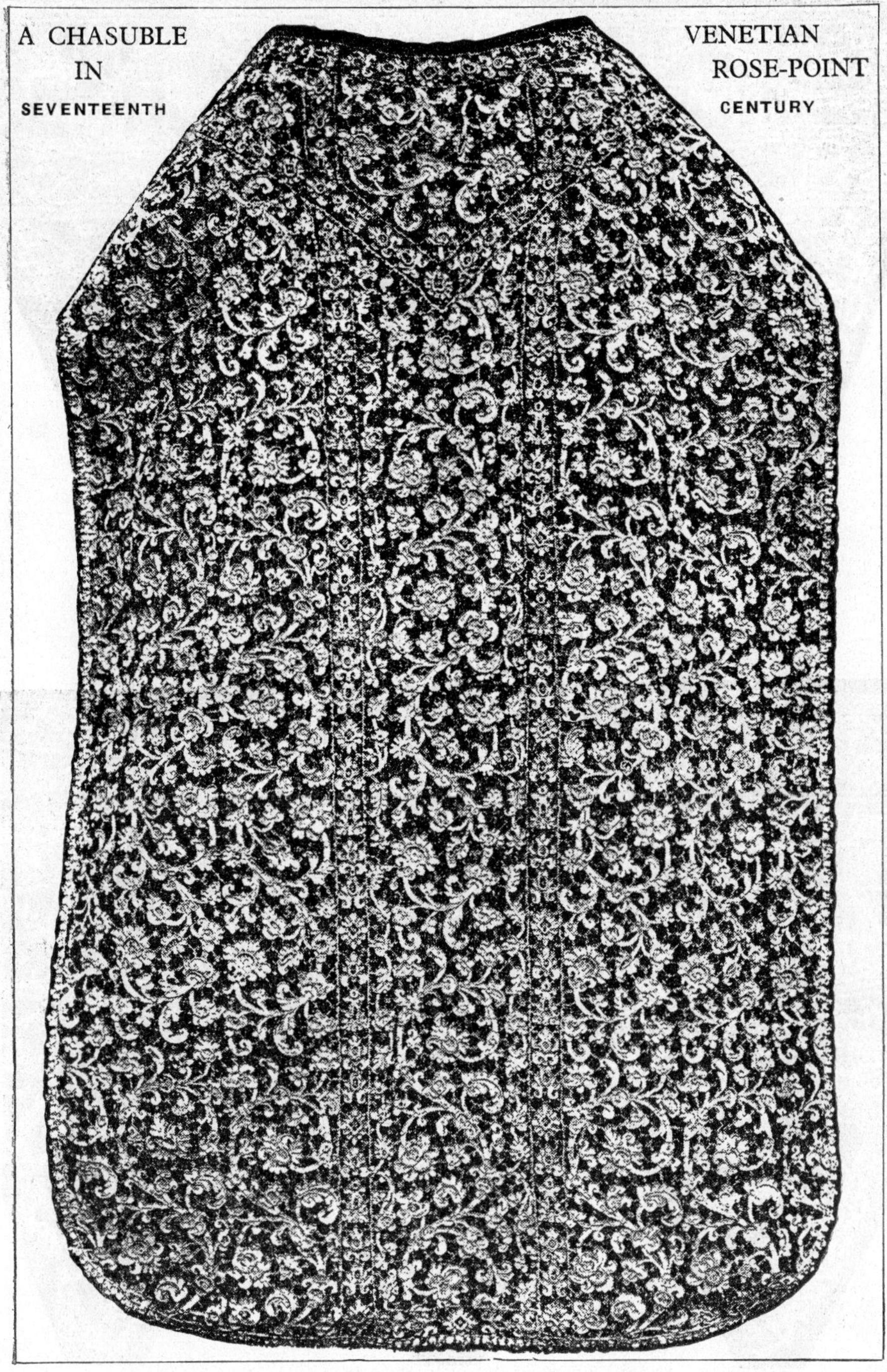

A CHASUBLE IN VENETIAN ROSE-POINT
SEVENTEENTH CENTURY

TWO VANDYKED BORDERS OF RETICELLA
AND PUNTO IN ARIA

ITALIAN SEVENTEENTH CENTURY

LATE SEVENTEENTH AND EIGHTEENTH CENTURIES

D

Above: Repeating floral sprigs and detached blossoms on a ground of fine mesh. *Below:* A beautifully executed border, made in France.

POINT D'ALENÇON

E. ALTAR FRONTAL OF POINT D'ARGENTAN. FRENCH. ABOUT 1700

POINT D'ARGENTAN LACE

E

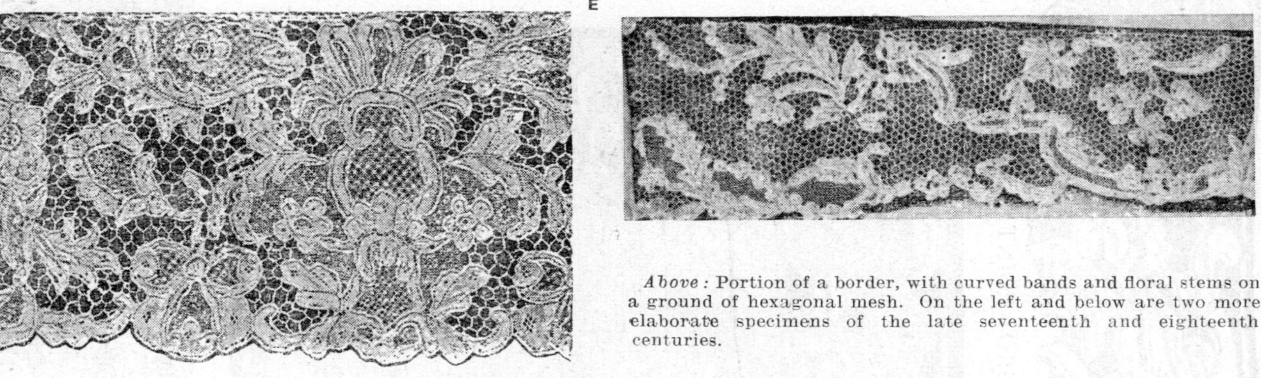

Above: Portion of a border, with curved bands and floral stems on a ground of hexagonal mesh. On the left and below are two more elaborate specimens of the late seventeenth and eighteenth centuries.

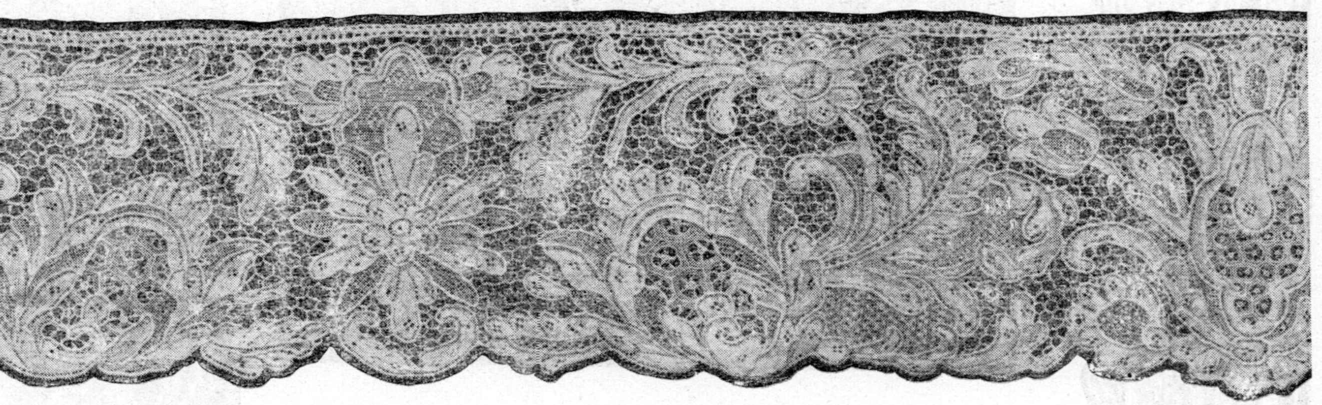

VENETIAN GROS POINT

F

RUFFLE AND BORDER

POINT DE FRANCE SEVENTEENTH CENTURY

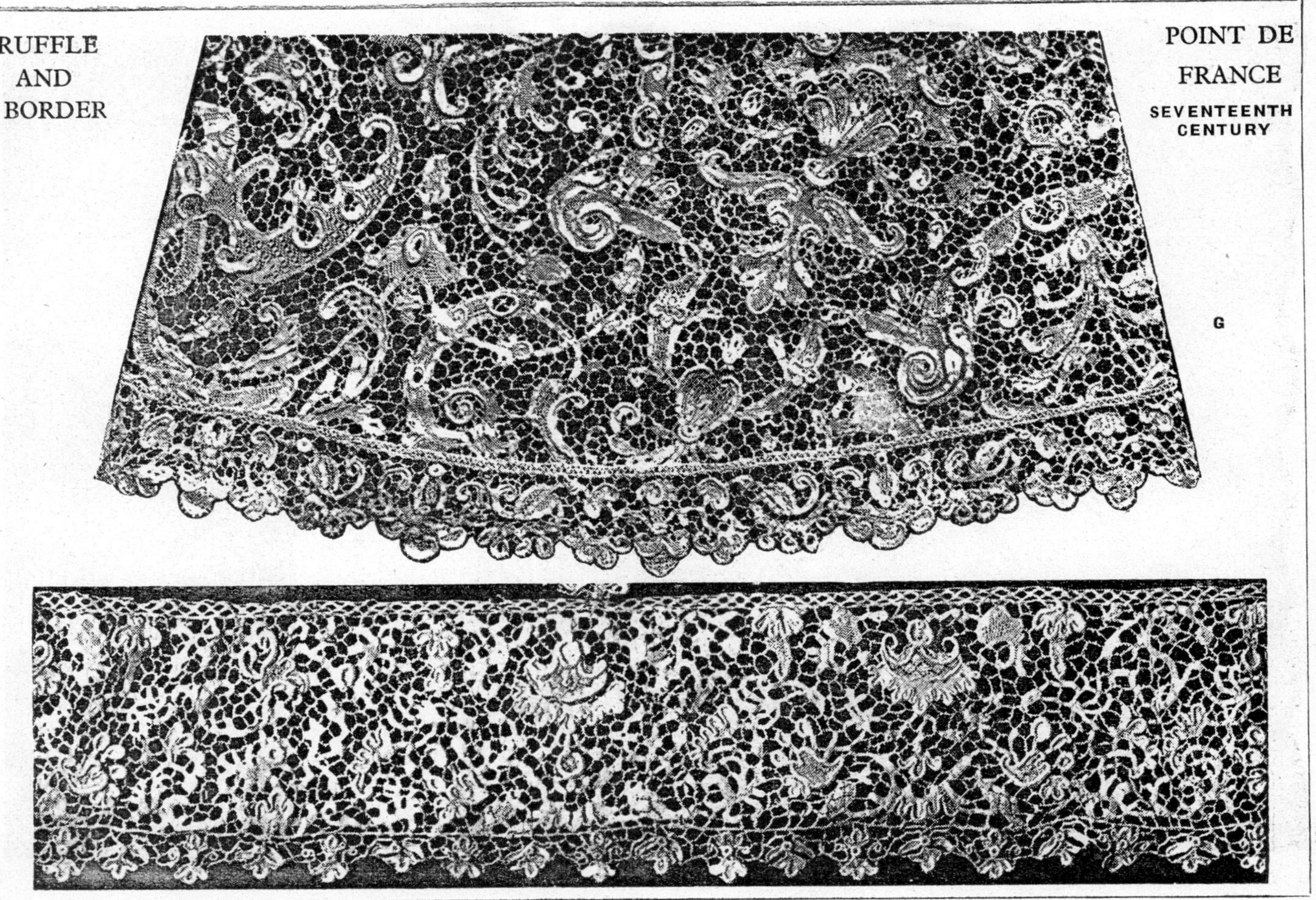

G

SILK NEEDLEPOINT LACE
ITALIAN SEVENTEENTH CENTURY

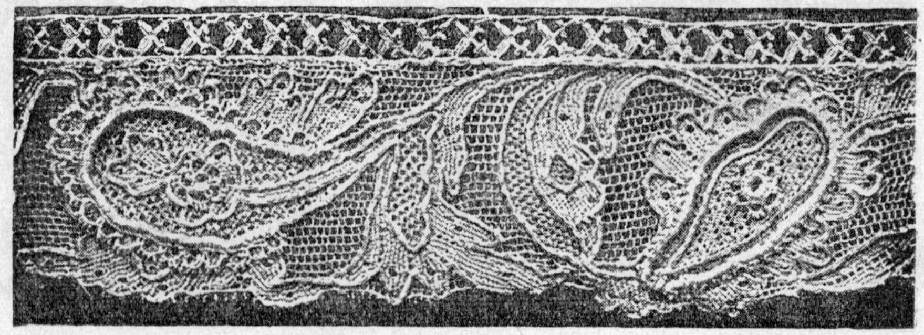

NEEDLEPOINT SILK LACE

Squares and Borders for ornamenting the Talith mantle or shawl worn during Jewish publish prayer.

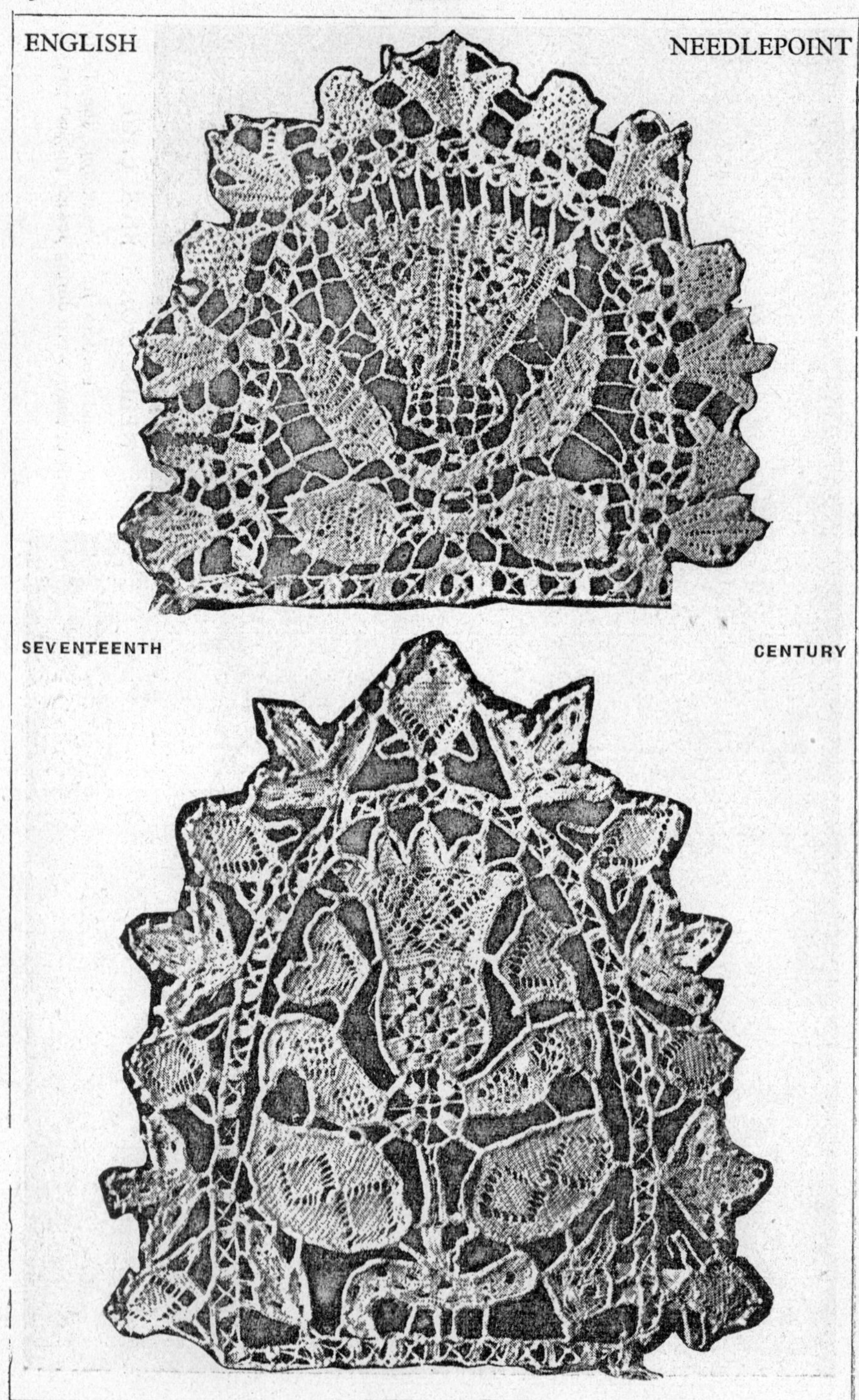
ENGLISH
NEEDLEPOINT
SEVENTEENTH
CENTURY

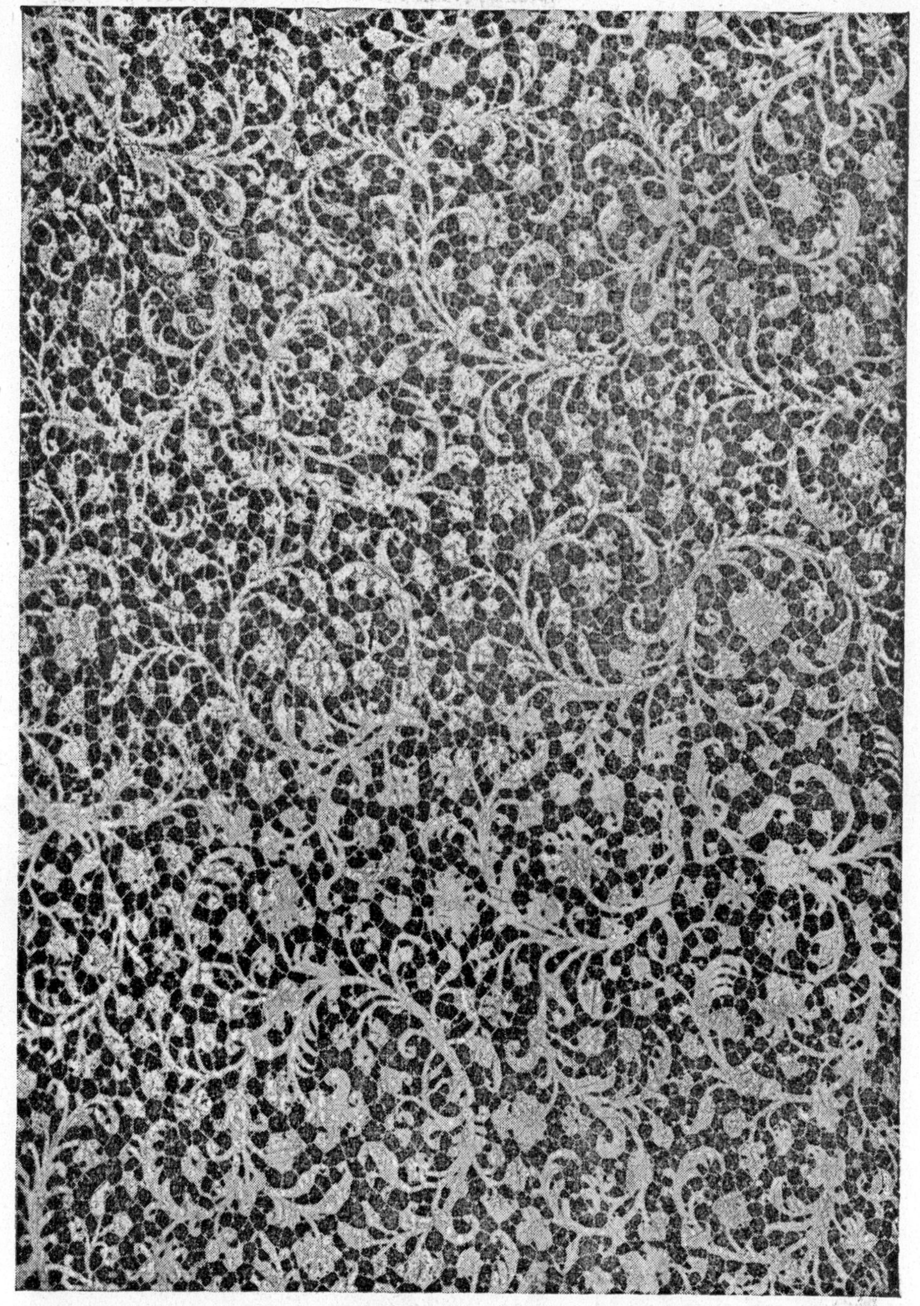

PART OF A FLOUNCE IN NEEDLEPOINT LACE. POINT PLAT DE VENISE

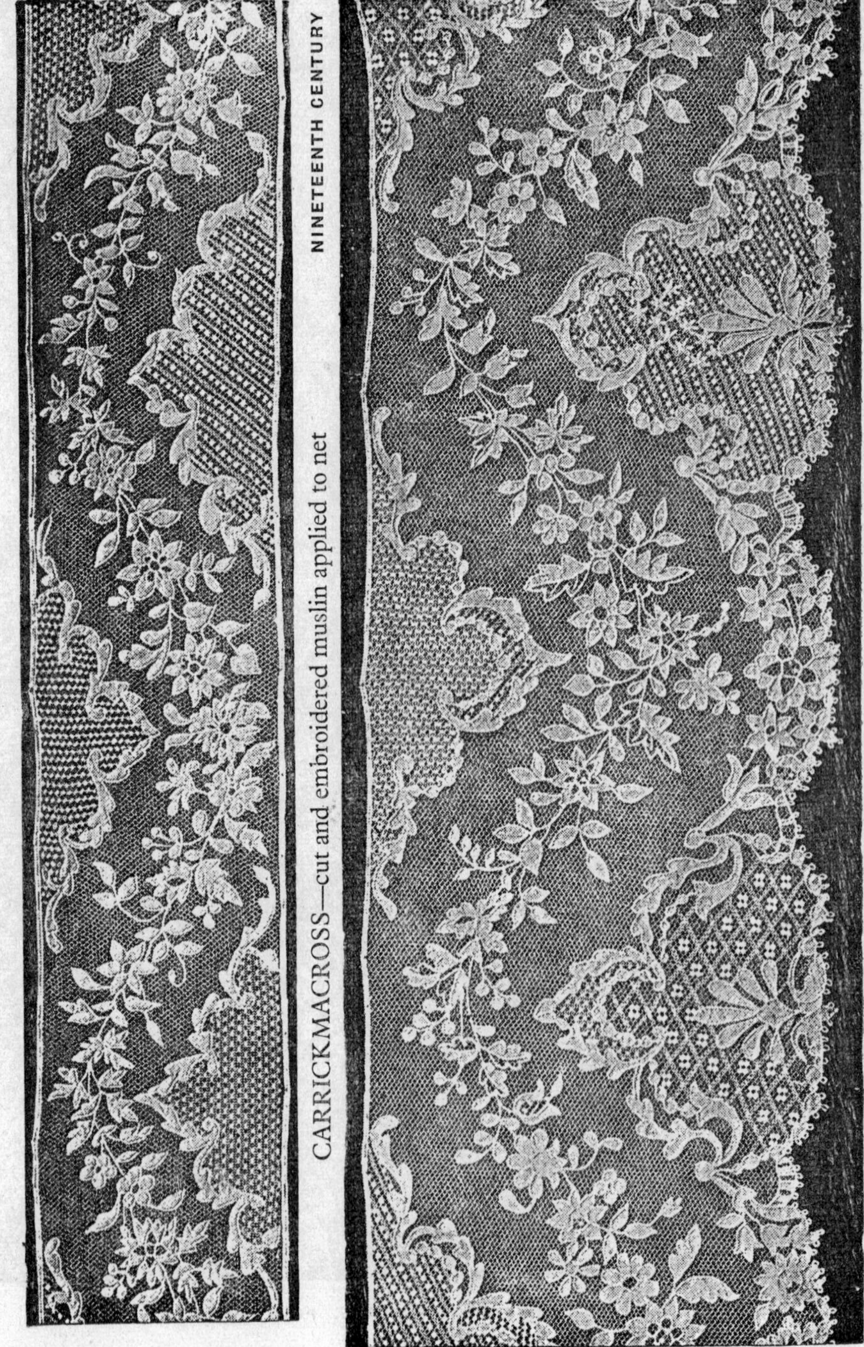

NINETEENTH CENTURY

CARRICKMACROSS—cut and embroidered muslin applied to net

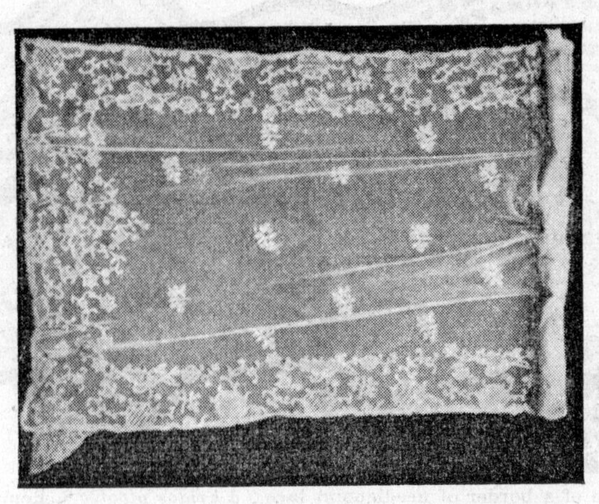

IRISH (OR LIMERICK)
NEEDLEPOINT LACE
19th Century

Portion of a border of needlepoint lace "*à brides picotée*". Reproduction of a Russian sixteenth-century design. Floral ornament introduced into a pattern of lozenges and circles.

Border of fine linen or cambric with pattern of floral and conventional ornament done in embroidery and drawn work. The more opaque portions, however, are done with applications (appliqué work) fastened at the back. This is called Indian work and is Danish eighteenth century. It is made in Londer, North Schleswig.

BOBBIN OR PILLOW-MADE LACE

In this class of lace there is no skeleton pattern as in needlepoint lace, but the fabric is made by twisting and plaiting the thread.

Early examples of the kind of work which ultimately developed into bobbin lace as we have it to-day, may be traced among the stuffs of the first centuries of the Christian era found in Egyptian burying grounds (A, p. 838).

The process of bobbin lace making is as follows: After the pattern has been drawn upon a strip of card, paper or parchment, (called "Down" in the English Midland Counties) it is pricked in small holes by an experienced worker and attached to the pillow, pins being put through the holes (C, p. 838). The thread is wound upon a narrow neck at the top of the bobbin, which is of wood, bone or metal (D, p. 838). The bobbins hang over the pillow, a separate one being required for each thread. By manipulating the bobbins with the hands the threads are twisted, plaited or crossed as required by the pattern, and thus the lace is produced. The solid part of the pattern is known as gimp or mat (Fr. *fond*); it has the general appearance of plain weaving like muslin or cambric (E, p. 839), and has a texture easily distinguished from the close rows of button-hole stitches which make up the toile of needlepoint lace.

In many classes the pattern is outlined, wholly or in part by a thicker white thread (*cordonnet*) as in Mechlin, Lille and Buckinghamshire laces (F. p. 840). Others have no outlining thread (E, p. 839). Most bobbin-made laces have the pattern and ground worked simultaneously, but sometimes the pattern is either made separately and applied afterwards to a net ground, as in Brussels and Devon appliqué (H, p. 841) or the ground is worked round the design, as in Brussels (G, p. 841).

The pattern is usually joined either by bars (*brides*) or by meshes (*réseaux*). The bars (I, p. 842) are sometimes decorated with small knots (picots). The mesh (G, p. 841) is more varied than that of needlepoint lace and the different classes can be recognised by peculiarities in their structure. Geometrical and diaper fillings (*modes à jours*) are found in the pattern of some laces, such as Brussels (the wavy band in G. p. 841), Mechlin, and Devonshire (the flowers in J, p. 841). The fillings are occasionally based on needlepoint patterns. There is a class of Brussels lace in which both needlepoint and bobbin work is combined, the former usually providing the pattern and fillings, and the latter the ground: it is known as "mixed lace" (K, p. 843). Net ground for bobbin lace was first made on the machine in the beginning of the nineteenth century, and has been increasingly used from that time. The pattern is made separately and applied to the net (H, p. 841).

Portion of a bag of netting in twisted and plaited wools, found at Ehnasya (Herakleopolis Magna) during the excavations of 1903-4. It probably dates back to the fifth century.

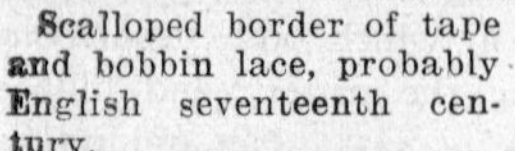

Scalloped border of tape and bobbin lace, probably English seventeenth century.

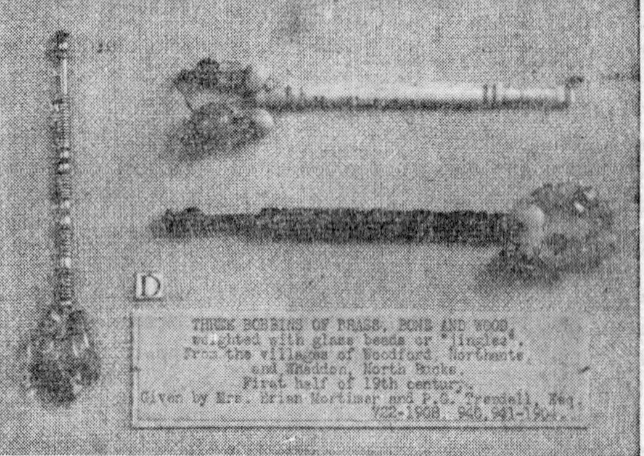

Above: a parchment pattern or "Down" for a border, pricked for use upon the pillow with a portion of the pattern worked in bobbin lace. The three bobbins, above, in D, are of bone, brass and wood and weighted with glass beads or jingles. From the villages of Woodford, Northants, and Whaddon, Bucks.

C

VALENCIENNES BOBBIN-MADE LACE

E

The border below is in pillow-made lace with obliquely arranged sprays of carnations and other floral devices, alternated with an obliquely arranged series of panels of different forms filled in with various "*modes*." Made in France in eighteenth century.

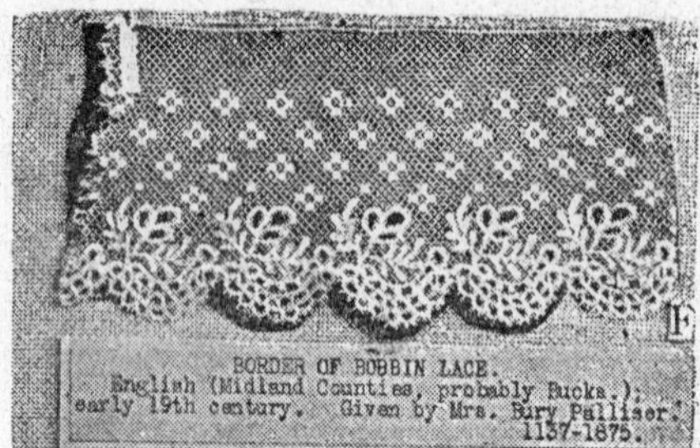

F
BORDER OF BOBBIN LACE.
English (Midland Counties, probably Bucks.),
early 19th century. Given by Mrs. Bury Palliser.
1137-1875.

BOBBIN LACE

A border of English—probably Buckinghamshire—lace, of the early nineteenth century.

F

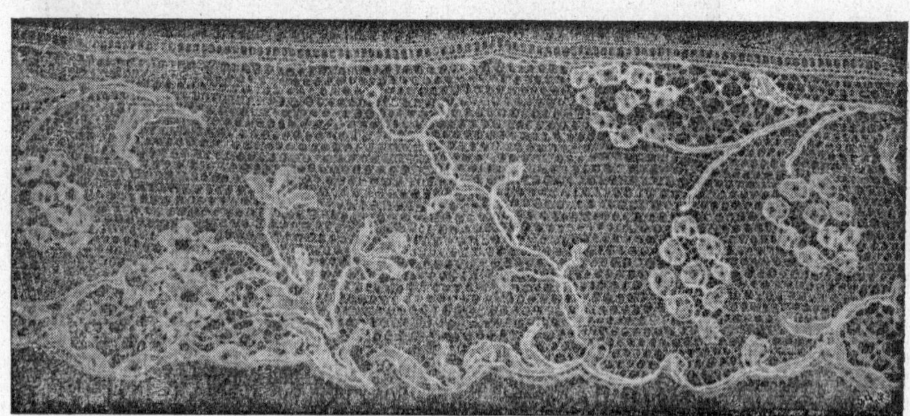

BUCKINGHAMSHIRE LACE

Here are two borders of pillow-made lace made in Buckinghamshire in the first half of the nineteenth century. The upper border has a repeating pattern of berried stems, diagonal interlaced stems, and (along the edge) floral stems, all on a ground of six-pointed star mesh. Ornamental star diaper in the fillings are used. The lower border has a repeating row of rounded compartments filled with diapered openwork in variegated and " point net " grounds, alternating with leaves on a small hexagonal mesh.

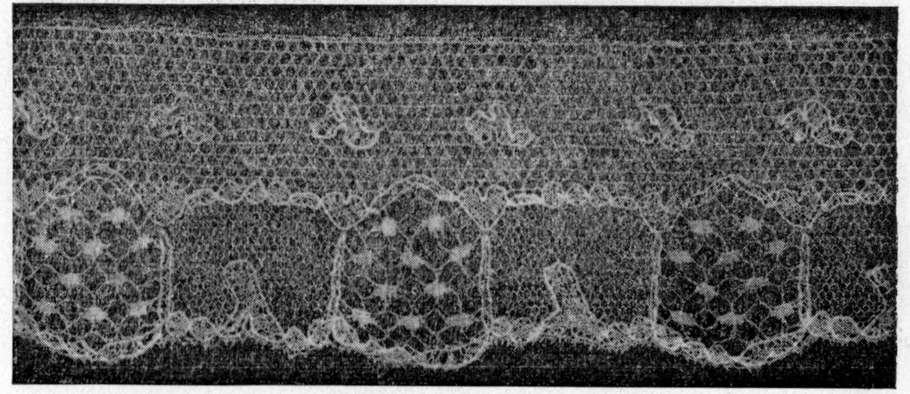

Cuff of bobbin-made lace applied to a ground of machine-made net. English; first half of the nineteenth century.

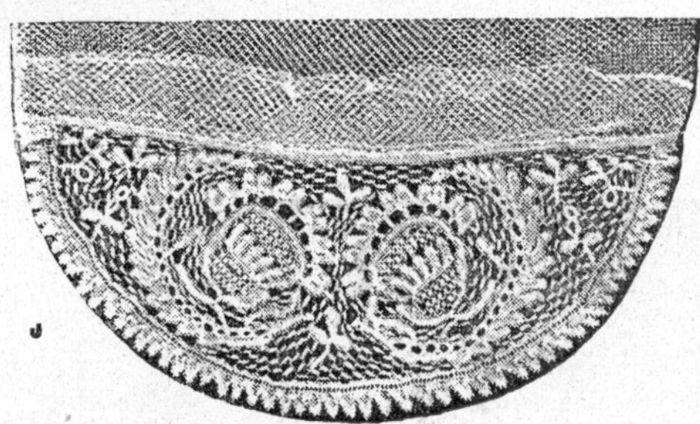

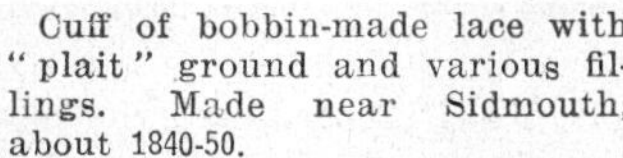

Cuff of bobbin-made lace with "plait" ground and various fillings. Made near Sidmouth, about 1840-50.

Border of bobbin-made lace. Brussels; middle of eighteenth century.

Below: Border of pillow-made lace. Horizontal wavy of large circular mesh, interlaced with a narrower band bearing leaves; floral devices with diaper fillings along the edge; ground of small hexagonal mesh. The cordonnet unusually prominent. Mechlin; second half eighteenth century.

ITALIAN SEVENTEENTH CENTURY

Border designs of pillow-made lace taken from the Vacher Cóllection. They are all Italian of the seventeenth century.

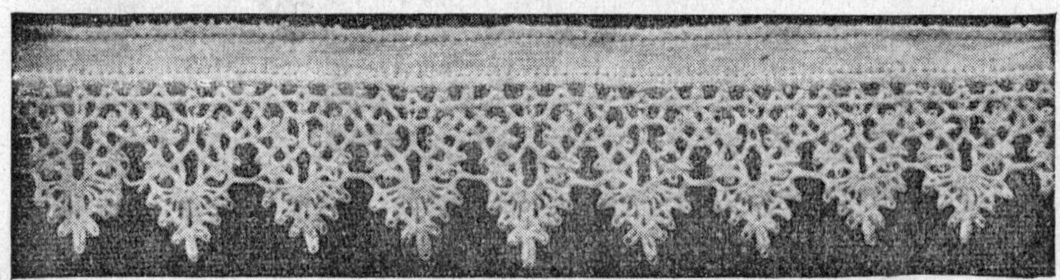

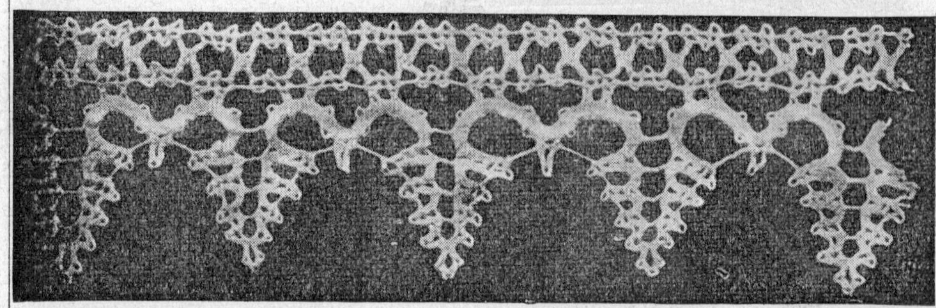

One motif from a flounce of mixed lace (needlepoint and bobbin) which was worked in Brussels in the first half of the eighteenth century.

MIXED LACES

K

On the left is a small section of a veil of Brussels mixed lace. The pattern is worked with the needle and applied to bobbin mesh.

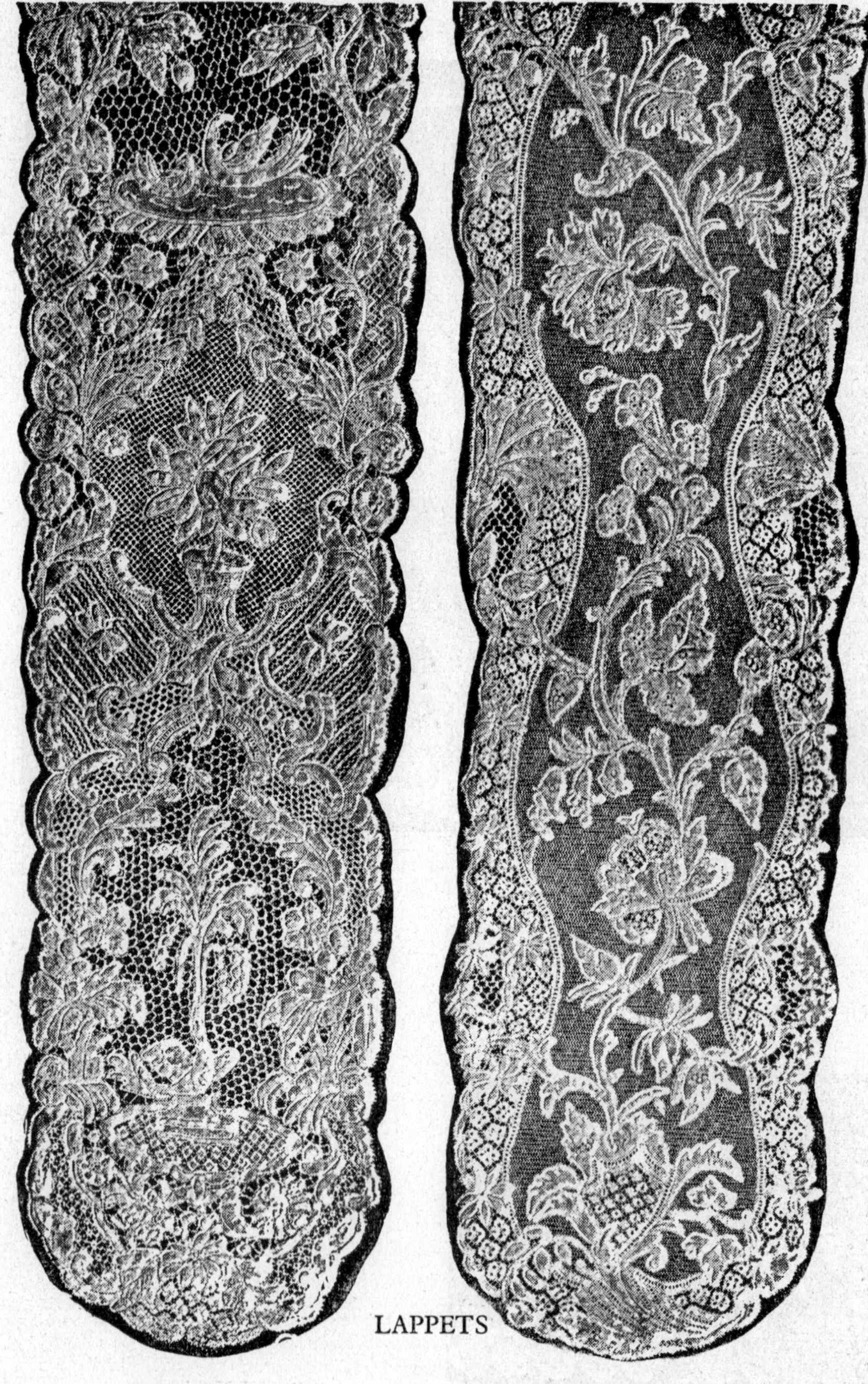

LAPPETS

BRUSSELS FIRST HALF EIGHTEENTH CENTURY

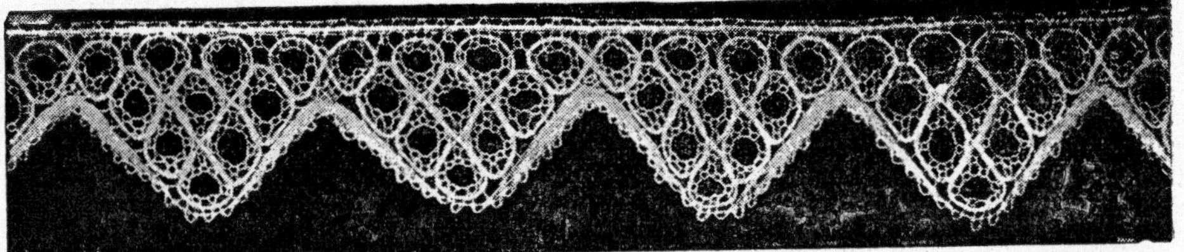

PILLOW-MADE LACES

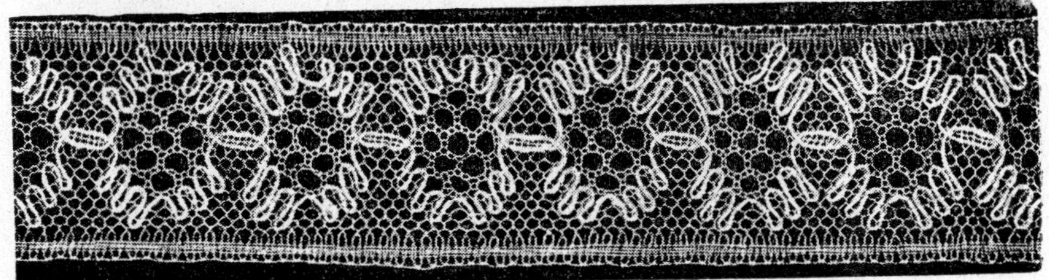

ENGLISH—1875

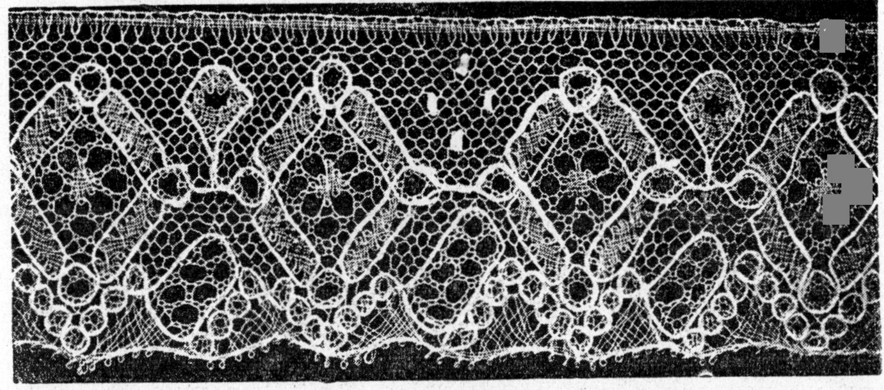

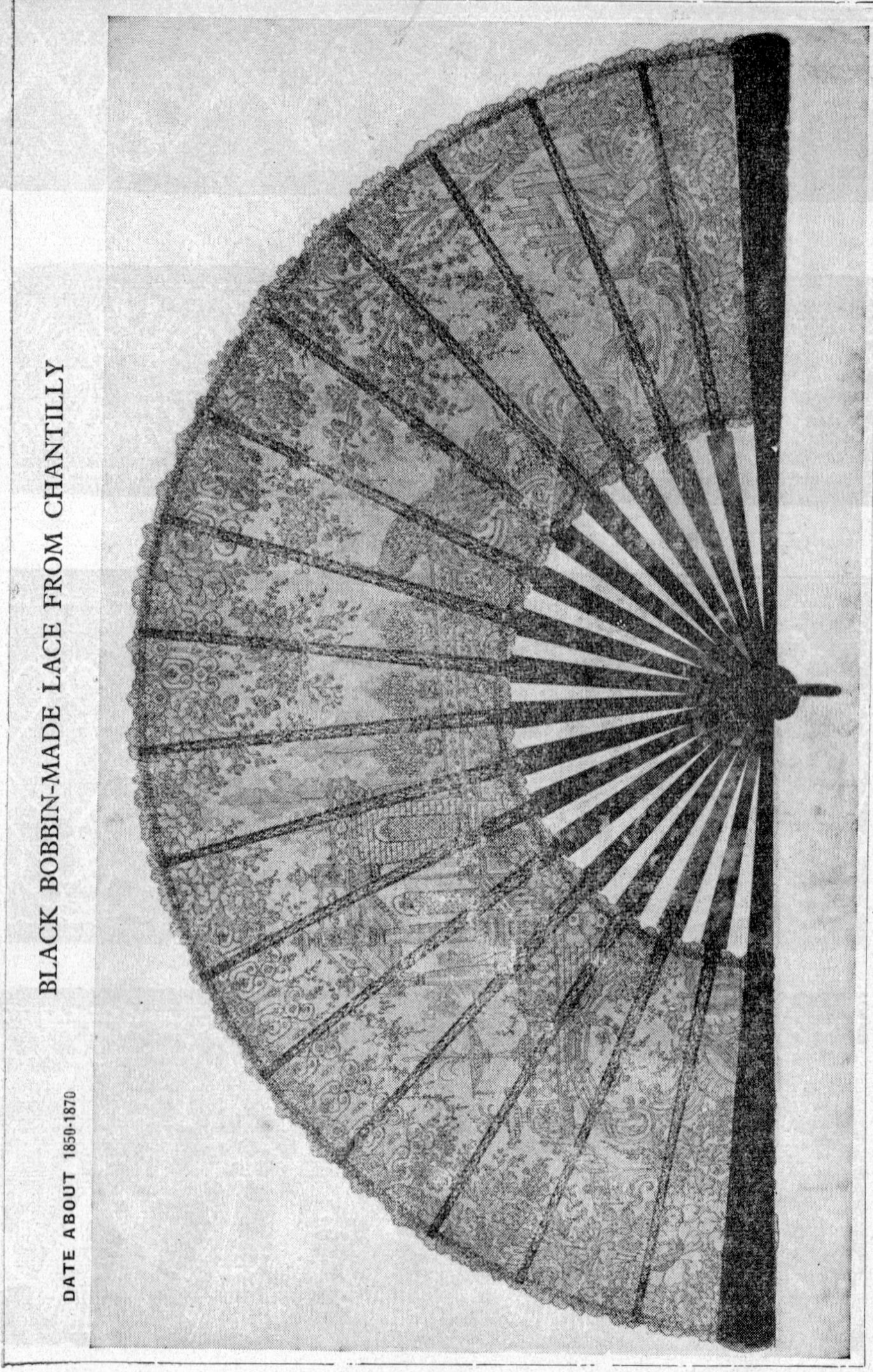

BLACK BOBBIN-MADE LACE FROM CHANTILLY

DATE ABOUT 1850-1870

BOBBIN LACE A RÉSEAU

Part of a Flemish flounce of the late seventeenth century, this lovely design contains some varied fillings.

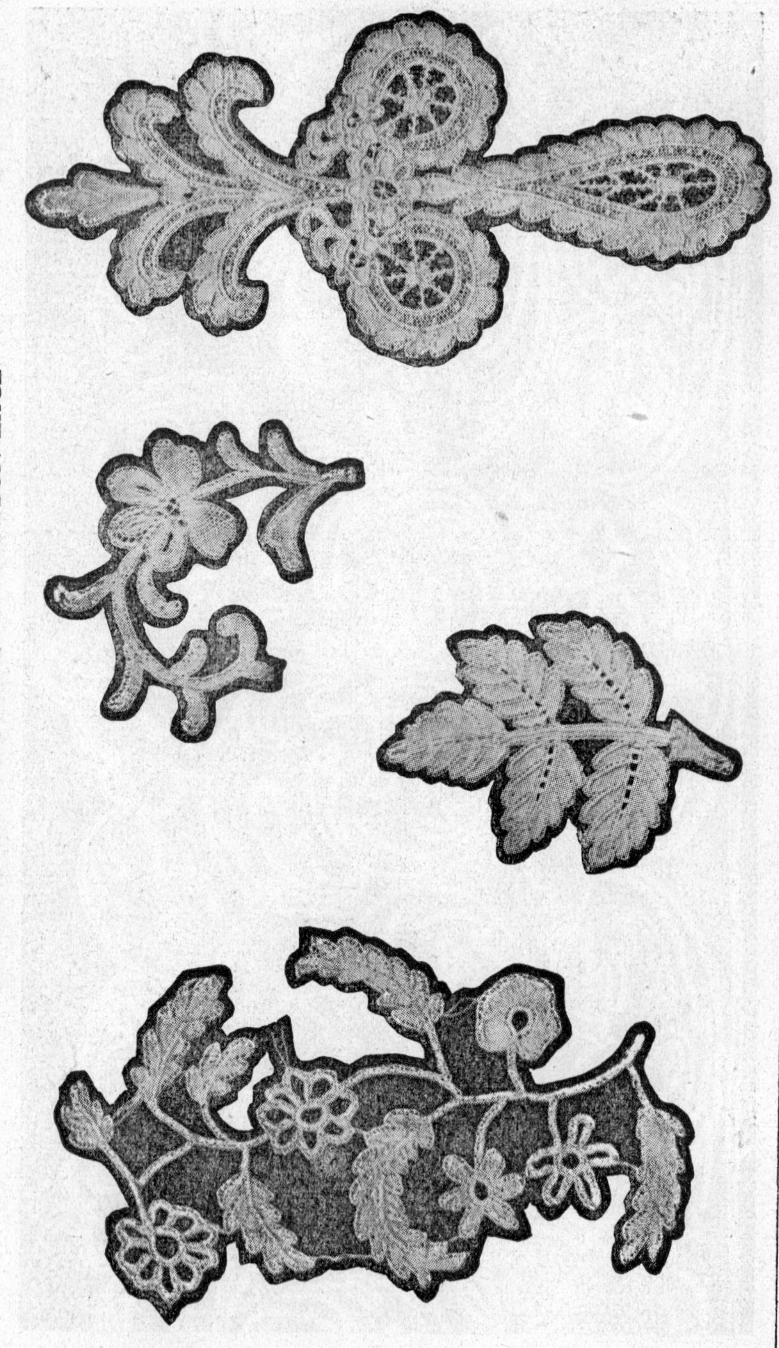

VARIOUS SPRIGS USED IN HONITON LACE

HONITON PILLOW-MADE LACE

TWO SPRIGS WITH MORE ELABORATE FILLINGS

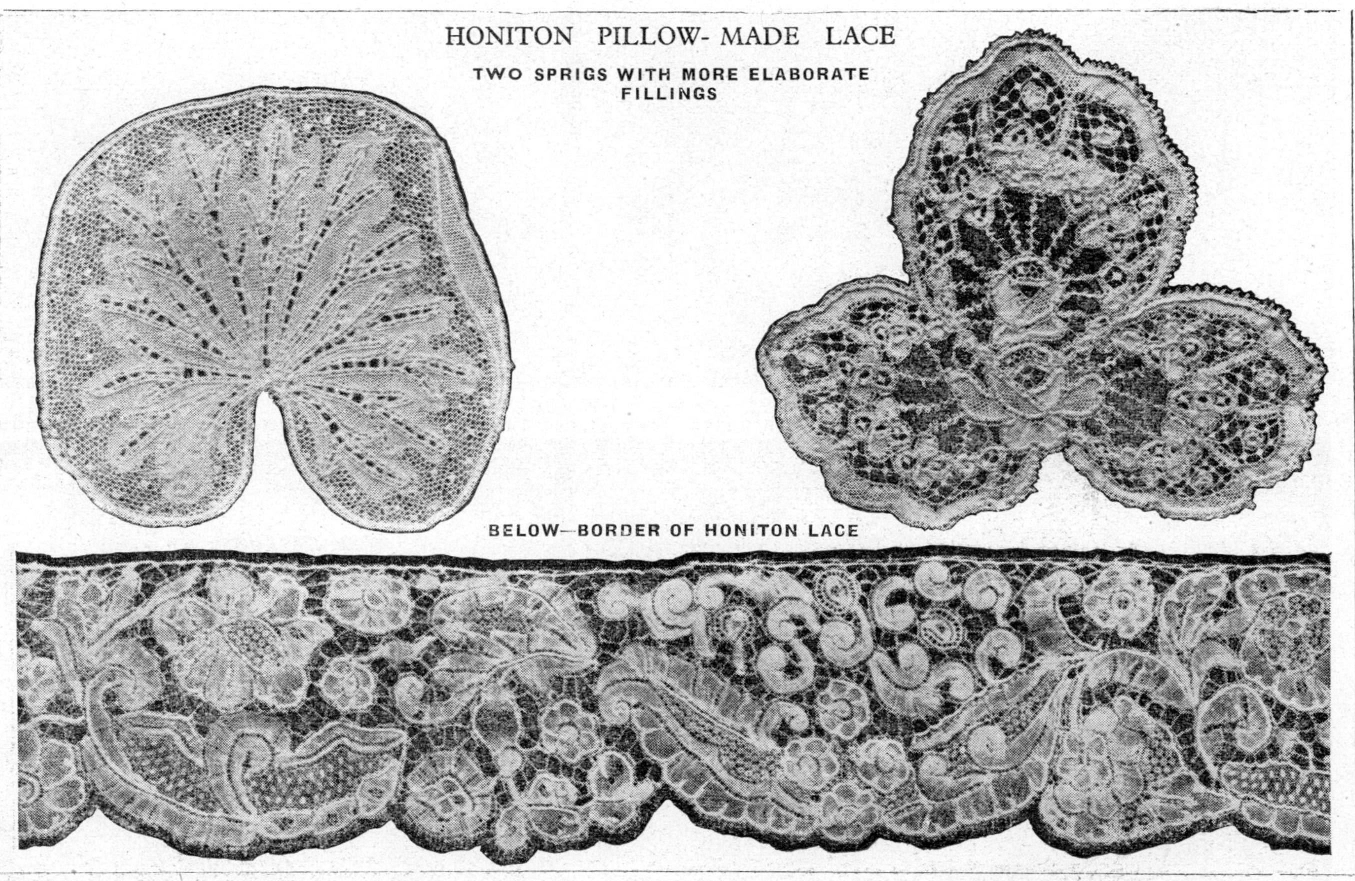

BELOW—BORDER OF HONITON LACE

ABOVE, BRUGES PILLOW-MADE LACE. NOTICE THE STEMS ARE UNITED BY BRIDES PICOTEES. BELOW, BORDER IN ANTWERP EIGHTEENTH CENTURY PILLOW-MADE LACE. "POTTEN KANT"

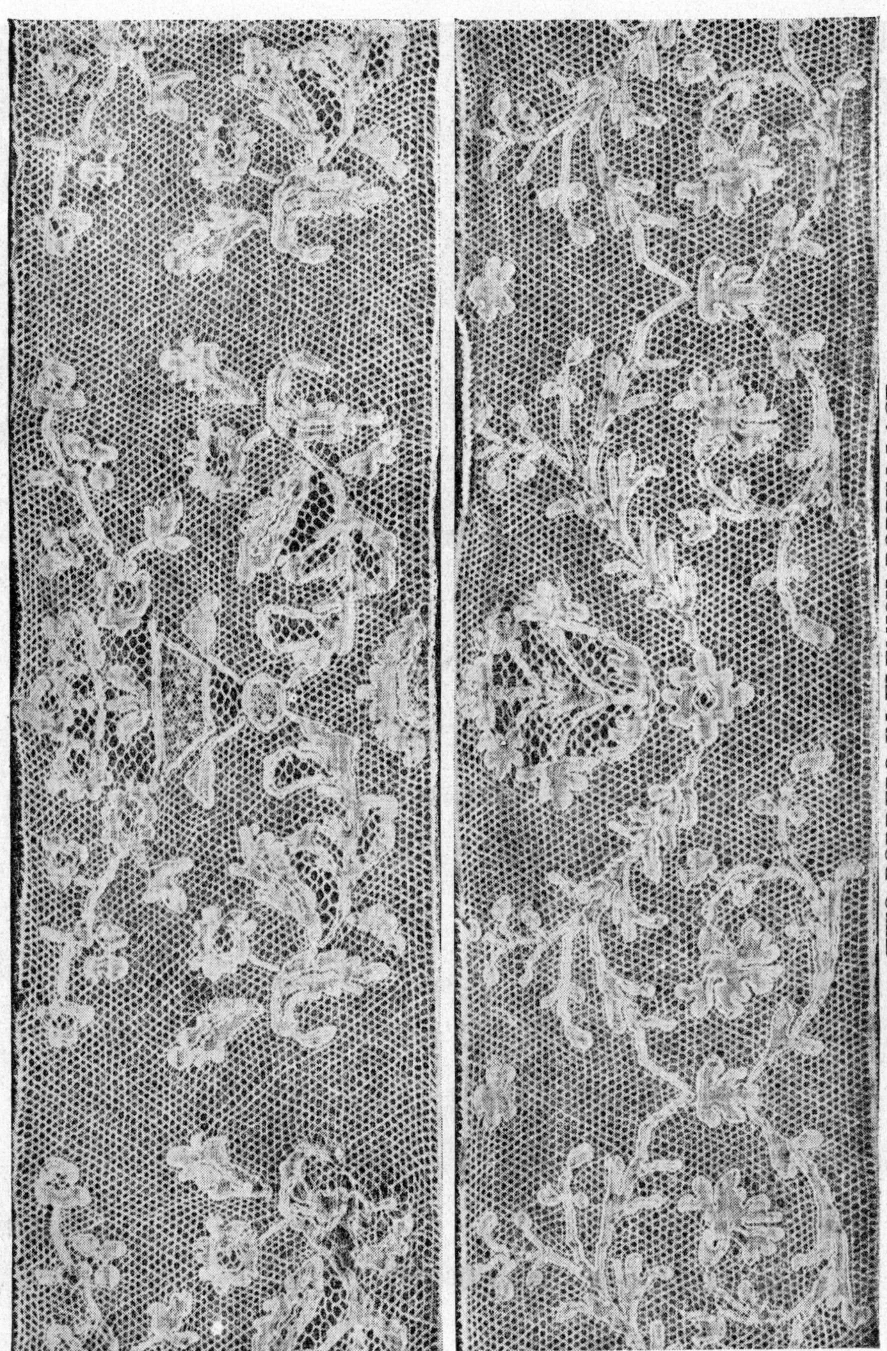

TWO BORDERS IN FLEMISH BOBBIN LACE

BOBBIN LACE À BRIDES MILAN, SEVENTEENTH CENTURY

TRIANGULAR SHAWL

Brussells Bobbin Lace applied to a ground of machine-made net.

AN ITALIAN SEVENTEENTH CENTURY VANDYKED BORDER OF MACRAME OR KNOTTED LACE

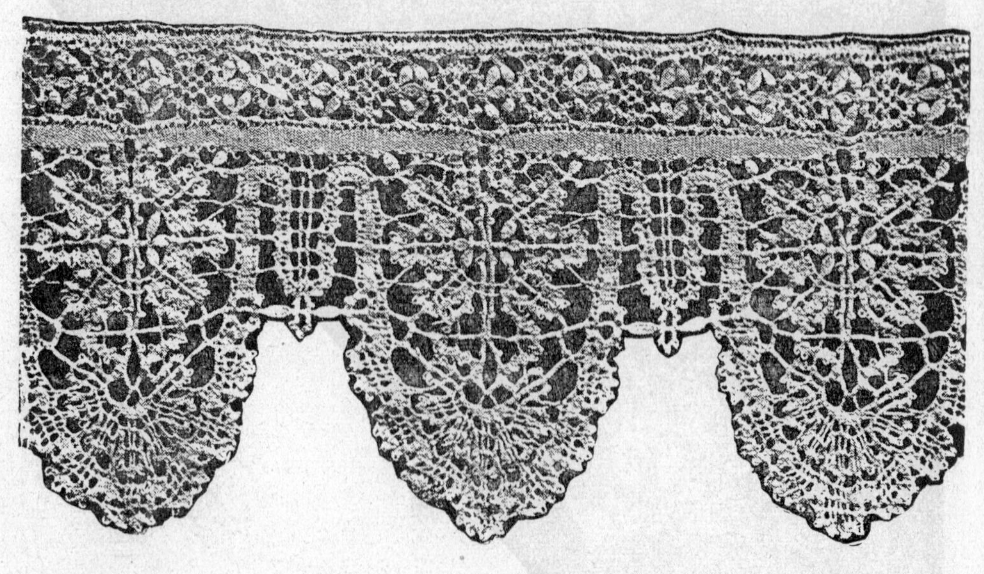

A GENOESE PIECE OF PILLOW-MADE LACE WITH A DEEP SCALLOPED BORDER SEVENTEENTH CENTURY

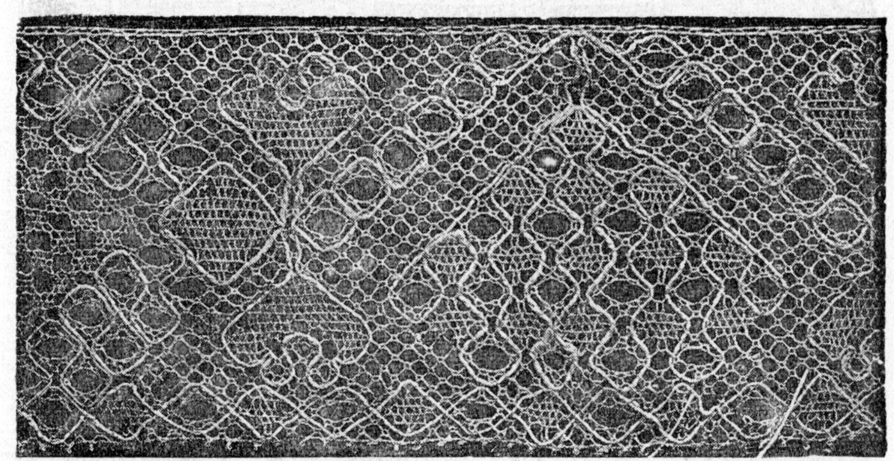

INSERTION OF PILLOW-MADE LACE OF GEOMETRIC PATTERN OUTLINED BY A THICK THREAD. MADE BY THE PEASANTS OF ERZEGEBIRGE. SAXON NINETEENTH CENTURY

AN ITALIAN SIXTEENTH CENTURY BORDER OF CUT LINEN, OUTLINED WITH SILVER GILT THREAD

LACIS OR DARNED NETTING

Part of an altar band which consists of six large panels of lacis or darned netting. This panel, as can be clearly seen, represents the Crucifixion. The other five are equally beautiful in work and design. Worked in France in the sixteenth century.

ANOTHER EXQUISITE PIECE OF DARNED NETTING

LACIS OR

These amusing and beautifully worked specimens contain some useful and decorative fillings. Darning stitch is used on knotted net. Spanish, seventeenth century.

DARNED NETTING

INDEX

D